Gateway 2000 Inc.
  http://www.gw2k.com
General Electric
  http://www.ge.com
General Motors Corp.
  http://www.gm.com
Golden Rule Insurance Company
  http://www.goldenrule.com
W. L. Gore Associates
  http://www.gore.com
Guidestar (The Donor's Guide to The Nonprofit Universe)
  http://www.guidestar.org
Hasbro
  http://www.hasbro.com
Honeywell Inc.
  http://www.honeywell.com
Hot Coupons Savings Club
  http://www.hotcoupons.com
InterActive Custom Clothes Company
  http://www.ic3d.com
International Accounting Standards Committee
  http://www.iasc.org.uk
International Brownie
  http://www.internationalbrownie.com
International Commerce Exchange Systems
  http://www.icesinc.com
International Organization for Standardization
  http://www.iso.ch
The Internet Business Network (A Web Guide to
    the Job Search)
      http://www.interbiznet.com/hunt/tools.html
Intuit Inc.
  http://www.intuit.com
IRS
  http://www.irs.ustreas.gov
JAMTV Music Network
  http://www.jamtv.com
JCPenney
  http://www.jcpenney.com
Jeep Home Page (Chyrsler Corp.)
  http://www.jeepunpaved.com
JobSmart (Job Search Guide)
  http://www.jobsmart.org
Joe Boxer
  http://www.joeboxer.com
Johnson & Johnson
  http://www.jnj.com
JumboSports
  http://www.jumbosports.com
Junkbusters
  http://www.junkbusters.com
Just For Feet
  http://www.feet.com
Juno Online Services
  http://www.juno.com
Kmart Corporation
  http://www.kmart.com
Levi Strauss
  http://www.levi.com
Lexus
  http://www.lexus.com/clapton
LifeSavers
  http://www.candystand.com
Lincoln Electric Co.
  http://www.lincolnelectric.com
Liz Claiborne
  http://www.lizclaiborne.com

M.Y.O.B. Accounting
  http://www.myob.com
Madam C. J. Walker Enterprises Inc.
  http://www.madamcjwalker.com
McDonald's
  http://www.mcdonalds.com
Microsoft
  http://www.microsoft.com
Microsoft Financial Forum
  http://www.microsoft.com/msft
Monarch Marking Systems
  http://www.monarch-marking.com
Money Hunter
  http://www.moneyhunter.com
The Monster Board–DSC Communications
  http://www.monster.com
MONY
  http://www.mony.com
Motorola
  http://www.motorola.com
MSBET & Microsoft joint venture
  http://www.msbet.com
Multimedia 2000
  http://www.m-2k.com
Music Boulevard
  http://www.musicblvd.com
MySki Inc.
  http://www.myski.com
Nantucket Nectars
  http://www.juiceguys.com
NASCAR
  http://www.nascar.com
National Association of Securities Dealers Automated
    Quotation System
      http://www.nasdaq.com
National Center for Employee Ownership
  http://www.nceo.org
National Fraud Information Center
  http://www.fraud.org
National Highway Traffic Safety Administration
  http://www.nhtsa.dot.gov
Netscape
  http://www.netscape.com
Netstock Direct
  http://www.netstockdirect.com
Network Associates
  http://www.networkassociate.com
New York Stock Exchange
  http://www.nyse.com
NordicTrack
  http://www.nordictrack.com
Nortel Northern Telecom
  http://www.nortel.com
OPEC (Organization of Petroleum-Exporting Countries)
  http://www.opec.org
Oracle Education
  http://www.oracle.com
Parent Time at Work
  http://www.parenttime.com
Pink Jeep Tours
  http://www.pinkjeep.com
PriceSCAN
  http://www.pricescan.com
Procter & Gamble
  http://www.pg.com
Prufrock Press
  http://www.prufrock.com

Contemporary Business 2000

Louis E. Boone

Ernest G. Cleverdon Chair of Business and Management

University of South Alabama

David L. Kurtz

The R. A. and Vivian Young Chair of Business Administration

University of Arkansas

SOUTH-WESTERN

™

THOMSON LEARNING

Australia • Canada • Mexico • Singapore • Spain
United Kingdom • United States

SOUTH-WESTERN
™
THOMSON LEARNING

Contemporary Business 2000
Louis E. Boone, David L. Kurtz

Publisher:
Mike Roche

Acquisitions Editor:
John Weimeister

Developmental Editor:
Tracy L. Morse

Market Strategist:
Lisé Johnson

Project Editor:
Kathryn Stewart

Art Director:
Bill Brammer

Project Manager:
Darryl King

Project Management:
Elm Street Publishing Services, Inc.

Printer:
RR Donnelley & Sons
Willard, OH

For permission to use material from
this text or product, contact us by
Tel (800) 730-2214
Fax (800) 730-2215
http://www.thomsonrights.com

Library of Congress Catalog Card
Number: 99-74473

ISBN: 0-03-026256-9

To the 2.9 million students around the globe who began their business studies using *Contemporary Business* in their classes, making it the most widely used business text in history

and

to the Text and Academic Authors Association, which awarded *Contemporary Business* the first William Holmes McGuffey Award for Excellence and Longevity.

Dear Fellow Introduction to Business Instructor:

The first course I ever taught was introduction to business. As a neophyte instructor, I found it to be a fascinating, often frustrating, and constantly challenging assignment. Questions were posed from every business discipline, causing me to often respond with, "I don't know the answer to that question, but I'll find out and let you know." It was a memorable experience, one that played an important role in my decision to remain in academia.

In fact, I liked everything about teaching the class except the textbook. It was one of the market leaders at the time, filled with lists and definitions, and appeared to cover the subject of business adequately. What it lacked was the heartbeat of business—its vitality, its ability to solve societal and ethical problems, its importance in determining the standards of living we enjoy, and its choices of meaningful careers in which each student could achieve personal and professional goals and contribute to society. I hoped that one day I would have the opportunity to create a book that would convey this to college students.

Years later I was fortunate enough to form a writing partnership with my talented friend and colleague Dave Kurtz. The result was *Contemporary Business*—a book that vaulted to market leadership within months of its first release and has never wavered from its position as the unquestioned leader in the introduction to business market. At last count, 2.9 million students have begun their academic careers in business using *Contemporary Business* as their text. We are also especially proud that our U.S. and Canadian colleagues who write college textbooks recently honored our text with the McGuffey Award as one of the best business texts written in the second half of the twentieth century.

Dave and I understood and practiced the concept of continuous improvement years before it became a management buzzword. We are convinced that leadership of any industry is accompanied by a commitment to make each new edition better than its predecessor. Rather than resting on the laurels of the success of the current edition, we practice the philosophy embodied in the statement, "First, we will be best. Then we will be first."

I have taught sections of these courses on a regular basis, using the classes as real-life laboratories in which to experiment with new chapter materials, new teaching approaches, and new assignments. Although Dave and I visit dozens of classrooms on college campuses throughout the nation and use market research feedback, check-off questions on mail questionnaires can never replace the immediacy of conducting classroom sessions and receiving feedback firsthand from students and other instructors.

The result of this classroom experimentation, combined with feedback from students and introduction to business professors at numerous other colleges and universities, is *Contemporary Business 2000*. The new edition responds to these requests:

- "We want more applied, 'how-to' practical information in the text—information our students can use immediately."
- "We want more emphasis on entrepreneurship as a viable career alternative for students."
- "We want more coverage of technology—and especially the Internet—as a key ingredient in America's success in the twenty-first century."
- "We want more emphasis on business ethics and social responsibility in the new edition."
- "We want more experiential, hands-on assignments for our students."

As Dave and I will demonstrate in the following pages, we have worked hard to serve our instructor and student customers by addressing these requests. We are confident that you will be delighted with the results.

Sincerely,

Louis E. Boone

NEW 2000 UPDATE

Throughout the publication history of *Contemporary Business*, currency has been a goal and driving force. But never before has the pace of change in business been so rapid. Innovative use of technology and the Internet, a new spirit of entrepreneurship, the critical importance of relationships with customers, and emphasis on ethics and social responsibility have revolutionized the face of business today. These changes have made it all the more important to offer students and instructors a current business text—more current than the standard three-year revision cycle allowed. The result is *Contemporary Business 2000*. This new edition, containing all new vignettes, new Web sites, and many new boxed features, allows instructors to involve their students in the excitement of today's business world. Here's just a sample of late-breaking events covered in *Contemporary Business 2000*.

- ▼ The ongoing legal battles of Microsoft and the U.S. Department of Justice

- ▼ The comeback of the VW Beetle

- ▼ The cyberspace merger between America Online and Netscape

- ▼ The fallout from the NBA basketball strike

- ▼ The frenzy over the Furby animated toy

- ▼ The successes of Sun Microsystems and its unconventional CEO, Scott McNealy

Contemporary Business 2000 is also offered in a new paperback format, making it more affordable for students. The book's retail price is approximately 35 percent less than the previous edition and well below the price of competing hardcover texts. An instructor's addendum is available on the *Contemporary Business* Web site that describes the differences between the hardcover and paperback.

New for *Contemporary Business 2000* is more Web support. Southwestern is committed to assisting adopters with Web-based education materials. Framework includes reading assignments, goals, self-quizzes, Web-based activities, and more. Your local Southwestern sales representative can provide you with more details.

CONTENT FEATURES

Emphasizing Technology

Contemporary Business 2000 embraces technology, inte-grating it into every aspect of the text and package, resulting in the most innovative, exciting product on the market.

A high-tech student preface includes a glossary of helpful Internet terms and information on getting online, search engines, private data sources, and the text's personal World Wide Web directory.

In-depth, practical coverage of technology begins early in Chapter 1 and is thoroughly integrated throughout succeeding chapters and in the package components.

The Boone & Kurtz Home Page connects the new-technology theme to the real world. Completely integrated with the text, the Web site plugs students into additional sources of information and teaches them how to use the Internet as a business tool. The site links professors to valuable teaching resources and educational information. A new *Web Instructor's Manual* also helps professors navigate through the site and use it effectively within their courses.

Web addresses are included in each chapter to give students access to additional online information. Each chapter opens with a vignette detailing a success story involving technology. Online addresses are included for the company. "Nothing but Net" end-of-chapter application exercises plug students into the Internet, sharpening student surfing skills.

Part V, "Managing Technology and Information," features a stronger emphasis on high-tech issues. The part now contains two technology chapters—one on businesses' use of technology and the Internet to remain competitive and one on the use of technology to manage information.

Chapter 17, "Using Technology and the Internet to Succeed in Business," gives students practical insight into how to most effectively use the new and emerging technology to get ahead in the business world. It describes how applications of new technologies are important keys in maintaining a competitive edge and taking advantage of global opportunities. Applications of new technologies ranging from e-mail, smart cards, and product design to human resource education and training and continuous improvement are treated here. Likely breakthroughs in new technology are also explored.

The second half of the chapter is devoted to one of the most important current technologies: the Internet. The roles played by the Internet in electronic commerce, research, job searches, and online selling are examined. In addition, the chapter looks at costs and sources of revenue from Web sites, describes the typical Internet user, and examines the problems facing business executives who rely heavily on the Internet in their organizations. Finally, the chapter discusses organizational communications through intranets and their advantages and disadvantages.

Practical applications featured in the chapter include:

▼ "Tips for Creating a Successful Web Site"

▼ "Navigating the Net"

▼ "Choosing the Right Internet Service Provider"

Appendix A, "Your Career in Business," is tied directly to the *Discovering Your Business Career* CD-ROM, as well as to relevant material on the Boone & Kurtz Web site.

Emphasizing Entrepreneurship as a Career Alternative

Contemporary Business 2000 has an underlying entrepreneurial theme, encouraging students to look at issues from the perspective of business owners. It also corrects the unbalanced emphasis on giant business found in most business texts by analyzing entrepreneurship as an alternative for business students. The text offers practical information to future entrepreneurs, equipping them with facts needed to succeed in business.

Entrepreneurship is introduced within the first pages of the text and then completely integrated throughout. Each chapter contains checklists, questionnaires, and self-scoring exercises, re-emphasizing key chapter concepts and helping students learn about their personal business style and their aptitude for entrepreneurial success. These practical, interactive features help students create a toolbox of information about themselves as future business executives. Most of the opening vignettes focus on entrepreneurs who have successfully applied emerging technologies to business challenges.

Part II, "Starting and Growing Your Business," gives students practical insight into two of the most critical stages of business ownership: starting and growing a new venture. The section explores strategies for avoiding the high failure rate associated with many new businesses.

Chapter 6, "Starting Your Own Business: The Entrepreneurship Alternative," is written from a "you" approach, placing students in the role of new entrepreneurs. It is completely integrated with the *Discovering Your Business Career* CD-ROM.

Emphasizing Business Success in the Relationship Era

Chapter 7, "Strategies for Business Success in the Relationship Era," combines material on business strategy and planning with a major new emphasis on relationships. Features include strategic alliances (in production, finance, human resources, communications/information systems,

marketing, international business), the relationship era in marketing, and roles played by databases.

Emphasizing Ethics and Social Responsibility

Continuing to lead the market in its emphasis on ethics and social responsibility, the new edition introduces the topics even earlier—within the first few pages of Chapter 1 and in Chapter 2, "Achieving Business Success by Demonstrating Ethical Behavior and Social Responsibility."

Ethical and societal issues are often best understood when various positions are examined through class discussions and assignments. A feature of each chapter is "Solving an Ethical Controversy," in which students are presented with an experiential activity related to an ethical dilemma. Some of the topics included are:

▼ Should Intel Be Baking Your Cookies Online?

▼ Should the Public Tolerate Child Labor?

▼ Should Whistle-Blowers Get a Share of the Money They Help Recover?

▼ Are Big Oil Companies Merging into Dangerous Giants?

▼ Should Company Auditors Act as Bean Counters or Gumshoes?

▼ Should Hedge Funds Expect to Be Rescued from Their Greed?

Greater Emphasis on the Applied, "How-To" Approach

The most common student suggestion for improving all business textbooks can be summed up as, "Give more real-life information that I can apply." In *Contemporary Business 2000,* we do just that.

▼ The new edition integrates a "how-to" approach in text chapters from chapter titles to new boxes and exercises.

▼ End-of-chapter Experiential Exercises and "Nothing but Net" Internet assignments move the student beyond memorization and focus on applications.

▼ "Business Tool Kits" placed throughout the text give students "how to" information they can apply immediately.

PEDAGOGY AND TEXT FEATURES

Focus on Essential Concepts

Each chapter includes 10 essential business terms, further emphasizing the most important concepts. Additional business terms are also highlighted in each chapter.

Skill Development Emphasis

SCANS (Secretary's Committee on Acquiring Necessary Skills) features continue to be integrated throughout the text, such as critical-thinking questions that are included at the end of boxed features in every chapter, career development exercises, video cases, Internet-based exercises, and practical tips. These features give students real-world feedback on specific topics.

Business Hall of Fame and Shame Boxes

"Business Hall of Fame" and "Business Hall of Shame" boxes in each chapter detail actual business strategies that scored big as well as those that flopped. Presented in a punchy, eye-grabbing format, these stories give students an inside view of the results of actual business decisions.

Solving an Ethical Controversy

"Solving an Ethical Controversy" boxes in each chapter highlight real-world ethics and diversity issues. These topics are excellent springboards for classroom discussions and debates.

Business Tool Kits

"Business Tool Kits," included in each chapter, equip students with hands-on business insight and information they can apply to their lives immediately. Topics include tips for creating a Web page, choosing software, and creating an electronic resumé.

Business Directory

The student-friendly "Business Directory" defines key terms in a highlighted box on the two-page spread in which they appear.

End-of-Chapter Activities

New end-of-chapter material includes Ten Business Terms You Need to Know, Questions for Critical Thinking, an Experiential Exercise, and Nothing but Net Web exercises.

Continuing Video Case

Hard Candy, the novel nail-polish company that shook up established industry giants, is the subject of the new Continuing Video Case that appears at the end of the text. Separate sections of the case focus on issues related to each section of *Contemporary Business 2000,* implementing new topics as students learn them. The accompanying video is also divided into parts corresponding to the text and the written case.

Custom-Made Modules

Three new four-color, 32-page modules are available separately or packaged with the text at **No Additional Charge.**

Hispanic Americans in Contemporary Business
Reflecting the increasing number of U.S. Hispanic-owned companies as well as burgeoning opportunities with Mexico-based operations, this new module highlights contributions from Hispanic American business owners and executives, features leadership success stories, discusses the impact of NAFTA, and explores demographic, employment trends and career opportunities for Hispanic Americans.

African Americans in Contemporary Business
Mirroring a more diverse marketplace and the increasingly powerful African American segment, this module explores opportunities for African Americans in today's business environment, analyzes employment trends and demographics, features African American business role models and leaders, details entrepreneurial success stories, and spotlights contributions by African Americans as they relate to U.S. business. This module was extensively reviewed by leading African American academic and business leaders.

In-Class Exercises and Technology Module
Tied directly to our increased technology emphasis, this innovative resource features detailed and practical tips for effectively navigating the Internet, includes interactive Web exercises, and focuses on the fast-paced advances in technology and their impact on business in the 21st century. In

addition, this interactive supplement features tips and ideas for cross-functional teaching, as well as additional exercises and cases focusing on issues affecting actual companies, enabling students to apply chapter concepts to hands-on, real-world exercises and experiences.

THE MOST COMPLETE AND INNOVATIVE SUPPORT PACKAGE ON THE MARKET

Boone & Kurtz's *Contemporary Business 2000* continues to lead the market with the most innovative, technologically advanced package and packaging available. Completely integrated with the text, this high-tech resource illustrates key chapter concepts with hands-on, real-world applications for students. For instructors and students, it provides support unrivaled by any package on the market. Along with cutting-edge, new features, the package also includes some of Boone & Kurtz's precedent-setting originals, revised and updated for this new edition.

NEW! Web Instructor's Manual

Created to help instructors integrate the Boone and Kurtz Web site into the course with ease, the *Web Instructor's Manual* includes detailed outlines of the Web site, instructor's teaching notes for company profiles and exercises, and detailed notes on how the instructor can integrate the Web site into the course.

Video Package

The innovative video package for the new edition integrates the book's technology, entrepreneurship, and societal themes. The videos take a problem-resolution approach, with problems and solutions featuring concepts directly from the text chapters. Custom produced for *Contemporary Business,* the videos were created in partnership with successful, well-known companies, giving students a real-world perspective of how business professionals meet the challenges of the new century. Here are some examples of the 21 end-of-chapter videos included in the new edition:

▼ Chapter 3, "Economic Challenges Facing Global and Domestic Business"
Video Case: Fossil—Watching the World
This designer and manufacturer of popular fashion watches has offices in both the United States and Hong Kong. The video examines new business challenges facing the firm now that Hong Kong has returned to Chinese authority.

▼ Chapter 6, "Starting Your Own Business: The Entrepreneurship Alternative"
Video Case: Two Artists or Two Executives? The Story of Two Women Boxing
Linda Finell and Julie Cohn launched this successful venture 14 years ago. Two Women Boxing creates one-of-a-kind handmade boxes, picture frames, and hand-decorated photo albums. In addition to their product lines, the two entrepreneurs are now licensing their designs to such outlets as Neiman Marcus, Silvestry, and Chronicle Books.

▼ Chapter 7, "Strategies for Business Success in the Relationship Era"
Video Case: Paradigm Simulation—Reality Bites in the Virtual World
Paradigm has enjoyed a mutually beneficial relationship with Nintendo, creating innovative 3-D software games such as *Pilot Wings*. In addition, Paradigm is now creating games for the Sega Channel and will soon launch its first game on the Internet.

▼ Chapter 17, "Using Technology and the Internet to Succeed in Business"
Video Case: A Search Engine Named Yahoo!
This inspiring video details how two young college students turned their hobby—collecting fun sites on the World Wide Web for their friends—into a tremendously successful business. That was April 1994. Today the two founders are multimillionaires, and their business is now a global Internet service.

▼ Chapter 18, "Using Technology to Manage Information"
Video Case: Human Genome Sciences
Founded by Harvard genetics guru William Hazeltine and a group of private investors, HGS is engaged in the competitive race to match components of DNA in the scientific quest to identify all of the genes in the human body. The team is striving to identify human genes and their functions. Collected database information will eventually be sold to pharmaceutical companies to help them develop treatments and cures for life-threatening diseases and illnesses.

Continuing Case Supported by Video

The new edition of *Contemporary Business* includes a special continuing video case featuring Hard Candy. Hard Candy, a cosmetics company for Generation Xers, was born when pre-med student Dineh Mohajer began mixing unusual nail polish colors in the bathtub of her apartment and selling them to trendy boutiques on Melrose Avenue. The firm's transition from a sole proprietorship to a full-blown (and highly profitable) global corporation is traced in the memorable video segments. This exciting video can be packaged with each copy of *Contemporary Business 2000*.

The continuing case feature is a new component of this new edition that students won't quickly forget.

Boone & Kurtz Web Site

The Internet Business Connection is located at www. contemporarybusiness.com. This online resource connects professors and students alike with countless business resources. From this site, users can select the home page for any chapter or appendix in the textbook. The individual home pages contain company profiles, exercises, numerous resources associated with chapter topics, links to other sites related to chapter material, interactive simulations for applicable chapters, and much more. For example, the "Reading Room" allows users to access online business magazines such as *Fortune, Forbes, Money,* and *BusinessWeek,* as well as the business sections of many regional and national newspapers such as *USA Today,* the *New York Times*, and the *Washington Post*. Additional online exercises help students review chapter materials. In addition, instructors are linked to teaching resources, bibliographies of articles related to text material, and ideas on how to use the Internet in class. The *Internet Business Connection* also includes a comprehensive Web page for Appendix A, "Your Career in Business." Students see links to over 30 sites where current business jobs are posted or sites for researching and locating employers. They also receive helpful tips to maximize their job searches, including specific search words or phrases they can use for each of the seven business careers explored in the *Discovering Your Business Career* CD-ROM. For faster browsing and convenience, users can download the *Internet Business Connection* and install it on their computers. It runs in a special Web browser inside the *Discovering Your Business Career* program.

Internet Guide

An *Internet Guide* can be packaged with each copy of *Contemporary Business 2000*. All students can be Internet savvy with this invaluable guide to the Internet. The handbook's Internet terms and popular Web site addresses—over 160 ranging from the American Stock Exchange to the White House—get students where they want to go on the Internet.

Discovering Your Business Career CD-ROM

This interactive, multimedia program guides students as they explore business career options such as accounting, corporate financial management, information systems, risk management/insurance, retail bank management, sales, and store operations. Offering practical insight, the CD-ROM walks students through the entire career-search process, from assessing their compatibility with different careers and determining the depth of their interest to effectively implementing a job search strategy. The program helps students pinpoint careers of interest based on their answers to questions about their preferences for specific job activities, as well as personal priorities about work environment, compensation, and advancement. For each potential business career, students can view a custom video summarizing what their responses reveal about how well the career suits them and also receive a three- to six-page report detailing how each of their responses on relevant items may or may not indicate a good career match. Students can access comprehensive profiles on a variety of careers, including videos, audios, and extensive text detailing skill requirements, compensation trends, and actual job responsibilities. A list of associations, directories, and other relevant information is also included. This CD-ROM can be packaged with each copy of *Contemporary Business 2000*.

PowerPoint/CD-ROM Media Active Presentation Software

Classroom lectures and discussions come to life with this innovative presentation tool. Extremely instructor friendly and organized by chapter, this program enables instructors to custom design their own multimedia classroom presentations, using overhead transparencies, figures, tables, and graphs from the text, as well as completely new material from outside sources.

Transparency Acetates, Masters, and Teaching Notes

Over 200 full-color overhead transparency acetates are available. The acetates—many of which are new to this edition—illustrate key concepts discussed in the text. Most are original, but some are copies of key text figures and graphs. Transparency masters highlight actual figures and graphics found in the text. A complete set of teaching notes is included for both the acetates and masters.

Distance-Learning Instructor's Resource System

In a continuing effort to provide the most innovative package system available and to meet the changing needs of this growing marketplace, Boone & Kurtz have provided Web-based materials for instructor's use in distance-learning courses. In addition, a *Distance-Learning Study Guide* is available for students.

Media Instructor's Manual

This separate media manual features easy-to-use guidelines to help instructors incorporate the videos and PowerPoint presentation software into lectures and classroom presentations. It also includes important information for each of the videos, including teaching objectives, a list of chapter concepts illustrated in the video, outlines of the videos, answers to in-text video case questions, and experiential exercises.

Instructor's Resource Manual

Instructors have asked for a more user-friendly resource, and we have delivered the most innovative *IRM* on the market. The *IRM* includes the following helpful sections for each chapter:

▼ Changes in this new edition

▼ New coverage

▼ New terms

▼ New features

▼ Internet addresses included in each chapter

▼ Annotated learning goals

▼ Lecture outline

▼ Ten business terms you need to know

▼ Other important business terms

▼ Answers to Business Hall of Fame/Shame critical-thinking questions

▼ Answers to review questions

▼ Answers to end-of-chapter critical-thinking questions

▼ Experiential exercises

▼ Teaching notes for Nothing but Net

▼ Answers to video case questions

▼ Additional teaching resources for chapter
  experiential exercises
  supplemental cases
  guest speaker suggestions

Supplemental Modules

Three separate supplemental modules—Quality, Diversity, and Business Math—provide additional coverage for instructors who want to further emphasize any of these areas.

Assessment Module

This unique module enables instructors to assess student mastery of text concepts. Organized by chapter, it includes chapter learning goals, review questions, essay questions, and unique assessment exercises.

Electronic Instructor's Manual and Study Guide

This innovative instructor resource system includes electronic versions of the *Instructor's Resource Manual* and *Study Guide* on disk.

Test Bank

Double- and triple-checked for accuracy, the revised and updated *Test Bank* includes 3,500-plus questions, more than half of which are new. Questions are keyed to chapter learning goals, text page number, and type of question (knowledge or application). Questions include multiple choice, true/false, and a short essay for each learning goal. Mini-cases with multiple-choice questions and critical-thinking questions emphasize the importance of the concepts presented in each chapter.

Computerized Test Bank

Available in IBM-, Windows-, and Macintosh-compatible formats, the computerized version of the printed *Test Bank* enables instructors to preview and edit test questions, as well as add their own. The tests and answer keys can also be printed in scrambled formats.

RequesTest and Online Testing Service

Dryden Press makes test planning quicker and easier than ever with this program. Instructors can order test masters by question number and criteria over a toll-free telephone number. Test masters will be mailed or faxed within 48 hours. Dryden can provide instructors with software to install their own online testing program, allowing tests to be administered over a network or on individual terminals. This program offers instructors greater flexibility and convenience in grading and storing test results.

Web-Based Stock Market Game

The fastest path to learning is through hands-on application, which is exactly what students gain when they use this interactive new program. Through this Web-based supplement, students create a stock portfolio they manage and manipulate throughout the course.

Computer Simulation

The computerized game *Chopsticks*—created by Professors Eugene J. Calvasina, James Leon Barton, Jr., Ava Honan, Richard Calvasina, and Gerald Calvasina of Auburn University—challenges students to develop and experience the business concepts presented in the text and to utilize frequently used business decision-making tools. The game is accompanied by an *Instructor's Manual* that provides instructions and student worksheets. The simulation game is available on disk for use with IBM and IBM-compatible PCs.

Web-Based Computer Cases Supplement and the B&K Business Disk

These innovative Web-based components are designed to assist instructors who want to include analytical problems as homework assignments or to use such tools as personal computers in the basic business course. The computer cases supplement includes three to five business problems and solutions per chapter, focusing on key concepts. The business disk includes complete programs for the computer cases and the solutions to each case.

Web-Based Portfolio of Business Papers

Available on the Boone & Kurtz Web site, this comprehensive collection of actual business documents helps students understand the variety of official papers required in a modern business organization. Teaching notes are included.

Study Guide

An invaluable tool for helping students master business concepts, the *Study Guide* includes a brief outline, experiential exercises, a self-quiz, cases, short-answer questions, and crossword puzzles for each chapter. Solutions appear at the end of the guide.

Alternate Study Guide

Answers and solutions are not included with this alternate guide. When required as a part of the course materials, instructors can assign homework from the guide, using it to evaluate how well students are retaining concepts covered in the text.

Computerized Self-Study

A computerized Windows-based study aid for students. Modified Test Questions are organized by chapter and give students the opportunity to test their knowledge of key chapter concepts. Available on a 3½-inch disk or as a downloadable file on the *Contemporary Business* Web site.

ACKNOWLEDGMENTS

The authors gratefully acknowledge the following colleagues who reviewed all or part of the new edition and its ancillaries. We are extremely grateful for the insightful comments of the following people:

Alison Adderly-Pitman
Brevard Community College

David Alexander
Angelo State University

Charles Armstrong
Kansas City Kansas Community College

Charles Beem
Bucks County Community College

Carol Bibly
Triton College

Steven E. Bradley
Austin Community College

Willie Caldwell
Houston Community College

Edward Friese
Okaloosa–Walton Community College

Stephen W. Griffin
Tarrant County Community College South

Annette L. Halpin
Beaver College

Nathan Himelstein
Essex County College

Eva M. Hyatt
Appalachian State University

Gloria M. Jackson
San Antonio College

Steven R. Jennings
Highland Community College

Bill Kindsfather
Tarrant County Community College

Charles C. Kitzmiller
Indian River Community College

Fay D. Lamphear
San Antonio College

Paul Londrigan
Mott Community College

James McKee
Champlain College

Linda S. Munilla
Georgia Southern University

George Otto
Truman College

Alton Parish
Tarrant County Community College

William E. Rice
California State University, Fresno

Catherine A. Sanders
San Antonio College

Gene Schneider
Austin Community College

Nora Jo Sherman
Houston Community College

James B. Stull
San Jose State University

The authors also would like to recognize the professors and individuals who participated in keeping the *Contemporary Business 2000* supplements an outstanding and innovative package:

Hal Babson
Columbia College

Jeanne Bartimus
University of South Alabama

Kathy Daruty
Los Angeles Pierce College

Douglas Hearth
University of Arkansas

Eric Sandburg
President of Career Design Software

Amit Shah
Frostburg State University

Raymond Shea
Monroe Community College

Bill Syvertsen
California State University, Fresno

Gary Thomas
Anne Arundel Community College

Roland D. Tollefson
Anne Arundel Community College

David Wiley
Anne Arundel Community College

The authors also would like to respectfully acknowledge and thank the professors and ancillary authors whose comments and efforts helped create a successful revision of the eighth edition of *Contemporary Business:*

James Leon Barton, Jr.
Auburn University

Robb Bay
Community College of Southern Nevada

Eugene J. Calvasina
Auburn University

Gerald Calvasina
Auburn University

Richard Calvasina
Auburn University

Rowland Chidomere
Winston–Salem State University

Robert Cox
Salt Lake Community College

Norman B. Cregger
Central Michigan University

Kathy Daruty
Los Angeles Pierce College

Jodson Faurer
Metropolitan State College at Denver

Blane Franckowiak
Tarrant County Community College

Milton Glisson
North Carolina AT&T State University

Don Gordon
Illinois Central College

Stephen Griffin
Tarrant County Community College, South

Douglas Heeter
Ferris State University

Paul Hegele
Elgin Community College

Tom Heslin
Indiana University, Bloomington

Ava Honan
Auburn University

Vince Howe
University of North Carolina, Wilmington

Geraldine Jolly
Barton College

Dave Jones
La Salle University

Kenneth Lacho
University of New Orleans

Thomas Lloyd
Westmoreland County Community College

Martin St. John
Westmoreland County Community College

Eric Sandburg
President of Career Design Software

Joan Sepic-Mizis
St. Louis Community College at Florissant Valley

Raymond Shea
Monroe Community College

E. George Stook
Anne Arundel Community College

Roland Tollefson
Anne Arundel Community College

Sheb True
Loyola Marymount University

Robert Ulbrich
Parkland College

W. J. Walters
Central Piedmont Community College

Tom Wiener
Iowa Central Community College

David Wiley
Anne Arundel Community College

Joyce Wood
Northern Virginia Community College

Gregory Worosz
Schoolcraft College

Last, but not least, we want to thank our good friends at our publisher and Elm Street Publishing Services. Our acquisitions editor, John Weimeister, our developmental editors Tracy Morse and Karen Hill, our project editors, Kathryn Stewart and Phyllis Crittenden, our designers, Bill Brammer and Melissa Morgan, our production managers, Darryl King and Barb Lange, our market strategist, Lisé Johnson, and our photo and permissions editors, Jan Huskisson and Abby Westapher, have been most supportive and helpful. We are especially appreciative of the numerous contributions of our research associates Jeanne Bartimus, Marlene Bellamy, Douglas Hearth, Carolyn Lawrence, and Nancy Moudry.

Business has gone high tech. And never has there been a more exciting time to study this dynamic field. New technological advances have created an industry of endless opportunities—limited only by business's creativity.

Contemporary Business 2000 is wired for the new high-tech advances, integrating a technology emphasis throughout the text and package. Internet, CD-ROM, multimedia—these are some of the new tools you'll use to learn about traditional and emerging business concepts and issues.

For example, *Contemporary Business* has an especially strong connection to the Internet, including its own student-friendly site on the World Wide Web. The Internet offers countless exciting opportunities for businesses. With Boone & Kurtz, you'll learn firsthand what an effective business tool this—and other high-tech applications—can be, as well as experience the intricacies of effectively navigating the Information Superhighway.

The Internet is literally the application of all business principles:

1. The Internet is all about advertising—from advertising goods and services to creating an image through the home page.

2. Many companies gather data over the Net—practical information about competitors, suppliers, and customers. Many firms include questionnaires on the Web for data gathering.

3. Companies can test-market new ideas or product and service enhancements over the Net.

4. Home pages often include e-mail addresses or links, offering another avenue for helpful information.

5. Legal issues are reviewed on the Web. Issues such as product liability or the Communications Decency Act may be investigated. Instructions are also offered for reporting consumer complaints to various agencies.

6. The Web opens the door to international companies or governments. It is especially insightful to investigate legal issues regarding business in other countries.

7. Many special-interest groups have home pages. Ethical and environmental issues, for example, are frequently reviewed.

8. The Web is a unique channel for distributing goods, services, and information.

9. Direct access to producers by consumers may significantly change the nature of selling.

10. The Internet may be used for job searches. Many companies post job openings on their home pages. Several online job search services are also available.

As you can see, the applications are endless. And *Contemporary Business* is your direct link to business innovation. Visit the Boone & Kurtz *Contemporary Business* Web site at www.contemporarybusiness.com

STUDENT GLOSSARY OF HELPFUL INTERNET TERMS

Bookmark. A browser feature that places selected URLs in a file for quick access.

FTP (file transfer protocol). A tool for transferring files between computers on the Internet, often used to transfer large files of statistics, scientific experiments, and full-text articles.

Gopher. A text-based Internet search engine developed by the University of Minnesota that provides subject access to files on the Internet through menus.

Home page. The first hypertext document displayed on a Web server. A home page is often a menu page with information about the developer and links to other sites.

HTML (hypertext markup language). Code in which World Wide Web documents are written and presented.

HTTP (hypertext transfer protocol). The protocol used by the Web to transfer hypertext documents.

Hypertext. Documents that contain links to other documents, allowing the user to jump from one document to another.

URL (uniform resource locator). Web address that gives the exact location of an Internet resource.

Usenet. A group of systems that enable users to exchange discussion on specific topics through news groups.

World Wide Web (WWW). A hypertext-based system for finding and accessing Internet resources.

HOW TO GET ONLINE

Learning to use the basic tools will make surfing the Net more profitable and enjoyable for you. Each site has an address, which is referred to as a URL, or uniform resource locator. Using a URL is a fast way to get to a site. Setting a bookmark makes getting to a useful site at a later time even faster. If you do not know a specific URL, you can use any of the various search engines (for example, Yahoo!, Infoseek) to conduct a search.

YOUR PERSONAL WORLD WIDE WEB DIRECTORY

Contemporary Business provides students with an in-text World Wide Web directory. Online addresses are included in the textbook for companies and organizations highlighted in extended-text examples, boxed features, opening vignettes, and photo illustrations. Company Web addresses are also listed alphabetically inside the front and back cover pages of the text.

For additional resources, you can reach the Boone & Kurtz *Contemporary Business 2000* home page at www.contemporarybusiness.com

Because the Internet is a constantly changing network of networks, no subject list is ever complete. Each day addresses change, new sites are added, and old sites disappear without warning. Following is a list of search engines and private data sources that provide links to numerous other sites relating to business and businesses themselves.

SEARCH ENGINES

If you don't know the URL for a site, you can use various search engines to perform a keyword search by developer or subject name. As with everything on the Internet, these search tools change daily, and new features are constantly added. The following search engines can help track down online information on a variety of topics:

Search.com (http://search.cnet.com/). This site gives access to more than 300 specialized indexes and search engines.

Metacrawler (http://www.go2net.com/). This tool submits your query to nine of the top search engines at once.

Altavista (http://www.altavista.com/). This service provides one of the largest search indexes on the Web.

Infoseek Guide (http://infoseek.go.com/). This search index includes millions of listings.

Yahoo! (http://www.yahoo.com/). This useful search index divides reference sites into logical groups.

GOVERNMENT DATA SOURCES

U.S. Census Bureau (http://www.census.gov/). This site provides free access to many census data reports and tables, including international census data from many countries.

U.S. Bureau of Economic Analysis (http://www. bea.doc.gov/). This site provides national and regional economic information, including gross domestic product by industry.

U.S. Bureau of Labor Statistics (http://stats.bls.gov/). This site gives access to the BLS survey of consumer expenditures, a report on how U.S. consumers spend their money.

Department of Commerce/STAT-USA (http://www. stat-usa.gov/). This subscription-based site provides access to hundreds of government-sponsored business research studies and other statistical information.

FedWorld (http://www.fedworld.gov/). This site provides a central access point for locating government information. If you need data from the government but don't know where to find it, start here.

PRIVATE DATA SOURCES

Knight-Ridder Information (http://www.dialog.com/). This extensive database provides access to thousands of business research reports, industry and competitor information, and trade publications. Although it proves itself an excellent source for secondary data of all types, a typical search can be expensive. Knowledge Index, available on CompuServe, provides access to many of the Dialog databases for an hourly fee.

Lexis-Nexis (http://www.lexis-nexis.com/). This is another extensive—and expensive—database of directories, trade publications, and legal information.

HOW TO CITE INTERNET SITES

If you plan to use the information you have retrieved from the Internet in a research paper or in homework assignments, you need to know how to cite the information correctly. Although formats are still being developed for the various types of electronic documents, new editions of most of the accepted style manuals have a section on citing electronic resources, including the Internet.

The University of Michigan's Internet Public Library has a list with links to recommend electronic information citation guides such as
http://www.uvm.edu/~ncrane/estyles,
which offers citation formats based on the forthcoming book by Li & Crane, *Electronic Styles: An Expanded Guide to Citing Information,* according to the Modern Language Association styles.

DISCOVERING YOUR BUSINESS CAREER CD-ROM

Included free with each new copy of *Contemporary Business 2000* by The Dryden Press is a CD-ROM titled *Discovering Your Business Career.* It contains three programs, each of which may be used in conjunction with your course: *Discovering Your Business Career, Career Design,* and *The Internet Business Connection.* Detailed instructions for these programs are included at the end of each part in the text.

Discovering Your Business Career

Discovering Your Business Career helps you learn about and assess your compatibility with seven major business career areas. They were selected not only to represent the diversity of business opportunities available but also for the number of jobs in these fields.

- ▼ Accounting
- ▼ Corporate financial management
- ▼ Information systems
- ▼ Risk management/insurance
- ▼ Retail bank management
- ▼ Sales
- ▼ Retailing

For each career, you receive broad guidance and practical advice on everything from clarifying the depth of your interest in that career to preparing and implementing an effective job search strategy.

The first step in your business career exploration is to complete a questionnaire. You rate a broad range of business-related job activities from "very appealing" to "very unappealing." For example, you rate the statement "Making financial forecasts about your company's profits based on the assumptions you have made about how many units will sell, the selling price, and the expenses." You also rate yourself according to ten broad career factors that measure your priorities about your work environment, compensation, and progression in your career. The program then matches your responses to specific business careers and indicates which may be of greatest interest to you. For each business career, you can view a personal video summarizing what your responses reveal about how well the career suits you. You can also read a detailed three- to six-page report explaining how each of your responses from the questionnaire may or may not indicate a good career match.

In addition to learning about your compatibility with different business careers, you can access complete career profiles about each of them. Through videos, multimedia slide shows, and extensive textual content, the profiles present a detailed, up-to-date picture of actual job responsibilities, career paths, and skills required to be successful. You also learn about current compensation levels and associations, directories, books, and other information about the business career of interest. To ensure that the profiles realistically reflect current job opportunities in the business field, researchers conducted extensive interviews with top professionals and executives from prominent companies, including AT&T, IBM, General Mills, Procter & Gamble, Ford, General Electric, Hewlett-Packard, McDonald's, Reebok, Bank of America, NationsBank, Chase Manhat-tan, Bankers Trust, Citicorp, PricewaterhouseCoopers, Arthur Andersen, KPMG Peat Marwick, JC Penney, Kimberly-Clark, USX Corp., John Hancock Mutual Life Insurance, Allstate Insurance, Neiman Marcus, Wal-Mart, Sears, and Kmart.

Career Design

Also included on the *Discovering Your Business Career* CD-ROM is a free copy of *Career Design,* the landmark career planning software program that is based on the work of John Crystal, the major contributor to the most widely read career book of all time, *What Color Is Your Parachute?,* by Richard N. Bolles. *Career Design* has received worldwide coverage and praise from both the business and computer press, including *BusinessWeek, Fortune, The Wall Street Journal, The Financial Times, The London Times, PC Magazine,* and *PC Computing.* The student version provides general career exercises and resources in the following sections:

- ▼ Interests—Uncovering your business interests.
- ▼ Skills—Identifying the strengths you offer a prospective employer, including technical skills achieved through formal training and education and nontechnical skills, such as leadership and communications.
- ▼ Entrepreneurship Quotient—Completing a questionnaire to determine your level of entrepreneurial orientation.
- ▼ Personal Finance—Finding out how much earning power you need. In a spreadsheet, you enter anticipated expenses upon graduation under such categories as "Insurance," "Loan Payments," and "Rent/Mortgage." The program then applies current federal and state income taxes to calculate the gross income before taxes that you must earn to maintain your chosen lifestyle.
- ▼ People Preferences—Identifying the types of people with whom you want to spend your time, including at work.
- ▼ Work Preferences—Identifying your preferred working conditions.
- ▼ Business Adventure—Writing about how you want to spend two weeks in a business-related activity, such as "Learning about the step-by-step process a bank or other lender follows in approving a multimillion-dollar loan for a large real estate project."
- ▼ *BusinessWeek* Article—Writing an imaginary article about what you or your future company has accomplished in the business world.

▼ Setting Goals—Clarifying your personal and professional direction by setting specific goals.

▼ Resumés—Preparing a resumé after comparing and choosing from one of three available formats: chronological, functional, or results oriented.

Internet Business Connection

The *Internet Business Connection* is the name of the Web site for *Contemporary Business*. From this site, you can select any chapter or appendix in the textbook. Each chapter and appendix has its own home page from which you can access company profiles, exercises, and resources associated with chapter topics. On the home page for the *Contemporary Business* Web site, you can select the "Reading Room" to access online business magazines such as *Fortune*, *Forbes*, *Money*, and *BusinessWeek*, as well as the business sections of many regional and national newspapers such as *USA Today*, the *New York Times*, the *Washington Post*, the *San Francisco Chronicle*, and more.

For faster browsing and convenience, you can download the *Internet Business Connection* and install it on your computer. It runs in a special Web browser inside the *Discovering Your Business Career* program.

The *Internet Business Connection* also includes a comprehensive Web page for Appendix A, "Your Career in Business." You have links to over 30 sites where current business jobs are posted or sites for researching and locating employers. You also receive helpful tips to maximize your job search, including specific search words or phrases you can use for each of the seven business careers in *Discovering Your Business Career*.

Together, *Discovering Your Business Career*, *Career Design*, and the *Internet Business Connection* offer an invaluable enhancement to your business course by enabling you to connect what you learn with exciting career opportunities in the field. Through the *Internet Business Connection*, you can seamlessly integrate the vast resources of the Web with what is covered in your course to bring the world of business closer to you.

Louis E. Boone, Ph.D., holds the Ernest G. Cleverdon Chair of Business and Management and serves as coordinator of the introductory business course at the University of South Alabama. He formerly chaired the Division of Management and Marketing at the University of Tulsa and has taught courses in management and marketing in Australia, Greece, and the United Kingdom.

Following recent major heart surgery, Dr. Boone has returned to active teaching, writing, and research. In addition to authoring numerous marketing and business texts and computer simulation games, he recently published *Quotable Business,* Second Edition (Random House, 1999). His current research focuses on event and sports management and marketing. Dr. Boone's research has been published in such journals as the *Journal of Business Strategy, International Journal of Management, Journal of Business Research, Sports Marketing Quarterly, Journal of Psychology, Business Horizons, Journal of Marketing,* and the *Journal of Business of the University of Chicago.* He is the 1999 recipient of the Outstanding Scholar Award from the University of South Alabama and is listed in *Who's Who in America.*

David L. Kurtz, Ph.D., is the R. A. and Vivian Young Chair of Business Administration at the University of Arkansas. He was formerly the head of the Department of Marketing and Transportation at Arkansas.

Prior to returning to his graduate alma mater, Dr. Kurtz held the Thomas F. Gleed Chair in Business and Finance at Seattle University. Earlier, he was department head at Eastern Michigan University. Dr. Kurtz has also taught at Davis & Elkins College and Australia's Monash University.

Dr. Kurtz has authored or co-authored 36 books and more than 120 articles, cases, and papers. His work has appeared in such publications as the *Journal of Business Research, Journal of Marketing, Journal of Retailing,* and numerous other well-known journals.

Dr. Kurtz has been active in many professional organizations including president of the Western Marketing Educator's Association, and vice-presidentships in the Academy of Marketing Science and the Southwestern Marketing Association. He is also the recipient of an honorary doctorate in pedagogy from Davis & Elkins College.

Contents in Brief

Contents

PART I
**BUSINESS IN A GLOBAL
ENVIRONMENT 2**

Opening Vignette
**Prospecting Online with
Levi Strauss**
Business Hall of Fame
**(Under) Feeding the Furby
Frenzy**
Business Hall of Shame
**Cinemex: Struggling to
Revamp Mexico's Movie
Industry**
Solving an Ethical
Controversy
**Should Intel Be Baking Your
Cookies Online?**
Business Tool Kits
- **Avoiding the Fine-Print
  Trap**
- **How to Line Up a Great
  Summer Job**
- **How to Develop Critical
  Thinking and Creative
  Skills**

Opening Vignette
**Microsoft: Predator or
Gentle Giant?**
Business Hall of Fame
**Bill Strickland: Modeling the
Future with Education,
Training, and Hope**
Business Hall of Shame
**Trouble Keeping an Eye on
the Ball at adidas**
Solving an Ethical
Controversy
**Should Whistle-Blowers Get
a Share of the Money They
Help Recover?**
Business Tool Kits
- **Before You Accept a Job,
  Review Your New
  Employer's Code of Ethics**
- **Protect Your Privacy**
- **How to Be Charitable
  without Being a Chump**

Opening Vignette
UPS Improves Worker Skills and Its Workforce
Business Hall of Fame
Dole Japan Delivers Fresh Produce and Lower Prices
Business Hall of Shame
Global Market and Local Greed Give OPEC Gas Pains
Solving an Ethical Controversy
The Growing Gap between Rich and Poor
Business Tool Kits
• **Using the Laws of Supply and Demand to Purchase a Car**
• **How to Survive an IRS Tax Audit**

Opening Vignette
Beetlemania Revisited
Business Hall of Fame
Asian Sources: Changing the Way Asia Does Business
Business Hall of Shame
Overseas Child Labor Clouds U.S. Business Ventures
Solving an Ethical Controversy
Who Favors China the Most?
Business Tool Kit
• **When in Rome . . . or Riyadh**

Business Tool Kits
- **Resources for Aspiring Entrepreneurs**
- **Think You Might Be a Good Entrepreneur?**

Opening Vignette
Time Warner Builds a Web of Customer Relationships
Business Hall of Fame
Just For Feet Makes Fun with "Shoppertainment"
Business Hall of Shame
Steering Car-Rental Companies toward Improved Customer Service
Solving an Ethical Controversy
Corporate Espionage or Pure Competition?
Business Tool Kits
- **Starting a Business? Have a Plan!**
- **How Good Are Your Networking Skills?**

PART III
MANAGEMENT: EMPOWERING PEOPLE TO ACHIEVE BUSINESS OBJECTIVES 262

Opening Vignette
Fun in the Sun with Scott McNealy of Sun Microsystems
Business Hall of Fame
Changing "Made in Germany" to "Made by Mercedes"
Business Hall of Shame
From Admired to Acquired: The Five-Year Plan at Rubbermaid

Opening Vignette
Streamline Offers a Lifestyle Solution
Business Hall of Fame
Bath & Body Works Cleans Up
Business Hall of Shame
Good-Bye to Good Buys at Woolworth
Solving an Ethical Controversy
Should Large Retail Chains Try to Censor the Music They Sell?
Business Tool Kit
- **How to Find the Right Independent Sales Rep for Your Product**
- **Attracting Customers on a Shoestring Promotion Budget**

Opening Vignette
Joe Boxer Sells Skivvies with "Guerrilla" Marketing
Business Hall of Fame
NASCAR Drives Home Sales for Sponsors
Business Hall of Shame
Swept Away
Solving an Ethical Controversy
Can Internet Marketers Ethically Solicit Business from Children?

Business Tool Kits
• **Choosing Software**
• **Are You Ready for 2000?**

Opening Vignette
**Finding Financial Figures for
Johnson & Johnson Online**
Business Hall of Fame
**Need an Accountant?
Consider a Virtual One**
Business Hall of Shame
**The Perils of Taking on Too
Much Debt**
**Solving an Ethical
Controversy**
**Should Company Auditors
Act as Bean Counters or
Gumshoes?**
Business Tool Kit
• **Remedies for the
Cash-Flow Blues**

**PART VI
MANAGING FINANCIAL
RESOURCES 654**

**Opening Vignette
Uncle Sam Levels the
Playing Field with EDGAR**
**Business Hall of Fame
Small Firms Can Bank on
New Services**
**Business Hall of Shame
ATM Fees—Making People
Pay to Use Their Own
Money**
**Solving an Ethical
Controversy**
**Are Credit Card Issuers
Responsible for Rising
Consumer Debt?**
Business Tool Kit
• **Tips from Two Venture
Capitalists**

Opening Vignette
Online Trading—Just a Keystroke Away with Ameritrade
Business Hall of Fame
Turning Customers into Investors
Business Hall of Shame
A Web of Deception
Solving an Ethical Controversy
Should Hedge Funds Expect to Be Rescued from Their Greed?
Business Tool Kit
• Selecting a Stockbroker

PART I | Business in a Global Environment

chapter 1

Business: Blending People, Technology, and Ethical Behavior

LEARNING GOALS

1. Describe the private enterprise system and the roles played by individual businesses, competitors, and entrepreneurs within the system.

2. Explain how the historical development of the U.S. economy continues to influence contemporary business.

3. Outline the challenges and opportunities that businesses face in the relationship era.

4. Describe how technology is changing the way businesses operate and compete.

5. Relate the importance of quality and customer satisfaction in efforts to create value for customers.

6. Explain how individual businesses and entire nations compete in the global marketplace.

7. Describe how changes in the workforce are leading to a new employer-employee partnership.

8. Identify the skills that managers need to lead businesses in the new century.

9. Explain how ethics and social responsibility affect business decision making.

10. List four reasons for studying business.

LEVISTRAUSS.CO

myski.co

DOCKERS.com

(pick one) [USA | CANADA | E

Prin

mercedes
—benz

Prospecting Online with Levi Strauss

Who would have believed it? A company with a brand name as well recognized as Coca-Cola, McDonald's, and Nike is scrambling to retain its customer base. The firm, born in 1873 in the aftermath of the California gold rush, enjoyed decades of sales and profit growth until the 1990s. By 2000, its share of the men's jeans market had dropped to 25 percent, down from 48 percent just ten years earlier.

A big factor in Levi's current problems is the vastly increased competition in the apparel industry. In addition to competing directly with brands like Lee and Wrangler, and trendier names like Old

Navy, The Gap, Tommy Hilfiger, and Calvin Klein, many of the retail stores that carry Levi's have begun offering their own branded merchandise. JCPenney, a leading Levi's outlet, also offers its Arizona brand, and Sears sells its Canyon River jeans.

Another problem resulted from a brand image that many teenagers and young adults considered stodgy. Teens don't want to wear the same brands their parents wear. And Levi's has been criticized for being slow to spot the fashion changes, illustrated by its failure to lead the recent trends for super wide-bottom slacks and cargo pants, which have large pockets on the thighs.

Although Levi's management hasn't pushed the panic button, changes are already under way. To hold down production costs, company-owned manufacturing plants in the United States and Canada are being replaced by lower-cost contract manufacturing companies in Mexico, Central America, and South America. Levi's has also offset some of its sales slippage in jeans by focusing on its successful line of casual and dress pants, Dockers and Slates. These brands have matched up well with the growing popularity of casual attire work policies where khakis—not jeans—can pull double duty at work and play.

To compensate for slippage on the product, focus on successful products

One major move by this longtime king of the denim empire is into the world of electronic commerce. How do you sell jeans on the Net, you ask? When you visit www.levi.com or www.dockers.com, you can get fashion tips from virtual salespeople, mix and match clothes in your own virtual dressing room, and even order your jeans in custom-tailored styles.

.WWW

www.levi.com
www.dockers.com

Once Levi's decided to focus more strongly on consumer needs, the jump to the Web was a logical move. Web sites offer more items than department stores can stock. They also make possible the much ballyhooed notion of mass customization—a production method that allows goods and services to be produced in lot sizes of just one or a few at a time. Want a new pair of jeans guaranteed to fit? Levi's Personal Pair jeans are sewn to your body measurements. These data are entered into a computer, which selects from 500 design choices to find your best match. The order travels via modem to the nearest Levi's factory where the jeans are made by altering standard Levi's patterns. For about $65, a customer can get a pair of personalized jeans in just three weeks.

This new focus on matching products to individual needs is reflected in the firm's advertising. In one recent print ad, a young dreadlock-sporting youth wears dark, baggy Levi's while standing on a sidewalk with a sign that reads, "Conformity Breeds Mediocrity."

To develop lasting relationships with its legions of customers in 76 markets worldwide, Levi's employs powerful tools like computer databases to provide continuing links in the form of direct-mail advertising and other promotions. For example, a recent mailing contained activity books and contest information to young customers to promote brand awareness and increase store traffic.[1]

CHAPTER OVERVIEW

The U.S. economy is riding high on a tremendous wave of prosperity that is likely to continue well into the 21st century. A quick glance at a few statistics illustrates the many benefits that these good times bring in people's lives:

▼ Over 95 percent of U.S. workers are employed, the highest level in almost a quarter-century.

▼ Total output of goods and services is growing at approximately 4 percent a year.

▼ Despite lost sales in markets affected by the Asian economic recession, U.S. corporate profits are up, and the millions of people who own shares of stock—either directly or through their retirement accounts—are beaming as the stock market continues to hit new all-time highs.

▼ In addition to balancing the federal budget, Congress has promised tax cuts of more than $135 billion over the next 5 years.

▼ High employment, low inflation, and growth in wages have combined to boost consumer confidence to record levels. As a result, sales of homes and durable goods are marching upward at a steady pace.

▼ Businesses are investing in new technology and improvements in order to take advantage of new consumer markets.

▼ In surveys, 90 percent of executives express confidence about the continued growth of the U.S. economy and nearly one-third plan to add workers to their labor pools.[2]

How does all this optimism affect you? Simply put, the economic growth opens doors of opportunity for those who are prepared to put ideas into action. Dineh Mohajer has provided another example of today's entrepreneurial spirit. A 23-year-old college student, Mohajer invested $200 to make and sell wildly colored nail polishes with funky names. Today, just 3 years later, her company, Hard Candy, is confronting cosmetics industry giants like Revlon and L'Oreal. And trusted names like Levi's are seeking new ways to compete through online sales and global manufacturing.

In the new century, everyone is facing new challenges posed by the technological revolution that is changing the rules of business. The combined power of telecommunications and computer technology is creating inexpensive, global networks that transfer voice messages, text, graphics, and data within seconds. These sophisticated technologies create new types of products, and they also demand new approaches to marketing existing products. Technology is also speeding the rate of change in the business world, where new discoveries rapidly outdate inventions created just months before.

Promotional messages, like the one from Merrill Lynch shown in Figure 1.1, illustrate the impact of technology on people's daily lives. Merrill Lynch, America's leading stock brokerage firm, is increasingly a global company. The ad shows how technology permits it to quickly locate information from experts in different countries and use it to advise its clients.

Innovative technologies are also globalizing today's business world. Businesses can now easily manufacture, buy, and sell across national borders. You can order a Big Mac or a Coke almost anywhere in the world, while Japanese and Korean companies manufacture most of the consumer electronics products sold in the United States. Mercedes Benz manufactures sport utility vehicles in Alabama, while many General Motors automobiles are assembled in Canada.

Figure 1.1 **Technology: Responding to Market Needs, Creating Global Markets, and Making Existing Products Obsolete**

HEAR THE ONE ABOUT THE OIL ANALYST FROM KARACHI WHO TALKED TO THE ECONOMIST IN SINGAPORE WHO CALLED THE FINANCIAL CONSULTANT IN AKRON TO ANSWER A QUESTION FOR SOMEONE IN SCHENECTADY?

Questions, questions, questions. In this interconnected world, there's certainly no shortage of them. How does X affect Y? How does Y affect Z? How does Z affect me?

Demystifying it all is something we're pretty good at. (So good, in fact, that our research team is ranked #1 by The Wall Street Journal *® and* Institutional Investor*.) With over 700 analysts, strategists and economists in 27 countries, we're constantly batting ideas and information around—from one person to the next, from one time zone to the next.*

The best of these ideas are downloaded daily to a Merrill Lynch Financial Consultant, who can align our global insights with your personal needs and goals.

Now, if you'll excuse us, Bangkok's on the line. **Merrill Lynch**

ml.com

This rapidly changing business landscape compels businesspeople to react quickly to shifts in consumer tastes and other market dynamics. Success requires creativity, split-second decision making, and innovative vision. Whether you decide to start your own business, as David Marcheschi did, work for a small, family-run business, or sign on with a large international corporation, your achievements will depend on your ability to maintain the constant pace of change in today's world.

Contemporary Business explores the strategies that allow companies to compete in today's interactive marketplace and the skills that you will need to turn ideas into action for your own career success. This chapter sets the stage for the entire text by defining *business* and revealing its role in society. The chapter's discussion illustrates how the private enterprise system encourages competition and innovation while preserving important individual freedoms. Later sections highlight the most important challenges and opportunities businesspeople will face in the 21st century.

WHAT IS BUSINESS?

What image comes to your mind when you hear the word *business?* Some people think of their jobs, others think of the merchants they patronize as consumers, and still others think of the millions of firms that make up the world's economy. This broad, all-inclusive term can be applied to many kinds of enterprises. Businesses provide the bulk of employment opportunities as well as the products that people enjoy.

Business consists of all profit-seeking activities and enterprises that provide goods and services necessary to an economic system. Some businesses produce tangible goods, such as automobiles, breakfast cereals, and computer chips; others provide services, such as insurance, music concerts, car rentals, and lodging.

Business drives the economic pulse of a nation. It provides the means through which standards of living improve. The United States leads the world in national, per-capita output of goods and services.

At the heart of every business endeavor is an exchange between a buyer and seller. A buyer recognizes a need for a good or service and trades money with a seller in order to obtain that product. The seller participates in the process in hopes of gaining profits—a critical ingredient in accomplishing the goals necessary to maintain constant improvement in standards of living.

Profits represent rewards for businesspeople who take the risks involved in blending people, technology, and information to create and market want-satisfying goods and services. In contrast, accountants think of profits as the difference between a firm's revenues and the expenses it incurs in generating these revenues. More generally, however, profits serve as *incentives* for people to start companies, expand them, and provide consistently high-quality, competitive goods and services.

Consider, for example, the role of profits in the U.S. newspaper industry over the past few years. In the early 1990s, newspapers saw their income from advertising drop as advertisers cut back because of the recession. At the same time, newspaper operating costs, especially the cost of paper, rose. The combination of dropping income and rising costs squeezed profits, and many newspapers were forced to make some tough decisions. The *Los Angeles Times,* for example, laid off 3,000 workers. Other newspapers simply closed up shop. By the mid-1990s, however, operating costs, including newsprint prices, had dropped again; as the economy improved, advertising revenues also increased. Once again, newspapers began to enjoy rising profits, allowing many of them to implement expansion plans. The *Los Angeles Times* is hiring again, and it has expanded its news coverage. Other papers have resumed marketing and community-relations programs they axed to cut costs in the early 1990s.[3]

Although the quest for profits is a central focus of business, businesspeople also recognize social and ethical responsibilities. To succeed in the long run, companies must deal responsibly with employees, customers, suppliers, competitors, government, and the general public.

Not-for-Profit Organizations

What characteristics link the National Football League, the U.S. Postal Service, the American Heart Association, and C-SPAN? For one, they are all classified as **not-for-profit organizations,** business-like establishments that have primary objectives other than returning profits to their owners. These organizations play important roles in society by placing public service above profits. Not-for-profit organizations operate in both the private and public sectors. Private-sector not-for-profits include museums, libraries, business associations, charitable and religious organiza-

Business Directory

business the profit-seeking activities of those engaged in purchasing or selling goods and services to satisfy society's needs and wants.

profits the financial rewards received by a businessperson for taking the risks involved in creating and marketing want-satisfying goods and services.

BUSINESS TOOL KIT

Avoiding the Fine-Print Trap

> "What the large print giveth, the small print taketh away."
> Anonymous

Big traps can lurk in tiny type. Whether you're leasing an apartment, renting a car, buying an airline ticket, or applying for a credit card, don't ignore the fine print at the end of the contract.

Contracts include more fine print than ever these days, because consumer protection laws are forcing companies to disclose progressively more details of their offers. You are bound to all terms of a contract you accept (except for blatantly illegal provisions) whether or not you read or understand these statements.

Worse, you don't even have to sign anything to be obligated. The first time you use a credit card, for example, you indicate agreement with all of the company's terms.

Before accepting any deal, therefore, pay attention to the details. Make sure you understand the full story about penalties and fees. Know what will happen if you pay a bill late, miss your airline flight, or fail to cancel a subscription when a free trial period ends. If you order anything online, be especially diligent about scrolling down until you come to the long legal documents at the end of the order form.

Most importantly, if you don't understand a clause or agreement, ask!

tions, and most colleges and universities. Additionally, government agencies, political parties, and labor unions are classified as not-for-profit organizations.

A good example of a not-for-profit organization is New York's Metropolitan Museum of Art. Like profit-seeking businesses, the Met must generate funds to cover its operating costs. Revenues come from a number of sources, including individual donations, memberships, government grants, gift-shop sales, and special fund-raising drives. The organization also uses such business techniques as advertising. The ad in Figure 1.2 describes a special exhibition of Florentine paintings. Such events provide added value to museum members and attract thousands of occasional and first-time visitors, who may become members.

Since 1970, the number of not-for-profit organizations in the United States has grown four times faster than the national economy as a whole. Excluding U.S. government agencies, 1.2 million not-for-profit organizations control more than $1 trillion in assets. These operations employ more people than the entire federal government and all 50 state governments combined.[4] Additionally, millions of volunteers work for them in unpaid positions. Not-for-profits find funding both

Figure 1.2 **The Metropolitan Museum of Art: A Private-Sector, Not-for-Profit Organization**

from private sources, including donations, and from government sources. They are commonly exempt from federal, state, and local taxes.

Although they focus on goals other than generating profits, staff members of not-for-profit organizations face many of the same challenges as those of profit-seeking businesses. For example, Andrea Rich, president of the Los Angeles County Museum of Art, runs her organization like a business. She must find ways to serve and satisfy the museum's customer groups, including visitors, taxpayers, and donors. Rich must also manage a large and diverse staff of employees, ensuring that everyone from the custodians to the art curators efficiently performs her or his job. In addition, Rich manages a $30 million annual operating budget.[5]

As in the world of profit-seeking businesses, the new century will bring changes to the not-for-profit sector. An aging and increasingly diverse population may require not-for-profits to find new ways of delivering services. Government funding is also declining, a trend that will force not-for-profit executives to develop new cost-cutting methods. Faced with increased competition for limited funding, not-for-profits will also have to boost their effectiveness at marketing and fund-raising. These changes and others will require leaders with strong business skills and experience.[6] Therefore, many concepts discussed in this book will apply to not-for-profit organizations as much as to profit-oriented firms.

Factors of Production

Capitalism, like other economic systems, requires certain inputs for effective operation. Economists use the term **factors of production** to refer to the four basic inputs: natural resources, capital, human resources, and entrepreneurship. Table 1.1 identifies each of these inputs and the type of payment received by firms and individuals who supply them.

Natural resources include all productive inputs that are useful in their natural states, including agricultural land, building sites, forests, and mineral deposits. For example, Hershey uses 700,000 quarts of milk a day in producing almost 33 million chocolate Kisses. The milk used in Hershey's Kisses alone keeps 50,000 dairy cows "employed" full-time.[7] Natural resources are the basic inputs required in any economic system.

Human resources are also critical inputs in all economic systems. Human resources include anyone who works, from the chief executive officer of a huge corporation to a self-employed auto mechanic. This category encompasses both the physical labor and the intellectual inputs contributed by workers. Figure 1.3 emphasizes the importance of human resources to organizational goals by depicting a concert hall in which different musical instruments indicate the various skills of the members of the orchestra.

Capital, another key resource, includes technology, tools, information, and physical facilities. These elements frequently determine whether a fledgling computer firm, like Compaq or Microsoft, becomes an industry leader or remains a small operation. *Technology* is a broad term that refers to such machinery and equipment as production lines, telecommunications, and basic inventions. Information, frequently improved by techno-

logical innovations, is another critical success factor, since both managers and operating employees require accurate, timely information for effective performance of their assigned tasks.

Money is necessary to acquire, maintain, and upgrade a firm's capital. These funds may come from investments by company owners, profits, or loans extended by others. Money then goes to work building factories; purchasing raw materials and component parts; and hiring, training, and compensating workers. People and firms that supply capital receive factor payments in the form of interest.

Entrepreneurship is the willingness to take risks to create and operate a business. An entrepreneur is someone who sees a potentially profitable opportunity and then devises a plan to earn those profits. One such entrepreneur created the wildly popular Furby discussed in the Business Hall of Fame box. Some entrepreneurs set up new companies and ventures; others, such as the executives at Levi Strauss, revitalize established firms by keeping the organizations open to market changes and expansion possibilities.

To see how one firm utilizes the factors of production, consider Arnold Lund's new business, Windflower Corp. Lund sees opportunity in wind. He's spent 20 years developing the technology for a turbine-powered windmill that can produce 10,000 kilowatt hours of energy a year, about the same amount used in an average home. Lund's employees and technicians (human resources) are already working on the first unit, priced at $10,000, for a home in Palm Springs, California. In addition to wind, Lund's firm will require steel and other natural resources to build the units. Lund sold another firm he owned in the early 1990s to raise the $2 million in capital he needed to develop and market the windmills. Although Lund is confident that his windmills will serve a market need, he admits that he is taking an enormous risk, just as other entrepreneurs before him have done.[8]

The next section looks at how the factors of production are allocated and used within the private enterprise system, the economic system in which U.S. businesses currently operate.

Table 1.1 Factors of Production and Their Factor Payments

Factor of Production	Corresponding Factor Payment
Natural resources	Rent
Human resources	Wages
Capital	Interest
Entrepreneurship	Profits

THE PRIVATE ENTERPRISE SYSTEM

No business operates in a vacuum. All operate within a larger economic system that determines how goods and services are produced, distributed, and consumed in a society. The type of economic system employed in a society also determines patterns of resource use. Some economic systems, such as communism, feature strict controls on business ownership, profits, and resource allocations, in order to accomplish government goals.

In the United States, businesses function within the **private enterprise system,** an economic system that rewards businesses for their ability to perceive and serve the needs and demands of consumers. A private enterprise system minimizes government interference in economic activity. Businesses that are adept at satisfying customers gain access to necessary factors of production and earn profits.

Another name for the private enterprise system is *capitalism.* Adam Smith, often identified as the father of capitalism, first described the concept in his book *The Wealth of Nations,* published in 1776. Smith believed that an economy is best regulated by the invisible hand of **competition,** the battle among businesses for consumer acceptance. Smith felt that competition among companies would assure consumers of receiving the best possible products and prices, because less efficient producers would gradually be driven from the marketplace.

This invisible hand concept is a basic premise of the private enterprise system. In the United States, competition regulates economic life. To compete successfully, each firm must find a basis for **competitive differentiation,** the unique combination of organizational abilities and approaches that sets a company apart from competitors in the minds of consumers. Eyeglasses retailer Lenscrafters has differentiated itself from competitors through service. Customers get their new lenses in about an hour. Wal-Mart uses discount pricing on brand name products to attract customers.

Businesses operating in a private enterprise system face a critical task of keeping up with changing marketplace conditions. Firms that fail to adjust to shifts in consumer preferences or ignore the actions of competitors leave themselves open to failure. Consider, for example, Dydee Diaper. For 60 years, the Boston-based company laundered and delivered cloth baby diapers to parents. As women entered the workforce in increasing numbers, however, busy working mothers began to prefer the convenience of disposable diapers. Dydee started losing customers to giant manufacturers like Kimberly-Clark and Procter & Gamble. Dydee, one of the last diaper services left in the country, recently filed for bankruptcy.[9]

Throughout this book, the discussion will focus on the tools and methods that 21st-century businesses will apply to compete and differentiate their goods and services. Each Business Hall of Fame feature explains how an individual businessperson or company has developed successful strategies for competitive differentiation. The book will also discuss many of the ways in which market changes will affect business and the free enterprise system in the years ahead. Chapter 3 focuses specifically on how businesses function within other economic systems.

| Figure 1.3 | Human Resources: A Critical Factor of Production |

Business Directory

factors of production basic inputs into the private enterprise system, including natural resources, human resources, capital, and entrepreneurship.

private enterprise system an economic system that rewards firms based on how well they match and counter the offerings of competitors to serve the needs and demands of customers.

competition the battle among businesses vying for consumer acceptance.

BUSINESS HALL OF FAME

(Under)feeding the Furby Frenzy

From Barbie dolls to teddy bears. From yo-yos to Cabbage Patch kids to Tickle Me Elmo. The steady stream of toys, gadgets, and gizmos keeps the toy industry on its toes—ready for innovation and growth. A recent toy fad is Furby, an interactive bundle of fuzz that speaks its own language (Fur-

bish); learns English phrases; and responds to touch, sound, and light. Creator Dave Hampton got his inspiration from the Tamagotchi virtual pet (the LED companion that dies without constant and intense nurturing). "That's not a pet," said Hampton. "I want to make something that kids can hold . . . something that would seem alive." He has delivered on that vision. Furbies sing, dance, laugh, snore, make rude noises, and talk to other Furbies. They even teach kids to talk Furbish.

Along with the demanding little furballs came *Furby frenzy*—whipped up by the media, which began hyping Furbies right after February's Toy Fair '98. Even though the toy wouldn't be ready until fall, shoppers were interested. In fact, parents were clamoring for Furbies before the toys were even shipped from the factory.

Some accuse Hasbro, Furby's manufacturer, of using fad marketing to create the intense demand. If true, Hasbro wouldn't be the first to use such tactics. Look at De Beers and others in the diamond cartel who deliberately produce fewer diamonds than they can just to drive prices up and make diamonds more desirable. Even the Ty toy company removes various models

of Beanie Babies from the market before demand is satisfied—supporting the belief among consumers that the inexpensively made stuffed animals have some kind of collector's value. Of course, retailers are perfectly happy with manufacturers who undersupply because they won't be stuck with unsold inventory.

However, Hasbro's Tiger Electronics unit (which makes Furbies) claims that it did not conspire to tighten supply. Tiger's publicist says that before September, retailers had ordered 1 million Furbies. Confident that the toy would sell well, Tiger manufactured 1.3 million. But, in fact, after all the media coverage had stirred up so much interest, closer to 5 million Furbies could have been sold. So people got caught up in Furby frenzy.

Whether the scarcity was intentional or unplanned, Hasbro wasn't making Furbies fast enough, and stores were running out of them before parents could say "kah a-tay" (Furbish for "I'm hungry"). That's when millions of shoppers attempted to find Furbies on the Internet. Some Web sites didn't even try to sell the few Furbies that were still available. eToys (www.etoys.com) gave away one Furby a day until Christmas. You just

Basic Rights within the Private Enterprise System

Certain rights critical to the operation of capitalism are available to citizens living in a private enterprise economy. These include the rights to private property, profits, freedom of choice, and competition, as shown in Figure 1.4.

The right to **private property** is the most basic freedom under the private enterprise system. Every participant enjoys the right to own, use, buy, sell, and bequeath most forms of property, including land, buildings, machinery, equipment, inventions, and various intangible kinds of property.

The private enterprise system also guarantees business owners the right to all profits (after taxes) earned by their

activities. Although a business is not assured of earning a profit, its owner is legally and ethically entitled to any income it generates in excess of costs.

Freedom of choice means that a private enterprise system relies on the potential for citizens to choose their own employment, purchases, and investments. They can change jobs, negotiate wages, join labor unions, and choose among many different brands of goods and services. People living in the capitalist nations of North America, Europe, and other parts of the world are so accustomed to this freedom of choice that they sometimes forget its importance. A private enterprise economy maximizes individual human welfare and happiness by providing alternatives. Other economic systems sometimes limit freedom of choice in order to accomplish government goals, such as increasing industrial production.

had to visit the site every day and sign up. Of course eToys was glad to have you pick up one or two other gift items while you were visiting. Some Web sites sold Furbies for as long as they had the toys in stock. For FAO Schwarz (www.faoschwarz.com), the stock of Furbies lasted until the day after Thanksgiving. Still other sites were inundated. At the Toys R Us site (www.toysrus.com), shoppers got only "network error" messages when they tried to search for Furbies.

Several sites did have Furbies a few days after Thanksgiving. At eGift (www.egift.com), for example, you could order a Furby for $147.95—some five times the suggested retail price. And before Christmas was over, some sites were charging as much as ten times the suggested $29.99. Even so, people were more than willing to pay for a guaranteed delivery and especially for a chance to avoid the malls and their Furby-frantic crowds.

The question is, does Furby mania "have legs"? Can the cuddly toy retain its popularity? Some owners are finding out that Furbies can be demanding and loud. On the *Today* show, Katie Couric asked Tiger publicist Marc Rosenberg, "Can you get them to shut up now?" Whether Furby joins the ranks of teddy bears, yo-yos, and Barbies depends on the toy's ability to turn fad appeal into the sticking power of a toy classic. Will Furby keep its hot-toy

status, or is Hasbro's hit already a has-been? The competition is stiff.

Challenging Furby are Anakin Skywalker and Darth Maul, along with other *Star Wars* prequel characters. Also in the running are the Furby-inspired interactive toys that not only say a few words but can even hold a conversation. Mattel's entry is the CD-ROM that lets kids drive and crash Hot Wheel cars on a Hollywood sound set. The World Wrestling Federation modeled the Stone Cold Steve Austin figure after its famous wrestler to protect a kid's room as a talking security system, with light sensor and motion detector. Not the least of Furby's challengers are PBS's Teletubbies (Tinky Winky, Dipsy, Laa-Laa, and Po), which are interactive and which sport an LED "tummy screen" in three colors.

So how will Furby fare? Can Furby fend off the *Star Wars* prequel characters and the Teletubbies? True, Furbies have flashier coats. Hasbro has spruced them up, giving them patterned fur in giraffe, tiger, Dalmatian, and snow leopard prints. But will new fur be enough?

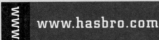
www.hasbro.com

Sources: Isabel Forgang, Kevin Penton, and Bill Hutchinson, "Furby Rules High-Tech Toys," *New York Daily News Online*, accessed at www.mostnewyork.com, February 9, 1999; Jason Ocampo, "Furby, PC Games Fuel Hasbro Profits," *Gamenews*, accessed at www.gamecenter, February 9, 1999; Benjamin Fulford, "Don't Flood the Market," *Forbes*, December 28, 1998, p. 56; "Flyin' Furbies," *People*, December 14, 1998, p. 88; Elizabeth Weise, "Stalking Rare Furbies in Web Wilderness," *USA Today*, Section D, December 2, 1998, p. 1; John Cloud, "How the Furby Flies," *Time*, November 30, 1998, pp. 84–85.

The private enterprise system also permits fair competition by allowing the public to set rules for competitive activity. For this reason, the U.S. government has passed laws to prohibit "cutthroat" competition—excessively aggressive competitive practices designed to eliminate competition. It also has established ground rules that outlaw price discrimination, fraud in financial markets, and deceptive advertising and packaging.

The Entrepreneurship Alternative

One of the options offered by capitalism is entrepreneurship. Indeed, entrepreneurial spirit beats at the heart of private enterprise. Individuals who recognize marketplace opportunities are free to use their capital, time, and talents to

pursue those opportunities for profit. The willingness of individuals to start new ventures drives economic growth and keeps pressure on existing companies to continue to satisfy customers. If no one were willing to take economic risks, the private enterprise system wouldn't exist.

The Small Business Administration reveals the extent to which entrepreneurial spirit fuels growth in the U.S. economy. Approximately 1,200 new businesses are launched every day, most of them small. The 20 million U.S. small businesses, defined by the SBA as companies with less than $6 million in net worth, create most of the new jobs in the country and are expected to grow at twice the rate of larger companies over the next 15 years. If U.S. small business constituted a separate economy, it would rank as the world's third-largest economic entity, behind the United States as a whole and Japan.[10]

Entrepreneurs often find novel ways to use natural resources, technology, and other factors of production. Englishman Simon Pratt, for example, saw an opportunity in a new invention, a tough, polyurethane bag that could be filled with liquids and still float. Since many countries suffer from severe fresh water shortages, he saw an opportunity to use tug boats to pull the bags full of fresh water to thirsty people around the world. Pratt figures that his firm, Aquarius Water Trading & Transportation Co., will accept nearly $40 million worth of contracts to deliver water over the next few years.[11]

Entrepreneurship is also important to existing companies in a private enterprise system. Large firms often encourage entrepreneurial thinking, hoping to benefit from enhanced flexibility, improved innovation, and new market opportunities. Take Bix Norman, a top-notch salesperson for office furniture manufacturer Herman Miller. He felt that his company was missing an opportunity by building only high-priced, premium-quality office furniture, ignoring the grow-ing number of small, home-based businesses. Norman convinced top management to let him start a new subsidiary that would manufacture a line of well-made but low-priced furniture. Last year, thanks to Norman's entrepreneurial insight and drive, the new division sold $200 million worth of desks, chairs, and bookcases.[12]

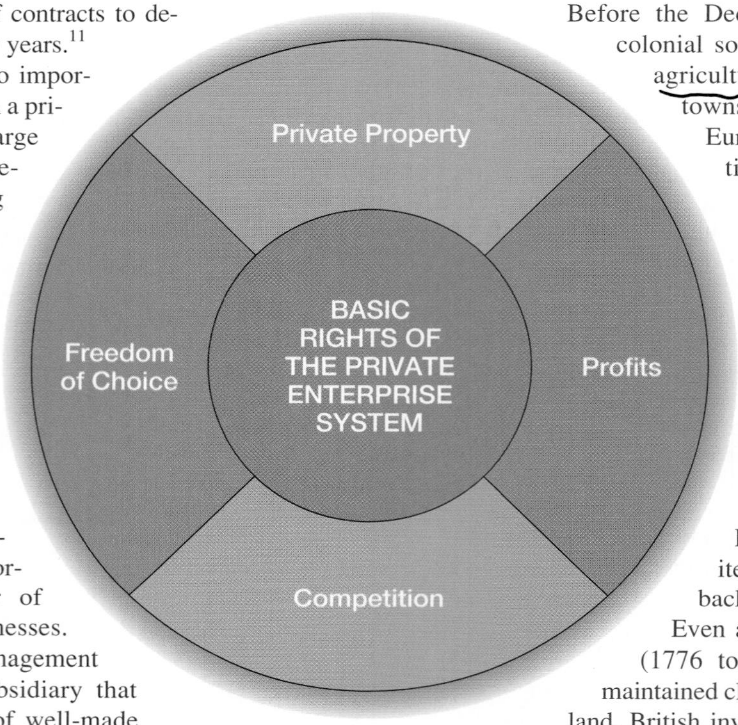

As the next section will explain, entrepreneurs have played a vital role in the history of American business. They have helped to create new industries, developed successful new methods for conducting business, and improved the U.S. standing in global competition. Chapter 6 returns to the subject of entrepreneurship and Chapter 5 looks more closely at how individuals start their own businesses.

SIX ERAS IN THE HISTORY OF BUSINESS

In nearly four centuries since the first European settlements appeared on the North American continent, amazing changes have occurred in the size, focus, goals, and use of technology by U.S. businesses. As Table 1.2 indicates, U.S. business history is divided into six distinct time periods:

(1) the colonial period, (2) the industrial revolution, (3) the age of industrial entrepreneurs, (4) the production era, (5) the marketing era, and (6) today's relationship era. The next sections describe how events in each of these time periods have influenced U.S. business practices.

The Colonial Period

Before the Declaration of Independence, colonial society emphasized rural and agricultural production. Colonial towns were small compared to European cities, and they functioned as marketplaces for farmers, craftsmen, doctors, bankers, and lawyers. The economic focus of the nation centered on rural areas, since prosperity depended on the output of farms and plantations. The success or failure of crops influenced every aspect of the economy.

Colonists depended on England for manufactured items as well as financial backing for infant industries. Even after the Revolutionary War (1776 to 1783), the United States maintained close economic ties with England. British investors continued to provide much of the financing for developing the U.S. business system, and this financial influence continued well into the 19th century.

Figure 1.4 **Basic Rights within a Private Enterprise System**

The Industrial Revolution

The industrial revolution began in England around 1750, moving business operations from an emphasis on independent, skilled workers who specialized in building products one by one to a factory system that mass-produced items by bringing together large numbers of semiskilled workers. The factories profited from the savings created by large-scale production, bolstered by increasing support from machines over time. As businesses grew, they could often purchase raw materials more cheaply in larger lots than before. Specialization of labor, limiting each worker to perform only one specific task in the production process, also improved production efficiency.

Influenced by these events in England, business in the United States began a time of rapid industrialization. Agriculture became mechanized, and factories sprang up in cities. During the mid-1800s, the pace of the revolution was increased as newly built railroad systems provided fast, economical transportation.

The Age of the Industrial Entrepreneur

Building on the opportunities opened by the industrial revolution, entrepreneurship increased in the United States during the late 19th century. Inventors created a virtually endless array of commercially useful products and new production methods.

Will fresh water soon become an internationally traded commodity? Entrepreneur Simon Pratt is betting on this possibility. Here, the water transporter stands on Aquarius's 200,000-gallon water bag off the Greek island of Aegina.

▼ Eli Whitney introduced the concept of interchangeable parts, an idea that would later facilitate mass production on a previously impossible scale.

▼ Robert McCormick designed a horse-drawn reaper that reduced the labor involved in harvesting wheat. His son, Cyrus McCormick, saw the commercial potential of the reaper and launched a business to build and sell the machine. By 1902, the company was producing 35 percent of the country's farm machinery.

▼ Cornelius Vanderbilt, J. P. Morgan, and Andrew Carnegie among others saw enormous opportunities waiting for anyone willing to take the risk of starting a new business.

▼ Cleveland bookkeeper John D. Rockefeller saved and borrowed to finance his own dry goods trading business. The business thrived and Rockefeller decided to go into oil refining. By age 31, he was well on his way to becoming one

of the richest men in the world. The company he founded, the Standard Oil Company, is now a multibillion-dollar global business.[13]

The entrepreneurial spirit of this golden age in business did much to advance the U.S. business system and raise the overall standard of living. That market transformation, in turn, created new demand for manufactured goods.

The Production Era

As demand for manufactured goods continued to increase during the early years of the 20th century, businesses focused even greater attention on the activities involved in producing those goods. Work became increasingly special-

Table 1.2	Six Eras in Business History	
Era	**Main Characteristics**	**Time Period**
Colonial	Primarily agricultural	Prior to 1776
Industrial revolution	Mass production by semiskilled workers, aided by machines	1760-1830
Industrial entrepreneurs	Advances in technology and increased demand for manufactured goods, leading to enormous entrepreneurial opportunities	Late 1800s
Production	Emphasis on producing more goods faster, leading to production innovations like assembly lines	Prior to 1920s
Marketing	Consumer orientation, seeking to understand and satisfy needs and preferences of customer groups	Since 1950s
Relationship	Benefits derived from deep, ongoing links with individual customers, employees, suppliers, and other businesses	Began in 1990s

ized, and huge, labor-intensive factories dominated U.S. business. Assembly lines, introduced by Henry Ford, became common business equipment. Business owners turned over their responsibilities to a new class of managers trained in operating established companies. Their activities emphasized efforts to produce ever more goods in quicker processes.

In 1917, U.S. Steel Co. was the largest company in America, with 286,000 workers producing 23 million tons of metal a year to meet the growing demand for industrial materials. The company operated blast furnaces, rolling mills, hopper cars, barges, coal mines, ships, and shipyards around the clock. In today's dollars, U.S. Steel's assets at the time would be worth $31 billion.[14]

During the production era, business focused attention on internal processes rather than external influences. Marketing was almost an afterthought, designed solely to distribute products generated by central company activities. Little attention was paid to consumer wants or needs. Instead, businesses tended to make decisions about what the market would get. For example, if you wanted to buy a Ford Model T automobile, you had no choice in color. Henry Ford's factories produced cars in only one color—black—because that decision simplified the manufacturing process.

The Great Depression of the early 1930s changed the shape of U.S. business yet again. As incomes nose-dived, businesses could no longer automatically count on selling everything they produced. Managers began to pay more attention to the markets for their goods and services, and sales and advertising took on new importance. During this period, *selling* was often synonymous with *marketing*.

Demand for all kinds of consumer goods exploded after World War II. Suddenly, consumers were buying again. At the same time, however, competition also heated up. Soon businesses began to think of marketing as more than just selling; they envisioned a process of determining what consumers wanted and needed and then designing products to satisfy those needs. In short, they developed a **consumer orientation.**

They said it

"If no one ever took risks, Michelangelo would have painted the Sistine Floor."

Neil Simon (1927-)
American playwright

Businesses throughout the United States formed marketing research departments to analyze consumers' desires before beginning actual production. Consumer choice skyrocketed. Today's automobiles no longer come just in black; instead, car buyers can choose from a wide range of colors.

Businesses also have discovered that they need to distinguish their goods and services from those of competitors. **Branding,** the process of creating an identity in consumers' minds for a good, service, or company, is one tool used by marketing oriented companies. A **brand** can be a name, term, sign, symbol, design, or some combination that identifies the products of one firm and differentiates them from competitors' offerings.

One of the early masters of branding was Ray Kroc, the founder of the McDonald's restaurant chain. Kroc insisted that every one of his restaurants follow the same operating procedures and offer similar menu items, reinforcing the nationwide image of the growing restaurant franchise in consumer minds across the country. Today, the golden arches are among the best-known company symbols in the world.

A more recent example of a successful consumer orientation and application of branding is General Motors' Saturn Corp. In the 1980s, most U.S. car manufacturers were struggling to compete with imports from foreign auto makers. GM created Saturn as a separate company to offer high-quality automobiles, but the new firm's real success derived not from its quality but from its ability to develop and implement a consumer orientation. For example, recognizing that many consumers hated buying a new car, Saturn took pains to improve the experience. Prospective car buyers entering a Saturn showroom don't face the high-pressure sales tactics normally associated with car salespeople. Instead, they are served by "sales consultants" who are trained to treat customers with respect. No one haggles over price. Saturn sets prices to satisfy customer expectations, while still allowing the firm to make a profit. As a result, nearly 87 percent of Saturn buyers say they would recommend Saturn to their friends.[15]

The marketing era has had a tremendous effect on the way business is conducted today. Even the smallest business owners recognize the importance of understanding what customers want and the reasons why they buy.

The Relationship Era

Contemporary business is poised on the cusp of a new age. Unlike the industrial revolution, which was powered by manufacturing advances, this new era is driven by advances in information technology. Powerful computers, online connections, and other technologies are helping businesses to form deep, direct links with their customers, employees, suppliers, and other organizations. During this new era, the relationship era, business will focus on developing and leveraging relationships for mutually beneficial returns.

Traditionally, business activities have focused on increasing the number of exchanges, or transactions, between buyers and sellers with only limited attention to communications and little or no ongoing relationships between the parties. The goal has simply been to get as many customers as possible to buy at least once. Techniques like price discounts, coupons, and prizes in cereal boxes influence short-term purchase decisions. However, firms are realizing the limitations of this approach for long-term operations. Not only is it an expensive and inefficient way to do business, but it builds little protection against competitors' efforts to attract customers to their goods and services.

Businesses gain several advantages by developing ongoing connections with customers. Since they can serve existing customers less expensively than they can find new ones, businesses that develop long-term customer relationships successfully reduce their overall costs. Long-term relationships with customers enable businesses to improve their understanding of what customers want and prefer from the company. As a result, businesses enhance their chances of sustaining real advantages through competitive differentiation.

USAA is already firmly entrenched in the relationship age. The San Antonio company began selling auto insurance in the 1930s to U.S. military officers stationed around the world. The company builds relationships with customers by paying careful attention to quality and service. A sophisticated computer database keeps track of USAA's interactions with its nearly 3 million customers. All customer information and correspondence is consolidated into each customer's electronic file. With one phone call to a customer service representative, a policyholder can make changes in or ask questions about any of his or her insurance policies without frustrating transfers from department

to department. The USAA representative immediately commands all of the information necessary to provide personal service to that customer.[16]

USAA also seeks to forge lifelong links with customers by finding products to fill their changing needs. In addition to auto, life, and homeowner's insurance, USAA customers can turn to the company for home mortgages, credit cards, and even purchases of jewelry and home furnishings. USAA has accomplished this impressive level of service by setting up a network of alliances with other businesses, which actually provide the goods and services. When a customer calls USAA to apply for a credit card or home mortgage, for instance, the call connects him or her to a USAA ally firm. USAA's partners must agree to meet the company's strict criteria for providing quality service at reasonable cost.[17]

USAA and other businesses have discovered that the relationship era is an age of connections. Connections, not just between businesses and customers, but also between employers and employees, technology and manufacturing, and separate companies, are fueling economic growth. The economies of countries around the world are also becoming increasingly interconnected, as businesses expand beyond their national boundaries. In this new global economy, techniques for managing networks of people, businesses, information, and technology are of paramount importance to business success.

Each new era in U.S. business history has forced managers to reexamine the tools and techniques they formerly used to compete. The relationship era is no different from the others. Tomorrow's managers will need creativity and vision to stay on top of rapidly changing technology and to manage complex relationships in the global business world. The rest of this chapter and other elements throughout the book explain some of the ways in which businesses are preparing for the fast-paced 21st century.

> ## They said it
>
> "You must learn from the mistakes of others. You can't possibly live long enough to make them all yourself."
>
> **Sam Levenson (1911-1980)**
> **American humorist**

MANAGING THE TECHNOLOGY REVOLUTION

As the last section discussed, the relationship era is driven by new technologies that are changing nearly every aspect of people's lives. To succeed in the 21st century, business leaders must understand how technology is changing the shape, not just of business, but of the world as a whole.

This insight can begin with a definition of **technology** as a business application of knowledge based on scientific discoveries, inventions, and innovations. In business, technology can streamline production, creating new opportunities for organizational efficiency. A factory may rely on automated machinery to produce finished products. In an office, computers may simplify the process of managing the information involved in running a business.

Technological breakthroughs such as supercomputers, laser surgery, and electric cars result in new goods and services for consumers, improved customer service, reduced prices, and more comfortable working conditions. Technology can make products obsolete, just as cassette tapes and CDs wiped out the market for vinyl records. It can also open up new business opportunities.

Changes in technology can also create whole new industries and new ways of doing business. Technological innovations ranging from voice recognition and scanners to advanced fiber optics and online services are playing critical roles in advancing nations' standards of living as they approach the next century.

The Internet

Perhaps the most talked about technological innovation of the past few years is the **Internet,** a worldwide network of interconnected computers that, within limits, lets anyone with access to a personal computer send and receive images and data anywhere. The roots of the Internet began when the U.S. Department of Defense created a secure military communications system in the late 1960s.

Over time, other government and business computer networks were also created and interlinked. In 1986, the National Science Foundation facilitated comprehensive connections among many of these computer networks by dedicating five supercomputers that allowed all of the various networks to communicate with each other.

In 1993, Internet usage began to spread to individual users with the development of the **World Wide Web (Web or WWW),** an interlinked collection of graphically rich information sources within the larger Internet. The Web has opened new opportunities for organizations and individuals to communicate their messages to the world on **Web sites,** the data pages of the WWW. Most Web sites offer some interactive elements. A user simply clicks on a highlighted word or picture to receive information—text, photographs, charts, or even a song or movie clip. The number of Web sites has increased at an astounding rate in recent years, from about 18,000 Web sites in 1995 to 740,000 today.[18]

Another Internet communications tool is electronic mail, commonly called **e-mail,** the electronic delivery of messages via Internet links. Using e-mail, individuals and businesses can instantly send messages and information around the globe. E-mail also allows for documents, pictures, and spreadsheets to be sent almost anywhere in the world. By the turn of the century, analysts expect more than 6.9 trillion e-mail messages to be sent annually.[19]

What does the Internet mean to industry? For one thing, it represents a huge community of prospective customers. Some 200 million users are now connected to the Internet, and 45 percent of them are expected to buy almost $100 billion in goods and services directly through Internet connections this year.[20] As Figure 1.5 shows, residents of most of the world's nations now have Internet access.

The Internet is also facilitating new interactive relationships between businesses and their customers. Instead of relying on intermediaries such as retailers, agents, and brokers to reach customers, businesses can now connect directly with customers. This tool may dramatically change traditional business practices in some industries. For example, what role will travel agents play when most customers learn to book their own reservations with hotels and airlines directly over the Internet? Also, automobile-related transactions on the Internet are now nearing $1 billion a year. In the future, car buyers may be able to order units directly from the factories, completely bypassing dealers.[21]

The Internet is also opening up new ways of interacting with customers, suppliers, and employees. Many firms have invested in **intranets,** closed network systems using Internet standards that allow for information sharing among employees, divisions, and geographically diverse locations. Other firms have created **extranets,** secure networks accessible from outside, but only by trusted third parties such as familiar customers or suppliers.

The Internet's interactive capability also allows businesses to customize their goods and services for individual customers around the world. Need a new pair of skis? MySki Inc. lets you design your own via the Internet. Skiers indicate their level of expertise, the conditions they encounter when skiing, the colors they prefer, and even personalized messages they want imprinted on their skis.

Business Directory

Internet a worldwide network of interconnected computers that, within limits, lets anyone with access to a personal computer send and receive images and data anywhere.

| Figure 1.5 | How Nations Compare in Internet Access and Freedom of Content |

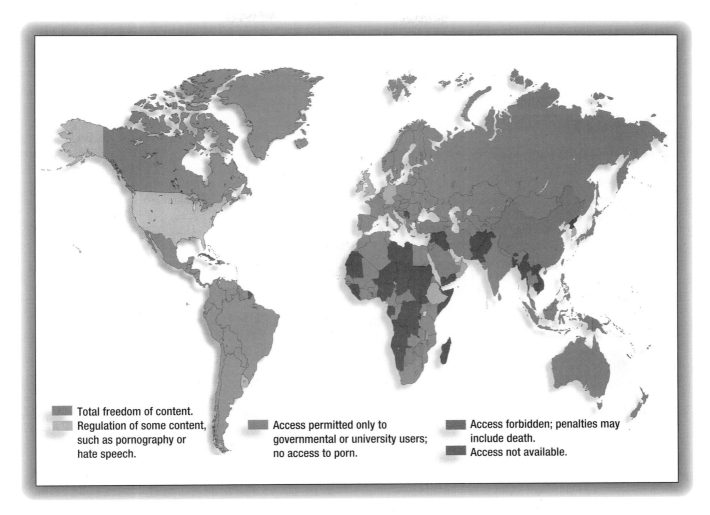

Total freedom of content.

Regulation of some content, such as pornography or hate speech.

Access permitted only to governmental or university users; no access to porn.

Access forbidden; penalties may include death.

Access not available.

www.evoski.com

MySki's Web site automatically creates an animated 3D preview. After a buyer places an order, the company makes a pair of skis according to the stated preferences. After 3 weeks, the new skis are delivered to the buyer's doorstep. Chris Jorgensen, president of MySki, says that skis are just the beginning. He has plans to open MySnowboard, My-Furniture, and MyCar Internet sites in the future.[22]

Chapter 17 will explain more about how businesses are managing technology, including Internet resources. Technology's role in various business functions is also a recurring theme throughout this book. Many of our Business Hall of Fame and Business Hall of Shame inserts report on firms' efforts to leverage technology for competitive advantage.

FROM TRANSACTION MANAGEMENT TO RELATIONSHIP MANAGEMENT

As the world enters the 21st century, a significant change is taking place in the ways companies interact with customers. Since the industrial revolution, most businesses have concentrated on building and promoting products in hopes that enough customers would buy them to cover costs and earn acceptable profits, an approach called **transaction management.**

In the relationship era, however, many businesses are taking a different, longer-term approach in their interactions with customers. These firms are seeking ways to actively nurture customer loyalty by carefully managing every interaction. They earn enormous paybacks for their efforts. A company that retains customers over the long haul reduces its advertising, sales, and account initiation costs. Since customer spending tends to accelerate over time, revenues also grow. Companies with long-term customers often can charge premium prices, and they find that many new customers come from loyal customer referrals.[23]

Increasingly, therefore, business focuses on **relationship management,** the collection of activities that build and maintain ongoing, mutually beneficial ties with customers and other parties. At its core, relationship management involves gathering knowledge of customer needs and preferences and applying that understanding to get as close to the customer as possible.

Hickory Farms, for example, fosters close ties with customers by building on its knowledge of individuals' preferences and needs. A central computer information system stores data about these preferences as a way to create ongoing ties with customers. If you sent gift baskets to friends and relatives last year, this year Hickory Farms will remind you who received your gifts, what you sent them, and even the wording of the accompanying greeting cards. All you need to do is let Hickory Farms know what gifts you want sent for this year and your gift-giving work is done. Hickory Farms customers who order regularly also work with personal sales representatives who are rewarded for satisfying individual customers.[24]

Hitachi Data Systems (HDS), a $2 billion computer equipment and service firm, has developed an even more comprehensive system of relationship management. The company invites an advisory panel of customers to regular, 3-day meetings with HDS executives and engineers. During the meetings, HDS gains first-hand feedback on service issues, product performance, and technological developments that help the company to stay ahead in a highly competitive, rapidly changing industry.[25] In a very real sense, HDS has moved its relationships with customers beyond buyer-seller interactions to a partnership in which customers have an important say in the company's future plans and direction.

Strategic Alliances and Partnerships

Businesses are also finding that they must form partnerships with other organizations in order to take full advantage of available opportunities. A **partnership** is an affiliation of two or more companies with the shared goal of assisting each other in the achievement of common goals. One such form of partnership between organizations is a **strategic alliance,** a partnership formed to create competitive advantage for the businesses involved.

For example, Bill Hanley knew that the only way to keep his business growing was to team up with his competitors. Hanley's company, Galileo Corp., manufactures fiber optic elements for military defense systems. In the early 1990s, when government defense spending fell to new lows, so did the demand for fiber optics. Hanley approached his top five local competitors and suggested they pool their resources and marketing efforts to capture a larger overall slice of the remaining defense fiber optics market. The companies joined together to form the Center for Advanced Fiber Optic Applications (CAFA). CAFA coordinates research and new product development among all member companies to win defense and international business for all of the partners in the alliance.[26]

Chapter 7 will take a closer look at other strategies that businesses are using to strengthen relationships with customers and other firms.

CREATING VALUE THROUGH QUALITY AND CUSTOMER SATISFACTION

Today's savvy consumers want the satisfaction of acquiring more than ordinary goods and services. Their demands extend beyond just low prices. Firms seeking to tighten bonds with customers must provide value to customers in order to earn their long-term loyalty.

Value is the customer's perception of the balance between the positive traits of a good or service and its price. Customers who feel that they have received value—that is, positive benefits for a fair price—are likely to remain satisfied and continue their relationships with a firm. However, when customers perceive an inequitable balance between benefits and price, they become dissatisfied and start to look for opportunities outside their relationship with the business. Value is also an important way to differentiate goods and services from competing offerings. A firm that provides real value to customers often enjoys superior advantages and wider opportunities in the marketplace.

Consider Mercedes Benz. You may not recognize the newest Mercedes Benz model offered for sale in Europe. The A140 is just 141 inches long with a tiny 82-horsepower engine. In fact, the car's only recognizable trait is the familiar three-pronged logo on the hood. Mercedes believes that customers will choose the A140 over similar, lower-priced offerings by Toyota, Chevrolet, and Volkswagen because they value the Mercedes reputation for qual-

They said it

"No sale is really complete until the product is worn out and the customer is satisfied."

Leon Leonwood Bean (1872-1967)
Founder of L. L. Bean outdoor-clothing company

Business Directory

customer satisfaction the ability of a good or service to meet or exceed buyer needs and expectations.

ity, service, and performance over competitors' price advantages—even for a Lilliputian Mercedes.[27]

Mercedes, like other companies, has discovered that customer value perceptions are often tied to **quality,** the degree of excellence or superiority of a firm's goods and services. Technically, quality refers to physical product traits, such as durability and performance reliability. However, quality also includes **customer satisfaction,** the ability of a good or service to meet or exceed buyer needs and expectations.

Technology wields a double-edged sword for customer satisfaction. On one hand, the use of technology can give a business the ability to improve interactions with customers. General Electric Medical Systems (GEMS), for example, is a $4 billion global manufacturer of high-tech medical equipment. GEMS customers, primarily large hospitals and clinics, were dissatisfied with the amount of training and support they were receiving. In response, GEMS set up its own television network to carry live training broadcasts via satellite directly to customer workplaces, which led to dramatic improvements in customer satisfaction.[28]

On the other hand, technologies like online communications, computerized engineering, and satellite communications have led customers to expect more from firms with which they do business. Customers are no longer content to wait for replies to their questions or complaints. They expect instant responses and personalized attention to their needs. They now insist on products that can perform expanded functions with improved reliability. Firms that do not keep up with customer expectations lose customers to rivals that do.

Businesses in all industries, therefore, face a common challenge of finding new ways to add value to customer interactions through increased customer satisfaction and quality. This statement introduces a recurring theme in this book—how businesses will compete in the relationship era. Chapter 7 focuses specifically on relationship management, and Chapter 12 discusses the specific methods by which businesses create value for their customers through quality and customer satisfaction.

COMPETING IN A GLOBAL MARKET

Businesses can no longer limit their sights to events and opportunities within their own national borders. The world's nations and their economies are developing increasing interdependence. To remain competitive, companies must continually search for both the most efficient manufacturing sites and the most lucrative markets for their products.

The global economy is currently expanding at an annual rate of about 4 percent. U.S. exports account for one-seventh of the world's exports, up from one-ninth in 1993. Major trading partners—led by Canada, Japan, Mexico, and China—are shown in Figure 1.6. The ten nations listed there purchase 64 percent of all U.S. exports. In addition,

Both shoppers and the retail outlets benefit from relationship management at Hickory Farms.

they account for two-thirds of all goods imported to the United States.[29] Recently, however, emerging economies in Latin America, eastern Europe, and Asia are presenting tremendous opportunities for trade. Rising standards of living in these countries have created increasing customer demand for the latest goods and services.

The prospects of succeeding in the global marketplace appeal to U.S. businesses, which can find huge markets outside North America. Of the world's 6 billion residents, less than 5 percent reside in the United States. U.S. giants such as Coca-Cola Co. and McDonald's have proved that they can duplicate their domestic success abroad, since 80 percent of both firms' sales come from non-U.S. customers. Similar sales patterns characterize Gillette, which generates two-thirds of annual sales from international markets, and Boeing, whose foreign sales account for 54 percent of its aircraft business. The largest U.S. exporters are shown in Table 1.3.

The United States is the world's leading exporter of cotton, wheat, fish, airplanes, fresh fruits, medical instruments, nuts, corn, soybeans, musical instruments, manufactured fertilizers, and movies. The United States even exceeds France in its exports of perfume.[30]

Figure 1.6	Top Ten U.S. Trading Partners

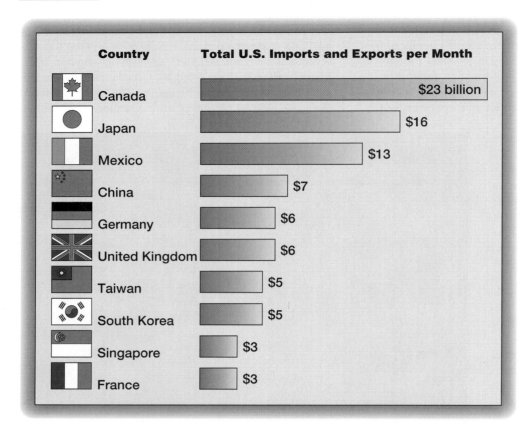

Country | **Total U.S. Imports and Exports per Month**
Canada	$23 billion
Japan	$16
Mexico	$13
China	$7
Germany	$6
United Kingdom	$6
Taiwan	$5
South Korea	$5
Singapore	$3
France	$3

Large corporations aren't the only businesses that export to the global market. Small and medium-sized businesses are increasingly active in foreign trade. An estimated 28 percent of these businesses are involved in some form of exporting activity. They enjoy faster growth in their revenues, profits, and employment than comparable, nonexporting firms.[31]

Going global helped to save Zippo Manufacturing. The maker of cigarette lighters faced stalled domestic sales tied to reductions in U.S. tobacco consumption. In response, Zippo's management targeted overseas markets, where smoking is still a socially acceptable practice and U.S. brand names are often valued. As a result, nearly 60 percent of Zippo's current sales are from overseas customers.

Many U.S. businesses are also finding that imported goods made by foreign manufacturers can create new oppor-

Mercedes Benz plans to parlay its reputation for luxury into a broader product line, ranging from this A140 subcompact to a U.S.-built sport utility vehicle. In seeking a broader market, the firm must avoid tarnishing its reputation among buyers of superluxury models.

tunities to satisfy the needs of domestic consumers. When an optometrist mentioned that he had difficulty finding eyeglass frames that fit the unique face shapes of African-Americans and members of other ethnic groups, Cynthia Bower saw an opportunity. Her company, Atlantic Optical Framewear, imports eyeglass frames from South America, Asia, and Africa and sells them through a network of domestic distributors.[32]

The United States also offers an attractive market for foreign competitors because of its size and high standard of living. Foreign companies like Matsushita, Mercedes Benz, Benetton, and Sun Life of Canada operate production, distribution, service, and retail facilities here. Foreign ownership of U.S. companies has increased as well. Pillsbury, MCA, and Firestone Tires are some well-known firms with foreign parents. Foreign investment in the United States means additional competitive pressures for domestic firms. One survey of U.S. firms found that 28 percent reported facing direct competition from non-U.S. companies.[33]

Productivity: Key to Global Competitiveness

Global competitiveness requires nations, industries, and companies to work efficiently at producing goods and services. As discussed earlier, firms need a number of inputs, or factors of production, in order to produce goods and services.

Productivity describes the relationship between the number of units produced and the number of human and other production inputs necessary to produce them. Pro-

Table 1.3	Top Ten U.S. Exporters		
Rank	**Company**	**Exported Products**	**Exports**
1	General Motors	Motor vehicles and parts, railroad locomotives	$16.1 billion
2	Ford	Motor vehicles and parts	11.9
3	Boeing	Commercial aircraft	11.8
4	Chrysler	Motor vehicles and parts	9.4
5	General Electric	Jet engines, turbines, plastics, medical systems	8.1
6	Motorola	Communications equipment	7.4
7	IBM	Computers	6.3
8	Philip Morris	Tobacco, beer, and food products	4.9
9	Archer Daniels Midland	Meats, vegetable oils	4.7
10	Hewlett-Packard	Measurement and computation products	4.7

ductivity is, therefore, a ratio of output to input. When a constant amount of inputs generates increased outputs, an increase in productivity occurs.

Total productivity considers all inputs necessary to produce a specific amount of outputs. Stated in equation form, it can be written as follows:

$$\text{Total productivity} = \frac{\text{Output (goods or services produced)}}{\text{Input (human/natural resources, capital)}}$$

Many productivity ratios focus on only one of the inputs of the equation: labor productivity or output per labor-hour. An increase in labor productivity means that the same amount of work produces more goods and services than before.

Productivity is a widely recognized measure of a company's efficiency. In turn, the total productivity of a nation's businesses has become a measure of its economic strength and standard of living. Economists refer to this measure as a country's **gross domestic product (GDP)**—the sum of all goods and services produced within its boundaries. GDP is based on the per-capita output of a country; in other words, total national output divided by the number of citizens. U.S. GDP is currently growing at an average rate of 2.7 percent a year. As Figure 1.7 shows, it remains the highest in the world.

However, some economists argue that this measure doesn't necessarily prove that the United States is the most productive or competitive nation in the world. They point out that Americans actually work longer hours and take fewer vacations than do workers in other countries. If national output is calculated on the basis of production divided by the total number of hours worked in a nation, France and Germany would show higher productivity levels and several other European countries would be close to the United States. In short, if Europeans simply worked longer hours, Americans would lag behind in productivity.[34]

Even though the United States leads the world in GDP, continued economic growth in countries such as Germany, China, and Japan has aroused fears about the global competitiveness of the United States. Some suggest that U.S. managers focus too much on short-term goals and devote insufficient attention to developing long-range plans for worldwide competition. Plant closings, business failures, and employee layoffs are seen as signs of the need to invest more in long-term research, development, and innovation in order to remain competitive in the global market.

Figure 1.7   **Nations with the Highest Gross Domestic Product**

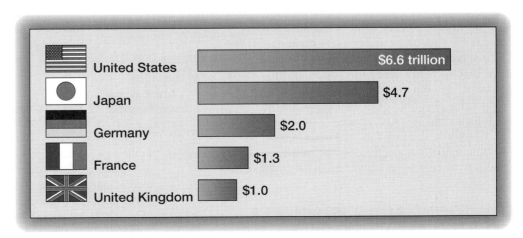

United States	$6.6 trillion
Japan	$4.7
Germany	$2.0
France	$1.3
United Kingdom	$1.0

BUSINESS HALL OF SHAME

Cinemex: Struggling to Revamp Mexico's Movie Industry

Mexico's moviegoers had gotten used to visiting dumpy, aging theaters and receiving poor service. The theater owners had grown accustomed to struggling under heavy government regulation, and the movie moguls had acquired a taste for controlling the industry. But all that changed when the government decided to privatize its state-owned movie company and deregulate the industry as a whole.

Young Mexican entrepreneur Miguel Angel Davila couldn't wait to take advantage of the decision. Along with two of his classmates from Harvard Business School, Davila saw a chance to introduce Mexican moviegoers to American-style cinema: multiplex theaters offering modern decor, comfortable seats, and state-of-the-art sound systems. So the three partners launched Cadena Mexicana de Exhibición—Cinemex.

Even as risky and difficult as it can be to start a new company in the United States, launching a startup in Mexico proved even tougher. For one thing, the old movie moguls were elitist and clubby, so financing was difficult to come by. One potential investor stated, "We don't need some Harvard MBAs with their Rolls Royce dreams telling us where to invest our money." In fact, Davila was turned down by every financial institution he asked. Luckily, foreign business vendors and a few wealthy Mexican investors saw more potential in the project, so Davila and his partners were able to raise $21.5 million.

When Cinemex opened its first two theaters in Mexico City's most elegant shopping districts, every night brought sell-out crowds. When Cinemex expanded into some of the poorer neighborhoods, people were at first intimidated by the theaters. But after Davila sent employees out on the sidewalk to invite folks in for a look, business soared in the new locations as well. Unfortunately, patrons weren't the

---

Education is another factor in judging a country's productivity and overall competitiveness. High school graduation rates in Japan, Germany, Canada, and the United Kingdom are now at or near U.S. levels. Meanwhile, the number of U.S. college graduates has risen only slightly over the past 20 years, while the number of graduates in Japan has skyrocketed. Finally, although the overall literacy rate of U.S. adults is comparable to that of other industrialized nations, the percentage of American adults falling into the lowest literacy level is higher than comparable figures for nearly every other developed nation. "There is good reason to believe that such low-level literacy is an impairment to our economic growth and competitive position," says Paul E. Barton of the Educational Testing Service.[35]

Chapter 4 examines these and other factors affecting global competitiveness, as well as the strategies employed by companies competing in the global market.

DEVELOPING AND SUSTAINING A WORLD-CLASS WORKFORCE

A skilled and knowledgeable workforce is an essential resource for keeping pace with the accelerating rate of change in today's business world. Employers need reliable workers to foster strong ties with customers and partners. They must build workforces capable of the productivity needed to compete in global markets. Business leaders are also beginning to realize that the brainpower of employees plays a vital role in a firm's ability to stay on top of new technologies and innovations.

A world-class workforce can be the foundation of a firm's competitive differentiation, providing important advantages over competing businesses. Building a world-class workforce is a difficult task, however, made all the more complex by the changing characteristics of workers as well as the effects of recent business history.

Preparing for Changes in the Workforce

In the new millennium, companies will face several trends that challenge their skills for managing and developing human resources. These trends include aging of the population, shrinkage in the pool of workers, increased mobility of workers, growing diversity, and the changing nature of work.

Aging of the Population Members of the baby boom generation, people born between 1946 and 1965, are nearing the peaks of their careers, and the oldest of them will begin

---

They said it

"Here's a good way to tell you have a bad professor. You ask the guy about *haiku* and he says, 'Oh, that's a guy pitching for the Yankees.'"

David Letterman
American comedian

only people that Davila and Cinemex had to deal with.

A powerful theater union sent gangs of roughnecks to block Cinemex employees from entering theaters. Davila was even shoved around by some of these thugs. The theaters received regular bomb threats, and during sold-out shows, mice were released in the theaters to panic the audiences.

Still unsatisfied, union bosses called on government friends to cause other trouble. For example, labor authorities scheduled detailed inspections of Cinemex's operations—not common practice, even in Mexico. The officials expected bribes, but Davila said no. "These mobsters had enjoyed political power for many years," he said of the union bosses. "They weren't going to roll over and play dead." But Cinemex prevailed when the Mexican labor department eventually ruled that the

company could work with any union it wanted.

In addition to bureaucrats and unions, Davila and his partners must face competition from imitators. Dallas-based Cinemark has recently built multiscreen theaters in smaller Mexican towns, and Organización Ramírez operates movie screens throughout the country. To maintain its edge, Cinemex focuses on making the movie-going experience as pleasant as it can be, even providing valet parking. Also, Cinemex offers online reservations for movies and other cultural events.

Davila still faces an occasional mouse panic. And he still has to deal with bureaucrats in the guise of tax auditors and fire inspectors. But Cinemex is helping Mexico change not only the way it sees movies but also the way it does business.

www.cinemex.com.mx

QUESTIONS FOR CRITICAL THINKING

1. Why do you think a businessperson today needs an understanding of a foreign country's culture, economy, and politics before entering into a venture there?

2. In what ways do you think the Internet can help a businessperson prepare for doing business in a foreign country?

Sources: José Aguayo, "Thugs, Bureaucrats, and Mice," *Forbes*, May 4, 1998, pp. 74–76; Cinemex Web site accessed at www.cinemex.com.mx, February 9, 1999.

---

retiring shortly after the new century begins. Employers will have to deal with issues arising from reliance on older workers, such as retirement, disability programs, retraining, and insurance benefits. By 2025, 62.2 million Americans will be senior citizens—nearly double today's number. As these elderly Americans leave the workforce, they will attract attention by businesspeople eager to earn profits by serving their needs. Figure 1.8 illustrates how airlines such as USAir cater to this age group by offering a variety of discount fares.

Retirement also creates human resource problems for thousands of businesses, because Generation Xers, those people born between 1966 and 1976, represent only 21 percent of the population compared to nearly 42 percent for baby boomers. Experts predict a decline in the number of available adult workers as the new century begins.

Management of retailer Mervyn's recognizes that Generation Xers will be tomorrow's managers and that

| Figure 1.8 | **USAir: Serving the Needs of Older Travelers** |

their attitudes about work differ from those of their predecessors. They value flexibility, training, and creative expression, so Mervyn's has developed a management training program to attract and keep Generation Xers. Trainees are allowed to choose their own pace as they work through the program, and development efforts pair them with experienced managers. After they graduate, they take responsibility for two or three departments in a store, supported by encouragement to apply new ideas and methods.[36]

Shrinking Labor Pool Throughout the 1980s and early 1990s, cost cutters at many large companies eliminated jobs as a way to boost profits. Now, managers face the opposite problem as the lowest unemployment rate in a quarter-century has led to a limited supply of skilled employees looking for jobs. In one study, nearly half of human resource executives at large and medium-sized companies reported difficulty finding workers. Most polled executives in mining, manufacturing, construction, and business and professional services expect the situation to worsen by 2000.[37]

The task of recruiting employees can be an even bigger challenge for small-business owners. Charles Whiteside owns Ana-Lab Corp., an environmental testing company in Kilgore, Texas, that employs 60 workers. Additional workers were needed, but those positions remained unfilled for several months. To attract more employees, Whiteside increased the firm's health insurance, sick leave, retirement, and education benefits. "There's not enough good employees for the demand," says Whiteside. "We pay a lot of overtime here because we don't have enough people."[38]

Increased Mobility of Workers Even after a firm's recruiters find the right employee for a job, the effort to keep that employee confronts them with increasing difficulties. Employees are no longer likely to remain with single companies for their entire careers. Men, in particular, are switching jobs faster than they did a decade ago.[39]

Fast-growing Cisco Systems, a manufacturer of computer network equipment, hires as many as 1,200 new employees a month. Cisco's trainers then concentrate on acclimating these workers to the firm in the hope that they will stay for the long term. Company systems track each new employee's orientation and ensure that each one starts with a fully functional workspace. Each new hire is assigned a "buddy," another employee who answers questions about working at Cisco and helps the newcomer to feel welcome.[40]

Increased Diversity Like the general population, the workforce is growing more diverse, a trend that will continue well into the next century. In 1980, ethnic minorities comprised just 18 percent of the U.S. population. By 2005,

members of these groups will represent 28 percent of the population, and by 2050, nearly 50 percent of Americans will belong to nonwhite ethnic groups. Hispanics and Asians represent the fastest-growing segments of the population.[41] Managers must be able to work effectively with diverse ethnic groups, cultures, and lifestyles in order to develop and retain a superior workforce for their company.

To benefit from diversity, executives of many companies develop explicit strategies to encourage and manage multiculturalism. As figure 1.9 explains, General Motors has an active program for recruiting minority employees. Inside the company, training programs help managers and workers to understand differences and similarities between various groups. Every GM division must spell out goals for encouraging diversity in its annual business plan.[42]

The Changing Nature of Work The United States is moving away from manufacturing as a basis for its economy and toward an economy based on service industries. This change will lead U.S. employers to rely increasingly heavily on service workers with sharp knowledge skills as well as manufacturing and technological skills. New work lifestyles are also becoming common elements of business life. The number of telecommuters who do their work at home for businesses located elsewhere has grown nearly 30 percent in the past 2 years.[43] Other employees are expecting employers to allow job flexibility so they can meet family and personal needs along with job-related needs.[44] Employers are also hiring growing numbers of temporary and part-time employees.[45]

Another business tool for staffing flexibility is **outsourcing,** contracting with another business to perform tasks or functions previously handled by internal staff members. In addition to reducing the continuing costs of hiring and training new employees, outsourcing can help a firm to compete by concentrating on the functions that pro-

Figure 1.9　**Reaping the Benefits of Diversity at General Motors**

"Going the extra mile.... that's what makes the GM team approach so rewarding."

Forget what you've heard about gigantic departments with big-time anonymity. Teamwork is the keystone of GM's global success today. We've knocked down the walls. Opened up a free exchange of ideas and information. Where you have the chance to make a real difference. And the better your ideas and information, the faster your rise up the corporate ladder (that's one thing we haven't changed).

To join the team with the driving difference, send your resume to: GM Education Relations, Fax: (313) 556-9165. For additional information, visit our website at: http://www.gm.com/edu_rel Teamwork that touches the world.

General Motors
An Equal
Opportunity
Employer

Southwest Airlines employees are recognized as one of the company's greatest assets. The company gives employees the power to satisfy customers on the spot—and to have fun while they do it.

vide competitive differentiation and delegating others that do not add to customer value. The Sabre Group, for example, handles all of US Airways' computer functions. Sabre operates the US Airways data processing center, maintains all company computers, and even manages the airline's internal computer network. This arrangement frees US Airways staff to turn their attention to the strategic issues of running an airline.[46] Outsourcing is a popular choice among companies in many other businesses, such as telemarketing, accounting, and even human resource management.

The New Employer-Employee Partnership
To handle the challenges of a changing workforce and to gain competitive advantage by fully utilizing employee talents, many employers are trying to form new types of relationships with employees. They emphasize creating an employer-employee partnership that recognizes and encourages workers' important contributions to providing value and satisfying customers.

Southwest Airlines CEO Herb Kelleher identifies the key to his company's success as its ability to build an intelligent and motivated workforce. Southwest achieves this goal by hiring service-oriented employees, treating them with respect, and creating a fun and challenging work environment. While rules and regulations are the basis for making decisions, Southwest employees are given latitude to make decisions that satisfy customers on the spot. Employees are encouraged to take active roles in suggesting and implementing new work methods and innovations. As a result, Southwest posts the best on-time performance record and receives the fewest customer complaints in the U.S. airline industry. "Competitors have tried and failed to copy us because they cannot copy our people," says Kelleher.[47]

Starbucks Coffee also treats employees as partners in the firm's success. The company offers stock options, dubbed "bean stock," to all employees at every level. If employees, through their efforts, make Starbucks more successful every year, their stock options increase in value. Starbucks CEO Howard Schultz credits the program with fostering a sense of ownership among employees that has encouraged them to submit innovative ideas about cutting costs, increasing sales, and creating value for customers.[48]

Reaping the Benefits of Diversity

As already discussed, today's workers come from many different ethnic, lifestyle, and age groups. Enlightened business leaders recognize the gain they receive from encouraging all of their employees to contribute their unique perspectives, skills, and experiences.

Diversity, blending individuals of different genders, ethnic backgrounds, cultures, religions, ages, and physical and mental abilities, can enrich a firm's chances of success.

Several studies have shown that diverse employee teams and workforces tend to perform tasks more effectively and develop better solutions to business problems than homogenous employee groups. This difference is due in part to the varied perspectives and experiences that foster innovation and creativity in multicultural teams.

Since nearly every business serves a diverse group of customers, diversity in its workforce can improve management understanding of customer needs and relationships with customer groups. Maybelline, for example, hoped to gain a share of the $55 million market for ethnic cosmetics by recruiting African-American, Hispanic, and Asian employees to develop product and marketing strategies for the new line. With their insights and input, Maybelline captured 41 percent of the ethnic cosmetics market.[49]

Also, practical managers know that attention to diversity issues can help them to avoid costly and damaging legal battles. Employee lawsuits alleging discrimination are now among the most common legal

> ## They said it
>
> "America is not like a blanket—one piece of unbroken cloth, the same color, the same texture, the same size. America is more like a quilt—many pieces, many colors, many sizes, all woven and held together by a common thread."
>
> Jesse Jackson (1941-)
> American civil rights leader

BUSINESS TOOL KIT

How to Line Up a Great Summer Job

Summer may seem like part of the distant future, but it's never too soon to start looking for a summer job that can give you a boost up the career ladder. Here are three tips for lining up a great summer job:

1. **Find an internship.** Prospective employers are impressed by students who have completed internships. Most colleges and universities maintain internship or career service offices. Professors might also provide leads. Not all internships are paid positions, but you can gain skills and experience worth the effort.

2. **Volunteer.** If you are an active volunteer, let prospective summer employers know about your experiences. If not, look for volunteer opportunities that fit your personality, skills, and career goals.

3. **Network.** Relationships with others may help you to land a great summer job. Let relatives, family, and friends know several months in advance what type of job you want. Find and join professional organizations in your area of interest. List 20 or 30 companies where you would like to work and write letters of introduction explaining your skills.

Source: Amy Lindgren, "Plan Now," *San Diego Union Tribune*, September 22, 1997, p. C2.

issues faced by employers. The median amount of compensation awarded in successful employee discrimination suits is now over $200,000.

Diversity and other issues related to human resource management will be discussed further in Part 3.

WANTED: A NEW TYPE OF MANAGER

Once, managers were encouraged to be "organization men," wearing identical gray flannel suits and working in a world of strict rules and rigid hierarchies. Companies no longer recruit only stereotyped, male managers; they look for someone with the ability to create and sustain a vision of how an organization can succeed. The 21st-century manager will need to apply critical thinking skills and creativity to business challenges, steer change, and manage an increasingly diverse workforce.

Importance of Vision

An important managerial quality needed in the 21st century is **vision**, the ability to perceive marketplace needs and what an organization must do to satisfy them. Business Hall of Fame illustrated, Dave Hampton created Furbies after seeing the Tamagotchi virtual pet and wanted to give kids something more. Another visionary entrepreneur is William Penzey, Jr. He started his spice-importing firm, Penzeys, Ltd., when he saw that consumers wanted exotic spices like Costa Rican cardamom pods and cinnamon sticks from Indonesia

and Vietnam—products that large spice companies refused to carry. Penzeys is now a $4-million-a-year mail-order business.[50]

The need for vision isn't limited to entrepreneurs. When Gary Mead took over as chief executive officer of La Quinta Inns in 1992, he didn't like what he saw. The hotel chain's units were in poor condition, and they offered even poorer service to customers. He knew that in order to compete, the firm's 248 hotels would need costly upgrades and repairs. Unfortunately, individual owner/managers of the properties didn't want to spend the money. Mead bought out all of La Quinta's independent franchisees in

Bill Penzey has built a $4 million business by selling exotic seasonings that big companies don't carry.

order to get the control he needed to fulfill his vision of a hotel chain offering consistent quality that would meet customers' demands. He then spent $270 million remodeling the properties, an investment that paid handsome dividends. Occupancy rates are up and profits have jumped 25 percent since 1996.[51]

Chapter 7 will explain how vision and the ability to turn ideas into action affect a firm's chances of success as part of the discussion of strategic planning.

Importance of Critical Thinking and Creativity

Critical thinking and creativity are essential characteristics of the 21st-century workforce. Businesspeople will need to look at a wide variety of situations, draw connections between disparate information, and develop future-oriented solutions.

Critical thinking is the ability to analyze and assess information in order to pinpoint problems or opportunities. The critical thinking process includes activities like determining the authenticity, accuracy, and worth of information, knowledge, and arguments. It involves looking beneath the surface for deeper meaning and connections that can help to identify critical issues and solutions. "In the past 20 years, the role of leadership has changed from being the person with the right answers to being the person with the right questions," explains Quinn Spitzer, CEO of consulting firm Kepner-Tregoe. To help you develop your critical thinking skills, critical thinking questions intended to stimulate discussion follow every Business Hall of Fame and Business Hall of Shame story and each chapter.

Creativity is the capacity to develop novel solutions to perceived organizational problems. While most people think of it in relation to artists, musicians, and inventors, they reveal a very limited definition. In business, *creativity* refers to the ability to see better and different ways of doing business. A computer en-

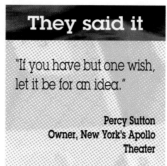

gineer who solves a glitch in a software program is executing a creative act; so is a mail-room clerk who finds a way to speed delivery of the company's overnight packages.[52]

In the highly competitive market for computer printers, even the most innovative manufacturers rely on creativity to devise novel ways to communicate with potential customers. Industry giant Hewlett-Packard used the amusing ad shown in Figure 1.10 to demonstrate the realism of its photo-quality images.

Communications systems manufacturer Lucent Technologies has developed an innovative way of fostering employee creativity through its IdeaVerse center. The center's purple walls, paintings on the ceiling, and beanbag chairs provide an environment where employees can nourish their creativity through seminars, books, videos, and speakers. The center also holds "ideation" sessions where groups of employees come together to brainstorm answers to particularly tough organizational problems.[53]

Creativity and critical thinking must go beyond generating new ideas, however; they must lead to action. In addition to creating an environment where employees can nurture ideas, managers must give them opportunities to take risks and try new solutions. The Business Tool Kit box contains tips on developing critical thinking and creative skills.

Figure 1.10	**Using Creativity to Communicate Product Superiority**

How to Develop Critical Thinking and Creative Skills

Open Your Mind

▼ Become aware of the need to improve your creativity.

▼ Recognize your routine patterns of thought and behavior.

Put Yourself in Someone Else's Shoes

▼ Pretend that you are a customer of a particular company and think of five things you would do to improve it.

▼ Repeat the exercise from the viewpoints of a sales representative for that company, an employee, and a dissatisfied customer.

Restate Issues in Reverse

▼ Name good ways for a company to *lose* customers.

▼ Name good reasons for *not* buying a product.

▼ List ways a company could destroy a good relationship with a customer or supplier.

Force Connections

▼ Select six photos of dissimilar items. Number the photos, roll a pair of dice, and match the two pictures with those numbers. Then create a statement that explains how these two items could be connected to create a new good or service.

▼ Select 50 nouns at random from a dictionary. Write each word on a card, shuffle the cards, draw two, and make a connection between the resulting pair of words.

Look for Inspiration in New Places

▼ Take a different route to school or work. What do you notice?

▼ Look for new ideas for goods or services in unusual places: an airport, doctor's office, theater, sporting event. What other sources can you identify?

Seek Multiple Solutions

▼ Choose a routine task that you frequently perform. Ask yourself, How else could I do this? What might happen if I were to do it another way?

Ability to Steer Change

Today's managers must guide their employees and organizations through the changes wrought by technology, marketplace demands, and global competition. Managers must be skilled at recognizing employee strengths and motivating people to move toward common goals as members of a team. Throughout this book, real-world examples demonstrate how companies have initiated sweeping change initiatives. Most, if not all, have been led by managers comfortable with the tough decisions that today's fluctuating conditions require.

Factors that require organizational change can come from both external and internal sources; successful managers must be aware of both. External forces might include feedback from customers, developments in the international marketplace, economic trends, and new technologies. Inter-

nal factors might arise from new company goals, emerging employee needs, labor-union demands, or production problems.

Apparel manufacturer Levi Strauss has compiled a long history of growth. Recently, however, the company found that consumers were becoming less loyal, retailers more demanding, and suppliers more numerous than before. As a result, Levi's management embarked on a companywide change program to prepare their firm for the 21st century. Top management set the goals, but the design and implementation of the transition was pushed down to middle managers and employees. Members of 20 teams composed of employees from different departments were asked to find new ways of moving products to stores, satisfying customers, and pleasing retailers. The 200 people on the 20 teams were designated as *change agents* responsible for explaining the new programs to their peers and following through to ensure achievement of goals. As the new programs were implemented, thousands of jobs were redesigned and many workers were asked to reapply for employment.

Thomas J. Kasten, a Levi's vice president, says that the changes weren't easy, but they've paid off in important gains. "There's no handbook for this stuff and I don't have a lot of personal experience to fall back on. I've had to dial up my personal learning quotient. But we're unearthing skills and talents that might not have surfaced otherwise."[54]

The role played by change agents is examined in more detail in Chapter 6. Teamwork is a major topic in Chapter 11.

MANAGING ETHICS AND SOCIAL RESPONSIBILITY

In recent years, headlines have been full of stories about misconduct by businesses and their employees. Texaco executives were caught on tape using derogatory terms to refer to African-Americans. A California firm illegally imported Mexican strawberries, resulting in thousands of elementary school students being exposed to hepatitis. Kathie Lee Gifford was compelled to apologize when news stories revealed that a line of clothing carrying her name was manufactured using child labor. These and other cases demonstrate the importance of ethics and social responsibility in business.

Business ethics refers to the standards of conduct and moral values involving right and wrong actions arising in the work environment. Poor ethical standards can lead to public image problems, costly lawsuits, high levels of employee theft, and a host of other expensive problems. Ethical decision making can also foster trust, a vital element of strong relationships with customers, employees, and other organizations.[55] It is particularly important for top executives to demonstrate ethical behavior, since studies have shown that employees emulate their behavior.[56]

Strong company and individual ethics are often the cornerstone of visionary companies. Drug manufacturer Johnson & Johnson has maintained a strong code of ethics for over 50 years. These ethical standards form a framework for decision making throughout the company. When bottles of Tylenol were found to have been laced with poison in the 1980s, for example, executives did not hesitate to recall the product or deal openly with the media, because their actions were guided by deeply ingrained principles.[57]

Working hand-in-hand with business ethics is **social responsibility,** a management philosophy that highlights the social and economic effects of managerial decisions. This chapter's ethical controversy box reports Internet companies' struggle to weigh their social responsibility against profit considerations as they decide what information to collect on Web surfers.

Businesses demonstrate their social responsibility in a variety of ways. Sounds True is a Boulder, Colorado, maker and distributor of audio tapes dealing with health, psychology, and spiritual topics. Through sponsorship of the Prison Audio Project, management encourages Sounds True customers to donate their used audio tapes to some 1.5 million U.S. prison inmates.[58] Phil J. Quigley, CEO of telecommunications giant Pacific Telesis Group, personally campaigned to get the company to donate $100 million to start Education First, a program with the goal of connecting all California public schools and libraries to the Internet.[59]

For managers and employees at Fujifilm, protecting the environment is both a social responsibility and an important company objective. The photo in Figure 1.11 shows Lita Lowder, Fuji's regulatory compliance coordinator, in front of South Carolina's Ace Basin, 350,000 acres of one of the most pristine and viable ecosystems in North America. Lowder and her 8,000 Fuji associates in the United States work to preserve and protect valuable natural resources.

Chapter 2 explores business ethics, social responsibility, and the influence of business on society as a whole in detail. Each chapter also presents a feature highlighting a current ethical controversy in business.

WHY STUDY BUSINESS?

As business moves into the 21st century, new technologies, population shifts, and shrinking global barriers are altering the world at a frantic pace. Businesspeople are catalysts for many of these changes, creating new opportunities for individuals who are prepared to take action. Studying contemporary business will help you to prepare for the future.

Throughout this book, you'll be exposed to the real-life stories of many businesspeople. You'll learn about the

Business Directory

business ethics standards of conduct and moral values involving right and wrong actions arising in the work environment.

social responsibility a management philosophy that highlights the social and economic effects of managerial decisions.

SOLVING AN ETHICAL CONTROVERSY

Should Intel Be Baking Your Cookies Online?

As a businessperson, you need to know as much about your audience as you can so your ads will grab attention and let you show off your product. But as a consumer, you need to know whether marketers can be trusted to collect and use the personal information they need without abusing your right to privacy. The Internet and its technology only intensify this dilemma.

Some Web sites leave *cookies* on your computer when you visit them. These user ID files are stored on your hard drive so that businesses can access data on you or your system and track your Web movements. Software-based security depends, in part, on how you enter information. And you can delete cookie files or even refuse to let them be deposited.

But Intel's new Pentium III chip contains an encoded serial number that can be read (like caller-ID) to trace any online communication to a single computer. Such hardware-based security reduces the chance of fraud, but critics are outraged over the power that such measures give marketers and over the loss of anonymity on the Internet. Intel was forced to disable the ID number as a consumer boycott brewed.

Privacy advocates see businesses stopping at nothing to get the data they want. In a *CIO* magazine poll, high-tech and business executives said it's more important to track customer information (64%) than to protect customer privacy (36%). A Federal Trade Commission survey, however, found that four out of five respondents were worried about how online information would be used.

? *Should Internet businesses be allowed to regulate themselves?*

PRO

1. More access to such consumer information as purchases and Web visits means more effective goods and services for consumers.

2. The Direct Marketing Association already puts privacy restrictions on its members and helps consumers take their names off members' lists, so no additional protection is needed.

3. Online businesses need to have the freedom to grow. Government regulation will only slow growth and increase the cost of doing online business.

4. Online businesses need a more secure ID system to enhance privacy by reducing the risk of credit-card fraud and identity theft.

CON

1. Companies may collect data for one reason but find other, more profitable ways of using it, such as selling to marketers.

2. To get free loot or play games, many kids think nothing of giving out personal data, which is used by some companies to market to the very young.

3. Web site marketers and software vendors could coerce people into releasing hardware serial numbers before allowing them access to popular programs and Web sites.

4. Invasion of privacy on the Internet is one more way people are losing control of personal information.

SUMMARY

Shoppers in cyberspace need to feel as comfortable doing business on the Web as they do on Main Street. Other than the Children's Online Privacy Protection Act, which will eventually provide some protection, we currently have no set of laws protecting privacy on the Internet. Some experts say that the government already collects data and consumers have no privacy now anyway, so they should "just get over it." But privacy advocates want to make sure that businesses won't be tempted to use personal data in public ways.

Sources: Robert Lemos, "The Dark Side of the Digital Home," *MSNBC*, accessed at www.msnbc.com, February 8, 1999; Laura Gibbons Paul, "Careful What You Click For," *Family PC*, accessed at www1.zdnet.com, January 11, 1999; Lauren Gibbons Paul, "Hook 'Em Early and Often," *Family PC*, accessed at www1.zdnet.com, February 9, 1999; Ted Bridis, "Intel Yields to Privacy Concerns," the Associated Press, February 9, 1999; Ted Bridis, "CIO Magazine Survey Shows Chief Information Officers Side with Intel, Picking Customer Data Over Privacy," PR Newswire, February 3, 1999; James Lardner, "Intel Even More Inside," *U.S. News & World Report*, February 8, 1999, p. 43.

range of business careers available and the daily decisions, tasks, and challenges that they face. By the end of the course, you'll understand how marketing, accounting, and human resource management work together to provide competitive advantage for firms. This knowledge will help you to become a more capable employee and enhance your career potential.

Perhaps working for someone else isn't your dream. Like Dave Hampton, Furby creator, you may see yourself as an **entrepreneur,** building your own business and controlling your own future. Entrepreneurs are willing to take risks to create and operate a business. As earlier sections have explained, entrepreneurship can bring tremendous rewards—and enormous risk. As you read each chapter, you

Figure 1.11 **Fujifilm: Doing Well by Doing Good**

One Fujifilm employee thinks it's no coincidence that our boxes are green.

Lita Lowder, Fuji Photo Film, Inc., Regulatory Compliance Coordinator, photographed in South Carolina's ACE Basin

When your products are used to capture the earth's beauty, you obviously don't want that beauty to disappear. That's why Fujifilm employs experts like Lita Lowder. She's just one of 8,000 associates, at 43 facilities across the country, helping us to meet safety and environmental requirements. Her work is part of the Fujifilm GreenCare Program, our multi-faceted effort to preserve and protect valuable natural resources. Our support of South Carolina's Ace Basin, 350,000 acres of the largest, most pristine and viable ecosystems in North America is one part of this effort. So the next time you see one of our green boxes, remember Lita Lowder and Fujifilm's other associates because, in addition to putting the film inside, we're making sure there will always be a place to use it. **FUJIFILM**

Reading about the mistakes of other entrepreneurs in the Business Hall of Shame features will help you to avoid repeating these costly errors. Additionally, Chapter 6 concentrates specifically on how to start your own business. The information in this book will lay the foundation for the practical skills you need to launch a successful venture.

Even if you do not plan on becoming a businessperson, your daily life will still be affected by business. Every time you shop at a grocery store, buy a car, or visit your bank, you interact with the business world. Each chapter examines the tools and tactics used by firms to gain your business. Understanding these concepts will help you to make well-informed consumer choices, whether you are buying a new CD player or stock in IBM.

Finally, the business world has the resources and capabilities to solve—or create—many of the world's problems. This book discusses many examples of how organizations have shaped the world. The questions for ethical discussion in each chapter will help you to understand the important influences of industry on society, government, and economics. Armed with this knowledge, you'll be prepared to help cure society's problems as they emerge during this new century.

As you can see, business affects nearly every facet of life. In Part 1 of this book we take a detailed look at the ethical and social responsibility issues facing contemporary business. Other chapters discuss how economics influences business and people's everyday lives. Later chapters focus on the challenges and opportunities faced by businesses competing in global markets.

will learn about successful entrepreneurs in the Business Hall of Fame features. These entrepreneurs can serve as valuable role models for you.

Business Directory

entrepreneur a risk taker in the private enterprise system.

SUMMARY OF LEARNING GOALS

1. Describe the private enterprise system and the roles played by individual businesses, competitors, and entrepreneurs within the system.

The private enterprise system is an economic system that rewards firms based on how well they match and counter competitors' goods and services. Competition in the private enterprise system ensures success for firms that satisfy consumer demands. Entre-

preneurs are the risk takers in the private enterprise system. If no one takes risks, no successful businesses emerge, and the private enterprise system will not function.

2. Explain how the historical development of the U.S. economy continues to influence contemporary business.

Contemporary business has benefited from the experiences and strengths of each era of business history. The production methods developed during the industrial revolution and the production era have helped U.S. businesses improve efficiency at producing goods. The emphasis on understanding and meeting consumer needs during the marketing era has given U.S. businesspeople insight into how to differentiate their goods and services in the global marketplace.

3. Outline the challenges and opportunities that businesses face in the relationship era.

Business in the 21st century will be driven by relationships. Managers will have to find the best way to connect people, technology, and ethics in order to form strong partnerships with customers, employees, and other organizations. Opportunities will include advances in technology and growth of global markets.

4. Describe how technology is changing the way businesses operate and compete.

Technology is the application of science and engineering to do practical work. New technologies are allowing businesses to provide new goods and services for consumers, improve customer service, lower prices, and enhance working conditions. However, technology is also changing the shape of some industries, while it creates entirely new industries. Technology also opens new questions about business ethics and social responsibility.

5. Relate the importance of quality and customer satisfaction in efforts to create value for customers.

Today's savvy consumers expect more than they received in the past. They are looking for goods and services with positive traits offered at fair prices, the essence of value. A customer's perception of value is tied to quality, the degree of excellence or superiority of a firm's goods and services. Quality also includes customer satisfaction, the ability of a good or service to meet or exceed buyer needs and expectations. If customers feel they have received value—that is, quality for a fair price—they are likely to remain satisfied and continue their relationships with a firm.

6. Explain how individual businesses and entire nations compete in the global marketplace.

Global competitiveness requires nations, industries, and companies to work efficiently at producing goods and services. *Productivity* is the term that describes the relationship between the number of units produced and the human and other production inputs needed to produce them. Productivity is a widely used measure of a company's efficiency. In turn, the total productivity of a nation's businesses has become a measure of its economic strength, standard of living, and ability to compete.

7. Describe how changes in the workforce are leading to a new employer-employee partnership.

Employers today face increasing diversity, an aging population, and the changing nature of work itself. These factors and others have led to shrinkage in the workforce, making it more difficult to find and keep the quality employees needed for successful competition. As a result, many businesses are striving to develop partnerships with their employees by recognizing and rewarding their contributions.

8. Identify the skills that managers need to lead businesses in the new century.

Because the workforce is changing, managers need to improve their abilities to coach, mentor, and nurture employees in order to avoid labor shortages and benefit from diversity. Managers in the new century will need vision, the ability to perceive marketplace needs and how their firm can satisfy them. Critical thinking skills and creativity will allow managers to pinpoint problems and opportunities and plan novel solutions. Finally, managers will be dealing with rapid change, and they will need skills to help steer their organizations through shifts in external and internal conditions.

9. Explain how ethics and social responsibility affect business decision making.

Business ethics are the standards of conduct and moral values involving right and wrong actions in the workplace. Businesses that set high ethical standards avoid public image problems, costly lawsuits, customer mistrust, and other expensive problems. They can also offer guidelines for executives and employees to apply in making decisions. Social responsibility is a management philosophy that highlights the social and economic effects of business decisions and actions. Socially responsible firms seek to give back to their communities, customers, and employees.

10. List four reasons for studying business.

Business influences nearly every aspect of society. An understanding of contemporary business provides an excellent foundation for building the skills and knowledge needed to handle the challenges and opportunities of the new millennium. Studying business will help you in at least four ways: (1) to learn about different business careers, (2) to assess the advantages and disadvantages of starting your own business, (3) to become a better-informed consumer and investor, and (4) to learn how business can contribute to solving many of the problems of society.

TEN BUSINESS TERMS YOU NEED TO KNOW

business	Internet
profits	customer satisfaction
factors of production	business ethics
private enterprise system	social responsibility
competition	entrepreneur

Other Important Business Terms

not-for-profit organization	extranet
natural resources	transaction management
human resources	relationship management
capital	partnership
entrepreneurship	strategic alliance
competitive differentiation	value
private property	quality
consumer orientation	productivity
branding	gross domestic product (GDP)
brand	outsourcing
technology	diversity
World Wide Web	vision
e-mail	critical thinking
intranet	creativity

REVIEW QUESTIONS

1. Why are profits important in a private enterprise system? Would entrepreneurs start organizations if they saw no opportunity for profit? Why or why not?
2. What is competitive differentiation? Pick three products that you use regularly and explain how the businesses that provide them have distinguished their products from competitors.
3. What is meant by the term *relationship era?* Give an example of a business or organization whose managers have found new ways to make connections with customers.
4. How is the relationship era different from the way business was conducted in each of the historical periods listed below? How is it the same?
   a. colonial era
   b. industrial revolution
   c. age of industrial entrepreneurs
   d. production era
   e. marketing era
5. What is meant by the term *productivity?* How is the concept of GDP related to productivity?
6. What is value, and what role does it play in consumer preferences and buying decisions? Can a poor-quality product have value to consumers?
7. What are the main challenges that businesspeople will face in building world-class workforces in the 21st century?
8. Explain the difference between critical thinking and creativity. Which do you think is more important in school? In business? In your personal life?
9. In newspapers and magazines, find at least three examples of how business ethics and social responsibility have affected specific business organizations' performances.
10. Does a country's education level affect its ability to compete in the global marketplace? Why or why not?

QUESTIONS FOR CRITICAL THINKING

1. To face the challenges and opportunities of the 21st century, businesses will need managers with vision, creativity, and critical thinking skills. How can a business determine whether a prospective employee has these characteristics before making the hiring decision? Write a list of interview questions through which an employer could evaluate a prospective employee's creativity. Do you think these skills are something that can be learned? Suggest ways in which businesses can encourage vision, creativity, and critical thinking in employees and managers. Do you think these characteristics are more important for managers in large companies or for entrepreneurs?
2. Discuss the ethical considerations of the following situations. What would you do if faced with these situations? Explain your reasoning in detail.
   a. You are a manager who has caught an employee stealing a box of pencils.
   b. You are placed in charge of your company's payroll department. You know it would be easy to write an extra company check to yourself.
   c. Your department is 3 days late in meeting a deadline for an important client, and you worry that you will be unable to fill the order. Should you make up an excuse so the client will give you more time or should you tell the truth and face the consequences? What should you tell your boss?
   d. You uncover information that shows your boss is illegally meeting with a competitor to set prices.
3. To encourage creativity among employees, Wal-Mart's head of store operations picks one product in which he sees untapped potential and then challenges employees to find ways to promote it and sell more of it. This month's pick is duct tape. Suggest a plan for promoting and selling duct tape. What new uses might you suggest to encourage customers to buy more duct tape? How would you display duct tape in the store to catch their attention?
4. Hispanic consumer groups recently threatened to boycott American Airlines after revelations that an airline training manual warned that Hispanic customers tended to drink heavily and cause disruptions during flights. Using the concepts in this chapter, devise a plan to help American Airlines deal with this situation. Be as specific as possible.

5. For years, Volvo had an image as a maker of boxy cars with a devotion to reliable performance and vehicle safety. Volvo customers were highly loyal, many of them middle-class families with children. After several years of poor sales, Volvo now plans to introduce a sporty new coupe and a racy convertible, with prices starting at $40,000, more than $20,000 higher than last year's models. Volvo believes that it can capture a share of the luxury car market now dominated by Mercedes Benz, BMW, and Lexus. Examine how Volvo will need to change its relationships with customers, employees, car dealers, and suppliers in light of this new strategy. How might customer perceptions of value, quality, and satisfaction change? Do you believe that Volvo's strategy will work? Why or why not?

Experiential Exercise

DIRECTIONS: Following is a list of workforce trends discussed in the chapter. Column 1 identifies the trends. Columns 2 and 3 ask you to anticipate how the trends might affect you and your career. Columns 4 and 5 are based on the answers you get when interviewing an employee who has been out of college and working full-time five or more years.

1. Trends	2. Potential Impact on My Career	3. My Strategies to Capitalize on These Trends	4. Impact on Person Interviewed	5. Company's Strategies to Manage Trends
a. Aging of the population				
b. Shrinking labor pool				
c. Increased mobility of workers				
d. Increased diversity				
e. Changing nature of work				

Nothing but Net

1. **The Internet.** To help you get the most out of the "Nothing but Net" exercises that appear at the end of every chapter, visit one of the Web sites listed here. If you're new to the Internet, list three things you learned that will help you develop your "surfing" skills. If you're a proficient Net surfer, list three items of information you learned that will help you improve your "surfing" skills.

www.pbs.org/uti/begin.html

www.msn.com/tutorial/default.html

2. **Code of Ethics.** Use your search engine to find the code of ethics for three organizations. One site that contains several codes of ethics is

www.arq.co.uk/ethicalbusiness/frsrc/susa.htm

At that site, choose "Business Ethics Resources on WWW."
Compare the three codes to determine their similarities and differences in focus, approach, language, and emphasis. Provide possible reasons for the similarities and differences you noticed. How might you benefit as an employee working for an organization with a code of ethics compared with one without a code of ethics?

3. **The New Employer-Employee Partnership.** Visit the Web site of a corporation you're interested in learning more about as a prospective employee. What assumptions can you draw about the company from its Web pages on job opportunities, employee benefits, and the like? Some possible Web sites follow:

Levi Strauss: www.levistrauss.com

Southwest Airlines: iflyswa.com/

Marriott Hotels Resorts and Suites: www.marriott.com/marriott/

Starbucks Coffee: www1.occ.com/starbucks/index.html

Hewlett-Packard: www.hp.com

Note: Internet Web addresses change frequently. If you do not find the exact sites listed, you may need to access the organization's or company's home page and search from there.

FAST TRACK TO SUCCESS

Every business is rooted in an entrepreneurial idea. Today, a growing number of entrepreneurs are finding themselves on the fast track to success by skillfully blending people, technology, and ethical behavior. Following are descriptions of five such companies.

YAHOO!

In 1994, as Ph.D. students at Stanford, Jerry Yang and David Filo began compiling lists of their favorite Web pages, which eventually led them to create a search engine called Yahoo! Today, nearly 2 million users access the Yahoo! site every day. Over the past few years Yahoo! has formed several important strategic alliances with Netscape, Softbank, the Village Voice, Fodor's, and MTV.

Yang and Filo are also giving back to the community. Not only does Yahoo! help promote the development of Internet education and programming, the company is connecting classrooms to the Internet, provides free educational seminars, and offers exposure for not-for-profit organizations on its Web sites.

PARADIGM ENTERTAINMENT

In 1990, three out-of-work engineers took their expertise in 3-D military computer simulations and found success offering it to a much broader user group. Forming a strategic alliance with Silicon Graphics, Paradigm has won accounts with organizations such as BMW, NASA, Chrysler, and Boeing. Paradigm is currently creating products for Nintendo, Disney, and Sega and will soon release its first game on the Internet.

Paradigm gives back to the community through a scholarship fund it has created for engineering students. The company also offers scholarship recipients a job with the company upon their graduation.

DREW PEARSON COMPANIES

Drew Pearson, former Dallas Cowboys Super Bowl Champ, is CEO of Drew Pearson Companies (DPC) one of the nation's top designers and manufacturers of sports caps. DPC is one of only six companies to have scored licenses with the NFL, NBA, MLB, and NHL. "We were the first to use computers in our design process," says President Ken Shead. "We could generate art that showed variation in designs—three-dimensional front and back views—something our competition had no clues as to how we were generating those looks." DPC also set itself apart by negotiating exclusive licensing agreements with non-sports companies such as Disney.

TWO WOMEN BOXING

Artists Julie Cohn and Linda Finnell's decidedly low-tech approach to design garnered their handmade line of journals, photo albums, baby books, and picture frames an account list including Neiman Marcus, Bergdorf's, and Barneys. But the company faced growth and competitive problems. According to Cohn, "As we got computerized, we were really able to analyze the cost of our business in more scrutinizing fashion."

Cohn and Finnell decided to focus their attention on their greatest strength—designing. In an effort to combat their limited manufacturing capabilities, they began licensing their designs to other mass market companies. Licensing has allowed the business to grow and the women to remain true to their management style without stressing their in-house staff.

HUMAN GENOME SCIENCES

Human Genome Sciences (HGS) was founded in 1992 by Harvard Medical School professor Dr. William Haseltine and a group of New Jersey venture capitalists. HGS's objective is to be the first to discover most human genes and use this knowledge to create new gene-based medicines to predict, detect, treat, and cure disease.

HGS shares its proprietary information with partners including SmithKline Beechman and Schering-Plough Corporation. HGS is entitled to licensing and research fees and receives royalty payments on products created by its partners. HGS also plans on developing its own therapeutic products. Dr. Haseltine asserts HGS's mission is to use the new gene technology to improve human health, not to alter genetic destiny.

Questions

1. Would you describe these businesses as entrepreneurial? Why or why not?

2. What role has technology played in the success of these businesses?

3. How do these businesses demonstrate their social responsibility?

chapter 2

Achieving Business Success by Demonstrating Ethical Behavior and Social Responsibility

LEARNING GOALS

1. Explain the concepts of business ethics and social responsibility.

2. Describe the factors that influence individual ethics and common ethical dilemmas in the workplace.

3. Explain how organizations shape ethical behavior.

4. Relate the ways in which government regulation affects business ethics and social responsibility.

5. Describe the responsibilities of business to the general public, customers, and employees.

6. Explain why investors and the financial community are concerned with business ethics.

7. Describe the ethical and social responsibility issues facing businesses in the global marketplace.

LOCKHEED MARTIN
http://www.lmco.co

FRAUD.

Unread | Total
0 | 6

U.S. DEPARTMENT OF
JUSTICE
www.usdoj.gov

microsoft.con

junkbusters.com
junkbusters.com
junkbusters.com
junkbusters.com

Microsoft: Predator or Gentle Giant?

A recent joke reveals much of the background surrounding the legal battles between the federal government and Microsoft Corp.: "In the U.S. government's fight with Bill Gates, I'm for the federal government. I always like to root for the little guy." Who hasn't heard of Bill Gates, the founder and CEO of software powerhouse Microsoft, whose company stock holdings have made him the world's richest man? To many, Gates is a folk hero of today's cyberspace economy, whose brains and business savvy enabled him to build a software monopoly and who is now being falsely accused by jealous rivals. To others, Gates and his company represent a fierce predator that wields its power to crush the competition.

Which group is right? If Microsoft has become a monopoly, its potentially uncompetitive clout can be countered by federal laws like the Sherman Antitrust Act and the Clayton Act, both described on page 50. The answer can be found by examining how Microsoft has been operating in the industry.

Microsoft makes Windows, the operating system that runs 90 percent of the world's personal computers. This advantage makes it difficult for other

companies to challenge the software giant because Windows is currently the door to the computer world. But rivals accuse Microsoft of throwing its weight around to monopolize the entire industry—forcing PC purchasers to buy products they don't want, dictating which business relationships other companies can enter into, and even offering questionable incentives. Although Microsoft executives express their right to compete forcefully in the marketplace, they deny any strong-arm tactics. And so the company finds itself in the federal courts, accused by the U.S. Justice Department of anticompetitive behavior.

While the government's responsibility is to protect consumer choice and preserve competition, Microsoft argues that the government is attempting to kill its ability to satisfy customers and compete successfully. Microsoft's position is that in bundling its own Internet Explorer browser with Windows 95, it was simply adding value to the software.

Product bundling isn't the only area of dispute. The Justice Department also questions some of Microsoft's contracts with Web site operators and Internet service providers. Web companies seeking top billing in the *Channels* section of Windows 98 were required to create Web pages whose appearance would deteriorate if viewed with a browser other than Explorer. Microsoft also asked these companies to avoid business with rival Netscape; Intuit is one such firm. The government claims that these contracts cut off key distribution channels for Netscape, but Microsoft says that PC users can easily find Netscape's product by downloading it from the Internet.

WWW.

www.microsoft.com
www.usdoj.com

The government points to other examples of unfair practices with respect to Netscape. Apple Computer execs claim that Microsoft threatened to withhold Microsoft Office for Macintosh unless Apple joined its war against Netscape. And the Justice Department claims that Microsoft offered Intuit $1 million to switch from Navigator to Internet Explorer. Microsoft labeled this an incentive. In fact, it argues that even though Netscape has lost market share, it still retains 40 percent of the total market. So Netscape is alive and offering consumers a competitive product.

Microsoft insists that it isn't a monopoly—and that the government simply doesn't understand the competition in today's global marketplace. After all, its industry dominance could be destroyed quickly by any programmer with a better idea. The rise of the personal computer 30 years ago cost IBM its overwhelming dominance. Will some high-tech giant slayer come looking for Microsoft?[1]

CHAPTER OVERVIEW

As discussed in Chapter 1, the underlying aim of most businesses is to serve customers at a profit. But the situation at Microsoft demonstrates that sole focus on profitability and beating the competition at any cost can have a dramatic downside. When does a company's self-interest conflict with society's and consumers well-being? And are seeking profits and upholding high principles of right and wrong mutually exclusive goals?

Today, a growing number of businesses of all sizes are answering "no." An organization that wants to prosper over the long term cannot do so without considering **business ethics,** the standards of conduct and moral values governing actions and decisions in the work environment. Business also must take a wide range of social issues into account, including how a decision will affect the environment, employees, and customers. A related term, *social responsibility,* refers to the philosophies, policies, procedures, and actions directed toward the enhancement of society's welfare as a primary objective. In short, businesses must find the delicate balance between doing what is right and doing what is profitable.

When that balance is skewed, they can experience serious consequences. Fruit

Business Directory

business ethics standards of business conduct and moral values.

and vegetable distributor Andrew & Williamson Sales found this out when an oversupply of Mexican-grown frozen strawberries filled its San Diego warehouse. When monthly storage fees for the fruit began cutting into the company's bottom line, the sales manager devised a plan to turn expense into profit. The frozen strawberries could be sold at discounted prices to school cafeterias across the country, except for one problem. Federal regulations require all fruit sold to schools to be domestically grown. Andrew & Williamson executives decided to disguise the Mexican-grown strawberries as domestically grown produce and sell them to schools through three independent food brokers.

The plan seemed to work well, until hundreds of Michigan school children became sick with hepatitis A. Government investigators quickly identified the source of the outbreak: All of the students had eaten frozen strawberries in their school cafeterias that had originated in the Andrew & Williamson warehouse. The company was forced to reveal that it had illegally sold Mexican strawberries to the schools. Most likely, an infected field worker in Mexico had inadvertently passed the disease to freshly picked strawberries. Several Andrew & Williamson executives were later indicted on criminal charges, and the company was left in financial ruin as a result of its unethical behavior.[2]

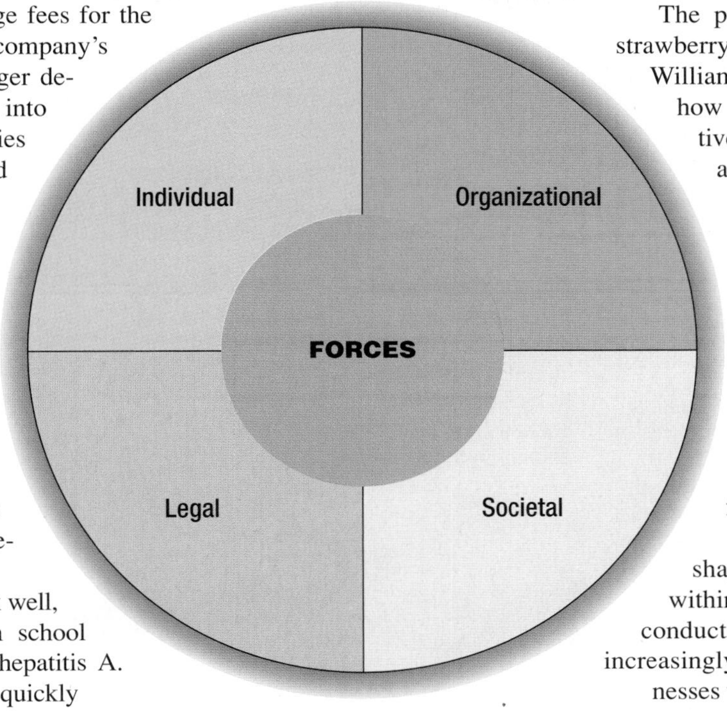

In business, as in life, deciding what is right or wrong in a given situation is not always a clear-cut choice. Businesses have many responsibilities—to customers, to employees, to investors, and to society as a whole. Sometimes conflicts arise in trying to serve the divergent needs of separate constituencies. Andrew & Williamson executives, for example, faced a conflict between the firm's desire for profits and its responsibility to customers and the law. In other cases, conflicts arise between ideal decisions and those that are practical in given situations.

As Figure 2.1 indicates, four main forces shape business ethics and social responsibility: individual, organizational, legal, and societal forces. Rather than oper-

Figure 2.1 **Forces Shaping Business Ethics and Social Responsibility**

> "The central business issue should be how to meet the needs of a group of people in a way that is fulfilling for employees, satisfying for customers, profitable for shareholders, and responsible in the community."
>
> **Mark S. Albion**
> American business writer

ating in a vacuum, each of the forces interacts with the other three, and the interactions powerfully impact both the strength and direction of each influence.

The problems resulting from the strawberry cover-up by Andrew & Williamson officials demonstrate how the ethical values of executives and individual employees at all levels can influence the decisions and actions a business takes. Throughout your business career, you will encounter numerous situations where you will need to weigh right and wrong before making a decision or taking action. Therefore, the discussion of business ethics begins by focusing on individual ethics.

Business ethics are also shaped by the ethical climate within an organization. Codes of conduct and ethical standards play increasingly significant roles in businesses where doing the right thing is both supported and applauded. This chapter will demonstrate how a firm can create a framework to encourage—and even demand—high standards of ethical behavior and social responsibility from its employees.

It is clear, however, that not all companies successfully set and meet the ethical standards of leading firms such as Nordstrom. As a protectionist move, federal, state, and local governments have enacted laws to regulate business practices. Many of these laws are examined in this chapter. It also considers the complex question of just what business owes to society and how societal forces mold the actions of businesses. Finally, it examines the influence of business ethics and social responsibility on global business.

INDIVIDUAL BUSINESS ETHICS

In today's business environment, individuals can make the difference in ethical expectations and behavior. As executives, managers, and employees demonstrate their personal ethical principles—or lack of ethical principles—the expectations and actions of those who work for them, as well as those who work with them, can change.

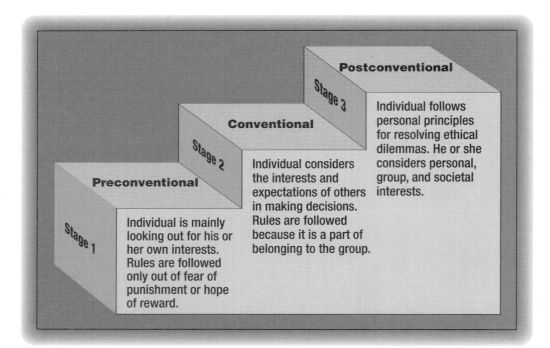

Figure 2.2 Stages of Moral and Ethical Development

What is the current status of individual business ethics in the United States? Although ethical behavior can be difficult to track or even define in all circumstances, evidence suggests that many individuals act unethically or illegally on the job. Take employee theft as an example. It is estimated that U.S. businesses currently lose over $120 billion a year from employee theft of everything from cash to paper clips. Nearly 60 percent of workers in one survey also admitted to "time theft" in such forms as coming in late to work, leaving early, or lying about sick days.[3]

Employee theft is not the only questionable behavior on the job. In one survey of American workers, nearly half admitted to committing one or more unethical or illegal acts on the job during the past year. The most common acts included cutting corners on quality (16 percent), covering up incidents (14 percent), and lying to or deceiving customers (9 percent).[4] Another study found that 30 percent of managers admitted to filing deceptive internal reports.[5]

Given these findings, it is apparent that nearly every employee, at every level, wrestles with ethical questions at some point or another. Some rationalize questionable behavior by saying "everybody's doing it." Others act unethically because they feel pressured to hold their jobs or meet performance quotas. Some, however, avoid unethical acts that don't mesh with their personal values and morals. In order to understand the differences in the ways individuals arrive at eth-

ical choices, the next section focuses on how personal ethics and morals are developed.

The Development of Individual Ethics

Individuals typically develop ethical standards in the three stages shown in Figure 2.2: the preconventional, conventional, and postconventional stages. In the preconventional stage, individuals primarily consider their own needs and desires in making decisions. They obey external rules only because they are afraid of punishment or hope to receive rewards if they comply.

In the second stage, the conventional stage, individuals are aware of and act in response to their duty to others, including their obligations to their family members, co-workers, and organizations. The expectations of these groups influence how they choose between what is acceptable and unacceptable in certain situations. Self-interest, however, continues to play a role in decisions.

The final, postconventional stage represents the highest level of ethical and moral behavior. The individual is able to move beyond mere self-interest and duty and take the larger needs of society into account, as well. He or she has developed personal ethical principles for determining what is right and can apply those principles in a wide variety of situations.

An individual's stage in moral and ethical development is determined by a huge number of factors. Past experiences help to shape responses to different situations. A person's family, educational, cultural, and religious backgrounds can also play a role. People can also have different styles of deciding ethical dilemmas, no matter what their stage of moral development. As Table 2.1 shows, one study suggests that men and women tend to use different techniques for resolving ethical situations.

To help you understand and prepare for the ethical dilemmas you may confront in your career, let's take a closer look at some of the factors involved in solving ethical questions on the job.

They said it

"First, there is the law. It must be obeyed. But the law is the minimum. You must act ethically."

IBM employee guidelines

Table 2.1	Ethical Gender Gap

Typical Ways Men Resolve Ethical Dilemmas:	Typical Ways Women Resolve Ethical Dilemmas:
– Primarily Respect Rights – Ask "Who Is Right?" – Value Decisiveness – Make Unambiguous Decisions – Seek Solutions That Are Objectively Fair – Rely on Rules – Are Guided by Logic – Accept Authority	– Primarily Respect Feelings – Ask "Who Will Be Hurt?" – Avoid Being Judgmental – Search for Compromise – Seek Solutions That Minimize Hurt – Rely on Communication – Are Guided by Emotion – Challenge Authority

On-the-Job Ethical Dilemmas

In the fast-paced world of business, you will sometimes be called to weigh the ethics of decisions that can affect not just your own future, but possibly the futures of your fellow workers, your company, and its customers. As already noted, it's not always easy to distinguish between what is right and wrong in many business situations, especially when the needs and concerns of various parties conflict.

Consider the situation that William Haggett, CEO of Bath Iron Works (BIW), found himself in after a quarterly meeting with his shipbuilding firm's top client, the U.S. Navy. After the meeting, Haggett discovered that one of the Navy consultants had accidentally left behind a 67-page document marked, "Business Sensitive." Scanning the document, Haggett realized it detailed a competitor's proposal for a project on which BIW also was bidding. Haggett not only read the competitor's proposal, he discussed the contents with subordinates and had the document copied. When a subordinate told BIW's president about Haggett's actions, the president went to Haggett and convinced him to return the proposal to the Navy's consultant. Although a Navy investigation cleared Haggett of any serious wrongdoing, his

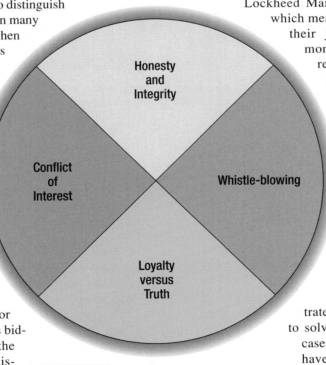

Figure 2.3 **Common Business Ethical Dilemmas**

(Honesty and Integrity; Conflict of Interest; Whistle-blowing; Loyalty versus Truth)

BIW colleagues pushed him to resign. "With the benefit of hindsight, I see it was a bad decision on my part," he later explained at a news conference.

Lockheed Martin CEO Norman Augustine found himself in a similar situation. The day before his firm's proposal for a large government contract was due to be turned in, a mysterious package arrived in the mail. It contained a copy of a competing proposal for the same contract. With the information in hand, he still had time to change Lockheed Martin's proposal in order to gain the upper hand at winning the contract. Augustine immediately turned the data over to the government and informed Lockheed Martin's competitor about what he had received. Lockheed Martin didn't win the contract, which meant that some employees lost their jobs and shareholders lost money. But Augustine didn't regret his decision. He recalls, "We helped establish a reputation that, in the long run, will draw us business."[6]

What would you do in a situation like this? Would you do whatever seemed necessary to make sure your company made the big sale? According to one recent survey, 98 percent of salespeople said they would do "anything" to close a sale.[7]

As these two stories illustrate, several avenues can be taken to solve ethical dilemmas. In many cases, each possible decision will have unpleasant consequences as well as positive benefits that must be evaluated. The ethical dilemma that confronted Haggett and Augustine is just one example of many different types of ethical questions encountered in the workplace. Figure 2.3 identifies some of the more common ethical dilemmas that business-people face.

Conflict of Interest A **conflict of interest** exists when a businessperson is faced with a situation where his or her decision may be influenced by the potential for personal gain. Bribes are one type of conflict of interest. Joseph Escalon, for example, worked for the Federal Aviation Administration (FAA) processing applications for commercial airline pilot licenses. A pilot for Asiana Airlines, who hadn't completed required flight checks or met FAA training and experience requirements, offered Escalon money and a free trip if he would rush the application through the certification process. Escalon accepted the bribe, but his actions were later revealed. He was sentenced to four months in prison and a $2,000 fine.[8]

Questions regarding conflicts of interest extend beyond bribery. Consider the debate at Wake Forest University's Bowman Gray School of Medicine. Several of the faculty members at the medical school also conducted research for R. J. Reynolds Tobacco Co. Their research was intended to determine whether the effects of nicotine from cigarette smoking were as dangerous as anti-tobacco activists claimed. Critics say the faculty members had a conflict of interest. On the one hand, they were working to train future doctors; on the other, they were accepting funding from a company which manufactures a product viewed as a major health threat.[9]

Honesty and Integrity Honesty and integrity are traits highly valued by employers. In a survey conducted by

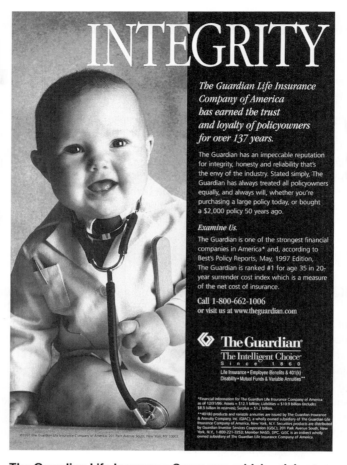

The Guardian Life Insurance Company, which celebrates its 140th birthday in 2000, highlights its strong reputation for integrity, honesty, and reliability in its promotional messages.

staffing firm Robert Half International, employers said the number one qualities they sought in job applicants were honesty and integrity.[10]

Integrity involves adhering to deeply felt ethical principles in business situations. It goes beyond being truthful—it means doing what you say you will do and accepting responsibility for mistakes.

Honesty is an ethical principle that permeates many work situations. Some people, for example, misrepresent their academic credentials and previous work experience on their resumes or job applications. Recent news stories have reported instances where individuals have misrepresented their military experience in order to qualify for burial in Arlington National Cemetery. One candidate withdrew from a political race after news reports surfaced that refuted his claims about a brother's racially motivated death during the civil rights struggles of the 1960s.

As already discussed, employee theft is an enormous expense for U.S. businesses. Research has shown that many employees also have few qualms about lying in order to protect themselves from punishment. Honesty is also a factor in developing strong customer relationships.

Loyalty versus Truth Businesspeople expect their employees to be loyal and to act in the best interests of the company. An ethical conflict can arise, however, when individuals must decide between loyalty to the company and truthfulness in business relationships. William Haggett and Norman Augustine both faced this issue in deciding how to handle situations where they had access to information about competitors' plans.

Whistle-Blowing When an individual does encounter unethical or illegal actions at

Business Directory

conflict of interest   a situation where a business decision may be influenced by the potential for personal gain.

whistle-blowing   an employee's disclosure to the media or government authorities of illegal, immoral, or unethical practices of the organization.

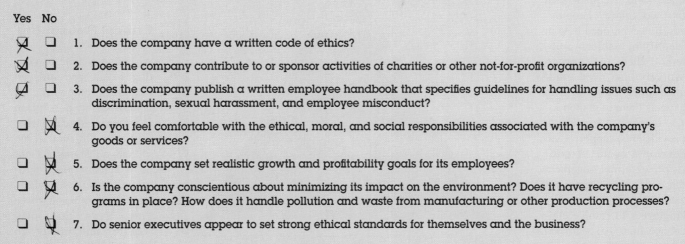

Before You Accept a Job, Review Your New Employer's Code of Ethics

How far would you go to satisfy your employer? If working for an ethical and socially responsible firm is important to you, look before you leap. Here are seven questions to help you evaluate how well a potential employer's ethical values mesh with your own.

Yes No

☑ ☐ 1. **Does the company have a written code of ethics?**

☑ ☐ 2. **Does the company contribute to or sponsor activities of charities or other not-for-profit organizations?**

☑ ☐ 3. **Does the company publish a written employee handbook that specifies guidelines for handling issues such as discrimination, sexual harassment, and employee misconduct?**

☐ ☑ 4. **Do you feel comfortable with the ethical, moral, and social responsibilities associated with the company's goods or services?**

☐ ☑ 5. **Does the company set realistic growth and profitability goals for its employees?**

☐ ☑ 6. **Is the company conscientious about minimizing its impact on the environment? Does it have recycling programs in place? How does it handle pollution and waste from manufacturing or other production processes?**

☐ ☑ 7. **Do senior executives appear to set strong ethical standards for themselves and the business?**

If you can answer "yes" to five or more of these questions, chances are you will find yourself working for an ethical and socially responsible firm.

---

work, he or she must decide what action to take. **Whistle-blowing** is the term for an employee's disclosure to the media or government authorities of illegal, immoral, or unethical practices of the organization. Nationwide Insurance agent John Askin faced an ethical dilemma in the early 1990s, and he decided that whistle-blowing was the only avenue available to him. Askin alleges that his boss gave him a map of Louisville, Kentucky, with a large *X* marked over several neighborhoods. Askin was told to avoid sales from these largely low-income, African American neighborhoods, but he refused and decided to alert government agencies. Although Nationwide has denied Askin's allegations, the Justice Department is investigating the company for illegally discriminating against minority groups.[11]

A whistle-blower must weigh a number of issues in the decision to come forward or not. Some may decide to try to work through internal channels within their organizations in order to correct the wrongdoing. If that fails, they must weigh the potential damages to the greater public good if they do not come forward. Although in many instances whistle-blowers are protected by state and federal laws, they may still experience dramatic retribution for their actions. For example, Mark Whitacre was an executive at Archer Daniels Midland (ADM) when he blew the whistle on his employer for illegally fixing grain prices. He cooperated with the FBI's investigation by se-cretly taping meetings over a 3-year period in which the alleged misdeeds occurred. ADM later fired Whitacre and accused him of embezzlement, effectively destroying his career.[12]

Obviously, whistle-blowing and other ethical issues arise relatively infrequently in firms with strong organizational climates of ethical behavior. The Business Tool Kit gives guidelines that will help you to evaluate a potential employer's ethics. The next section examines how a business can develop an environment that discourages unethical behavior among individuals.

HOW ORGANIZATIONS SHAPE ETHICAL CONDUCT

No individual makes decisions in a vacuum. Choices are strongly influenced by the standards of conduct established within the organizations where people work. Most ethical lapses in business reflect the values of the firms' corporate cultures.

As shown in Figure 2.4, development of a corporate culture to support business ethics happens on four levels: ethical awareness, ethical reasoning, ethical action, and ethical leadership. If any of these four factors is missing, the ethical climate in an organization will weaken.[13]

Ethical Awareness

The foundation of an ethical climate is ethical awareness. As we've already seen, ethical dilemmas occur frequently in the workplace. Employees, however, need help in identifying ethical problems when they occur. Workers also need guidance about how the firm expects them to respond.

One way for a firm to provide this support is to develop a **code of conduct,** a formal statement that defines how the organization expects and requires employees to resolve ethical questions. An estimated 73 percent of companies have such codes of conduct in place.[14]

At the most basic level, a code of conduct may simply specify ground rules for acceptable behavior, such as identifying the laws and regulations that employees must obey. Other companies, however, use their codes of conduct to identify key corporate values and provide frameworks that guide employees as they resolve moral and ethical dilemmas.

Telecommunications giant Nortel views its corporate code of conduct as a way to put the firm's core values into practice. The company's code identifies the commitments the firm has made to five groups of stakeholders: employees, customers, suppliers, shareholders, and the global community in which the company operates. Nortel executives sought input and feedback from employees in developing the code. Over 36 discussions were held with groups of employees to pinpoint ethical areas where employees wanted and needed guidance. The company placed a draft of the code on its employee

www. www.nortel.com/cool/ethics/home.html

| Figure 2.4 | Structure of an Ethical Environment

- Ethical Leadership
- Ethical Action
- Ethical Reasoning
- Ethical Awareness

intranet, allowing all 63,000 Nortel employees to comment. After the code was finalized, Nortel posted it at the company's Web site.[15]

Ethical Reasoning

Although a code of conduct can provide an overall framework, it cannot detail a solution for every ethical situation. Recall that some ethical questions do not have clear black-and-white answers. Many ethical dilemmas involve gray areas that may require individuals to sort through several options and potential consequences. Businesses must provide the tools employees need to evaluate these options and arrive at suitable decisions.

Many firms have instituted ethics training programs. Although some observers debate whether ethics can actually be taught, this training can give employees an opportunity to practice applying ethical values to hypothetical situations as a prelude to applying the same standards to real-world situations. At MONY insurance, everyone in the company, including senior management, must attend an ethics training course that focuses on specific situations employees might encounter in their jobs.[16]

www. www.mony.com

Lockheed Martin hired a consulting firm to develop an ethics training game called "The Ethics Challenge" based on the popular comic-strip characters Dilbert and Dogbert. Teams move game pieces around a board that resembles different parts of an office. As they move toward the finish line, teams must solve ethical problems from sample cases. The company believes that the board game encourages employees not only to discuss ethical situations but also to arrive at ethical choices working as a group.[17]

Business Directory

code of conduct a formal statement that defines how the organization expects and requires employees to resolve ethical questions.

Ethical Action

Codes of conduct and ethics training help employees to recognize and reason through ethical problems. However, firms must also provide structures and approaches that allow decisions to be turned into ethical actions.

Goals set for the business as a whole and for individual departments and employees can affect ethical behavior. A firm whose managers set unrealistic goals for employee performance may find an increase in cheating, lying, and other misdeeds, as employees attempt to protect themselves. One study of unethical behavior on the job found that 56 percent of workers who did misbehave felt pressured to do so because of stress in the workplace.[18] Wetherill Associates, a Pennsylvania auto-parts distributor, tries to avoid this problem by not setting sales goals for its salespeople.

Other companies encourage ethical action by providing support for employees faced with dilemmas. One common tool is an employee hotline, a telephone number that employees can call, often anonymously, for advice or to report unethical behavior they have witnessed. Some companies also create ethics officers, individuals responsible for guiding employees through potential ethical minefields.

Nortel employees can call AdviceLine to discuss any questions they have regarding the company's code of conduct. In each region around the globe where Nortel operates, a local employee conducts classes on ethical behavior. Nortel believes that this helps to personalize each employee's relationship with the company by providing one-on-one access to a corporate business ethics representative.[19]

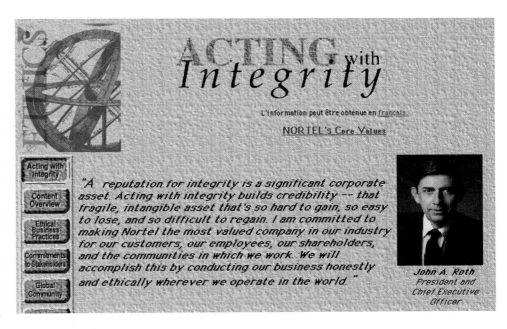

"A reputation for integrity is a significant corporate asset. Acting with integrity builds credibility -- that fragile, intangible asset that's so hard to gain, so easy to lose, and so difficult to regain. I am committed to making Nortel the most valued company in our industry for our customers, our employees, our shareholders, and the communities in which we work. We will accomplish this by conducting our business honestly and ethically wherever we operate in the world."

John A. Roth
President and Chief Executive Officer

Ethical Leadership

Executives must not only talk about ethical behavior but also demonstrate it in their actions. This principle requires that they be personally committed to the company's core values and be willing to base their actions on them.

However, ethical leadership should also go one step further and charge each employee at every level with the responsibility for being an ethical leader. As such, each individual should be aware of transgressions and be willing to defend the organization's standards.

Unfortunately, not all organizations are able to build this solid framework of business ethics. The Business Hall of Shame discusses what can happen when companies assume that others share their ethical concerns. Because the damage from ethical misconduct can powerfully affect a firm's stakeholders—customers, investors, employees, and the public—pressure is exerted on businesses to act in acceptable ways. The next section examines the legal and governmental forces that are designed to safeguard society's interests when businesses fail at self-regulation.

CONTROLLING BUSINESS BEHAVIOR THROUGH GOVERNMENT REGULATION

Although few would disagree that businesses should act ethically and responsibly, it is clear that not all companies behave this way. When businesses fail to regulate their own actions, consumers and other businesses can suffer serious consequences. Because of this threat, federal, state, and local governments sometimes step in to regulate business activity. Many of the major federal laws affecting business are listed in Table 2.2. Legal protections for employee safety and equal employment opportunities are covered later in this chapter. Many of the laws that affect specific industries or individuals are described in other chapters. For example, legislation affecting international business operations is discussed in Chapter 4. Laws designed to assist small businesses are examined in Chapter 5. Laws related to formation and operation of labor unions are described in Chapter 11. Finally, legislation related to banking and the securities markets is discussed in Chapters 20 and 21.

The history of government regulation in the United States can be divided into three phases: regulation of competition, consumer protection, and deregulation. Because an understanding of the political and legal environment in

Table 2.2   Major Federal Laws Affecting Business

Date	Law	Description
A. LAWS TO MAINTAIN A COMPETITIVE ENVIRONMENT		
1890	Sherman Antitrust Act	Prohibits restraint of trade and monopolization; delineates a competitive marketing system as national policy.
1914	Clayton Act	Strengthens the Sherman Act by restricting such practices as rice discrimination, exclusive dealing, tying contracts, and interlocking boards of directors where the effect {may be to substantially lessen competition or tend to create a monopoly."
1914	Federal Trade Commission Act	Prohibits unfair methods of competition; established the Federal Trade Commission, an administrative agency that investigates business practices and enforces the FTC Act.
1938	Wheeler-Lea Act	Amended the FTC Act to further outlaw unfair practices and give the FTC jurisdiction over false and misleading advertising.
1950	Celler-Kefauver Antimerger Act	Amended the Clayton Act to include major asset purchases that decrease competition in an industry.
1992	American Automobile Labeling Act	Requires a vehicle's manufacturer to provide a label informing consumers of where the vehicle was assembled and where its components originated.
B. LAWS TO REGULATE COMPETITION		
1936	Robinson-Patman Act	Prohibits price discrimination in sales to wholesalers, retailers, or other producers; prohibits selling at unreasonably low prices to eliminate competition.
1937	Miller-Tydings Resale Price Maintenance Act	Exempts interstate fair trade contracts from compliance with antitrust requirements. Repealed by passage of the Consumer Goods Pricing Act in 1975.
1993	North American Free Trade Agreement (NAFTA)	International trade agreement between Canada, Mexico, and the United States designed to facilitate trade by removing tariffs and other trade barriers among the three nations.
C. LAWS TO PROTECT CONSUMERS		
1906	Federal Food and Drug Act	Prohibits adulteration and misbranding of foods and drugs involved in interstate commerce; strengthened by the Food, Drug, and Cosmetic Act (1938) and the Kefauver-Harris Drug Amendment (1962).
1958	National Traffic and Safety Act	Provides for the creation of safety standards for automobiles and tires.
1966	Fair Packaging and Labeling Act	Requires disclosure of product identification, name and address of manufacturer or distributor, and information on the quality of contents.
1967	Federal Cigarette Labeling and Advertising Act	Requires written health warnings on cigarette packages.
1968	Consumer Credit Protection Act	Truth-in-lending law requiring disclosure of annual interest rates on loans and credit purchases
1970	Fair Credit Reporting Act	Gives individuals access to their credit records and allows them to change incorrect information.
1970	National Environmental Policy Act	Established the Environmental Protection Agency to deal with various types of pollution and organizations that create pollution.
1971	Public Health Cigarette Smoking Act	Prohibits tobacco advertising on radio and television.
1972	Consumer Product Safety Act	Created the Consumer Product Safety Commission with authority to specify safety standards for most products.
1975 1977	Equal Credit Opportunity Act	Bans discrimination in lending practices based on sex and marital status (as of 1975) and race, national origin, religion, age, or receipt of payments from public-assistance programs (as of 1977).
1990	Nutrition Labeling and Education Act	Requires food manufacturers and processors to provide detailed nutritional information on the labels of most foods.
1990	Children's Television Act	Limits the amount of advertising to be shown during children's television programs to not more than 10.5 minutes per hour on weekends and not more than 12.0 minutes per hour on weekdays.
1990	Americans with Disabilities Act (ADA)	Protects the rights of people with disabilities; makes discrimination against the disabled illegal in public accommodations, transportation, and telecommunications.
1993	Brady Law	Imposes a 5-day waiting period and a background check before a gun purchaser can take possession of the gun.
D. LAWS TO DEREGULATE SPECIFIC INDUSTRIES		
1978	Airline Deregulation Act	Grants considerable freedom to commercial airlines in setting fares and choosing new routes.
1980	Motor Carrier Act and Staggers Rail Act	Significantly deregulates the trucking and railroad industries by permitting them to negotiate rates and services.
1996	Telecommunications Act	Significantly deregulates the telecommunications industry by removing barriers to competition in local and long-distance phone and cable television markets.

which business decisions are made is closely linked to ethics and social responsibility, the following sections examine how each of these regulatory phases has shaped, and still influences, the business landscape.

Regulation of Competition

As Chapter 1 showed, competition is the cornerstone of a private enterprise economy. During the late 19th and early 20th centuries, however, government became concerned that power in many industries was too concentrated in the hands of small numbers of companies. These large, industry-controlling companies not only stifled competition, but they also had little incentive to act ethically. In response, the federal government began to intervene to regulate competition and commercial activities.

Some industries, such as electric utilities, became regulated. Throughout most of this century, government regulations allowed only one power company in a given market. Regulators reasoned that the large capital investment required to construct electric transmission lines made this type of regulation appropriate. In a **regulated industry,** competition is either limited or eliminated, and close government control is substituted for free competition. In most cases, regulated industries are those closely tied to the public interest where competition would be wasteful or excessive.

The second form of government regulation, enactment of statutes, has led to both state and federal laws that affect competition and various commercial practices. Over a century ago, the federal government began to regulate competition with the Sherman Antitrust Act of 1890. This act prohibits any contract or conspiracy that tends toward restraint of trade. It also declares illegal any action that monopolizes or attempts to monopolize any part of commerce.

Another major federal law, the Clayton Act of 1914, forbids such trade restraints as tying contracts, interlocking directorates, and certain anticompetitive stock acquisitions. A tying contract requires the exclusive dealer for a manufacturer's products to carry other, perhaps unwanted products in inventory. In interlocking directorates, competing companies have identical or overlapping boards of directors. The Clayton Act also forbids any purchase of another company's stock that reduces competition.

Both the Sherman Act and the Clayton Act are enforced by the Antitrust Division of the U.S. Department of Justice. Violators are subject not only to criminal fines or imprisonment but also to civil damage suits by competitors or other parties. In some cases, the government allows the accused firm to enter into a consent order, under which it agrees voluntarily to cease the conduct that the government alleges is inappropriate. The Celler-Kefauver Antimerger Act (1950) amended the Clayton Act to prohibit major asset purchases that decrease competition in an industry.

This chapter began by describing the antitrust suit recently filed by the Department of Justice against Microsoft for alleged tying contract violations. Microsoft imposed a requirement on personal computer makers that wanted to include its Windows software with their machines to also include Microsoft's Internet Explorer software. Among the companies testifying against Microsoft were Compaq and Netscape. Microsoft, however, argued that because its Internet Explorer was not a separate product but a new feature of Windows, it was not subject to the tying contract prohibition.[20]

The Federal Trade Commission Act of 1914 banned unfair competitive practices and set up the Federal Trade Commission (FTC) to administer various statutes that apply to business. The powers and investigative capacities of the FTC have grown rapidly over the years; today, it is the major federal regulatory and enforcement agency to oversee competitive practices. The FTC can sue violators or enter into consent orders with those that agree to cease questionable practices.

During the Great Depression of the 1930s, other laws aimed at protecting competitors were enacted when independent merchants felt the need for legal protection against competition from larger chain stores. Federal legislation enacted during this period included the Robinson-Patman Act and the Miller-Tydings Resale Price Maintenance Act.

www.ftc.gov

Business Directory

regulated industry an industry in which competition is either limited or eliminated, and government monitoring substitutes for market controls.

BUSINESS HALL OF SHAME

Trouble Keeping an Eye on the Ball at adidas

Everyone knows that to succeed in sports, you have to keep your eye on the ball. The same is true for succeeding in business, especially when the business is making sports equipment. Just ask adidas. The German sports manufacturer learned firsthand about what happens when you don't watch the ball—adidas was sued by laborer Bao Ge for the pain and suffering he endured while being forced to manufacture adidas soccer balls in a Chinese prison under the worst conditions of exploitation and torture.

The sports-equipment manufacturer has always taken great pride in how closely it monitors its production process. For example, when rival Nike lost sales due to media reports that its products were made in Asian factories with poor labor conditions, adidas reemphasized it code of conduct. The company joined 58 global sports-equipment makers in an agreement to curtail the use of children to produce soccer balls. And when CEO Robert Louis-Dreyfus first heard about adidas soccer balls being sewn in Chinese prisons, he promised, "If it turns out that even one item was made by slave labor or in a prison camp, heads will roll—maybe even my own."

How could this happen to such a diligent company? Maybe adidas wasn't watching the ball closely enough. Several Chinese manufacturers produce balls for adidas. Shanghai Union, one of China's oldest and largest sports-ball makers, says it makes adidas-brand balls for Japan's Molten Corp., which is licensed to manufacture and market adidas balls in Japan. However, adidas says that its contract with Molten "demands that they don't use child or prison labor." Likewise, Molten says subcontractor Shanghai Union assures that no prison labor is used on adidas soccer balls. But, Molten adds, it can't be certain those assurances are true. "We

This text covers many other specific business practices regulated by government in other sections and in Appendix C, Business Law.

Consumer Protection

Although the objective of consumer protection underlies most business-oriented laws—including the Sherman Act and the Clayton Act—many of the major consumer-oriented laws have been enacted during the past 40 years.

Federal and state legislation plays a major role in regulating product safety. The Consumer Product Safety Act of 1972 created a powerful regulatory agency called the Consumer Product Safety Commission (CPSC). The agency has the authority to ban products without court hearings, order recalls or redesigns of products, and inspect production facilities, and it can charge managers of negligent companies with criminal offenses. Other federal laws, such as the Poison Prevention Packaging Act of 1970, set guidelines for product labels of manufacturers in various

industries. Additionally, the dramatic rise in product liability lawsuits over the past two decades has pushed businesses in all industries to pay greater attention to customer safety issues.

A later section takes a closer look at consumer protection issues as part of a discussion of businesses' social responsibilities to customers.

Deregulation

Deregulation, the movement toward eliminating legal restraints on competition in various industries, has significantly reshaped the legal environment for many industries in the last two decades. Considerable controversy continues to surround the government's role in regulating the actions of businesses and the benefits of allowing industries to compete without intense government control.

During this phase, the federal government has worked to increase competition in a number of industries, including telecommunications, utilities, transportation, and banking, by discontinuing many regulations and permitting firms to expand their service offerings to new markets. The trend toward deregulation started in 1978 with the Airline Deregulation Act, which encouraged competi-

Business Directory

deregulation a regulatory trend toward elimination of legal restraints on competition.

have a subcontracting agreement with Shanghai Union . . . nothing more. We can't be too inquisitive about them," says Molten's Hidesuke Kuriki.

Because stitching together 32 panels for one soccer ball is highly labor intensive, it is common practice in China to send the handwork out to rural areas where labor costs are low. However, when a company contracts hand labor with a Chinese factory, it is difficult to be sure that none of the work is being done by prisoners. Once raw materials are delivered to workshops in China, you can't be sure where the actual work is being done, says Frank Change, whose Shanghai-based Mortex Ltd. makes adidas soccer balls for export to Europe. As Chang points out, "Unless you have somebody there who watches when they sew, there's no way anyone can control that."

To its credit, adidas has canceled all orders for Chinese-made soccer balls. But the embarrassment the company has endured over this incident is a lesson for any company that contracts work in a country as poorly regulated as China. It's also a lesson to any businessperson: When ethics are involved, you really do have to keep your eye on the ball.

QUESTIONS FOR CRITICAL THINKING

1. Discuss the ethical and social values involved in manufacturing products under poor labor conditions. How could adidas have made sure that its soccer balls would not be produced in prisons? Would any of these actions cut into adidas's profits?

2. When adidas canceled its orders for Chinese soccer balls, the decision was applauded by the Brussels-based International Textile, Garment and Leather Workers' Federation, whose member unions represent people employed in the production of soccer balls. Do you think the approval was based on the federation's concern for the human rights of all workers? Or was the move a chance for its members to get more work? Defend your answer.

Sources: Bao Ge, "I Miss My Cellmates in the Prison," Digital Freedom Network, accessed at www.dfn.org, February 9, 1999; "adidas Cancels All Football Orders from China," Hong Kong Voice of Democracy, July 29, 1998, accessed at www.democracy.org.hk; and "Questions about Prison Labor Hits adidas," *The Wall Street Journal*, June 26, 1998, p. A13.

tion among airlines by allowing them to set their own rates and to add or abandon routes based on profitability.

Critics of deregulation often point out negative effects of the trend. Some say that deregulation may lead to increasing prices as competitors are eliminated. Others suggest that firms may sacrifice safety in the name of competition. All of these issues are legitimate concerns.

The latest industry undergoing deregulation is the electric utility industry. With 198 investor-owned utilities in the United States, it is also the largest industry to be deregulated so far. California became the first state to totally open electricity sales to free competition. Consumers and businesses can now choose to buy from several different electricity suppliers, either locally or from other states. Several months before deregulation, industry giant Enova began an intensive television advertising campaign in order to convince consumers to use its services. Other state regulatory agencies are poised to follow California's lead. Supporters claim that deregulation will slash consumer and business electricity costs by 20 to 30 percent over the next 5 to 10 years. Critics, however, say that savings are likely to be much smaller, especially for residential users.[21]

Government Regulation of Cyberspace

The newest regulatory frontier is the Internet. Regulation of business on the Internet is a major issue facing govern-

ments and businesses around the world. The Internet is a borderless market; for it to function as a global marketplace, governments must work together to develop a stable economic and legal environment in which firms can operate freely, regardless of jurisdiction. Policies such as encryption (coding) of sensitive information, regulation, and electronic payments can't be decided separately by each country.

To that end, the Clinton administration recently released its *Framework for Global Electronic Commerce.* The framework acknowledges that cyberspace is very different from traditional communications media, and many current laws may no longer be appropriate for it. The European Union and the United States support a market-driven approach to electronic commerce. The framework emphasizes self-regulation by the private sector rather than government restrictions. Among the recommendations are:

▼ Declaring the Internet a tariff-free environment for cross-border transactions

▼ Developing and implementing a consistent global commercial and legal framework for electronic commerce. Contracts, rather than laws, should govern e-commerce

▼ Protecting copyrights, patents, and trademarks

▼ Protecting privacy of personal data, especially with regard to children, through self-regulation rather than censorship.[22]

BUSINESS TOOL KIT

Protect Your Privacy

A recent investigation by *Money* magazine found that today's consumers face a very real threat to their privacy. Many companies resell data about their customers to other businesses. Criminals also can illegally obtain facts about you by hacking into computer databases. As a result, details such as your address, bank account numbers, buying patterns, and other personal information may be in the hands of more people than you think. Here are five tips to protect your privacy:

1. When buying over the Internet, be sure your order is encrypted, so the information you provide cannot be read by computer hackers.

2. Put your name on the Direct Marketing Association's free Mail Preference List. This step will cut down unsolicited mailings from marketers who've obtained your name and address from other companies. The DMA's address is P.O. Box 9008, Farmingdale, NY 11735. To cut down on unwanted e-mail solicitations, try registering with Junkbusters:

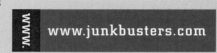 www.junkbusters.com

3. On the job, avoid sending personal e-mail or accessing nonwork-related Internet sites. Employers have the right to monitor any communications sent over office computers, and many do so.

4. Many Web sites place "cookies" into visitors' computers. A cookie keeps track of every site you visit and reports the information back to the original site. If you don't want a Web operator to keep tabs on your surfing, go to your computer's Find or Search feature, type in *COOKIES*, and then delete the text file.

5. At least once a year, order your credit report from a major credit bureau such as Trans Union (610–690–4909), or Equifax (770–612–2500). Check for any inaccuracies or false charges that may indicate someone has illegally gained access to your account.

Source: Ann Reilly Dowd, "Protect Your Privacy," *Money*, August 1997, p. 104.

Reaching an internationally agreed upon system for Internet communication and transactions will take years. Many international alliances, trade blocs, and treaties may affect Internet business, as well. Chapter 17 looks more closely at the issues surrounding Internet commerce. The Business Tool Kit discusses measures by which individual Internet users can protect their sensitive information.

ACTING RESPONSIBLY TO SATISFY SOCIETY

A second major issue affecting business is the question of social responsibility. In a general sense, **social responsibility** is management's acceptance of the obligation to consider profit, consumer satisfaction, and societal well-being of equal value in evaluating the firm's performance. It is the recognition that business must be concerned with

the qualitative dimensions of consumer, employee, and societal benefits as well as the quantitative measures of sales, revenue, and profit, by which business performance is traditionally measured.

As Professors James F. Engel and Roger D. Blackwell point out, social responsibility is a concept easier to measure than business ethics:

Actions alone determine social responsibility and a firm can be socially responsible even when doing so under coercion. For example, the government may enact rules that force firms to be socially responsible in matters of the environment, deception, and so forth. Also, consumers, through their power to repeat or withhold purchasing, may force businesses to provide honest and relevant information, fair prices, and so forth. To be ethically responsible, on the other hand, it is not sufficient to act correctly; ethical intent is also necessary.[23]

Historically, a company's social performance has been measured by its contribution to the overall economy and the employment opportunities it provides. Variables such as wage payments often serve to indicate social per-

Business Directory

social responsibility management's acceptance of the obligation to consider profit, consumer satisfaction, and societal well-being of equal value in evaluating the firm's performance.

formance. While profits and employment remain important, today many factors contribute to an assessment of a firm's social performance. These include providing equal employment opportunities; respecting the cultural diversity of employees; responding to environmental concerns; providing a safe, healthy workplace; and producing safe, high-quality products.

A business is also judged by its interactions with the community. Many corporations highlight charitable contributions and community service in their annual reports to demonstrate their social responsibility. Among them:

- ▼ Ford recently paid about $1 million to sponsor an episode of the television show *Murphy Brown* dealing with breast cancer. Public service ads focused on the disease, its detection, and cure.

- ▼ AT&T is active in the Partnership for a Drug-Free America. An example of drug education and awareness programs sponsored in part by AT&T is shown in Figure 2.5.

- ▼ Johnson & Johnson gives the World Wildlife Fund a cut from sales of a special line of children's toiletries.

- ▼ American Express credit card users generated $22 million for Share Our Strength, a poverty-relief charity aimed at providing food for low-income households.[24]

Some firms measure social performance by conducting **social audits,** formal procedures that identify and evaluate all company activities that relate to social issues such as conservation, employment practices, environmental protection, and philanthropy. The social audit informs management about how well the company is performing in these areas. Based on this information, management may take steps to revise current programs or develop new ones.

Outside groups may conduct their own evaluations of businesses. Various environmental, religious, and public-interest groups have created standards of corporate performance. Reports on many of these evaluations are available

| Figure 2.5 | **AT&T Contributions to the Partnership for a Drug-Free America** |

Her dreams don't have to be limited by her reality.

The reality is that she witnesses a lot of drug abuse. She finds it in her neighborhood, at her school, and in the park. But thanks to the Partnership for a Drug-Free America, this reality doesn't have to define her future. Through drug education and awareness programs, sponsored in part by AT&T, children are learning how drugs can weaken ambition and take away dreams. They are about to discover the power of their own determination and how to use it in the fight against drugs. AT&T and the Partnership for a Drug-Free America are helping them realize their potential. The reality is that every child has the right to dream.

AT&T and the Partnership for a Drug-Free America are giving children back their childhood.

© 1996 AT&T

to the general public. The Council on Economic Priorities produces publications such as *The Better World Investment Guide,* which recommends basing investment decisions on companies' track records on various social issues, including environmental impact, nuclear weapons contracts, community outreach, and advancement of women and minorities. Other groups have used the Internet to publicize their evaluations and criticisms of the social responsibility of firms.

Many firms find that consumers evaluate their social track records in financial decisions, that is, by either buying or not buying the firms' goods and services. One study, for example, reported that 75 percent of consumers surveyed said they wouldn't buy, no matter what the price, from firms they considered socially irresponsible.[25] Other consumer groups organize boycotts of companies they find to be socially irresponsible. In a boycott, consumers refuse to buy a company's goods or services.

The *Boycott Quarterly,* a Seattle-based publication, reports that some 800 products currently are being boycotted by consumer activists. The AFL-CIO recently asked its members to boycott 20 companies it believes to have unfriendly policies against unions.[26]

As Figure 2.6 shows, the social responsibilities of business can be classified according to its relationships to the general public, customers, employees, and investors and the rest of the financial community. Many of these relationships extend beyond national borders.

Responsibilities to the General Public

The responsibilities of business to the general public include dealing with public-health issues, protecting the environment, and developing the quality of the work force. Additionally, many would argue that businesses have responsibilities to support charitable and social causes and organizations that work toward the greater public good. In other words, they should give back to the communities in which they earn profits. This is called **corporate philanthropy.**

Figure 2.7 summarizes these four responsibilities, which are discussed in the sections that follow. The Business Tool Kit on how to be charitable suggests some criteria for choosing these actions.

Public-Health Issues One of the more complex issues regarding business ethics and social responsibility to the general public revolves around public health. Central to this debate is the question of what businesses should do about products that are inherently dangerous. For example, tobacco products represent a major health risk, contributing to the incidence of heart disease, stroke, and cancer among smokers. Furthermore, families and co-workers of smokers share this danger, as well, since their exposure to secondhand smoke increases their risks for cancer, asthma, and respiratory infections. Substance abuse, including alcohol abuse, is another serious public-health problem worldwide. Motor vehicle accidents are a major killer, and drunk drivers cause many serious crashes. Alcohol abuse has also been linked to serious diseases such as cirrhosis of the liver. Other public-health dangers are posed by fatty foods, TV violence, handguns, and even motorcycles.

A second health-related question that businesses must answer involves the protection of vulnerable groups. Consider, for example, that 80 to 90 percent of smokers begin the habit before age 18. Over the last 5 years, the number of high school students who smoke has increased each year.[27] These young people will become tomorrow's work force, and their smoking habits will predispose them to a multitude of health problems. The tobacco industry has been repeatedly criticized for using advertisements aimed at children and teens. Until 1999, Joe Camel, for example, a cartoon figure used to promote Camel cigarettes, was one of the most widely recognized advertising symbols among young children. Absolut vodka ads have even become collector's items for many teens, raising concerns that the company is encouraging underage drinking. Both alcohol and tobacco companies have been criticized for targeting ethnic and racial minorities in their advertising.

Many consumers view both alcohol and tobacco advertising, whether aimed at adults or young people, as socially irresponsible. Some brewers have tried to counter these views by sponsoring advertising campaigns that promote moderation. Even firms who are not in these industries have faced controversy over this issue. For instance, the *San Francisco Bay Guardian* was recently picketed by anti-tobacco activists for accepting advertising from tobacco companies, even though the newspaper's editorial coverage had strongly criticized the tobacco industry in the past.[28]

Many of these concerns were highlighted in a huge $246 billion settlement between the tobacco industry and the state attorneys general. The industry agreed to make these payments to the states over 25 years. The money will be used to reimburse state governments for health-care costs of smoking-related illnesses and to fund smoking-education programs. Additionally, the tobacco firms agreed that they would not use humans or cartoons in ads, effectively killing off Joe Camel and the Marlboro Man. Tobacco ads, already banned on radio and television, may be placed only in newspapers, direct-mail pieces, and adult magazines. Transit and billboard advertising—which as recently as 1998 had totaled $150 million in the United States—are now prohibited. The tobacco settlement is likely to have repercussions for all products deemed dangerous to public health.[29]

Businesses also face challenges when dealing with the consequences of diseases like AIDS, a devastating virus that breaks down the body's ability to defend itself against illness and infection. AIDS is especially dangerous because, on average, 5 years pass between a person's first exposure to the virus and actual development of the disease. During this period, people may not show any symptoms, and they probably don't even know they have the infection, but they are still carriers who can transmit the disease to others. This large pool of unknown carriers accounts for the rapid spread of the disease.

AIDS has forced companies to educate their workers about how to deal with employees and customers who have the deadly disease. Health care for AIDS patients can be incredibly expensive, straining the ability of small companies to pay for health-care coverage. Do companies have the right to test potential employees for the AIDS

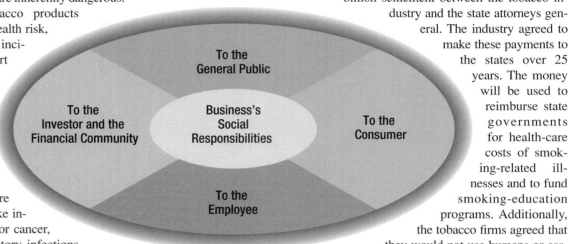

Figure 2.6 **Responsibilities of Business**

They said it

"Joe Camel is dead. He had it coming."

Bruce Reed
Assistant to President Clinton for domestic policy

virus and avoid this expense? Some people believe that this screening would violate the rights of job applicants; others feel that a firm has a responsibility not to place AIDS patients in jobs where they could infect members of the general public. These are difficult questions. In resolving them, a business must balance the rights of individuals against the rights of society in general.

Protecting the Environment Businesses affect the world's fragile environment in a variety of ways. They consume huge amounts of energy, which increases the burning of

Figure 2.7 **Business Responsibilities to the General Public**

Consideration of Public Health
AIDS
Smoking
Alcohol Abuse

Developing the Quality of the Work Force
On-the-Job Training
Education Benefits

Protecting the Environment
Avoiding Pollution
Recycling

Corporate Philanthropy
Monetary Donations to Charitable and Social Organizations
Supporting Employee Volunteer Efforts
Donating Goods to Charitable and Social Organizations

fossil fuels such as coal and oil for energy production. This activity introduces carbon dioxide and sulfur into the earth's atmosphere, substances that many scientists believe will result in dramatic climate changes over the next century. Meanwhile, the sulfur from fossil fuels combines with water vapor in the air to form sulfuric acid. The acid rain that results kills fish and trees and pollutes ground water. Wind can carry the sulfur around the entire globe. Sulfur from factories in the United States is damaging Canadian forests, and pollution from London smokestacks has been found in the forests and lakes of Scandinavia. Other production and manufacturing methods leave behind large quantities of waste materials that can further pollute the environment and fill already bulging landfills.

Pressures from government and the public have caused many businesses to reevaluate their impact on the environment. For many managers, finding ways to minimize the **pollution** and other environmental damage caused by their products or operating processes has become an important economic, legal, and social issue.

Perhaps no industry better demonstrates the changing relationship between business and the environment than the oil industry. When Royal Dutch/Shell Oil first explored the Amazon in search of oil in the mid-1980s, the company paid little attention to environmental issues. Workers cut

They said it

"Air pollution is turning Mother Nature prematurely gray."

Irv Kupcinet (1912 –)
American newspaper columnist

more than 1,250 miles of trails and roads through the rain forest, and mud and garbage from well drilling were dumped into rivers. After being strongly criticized by environmentalists for these and other actions, Royal Dutch/Shell promised Peru it would be more responsible in future natural gas projects. The firm has hired an anthropologist and a team of biologists from the Smithsonian Institute to survey the native plant and animal populations. This information will be used to return the project site to its natural state when the gas fields have been exhausted. To avoid road cutting, workers and equipment are shuttled into the site by air at a cost of $10,000 an hour. Special equipment is used to recycle potentially toxic waste, and whatever can't be treated or reused is hauled off the site.[30]

As Figure 2.8 points out, the world's rain forests are disappearing at the rate of an acre per second. Both socially conscious, profit-seeking firms like Mobil and not-for-profit organizations like the World Wildlife Fund are working to reverse this trend and to inform the world's citizens of the value of the rain forests to every individual.

Many consumers have more favorable impressions of environmentally conscious businesses; in fact, they often prefer to buy from such firms. To target these customers, companies use *green marketing,* a marketing strategy that promotes an environmentally safe product. For example,

Figure 2.8 **Protecting the Rain Forest and the World's Oceans**

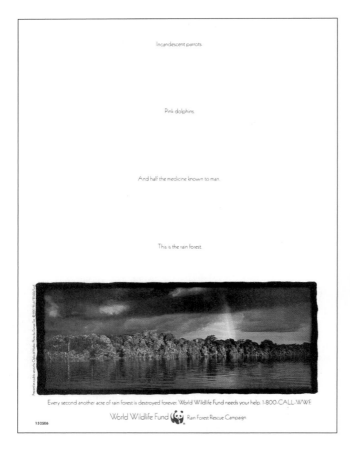

one office manager chose Northeast Utilities for her company's electric supplier because it draws most of its power from hydroelectric dams rather than coal and nuclear plants. Choosing Northeast costs about $10 more a month but it "fits our environmental concerns."[31]

However, a business cannot simply claim that its goods or services are environmentally friendly. In 1992, the Federal Trade Commission issued guidelines for businesses to follow in making environmental claims. A firm must be able to prove that any environmental claim made about a good or service has been substantiated with reliable scientific evidence. Additionally, as shown in Figure 2.9, the FTC has given specific directions about how various environmental terms may be used in advertising and marketing.

Environmental concerns can lead to new technologies. General Motors, Honda, Toyota, and Ford, for instance, have developed electric cars that they hope will eventually

The need to be cool: The Mississippi State Department of Health uses part of the state's $3.4 billion settlement with the tobacco industry in an attempt to sway nonsmoking teens from ever picking up the habits of smoking or dipping (chewing) tobacco. The billboards appeal to a tried-and-true staple of high school worries—image.

How to Be Charitable without Being a Chump

Although your firm may be staffed with Good Samaritans, plenty of unscrupulous people are willing to take advantage of your good intentions. If you are unfamiliar with a charity, but think it's something you might like to support, first find out what the group does in your area. Then look for the following warning signs that can expose scams. If you encounter any of these practices, take a much closer look before shelling out a donation.

▼ *Solicitations designed to make you cry, not think.* Charities should provide specific information about their programs. If you're not sure what they intend to do with your money, call the group and ask.

▼ *Vague claims of charity donations from sales of a service or good.* Typically, less than 10 percent of the purchase price goes to the charity.

▼ *Requests for donations in cash.* Almost always a bad idea. Cash donations can be pilfered or lost, and there's no record of your contribution for tax purposes.

▼ *Phone solicitors who want personal financial information, such as your credit card or checking account numbers.* Ask the caller to mail you information, and hang up on anyone who tries to pressure you into making a donation right away. Honest charities willingly wait.

A valuable source of information to help givers find charities that suit their needs is Guidestar. Using IRS data, this service provides online reports detailing the finances and programs of more than 600,000 charities.

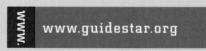 www.guidestar.org

Source: Warning signs reported in Sandra Block, "Warning Signs Can Expose Scams," *USA Today*, December 5, 1997, p. 4B.

---

replace now-standard gas-burning vehicles. The automakers are pushing development of electric vehicles in response to government efforts to curb pollution. California regulators have mandated that, by 2003, 10 percent of the new cars and trucks sold in the state must be electric vehicles. New York and Massachusetts have enacted similar regulations, and ten other states plus the District of Columbia are considering similar laws.[32]

Another solution gaining acceptance among businesses is **recycling**—reprocessing used materials for reuse. Recycling could provide much of the raw material that manufacturers need, thereby conserving the world's natural resources and reducing the need for landfills. Several industries are experimenting on and developing ways to use recycled materials.

Take old tires like those shown in Figure 2.10, for example. At least one-third of the rubber in every tire comes from a tree, and with an estimated 800 million used tires in dumps across the United States, the importance of finding a use for them is two-fold: save trees and clean up the environment. Recently, entrepreneurs have been coming up with inventive new uses for recycled tires, from tarp anchors and planters to shoe soles and jungle gyms. In fact, uses

have been found for over 75 percent of all waste tires: Over 100 factories supplement coal fuel by burning tires; 150 million tires each year are used making cement, paper, electricity, lime, iron, and copper; the ground-rubber market consumes another 12 million tires a year; and tire fuel is expected to gain wider acceptance in the near future.[33]

Developing the Quality of the Work Force In the past, a nation's wealth has often been based on its money, production equipment, and natural resources. A country's true wealth, however, lies in its people. An educated, skilled work force provides the intellectual know-how required to develop new technology, improve productivity, and compete in the global marketplace. It is becoming increasingly clear that in order to remain competitive, U.S. business must assume more responsibility for enhancing the quality of its work force. Since 1991, hotel chain Marriott Corp. has trained over 600 former welfare recipients as entry-level employees. The following Business Hall of Fame box

Business Directory

recycling reprocessing of used materials for reuse.

Figure 2.9 FTC Guidelines for Environmental Claims in Green Marketing

In July 1992, the Federal Trade Commission spelled out exactly how various terms should be used in marketing and advertising to avoid misleading consumers about a product's environmental friendliness.

If a business says a product is...	The product or package must...
Biodegradable	break down and return to nature in a reasonably short period of time.
Recyclable	be entirely reusable as new materials in the manufacture or assembly of a new product or package.
Refillable	be included in a system for the collection and return of the package for refill. If consumers have to find a way to refill it themselves, it is not *refillable*.
Ozone Safe/Ozone Friendly	must not contain any ozone-depleting ingredient.

reveals how successful corporate-sponsored training and employment programs can be.

Most new jobs require college-educated workers. Many professions demand as much as 10 years of study beyond high school, and even the least-skilled jobs require certain levels of reading, computing, and thinking abilities. Business must encourage students to stay in school, continue their education, and sharpen their skills. Companies must also encourage employees to learn new skills and remain competitive.

An added benefit of supporting educational initiatives may be a more positive image in the eyes of customers. How can a company improve its image? According to a recent survey, over 70 percent of respondents recommended donating school materials and equipment, supporting literacy programs for children and adults, and supporting part-time work programs for kids.[34]

Organizations also face enormous responsibilities for helping women, members of various cultural groups, and those who are physically challenged to contribute fully to the economy. Failure to do so is not only a waste of over half of the nation's work force, but it can also have a devastating impact on a firm's public image. Firms such as Lockheed Martin use messages like the one in Figure 2.11 to communicate the importance of diversity to continued leadership in cutting-edge technologies.

However, newspaper and television news reports all too often include stories of firms facing negative consequences from diversity issues. When West Coast electric utility Enova Corp. recently proposed a $4.3 billion merger

with Pacific Enterprises, it faced strong questioning about its ethnic diversity record. Minority advocacy groups argued that the firm had lagged far behind other utilities in diversifying the ethnic makeup of its management and in supporting economic development efforts for low-income communities.[35]

Oil giant Texaco had its own diversity crisis. When top company executives were exposed for using derogatory terms when referring to African Americans, the firm faced public outrage and threats of boycotts. Several employees filed a class-

Figure 2.10 Recycling Old Tires for New Uses

Figure 2.11 **Lockheed Martin: Offering Career Opportunities as Diverse as Its Employees**

IMAGINE IF IT HAD BEEN PAINTED IN ONLY ONE COLOR.

Monet's art celebrated color, fresh perspectives and striking diversities. At Lockheed Martin, we believe wholeness comes from diversity. And in diversity, a range of insights and viewpoints that leads to creative solutions. Solutions that set Lockheed Martin apart. To continue our leadership role in cutting edge technologies, we're committed to having a diverse work force. ♦ Positions are available for experienced personnel. The corporation also has more than 1,000 entry-level career opportunities for recent college graduates in engineering. If you'd like to work for a company where the opportunities are as diverse as the employees, fax or send your resume to Lockheed Martin listed below.

LOCKHEED MARTIN

©1997 Lockheed Martin Corporation

- ♦ Manager Internal Audit
- ♦ Senior Internal Auditors
- ♦ Information Technology Auditors (IT)
- ♦ Senior Accountant of Financial Reporting
- ♦ Associate Benefits Analyst
- ♦ Senior Accountant of Consolidation and Analysis
- ♦ Executive Secretary

Please fax your resume to Dept. 0A9704b, (800) 461-5789, or mail to: Lockheed Martin Corporation, Box 8048, Dept. 0A9704b, Bldg. 10/Rm. 1019, Philadelphia, PA 19101

action lawsuit against Texaco, alleging that the company discriminated against African American employees in its promotion and performance appraisal practices.

Corporate Philanthropy As pointed out in Chapter 1, not-for-profit organizations play an important role in society by serving the public good. They provide the human resources that enhance the quality of life in communities around the world. In order to fulfill this mission, however, many not-for-profit organizations rely on financial contributions from the business community. Businesses receive substantial pressure from government and consumers to lend this support. They respond by donating over $8 billion each year to not-for-profit organizations. This **corporate philanthropy** includes cash contributions, donations of equipment and products, and supporting the volunteer ef-

forts of company employees.[36] Local cultural organizations are likely to be the most frequent recipients of corporate generosity. The most recent data indicate that 61 percent of surveyed companies reported such contributions. Adopt-a-school programs were a close second in popularity, followed by community development and housing and job training programs.[37] As Table 2.3 shows, the range of programs supported by corporate giving is very broad.

Corporate philanthropy can have many positive benefits beyond the purely altruistic rewards of giving. Among the benefits are higher employee morale, enhanced image, and improved customer relationships.[38] Hanna Andersson, a mail-order children's wear firm, donates 5 percent of its profits to charity, far above the national corporate giving average of 1 percent. Additionally, the firm invites customers to send back outfits that their children have outgrown. The company then donates the clothing to needy families. In return, the customer gets a 20 percent discount on the next purchase. More than 3,000 "Hannadowns" pour into corporate headquarters each month.[39]

In an effort to maximize the benefits of corporate giving in an era of downsizing, businesses have become more selective of the causes and charities they choose to support. Many seek to align their marketing efforts with their charitable giving. This is known as *cause-related marketing*. Boston Market, for example, conducted a great deal of research before giving its financial support to Y-Me's hotline number at all of its stores and providing free meals for chemotherapy patients. "We chose this because breast cancer affects the whole family. . . . Our business is about families, and we want to do something to help them," says Robin Showdeir, Boston Market's director of cultural relations.

Working Assets, a San Francisco provider of credit cards and long-distance phone service, asks its customers to decide which causes are important to them. Each of the firm's 260,000 customers votes on how much the company should give each of the 200 not-for-profit organizations that Working Assets supports. Last year, Working Assets contributed $2.5 million to not-for-profit organizations and causes chosen by its customers.

Another form of corporate philanthropy is volunteerism. In their roles as corporate citizens, thousands of businesses encourage their employees to contribute their efforts to projects as diverse as Habitat for Humanity, local literacy programs, and Red Cross blood drives. In addition

Business Directory

corporate philanthropy the act of an organization giving something back to the communities in which it earns profits.

BUSINESS HALL OF FAME

Bill Strickland: Modeling the Future with Education, Training, and Hope

At 17, Andy Karaman is thinking about college. Typical for someone at that age, right? Not necessarily. Andy will be the first in his family to attend college, the first to dream of a career in art.

Janine Johnson is planning on owning her own restaurant. A single mother of four on welfare, she will soon complete a course in culinary arts. Commuting two hours each way, she spends her days studying to become a chef.

What inspires these people to follow their dreams? Bill Strickland says, "You start with the perception that the world is an unlimited opportunity." And that's just what he did. When he began the Manchester Craftsmen's Guild (MCG) and took over the Bidwell Training Center (BTC), Strickland began reshaping the business of social change. With a combined staff of 110 and a budget over $6 million, both programs offer support, training, and hope—all free of charge.

Strickland knows what it's like to feel hemmed in by life. A 16-year-old black kid in a decaying neighborhood, he wanted out but couldn't find the way. Then opportunity knocked one day as he looked from a dark hallway through a doorway into a sunlit classroom and saw a man absorbed in shaping a vessel out of a rotating mound of clay. That doorway led to a "whole range of possibilities and experiences I had not explored." He walked in and introduced himself to ceramics teacher Frank Ross, who became his mentor for the next 20 years. Ross taught Strickland about pottery—and much more. Strickland remembers, "He said, 'You have the talent and the resources to take control of your life,' and I believed him. I saw a radiant, hopeful image of how the world ought to be."

Two years later, Strickland entered college, where in 1968—before he had even graduated—he decided to do something to bring hope back to the streets. He opened MCG, and after-school program that uses art to teach life skills to at-risk school kids—the same program that Andy Karaman attends. In 1971, Strickland was asked to take over BTC, a partnership program with local companies that trains adults for real work in real jobs—the same program that offers Janine Johnson training and support.

Using these two programs, Strickland is rebuilding his community from two directions: getting troubled kids into college and giving adults career training. In 1983, with only $112 in the bank, Strickland launched a fundraising drive to construct an $8-million building to house these rapidly growing programs. The effort took three years, but the contacts he made have lasted much longer.

Strickland's loyal supporters include former president George Bush (who named Strickland to the board of the National Endowment for the Arts), Hillary Clinton, Harvard Business School, Harvard Graduate School of Education (where Strickland serves as an adjunct faculty member), San Francisco Mayor Willie Brown and jazz musician Herbie Hancock (who are replicating Strickland's programs in San Francisco), and the MacArthur Foundation (that awarded Strickland a $295,000 "genius" grant in 1996).

to making tangible contributions to the well-being of fellow citizens, such programs generate considerable public support and goodwill for the companies and their employees. In some cases, the volunteer efforts occur mostly during off-hours for employees. In other instances, the firm permits its work force to volunteer during regular working hours. Chemical giant Hoechst Celanese executives are shown taking time off from a meeting to help renovate a North Carolina facility for adults with special needs in Figure 2.12.

Table 2.3	Favorite Charities of Selected Companies	
Company and Date Program Started	**Cause**	**Total Amount Donated**
Avon (1993)	Breast cancer awareness	$22 million
American Express (1993)	Hunger relief and prevention	$20 million
Chevrolet (1989)	Tree planting and urban forestry	$5 million
Ralston Purina (1990)	Endangered species preservation	$3.5 million
Estée Lauder (1993)	Breast cancer research	$2.2 million
Visa USA (1996)	Children's literacy	$1 million
Sterling Vineyards (1992)	Public land conservation	$400 thousand
Quaker (1996)	Breast cancer research	$160 thousand

Both MCG and BTC are success stories. Over the past five years, 75 to 80 percent of the kids in the MCG program have gone on to college, and 78 percent of the adults who graduate from BTC find jobs. Strickland continues to strengthen these programs by never losing sight of the possibilities and expanding on them. For example, he oversees a jazz concert hall, a Grammy Award–winning record label, and a food-services company, and he has begun a new national effort to teach not-for-profit leaders how to think like entrepreneurs. As he pursues diverse directions such as fund-raising, franchising, and real-estate development, Strickland shows his flair for mixing profit and not-for-profit goals to shape social miracles for folks like Andy Karaman and Janine Johnson.

QUESTIONS FOR CRITICAL THINKING

1. Do you agree with Bill Strickland's suggestion that self-perception controls what people do in life by determining what opportunities they choose or refuse? Defend your answer.

2. Strickland successfully recruits profit-seeking companies to work with not-for-profit organizations. Beside the good feelings they get from helping others, what benefits do the for-profit companies receive from these joint efforts?

3. As Mayor Willie Brown and jazz musician Herbie Hancock try to replicate Strickland's programs in San Francisco, can they expect their programs to be as successful as the original without the inspiration of Strickland himself? In other words, can they replicate Strickland's vision and enthusiasm as well as his programs? Explain your answer.

Sources: Ryan Rhea, "Social Visionary and Entrepreneur Bill Strickland to Deliver an Address as Part of Washington University's Assembly Series," News & Information, Office of Public Affairs, accessed at wupa.wustl.edu, February 9, 1999; Bidwell Training Center home page, accessed at www.realpittsburgh.com, February 23, 1999; and Sara Terry, "Genius at Work," *Fast Company*, September 1998, pp. 170–181.

Responsibilities to Customers

Businesspeople share a social and ethical responsibility to treat their customers fairly and act in a manner that is not harmful to them. Auto-safety advocate Ralph Nader first pioneered this idea in the late 1960s. Since then, **consumerism**—the public demand that a business consider the wants and needs of its customers in making decisions—has gained widespread acceptance. Consumerism is based on the belief that consumers have certain rights. The most frequently quoted statement of consumer rights was made by President John F. Kennedy in 1962; it included the rights to be safe, to be informed, to choose, and to be heard. Numerous state and federal laws have been implemented since then to protect these rights.

The Right to Be Safe Contemporary businesspeople must recognize obligations, both moral and legal, to ensure the safe operation of their products. Consumers should feel assured that the goods and services they purchase will not cause injuries in normal use. *Product liability* refers to the responsibility of manufacturers for injuries and damages caused by their products. Products that lead to injuries, either directly or indirectly, can have disastrous consequences for their makers. Dow Corning, for instance, was ordered to pay millions of dollars in damages for injuries to women from the silicone in breast implants it manufactured. The company eventually had to declare bankruptcy. Dow Corning's parent company, Dow Chemical, was also held liable for damages from the breast implants, even though the parent company argued that it had never made silicone, tested it for human use, or claimed it was safe.[40]

Many companies put their products through rigorous testing to avoid safety problems. Still, testing alone cannot foresee every eventuality. Companies must consider all possibilities and provide adequate warning of potential dangers. Although Mattel has a strict testing program for its toys, the company did not recognize the real-world threat one doll would pose. The Cabbage Patch Snacktime dolls were designed to gobble meals of fake carrots and French fries, but they ended up chewing on children's hair, as well. After reports of 35 hair-eating episodes, the Consumer Product Safety Commission urged Mattel to issue a warning about the danger, along with instructions for disabling the dolls, on packages.[41]

When a product does pose a threat to customer safety, a responsible manufacturer responds quickly to either repair the problem or recall the dangerous product. For example, when defective cranks on mountain bikes made by Shimano American Corp. caused 22 injuries, the 76-year-old company voluntarily recalled millions of mountain bikes worldwide.[42]

Safety planning is now a vital management issue for many businesses. Companies and industry associations have sponsored voluntary improvements in safety standards. Consider Jack-in-the-Box. After an outbreak of food-related illnesses and deaths was linked to undercooked hamburgers in its restaurants, the firm aggressively sought to tighten internal safety measures. The company also pushed for new state and federal laws to improve food-handling safety throughout the restaurant industry.[43]

The Right to Be Informed Consumers should have access to enough education and product information to make responsible buying decisions. In their efforts to promote and sell their goods and services, companies can easily neglect consumers' right to be fully informed. The Federal Trade Commission and other federal and state agencies have established rules and regulations that govern advertising truthfulness. These rules prohibit businesses from making unsubstantiated claims about the performance or superiority of their goods or services. They also require businesses to avoid misleading consumers. Businesses that fail to comply face scrutiny from the FTC and consumer protection organizations.

A television ad for General Motors' Chevrolet S-Blazer, for example, promoted a 2-year lease for $1,360 down and $299 a month. Further information about costs

Figure 2.12	**Volunteerism: A Growing Form of Corporate Philanthropy**

There Is More Than One Way To Climb The Corporate Ladder.

When Hoechst Celanese executives climbed these ladders armed with hammers and paint brushes, it was really no surprise. They had taken time off from a meeting to renovate the Nevins Center, a North Carolina facility for adults with special needs. This is just one of the many ways Hoechst Celanese men and women volunteer to improve the quality of life in the communities in which they live and work.

Whether they are educating schoolchildren on science or senior citizens on health care, our employees are dedicated to helping people and making a real difference. And that's really no surprise either. Because being a good corporate citizen is an important part of who we are at Hoechst Celanese.

Hoechst Celanese

Hoechst

The Name Behind The Names You Know

The Hoechst name and logo are registered trademarks of Hoechst AG

and restrictions was shown in light-colored fine print that appeared on the television screen for just 5 seconds. The FTC said this ad was misleading, because consumers were not adequately informed about the full costs associated with leasing the vehicle. GM wasn't the only automobile company to experience the FTC's wrath, which labeled the industry "deplorable."[44]

The Food and Drug Administration (FDA), which sets standards for advertising conducted by drug manufacturers, recently eased restrictions for prescription drug advertising on television. In print ads, drug makers are required to spell out potential side effects and the proper uses of prescription drugs. Because of the requirement to disclose this information, prescription drug television advertising was limited. Now, however, the FDA says drug ads on radio and TV can directly promote a prescription drug's benefits if they provide a quick way for consumers to learn about side effects, such as displaying a toll-free number or Internet address.[45]

The ad for Prozac shown in Figure 2.13 includes over six paragraphs of information—considerably less than the pageful of tiny type that was once required. Recently, however, the Food and Drug Administration reduced the amount of information that prescription drug advertisers must provide in all ads for potential patients about the medical effects of using certain drugs.

The responsibility of business to preserve consumers' right to be informed extends beyond avoiding misleading advertising, however. All communications with customers—from salespeople's comments to warranties and invoices—must be controlled to clearly and accurately inform customers. Sears recently agreed to refund at least $100 million to customers who were pressured to pay off their credit card debts even though they were protected by bankruptcy laws. When a person declares bankruptcy, the companies to which they owe money must work through the bankruptcy court to arrange payment. Instead, Sears went directly to its 200,000 customers who had declared bankruptcy and demanded payment, failing to inform them that they did not legally have to pay.[46]

The Internet raises new issues about the right to be informed. The online world is ripe for misleading or deceptive marketing claims. The National Consumers League, a consumer protection organization, notes that complaints against Internet marketers more than tripled in 1997. The most common complaints are extravagant promises, suspiciously low prices, or undelivered merchandise. The league has set up a Fraud Watch Web site to warn Internet users of marketing scams.[47] In one case, customers paid for reconditioned phone equipment purchased through the Internet from KRW Internet Sales & Marketing, but they never received the products. The Denver street address displayed by the firm on its Internet site turned out to be a private mail drop, and phone numbers listed there were disconnected local numbers.[48]

www. www.fraud.org

Despite strict product testing by Mattel, the company was forced to issue a public warning about the Cabbage Patch Snacktime Kids doll, which nibbles on plastic French fries, as shown here, as well as on children's hair.

To protect themselves against claims of insufficient disclosure, businesses often include warnings on products. As Figure 2.14 shows, sometimes these warnings go far beyond what a reasonable consumer would expect.

The Right to Choose Consumers have the right to choose which goods and services they need and want to purchase. Socially responsible firms attempt to preserve this right, even if they reduce their own sales and profits in the process. Other companies, however, are not as ethical about protecting a consumer's right to choose.

Consider, for example, what happened to Louis Poggi, who had an account with the stock brokerage firm Investors Associates. When he received a telephone call from a salesperson at Investors Associates trying to sell him stock, Poggi turned down the offer. A few weeks later he was surprised to learn that the salesperson had purchased 1,000 shares of the

Figure 2.13 **Informing Consumers about the Side Effects of Prescription Drugs**

Figure 2.14 **Wacky Warning Labels**

The number of product liability lawsuits has skyrocketed in the past decade. To protect themselves, businesses have become more careful about including warnings on products. However, some companies may go overboard, as demonstrated by these actual product warning labels:

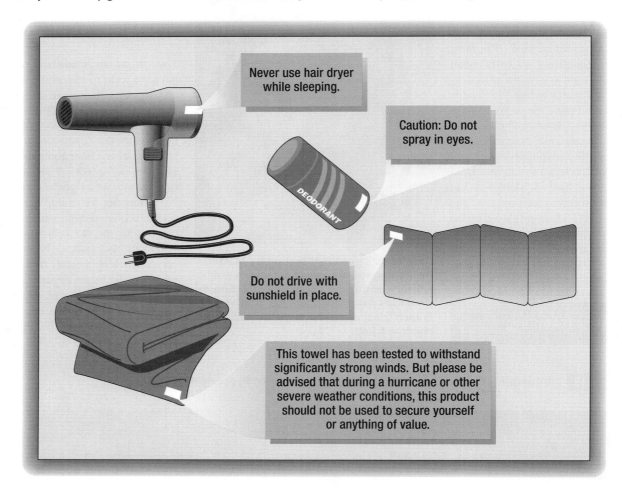

stock in Poggi's name and was demanding payment. State regulators, who canceled Poggi's "purchase" and other unauthorized transactions, estimate that over a 2-year period, Investors Associates used similar tactics to relieve unsuspecting customers of more than $10 million.[49]

Since the long-distance telephone industry has been deregulated, many customers have also been the victims of fraud. Several unscrupulous long-distance carriers have duped customers into switching their service through an unsavory practice called *slamming*. The firms induce customers to sign contest-entry forms that contain less-than-obvious wording saying they agree to be switched. In other cases, long-distance companies have switched customers without their consent after making telemarketing calls to them.

The Right to Be Heard Consumers should be able to express legitimate complaints to appropriate parties. Many companies exert considerable effort to ensure full hearings for consumer complaints. Ford Motor Co., for example, has set up a consumer appeals board to resolve service complaints. Similarly, The Custom Foot, a men's and women's shoe store chain, places high value on satisfying customers. Each pair of Custom Foot shoes is made to order according to individual customer preferences and measurements. After every sale, a store representative calls each customer to make certain that no problems or complaints have arisen since he or she received the products. The Custom Foot then uses this feedback to fine-tune its sales and production processes.[50]

Responsibilities to Employees

As Chapter 1 explained, one of the most important business resources is an organization's work force. Companies that are able to attract skilled and knowledgeable employees are better able to meet the challenges of competing on a global basis. However, in return, businesses have wide-ranging responsibilities to their employees. These include workplace safety, quality of life issues, avoiding discrimination, and preventing sexual harassment and sexism.

Workplace Safety In the earliest part of the 20th century, few businesses paid much attention to the safety of their workers. In fact, most business owners viewed employees as mere cogs in the production process. Workers, often very young children, toiled in frequently dangerous conditions. In 1911, 146 people, mostly young girls, died in a fire at the Triangle Shirtwaist Factory in New York City. Contributing to the massive loss of life were the sweatshop working conditions at the factory, including overcrowding, blocked exits, and a lack of fire escapes. The horrifying tragedy forced businesses to begin to recognize their responsibility for their workers' safety.

The safety and health of workers while on the job is now an important business responsibility. The Occupational Safety and Health Administration (OSHA) is the main federal regulatory force in setting workplace safety and health standards. These mandates range from broad guidelines on storing hazardous materials to specific standards for worker safety in industries like construction, manufacturing, and mining. OSHA tracks and investigates workplace accidents and has the authority to fine employers who are found liable for injuries and deaths that occur on the job. While businesses are required to comply with many OSHA regulations, ultimately each company's management must set standards and implement programs to ensure that workers are kept safe in the workplace.

Executives at Georgia-Pacific, for example, had a serious safety problem. Accident rates in the forest-products company's paper mills, sawmills, and plywood factories were high, averaging nine serious injuries per 100 employees each year. Twenty-six workers died on the job between 1986 and 1990. To reduce accidents among the company's 47,000 workers, Georgia-Pacific launched a safety crusade.

One of the first changes executives sought was a transformation in employee and management attitudes. Previously, employees took dangerous risks in operating machinery, because they felt pressured by management to get products out at any cost. Management made it clear that safety would begin to take priority. Workers who spot a potential safety problem can now shut down production lines. Intensive training sessions are held throughout the company on a regular basis, reinforcing the message that safety comes first. Managers are held accountable for the safety records of their departments, and safety success stories are beamed via the company's SafeTV cable network to 350 Georgia-Pacific sites around the United States. The result? By 1996, nearly 80 percent of the company's plants operated without injuries, and no employees died on the job. The company's sawmills are now about 70 percent safer than the industry average.[51]

Quality of Life Issues Balancing work and family is becoming harder for many employees. They find themselves squeezed between working long hours and handling childcare problems, caring for elderly parents, and solving other family crises. In a recent survey of 12,000 workers, only 49 percent said they could have a good family life and still get ahead at work.[52] Those juggling work with life's other demands aren't just working mothers. Childless couples, single people, and men all expressed frustration with the pressures of balancing work and family. Helping workers find solutions to these quality of life issues has become an important concern of many businesses, but finding answers isn't always easy. A recent *Business Week* survey ranked five firms at the top of the "family friendly" ranking. Table 2.4 lists the most family-oriented firms and their strongest family-friendly characteristics.

Some companies offer flexible work arrangements to support employees. Hewlett-Packard Co. has redesigned jobs in several units in order to allow employees to work from home, work part-time, or work shortened work weeks. All managers at First Chicago NBD Corp. are required to submit written plans specifying how employee job flexibility can be increased. At Baxter Export, the international shipping division of medical equipment maker Baxter International, 30 percent of workers telecommute, share jobs, or work part-time.[53]

Table 2.4	Top Five Family-Friendly Firms	
Company	**Grade**	**What It Does Right**
MBNA America	A	Strong family friendly culture and programs
Motorola	A−	Continuous communication through Intranet
Barnett Banks (now Nationsbank)	A−	On-site primary school, car cleaning
Sequent Computer Systems	A−	On-site kindergarten, first grade
First Tennessee Bank	A−	Measures effect of work-family strategies on profits

Table 2.5	Laws Designed to Ensure Equal Opportunity
Law	**Key Provisions**
Title VII of the Civil Rights Act of 1964 (as amended by the Equal Employment Opportunity Act of 1972)	Prohibits discrimination in hiring, promotion, compensation, training, or dismissal on the basis of race, color, religion, sex, or national origin.
Age Discrimination in Employment Act of 1968 (as amended)	Prohibits discrimination in employment against anyone aged 40 or over in hiring, promotion, compensation, training, or dismissal.
Equal Pay Act of 1963	Requires equal pay for men and women working for the same firm in jobs that require equal skill, effort, and responsibility.
Vocational Rehabilitation Act of 1973	Requires government contractors and subcontractors to take affirmative action to employ and promote qualified disabled workers. Coverage now extends to all federal employees. Coverage has been broadened by the passage of similar laws in more than 20 states, and through court rulings, to include persons with communicable diseases, including AIDS.
Vietnam Era Veterans Readjustment Act of 1974	Requires government contractors and subcontractors to take affirmative action to employ and retain disabled veterans. Coverage now extends to all federal employees and has been broadened by the passage of similar laws in over 20 states.
Pregnancy Discrimination Act of 1978	Requires employers to treat pregnant women and new mothers the same as other employees for all employment-related purposes, including receipt of benefits under company benefit programs.
Americans with Disabilities Act of 1990	Makes discrimination against the disabled illegal in public accommodations, transportation, and telecommunications; stiffens employer penalties for intentional discrimination on the basis of an employee's disability.
Civil Rights Act of 1991	Makes it easier for workers to sue their employers for alleged discrimination. Enables victims of sexual discrimination to collect punitive damages; includes employment decisions and on-the-job issues such as sexual harassment, unfair promotions, and unfair dismissal. The employer must prove that it did not engage in discrimination.
Family and Medical Leave Act of 1993	Requires all businesses with 50 or more employees to provide up to 12 weeks of unpaid leave annually to employees who have had a child or are adopting a child, or are becoming foster parents, who are caring for a seriously ill relative or spouse, or who are themselves seriously ill. Workers must meet certain eligibility requirements.

Other firms offer benefits such as subsidized child care or on-site education and shopping to assist workers trying to balance work and family. At MBNA, bank employees can bring their children to the company's on-site day-care center, get their clothes tailored in the office, and work out in the firm's fitness center.[54]

Another solution has been to offer **family leave** to employees who need to deal with family matters. The Family and Medical Leave Act of 1993 requires every business with 50 or more employees to provide up to 12 weeks of unpaid leave annually for an employee who has a child or is adopting a child, who is becoming a foster parent, caring for a seriously ill relative or spouse, or who is seriously ill. Workers must meet certain eligibility requirements. Employers must continue to provide health benefits during the leave and guarantee that employees will return to equivalent jobs. The issue of who is entitled to health benefits can also create a dilemma as companies struggle to balance the needs of their employees against the staggering costs of health care.

> **They said it**
>
> "It doesn't matter if a cat is black or white, so long as it catches mice."
>
> Deng Xiaoping (1904–1997)
> Chinese premier

Ensuring Equal Opportunity on the Job Businesspeople face many challenges managing an increasingly diverse work force in the 21st century. By 2050, ethnic minorities and immigrants will make up nearly half of the U.S. work force. Businesses will also need to find ways to responsibly recruit and manage older workers, disabled workers, and workers with varying lifestyles. All of these groups deserve the right to work in an environment that is nondiscriminatory.

An effective diversity effort requires commitment from top management and the involvement of employees at all levels. One firm that has actively sought to manage and benefit from diversity is CoreStates. The bank's CEO, Terrence A. Larsen, initiated the effort after he noticed problems with interactions between various employee groups. At the company's annual employee meeting, he announced he would no longer tolerate bigotry, sexism, or infighting between employees with different backgrounds. He appointed a senior vice president in charge of diversity and change management, tasking her with encouraging awareness of diversity issues. For example, all CoreStates managers must attend a 5-day training program that helps them understand how individual, group, and organization attitudes and expectations affect relationships and communications between diverse groups. The company also encourages employees to establish networks based on their diverse interests and concerns. Currently, there are networks for senior-level women, people of color, gays and lesbians, and white males.[55]

To a great extent, efforts at managing diversity are regulated by law. The Civil Rights Act (1964) outlawed many kinds of discriminatory practices, and Title VII of the act specifically prohibits discrimination in employment. As shown in Table 2.5, other nondiscrimination laws include the Equal Pay Act (1963), the Age Discrimination in Employment Act (1967), the Equal Employment Opportunity Act (1972), the Pregnancy Discrimination Act (1978), the Civil Rights Act of 1991, and numerous executive orders. The Americans with Disabilities Act (1990) protects the rights of physically challenged people. The Vietnam Era Veterans Readjustment Act (1974) protects the employment of veterans of the Vietnam war.

The **Equal Employment Opportunity Commission (EEOC)** was created to increase job opportunities for women and minorities and to help end discrimination based on race, color, religion, disability, sex, or national origin in any personnel action. The EEOC can help employers set up programs to increase job opportunities for women, minorities, the disabled, and people in other protected categories. Part 3 takes a closer look at diversity and employment discrimination issues as part of a discussion of human resource management.

Sexual Harassment and Sexism Every employer has a responsibility to ensure that all workers are treated fairly and are safe from sexual harassment. **Sexual harassment** refers to unwelcome and inappropriate actions of a sex-

The Women's Bureau of the U.S. Department of Labor publishes information and offers a toll-free number and regional centers to help employees deal with sexual harassment at work. The brochure shown describes sexual harassment and explains how to handle it.

ual nature in the workplace. It is a form of sex discrimination that violates the Civil Rights Act of 1964, which gave both men and women the right to file lawsuits for intentional sexual harassment.

Over 10,000 sexual harassment complaints are filed with the Equal Employment Opportunity Commission each year, and thousands of other cases are either handled internally by companies or never reported. Research shows that 90 percent of *Fortune* 500 firms have dealt with complaints about sexual harassment, more than one-third of them have been sued at least once, and a quarter of them have been sued repeatedly.[56] In another study, 88 percent of 9,000 women surveyed said they had been sexually harassed on the job one or more times.[57]

Sexual harassment is divided into two types. The first category occurs when an employee is pressured to comply with unwelcome advances and requests for sexual favors in return for job security, promotions, and raises. Sexual harassment can also result from a hostile work environment in which an employee feels hassled or degraded because of unwelcome flirting, lewd comments, or obscene jokes. The

Business Directory

sexual harassment inappropriate actions of a sexual nature in the workplace.

SOLVING AN ETHICAL CONTROVERSY

Should Whistle-Blowers Get a Share of the Money They Help Recover?

Few on-the-job ethical dilemmas are more gut wrenching than the issue of what an employee can do about a company engaged in illegal, immoral or unethical practices—especially when the infractions are ongoing and the company refuses to change. For some employees, the potential damage to the public good outweighs their loyalty to the organization, and they turn to the media or government authorities to expose the wrongdoing and correct it. But the act of whistle-blowing often exerts a steep price for the person who actually blows the whistle—ostracism by fellow workers and, frequently, dismissal when the employer finds out.

Rob Merena, a SmithKline Beecham billing analyst in Collegeville, Pennsyl-

vania, got nowhere in reporting improper charges being billed to the U.S. government. When he called the government fraud hot line, he was referred to the office of the U.S. Attorney in Philadelphia. He agreed to continue working undercover for another 18 months and then assist the FBI and other government agencies in reviewing subpoenaed SmithKline Beecham documents and computer files. All the while, he was sworn to secrecy, and all the while he paid a high price for his cooperation.

Once Merena's role in the investigation became known to his superiors, he lost his $60,000-a-year job. He fell deeply into debt and had trouble supporting his family. And friends from SmithKline began to shun him. The stress became overwhelming. He suffered panic attacks, and his wife often cried herself to sleep.

Then the nearly-broke Merena dis-

covered something about whistle-blowers that he had not known before. In cases involving the federal government, whistle-blowers can receive as much as 30 percent of recovered funds. Merena asked for his share of the settlement, but the Justice Department said no—he didn't deserve the money because his contribution wasn't all that helpful and only added to a case that was already in progress. So Merena went back to court, this time to fight his former ally—the U.S. government.

Ultimately, Merena prevailed and received an award of $52 million. Although the federal government paid $9.7 million, its attorneys appealed the rest. But Merena joined the ranks of millionaires and could potentially receive millions more. However, he is still having trouble finding a job, because he has to tell prospective employers why he left SmithKline.

When asked about regrets, Merena

courts have ruled that allowing sexually oriented materials like pinup calendars and pornographic magazines at the workplace can create a hostile atmosphere that interferes with an employee's ability to do the job. Employers are also legally responsible to protect employees from sexual harassment from customers and clients.[58] The EEOC's Web site informs employers and employees of criteria for identifying sexual harassment and how it should be handled in the workplace.

In one highly publicized case, female workers at Mitsubishi Motors Corp.'s Illinois factory charged that male co-workers routinely groped and grabbed at them. Some women said they were forced to have sex in order to win jobs. Pornographic drawings with the women's names on them were passed among workers on the assembly line. The company had no formal mechanism in place to allow employees to complain about sexual harassment. Those who objected informally found themselves shut out of job opportunities. To settle the resulting lawsuit, the company agreed to pay an estimated $9.5 million in damages to 23 female workers. Lawsuits filed by other female Mitsubishi workers could cost the company as much as $5 million more.[59]

www.eeoc.gov

To avoid sexual harassment problems, many firms have established policies and employee education programs aimed at preventing such violations. An effective harassment prevention program should include:

▼ Issuing a specific policy statement prohibiting sexual harassment

▼ Developing a complaint procedure for employees to follow

▼ Creating a work atmosphere that encourages sexually harassed staffers to come forward

▼ Investigating and resolving complaints quickly, and taking disciplinary action against harassers

Unless all of these components are supported by top management, sexual harassment is difficult to eliminate.

Sexual harassment is often part of the broader problem of **sexism**—discrimination against members of either sex,

takes his time before responding: "No, I want to see this through to the end now. I'm thankful, though, that I didn't know the process before going into this."

? Should Whistle-Blowers Benefit Financially from Their Actions?

PRO

1. When whistle-blowers report their employers to the media or government agencies, they pay a high price emotionally, financially, and professionally. They deserve a generous reward for their courage.

2. Even though employers, media firms, and government agencies have funds to cover the soaring legal expenses, whistle-blowers have no means of recovering their legal fees unless they receive a share of the settlement.

3. Without some fallback protection from the employer's retribution, the loss of income and security, and the anger and cruelty of fel-

low workers, honest workers may be forced to close their eyes and refuse to speak out against illegal or unethical practices on the job.

CON

1. The federal government should not have to pay significant amounts to whistle-blowers whose assistance is limited in scope or usefulness.

2. Adding jackpot payoffs for actions traditionally associated with good citizenship could turn otherwise honest, hard-working people into greedy bounty hunters who waste everyone's time with undeserving or unimportant cases.

3. It isn't fair to the American people for whistle-blowers to become millionaires for simply telling the truth about a company's questionable business practices. People should not need a reward for doing the right thing.

SUMMARY

Do large case awards help whistle-blowers weather the storm? Or does the money actually encourage employees to blow the whistle on their employers when the issue could have been resolved through internal channels? Whistle-blowers helped the government recover more than $1 billion during the past decade. Surely the emotional, financial, and professional price they endure is worth some kind of recompense. But should that reward make whistle-blowers rich beyond their dreams?

Sources: "Blue Cross Whistle-Blower Gets $29M," *The Associated Press*, January 27, 1999; Tom Lowry, "Whistle-Blower Now Fighting Former Allies," *USA Today*, November 9, 1998, p. 15B; and "Expert Says Georgia Law a 'Cardboard Shield,'" *Atlanta Journal*, April 12, 1998, accessed at www.accessatlanta.com.

but primarily affecting women. Some examples of sexism are blatant, as when a woman earns less than a male colleague in the same job, or when a male employee gains a promotion over a better-qualified female. Other instances are more subtle; the only female in a work group may not be introduced to a client or may not get a work assignment.

One important sexism issue concerns equal pay for equal work. On average, women in the United States earn 71 cents for every dollar earned by men. In the course of a working lifetime, this disparity adds up to a gap of $420,000. This data actually represents an improvement; in 1980, women's wages averaged 64 percent of men's. The gap is closing only partly because of gains in women's salaries; the rest is due to a decline in men's earnings. Female high-school graduates still earn less than men who quit school before the ninth grade.[60]

Responsibilities to Investors and the Financial Community

Although a fundamental goal of any business is to make a profit for its shareholders, investors and the financial com-

munity demand that businesses behave ethically as well as legally in handling their financial transactions. When businesses fail in this responsibility, thousands of investors and consumers can suffer.

For example, in the early 1990s, banks and savings and loan institutions (S&Ls) were failing at the highest rate since the Great Depression of the 1930s. All too often, the problems resulted because bank executives approved too many high-risk investments. The banks used their deposits to finance real estate developers, third-world governments, and corporate buyouts. When the borrowers couldn't repay the loans, the banks failed. Federal deposit insurance covered most depositors' losses at the failed banks and S&Ls. However, these payments cost the government, and ultimately taxpayers, billions of dollars.

Both state and federal government agencies currently protect investors from abuses such as land fraud. As Figure 2.15 points out, personal finance magazines such as *Kiplinger's* also play an important role in alerting investors to such abuses.

The Securities and Exchange Commission is the federal agency responsible for investigating suspicions that publicly traded firms engaged in unethical or illegal finan-

Figure 2.15   **Protecting Investors from Unethical Practices**

Without 50 years of Kiplinger's, there's no telling where people would've sunk their money.

Great Investment - Just over 30 acres.
Plenty of trees. Right on the water.
Priced to sell. (303) 555-2940

WE DELIVER SUBSTANCE.

cial behavior. Often investigations arise when a business uses faulty accounting practices that inaccurately portray its financial resources and profits to investors. For example, Pinnacle Micro, a maker of computer storage devices, suffered from falling profits for several years. The SEC found that the company tried to hide its losses by counting sales that were actually made the following year in its current-year sales figures. This maneuver made it appear that the firm had met its annual sales goals when it really hadn't. As a result of these and other accounting problems, the SEC fined the company and ordered it to release revised accounting records that correctly showed its weak profits. Three of the company's officers were also fined for their role in the situation. Chapter 19 discusses accounting practices further.

Businesses also behave unethically when they mislead investors about potential opportunities. Consider Bre-X Minerals. The company claimed that it had found a deposit of 71 million ounces of gold, worth $24 billion, in a rain forest in Indonesia. Hearing the news, investors drove the stock price for Bre-X to record levels. However, reports soon revealed that the company had actually placed 60 ounces of gold into a sample taken at the mining site in order to support its discovery claims. In reality, exploration had found no gold. Bre-X became the focus of a criminal investigation, and shareholders sued the company for providing false information to investors.

Bre-X is not the only business to face charges in court. As this chapter's Solving an Ethical Controversy described, SmithKline Beechan was placed under investigation for Medicare fraud. The company eventually settled with the Justice Department for $325 million, which was the largest award ever in a whistle-blower case.

ETHICS AND SOCIAL RESPONSIBILITY IN THE GLOBAL MARKETPLACE

Expanding globally can open new dilemmas about a firm's ethics and social responsibility. Global corporations need to carefully evaluate the cultures of the countries where they do business. Individual cultures may not only have different standards of right and wrong but also different conceptions of how misdeeds should be treated. In many countries, bribes and kickbacks are considered part of doing business. Solving ethical problems in foreign countries may require flexibility and creativity.

Consider the ethical dilemma Jerry Torma faced. Torma spent 4 years working in the Middle East as director of international compensation for Nordson Corp. Local officials demanded that he provide "facilitating payments" before they would process work permits for the company. Other foreign firms had agreed to pay these bribes. Torma, however, took a different approach. He explained to the officials that he wasn't permitted to pay bribes and suggested they work together to find a different solution. In talking with one official, Torma discovered that a monumental backlog of paperwork awaited the official's staff. Torma suggested that he provide the assistance of a secretary to help clear the backlog instead of paying a bribe. This solution was legal, ethical, and satisfactory to both parties.[61]

Global firms also face quandaries about their responsibilities to workers in countries where commitments to social responsibility for employees are often weaker than those of domestic firms. In many countries, government agencies and others exert little or no control over the conditions in which workers toil. The average worker may only earn a few dollars a week, and child labor is considered an acceptable practice. When U.S. manufacturers do business in these countries, or purchase products manufactured in them, they can violate the social responsibility expectations of U.S. consumers. These firms must balance their needs for low-cost labor with their responsibilities toward human rights.

For example, the U.S. Department of Labor reports that 80 percent of the soccer balls sold in the United States were made with child labor in Pakistan. Reebok, a major importer of soccer balls from Pakistan, has vowed that it will purchase soccer balls made only in factories that use adult labor. To verify this position, Reebok has hired an accounting firm to audit factory records. The company also invited human rights observers to visit and interview workers on a regular basis. Finally, Reebok has also committed to support training programs for children who were previously employed in Pakistani soccer ball factories. In the United States, the company's soccer balls will carry a label reading, "Human rights guarantee: No child labor used."[62]

Nike was also forced to confront this dilemma recently when reports revealed that most of the company's products were manufactured in foreign factories where workers were paid only pennies a day. Nike issued requirements for wages and working conditions in factories wishing to do business with the company. The company severed ties with several Asian factories that failed to meet these standards. Critics still contend, however, that Nike should pay its foreign workers wages comparable to those earned by workers in the United States.[63]

To confront these issues, the Council on Economic Priorities (CEP), a public-interest group based in New York, has joined with a group of influential companies including Avon, Toys 'R' Us, and Eddie Bauer to launch a program called *Social Accountability 8000* (SA 8000). The group has outlined standards for employers to follow in hiring workers abroad. Among the proposed labor standards, participating companies would agree to:

▼ Avoid using child or forced labor

▼ Provide safe working environments

▼ Respect workers' rights to unionize

▼ Require no more than 48-hour work weeks

▼ Pay wages sufficient to meet workers' basic needs[64]

WHAT'S AHEAD

As this chapter has shown, the decisions and actions of businesspeople are often affected by outside forces such as the legal environment and society's expectations about business responsibility. Firms also are affected by the economic environments in which they operate. The next chapter discusses the broad economic issues that influence businesses around the world. Our discussion will focus on how factors such as supply and demand, unemployment, inflation, and government monetary policies pose both challenges and opportunities for firms seeking to compete in the global marketplace.

SUMMARY OF LEARNING GOALS

1. Explain the concepts of business ethics and social responsibility.

Business ethics refers to the standards of conduct and moral values that govern actions and decisions in the workplace. Businesspeople must take a wide range of social issues into account when making decisions. *Social responsibility* refers to management's acceptance of the obligation to consider profit, consumer satisfaction, and societal well-being of equal value in evaluating the firm's performance.

2. Describe the factors that influence individual ethics and common ethical dilemmas in the workplace.

Among the many factors shaping individual ethics are past experience, peer pressure, and organizational culture. Individual ethics are also influenced by family, cultural, and religious standards. Additionally, the culture of the organization where a person works can be a factor. Common on-the-job ethical situations faced by individuals include conflicts of interest, loyalty to one's employer, bribery, and whistle-blowing.

3. Explain how organizations shape ethical behavior.

Employees are strongly influenced by the standards of conduct established and supported within the organizations where they work. Businesses can help shape ethical behavior by developing codes of conduct that define their expectations. Organizations can also use this training to develop employees' ethics awareness and reasoning. Executives must also demonstrate ethical behavior in their decisions and actions in order to set examples for employees to follow.

4. Relate the ways in which government regulation affects business ethics and social responsibility.

Because businesses sometimes fail to regulate their own actions, federal, state, and local governments may step in to regulate business activity. The federal government regulates competition and commercial activities. In a regulated industry, competition is either limited or eliminated, substituting close government control for free competition. Laws have also been enacted to protect against unfair competition and to protect consumers. Deregulation has significantly reshaped the legal environments in many industries in the last two decades.

5. Describe the responsibilities of business to the general public, customers, and employees.

The responsibilities of business to the general public include dealing with public-health issues, protecting the environment, and developing the quality of the work force. Additionally, many would argue that businesses have a social responsibility to support charitable and social causes in the communities in which they earn profits.

Business also has a social and ethical responsibility to treat customers fairly and act in a manner that will not harm them. Ultimately, businesses themselves are responsible for protecting consumers' rights. Among the rights of consumers that businesspeople should uphold are the rights to be safe, to be informed, to choose, and to be heard.

A firm's employees are an important resource, and businesses have wide-ranging responsibilities to their workers. They must make sure that the workplace is safe for employees. Businesses must also address quality of life issues by helping workers find solutions to problems such as how to balance work and family requirements. Employees also deserve the right to work in nondiscriminatory environments, so businesses must manage diversity. Finally, employers have a responsibility to ensure that all workers are treated fairly and are safe from sexual harassment.

6. Explain why investors and the financial community are concerned with business ethics.

Investors and the financial community demand that businesses behave ethically as well as legally in handling their financial transactions. They must be honest in reporting their profits and financial performance in order to avoid misleading investors. The Securities and Exchange Commission is the federal agency responsible for investigating suspicions that publicly traded firms have engaged in unethical or illegal financial behavior.

7. Describe the ethical and social responsibility issues facing businesses in the global marketplace.

Global expansion opens new dilemmas about a firm's ethics and social responsibility. Individual cultures may not only have different standards of right and wrong but also different concepts of how misdeeds should be treated. Bribes and kickbacks are considered part of doing business in many countries. Other countries may have different expectations of a firm's social responsibilities. Solving ethical problems in foreign countries may require flexibility and creativity.

TEN BUSINESS TERMS YOU NEED TO KNOW

business ethics	deregulation
conflict of interest	social responsibility
whistle-blowing	recycling
code of conduct	corporate philanthropy
regulated industry	sexual harassment

Other Important Business Terms

integrity

social audit

pollution

consumerism

family leave

Equal Employment Opportunity
Commission (EEOC)

sexism

REVIEW QUESTIONS

1. What do the terms *social responsibility* and *business ethics* mean? Cite an example of each. Discuss the current status of social responsibility and business ethics practices in U.S. industry.

2. Explain how individuals' actions can be shaped by an organization's traditions and expectations. Do you agree or disagree that a company where ethical behavior is expected tends to have fewer problems with employee misconduct than firms with other expectations? Why or why not?

3. Does self-regulation deter government regulation in matters of social responsibility and business ethics? Why or why not?

4. How does government regulate both competition and specific business practices? Describe specific regulations with which businesspeople should be familiar. What is deregulation? What are its advantages and disadvantages?

5. What are the responsibilities of business to the general public? Cite specific examples.

6. What basic consumer rights does the consumerism movement try to assure? How has consumerism improved the contemporary business environment?

7. What is meant by discrimination? How can organizations ensure equal opportunity on the job?

8. Distinguish between sexual harassment and sexism. Cite examples of each. How can firms avoid these problems?

9. What are a firm's responsibilities to its investors and the financial community? What can happen when a firm fails to meet these responsibilities?

10. List some of the ethical dilemmas that people in international businesses may encounter.

QUESTIONS FOR CRITICAL THINKING

1. Al "Chain Saw" Dunlap made most businesspeople's "Bosses from Hell" list for his willingness to eliminate thousands of jobs in pursuit of corporate profit. When Dunlap was CEO of Kimberly Clark's Scott Paper division, he eliminated the company's $5 million annual corporate philanthropy budget as part of his efforts to cut costs and boost the company's profits. Before the Sunbeam Corp. board of directors fired him from his next job, Dunlap vetoed that company's $1 million annual giving program, too. His explanation: "The purest form of charity is

to make the most money you can for shareholders and let them give to whatever charities they want."
   a. Do you agree with Dunlap's point of view? Why or why not?
   b. What positive and negative effects might Scott Paper and Sunbeam experience from eliminating their corporate philanthropy budgets?
   c. Are most consumers aware of the corporate contributions of specific companies?

2. "Everybody exaggerates when it comes to selling products, and the consumer ought to take that with a grain of salt," said one advertising executive recently in response to a complaint filed by the Better Business Bureau about misleading advertising. "Don't we all have a brain, and can't we all think a little bit?"
   a. Discuss the consumer's responsibility in sorting the information provided by businesses seeking to market their products. If a consumer fails to carefully read an instruction manual and is injured, who do you think should be responsible?
   b. Do you agree or disagree with the statement that all businesses exaggerate when selling, advertising, and marketing products? Find at least two advertisements that support your argument.

3. Write a personal code of ethical conduct that details your own feelings about ethical issues such as lying, stealing, taking bribes, and hurting others. How will you handle situations where the ethics are not clear-cut? Do you think your code of conduct will be different 5 years from now? In 10 years? In 20 years? Would you take action that didn't fit with your code of conduct if your employer made it a requirement for advancing in your job? If you were offered a large sum of money? What role will your personal ethics play in deciding your choice of career and acceptance of a job?

4. Suppose that you own a small company with 12 employees. One of them tells you in confidence that he has just found out he has AIDS. You know that health-care costs for AIDS patients can be disastrously high, and this expense could drastically raise the health insurance premiums that your other employees must pay. What are your responsibilities to this employee? To the rest of your staff? Explain.

5. Evaluate the potential ethical and social issues facing the listed organizations. If possible, make recommendations for how the organizations should handle or avoid specific issues.
   a. Ford Motor Company
   b. Real estate developers
   c. the American Heart Association and the American Lung Association
   d. Jenny Craig Weight Loss Centers
   e. IBM

Experiential Exercise

Directions: At the end of the chapter section titled *Ethical Reasoning,* you learned about Lockheed Martin's ethics training program, "The Ethics Challenge," based on the popular comic-strip characters Dilbert and Dogbert. The following exercise provides a sampling of the complete board game by beginning with an overview of the game's *Ethical Decision Making Model* and giving you two of the fifty case studies to solve. Either work alone or as a member of a group to complete this exercise. (If you were involved in the ethics training sessions at Lockheed Martin, you would probably be one member in a group of five to seven individuals.)

1. Use the *Ethical Decision Making Model* to help you select the best option in the two case studies presented below. In addition to answers designated A, B, C, and D, each case includes a Dogbert answer, which is worth zero points, since it usually is the worst thing you could possibly do. Some answers are better than others and will rate point values between 0 and 5. Circle your choices after you have read the case studies.

2. Following the second case study is a section titled *Leader's Comments*. Read this section after you've selected your answers because it will explain the rationale for each potential answer and provide the points assigned to each response.

Ethical Decision Making Model
1. Evaluate information.
2. Consider how your decision might affect stakeholders (employees, customers, communities, shareholders, suppliers).
3. Consider what ethical values are relevant to the situation (honesty, integrity, respect, trust, responsibility, citizenship).
4. Determine the best course of action that takes into account relevant values and stakeholders' interests.

CASE FILE NUMBER: 18
Category: Quality Assurance
Setting the Standard: Responsibility

You work in Quality Assurance. You rejected some parts as not conforming to specifications, but your manager told you to accept the parts "as is." You don't agree with the decision. What do you do?

Potential Answers:
A. Do nothing. It's the manager's decision to make.
B. Discuss it with your manager.
C. Call the Ethics HelpLine.
D. Ask the engineers who are responsible for the specification to clarify the situation.
Dogbert: Gripe about it to everybody in the cafeteria.

CASE FILE NUMBER: 39
Category: Employee Recognition Program
Setting the Standard: Honesty

A work team submits a suggestion to the suggestion program. In the meantime, some employees on the team are laid off. The suggestion has been adopted. How do you distribute the award payment?

Potential Answers:
A. Divide it equally among the members of the team still employed.
B. Divide it among all former team members, whether they're still working or not.
C. If the remaining team members agree, donate the check to a charity.
D. Divide the check among all the current employees. If the former employees find out about the award, they can call and request their share.
Dogbert: Declare yourself the winner.

Leader's Comments: Case File Number 18
A. 0 points. If you have a concern, don't ignore it.
B. 5 points. This is your opportunity to explain your concern to your manager. The manager may have justification for accepting the part—some decisions are based on judgment or experience. Then, if you're still concerned, call the Ethics HelpLine.
C. 4 points. This is always a good idea, especially if you are uncomfortable resolving the situation with your manager.
D. 3 points. The engineers may give you technical information that resolves your concern.

Leader's Comments: Case File Number 39
A. 0 points. This deliberately cheats the former employees out of their share of the award.
B. 5 points. This is the only fair solution. This way everyone who earned a share gets a share.
C. 2 points. Better than A, but it still excludes the laid-off workers.
D. 0 points. Put yourself in the shoes of the laid-off workers. How would you feel if you were excluded?

Source: Lockheed Martin's 1997 ethics awareness training module, *The Ethics Challenge*.

Nothing but Net

1. **Social Responsibility.** The Business for Social Responsibility (BSR) is an organization for companies of all sizes and sectors. BSR's mission is to help its members achieve long-term commercial success by implementing ethical policies and practices and meeting their responsibilities to all who are affected by their decisions. Visit BSR's fact sheet at

   www.bsr.org/bsrfacts.htm

   and answer the following questions:
   (a) How many member companies belong to BSR?
   (b) What are BSR's areas of expertise?
   (c) What benefits do member companies receive for their BSR dues?

2. **Ethics.** Select a topic, such as whistle-blowing at Archer Daniels Midland

   condor.depaul.edu/ethics/adm.html

   or The Body Shop's ethics controversy

   www.arq.co.uk/ethicalbusiness/archive/bodyshop/index.htm

   then use your search engine to find information to write a 1- to 2-page analysis of your selected topic. Another source for topic ideas is DePaul University's Institute for Business & Professional Ethics at

   condor.depaul.edu/ethics/prob1.html

   which provides links regarding specific issues or problem areas.

3. **Protecting the Environment.** Visit a Web site of a company committed to protecting the environment. Two such sites are Goodyear and The Gap:

   www.goodyear.com/about/enviro/balance.html

   www.gap.com/company/comm.env.policy.asp

   Identify (a) the specific challenges facing the company you have chosen and (b) the strategy and accomplishments of the company regarding its efforts to protect the environment.

Note: Internet Web addresses change frequently. If you do not find the exact sites listed, you may need to access the organization's or company's home page and search from there.

CONTRIBUTING TO THE COMMUNITY—
LA MADELEINE

What is a socially responsible corporation? How do the concepts of corporate vision and community contribution fit? Patrick Esquerré states that his French bakeries are not part of a restaurant chain. Rather he describes each of them as "a French bakery on the corner" that provides a homey place to eat for its "guests."

Esquerré's vision of la Madeleine is "to be as close as possible to our guests, and to our associates—the people working inside the company—in order to inspire whatever needs to be done to make them feel good, to make each person feel special." What does this mean in terms of actions? Esquerré actually designed the first la Madeleine bakery and restaurant by listening to people who walked by as construction began. When they commented that they hoped there would be a wood burning stove, he made sure there was. When he asked passersby about what they thought a French bakery should have and they answered "wood beams in the ceiling," these were installed as well.

Esquerré sees his guests as the leaders of the organization. His customers decide what they want, how they want it, and even at what price. How does he view his own job? "My job is to listen to these leaders; to adapt to their tastes as much as I can without compromising on key issues; and, to surprise them by going beyond what they expect."

This unique leader sees his "guests" and associates (employees) as part of his family. One of Esquerré's priorities is to make sure that his associates are recognized for their good work as often as possible. It is important to him, for example, that associates know there is a chance for advancement and promotion within their firm. In addition, he uses a bonus plan to reward excellent performance and to increase motivation. Perhaps even more important is the fact that as part of the "orientation" program, all managers who begin a career at la Madeleine are taken to France to be given an opportunity to experience French life. This experience helps to guide them in their jobs. Managers-of-the-Year are rewarded with a free trip to France with their spouses. The managers at la Madeleine are those very people who must listen, adapt, and surprise their guests!

Esquerré also pays attention to the needs of the communities in which the bakeries are located. He and his associates regularly participate in local fundraising activities. Bill Buchanan, one of Esquerré's managers, commented, "The environment that Patrick Esquerré provides for everyone is one in which you can be successful, care for others, and give back to the community in particular—this has made an impact on my own management style, as well as how I conduct my life."

One of the company's programs is a joint effort between the local Public Broadcasting Service station, la Madeleine, and the local food bank. Esquerré makes a fresh food donation to the neighborhood food bank equivalent to 50 percent of total PBS pledges. This tends to increase overall giving to PBS as people understand that the value of their donations is increased through the program. The company has donated over $200,000 of food in a given year.

Contributions, however, are not the only way that la Madeleine is involved in community efforts. Esquerré, along with other managers, frequently takes truckloads of baked goods into the streets to feed the homeless. One manager noted that he had gone with Patrick Esquerré on a weekend to the parking lot right behind City Hall in Dallas to hand out food, coffee, and orange juice to people "who have no other means."

Does la Madeleine have no concern about its bottom line? The corporate philosophy is that you worry about the bottom line by focusing on the top—building sales and maintaining strong involvement with the community, making sure that people want to come to your bakery. Rather than focusing on the short run, la Madeleine and Patrick Esquerré focus on community and the long run—in doing so, he has developed a highly successful and growing enterprise.

Questions

1. Describe the ways that la Madeleine shows the philosophy of community social responsibility. What other responsibilities to the general public may be appropriate for la Madeleine?

2. How does la Madeleine show its responsibility to its customers? To its employees? Explain.

3. Give an example of a firm in your own community that you feel is socially responsible. How has this affected their success in their location?

Sources: L. Stones and K. Lynn, "Entrepreneurism + Customer Service = Success," *Management Review* (November 1993), 38–44.

chapter 3

Economic Challenges Facing Global and Domestic Business

LEARNING GOALS

1. Distinguish between microeconomics and macroeconomics.

2. List each of the factors that collectively determine demand and those that determine supply.

3. Compare supply and demand curves and explain how they determine the equilibrium price for a good or service.

4. Contrast the three major types of economic systems.

5. Identify the four different types of market structures in a private enterprise system.

6. Identify the major factors that guide an economist's evaluation of a nation's economic performance.

7. Compare the two major tools used by a government to manage the performance of its national economy.

8. Describe the major global economic challenges of the 21st century.

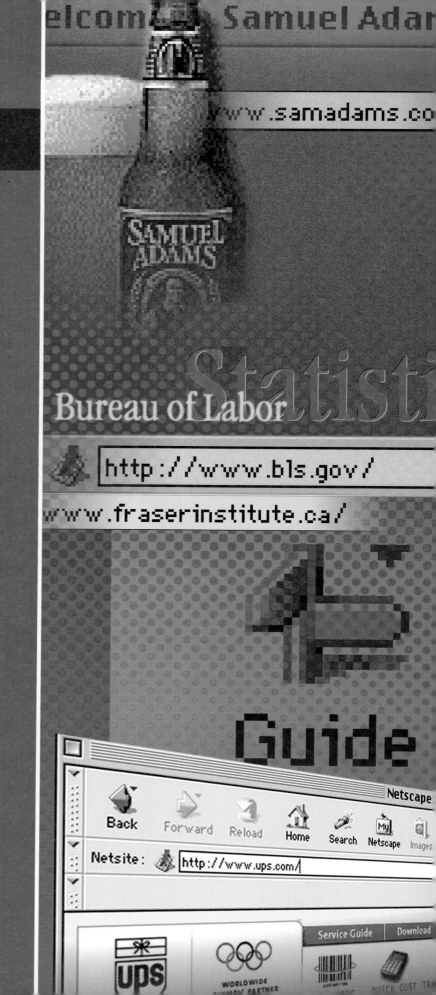

UPS Improves Worker Skills and Its Workforce

Package-handling giant United Parcel Service (UPS) has reaped the benefits of recent economic prosperity in the form of strong demand. At the same time, UPS has been forced to find innovative ways to attract and retain the human resources it needs. With unemployment rates below 4.5 percent and Help Wanted signs everywhere, UPS discovered that above-average compensation and an attractive benefits package was not sufficient to attract the people needed to service the firm's growing business. Then UPS management chose a new approach aimed at accomplishing more than simply filling

its personnel roster. It became a founding member of the Welfare to Work Partnership, a federal program aimed at reducing the nation's welfare rolls.

Susan Miller represents one of many success stories. Hired on a part-time basis as a package handler, Miller worked hard to leave the welfare rolls and return to work—something she sees as an important example for her three small children. She quickly earned the respect and trust of both management and her coworkers. Promotion to supervisor soon followed, and today she is responsible for training new-hires at the Atlanta hub.

But the Welfare to Work Partnership has not been problem free. When participants couldn't find public transportation to the UPS distribution center near Philadelphia International Airport, the firm arranged for two school buses to carry workers back and forth. Later it convinced the metro bus system to extend routes directly to the terminal by agreeing to subsidize any bus that didn't break even. Today, 53 buses make the trip 24 hours a day, and all of them are profitable.

The buses aid UPS employees in nonwork activities. For example, Tiffany Smith, a 21-year-old package sorter, rides the bus to the terminal to take classes for her general equivalency diploma. Taught at the airport by local college professors, these classes are paid for by UPS.

Nowhere was worker education more important to UPS than at its Louisville hub in Kentucky. The company needed to hire 6,000 more workers to fill the midnight shift, but Louisville's unemployment rate was already so low that consideration was being given to relocating the facility to a place with a larger applicant pool. Then someone came up with a unique employee benefit: night-shift workers would receive free tuition at their choice of three local colleges. Although it cost the employer approximately $1,500 per semester for each participant, the offer proved a real crowd-pleaser. The following semester began with 700 UPS workers participating.

WWW.

www.ups.com

The welfare-to-work effort is great for the employee participants but it also produces hundreds of capable workers for the employers. "I have been pleasantly surprised," says UPS CEO James P. Kelly. In just the first six months, UPS retained 88 percent of its welfare employees (compared with a previous rate of 60 percent) in Philadelphia. Of equal importance is the fact that UPS experienced no decline in productivity.

Much of the additional recruitment and training costs are covered in the form of federal tax credits of up to $8,500 for each welfare recipient hired. But the payoff comes in many ways. The nation's welfare caseload has plummeted more than 30 percent over the past four years. Companies like UPS have gained productive employees, and former welfare recipients have acquired skills capable of freeing them from the cycle of poverty. As Pamela Brown, one of UPS's many success stories, puts it, "Moving off welfare is like climbing a mountain with your head held high."[1]

CHAPTER OVERVIEW

At UPS, the training and assistance that workers receive benefit both the company and society in general. Employees are a resource that a company uses to produce its goods and services. In return, empoyees gain wages, skills, and—in the Welfare to Work Partnership program—education that improves individuals' lives and raises the overall quality of the workforce.

Looking at the exchanges that companies and societies make as a whole, we are speaking of their **economic sys-**

clothing supplier, he is particularly attracted to the suit shown in Figure 3.1. This one person with a single purchase has involved himself in international trade by choosing the Italian-made Ermenegildo Zegna suit over the U.S.-made Hilfiger brand. Businesses also make economic decisions when they choose how to use human and natural resources, invest in machinery and buildings, and form partnerships with other firms.

Economists refer to the study of small economic units, such as individual consumers, families, and businesses, as

---

| **Figure 3.1** | **Making Economic Choices between Domestic and Imported Products** |

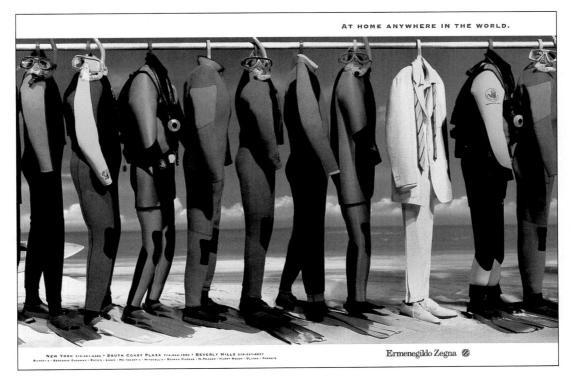

AT HOME ANYWHERE IN THE WORLD.

NEW YORK 212-421-4488 • SOUTH COAST PLAZA 714-668-1934 • BEVERLY HILLS 310-247-8827

Ermenegildo Zegna ⬢

---

tems, that is, the combination of policies and choices a nation makes to allocate resources among its citizens. Countries vary in the ways they allocate scarce resources.

Economics, the social science analyzing the choices made by people and governments in allocating scarce resources, affects each of us, since everyone is involved in producing, distributing, or simply consuming goods and services. In fact, your life is affected by economics every day. When you decide what goods to buy, what services to use, or what activities to fit into your schedule, you are making economic choices.

The choices you make often are international in scope. Consider, for example, a man who decides to buy a new suit. Even though he has leaned toward Tommy Hilfiger as his

microeconomics. On a broader level, however, government decisions about the operation of the country's economy also affect you, your job, and your financial future. When the U.S. Congress decided to reduce military spending in the early 1990s, for example, many military bases were closed, affecting the financial well-being of businesses and individuals in surrounding communities. The study of a country's overall economic issues is called **macroeconomics.** (*Macro* means *large.*) This discipline addresses such issues as how an economy maintains and

Business Directory

economics   social science analyzing the choices made by people and governments in allocating scarce resources.

allocates resources and how government policies affect people's standards of living.

Chapter 1 explained the increasing interdependence of the world's nations and their economies. As a result, macroeconomics also examines not just the economic policies of individual nations, but the ways in which those individual policies affect the world's economy overall. Remember, though, that microeconomics and macroeconomics are interrelated disciplines—large macroeconomic issues reflect the small decisions made every day by individuals, families, and businesses.

This chapter introduces economic theory and the economic challenges facing individuals, businesses, and governments in the global marketplace. This discussion begins with the microeconomic concepts of supply and demand and their effect on the prices people pay for goods and services. Next, the various types of economic systems are explained along with tools for comparing and evaluating their performance. The chapter then examines the ways in which

governments seek to manage economies in order to create stable business environments in their countries. The final section in the chapter looks at some of the driving economic forces that will affect people's lives in the early years of the 21st century.

MICROECONOMICS: THE FORCES OF DEMAND AND SUPPLY

A good way to begin the study of economics is to look at the economic activities and choices of individuals and small economic units such as families and firms. These economic actions determine both the prices of goods and services and the amounts sold. Microeconomic information is vital for a business, because its survival depends on selling enough of its products at prices high enough to cover expenses and earn profits. This information is also important to consumers, whose well-being may depend on the prices and availability of needed goods and services.

At the heart of every business endeavor is an exchange between a buyer and a seller. A buyer recognizes that he or she has a need or wants a particular good or service and is willing to pay a seller in order to obtain it. The seller is motivated to participate in the process by the anticipated financial gains from selling the good or service. The exchange process, therefore, involves both demand and supply. **Demand** refers to the willingness and ability of buyers to purchase goods and services at different prices. The other side of the exchange process is **supply,** the willingness and ability of sellers to provide goods and services for sale at different prices.

Understanding the factors that determine demand and supply, as well as how the two interact, can help you to understand many of the actions and decisions that individuals, businesses, and government make. This section takes a closer look at these concepts.

| **Figure 3.2** | **Consumer Preferences, Incomes, and the Prices of Substitute Products: Factors Affecting Demand for Automobiles** |

Business Directory

demand willingness and ability of buyers to purchase goods and services.

supply willingness and ability of sellers to provide goods and services for sale.

Factors Driving Demand

For most people, economics amounts to a balance between unlimited wants and limited financial means. Because of this dilemma, each person must make choices about how much available money to save and how much to spend, as well as how to allocate that spending among all the goods and services competing for attention. This continuing effort to overcome the unlimited wants/limited means dilemma caused one writer to refer to economics as *the dismal science*.

Even though you may be convinced that the Jeep Wrangler shown in Figure 3.2 is the perfect answer to your automotive needs, a quick perusal of the required monthly payments may force you to compromise with a less expensive Suzuki Samurai. Even if you can afford the monthly payments on the Jeep, you may still select the more economical Samurai and spend the money you save on new clothes, a trip to Disney World, or a more expensive apartment with an extra bedroom. Demand, therefore, is driven by a number of factors that influence how people decide to spend their incomes.

Price is one of the most important factors influencing demand. In general, as the price of a good or service goes up, people buy diminishing amounts. In other words, as price rises, the quantity demanded declines. At lower prices, consumers are generally willing to buy more of a good. A **demand curve** is a graph of the amount of a product that buyers will purchase at different prices. These curves typically slope downward, reflecting the fact that lower and lower prices typically attract larger and larger purchases.

If you have shopped for a personal computer in recent months, you have encountered the steep decline in prices for these products—and the resulting impact on sales. Tumbling component costs allowed manufacturers like Compaq, Dell, Gateway, and Hewlett-Packard to offer ultra-cheap PCs with expanded power and features. As consumers discovered that

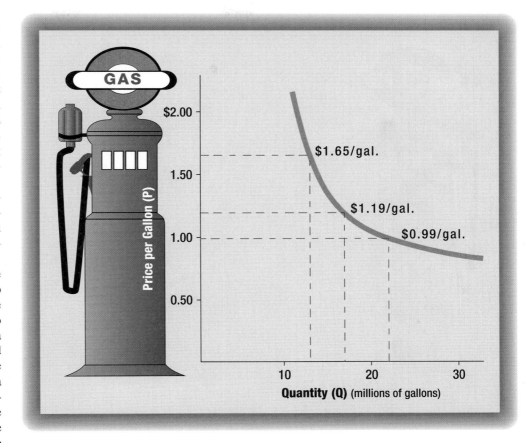

Figure 3.3   **Demand Curve for Gasoline**

for around $800 they could get a computer with Intel's latest Pentium chip, the Windows 95 operating system, a speedy modem, and CD-ROM drives, they rushed into the market. Currently, two of every five PCs sold in the United States carry retail prices below $1,000. By 2000, prices for basic PCs had dropped below $500, making it possible for over 50 percent of the nation's households to own at least one.[2]

Gasoline provides another good example of how demand curves work. Figure 3.3 shows a possible demand curve for the total amount of gasoline that people will purchase at different prices. When gasoline is priced at $1.19 a gallon, for example, drivers may fill up their tanks once or twice a week. At $1.65 a gallon, however, many of them may start economizing. They may make fewer trips, start carpooling, or ride buses to work. The quantity of gasoline demanded at $1.65 a gallon, therefore, is lower than the amount demanded at $1.19 a gallon. The opposite happens at $0.99 a gallon. Some drivers may decide to top off their tanks more often than they would at a higher price; they may also decide to take cross-country motoring vacations or drive to school

They said it

"You can make even a parrot into a learned economist by teaching him two words: supply and demand."

Anonymous

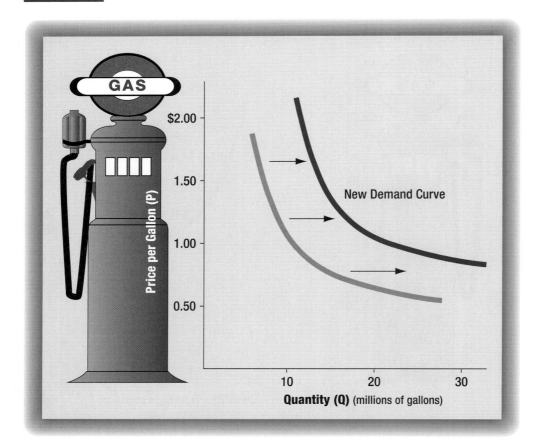

Figure 3.4 **Shift in the Demand Curve for Gasoline**

For example, record amounts of gasoline were consumed last year. As the popularity of gas-guzzling vehicles like sport-utility vehicles grew, Americans used more gasoline. In addition, many consumers in developing countries like India and China found themselves able to afford to buy cars for the first time, increasing the demand for gasoline at all prices. Figure 3.4 shows how the increased demand for gasoline worldwide has created a new demand curve. The new demand curve shifts to the right of the old demand curve, indicating that overall demand has increased at every price. A demand curve can also shift to the left when the demand for a good or service drops.

While price is the underlying cause of movement along a demand curve, many factors can combine to determine the overall demand for a good or service.

instead of taking the bus. As a result, more gasoline is sold at $0.99 a gallon than at $1.19 a gallon.

Economists make a clear distinction between changes in the quantity demanded at various prices and changes in overall demand. A *change in quantity demanded,* such as the change that occurs at different gasoline prices, is simply movement along the demand curve. A *change in overall demand,* on the other hand, results in an entirely new demand curve.

These include customer preferences and incomes, the prices of substitute and complementary products, the number of buyers in a market, and the strength of their optimism regarding the future. Changes in any of these factors will produce a new demand curve.

Take a change in income as an example. Rising incomes are likely to permit firms to sell more products at every price, causing the demand curve to shift to the right. By contrast, a significant increase in film prices may re-

Table 3.1 **Expected Shifts in Demand Curves**

Factor	Demand Curve Shifts	
	to the Right IF:	to the Left IF:
Customer preferences	increase	decrease
Number of buyers	increases	decreases
Buyers' incomes	increase	decrease
Prices of substitute goods	increase	decrease
Prices of complementary goods	decrease	increase
Future expectations become more	optimistic	pessimistic

duce overall demand for complementary goods like cameras. Table 3.1 describes how a demand curve is likely to respond to each of these changes.

For a business to succeed, management must carefully observe the factors that may affect demand for the goods and services it hopes to sell. In setting prices, for example, firms often try to predict how the chosen levels will influence the amounts they sell. Businesspeople also try to influence overall demand through advertising, sales calls, product enhancements, and other marketing techniques.

Factors Driving Supply

Important economic factors also affect supply, the willingness and ability of businesses to provide goods and services at different prices. Just as consumers must make choices about how to spend their incomes, businesses must also make decisions about how to use their resources in order to obtain the best profits.

Obviously, sellers would prefer to command high rather than low prices for their goods or services. A **supply curve** graphically shows the relationship between different prices and the quantities that sellers will offer for sale, regardless of demand. Movement along the supply curve is the opposite of movement along the demand curve. That is, as price rises, the quantity sellers are willing to supply also rises. At progressively lower prices, the quantity supplied decreases. In Figure 3.5, for example, a possible supply curve for gasoline shows that increasing prices for gasoline should bring increasing supplies to market, as oil companies are motivated by the possibility of earning growing profits.

Businesses require certain inputs in order to operate effectively to produce their goods and services. These inputs, called **factors of production,** include natural re-

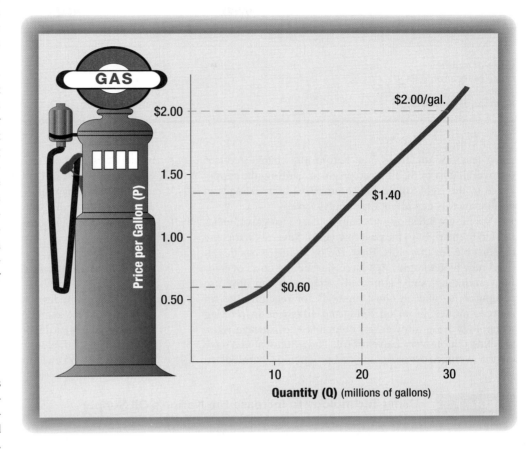

Figure 3.5   **Supply Curve for Gasoline**

sources, capital, human resources, and entrepreneurship. *Natural resources* include everything that is useful in its natural state. Examples of natural resources include land, building sites, forests, and mineral deposits. *Human resources* include the physical labor and intellectual inputs contributed by workers. *Capital* refers to resources such as technology, tools, information, physical facilities, and financial capabilities. Finally, the fourth factor of production, *entrepreneurship,* is the willingness to take risks to create and operate a business.

Factors of production play a central role in determining the overall supply of goods and services. A change in the cost or availability of any of these inputs can shift the entire supply curve, either increasing or decreasing the amount available at every price. For example, if the cost of raw materials (natural resources) rises, producers may respond by lowering production levels, shifting the supply curve to the left. On the other hand, if an innovation in the production process allows them to turn out more products

DID YOU KNOW?

How long it takes to manufacture a: McDonald's Big Mac, 21 seconds; Chevrolet Corvette, 40 hours; commuter airplane, 18,000 hours.

Table 3.2	Expected Shifts in Supply Curves		
		Supply Curve Shifts	
Factor		to the Right IF:	to the Left IF:
Costs of inputs		decrease	increase
Costs of technologies		decrease	increase
Taxes		decrease	increase
Number of suppliers		increases	decreases

using less raw materials than before, the change reduces the overall cost of the finished products, shifting the supply curve to the right. Table 3.2 summarizes how changes in various factors can affect the supply curve.

As Figure 3.6 shows, the supply curve for gasoline has shifted to the right in the past few years. Several factors are responsible for this shift. First, the oil industry has developed new technologies that have slashed the costs of finding, producing, and refining oil. Engineers can now use computers to plan the best methods for reaching the resources hidden in an oil field, and advances in refining technology have allowed oil companies to squeeze more gasoline out of every barrel of oil. These innovations have cut the average cost of finding and producing a barrel of oil

by about 60 percent over the past 10 years. At the same time, new sources of oil are opening up. Special sensors use magnetic imaging to peer ahead of drills as they move underground, finding the least expensive routes to new oil sources both underground and under the sea.[3]

How Demand and Supply Interact

Separate shifts in demand and supply have obvious effects on prices and the availability of products. In the real world, however, changes do not alternately affect demand and supply. Several factors often change at the same time— and they keep on changing. Sometimes such simultaneous

Figure 3.6   **Using Technology to Increase the Nation's Oil Supply**

BUSINESS TOOL KIT

Using the Laws of Supply and Demand to Purchase a Car

Looking for a great deal on a car? You can save thousands of dollars by applying the laws of demand and supply when shopping the car lots. Here are three ways to save:

1. *Buy a model that is out of season.* Demand for four-wheel-drive vehicles tends to drop in the summer months in northern regions of the country. As soon as the snow starts to fall, prices typically rise 5 percent to 10 percent. On the other hand, if your heart is set on a convertible, shop in the winter when demand has declined. Once spring arrives, demand for convertibles will rise, driving up prices.

2. *Shop during times of high supply.* Dealers are much more willing to negotiate especially if their lots are overstocked. Avoid the most popular models if you want to save money. Another trick is to shop in early fall, right after next year's models arrive in dealer showrooms. Many dealers still have plenty of the current models on their lots, and they bargain vigorously about price to sell them.

3. *Consider used cars from expired leases.* An increasingly common response to sticker shock is to lease, rather than purchase, new autos. A typical 36-month lease includes an annual 12,000-mile limit with stiff financial penalties for drivers who exceed these limits. As a result, the used-car market is often flooded with relatively low-mileage, well-maintained used cars. The availability of thousands of such cars has driven down used-car prices 5 percent to 10 percent over the past year in several models.

changes in multiple factors cause contradictory pressures on prices and quantities. In other cases, the final direction of prices and quantities reflects the factor that has changed the most.

Figure 3.7 shows the interaction of both supply and demand curves for gasoline on a single graph. Notice that the two curves intersect at *P.* The law of supply and demand states that prices (*P*) are set by the intersection of the supply and demand curves. The point where the two curves meet identifies the **equilibrium price,** the prevailing market price at which you can buy an item.

If the actual market price differs from the equilibrium price, people tend to make economic choices that restore the equilibrium level. For instance, if oil companies lower their prices below equilibrium, drivers are likely to increase their gasoline use and quickly snap up all of the available supply. As sellers renew their stocks, they are likely to mark up the price so they can increase their profits. On the other hand, if merchants mark their

prices too high, some buyers will drop out of the market entirely, and others will reduce their purchases of the product. Sellers must then compete with each other for

Figure 3.7 **Law of Supply and Demand**

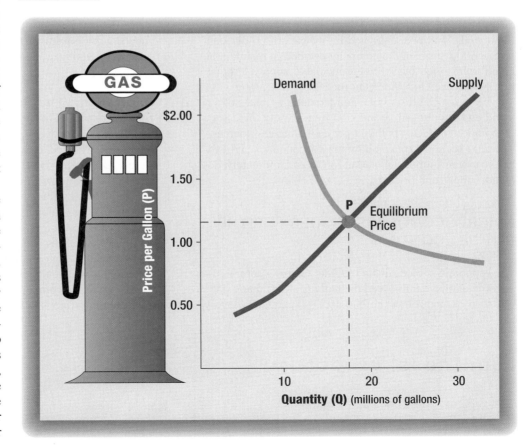

Table 3.3   Types of Competition

| Characteristics | Types of Competition | | | |
	Pure Competition	Monopolistic Competition	Oligopoly	Monopoly
Number of competitors	Many	Few to many	Few	No direct competition
Ease of entry into industry by new firms	Easy	Somewhat difficult	Difficult	Regulated by government
Similarity of goods or services offered by competing firms	Similar	Different	Similar or different	No directly competing products
Control over price by individual firms	None	Some	Some	Considerable in a pure monopoly; little in a regulated monopoly
Examples	Small-scale farmer in Mississippi	Hallmark card shop	McDonnell Douglas	De Beers

customers by lowering their prices to the point at which they can sell all of their supplies, which is the equilibrium price.

General Motors' Saturn automobile division recently faced a supply-demand imbalance that required management's attention. A 10 percent sales decline during 1997 left Saturn dealers with an 84-day supply of unsold models, far more than the desired 65-day supply. One option management considered, but quickly rejected, was a price reduction. Executives feared a backlash from existing customers who had been attracted by the Saturn no-discount price policy. Instead, the company decided to maintain an equilibrium price by shrinking available supply. Production was slashed by 19 percent for 1998.[4]

As the earlier discussion pointed out, the forces of demand and supply can be affected by a variety of factors. One important factor is the larger economic environment. The next section explains how macroeconomics and economic systems influence market forces and, ultimately, demand, supply, and prices.

MACROECONOMICS: ISSUES FOR THE ENTIRE ECONOMY

The economic choices made by Fidel Castro's communist government have influenced the daily life of Cubans since Castro took control in the late 1950s. Like Cuba, every country faces decisions about how to best use the four basic factors of production. Each nation's policies and choices help to determine its economic system.

The political, social, and legal environments differ in every country. Therefore, no two countries have exactly the same economic system. In general, however, economic systems can be classified into three categories: private enterprise systems, planned economies, or combinations of the two referred to as *mixed economies*. As business becomes an increasingly global undertaking, it is important to understand the primary features of the various economic systems operating around the world.

Capitalism: The Private Enterprise System and Competition

Most industrialized nations operate economies based on the **private enterprise system,** also known as *capitalism* or a *market economy*. A private enterprise system rewards businesses for meeting the needs and demands of consumers. Government tends to favor a "hands off" attitude toward controlling business ownership, profits, and resource allocations. Instead, competition regulates economic life, creating opportunities and challenges that businesspeople must handle in order to succeed.

The relative competitiveness of a particular industry is an important consideration for every firm, because it determines the ease and cost of doing business within that industry. Four basic degrees of competition take shape in a private enterprise system: pure competition, monopolistic competition, oligopoly, and monopoly. Table 3.3

Business Directory

private enterprise system   economic system in which business success or failure depends on how well firms match and counter the offerings of competitors; also known as *capitalism* or a *market economy*.

highlights the main differences between these types of competition.

Pure competition is a market structure, like that of small-scale agriculture, in which large numbers of buyers and sellers exchange homogeneous products so no single participant has a significant influence on price. Instead, prices are set by the market itself as the forces of supply and demand interact. Firms can easily enter or leave a purely competitive market, because no single company dominates. Also, in pure competition, buyers see little difference between the goods and services offered by competitors.

Agriculture is probably the closest modern example of pure competition. The grain grown and sold by one farmer is virtually identical to that sold by others. Over the next few years, U.S. agriculture is expected to move even closer to pure competition as Congress phases out federal price guarantees and subsidies. Farmers will now need to pay even closer attention than they have in the past to actual market demand in deciding which products to grow. Even though Harry Stephens' family has raised cotton in Arkansas since before the Civil War, he switched to growing corn on part of his property last year. Stephens decided to respond to a shortage of corn that drove up the commodity's price.[5]

Monopolistic competition is a market structure, like that for retailing, in which large numbers of buyers and sellers exchange relatively well-differentiated (heterogeneous) products, so each participant has some control over price. Products can be differentiated from competing offerings on the basis of price, quality, or other features. A firm can relatively easily begin or stop selling a good or service in an industry that features monopolistic competition. Indeed, the success of one seller often attracts new competitors to such a market. Individual firms also have some control over how their individual goods and services are priced.

The market for beer is an example of monopolistic competition. Consumers can choose from hundreds of beer brands. Brewers try to make their products stand out using advertising, pricing, packaging, and different brewing techniques. Jim Koch, founder of Samuel Adams Brewery, built his company by persuading beer drinkers to pay a premium price for a high-quality, American-brewed beer. To convince consumers of the beer's superiority over competing offerings, the company's Web site explains how Samuel Adams is brewed and highlights its high standards of product freshness. The site also educates visitors about the different tastes of the firm's 15 beer varieties. The brand's success has produced a host of imitators, as competitors have rushed to introduce their own beers.[6]

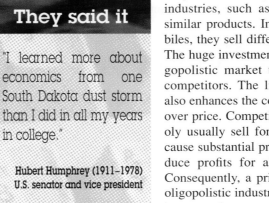

www.samadams.com

An **oligopoly** is a market situation, like those in the steel and airline industries, in which relatively few sellers compete, and where high start-up costs form barriers to keep out new competitors. In some oligopoly industries, such as steel, competitors offer similar products. In others, such as automobiles, they sell different models and features. The huge investment required to enter an oligopolistic market tends to discourage new competitors. The limited number of sellers also enhances the control these firms exercise over price. Competing products in an oligopoly usually sell for quite similar prices, because substantial price competition would reduce profits for all firms in the industry. Consequently, a price cut by one firm in an oligopolistic industry will typically be met by its competitors.

Consider the U.S. airline industry. A recent competitive move by Delta Air Lines is illustrated in Figure 3.8. Delta's management realizes that if it were to reduce its fares for flights from Atlanta to Toronto, other competitors such as American and United would quickly match the new

> **They said it**
>
> "I learned more about economics from one South Dakota dust storm than I did in all my years in college."
>
> **Hubert Humphrey (1911–1978)**
> **U.S. senator and vice president**

fares. Most airlines offer quite similar services, so Delta tries to differentiate itself by offering passenger convenience in the form of nonstop flights to cities like Montreal, Toronto, and Vancouver. In addition, the airline provides 1,339 Canadian one-stop connections from over 160 U.S. cities.

The sizes of current competitors and the financial investment required to join them pose extremely difficult obstacles for new airlines trying to break into the industry. Passage of the Airline Deregulation Act of 1978 has prompted more than 200 fledgling airlines to try to take on the established industry players, but only a handful have survived. One exception is Reno Air, which benefited by forming a strategic partnership with American Airlines to take over several of its shortest routes. Even though Reno has been operating for more than 5 years, it continues to get by with razor-thin profit margins, as its management struggles to build an expensive infrastructure of planes, airport facilities, skilled personnel, and reservation centers.[7]

www.renoair.com

The final type of market structure is a **monopoly,** in which a single seller dominates trade in a good or service for which buyers can find no close substitutes. A *pure monopoly* occurs when a firm possesses unique characteristics so important to competition in its industry that they serve as barriers to prevent entry by would-be competitors. Many firms create short-term monopolies when research breakthroughs permit them to receive exclusive patents on new products. In the pharmaceuticals industry, drug giants like Merck, Pfizer, and Pharmacia & Upjohn invest billions in research and development programs. Their successful efforts are rewarded through temporary monopolies created by patent laws. The Business Hall of Shame discusses how prices and supply can be controlled by a cartel—specifically the Organization of Petroleum Exporting Countries. Cooperation is central to control, however.

Other than temporary monopolies granted through patents, most pure monopolies are prohibited in the United States through antitrust legislation such as the Sherman Act and the Clayton Act. Much more common are *regulated monopolies,* in which a local, state, or federal government grants exclusive rights in a certain market to a single firm. Public utilities, such as the power company advertised in Figure 3.9, are included in this category. Pricing decisions—particularly rate-increase requests—are subject to control by regulatory authorities such as state public service commissions. In recent years, governments have adopted a policy of encouraging increased competition in industries previously considered to be regulated monopolies. Long-distance telephone service, cable television, cellular phones, even local telephone service and electrical service have been deregulated, and entry barriers have been removed to encourage new competition.

Planned Economies: Communism and Socialism

In a **planned economy,** strict government controls determine business ownership, profits, and resource allocation to accomplish government goals rather than those set by individual businesses. Communism and socialism are both forms of planned economies.

The writings of Karl Marx in the mid-1800s formed the basis of communist theory. Marx believed that private enterprise economies created unfair conditions and led to worker exploitation, because business owners controlled most of society's resources and reaped most of the economy's rewards. Instead, he suggested an economic system where all property would be shared equally by the people of a community under the direction of a strong central government. Thus, **communism** is an economic system in which private property is eliminated, goods are owned in common, and factors of production and production decisions are controlled by the state.

Marx believed that elimination of private ownership of property and businesses would ensure the emergence of a classless society that would benefit all. Each individual would contribute what

| Figure 3.8 | **Competing in the Oligopolistic Airline Industry by Offering Nonstop Service to Seven Canadian Cities** |

Heading North For Canada With 58 Nonstops Every Day.

The next time business takes you to Canada, fly the airline that has dozens of nonstops leaving for seven cities north of the border every day. And with 1,339 daily one-stop connections, from over 160 cities in the U.S., Delta's extensive hub system can get you to Canada with ease. From the U.S. to Toronto, Montreal, Vancouver, Calgary, Edmonton, Ottawa and Quebec City, chances are Delta has a flight leaving whenever you'd like to go. **△ Delta Air Lines**
You'll love the way we fly.

Visit our web site at http://www.delta-air.com

he or she could, and resources would be distributed according to each person's needs. Under communism, the central government owns the means of production, and the people work for state-owned enterprises. The government determines what people can buy, because it dictates what is produced in the nation's factories and farms.

Many nations adopted communist economic systems during the 20th century in an effort to improve quality of life for their citizens. In practice, however, communist governments often give people little or no freedom of choice in selecting jobs, purchases, or investments. Communist governments often make mistakes in planning the best uses of resources in order to compete in the growing global marketplace. Government-owned monopolies often suffer from inefficiency.

Consider the former Soviet Union, where large government bureaucracies controlled nearly every aspect of daily life. Shortages became chronic, because producers felt little or no incentive to satisfy customers. The quality of goods and services also suffered for the same reason. When Mikhail Gorbachev was selected as the last prime minister of the dying Soviet Union, he took strides to improve the quality of Soviet-made products. Gorbachev authorized an exhibition of shoddy and defective goods produced by the Soviet workers, including a whole consignment of boots with high heels attached to the toes.

Effectively shut out of trading in the global marketplace and caught up in a treasury-depleting arms race with the United States, the Soviet Union faced severe financial problems. Eventually these economic crises led to the collapse of Soviet communism and the breakup of the Soviet Union itself.

A second type of planned economy, socialism, is characterized by government ownership and operation of all major industries. This system shares some common beliefs with communism, in that socialists assert that major industries are too important to a society to be left in private hands and that government-owned businesses can serve the public's interest better than can private firms. However, socialism also allows private ownership in industries considered less crucial to social welfare, like retail shops, restaurants, and certain types of manufacturing facilities.

What's Ahead for Communism? Many formerly communist nations have undergone dramatic changes in recent years. Some of the most exciting developments have occurred in the republics that formerly composed the Soviet Union. These new nations have restructured their economies by introducing Western-style private enterprise systems. By decentralizing economic planning and sweetening incentives for workers, they are slowly shifting to market-driven systems.

Economic reforms in these countries haven't always shown smooth progress. Although many have opened their arms to Western entrepreneurs and businesses, these investors have often encountered difficulties such as official corruption, crime, and the persistence of bloated bureaucracies. Reducing the power of government-operated monopolies has also proved a difficult challenge. In Russia, for example, three sprawling monopolies still control the gas, electricity, and rail industries. Close links to government officials and preferential tax breaks obstruct plans for new competitors to enter these markets. The power of these monopolies gives them a stranglehold on prices that critics say is blocking free-market capitalism in Russia. Reformers are pushing for changes that would force these

| **Figure 3.9** | **The Utility Industry: Evolving from Regulated Monopoly to Competitive Marketplace** |

IN ALABAMA, WE HAVE THE POWER TO BUILD A BETTER FUTURE FOR EVERYONE.

All things being equal, most opportunities aren't. But one state that works most aggressively to create equal opportunities for everyone is Alabama. We do it by helping to create as many jobs, in as many fields, as possible. In the past few years alone, Alabama Power has worked with other state agencies to help approximately 3,800 companies relocate here, creating almost 100,000 new jobs and training opportunities for Alabama citizens. In the same spirit, Alabama Power is especially proud to lend additional support to minority businesses. Our Mentorship Program and Minority/Female Business Development Program are among the most lauded in the nation.

So, the possibilities should seem clear. In moving or expanding your business to Alabama, you'll not only enjoy some of the lowest electric prices in the nation, you'll help us create an environment where everyone can rise to their best. There's only one way to provide that kind of opportunity. And that's by working together to create it. We invite you to join us. If you are interested in relocating or expanding your business, call Alabama Power, 1-800-990-APCO.

ALABAMA POWER
A SOUTHERN COMPANY

Business Directory

communism planned economic system in which private property is eliminated, goods are owned in common, and factors of production and production decisions are controlled by the state.

socialism planned economic system characterized by government ownership and operation of all major industries.

and other Russian companies to improve efficiency and respond to market demands. For example, Unified Energy Systems, which controls all electricity transmission in Russia, has recently been forced to reduce its prices and open up its market to competitors.[8]

Today, communism remains firmly entrenched in just a few countries, like the People's Republic of China, North Korea, and Cuba. Even these staunchly communist countries, however, show signs of growing openness toward some of the benefits of private enterprise as possible solutions to their economic challenges.

In China, for example, about half of the 118,000 state-run manufacturing enterprises lost money last year. China's 123 auto assembly plants produce about 1.5 million vehicles a year, less than one-sixth the number of vehicles manufactured in the United States by the Big Three automakers. Other Chinese industries face enormous overcapacity, because too many factories make the same goods.

To solve these problems, China's President Jiang Zemin hopes to sell thousands of government-owned factories to private investors. A bankrupt rubber plant, for example, was recently sold for $12 million to a private Shanghai investment group. In addition, Jiang plans to set up national health and retirement programs that would release state companies from the high costs of providing health care, pensions, and housing. The government is also simplifying the process for Chinese citizens to buy their own homes.[9]

Another symbol of China's changing economic strategy has accompanied the 1997 return of Hong Kong to Chinese rule. Jiang's government has promised that Hong Kong's businesses will continue to operate in a private enterprise economic system.

The dramatic end of the Soviet Union in the early 1990s is symbolized by the removal of the statue of Vladimir Lenin, leader of the Russian Revolution of 1917 and the first Soviet premier.

Mixed Market Economies

Private enterprise systems and planned economies adopt basically opposite approaches to operating economies. In practice, however, most countries implement **mixed market economies,** economic systems that display characteristics of both planned and market economies in varying degrees. For example, government-owned firms sometimes operate alongside private enterprises.

France has blended socialist and free enterprise policies for hundreds of years. The country's banking, automobile, utility, aviation, steel, and railroad industries have traditionally been run as nationalized industries, controlled by the government. Meanwhile, a market economy flourishes in other industries. Over the past two decades, the French government has loosened its reigns on state-owned companies, inviting both competition and private investment into industries previously operated as government monopolies.[10]

The proportions of private and public enterprise can vary widely in mixed economies, and the mix frequently changes. Like France, over 50 countries have converted government-owned companies into privately held firms in a trend known as **privatization.** Governments may privatize state-owned enterprises to improve their economies, believing that private corporations can manage and operate the businesses more cheaply and efficiently than government units can. Selling these enterprises also helps governments to raise badly needed funds.

For example, the Brazilian government recently privatized its railroad system, selling the 2,760-mile network to a consortium of industrial and mining companies for $146 million. The new owners plan to invest an additional $136 million in the railway, boosting its competitive strength against the trucking and inland waterway systems and benefiting the entire Brazilian economy. During the last decade, Brazil has also sold its five biggest government-run steel mills to private investors, generating a cash infusion of $5.6 billion in the process.[11]

Table 3.4 compares the three alternative economic sys-

Business Directory

mixed market economy economic system that combines characteristics of both planned and market economies in varying degrees, including the presence of both government ownership and private enterprise.

| Table 3.4 | Comparison of Alternative Economic Systems | | | |

| System Features | Capitalism (Private Enterprise) | Planned Economies | | Mixed Economy |
		Communism	Socialism	
Ownership of enterprises	Businesses are owned privately, often by large numbers of people. Minimal government ownership leaves production in private hands.	The government owns the means of production with few exceptions, like small plots of land.	Basic industries are owned by government, but private owners operate some small-scale enterprises.	A strong private sector blends with public enterprises. The private sector is larger than that under socialism.
Management of enterprises	Each enterprise is managed separately, either by its owners or by people who represent the owners, with minimal government interference.	Centralized management controls all state enterprises in line with 3- to 5-year plans. Planning now is being decentralized.	Significant government planning pervades socialist nations. State enterprises are managed directly by government bureaucrats.	Management of the private sector resembles that under capitalism. Professional managers are also common in state enterprises.
Rights to profits	Entrepreneurs and investors are entitled to all profits (minus taxes) that their firms earn. However, they are expected to operate in a socially responsible manner.	Profits are not acceptable under communism.	Only the private sector of a socialist economy generates profits.	Entrepreneurs and investors are entitled to private-sector profits, although they often must pay high taxes. State enterprises also typically are expected to break even or to provide financial returns to the government.
Rights of employees	The rights to choose one's occupation and to join a labor union have long been recognized.	Employee rights traditionally were limited in exchange for promised protection against unemployment.	Workers have the right to choose their occupations and to join labor unions. However, the government influences career decisions for many people.	Workers have the right of job choice and labor-union membership. Unions often become quite strong in these countries.
Worker incentives	Considerable incentives motivate people to perform at their highest levels.	Incentives are emerging in communist countries.	Incentives usually are limited in state enterprises, but do motivate workers in the private sector.	Capitalist-style incentives operate in the private sector. More limited incentives influence public-sector activities.

tems on the basis of ownership and management of enterprises, rights to profits, employee rights, and worker incentives.

EVALUATING ECONOMIC PERFORMANCE

Ideally, an economic system should provide two important benefits for its citizens: a stable business environment and sustained growth. In a stable business environment, the overall supply of all goods and services is aligned with the overall demand for all goods and services. No wild fluctuations in price or availability complicate economic decisions. Consumers and businesses not only have access to ample supplies of desirable goods and services at affordable prices, but they also have money to buy the items they demand.

Growth is another important economic goal. An ideal economy incorporates steady change directed toward continually expanding the amount of goods and services

BUSINESS HALL OF SHAME

Global Market and Local Greed Give OPEC Gas Pains

Oil has long been considered black gold the world over. Indeed, in the early 1970s, U.S. consumers were paying exorbitant prices at the gas pump for the precious commodity. Why? Because the Organization of Petroleum Exporting Countries (OPEC), an oil cartel of 11 countries formed in 1960, restricted oil production to increase profits. For years, OPEC regulated the production, pricing, and marketing of oil and too often used its power unfairly. More recently, however, OPEC has lost some of its control over the oil market, and Americans have enjoyed some of the lowest gas prices at the pump in a quarter century.

Currently, OPEC members include Iran, Iraq, Kuwait, Saudi Arabia, Venezuela (the founding five), and six others: Algeria, Indonesia, Libya, Nigeria, Qatar, and the United Arab Emi-

rates. OPEC's stated mission is to coordinate and unify member petroleum policies to ensure (1) the prosperity of petroleum producers, (2) the availability of oil to consumers, and (3) the fair return on capital to investors. Twice a year, OPEC ministers meet to analyze the oil market and review predictions for world conditions. From this information, they determine whether oil production should be decreased or increased.

The world runs on energy, and oil remains the most popular fuel. Oil prices affect the price of transportation, the cost of producing goods and services, and the availability of food, water, and shelter. OPEC's member countries currently produce about 40 percent of the world's crude oil. Although the cartel doesn't fully control the oil market, its exports make up roughly 60 percent of the oil traded internationally.

But the market is changing as oil gushes from new suppliers all over the world. If OPEC were to cut production now, consumers would simply turn to

other suppliers for their energy needs. The oil market has been greatly enhanced by today's information technologies such as computer visualization to reveal potential reserves deep underground. This makes finding oil easier, lowers research and exploration costs, and increases the amount of oil available.

As oil producers recognize the wealth that lies in oil revenues, they are focusing more than ever before on finding oil. Suddenly, countries formerly closed to outside companies now are inviting foreigners to join in exploration and production efforts. Saudi Arabia recently asked seven U.S. oil companies to bid on new oil and gas projects. Iranians and Kuwaitis have also been talking with foreign investors—and promising long-terms access to oil reserves.

Although today's swiftly changing environment should encourage OPEC members to cooperate more than ever, many members continue to make decisions dictated by self-interest and

produced from the nation's resources. Growth leads to expanded job opportunities, improved wages, and a rising standard of living.

Flattening the Business Cycle

In reality, however, a nation's economy tends to flow through various stages of a business cycle, including prosperity, recession, depression, and recovery. No true economic depressions have occurred in the United States since the 1930s, and most economists believe that society is capable of preventing future depressions through effective economic policies. Consequently, they would expect a recession to give way to a period of economic recovery.

Both business decisions and consumer buying patterns differ at each stage of the business cycle. In periods of economic *prosperity* such as the late 1990s, unemployment remains low, strong consumer confidence

They said it

"It's a recession when your neighbor loses his job; it's a depression when you lose your own."

Harry S. Truman (1884–1972)
33rd president of the
United States

about the future lead to record purchases, and businesses expand to take advantage of marketplace opportunities. During *recessions*—cyclical economic contractions that last 6 months or longer—consumers frequently postpone major purchases and shift buying patterns toward basic, functional products carrying low prices. Businesses mirror these changes in the marketplace by slowing production, postponing expansion plans, and reducing inventories. Should the economic slowdown continue in a downward spiral over an extended period of time, the economy falls into *depression*. Many Americans grew up hearing stories from their grandparents who lived through the 1930s haunted by the specter of joblessness (a 25 percent unemployment rate at one point), idle factories, and despair about the future.

In the *recovery* stage of the business cycle, the economy emerges from recession and consumer spending picks up steam. Unemployment begins to decline, as business ac-

greed. For example, as the world's largest producer, Saudi Arabia doesn't relish cutting production as a means of increasing world prices when such action would merely encourage some other country to seize the business it turns down. In fact, many observers feel that the Saudis would rather increase production. Although this would drive down world prices and hurt the Saudis, it could ruin the new high-cost competitors from the Caspian Sea and West Africa. And despite OPEC agreements to cut production, the temptation for cash-strapped members is to ship more oil, further weakening the cartel.

Oil's role in the energy market may shrink, but it will long remain the world's largest source of energy. And OPEC will continue to wield its power simply because it controls over three-fourths the world's crude oil reserves. The oil cartel is no longer polishing its cache of black gold as the oil market becomes glutted with new competitors. Experts point out that the market—not OPEC—is finally gaining power in an energy-starved world.

www.opec.org

QUESTIONS FOR CRITICAL THINKING

1. **Iraq is sitting on nearly as much oil as Saudi Arabia. Some analysts think that once political sanctions are ended, Iraq's fields will be rebuilt and could start producing between 6 million and 8 million barrels a day—rivaling Saudi Arabia. What effect do you think such a development might have on the OPEC cartel?**

2. **Some observers think that survival among OPEC members depends on a "careful balancing of interests." What do experts mean by this phrase? Relate your answer to the way the oil cartel must operate to secure agreement from its members.**

Sources: "A Brief History of OPEC," OPEC Web site, accessed at www.opec.org, February 9, 1999; "Growing Economic Malaise to Shrink Oil Demand—IEA," Reuters Limited, February 9, 1999; "UAE: Include Iraq in OPEC Decision," The Associated Press, February 7, 1999; David Ignatius, "Where the Oil Is," *Washington Post*, February 7, 1999, p. B7; and Daniel Yergin and Joseph Stanislaw, "How OPEC Lost Control of Oil," *Time.com*, April 6, 1998, accessed at cg.pathfinder.com/time/magazine.

tivity accelerates and firms seek additional workers to meet growing production demands. Gradually, the concerns of recession begin to disappear, and consumers begin to purchase more discretionary items such as vacations, new automobiles, and other extravagances.

Economists observe several indicators to measure and evaluate how successfully an economic system provides both stability and growth. These variables include productivity as measured by gross domestic product (GDP), rate of inflation or deflation, employment levels, and relative economic freedom.

Productivity and the Nation's Gross Domestic Product (GDP)

An important concern for every economy is **productivity,** the relationship between the goods and services produced in a nation each year and the human work and other production inputs necessary to produce them. In general, as productivity rises, so does an economy's growth and the wealth of its citizens. In a recession, productivity declines or stagnates.

Chapter 1 explained that a commonly used measure of productivity is a country's **gross domestic product (GDP),** the sum of all goods and services produced within a nation's boundaries each year. Economists calculate per-capita GDP by summing the total output of all goods and services produced within a country and then dividing that output by the number of citizens. GDP is an important indicator for measuring a country's business cycle, since a shrinking GDP indicates a recession. As the economy again begins to expand, GDP reflects this growth.

GDP in the United States is tracked by the Bureau of Economic Analysis, a division of the U.S. Department of Commerce. Current updates and historical data on the GDP are available at the BEA's Web site.

www.bea.doc.gov/

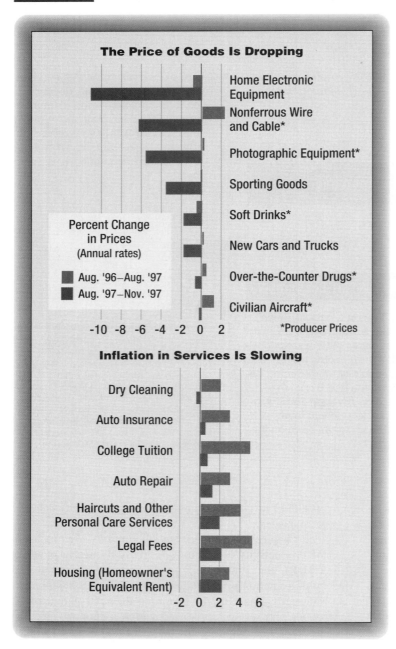

Figure 3.10 **New Patterns in Price Changes**

In extreme cases, **hyperinflation** occurs—an economic situation characterized by soaring prices. In 1993, for example, Ukrainian consumers suddenly saw the price of food, clothes, and housing rise 5,000 percent![12]

Inflation devalues money as persistent price increases reduce the amount of goods and services people can purchase. The most severe inflationary period in the United States in the last half of the 20th century peaked in 1980 when general price levels rose 13.6 percent. In recent years, however, inflation worries have gradually been replaced with a phenomenon of falling prices. In fact, goods prices, excluding food and energy, have actually declined since mid-1997. As Figure 3.10 shows, shoppers are discovering big price reductions in products ranging from home electronic equipment and sporting goods to a six-pack of Cokes and a new Nissan Altima. Even services, long characterized by relatively high rates of inflation, are experiencing slowing price hikes.

Increased productivity that results in falling prices can have a major positive impact on an economy. In a low-inflation environment, businesses can make long-range plans without the constant worry of sudden inflationary shocks. Low interest rates encourage them to invest in research and development and capital improvements, both of which are likely to produce productivity gains. Consumers can purchase growing stocks of goods and services with the same amount of money, and low interest rates encourage major acquisitions like new homes and autos.[13]

In the United States, changes in price levels are tracked by the **Consumer Price Index (CPI),** which measures the monthly average change in prices of goods and services. The federal Bureau of Labor Statistics (BLS) calculates the CPI monthly based on prices of a *market basket*—a compilation of the goods and services most commonly purchased by urban consumers. Figure 3.11 shows the categories included in the CPI market basket.[14]

www.stats.bls.gov

Each month, BLS representatives visit thousands of stores, service establishments, rental units, and doctors' offices all over the United States to price the multitude of items in the CPI market basket. This data is then compiled to create the CPI. Thus, the CPI provides a running measurement of consumer price changes. Critics charge, however, that the CPI may actually overstate inflation by not

Price-Level Changes

The general level of prices is another important indicator of an economy's stability. For most of the 20th century, economic decision makers have concerned themselves with **inflation,** rising prices caused by some combination of excess consumer demand and increases in the costs of raw materials, component parts, human resources, and other factors of production. The first type is referred to as *demand-pull inflation;* the second is called *cost-push inflation.*

fully accounting for changes in the goods that people buy. The *Producer Price Index (PPI)* is another economic indicator used to track the prices that business buyers pay for the goods their firms use in manufacturing.

Although falling prices might seem like a positive economic indicator, this is not necessarily true. Deflation resulting from productivity gains benefits both producers and consumers. For example, a wave of consumer pessimism about the future might induce people to postpone purchases, increase savings, and restrict spending to wait out the expected crisis. Businesses, stuck with inventories they are unable to sell, may respond by reducing prices in an effort to generate needed funds. Such a situation severely restricts profits, prompting management decision makers to scale back production plans. The result may be job layoffs, declines in the value of personal investments such as homes, and other problems of slow growth or even a recession.[15]

Employment Levels

Consumers need money in order to purchase the goods and services produced in an economy. Because most consumers earn the money they spend by working, the number of people in a nation who currently have jobs is an important indicator of both overall stability and growth. People who are actively looking for work but unable to find jobs are counted in unemployment statistics.

Economists refer to a nation's **unemployment rate** as an indicator of its economic health. The unemployment rate is usually expressed as a percentage of the total work force. The total labor force includes all people who are willing and available to work at the going market wage, whether they currently have jobs or are seeking work. The U.S. Department of Labor, which tracks unemployment rates, also includes so-called *discouraged workers* in the total labor force. These individuals want to work but have given up looking for jobs.

www.dol.gov

Unemployment can be grouped into the four categories shown in Figure 3.12: frictional, seasonal, cyclical, and structural unemployment. *Frictional unemployment* applies to members of the work force who are temporarily not working but are looking for jobs. This pool of potential workers includes new graduates, people who have left jobs

for any reason and are looking for others, and former workers who have decided to return to the labor force. *Seasonal unemployment* is the joblessness of workers in a seasonal industry. Construction workers, farm laborers, and retail clerks often must contend with bouts of seasonal unemployment.

Cyclical unemployment includes people who are out of work because of a cyclical contraction in the economy.

| Figure 3.11 | Consumer Price Index Market Basket |

Category	Examples
Food and Beverages	breakfast cereal, milk, coffee, wine, chicken, snacks
Housing	rent, fuel oil, furniture
Apparel	men's shirts, women's dresses, jewelry
Transportation	automobiles, airline fares, gasoline
Medical Care	prescription drugs, medical supplies, doctor's office visits, eyeglasses
Recreation	television, pets and pet products, sports equipment, movie tickets
Education	tuition, postage, telephone service, computers
Other Goods and Services	tobacco, haircuts

During periods of economic expansion, overall employment is likely to rise, but during economic slowdowns such as recessions, unemployment levels commonly rise. At such times, even workers with good job skills may face temporary unemployment.

Structural unemployment applies to people who remain unemployed for long periods of time, often with little hope of finding new jobs like their old ones. This situation may arise because these workers lack the necessary skills for available jobs or because the skills they have are no longer in demand.

Relative Economic Freedom

Some economists have suggested another way to measure and compare the world's economies. They advocate looking at the *relative economic freedom* enjoyed in each country.

The Fraser Institute, a Canadian economic think tank, recently developed a formula for comparing economic variables that combines inflation rates, government regulation, taxation, and restrictions on trade to determine final rankings. The most recent study ranked Hong Kong as highest in the world in relative economic freedom. Other countries in the top ten included, in order, Singapore, New Zealand, the United States, the Indian Ocean island of Mauritius, Switzerland, the United Kingdom, Thailand, Costa Rica, and Malaysia. Singapore's second-place ranking is evidence of the statistic's focus on economic—rather than political—freedoms. The Business Hall of Fame examines Dole's foothold in Japan's tightly restricted agricultural industry.

In last place among 115 nations ranked in the study is Algeria. Other nations at the bottom of the list are Croatia, Ukraine, and Albania. A country's per-capita income and its economic growth appear to be closely related to economic freedom. For example, Hong Kong, the highest ranked nation, also has the highest per-capita GDP.[16] To determine the rankings of countries you have visited or plan to visit, contact the Fraser Institute Web site.

www.fraserinstitute.ca/

MANAGING THE ECONOMY'S PERFORMANCE

Besides just measuring economic growth and evaluating stability, economists provide tools that governments use to manage their countries' economic performance. A national government can use both monetary policy and fiscal policy to fight inflation, increase employment levels, and encourage growth.

Monetary Policy

A common method of influencing economic activity is **monetary policy,** government action to increase or decrease the money supply and change banking requirements and interest rates to influence spending by altering

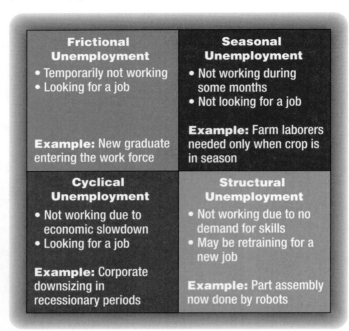

Figure 3.12 **Four Types of Unemployment**

Frictional Unemployment
- Temporarily not working
- Looking for a job

Example: New graduate entering the work force

Seasonal Unemployment
- Not working during some months
- Not looking for a job

Example: Farm laborers needed only when crop is in season

Cyclical Unemployment
- Not working due to economic slowdown
- Looking for a job

Example: Corporate downsizing in recessionary periods

Structural Unemployment
- Not working due to no demand for skills
- May be retraining for a new job

Example: Part assembly now done by robots

bankers' willingness to make loans. An *expansionary monetary policy* increases the money supply in an effort to cut the cost of borrowing, which encourages business decision makers to make new investments, in turn stimulating employment and economic growth. By contrast, a *restrictive monetary policy* reduces the money supply to curb rising prices, overexpansion, and concerns about overly rapid economic growth.

In the United States, the Federal Reserve System ("the Fed") is responsible for formulating and implementing the nation's monetary policy. It is headed by a chairman (currently Alan Greenspan) and a Board of Governors, each of whom is appointed by the president. All national banks must be members of this system and keep some percentage of their checking and savings funds on deposit at the Fed.

The Fed's Board of Governors uses a number of tools to regulate the economy. By changing the required percentage of checking and savings accounts that banks must deposit with the Fed, the governors can expand or shrink funds available to lend. The Fed also lends money to member banks, which, in turn, make loans (at higher interest rates) to business and individual borrowers. By changing the interest rates charged to commercial banks, the Fed affects the interest rates charged to borrowers, and consequently their willingness to borrow.

The Federal Reserve has a number of other monetary policy tools at its disposal. Each of these is described in detail in Chapter 20, where Table 20.4 indicates the effect of a change in each tool on the economy.

Fiscal Policy

Governments also influence economic activities through taxation and spending decisions. Through revenues and expenditures, the government implements **fiscal policy,** the second technique that officials use to control inflation, reduce unemployment, improve the general welfare of citizens, and encourage economic growth. Increased taxes may restrict economic activities, whereas lower taxes and increased government spending usually boost spending and profits, cut unemployment rates, and fuel economic expansion.

Each year the president prepares a budget for the federal government, a plan for how it will raise and spend money during the coming year, and presents it to Congress for approval. A typical federal budget proposal undergoes months of deliberation and numerous modifications before receiving approval. The major sources of federal revenues and categories of expenditures are shown in Figure 3.13.

The federal budget includes a number of different spending categories, ranging from defense and social security to interest payments on the national debt. The decisions about what to include in the budget have a direct effect on various sectors. During a recession, the federal government may approve major spending on interstate highway repairs to improve transportation and increase employment in the construction industry. A decision to invest new federal funds in job-training programs often pays off in productivity gains produced by enhancing the skills of the workforce.

As Malaysia develops from a small, agricultural economy to a newly industrialized nation, its government is taking steps to ensure that the country's infrastructure components of transportation, power generation, and communications keep pace. As Figure 3.14 describes, YTL Corp. feels the direct effects of government spending decisions aimed at infrastructure improvements. Since 1955, the company, based in Kuala Lumpur, has participated in major projects in construction, hotels and resorts, manufacturing, and power generation.

Taxes, fees, and borrowing are the primary sources of government funds to cover the costs of the annual budget. Both the overall amount of these funds and the specific combination of them have major effects on the economic well-being of the nation. One way governments raise money is to impose taxes on

Ranked first in economic freedom, both business managers and tourists have long included Hong Kong among the world's great cities. Blessed with free trade, one of the world's great harbors, and a new state-of-the-art international airport, Hong Kong is the premier gateway to business in China and Southeast Asia.

sales and income. Increasing taxes reduce people's incomes, leaving them with less money to spend. Such a move can reduce inflation, but overly high taxes can also slow economic growth.

Taxes don't always generate enough funds to cover every spending project the government hopes to undertake. When the government spends more than the amount of money it raises through taxes, it creates a **budget deficit**. To cover the deficit, the U.S. government has borrowed money by offering Treasury bills, Treasury notes, and Treasury bonds for sale to investors. All of this borrowing comprises the **national debt.** Currently, the U.S. national debt is about $5.5 trillion, or approximately $20,000 for every U.S. citizen.[17]

In recent years, both citizen groups and politicians have called for a halt to the long-time practice of borrowing to fund government spending in excess of its income. Instead, a growing commitment has targeted a **balanced budget,** in which the total revenues raised by taxes equal total proposed spending for the year. Even though the federal government spent more money than it received from taxes and fees during every year of the 1970s, 1980s, and most of the 1990s, over half of the nation's state governments are required by their constitutions to balance their annual budgets. By 1999, the federal government accomplished a feat not experienced since 1969—a balanced

Business Directory

monetary policy government action to increase or decrease the money supply and change banking requirements and interest rates to influence bankers' willingness to make loans.

fiscal policy government spending and taxation decisions designed to control inflation, reduce unemployment, improve the general welfare of citizens, and encourage economic growth.

budget deficit funding shortfall that results when the government spends more than the amount of money it raises through taxes and fees.

Figure 3.13   **The Federal Budget: Where the Money Comes From and Where It Goes**

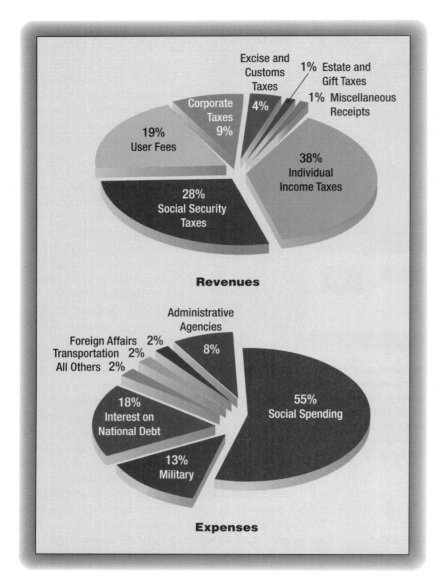

nomic indicators painted a very positive picture of sustained growth and relative economic stability.

Continuing Growth The U.S. GDP is enjoying a strong cycle of growth. Fueling much of this growth is the continuing expansion of companies in high technology industries, such as software publishers and computer manufacturers. Corporate profits rose 14 percent last year, signaling not only an increase in productivity but strong payoffs from investments in expansion programs. Investors have responded by pushing the U.S. stock market to historic highs.[18]

For individual businesses, the continued growth of the economy opens new doors. Consider the experience of Bobbi's Sweet Surrender, a small baker of gourmet cookies, cakes, and brownies in southern California. When economic growth slowed early in the decade, the company had trouble selling its fancy baked goods. "Things were really tight and people weren't buying gourmet products," explains owner Bobbi Cameron.

In today's economic climate, however, sales have exploded as consumers once again have enough disposable income to splurge on premium-priced baked goods. The company's overall cookie production grew to 400,000 pounds last year, and Cameron expects next year to be her biggest ever. "Before, we were trying to get business," she says. "But what's nice is people are now calling us about our products."[19]

Inflation in Check In recent years, both the CPI and PPI have reported little or no inflation in the U.S. economy. The CPI rose just 1.8 percent in 1998, compared with 3.3 percent the year before and 6.0 percent in 1990. The PPI actually dropped 1.2 percent, as energy costs declined. Given suggestions that the CPI may actually overstate inflation by not fully accounting for changes in the goods people buy, the U.S. inflation rate in 1997 may actually have been close to zero with deflation a reality in 1998.[20]

budget. This goal was reached through a combination of healthy tax-income driven by a prosperous economy and significant spending cuts in such areas as defense and welfare payments.

The U.S. Economy: These Are the Good Old Days

For most of the 1990s, the U.S. economy has experienced the strongest wave of prosperity in nearly a quarter-century. For many individuals and businesses in America, these *are* the good old days, ripe with economic opportunity. As *Contemporary Business* went to press, current eco-

Strong Employment U.S. firms employ more people now than at any time in the last 25 years. In recent years, the national unemployment rate has remained below 5 percent. However, some companies and industries are still making structural changes to their employment practices. Eastman Kodak, AT&T, and JCPenney are just three of several U.S. businesses that have recently announced major job cutbacks reducing each firm's workforce by at least 4,000 employees. Toymaker Hasbro also recently announced plans to cut 20 percent of its worldwide workforce and close several factories. Industry analysts noted that the toy industry is changing as children's interests shift toward computer games. As a result, Hasbro is reevaluating its human resource needs and eliminating numerous manufacturing positions through automation.[21]

Shrinking Budget Deficit
The strong economy also helped the federal government to accomplish its goal of balancing the budget. Three decades passed between the 1969 balanced budget and the slight budget surplus of 1999. As Figure 3.15 indicates, several factors contributed to this achievement. First, the Clinton administration has reduced government spend-

Figure 3.14 **Government Spending Aimed at Infrastructure Improvements**

Over the next decade, Asia will spend over US$273 million a day on infrastructure projects. (How can you get an overview of the latest developments?)

YTL's home is in Malaysia, a country whose government targets the economy to grow 7% annually until the year 2020. That growth is being made possible largely by the continuing development of the country's modern infrastructure.

YTL's skills have grown in step with Malaysia's development from a small agricultural economy to a newly industrialised nation.

From a modest construction start-up in 1955, we have since participated in many infrastructure projects in Malaysia, culminating in our recent appointment as the country's first Independent Power Producer.

Since 1955, the YTL Group has been a leader in the develop-

ment of the infrastructure so necessary for the continued successful expansion of Malaysia's economy; in construction contracting, property development, hotels and resorts, manufacturing and power generation.

Newly emerging economies throughout Asia are destined to replicate Malaysia's economic success. Ambitious nations need companies with local knowledge.

If you want an experienced partner in your quest to help build the rest of the Asian region, talk to us.

Working for the advancement of infrastructure since 1955

YTL

YTL Corporation Berhad, 55 Jalan Bukit Bintang, 55100 Kuala Lumpur, Malaysia. Fax: 603-2421477

ing, slashing the deficit by more than $400 billion over 5 years. The strong economy has helped, too. As businesses' earnings grow, they pay increasing tax bills. In fact, estimates suggest that the federal government will collect an extra $225 billion in tax revenues over the next 5 years.[22]

All these indicators show that, at present, the U.S. economy retains its recent strength. However, future prosperity is not guaranteed. With inflation levels near zero, some analysts worry about deflationary pressures that might force businesses to charge lower prices than they can justify by savings from increasing productivity. At the same time, the low unemployment rate is pressuring employers to raise wages in order to attract and keep workers. Proposals to increase the minimum wage above the $5-per-hour level are favored by many economists and government officials as one means of reducing the growing gap between rich and poor. Critics of the proposal worry that raising human resource costs would cause profits to drop, forcing firms to lay off workers and slowing overall economic growth. The final section of this chapter examines some other economic challenges that may lie ahead.

GLOBAL ECONOMIC CHALLENGES OF THE 21ST CENTURY

Businesses face a number of important economic challenges in the coming century. As the economies of countries around the globe become increasingly interconnected, governments and businesses must compete throughout the world. Although no one can predict the future, both governments and businesses will likely need to successfully meet several challenges to maintain their global competitiveness. This section overviews challenges such as the continuing shift toward a global information economy, the aging of the world's population, continuing emphasis on improving quality and customer service, and efforts to enhance the competitiveness of every country's workforce.

The Shift toward a Global Information Economy

The economic growth that began in the industrial revolution of the late 1700s was driven by manufacturing advances that enabled businesses to speed mass production of goods. The economic growth of the 21st century, however, will be propelled by technological advances that enable businesses to enhance the effectiveness of their use, management, and control of information. In the information economy, businesses are working smarter than before, using brains, not brawn, to push economic growth.

American companies are leading the information revolution. Nearly 60 percent of U.S. workers are employed in information-intensive jobs, rather than in traditional labor-intensive positions.[23] Computers enhance productivity in sectors from agriculture to factories. In fact, U.S. businesses and consumers spent an average of $850 per person

BUSINESS HALL OF FAME

Dole Japan Delivers Fresh Produce and Lower Prices

If you like apples and you happen to live in Japan, you'd better be prepared to pay dearly. In Tokyo, an apple costs $5. "Why so much?" you ask. The primary reason is the large number of middlemen who operate between the orchard and the Japanese consumer, each of them receiving a share of the final price. The system is both inefficient and expensive, but it has remained impenetrable for hundreds of years. But Dole Japan, a subsidiary of Dole Foods, has broken through the layers of intermediaries and lowered the price of fresh produce in the Land of the Rising Sun.

Both retailers and Japanese consumers are benefitting from Dole's streamlined distribution system. Prices on locally grown fresh produce have been slashed 25 percent.

Agricultural deregulation played a major role in the price cuts. It permitted Dole to introduce contract growing to local producers of broccoli, tomatoes, cabbage, radishes, carrots, lettuce, and melons. Prior to deregulation, growers had to sell their output to their cooperatives. In fact, when tomato farmer Chikashi Matsunaga tried to sell his output on his own, the co-op kicked him out, making it virtually impossible for him to find a buyer. Since deregulation, he has been able to sell all the tomatoes he can grow to Dole Japan. Says Matsunaga, "We just deliver tomatoes in large containers and Dole does the rest of the work. Dole also sets prices in advance so we know we can cover costs and earn a living."

Dole Japan has been working at removing unnecessary links in Japan's food chain for over a decade. In addi-

tion to reducing prices, slashing the number of middlemen in the distribution channel gives Dole greater quality control of the produce it distributes to supermarket shelves. With some 15 fresh-cut fruit and vegetable centers in Japan, the company can deliver items such as precut salads to any store in the country within three hours.

The Japanese government traditionally has protected its farmers, distributors, and retailers with regulation, import restrictions, and numerous other barriers to open competition—even though it knew that Japanese consumers paid more for products than their counterparts in other nations. But times are changing and since Japan grows only 42 percent of its food—the lowest ratio among large industrial nations—it is imperative that it have access to food sources located outside the country. In addition, 40 percent of Japanese farmers are now 65 or older, adding to concerns that the Japanese government must take action to secure a strong food industry. Observers expect a revision in the government's Agriculture Basic Law to permit corporations to till the land. Rules governing retail operations have already been relaxed.

With more deregulation likely in the near future, Dole is in a great position to supply Japan's increasing need for affordable and available produce. The firm's goal has been stated as "to have the industry's finest distribution system deliver the highest quality product at the most efficient cost structure." In short, Dole is committed to providing more efficient food distribution in Japan and around the world.

 www.dole.com

QUESTIONS FOR CRITICAL THINKING

1. The falling barriers against foreign competitors are likely to encourage other non-Japanese companies to enter the market to compete not only with the Japanese firms but also with Dole. Is this influx of non-Japanese producers likely to hurt Dole's position? Explain your answer.

2. In today's global economy, how are each of the following likely to affect Dole's operations in Japan?

   a. the recent Russian economic collapse, which reduced demand for bananas

   b. Hurricane Mitch, which devastated Dole's Central American fruit-farming operations.

Sources: "Dole Asia," Dole's Web site, accessed at www.dole.com, February 9, 1999; and Neil Weinberg, "Upsetting the Apple Cart," *Forbes*, December 14, 1998, pp. 210, 212.

How to Survive an IRS Tax Audit

The federal agency most responsible for collecting funds that finance government expenditures is the Internal Revenue Service (IRS). Although your chance of the IRS auditing your tax return is about 1 in 100, just the thought of an audit is enough to make taxpayers shudder. President Clinton and both houses of Congress support an IRS reform law designed to shift the agency's focus to improving the government's understanding and problem-solving ability from the taxpayer's point of view. Even so, tax audits rank among life's least pleasant events.

If you are called for an audit, the IRS will thoroughly examine your tax return to evaluate the accuracy of all information you have provided. These five tips will help you to survive an IRS audit:

1. *Be prepared.* The IRS will give you time to gather relevant records. Go through your tax file and find proof of the information you used to prepare the tax return being audited. In general, you should save this information for at least 3 years. If, during the audit, you find you don't have needed information, you have the right to postpone the audit in order to complete further preparations.

2. *Ask for a correspondence audit.* Not all audits need to be conducted face-to-face. Many taxpayers reduce the stress of their dealing with IRS auditors by exchanging information via the mail. This is called a *correspondence audit.*

3. *Don't volunteer any additional information.* Most audits look at specific areas of your tax return. If, however, you raise another issue during the audit, the auditor can investigate it. Therefore, keep your answers as brief and specific as possible.

4. *Everything is negotiable.* If the audit shows that you owe additional taxes, along with penalties and interest, ask the auditor if the IRS will accept less than the full amount. The IRS also frequently waives or reduces penalties.

5. *Never sign when you don't agree.* The auditor will ask you to sign a form after completion of the audit. If you don't agree with the auditor's findings, you don't have to sign the form. Signing the form may limit your rights to future appeals.

Source: "IRS Head Proposes Major Overhaul," *USA Today,* January 28, 1998, p. B1; and Louis E. Boone, David L. Kurtz, and Douglas Hearth, *Planning Your Financial Future* (Fort Worth, Tex.: Dryden Press, 1997), p. 180.

on information technology in a recent year—eight times the global average of $98.[24] That trend adds up to some $420 billion a year, $282 billion on computer hardware alone.[25]

Investments in information technology have paid off for U.S. businesses by increasing their global competitiveness. Worker productivity is rising, customer service is improving, and production costs in many industries are shrinking or remaining constant. Consider Bethlehem Steel's experience. Through the 1980s, the steel manufacturer struggled to compete with foreign competitors with lower production costs—especially labor costs. Since then, Bethlehem Steel has invested almost $6 billion to modernize its facilities. Much of this amount paid for new technologies to reduce the amount of human labor required to produce steel. The firm needed 7 worker-hours of labor to produce a ton of steel 10 years ago. Today, thanks to its modernization investments, Bethlehem Steel can produce a ton of steel with only 3 hours of human resource inputs.[26]

The growth of information technology has fueled U.S. economic growth in another way. During the past 3 years, 27 percent of America's GDP growth came from such high-technology sectors as computer manufacturers, software designers, and telecommunications firms.

Figure 3.15 **How the Federal Government Reduced Budget Deficits by $534 Billion over 5 Years and Balanced the Budget**

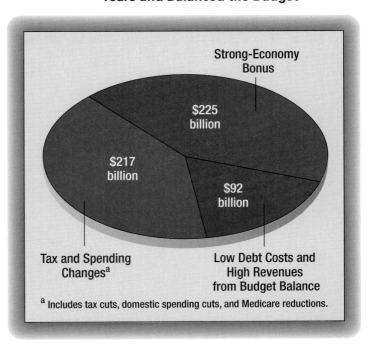

Strong-Economy Bonus
$225 billion
$217 billion
$92 billion
Tax and Spending Changes[a]
Low Debt Costs and High Revenues from Budget Balance
[a] Includes tax cuts, domestic spending cuts, and Medicare reductions.

SOLVING AN ETHICAL CONTROVERSY

The Growing Gap between Rich and Poor

Framingham, Massachusetts, is a town with a split personality. Residents on the town's north side, many employed by the area's growing high-technology industries, live in relative affluence in colonial-style homes on attractive, tree-lined streets.

Venture into Framingham's south side, however, and a different picture emerges. The area was once home to generations of blue-collar workers employed by the town's manufacturing plants, but most of these employers have moved or simply gone out of business. Now the south side is filled with decaying buildings occupied by families barely scraping by on low-paying jobs or welfare. Most south-side

residents see little chance of bettering their lives.

"Framingham was one of the places where we always saw people moving up the rungs on the ladder," explains Robert Reich, former U.S. labor secretary. "The reality today is that those rungs are much farther apart. And what is happening in Framingham is happening across the country."

Despite strong U.S. economic growth, the gap between the 20 percent of U.S. families with the highest incomes and the 20 percent at the lowest income levels has widened significantly over the last 20 years. Families at the top level saw their incomes increase 30 percent during this time, from $27,000 to $117,000. Meanwhile, wages among the bottom 20 percent dropped 21 percent, to an annual average of just $9,250.

The government could implement several policy options to narrow the gap, such as offering tax breaks to those at lower-income levels or tightening trade agreements with other countries in order to keep low-end manufacturing jobs from moving to foreign facilities. The government could also raise the minimum wage again or increase welfare benefits. As the income gap widens, the controversy grows over whether the government should take these or other actions to close it.

 Should the Government Intervene to Narrow the Income Gap?

PRO

1. An economic system owes its members some share in its prosperity. Those without skills should not

---

This contribution to the nation's economic growth is seven times greater than GDP gains coming from the U.S. auto industry.[27]

Even though the United States leads the world in information technology, several emerging trends may threaten the benefits the country derives from this leadership position. First, other countries are adapting these information technology advances in their own industries, which may reduce the competitive advantage currently enjoyed by the United States. Also the U.S. economy is becoming increasingly dependent on the continued growth of high-technology industries. A downturn in demand for these goods and services could negatively affect the entire economy. This dependence puts added pressure on U.S. companies to stay on top of technology development.[28]

Effect of an Aging Population

Most nations are experiencing some graying of their populations. In the United States, the median age has reached 35, and the baby boomers, people born between 1946 and 1965, comprise the largest population

> **They said it**
>
> "The factory of the future will have only two employees, a man and a dog. The man will be there to feed the dog. The dog will be there to keep the man from touching the equipment."
>
> Warren G. Bennis (1925–)
> American business writer

group. These people will approach retirement age over the next two decades. By 2025 over 62 million Americans will be 65 or older—nearly double today's number.

First, as this huge group ages, the need for health care, social security, and other support services is likely to grow. This trend could put budgetary pressure on governments, as they struggle to meet these changing demands.

Employers will also have to deal with pressing issues due to the aging of their workforces: retirement, worker disabilities, and insurance. As the baby boomers begin to retire, U.S. businesses will also need to find ways to replace their skills in the workplace. Generation Xers, people born between 1966 and 1976, are a much smaller population group, so employers face the possibility of significant labor shortages early in the 21st century.

Demand for many goods and services will also change as the baby boomers age. Retired consumers will probably demand fewer large homes, sport-utility vehicles, child-care services, and bank loans. They will, however, have a growing need for medical care, insurance, travel services, and retirement housing. As Figure 3.16 illustrates, successful

be sacrificed to increase business firms' profits. Instead, a fair economic system trades some growth for economic fairness among all members. "The widening income gap shows that the distribution of the benefits of economic growth has gone awry," says Harvard University economics professor Richard Freeman.

2. Income inequality is a form of discrimination. Wages paid to minority groups and women tend to be significantly lower than those earned by white males.

CON

1. Income inequality is not an inherent problem. Rather, it is capitalism's way of rewarding those who have invested time and effort to develop skills and knowledge. "Rich people are becoming richer because they have some special talent in a global economy," says Dan Mitchell of the Heritage Foundation.

2. Cutting income inequality through programs like welfare is not fair to those who have worked their way up the economic ladder. Why should their tax dollars support people who have not made the same effort?

SUMMARY

In Framingham, social service agencies dispense benefits like subsidized housing, welfare, food stamps, and Medicaid to the city's south-side poor. Meanwhile, in the kitchen of their large house on the north side, David Walsh and his wife mourn the changes in the town where they have lived for 25 years. "Framingham has become two towns," says Walsh. "Where we live is a wonderful, safe, suburban neighborhood. The south side used to be for people on the lower rungs of the ladder, climbing up. That's not true anymore. When you go over there now, there's prostitution, drugs, crime, families that are broken. These are people who are falling off the ladder, not climbing up."

Sources: Alice Ann Love, "Social Security Narrows Income Gaps," The Associated Press, April 9, 1999; Del Jones, "Family Income Disparity Increases: Gap Broadens between Richest, Poorest," *USA Today,* December 17, 1997, p. 4B; Gene Koretz, "Economic Trends: The Unhealthy U.S. Income Gap," *Business Week,* November 10, 1997, p. 22; and Charles M. Sennott, "Framingham USA: The Income Gap," *Boston Globe,* special series, July 20–22, 1997.

businesses will respond to these changing marketing opportunities.

Companies that currently offer goods and services geared toward the needs of young consumers aren't likely to disappear, of course, but they may need to adjust their strategies. They may, for example, shift their focuses toward overseas markets to find continued growth. Many Asian countries have relatively large numbers of young consumers who could fill the gap left by the aging U.S. baby boom generation.

Improving Quality and Customer Service

Ongoing improvements in product quality and customer service will continue to require close attention by companies hoping to compete in the global economy of the 21st century. Although technology can help firms to develop exciting new products, poor quality can cause failures when the products hit the market. For example, Seattle-based Virtual i-O Corp. developed a new technology for virtual reality headsets, the computer output systems that give customers three-dimensional virtual reality journeys. The new technology received high marks and attracted millions of dollars from investors. But Virtual i-O eventually declared bankruptcy because poor product quality limited the value of its products to consumers. "It didn't stand up to the abuse that happens on the retail floor, so a lot of demos didn't work," explained one industry analyst.[29]

On the other hand, Kirk Perron's obsession with product quality made his Jamba Juice business flourish. Perron launched the first store selling his nutritious milkshake-like fruit drinks in 1990. Even though the new venture exceeded his highest expectations, he purposely limited the number of stores the company opened so he could personally monitor product quality. "I just could not see a future with, say, 100 stores," Perron says. "It would have been total chaos." Perron acknowledges that preserving high quality also requires "leveling out Mother Nature's uncontrolled inconsistencies." To accomplish this, the company buys the best fruit at the peak of the season and then freezes the ingredients for future use. When a particularly tasty variety of red peach became available, for example, Perron bought the entire crop.[30]

Customer service is the crucial aspect of a competitive strategy that defines how a firm treats its customers. Businesses show that they value exceptional customer service when they create the easiest possible systems for customers to order and receive their products. They also design systems such as customer-service hot lines to resolve product-related customer complaints. Even marketers of such basic products as Pizza Hut pizzas list toll-free

| Figure 3.16 | AIG Financial Services: Responding to an Aging Population |

customer satisfaction numbers on their packages as communication channels for customer complaints and problems needing management attention.

When Harold Lewis assumed the reins as CEO of Childtime Children's Centers in 1991, the chain of childcare facilities was teetering on the edge of failure. Childtime's problem did not result from a shortage of potential customers; Americans spend $40 billion a year on child care. But the firm's financial statements showed losses or scant profits at most of the centers.

Lewis decided to emphasize customer satisfaction through a combination of quality improvements and enhanced communications with parents. A team of specialists strengthened the Childtime curriculum, and parents received information documenting the changes. Employees working with infants were required to wear disposable hospital booties over their shoes, a visible evidence of the sanitary environments provided at the child-care centers. Communications with parents increased in frequency and information content, and staff members issued report cards for children several times a year. By stressing customer service through these and other methods, Childtime has reached annual sales of $95 million, added new centers, and almost freed itself of debt.

Software designer PeopleSoft is another company benefiting from its management decision to organize operations around providing exceptional service. The firm's 300 account executives act as liaisons between business customers and internal staff members. They aren't paid commissions for the number of products they sell to customers. Instead, their performance evaluations and pay are tied to measures of customer happiness and loyalty. Their primary goal is to establish easy ways for customers to install and use PeopleSoft products. Account executives strive to understand every aspect of their customers' businesses so they can quickly solve problems that those firms face. They act as the customers' voices within the company. "The account manager is really our differentiator," says PeopleSoft's vice president of customer services. "It's the glue that holds PeopleSoft and the customer together."[31]

Maintaining the Competitiveness of the Workforce

Like PeopleSoft, thousands of businesses have discovered that human resources are replacing factories and machines as a decisive competitive factor. "The only way we can beat the competition is with people," notes Chrysler CEO Robert Eaton. "That's the only thing anybody has. Your culture and how you motivate and empower and educate your people is what makes the difference." Success hinges on whether or not a company creates an environment that encourages employees to innovate and follow up on new ideas. Internal systems must then quickly move new ideas through product development and into the marketplace.

Just adding new equipment is not enough. Workers must be trained in effective use of these resources. Employees must have the skills to control, combine, and supervise work operations, and they must be motivated to provide the best-quality products and highest levels of customer service.

The skills and education levels that businesses demand of their workforces are changing in the information economy. Effective workers must now be able to ask appropriate questions, define problems, combine information from many different sources, and deal with topics that stretch across disciplines and cultures. Companies are investing in training programs in order to develop the worker skills they need. U.S. employers spent an estimated $55 billion on formal employee training programs in 1995, and 69 percent of U.S. firms with 65 or more employees reported in a recent study that they are substantially increasing spending on employee training.[32]

The RJ Lee Group is a Pennsylvania company that uses computer-controlled scanning microscopes and other high-tech devices to analyze crime-scene materials for police departments. The company is expanding, but so are its competitors. "The only way to survive is to make your people work smarter and make them more productive," says owner Richard J. Lee. To accomplish that goal, Lee requires all of his technical people to be trained to handle the tasks of jobs other than their own. He also expects computer literacy of everyone in the company, so they can understand and use the company's state-of-the-art internal computer network.[33]

Other companies are joining forces to improve the competitive strength of their workforces. When phone giant Ameritech had trouble finding qualified workers in Cleveland, the company formed a coalition called the Jobs & Work Force Initiative. The task force has involved more than 100 companies in activities aimed at raising the skill levels of Cleveland's workforce. Ameritech's executives are also backing a statewide School-to-Work Program throughout Ohio that makes sure real-world training is part of the curricula at all 2-year and 4-year colleges in the state. The schools are encouraged to include instruction in computer use and customer service in their course offerings.[34]

But business efforts alone are not sufficient to ensure a skilled workforce. As the Business Hall of Fame demonstrated, Ireland's economic success is largely tied to government investment in education and training. In today's global marketplace, similar government initiatives may be required from other countries seeking to develop competitive workforces.

Education levels in the United States have grown over the past two decades. Between 1984 and 1994, the number of people enrolled in both 2-year and 4-year colleges rose 17 percent. By 2005, nearly 4 million more students will be graduating each year than in 1985. Increasingly, education is a critical requirement for any high-paying job. Workers with high-school diplomas, for example, now earn an average of $31,081 a year, while college graduates receive nearly twice as much, $61,008. As Table 3.5 shows, the fastest-growing jobs in the United States demand postsecondary education.

CREATING A LONG-TERM GLOBAL STRATEGY

No country is an economic island in today's global economy. Not only has an ever-increasing stream of goods and services crossed national borders, but many businesses have become true multinational firms, operating manufacturing

Table 3.5	Jobs on the Fast Track			
Career	Description	Entry Salary	Top Salary	Minimum Education
Accounting Business Valuator	Determine the value of business assets	$30,000	$200,000	Bachelor's in accounting, CPA certification
Bank Financial Planner	Recommend investments, manage portfolios	20,000+	175,000	Bachelor's in finance, MBA preferred
Communications Crisis Specialist	Public relations for handling corporate crises	23,000	76,000	Bachelor's in P.R., journalism, or communications
Computer Engineer	Design computer hardware	55,000	79,000+	Bachelor's in software systems, computer engineering, or math
Human Resources Training Specialist	Train workers	31,400	73,900	Bachelor's or master's in business, computers, education, or psychology

plants and other facilities around the world. As global trade and investments grow, the economic events in one country can reverberate around the globe.

Consider, for example, how Asia's recent economic woes may affect business in the United States. Starting in mid-1997, financial markets in Thailand, Indonesia, South Korea, and Japan tumbled. The U.S. stock market reacted with a drop of its own amid fears of shrinking revenues for companies that had invested heavily in Asia. Although the U.S. stock market quickly rebounded, analysts predict that ongoing problems in Asia will continue to affect U.S. businesses by weakening the Asian market for U.S.-made goods such as computers, electronics, and consumer goods. U.S. manufacturers that have built up manufacturing capacity in expectation of growth in Asian markets may find themselves oversupplied, eventually forcing layoffs.[35]

Still, global expansion can offer huge opportunities to U.S. firms. As mentioned in Chapter 1, U.S. residents account for only 4 percent of the world's 6 billion people.

Growth-oriented companies can't afford to ignore the world market outside their native countries. Other U.S. businesses are benefiting from the lower labor costs in other parts of the world, and some are finding successful niches importing goods made by foreign manufacturers. The biggest challenge for U.S. businesses in the 21st century is to develop long-term strategies for global competitiveness that minimize risk while maximizing these opportunities.

WHAT'S AHEAD

Chapter 4 will focus on the global dimensions of business. The chapter will review the key concepts of doing business internationally and examine how nations can position themselves to benefit from the global economy. Then, it will describe the specific methods used by individual businesses to expand beyond their national borders and compete successfully in the global market.

SUMMARY OF LEARNING GOALS

1. Distinguish between microeconomics and macroeconomics.

Microeconomics is the study of economic behavior among individual consumers, families, and businesses whose collective behavior in the marketplace determines the quantity of goods and services demanded and supplied at different prices. By contrast, macroeconomics is the study of the broader economic picture and how an economic system maintains and allocates its resources; it focuses on how a government's monetary and fiscal policies affect the overall operation of an economic system.

2. List each of the factors that collectively determine demand and those that determine supply.

Demand is the willingness and ability of buyers to purchase goods and services at different prices. Factors that collectively determine overall demand for a good or service include customer preferences, number of buyers and their incomes, the prices of substitute goods, the prices of complementary goods, and consumer expectations about the future. Supply sums up the willingness and ability of businesses to offer goods and services for sale at different prices. Overall supply is determined by the costs of inputs (natural resources, capital, human resources, and entrepreneurship), costs of technology resources, taxes, and the number of suppliers operating in the market.

3. Compare supply and demand curves and explain how they determine the equilibrium price for a good or service.

A demand curve is a graph showing the amount of a good or service buyers will purchase at different prices. Since buyers likely will demand increasing quantities of a good at progressively lower prices, demand curves usually slope downward as they move to the right. By contrast, a supply curve is a schedule of the amounts of a good or service that businesses will offer for sale at different prices. Since sellers will likely make progressively more goods and services available as prices rise, supply curves usually slope upward as they move to the right. The interaction of the supply and demand curves determines the equilibrium price, the price at which the quantity supplied by sellers is precisely equal to the quantity demanded.

4. Contrast the three major types of economic systems.

Each of the world's national economies can be classified as either a private enterprise economy, a planned economic system such as communism or socialism, or a mixed market economy. A private enterprise system is characterized by individuals and private businesses pursuing their own interests without undue governmental restriction; by private ownership of factors of production; by investment decisions made by private industry rather than by government decree; and by determination of prices, products, resource allocation, and profits through competition in a free market. In a planned economy, the government exerts stronger control over business ownership, profits, and resources in order to accomplish government—rather than individual—goals. Communism is an economic system without private property; goods are owned in common, and factors of production and production decisions are controlled by the state. Socialism, another type of planned economic system, is characterized by government ownership and operation of all major industries. The final type of economic system, a mixed market economy, blends government ownership and private enterprise, combining characteristics of both planned and market economies.

5. Identify the four different types of market structures in a private enterprise system.

Four basic models characterize competition in a private enterprise system: pure competition, monopolistic competition, oligopoly, and monopoly. Pure competition is a market structure, like that in small-scale agriculture, in which large numbers of buyers and sellers exchange homogeneous products, so no single participant has a significant influence on price. Monopolistic competition is a market structure, like that in retailing, in which large numbers of buyers and sellers exchange relatively well-differentiated (heterogeneous) products, so each participant has some control over price. Oligopolies are market situations, like those in the steel and airline industries, in which relatively few sellers compete, and where high start-up costs form barriers to keep out new competitors. The final market structure is a monopoly, in which only one seller dominates trade in a good or service, for which buyers can find no close substitutes. Local water utilities and firms that hold exclusive patent rights on significant product inventions are examples.

6. Identify the major factors that guide an economist's evaluation of a nation's economic performance.

Economists consider several economic indicators to measure and evaluate the success of an economic system in providing a stable business environment and sustained growth. A nation's productivity is evidence of its economic strength and competitiveness. Gross domestic product (GDP), the market value of all goods and services produced within a nation's boundaries each year, is a commonly used measure of productivity. Changes in general price levels—inflation, price stability, or deflation—are important indicators of an economy's general stability. The U.S. government measures price-level changes by the Consumer Price Index (CPI). A nation's unemployment rate is an indicator of both overall stability and growth. The unemployment rate shows the number of people actively seeking employment who are unable to find jobs as a percentage of the total labor force. A final factor is the relative economic freedom enjoyed by individuals and private businesses in a nation.

7. Compare the two major tools used by a government to manage the performance of its national economy.

The various tools used by government officials to influence the economy can be categorized as elements of either monetary policy or fiscal policy. Monetary policy encompasses a government's efforts to control the size of the nation's money supply. Various methods of increasing or decreasing the overall money supply affect interest rates and therefore impact borrowing and investment decisions. By changing the size of the money supply, government can encourage growth or control inflation. Fiscal policy, the second government tool, involves decisions regarding government revenues and expenditures. Changes in government spending affect economic growth and employment levels in the private sector. However, government must also raise money, either through

taxes or through borrowing, to finance its expenditures. Since tax payments represent funds that might otherwise have been spent by individuals and businesses, any taxation changes also affect the overall economy.

8. Describe the major global economic challenges of the 21st century.

Business in the 21st century is likely to be propelled by technological advances that enable businesses to enhance the effectiveness of their use, management, and control of information. A highly trained workforce is an essential requirement for businesses that want to take advantage of this change. A second important economic challenge involves dealing with the effects of an aging population. Both government and business must be prepared to accommodate changing demands in health care, social security, and other support services. Customer service and quality remain vital ingredients for competitive superiority in the global market. A final factor in gaining competitive advantage is a competitive workforce. Both government and business must formulate effective plans for developing the skills and knowledge of workers in the 21st century.

TEN BUSINESS TERMS YOU NEED TO KNOW

economics	socialism
demand	mixed market economy
supply	monetary policy
private enterprise system	fiscal policy
	budget deficit
communism	

Other Important Business Terms

economic system	planned economy
microeconomics	privatization
macroeconomics	productivity
demand curve	gross domestic product (GDP)
supply curve	inflation
factors of production	hyperinflation
equilibrium price	Consumer Price Index (CPI)
pure competition	unemployment rate
monopolistic competition	national debt
oligopoly	balanced budget
monopoly	

REVIEW QUESTIONS

1. Imagine that you own a donut shop. Draw a supply and demand graph that estimates what will

happen to demand, supply, and the equilibrium price if these events occur:

   a. A major medical report states that eating donuts appears to reduce the likelihood of heart disease.
   b. Consumer incomes decline.
   c. The price of flour falls.
   d. The government imposes a tax on donut production.
   e. Four new donut shops open for business in your area.
   f. The Consumer Price Index shows a sharp jump in prices.

2. Compare the three major types of economic systems: private enterprise system, planned economies, and mixed market economies. Discuss the current status of each of these economic systems in the world. What potential benefits does each system offer? What negatives are associated with each system?

3. The four basic types of competition are pure competition, monopolistic competition, oligopoly, and monopoly. What type of competition does each of these companies face in its industry?

   a. Texaco
   b. McDonald's
   c. America Online
   d. Fred and Susan Smith's 640-acre Iowa farm
   e. Amtrak
   f. Your local water utility

4. Distinguish between inflation and deflation. Explain the difference between cost-push inflation and demand-pull inflation. Evaluate the economic indicators used by the U.S. government to measure price-level changes. Is deflation always a positive development?

5. Match the following descriptions with the type of unemployment they represent: (a) frictional, (b) seasonal, (c) cyclical, and (d) structural unemployment.

   _____ A factory worker suffers a temporary layoff because of slow sales.

   _____ A steelworker loses his job when a mill permanently closes.

   _____ An amusement park employee is laid off at the end of the summer.

   _____ A recent graduate searches for an entry-level job.

6. Distinguish between monetary policy and fiscal policy. How does each operate to regulate the economy? Cite specific examples. Explain the effects of both monetary policy and fiscal policy on your daily life.

7. Define the term *information economy*. How do the concerns of business differ in an information economy from those in a manufacturing economy?

8. Explain the contributions of quality and customer service to a nation's economic health. How does each help a firm to differentiate itself from competitors?

9. Explain how the development of a competitive national workforce affects the economy. How can the U.S. government and U.S. firms contribute to the development of a competitive workforce?

10. Discuss the importance of developing a long-term global strategy.

QUESTIONS FOR CRITICAL THINKING

1. Economics has been called "this dismal science." Do you agree or disagree? Support your arguments. Identify at least five ways that economics affects your daily life.

2. Identify, as specifically as possible, the factors most likely to affect demand, supply, and equilibrium price in the listed industries. If you were an executive of a company in these industries, how would you monitor changes for each factor?

   a. The personal computer industry
   b. The fast-food restaurant industry
   c. The automobile manufacturing industry
   d. The banking industry

3. Must a small business owner whose firm only operates locally remain aware of overall supply and demand trends in the national market for the firm's goods or services? Why or why not? How can supply and demand principles help small business owners to identify potential business opportunities?

4. Review the economic indicators discussed in this chapter. If you were president of the United States, what would you consider the most important indicator of the economy's overall health? Why? Discuss how both monetary and fiscal policies could affect this indicator.

5. Assume that you are chief economic advisor to the president of the United States, and you are convinced that the economy is entering a period of recession. What economic indicators would you cite to support your belief? What actions would you recommend that the president take? Should the federal government always intervene in a recession? Why or why not?

Experiential Exercise

Background: The most phenomenal movie success in recent memory is *Titanic*. Its high-priced production, compelling story line, and string of awards quickly propelled it into first place as the biggest money-making film of all time. Within a matter of weeks following its release, *Titanic* passed longtime box-office leaders like *Star Wars, E.T. The Extra-Terrestrial,* and *Jurassic Park*—and revenue continues to pour in.

Directions: Assume you are a decision-maker at a local theater and must determine the ticket price your theater should charge for an evening showing of *Titanic*. Based on the following assumptions, plot your theater's supply curve on the graph provided in this exercise and label it "supply curve."

Quantity	Price
250	$4.00
325	$6.00
400	$8.00

Using the following assumptions, plot your customers' demand curve on the graph in this exercise and label it "demand curve."

Quantity	Price
450	$4.00
350	$6.00
225	$8.00

Determine the point at which the quantity of theater tickets your company is willing to supply equals the quantity of theater tickets the customers in your area are willing to buy, and label that point "equilibrium price."

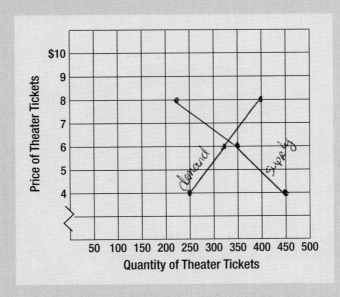

Equilibrium Price of Theater Tickets

Nothing but Net

1. **Competition.** Assume you have a $2,000 budget to purchase any computer products you want. Visit

   www.zdnet.com/netbuyer/

   and conduct a search on the products you wish to purchase. After you key in information to define your requirements, this Web site will comparison shop for you at some 75 computer product vendors. The site provides you with a wealth of information about what competitors have to offer. Web sites such as these provide you with what you need to know to buy the best products at the best prices.

2. **Privatization.** Use any Web search engine and key in the word "privatization." Find a site that provides information related to an area of privatization that is of interest. For example,

   www.socialsecurity.org/

   is the Cato Institute's Web page on social security privatization. Once you've selected a specific privatization area, write a brief summary that includes at least three problems that are/were driving forces toward privatization and explain the privatization plan. If you select a privatization area that has not yet happened (e.g., social security), write your summary from the perspective of what problems exist that privatization could solve and how proponents suggest privatization should be implemented. On the other hand, if you choose an existing privatization plan (e.g., the Brazilian government's recent privatization of its railroad system), write from the perspective of why privatization was necessary and how privatization was implemented.

3. **Gross Domestic Product (GDP).** The Social Sciences Data Center of the University of Virginia provides NIPA (National Income and Product Accounts) data at

   www.lib.virginia.edu/ssdcbin/nipabin/level1.cgi

   Visit this site to submit a request for a line chart illustrating GDP in billions of dollars for any length of time from 1959 to the most recent quarter for which data is available.

Note: Internet Web addresses change frequently. If you do not find the exact sites listed, you may need to access the organization's or company's home page and search from there.

VIDEO CASE 3

FOSSIL—KEEPING WATCH ON A GLOBAL BUSINESS

For being only a 14-year-old company, founded by a 23-year-old, Fossil, Inc., located in Richardson, Texas, has emerged as a leader of the fashion watch industry. In the early 1980s Tom Kartsotis was selling hard-to-get tickets for sporting events and concerts. This ticket-scalping business taught him important lessons in marketing. Tom's older brother Kosta, at the time a merchandise executive for a large Dallas department store chain, told him about the large profit margins being earned on importing retail goods from the Far East—in particular, the increasing trend of moderately priced watches pioneered by Swiss-owned Swatch. Taking Kosta's suggestion, Tom went to Hong Kong, where he hired a manufacturer to make 1,500 watches, which he sold to local department stores and boutiques. Fossil was born.

To carve his own niche in the fashion watch industry, Tom came up with a retro theme to differentiate his watches from Swatch or Guess. Inspiration for the watch designs comes largely from old magazines of the 1940s and 1950s.

Today Fossil designs, develops, markets, and distributes fashion watches, leather accessories, and sunglasses principally under the Fossil, FSL, and RELIC brand names. Fossil has sales and distribution centers in the United States, Germany, Italy, Japan, Spain, Hong Kong, Canada, Mexico, and the United Kingdom. This network of distributors offers Fossil products to over 50 countries.

Although Switzerland was known for watch manufacturing, Hong Kong has emerged as the center of the watch industry today. "The reason we picked Hong Kong is twofold," says Gary Bolinger, senior vice president of international sales and marketing. "One, the infrastructure is there. To be able to deliver and assemble goods, and get it out of the country in a timely manner. And secondly the mentality of the Hong Kong people that they can get anything done."

With Hong Kong's return to China in July 1997, there has been much speculation about its impact on businesses. "I have been back twice since the turnover and can safely say that from our business point of view in watch manufacturing there has been no change in that turnover," says Dermott Bland, senior vice president of watch products.

"There have been few changes with regards to exporting and importing, but in the majority, there have been improvements."

Fossil forges ahead with the challenges of anticipating fashion trends, managing product changes, taking the American image global, diversifying with other product lines. Recently, Fossil paired up with London Fog for the production and marketing of Fossil outerwear in the United States.

Questions

1. What type of market structure exists in the fashion watch industry? Explain.

2. How would you classify the economic systems of China? Hong Kong? What impact do you think the return of Hong Kong to China might have on companies like Fossil?

3. What global economic challenges do companies like Fossil and countries that Fossil does business with need to successfully meet to maintain their global competitiveness?

chapter 4

Competing in Global Markets

LEARNING GOALS

1. Explain the importance of international business and the main reasons why nations trade.

2. Discuss the relationship of absolute and comparative advantage to international trade.

3. Describe how nations measure international trade and the significance of exchange rates.

4. Identify the major barriers that confront global businesses.

5. Explain how international trade organizations and economic communities reduce barriers to international trade.

6. Compare the different levels of involvement used by businesses when entering global markets.

7. Describe the types of international organizational structures available to businesses.

8. Distinguish between a global business strategy and a multidomestic business strategy.

Beetlemania Revisited

As Yogi Berra would say, "It's *déjà vu* all over again." From "Love Bug" to retro-chic. From planned economy to affordable luxury. From Germany through Mexico—the Volkswagen Beetle has come a long way. It's back, and its brought with it all the magic and nostalgia from the past. The old Beetle of the 1960s and 1970s was more than a car. It was a trusted friend, a component of its owner's personality, and a link to youth that Baby Boomers still talk about with affection. The Beetle was the commuter car that offered solid transportation to an entire generation. It was simple, durable, and inexpensive. Its high gas mileage let owners survive gasoline shortages and soaring prices of the 1970s. By 1968, Americans had bought 399,674 Bugs, making it the leading import in the United States. But within a decade, the Beetle was being supplanted by a host of Japanese imports with names like Honda, Nissan, and Toyota, and the Volkswagen faded into obscurity.

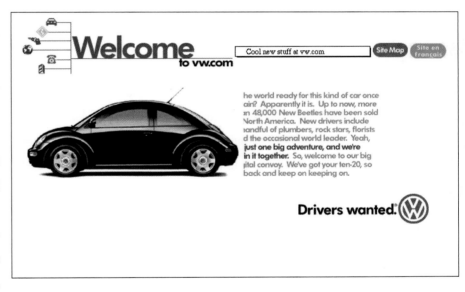

Now it's back for the 21st century and U.S. car dealers can't keep the new Beetle in stock. A quick glance is all you need to recognize that it's the real deal. The body contains front and rear smiles, the dashboard sports a flower vase, and the interior still offers a large assist handle above the glove compartment.

The new model does contain a few basic differences. Front-wheel drive replaces the old rear-wheel approach. A new 2-liter 4-cylinder engine with 115 horsepower is a welcome improvement over the tiny original 48-horsepower version. The new Beetle is 3 inches taller, 4.6 inches longer, and the trunk has been moved from the front to the back. Perhaps the biggest change is the sticker price—$800 in 1949 to between $15,000 and $18,000 today.

WWW.
www.vw.com

But the difference between the two generations extend beyond horsepower, inches, and price. Buyers won't overlook the up-to-date technology in new features such as standard air conditioning and optional CD player. In fact, the new Beetle is a thoroughly modern creation that is not only functional but also packed with plenty of creature comforts and the latest advancements in safety.

Standard features include such techno-comforts as a pollen and odor filter, a six-speaker stereo, an antitheft alarm system, halogen headlamps, and four-wheel disc brakes. State-of-the-art safety features include energy-absorbing crush zones, dual air bags, and front-seat-mounted side air bags. And for just a bit more cash, you can choose one-touch power windows, cruise control, fog lamps, a folding center armrest, 16-inch alloy wheels, leather seating with heatable front seats, and a three-spoke leather-covered steering wheel.

The old Beetle would rust with envy. Its new namesake is built to the highest standards with unmatched body rigidity. The new Beetle's bumpers and fenders are even made using a dent-resistant plastic. And, best of all, it is no slouch in road tests. The sporty little car rewards its driver with the performance and fun expected from a modern German-engineered car.

The Beetle's cute-as-a-bug image has U.S. consumers pressing their noses against showroom windows, eager for their 30-year-old friend who has come out of the past. True, the Bug now has a little less flower and a little more power. It promises to deliver Volkswagen's most advanced technology and a little more sunshine, along with 48 miles to the gallon. The original Beetle was designed by Ferdinand Porsche in 1935 Germany as a German car for the German masses. Now, designed in Germany and assembled in Mexico for U.S. and other car buyers, the Volkswagen Beetle is truly a product of international business.[1]

CHAPTER OVERVIEW

Consider for a moment how many products you used today that came from outside the United States. Maybe you drank Brazilian coffee with your breakfast, wore clothes manufactured in Honduras or Malaysia, drove to class in a German or Japanese car fueled by gasoline refined from Venezuelan crude oil, and watched a movie on a television set assembled in Mexico for a Japanese company like Sony. A fellow student in France may be wearing Levi's jeans, using an IBM or Compaq computer, and drinking Coca-Cola.

Figure 4.1 **The World of Coca-Cola**

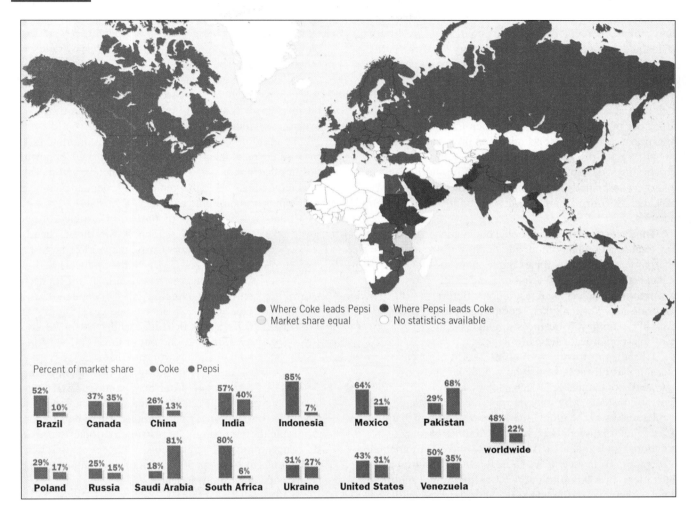

● Where Coke leads Pepsi ● Where Pepsi leads Coke
○ Market share equal ○ No statistics available

Percent of market share ● Coke ● Pepsi

Brazil 52% / 10%
Canada 37% / 35%
China 26% / 13%
India 57% / 40%
Indonesia 85% / 7%
Mexico 64% / 21%
Pakistan 29% / 68%
worldwide 48% / 22%

Poland 29% / 17%
Russia 25% / 15%
Saudi Arabia 18% / 81%
South Africa 80% / 6%
Ukraine 31% / 27%
United States 43% / 31%
Venezuela 50% / 35%

Like Volkswagen, Levi Strauss, IBM, Sony, and Coca-Cola, most U.S. and foreign companies recognize the importance of international trade to their future success. As Chapter 1 explained, economic interdependence is increasing throughout the world as companies seek additional markets for their goods and services as well as the most cost-effective locations for production facilities. No longer can businesses rely only on sales in domestic markets. Today, foreign sales are essential to U.S. manufacturing, agricultural, and service firms, providing new markets and profit opportunities. Foreign companies also seek out new markets.

Thousands of products cross national borders every day. The computers that U.S. manufacturers sell in France are **exports,** domestically produced goods and services

sold in markets in other countries. **Imports** are foreign-made products purchased by domestic consumers. International trade now accounts for almost 25 percent of the U.S. gross domestic product, compared with about 5 percent 25 years ago. U.S. exports exceed $925 billion each year, while annual imports total $1.3 trillion. That total amounts to three times the nation's imports and exports as recently as 1990.

For soft-drink giant Coca-Cola, global markets mean global profits. As Figure 4.1 shows, Coke is a dominant

Business Directory

exports domestically produced goods and services sold in markets in other countries.

imports foreign goods and services purchased by domestic consumers.

brand on every continent. Although its U.S. market share is an impressive 43 percent, it enjoys even better positions abroad, with virtual monopolies marked by market shares of 80 percent or higher in countries like South Africa and Indonesia. In fact, $4 of every $5 Coke earns come from overseas sales. By contrast, its major competitor Pepsi lags far behind in the international marketplace. With the exception of Canada, foreign sales don't produce a dime in profits for Pepsi. The chief reason for this difference in results appears to be Coca-Cola's continuing investment in distribution and other physical resources for getting its products within arm's reach of its customers; instead, Pepsi relies on creative promotions. One observer described soft-drink operations in emerging markets: "Soft drinks are much less about branding than logistics."[2]

Transactions that cross national boundaries may expose a company to an additional set of environmental factors—for example, new social and cultural practices, economic and political environments, and legal restrictions. Before venturing into world markets, companies must adapt their domestic business strategies and plans to accommodate these differences.

This chapter travels through the world of international business to see how both large and small companies approach globalization. First, it considers why nations trade, the importance and characteristics of the global marketplace, and how nations measure international trade. It then examines barriers to international trade that arise from cultural and environmental differences. To reduce these barriers, countries turn to organizations that promote international trade and multinational agreements designed to encourage trade. Finally, the chapter looks at the strategies firms implement for entering global markets and how they develop international business strategies.

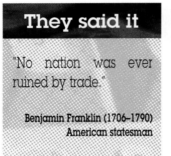

They said it

"No nation was ever ruined by trade."

Benjamin Franklin (1706–1790)
American statesman

WHY NATIONS TRADE

As domestic markets mature and sales growth slows, companies in every industry recognize the increasing importance of efforts to develop business in other countries. McDonald's opens restaurants in Latin America; Nike designs soccer shoes for Brazilians; Wal-Mart tempts Chinese shoppers with a wide selection of merchandise at discount prices. These and other U.S. companies are taking advantage of the interest shown by foreigners in their goods and services. Likewise, the U.S. market, with the world's largest purchasing power, attracts thousands of foreign companies to American shores. Large populations, substantial resources, and rising standards of living are boosting the attractiveness of many countries as targets for U.S. exports and imports.

International trade is vital to a nation and its businesses because it boosts economic growth. The economies of developing nations that encourage international trade grow at an average rate of 4.5 percent a year, compared to only 1 percent for those that resist trade with other countries. The same holds true for industrialized nations. Those that encourage trade saw their economies expand an average of 2.3 percent in a recent year, while business growth averaged only 0.7 percent in those with restrictive policies.

In addition, companies in nations that promote global trade can expand their markets, seek out growth opportunities in other nations, and achieve production and distribution economies. They also reduce their dependence on the economies of their home nations.

"The growth markets of the world are clearly overseas," believes John F. Smith, Jr., head of General Motors Corp., the world's largest automaker. As GM's share of the U.S. light-vehicle market has declined, its focus has shifted to overseas sales of models like the Opel Corsa. In an average year, Smith's firm sells 800,000 Corsas to drivers in 75 countries. In fact, one out of three GM vehicles is sold outside North America.[3]

GM is in the midst of implementing a $2.2 billion "four-plant strategy" for its operations in Argentina, Poland, China, and Thailand to take advantage of local sales opportunities. These new factories represent the company's largest international expansion. By concentrating its investments in the developing world, GM intends to establish 50 percent of its manufacturing capacity outside North America.[4]

www. **www.gm.com**

International Sources of Factors of Production

The General Motors global expansion strategy fits into a larger picture of why nations trade, and in particular, why they target partners in specific countries. Availability of comparably cheap or experienced labor and availability of natural resources, raw materials, and capital—the basic factors of production—influence a company's decision to invest in a foreign country. For example, expertise in titanium technology led Western manufacturers of golf equipment to Russia. Privately owned Metal-Park Co., a converted Soviet missile factory, now processes titanium to produce thousands of golf clubs for U.S. and Asian companies such as Taylor Made Golf Co. in Carlsbad, California.[5]

International trade also boosts employment and wages in the home country. More than 12 million U.S. workers—about one of every 10 members of the nation's workforce—produce goods or provide services for export. Rather than losing their jobs or taking wage cuts, domestic workers who hold export-related jobs earn an average of 15 percent more than the average wage. In the U.S. economy, every additional $1 billion of export sales supports an average of 20,000 jobs.[6]

Other key factors in choosing overseas markets include favorable regulatory conditions and healthy business climates. Trading with other countries also allows a company to spread risk; while the business cycle of a given market is at a low point, another may be enjoying brisk economic activity. For example, U.S. companies turned their attention to the Pacific Rim countries while Europe was in a recession, increasing exports to Europe again when economic activity there picked up. Later sections of the chapter discusses how these elements affect businesses.

Size of the International Marketplace

In addition to their pursuit of production factors such as human and natural resources, entrepreneurship, and capital, companies are attracted to international business by the sheer size of the marketplace. Of the world's 6 billion inhabitants, just over 20 percent live in relatively well-developed countries. The remaining 4.7 billion live on lower incomes in less-developed countries. The gap between these two groups will increase even more in the coming years due to significant differences in birth rates. Population growth in developed nations is only about 0.4 percent per year, five times slower than the 2 percent growth occurring in developing nations.

As developing nations expand their involvement in international trade, the potential for reaching new groups of customers dramatically increases. Firms looking for new sales are inevitably attracted to giant markets like China and India, with populations of 1.2 billion and 950 million, respectively. However, people alone are not sufficient to create a market. Purchasing power is also required. As Table 4.1 shows, population size is no guarantee of economic prosperity. Only two of the ten most populous countries appear on the list of those with the highest per-capita gross domestic product (GDP).

Even though people in the developing nations have lower per-capita incomes than those in the highly developed economies of North America and western Europe, their huge populations do represent lucrative markets. However, the high-income segments of those populations may amount only to small percentages of all households. For example, although India's people receive a low $330 per-capita income, that nation's growing middle class represents a huge potential target market for foreign businesses. An estimated 200 million Indians earn incomes comparable to those in the United States and Canada.[7]

Many developing countries have posted high rates of annual GDP growth, such as China with over 9 percent a year and India, Poland, and Turkey, each with over 6 percent. These markets represent opportunities for global businesses, even though their per-capita incomes lag behind those in more developed countries. Dozens of international firms are currently establishing operations in these countries to position themselves to benefit from local sales driven by rising standards of living.

Developing sophisticated systems of trade and industrial relations lifts the standard of living for a country's population, making it an even more desirable trading partner. A good example is Singapore. Once considered a developing nation, the tiny island country has used its newfound ability to produce competitively priced goods and services to earn industrialized nation status with a per capita gross domestic product of $22,900.[8]

Table 4.1	The World's Top Ten Nations Based on Population and Wealth		
Country	**Population (in millions)**	**Country**	**Per-Capita GDP**[a]
China	1,210	Luxembourg	$33,200
India	950	United States	28,500
United States	270	Japan	23,800
Indonesia	207	United Arab Emirates	23,600
Brazil	163	Switzerland	23,500
Russia	148	Norway	23,300
Pakistan	129	Singapore	22,900
Japan	126	Belgium	22,400
Bangladesh	123	Denmark	22,400
Nigeria	104	France	21,700

[a]Measured in U.S. dollars.

BUSINESS HALL OF FAME

Asian Sources: Changing the Way Asia Does Business

For years, a slow boat to China described the only option for international traders looking to import exotic products from the Far East. Too often, Asian business transactions depended on a company blindly trusting middlemen and go-betweens. Indeed, trade with these countries was often a dark business, reminiscent of Humphrey Bogart in *The Maltese Falcon*.

Fortunately, that is no longer the case. Although business travelers will agree that trips to Hong Kong, Singapore, or Beijing often are tiring and time consuming, they now have the resources of the Web to gain immediate access to companies in foreign markets without ever leaving home. In addition, cyber-companies now offer many specialized services that facilitate trade, such as providing Western buyers and Eastern suppliers a place to do business. Asian Sources does just that.

Acting as a gateway for electronic commerce, Asian Sources provides trade-matching services in an environment where differences in time, language, and physical distance present no barriers. Based in Hong Kong, Manila and Singapore, the company serves importers around the world and boasts of its unrivaled understanding of Asian business practices. After all, they will tell you, "Asia is our home."

Asian Sources gives practical advice to suppliers, suggesting which computer systems to install and how to connect to the Internet. It has even negotiated special Internet deals for customers with AT&T in Hong Kong and IBM Global Network in Taiwan. CEO Sarah Benecke says the company's objective is to "help Asian companies meet the challenges of electronic commerce and emerge more efficient and competitive." She believes that e-commerce is no longer an option to be chosen or ignored. Companies that want global business have to get wired now.

Suppliers can also use the services of Asian Sources to create their Web sites. An Asian Sources account executive visits a company, enters product information into a notebook PC, and photographs the products with a digital camera. These data are then uploaded

MAJOR WORLD MARKETS

As Figure 1.6 showed, the major trading partners of U.S. firms are the country's northern and southern neighbors, Canada and Mexico. Other important global partners include Japan, China, Germany, and the United Kingdom.

More than coincidence ensures that these countries represent the world's major market regions: North America, western Europe, the Pacific Rim, and Latin America. These regions encompass not only western Europe and Japan, but also such emerging markets as India, Malaysia, and Vietnam. As Figure 4.2 shows, many of the world's most attractive emerging markets are located in Latin America and around the Pacific Rim.

North America With a combined population of about 400 million and a total GDP exceeding $9 trillion, this region represents one of the world's most attractive markets. The United States—the single largest market in the world and the most stable economy—dominates North America's business environment. Home to less than 5 percent of the world popula-

Figure 4.2	Emerging Markets for the 21st Century

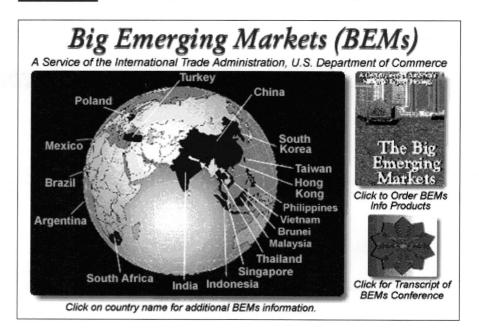

to Asian Sources and used to set up the supplier's virtual showroom. The site goes up on the Web overnight, faster than anyone has ever reached the world market before.

www.asiansources.com

In addition to its basic services, Asian Sources has introduced Private Buyer Catalogs that list the specific products an importer is interested in buying. When an Asian supplier advertises a new product through Asian Sources, the product specifications are automatically e-mailed to the appropriate buyer. The company targets big buyers, such as Ace Hardware, Toys 'R' Us, and Federated Department Stores (parent company to Bloomingdale's and Macy's). These large companies use the services of Asian Sources to find foreign products to stock in their domestic stores. Similarly, Asian suppliers look to Asian Sources to help them find outlets for their products.

Traditional product-sourcing techniques still rely on physical trips to Asia. Each year buyers congregate to meet new suppliers and check out their newest offerings. Asian Sources helps both buyers and sellers during these annual visits by initiating communication between all parties. This service strengthens ties and can even help eliminate the need for trips altogether.

By combining electronic commerce technology, the immediacy of the Internet, and the trust of strategic alliances, Asian Sources is easing business transactions around the globe. The company is doing more than just changing the way Asia does business—it is encouraging and increasing international business as a whole.

Sources: Asian Sources Web site, accessed at www.asiansources.com, February 9, 1999; and Carol Memmott, "Net Saves Time, Opens Door to Asian Market," *USA Today*, November 16, 1998, p. 8E.

QUESTIONS FOR CRITICAL THINKING

1. By using a Web site to advertise their products, suppliers are likely to get many small orders from small companies. Would this be a problem for suppliers? Explain.

2. Asian Sources is beginning to charge suppliers for sending product details to buyers. By paying, suppliers can post their products in a private environment to specific buyers—an improvement for suppliers. How will the new system help buyers? Explain your answer.

---

tion, the country's $8 trillion GDP represents about one-fifth of total world output. Major U.S.-based corporations like Citicorp., General Electric, and Disney maintain sizable investments both around the world and in North America.

Canada's business organizations, while often overshadowed by U.S. competitors, still have a major international presence, with companies like Bell Canada investing in Latin America.[9] Canada's international trade totals about $400 billion. Because trade with the United States now accounts for two-fifths of Canada's GDP, its economy is extremely vulnerable to events in the U.S. economy.[10]

South of the border, Mexico is another country moving from developing-nation to industrial-nation status, thanks to low-cost labor and the North American Free Trade Agreement (NAFTA). Stretching 2,100 miles from the Pacific Ocean to the Gulf of Mexico, the U.S.-Mexican border is home to 1,500 *maquiladoras,* foreign-owned manufacturing plants that produce products for export. Tijuana has become the television manufacturing capital of the world. Sanyo Electric moved its North American headquarters from New York to San Diego to be close to its Tijuana plant. Cincinnati-based Baldwin Piano & Organ Co. employs 270 workers in its Juarez factory, across the border from El Paso.[11]

Mexican products are also competing effectively in the U.S. market. In 1998, U.S. sales of Corona surpassed those of long-time market leader Heineken making it the leading import brand of beer.

Western Europe Western Europe, particularly Germany, the United Kingdom, France, and Italy, is a sophisticated and powerful industrial region with a combined GDP comparable to that of the United States. The European Union, an economic community created in 1992 and discussed later in this chapter, has solidified the importance of this market. Royal Dutch Shell, Nestlé, Daimler Benz, and Glaxo Wellcome are international companies with headquarters in this region.

Significant investments from around the world are flowing into European nations, as foreign companies locate manufacturing and distribution facilities across the continent. In Britain, where traditional industries such as shipbuilding and coal mining have declined, foreign manufacturers are establishing themselves. Japan's Nissan Motor Co. set up an auto-assembly plant in the northeastern region of Sunderland to turn out 250,000 Primeras and Micras each year, making it one of Europe's three largest car-production facilities.

One growth industry currently making inroads in Britain is electronics. Scotland's equivalent of California's Silicon Valley, Silicon Glen, is located between Glasgow and Edinburgh. IBM, Compaq Computer, Hewlett-

Packard, and Sun Microsystems operate factories there, and Germany's Siemens is spending $1.8 billion on a new semiconductor plant that will employ 1,500 people.[12]

One of France's major economic assets is a large supply of well-trained, high-tech talent. French levels of formal education are second only to those in the United States, and France has supplied U.S. high-tech industries with such notable executives as 3Com CEO Eric Benhamou and Borland founder Philippe Kahn.[13] To attract foreign investors, the French government emphasizes the availability, expertise, and flexibility of its country's workforce in promotions such as the one shown in Figure 4.3.

Even the nearby countries of eastern Europe are considered excellent growth prospects for international businesses. Following the fall of communism, the former Soviet-bloc countries have opened their borders to international trade. They are also modifying their legal, political, and economic environments to improve conditions for development of market economies. A good example is Germany's eastern neighbor. Poland's GDP growth rate exceeds 6 percent per year, making it one of Europe's fastest-growing economies. U.S. exports to Poland have passed the $1 billion mark, up 56 percent since 1992.[14]

The Pacific Rim Australia, China (including Hong Kong), Indonesia, Japan, Malaysia, the Philippines, Singapore, South Korea, and Taiwan are the major nations of this large and growing region. As recently as 1996, the combined exports of Japan, China, and Hong Kong totaled $743 billion and U.S.-Asian trade was $210 billion. The industries that fuel Asian economies—electronics, automobiles, and banking—are strong competitors to U.S. companies.[15]

The euphoria once associated with rapid Asian growth rates faded in 1997, as the region faced what Singapore Prime Minister Goh Chok Tong called, "Asia's worst crisis since the Second World War." A combination of poorly regulated banking activities and an influx of investment dollars from westerners eager to participate in the region's economic growth led to a series

of bad loans for highly speculative real estate ventures. As business failures increased, nervous local and foreign investors began to pull their money out of banks, and real estate values plummeted, leaving the economies of Indonesia, Malaysia, South Korea, and Thailand in shambles.[16]

During the 5 years prior to this economic crisis, U.S. exports to Asia's ten largest markets had increased at an annual rate of 10 percent. This growth can be attributed to three factors:

▼ Asia's fast-growing economies created local markets where U.S. goods and services were in strong demand.

▼ Liberalized trade policies in the region removed many barriers to importing American products.

▼ Foreign investment in Asian countries accelerated, especially by U.S. companies.[17]

China is perhaps the most remarkable success story among a number of Pacific Rim nations with successes of their own. Until recently, China was known as a leading exporter of low unit-value goods like toy dolls and clothing. Today, however, it is challenging both the United States and Japan with its capabilities for low-cost production of high-tech products. Its exports of high-tech goods leaped 75 percent over the past 4 years, making China the world's second fastest-growing economy.[18]

Despite inevitable and periodic declines in the region's economies, Asia's technology-driven markets, rapid urbanization, and growing middle class make it a significant market for U.S. goods and services.

Latin America Latin American countries, in particular Brazil and Argentina, are attracting an unprecedented flow of foreign direct investment. Privatization of port facilities, railways, telecommunications, mining, and energy has contributed important motivation to attract new industry. Another stimulant is the 1995 formation of the MERCOSUR,

Figure 4.3 **Attracting Foreign Investments to France by Emphasizing Local Workforce Strengths**

a cooperative attempt by Argentina, Brazil, Paraguay, and Uruguay to reduce trade barriers. The United States is the MERCOSUR's largest trading partner.

These moves to encourage international investment and trade are a dramatic change from the past, when foreign companies stayed away from Latin America, fearing its political and economic volatility. In addition, the area had compiled a poor record for innovation. Latin American firms spend very little on research and development and avoid active participation in new industries, due in part to difficulties in obtaining start-up capital.

Some of these conditions are changing, however. Pay television is gaining popularity, creating opportunities for local programming in Spanish and Portuguese. Privatization of telecommunications is creating some local technology companies. In Chile, Fundacio Chile, a technology transfer center, has developed new industries such as salmon farming (in which Chile now ranks second in the world), berry growing, and furniture making. The investment firm Cresud is investing in Argentina's farms and looking at growing activity in beef processing and marketing since U.S. restrictions on beef imports from the country have been lifted.[19]

Latin America is a big market for high-technology products. Microsoft sells $500 million in software in Latin America, and the total is soaring. "We are experiencing 30 to 40 percent growth every year," says Alessandro Annoscia, Microsoft's enterprise customer manager for Latin America. "We believe the region is underinvested still in the information technology business."[20]

As trade barriers slip away and governments and economies stabilize throughout the region, Latin America is becoming home to a growing contingent of multinationals and competing strongly in areas such as electric utilities. "Latin America is for big players now," says Ricardo Alvial Muñoz, investor relations director for the Chilean energy conglomerate Enersis. Enersis, Latin America's largest private-sector electricity firm, provides electric power to 32 million people in the region.[21]

Absolute and Comparative Advantage

Few countries can produce all the goods and services needed by their people. For centuries, trading has been the way that countries can meet those needs. If a country can focus on producing what it does best, it can export surplus domestic output and buy foreign products that it lacks or cannot efficiently produce. The potential for foreign sales of a particular good or service depends largely on whether the country has an absolute advantage or comparative advantage.

A country has an *absolute advantage* in making a product for which it can maintain a monopoly or that it can produce at a lower cost than any competitor. For centuries, China enjoyed an absolute advantage in silk production. This luxurious fabric was woven from fibers recovered from silkworm cocoons, making it a prized raw material in high-quality clothing such as the silk neckties shown in Figure 4.4. Demand among Europeans for silk led to establishment of the famous *silk road,* a 5,000-mile link between Rome and the ancient Chinese capital city of Xian.

Absolute advantages are rare these days. One good current example is the diamond-mining industry in Russia and South Africa. However, some countries manage to approximate absolute advantages in some products: Middle Eastern countries' control over oil can endanger U.S. supplies when a threat of war or political unrest emerges. The Brazilian and Colombian dominance in coffee production can create price surges when crop damage limits harvests.

By contrast, a nation can develop a *comparative advantage* in a product if it can supply it more efficiently and at a lower price than it can supply other goods, compared to the outputs of other countries. China has long held a comparative advantage in producing toys and clothing due to very low labor costs. On the other hand, Japan has maintained a comparative advantage in producing electronics by preserving efficiency and technological expertise. U.S. exports reflect the country's highly industrialized environment and variety of natural resources. U.S. firms export cars, computers,

Figure 4.4 **Silk: Source of Ancient China's Absolute Advantage**

and grain overseas, and they import clothing, oil, and television sets.

MEASURING TRADE BETWEEN NATIONS

Clearly, engaging in international trade provides tremendous competitive advantages to both the countries and companies involved. Any attempt to measure global business activity requires an understanding of the concepts of the balance of trade and balance of payments. Another important factor is currency exchange rates.

A country's **balance of trade** is the relationship between its exports and imports. If a country exports more than it imports, it achieves a favorable balance of trade, called a *trade surplus.* If it imports more than it exports, it produces an unfavorable balance of trade, called a *trade deficit.* The United States has run a trade deficit every year since 1976. Despite being the world's top exporter, the U.S. economy feels an even greater appetite for foreign-made goods. The trade deficit peaked in 1987 at $152 billion, dropped to $28 billion by 1991, and crept up to $114 billion in 1997.[22]

As Figure 4.5 shows, the export total for 1997 of $78 billion was more than offset by imports that topped the $1 trillion mark for the first time. Almost all of this deficit results from trade with Japan ($56 billion) and China ($50 billion). China is expected to surpass Japan prior to 2000 as the country with which the United States has its largest trade deficit. In addition, the trade deficit will continue to grow due to Asia's economic problems.[23]

A nation's balance of trade plays a central role in determining its **balance of payments**—the overall flow of money into or out of a country. Other factors also affect the balance of payments, including overseas loans and borrowing, international investments, profits from such investments, and foreign aid payments. Figure 4.6 illustrates the components of a country's balance of payments. A favorable balance of payments, or a *balance of payments surplus,* brings more money into a country than out of it. An unfavorable balance of payments, or *balance of payments deficit,* takes more money out of the country than enters it.

Major U.S. Exports and Imports

The United States, with combined exports and imports of $2 trillion, leads the world in international trade activity. Table 4.2 shows the top ten categories of goods exchanged by U.S. exporters and importers.

With $150 billion in annual imports from the United States, Canada is the largest single-country market for U.S. exports. The Pacific Rim countries as a region account for over $200 billion in annual U.S. imports.[24] While the United States imports more goods than it exports, the opposite is true for services. U.S. exporters sell more than $235 billion in annual service exports, about half of the total from travel and tourism—money spent by foreign nationals visiting the United States. U.S. service exports include business and technical services such as engineering, financial services, computing, legal services, and entertainment. Others involve technologies developed by U.S. firms that earn royalties and licensing fees from users abroad. Many service exporters are well-known companies, like American Express, American Airlines, America Online, AT&T, Citibank, Walt Disney, Allstate Insurance, and Federal Express, as well as retailers such as Foot Locker, The Gap, Office Depot, Toys 'R' Us, and PriceCostco warehouse clubs.

| **Figure 4.5** | **U.S. International Trade in Goods and Services** |

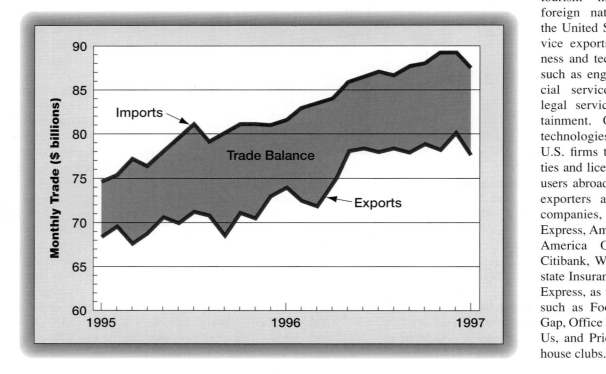

As developing nations industrialize, they often call on the expertise of U.S. financial and legal professionals. For example, when China's state-owned corporations needed to raise funds in international markets, accounting firm Arthur Andersen sent over 1,000 professionals to bring U.S. accounting standards to the country.[25]

Entertainment is a major growth area for U.S. service exports. "The North American market is basically saturated," says Daniel Friego, director of Buena Vista Studio's European distribution. Buena Vista, a Disney division, is not only exporting its U.S. movies to Europe and Asia, but it also produces feature films specifically for local audiences. "Internationally, we're seeing more people going to the movies," says Friego.[26]

The Discovery Channel also takes its TV shows worldwide to create a global television network. It reaches over 87 million subscribers in 90 countries, from New Zealand to Saudi Arabia. As Figure 4.7 indicates, the Discovery Channel's blend of science and technology, world cultures, nature, and adventure stories is a successful formula for attracting audiences around the globe, including 35 million Latin American viewers. Discovery's Cartoon Network is Asia's most popular children's network, seen in over 9 million homes and broadcast in three languages: English, Mandarin, and Thai. The Cartoon Network also has 5 million fans in Latin America and another 31 million in Europe.[27]

U.S. annual imports worth more than $1 trillion rank the country as the world's leading importer. American tastes for foreign-made goods, reflected by the huge trade deficits with the consumer-goods exporting nations of China and Japan, also extend to European products. Last year, the 15 EU countries shipped $6.5 billion of consumer-ready foods like cheese, liquor, and chocolate to U.S. buyers.[28]

U.S. economic growth is luring even more companies to try their luck in this market. "The U.S. market is huge, and

Figure 4.6 **Balance of Payments Components**

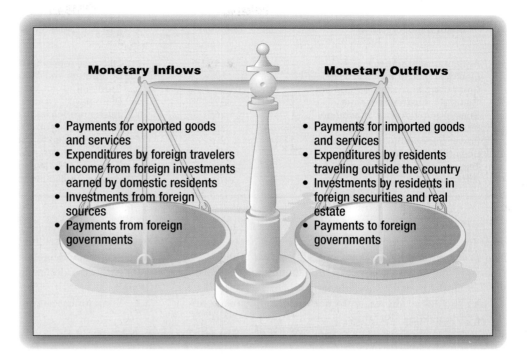

we can't afford not to be there," says Mitsuo Hama, general manager of Rheon Automatic Machinery Co., a Japanese manufacturer of pasta-making machines. Rheon hopes to triple its exports to the United States by 2000. Similarly, another Japanese firm, Iris Ohyama Co., is exporting its flower pots, storage containers, and garbage bins to retailers like Staples and Target. The plastics company's $60 million in revenues from U.S. sales represent 10 percent of its total revenues, allowing it to survive in the face of Japan's economic downturn. "To survive," says owner Kentaroh Ohyama, "you have to succeed internationally."[29]

Exchange Rates

A nation's **exchange rate** is the rate at which its currency can be exchanged for the currencies of other nations. Each currency's exchange rate is usually quoted in terms of an-

Business Directory

balance of trade surplus or deficit relationship between a nation's exports and imports.

balance of payments surplus or deficit flow of money into or out of a country.

exchange rate value of one nation's currency relative to the currencies of other countries.

Table 4.2	Top Ten U.S. Exports and Imports			
	Major Export Product	Amount (billions)	Major Import Product	Amount (billions)
1.	Agricultural products	$59	1. Electrical machinery	$76
2.	Electrical machinery	57	2. Computers and office equipment	67
3.	Computers and office equipment	36	3. Crude oil	51
4.	General industrial machinery	27	4. Clothing	42
5.	Specialized industrial machinery	26	5. Telecommunications equipment	34
6.	Motor vehicle parts	25	6. Agricultural products	33
7.	Power generating equipment	22	7. Cars produced in Canada	25
8.	Scientific instruments	21	8. General industrial machinery	25
9.	Telecommunications equipment	20	9. Power generating equipment	23
10.	Airplanes	19	10. Cars produced in other countries (not Canada)	22

other important currency, for example, the number of Mexican pesos needed to purchase one U.S. dollar. Table 4.3 compares the values of several national currencies against the U.S. dollar over a 12-month period.

As the table shows, currency values fluctuate, or "float," depending on the supply and demand for each currency in the international market. In this system of *floating exchange rates,* currency traders create a market for the world's currencies based on each country's relative trade and investment prospects. In theory, this market permits exchange rates to vary freely according to supply and demand. In practice, exchange rates do not float in total freedom. National governments often intervene in the currency markets to adjust the exchange rates of their own currencies. Also, nations form currency blocs by linking their exchange rates to each other, and many governments practice protectionist policies that seek to guard their economies against trade imbalances. **Devaluation** describes a fall in a currency's value relative to other currencies or to a fixed standard. The dramatic changes in the value of the South Korean and Thai cur-

rencies shown in Table 4.3 are examples of devaluations. Each currency decreased to about half of its former value relative to the dollar due to the recent economic crisis in Asia.

Sometimes, national governments take deliberate action to devalue their currencies as a way to increase exports. Although devaluation may not change the price of a U.S.-made product, a buyer in Austria receives a de facto price cut due to a devaluation of the U.S. dollar, because he or she would gain more dollars for the same amount of Austrian schillings. Not only would U.S. goods sell for lower prices abroad, but foreign tourists would find that American vacations would cost less, too. At the same time, the U.S. currency devaluation would force U.S. consumers to pay more than before for imported products. American companies would also find foreign goods more expensive, while foreign firms would be attracted to cheaper U.S. products.

Exchange rate changes can quickly wipe out or create a competitive advantage, so they are important factors in decisions about whether or not to invest abroad. If the

Figure 4.7 **Entertainment: A Major U.S. Service Export**

dollar rises in price relative to the yen, for instance, a dollar will buy more yen. For example, in 1995, it took 84 yen to buy one U.S. dollar. By 1998, the value had dropped to almost 130 yen per dollar. As a result, Japanese products became less expensive than before the change. Japanese exports to the United States increased, and U.S. firms faced greater competition.[30]

Currencies that owners can easily convert into other currencies are called *hard* currencies. Examples include the U.S. dollar, British pound, Japanese yen, and Swiss franc. The Russian ruble and many eastern European currencies are considered *soft* currencies, because

Table 4.3	Foreign Exchange Rates for Selected Currencies		
Country	**Currency Unit**	**1997 Exchange Rate (per U.S. dollar)**	**1998 Exchange Rate (per U.S. dollar)**
Canada	Dollar	1.3	1.4
China	Yuan	8.3	8.3
France	French franc	5.4	6.1
Germany	Deutsche mark	1.6	1.8
India	Rupee	36.0	39.0
Italy	Lira	1,568.0	1,790.0
Japan	Yen	118.0	127.0
Mexico	Peso	7.8	8.6
South Korea	Won	854.0	1,564.0
Switzerland	Swiss franc	1.4	1.5
Thailand	Baht	26.0	45.0
United Kingdom	Pound	0.59	0.63

they cannot be readily converted. Exporters that trade with these countries often prefer to barter, accepting payment in oil, timber, or other commodities that they can resell for hard currency payments.

BARRIERS TO INTERNATIONAL TRADE

All businesses encounter barriers in their operations, whether they sell only to local customers or trade in international markets. For example, national food chains distribute different products to rural U.S. stores than to large chain stores in major cities. These differences and difficulties are multiplied many times over for businesses with international operations. International companies may also have to reformulate their products to accommodate different tastes in new locations. Frito-Lay exports cheeseless Cheetos to Asia, while Domino's Pizza offers pickled ginger pizzas at its Indian fast-food restaurants.

In addition to social and cultural differences, companies engaged in international business also face economic barriers as well as legal and political ones. Some of the hurdles shown in Figure 4.8 are easily breached, while others require major changes in a company's business strategy. To successfully compete in global markets, companies and their managers must understand not only how these barriers affect international trade but also how to overcome them.

Social and Cultural Differences

Understanding and respecting social and cultural differences, ranging from language to customs to educational background to religious holidays, is a critical part of the process leading to international business success. Businesspeople armed with knowledge of host countries' cultures, languages, social values, and religious attitudes

| Figure 4.8 | **Barriers to International Trade** |

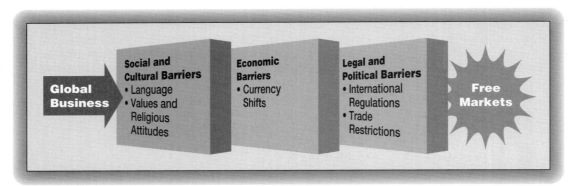

come well equipped to the negotiating table. Acute sensitivity to such elements as attitudes, forms of address and dress, body language, and timeliness also help them to win customers and achieve their business objectives. Without this knowledge, companies may discover that their goods and services will not appeal to customers in foreign countries. The Business Tool Kit provides advice on avoiding social and cultural blunders when doing business abroad.

Language Understanding a business colleague's local language is a critical factor in international business. Companies and their representatives must not only choose correct and appropriate words, but they must also translate words correctly to convey the intended meanings. Companies may need to rename products or rewrite slogans for foreign markets. Imagine the reaction in Japan when Microsoft's marketing tag line, "Where do you want to go today?" was translated, "If you don't know where you want to go, we'll make sure you get taken."[31]

Potential communication barriers include more than mistranslation. Companies may present messages through inappropriate media, overlook local customs and regulations, or ignore differences in taste. For example, *Good Housekeeping* does not try to export the same magazine it sells in the United States. "That would be cultural suicide," according to editor-in-chief Ellen Levine. For the Japanese market, *Good Housekeeping* changed the content to avoid articles about idealized America and eliminated its Seal of Approval, which confused Japanese women. The magazine hired Japanese writers to produce stories that appealed to that country's readers, usually younger than its typical U.S. readers. In addition, *Good Housekeeping* needed to print the magazine on higher-quality paper than it used for the U.S. version to appeal to Japanese readers.[32]

Values and Religious Attitudes Even though today's world is shrinking in many ways, people in different countries do not necessarily share the same values or religious attitudes. Marked differences remain in workers' attitudes between traditionally capitalist countries and those adopting new capitalist systems and even among traditionally capitalist countries.

For example, U.S. society places a different value on the labor force than attitudes common in Europe. U.S. employees often receive no paid vacation benefits during their first year of employment and then get 2 weeks vacation, working up to 3 or 4 weeks over many years. In Europe, the standard vacation time is 5 to 6 weeks per year. A U.S. company that opens a manufacturing plant in Europe would not be able to hire any workers without offering vacations in line with local business practices.

U.S. culture promotes national unity tolerant of regional differences. The United States is viewed as a national market with a single economy. European countries that are part of the 15-member European Union are trying to create a similar marketplace. However, many resist the idea of being European citizens first and British, Italian, or French citizens second. British consumers differ from Italians in important ways, and U.S. companies that fail to recognize this variation will run into problems with brand acceptance.[33]

DID YOU KNOW?

Press reports have chronicled some classic international snafus resulting from faulty translations:

▼ In South America, Parker Pen Co. once indicated by mistake that its product would prevent unwanted pregnancies.

▼ Although the name of Chevy's Nova model literally means "star" in Spanish, Puerto Rican car buyers shunned it. When spoken aloud, it sounds like *no va*, which means "It doesn't go."

▼ In Japan, Ronald McDonald's name changed to Donald McDonald to make it easier to pronounce.

When in Rome . . . or Riyadh

When managers venture overseas, they are moving into mysterious cultural waters. Unless they research the customs of the countries they visit, they risk making major etiquette mistakes—and losing sales in the process. Here are some tips to help you avoid offending your international business colleagues, whether you are in Europe or the Middle East.

▼ *Gift giving* Some gifts that are commonly exchanged in the United States are associated with funerals elsewhere: flowers in Ghana and clocks in China, for example. If you express your admiration for a Ming vase while dining at the home of a Chinese colleague, the host will probably give it to you, as he believes it his responsibility to take care of your every wish. He will expect you to reciprocate in kind. In Latin America and throughout Asia, gifts of knives and handkerchiefs mean that the givers wish hardship on the recipients. Presenting gifts with the left hand in Moslem cultures is taboo, since it is believed to be the unclean hand.

▼ *Negotiating styles* In China, a signed contract is viewed as acknowledging an agreement to work together, not the final deal. A Chinese businessperson may want to change the terms. Indonesian and Japanese people desire to avoid confrontation and say *no* many ways, so understanding requires careful listening.

▼ *Scheduling* Don't arrive late for meetings in the Netherlands, as Dutch executives prize punctuality. In Russia, however, meetings often start late and run hours longer than expected, so allow flexibility in your schedule.

▼ *Gestures* The gesture of drawing a finger across one's throat means "I love you" in Swaziland, an interpretation far removed from its U.S. meaning. The gesture with the thumb and forefinger making a circle means "A-OK" in the United States, but it is considered obscene in Brazil.

▼ *Shaking hands* In Europe, businesspeople shake hands when they meet even after being apart for short periods, such as lunch breaks. The style of the handshake is also an important consideration. The French and Japanese expect one firm shake, and a Japanese handshake may include a slight bow. Arab and Latin American businesspeople typically favor lighter and more lingering handshakes. Ending the handshake too soon could be interpreted as a rejection.

Gifts bring particularly important risks, but what constitutes a good gift? Two general suggestions are gifts that reflect your home country—things like coffee-table books with photos of U.S. cities and landscapes and uniquely American fare such as maple syrup, Southern barbecue sauce, a baseball cap from a local team, a jacket from a well-known university, or a souvenir from the local golf course. (Just make sure that there are no "Made in Taiwan" labels on the bottom!) In Japan, difficult-to-find items like a basket of U.S.-grown citrus fruits make excellent gifts. A small, silver compass makes a wonderful gift for Muslim associates. No matter where in the world they may be, they can always locate Mecca and perform daily prayers.

Sources: Dean Foster, "The Gift that Keeps on Grating," *Brandweek*, February 23, 1998, p. 21; "Five Tips for International Handshaking," *Sales and Marketing Management*, July 1997, p. 90; and Nicole Crawford, "When in Ghana, Hold the Flowers," *Promo*, September 1997, p. 132.

Whirlpool, the U.S. appliance manufacturer, discovered that European value differences affected acceptance of its products. Company managers were surprised to learn that Scandinavians wanted washing machines that would spin-dry clothes much more thoroughly than those sold in southern Italy, where consumers prefer to dry clothes naturally, taking advantage of their warm weather.

Companies like Whirlpool can learn from disappointing experiences and rethink their strategies. While intent on maintaining its global manufacturing plan, Whirlpool restructured its European operations and laid off almost 8,000 employees. By 1998, total net earnings had doubled those of the previous year. Company officials credited the profit increase to improved European operations.[34]

Because religion plays an important role in every society, businesspeople must cultivate sensitivity to the dominant religions in countries where they operate. Understanding religious cycles and the timing of major holidays can help to prevent embarrassing moments when scheduling meetings, trade shows, conferences, or events such as the dedication of a new manufacturing plant. For example, people doing business in Saudi Arabia must take into account the month-long Ramadan observance, when companies do no work after noon. Friday is the Moslem Sabbath, so the Saudi work week runs from Saturday through Thursday.[35]

Companies can unknowingly offend members of religious groups. Nike's Summer Hoops basketball shoes sported the word "air" written in stylized script with flame-like letters, as shown in Figure 4.9. Moslems complained that the logo looked like the Arabic word for Allah, or God, and the Council on American-Islamic Relations threatened a worldwide boycott. Nike recalled the shoes and discontinued production.[36]

Economic Differences

Business opportunities are flourishing in densely populated countries such as China and India, as local consumers eagerly buy Western products. While such prospects might tempt American firms, managers must first consider the economic factors involved in doing business in these markets. A country's size, per-capita income, and stage of economic development are among the economic factors to consider when evaluating it as a candidate for an international business venture.

Perspective: Global.
Language: Local.
Space: Available.

In 1998, the popular newsmagazine *Time* launched a Latin American edition. While the Spanish-language edition reported on such global issues as cloning, the decidedly Latin American focus of the new magazine generated sales of over 800,000 copies.

Along with these factors, businesses should also consider a country's infrastructure. **Infrastructure** refers to basic systems of communication (television, radio, print media, telecommunications), transportation (roads and highways, railroads, airports), and energy facilities (power plants, gas and electric utilities). These economic factors are more critical in developing countries. People in Japan enjoy a high standard of living. They live in a society with a well-established infrastructure and a per-capita GDP of about $24,000. Their neighbors in China, where the per-capita GDP is only $3,200, live in much more primitive conditions, and few families have telephone and electric service.

The need for improving national infrastructures is a priority of such global firms as telecommunications giant AT&T, as shown in Figure 4.10. AT&T provides long-distance service to every country and territory in the world—280 total—and has operations and business alliances in over 30 countries, providing satellite, digital, and wireless communication services.

Despite growing similarities in infrastructure, when crossing borders the world over, people encounter basic economic differences: national currencies. Although many countries trade in U.S. dollars, firms may trade in the local currency—for example, the Mexican peso, Chinese yuan, Indonesian rupee, Swiss franc, Japanese yen, and English pound. Foreign currency fluctuations may present added problems for global businesses.

Currency Shifts As explained earlier in the chapter, the values of the world's major currencies fluctuate in relation to each other. The recent financial crisis in Asian markets has shown how exchange rates affect the economic environment for businesses. As exchange rates in many Asian countries dropped, people who owned U.S. dollars were able to buy more than they could have before the changes. This development brought an advantage to U.S. residents who dreamed of relaxing on vacations to Bali as well as to businesses importing clothing made in China and Korea. With the increasing value of the dollar compared to local currencies, tourists pay significantly less for hotel rooms and food than if they were traveling when the value of the dollar had fallen.

Residents, local businesses, and U.S. firms depending on Asian sales found themselves in much less fortunate circumstances. Vans Inc., a shoemaker with substantial Asian export sales, cut its workforce by 30 percent in response to sharply reduced sales there, particularly in Japan. San Diego-based Qualcomm, a company that supplies wireless telecommunications systems to Asia and developing countries, laid off 700 employees following cancellation of orders for circuit components from South Korea.[37]

Political and Legal Differences

Similar to social, cultural, and economic differences, legal and political differences in host countries can pose barriers to international trade. Indonesian laws prohibit foreign firms from creating their own wholesale or retail distribution channels, forcing outside companies to work through local distributors. Brazilian law requires foreign-owned manufacturers to buy most of their supplies from local vendors. Managers involved in international business must be well-versed in legislation that affects their industries if they want to compete in today's world marketplace.

Some countries impose general trade restrictions. Others have established detailed rules that regulate how foreign companies can do business. The one consistency among all countries is the striking lack of consistent laws and regulations governing the conduct of business.

Political Climate An important factor in any international business investment is the stability of the political climate. The political structures of many nations promote stability similar to that in the United States. Other nations, such as Iraq, Congo, and Bosnia, feature quite different—and frequently changing—structures. Host nations often pass laws designed to protect their own interests, often at the expense of foreign businesses. In South Korea, for example, government subsidies benefit domestic consumer electronics producers, and government restrictions limit imports of electronic equipment.

During the past decade, the political structures of Russia, Turkey, the former Yugoslavia, Hong Kong, and several eastern European countries (including the Czech Republic and Poland) have seen dramatic changes. Such political changes almost always bring changes in the legal environment. Hong Kong is an example of an economy where political developments produced changes in the legal and cultural environments.

Hong Kong Reunited
In 1997, Hong Kong ended its status as a British colony and rejoined the People's Republic of China. As Figure 4.11 suggests, this tiny former seaport colony on the southern edge of China is blessed with a rich culture, one of the world's great ports, and an energetic, entrepreneurial population. Previously considered the freest economy in the world, Hong Kong has entered a period of uncertainty as both local and Western businesses have worried about dealing with the Chinese government with its penchant for tight control.[38]

In the months following the takeover, business as usual continued in Hong Kong, and China seemed more interested in continued business success for the former colony than in promoting any ideological changes. A few changes were implemented, such as switching from English to Chinese as the official language. In addition, some traditional legal premises changed with the extension of Chinese laws to Hong Kong. Chinese law operates on the principle that you cannot do something unless the law says you can. In Hong Kong, residents had previously operated on the principle that they could do anything not prohibited by law.[39]

Figure 4.9 **Nike: Discontinuing a Potentially Offensive Shoe Design**

Nike's "Air" logo

The Arabic word for Allah

Figure 4.10 **Telecommunications: Critical Component of a Nation's Infrastructure**

Have you ever studied with a classmate thousands of miles away?

In the near future you'll share your classroom with students thousands of miles away. Using powerful, two-way sound and video hook-ups. That will let you study with anyone who shares your interests. No matter where they are.

The world-wide classroom. The company that will bring it to you is AT&T.

YOU WILL

AT&T

Legal Environment When conducting business internationally, managers must be familiar with three dimensions of the legal environment: U.S. law, international regulations, and the laws of the countries where they plan to trade. Some laws protect the rights of foreign companies to compete in the United States. Other laws dictate actions allowed for U.S. companies doing business in foreign countries.

For example, the 1978 *Foreign Corrupt Practices Act* forbids U.S. companies from bribing foreign officials, political candidates, or government representatives. This act, passed by Congress in a rush to clean up Watergate-era misdeeds, prescribes fines and jail time for American managers who are aware of illegal payoffs. By contrast, French and German laws not only decline to prohibit payments of bribes to foreign officials, but they allow tax deductions for these expenses.[40]

Still, official corruption is an international problem. Its pervasiveness, combined with U.S. prohibitions, creates a difficult obstacle for Americans who want to do business in many foreign countries. Chinese pay *huilu,* and Russians rely on *vzyatka.* In the Middle East, palms are greased with *baksheesh,* while a bribe in Mexico is called *una mordida*—"a bite." Figure 4.12 compares 53 countries based on surveys of perceived corruption.[41]

The *Helms-Burton Act,* a controversial law enacted in 1996, is another example of a legal barrier to international commerce. The act imposes trade sanctions against Cuba and permits U.S. companies and citizens to sue foreign companies and their executives that use assets expropriated from U.S. owners to do business in Cuba. It also denies U.S. visas to executives of firms facing lawsuits for violating the act.

The growth of e-commerce with the unfolding information age has introduced new elements to the legal climate of international business. Ideas, patents, brand names, trademarks, copyrights, and other intellectual property are difficult to police given the availability of information on the Internet. However, some countries are

Figure 4.11 **Hong Kong's Changing Political Environment**

adopting laws to protect information obtained by electronic contacts. For example, Malaysia's Computer Crimes Act carries stiff fines and long jail terms for those convicted of illegally accessing computers and using information that passes through them. China also restricts use of the Internet with the stated objective of "protecting national security and social stability."[42] The United States is taking a less restrictive stance on regulating e-commerce, favoring a market-determined approach. This chapter's Solving an Ethical Controversy discusses another element of the legal environment for trade with China.

International Regulations To regulate international commerce, the United States and many other countries have ratified treaties and signed agreements that dictate the conduct of international business and protect some of its activities. The United States has entered into many *friendship, commerce, and navigation (FCN) treaties* with other nations. Such treaties address many aspects of international business relations, including the right to conduct business in the treaty partner's domestic market. Other international business agreements concern product standards, patents, trademarks, reciprocal tax policies, export controls, international air travel, and international communications.

Many types of regulations affect the actions of managers doing business in international markets. Worldwide producers and marketers must not only maintain required minimum quality levels for all the countries in which they operate, but they must also comply with numerous specific, local regulations. For example, the European Union has introduced a standardized system of presenting ecological information on labels for certain products. Other European regulations deal with information and privacy issues. The Data Protection Act in the United Kingdom, for instance, restricts the ways in which direct marketers can use computer-generated lists for promotional campaigns.

| Figure 4.12 | **Corruption in Business and Government: The Clean and the Sleazy** |

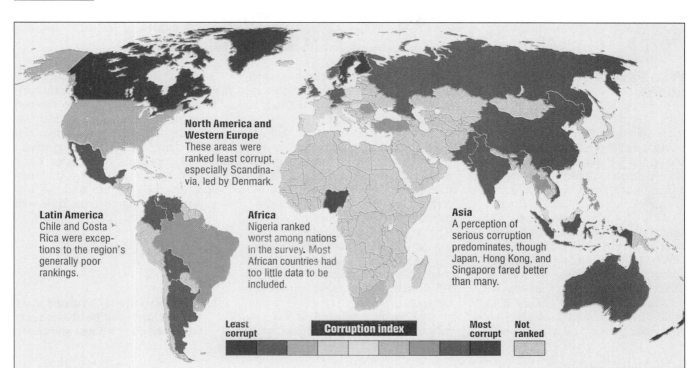

Host-country laws also influence the international efforts of foreign companies. Borg-Warner, a Chicago-based auto parts manufacturer, was a recent victim of Chinese laws because of an ill-fated venture with a local partner, SATF. The planned joint effort ended when Borg-Warner learned that its supposed partner was actually opening a rival transmission factory. Borg-Warner sued in Chinese courts and lost. SATF's countersuit was successful, resulting in the Chinese firm being awarded all of Borg-Warner's $2.2 million investment in the project. To make matters worse, the U.S. firm was not informed of the result until after the deadline for filing appeals.[43]

To avoid problems resulting from unfamiliarity with local or international laws affecting trade, firms often rely on expertise provided by government agencies and private consultants. Figure 4.13 describes how the international management advisor Arthur Andersen guided a U.S. firm through a maze of foreign business and tax regulations.

Software piracy offers an example of huge problems that can result from the lack of international regulations. Chinese outlaws illegally reproduce U.S. software as well as music and movies, costing American firms billions of dollars in lost revenues. Latin America is another area with rampant piracy: Of every $100 in software sales there, an estimated

$68 goes to pirates. Microsoft manager Alessandro Annoscia estimates that without piracy, the company's Latin American sales would be over $1 billion, rather than $500,000. He is optimistic that the company is making progress, though. Mexico, in particular, has enacted strong antipiracy laws.[44]

Types of Trade Restrictions

Trade restrictions such as tariffs and administrative procedures create additional barriers to international business. They may limit consumer choices while simultaneously increasing the costs of foreign-made products. Trade restrictions are also imposed to protect citizens' security, health, and jobs; for example, a government may limit exports of strategic and defense-related goods to unfriendly countries to protect its security. Bans on imports of insecticide-contaminated farm products protect health. Restrictions on imports protect domestic jobs in the importing country.

Trade restrictions grow out of a country's legal structure, often in response to the political environment. Some restrictions, such as those applied by the U.S. government to deter trade with Iraq and Cuba, are intended to punish or protest countries' political actions. Other restrictions

SOLVING AN ETHICAL CONTROVERSY

Who Favors China the Most?

Every year, questions about trade with China incite predictable drama. Should the U.S. government grant the world's largest country—and the last major communist power—most-favored-nation (MFN) trading status?

With U.S.-China trade totaling $65 billion, it is not surprising that global business giants like Boeing, General Motors, TRW, and United Technologies lobby hard each year to continue China's MFN status. Each has invested hundreds of millions of dollars there, and future deals could be at stake. Last year, Boeing lost a $1.5 billion jet order

to Europe's Airbus Industrie because, in the words of China's premier Li Peng, "They do not attach political strings to cooperation with China."

In reality, most opposition to MFN status for China has nothing to do with trade. Efforts to revoke it have traditionally focused on concerns about human rights, political freedom, and use of prison labor in factories. More recent allegations of wrongdoing involve possible illegal political contributions during the 1996 U.S. presidential elections. Opponents want to deny MFN treatment as a way to punish China or at least force it to improve its human rights record.

But how big a deal is most-favored-nation status? The name implies more

beneficial treatment than a country actually experiences. MFN status qualifies the trading partner for low import taxes and streamlined negotiating processes. However, every nation but seven currently has this designation. Only Afghanistan, Cuba, Laos, Montenegro, North Korea, Serbia, and Vietnam lack MFN status, and the U.S. government currently bans trade with three others—Iran, Iraq, and Libya.

Should China Have MFN Trade Status?

PRO

1. As global powers, China and the United States must be able to trade with each other without erecting

---

Figure 4.13   **Using Consultants to Avoid International Legal Problems**

barriers designed to achieve objectives unrelated to trade.

2. Building business and economic ties—and therefore creating jobs—is one way of improving human rights.

3. Since other countries are already actively pursuing investments in China, denying MFN status would benefit U.S. business competitors, should China retaliate.

4. China's population of 1.25 billion is a potentially huge consumer market. The United States should not risk access to these potential sales by undermining trade relations.

5. With Hong Kong now under Chinese control, failure to renew MFN status could put valuable, long-term business relationships at risk.

CON

1. The Chinese government has made no move toward halting human-rights violations against its people. Withdrawing MFN status could force changes, if the country's leaders believe their economy might suffer.

2. China is a known dealer of weapons to "rogue states" around the world and should be punished for these sales.

3. The United States runs a huge trade deficit with China, in part because that nation uses unfair trading practices. The U.S. government should end China's MFN status until those practices are discontinued.

SUMMARY

Because China's MFN status is as much a political litmus test as a practical trade matter, annual debates over the issue will continue to pit human-rights protesters against business interests. Human-rights advocates want to use the annual waiver to get China's leaders to improve their record. Big business wants to continue economic ties with the country to generate sales and maintain the flow of profits.

Sources: Donna Smith, "Daley Sees Uphill Battle on China in U.S. Congress," Reuters Limited, April 15, 1999; Paul Magnusso, "China: The Great Brawl," *Business Week*, June 16, 1997, pp. 32-34; Bill Nichols, "This Year, Sharper Edge to Trade Debate," *USA Today*, May 20–21, 1997, p. 7A; and Greg McDonald, "China Trade Status Survives in House," *Houston Chronicle*, June 24, 1997.

---

are imposed to promote trade with certain countries. Still others protect countries from unfair competition. Table 4.4 summarizes the arguments for and against trade restrictions.

Regardless of the political reasons for trade restrictions, most take the form of tariffs. In addition to tariffs, governments impose a number of nontariff—or administrative—barriers. These include quotas and embargoes.

Tariffs Tariffs are taxes, surcharges, or duties on foreign products. Governments assess two types of tariffs—revenue and protective tariffs—both of which make imports more expensive for domestic buyers. Revenue tariffs generate income for the government. For example, upon returning home, U.S. leisure travelers who bring back goods are taxed 10 percent of the amount in excess of $400. This duty goes directly to the U.S. Treasury. The sole purpose of a protective tariff is to raise the retail price of imported products to match or exceed the prices of similar products manufactured in the home country.

Many Americans prefer luxury German and Japanese cars to comparable American cars. If the United States imposed a protective tariff on foreign-made automobiles, the objective would be to boost the financial incentive to buy domestic cars. Current U.S. tariffs discourage importing such luxury goods as Rolex watches. In other words, protective tariffs seek to level the playing field for local competitors.

Nontariff Barriers Nontariff, or administrative, trade barriers restrict imports in more subtle ways than tariffs. These measures may take such forms as customs barriers, quotas on imports, unnecessarily restrictive standards for imports, and export subsidies. Because many countries have recently substantially reduced tariffs or eliminated them entirely, these nontariff barriers are increasingly used to boost exports and control flows of imported products. For example, pharmaceutical companies wait 4 years on average for approval to import drugs to Japan. During this time, a Japanese drug company gains time to develop a local version of the product.

Customs regulations can also create trade barriers. France tried to protect its manufacturers of videocassette recorders by requiring all imported VCRs to pass through one customs station at Poitiers. Located in the middle of the country, the station was hard to reach, open only a few

Business Directory

tariff tax imposed by the importing country on goods that cross its borders.

Table 4.4	Arguments For and Against Trade Restrictions

For 👍	Against 👎
Protect national defense and citizens' health	Raise prices for consumers
Protect new or weak industries	Restrict consumer choices
Protect against a practice called *dumping,* in which products are sold for less abroad than in the home market, competing unfairly with domestic goods.	
Protect domestic jobs in the face of foreign competition	Result in loss of jobs
Retaliate for another country's trade restrictions	Cause inefficient allocations of international resources

days each week, and staffed by only a few customs officials who insisted on inspecting individual packages. This totally legal system caused major delays in processing VCR imports.[45]

Quotas limit the amounts of particular products that countries can import during specified time periods. Limits may be set as quantities (number of cars or bushels of wheat) or as values (dollars worth of cigarettes). Governments regularly set quotas for agricultural products and sometimes for imported automobiles.

Quotas help to prevent **dumping,** a practice that developed during the 1980s. In one form of dumping, a company sells products abroad at prices below their costs of production. In another, a company exports a large quantity of a product at a lower price than the same product in the home market and drives down the price of the domestic product. Dumping benefits domestic consumers in the importing market, but it hurts domestic producers. It also allows companies to gain quick entry to foreign markets.

While charges of dumping are difficult to prove, countries may establish quotas if they suspect it. In addition to establishing quotas, companies can protect themselves against dumping by requesting that their government impose an antidumping duty, thus offsetting the cost advantage of the foreign good.

More severe than a quota, an **embargo** imposes a total ban on importing a designated product or a total halt to trading with a particular country. In addition to their punitive effects, embargoes can protect citizens' health. Embargo durations can vary. The U.S. government imposed an embargo on trade with Cuba in 1960, 2 years after a successful revolution led by Fidel Castro. Cuban exports such as sugar and cigars were not permitted to enter the United States, and U.S. companies were prohibited from investing in Cuba. The 1991 embargo imposed on Iraq in response to its invasion of Kuwait prohibits imports of Iraqi oil to the United States.

Another form of administrative trade restriction involves **exchange controls.** Imposed through a central bank or government agency, exchange controls affect both exporters and importers. Firms that gain foreign currencies through exporting are required to sell them to the central bank or another agency. Importers must buy foreign currencies to pay for their purchases from the same agency. The exchange control authority can then allocate, expand, or restrict foreign exchange to satisfy national policy goals.

REDUCING BARRIERS TO INTERNATIONAL TRADE

While tariffs and administrative barriers still restrict trade, overall the world is moving toward free trade. Several types of organizations ease barriers to international trade. These include groups that monitor trade policies and practices and institutions that offer monetary assistance. Another type of federation designed to ease trade barriers is the multinational economic community, such as the European Union. This section looks at the roles these organizations play.

Business Directory

World Trade Organization (WTO) institution with 132 members that succeeds GATT in monitoring and enforcing trade agreements.

Organizations Promoting International Trade

For the 50 years of its existence, the **General Agree-**

ment on Tariffs and Trade (GATT), an international trade accord, sponsored a series of negotiations, called *rounds,* that substantially reduced worldwide tariffs and other barriers. Major industrialized nations founded the multinational organization in 1947 to work toward reducing tariffs and relaxing import quotas. The last set of negotiations (the Uruguay Round) cut average tariffs by one-third, in excess of $700 billion, reduced farm subsidies, and improved protection for copyright and patent holders. In addition, international trading rules now apply to various service industries, with specific details yet to be resolved. Finally, the new agreement established the **World Trade Organization (WTO)** to succeed GATT. This new organization includes representatives from 132 countries.

World Trade Organization Since 1995, the WTO has monitored GATT agreements among the member nations, mediated disputes, and continued the effort to reduce trade barriers throughout the world. Unlike provisions in GATT, the WTO's decisions are binding on parties involved in disputes.

Trade officials continue to debate the direction for WTO. After the years since its founding, the WTO still faces many problems. Telecommunications is a major area of discussion, with developed countries keen to protect their companies' products. Barriers to providing telecommunications services were lifted in 1998 with implementation of the WTO's agreement to liberalize international trade in basic telecommunications services. Over half of WTO members agreed to open their domestic markets to foreign companies. The agreement covers voice and cellular telephony, data transmission, telex, facsimile, fixed and mobile satellite systems, and paging and personal communications systems.[46]

www.wto.org

World Bank Shortly after the end of World War II, industrialized nations formed an organization to lend money to less-developed and developing countries. The **World Bank** primarily funds projects that build or expand nations' infrastructure networks such as transportation, education, and medical systems and facilities. The World Bank and other development banks provide the largest source of advice and assistance to developing nations.

The World Bank received criticism recently for its support of Asian countries suffering from that region's economic crisis. It was chastised, in particular, for lending

huge amounts of money to Indonesia in spite of reports of extensive government corruption.[47]

International Monetary Fund Established 1 year after the World Bank, the **International Monetary Fund (IMF)** was created to promote trade through financial cooperation, in the process eliminating barriers. The IMF makes short-term loans to member nations that are unable to meet their budgetary expenses.

It operates as a lender of last resort for troubled nations.[48] In exchange for these emergency loans, IMF lenders frequently extract significant commitments from the borrowing nations to address the problems that led to the crises. These steps may include curtailing imports or even devaluing currency.[49]

Throughout its existence, the IMF has worked to prevent financial crises by warning the international business community when countries encounter problems meeting their financial obligations. Often, the IMF lends to countries to keep them from going into default on prior debts and to prevent economic crises in particular countries from spreading to other nations.

> ## They said it
>
> "The next time you see a headline about the IMF lending some country a billion dollars, think about it this way. If you spent $100,000 every day of the week, it would take you more than 27 years to spend a billion dollars."
>
> **Anonymous**

International Economic Communities

International economic communities reduce trade barriers and promote worldwide economic integration. In the simplest approach, countries may establish a *free-trade area* in which they trade freely among themselves without tariffs or trade restrictions. Each maintains its own tariffs for trade outside this area. A *customs union* sets up a free-trade area and specifies a uniform tariff structure for members' trade with nonmember nations. In a *common market,* or economic union, members go beyond a customs union and try to bring all of their government trade rules into agreement. These partnerships succeed in varying degrees.

One example of a free-trade area is the **North American Free Trade Agreement (NAFTA)** enacted by the United States, Canada, and Mexico. Other examples of regional trading blocs include the MERCOSUR customs union (joining Brazil, Argentina, Paraguay, Uruguay, Chile, and Bolivia), and the 10-country ASEAN (Association of South East Asian Nations). To ensure continuing success in meeting its goal of creating peace, stability, and prosperity, ASEAN holds annual meetings where members review developments and give directives for meeting economic and political challenges. Figure 4.14 shows the size of these new economic communities.

Figure 4.14   **NAFTA, MERCOSUR, and ASEAN Free-Trade Areas**

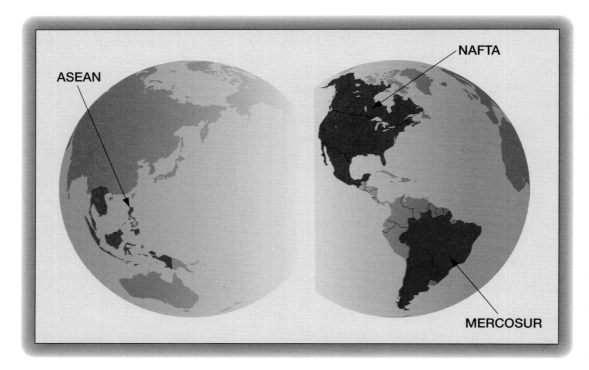

date. Trade between the partners has increased steadily (up 44 percent since 1994), and U.S. exports to Mexico have increased 37 percent, despite the 1994 peso devaluation and subsequent recession in that country. Mexican tariffs on U.S. exports were reduced from 10 percent to 2.9 percent, and U.S. firms now supply more than 75 percent of all Mexican imports.[50]

With the Mexican economic problems and almost 10 years

NAFTA

The North American Free Trade Agreement (NAFTA) became effective in 1994, creating the world's largest free-trade zone with the United States, Canada, and Mexico. By eliminating all trade barriers and investment restrictions among the three nations over a 15-year period, NAFTA opens more doors for free trade. The agreement also eases regulations governing trade in services, such as banking, and establishes uniform legal requirements for protection of intellectual property.

The three signatory countries can trade with one another without tariffs or other trade barriers, simplifying shipments of goods across the partners' borders. Standardized customs and uniform labeling regulations create economic efficiencies and smooth import and export procedures.

By eliminating trade barriers, NAFTA expands choices of products and suppliers for consumers. Domestic producers in the United States, Canada, and Mexico have gained free access to a larger market. Many items are produced at lower per-unit costs than before NAFTA, because companies are able to plan for larger volumes of output.

NAFTA's Effect on the United States, Canada, and Mexico Although NAFTA was approved based on prospects of expanding exports, generating new jobs, and ensuring consumers in all three nations of the best quality products at the best prices, it has produced mixed results to

remaining before all trade barriers must disappear, no clear picture has yet emerged of the overall effect of NAFTA. Pre-NAFTA tariffs, particularly on Mexican goods, were already low, and many U.S. factories had moved to Mexico and other nations prior to 1995. China continues to lead the world in U.S. imports, and Mexico has replaced Japan as the second-largest market for U.S.-made products.[51]

As noted earlier, NAFTA has brought billions of dollars in direct foreign investment to the U.S.-Mexican border region. Because of the gradual elimination of tariffs on goods made or assembled in North America and traded among the three countries, NAFTA encourages companies to locate in North America while maintaining competitiveness.[52]

NAFTA's Effect on Jobs Another promised NAFTA benefit was job creation and increased wages in all three nations. U.S. jobs supported by exports to Mexico and Canada have grown by 300,000, a net gain of almost 185,000. In addition, new markets on both sides of the border have been opened. Since NAFTA was signed into law, California's exports to Mexico increased almost 50 percent. The state's export trade to Mexico supports an estimated 126,000 California jobs. For example, Mexico now represents the largest foreign market for San Diego companies (42 percent of all exports).[53]

Expanding NAFTA to Other Countries The promised success of NAFTA encouraged the Clinton administration to pursue initiatives expanding the agreement to other countries in the Americas. Chile is the most likely candidate to be added, which would broaden NAFTA's scope to make AFTA, the American Free Trade Agreement. Supporters of this expansion effort believe this growth will lead to a free-trade zone for the entire Western Hemisphere.

European Union

Perhaps the best-known example of an international economic community is the **European Union (EU).** The European Union combines 15 countries, 350 million people, and a total GDP of $5 trillion to form a huge common market. Several eastern European countries and former Soviet republics have also applied for EU membership.

To achieve its goal of a borderless Europe, the EU intends to remove all barriers to free trade among its members. This highly complex process involves standardizing business regulations and requirements, standardizing import duties and taxes, and eliminating customs checks, so that companies can transport goods from England to Italy as easily as from New York City to Boston.

Beginning in 1999, the EU plans to form an Economic and Monetary Union (EMU) and introduce the euro to replace currencies like the French franc and Italian lira. Potential benefits include eliminating the economic costs of exchanging one currency for another and simplifying price comparisons.[54] However, not all of the 15 EU members will be part of the EMU. Britain, Sweden, and Denmark have opted not to join. Their reasons for opposing the euro include histories of successful international commerce and nationalistic feelings.

To take advantage of the EU's move toward trade liberalization, the United States and the European Union are currently involved in negotiations to reduce transatlantic trade barriers. Although transatlantic trade is relatively free already, barriers remain in a number of industries. U.S. policies restrict shipping and textiles, and those in the EU limit agricultural and audiovisual products.[55]

GOING GLOBAL

While expanding into overseas markets offers increased profit potential and marketing opportunities, it also introduces new complexities to a firm's business operations. Before making the decision to go global, a company faces a number of key decisions, including:

▼ Determining which foreign market(s) to enter

> **They said it**
>
> "Don't overlook the importance of worldwide thinking. A company that keeps its eye on Tom, Dick, and Harry is going to miss Pierre, Hans, and Yoshio."
>
> **Al Ries (1929–)**
> **American advertising executive**

▼ Analyzing the expenditures required to enter a new market

  ▼ Deciding on the best way to organize the overseas operations

These issues vary in importance depending on the level of involvement a company chooses. For example, education and worker training in the host country is much more important for a bank planning to open a foreign branch or an electronics manufacturer building an Asian factory than to a firm that is simply planning to export American-made products.

The choice of which markets to enter usually follows extensive research focusing on local demand for the firm's products, availability of needed resources, and ability of the local workforce to produce world-class quality. Other factors include existing and potential competition, tariff rates, currency stability, investment barriers, and even possible corruption in the customs service.[56]

A variety of government and other sources are available to facilitate this research process. A good starting place is the *CIA World Factbook,* which contains country-by-country information on geography, population, government, economy, and infrastructure.

www. www.odci.gov/cia/publications

U.S. Department of Commerce counselors at the agency's 68 district offices offer a full range of international business advice, including computerized market data and names of business and government contacts in over 60 countries. As Table 4.5 shows, the Internet has simplified the process of gathering international trade information.

Levels of Involvement

After the company has completed its research and decided to enter a foreign market, it can choose one or more of the entry strategies shown in Figure 4.15:

▼ Exporting or importing

▼ Entering into contractual agreements like franchising, licensing, and subcontracting deals

▼ Direct investment in the foreign market through acquisitions, joint ventures, or establishing an overseas division.

While the company's risk increases with the level of its involvement, so does its overall control of all aspects of

Table 4.5	International Trade Research Resources on the Internet
Web Site and Address	**General Description**
Asia, Inc. www.asia-inc.com	Covering business news in Asia, this Web site features articles on Asian countries from India to Japan.
Europages www.europages.com	This resource offers a contact tool and directory of Europe's top 150,000 companies from 25 European countries.
Mexico Business www.nafta.net/mexbiz	Leading information source on doing business in and with Mexico, including a guide to key Mexican companies.
Doing Business in Canada www.tpusa.com/naft/nafta-facts/canada/html	This site offers comprehensive information on how to trade with our northern neighbor.
World Trade Organization gatekeeper.unicc.org/wto	This resource provides details on the trade policies of various governments.
STAT-USA www.stat-use.gov	This massive resource lists trade and economic data, information about trends, daily intelligence reports, and background data. Access requires a paid subscription to the service.
U.S. Business Advisor bacchus.fedworld.gov/index2.html	This one-stop resource gives access to a full range of federal government information, services, and transactions.
U.S. State Department Travel Warnings travel.state.gov/travel-warnings.html	The State Dept. lists its latest travel warnings about conditions that may affect safety abroad, supplemented by a list of consulate addresses and country information.

producing and selling its good or service. Companies frequently combine more than one of these strategies in a single country. In Brazil, Wal-Mart owns five retail stores but depends on contract truckers or its suppliers for local delivery of most of the goods it imports to these stores.[57]

Importers and Exporters When a firm brings in goods produced abroad to sell domestically, it is an importer. Likewise, companies are exporters when they produce goods at home and sell them in overseas markets. This strategy provides the lowest level of international involvement, with the least risk and control.

An importer must assess the local demand for a product before importing it from another country. Baltimore-based Sweet-N-Spicy Foods has targeted West Indians living in the Washington, D.C. metropolitan area who are nostalgic for the flavors of their homeland. The company ships in 200 different types of Caribbean fruits and vegetables like callaloo, peppers, thyme, and yams from Jamaica each week. Co-owner Mike Chin estimates that Sweet-N-Spicy spends approximately $1,000 a week on transportation to import the food, and depends on a number of different Jamaican suppliers to fill each order.[58]

Exports are frequently handled by special intermediaries called *export trading companies*. These firms search out competitively priced local merchandise and then resell it abroad at prices high enough to cover expenses and earn profits. When a retail chain like Dallas-based Pier One Imports wants to purchase West African products for its store shelves, it may contact an export trading company operating in a country such as Ghana. The local firm is responsible for quality assurance, packaging the order for trans-Atlantic shipment, arranging transportation, and handling the customs paperwork and other steps required to move the product from Ghana to the United States.

Firms engage in exporting of two types: indirect and direct exporting. A company engages in *indirect exporting* when it manufactures a product, such as an electronic component, that becomes part of another product that is sold in foreign markets. The second method, *direct exporting,* occurs when a company seeks to sell its product in markets outside its own country. Often the first step for companies entering foreign markets, it is the most common form of international business. Firms that find success in exporting their products may then move on to other entry strategies.

In addition to dealing with export trading companies to reach foreign markets, novice exporters may choose two other alternatives: export management companies and offset agreements. Rather than simply relying on an export trading company to assist in locating foreign products or foreign markets, an exporting firm depends on an *export management company* for advice and expertise. These international specialists help the first-time exporter with paperwork, making contacts with local buyers, and compliance with local laws governing labeling, product safety, and performance testing. At the same time, the exporting firm retains much more control than would be possible with an export trading company.

An *offset agreement* matches a small business with a major international firm. It basically makes the small firm a subcontractor to the larger one. Such an entry strategy helps a new exporter by allowing it to share in the larger company's international expertise. The small firm also benefits in such important areas as international transaction documents and financing.

Countertrade An estimated 15 to 30 percent of all international trade involves payments made in the form of

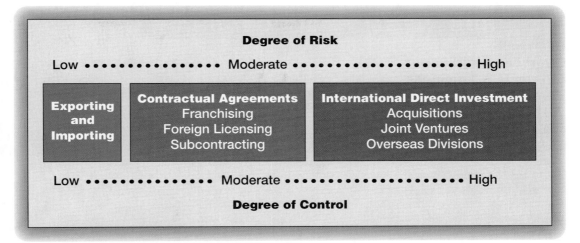

Figure 4.15 **Levels of Involvement in International Business**

local products, not currency. This system of international bartering agreements is called **countertrade.**

A common reason for resorting to international barter is inadequate access to needed foreign currency. To complete an international sales agreement, the seller may agree to accept part of the purchase cost in currency and the remainder in other merchandise. Since the seller may decide to locate a buyer for the bartered goods prior to completing the transaction, a number of international buyers and sellers frequently join together in a single agreement.

Countertrade may often be a firm's only opportunity to enter a particular market. Many developing countries simply cannot obtain enough credit or financial assistance to afford the imports that their people want. Countries with heavy debt burdens also resort to countertrade. Russian buyers, with their country's so-called *soft currency,* may resort to trading local products ranging from crude oil to diamonds to vodka as payments for purchases from foreign companies unwilling to accept Russian rubles. Still other countries, such as China, may restrict imports. Under such circumstances countertrade may be the only practical way to win government approval to import needed products.

Contractual Agreements Once a company, large or small, gains some experience in international sales, it may decide to enter into contractual agreements with local parties. These arrangements can include franchising, foreign licensing, and subcontracting.

Franchising Common among U.S. companies, franchising can work well for companies seeking to expand into international markets, too. A **franchise,** as described in detail in Chapter 5, is a contractual agreement in which a wholesaler or retailer (the franchisee) gains the right to sell the franchisor's products under that company's brand name if

it agrees to the related operating requirements. The franchisee can also receive marketing, management, and business services from the franchisor. While these arrangements are common among leading fast-food brands such as Pizza Hut, McDonald's, and KFC, other kinds of service providers often look to franchising as an international marketplace option.

Coverall North America is one of them. Specializing in commercial janitorial services, Coverall has 3,500 franchises worldwide. Founder Alex Roudi determined to take the concept overseas soon after his company's 1985 launch. He has shown considerable adaptability to make the concept work. Each country presents a different environment, with its own set of labor and tax laws. Differences in cultural constraints include varying attitudes toward entrepreneurs. In the Middle East, people going into business for themselves, including franchisees, must have sponsors.[59]

Foreign Licensing In a **foreign licensing agreement,** one firm allows another to produce or sell its product, or use its trademark, patent, or manufacturing processes in a specific geographic area. In return, the firm gets a royalty or other compensation.

Licensing can be an advantageous choice for a small manufacturer anxious to launch a well-known product overseas. Not only does it get a market-tested product from another market, but it must raise little or no investment to begin operating. The arrangement can also allow entry into a market otherwise closed to imports due to government restrictions.

For many years, Famous Trails, a small San Diego sporting goods manufacturer, had an agreement with Mitsubishi to sell Famous Trails products in Japan. When the company decided to go in a different direction and stopped

BUSINESS HALL OF SHAME

Overseas Child Labor Clouds U.S. Business Ventures

While his Western counterparts find themselves in middle-school classrooms, on local playgrounds, or at the library, the Bangladeshi preteen shown here spends his days in the factory working for a few cents per hour to help support his family. The use of exploited workers, including children, in foreign factories is a touchy issue for many well-known firms. Nike, Minute Maid, Wal-Mart, and Disney are just a few of the companies that find this issue discomforting, complicated by their dependence on subcontractors who may not work under their direct supervision.

Consumers like the No Sweatshop Coalition in New York see a straightforward issue. These women want nothing to do with clothing made by exploited workers, including children. To clearly demonstrate their point, they have organized events like "Let's Go No Sweatshopping," in which they ask selected storekeepers about the conditions under which garments offered for sale were made.

According to International Labor Organization (ILO) standards, the minimum age for employment should not

be less than 15 years old. A minimum age of 14 is allowed in countries with poorly developed economic and edu-

---

manufacturing in the United States, Mitsubishi approached its management with an offer to license various products in Japan under the Famous Trails logo. Mitsubishi now distributes backpacks, sweatshirts, and other popular items to Japanese department stores, and Famous Trails receives a percentage of the licensee's income from sales.[60]

Subcontracting The third type of contractual agreement, **subcontracting,** involves hiring local companies to produce, distribute, or sell goods or services. This move allows the foreign firm to take advantage of the subcontractor's expertise in local culture, contacts, and regulations. Subcontracting works equally well for mail-order companies, which can farm out order fulfillment and customer service functions to local businesses. Manufacturers practice subcontracting hoping to save money on import duties and labor costs, and businesses go this route to market products best sold by locals in a given country.

Ed Anderson invented a doughnut machine that evolved into a business called Lil' Orbits. Originally designed for American fairs, he thought the machines might generate international success. In 1987, after placing a small ad in a U.S. Department of Commerce publication, he received a huge number of responses. Instead of going overseas himself to find customers, Anderson hired foreign distributors to sell what has grown to a line of seven machines, as well as doughnut mix. With 42 people working

on his company's behalf, Lil' Orbits can now be bought in more than 80 countries.[61]

However, companies cannot always control their subcontractors' business practices. The Business Hall of Shame discusses how several major U.S. companies found themselves in an embarrassing position, because subcontractors used child labor to manufacture clothing.

International Direct Investment Investing directly in production and marketing operations in a foreign country is the ultimate level of global involvement. Over time, a firm may develop experience and success in conducting business in other countries through exporting and contractual agreements. Its managers may then decide to establish manufacturing facilities in those countries, open branch offices, or buy ownership interests in local companies in desirable markets.

An *acquisition* allows a company to purchase another existing company in the host country. In 1997, Wal-Mart spent $1.2 billion to buy Cifra, Mexico's largest retailer. Originally, the two companies formed a partnership that included 145 stores and restaurants. Then Wal-Mart bought out Cifra's position and took complete control of the retail operation.[62]

Joint ventures, like Wal-Mart's initial arrangement with Cifra, allow companies to share risks, costs, profits, and management responsibilities with one or more host country nationals. In 1997, NBC joined forces with Tele-

cational facilities. Economic exploitation of children is also a violation of United Nations rules. Yet the ILO places the number of illegal child laborers at between 100 and 200 million, most of them in Asia.

Although the most highly publicized finger-pointing involved Wal-Mart's line of clothing endorsed by TV personality Kathie Lee Gifford, allegedly produced by Honduran children, other U.S. firms have also been under scrutiny. The Gap has been accused of selling clothing made in Salvadoran sweatshops that employ young workers. Levi Strauss is currently investigating reports that its clothing is supplied by an independent contractor employing young girls from Bangladesh.

"The sad fact is that far too many of the products we may buy for loved ones . . . are made by the sweat and toil of children," says Iowa's U.S. Senator Tom Harkin. Harkin recently endorsed a U.S. Labor Department proposal that U.S. retailers should voluntarily launch labeling programs guaranteeing that the goods they sell are not made by children.

Companies relying on foreign production of their products are also banding together to stop child-labor practices. In 1997, Reebok, Nike, and other sporting goods companies announced that they would continue to purchase Pakistani-made soccer balls only if the suppliers provided assurances that they were not made by children.

Confidence in such a belief would require strict monitoring, however, and a commitment to crack down on overseas subcontractors and factories that exploit their workforces. As Reebok CEO Paul Fireman remarked about his industry's efforts, "Unless everyone is playing with a ball that's free of child labor, this thing is a farce."

visa S.A. de C.V. in Mexico City to distribute NBC's two cable networks in Mexico. Under the agreement, Sky Mexico, a satellite direct-broadcast operation, will broadcast MSNBC and CNBC throughout the country.[63]

By setting up an *overseas division,* a company can conduct a significant amount of its business overseas. This strategy differs from that of a multinational company in that a company with overseas divisions remains primarily a domestic organization with international operations. Its focus stays on the domestic market of the home country.

From Multinational Corporation to Global Business

A **multinational corporation (MNC)** is an organization with significant foreign operations. As Table 4.6 shows, firms headquartered in the United States and Japan dominate the list of the world's largest multinationals. Of the top 20 multinational corporations, only Royal Dutch/Shell (with headquarters divided between Britain and the Netherlands) and Germany's Daimler-Benz locate their head offices outside the United States or Japan. The

United States is home to one-third of the top 500 MNCs, followed by Japan with 25 percent, and France and Germany with about 8 percent each. Such well-known U.S.-based firms as IBM, Wal-Mart, General Electric, AT&T, and Mobil are included among the 20 largest MNCs.

Since the 1960s, when the first concerns surfaced about their influence on international business, multinationals have undergone a number of dramatic changes. For one, they are no longer almost exclusively U.S. phenomena. Today's MNC is just as likely to be based in Japan (Sony, Nissan, and Matsushita, for example), Germany (DaimlerChrysler, Bayer, or BASF), or Great Britain (British Petroleum, Cadbury Schweppes, or Glaxo Wellcome). Additionally, multinationals integrate capital, technologies, and even ideas from within their various global operations. These operations no longer function as distant market outposts.

Many U.S. multinationals, including Nike and Wal-Mart, have expanded their overseas operations, because

Business Directory

multinational corporation (MNC) firm with significant operations and marketing activities outside its home country.

Table 4.6	The World's Top Ten Multinationals	
Rank and Company	**Corporate Headquarters**	**Revenues (in billions)**
1. General Motors Corp.	United States	$168
2. Ford Motor Co.	United States	147
3. Mitsui	Japan	145
4. Mitsubishi	Japan	140
5. Itochu	Japan	136
6. Royal Dutch/Shell	United Kingdom/ Netherlands	128
7. Marubeni	Japan	124
8. Exxon	United States	119
9. Sumitomo	Japan	119
10. Toyota	Japan	109

they feel that domestic markets are peaking and foreign markets offer greater sales and profit potential. Also multinationals employ large numbers of foreign workers compared to their U.S.-national workforces. While foreign workers provide low-cost labor in some regions, many multinationals are locating high-tech facilities in countries with large numbers of technical-school graduates.

India's wealth of engineering talent has made it a popular country for technology-oriented companies. As Figure 4.16 points out, companies like Motorola are making substantial investments in nations sometimes labeled *developing countries.* "We are in India because that's where a lot of talent is," says Amreesh Modi, head of Motorola's Global Software Division. The communications and computer giant is also in other nations—from Brazil to China.[64]

As multinationals contribute to a global economy, they reap the benefits of the global marketplace. Chinese consumers love Kentucky Fried Chicken. Consumers in countries as geographically and culturally distant as Saudi Arabia and Canada shave with Gillette's razor blades, wash clothes with Procter & Gamble's Tide detergent, and use computers with Intel chips inside. Half of Procter & Gam-

ble's revenues and one-third of its net profits come from global operations. The multinational's Joy dishwashing liquid is a market leader in Japan.

Figure 4.16 Direct Investment by a Communications/Computer Multinational

INTERNATIONAL ORGANIZATION STRUCTURES

The decision to go global must be followed by a series of additional decisions that specify the most appropriate organization structure for the expanded operation. The level of involvement in international business is a key factor in these decisions. While a firm engaged in simple export activities may be best served by an export trading company, another company with extensive overseas sales may establish its own sales force for each country in which it operates. Figure 4.17 lists the alternative international organization structures that global business firms typically adopt.

Independent Agents

One method of entering international markets avoids the need to commit a major investment for developing and maintaining an overseas sales force: Use **independent agents.** These marketing intermediaries serve as independent sales forces in foreign markets, earning commissions on sales they book. They typically make sales calls on prospective customers, collect payments, and ensure customer satisfaction. Most cover limited geographic markets and hold down costs by representing multiple companies that produce related, noncompeting products.

Companies entering new foreign markets frequently rely on independent agents for several reasons:

▼ They understand their target markets, including customs and local environments.

▼ They represent minimal-risk entry alternatives for first-time exporters. If the firm is unhappy with an independent representative, it can terminate the relationship, usually at a low cost.

▼ Since most exporter-independent agent agreements specify compensation based on sales, they limit financial risks.

Exporters considering distributing through independent agents can secure names of local agents in various countries by contacting state export bureaus of the U.S. Department of Commerce. These agencies can also assist in developing sales agreements.

Figure 4.17   **International Organization Structure Alternatives**

depend on sales of the licensed products for their revenues. Because they invest more resources in the product than independent agents would, they often provide more effective representation in foreign markets.

Licensing agreements are relatively inexpensive and easy to create. The license holder is familiar with the target market, and the exporting company can draw on its experience and expertise instead of spending money researching the market and culture.

Licensing agreements bring an important limitation, however: They usually specify long time periods. A company that wants to attract the best license holder in a market typically must grant exclusive rights to the product for a 5-year period or even a longer time. While firms may benefit from such time commitments if license holders provide effective support, these contracts are difficult to terminate if the license holders prove ineffective partners.

Branch Offices

A branch office involves a different kind of commitment to foreign investment by a company. Instead of relying on a third party, the firm establishes its own overseas facility. In this way, it both improves its control and strengthens its presence in the host country.

To maintain a branch office in another country, a firm must develop an understanding of both the local market and its culture. This requirement demands a more extensive investment in time and experience than working with an independent agent or licensee. Many firms choose to combine branch offices and licensing agreements. The two strategies can complement each other, since license holders provide access to the local market, and the branch office can oversee the activities of the license holder.

Licensing Agreements

Some firms try to secure international sales revenues without making significant foreign investments by licensing their products, brand names, or production processes to other firms. The Famous Trails licensing agreement with Japan's Mitsubishi discussed earlier is a good example. This arrangement gives the firm receiving the license exclusive rights to use the production process or manufacture and/or market the product in a specified market. In return, the firm granting the license typically receives an upfront fee plus ongoing royalties based on a percentage of product sales.

Licensing agreements can be advantageous deals for companies seeking to enter foreign markets. License holders are usually relatively large, well-known companies that

Strategic Alliances

Similar to a joint venture, a **strategic alliance** is an international business strategy in which a company finds a partner in the country where it wants to do business. These partnerships can create competitive advantages in new markets by allowing the parties to combine resources and capital into new, jointly owned business ventures. Both the

Figure 4.18   **Global Business through Strategic Alliances**

risks and profits are shared, firms maintain control over their international activities, and they benefit from the local market expertise of their partners.

This kind of partnership has been increasing at an esti- mated rate of 20 percent a year. This trend is likely to con- tinue since a number of countries, including Mexico and China, have implemented laws that require foreign firms doing business in their countries to work through such al- liances.

In the ad shown in Figure 4.18, the Italian telecommu- nications giant STET/Telecom emphasizes the strengths it brings to the strategic alliances in which it participates. In 1997, for example, it formed an alliance with AT&T to de- liver telecommunications services in Latin America. Both parties chose this international organization structure, be- cause it allowed them to build on their complementary strengths to establish a strong presence.[65]

Direct Investment

Unlike strategic alliances, a firm makes a **direct invest- ment** in a foreign market when it buys an existing com- pany or establishes a factory, retail outlets, or other facili- ties there. Direct investment entails the most complete involvement in foreign trade, but it also brings the most

risk. Companies that invest directly in other countries must consider a number of issues discussed in this chapter, in- cluding the cultural environments, political stability, labor markets, and currency stability they will likely encounter.

As Figure 4.19 shows, U.S. companies—the most ac- tive in international direct investments—allocated about half of their $90 billion in total direct investment to Eu- rope. The U.S. market is also a popular investment location for foreign firms, which recently invested almost $85 mil- lion in projects ranging from a Mercedes-Benz assembly plant to the Seattle Mariners major league baseball team.

Some countries, eager to encourage foreign invest- ment, are not just accepting overseas involvement, they are helping to facilitate it. In China, the Beijing government contracted with partners in Singapore to develop an indus- trial park in Suzhou, near Shanghai. In business since 1994, the Suzhou Industrial Park has received investment commitments from such major international corporations as RJR Nabisco, Samsung Electronics, Black & Decker, and Eli Lilly.[66]

An interesting twist on international direct investment is Mexico's *maquiladora* plants, mentioned earlier in the chapter. Established in border cities like Tijuana, Juarez, and Nuevo Laredo, these foreign-owned factories hire low- wage Mexican workers to produce products at low cost, mostly for sale across the U.S. border. In Tijuana alone,

560 *maquiladoras* are currently operating. To sweeten incentives for such investments, the Mexican government allows manufacturers to import needed components without paying import duties.

Companies that have taken advantage of this innovation include Japanese multinationals Sony and Sanyo, as well as Korea's Samsung, Hyundai, and LG Electronics. Samsung recently spent $212 million to build a television and computer-monitor plant in a former olive grove. The company plans to spend another $580 million to expand the plant, which will eventually employ 9,300 people.[67]

Figure 4.19 **Destinations of Direct Investment Dollars**

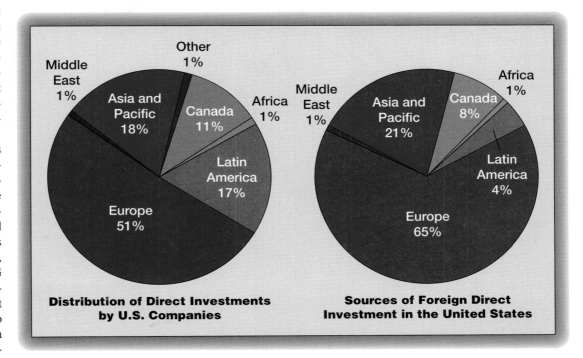

Distribution of Direct Investments by U.S. Companies

Middle East 1% · Asia and Pacific 18% · Other 1% · Canada 11% · Africa 1% · Latin America 17% · Europe 51%

Sources of Foreign Direct Investment in the United States

Middle East 1% · Asia and Pacific 21% · Canada 8% · Africa 1% · Latin America 4% · Europe 65%

DEVELOPING A STRATEGY FOR INTERNATIONAL BUSINESS

In developing a framework within which to conduct international business, managers must first evaluate their corporate objectives, organizational strengths and weaknesses, and strategies for product development and marketing. They can choose to combine these elements in either a global strategy or a multidomestic strategy.

Global Business Strategies

A **global business (or *standardization*) strategy** specifies a standardized, worldwide product and marketing strategy. The firm sells the same product in essentially the same manner throughout the world. Many companies simply modify their domestic business strategies by translating promotional brochures and product-use instructions into the languages of the host nations.

Ford Motor Co. created a single development organization when it launched its Ford 2000 global strategy. It merged its regional U.S., European, Asian, and Latin American operations into a single, worldwide company that adopts the best practices from all over the world. Ford management's goal is to create cars in standardized categories to be sold worldwide, reducing the company's costs dramatically by engineering products only once, rather than multiple times for different markets. For example, instead of making two similar four-cylinder engines, one for North America and one for Europe, the company will build one power unit for both markets.

Ford's Ka, a minicar built to compete in price-sensitive markets, was developed in a record time of just over 2 years. To reduce retooling and other start-up costs, the Ka uses the Ford Fiesta chassis and a number of other pre-assembled components. Following early marketplace success, Ford introduced a sister car, the Puma coupe. Spain was selected for the first Ka assembly plant; the second was located in Brazil.

Introduction of the coupe version of the Ka shows that Ford executives will not ignore customer preferences.

Business Directory

global business strategy reliance on a standardized marketing mix that guides marketing decisions with minimal modifications in all of a firm's domestic and foreign markets.

However, by consolidating engine and transmission options and recycling existing platform types, the company intends to move quickly and efficiently into new ventures. At least 50 percent of all Ka components were originally designed for other Ford models.[68]

A global marketing perspective can be appropriate for some goods and services and certain market segments that are common to many nations. The approach works for products with universal appeal, like Coca-Cola, and for luxury items like jewelry.

Multidomestic Business Strategies

Under a **multidomestic business (or *adaptation*) strategy,** the firm treats each national market in a different way. It develops products and marketing strategies that appeal to the customs, tastes, and buying habits of particular national markets. Software maker Microsoft pursues a multidomestic strategy by adapting its products for specific markets. It must design software to support different languages and writing styles, an especially daunting challenge when languages differ from English even in their alphabets, as do Arabic, Hebrew, Russian, Chinese, and Japanese. Microsoft also hires mostly local managers for its overseas operations, which span 60 countries. "That's key," says CEO Bill Gates. "It sends the wrong message to have a foreigner come in and run things." Microsoft sets up partnerships with small, local companies that know how to sell in their markets, creating a multidomestic strategy that is working. Overseas sales now account for 57 percent of revenues, with sales growth in China, India, and Southeast Asia topping 55 percent a year.[69]

Sources of Export Assistance

Regardless of the global business strategy that a company chooses, it may require export assistance. Companies can tap a variety of resources for this help. For example, the U.S. Department of Commerce maintains a toll-free information hot line (1–800–872–8723) that describes various federal export programs.

www.ita.doc.gov

Companies can also seek advice from trade counselors at the Commerce Department's 68 district offices, who can offer information about exporting, computerized market data, and names of contacts in more than 60 countries. Some of these services are free; others are reasonably priced.

▼ *National Trade Data Bank.* This large database, updated monthly, collects market reports on foreign demand for specific products. It is available at Commerce Department district offices or by subscription.

▼ *Agent/distributor services.* This search service helps companies to locate overseas distributors for their products.

▼ *Commercial News USA.* This monthly export catalog/magazine promotes U.S. goods and services to 100,000 international buyers in over 150 countries. An electronic version now on the Web helps foreign importers to find American companies.

www.cnewsusa.com

▼ *Catalog and video shows.* This service displays companies' catalogs or demonstration videos at shows held at U.S. consulates or embassies. Shows are oriented toward particular industries, such as medical supplies or marine equipment.

▼ *Matchmaker missions.* Sponsored visits help U.S. firms in specific industries to meet potential customers in foreign countries.

▼ *Trade shows.* Commerce Department-sponsored trade shows in other countries create effective forums for obtaining market information and meeting customers.

WHAT'S AHEAD

As this chapter has shown, both large and small businesses are relying on world trade almost as much as are major corporations. Chapter 5 examines the special advantages and challenges that small-business owners encounter. A critical decision facing any new business is the choice of the most appropriate form of business ownership. Chapter 5 examines the major ownership structures—sole proprietorship, partnership, and corporation—and assesses the pros and cons of each one. The chapter closes with a discussion of recent trends affecting business ownership, such as the growing impact of franchising and business consolidations through mergers and acquisitions.

Business Directory

multidomestic business strategy reliance on market segmentation to identify specific foreign markets and tailor the marketing mix to match their specific traits.

SUMMARY OF LEARNING GOALS

1. Explain the importance of international business and the main reasons why nations trade.

The United States is both the largest importer and the largest exporter in the world, although less than 5 percent of the world's population lives within its borders. With the increasing globalization of the world's economies, the international marketplace offers tremendous opportunities to U.S. and foreign businesses to expand into new markets for their goods and services. Doing business globally also provides new sources of materials and labor. Trading with other countries also reduces a company's dependence on economic conditions in its home market. Countries that encourage international trade enjoy higher levels of economic activity, employment, and wages than those that restrict it. The major world markets are North America, western Europe, the Pacific Rim, and Latin America. Emerging markets such as China and Brazil will become increasingly important to U.S. businesses over the next decade.

2. Discuss the relationship of absolute and comparative advantage to international trade.

Countries usually benefit if they specialize in producing certain goods or services. A country has an absolute advantage if it holds a monopoly or produces a good or service at the lowest cost. It has a comparative advantage if it can supply a particular product more efficiently or at a lower cost than it can produce another item.

3. Describe how nations measure international trade and the significance of exchange rates.

Companies measure the level of international trade by calculating trade surpluses or deficits, that is, the balance of trade, which represents the difference between exports and imports. The term *balance of payments* refers to the overall flow of money into or out of a country, including overseas loans and borrowing, international investments, profits from such investments, and foreign aid. An exchange rate is the value of a nation's currency relative to the currency of another nation. Currency values typically fluctuate, or "float," relative to the supply and demand for specific currencies in the world market. When the value of the dollar falls compared to other currencies, the cost of U.S. goods abroad declines, and demand for exports may rise. An increase in the value of the dollar raises the prices of U.S. goods sold abroad, but it reduces the prices of foreign goods sold in the United States.

4. Identify the major barriers that confront global businesses.

Businesses face several types of obstacles in the global marketplace. Companies must be sensitive to social and cultural differences, such as languages, values, and religions, when operating in other countries. Economic differences include standards of living and levels of infrastructure development. Legal and political barriers are among the most difficult to breach. Each country sets its own laws regulating business practices. Trade restrictions like tariffs and administrative barriers also present obstacles to international business.

5. Explain how international trade organizations and economic communities reduce barriers to international trade.

Many international organizations seek to promote international trade by reducing barriers. The list includes the World Trade Organization, World Bank, and International Monetary Fund. Multinational economic communities remove barriers to flows of goods, capital, and people across the borders of member nations. The two major economic communities are the North American Free Trade Association (NAFTA) and the European Union (EU).

6. Compare the different levels of involvement used by businesses when entering global markets.

Exporting and importing, the first level of involvement in international business, entails the lowest degree of both risk and control. Companies may rely on export trading or management companies to assist in distribution of their products. Contractual agreements such as franchising, foreign licensing, and subcontracting offer additional, flexible options. Franchising and licensing are especially appropriate for services. Companies may also choose local subcontractors to produce goods for local sales. International direct investment in production and marketing facilities provides the highest degree of control but also the greatest risk. Firms make direct investments by acquiring foreign companies or facilities, forming joint ventures with local firms, and setting up their own overseas divisions.

7. Describe the types of international organizational structures available to businesses.

Once a company's managers decide on the desired level of international involvement, they must choose the appropriate organization structure for their overseas venture. An independent agent represents an exporter in a foreign market. A license holder makes a larger investment in the product than an independent agent, perhaps motivating better representation for the product. However, licensing arrangements require longer time commitments than working with independent agents. Branch offices are units of an international firm located in foreign countries. Strategic alliances are joint ventures with local companies that combine resources and capital to create competitive advantage.

8. Distinguish between a global business strategy and a multidomestic business strategy.

A company that adopts a global (or standardization) strategy develops a single, standardized product and marketing strategy for implementation throughout the world. The firm sells the same product in essentially the same manner throughout the world. Under a multidomestic (or adaptation) strategy, the firm develops a different treatment for each national market. It develops products and marketing strategies that appeal to the customs, tastes, and buying habits of particular national markets.

TEN BUSINESS TERMS YOU NEED TO KNOW

exports

imports

balance of trade

balance of payments

exchange rate

tariff

World Trade Organization (WTO)

multinational corporation (MNC)

global business strategy

multidomestic business strategy

Other Important Business Terms

devaluation

infrastructure

quota

dumping

embargo

exchange control

General Agreement on Tariffs and Trade (GATT)

World Bank

International Monetary Fund (IMF)

North American Free Trade Agreement (NAFTA)

European Union (EU)

countertrade

franchise

foreign licensing agreement

subcontracting

joint venture

independent agent

strategic alliance

direct investment

maquiladora

REVIEW QUESTIONS

1. Summarize the major reason nations and businesses engage in international trade.
2. Distinguish between the concepts of absolute advantage and comparative advantage. Cite examples of both.
3. Can a nation have a favorable balance of trade and an unfavorable balance of payments? Defend your answer.
4. Explain how exchange rates are established. What factors can affect them?
5. Describe three types of barriers that firms may face in international business. Give an example of each.
6. Explain the difference between a revenue tariff and a protective tariff. What other types of trade restrictions affect international trade?
7. Identify three international organizations or economic communities and explain how they reduce barriers to international trade.
8. Explain the different levels of involvement in international business and give an example of each.

9. Differentiate between various types of international organizational structures that firms can use to go global.
10. How does a firm that follows a multidomestic strategy operate in the global marketplace?

QUESTIONS FOR CRITICAL THINKING

1. Now that the Internet has opened up the opportunity for borderless trade, what impact do you think it will have on how countries set trade standards?
2. In recent years, what countries have proved to be more risky markets for foreign investment? Why? Use examples of cultural, economic, political, and legal factors to explain your choices.
3. China took over Hong Kong in 1997, creating uncertainty in global markets, especially the United States, about the future of trade relations with one of the world's most prosperous and friendly nations. Identify some practices that H. C. Tung, Hong Kong's new leader, might use to minimize the effect of political differences on international business. What can the United States do to maintain strong business relations with Hong Kong?
4. Over the past 50 years, the World Bank and the IMF have helped many developing countries enter and maintain their positions in the world of international business, even when governments of those countries were known to be corrupt. One such country is Indonesia, which now has a significantly more advanced infrastructure and is a major player in international trade. Indonesia, along with its neighbors, has suffered from Southeast Asia's recent economic crisis. Many world leaders do not support efforts of the World Bank and the IMF to shore up the economy.

   Do you think it is important to provide monetary support to such countries even if government corruption exists? Describe some consequences on the world marketplace that might result from lending such support.
5. Although large multinationals receive the lion's share of attention for going global, small business exports are a growing trend. U.S. exercise video company Kresics Inc. recognized that the U.S. market was saturated by competition from superstars like Cindy Crawford and Richard Simmons. After learning that only about 10 commercial exercise videos were available in Japan, company president Krescenthia David pulled most of her products from U.S. store shelves, remade them for the Japanese market, and began exporting them. Now 90 percent of Kresics's sales are to Japan. Discuss the risks and opportunities that Kresics and other small businesses face when they enter overseas markets.

Experiential Exercise

Directions: This exercise helps you assess your global awareness. Answer the following ten questions to test your knowledge.

1. List the six countries that contain one-half the total population of the world:
   1.
   2.
   3.
   4.
   5.
   6.
2. The five most commonly spoken languages are:
   1.
   2.
   3.
   4.
   5.
3. How many of the world's languages have at least 1 million speakers?
   a. 73
   b. 123
   c. 223
4. How many nations were there in 1992?
   a. 288
   b. 188
   c. 88
5. Which nation is home to the largest number of commercial banks?
6. Between 1960 and 1987, the world spent approximately $10 trillion on health care. How much did the world spend on the military?
   a. $7 trillion
   b $10 trillion
   c. $17 trillion
   d. $25 trillion
7. According to the United Nations, what percentage of the world's work (paid and unpaid) is done by women?
   a. 33%
   b. 50%
   c. 67%
   d. 75%
8. According to the United Nations, what percentage of the world's income is earned by women?
   a. 10%
   b. 30%
   c. 50%
   d. 70%
9. The nations of Africa, Asia, Latin America, and the Middle East, often referred to as the Third World, contain about 78 percent of the world's population. What percentage of the world's monetary income do they possess?
   a. 10%
   b. 20%
   c. 30%
   d. 40%
10. Americans make up approximately 5 percent of the world's population. What percentage of the world's resources do Americans consume?
    a. 15%
    b. 25%
    c. 35%
    d. 45%

Answers

1. China (1.1 billion)
   India (882 million)
   United States (256 million)
   Indonesia (185 million)
   Brazil (151 million)
   Russia (149 million)
2. Mandarin
   English
   Hindi
   Spanish
   Russian

3. c. 223
4. b. 188
5. Japan
6. c. $17 trillion
7. c. 67%
8. a. 10%
9. b. 20%
10. c. 35%

Source: Adapted from Jan Drum, Steve Hughes, and George Otere, "State-of-the-World Test," in *Global Winners*. (Yarmouth, ME): Intercultural Press, Inc., 1994.

Nothing but Net

1. **Going Global.** One company that has made its mark on every continent, except Antarctica, is McDonald's, with over 22,000 restaurants in 109 countries. Check out their international Web site at the address listed and record five interesting facts you learned about McDonald's international operations.

   www.mcdonalds.com/surftheworld/index.html

2. **The World Bank.** Visit the World Bank's Web site and locate the section that provides information on the countries and regions the World Bank serves. Select a country that interests you and report on the projects funded by the World Bank there.

   www.worldbank.org

3. **European Union.** Use your search engine to find the latest information related to the new euro currency discussed in this chapter. The Web site listed provides many links to EU information. Select an additional EU topic to explore and summarize your findings in a one-page report.

   www.lib.berkeley.edu/GSSI/eu.html

Note: Internet Web addresses change frequently. If you do not find the exact sites listed, you may need to access the organization's or company's home page and search from there.

VIDEO CASE 4

PIER 1 IMPORTS—PLANNING FOR WORLDWIDE GROWTH

By mid-1996, Pier 1 Imports was on its way to record sales and earnings. An exciting new merchandise mix combined with the company's first television advertising campaign, had dramatically increased store traffic. Shoppers were attracted to retail stores vastly different from the Pier 1 of the early 1980s.

The old Pier 1 struggled with a disappointing merchandise selection and an outdated image. To turn the retail chain around, its board of directors brought in a new CEO, Clark Johnson. The strategic plan he and his management team devised in 1985 centered around an ambitious program to double the number of Pier 1 stores.

Other components of the plan included upgrades and expansion of merchandise offerings and investments of $27 million in new corporate systems aimed at improving efficiency. For example, new inventory systems enabled the company to reduce inventory levels in the stores and distribution centers. Customer service has been greatly enhanced by more sophistcated store checkout equipment that facilitates price checking, credit-card processing, and communications with other stores. But nowhere has the investment in systems had a greater payoff than in the logistics area. Beginning with order entry in foreign countries, through shipment from the company's six massive distribution centers to company stores, merchandise is monitored each step of the way, providing a significant increase in cost-effectiveness.

Has Pier 1's growth been a smooth process? Hardly! In 1990, as the U.S. economy slowed down, so did consumer buying. Like other retailers, Pier 1 focused on controlling costs and increasing the efficiency of its operations. By 1992, however, on Pier 1's 30th anniversary, record earnings were again reported. During the early 1990s, Pier 1 once again invested in an extensive strategic planning process.

What are management's current plans for their organization? In a corporate document entitled *A Strategy for Profitable Worldwide Growth,* management states that "Pier 1 Imports will expand its North American retail operations to 900 stores by the year 2000 and enter new worldwide retail markets through direct investment and partnerships." Other strategic goals for the year 2000 include:

▼ Achieve $1.25 billion in sales and produce $75 million in net income.

▼ Introduce Pier 1 stores internationally with direct investment in selected countries.

▼ Expand the Pier 1 market presence in Southeast Asia, Mexico, and Central and South America through franchise agreements and joint ventures.

▼ Enter new specialty retail markets in North America to be chosen using several specific and consistent criteria.

▼ Establish a major procurement, logistics, and distribution presence in Singapore to reinforce the company's international sourcing capacity.

With goals and a strategic plan in place, Pier 1 Imports' management believes that the company's focus is clear. "When 2000 arrives, our goal is to look back and verify:

▼ We defined a clear strategy and executed it well through the end of the 1990s.

▼ We produced long-term financial results that exceeded expectations.

▼ We identified global opportunities along the way, moved decisively, and increased the intrinsic value of Pier 1 Imports.

▼ We remained sensitive to each market area and adapted readily to customer wants and needs.

▼ We focused clearly on our basic strategy of profitable growth through market expansion, new store openings, maximizing profitability of existing units, motivating our associates, and remaining dedicated to our customers."

Building on their past successes, Pier 1 Imports is committed to achieving these goals.

Questions

1. What barriers to global business is Pier 1 Imports likely to encounter? Explain.

2. Describe Pier 1 Imports' corporate strategy. Give examples of how these goals can be achieved throughout the organization.

3. Distinguish between a global strategy and a multinational strategy. Where does Pier 1 Imports fit?

4. What are the different approaches to doing business abroad? Which of these are being pursued by Pier 1 Imports?

PART I

Careers in Business

INTRODUCTION

Included with *Contemporary Business* is a CD-ROM titled "Discovering Your Business Career." After following the installation instructions in the "Read Me" file on the CD-ROM, you will have placed two programs on your computer: *Discovering Your Business Career* and *Career Design*. Both of these programs are placed in the program group called "Career Assistance."

Discovering Your Business Career helps you learn about and assess your compatibility with a wide range of careers in the business world:

- ▼ Accounting
- ▼ Corporate financial management
- ▼ Information systems
- ▼ Risk management/insurance
- ▼ Retail bank management
- ▼ Sales
- ▼ Store operations

As you explore each career, you will receive broad guidance and practical advice on everything from clarifying the depth of your interest in a particular business career to preparing and implementing an effective job search strategy.

You will also be able to access complete career profiles about each area. Through videos, multimedia slide shows, and extensive textual content, the profiles present a detailed, up-to-date picture of current compensation levels, job responsibilities, career paths, and skills required to be successful in that career. Exercises related to those careers begin in the "Careers in Business" section for Part 4. The *Internet Business Connection*, an integrated part of the program, links you to relevant Web sites for learning more about each business career, including current job opportunities.

The *Career Design* program offers a series of exercises based on the work of John Crystal, the major contributor to the best-selling career book of all time, *What Color Is Your Parachute*, by Richard N. Bolles. These exercises help you:

- ▼ Decide on a major.
- ▼ Identify your best skills.

- ▼ Discover what career to pursue.
- ▼ Find out if starting a business may be your appropriate career path.
- ▼ Determine your key preferences for co-workers and working conditions.
- ▼ Create a custom resumé that stands out from others.
- ▼ Develop communication skills by organizing your thoughts in writing.

As the new century proceeds, the pace of change in the business world will continue to accelerate and students who know what careers they want to pursue will enjoy a dramatic advantage. The best way to ensure that you land the right job when you graduate is to start your career preparations now. Begin by learning how to match your individual abilities and interests to specific career alternatives. Based on this knowledge, you will be able to create an academic plan that will result in securing that first job in your career path. Your instructor and the "Business Career Exercises" will help you to accomplish this.

In the following section, and at the end of every part in *Contemporary Business,* you will find instructions for completing "Business Career Exercises" using the free CD-ROM provided with your text. These exercises show you how to apply what you learn in the course to your career.

BUSINESS CAREER EXERCISES

Career Questionnaire

The first step in your business career exploration is to complete a questionnaire in which you rate a broad range of business-related job activities. For example, you rate from "very appealing" to "very unappealing" the statement, "Making financial forecasts about your company's profits based on the assumptions you have made about how many units will sell, the selling price, and the expenses." You also rate yourself according to ten broad career factors that measure your priorities about your work environment, compensation, and progression in your career.

In later sections of the book, you'll learn how to connect the results of this questionnaire with the business subjects you're currently studying. For example, when studying marketing, you'll discover what the questionnaire reveals about your interest in marketing careers such as sales.

How to Locate the Exercise Launch *Discovering Your Business Career* from the "Career Assistance" program group. Then select "Questionnaire" in the upper right corner of the main menu.

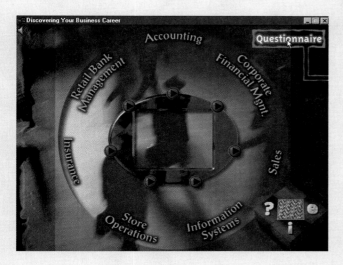

Interests and Fascinations

Anything that interests you can be an important clue about your career direction, and this exercise helps you clarify those interests. When you are asked to list your interests, take the program's advice and type in as many of your interests as you can, regardless of whether you think they are job related. Since your introductory business course provides a unique opportunity to discover what areas of business fascinate you, start this exercise by reviewing the chapters you have completed so far and write down any topics of interest. Then add these to your "Interests and Fascinations" list on the computer.

This exercise will help you to:

▼ Discover and keep track of your interests throughout the course.

▼ Understand that choosing a career that interests you can result in better pay and job satisfaction.

▼ Get a start in finding out what major to choose.

How to Locate the Exercise Launch *Career Design* from the "Career Assistance" program group. Then select "Navigation" from the menu at the top of the screen, followed by "Career Sections" and then "Interests."

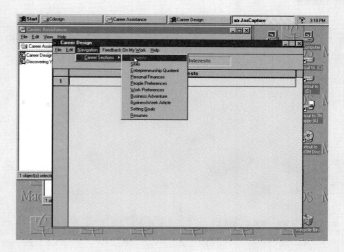

Business Adventure

Now that you have completed the "Interests and Fascinations" exercise, here is another one that helps you discover even more about what you want. This exercise stimulates your imagination about the things you would like to do in the field of business. The more you write, the better.

This exercise will help you to:

▼ Discover some of your interests in the business world.

▼ Feel encouraged to actively pursue your dreams.

▼ Clarify your goals and determine what areas of life are important to you.

▼ Stimulate your thinking about what you want to accomplish in your life.

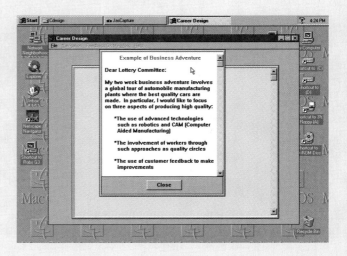

How to Locate the Exercise Launch *Career Design* from the "Career Assistance" program group. Then select "Navigation" from the menu at the top of the screen, followed by "Career Sections" and then "Business Adventure."

PART II | Starting and Growing Your Business

chapter 5

Options for Organizing Small and Large Businesses

LEARNING GOALS

1. Define *small business,* and identify the industries in which most small firms are established.

2. Explain the economic and social contributions of small business.

3. Compare the advantages and disadvantages of small business.

4. Describe how the Small Business Administration assists small-business owners.

5. Explain how franchising can provide opportunities for both franchisors and franchisees.

6. Identify and explain the three basic forms of business ownership and the advantages and disadvantages of each form.

7. Identify the levels of corporate management.

8. Describe recent trends in mergers and acquisitions.

9. Differentiate among private ownership, public ownership, and collective ownership (cooperatives).

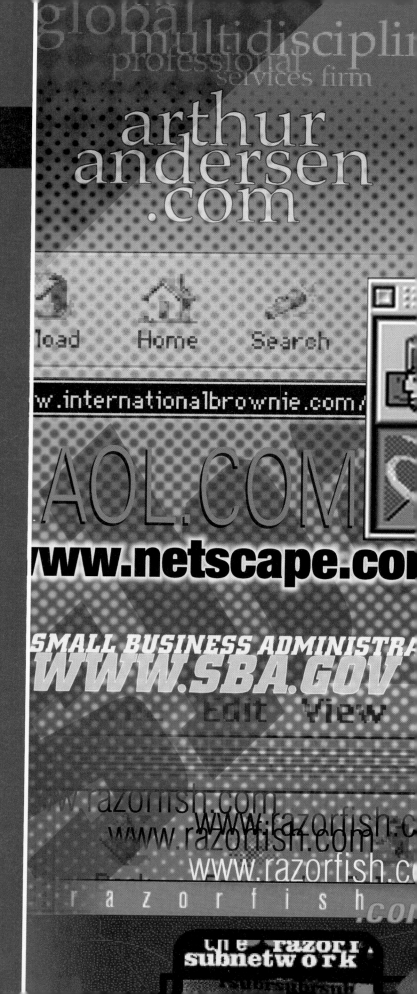

America Online Buys More Real Estate in Cyberspace

Ask any real estate specialist the three most important words in that profession and you're most likely to hear "Location, location, location." These factors come into play when buying and selling real estate in town, in the suburbs, or out in the country. They also apply to cyberspace, and giant Internet provider America Online (AOL) knows it. With 16 million subscribers, AOL boasts the largest online population on earth. It has also designed the Web's largest virtual shopping mall, with 400 stores ranging from J. Crew to J & R Computer World. These tenants pay AOL millions (some of them $50 million and more) for their prime location. So what more could AOL want? A lot more.

Whether large or small, most business organizations seek growth as a means of accomplishing their objectives to their owners, customers, and employees. But once you've grown into a huge company, the question becomes one of how to grow even bigger. Rather than spending years of plowing more and more funds into the firm to finance growth, a number of firms decide to expand their operations by acquiring the strengths provided by other companies. In short, they purchase (acquire) another company, or they merge with one or more companies.

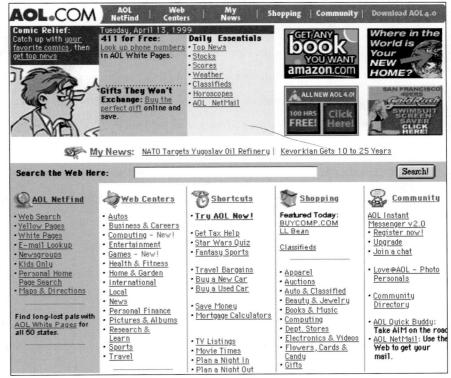

Successful mergers and acquisitions strengthen all the parties involved. But even proposed combinations that look great on paper involve considerable risk, and a doomed business marriage results in large and lasting costs to everyone.

AOL's management realized that their company had been remarkably successful within the space of a few years. They also knew that their firm needed to widen its lead and expand its areas of operation. Already a success at creating an attractive online experience for new Web surfers (who can barely plug in their PCs), AOL needed to attract an even larger audience willing to spend more shop-

www.aol.com
www.netscape.com

ping money on the Web. Although it occupied the number one advertising spot on rival Microsoft's Channels section of Windows 98, AOL needed an even better location.

Already leasing virtual real estate to tenants and helping them promote their shopping sites, AOL needed to help these tenants build their commerce service with powerful software. But in most cases, the company had neither the resources nor the expertise to satisfy its needs for growth. So how did AOL solve its problem? It bought Netscape—lock, stock, and browser.

Netscape is best known for its Internet browser. The 1994 launch of its Navigator 1.0 marked a major change in the world of e-commerce. With the click of a mouse, the Internet was accessible to people at home as well as at work. Netscape's software was improving people's lives—and with more than just its browser. It also included industrial-strength Web tools and "back-office" e-commerce programs to help companies do business and make sales over the Web. Then there's the Netcenter portal. A *portal* is a full-service Web site, an online launching pad, entertainment network, and shopping mall rolled into one. A first stop for most Web surfers, portals offer search engines, shopping areas, and other services that attract a lot of traffic.

Talk about location! Netcenter is one of the most heavily visited portals on the Web, mainly because it automatically pops up whenever someone clicks to open a Netscape browser. (Even though users can easily change that automatic setting, they either don't know that or don't care.) With 9 million registered users, Netcenter's traffic numbers are mind-boggling.

America Online bought it all—the browser, the software (and the programmers to go with it), and Netcenter (the location of locations)—for $10 billion. The fit looks good. First, with netscape.com, aol.com, and the AOL service itself, the company's audience now numbers in the tens of millions. Second, Netcenter balances AOL's heavy evening and weekend use by the home market with more white-collar traffic, which is the heaviest on weekdays from 9 to 5. Third, AOL now has the option of switching its built-in browser from rival Microsoft's Internet Explorer to Netscape's Navigator. And fourth, but far from the least, AOL now has the software and expertise to plunge into e-commerce, not only with its current tenants but also with the tenants that will be moving into its ever-expanding shopping mall. Consumer advocates criticize the acquisition as further concentration of an already too small Internet software industry. But with forecasts for e-shopping ranging from dramatically huge to overwhelmingly huge (from tens to hundreds of billions of dollars within three or four years), securing the real estate now seems like a good idea.[1]

CHAPTER OVERVIEW

If you have ever thought of operating your own business, you are not alone. In fact, on any given day in the United States, more people are trying to start new businesses than are getting married or having children. However, before entering the world of contemporary business, an entrepreneur needs to understand its framework.

Like America Online, every business owner must choose the type of legal ownership that best meets the company's needs. Several variables affect the choice of the best way to organize your business:

▼ How easily can you form this type of organization?

▼ How much financial liability can you afford to accept?

▼ What financial resources do you have?

▼ What strengths and weaknesses do you see in other businesses in the industry?

▼ What are your own strengths and weaknesses?

This chapter begins with a focus on small-business ownership, including a discussion of the advantages and disadvantages of small-business ventures and a look at the services provided by the U.S. government's Small Business Administration. The role of women and minorities in small business is discussed in detail as well as global opportunities for small-business owners. The chapter then turns to an overview of the three types of private business ownership—sole proprietorships, partnerships, and corporations. Next, the chapter takes an in-depth view of the structures and operations typical of large corporations. Finally, it reviews the trends in business with a fresh look at mergers, acquisitions, and multinational corporations. The chapter ends with an explanation of public and collective ownership.

MOST BUSINESSES ARE SMALL BUSINESSES

Although many people associate the term *business* with international giants like Exxon,

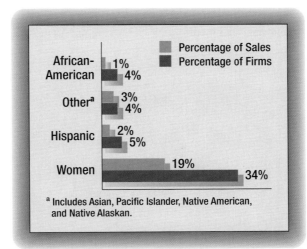

Figure 5.1

Women and Minority Ownership of U.S.-Based Small Businesses

- Percentage of Sales
- Percentage of Firms

African-American: 1% / 4%
Other[a]: 3% / 4%
Hispanic: 2% / 5%
Women: 19% / 34%

[a] Includes Asian, Pacific Islander, Native American, and Native Alaskan.

Citibank, Wal-Mart, and General Electric, 19 of every 20 businesses in the United States employ fewer than 50 people. Of all the new businesses started last year, 20 percent are one- or two-person operations.

Small business is also the launching pad for entrepreneurs from every sector of the U.S. economy. As Figure 5.1 indicates, one-third of the nation's 17 million small businesses are owned by women. Hispanic-owned businesses account for 5 percent of all U.S. small businesses, and African-Americans own another 4 percent. In total, small businesses generate annual sales of over $3 trillion.

What Is a Small Business?

How do you distinguish a small business from a large one? Is sales the key indicator? What about market share or number of employees? The Small Business Administration (SBA), the federal agency most directly involved with this sector of the economy, considers a **small business** to be a firm that is independently owned and operated and is not dominant in its field.[2] The SBA also considers annual sales and number of employees in some industries to identify small businesses.

▼ A manufacturer is considered a small business if it employs fewer than 1,500 workers; a small wholesaler can employ no more than 100 workers.

▼ A retailer can generate up to $14.5 million in annual sales and still be considered a small business.

Quantitative standards such as maximum sales, market share, or number of employees frequently determine qualifications for loan programs developed to assist small businesses or procurement programs attempting to encourage proposals from them.

Business Directory

small business firm that is independently owned and operated, not dominant in its field, and meets certain size standards for income or number of employees.

Typical Small Business Ventures

For decades, small businesses have competed against some of the world's largest organizations as well as multitudes of other small companies. Judi Jacobsen, owner of Madison Park Greetings, is motivated by the competition from card giants Hallmark and American Greetings. Jacobsen and her 35 employees have found so much success with a line of 400 boutique greeting cards that she recently was named Small Business Person of the Year by the Small Business Administration. Her motto is, "Try to keep ahead of the trends and find your niche."[3]

For centuries, retailing and service establishments have remained the most common nonfarming small businesses. Take Longfellow's Wayside Inn in Sudbury, Massachusetts. Although only one U.S. business in four has celebrated its 25th anniversary, the Wayside Inn has been serving "man, woman, and beast" since the early 1700s and is probably the oldest home-grown business in the United States.[4] As Figure 5.2 indicates, small businesses dominate four industries: business services, eating and drinking establishments, wholesale trade—durable goods, and special trade contracting.

Giant card-makers didn't hinder Judi Jacobsen of Madison Park Greetings.

Retailing is another important industry for today's small businessperson. General merchandising giants like Wal-Mart, Kmart, and Sears may be the best-known retailing firms, but small, privately owned retail stores outnumber them. Small-business retailing includes stores that sell shoes, jewelry, office supplies and stationery, apparel, flowers, drugs, convenience foods, and thousands of other products. In fact, one-fifth of the nation's women-owned small businesses compete in the retail sector. Becky and Mike Busath are a good example. The two business partners turned Becky's love of baking bread into a successful small business by opening the Stone Ground Bread Company in San Antonio, Texas, where they sell whole-grain bread made fresh every day.[5]

Most farming is still the work of small businesses. The family farm is a classic example of a small-business operation; it is independently owned and operated, with relatively few employees, but with substantial reliance on unpaid, family labor. In fact, family-owned businesses are once again a popular form of business ownership, as retiring baby boomers and their Generation X children join forces.

▼ Julia (JJ) Gonson and her dad, Don, started their own record label, Undercover, with $6,000 in savings from JJ and another $30,000 investment from Don. Their first product, a cover album of David Bowie songs, sold 7,000 copies and recouped its $15,000 cost. Six more CDs were released in 1998.

▼ Barry Levin, a 64-year-old Bostonian, and his son Gregg will generate $1 million in sales this year from what Barry considered a dumb idea: making the brim of a baseball cap curve the right way when worn backward. Gregg educated his father on the number of people who wear caps and showed him a plastic gizmo he had designed that would perfectly bend the cap's visor. Today their company, The Perfect Curve, has 250 accounts at 350 sporting goods and specialty cap stores.[6]

One of every two companies is a **home-based business**—operated from the residence of the business owner. This arrangement is especially popular for fledgling firms; 57 percent of firms with revenues of $25,000 or less are home-based companies, contrasted with only 5 percent of the firms generating sales of $1 million or more.

Home-based businesses are not only widespread, but their number is rapidly growing. Today, more than 14 million people are self-employed, and 15 million Americans earn extra income from part-time work at home.[7] Home-based business owners earn six-figure annual incomes in several industries, including business brokers, business plan writers, desktop video producers, executive searchers, export agents, home inspectors, and management consultants. A major factor in the growth of home-based businesses is the increased availability of personal computers and such communications devices as fax machines, low-cost photocopiers, and electronic mail.

Many new-technology firms, those that design, produce, and market scientific innovations, begin as small businesses. Razorfish, a New York City company devoted to designing elegant Web sites, began small and later merged with another small company, avant garde interactive advertising firm Avalanche Systems. Even today, the successful combination has only a total of 85 employees.[8]

American business history is filled with inspirational stories of great inventors who launched companies in barns, garages, warehouses, and attics. For young visionaries like Apple Computer founders Stephen Jobs and Steve Wozniak, the logical option for transforming their technical idea into a commercial reality was to begin work in a family garage. The Business Tool Kit on page 167 offers tips on operating a home-based business. The impact of today's entrepreneurs, including home-based businesses, is discussed in more depth in Chapter 6.

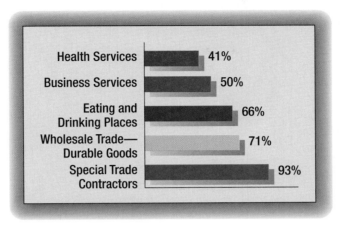

Figure 5.2   Top Five Industries for Small Business

Health Services — 41%
Business Services — 50%
Eating and Drinking Places — 66%
Wholesale Trade—Durable Goods — 71%
Special Trade Contractors — 93%

tion levels than do employees of larger firms.[10]

Creating New Industries

Small businesses make tremendous contributions to the U.S. economy and society as a whole. A later section of this chapter will examine in more detail the opportunities that small businesses offer for women and minorities. The small-business sector also gives entrepreneurs an outlet for developing their ideas and perhaps for creating entirely new industries. Many of today's successful high-tech firms—Netscape, Cisco Systems, Yahoo!, and Dell Computer—began as small businesses.

Another contribution of small business is its ability to provide needed services to the larger corporate community. The movement toward corporate downsizing that began in the early 1990s created a demand for other businesses to perform activities previously handled by company employees. Outsourcing such activities as security, employee benefits management, maintenance, and logistics created opportunities that were often filled by employees of small businesses.

Attracting New Industries Urban planners realize the importance of small businesses to their cities, and successful revitalization programs have improved conditions in depressed areas by attracting new industries. Fort Myers, Florida, more than doubled its population by attracting young professionals and small-business owners. Downtown Houston experienced a revival when Bellaire Boulevard was converted into a line of strip-mall stores to accommodate the increasing number of Asians, Hispanic Americans, and African-Americans who now constitute two-thirds of the city's population.[11]

CONTRIBUTIONS OF SMALL BUSINESS TO THE ECONOMY

Small businesses form the core of the U.S. economy, accounting for 52 percent of all sales and half of the private gross domestic product. They account for 99.7 percent of all U.S. employers, with 54 percent of the nation's private workforce.[9]

Even more impressive is the number of new jobs created each year by small businesses. While recent employment data reveal that giant firms employing 500 or more people actually reduced their total staffing, industry sectors dominated by small businesses created almost two-thirds of all new jobs. As Figure 5.3 reveals, tiny firms with one to four employees created 49 percent of the nation's new jobs.

Even if you never plan to start your own business, you will probably work for a small business at some point in your career. If you're looking for your first job, chances are a small business will provide it. Small firms generate two-thirds of all first-time employment opportunities. And once you get hired by a small business, you may just decide to stay for the long haul. Recent research studies report another important finding of interest to new employees: People who work for small businesses report higher job satisfac-

Gregg Levin convinced his father, Barry, to go into business with him selling a plastic ball-cap-bending gizmo called The Perfect Curve.

But how do cities make these areas such attractive locations? Among the most important qualities reported by entrepreneurs deciding to relocate in previously neglected urban areas are available workers, inexpensive facilities, strong markets, availability of government-funded worker-training programs, funding sources, and positive attitudes shown by city officials and local community groups regarding the businesses.

Figure 5.3 Importance of Small Businesses in New-Job Creation

The Small Business Administration (SBA) reports that small firms produce twice as many product innovations per employee as larger firms. In addition, they obtain more patents per sales dollar than larger businesses do, which indicates that small businesses make more discoveries. The airplane, audiotape recorder, double-knit fabric, optical scanner, personal computer, soft contact lens, and the zipper are all important 20th-century innovations that were developed by small businesses.[13]

ADVANTAGES OF A SMALL BUSINESS

Small businesses are not simply smaller versions of large corporations. They differ greatly in forms of organization, market positions, staff capabilities, managerial styles, organizational structures, and financial resources. But these differences usually seem like strengths to small-business owners, who find many advantages in operating small businesses as compared to working within large, powerful, multinational corporations. As Figure 5.4 indicates, the four most important advantages are innovation, superior customer service, lower costs, and opportunities to fill isolated niches.

Innovation

In order to compete effectively with giant corporations backed by massive resources, small firms often have to find new and creative ways of conducting business. The Business Hall of Fame box reports one case of a company that took its public securities offerings to the Internet. Vulcan Breweries offered stocks directly to the public over the Web, where the experiment both succeeded and failed.

Small businesses are often fertile ground in which to plant innovative ideas for new goods and services. After Neil Senturia had difficulty accessing online services when he was traveling, his California-based Atcom/Info developed the Cyberbooth. Travelers can now use Atcom's Internet kiosks to visit the Internet and read their e-mail at 167 airports, convention centers, and hotels.[12]

Superior Customer Service

A small firm can often operate with greater flexibility than can a large corporation, allowing it to tailor its product line and services to the needs of its customers. InterActive Custom Clothes does that—literally—for its customers. Consumers can visit InterActive's Web site, answer a few questions including their body measurements, and have their own custom-tailored jeans made within an hour. InterActive's computer program uses artificial intelligence to transmit the personal specifications to a machine that cuts the 19 pieces of cloth that make up a pair of jeans. Among the options are colored rivets, leather labels, novelty buttons, and a wide selection of fabrics. To get this kind of service a few years ago, says co-founder Peter del Rio, "You would have your clothes made by a master tailor. Now you have your own virtual master tailor."[14]

www.ic3d.com

Low Costs

Small firms can often provide goods and services at prices that large firms cannot match. Small businesses usually minimize overhead costs—costs not directly related to providing specific goods and services—allowing them to earn profits on low prices.

A typical small business sets up a lean organization with a small staff and few support personnel. The limitation on overhead costs made possible by maintaining a small permanent staff can provide a

Innovation	Superior Customer Service
Example: Start-up business to offer online grocery shopping and delivery	Example: Free alterations on clothing purchases from a small boutique
Lower Costs	**Isolated Niches**
Example: Small retailer who can prepare sales flyers on a personal computer	Example: Retail store that specializes in selling products designed for left-handed consumers

Figure 5.4 Advantages of Small-Business Ownership

Ten Keys to Succeeding in a Home-Based Business

Home-based business owners often face unique challenges. The following tips can help you get a home-based business off to a good start:

1. Make certain your business won't be violating local zoning or other regulations.

2. Select a space that can be dedicated exclusively to your business.

3. Establish a regular work schedule.

4. Set up at least one phone line strictly for your business. If you'll be using a fax or modem, a second business telephone line is a good idea.

5. Invest in basic equipment like a computer with modem, a quality printer, and a fax machine.

6. Present your business positively by purchasing quality letterhead, business cards, and marketing materials.

7. Protect your business from disaster by purchasing business insurance.

8. Set up a recordkeeping system to track accounts, expenses, and income.

9. Join a professional organization or a home-based business owners' association to network and prevent isolation.

10. Set boundaries for family or roommates about interruptions and distractions when you are working.

Source: "The Ultimate Home-Based Business Guide," *Business Start-Ups*, September 1997, pp. 37–38.

distinct advantage for a small business. Instead of hiring high-income attorneys and accountants as permanent staff members, small-business owner-managers typically hire them when needed for special projects or as outside consultants. This approach typically helps to restrain payroll costs for the small business.[15] The ad in Figure 5.5 highlights the benefits gained by small businesses when they contract as needed with outside professionals.

Another source of cost savings is the quantity and quality of work performed by the business owner. Entrepreneurs typically work long hours with no overtime or holiday pay. In addition, their family members frequently contribute services at little or no pay as bookkeepers, laborers, receptionists, production assistants, and delivery personnel.

Even a small business like InterActive Custom Clothes can provide one-on-one service to its customers using the World Wide Web. At this site, customers can make their selections and place orders for jeans tailored to their measurements.

Low overhead also helps to keep the costs of small business operations at minimal levels. Many such businesses avoid rent and utility expenses by operating out of the owners' homes. In addition, these firms often carry little or no inventory, further reducing total operating costs.

Filling Isolated Market Niches

Large, growth-oriented businesses tend to focus on large segments of the overall market. The growth prospects of small market niches are simply too limited and the expenses involved in serving them too great to justify the required time and effort. Because high overhead costs force large firms to set minimum sizes for their target markets, small, underserved market niches have always attracted small businesses willing and able to serve them.

Figure 5.5 **Reaping the Benefits of Hiring Outside Professionals**

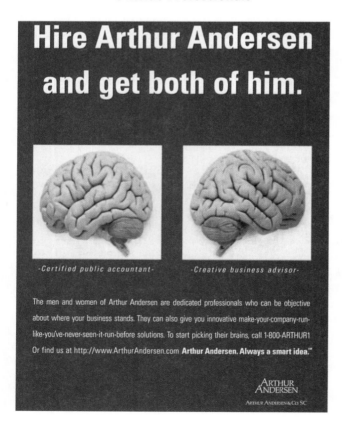

In addition, certain types of businesses favor small organizations. Many service businesses illustrate this point. Finally, economic and organizational factors may dictate that an industry consist primarily of small firms. Upscale restaurants and personal shopping services are typically small business operations.

Former high school teacher Joel McIntosh found an isolated niche when he tried to locate educational materials to use in his classes for gifted children in Waco, Texas. After deciding that available materials were inadequate, he used simple desktop publishing equipment to publish and distribute magazines and books to help other teachers and parents of gifted children. Although still a small business, McIntosh's Prufrock Press has grown to become one of the largest independent education publishers.[16]

 www.prufrock.com

DISADVANTAGES OF A SMALL BUSINESS

Although small businesses bring a number of strengths to the competitive marketplace, they also have a variety of

Vulcan Breweries is only offering two sensational new brews -- Vulcan Beer, a crisp pilsner-style beer, and Vulcan Hefe Weizen, an unfiltered German-style wheat beer --

For additional information not found in this web site, we encourage you to call us at 800-972-8729 or email us.

Also visit Where the Money Goes...

tracted to raise $5 million. It was slow going at first, with only 70,000 shares sold for a grand total of $130,000. Since international stock buyers aren't limited by U.S. laws, Vulcan also enticed buyers from as far away as Russia.

But the unorthodox method of raising money produced unexpected benefits. Hundreds of stockholders are now actively promoting the company. "Those $185-a-whackers are becoming mini-reps for the company," explains Busby. They are asking their grocers to carry the beer, convincing their friends to buy it, and complaining when it's unavailable. In its home market of Birmingham, Vulcan's products are now outselling Abita—previously the best-selling microbrewery in the South—and beating Jack Daniel's beer for market share.

The Internet may not yet be the sales channel of choice for most firms seeking to sell stock, but it has been a great start for Vulcan's expansion plans. The little microbrewer is on the leading edge of companies offering stock to micro-investors on the Net.

QUESTIONS FOR CRITICAL THINKING

1. **If banks are reluctant to lend to small businesses, why are investors willing to risk their money on these ventures? Explain your answer.**

2. **Could Vulcan have come closer to their $5 million goal by setting their minimum commitment higher—say $100,000? Explain.**

Sources: Birmingham Brewmasters Web site, accessed at www.bham.net, February 25, 1999; and Verna Gates, "Brewing a Small Cap Marketing Coup," *Business Alabama Monthly*, February 1998, pp. 17–19.

---

disadvantages in competing with larger, better established firms. A small business may find itself especially vulnerable during an economic downturn, since it may have accumulated fewer resources than its larger competitors to cushion a sales decline.

The primary disadvantages facing today's small businesses include management shortcomings, inadequate financing, and government regulations. These issues—quality and depth of management, availability of financing, and ability to wade through government rules and requirements—are so important that firms with major deficiencies in one or more areas often find themselves in bankruptcy proceedings. As Figure 5.6 shows, almost one new business in four will permanently close its doors within 2 years of opening them, and 62 percent will fail within the first 6 years of operation. While highly motivated and well-trained business owner-

managers can overcome these potential problems, they should analyze all of these issues before starting new companies.

Management Shortcomings

Among the most common discoveries at a post mortem examination of a small-business failure is inadequate management. Business founders often possess great strengths in specific areas such as marketing or interpersonal relations, but they suffer from hopeless deficiencies in others

Figure 5.6 **Business Failures**

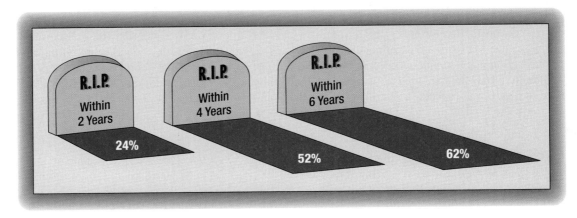

R.I.P. Within 2 Years — 24%

R.I.P. Within 4 Years — 52%

R.I.P. Within 6 Years — 62%

The Five Best Businesses to Start from Your Dorm

Are you anxious to get started in the world of business? Do you want to accumulate some real-world experience, build your resume, or simply make some money? The following suggestions may be just the ticket to making your next school term happier, busier, and richer than this one.

▼ *Web-Site Developing.* Three Boston University roommates began by using their own computers and university scanners to help a local hair salon launch a Web site. Their company, Net One, earned over $80,000 in 1998.

▼ *Resumé Writing.* Armed with a good $1,000 graphics software program such as Quark Xpress or PageMaker and a way with words, you can earn between $10 and $15 per hour.

▼ *Computer Repair.* Almost one-third of the nation's 15 million college students own personal computers. Students who know how to repair these machines when they go on the blink can earn between $10 and $20 per hour.

▼ *Word Processing.* A student with good typing skills, a personal computer, and a printer can earn money charging flat fees for completed projects or a set price per page. Pass out flyers in the community to inform local companies of your business.

▼ *Laundry Pickup and Delivery.* Contact local laundries to obtain a bulk discount, then offer pickup and delivery service to student customers who are charged the same amount they would pay if they brought in the laundry themselves. A 50-customer list can generate $150 per week.

For peer support, business resources, and contacts with other entrepreneurs around the world, contact the Young Entrepreneurs Network in Boston at (617) 867–4690 or visit their Web site:

www.idye.com

Source: Business suggestions in Frances Huffman, "Most Likely to Succeed," *Business Start-Ups*, March 1998, pp. 54–59.

like finance or order fulfillment. Large firms recruit trained specialists to manage individual functions; small businesses frequently rely on small staffs who must be adept at varied skills.

An even worse result frequently occurs when people go into business with little, if any, business training. Some new businesses are begun almost entirely on the basis of what seems like a great idea for a new product. Managers assume that they will acquire needed business expertise on the job. All too often, the result is business bankruptcy.

If you are seriously contemplating starting a new business, heed a word of warning: learn the basics of business *first*, and *second*, recognize your limitations. Although most small-business owners recognize the need to seek out the specialized skills of accountants and attorneys for financial and legal assistance, they often hesitate to turn to consultants and other advisors for assistance in areas where they lack knowledge or experience.

Nouveau Contemporary Goods, a Baltimore retail outlet selling everything from greeting cards to furniture, grew much faster than owners Steve Appel and Lee Whitehead ever anticipated. Since 1996, the store has doubled its staff as sales have climbed to $1.2 million. Since neither partner brought any retailing experience to the venture, they agreed that they needed help to manage such rapid change. The partners brought in a retail consultant to help them plan future strategies and develop retailing skills of employees and managers.[17]

Founders of new businesses frequently struggle with an ailment that might be called "the rose-colored-glasses" syndrome. Filled with excitement about the potential of newly designed products, they may neglect important details like marketing research intended to determine whether potential customers share their excitement. Someone considering launching a new business should first determine whether the proposed product meets the needs of a large enough market and whether they can convince the public of its superiority over competing offerings.

International Brownie founder Cindy Rice almost talked herself out of implementing her business idea before even starting. The future gourmet brownie entrepreneur started worrying when she noticed a retail store in a nearby shopping mall selling trays of brownies that looked just like the ones she planned to sell. "When I saw products that were similar to mine, I used to be afraid they were going to take away my customers. Then I realized that what it really meant was that there's a market out there for my product." To help distinguish her products, which she sells via the Internet and direct-mail orders, from those of competitors, Rice emphasizes superior product quality and unparalleled customer service.[18]

www.internationalbrownie.com

Inadequate Financing

Another leading cause of small-business problems is inadequate financing. In too many instances, entrepreneurs start new businesses assuming that their firms will generate enough funds from the first month's sales to finance continuing operations. Building a business takes time, though. Employees must be trained, equipment purchased, deposits paid for rent and utilities, and marketing dollars must be spent to inform potential customers about the new firm and its product offerings. Unless the owner has set aside enough funds to cover cash shortfalls during the first several months in which the business is becoming established, the venture may collapse at an early stage.

After surviving the cash crunch that often accompanies the first months of operation, a business must confront another major financial problem: uneven cash flows. For most small and large businesses, cash inflows and outflows do not display even patterns; instead, they fluctuate greatly at different times of the year. Small retail outlets frequently generate much of their annual sales revenues during the December holiday period. Florists make most of their deliveries during three holidays: Valentine's Day, Easter, and Mother's Day. Large firms may build up sufficient cash reserves to weather periods of below-average sales, or they can turn to banks and other lenders for short-term loans; new business start-ups often lack both cash balances and access to sources of additional funds.

With no track record and few assets to pledge as collateral, the owners of a small business usually discover that banks are highly reluctant to make business loans. As Table 5.1 shows, personal savings or personal loans made by owners provide the primary sources of start-up funding.

Irwin Simon took out a second mortgage on his home to raise the money he needed to buy a kosher frozen-food business. But the risky decision paid off. Simon's Hain Food Group eventually grew into a $65-million-a-year business success.[19]

Small-business owners also rely heavily on credit cards as a source of short-term— but high-cost—financing. A recent survey revealed that 39 percent of all small-business owners use their personal credit cards for business purposes. The heaviest users of credit cards for business financing are tiny firms with fewer than 10 employees.[20]

Banks often provide limited funding for small companies that meet stringent criteria. In addition, the high risks and relatively high processing expenses involved in making small loans often cause lenders to charge high interest rates to small-business borrowers. Only one business loan in five made by U.S. commercial banks is for less than $100,000.[21] The five banks ranked highest among small-business borrowers are Wells Fargo, NationsBank, Keybank, Bank One, and First Union National Bank.[22]

Some business pioneers take unusual approaches to scaling obstacles between themselves and new-business financing—and this kind of innovation can lead to handsome payoffs. Henry Gibson is a good example. Gibson is one of 30 owners of the Big Wash, a highly successful

They said it

"Being in your own business is working 80 hours a week so that you can avoid working 40 hours a week for someone else."

Ramona E. F. Arnett
President, Ramona
Enterprises, Inc.

Table 5.1	Sources of Start-Up Funding	
Source of Funds	**Percentage of Business Owners Obtaining at Least Some of Their Start-up Funds from This Source**
Personal savings	72%[a]
Banks	45
Friends and/or relatives	28
Individual investors (not friends or relatives)	10
Government-guaranteed loans	7
Venture capital firms	1

[a] Total exceeds 100 percent due to use of multiple sources of funding by some firms.

Washington, D.C. laundry. Gibson knew it would not be easy to raise the $250,000 needed to set up a coin-operated laundry, so he thought about what a giant business would likely do in his place. Then he settled on his big idea—he would sell shares of stock in the venture at $100 each. Many of the first investors were fellow church members, others were neighbors who knew and believed in Gibson's ability and the need for a convenient laundry. Most of them could afford to buy only one share, but few bought as many as 50. Once Gibson had raised $30,000, he applied for a loan from a local bank and raised $60,000 in grants from seven different foundations. Today, Big Wash is an unquestioned success, having already returned its owners $175 for each share they own. Gibson has also been rewarded for all his efforts. As he puts it, "It's the best thing I've ever done."[23]

Government Regulation

Small-business owners often complain bitterly of excessive government regulation and red tape. Paperwork costs alone account for billions of small-business dollars each year. A large company with a substantial staff can usually cope better with requirements for forms and reports. Many experts within and outside government recognize the need to reduce the paperwork required of small businesses, since they simply lack the capabilities to handle the burden. Small businesses often struggle to absorb the costs of government paperwork because of their slim profit margins. Some small firms close down for this reason alone.

Taxes are another burdensome expense for a small business. In addition to state and federal income taxes, employers must pay taxes covering workers' compensation insurance and unemployment benefits.

INCREASING THE LIKELIHOOD OF BUSINESS SUCCESS

How can a prospective owner gain the numerous advantages of running a small business while also avoiding the

disadvantages? Successful entrepreneurs make two critical recommendations:

▼ Develop a business plan.

▼ Use the resources provided by such agencies as the Small Business Administration and local business incubators for information, advice, funding, and networking opportunities.

They said it

"Banks will lend you money if you can prove you don't need it."

Mark Twain (1835-1910)
American author

Creating a Business Plan

Creating a business plan represents perhaps the most important task that an entrepreneur faces. An effective business plan can make the difference between a company that succeeds and one that fails. A **business plan** is a written document that provides an orderly statement of a company's goals, the methods by which it intends to achieve those goals, and the standards by which it will measure achievements.

Plans give a sense of purpose to an organization. They provide guidance, influence, and leadership, as well as communicating ideas about goals and the means of achieving them to associates, employees, and others. In addition, they set standards against which achievements can be measured. Planning usually works best when the entire organization participates in the process. Planning can combine good ideas presented by employees and communicate information while making everyone feel a part of the team.

Although no one format best suits all situations, a good small-business plan will include a detailed time frame for achieving specific goals, projections of money flows (both income received by the business and funds disbursed to pay expenses), and units for measuring achievement. A business plan should also cover the methods by which the firm will achieve specific goals, procedures it will follow, and values that define important standards for conduct. Perhaps most importantly, the plan should always be open to revision.

Before writing a business plan, a business owner should answer some questions:

▼ How would you explain your idea to a friend?

▼ What purpose does your business serve? How does your idea differ from those behind existing businesses?

Business Directory

business plan written document that provides an orderly statement of a company's goals, the methods by which it intends to achieve those goals, and the standards by which it will measure achievements.

▼ What is the state of the industry you are entering? Who will be your customers or clients?

▼ How will you market the firm's goods or services?

▼ How much will you charge?

▼ How will you finance your business?

▼ What characteristics qualify you to run this business?

Give special attention to the name of your proposed business. Does the name reflect the firm's goals? Is it already registered by someone else? Does it convey any hidden meanings to other people? What does it mean phonetically in other languages? Is it offensive to any religious or ethnic groups?

Be sure to do adequate research. Trade journals are excellent sources of industry-related information. The Small Business Development Centers (SBDC) on many college campuses, the Small Business Administration in Washington, D.C., many local Chambers of Commerce, and your local library can also assist in this research. You may gain useful insights by talking to suppliers in the industry and to local licensing authorities. How many similar businesses have succeeded? How many have failed? Why? What risks are specific to your industry? What markups are typical in the industry's pricing structure? What are common levels of expenses and profit percentages?

Components of a business plan typically include:

▼ An executive summary should answer the who, what, why, when, where, and how questions for the business in brief. (Although the summary appears early in the plan, it probably should be the last element written.)

▼ An introduction should give a general statement of the concept, purpose, and objectives of the proposed business, along with an overview of the industry. This element should include a brief description of the owner's education, experience, and training, with references to a resume included later in the plan.

▼ A marketing section should describe the firm's target market, its anticipated competitors, and plans for distri-

bution, advertising, pricing, and locations of facilities. This section should cover the background of the industry and industry trends as well as the potential of the new venture. It should also point out any unique or distinctive features of the business and explain the reasons for choosing a particular start-up date.

▼ The marketing section should also cover equipment rental, leasing, or purchase costs, and the influences of traffic volume, neighboring businesses, demographics, parking, accessibility, and visibility. Further discussion should review labor costs, utility access and rates, police and fire protection, zoning restrictions, and other government rules and regulations.

▼ Another section should detail an operating plan forecast, a plan for obtaining capital, and a description of plans for spending funds.

▼ A section should estimate assets and liabilities and analyze when the firm will reach the break-even point (the level of sales at which revenues equal costs).

▼ A plan written to obtain funding should include resumes of the principals of the business.

A business plan should cover some other topics, as well, including whether the firm will be organized as a sole proprietorship, partnership, or corporation; when it will need to hire employees and what job descriptions will guide their work; the lines of authority in the business; a risk management plan, including detailed information on insurance; a list of suppliers and methods for assessing their reliability and competence; and a policy for extending credit to customers.

Since business plans are essential tools for securing outside funds, the financial section requires particular attention to detail. As Lucien Campolo, co-founder of Miami-based suntan-oil producer South Beach Sun Co., explains, "If you wait until you have enough money to take a shot at starting your own business, you'll be waiting your entire life. You need to put together the plan, put together the idea, and just get started."[24]

If the plan becomes part of a request for financing, the banker will examine the owner's management

At 28, Kelly and Lucien Campolo proved what they've known all along: Sun-care products are hot stuff.

skills and experience, the risk of the enterprise, available collateral, and the ability to repay the loan. Potential outside investors are more likely to evaluate the potential for profits and growth and place less emphasis on downside risks.

If certain assumptions underlie the body of the plan, tie them into the financial section. A plan for two outlets, for example, should provide cash-flow projections that show how the firm will pay their costs. Deal with both significant and insignificant variables. The bankers or investors who analyze a plan may not know whether your firm will spend $250 or $25,000 to install an exotic, high-tech part, but they will know that a telephone system for 50 people will cost more than $250 per month. Carelessness with seemingly insignificant variables can undercut credibility.

Itemize monthly expenses rather than simply projecting annual amounts. A firm with $100,000 in annual costs may not spend exactly $8,333 each month. It must pay some expenses monthly and some once each year. An owner who must cover several large, annual payments at the beginning of the year will be running back to financiers in the first month to explain problems with the cash-flow projection—not a good way to start.

In addition to cash-flow projections, a business plan should project a detailed profit-and-loss statement. It must also state all assumptions it makes about the conditions under which the firm will operate. The Business Hall of Shame discusses how assumptions about a market may prove disastrously wrong.

The assembled plan should include a table of contents so that readers can turn directly to the parts that most interest them. Make sure that the plan is presented in an attractive and professional format.

Small Business Administration

A number of invaluable resources for small businesses are provided by the Small Business Administration (SBA). The SBA is the principal government agency concerned with helping small U.S. firms. It is the advocate for small businesses within the federal government. About 4,000 employees staff the SBA's Washington headquarters and its regional and field offices. Its primary operating functions include providing financial assistance, aiding in

government procurement matters, and providing management training and consulting.

 www.sba.gov

Financial Assistance from the SBA Contrary to popular belief, the SBA seldom provides direct business loans. Its major financing contributions are the guarantees it provides for small-business loans made by private lenders, including banks and other institutions. Direct SBA loans are available in only a few special situations, such as natural disaster recovery and energy conservation or development programs. Even in these special instances, a business applicant must contribute at least 30 percent of the proposed project's total cost in cash, home equity, or stocks in order to qualify.

The SBA also guarantees *microloans* of less than $25,000 to very small firms. These loans are available from more than 100 sources throughout the United States, most of them not-for-profit business development groups. Other sources of microloans include the federal Economic Development Administration, some state governments, and certain private lenders, such as credit unions and community development groups.

Small business loans are also available through an SBA-licensed organization called a **Small Business Investment Company (SBIC).** SBICs can borrow up to four times the amount of their capitalization from the federal government and use the funds to make loans. Last year, they loaned $2.4 billion to small businesses for equity capital and other financial needs. SBICs are also likely to be more flexible than banks in their lending decisions. Well-known companies that used SBIC loans for start-up financing include Apple Computer, Callaway Golf Company, America Online, Federal Express, Intel, and Sun Microsystems.[25]

www.ace-net.sr.unh.edu/

Another financial resource underwritten by the SBA is the Angel Capital Electronic Network (ACE-Net), which matches entrepreneurs looking for start-up capital with potential investors. Entrepreneurs post information about their businesses on ACE-Net's Web site, where potential investors can review it. Interested parties contact the firms. The goal is

They said it

"To open a business is very easy; to keep it open is very difficult."

Chinese proverb

Business Directory

Small Business Administration (SBA) federal agency that assists small businesses by providing management training and consulting, financial advice, and support in securing government contracts.

Table 5.2   Programs and Services of the Small Business Administration

A. BUSINESS COUNSELING AND TRAINING

Small Business Development Center (SBDC)
Over 900 SBDCs provide management and technical assistance to small businesses and would-be entrepreneurs. They are cooperative efforts among the SBA, the academic community, the private sector, and state and local governments.
Service Corps of Retired Executives (SCORE)
Nationwide, 12,400 SCORE volunteers in nearly 400 chapters provide expert advice, based on years of firsthand experience and shared knowledge, on virtually every phase of business.
Business Information Center (BIC)
BICs offer small-business owners access to state-of-the-art computer hardware and software as well as counseling by SCORE volunteers.
Women's Network for Entrepreneurial Training (WNET); Veterans' Entrepreneurial Training (VET); and Office of Native American Affairs (ONAA)
These three programs provide in-depth entrepreneurial training for women, veterans, and Native Americans. Resources include workshops and mentoring programs.

B. LENDING PROGRAMS

Women's and Minority Prequalification Loans
These programs enable the SBA to prequalify a loan guaranty for a woman or minority business owner before approaching a lender. The program focuses on an applicant's character, credit, experience, and reliability rather than collateral.
FA$TRAK
A new loan program, piloted with selected banks nationwide, FA$TRAK provides additional incentive to lenders to make small-business loans.
7(m) MicroLoan
The MicroLoan program provides short-term loans ranging from under $100 to $25,000 for small-scale financing purposes such as inventory, supplies, and working capital.

C. INTERNATIONAL TRADE ASSISTANCE

U.S. Export Assistance Center (USEAC)
USEACs combine in single locations the trade-promotion and export-finance resources of the SBA, the U.S. Department of Commerce, and the Export-Import Bank of the United States.

D. FEDERAL GOVERNMENT PROCUREMENT

Prime Contracting and Subcontracting
This program increases opportunities for small businesses in the federal acquisition process. It initiates small-business set-asides, identifies new small-business sources, and counsels small firms on how to do business with the federal government.

---

to help businesses seeking smaller amounts of capital than those typically handled by venture capital firms.[26]

Other Specialized Assistance Although government purchases represent a sizable market, small companies have difficulty in competing for this business with giant firms, which employ specialists to handle the volumes of paperwork involved in preparing proposals and completing bid applications. Today, many government procurement programs specifically set aside shares for small companies; an additional SBA role involves assisting small firms in securing these contracts.

A **set-aside program** specifies that certain government contracts (or portions of those contracts) are re-

stricted to small businesses. Every federal agency with buying authority must maintain an Office of Small and Disadvantaged Business Utilization to ensure that small businesses receive a reasonable portion of government procurement contracts.

In addition to financial advice and guaranteed loan programs, the SBA provides a variety of other services to small businesses, including toll-free telephone numbers and online resources to answer questions. It offers hundreds of publications at little or no cost, and it sponsors popular conferences and seminars. Table 5.2 summarizes several of the programs that the SBA currently offers to small-business owners.

Pat Creedon turned to the Service Corps of Retired Executives (SCORE) for help when her 5-year-old electrical contracting firm, Creedon Controls, encountered cash flow problems. Customers owed money but were not paying their bills on time; in turn, Creedon was struggling to meet her company's financial obligations. A SCORE counselor helped Creedon to write a business plan that enabled her to double the firm's credit line to $100,000. With the larger credit line, Creedon was better able to ride out periods when accounts didn't pay on time.[27]

Business Incubators

In recent years, local community agencies interested in encouraging business development have implemented a concept called a **business incubator** to provide low-cost, shared business facilities to small, start-up ventures. A typical incubator might section off space in an abandoned plant and rent it to various small firms. Tenants often share secretaries, copiers, and other business services.

About 600 business incubator programs now operate nationwide. Some are operated by industrial development authorities, others by not-for-profit organizations, colleges and universities, or even by private investors. These facilities offer management support services and valuable management advice from in-house mentors.

Some incubator programs specialize in particular industries or types of businesses. The Entergy Arts Business Center in New Orleans offers a place where artists and graphic designers can gain expert advice about running businesses. Jocelyn Burrell, an artist specializing in jewelry, metal, and mixed media, finds that Entergy

| Figure 5.7 | **Large Firms Providing Specialized Services for Small Businesses** |

gives her a chance to network with others running art businesses and find new markets for her work.[28]

Large Corporations Assisting Small Businesses

Corporate giants often devise special programs aimed at solving small-business problems. In doing so, they are not acting out of humanitarian interests. Instead, they recognize the size of the small-business market, its growth rate and buying power, and the financial rewards for firms that support small businesses. Figure 5.7 provides an example of a large company attempting to meet this challenge. AT&T offers custom-tailored assistance in designing and operating a Web site. First Union Bank also offers small businesses easy-to-use financial services complete with 24-hour loan approvals, account statements faxed daily, and automatic transfers of surplus cash into interest-paying accounts.

Wal-Mart is another international giant familiar with the expression, "One hand washes the other." The world's largest retailer has long supported small businesses. The Wal-Mart Innovation Network (WIN) and the Support American Made Products program have already helped more than 3,000 inventors and entrepreneurs by evaluating their products and prototypes for possible distribution by the chain. To determine Wal-Mart's interest in adding your product to its store offerings, call 1-501-273-4000 and ask the WIN representative to send you an application form. Return the application with detailed company information, a $175 evaluation fee, and a prototype of your product. Within 60 days, WIN evaluators will send you a detailed critique covering issues like product quality, packaging, service capacity, capitalization levels, and a decision on whether your product will be placed on Wal-Mart shelves.

These efforts not only help small businesses; they are also pivotal in Wal-Mart's success. Gerald Udell, ad-

Business Directory

business incubator organization that provides low-cost, shared facilities to small, start-up ventures.

ministrator of both programs, points out, "Wal-Mart doesn't want to end up with empty shelves."[29]

SMALL-BUSINESS OPPORTUNITIES FOR WOMEN AND MINORITIES

The thousands of new business start-ups each year include growing numbers of women-owned firms as well as new businesses launched by African-Americans, Hispanics, and members of other minority groups. These entrepreneurs see small-business ownership and operation as an attractive and lucrative alternative to working for someone else. Figure 5.8 shows the types of businesses commonly owned by women and minorities.

Women-Owned Businesses

In the United States today, nearly 8 million women-owned firms provide jobs for 16 million people—more than are employed by the Fortune 500 industrial firms. Two of the largest women-owned businesses in the United States are packaged-food giant Beatrice Foods and Raley's, a supermarket chain.

Increasing numbers of women are starting their own companies for several reasons. Some may leave large corporations when they feel blocked from opportunities for advancement, that is, when they hit the so-called *glass ceiling*, as discussed in Chapter 9. Other women may want flexible working hours so they can spend time with their families. Still others may have lost their jobs when their employers downsized or left because they became frustrated with the bureaucracies in large companies.

Of all the minority classifications in the United States, minority women-owned firms have far outpaced others in their growth. During the past 20 years, the number of minority-owned firms grew 47 percent. During this same time, women-owned firms almost doubled that rate at 78 percent, while businesses owned by minority women grew at an astounding 153 percent.[30]

Over half of women-owned firms are service businesses, and another 18 percent are retail stores—many of them competing in segments traditionally dominated by men.[31] Louisa Hechavarrias took out a $2,000 loan to open Friendly Auto Glass, a mobile windshield repair company. She runs the firm from her home, keeping her

costs low at the same time she keeps tabs on her three young children.[32]

Along with this strong growth, women have been able to establish a powerful support network in a relatively short time. Many nationwide business assistance programs serve only women. In Boston, the Center for Women & Enterprise offers training and workshops; in Chicago, the Women's Business Development Center instructs female would-be business owners on matters of financing; in San Francisco, the Women's Initiative for Self Employment not only provides bilingual entrepreneurship training, but also offers technical assistance and financing to low-income women.[33]

Hispanic-Owned Businesses

Hispanics are the nation's largest group of minority business owners. During the past decade, the Hispanic population and the number of Hispanic-owned businesses have more than doubled. Many economists foresee even more growth ahead for this sector, especially as trade between the United States and Latin America increases with the implementation of NAFTA.

Despite their progress, Hispanic entrepreneurs, like other minority business owners, still face some obstacles. Minority entrepreneurs tend to start businesses on a smaller scale and have more difficulty finding investors than white entrepreneurs. Some industry analysts believe

Figure 5.8 **Types of Businesses Owned by Minorities and Women**

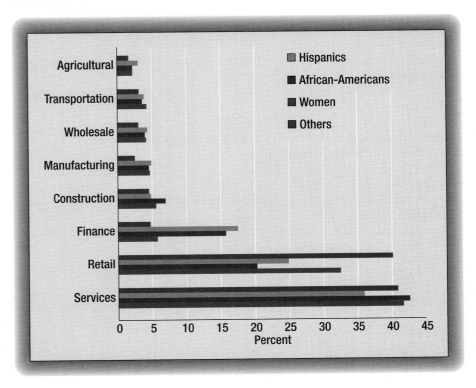

BUSINESS HALL OF SHAME

Closing Day at Centaur Zone Cafe

When W. David Waters opened the Centaur Zone Cafe in Honolulu, he dreamed of growing his new company into an international franchise of coffeehouses. "I thought we'd either be an overnight sensation or we'd flop," he remembers. But when closing day came a short year later, he recalls, "It was nothing romantic. It just sort of opened and just sort of closed."

Waters was full of confidence when he started out and expected to be a success. Failure was not in his vocabulary. With a dual degree in international management and finance, he knew where to start. He began by conducting research.

Waters thought downtown Honolulu would be an excellent location

for a coffeehouse. He saw two types of customers there: the artsy crowd from the Hawaii Theatre located across the street from his proposed location and the wealthy Asian students from Hawaii Pacific University, just around the corner. Tourists were also expected to add to his clientele. After talking with other coffeehouse owners, a representative from SCORE (Service Core of Retired Executives), and the director of a national coffee organization, Waters wrote up his business plan.

Next, he went in search of start-up capital. He combined $10,000 from his own savings and credit cards with $13,000 from a Japanese investor. But his greatest support came from his father, who loaned him $20,000. With the planning and financing taken care of, Waters signed the lease on the downtown location he had chosen for

the Centaur Zone Cafe. He painted and decorated the cafe with used furniture reupholstered in animal prints and purple velvet. While he was fixing up the place, people kept stopping by, eager for the cafe to open. "We thought once the doors opened, people would come in," says Waters.

Finally, the Centaur Zone officially opened. But the first day was slow and depressing. Waters also hoped that many of the people attending a dance performance that night at the Hawaii Theatre would stop in for a cup of coffee after the show. "We passed out fliers, and we bought all these desserts," explains Waters. "The theater closed, and everybody just walked by. Less than 10 people came in. It was so embarrassing."

Eventually, word-of-mouth spread to the university campus, and college students began hanging out at the

that minority entrepreneurs have more trouble buying franchises. Even today, minorities own only 5 percent of U.S. franchise businesses, just one-fourth the amount expected based on their proportion of the total U.S. population. Ask Susan Kezios, president of Women in Franchising, a Chicago-based association that provides services for women and minorities who are interested in franchising opportunities. Minority groups, says Kezios, are "the last markets on franchisors' list of priorities."[34]

Businesses Owned by African-Americans and Members of Other Minority Groups

In recent years, the number of black-owned businesses has almost doubled—twice the growth of U.S. businesses overall. In fact, the 100 largest black-owned companies together generated revenues of over $14 billion last year.[35]

A few years ago, Charles Hardesty became one of the 7

million Americans each year who realize their dream of business ownership. Every Friday night, Hardesty would drive 4 hours to the Atlantic coast, buy 600 pounds of fresh shrimp, and return to spend weekends at a Winston-Salem, North Carolina flea market. When Hardesty learned that one of his customers wanted to sell his seafood restaurant, he decided to change careers. Pooling his life savings and a bank loan, Hardesty came up with $18,000 and the Forsyth Seafood Cafe was born. Since then he has opened a second seafood restaurant and rakes in $700,000 in sales each year.[36]

THE FRANCHISING ALTERNATIVE

The franchising concept has played a major role in the growth of small business. **Franchising** is a contractual business arrangement between a manufacturer or another supplier and a dealer. The contract specifies the methods by which the dealer markets the good or service of the supplier. Franchises can involve both goods and services; some of the best known are Domino's, McDonald's, and Subway.

Starting a small, independent company can be a

Business Directory

franchising contractual agreement that specifies the methods by which a dealer can produce and market a supplier's good or service.

cafe. After three weeks, the business broke even. "We were making enough money to pay the rent and electricity," says Waters, "but not enough for me to pay my own bills." But when summer came, the students went home, and business dropped again. He got an extension on his rent until fall, but by that time, Hawaii's economic downturn was taking its toll. Then the financial crisis hit Asia, and tourism slowed. The cafe was hit hard. After only a year, the Centaur Zone Cafe closed its doors. "Until the end," explains Waters, "we thought something miraculous would happen."

So what happened to Waters's business plan? Business consultant Sam Slom thinks that Waters's basic assumptions weren't realistic. For one thing, unlike malls, "downtown areas are more transient," explains Slom. In addition, Slom points out that the costs of doing business in Hawaii are high as a result of such mandatory employee benefits as medical, workers' compensation, unemployment insur-

ance, and liability costs, which can add 50 percent to payroll costs. But Waters's biggest mistake, according to Slom, was "underestimating the consequences of Hawaii's worst-in-the-nation business and tax climate, "which had crushed big and small businesses alike and broken many able entrepreneurs during the past decade.

Would Waters someday consider starting another business? He says yes. After all, someone once described a successful entrepreneur as a person who has already experienced at least three business failures.

QUESTIONS FOR CRITICAL THINKING

1. When asked about his experience with the Centaur Zone Cafe, Waters says, "I never dreamed we would just drag along, hanging on to tidbits of hope here and there. It was emotionally and psychologically trying." The times were tough, he says, "part of me kept

wanting to go on. Closing wasn't my choice." Why do you think he was unable to see the writing on the wall? Explain your answer.

2. How could Waters have more fully investigated the likelihood of getting customers in the Centaur Zone? Would more research have helped? What about surveys or personal interviews?

Sources: Cheryl McManus, "Uh-Oh: Business Failures Up," *Inc.*, January 1999, p. 79; and Janean Chun, "Out of Business," *Entrepreneur*, August 1998, pp. 12–13.

---

risky, time-consuming endeavor, but franchising can reduce the amount of time and effort needed to expand. For instance, Ken Rosenthal knew he wanted to start a bakery, but he also knew he wanted to avoid the long hours that this service-oriented business frequently requires. "I'll never forget one story," he recalls. "This guy was working around the clock. He'd come home, get in the shower, turn on the water, and sit on the floor to rest. And when the hot water ran out and the shower ran cold, it was time to go back to work." When Rosenthal opened a bakery/cafe called the Saint Louis Bread Company, he planned from the beginning to franchise his concept. With a franchise, comments the company's CEO David Hutkin, "You give away a big percentage, and you don't make as much money, but it's a cheaper way to grow."

Thanks to franchising, in just 10 years, the Saint Louis Bread Company has grown from one cafe to more than 17 today. Rosenthal keeps two large notebooks filled with inquiries from 400 potential franchisees. Notes Myron Klevens, one of Rosenthal's partners. "We'd like to be kind of the itsy-bitsy spider—here's St. Louis, and here's someplace else, here's someplace else, and sort of link them all up."[37]

The Franchising Sector

Franchising started just after the Civil War, when the Singer Company began to franchise sewing-machine outlets. The concept became increasingly popular after 1900 within the

With a new restaurant to go with their seafood market and takeout grill, Charles A. Hardesty and his wife, Virginia, are satisfying their appetite for business growth.

| Figure 5.9 | **Franchises in the Service Sector** |

Every 12 hours we give birth to a business owner.

The ServiceMaster family of companies welcomes you into the franchise world the right way. For over 65 years we've helped franchisees grow up to be healthy, strong businesses. With the support we provide, they skip right past the crawling stage and hit the ground running.

Twice every business day, a new franchise within our group of companies opens its doors, giving birth to another potential success story. It's no wonder-you'll be born into a business family with 5 leading franchise brands, a Fortune 500 parent and relations with 6.5 million customers. Let's talk about your due date in this exciting world. Give us a call.

AMERISPEC — As North America's premier provider of home inspection services, AmeriSpec is over 280 franchises strong and still expanding in a billion-dollar, high-growth industry. www.svm.com

FURNITURE MEDIC — The Furniture Medic experts revolutionized furniture repair and restoration by developing a patented process and products for on-site service-an exciting ground floor opportunity. www.furnituremedic.com

merry maids — Merry Maids-the most recognized name in residential home cleaning-has been rated the number one franchise company in a rapidly growing category by *Money*, *Success* and *Entrepreneur* magazines. www.merrymaids.com

ServiceMASTER Clean — America's leading service provider in the 25 billion-dollar cleaning industry, ServiceMaster is the preferred choice for commercial and residential carpet cleaning, disaster restoration and janitorial services. www.servicemaster.com

TERMINIX — Terminix, the pioneer in termite control, is the leading termite and pest control brand worldwide protecting homes and businesses with the most advanced treatment methods. www.terminix.com

1-888-OWN NOW 5
(1-888-696-6695)

Quality Service Network

automobile industry. Automobile travel led to demands for gasoline, oil, and tires; makers of all of these commodities franchised dealers to distribute them. Soft-drink and lodging firms offered additional popular franchises.

Quality Service Network is one of the largest franchisors of consumer and business services. Included in its portfolio of franchise alternatives are a termite and pest control firm (Terminix), a home inspection company (AmeriSpec), a furniture repair and restoration business (Furniture Medic), Merry Maids residential home cleaning, and commercial and residential carpet-cleaning specialist Servicemaster Clean. As Figure 5.9 points out, the company is growing at the rate of one new business every 12 hours.

The franchising concept continues its rapid growth. Total U.S. sales from franchising are expected to top $1 trillion by 2000. Franchising is also popular overseas. In Australia, for example, franchise sales topped $60 billion in 2000.

Franchising Agreements

The two principals in a franchising agreement are the franchisee and the franchisor. The dealer is the *franchisee*, a small-business owner who contracts to sell the good or service of the supplier—the *franchisor*—in exchange for some payment (usually a flat fee plus future royalties or commissions). The franchisor typically provides building plans, site selection help, managerial and accounting systems, and other services to assist the franchisee. The franchisor also provides name recognition for the small-business owner who becomes a franchisee. This public image is created by advertising campaigns, and the franchisee typically contributes to cover such costs.

The franchisee purchases both tangible and intangible assets from the franchisor. A franchisor may charge a management fee in addition to its initial franchise fee and a percentage of sales or profits. Another may require contributions to a promotional fund. Total costs can vary over a wide range. Start-up costs for a Wendy's fast-food restaurant can run anywhere from $805,000 to $1.3 million. By contrast, start-up costs for a coverall cleaning service franchise average $2,500.

Many franchisors provide some type of training for new franchisees and their employees. The Saint Louis Bread Company, for example, offers 56 training modules on topics such as "Espresso Standards" and "Product Packaging"; workers who hold different positions within a franchise must complete different combinations of modules.

Benefits and Problems of Franchising

As for any other business property, the buyer of a franchise bears the responsibility for researching what he or she is buying. Poorly financed or poorly managed franchise systems offer opportunities no better than those in poorly financed or poorly managed independent businesses. Thousands of franchise businesses close each year, and estimates of franchise failure rates range from 30 percent to 50 percent. The franchising concept does not eliminate the risks of a potential small-business investment; it merely adds alternatives.

Advantages of franchises include a prior performance record, a recognizable company name, a tested management program, and business training. An existing franchise has posted a performance record on which the prospective buyer can base comparisons and judgments. Earlier results can indicate the likelihood of success in a proposed venture. In addition, a widely recognized name gives the franchisee a tremendous advantage; car dealers, for instance, know that their brand-name products will attract particular segments of the market. A tested management program usually allows the prospective franchisee to avoid worrying about setting up an accounting system, establishing quality control standards, or designing employment application forms. In addition, some franchisors offer valuable business training. McDonald's, for instance, teaches the basics of operating a franchise at its Hamburger University in Oak Brook, Illinois.

On the negative side, franchise fees and future payments can be a very expensive cost category. International fast-food giant McDonald's continues to add new franchisees, both in the United States and abroad. The fast-food pioneer has made successful efforts to achieve diversity in franchise ownership. Today, one McDonald's franchise in eight is black-owned. These restaurants employ 65,000 workers and generate annual revenues of $1.1 billion.[38] Messages such as the one shown in Figure 5.10 to potential McDonald's owners demonstrate the firm's commitment to attracting additional women and minority owners.

As a general rule, however, the typical owner of a franchise with the tested management system, proven performance record, and globally recognized brand name of a McDonald's will spend between $400,000 and $600,000, depending on the location, in start-up costs. Among people able to pass this obstacle, less than one applicant in ten will be awarded a franchise.

For another potential drawback, the franchisee is judged by the actions of his or her peers. A successful franchise unit can lose customers if other units of the same franchise fail. A strong, effective program of managerial control is essential to offset any bad impressions created by unsuccessful franchises.

Finally, someone who is considering buying a franchise must think first about whether he or she has the right personality for the endeavor. Chapter 6 features an in-depth discussion of the basic characteristics that entrepreneurs should bring to their new endeavors.

SMALL BUSINESS GOES GLOBAL

Traditionally, a very small percentage of U.S. businesses were involved in importing and exporting. International businesses confronted high costs and many other challenges, including cultural, legal, and economic barriers.

Figure 5.10 **High Franchise Fees and Stringent Management Requirements: Significant Hurdles for People Who Want to Own Well-Known Franchises**

But this situation is quickly changing as global involvement in contemporary business is fast becoming synonymous with electronic commerce and the Internet. A small business can enter new markets today as easily as getting a Web address and setting up a home page.

A recent survey of more than 700 U.S. small businesses revealed that they tend to target markets that conduct business in English; also, they prefer one-on-one relationships and work under favorable trade agreements. Canada is the most favored nation to receive goods and services from U.S. small-business exporters.[39]

Role of the Internet in International Expansion

Some small businesses generate much of their annual revenue from overseas sales. Suzanne Southard, for example, started Texas Trading to export clothes, accessories, sports equipment, and snack food to Swedish consumers. Last year, she shipped more than $30,000 worth of goods to Sweden from her home-based office in Dallas.

Kris Olson's ski clothing firm, Beater Wear, uses its Web site as a promotional tool for extending the selling season from 5 months to year-round. Via the Internet, Olson can expose his small business to consumers in the Southern Hemisphere, where the seasons are reversed from those in the Northern Hemisphere. The Beater Wear Web site now receives 2,700 visits a day and has dramatically increased its position in its industry. Ski magazines now promote Beater Wear in exchange for commissions on resulting product sales.[40]

www. **www.beater.com**

Even if they don't maintain Web sites, the Internet can be an important information resource for companies hoping to sell their goods and services in other countries.

By surfing the WWW, small-business owners can find leads on potential customers, gather information about overseas markets, and pinpoint government restrictions. Table 5.3 lists some of the many trade and exporting resources available on the Internet.

Licensing as a Growth Strategy

As the previous chapter discussed, licensing is a relatively simple way to enter a foreign market. Under a *licensing agreement,* one firm allows another to use its intellectual property in exchange for compensation in the form of royalties. Examples of intellectual property include trademarks, patents, copyrights, and technical know-how. For instance, a firm that has developed a new type of packaging might license the process to foreign companies.

Licensing can be a very lucrative opportunity for a small business that targets collector products. Nearly 14 million American households are collector households, and half of those include children. Top collector items for young girls are dolls and stuffed animals, while boys prefer sports cards and miniature cars. Kristin Edstrom, licensing manager for Ty Inc., marketer of the popular Beanie Babies, has taken licensing to the limit. Ty is developing a licensed fan club program and newsletter and discussing publishing, TV, and film deals with potential licensees.[41]

Figure 5.11 **Forms of Business Ownership**

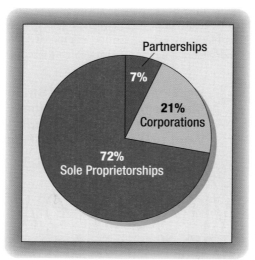

Exporting through Intermediaries

Sometimes a small firm can achieve exporting success by teaming up with another firm that can provide services it cannot afford on its own. An *export management company* is a domestic firm that specializes in performing international marketing services as a commissioned representative or distributor for other companies. Another option for a small firm is to purchase needed goods and sell its products internationally through an *export trading company,* a general trading firm that plays varied roles in world commerce, in turn importing, exporting, countertrading, investing, and manufacturing.

ALTERNATIVES FOR ORGANIZING A BUSINESS

Every business fits one of three categories of legal ownership: sole proprietorships, partnerships, and corporations. As Figure 5.11 shows, sole proprietorships are the most common form of business ownership. However, the simple *number* of firms organized according to each model may overstate the importance of sole proprietorships and understate the role of corporations in generating revenues, producing and marketing goods and services, creating jobs, and paying taxes. After all, General Motors is only one of the corporations represented in Figure 5.11,

Table 5.3	Small-Business Online Exporting Resources

U.S. Department of Commerce International Trade Administration
This agency offers answers to the most frequently asked questions about international trade and provides information about markets around the world.

www.ita.doc.gov.

Export-Import Bank of the United States
The Eximbank offers information about obtaining working capital, direct loans, and export insurance.

www.exim.gov.

U.S. Small Business Administration
The SBA offers information on funding sources for exporting firms.

www.sba.gov.

Bureau of Export Administration
This agency provides data about the licenses required to export technology products.

Table 5.4	Comparing the Three Major Forms of Private Ownership			
Form of Ownership	**Number of Owners**	**Liability**	**Advantages**	**Disadvantages**
Sole proprietorship	One owner	Unlimited personal liability for business debts	1. Owner retains all profits 2. Easy to form and dissolve 3. Owner has flexibility	1. Unlimited financial liability 2. Financing limitations 3. Management deficiencies 4. Lack of continuity
Partnership	Two or more owners	Personal assets of any operating partner at risk from business creditors	1. Easy to form 2. Can benefit from complementary management skills 3. Expanded financial capacity	1. Unlimited financial liability 2. Interpersonal conflicts 3. Lack of continuity 4. Difficult to dissolve
Corporation	Unlimited number of shareholders; up to 75 shareholders for S corporations	Limited	1. Limited financial liability 2. Specialized management skills 3. Expanded financial capacity 4. Economies of large-scale operations	1. Difficult and costly to form and dissolve 2. Tax disadvantages 3. Legal restrictions

but its impact on the nation's economy exceeds the collective effect of thousands of small businesses organized as proprietorships.

Each form offers unique advantages and disadvantages, as outlined in Table 5.4. As actor Burt Reynolds discovered a few years ago, these characteristics must be considered very carefully before launching any new business. Reynolds did not organize a restaurant venture as a corporation, leaving him personally liable for $28 million committed for leases and equipment. This section will also briefly examine S corporations, limited-liability partnerships, and limited-liability companies—three specialized organizational forms designed to overcome certain limitations of the traditional ownership structures.[42]

Sole Proprietorships

The most common form of business ownership, the **sole proprietorship** is also the oldest and the simplest, because no legal distinction separates the sole proprietor's status as an individual from his or her status as a business owner. Although sole proprietorships are common in a variety of industries, they are concen-

trated primarily among small businesses such as repair shops, small retail outlets, and service organizations, like painters, plumbers, and lawn-care specialists.

Sole proprietorships offer advantages that other business entities cannot. For one, they are easy to form and dissolve. (Partnerships are also easy to form, but difficult to dissolve.) A sole proprietorship gives the owner management flexibility and the right to retain all profits, except what goes to the government for personal income taxes. Retention of all profits and responsibility for all losses give sole proprietors the incentive to maximize efficiency in their operations.

Minimal legal requirements simplify entering and exiting a sole proprietorship. Usually the owner must meet only a few legal requirements for starting one, including registering the business or trade name at the county courthouse (to guarantee that two firms do not use the same name) and taking out any necessary licenses. (Local governments require certain kinds of licenses of restaurants, motels, retail stores, and many repair shops.) Some occupational licenses require firms to carry specific types of insurance, such as liability coverage.

Business Directory

sole proprietorship   form of business ownership in which the company is owned and operated by a single person.

The ease of dissolving a business set up as a sole proprietorship is an attractive feature for certain types of enterprises. This is a particularly important benefit for temporary businesses set up to handle just a few transactions. For example, someone could create a business to organize a single concert at a local arena.

Ownership flexibility is another advantage of a sole proprietorship. The owner can make management decisions without consulting others, take prompt action when needed, and keep trade secrets where appropriate. You've probably heard people say, "I like being my own boss." This flexibility leads many business owners to prefer the sole proprietorship organization form.

A disadvantage of the sole proprietorship form comes from the owner's financial liability for all debts of the business. Also, the business must operate with financial resources limited to the owner's personal funds and money that he or she can borrow. Such financing limitations can keep the business from expanding. For another disadvantage, the owner must handle a wide range of management and operational tasks; as the firm grows, the owner may not perform all duties with equal effectiveness. Finally, a sole proprietorship lacks long-term continuity, since death, bankruptcy, retirement, or a change in personal interests can terminate it.

Partnerships

Another option for organizing a business is forming a partnership. The Uniform Partnership Act, which regulates this ownership form in most states, defines a **partnership** as an association of two or more persons who operate a business as co-owners by voluntary legal agreement. The partnership has been a traditional form of ownership for professionals offering services, such as physicians, lawyers, and dentists.

Partnerships are easy to form; as with sole proprietorships, the legal requirements involve registering the business

Figure 5.12 **Using Life Insurance on Partners to Achieve Business Continuity**

INSURANCE FOR THE UNEXPECTED.
INVESTMENTS FOR THE OPPORTUNITIES?

John Hancock

WORLDWIDE SPONSOR

If your partner dies, will your business be far behind?

As difficult as it would be to suffer the tragedy of losing a partner, consider that without

the proper plan, you could also lose control of your business. However, there is a way to prepare for something so

unthinkable. We will show you how to use life insurance to help fund a buy-sell agreement that will allow

you to maintain control of your business. How? With the proceeds from life insurance, you'll have the funds to

buy out your partner's heirs and retain control of your company. To find out more, call

1-800-508-1495, ext. 211 and we'll put you in touch with our **Business Planning Group.**

John Hancock Mutual Life Insurance Company, Boston, MA 02117   CP-AD7 1/97

name and taking out the necessary licenses. Partnerships also offer expanded financial capabilities when each partner invests money. They also usually increase access to borrowed funds as compared to sole proprietorships.

Another advantage is the opportunity for professionals to combine complementary skills and knowledge. Larry Meltzer and Robert Martin, for example, are co-owners of Meltzer & Martin Public Relations in Dallas. "Larry is more creative and I'm more strategic," explains Martin. So Martin focuses on management issues like accounting and human resource management, while Meltzer spends most of his time working with clients to develop effective public relations campaigns. Sharing responsibilities in this way helps them to play off each other's strengths to boost the success of their business.[43]

Like sole proprietorships, most partnerships have the disadvantage of unlimited financial liability. Each partner bears full responsibility for the debts of the firm, and each is legally liable for the actions of the other partners. Partners must pay the partnership's debts from their personal funds if its debts exceed its assets. Breaking up a partnership is also a much harder undertaking than dissolving a sole proprietorship. Rather than simply withdrawing funds from the bank, the partner who wants out must find someone to buy his or her interest in the firm.

In many states, partners can minimize some of these risks by organizing as a *limited liability partnership*. In many respects, such a partnership resembles a general partnership, but laws limit the liability of the partners to the value of their investments in the company.

The death of a partner also threatens the survival of a partnership. A new partnership must be formed, and the estate of the deceased is entitled to a share of the firm's value. To ease the financial strains of such events, business planners recommend life insurance coverage for each partner combined with a buy-sell agreement. As Figure 5.12 points out, the insurance proceeds can repay the deceased partner's heirs and allow the surviving partner to retain control of the business.

Partnerships are also vulnerable to personal conflicts.

Personal disagreements may quickly escalate into business battles. Good communication is the key to resolving conflicts before they damage a partnership's chances for success or even destroy it. Tim Wagner and his partner learned this lesson when they joined forces to buy Webster's, a Milwaukee bookstore-cafe combination. Although the two had been close friends for years, the pressures of running a business together led to unexpected conflicts. "He felt if he was working, I should be working," recalls Wagner. "But what he failed to realize is that I'd work through the night doing the books after he left for the day." Eventually, the two started avoiding each other, the business failed, and for several years, the partners were unable to resume their friendship.[44]

Corporations

A **corporation** is a legal organization with assets and liabilities separate from those of its owner(s). (Regular corporations are sometimes referred to as *C corporations* to distinguish them from other types.) Although even the smallest business can choose the corporate form of organization, most people think of large companies when they hear the term *corporation*. In truth, many corporations are extremely large businesses. Some of the products made by General Motors, the nation's largest corporation, are shown in Figure 5.13.

GM is joined on the list of the nation's largest firms by its U.S.-based auto rival Ford Motor Co. In addition, the list contains two oil companies (Exxon and Mobil), retail giant Wal-Mart, General Electric, IBM, AT&T, and tobacco and food-products producer Philip Morris. Each of the ten companies produces annual revenues over $50 billion. GM generates sales of $1 billion *every two days!*[45]

The corporate ownership form offers considerable ad-

Figure 5.13 **General Motors: America's Largest Corporation**

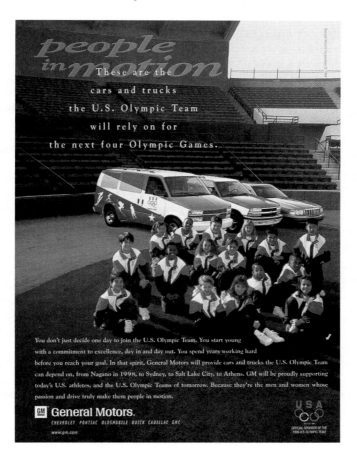

vantages. First, because a corporation acquires the status of a separate legal entity, the stockholders take only limited financial risk; if the firm fails, they lose only the amounts they have invested. The limited risk of corporate ownership is clearly reflected in corporate names throughout the world. While many U.S. and Canadian corporations include the *Inc.* designation in their names, British firms favor the *Ltd.* abbreviation to publicize their *limited* liability. In Australia, the abbreviation for *Proprietary Limited—Pty. Ltd.*—is frequently included in corporate names.

Corporations offer other advantages. They can draw on the specialized skills of many employees, unlike sole proprietorships and partnerships, for which managerial skills are usually confined to the abilities of the owners. They gain expanded financial capabilities from opportunities to offer direct outside investments such as stock sales.

The large-scale operation permitted by corporate ownership also brings several advantages. Employees can specialize in their most effective tasks. A large firm can generate internal financing for many projects by transferring money from one part of the corporation to another. Long manufacturing runs usually promote efficient production and allow the firm to charge low prices that attract customers.

One disadvantage for a corporation is the potential for double taxation of corporate earnings. After a corporation pays federal, state, and local income taxes on its profits, its owners (stockholders) also pay personal taxes on any distributions of those profits they receive from the corporation in

Business Directory

partnership form of business ownership in which the company is operated by two or more people who are co-owners by voluntary legal agreement.

corporation business that stands as a legal entity with assets and liabilities separate from those of its owner(s).

the form of stock dividends. Figure 5.14 shows how this process works.

Corporate ownership also involves some legal issues that sole proprietorships and partnerships do not encounter. The number of laws and regulations that affect corporations has increased dramatically in recent years.

A number of firms have implemented modified forms of the traditional corporate and partnership structures to avoid double taxation of business income while achieving (or retaining) limited financial liability for their owners. Businesses that meet certain size requirements (including ownership by no more than 75 shareholders) may decide to organize as *S corporations* (or *subchapter S corporations*). These firms can elect to pay federal income taxes as partnerships while retaining the liability limitations typical of corporations.

Laws in 47 states allow business owners to form **limited liability companies (LLCs)** to secure the corporate advantage of limited liability while avoiding the double taxation characteristic of corporations. An LLC is governed by an operating agreement that resembles a partnership agreement, except that it reduces each partner's liability for the actions of the other owners.

Changing Legal Structures to Meet Changing Needs

Someone planning to launch a new business must consider dozens of factors before deciding on an appropriate legal form. These include:

▼ Personal financial situations and the need for additional funds for the business start-up and continued operation

▼ Management skills and limitations

▼ Management styles and capabilities for working with partners and other members of top management

▼ Concerns about personal liability exposure

Although the legal form of organization is a major decision facing new business owners, they need not treat it as a permanent decision. Over time, changing conditions such as business growth may prompt the owner of a sole proprietorship or group of partners to switch to a more appropriate form. That's what Deborah Williams did.

Williams launched Black Cat Computer Wholesale as a sole proprietorship, but when the firm started to grow by leaps and bounds, she recognized the need for a change. "The main thing I was worried about was limiting my personal liability," she says, so she switched to an S corporation. It wasn't long, however, before Black Cat's growth caused other concerns. Williams needed financing to fund the firm's rapid expansion. After weighing the advantages and disadvantages, she decided to change once again to a C corporation. "My real goal was to create a broader base of financing for the company."[46]

ORGANIZING AND OPERATING A CORPORATION

One of the first decisions in forming a corporation is determining where to locate its headquarters and where it will do business. This section describes the various types of corporations and considers the options and procedures involved in incorporating a business.

Types of Corporations

Corporations fall into three categories: domestic, foreign, or alien corporations. A firm is considered a **domestic corporation**

Figure 5.14 **Double Taxation: A Disadvantage of the Corporate Form of Organization**

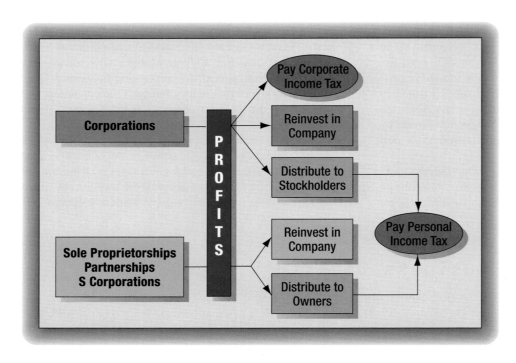

in the state where it is incorporated. When a firm does business in states other than the one where it has filed incorporation papers, it is registered as a **foreign corporation** in each of those states. A firm incorporated in one nation that operates in another is known as an **alien corporation** where it operates. Some firms operate under all three forms of incorporation.

Johnson Products Inc., a maker of personal-care products for African-Americans, operates as a domestic, foreign, and alien corporation. The company is incorporated in Delaware, where it is a domestic corporation, but its headquarters are in Chicago, where it operates a large plant as a foreign corporation. The firm also operates overseas as an alien corporation, with sales and distribution centers in Great Britain and other European countries.

A fourth category of corporations was discussed in the previous chapter. *Multinational corporations* are firms with significant operations and marketing activities outside their home countries. Examples include General Electric, Siemens, and Mitsubishi in heavy electrical equipment and Timex, Seiko, and Citizen in watches.

The Incorporation Process

Suppose that you decide to start a business, and you believe that the corporate form offers the best way to organize it. Where should you set up shop? How do you establish a corporate charter? The following paragraphs discuss the procedures for creating a new corporation.

Where to Incorporate Location is one of the most important considerations for any small-business owner. While most small and medium-sized businesses are incorporated in the states where they do most of their business, a U.S. firm can actually incorporate in any state it chooses. The founders of large corporations, or of those that will do business nationwide, often compare the benefits provided in various states' laws to corporations in various industries. The favorable legal climate in Delaware has prompted a large number of major corporations to incorporate there.

Figure 5.15 **States Considered Best—and Worst—for Incorporating a Manufacturing Firm**

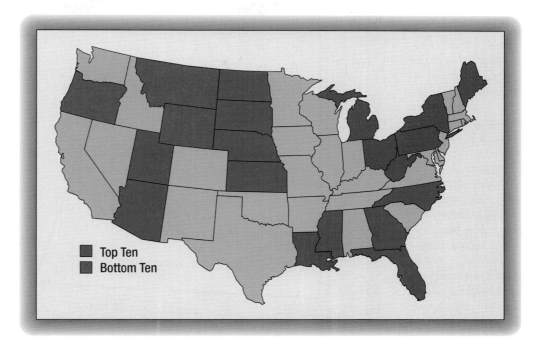

Top Ten
Bottom Ten

Figure 5.15 shows the ten states considered to be the best choices for incorporating a manufacturing firm as well as the ten states at the bottom of the list.

The Corporate Charter Each state mandates a specific procedure for incorporating a business. Most states require at least three *incorporators*—the individuals who create the corporation—which opens incorporation possibilities to small businesses. Another requirement demands that a new corporation adopt a name dissimilar from those of other businesses; most states require that the name must end with the words *Company, Corporation, Incorporated,* or *Limited* to show that the owners have limited liability. Figure 5.16 lists ten elements of the articles of incorporation that are requirements in most states for chartering a corporation.

The information provided in the articles of incorporation form the basis on which a state grants a **corporate charter,** a legal document that formally establishes a corporation. After securing the charter, the owners articulate the company's bylaws, which describe the rules and procedures for its operation.

Corporate Management

Figure 5.17 illustrates the levels of management in a corporation. **Stockholders** are owners; they acquire shares of stock in the corporation and, therefore, become part owners of it. Some companies, such as family businesses, are owned by relatively few stockholders, and the stock is generally unavailable to outsiders. In such a firm, known as a *closed corporation* or *closely held corporation,* the stockholders also control and manage all activities. In contrast, an *open corporation* sells stock to the general public, establishing diversified ownership, and often leading to larger operations than those of a closed corporation.

Stock Ownership and Stockholder Rights Corporations usually hold annual stockholders' meetings during which managers report on corporate activities and stockholders vote on any decisions that require their approval, including elections of officers.

Shares are usually classified as common or preferred stock. Although owners of *preferred stock* have limited voting rights, they are entitled to receive dividends before common-stock holders and, in the event of a corporate dissolution

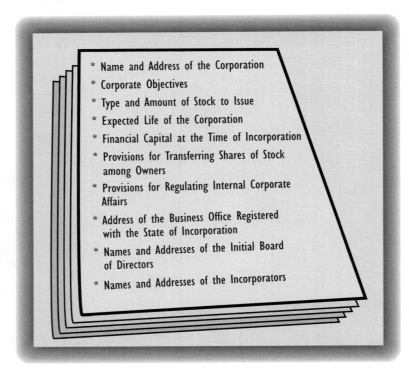

Figure 5.16 **Articles of Incorporation**

* Name and Address of the Corporation
* Corporate Objectives
* Type and Amount of Stock to Issue
* Expected Life of the Corporation
* Financial Capital at the Time of Incorporation
* Provisions for Transferring Shares of Stock among Owners
* Provisions for Regulating Internal Corporate Affairs
* Address of the Business Office Registered with the State of Incorporation
* Names and Addresses of the Initial Board of Directors
* Names and Addresses of the Incorporators

would have first claims on assets once debtors are repaid. Owners of *common stock* have voting rights but only residual claims on the firm's assets; that is, they are last to receive any income distributions (dividends). Since one share is worth only one vote, small stockholders generally have little influence on corporate management actions. The various types of common and preferred stock are described in detail in Chapter 21.

Board of Directors Stockholders elect a **board of directors**—the governing body of a corporation. The board sets overall policy, authorizes major transactions involving the corporation, and hires the chief executive officer (CEO). Most boards include both inside directors (corporate executives) and outside directors, people who are not employed by the organization. Sometimes, the corporation's top executive also chairs the board. Generally, outside directors are also stockholders.

"At the dawn of a new millennium, the mission of the Sydney Organising Committee for the Olympic Games is to deliver to the athletes of the world and to the Olympic movement, on behalf of all Australians, the most harmonious, athlete-oriented, technically excellent and culturally enhancing Olympic Games of the modern era."

For the second time in the past 50 years, the Summer Olympics return to the Land Down Under. In 1956, Melbourne hosted the games; now the torch has passed to Australia's largest city.

Corporate Officers The CEO and other members of top management, such as the chief operating officer (COO), chief information officer (CIO), and chief financial officer (CFO), make most major corporate decisions. Managers at the next level down the hierarchy, middle management, handle the ongoing operational functions of the company. At the bottom tier of management, supervisory personnel coordinate day-to-day operations, assign specific tasks to employees, and often evaluate workers' job performance. The activities and responsibilities of managers at various levels in the organization are described in detail in Chapter 8.

Employee-Owned Corporations

Another alternative in creating a corporation is *employee ownership,* in which workers buy shares of stock in the company that employs them. The corporate organization stays the same, but most stockholders are also employees.

Science Applications International Corp. (SAIC) has achieved dramatic success under this form of corporate organization. SAIC's 25,000 employees own 90 percent of the San Diego firm, and the other 10 percent is owned by former employees. Says one owner-manager, "When I'm making a decision, I don't just make it as a manager, I make it as an owner."[47]

Although the popularity of this form of corporation is growing, almost one-quarter of all employee-owned firms fail. Employee ownership doesn't solve every problem. The employees of United Airlines, for example, engineered a stock buyout in 1994. Since the buyout, sales and profits have risen, but United's top management continues to experience labor disagreements with employee-owners.[48] Employee-owned firms are discussed in more detail in Chapter 11.

Not-for-Profit Corporations

The same business concepts that apply to firms whose objectives include earning profits also apply to *not-for-profit corporations*—which pursue primary objectives other than returning profits to owners.

Over 1 million not-for-profits operate in the United States, employing well over 10 million people and generating an estimated $300 billion in revenues each year. Most states' laws set out separate provisions dealing with the organization structures and operations of not-for-profit corporations. These organizations do not issue stock certificates, since they pay no dividends to owners, and ownership rarely changes. They are also exempt from paying income taxes. This sector includes museums, libraries, religious and human-service organizations, private secondary schools, health-care facilities, symphony orchestras, zoos, and thousands of other groups such as government agencies, political parties, and labor unions.

Perhaps the best known international not-for-profit runs the Olympic games. Several industry-leading international companies, including Kodak, IBM, Coca-Cola, McDonald's, Xerox, Visa, and UPS, donate expertise, technology, resources, and revenue. The average price for a multinational Olympic sponsorship is $50 million in cash, equipment, and services. Between 1997 and 2000, more than $3.5 billion will be generated through sales of broadcast rights fees, sponsorships, and other marketing programs. The International Olympic Committee redistributes these funds to support athletic training and competition. Around $300 million goes to National Olympic Committees for administrative expenses, sports development, and travel to the games. More than $130 million goes to the seven Winter Sports Federations and 28 Summer Federations to promote their sports. The Olympic cities also help to support the games. The 2000 Sydney Summer Olympics and the 2002 Winter Olympics in Salt Lake City, Utah, will donate more than $23 million worth of accommodations to Olympic athletes and officials.[49]

Figure 5.17 Levels of Management in a Corporation

```
┌─────────────────────────────────┐
│         STOCKHOLDERS            │
│   • Buy shares in corporation   │
│   • Elect board of directors    │
└─────────────────────────────────┘
                 │
                 ▼
┌─────────────────────────────────┐
│       BOARD OF DIRECTORS        │
│   • Sets overall policy         │
│   • Authorizes major transactions │
│   • Hires CEO                   │
└─────────────────────────────────┘
                 │
                 ▼
┌─────────────────────────────────┐
│        TOP MANAGEMENT           │
│   Chief Executive Officer (CEO) │
│   Chief Operating Officer (COO) │
│   Chief Financial Officer (CFO) │
│   • Manage overall operations   │
│   • Make major decisions        │
│   • Introduce major changes     │
└─────────────────────────────────┘
                 │
                 ▼
┌─────────────────────────────────┐
│       MIDDLE MANAGEMENT         │
│        Branch Managers          │
│         Plant Managers          │
│      Division Heads/Directors   │
│   • Manage operations           │
│   • Serve as liaisons between top management and other levels │
└─────────────────────────────────┘
                 │
                 ▼
┌─────────────────────────────────┐
│     SUPERVISORY MANAGEMENT      │
│          Supervisors            │
│        Department Heads         │
│   • Coordinate day-to-day operations │
│   • Supervise employees         │
│   • Evaluate staff performance  │
└─────────────────────────────────┘
```

WHEN BUSINESSES JOIN FORCES

Today's corporate world features many complex unions of companies, not always in the same industry or even in the

| Figure 5.18 | **Billions of Dollars in U.S. Mergers and Acquisitions** |

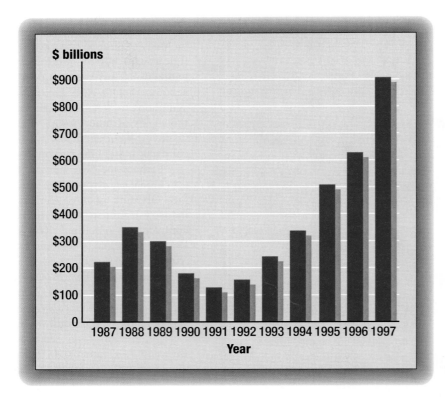

▼ Citicorp and Travelers Insurance: $73 billion

▼ Ameritech and SBC Communications: $72 billion

▼ GTE and Bell Atlantic: $71 billion

Says one industry analyst, "Business is almost scary in its intensity."[50] Figure 5.18 shows the recent, dramatic rise in mergers and acquisitions.

The terms *merger* and *acquisition* are often used interchangeably, but their meanings differ. In a **merger,** two or more firms combine to form one company; in an **acquisition,** one firm purchases the property and assumes the obligations of another. Acquisitions also occur when one firm buys a division or subsidiary from another firm. Many mergers and acquisitions cross national borders, as managers attempt to enter new markets and improve global competitiveness for their companies.

Mergers can be classified as vertical, horizontal, or conglomerate mergers. A **vertical merger** combines firms operating at different levels in the production and marketing process. A vertical merger pursues one of two primary goals: (a) to assure adequate flows of raw materials and supplies needed for a firm's products, or (b) to increase distribution. Software giant Microsoft Corp. is well-known for merging with small firms that have developed products with strong market potential. Large petroleum companies often try to reduce the uncertainty of their future petroleum supplies by acquiring successful oil and gas exploration firms. To enhance distribution opportunities, Disney's merger with the ABC television network provided Disney with an additional outlet for its film and television productions.

A **horizontal merger** joins firms in the same industry that wish to diversify, increase their customer bases, cut costs, or offer expanded product lines. When Chemical Bank and Chase Manhattan merged in 1996, the two companies had a total of 75,000 employees and 600 branches. By eliminating overlapping branches and divisions, the new company plans to operate with just 500 branches and reduce its workforce by 12,000 employees.[51]

same country. Many well-known firms have changed owners, become parts of other corporations, or split into smaller units. Current trends in corporate ownership include mergers and acquisitions and joint ventures.

Mergers and Acquisitions

Merger mania hit U.S. corporations in the 1980s, and it continues today, setting new records for the number of mergers and acquisitions. The 11,000 mergers during the past year involved companies considered household names with price tags in the billions. Consider just a few:

▼ Mobil and Exxon; $74 billion

Business Directory

merger combination of two or more firms to form one company.

acquisition procedure in which one firm acquires the property and assumes the obligations of another.

A **conglomerate merger** combines unrelated firms. The most common reasons for a conglomerate merger are to diversify, to spur sales growth, or to spend a cash surplus that might otherwise make a firm a tempting target for a takeover effort. Conglomerate mergers may join firms in totally unrelated industries. Consider Metromedia International Group Inc., a venture that combines movie-maker Orion Pictures, several eastern European telecommunications companies, and Actava Group, the maker of Snapper lawn mowers. Even apparently related companies may not fit well together after a merger or acquisition, however. Solving an Ethical Controversy discusses the pros and cons of the recent increased merger activity.

Joint Ventures—Specialized Partnerships

A **joint venture** is a partnership between companies formed for a specific undertaking. Sometimes, a company enters into a joint venture with a local firm or government, sharing the operation's costs, risks, management, and profits with its local partner. As discussed in the previous chapter, joint ventures offer particularly attractive ways for small firms to conduct international business, since they bring substantial benefits from partners already operating inside the host countries.

PUBLIC AND COLLECTIVE OWNERSHIP

While most business organizations are owned privately by individuals or groups of people, municipal, state, or national governments own some firms. Also, groups of people collectively own some companies. Public ownership is common in many industries, both in the United States and abroad.

Public Ownership

One alternative to private ownership is some form of **public ownership,** in which a unit or agency of government owns and operates an organization. In the United States, local governments often own parking structures and water systems. The Pennsylvania Turnpike Authority operates a vital highway link across the Keystone state. The federal government operates Hoover Dam in Nevada to provide electricity over a large region.

Government-Owned Corporations

Sometimes, public ownership results when private investors are unwilling to invest, fearing a high probability of failure. This situation occurred with the rural electrification program of the 1930s, which significantly expanded utility lines in sparsely populated areas. At other times, public ownership has replaced private ownership of failed organizations. Certain functions, such as municipal water systems, are considered so important to the public welfare that governments implement public ownership to protect citizens from problems. Finally, some nations have used public business ownership to foster competition by operating public companies as competitive business enterprises. In Bogota, Colombia, the government runs a TV and radio network, Instituto Nacional de Radio & Television, that broadcasts both educational and commercial programs. Public ownership remains common abroad, despite a general trend toward privatization.

Customer-Owned Businesses: Cooperatives

Another alternative to traditional, private business ownership is collective ownership of a production, storage, transportation, and/or marketing organization. Such collective ownership establishes an organization referred to as a **cooperative** (or co-op) whose owners join forces to collectively operate all or part of the functions in their industry.

Cooperatives allow small businesses to obtain quantity purchase discounts, reducing costs and enabling the co-op to pass on the savings to its members. Marketing and advertising expenses are shared among members, and the co-op's facilities can also serve as a distribution center.

Cooperatives are frequently found in small farming communities, but they also serve the needs of large growers of specific crops. For instance, Blue Diamond Growers is a cooperative that represents California almond growers. Retailers have also established co-ops. Ace Hardware is a cooperative of independent hardware store owners. Financial co-ops, such as credit unions, offer members higher interest rates on deposits and lower interest rates on loans than other institutions could provide.

WHAT'S AHEAD

The next chapter shifts the book's focus to the driving forces behind new-business formation: entrepreneurs. It examines the differences between a small-business owner and an entrepreneur and identifies certain personality traits typical of entrepreneurs. The chapter also details the process of launching a new venture, including identifying opportunities, locating needed financing, and turning good ideas into successful businesses. Finally, the chapter explores a method for infusing the entrepreneurial spirit into established businesses—intrapreneurship.

SOLVING AN ETHICAL CONTROVERSY

Are Big Oil Companies Merging into Dangerous Giants?

Every student of U.S. history is familiar with the great monopolies of the late 1800s. John D. Rockefeller and J. Paul Getty are remembered as the oil barons who became two of the most powerful men in America. With the Sherman Antitrust Act, however, monopolies were broken up and competition was restored. Yet, over the past century, as business became more globalized, the industry again found itself in the hands of another oil-production monopoly: the Organization of Petroleum Exporting Countries (OPEC). One way U.S. oil companies staved off OPEC's stranglehold was to merge. Some experts are now questioning whether merger is merely another term for monopoly.

Facing fierce competition on one side and low prices on the other, oil companies are pumping themselves up, growing stronger and bigger. French oil giant Tatal has purchased Belgium's Petrofina for $11.6 billion, creating the world's sixth largest publicly traded oil group. British Petroleum has joined with Amoco in a $55 billion union. U.S. oil firms created the largest oil company in the world when Exxon acquired Mobil for $73.7 billion.

To understand the reason behind the increase in mergers and acquisitions requires a view of the environment surrounding the oil industry. By the turn of the century, crude oil prices had reached a 12-year low as a result of an enormous surplus. The troubled economy in Asia caused oil consumption to drop by 750,000 barrels a day, but oil companies continued producing a million barrels a day more than were being sold. Just finding places to store all the surplus has become a problem. OPEC has made several attempts to cut production, but cheating among its members kept production up and prices down. The market is so saturated that even OPEC has been unable to boost prices.

For U.S. companies, cutting produc-

tion would mean financial disaster. Instead, they are merging to cut overhead costs and squeeze out more profits. That is what Exxon and Mobil are attempting by pooling resources to cover increasingly high costs of exploration in areas such as West Africa and the Caspian Sea, both geographically remote and politically risky. In addition, the combined companies will be able to compete on the world market with other megacompanies.

But critics of the merger wonder whether such a large company will be too powerful, control the market, and thus destroy competition. After all, both Exxon and Mobil are the offspring of Rockefeller's much-feared Standard Oil monopoly (broken up by the U.S. government in 1911). Experts question whether Exxon–Mobil will again be the monopoly its parent was. Supporters claim that the world has changed since Rockefeller's time, that these companies would have trouble surviving without the merger, and that competition can only be served by such consolidation.

? *Should Oil Giants Such as Exxon and Mobil Be Allowed to Merge?*

PRO

1. Mergers are good for U.S. business since larger companies can compete better in foreign markets.

2. Oil mergers reduce the number of players in an industry where too many firms are already fighting for an ever-shrinking prize.

3. Frequently, mergers result in healthier companies that can run more efficiently and thus pass cost savings along to customers.

4. Such mergers are necessary attempts to survive the dwindling roles played by oil firms in the U.S. and global markets.

CON

1. Megamergers destroy healthy competition because fewer players

have more say in controlling production and setting prices.

2. Consumers eventually pay for such mergers with higher prices.

3. As other oil companies compete with the newly merged giants, they will have to consolidate further, leaving even fewer players.

4. Such mergers often force retail service stations to go out of business.

5. Such mergers result in job loss, mostly white-collar. Even the unions agree: "These deals are seldom good for workers."

SUMMARY

During the 1970s, when gas prices soared, the Exxon–Mobil merger would never have survived the regulatory obstacles. But the Federal Trade Commission thinks differently today. Big isn't so bad any more. Many observers believe that you can still have healthy competition with only a few companies.

Moreover, oil is an industry in decline. In Rockefeller's time, petroleum was a cutting-edge energy source and the Standard Oil monopoly controlled 84 percent of the U.S. petroleum market. Today, as the largest oil company in the world, Exxon–Mobil controls some 22 percent of U.S. gasoline sales.

Finally, globalization has changed the structure of industries. Companies can no longer succeed by looking at national markets. Oil companies no longer compete with one another; they compete with all industries, across all borders. American firms like Exxon and Mobil need the flexibility of mergers to compete overseas.

Sources: "Van Miert Says BP/Mobil Problem in Exxon Merger," Reuters Limited, February 24, 1999; Phillip J. Longman and Jack Egan, "Why Big Oil Is Getting a Lot Bigger: Exxon, Mobil, and Rockefeller's Legacy," *U.S. News & World Report*, December 14, 1998, pp. 26–28; Elliot Blair Smith, "Reinventing Monopolies?" *USA Today*, December 3, 1998, pp. 1B–2B; and Thor Valdmanis and Tom Lowry, "$74B Deal Largest Ever," *USA Today*, December 2, 1998, pp. 1B–2B.

SUMMARY OF LEARNING GOALS

1. Define *small business* and identify the industries in which most small firms are established.

A small business can adopt many profiles, from a part-time, home-based business to a company with several hundred employees. A small business is a firm that is independently owned and operated, is not dominant in its field, and meets industry-specific size standards for income or number of employees. Small businesses operate in every industry, but retailing, services, and construction feature the highest proportions of small enterprises.

2. Explain the economic and social contributions of small business.

Small businesses create most of the new jobs in the U.S. economy and employ the majority of U.S. workers. They provide valuable outlets for entrepreneurial activity and often contribute to creation of new industries or development of new business processes. Women and minorities find small-business ownership to be an attractive alternative to the sometimes limited opportunities available to them in large firms. Small firms may also offer enhanced lifestyle flexibility and opportunities to gain personal satisfaction.

3. Compare the advantages and disadvantages of small business.

Small firms can often operate with greater flexibility than larger corporations can achieve. This flexibility allows smaller businesses to provide superior customer service, develop innovative products, and fill small market niches ignored by large firms. However, small businesses also must operate with fewer resources than large corporations can apply. As a result, they may suffer from financial limitations and management inadequacies. Taxes and government regulation can also impose excessive burdens on small businesses.

4. Describe how the Small Business Administration assists small-business owners.

The U.S. Small Business Administration helps small-business owners to obtain financing through a variety of programs that guarantee repayment of their bank loans. The SBA also assists women and minority business owners in obtaining government purchasing contracts. It offers training and information resources, so business owners can improve their odds of success. Finally, the SBA advocates small-business interests within the federal government.

5. Explain how franchising can provide opportunities for both franchisors and franchisees.

A franchisor is a company that sells the rights to use its brand name, operating procedures, and other intellectual property to franchisees. Franchising helps business owners to expand their companies' operations with limited financial investments. Franchisees, the individuals who buy the right to operate a business using the franchisor's intellectual property, gain a proven business system, brand recognition, and training and other support from the franchisor.

6. Identify and explain the three basic forms of business ownership and the advantages and disadvantages of each form.

A single person owns and operates a sole proprietorship. While sole proprietorships are easy to set up and offer great operating flexibility, the owner remains personally liable for all of the firm's debts and legal settlements. In a partnership, two or more individuals agree to share responsibility for owning and running the business. Partnerships are relatively easy to set up, but they do not offer protection from liability. Additionally, partnerships often experience problems when partners fail to communicate or forge effective working relationships. When a business is set up as a corporation, it becomes a separate legal entity. Individual owners receive shares of stock in the firm. Corporations protect owners from legal and financial liability, but double taxation reduces their revenues.

7. Identify the levels of corporate management.

Stockholders, or shareholders, own a corporation. In return for their financial investments, they receive shares of stock in the company. The number of stockholders in a firm can vary widely, depending on whether the firm is privately owned or makes its stock available to the public. Shareholders elect the firm's board of directors, the individuals responsible for overall corporate management. The board has legal authority over the firm's policies. A company's officers are the top managers who oversee its operating decisions.

8. Describe recent trends in mergers and acquisitions.

After a decline in the early 1990s, U.S. corporations are now spending record amounts on mergers and acquisitions. These business combinations occur worldwide, and companies often merge with or acquire other companies to aid their operations across national boundaries. Vertical mergers help a firm to ensure access to adequate raw materials and supplies for production or to improve its distribution outlets. Horizontal mergers occur when firms in the same industry join in an attempt to diversify or offer expanded product lines. Conglomerate mergers combine unrelated firms, often as part of plans to spend cash surpluses that might otherwise make a firm a takeover target.

9. Differentiate among private ownership, public ownership, and collective ownership (cooperatives).

Managers or a group of major stockholders sometimes buy all of a firm's stock. The firm then becomes a privately owned company, and its stock is no longer publicly traded. Some firms allow workers to buy large blocks of stock, so the employees gain ownership stakes. Municipal, state, and national governments also own and operate some businesses. This public business ownership has declined, however, through a recent trend toward privatization of publicly run organizations. In a cooperative, individuals or companies band together to collectively operate all or part of an industry's functions. The cooperative's owners control its activities by electing a board of directors from their members. Cooperatives are usually set up to provide for collective ownership of a production, storage, transportation, or marketing organization that is important to an industry.

TEN BUSINESS TERMS YOU NEED TO KNOW

small business

business plan

Small Business Administration (SBA)

business incubator

franchising

sole proprietorship

partnership

corporation

merger

acquisition

Other Important Business Terms

home-based business

Small Business Investment Company (SBIC)

set-aside program

limited liability company (LLC)

domestic corporation

foreign corporation

alien corporation

corporate charter

stockholder

board of directors

vertical merger

horizontal merger

conglomerate merger

joint venture

public ownership

cooperative

REVIEW QUESTIONS

1. Explain the meaning of the term *small business*. Discuss the differences between a small business and a large business. What advantages does each offer? What challenges does each type face?
2. How does small business contribute to a nation's economy?
3. The chapter notes that a written business plan can make the difference between success and failure in a new business venture. Develop a brief outline of a business plan, including the major components described in this chapter. Refer to your outline to explain the relationship between an effective plan and business success.
4. What is a franchise? What benefits does franchising provide to a franchisor? Why is franchising attractive to franchisees? Suggest ways in which franchisors and franchisees can improve the effectiveness of franchising for both parties.
5. What is a sole proprietorship? Why is this form of business ownership the most popular one? Discuss the advantages and disadvantages of sole proprietorships.
6. What is a partnership? What advantages and disadvantages characterize this form of business ownership, and how can partners minimize the disadvantages?
7. What is the primary advantage of the corporate form of business ownership? Discuss the differences among a C corporation, an S corporation, and a partnership organized as a limited liability company.
8. How does a corporation operate? What roles do shareholders, the board of directors, top manage-

ment, middle management, and supervisory management play?
9. Discuss the different types of mergers. List reasons why a firm's management might decide to merge with another company.
10. What is a cooperative? How does it differ from other business entities?

QUESTIONS FOR CRITICAL THINKING

1. You are considering buying a small Oregon partnership that manufactures high-pressure laminated particleboard used to make office cubicles. The firm enjoys an excellent reputation for high-quality products and provides superior customer service and quick turnaround on orders. The firm's two partners currently handle most marketing and sales contacts. Since they have to devote most of their time to running the company, they rely primarily on word-of-mouth recommendations to generate orders. Consequently, the company is currently running at 30 percent of its plant capacity. Production facilities are under long-term leases, and the firm's 35 employees have pledged to stay on after the sale is completed. Last year, the firm earned $522,000 in profits on $2 million in sales. The owners are asking $3.4 million for the company, including $1 million worth of finished inventory.

   What additional information would you need in order to make a purchase decision? What are some sources of financing that you could realistically tap to buy the company? What major challenges would you expect to encounter in running this firm? Suggest how you would overcome these challenges.
2. Choose a small-business owner in your area and interview him or her about the experience of owning one's own business. What advice would this person give about starting a business? What mistakes do new business owners commonly make? Share your findings with the class.
3. Although a rising number of small firms export products to other countries, more than half of small businesses still are not participating in the global marketplace. Why don't more small U.S. firms export their products? What changes would encourage them to do so, in your opinion? Is going global really an option for every small business?
4. Assume that you are involved in establishing the businesses listed here. What form of ownership would you propose for each? Explain your reasoning for each choice by discussing the advantages and disadvantages of each form of ownership.
   a. dry cleaning franchise in New Orleans
   b. Toledo Mud Hens minor league baseball team
   c. Miami-based management consulting firm
   d. Small foundry outside Pittsburgh, Pennsylvania
5. What steps are necessary to set up a corporation in your state or locality? Do these procedures differ from requirements elsewhere? If so, how?

Experiential Exercise

DIRECTIONS: Using this chapter's Business Tool Kits, answer the following questions:

1. From "The Five Best Businesses to Start from Your Dorm" on page 170, select the business idea that you believe you could successfully implement. If none of these ideas is suited to your interests or abilities, select one with which you are confident.
2. Turn to "Ten Keys to Succeeding in a Home-Based Business" on page 167 and circle the tips that are relevant to the business idea you chose in Step 1
3. Turn to the chapter section titled "Creating a Business Plan," beginning on page 172, and think through the answers to the questions included in this section. Outline the components that your business plan should include.

Nothing but Net

1. **Home-Based Businesses.** Assume you are looking for information about starting a home-based business. Find a Web site, such as the one listed, which provides information about home-based business opportunities. Select a home-based business opportunity suited to your interests, skills, and aptitudes that you believe would be a good money-making opportunity. In addition, identify the business tools available at the Web site that could help you get started and prepare a three- to five-minute oral report to be given either in a small-group discussion or to the entire class.

   www.getbuzy.com/

2. **Minority- and Women-Owned Businesses.** The U.S. Small Business Administration provides information and support services for minority- and women-owned businesses. Visit the two Web sites listed and find out what is available through these offices. Compare each mission statement and summarize in one sentence the common purpose between these two agencies of the federal government.
   Office of Women's Business Ownership:

   www.sba.gov/womeninbusiness/

   Office of Minority Enterprise Development:

   www.sba.gov/MED/

3. **Incorporating.** Use a search engine to find information about incorporating in your home state or any other state that interests you. Sites such as the one listed provide information and fee-based services for incorporating your business online. Answer at least one of the following questions:
   (a) What are three uses of a corporation's employer tax ID number?
   (b) What is the filing fee for incorporating in the state you chose?
   (c) Which states have the highest filing fees?
   (d) Which states have the lowest filing fees?

   incorporate-usa.com/index.html

Note: Internet Web addresses change frequently. If you do not find the exact sites listed, you may need to access the organization's or company's home page and search from there.

LOST ARTS—
FINDING SUCCESS THROUGH RESTORATION

Five years ago, while working on furnishing a multimillion dollar house, Gary, deLarios needed a place to do the work and manage the creative art of many artisans. Lost Arts was created. The founder and owner, Gary deLarios says, "the idea behind Lost Arts was to have control over large-scale projects and have many craftsmen under one roof learning from each other. There are few people in the world who do this type of work. We actually have to get the books, do the research, and get out and try to understand and work the medium and the material." The craftsmen at Lost Arts combine today's technology with ancient techniques to speed the creative process of creating "functional art."

Today, Lost Arts operates in the Dallas/Fort Worth area, specializing in design, fabrication, and installation of custom architectural and decorative accessories. The company was founded by Gary deLarios as a sole proprietorship working for one primary client for whom quality, not cost, was the main concern. Moving from one client to several now, "the company must be commercially viable and find a balance between cost and quality in this functional art business," says deLarios.

Other products and services provided by Lost Arts include design consultation and drafting; hand-forged custom architectural hardware; custom interior and exterior light fixture fabrication; glasswork; custom wood-working, including expert wood carving; decorative ironwork; railings; balustrade and metal casting. Lost Arts works on a number of one-of-a-kind projects such as the Historical City Park in Dallas, Texas where craftsmen recreated the entire city, providing a hands-on exhibit of the parks.

For Gary and his brother Patrick, control over projects and having a reputation for providing quality products are important factors in running their small business. With only 10 expert employees, motivation becomes a constant battle. Says deLarios, "two foremost challenges in this business are: organization, that is, having 50 to 70 projects going at one time and having the manpower and materials to make each an artistic creation and, two, cost effectiveness in production, that is, balancing the cost and the quality and keeping the employees happy."

Gary deLarios has a hands-on management philosophy and believes that one must have patience and persistence to succeed. Above all, people must love what they do for a living. "Do work that you believe in, not purely for money," says Gary, "You have to love it to excel." The company has relied on word-of-mouth and has never advertised, yet has more business than it can handle. With gross sales under a million and climbing, and an expanding client base, Lost Arts is looking to modify its form of ownership.

Questions

1. What are the advantages and disadvantages of Lost Arts' current form of ownership?

2. As the company grows, which ownership form would you recommend? Why?

3. What are the advantages and challenges for Gary deLarios in his small business?

chapter 6

Starting Your Own Business: The Entre- preneurship Alternative

LEARNING GOALS

1. Define the term "*entrepreneur,*" and distinguish among an entrepreneur, a small-business owner, and a manager.

2. Identify three different types of entrepreneurs.

3. Explain why people choose to become entrepreneurs.

4. Discuss conditions that encourage opportunities for entrepreneurs.

5. Describe the role of entrepreneurs in the economy.

6. Identify personality traits that typically characterize entrepreneurs.

7. Discuss the process of starting a new venture.

8. Explain how organizations promote intrapreneurship.

Amazon.com: Building the Best Buying Experience on the Web

"We're trying to build the most customer-centric company in the world," says Jeff Bezos, founder and CEO of Amazon.com. Back in 1994, Bezos was working on Wall Street and discovered that Web usage was growing 2300 percent a year. He knew the Internet would soon be everywhere, and he wanted to be part of it. Since then he has been passionately building the kind of company he envisioned—not by *aspiring* to be a corporate model but by *creating* that model. Indeed, the Amazon.com corporate philosophy is simple: "If it's good for our customers, it's worth doing." Bezos wants people to come to Amazon.com, find what they want, discover things they didn't know they wanted, and leave feeling they have a favorite place to shop. In short, Bezos wants Amazon.com to be the best buying experience on the Web.

He started by selling books because he determined that they are the number-one product to

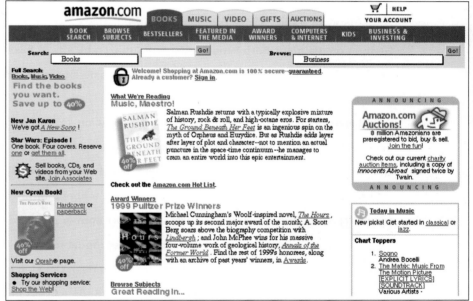

sell on the Internet. In 1995 Amazon.com sold books out of a garage to a handful of customers. Today, the company offers millions of books and other items: music CDs, videos, and gifts—not to mention secure credit card payment, personalized recommendations, and streamlined ordering. Even though the company has yet to turn a profit, Amazon.com has become one of the "blue-chip" Internet stocks.

But as successful as his company has become, Bezos is not standing still. "Our customers are loyal right up to the moment someone offers them better service," says Bezos. So he continues to build and expand the company. "What we're trying to do is invent the future of e-commerce," says Bezos, revealing his goal to build not just a better bookstore but a global online retailing operation. And before you can say "innovation," he's on his way.

Amazon.com has already expanded in myriad directions: It operates Planet All (www.planetall.com), a Web-based address book, calendar, and reminder service. And it operates the

Internet Movie Database (www.imdb.com), a comprehensive source of information on more than 150,000 movies and entertainment programs and 500,000 cast and crew members dating from 1892 to the present. In addition, the company has accepted into its "Associates" program Sun Entertainment Holding Corporation (www.sunrecords.com). Based in Nashville, Sun has the exclusive world-wide rights to some 7,000 master recordings by artists including Johnny Cash, Jerry Lee Lewis, and Elvis Presley. Sun's customers are able to purchase music and merchandise from Sun's own extensive library or access

WWW. www.amazon.com/exec/obidos/subst/home/home.html

Amazon's vast selection. In addition, Sun earns a commission on Amazon.com purchases from anyone who goes there from Sun's Web site.

Nor has the company neglected the *global* part of Bezos's goal. Amazon.com has launched operations in both England and Germany, going head-to-head with rival Barnes & Noble and its partner, German media giant Bertelsmann AG. The Amazon.uk site is based in Slough, England, and carries a catalog of 1.2 million U.K. titles. The Amazon.com.de site is based in Regensburg, Germany, and features 335,000 German titles.

Closer to home, the company invested $5 million to buy a 7 percent stake in Geoworks, which delivers Internet-based content over wireless devices. In the deal, Amazon.com acquired the services and know-how of the 19 software engineers based in Geoworks' Seattle office. The company also has a 46 percent stake in Drugstore.com, which offers a lineup of prescription and nonprescription drugs, cosmetics, and personal-care products. Drugstore.com is promoted on the Amazon.com site.

The company has become an entrepreneurial model for Net wannabes. Just some of the startups copying Amazon.com include Netgrocer.com (groceries), Cooking.com (cookware and specialty foods), Sportscape.com (sporting goods), and FreshFlowerSource (fresh flowers). Of course, that doesn't count out the giant book retailers establishing their own cyber-shopping sites. Bezos is the consummate entrepreneur, working hard to lengthen his lead. Without question, Amazon.com is the benchmark for buying on the Web.[1]

CHAPTER OVERVIEW

Like millions of people, you'd probably love to start and run your own company. Perhaps you've spent time trying to come up with an idea for a business you could launch. If you've been bitten by the entrepreneurial bug, you're not alone. More than ever, people like Amazon.com's Jeff Bezos are choosing the path of entrepreneurship for their careers.

How do you become an entrepreneur? Experts advise that aspiring entrepreneurs should learn as much as possible about the pleasures and pitfalls of entrepreneurship before striking out on their own. By reading newspaper and magazine articles and biographies of successful entrepreneurs, you'll learn how they handled the challenges of starting up their businesses. Advice you need to launch and grow a new venture abounds. Some resources are listed in the Business Toolkit box.

BUSINESS TOOL KIT

Resources for Aspiring Entrepreneurs

Effective entrepreneurs know where to get information and advice. "If I had to name the single characteristic shared by all the truly successful people I have met over a lifetime, I would say it is the ability to create and nurture a network of contacts," says Harvey Mackay, best-selling author and founder of Mackay Envelope Corp. His advice to aspiring entrepreneurs: "Don't suffer from 'call reluctance.' Pick up the phone or your pen, and ask for the advice you need."

A first step in becoming part of the entrepreneurial network is gathering information. Here are some ideas to get you started:

Subscribe to Magazines
Publications such as *Entrepreneur, Success, Inc., Nation's Business,* and *Black Enterprise* are loaded with articles about entrepreneurs and their experiences and insights on launching new ventures.

Read Books
Your local library and bookstore offer titles such as *How to Start Your Own Business without Losing Your Shirt, The Entrepreneurial Family, The Student Entrepreneur's Guide, The Home-Based Entrepreneur, The Woman Entrepreneur,* and *For Entrepreneurs Only.* Many successful entrepreneurs have written books explaining how they built their businesses, what unexpected obstacles they encountered, and how they dealt with those problems.

Use the Internet
For a catalog of books on entrepreneurship and a review of each title, visit The Entrepreneur's Wave (http://www.en-wave.com). The Entrepreneur's Mind (http://www.benlore.com/index.html) and Entrepreneurial Edge Online (http://www.edgeonline.com) are online magazines that give real-life stories from successful entrepreneurs and advice from business experts. The Entre-World Web site (http://www.entreworld.org) provides information you need to start, run, and grow a business. Black Enterprise Online (http://www.blackenterprise.com) includes career-oriented content for college students. Each month, the First American Group Purchasing Association site (http://www.firstgpa.com) lists its choices of the ten most valuable sites for entrepreneurs.

www. www.en-wave.com
www.benlore.com/index.html
www.edgeonline.com
www.entreworld.org
www.blackenterprise.com
www.firstgpa.com

Contact Trade Associations
For information on specific businesses or industries that interest you—for example, retailing—look in *The Encyclopedia of Associations.* Your library has a copy of this reference book, which covers some 20,000 industries. It includes organizations for entrepreneurs, such as:

▼ Association of Collegiate Entrepreneurs, Wichita State University, Center for Entrepreneurship, 1845 Fairmount, Wichita, Kansas, 67260–0147. Phone: 316–689–3000.

▼ The Entrepreneurship Institute, 3592 Corporate Drive, Suite 101, Columbus, Ohio, 43231. Phone: 614–895–1153.

▼ Association of African-American Women Business Owners, P.O. Box 13858, Silver Spring, Maryland, 20911–3858. Phone: 301–585–8051.

▼ Young Entrepreneurs' Organization, 1010 North Glebe Road, Suite 600, Arlington, Virginia, 22201. Phone: 703–527–4500.

▼ International Directory of Young Entrepreneurs, Boston, Massachusetts. Phone: 617–562–8616.

Source: Harvey Mackay quote from Robert McGarvey, "Words from the Wise," *Entrepreneur,* May 1997, pp. 152, 154.

This chapter focuses on pathways for entering the world of entrepreneurship, describing the increasingly important role that entrepreneurs play in the economy and explains why a growing number of people choose this area of business. It discusses the characteristics that help entrepreneurs to succeed and the ways they start new ventures and ends with a discussion of methods by which large companies try to incorporate the entrepreneurial spirit within their organizations.

WHAT IS AN ENTREPRENEUR?

You learned in Chapter 1 that an **entrepreneur** is a risk taker in the private enterprise system, a person who seeks a profitable opportunity and takes the necessary risks to set up and operate a business. Many entrepreneurs start their businesses from scratch, but you don't have to launch your own company to be considered an entrepreneur. Consider Ray Kroc, founder of McDonald's. He started by buying a small hamburger shop and grew this small venture into a multibillion-dollar global business.

Entrepreneurs differ from small-business owners. Rieva Lesonsky, editor of *Entrepreneur* magazine, says,

> Merely owning a business does not make you an entrepreneur, it makes you a small-business owner.... Entrepreneurs don't only own their businesses, they run them. Entrepreneurship is not a theoretical mind game but a hands-on, up-to-the-elbows, down-in-the-dirt experience. You cannot be an absentee entrepreneur.... [2]

William Wetzel, a University of New Hampshire professor, confirms the difference. "It's totally inappropriate to equate small-business founders and entrepreneurs. One's looking for an income. The other has the intention of building a significant company that can create wealth for the entrepreneur and investors."[3]

Entrepreneurs also differ from managers. Managers are employees who direct the efforts of others to achieve an organization's goals. They use the resources of their organizations—employees, money, equipment, and facilities—to accomplish their work. In contrast, entrepreneurs pursue their own goals and take the initiative to find and organize the resources they need to start their ventures. For example, raising money to back a new venture is one of the entrepreneur's greatest challenges.

Studies of entrepreneurs have identified certain personality traits and behaviors common to them that differ from those required for managerial success. One of these traits is the willingness to assume the risks involved in starting a new venture. Some managers leave jobs with other firms to start their own companies and become successful entrepreneurs. Other managers find that they lack the characteristics required to start and grow a business. Entrepreneurial characteristics are examined in detail in a later section of this chapter.

CATEGORIES OF ENTREPRENEURS

A set of distinct categories comes from the Center for Entrepreneurial Leadership at the State University of New York at Buffalo: classic entrepreneurs, intrapreneurs, and change agents.[4]

Classic entrepreneurs identify business opportunities and allocate available resources to tap those markets. The story of David Marcheschi exemplifies the actions of a classic entrepreneur. Deciding as a college student to market a caffeinated bottled water drink, he graduated and began looking for a chemist to produce a formula for his product, Water Joe. Marcheschi formed a partnership with a bottling company that agreed to distribute the drink, and after only a year of production, sales had reached $12 million. The innovation is a hit not only with college students, but also with truck drivers, athletes, and band members. Marcheschi says that some customers buy Water Joe to make lemonade and orange juice. Some even use it to brew their coffee.[5]

Intrapreneurs are entrepreneurially oriented people who seek to develop new products, ideas, and commercial ventures within large organizations. For example, 3M Company continues to develop innovative products by encouraging intrapreneurship among its personnel. Some of 3M's most successful products began as inspirations of intrapreneurs. Art Frey invented the Post-It Note, and intrapreneurs Connie Hubbard and Raymond Heyer invented the Scotch-Brite Never Rust soap pad. Intrapreneurship will be discussed later in this chapter.

Change agents, also called *turnaround entrepre-*

Business Directory

entrepreneur a person who seeks a profitable opportunity and takes the necessary risks to set up and operate a business

classic entrepreneur a person who identifies a business opportunity and allocates available resources to tap that market

intrapreneur an entrepreneurially oriented person who develops innovations within the context of a large organization

change agent a manager who tries to revitalize an established firm to keep it competitive

neurs, are managers who seek to revitalize established firms in order to keep them competitive in the modern marketplace. Joanna Lau is a change agent who turned around Bowmar/ALI, a manufacturer of electronic systems for the defense industry and a firm in bad shape. "We were dying on the vine," said one employee. Close to losing its remaining three customers due to poor product quality and delivery performance and operating at a loss of $1.5 million, Bowmar charted a new course when Lau and a group of employees bought the company and renamed it Lau Technologies. As the company's new owner, Lau visited customers, promising them improved product quality and timely delivery. She followed through on her promise by establishing a total quality management program and financial controls to improve cash flow and reduce company debt. Lau broadened the company's product and customer base by entering the nondefense business of digital imaging. Within 5 years, she transformed the company into a profitable venture with $60 million in sales.[6]

REASONS TO CHOOSE ENTREPRENEURSHIP AS A CAREER PATH

If you had to choose between getting a job or starting your own company, which option would be more appealing to you? According to the Small Business Administration (SBA), about 30 percent of the U.S. population is "always thinking about starting a business," and 4 percent of all working-age adults—7 million people—are actively involved in starting new ventures at any one time.[7] Since the early 1980s, some have observed a heightened interest in entrepreneurial careers, spurred in part by publicity celebrating the successes of entrepreneurs like Sam Walton, Martha Stewart, Bill Gates, and Steve Jobs.

The popularity of entrepreneurship is likely to continue. Today's teenagers and preteens say they would rather start their own companies than work for others. Business educators are calling this young group *Generation E,* emphasizing their prospects as future entrepreneurs. A 1996 Gallup poll conducted for the Center for Entrepreneurial Leadership found that 7 of 10 high school students want to start and run their own businesses. "The kids believe their only chance in life is to make a job, not take a job," says Dr. Marilyn Kourilsky, the center's vice president. "They see job security as an issue with their parents . . . [and] they want to be their own boss."[8] People choose to become entrepreneurs for many different reasons. Some are motivated by dissatisfaction with the organizational world, citing desires to escape unreasonable bosses or insufficient rewards and recognition as motives to start their own firms. Other people, like David Marcheschi, start businesses because they believe their ideas represent opportunities to fulfill customer needs. The following motives are often cited as major reasons why people become entrepreneurs.

Typifying a classic entrepreneur, David Marcheschi identified a business opportunity and launched a company to market Water Joe, an innovation that satisfies the desire of people who want the stimulative effect of caffeine without its flavor.

Desire to Be One's Own Boss

Self-management is the motivation that drives many entrepreneurs. In *Inc.* magazine's annual survey of America's top 500 fastest-growing companies, 41 percent of the CEOs cited the same main reason for starting companies: "to be my own boss or to control my own life."[9] The CEOs' top reasons for becoming entrepreneurs are listed in Table 6.1.

Table 6.1	Five Most Common Reasons for Starting a New Firm
To be my own boss or to control my own life	41%
To make money	16
To create something new	12
To prove I could do it	9
Because I was not rewarded at my old job	6

T. J. Rodgers, CEO of Cypress Semiconductor, knew he'd be his own boss one day. His entrepreneurial urge resulted from the mismanagement he saw at the construction companies where he worked during his high school years. "I've never liked taking orders from morons," says Rodgers. After graduating from college, Rodgers resolved that he'd be CEO of his own firm by the time he was 35. He achieved his personal goal, launching his microchip manufacturing firm as its only employee and growing it into a $600 million company.[10]

Financial Success

Entrepreneurs are wealth creators. Many start their ventures with the specific goal of creating a profitable business and reaping its financial rewards. They believe they won't get rich by working for someone else. "We were brought up to believe that it's better to make 50 cents for yourself than a buck for someone else," says Staci Munic Mintz. While both in their mid-20s, Mintz and her brother started Little Miss Muffin, a company that sells low-fat, low-cholesterol muffins and other bakery items to coffee houses and espresso bars. After a year in business, Little Miss Muffin had 400 customers and earned revenues of $1.5 million.[11]

Although entrepreneurs often mention financial rewards as a motive for starting their businesses, experts advise that a desire to make a pot of gold shouldn't be the entrepreneur's primary motivation. Venture capitalist Barry Weinman says, "We won't work with people who just talk about getting rich. If you're just looking for a windfall, go play the lottery."[12] Professor Jon Goodman, who directs the entrepreneurial program at the University of Southern California, agrees. "I've worked with hundreds of entrepreneurs, and I've never met one who said, 'I want to get rich,' who did," says Goodman. "The successful ones say, 'I want to find a way to do animation faster,' or 'I'm really interested in adhesion.'"[13]

Job Security

The millions of people who have lost their jobs due to downsizing give another reason that workers, especially those of the younger generation, are attracted to entrepreneurship. From 1990 to 1995, for example, companies dismissed some 17.1 million employees, and the downsizing trend is expected to continue.[14] In the wake of that trend, people are opting to create their own job security.

Sidney Warren explains, "With all the downsizing going on, there isn't even the appearance of security in corporate America."[15] The 32-year-old left a full-time job to buy a TCBY Treat/Mrs. Fields Cookies cofranchise with two of his friends. A recent survey indicated that most new businesses are started by young people in the 25-to-34 age group.[16] Figure 6.1 shows the percentages of new ventures started by people in different age groups.

Although many prospective employees see little job security in working for others, lack of security is also an issue for entrepreneurs. Clearly, many new ventures fail, but studies on the failure rate for startups have produced different results. Those done by the SBA indicate that 24 percent of new ventures dissolve within 2 years, and 52 percent fold within 4 years. After tracking 3,000 startups over a 3-year period, another study recently found that 77 percent of the firms were still in business, 19 percent had folded, and 4 percent had been sold.[17]

They said it

"The most exhilarating, exciting, and empowering business experience you can have is being an entrepreneur, even though it is as tough and risky a task as you can undertake."

Earl G. Graves, founder and publisher of *Black Enterprise* magazine

Quality of Life

Entrepreneurship is an attractive career option for people seeking to improve their quality of life. Susan Lammers, a mother of two young children, left her management job at Microsoft to start her own educational software company, Headbone Interactive. "I felt constrained by the system," says Lammers. "They wanted work and family separated, but I wanted them integrated—like the family farm of the agricultural age." Lammers located Headbone's office 5 minutes away from her kids' school so she can participate in their class parties and activities. She's made Headbone a family-friendly workplace, allowing her employees to work flexible hours and to bring their kids to the office.[18]

THE ENVIRONMENT FOR ENTREPRENEURS

If you feel motivated to start your own company, conditions have never suited entrepreneurship better than they do today. For one improvement, society now accepts entrepreneurship as a respectable career choice. "The public's perception of people who start their own companies has dramatically improved," says Bill Sahlman, professor of business administration at Harvard Business School. "They're not outcasts anymore. They're in the mainstream."[19] Jim McCann, founder of 1-800-FLOWERS, explains the change in society's attitude between when he started his company in the late 1970s and today:

> As a person who grew up in a mostly blue collar community, where my parents were products of the postwar era, all I heard at the time was "Get a job with a big company, a secure company. Even get a civil service job." Being an entrepreneur is much more culturally acceptable now than it was. It's a worthwhile, laudable, realistic career alternative for so many people. Today people say, "I want to work in an entrepreneurial environment." Twenty years ago, believe me, you didn't have many people saying that.[20]

The movement of entrepreneurship toward the business mainstream began in the early 1980s after Steve Jobs of Apple Computer and other high-tech entrepreneurs gained national attention by going public— that is, selling stock in their companies. Today's entrepreneurs are reaping the benefits from growing interest among investors, as discussed later in the chapter. Investors now eagerly back new ventures, making more money more available than before, helping entrepreneurs to find funds to back their startups. In addition to changing public attitudes towards entrepreneurs and the growth in financing options, other factors that support and expand opportunities for entrepreneurs include globalization, education, information technology, and demographic and economic trends.

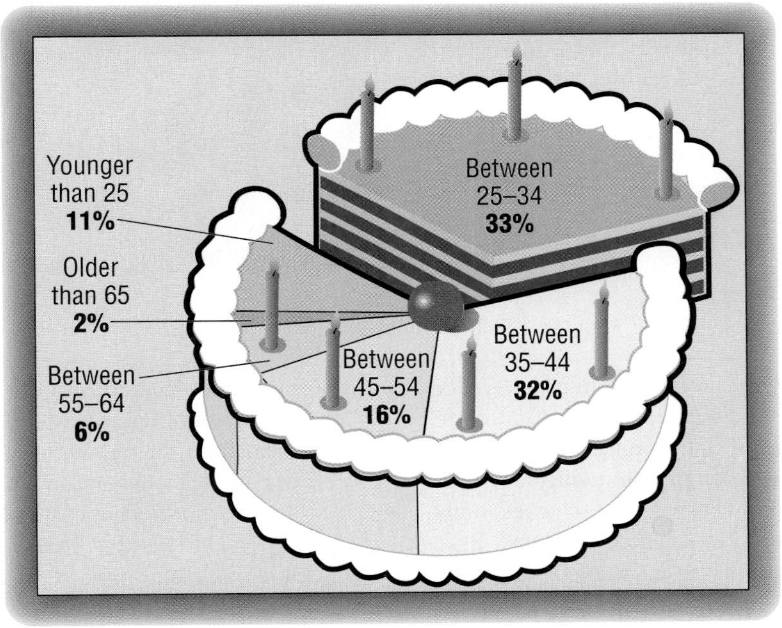

Globalization

The globalization of business described in the first four chapters of this book has created many opportunities for entrepreneurs. Entrepreneurs are marketing their products abroad and hiring international talent. For example, Jonathan Strum uses the Web-design services of another entrepreneur in Caracas, Venezuela. Strum's startup, Interactive Marketing Partners, is an Internet marketing, design, and development company based in Los Angeles. "Not long ago I would have thought depending on a firm in Caracas for the services we need for our business was outlandish," Strum says. "Now I am importing all my graphic design and most of my programming from overseas."[21]

Entrepreneurs are also forming business partnerships with others like themselves to expand their businesses around the globe. When Ingenico, a French firm that markets smart-card readers, wanted to expand into Australia, China, Singapore, Germany, Russia, and the United States, the company formed strategic alliances with local entrepreneurs in these countries to set up subsidiaries. Gerard Compain, Ingenico's managing director, says, "I wasn't interested in hiring managers. Since we're a relatively small company, I can't bring these people to Paris every month to take their orders." With entrepreneurs, says Compain, "we say, 'Let's go.' Entrepreneurs do things in a way that's smarter, quicker, and simpler. These people know their countries better than we do. And they know how to design and sell products for those markets." Compain's strategy of teaming up with global entrepreneurs helped Ingenico to double its sales within 2 years.[22]

Figure 6.1 **Percentage of Startups by Age Group**

Younger than 25 **11%**

Older than 65 **2%**

Between 55–64 **6%**

Between 45–54 **16%**

Between 35–44 **32%**

Between 25–34 **33%**

Education

The past two decades have brought tremendous growth in the number of educational opportunities for would-be entrepreneurs. Today, some 400 U.S. colleges offer classes in starting and running a business, up from 16 in 1970, and about 125 schools have organized entrepreneurship curricula.[23] Some college programs invite students to apply the practices they learn in the classroom in real-life business settings. For example, at Babson College in Wellesley, Massachusetts, students work with mentors in Boston-area startups.

BUSINESS HALL OF FAME

Selling Cars the High-Tech Way

Pete Ellis followed in the footsteps of his father, who owned a car dealership. At 16, Ellis sold his first car; at 24, he owned his first car dealership. He grew his business into a network of 16 dealerships and related businesses in Arizona and California. Car sales started declining in the early 1990s, however, forcing Ellis to sell or simply to close all of his dealerships. In 1994, he filed for Chapter 7 bankruptcy, losing two houses and $15 million.

Out of a job at 48, Ellis started playing on the Internet using his home computer when he got the idea of selling cars online. In March 1995, he launched Auto-By-Tel (ABT), a car-buying service, online with Prodigy. He hoped the service would generate 50 buyer requests a day. "But on the fourth day, we got 1,348 requests for cars," says Ellis. "That's when we realized this is the way mainstream America wants to buy cars."

Ellis says he started ABT because he never liked the way the car-selling industry worked. "I've always thought the model was wrong—too many unpleasant practices for customers," says Ellis. "I hated my dealerships. I hated the way there would be 20 salesmen waiting to jump on the next customer who walked in the door."

With ABT, Ellis is challenging the auto industry's traditional way of selling cars. He cites information technology as the key factor in changing the balance of power in car buying from the manufacturers and dealers to consumers. "I see the Internet as destroying the old structure," says Ellis. With the Internet, consumers have access to the true costs of cars.

ABT targets serious car buyers who want specific car models. It invites

Many organizations have sprouted up in recent years to teach entrepreneurship to young people. The Center for Entrepreneurial Leadership offers training programs for learners from kindergarten through community college. The center's Entreprep summer program teaches high school juniors how to start and manage a company. Students in Free Enterprise (SIFE) is a national not-for-profit organization in which college students, working with faculty advisors, teach grade school and high school students and other community members the value of free enterprise and entrepreneurship. The San Francisco Renaissance Entrepreneurship Center is a not-for-profit organization offering entrepreneurship training—from introductory to advanced—to disadvantaged students. The Renaissance program supports its entrepreneurs with a business incubator and a financial resource center that links startups with banks and other funding sources.

Information Technology

The explosion in information technology has been one of the biggest boosts for entrepreneurs. As computer and communications technologies have merged, accompanied by dramatically falling costs, entrepreneurs have gained tools that help them to compete with large companies. The Business Hall of Fame box describes how an entrepreneur has created an Internet-based business that is challenging one of America's biggest and most traditional industries.

Information technology helps entrepreneurs to work quickly and efficiently, provide attentive customer service, increase sales, and project professional images. Merchant of Vino Corp., a retailer of fine wine, food, and gift baskets, attributes increases in its customer satisfaction rating to a new bar-coding system and customized software that captures detailed buyer information. Information technology, says Merchant President Marc Jonna, "has increased our customer service tremendously because we don't run out of stock as often. Our customers are delighted because we're more in tune with their buying habits."[24]

Demographic and Economic Trends

Demographic trends, such as the aging of the U.S. population and the growth of dual-income families, create opportunities for entrepreneurs to market new goods and services. Gail Sharp and Nancy Bible left their jobs to launch a day spa, riding the wave of a growing industry built on relieving working women's rising stress levels and tighter

these savvy car shoppers to research vehicles on the Internet and, when they find the cars they want, to fill out purchase requests. ABT sends the requests to the nearest of its nationwide network of some 2,400 dealers. Within 24 to 48 hours after receiving the request, dealers must give buyers a low, haggle-free price quote on new cars, used cars, and leases over the phone. Buyers then pick up their cars at their convenience. By forming strategic alliances with Chase Manhattan Bank, Key Corp., Triad Financial, GE Capital, and American International Group, ABT also offers its customers auto insurance, leasing, and financing.

Auto-By-Tel makes money by charging dealers annual and monthly fees. In return, dealers electronically receive customer purchase requests in their exclusive territories. According to Ellis, ABT can reduce dealers' costs in selling a car by 80 percent. For each new car they sell, dealers typically spend $225 on marketing and $820 in personnel costs. Dealers also benefit

with increased sales. Atamian Honda Volkswagen in Tewksbury, Massachusetts, claims that its link with ABT has boosted unit sales by 40 percent each month and that the ABT sales cost 70 percent less than its traditional sales. "These people who come through ABT represent found business for us," says Sherry Atamian, director of operations. "It's delusional to think we'd get it otherwise." Atamian says dealers have to embrace the ABT program "because the auto industry is changing to being customer driven."

According to Ellis, ABT's mission is "to put ourselves in a consumer-advocacy position" and "to give our dealers a total survival package to keep them in business and profitable for years to come." ABT's rapid growth since it started in 1995 indicates that the company is achieving its mission. Sales of $274,000 in 1995 have grown to more than $15 million. ABT is certainly a hit with consumers. It gets some 4 million hits each month on its Web site (http://www.autobytel.com),

along with more than 85,000 purchase requests per month.

 www.autobytel.com

QUESTIONS FOR CRITICAL THINKING

1. Do you agree with Pete Ellis's statement that the Internet is destroying the traditional way dealers sell cars? Why or why not?

2. Would you buy a car on the Internet? As a car buyer, what would you like and dislike about ABT's Internet service?

Sources: Joanna Glasner, "Autobytel Shares Race Upward," Wired News, March 26, 1999, accessed at www.wired.com; Edward O. Welles, "Burning Down the House," *Inc.*, August 1997, pp. 66–73; and Lynn Beresford, "Full Speed Ahead," *Entrepreneur*, June 1997, pp. 112–113.

time constraints. "People don't have time to get away for a weekend," says Sharp, "but a few hours—that's doable." Sharp and Bible teamed up with Aveda, a cosmetics and body-care company, to open the TallGrass Aveda Day Spa in Evergreen, Colorado, generating terrific customer response. Within 2 years of launching the day spa, the company earns a profit on revenues of $1 million.[25]

David Birch, founder of the economic research firm Cognetics Inc., sees a shift from an industrial economy to a knowledge-based economy. Birch believes that entrepreneurial firms can compete effectively in an economy based on knowledge "because the cost of producing knowledge is very low."[26]

Consider the rapid growth of The Princeton Review, a service that offers classes to prepare high school students for the Scholastic Aptitude Test, a college entrance exam. Entrepreneur John Katzman started this business at the age of 21 and quickly began franchising it. The classes are now offered at 600 locations throughout the United States. With revenues of $70 million, The Princeton Review has complemented its classes with books and software designed to help students make the transition from high school to college. Brisk demand for the firm's offerings has convinced Katzman to redefine his business as "a cross-media education company." He plans to add other courses geared to students

taking licensing tests, such as medical boards, and classes for professionals who want to change their careers.[27]

Entrepreneurship around the World

The growth in entrepreneurship is a worldwide phenomenon. The motto of the 1997 World Economic Forum was "Entrepreneurship in the global public interest." At the conference, the world's most influential business and political leaders discussed how their countries could support entrepreneurial activity. The role of entrepreneurs is growing in most industrialized and newly industrialized nations and in the emerging free-market countries in eastern Europe. In France, for example, 52 percent of new jobs are attributed to startups.[28] In Poland, some 2 million entrepreneurs have started companies since 1989.[29]

Most nations look to the United States as a model for a climate that encourages entrepreneurship. "What we need is a few Bill Gateses in Europe," says David de Pury, who resigned as co-chairman of ABB, one of Europe's largest industrial firms, to start his own financial services company. "The European dream is still to get a cozy job in a big company. We need to change that dream."[30] Until very recently, landing a safe job in a big company was also the dream of Japanese students entering the workforce. But slowing economic growth in Japan and European countries has sparked interest in entrepreneurship as a way to stimulate economic renewal.

Entrepreneurs abroad struggle harder to start businesses than do their U.S. counterparts. Matthias Zahn, a German entrepreneur, says that European startups lack the "food chain" needed to launch new ventures—the educational, financial, and information technology support available in the United States.[31] Other obstacles include government regulations, high taxes, and political attitudes that favor big business. "Owners of startups have virtually no access to bank loans," says Peter Kramer, a German entrepreneur. As president of Europe's 500, a group of the European Union's fastest-growing small businesses, Kramer is leading an effort to establish an environment in which entrepreneurs can flourish.[32]

Among women, entrepreneurship is on the rise throughout the world, according to the Women's Entrepreneurism Worldwide Survey. The survey covered new-venture activity over a 5-year period for 16 countries in the Americas, Europe, Africa, and the Asia-Pacific region. Survey results indicate several major reasons why women start their own firms: economic necessity, high unemployment rates, and the lack of well-paying jobs. Women entrepreneurs in the United States, however, cited greater freedom and flexibility over their careers and few advancement opportunities to top positions in the organizational world as reasons for becoming entrepreneurs.[33]

THE INFLUENCE OF ENTREPRENEURS ON THE ECONOMY

From Thomas Edison's development of the phonograph to the birth of the Apple microcomputer in Steve Jobs's garage, American entrepreneurs have given the world goods and services that have changed the way people live, work, and play. The list includes ball-point pens, Netscape Navigator software, fiberglass skis, Velcro fasteners, the Yahoo! Internet directory, FedEx delivery service, and Big Mac hamburgers. In addition to creating major innovations, entrepreneurs play a significant role in the economy by creating jobs and providing opportunities for women and minorities.

Innovation

Entrepreneurs create new products, build new industries, and bring new life to old industries. Innovators David Filo

and Jerry Yang invented a new industry when they launched Yahoo!, a service that helps people locate Web sites that interest them. "This company isn't really about technology," says Yang. "It's about solving people's basic needs for efficiency, effectiveness, and simplicity." Yahoo! was an instant hit with Web surfers, and competitors like Lycos and Excite quickly entered the search engine industry.[34]

Some innovators take an old industry and reshape it. Almost 30 years ago, entrepreneurs Herb Kelleher, a lawyer, and Rollin King, a pilot, founded a new airline based on their vision "that people could fly affordably and have fun along the way." Their innovations include serving passengers peanuts rather than meals, eliminating assigned seating, and encouraging employees to have fun while they work and to entertain passengers. A study by the U.S. Department of Transportation credits Southwest Airlines as the "principal driving force for changes occurring in the airline industry."[35]

DID YOU KNOW?

The Department of Commerce considers these ten countries the most attractive for global business in the twenty-first century: China, Brazil, South Africa, India, Mexico, Indonesia, South Korea, Thailand, Argentina, and Poland.

Job Generation

Entrepreneurs are a vital source of new jobs. Since launching Yahoo! in 1995, Filo and Yang have hired 225 employees. Today, Southwest Airlines has a staff of more than 25,000 employees. As large firms continue to downsize, more new jobs are being generated by entrepreneurships in the United States. Research on job generation and entrepreneurial activity has found that fast-growing startups—about 3 percent of all small firms—have become the principal job creators in the United States. These companies, called *gazelles,* created about 97 percent of the new jobs in the United States between 1991 and 1995. Rapid growth by startups will continue to be a significant source of job creation in the future.[36]

Diversity

Entrepreneurship offers economic opportunities for women and minorities, who often find themselves excluded from well-paying jobs with career advancement opportunities in the corporate world. Discontented with her career prospects, Lolita Sweet, an African-American woman, decided to start a San Francisco limousine service called BAYE Limousines (*BAYE* stands for Bay Area Young Entrepreneurs). For Sweet, building a successful company means developing a diverse workforce. "Our staff is like the United Nations," says Sweet. As a member of the National Foundation for Teaching Entrepreneurship,

Sweet spends two days each week teaching minority students how to start and run a business.[37]

The number of women- and minority-owned startups has grown tremendously in recent years. Hispanic-owned businesses have grown from 100,000 to more than 1 million during the past 18 years.[38] According to U.S. Census Bureau statistics, African-Americans created more than 200,000 new enterprises between 1987 and 1995, a 46 percent increase. Of the 1.3 million new business startups in a recent year, women owned 32 percent.[39]

Realizing the value of both women- and minority-owned startups in creating jobs and promoting diversity, many large companies have developed diversity programs that help these entrepreneurs get startup capital, subcontracts, and other assistance. Eastman Kodak, General Motors, Arthur Andersen, JCPenney, Toyota, and Pacific Gas & Electric are large firms that offer supplier diversity programs. The United Airlines ad in Figure 6.2 illustrates the importance of minority suppliers to the airline's global success. Large companies frequently advertise in magazines like *Black Enterprise* and *Hispanic,* encouraging readers to contact their directors of supplier diversity for information about their diversity programs.

| Figure 6.2 | United Airlines: A Supporter of Minority Suppliers |

mon characteristics. In addition to having similar motivations entrepreneurs share family backgrounds and personality traits.

A recent study revealed that parents' occupations directly influence the likelihood that their children will become entrepreneurs. According to the study, 32 percent of sons with entrepreneurial fathers started their own businesses compared to only 12 percent of sons whose dads were not entrepreneurs. Similarly, 24 percent of daughters with entrepreneurial mothers became entrepreneurs compared to 13 percent of daughters whose mothers weren't entrepreneurs. The study found that most children of entrepreneurial parents started businesses in industries different from those of their parents. It also revealed that while parents' financial support affected their children's decisions to become entrepreneurs, children were most influenced by their parents' attitudes and values, such as the desire to be one's own boss.[40]

"I just always knew that I was going to have my own company or be my own boss someday," says Theodore Waitt, founder of Gateway 2000, a personal computer manufacturer. Waitt's father was an entrepreneurial role model. He discouraged his son from joining the family cattle feedlot business because opportunities there were diminishing due to changes in the industry. But he infused his son with his entrepreneurial spirit. "My father probably could have made more money working for somebody else, but he refused to do that," says Waitt, who started his business at 22 in the family barn.[41]

Researchers have associated many personality traits with successful entrepreneurship. They say entrepreneurs are inquisitive, passionate, self-motivated, honest, courageous, flexible, intelligent, and reliable people. The eight

CHARACTERISTICS OF ENTREPRENEURS

From the examples of entrepreneurship you've read so far, you're probably beginning to think that people who strike out on their own are a different breed. However, researchers found that successful entrepreneurs share com-

| Figure 6.3 | **Characteristics of Entrepreneurs** |

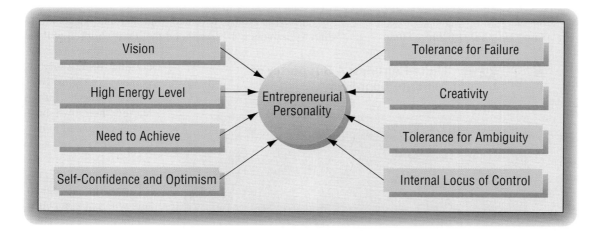

traits summarized in Figure 6.3 are especially important for people who want to succeed as entrepreneurs.[42]

Vision

Entrepreneurs begin with visions or overall ideas for their businesses, and then they passionately pursue these visions. For example, Bill Gates and Paul Allen launched Microsoft with the vision of a computer on every desk and in every home, all running Microsoft software. Their vision has helped Microsoft to become the world's largest marketer of computer software. It has guided the company and provided clear direction for employees as Microsoft has grown, adapted, and prospered in an industry characterized by tremendous technological change. Since the company's founding in 1975, it has grown from a two-person startup to a global industry leader with more than 21,000 employees and $10 billion in revenues. When people ask him about the secret to Microsoft's success, Gates says, "I think the most important element was our original vision."[43]

High Energy Level

Entrepreneurs willingly work hard to realize their visions. Starting and building a company requires an enormous amount of hard work and long hours. Some entrepreneurs work full-time at their regular day jobs and spend weeknights and weekends in launching their startups. Many commonly devote 14-hour days 7 days a week to their new ventures. Patricia Gallup, cofounder and CEO of PC Connection, a mail-order vendor of PCs and peripherals, offers this advice to budding entrepreneurs: "Work all the time. Dream about work."[44]

Sue Szymczak, founder and CEO of Safeway Sling USA, attributes the success of her company to the sweat equity she invested in it. Safeway manufactures nylon and polyester slings for construction cranes, an industry dominated by males. Through hard work and by making top-quality products, Szymczak built one of the most successful firms in her industry. She says, "You can take people like myself who came from a very poor background, with only a high school education, and if you're willing to work yourself nearly to death and risk everything you have, you can succeed."[45]

Need to Achieve

Entrepreneurs work hard because they want to excel. Their strong competitive drives help them to enjoy the challenge of reaching difficult goals and promotes dedication to personal success. Deborah Dolman's need to achieve led her from a job as a court reporter to an entrepreneur running her own court-reporting service. When she noticed increased interest in videotaped court reporting, she hired a sound engineer to develop a videotape system and launched a new company, Dolman & Associates, to market the patented, voice-activated product. "I was extremely undercapitalized from the beginning," Dolman says, "but I told myself, 'I'm going to take my last penny if necessary to get this thing developed.' . . . I never thought of giving up." Not only is Dolman's new venture a success, but she won the Michigan Outstanding Minority Entrepreneur Award and the top prize in Michigan's annual New Product Award competition for her technical innovation.[46]

Self-Confidence and Optimism

Entrepreneurs believe in their ability to succeed, and they instill their optimism in others. Consider Shirley Halperin, publisher of the alternative music magazine *Smug.*"I'm very good at knowing what music people are listening to and what people want to read about," says Halperin. "I know that one day I will be a big publishing person of some kind. I have the ideas and the will to keep going." Halperin's self-confidence and optimism sustain her loyal group of 30 writers, photographers, editors, and designers who work with no pay. One photographer says, "It's so obvious to me that she's going to make it. When she does get big, I want to be right alongside her."[47]

Tolerance for Failure

Entrepreneurs view setbacks and failures as learning experiences. They're not easily discouraged or disappointed when things don't go as planned. "I call my failure my M.B.A.," says Mark Kvamme. With a partner, he started International Solutions with a vision of selling non-English keyboards to foreign computer users in the United States and distributing Macintosh software to international customers. Kvamme had a great idea, and sales climbed quickly to $3 million, but performance quickly turned sour on him. Two of the company's largest customers went bankrupt, and Macintosh sales started to decline. Worse yet, the company never developed adequate control of finances, leaving it with poor systems for keeping track of money made and spent. Kvamme, then 24, dissolved the business and paid back his creditors and vendors by selling his office furniture and running product promotions. "I learned so much more about business when my company was going down than when it was thriving," says Kvamme. As one lesson, he warns entrepreneurs not to rely on one product line or customer and to recognize the importance of controlling costs.

Kvamme and two friends started a new company, CKS Group, a successful ad agency with $130 million in sales that's earned a reputation as the most innovative firm in the business. Kvamme attributes the success of his second venture to his first failure: "A big reason this company came together was that I failed and learned from it," he says.[48]

Creativity

Entrepreneurs typically conceive new ideas for goods and services, and they devise innovative ways to overcome difficult problems and situations. Working as a computer consultant in Columbus, Ohio, Tony Wells always heard questions from customers about where they could get training on new software. Wells asked national software makers the same questions and got this answer: The city was too small to support a training center. He solved the problem by launching Knowledge Development Center, a facility that software firms can rent to provide training classes for their

products. Four banks refused to loan Wells the money to start his company, so he mortgaged his house, maxed out his credit cards, and depleted his savings. With money in short supply, Wells devised creative solutions to keep his company operating. One of them was bartering for services he needed but couldn't afford. For example, he traded muffins baked by his brother-in-law, a chef, with another office in his building in return for use of its photocopying machine. Bartering helped Wells to limit his expenses while he built his business.[49]

Tolerance for Ambiguity

Entrepreneurs take in stride the uncertainties associated with launching a venture. Lillian Vernon, founder and CEO of the mail-order company named after her, says, "The biggest lesson every entrepreneur has to understand: Always expect the unexpected—and be prepared to deal with whatever surprises come your way."[50]

Dealing with unexpected events is the norm for most entrepreneurs. Take Kay Meurer. She started her business, Discount Office Interiors, and filled her building with surplus furniture. One day she banked the check for a huge $50,000 sale while "dancing on Cloud Nine." The next day, her building burned to the ground. She lost all her inventory, including the furniture for her big sale, and had to tell the customer to stop payment on his check. Then she learned, with horror, that she was suspected of causing the fire. The police investigating the fire found a gas can next to a huge pile of cardboard boxes on Meurer's loading dock. "My insurance agent wouldn't even talk to me," says Meurer. She wondered how she would prove that she didn't set the fire. A week later the police found the real arsonist, and later Meurer found a new site and reopened her store, which is thriving with $2 million in sales. "No matter what happens," says Meurer, "you've got to do what has to be done."[51]

Internal Locus of Control

Entrepreneurs believe that they control their own fates, so they are said to have an internal locus of control. You won't find an entrepreneur gazing into a crystal ball or looking for a four-leaf clover—they take personal responsibility for the success or failure of their actions rather than believing in luck or fate. They don't make excuses for their shortcomings, nor do they blame others for setbacks and failures. "As entrepreneurs, we are our own biggest obstacle," says Giselle Briden. "The only limits to our success are the ones we put in our own head." After Briden's first business

> **They said it**
>
> "Smart entrepreneurs . . . give their employees the freedom to make decisions so the workers can experience the thrill of being a part of a winning team."
>
> Richard J. Egan,
> CEO of EMC Corp.

BUSINESS HALL OF SHAME

Failure Is Forgiven, Fraud Isn't

Entrepreneurs should feel no shame about failing. Failure may bruise egos, but the damage often is not bad enough to prevent them from trying again and doing better work the second time. Nowhere is failure more acceptable than in the high-tech industry. Investors who finance high-tech startups aren't bothered by failure, either. "Investors here always look at the cup as half full, not half empty," says Ann

Winblad, a software venture capitalist. "They are willing to take chances on entrepreneurs who've made mistakes."

Some investors even prefer to finance failed entrepreneurs. Venture financier Mike Child explains why: "A lot of investors don't like to back guys out of big companies who haven't failed. They haven't learned the issues of meeting payroll, raising money, budgeting for R&D. They just don't know how to run a startup. People who have failed are hungrier and have a keener understanding of the product-market timing interface."

The only way to truly fail as a high-tech entrepreneur is to commit fraud. Writer Geoff Baum says, "Don't bother looking for more VC backing if you cook the books. The industry never rewards entrepreneurs and executives who are caught lying, stealing, or cheating. Ever."

Consider the founder of Platinum Software, which makes accounting software for business customers. The founder and five Platinum executives, including the chief financial officer, were caught committing fraud and found liable for illegally manipulating

---

flopped, she and a partner founded The Magellan Group, a promotion firm that arranges appearances for Anthony Robbins, Deepak Chopra, and other celebrity speakers.[52]

After reading this summary of typical personality traits, maybe you're wondering if you have what it takes to become an entrepreneur. Take the test in the Business Toolkit box later in this chapter to find out. Your results may help you to determine whether you would be successful in starting your own company.

STARTING A NEW VENTURE

The examples of entrepreneurs presented so far have introduced many ways to start a business. This section discusses the process of choosing an idea for a new venture and transforming the idea into a working business.

Selecting a Business Idea

The two most important considerations in choosing an idea for your business are (1) finding something you love to do and are good at doing and (2) determining whether your idea can satisfy a need in the marketplace. You'll willingly work hard doing something you love, and the experience will bring you personal fulfillment. The old adages "Do what makes you happy" and "To thine own self be true" are the best guidelines for deciding on a business idea. Success also depends on customers, though, so ensure that your idea has merit in the marketplace.

Jackie Bazan launched her business, Bazan Entertain-

ment Marketing, by combining what she loves to do with a marketplace need. First she focused on what she enjoyed doing. For Bazan, that meant "not only working in the film industry but also limiting my business to marketing and publicity for African-American and other minority-made and -oriented films." Bazan found a small market niche that needed her services. Her company has handled the marketing and publicity for Spike Lee's films *Get on the Bus* and *4 Little Girls* and for the Oscar-winning boxing documentary *When We Were Kings*.[53]

The following guidelines may help you to select an idea that represents a good entrepreneurial opportunity for you:[54]

▼ List your interests and abilities. Include your values and beliefs, your goals and dreams, things you like and dislike doing, and your job experiences.

▼ Make another list of the types of businesses that match your interests and abilities.

▼ Read newspapers and business and consumer magazines to learn about demographic and economic trends that project needs for products that no one yet offers.

▼ Carefully evaluate existing goods and services looking for ways you can improve on them.

▼ Decide on a business that matches what you want and offers profit potential.

▼ Conduct marketing research to determine whether your business idea will attract enough customers to earn a profit.

required reports of financial information, according to the Securities and Exchange Commission. The executives cooked Platinum's books by declaring revenues for products the company hadn't yet shipped. For example, an independent auditor found that Platinum claimed revenues for one accounting period of $9.3 million, when its real revenues reached only $6.8 million. The company not only falsified its financial statements, but used the inflated revenues to influence stock trades.

The financial misconduct had devastating effects. Investors lost millions of dollars, Platinum's stock price plummeted, some 100 company employees lost their jobs, the firm posted seven

straight quarterly losses in revenues, and it limped into the future with a tarnished reputation.

Under the leadership of a new CEO, Platinum is trying to rebuild its image and its sales after settling a $17 million class-action suit. As for the company's founder, the SEC banned him from holding an office in a public company for 10 years. He was fined $100,000 and ordered to pay $1.25 million to settle shareholder lawsuits.

QUESTIONS FOR CRITICAL THINKING

1. Do you think Platinum's CEO got off too easily by just paying fines and being barred from holding an

officer position? Do other students agree with your position?

2. Tolerance for failure is one of the entrepreneur's defining characteristics, but the need to achieve is another. How do you think an entrepreneur balances these two characteristics? Where did the balance tip in Platinum's case?

Sources: "Platinum Software Corporation Named among the Fastest-Growing Windows ISVs," PR Newswire, April 19, 1999; Geoff Baum, "Bouncing Back," *Forbes ASAP*, June 2, 1997, pp. 49–52; Geoff Baum, "When Losers Really Are Losers," *Forbes ASAP*, June 2, 1997, p. 52; Rochelle Garner, "In Need of a Shine," *PC Week*, January 22, 1996, p. A9; and Sam Whitmore, "Platinum Problems Should Spur Wall Street Reforms," *PC Week*, June 6, 1994, p. A13.

▼ Learn as much as you can about the industry in which your new venture will operate, your merchandise or service, and your competitors. Read surveys that project growth in various industries.

Most new ventures are formed to solve problems that people have experienced either at work or in their personal lives. For example, Kristin Roach, an avid snowboarder, started her business because she was frustrated with the choice of unisex outfits then available for snowboarders. The apparel was ill-fitting and uncomfortable because it wasn't designed for women's bodies. Roach dropped out of college to launch Kurvz Extremewear, selling comfortable, stylish, and colorful outfits for women snowboarders.[55]

An entrepreneur's need for marketing research varies depending on the business idea, industry, and competitive conditions. An innovative idea with an unproven potential customer base may require

more research than a proposal to improve an existing product. Jens Molbak conducted research to determine if a large enough customer base would welcome his novel idea of marketing a coin-sorting machine. Molbak's research consisted of asking people at grocery stores what they did with their change. "We talked to 1,500 people, and it turned out that three out of four had coins at home, with an average of about $30 at any one time," says Molbak. From this research, Molbak estimated that Americans nationwide stored about $8 billion of coins at home. These results convinced him to proceed with development of his Coinstar machine, which would accept coins in a hopper and return a voucher redeemable for cash at participating grocery stores. Molbak earns a profit on each transaction because the machine keeps 7.5 cents of each dollar it processes. Molbak has installed Coinstar machines in more than 2,000 stores, and the average customer, as his research predicted, deposits $30 worth of coins to be sorted.[56]

Customers love Jens Molbak's innovation, which sorts their stashes of coins and gives them vouchers redeemable for cash.

B U S I N E S S   T O O L   K I T

Think You Might Be a Good Entrepreneur?

Answer *yes* or *no* to the following questions:

Yes No

❑ ❑   1. Are you a first-generation American?

❑ ❑   2. Were you an honor student?

❑ ❑   3. Did you enjoy group functions in school—clubs, team sports, even double dates?

❑ ❑   4. As a youngster, did you frequently prefer to spend time alone?

❑ ❑   5. As a child, did you have a paper route, a lemonade stand, or some other small enterprise?

❑ ❑   6. Were you a stubborn child?

❑ ❑   7. Were you a cautious youngster, the last in the neighborhood to try diving off the high board?

❑ ❑   8. Do you worry about what others think of you?

❑ ❑   9. Are you in a rut, tired of the same routine every day?

❑ ❑ 10. Would you be willing to invest your savings—and risk losing all you invested—to go it alone?

❑ ❑ 11. If your new business should fail, would you get to work immediately on another?

❑ ❑ 12. Are you an optimist?

Answers

1. Yes = 1, No = minus 1
2. Yes = minus 4, No = 4
3. Yes = minus 1, No = 1
4. Yes = 1, No = minus 1
5. Yes = 2, No = minus 2
6. Yes = 1, No = minus 1
7. Yes = minus 4, No = 4. (If you were a very daring child, add another 4 points.)
8. Yes = minus 1, No = 1
9. Yes = 2, No = minus 2
10. Yes = 2, No = minus 2
11. Yes = 4, No = minus 4
12. Yes = 2, No = minus 2

Add up your total score. A score of 20 or more points indicates strong entrepreneurial tendencies. A score between 0 and 19 points suggests some possibility for success as an entrepreneur. A score between 0 and minus 10 indicates little chance of successful entrepreneurship. A score below minus 11 indicates someone who's not the entrepreneurial type.

Source: This test was designed by John R. Braun, now a psychologist with CHE Senior Psychological Services, and the Northwestern Mutual Life Insurance Company.

If you're an inventor-entrepreneur like Molbak, you'll need to secure a patent for your product. The Web site, Obtaining a Patent and Invention Development, http://www.bosbbb.org/lit/0022.html presents basic information about applying for a patent and commercializing your invention. It also lists names and addresses of organizations and other resources that can help you to turn an idea into a business.

 www.bosbbb.org/lit/0022.html

In addition to starting a new business from scratch, aspiring entrepreneurs can choose two more popular options: buying existing businesses and buying franchises.

Buying an Existing Business Some entrepreneurs prefer to buy established businesses rather than assuming the risks of starting new ones. Buying an existing business brings many advantages: Employees already in place serve established customers and deal with familiar suppliers, the good or service is known in the marketplace, and the necessary permits and licenses are already secured. It's also much easier to get financing for an existing business. Some sellers may even help the buyers by providing financing and offering to serve as consultants.[57]

To find businesses for sale, contact your local Chamber of Commerce as well as professionals such as lawyers, accountants, and insurance agents. Most people want to buy healthy businesses, while turnaround entrepreneurs enjoy the challenge of buying unprofitable firms and making them generate profits, as mentioned earlier in the chapter.

Buying a Franchise Like buying an established business, a franchise offers a less risky way to begin a business than starting your own firm. But franchising still involves risks of its own. You must do your homework, carefully analyzing the franchisor's terms and capabilities for delivering the support it promises. Energetic preparation helps to ensure that your business will earn a profit and grow.

Although a franchisee must agree to follow the procedures mandated by the franchisor, entrepreneurs can still find ways to inject their creativity into their franchises and make them grow. Consider LaVan Hawkins, who runs 14 Burger King outlets; in partnership with Black Entertainment Television, he plans to operate 475 by 2000. Hawkins learned the fast-food business starting from the bottom by scrubbing toilets and worked his way up to become manager of a Burger King outlet. Since acquiring a franchise of his own, he's made millions of dollars by tailoring the product formulas to the tastes of his customers—inner-city African-Americans. He serves banana shakes and Cajun fries in restaurants lit up with Klieg lights and neon. Customers listen to hip-hop and R&B music. Hawkins wants his restaurants to represent a symbol of hope for inner-city kids. He offers his employees stock options and helps them along career paths to become owner-operators. Although Hawkins's restaurants seem quite different from typical Burger King outlets, they bring in twice the revenue of an average unit.[58]

Creating a Business Plan

In the past, most entrepreneurs launched their ventures without creating formal business plans. While planning is an integral part of managing in the corporate world, entrepreneurs traditionally have favored seat-of-the-pants management. As Amar Bhide, who teaches entrepreneurship at the Harvard Business School, explains:

[A] comprehensive analytical approach to planning doesn't suit most startups. Entrepreneurs typically lack the time and money to interview a representative cross section of potential customers, let alone analyze substitutes, reconstruct competitors' cost structures, or project alternative technology scenarios. In fact, too much analysis can be harmful; by the time an opportunity is investigated fully, it may no longer exist. A city map and restaurant guide on a CD may be a winner in January but worthless if delayed until December.[59]

Jennifer Barclay built a thriving business quickly and without a plan in order to take advantage of an unexpected opportunity.

Jennifer Barclay's experience confirms Professor Bhide's observation. Working in her dad's garage, Barclay crafted handmade T-shirts and sold them at local art fairs. While attending a wholesale fashion show, she unexpectedly received orders for 6,000 pieces of clothing. Then 18 years old, Barclay moved quickly to seize the opportunity of filling the orders, launching Blue Fish Clothing Inc. as a producer of apparel from natural fibers. In the process, she raised capital to buy materials and equipment, found a manufacturing site, and hired employees to make the clothing. Barclay had no time to write a business plan. "If you overanalyze everything, you see how difficult it could be," she says. "It holds people back from [acting on] the wonderful ideas within them." With a strong belief in her one-of-a-kind clothing, Barclay has increased company revenues each year by 35 percent. Blue Fish Clothing is now sold at more than 600 retail stores and boutiques, including Nordstrom and Neiman Marcus.[60]

Although the planning process for entrepreneurs differs from a major company's planning function, today's entrepreneurs are advised to construct business plans following the guidelines presented in Chapter 7. Entrepreneurial business plans vary depending on the type of startup, but the basic elements of such a plan—stating company goals, outlining sales and marketing strategies, and determining financial needs—apply to all types of ventures.

For information about writing a business plan, visit the EntreWorld Web site (http://www.entreworld.org) and click on The Business Plan: Your Blueprint for the Future. The information there covers researching and writing your plan, as well as presenting it to financing sources. To see a sample business plan, visit the page labeled *A Sample Business Plan* at http://www.morebusiness.com/bplan. For an online tutorial in creating a plan, visit http://www.americanexpress.com/smallbusiness/resources/starting/biz_plan/index.html. This site includes an interactive Try It Yourself section that lets you create a plan for a startup and then gives feedback.

Finding Financing

How much money will you need to start your business and where will you get it? Requirements for **seed capital,** funds to launch a company, depend on the nature of your business and the type of facilities and equipment you need. A survey of successful entrepreneurs revealed that they raised an average of $25,000 to start their businesses.[61]

The vast majority of entrepreneurs rely on personal savings, advances on credit cards, and funds from partners, family members, and friends to fund their startups. New ventures secure funds in two forms: debt financing and equity financing.

Debt Financing When entrepreneurs use **debt financing,** they borrow money that they must repay. Loans from banks, finance companies, credit card companies, and family and friends are sources of debt financing. While many entrepreneurs charge business expenses to personal credit cards because it's an easy way to pay, high interest rates make this source of funding an expensive choice. For example, annual interest charges on a credit card can run as high as 20 percent, while a home equity loan (borrowing against the value of a home) currently charges a more reasonable 8½ percent.

www.americanexpress.com/smallbusiness/resources/starting/biz_plan/index.html

Still, credit card financing is a viable option for entrepreneurs who expect to grow quickly and know that they can pay off their debt in a short time. Brothers Thomas and Kevin Lane chose this option. They got their idea to produce custom-made baseball bats when Kevin, a pitcher for a minor league affiliate, heard his teammates complain about the poor quality of their bats. The brothers asked their father, a skilled carpenter, to craft several bats for the players to try out.

The players loved the custom bats, but the Lanes waited for approval of their use in the major leagues before taking a $20,000 cash advance on their credit cards to buy the equipment they needed to launch Carolina Clubs. As they expected, "We can't keep up with demand," says Thomas.[62]

Many banks turn down requests for loans to fund startups, fearful of the high risk such ventures entail. Only a small percentage of startups raise seed capital through bank loans, although some new firms can get the SBA-backed loans, as discussed in Chapter 5. While friends, family members, and credit card companies probably won't ask to see a business plan, bank loan officers will. They will also evaluate your credit history. Since a startup has not yet established a business credit history, banks often base lending decisions on evaluations of entrepreneurs' personal credit histories. Banks are more willing to make loans to entrepreneurs who've been in business for a while, show a profit on rising revenues, and need funds to finance expansion. Even then, as the Solving an Ethical Controversy box illustrates, entrepreneurs face serious challenges obtaining bank loans.

DID YOU KNOW?

Spike Lee financed his first film using his credit card.

Equity Financing When entrepreneurs secure **equity financing,** they invest their own money along with funds

Business Directory

seed capital initial funding needed to launch a new venture

debt financing borrowed funds that entrepreneurs must repay

equity financing funds invested in new ventures in exchange for part ownership

supplied by people and firms that become co-owners of the startups. An entrepreneur does not have to repay equity funds. In exchange for their financial investments, equity investors receive part ownership in the business. Sources of equity financing include family and friends, business partners, venture capital firms, and private investors.

Teaming up with a partner who has funds to invest may benefit an entrepreneur with a good idea and skills but no money. When designer Tommy Hilfiger needed financing for his clothing business, he formed a partnership with Silas Chou, owner of Hong Kong's oldest textile firm, who invested funds and supplied manufacturing expertise. Hilfiger and Chou shared the goal of rapidly growing the business. During the first year of their partnership, they generated sales of $25 million.

Venture capitalists are business organizations or groups of private individuals that invest in new and growing firms. Venture capital supports only a very limited number of startups, because these investors expect very high rates of return, from 28 percent to 40 percent, in short time periods, typically 5 years. Consequently, they invest in firms in fast-growing industries such as technology and communications. One venture capitalist says, "If there's no possibility you're going to hit the $25 million benchmark within 5 years, it's simply a waste of time to pursue institutional venture capital."[63]

A larger group of entrepreneurs consists of angel investors. **Angel investors** are wealthy individuals willing to invest money directly in new ventures for equity stakes. They invest more capital in startups than do venture capitalists. From 90 percent to 100 percent of angel capital is invested in new ventures, compared to just 10 percent of that distributed by venture capitalists. Many angel investors are themselves successful entrepreneurs who want to help aspiring business owners by providing funding that would have helped them when they were launching their businesses. Angel investors back a wide variety of new ventures. Some invest only in certain industries, some invest only in startups with socially responsible missions, and some prefer to back only women entrepreneurs.

Because entrepreneurs have trouble finding wealthy private investors, angel networks form to match business angels with startups in need of capital. One angel network, Investors' Circle, holds conferences twice a year to consider presentations made by entrepreneurs. Investors' Circle provided the financing that saved Kermit Heartstrong's new business, Word Origin Inc., which makes educational board games and puzzles for children. Loans and other capital from Heartstrong's friends and family weren't enough to finance his production for the holiday season. After giving a presentation about his company and his need for cash at an Investors' Circle conference, Heartstrong received a total of $1.5 million in investment capital from 12 different business angels.[64]

As entrepreneurs start their businesses, they spend much of their time seeking and securing financing. Most company founders perform all the activities needed to operate their businesses because they don't have enough money to hire employees. Most entrepreneurs begin as sole proprietors working from their homes. After their initial startup periods, however, entrepreneurs must make many management decisions as their companies begin to grow. They must establish legal entities, buy equipment and choose facilities and locations, assemble teams of employees, and ensure compliance with a host of government regulations. These challenges will be discussed in other chapters throughout this book.

INTRAPRENEURSHIP

Large, established companies try to retain the entrepreneurial spirit by encouraging **intrapreneurship,** the process of promoting innovation within their organizational structures. Today's fast-changing business climate compels large firms to continually innovate in order to maintain their competitive advantages. Entrepreneurial environments created within companies such as 3M, Thermo Electron, Xerox, and Intuit can help these larger firms retain valuable employees who might otherwise leave their jobs to start their own businesses.

Large companies support entrepreneurial activity in varied ways. One leader in this area, 3M Corp., has established companywide policies and procedures that give employees personal freedom to explore new products and technologies. For example, 3M allows its 8,000 researchers to spend 15 percent of their time working on their own ideas without approval from management. Even 3M's hiring process is designed to select innovative people as employees. The company has developed a personality profile of characteristics shared by its top creative scientists. Based on the profile, 3M

Business Directory

venture capitalists a business firm or group of individuals that invests in new and growing firms

angel investors wealthy individuals who invest directly in a new venture in exchange for an equity stake

intrapreneurship the process of promoting innovation within an organization's structure

SOLVING AN ETHICAL CONTROVERSY

Should Banks Lend to Firms with Dual Bottom Lines?

Bagel Works of Keene, New Hampshire, makes bagels and sells them through its own chain of cafes. In business for 9 years, the company proudly defines itself as a socially responsible firm. It recognizes dual bottom lines: It measures success according to the profits it earns and the benefits it brings to employees, the community, and the environment.

Each year, Bagel Works donates about $10,000 worth of bagels to community organizations. It uses environmentally safe—though often expensive—organically grown ingredients to make its bagels. The company treats its employees well by providing them with programs such as gainsharing, in which they receive financial rewards when they meet performance targets.

Bagel Works wanted to expand its headquarters facility and open a cafe in another city. It planned for the expansion by setting aside some cash reserves and raising $500,000 in equity funding, but the company still needed more funds to finance the expansion. Jennifer Pearl, a founder and managing partner, and Richard French, the

company's president, asked their bank for a loan. Unfortunately, Bagel Works didn't show the kind of bottom line that the bank wanted to see. On sales of $3.5 million, the company was showing operating losses.

"The bank loan officer really struggled with the fact that we were incurring these extra expenses [for socially responsible practices] while we weren't making money as a company," says Pearl. The banker wanted Pearl and French to change their principles, but they refused to compromise their social goals just to show a profit.

? *Should Banks Give Loans to Firms that Emphasize Social as Well as Profit Goals?*

PRO

1. In the long term, socially responsible firms are stronger and ultimately more profitable than more self-oriented companies. Financial incentives like gainsharing decrease employee turnover and reduce the costs of recruiting and training new employees. Product donations to community groups benefit financial performance by increasing customer loyalty and enabling potential customers to sample the products.

2. Expansion periods are tough times for all businesses. Entrepreneurs incur as much risk during growth spurts as at their initial startups. Companies commonly show losses when they are trying to grow. Lenders should be more concerned about strong sales revenues, which indicate that a firm is satisfying its customers, rather than about profits or losses.

CON

1. A firm should strive to treat its employees and community well, but not at the expense of earning a profit. When socially responsible practices hurt a company's net profits, the company should shift its focus to earning money rather than doing good. After all, banks are in business to earn a profit by lending money and charging interest to other profitable firms.

2. While entrepreneurs are prone to take calculated risks, bankers are much more conservative risk takers. They properly avoid the risk of lending money to companies with operating losses. If the company can't repay the loan, the bank loses money.

---

has crafted questions and scenarios that help company interviewers to gauge the creative skills of job candidates.

In addition to its traditional product development approach, in which managers and researchers work together to develop products, 3M implements two intrapreneurial approaches: skunkworks and pacing programs. One skunkworks project produced 3M's Post-It Notes. Such a project is initiated by an employee who conceives an idea and then recruits resources from within 3M to turn it into a commercial product. Pacing programs are company-initiated projects that focus on a few products and technologies in which 3M sees potential for rapid marketplace winners. The company provides financing, equipment, and people to support such pacing projects. The Scotch-Brite Never Rust wool soap pad was a successful 1990s pacing

project. Within 2 years of its introduction, the pad captured a market share above 17 percent.[65]

A large company that wants to nurture intrapreneurs faces a difficult challenge in dealing with the differences between managers and entrepreneurs. William F. O'Brien, president of Starlight Telecommunications, explains:

> There is a natural tension between the way corporate managers think and the way entrepreneurs think. Many executives at large companies work long and hard to achieve reliability and stability within their organization, and may seem overly cautious to the entrepreneur. The entrepreneur's calls for rapid change and willingness to accept risk, on the other hand, can be threatening to the executive.[66]

SUMMARY

Jennifer Pearl and Richard French are members of the new generation of entrepreneurs who care about their employees, their communities, and the environment. These young entrepreneurs "run their businesses like they would run a family. Money is not your No. 1 focus," says Jennifer Kushell, president of the Young Entrepreneurs Network.

Bagel Works eventually found a bank that believed in its dual bottom lines and was willing to lend the company $681,000 to finance its expansion plans. Pearl and French met David Berge, a vice president of Vermont National Bank, at a community event.

David Berge (center), vice president of Vermont National Bank, loaned money to Richard French and Jennifer Pearl's company, helping them to maintain their dual bottom lines.

They persuaded Berge to take a risk on their company, even though it was losing money.

Berge viewed Bagel Works's social programs differently from the firm's first banker. "A company that treats its workers right is probably going to treat its lender right," says Berge. He adds, "Committed workers tend to make a higher-quality product. High quality means a better reputation in the community." The banker was also impressed with the way Bagel Works planned ahead for its expansion by saving cash and raising equity, citing those precautions as signs of responsible management. Finally, talking with Pearl and French about the importance to them of their social programs convinced Berge that he could build a relationship of trust with them.

The funding for the Bagel Works loan came from Vermont National's Socially Responsible Banking (SRB) Fund. Deposits in the SRB Fund are made by people throughout the United States and 16 countries who want their money

to support businesses with social as well as profit goals. According to Berge, who is a director of the fund at Vermont National, the quality of SRB loans is better than that of the bank's other loans. SRB loan customers have a 0 percent delinquency rate on commercial loans of more than 90 days.

Pearl credits Vermont National Bank with helping Bagel Works "get over some of the financial obstacles that we were facing at the time." Company sales continue to climb, and today Bagel Works is turning a profit.

QUESTIONS FOR CRITICAL THINKING

1. Suppose you are a bank loan officer and Jennifer Pearl and Richard French visit your office and ask you for a loan. How much weight would social responsibility goals hold in your decision to grant or deny their request?

2. Would you deposit money in a savings account like the SRB Fund? Why or why not?

Sources: Sam Barry, "Of Bagels, Business, and Bottom Lines," Co-op America Web site, accessed at www.coopamerica.org, April 20, 1999; Rieva Lesonsky, "The Right Path?" *Entrepreneur*, March 1997, p. 6; Sharon Nelton, "Loans with Interest—and Principle," *Nation's Business*, January 1997, pp. 22, 24; and "Talking about Her Generation," *U.S. News & World Report*, September 23, 1996, p. 67.

O'Brien's insight is based on a personal experience. Before launching Starlight, he worked for GTE, the giant telecommunications firm. In charge of GTE's African sales, O'Brien and a colleague, Pete Nielsen, wanted to set up a new venture within the company to compete with the small, locally based telephone companies in Africa that were taking market share from large firms. Encouraged by a sponsor within the firm to develop a business plan for their idea, O'Brien and Nielsen performed their regular jobs and worked nights and weekends on their plan, completing it in 6 months and receiving approval for funding from GTE's new venture group. Then they waited 18 months as their plan moved through the final approval process. During that time, the main

sponsor for their idea retired, and the successor didn't like the idea, nor did he want to lose O'Brien and Nielsen as employees to a new venture. Ultimately, GTE pulled the plug on their idea. O'Brien and Nielsen resigned to form Starlight, which offers telephone service in Somalia and Uganda and plans to expand service in other African countries.

From the perspective of a disappointed intrapreneur, O'Brien has developed the following guidelines for large firms that want to encourage employee intrapreneurship:

1. Identify and disseminate companywide goals relating to new ventures, and encourage managers to support spin-offs that advance those goals.

2. Protect and reward employees who identify new business ideas.

3. Quickly move proposals for new ventures through the approval process.[67]

Recognizing that entrepreneurial employees often leave to form their own startups, some companies actually encourage employees to take the plunge. Several divisions of Lockheed-Martin, the $26 billion defense contractor, offer an Entrepreneurial Leave of Absence Program. The program allows an employee with a new venture idea to take a 2-year, unpaid leave to start the business. After the 2-year period, the employee can leave permanently or hire managers to run the new company and return to work to invent something else. For about a 10 percent stake in the startup, Lockheed-Martin invests about $250,000 in financing the new venture and the company also provides incubator space, management advice, and leads to help identify potential investors. Tim Scott, the first employee to try the leave program, launched Genase LLC, a firm that creates and sells an enzyme for stonewashing denim fabric. Scott decided not to return to Lockheed-Martin. Speaking as a true entrepreneur, Scott said, "I decided that working on my own is what I really want to do."[68]

SUMMARY OF LEARNING GOALS

1. Define the term "entrepreneur," and distinguish among an entrepreneur, a small-business owner, and a manager.

Unlike small-business owners, entrepreneurs own and run their businesses with the goal of building significant firms that create wealth and add jobs. Entrepreneurs are visionaries. They identify opportunities and take the initiative to quickly gather the resources they need to start their businesses. Managers use the resources of their companies to achieve the goals of those organizations.

2. Identify three different types of entrepreneurs.

The three categories are classic entrepreneurs, intrapreneurs, and change agents. A classic entrepreneur identifies a business opportunity and allocates available resources to tap that market. An intrapreneur is an employee who develops a new idea or product within the context of an organizational position. A change agent is a manager who tries to revitalize an existing firm to make it a competitive success.

3. Explain why people choose to become entrepreneurs.

People choose this kind of career for many different reasons. Reasons most frequently cited include desires to be one's own boss, to achieve financial success, to gain job security, and to improve quality of life.

4. Discuss conditions that encourage opportunities for entrepreneurs.

A favorable public perception, availability of financing, the falling cost and widespread availability of information technology, globalization, entrepreneurship education, and changing demographic and economic trends all contribute to a fertile environment for people to start new ventures.

5. Describe the role of entrepreneurs in the economy.

Entrepreneurs play a significant role in the economy as a major source of innovation and job creation. Entrepreneurship also provides many opportunities for women and minorities, who may encounter limits to their progress in established businesses.

6. Identify personality traits that typically characterize successful entrepreneurs.

Successful entrepreneurs share several typical traits, including vision, high energy level, need to achieve, self-confidence and optimism, tolerance for failure, creativity, tolerance for ambiguity, and internal locus of control.

7. Discuss the process of starting a new venture.

Entrepreneurs must select an idea for their business, develop a business plan, obtain financing, and organize the resources they need to operate their startups.

8. Explain how organizations promote intrapreneurship.

Organizations encourage entrepreneurial activity in a variety of ways. Hiring practices, dedicated programs such as skunkworks, and entrepreneurial leaves of absence encourage innovation within large firms.

TEN BUSINESS TERMS YOU NEED TO KNOW

entrepreneur	debt financing
classic entrepreneur	equity financing
intrapreneur	venture capitalist
change agent	angel investor
seed capital	intrapreneurship

REVIEW QUESTIONS

1. Distinguish between entrepreneurs, small-business owners, and managers. Which of these three would you choose as a career? Give a reason for your choice.
2. What are the three categories of entrepreneurs? How do they differ?
3. List some reasons why people become entrepreneurs. If you chose to start up your own company, what would be your primary motive for doing so?
4. Name six conditions that benefit people who want to start new ventures today.
5. Why can Americans launch new firms more easily than Europeans can?
6. What benefits do entrepreneurs bring to the economy?
7. Describe eight characteristics attributed to successful entrepreneurs. In your opinion, which trait is the most important determinant of success?
8. What two factors are most important in selecting an idea on which to base a startup?
9. Explain the differences between debt financing and equity financing. Give an example of each type of financing.
10. What is intrapreneurship? How do entrepreneurs and intrapreneurs differ?

QUESTIONS FOR CRITICAL THINKING

1. People thought that Mark Scatterday was crazy when he told them about his new-venture idea of putting birdseed into a balloon and selling the product for $10. But Scatterday forged ahead anyway, launching Pro-Innovative Concepts to make and market The Gripp, a patented squeeze ball that's bringing in revenues of more than $5 million. What characteristics of entrepreneurs do you think helped Scatterday to succeed in his new venture?
2. Many entrepreneurs choose to start their own businesses because they prefer to be their own bosses. Would you rather work for someone else or be your own boss? What are some advantages and disadvantages of each option?
3. Suppose that the principal of the high school from which you graduated called to ask if you would give a talk on entrepreneurship as a career option during the school's annual career day. The principal worries that many high school students say they want to be entrepreneurs but few realize what this choice involves. What advice would you give to these students?
4. Think of something you love to do—a personal interest or a hobby—that has the potential of being turned into a business. How would you go about determining whether your idea would satisfy enough customers to make it a profitable business?
5. You have just announced to your family members that you're going to start your own business. Your family members are delighted with your decision, as you'll be the first entrepreneur in the family. They have all read stories in newspapers and magazines about the overnight successes of entrepreneurs and are excited about the prospect of having a millionaire in the family. Before you even ask, they offer you money to start your company. No one in your family has ever invested in a business before, so you have to explain to them the difference between debt financing and equity financing. As an entrepreneur, you are optimistic that your business will succeed. But you are also realistic and know that your first venture brings many risks. You are concerned that if your business fails, it will cause family problems because you may not be able to pay back debt financing and family members will lose money they invest as equity financing. How would you resolve this issue?

Experiential Exercise

Directions: To learn more about the entrepreneurial experience, interview a successful entrepreneur either by telephone or in person. The person you interview should have a minimum of three years' entrepreneurial experience. Report your findings in a format requested by your instructor. Possibilities include (1) give a 3- to 5-minute oral report in class, (2) write a 2- to 3-page paper, or (3) compare your findings during a small group discussion with others in your class who have also completed this assignment.

Following are some questions you may use for your interview. Feel free to add to or delete from this list or to prepare another list with questions of your own. Your goal in this exercise is to get firsthand information about the entrepreneurial experience to help you determine whether entrepreneurship might be a career path for you.

1. Entrepreneurs begin with visions, or overall ideas for their businesses, and then they passionately pursue those visions. Describe the vision you had for your organization.
2. Did you start a business with your own idea, buy an established business, or buy a franchise? If you started a business based on your own idea, answer this question: In selecting your business idea, were you able to find something you love to do and are good at doing? How did you determine that your idea would fill a need in the marketplace?
3. Researchers have associated many personality traits with successful entrepreneurship. Which of these describe you? Which trait do you think contributed most to achieving your success? Explain why the trait you selected contributed so much to your success.

   ▼ Vision

   ▼ High energy level

   ▼ Need to achieve

   ▼ Self-confidence and optimism

   ▼ Tolerance for failure

   ▼ Creativity

   ▼ Tolerance for ambiguity

   ▼ Internal locus of control

4. Describe your typical workweek schedule, indicating what time your workday begins and ends and how many days per week you typically work.
5. Describe a setback or failure and how you responded to it.
6. Did you ever take a class or enroll in a program that taught you how to start and run a business?
7. Did you have a documented "Business Plan"? If yes, approximately how many hours did it take you to prepare it? Did you use it to explain and sell your business idea? Was it necessary to get the financing you needed?
8. Did you budget enough for your start-up costs? If not, what expenses did you not plan for that created a cash-flow problem?
9. Explain the procedure you followed to find financing for your new business. Did the process take more or less time than you anticipated? Was finding financing easier or harder than you expected? What's the best advice you can give a person who is seeking financing for starting a new business?
10. What's the most important entrepreneurial idea or advice that you would want to convey to college students contemplating going into business for themselves?

Nothing but Net

1. **Venture capitalists.** Assume you are seeking financing for an entrepreneurial venture and need to check the availability of possible funding. Visit the Web site called America's Business Funding Directory at

    www.businessfinance.com.

    According to the information applicants provide for the search, list the criteria venture capitalists consider when evaluating your capital request. After reviewing the procedure for using this Web site to locate funding sources, examine the tools, references, and resources also available at this site that can help you grow and keep your business strong.

2. **Creativity.** One of the characteristics of entrepreneurs is creativity. Use your search engine to find Web sites related to creativity or visit "Mind-Brain Links" at

    www.tiac.net/users/seeker/brainlinks.html.

    Present a 3- to 5-minute report to your classmates summarizing the most useful and interesting ideas you found that relate to entrepreneurs and creativity.

3. **Franchise opportunities.** On the Internet, you will be able to find a great deal of information about franchising opportunities available for entrepreneurs. Use your Internet search engine to locate a site such as "The Franchise Handbook: On-Line" at

    www.franchise1.com/franchise.html

    or "Business Opportunities Handbook: On-Line" at

    www.ezines.com.

    Select three franchise opportunities that are interesting to you and prepare a table where you can compare information related to each franchise. Across the top of the page list the franchises you've selected; down the left column list information categories provided below (or create your own categories of information); then fill in the columns with the information related to each franchise.

    ▼ Franchising since

    ▼ Number of franchised units

    ▼ Number of company-owned units

    ▼ Franchise fee

    ▼ Capital requirements

    ▼ Training and support provided

Note: Internet Web addresses change frequently. If you do not find the exact sites listed, you may need to access the organization's or company's home page and search there.

TWO ARTISTS OR TWO EXECUTIVES?
THE STORY OF TWO WOMEN BOXING

In 1983, a new venture was born when artist Linda Finnell was commissioned by a non-profit photography gallery to make boxes to be used as artists' portfolios. With her best friend and fellow artist, Julie Cohn, these two women handmade each box while sitting in the middle of Linda's living room. For three more years, the two friends worked together making and selling boxes, cards, and small books before deciding to hire a small number of employees and expand into a retail business. However, hiring employees was a big step. As Julie remarked, "We never thought it would be the way it is right now. I think we really thought it would be the Julie and Linda club forever."

As artists, both women had experienced the challenges, frustrations, and rewards of creating art and then negotiating with galleries for its display and sale. In the mid-80s, Julie and Linda decided that by focusing their joint energy on a business, they could create the life they wanted. They would be the design force behind the art products made by their company, and from the business, they would attain stable, and later, growing incomes. Starting with a capital infusion of only $400, by the early 1990s, the company was grossing nearly half a million dollars.

The early years meant a lot of hard selling as well as finding contract sales representatives to handle additional geographic regions and trade shows at which their company's work was displayed. Once a part-time office manager was hired along with more women in production, Julie and Linda increased the amount of time they spent on designing new products. Still, the day-to-day business details demanded their attention.

Because of the small, family-like nature of Two Women Boxing, policies regarding employees tended to be set with the employees' needs in mind. The women on the production line have always worked at their own pace and set their own schedules. This, in part, fits well with the nature of one-of-a-kind handicrafts. On the other hand, as the demand for higher volume and rapid delivery has increased, this type of flexibility is more costly to the business. A new piece rate pay system provides an incentive for helping to meet the production schedule. Currently, the production manager is working to create production jobs with more autonomy. This means that the employees are beginning to handle the ordering of materials, shipping, and some design elements. This new system clearly demands a fairly high level of cross-training, something that has always been part of this small firm. But it also demands more of the employees. As Julie noted, "The people who will work out well are the self-starters."

The pull between a completely employee-centered work environment and the needs of the business has at times created tension for the owners. "That's been one of the hardest things in the business—to be an employer and to try to play out both sides of what it must be like to be the person who's trying not to hand down rules, but to create a working structure," according to Julie.

By 1996, Two Women Boxing and its founders had hired a small staff of professional managers: two full-time office managers and a production manager. Still, as long as the company maintained a production orientation, Julie and Linda were called upon to handle management, marketing, supplier, and financial concerns. And that's not what they want any longer. These two entrepreneurs "started the business to support their art," and that's what they are working to get back to. Julie and Linda are consciously moving the business away from manufacturing and toward the design side. They are licensing their designs to companies, like Fitz and Floyd of Dallas and Sylvestrie, that make china, giftware, and other "tabletop" items. Although they are proud of their company's work in manufacturing—the competition and costs make it less fun—the design side is their joy. Julie and Linda have been forward thinking over the years and have continuously analyzed the direction of their business. They are therefore well-prepared to move forward on this repositioning of their business.

Questions

1. What are the advantages and disadvantages of owning a small business? Apply these to Two Women Boxing and explain your decisions.

2. What are some of the characteristics of an entrepreneur? Give examples of how these characteristics apply to Two Women Boxing.

3. As the company grows, where could Two Women Boxing find the financing?

4. How would you go about starting your own business? How would it differ from Two Women Boxing?

chapter **7**

Strategies for Business Success in the Relationship Era

LEARNING GOALS

1. Explain the role of vision in business success.

2. Describe the major benefits of planning.

3. Distinguish among strategic planning, tactical planning, and operational planning.

4. Explain the six steps in the strategic planning process.

5. Identify the components of SWOT analysis and explain its role in assessing a firm's competitive position.

6. Describe the importance of relationships with customers, suppliers, employees, and others in achieving a company's objectives.

7. Explain the core elements of buyer-seller relationships.

8. Identify strategies and tactics for building and sustaining relationships with other organizations.

Time Warner Builds a Web of Customer Relationships

Time Warner seems to possess the ingredients needed to become much more than just another Web retailer. After all, this media giant includes divisions as diverse as motion-picture production, Columbia House music clubs, the Book-of-the-Month Club, a collection of cable channels, the Atlanta Braves, and magazines like *Time, Fortune,* and *People*. With inventory like this, Time Warner should be able to build a superstore in cyberspace.

A few short years ago, the Internet was seen as a novelty with little practical application. Too many barriers existed—from concerns about credit-card purchasing to amateurish Web sites—for all but the bravest consumers to purchase anything online. Today, a whole new self-service economy is growing and what was previously unthinkable to companies like Time Warner became not only doable but lucrative.

Catalog giant Spiegel is one example of a company that has boarded the Internet train. While its Internet sales currently account for less than 5 percent of total revenues, they have grown fivefold over the past three years. Spiegel's traditional mail-order and telephone sales from its catalog have plunged over this same period. Dell Computer shoppers spend $3 million a day buying computers from its Web site. Even more important to the Austin, Texas-based company is the fact that direct sales allow Dell to avoid payments to retailers, giving it a 6 percent advantage over its competitors. Although many well-known Internet-based firms are awash in red ink, Eddie Bauer has been generating profits from Web sales of its outdoor clothing since 1997. Of the 2,000 commerce-related sites recently surveyed, nearly half are profitable and an additional 30 percent expect to be within two years. Even though online sales currently account for a tiny share of total U.S. sales, they are impressive in dollar amounts. Internet consumer sales in 2000 reached $20 billion, and online commerce between companies was $175 billion.

Time Warner is not without Web experience. Back in 1994, the company invested heavily to develop Pathfinder, which offered online versions of *Time, Fortune,* and other magazines. The original strategy was to generate revenues from advertisers eager to purchase space and from consumers seeking access to the site. But the venture proved disappointing, as consumers flocked to the site but balked at paying for the privilege. Other cybercompanies (including CDnow and Amazon.com) share Time Warner's experience of spending heavily for years in an effort to draw traffic to their sites but have yet to turn a profit.

www.

www.studiostores.warnerbros.com

Nevertheless, Time Warner is promising to take online retailing to a new level, capitalizing on its vast mail-order experience to quickly turn its cyber superstore into a profitable business. Indeed, the company has an enviable mail-order reputation. Using television ads and toll-free numbers, Time Warner is adept at getting viewers to the phone to buy products "they didn't know they wanted or needed," says Time Inc. CEO Don Logan. The firm is one of the largest U.S. Postal Service customers, already selling more than $2 billion worth of books, videos, and CDs through its Book-of-the-Month Club, Time-Life operations, and Columbia House record club. Its huge mail-order infrastructure should be invaluable for its online superstore, especially since it can tap an existing database of 60 million customers and existing workforce of thousands of employees in huge warehouses located in Indiana, Pennsylvania, and Virginia.

But can all of this be translated to the Internet? Do the typical appeals used in mail-order marketing sustain the relationship that cybershoppers are looking for on the Web? Bauer executive Judy Neuman says the Net "makes you think very differently about your customers." Cybercommerce is about more than building business; it's about more than building a new environment of convenience and speed. It's about relationships. As CDnow's Rod Parker puts it, "You can't reach and grab people." On the Net, soft sell rules. "You want to invite customers in and be of service to them."

Time Warner is starting its retail site off by restricting product offerings to its own items, such as Madonna CDs, Batman videos, Time-Life history books, and Tweety Bird boxers. But the firm has supersize plans—eventually even to sell entertainment merchandise of rival companies. As part of its overall effort, it is promoting the Web sites of other Time Warner units such as Warner Bros. Studio Stores and Atlantic Records. And it already has another advantage: Pathfinder. Consisting of dozens of other sites, Pathfinder attracts 1 billion page-views a month, giving Time Warner considerable power to direct traffic to its cybersuperstore. Other Internet retailers must pay millions to be promoted on popular Web sites (one of the major reasons these cybersellers have such difficulty showing a profit).

The new Net economy offers us the products we want when we want them. More and more cybershoppers are becoming accustomed to online price comparisons, automatic grocery shopping, and 24-hour service. The shopping malls of the 1980s and 1990s redefined how we shopped and even how we spent our time. If Time Warner can offer the types of relationships and shopping experiences that cybershoppers are looking for, its Internet superstore will play a key role in reshaping our shopping habits and expectations yet again.[1]

CHAPTER OVERVIEW

Success in today's business world doesn't just happen. Many factors play a role in a firm's ability to survive, grow, and achieve profitability. Chief among these factors is the ability to envision how a business can satisfy marketplace needs. Effective planning helps managers to meet the challenges of a rapidly changing business environment and to develop strategies to guide a company's future. This management activity involves setting goals and then preparing and implementing plans to reach those goals.

Like Time-Warner, many businesses now include building and managing relationships as core elements in their overall visions and plans. Instead of looking for ways to merely increase transactions with customers, they now focus their management efforts on the broader aim of forging strong, ongoing bonds with customers, employees, and other businesses.

This chapter begins by examining how successful organizations use strategic planning to turn visions into reality. It then explores some of the tools that companies are using to strengthen their links with customers, vendors, employees, and other important stakeholder groups.

THE NEED FOR VISION

As Chapter 1 discussed, business success almost always begins with a **vision,** a perception of marketplace needs and the methods by which an organization can satisfy them. Vision serves as the building block of a firm's actions, helping to direct the company toward opportunity and competitive differentiation. Michael Dell's idea of selling custom-built computers directly to consumers, for example, helped to distinguish Dell from hundreds of other computer industry startups.

Although it is critical to entrepreneurial success, vision isn't just for startup companies. Vision helps established companies to unify the actions of far-flung divisions, keep customers satisfied, and sustain growth.

St. Louis–based Monsanto Co. had long operated as a textile and chemical manufacturer similar to its larger competitor DuPont until Robert Shapiro, the firm's chief executive officer, conceived a different vision for his company. He viewed Monsanto as a biotech firm dedicated to improving human health and protecting the environment by developing what he termed "planet friendly" products. This refocused vision has led the multinational firm to sell off some divisions, acquire successful products such as Equal sugar substitute, and change the direction of others. New products are being developed to fulfill the vision, such as genetically altered vegetable seeds that allow farmers to reduce their use of pesticides. This vision of the future is already paying off in expanded sales and profits and the prices investors are willing to pay for shares of Monsanto stock.[2]

Vision must be focused and yet flexible enough to adapt to changes in the business environment. Retail giant Sears strayed from its department store origins through a series of misguided acquisitions and diversification moves into financial services, real estate, and insurance. Soon, billion-dollar annual profits had turned into losses, and customers began staying away in droves. The Sears board of directors hired a new CEO, Arthur Martinez, to return the firm to its original vision as a reliable retailer offering strong consumer brands. Martinez sold off such subsidiaries as Allstate Insurance, the Discover credit card, and the Coldwell Banker real estate operation. Even though his firm's hardware and appliance brands had maintained strong customer loyalty, particularly among male shoppers, Sears needed to do more to win back female customers turned off by the firm's stodgy retail image. Martinez and his executive team revitalized the Sears image through improved merchandise selection, store redesign, and an advertising campaign inviting consumers to "come see the softer side of Sears." Figure 7.1 illustrates this new image aimed at enhancing growth in sales and profits at Sears.[3]

As these examples demonstrate, however, vision is only the first step along an organization's path to success. While a clear picture of a firm's purpose is vitally important, it takes careful planning and action to turn a business idea into reality. As Nolan Bushnell, founder of Atari, once said, "Everyone who's ever taken a shower has an idea. It's the person who gets out of the shower, dries off and does something about it who makes the difference."[4] The next section takes a closer look at the planning and implementation process.

THE IMPORTANCE OF PLANNING

Managers at the Todo Loco Mexican restaurant were convinced that their new food package was a winner. The product, dubbed "Wraps," was a series of gourmet food entrees, each one wrapped up in a flavored tortilla. Consumer response was so favorable that Todo Loco's owners raised enough money to open 16 stores in their Seattle home market and several more in other West Coast locations, including California.

Business Directory

vision a perception of marketplace needs and methods by which an organization can satisfy them.

| Figure 7.1 | **Fashionable Clothing as Well as Building Supplies: The New "Softer Side" of Sears** |

"I went in for insulation."

"And left with a warm fuzzy feeling."

Come see the softer side of SEARS

©1997 Sears, Roebuck and Co. Prices may vary in Alaska, Hawaii and Puerto Rico.

But Wraps did not prove to be a success, at least not for Todo Loco. Competitors found the idea easy to copy, and the new restaurant chain quickly encountered stiff competition from imitators. In addition to regional competitors, international fast-food franchises such as Taco Bell and Wendy's introduced their own versions of the product, and Todo Loco found itself losing money. Expensive marketing efforts didn't work, and layoffs and store closings soon followed. Finally, the company sold several of its remaining restaurants to competitors and closed the rest. Just 3 years after inventing the Wraps concept, Todo Loco was out of business.[5]

Todo Loco's experience underscores the importance of planning based on a realistic assessment of opportunities combined with a clear-sighted evaluation of company strengths and competitive threats.

Planning is the process of anticipating future events and conditions and determining courses of action for achieving organizational objectives. Effective planning can help a business to crystallize its vision, avoid costly mistakes, and seize opportunities. As Todo Loco management discovered, effective planning requires an evaluation of the business environment and a well-designed road map of the actions needed to lead a firm forward.

A typical outcome of the planning process is the creation of a formal written document called a **business plan.** The business plan states the firm's objectives and specifies the activities and resources required to achieve them. It also includes details about the markets in which the firm plans to compete, its financial resources, and the competitive situation facing each of its products. Both new and existing companies create business plans, but these documents are particularly important for entrepreneurial ventures.

Types of Planning

Planning can be categorized by scope or breadth. Some plans are very broad and typically long-range, focusing on key organizational objectives. Other types of plans specify how the organization will mobilize to achieve these objectives. Table 7.1 explains these basic types: strategic, tactical, operational, adaptive, and contingency planning.

Strategic Planning **Strategic planning**—the most far-reaching level of planning—is the process of determining the primary objectives of an organization and then adopting courses of action and allocating resources to achieve those objectives. Strategic planning evaluates conditions through a wide-angle lens to determine the long-range goals of the organization. British Airways' strategic plan, for example, calls for transforming the air carrier from a British company into a global operator serving increased international routes and distinguishing itself from competitors by offering superior service.

Table 7.1	Types of Plans	
Type	**Description**	**Example**
Strategic	Establish overall objectives; position the organization within its environment for time periods ranging from short-term to long-term	Chase Manhattan's plans to become the largest U.S.-based financial institution by merging with Chemical Bank
Tactical	Implement activities and resource allocations, typically for short-term periods	McDonald's efforts to slow Burger King's growth by introducing a clone of the Whopper, BK's flagship brand
Operational	Set quotas, standards, or schedules to implement tactical plans	Requirement to handle grievances within 48 hours of receipt
Adaptive	Ensure flexibility for responding to changes in the business environment by developing scenarios to take advantage of potential opportunities or respond to foreseeable problems	Nike's investigation of moving its athletic shoe production from Asia to Mexico following the passage of NAFTA
Contingency	Prepare for emergencies	Burger King's ban of beef purchases from Hudson Foods after discovery of *E. coli* contamination at a Nebraska packing plant

Tactical Planning **Tactical planning** involves implementing the activities specified by strategic plans. Tactical plans guide the current and near-term activities required to implement overall strategies. Although strategic and tactical plans apply to different time frames, both contribute to the achievement of organizational objectives. Four key activities are outlined in British Airways' tactical plan:

▼ Develop an international marketing plan

▼ Help employees understand the firm's global vision

▼ Learn from the experiences of other airlines to improve service

▼ Form partnerships with other airlines to expand the route network

Operational Planning **Operational planning** creates the detailed standards that guide implementation of tactical plans. This activity involves choosing specific work targets and assigning employees and teams to carry out plans. Unlike strategic planning, which focuses on the organization as a whole, operational planning often centers on developing and implementing tactics in specific functional areas such as production, human resources, or marketing. Operational plans may state quotas, standards, or schedules. At British Airways, the operational planning process led the firm to develop a new identity program. All planes received new paint jobs displaying logos designed by artists around the world. Onboard its aircraft, British Airlines set new standards for service that included sensitivity to the cultural differences of passengers from diverse societies around the world.

Adaptive Planning All planning, whether at the strategic, tactical, or operational level, needs to develop courses of action fluid and forward-looking enough to adapt to changes in the business environment. To succeed in the volatile business world, companies must emphasize focus and flexibility in their plans. They must practice **adaptive planning.**

In emphasizing focus for planning, managers identify and then build on the company's strongest capabilities. British Airways, for example, already had established a superior reputation for ensuring passenger comfort, and that strength became a key point in differentiating the airline as a global carrier.

To emphasize flexibility in planning, managers must develop scenarios of potential future activities to prepare the firm to take full advantage of opportunities as they occur. British Airways bought large shares in several European airlines specializing in low-cost travel. These investments were intended to allow the airline to take advantage of the growth in consumer demand for low-priced flights.[6]

Contingency Planning As the first news reports confirmed the tragic death of Princess Diana, Weight Watchers President Kent Kreh realized that his company faced a major crisis. Unless he and his management team acted quickly, the problem could permanently damage his company. A few months earlier, Weight Watchers had hired Diana's former sister-in-law, the Duchess of York, as a celebrity endorser. Ads and brochures featuring her likeness had been prepared the same week the Princess of Wales died in a car accident after being chased by photographers. The ad campaign's headline proclaimed that losing weight is "harder than outrunning the paparazzi."

> **They said it**
>
> "No plan can prevent a stupid person from doing the wrong thing in the wrong place at the wrong time—but a good plan should keep a concentration from forming."
>
> Charles E. Wilson (1890–1961)
> U.S. Secretary of Defense during
> the Eisenhower Administration

All ads were pulled and Weight Watchers asked its advertising agency to begin work immediately on a new campaign.[7]

Planning cannot always foresee every possibility. Threats such as terrorism, natural disasters, and rapid economic downturns can throw even the best-laid plans into chaos. To handle the possibility of business disruption from negative events like these, many firms are turning to a contemporary innovation in planning, **contingency planning,** which allows a firm to resume operations as quickly and as smoothly as possible after a crisis while openly communicating with the public about what happened. This planning activity involves two components: business continuation and public communication. Many firms have developed management strategies to speed recovery from accidents such as airline crashes, factory fires, chemical leaks, product tampering, and product

Sarah, The Duchess of York

Contingency planning at Weight Watchers began immediately after the tragic and unexpected death of Princess Diana, former sister-in-law of celebrity endorser the Duchess of York. Out of respect for the Princess of Wales and her family, the company withdrew this ad and initiated a new ad campaign.

critical gesture, since early honesty means so much in the court of public opinion. A crisis management plan must ensure that the firm faces the public and makes amends. These steps may range from simple product replacements to payments of medical or monetary claims. Finally, the underlying cause of the problem must be determined and systems established to make certain that it does not recur. Hiring a highly regarded, independent research group to determine what caused the problem is recommended as a method of ensuring objectivity.

Planning at Different Organizational Levels

Although managers spend some time on planning virtually every day, the total time spent and the type of planning done differ at different levels of management. As Table 7.2 points out, members of top management, including a firm's board of directors and chief executive officer, spend a great deal of time on long-range planning, whereas middle-level managers and supervisors focus on short-term, tactical planning. Employees at all levels can benefit themselves and their company by making plans to meet their own goals.

failure. Contingency planning is more important now than ever; over half of the worst industrial accidents in this century have taken place since 1977.

A contingency plan usually designates a chain of command for crisis management, assigning specific functions for particular managers and employees in an emergency. Contingency planning also involves training workers to respond to emergency events, improving communications systems, and recovering the use of technology such as computer records and telecommunications systems. Additionally, contingency plans look at issues of safety and accident prevention to minimize the risk of crises in the first place.

Another important aspect of contingency planning is setting up a system for communicating with the media and public during and after a crisis. When a crisis occurs, the firm involved must quickly tell the truth. Accepting responsibility, even at the cost of short-term profitability, is a

Planning and the Other Managerial Functions

Each step in planning incorporates more specific information than the last. From the global mission statement to general objectives to specific plans, each phase must fit into a comprehensive planning framework. The framework also must include narrow, functional plans aimed at individual employees and work areas and relevant to individ-

Table 7.2	Planning at Different Management Levels	
Primary Type of Planning	**Managerial Level**	**Examples**
Strategic	Top management	Organizational objectives, fundamental strategies, long-term plans
Tactical	Middle management	Quarterly and semiannual plans, departmental policies and procedures
Operational	Supervisory management	Daily and weekly plans, rules and procedures for each department
Adaptive	All levels	Ongoing, flexible plans; quick response to changes in the environment
Contingency	Primarily top management, but all levels contribute	Ongoing plans for actions and communications in an emergency

ual tasks. These plans fit within the firm's overall planning framework, allowing it to reach objectives and achieve its mission. Planning is a key managerial function and planning activities extend into each of the other functions—organizing, directing, and controlling.

Organizing Once plans have been developed, the next step in the management process typically is *organizing*—the means by which managers blend human and material resources through a formal structure of tasks and authority. This activity involves classifying and dividing work into manageable units by determining specific tasks necessary to accomplish organizational objectives, grouping tasks into a logical pattern or structure, and assigning these elements to specific positions and people.

Included in the organizing function are the important steps of staffing the organization with competent employees capable of performing the necessary tasks and assigning authority and responsibility to these individuals. The organizing process is discussed in detail in the next chapter.

Directing Once plans have been formulated and an organization has been created and staffed, the management task focuses on *directing*, or guiding and motivating employees to accomplish organizational objectives. Directing includes explaining procedures, issuing orders, and seeing that mistakes are corrected.

The directing function is an especially important responsibility of supervisory managers. To fulfill their responsibilities to get things done through people, supervisors must be effective leaders. However, middle and top managers also must be good leaders and motivators, and they must create an environment that fosters such leadership. These topics are discussed in detail in Chapters 8, 9, and 10.

Controlling *Controlling* is the function of evaluating an organization's performance to determine whether it is accomplishing its objectives. The basic purpose of controlling is to assess the success of the planning function. The four basic steps in controlling are to establish performance standards, monitor actual performance, compare actual performance with established standards, and, if perfor-

mance does not meet standards, determine why and take corrective action. Controlling is discussed in detail in the chapters of Part 3 and Part 5.

THE STRATEGIC PLANNING PROCESS

Strategic planning often makes the difference between an organization's success and failure. Strategic planning has formed the basis of many fundamental management decisions:

▼ PepsiCo's decision to combine its rapidly growing Pepsi-Cola soft drink and Frito-Lay snack foods divisions and reorganize its Taco Bell, KFC Corp., and Pizza Hut operations within a separate restaurant division

▼ Internet provider America Online's decision to acquire rival CompuServe

▼ Motorola's decision to abandon the consumer-goods market and concentrate on industrial products

Successful strategic planners typically follow the six steps shown in Figure 7.2.

To demonstrate how the strategic planning process works, the discussion in this section follows one business through an entire planning cycle. The company is JumboSports, the second largest sporting goods retailer (behind The Sports Authority) in the United States. At the start of the strategic planning process, however, JumboSports had suffered through several years of disappointing performance and management was searching for ways to return to profitability.

Defining the Organization's Mission

Earlier discussion in this chapter pointed out the importance of an underlying vision for an organization. The first step in strategic planning is to translate the firm's vision into a

| Figure 7.2 | **Steps in the Strategic Planning Process** |

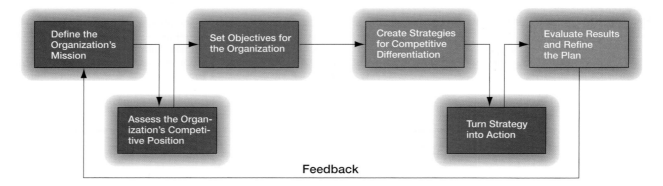

mission statement. A **mission statement** is a written explanation of an organization's business intentions and aims. It is an enduring statement of company purpose, highlighting the scope of operations, the market it seeks to serve, and how it will attempt to set itself apart from competitors. A mission statement guides the actions of people inside the firm and informs customers and other stakeholders of the company's underlying reason for existence. After creating the mission statement, a business should share it with employees, suppliers, partners, shareholders, and customers.

JumboSports's executive team developed a mission statement just 21 words long: "To be the number one sporting goods superstore retailer in each market it serves by focusing on service, selection, and value."

Other companies develop longer mission statements. Coffee retailer Starbucks sums up its mission this way:

> To establish Starbucks as the premier purveyor of the finest coffee in the world while maintaining our uncompromising principles as we grow. Starbucks accomplishes this mission with the help of five guiding principles:

> 1. Provide a great work environment and treat each other with respect and dignity.

> 2. Apply the highest standards of excellence to the purchasing, roasting, and fresh delivery of our coffee.

> 3. Develop enthusiastically satisfied customers all of the time.

> 4. Contribute positively to our communities and our environment.

> 5. Recognize that profitability is essential to our future success.

The Beckman Instruments mission statement shown in Figure 7.3 illustrates how the manufacturer of scientific laboratory equipment has transformed its corporate vision into a more precise definition of its mission. Beckman's mission statement identifies the broad range of customers it hopes to serve and stresses its aims for meeting the needs of employees and investors.

Although mission statements may seem simple, their development can be one of the most complex and difficult aspects of strategic planning. Completing these statements requires detailed consideration of company values and vision. Effective mission statements state specific, achievable, inspiring principles. They avoid empty promises, ego-stroking, and unrealistic statements.

Assessing Competitive Position

Once a mission statement has been created, the next step in the planning process is to assess the firm's current position in the marketplace. This phase also involves an examination of the factors that may help or hinder the organization in the future. Two frequently used tools in this phase of strategic planning are SWOT analysis and forecasts of future sales performance.

SWOT Analysis A **SWOT analysis** is an organized method of assessing a company's internal *s*trengths and *w*eaknesses and its external *o*pportunities and *t*hreats. The basic premise of this review assumes that a critical internal

Starting a Business? Have a Plan!

Poor planning has been the downfall of many a would-be entrepreneur. The truth is, every business no matter how new or how small needs a business plan.

Business plans are essential tools for raising money. Most banks and venture capitalists won't lend money to a new business until they become convinced that their investments will likely generate favorable returns.

A good business plan also saves time, stress, and wasted action by spelling out the exact actions to turn a business dream into reality. It helps to minimize mistakes and set priorities for using resources. Finally, the process of business planning helps entrepreneurs to gain realistic insights into the challenges that lie ahead.

What should an entrepreneur's business plan contain? Here's a short list of questions it should answer.

1. **How feasible is your business?**

   Take a realistic look at the challenges and opportunities that lie ahead and compare them to your firm's strengths and weaknesses.

   What business are you in? _____

   What good or service will you offer buyers? _____

   Who are your potential customers? _____

   What is the size of your market? _____

   Who are your competitors? _____

   What are their strengths and weaknesses? _____

   What other factors will affect your potential for success? _____

2. **What's your competitive advantage?**

   Specify your vision for your company.

   What is your firm's mission? _____

   How will you position your good or service to differentiate it from competitors? _____

   What benefits will your good or service provide to customers? _____

   What tactics will you use for marketing, human resources, operations, technology? _____

   _____

3. **What's your financial potential?**

   Determine your income and profit potential based on your sales forecasts.

   Want more information? For a downloadable template of a business plan, you can visit the Money Hunter Web site. The Small Business Administration (SBA) also offers a detailed tutorial on writing a business plan and shareware files outlining business plan elements.

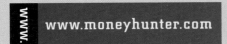
www.moneyhunter.com

www.sbaonline.sba.gov

and external study of reality will lead managers to select the appropriate strategy for accomplishing their organization's objectives. SWOT analysis encourages a practical approach to planning based on a realistic view of a firm's situation and scenarios of likely future events and conditions. The framework for a SWOT analysis is shown in Figure 7.4.

To evaluate the firm's strengths and weaknesses, the planning team may examine each functional area such as human resources, finance, marketing, and information technology. Entrepreneurs may focus analysis on the individual skills and experience they bring to a new business.

Large firms may also examine strengths and weaknesses of individual divisions and geographic operations. Usually, planners attempt to look at strengths and weaknesses in relation to those of other firms in the industry.

JumboSports management identified several strengths and weaknesses during its strategic planning process. Among its major strengths was a strong network of 85 U.S. outlets, each offering a broad selection of competitively priced sports apparel and equipment. Sales were second only to those of the market leader, The Sports Authority. However, these strengths were countered by significant

| **Figure 7.3** | **Vision, Values, and Mission of Beckman Instruments** |

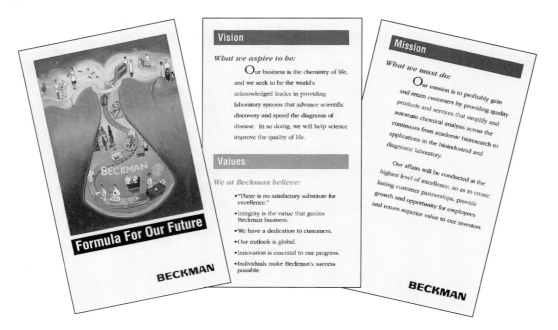

mountable difficulties. A SWOT analysis is a useful tool in the strategic planning process, because it forces management to look at factors both inside and outside the organization. SWOT analysis examines not only the current picture but also necessary current actions to prepare for likely future developments.

Forecasting A second tool used to assess the firm's competitive position and a complement to SWOT analysis is **forecasting,** the process of estimating or predicting a company's future sales or income. Forecasts can focus on the short term (under 1 year), intermediate term (1 to 5 years) or long term (over 5 years).

Qualitative forecasting methods are subjective techniques. The company might ask salespeople, managers, executives, or outside consultants to suggest likely levels of short-term sales. Some businesses also survey their customers about purchasing plans and develop forecasts based on the data collected. Because they rely on subjective assessments, qualitative forecasts are limited in their usefulness, and most firms use them only for very short time periods.

areas of weakness. Since stores carried different names—Sports Unlimited and JumboSports—in different markets, the chain had developed no national image. The company had no automated inventory control system, which meant that store managers had problems receiving merchandise quickly. Employee training tended to be lackluster and hampered store managers' efforts to provide attentive customer service. These weaknesses combined to produce an overall financial weakness, as the firm posted several years of back-to-back financial losses.[8]

SWOT analysis continues with an attempt to define the major opportunities and threats the firm is likely to face within the time frame of the plan. Environmental factors such as market growth, regulatory changes, or increased competition are all considered. For example, JumboSports saw moderate growth in the sales of sporting goods as an opportunity to improve its revenues. However, consolidation and increased competition in the sporting goods industry posed a very real threat.[9]

If a firm's strengths and opportunities mesh successfully, it gains competitive leverage in the marketplace. On the other hand, if internal weaknesses prevent a firm from overcoming external threats, it may find itself facing insur-

Product designers at Wrangler began forecasting by surveying women about what they wanted—and didn't want—in their jeans. A large percentage of respondents suggested that they would be more likely to buy jeans if the back pockets were eliminated. The result was Wrangler's new line of bareback jeans shown in Figure 7.5.

Quantitative forecasting uses historical data and mathematical models to predict how the firm will perform. For example, a business may track sales performance over a period of time, look for ongoing trends, and forecast future growth or declines based on the identified trends. This method is called *trend analysis.*

Forecasts are important because they guide the planning process and support decision making. They can help managers to pinpoint potential opportunities and threats

Business Directory

objectives specific performance targets that an organization hopes to accomplish.

that may interfere with the company's plans. On the other hand, they can become outdated and may require revisions due to environmental changes.

Setting Objectives for the Organization

After defining the company's mission and examining factors that may affect its ability to fulfill that mission, the next step in planning is to develop objectives for the organization. **Objectives** set guideposts by which managers define the organi-

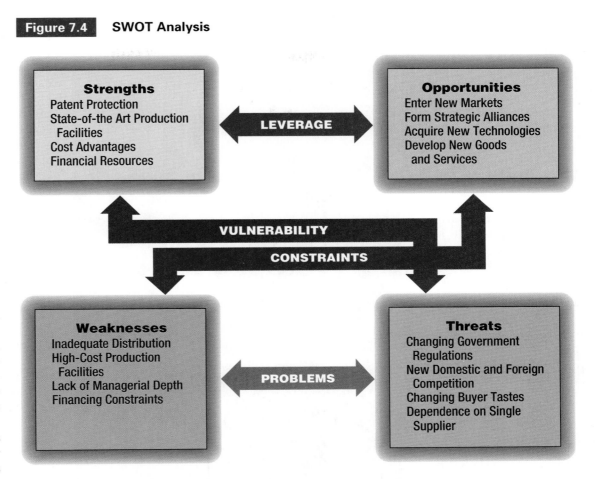

Figure 7.4 **SWOT Analysis**

Strengths
Patent Protection
State-of-the Art Production Facilities
Cost Advantages
Financial Resources

Opportunities
Enter New Markets
Form Strategic Alliances
Acquire New Technologies
Develop New Goods and Services

LEVERAGE

VULNERABILITY

CONSTRAINTS

Weaknesses
Inadequate Distribution
High-Cost Production Facilities
Lack of Managerial Depth
Financing Constraints

PROBLEMS

Threats
Changing Government Regulations
New Domestic and Foreign Competition
Changing Buyer Tastes
Dependence on Single Supplier

zation's desired performance in such areas as profitability, customer service, and employee satisfaction. While the mission statement delineates the company's goals in general terms, objectives are more concrete statements. More and more businesses are setting explicit objectives for performance standards other than profitability. As public concern about environmental issues mounts, many firms find that operating in an environmentally responsible manner pays off in good relations with customers. Others channel some of their profits into socially responsible causes, such as funding educational programs and scholarships. Today's businesses offer many additional examples:

▼ In addition to profitability and growth objectives, sports apparel manufacturer Russell Corp. has elaborated a variety of social objectives, including operating a "Stay in School" program aimed at high school students.

▼ An important Procter & Gamble objective is the development of disposable diapers that break down in industrial solid-waste programs.

▼ Rubbermaid has achieved growth objectives by acquiring Little Tikes, a toy company;

Con-Tact, a well-known maker of adhesive coverings; Gott Corp., with its line of insulated containers; Seco Industries, a floor-care products company; and MicroComputer Accessories, a supplier of accessories for personal computers.

JumboSports CEO Stephen Bebis and his management team knew that their firm would fulfill its mission only if they set some tough objectives. The primary objective was to return the company to profitability within 18 months by increasing sales and reducing expenses. Another objective was to build consumer awareness of the company's stores. The team also set standards for service, employee training, and merchandise control.[10]

Creating Strategies for Competitive Differentiation

Developing a mission statement and setting objectives point a business toward a specific destination. To get there, however, the firm needs to map the strategies it will follow to compete with other companies pursuing similar missions and objectives. The underlying goal of strategy development is **competitive differentiation,** the unique combination of a company's abilities and approaches that place it ahead of competitors. Common sources of competitive differentiation include human resources, product innovation, technology, and financial management. Figure 7.6 shows how some firms have leveraged these sources of differentiation to their advantage. The "Solving an Ethical Controversy" box in this chapter discusses some of the challenges faced in gaining a competitive edge. A later section of the chapter examines how firms achieve competitive differentiation through relationship management strategies.

Strategists at Jumbo-Sports made some difficult choices in deciding how to differentiate their firm. First, the executive team realized the need to scrap the previous strategy of increasing sales by adding stores, at least temporarily, because of its high cost. Second, the company could no longer avoid strategic applications of technology. Improvements in merchandising and inventory costs required investments in updated computer systems. Most importantly, however, management decided that to reach previously set objectives for increased sales and customer awareness, they would have to build a unified brand image and reputation for the entire company.[11]

| Figure 7.5 | Using Customer Surveys to Forecast New-Product Sales |

must begin to put strategy into action by identifying the specific methods and deploying the resources needed to implement the intended plans.

To implement its strategy of building a unified, companywide image, management replaced the jumble of names that had been used on the firm's 85 retail outlets with the JumboSports name. Accompanying the name change, interior redesigns added color changes for signage and employee attire. A series of television, radio, and print ads also helped to build awareness of the new JumboSports image. In addition, a new JumboSports Web page was launched.

Next on the strategic agenda was a project to replace the company's poor inventory-management system. A new computerized system enabled Jumbo Sports buyers to track inventory at each store and minimize out-of-stock situations by quickly resupplying needed products. It also cut the costs involved in ordering and shipping merchandise.

To improve customer service, JumboSports launched an employee training program dubbed *JumboSports College.* Special programs conducted at headquarters and in individual stores communicated product information to managers and employees and focused on customer-service skills. JumboSports addressed the profitability problem by designing a management compensation program that rewarded executives and store managers who met predetermined objectives for improving store profitability.[12]

Implementation: Turning Strategy into Action

Once the first four phases of the strategic planning process are complete, managers face even bigger challenges. They

WWW
www.jumbosports.com

Business Directory

competitive differentiation the unique combination of a company's abilities and approaches that will place it ahead of competitors.

Monitoring and Adapting Strategic Plans

The final stage in the strategic planning process, closely

linked to implementation, consists of monitoring and adapting plans when actual performance fails to match expectations. Monitoring involves establishing methods of securing feedback about actual performance. Common methods include comparisons of actual sales and market share data to forecasts, information received from supplier and customer surveys, complaints received on the firm's customer hot line, and reports prepared by staff members within production, finance, marketing, and other company departments.

| Figure 7.6 | **Sources of Competitive Advantage** |

Source	Example
Human Resources	Central Parking Corp. only hires college graduates to manage the company's public parking lots. The managers help institute formal management systems, sell new customers, and improve customer satisfaction.
Product Innovation	Cosmetic manufacturer Hard Candy developed a line of nail polishes in unusual shades. The company relies on a continual stream of new, innovative product shades to compete with large manufacturers like Revlon.
Technology	Federal Express has used technology to set itself apart from competitive delivery firms. Each shipment is bar-coded so FedEx customers can receive up-to-the minute status reports over the phone or through the Internet. Investments in technology also lead to higher productivity in FedEx's Louisville, Kentucky, distribution center.
Financial Management	Ross Stores Inc. purchases and sells end-of-season merchandise. Company buyers actively negotiate with manufacturers to get the lowest cost of goods. Tight controls on operating expenses also keep prices low. The savings translate into low prices for customers, a key advantage in the highly competitive retail market.

Ongoing use of such tools as SWOT analysis and forecasting can help management to adapt objectives and functional plans as changes occur. An increase in the price of a key product component, for instance, could dramatically affect the firm's ability to maintain planned prices and still earn acceptable profits. An unexpected strike by UPS may disrupt shipments of products to retail and industrial customers. In each instance, the original plan may require modification to continue to guide the firm toward achievement of its objectives.

The JumboSports turnaround plan produced mixed initial results. Some major strides were made in building a companywide brand image, correcting operating problems, and improving customer service. However, profits remained elusive as the company continued to pile up months of operating losses. CEO Bebis and his executive team continued to monitor feedback received from different sources, but they remained convinced that their strategic plan would ultimately return the firm to profitability. The continuing increase in the number of rivals in an already competitive sporting goods industry worried management, but they were confident that fine-tuning their planning and implementation efforts would result in profitable operations by 2000.[13]

The JumboSports World Wide Web home page reflects its new corporate image that was created when the company changed the names of all of its 85 stores to JumboSports.

SOLVING AN ETHICAL CONTROVERSY

Corporate Espionage or Pure Competition?

Nearly every business keeps tabs in some way on competitors' products, prices, and advertising. Strategic planning would be almost impossible without this kind of information. At what point, however, does gathering competitive intelligence cross an ethical line?

Kodak's research and development team was working on a design for disposable cameras when they uncovered some important competitive information. They learned that arch-rival Fuji was planning to launch its own version of a disposable camera in the near future. Kodak rushed development in order to launch its camera just one day before Fuji. The move gave Kodak the lion's share of media coverage and left Fuji as an also-ran in the minds of consumers and retailers.

Competitive information took on a different slant for General Motors when a high-ranking executive resigned and took a position in Volkswagen's headquarters in Germany. According to a lawsuit filed by General Motors against VW, the executive shared GM's product plans and strategies with his new employer, resulting in unfair competitive advantage for VW. The German firm ended up paying $100 million in damages and firing the former GM ex-

ecutive. The GM case is only the tip of the iceberg in the automotive industry. Over 25 industrial espionage lawsuits are currently active in Michigan courts alone. Other recent suits involving well-known companies include *Campbell* v. *Heinz*, *Informix* v. *Oracle*, *Dow* v. *GE*, and *Cadence* v. *Avant*.

 Is gathering competitive intelligence an ethical practice?

PRO

1. Most intelligence-gathering activities don't break the law. When a company prints a brochure, sets up a Web page, or runs a commercial on TV, it willingly shares information with the world. If businesses analyze publicly available information for insights about a competitor's plans and strategies, they are within their rights.

2. Gathering competitive intelligence is just good business sense. Managers can't make decisions about their own strategies in a vacuum. They need information about what other companies in the industry are planning and what methods they're using.

CON

1. Many of the tactics used to collect competitive information lie in ethical and legal gray areas. For ex-

ample, representatives of some companies have rummaged through the trash bins of rivals, cracked computer codes, and even placed electronic bugging devices in order to collect competitive intelligence.

2. Some studies estimate that industrial espionage costs U.S. firms as much as $2 billion a month in lost sales and wasted research and development.

3. Passage of the Economic Espionage Act of 1996 makes stealing trade secrets a federal crime with penalties of up to 15 years in prison and up to $500,000 in fines for each person convicted. Although the law has not yet been tested in the courts, some believe that the collection and use of certain types of competitive intelligence fall within the bill's jurisdiction.

Sources: Daniel Eisenberg, "Eyeing the Competition," *Time*, March 22, 1999, accessed at www.pathfinder.com; "CI Success Stories," downloaded from Fuld & Company Web site, www.fuld.com, August 16, 1997; Stan Crock and Jonathan Moore, "Corporate Spies Feel a Sting," *Business Week*, July 14, 1997, p. 76; and Stephen H. Miller, "Economic Espionage: Now It's a Federal Case," *Competitive Intelligence Review*, Spring 1997.

RELATIONSHIP MANAGEMENT STRATEGIES

As explained in the earlier discussion, a big part of the strategic planning process revolves around deciding how to best use the organization's capabilities in light of market opportunities and threats. The past decade has brought rapid change to most industries, as customers have become better-informed and more demanding purchasers through closely comparing competing goods and services. They expect, even demand, new benefits from the companies that supply them, making it harder for firms to gain competitive advantage based on product features alone.

Meanwhile, most businesses have traditionally focused on **transaction management,** characterized by buyer and seller exchanges with limited communications and little or no ongoing relationship between the parties. In transaction management, the goal is simple: Negotiate hard with suppliers to secure the least expensive raw materials and components, then build products and find customers to buy them at prices high enough to cover costs and still earn a profit.

In today's hyper-competitive era, however, businesses need to find new ways of relating to customers if they hope to maintain long-term growth. Instead of keeping customers at arm's length, businesses are developing strate-

BUSINESS HALL OF FAME

Just For Feet Makes Fun with "Shoppertainment"

In an industry plagued by too many retail stores and lagging sales of high-priced licensed merchandise, Just For Feet is a big exception. The Birmingham, Alabama–based firm operates superstores that specialize in brand-name athletic and outdoor footwear and apparel. But they are far more than just stores. Each Just For Feet outlet is a giant indoor playground for adults and kids, creating a new and exciting shopping experience. As company founder and CEO Harold Ruttenberg puts it, "We take our cue from Walt Disney, a master at making people smile."

Today's sports shoppers are bored—by the hassle of shopping and by the sameness of merchandise. They can turn to giant box stores like Sports Authority and Academy Sports, place orders from mail-order catalogs, or buy on the Internet. How can an independent retailer compete? Just For Feet stands out by offering something called *shoppertainment*, mixing merchandising techniques with entertainment. By making shopping more fun, more educational, and more interactive, Ruttenberg's firm is establishing a new kind of customer relationship.

The typical Just For Feet store features an indoor basketball court, a wall of video screens, laser light shows, a hot dog stand, and athletic events. "During Wimbledon, we invited the public to watch the matches on the big screen, and we served them doughnuts and coffee," says Ruttenberg. "That was ten years ago. Now we have our own restaurants." The smile campaign is working wonders. Despite increasing competition in the athletic shoe industry, Just For Feet is posting record sales. Its 84 U.S. superstores recently posted annual sales of $600 million—a healthy jump from its 1993 sales of $23 million.

The possibilities for shoppertainment are limited only by the entrepreneur's imagination. Whether it's hands-on product testing, expert advice, in-store food, or special events like slide shows, book signings, lectures, and free classes, most customers like to participate. Experts caution that whatever retailers choose to do, they make sure the entertainment is compatible with their products and their store image. And they must always remember that no entertainment events can make up for poor-quality or inappropriate merchandise, uncompetitive prices, or poor customer service. Top-quality products offered at a fair price with stellar service are essential for success.

Just For Feet succeeds by meeting customers with smiling faces and offering them a sensory roller coaster ride. But the company also offers a huge selection of top merchandise. It claims the world's largest shoe wall, with 3,000 to 4,000 styles of athletic and outdoor shoes. Plus, Just For Feet offers superior customer service. For example, the company invests time and money training its staff. The people at Just For Feet know that entertainment will get customers to come in. They also know that, to succeed, Just For Feet must offer great value.

QUESTIONS FOR CRITICAL THINKING

1. Suppose you went into business to sell used textbooks. Your store is in a small but charming building close to campus. What shoppertainment ideas could build an exciting relationship with customers?

2. What potential drawbacks exist in the use of shoppertainment to attract customers? Can you envision problems with a hobby shop encouraging customers to test their skills with display models? Explain.

Sources: "Just For Feet, Inc., Announces Record Sales and Comp Stores Sales for the Fourth Quarter," Just For Feet press release, February 2, 1999, accessed at www.feet.com; and Carla Goodman, "That's Entertainment," *Entrepreneur*, December 1998, pp. 124–131.

gies and tactics that draw them into a tighter connection with their customers. Such webs may expand to include stronger bonds with suppliers, employees, and even, in some cases, competitors. Many firms, therefore, are turning their attention away from managing transactions to the broader issues of **relationship management**. Relationship management can be defined as a firm's activities dedicated to building and maintaining ongoing, mutu-ally beneficial ties with customers, suppliers, employees, and other partners. Unlike transaction management, relationship management targets a more complex goal than just producing goods and services and finding buyers for

Business Directory

relationship management a firm's activities that build and maintain ongoing, mutually beneficial ties with customers, suppliers, employees, and other partners.

them. As Figure 7.7 shows, relationship management seeks to find suppliers and buyers, build relationships with them, and continually fill their needs by creating customer-tailored goods and services.

The emphasis on managing relationships instead of completing transactions often leads to some unique partnerships. The following list reviews a few of the ways businesses are using relationships to reach corporate goals.

▼ *Partnering with customers* Homeowners thinking about putting tile down in their bathrooms or hanging new wallpaper in the living room can get more than supplies for their jobs at Home Depot. The chain's 500-plus stores run weekend how-to seminars that teach customers the skills they need to do home repair and remodeling jobs themselves. Store sales associates prowl the aisles offering advice and tips to do-it-yourself shoppers. Many stores even offer to send interior design consultants out to customers' homes. Working with customers helps Home Depot to ring up $24 billion in sales each year.[14]

▼ *Partnering with suppliers* Ruth Owades says she wouldn't be in business without her suppliers. Owades's firm Calyx & Corolla is a catalog company that sells fresh flowers to customers across the country. To make sure that the highly

perishable products reach customers in peak condition, she formed partnerships with wholesale growers and Federal Express. These partners helped her to devise packaging and shipping methods for efficient delivery of her flowers. When a customer places an order, Calyx & Corolla's growers are alerted and send the order out via Federal Express for next-day arrival.[15]

▼ *Partnering with other businesses* Cardinal Laboratories' new Crazy Dog pet shampoos and sprays were instant hits with customers. In fact, customers clamored for additional products. Since Cardinal's factory wasn't geared to produce them, management invited five small manufacturers to partner with the firm. Each business developed and manufactured new products—from dog toys to pet food—which were marketed jointly under the Crazy Dog label. All six of the partners then split the profits.[16]

▼ *Partnering globally* When General Electric decides to sell appliances in a new country, one of its first moves is to team up with a local company that understands the market. In Japan, its partnership with a large retailer helped to cut the cost of distribution, allowing GE to sell its products at far lower prices than it could have achieved alone. In the first month, GE sold 20,000 appliances.[17]

By presenting weekend "how-to" seminars that teach customers to do home repairs and remodeling jobs themselves, Home Depot uses relationships to increase customer satisfaction.

Relationship Strategy Benefits

Relationship strategies help all parties involved. In addition to mutual protection against competitors, businesses that forge solid links with suppliers and customers are often rewarded with lower costs and higher profits than they would generate on their own. Long-term agreements with a few high-quality suppliers frequently reduce a firm's production costs. Unlike one-time sales, these ongoing relationships encourage suppliers to offer preferential treatment to their customers, quickly adjusting shipments to accommodate changes in orders and correcting any quality problems that might arise.

Any manager will also agree that a firm must spend much more to continually find new customers than it would spend to keep loyal customers. In fact, attracting a new customer can cost as much as five times more than keeping an existing one. Not only do marketing costs go down, but long-term customers usually buy more, require less service, refer other customers, and provide valuable feedback.

Because of these factors, one of the most important measures in relationship management is the **lifetime value of a customer**: the revenues and intangible benefits (referrals, customer feedback, etc.) that a customer brings to the seller over the average lifetime of the relationship, less the amount the company must spend to acquire, market to, and service that customer. Taco Bell, for example, estimates that the lifetime value to the com-

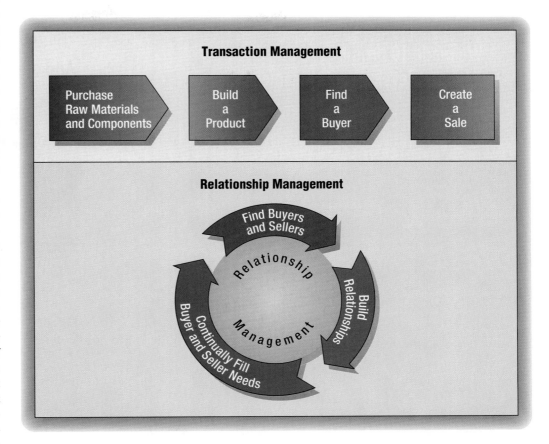

Figure 7.7 **Transaction Management versus Relationship Management**

pany of a loyal customer is $11,000. To retain as many of these valuable relationships as possible, Taco Bell managers take steps to listen to their customers. In a typical year, the fast-food restaurant chain surveys 800,000 of them.[18]

Customers also benefit from strong relationships with their suppliers. Purchasers who repeatedly buy from one business may find that they save time and gain service quality as the business learns their specific needs. Some relationship-oriented companies also customize goods and services based on customer preferences. Because many businesses now choose to reward loyal customers with discounts or bonuses, some customers may even find that they save money by developing long-term relationships.

Businesses like General Electric that choose to form alliances with other firms also reap rewards. The alliance partners combine their capabilities and resources to accomplish goals that they

could not reach on their own. Additionally, alliances with other firms may help businesses to develop the skills and experience they need to successfully enter new markets or improve service to current customers.

The discussion that follows concentrates on the specific strategies, tools, and tactics through which businesses can develop and manage partnerships for competitive advantage. First, the section examines the techniques organizations use to build long-lasting relationships with their customers. Then it discusses how choosing the right partners for business alliances can help firms to reach their objectives.

Business Directory

lifetime value of a customer the revenues and intangible benefits that a customer brings to a seller over the average lifetime of the relationship, less the amount the company must spend to acquire, market to, and service the customer.

| Figure 7.8 | The Contax Camera: Making—and Keeping—Promises |

Kyocera elaborated ten promises to combine the best elements of German and Japanese technology to produce a camera with unparalleled optical characteristics for discerning photographers. Refined viewfinder, focus, and film handling mechanisms ensure exemplary performance for a user who is unwilling to compromise for the sake of reducing cost.

FOUNDATIONS OF BUYER-SELLER RELATIONSHIPS

At the heart of any successful relationship management strategy is the buyer-seller relationship. In order to build that relationship, a business must nurture its links with customers. This section focuses on the core elements of the buyer-seller relationship: the three promises that form the basis of buyer-seller relationships and the four dimensions involved in building that relationship.

Promises in Relationship Management

Promises are the building blocks of successful buyer-seller relationships, whether the buyers are individuals or other companies. Businesses make promises to parties outside their organizations, within their organizations, and in their interactions with customers. This network of promises defines the buyer-seller relationship. Therefore, managing those promises is a central element of efforts to nurture loyalty and trust.

Making Promises Businesses make a variety of promises to their customers, including lower prices, better quality, and more exceptional service than competitors offer. A company must carefully ensure that the promises it communicates to customers are both realistic and consistent with one another.

To satisfy professional photographers, Japanese camera manufacturer Kyocera made ten promises outlined in Figure 7.8. These principles underlie the design of the firm's Contax model, a blend of German artisan culture and Japanese high-tech performance. Camera purists seeking unparalleled quality rank this camera as the Stradivarius of photography tools.

Enabling Promises A relationship management strategy will succeed only if a firm has set up the procedures, systems, and internal capabilities that enable it to fully meet its promises. This condition requires recruiting talented employees and providing them with the tools, training, and motivation they need to achieve effective performance. When businesses do not sell directly to customers, they must make sure that the intermediaries between their own organizations and customers do not hinder their relationships.

For example, although Toyota automobiles have built a favorable reputation for quality and reasonable prices, company research showed that customers were turned off by their experiences at Toyota dealerships. Toyota studied the customer service practices of leaders in other industries, including L. L. Bean and Citibank, to develop new standards for dealer-customer interactions. New customer-service training programs were also implemented at dealerships. The new initiatives were designed to keep customers coming back to Toyota for subsequent car purchases.[19]

Keeping Promises Every time a customer interacts with a business, the transaction reaches a moment of truth, when the seller must meet or surpass customer expectations. The moment of truth typically occurs when the business provides a good or service and the customer receives it. A company that fails to keep its promises at this point in the exchange process destroys any hope of forging a continuing buyer-seller relationship.

Four Dimensions of Buyer-Seller Relationships

Although making, enabling, and keeping promises are crucial elements in creating a relationship with a buyer, other factors also influence the attachment between buyer and seller. The firm needs to develop emotional links with its customers, as well. Figure 7.9 highlights four key dimensions of building these linkages: bonding, empathy, reciprocity, and trust.

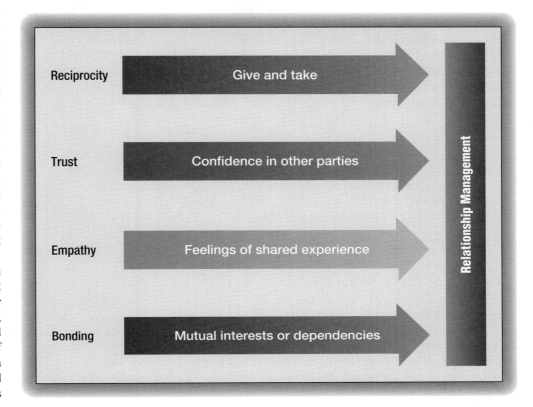

Figure 7.9 **Dimensions of Buyer-Seller Relationships**

Reciprocity — Give and take

Trust — Confidence in other parties

Empathy — Feelings of shared experience

Bonding — Mutual interests or dependencies

Relationship Management

Bonding A long-term relationship between buyer and seller requires a *bond* that joins the two. Mutual interests or dependencies must be identified and satisfied in order to cement the relationship. Customers with strong bonds to a business are more likely to remain committed to continuing their relationships with the firm.

DaimlerChrysler uses bonding strategies to reinforce the attachment many Jeep owners feel toward their vehicles and the company. Throughout the year, it sponsors events designed to foster a feeling of belonging. During these Jeep Jamborees, customers travel together on exciting off-road adventures in destinations like Utah and Colorado. Jeep's World Wide Web site gives full coverage to the twists and turns encountered during each jamboree.

WWW **www.jeepunpaved.com**

Each year, more than 6,000 people also travel to Camp Jeep in Colorado's Camp Hale. During the 3-day camp, Jeep owners, accompanied by their families and friends, learn the basics of off-highway driving and participate in activities like white-water rafting and rock-climbing.[20] Jeep 101 is the newest of DaimlerChrysler's programs. Owners and prospective owners drive through a course that

BUSINESS HALL OF SHAME

Steering Car-Rental Companies toward Improved Customer Service

Many travelers encounter the worst experiences of their trips after they reach their destinations. Trudging over to the counters of car-rental agencies, they begin the long and frustrating process of renting cars.

Short-term auto rentals are up 25 percent since 1992, but many customers complain that car-rental companies like Avis, Hertz, and National still lag far behind other industries in their emphasis on nurturing customer relationships. In fact, consumer ratings of the service, convenience, and availability benefits they receive from auto-rental firms have slipped steadily since 1995. Big gripes include long waits, hassles at the counter over insurance and gas, and bills that are all but impossible to decipher. "They're like, 'You booked with me. Now drop dead,'" grumbles one business traveler.

The problems stem from years of struggling to increase sales transaction by transaction. Promotional tools like discount coupons, bargain rates, and tie-ins with airline frequent flyer programs have done little to encourage long-term bonds with customers. Employees have found weak incentives to improve service, because most auto-rental firms tie compensation to sales levels instead of service objectives.

simulates trail conditions in the wilderness. They're accompanied by experienced Jeep guides who explain the capabilities of Jeep vehicles. This year, Jeep 101 programs are scheduled in five major cities. "All three programs provide a peak experience that links the owner emotionally to both the activity and their vehicle," says General Manager Martin R. Levine.[21]

Empathy Empathy is the ability to see a situation from the perspective of another party. Understanding customer needs and motivations helps businesses to improve the effectiveness of their goods, services, and programs. Empathy also encourages customer loyalty by reassuring them that the company cares about their concerns.

Patients of health maintenance organizations (HMOs), for example, often complain of feeling dehumanized when they contact their health-care providers for help or information. Connecticut-based Oxford Health Plans recognized this problem and restructured its customer service operation. Previously, different customer service representatives handled different types of inquiries. Now, however, every Oxford Health Plan customer is assigned to a dedicated service manager who handles all of her or his problems and responds to all questions. Because each dedicated service manager serves the same patients on an ongoing basis, Oxford staff members personalize the service they provide and establish stronger relationships with individual patients.[22]

Reciprocity Give-and-take, or *reciprocity*, is a part of every relationship. One party makes allowances and grants favors to the other in exchange for the same treatment when a need arises. In business relationships, this give-and-take process weaves a web of commitment between buyer and seller, binding them ever closer together.

Kingsway Paper is not the lowest-cost supplier of paper shopping bags, but the specialized services it renders to its retail customers more than justify the difference in price. The firm tracks each customer's usage patterns and shipments and then creates a

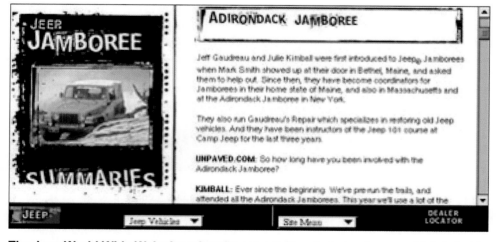

The Jeep World Wide Web site advertises the Adirondack Jamboree, which is held in New York. Jeep owners attending this Jamboree or others in locations such as Utah, or Colorado experience a bonding, which helps to form the attachment they feel toward their vehicles.

The low-price battles between auto-rental companies have also slashed industry profits. As a result, few companies can invest in the new computer systems and employee training programs needed to boost the efficiency of their service. Rental companies have also tried to keep expenses under control by purchasing inexpensive, relatively unpopular car models from automobile manufacturers.

Some companies are trying to stem the tide. National recently launched an employee training program to improve customer care. Alamo is adding airport kiosks that let customers handle transactions over electronic links. Budget has started offering Harley-Davidson motorcycles and convertibles in order to attract customers. A number of mergers have also consolidated the industry. Whether these measures will convince travelers that the firms have changed remains to be seen.

QUESTIONS FOR CRITICAL THINKING

1. **How has the auto-rental industry violated the principles of relationship management?**
2. **What specific strategies and tactics would you recommend to ex-** ecutives in the car-rental industry to help improve customer satisfaction and service?
3. **How could the auto-rental industry use business-to-business partnerships to improve performance?**

Sources: "Thrifty Named Top Car Rental Company by *Entrepreneur* Magazine for Sixth Straight Year," PR Newswire, April 19, 1999; Lisa Miller, "Car Rental Industry Promises that Things Will Improve. Really," *The Wall Street Journal*, July 17, 1997, p. A1; and "Limited Mileage," *The Economist*, January 18, 1997, p. 63.

customized report showing the order placement times and quantities that would minimize the company's funds tied up in inventory as well as its shipping and handling costs. Even though Kingsway's products cost up to 7 percent more than those of competitors, customers are willing to pay the difference in exchange for the special services Kingsway offers.[23]

Trust The glue that holds a relationship together is *trust*. Trust is one party's confidence that it can rely on the other's integrity to deliver what it promises. When a business follows through on its commitments to customers, trust grows and allegiance is fortified.

Seattle-based Costco is a master at nurturing customer trust. A recent survey found that 75 percent of the warehouse club's members say they trust Costco implicitly to sell quality products. In fact, they trust Costco enough to pay a $35 a year membership fee for the right to shop there. Costco protects this trust by forging ties with the manufacturers of the products it sells. The retailer even gets involved in its suppliers' production and distribution methods in an effort to enhance customer value. Over the past few years, Costco has pressed its suppliers to improve its fresh salmon fillets by trimming fat, removing bones, and removing skin. It also began buying directly from suppliers in Canada and Chile, shaving prices to $4.79 a pound, about half what local supermarkets charge. Not surprisingly, Costco now sells about 9 million pounds of salmon fillets a year.[24]

MANAGING RELATIONSHIPS WITH BUYERS

Every business establishes relationships of some kind with its customers. The intensity of these relationships varies depending on the type of good or service the company provides and the manner in which it is delivered. Purchases that involve greater risk for the buyer tend to increase the intensity of the relationships.[25]

Relationship intensity can be represented as a continuum of customer commitment to the firm. As shown in Figure 7.10, the strength of commitment between the parties grows as an individual or firm progresses from the lowest level to the highest level in this continuum. At the same time, the likelihood of a business continuing a long-term relationship with its customers also increases. Relationship management seeks to move customers along this continuum whenever it can.

The First Level of Buyer Commitment

At the lowest level of customer commitment, buyer and seller share only a short-term and superficial relationship. Consumers may see little or no distinctions among the offerings provided by different firms. Although they expect quality goods and services at this level, they have little incentive or desire to remain committed to a particular firm. At this level of commitment, customers make choices based on fundamental considerations like price or product features rather than feelings of bonds to a particular firm. Manufacturers of products like toothpaste, soup, laundry detergent, and gasoline generally operate at this level of customer commitment.

Firms seeking to improve this weak customer commitment usually focus their efforts on pricing and other financial considerations to motivate customers to enter into buying relationships. Examples include United Airlines' Mileage Plus frequent-flyer program, the Discovery Card's offer of cash back for every purchase made with the credit card, and value meal promotions at fast-food outlets.

Programs like these offer only a low probability of creating long-term buyer commitment. Although frequent-flyer programs like that offered by United Airlines do offer added value to consumers, they are easily duplicated by competitors, so they do very little to convince buyers to remain loyal to the sponsoring firms over time. A seller must offer more than a low price or other financial incentive to create a long-term relationship with a buyer.

The Second Level of Buyer Commitment

Relationship intensity increases at the second level of buyer commitment to a business. Interactions between buyers and sellers often involve *social* exchanges based on deeper links than the financial motivations of the first level. Consumers begin to believe that they receive unique benefits by continuing their relationships with a particular firm. They are motivated by their perceptions of attentive service, some product customization by the seller to meet their needs, or intangible benefits like a sense of belonging derived from doing business with the firm.

Like Jeep, Harley-Davidson uses social relationships to strengthen customer bonds. Local dealers sponsor Harley Owners' Groups (HOGs), and the company includes a 1-year free membership with each motorcycle it sells. Harley-Davidson also makes a complete line of accessories and apparel to encourage customers to live the Harley lifestyle.[26] Similarly, Mitre, a well-known soccer equipment manufacturer, invites customers to join Club Mitre. Members receive newsletters that highlight soccer tournaments and offer game tips from soccer professionals.

In other cases, the bonds that customers feel for a particular company can be strengthened by creating an emotional link with a cause or charity important to them. For example, New Jersey–based Catholic Telecom offers long-distance and Internet service to Roman Catholics worldwide. The firm offers added value to its customers by contributing 3 cents of every dollar it receives to the Catholic church and not-for-profit charities related to it.[27]

The Third Level of Buyer Commitment

At the highest level of buyer commitment, the buyer-seller social relationship is transformed into structural changes that forge true partnerships. The buyer and seller find themselves working closely together, developing a dependence on one another that continues to grow over time. Sellers become intimately aware of buyer needs at this level. Buyers hesitate to switch to another company, because they would then have to educate the new seller about their requirements. They see themselves as receiving value-added benefits and specialized services that cannot be found elsewhere.

Fashion retailer Saks Fifth Avenue nurtures customer commitment with its Fifth Avenue Clubs. Customers are invited to special personal shopping areas set up away from the stores' main sales floors. While they enjoy refreshments and other amenities, specially trained store associates work with them to identify their wardrobe needs. The associates then put together selections for the customers to approve. When a personal shopper notes the arrival of new merchandise that matches a customer's preferences, the staff member contacts the customer. "We're there only to

| Figure 7.10 | **Three Levels of Buyer Commitment** |

spoil you," explains Saks's personal shopper supervisor Susan Olden. "We know your figure flaws, what you'd like for lunch, your favorite fitter, and the length of your sleeve." In one case, Saks's personal shoppers put together an entire business wardrobe in 2½ hours for an executive whose suitcase had been stolen en route to London.[28]

Businesses that sell to other businesses also reach high levels of customer commitment by forging partnerships with customers. Process Products Ltd., a maker of nuts, bolts, and other small parts used in manufacturing, places its own employees at the factories of major customers. These representatives help to specify and order the parts that the customers require, a service that adds value for customers by eliminating the cost of assigning this task to their own staff. The service also binds them closer to Process Products.[29]

Tools for Nurturing Customer Relationships

Although relationship management has important benefits for both customers and business, most relationship-oriented businesses quickly discover that not all customers justify equally vigorous treatment. Some customers generate more profitable business than others. An often-quoted standard asserts that 20 percent of most firms' customers account for 80 percent of their sales and profits. A customer in this category undoubtedly has a higher lifetime value than a customer who buys only sporadically or makes only small purchases.

While businesses shouldn't ignore any customer, of course, their objectives and tactics for managing relationships with individual customers often reflect the overall value to the firm of the resulting business. A firm may choose to custom-manufacture goods or services for high-value customers while working to increase repeat sales of stock products to less valuable customers. An important task in developing relationship strategies, therefore, is to differentiate between customer groups when seeking ways to pull each one closer to an intense

Table 7.3	Tools for Developing Customer Relationships
Area	**Specific Tactics**
Marketing	Frequency marketing programs
	Affinity programs
	Co-marketing
	Co-branding
Human resources	Employee selection, training, and retention programs
Production	Customization
	Mass-customization
Technology	Internet and extranets
	Electronic data interchange
	Customer databases

commitment to the firm. The firm can then choose the particular tactics that suit each customer group.[30]

Table 7.3 illustrates some of the tools businesses can use to accomplish their relationship goals. Some of these tactics are suitable for developing relationships with individual consumers, others for developing relationships in business-to-business makets, and some are suitable for both.

Marketing Popular techniques through which firms try to build and protect customer relationships include frequent-buyer and frequent-user programs. Such a marketing initiative, commonly known as a **frequency marketing** program, rewards purchases with cash, rebates, merchandise, or other premiums. Catalog retailer Eddie Bauer enrolls customers in its Rewards program. Members earn 10 points for every dollar they spend on store or catalog purchases. When they collect 5,000 points, they receive a $10 discount on future purchases. Rewards members also receive Eddie Bauer fashion newsletters and opportunities to earn other special bonuses.[31] Hallmark Cards has launched a similar frequency marketing program that awards points to customers for every purchase and then distributes certificates to those who

The Fifth Avenue Clubs at Saks Fifth Avenue department stores provide their busy male and female clients with efficiency, speed, and personal service, which builds a structural relationship between the seller and the buyer.

reach purchase goals. Company research shows that customers in the program spend an average of 70 percent more than others each time they visit Hallmark stores.[32]

Affinity programs are another tool for building emotional links with customers. An **affinity program** is a marketing effort sponsored by an organization that solicits involvement by individuals who share common interests and activities. Affinity programs are common in the credit card industry. For example, SunTrust Bank offers a Professional Golf Association (PGA) Tour MasterCard. American Express competes directly by offering its own American Express Golf Card.[33] General Motors' Concept Cure line of vehicles is another example of an affinity program. GM promises to donate a percentage of the proceeds from new-car sales to breast-cancer research.[34]

Many businesses have also used co-marketing and co-branding for some time. In a **co-marketing** deal, two businesses jointly market each other's products. Many personal computer manufacturers use co-marketing to promote the Intel Pentium processors in their machines. The PC makers gain credibility through their association with the high-quality, cutting-edge reputation of Intel Corp., and Intel benefits by having its name appear in more places and more often than it could achieve on its own.

When two or more businesses team up to closely link their names for a single product, **co-branding** occurs. Several restaurant companies have joined forces to house more than one restaurant choice under one roof. Inside many Subway or Blimpies restaurants, you can also order a frozen yogurt from a stand run by the TCBY frozen yogurt chain.[35] Nestlé USA and Frito-Lay teamed to develop Pretzel Flips, a co-branded candy snack combining Nestlé's chocolate and Frito-Lay's Rold Gold Pretzels.[36] Toymaker Hasbro and sunscreen maker Nantucket Gold developed a line of kid-targeted sunblock products that feature the Playskool logo.[37] The chapters on marketing management in Part IV will focus on additional marketing tools that can help firms

| Figure 7.11 | **Building Successful Relationships through Human Resources** |

The right relationship begins with the right people.

The way we see it, everything that makes us unique, makes our work force that much stronger in a diverse world. Our commitment is to create an environment in which the best people do their best work, and that means building a global organization in which differences are respected and valued. We recognize that this goal is a challenging one, and we know we're not there yet. But our candor is matched only by our determination in reaching this goal — to cultivate a broader base of people whose differences can help to create successful relationships for ourselves and with our clients.

CHASE. The right relationship is everything.

© 1997 The Chase Manhattan Corporation.

> "A little reciprocity goes a long way."
>
> Malcolm Forbes (1919–1990)
> American publisher

to build more solid customer relationships.

Human Resources As mentioned earlier, a firm can fulfill the promises it makes to its customers only through properly trained and equipped employees. Most relationship-oriented organizations try to develop human resource tactics to support their relationship management initiatives. Financial institutions, like Chase Manhattan Bank and Boston-based Fleet Capital Corp. build long-term relationships with customers on a foundation of long-term relationships with employees. The banks' training programs help employees to understand the firms' missions and empathize with customer needs. The banks have also redesigned their employee compensation and rewards systems to encourage employee loyalty.[38] This commitment to serve customers with highly-trained, motivated employees is illustrated in Figure 7.11.

Entrepreneur Steve Lauer owns and operates 31 Subway franchises. "Everything is based on getting and keeping good employees," he says. "You have to focus on your employees before you can serve customers." When Lauer hires managers for his restaurants, he looks for people with positive personalities and attitudes. He knows the managers will have a big impact on how employees feel about their jobs—and how they treat customers. "I look for managers who can make coming to work fun. Employees who are happy at their jobs are more likely to make customers happy."[39]

The next four chapters take a closer look at the tactics for human resource management that promote development of a solid workforce that effectively serves customers.

Production Adapting production processes to meet customer needs is an important component of relationship management. In some industries, the ability to customize a good or service to suit the individual requirements of customers offers competitive advantage. Salespeople for Nordstrom Valves carry laptop computers that run specially

How Good Are Your Networking Skills?

The old saying, "It's not what you know but who you know" is more accurate today than it ever was. Networking, or parlaying your social, business, and educational connections into helpful relationships, can often provide invaluable assistance in business. How good are your networking skills? To find out, check the appropriate line to the left of each of the following ten questions.

Yes No

☐ ☐ 1. I treat everyone I meet with respect and honesty.

☐ ☐ 2. I believe I have skills and experience that are worth sharing with others.

☐ ☐ 3. I take an active role in learning about other people's interests.

☐ ☐ 4. I'm able to remember other people's interests when I meet them for a second or third time.

☐ ☐ 5. I enjoy introducing people to one another.

☐ ☐ 6. When I join a club or organization, I don't mind taking on responsibility.

☐ ☐ 7. I am a good team player.

☐ ☐ 8. When someone does something especially nice or helpful for me, I make it a point to thank them with a personal note or follow-up phone call.

☐ ☐ 9. I keep in touch with friends, teachers, employers, and co-workers from my past.

☐ ☐ 10. I'm a good listener.

Interpreting Your Answers

If you answered Yes three times or less, your networking skills need work. To build solid networking relationships you have to be willing to give before you expect to receive. Answering Yes four to seven times means that you recognize the importance of developing bonds with others, but you're still uncertain about how to develop them. If you answered Yes eight to ten times, congratulations! You understand some of the key factors involved in creating a network of contacts who will be willing to help you in the future.

For more information on networking, read *The Secrets of Savvy Networking* by Susan Roane, Warner Books, 1993.

---

designed software. When salespeople meet with customers the computer program allows them to customize the design of the tire products on the spot. Customers can instantly see a product simulation and receive data on the cost of buying and using the finished product. Nordstrom customers are willing to pay prices 15 to 20 percent higher than those of competing products in order to buy customized products.[40]

Some businesses plan the locations of their factories to strengthen customer relationships. Nypro Inc. is a Massachusetts firm that produces plastic products through injection molding. In order to reinforce bonds with its major customers, Nypro has built dedicated factories close to their sites. Nypro's Oregon plant is only 3 miles from one of its largest customers, Hewlett-Packard. The facility was even designed with space for a development center to be used by Hewlett-Packard engineers.[41]

Some businesses strive for **mass-customization,** a production method that allows for mass production of goods and services in lot sizes of one or just a few at a time. Want a new pair of jeans guaranteed to fit? Levi Strauss' Personal Pair jeans can be personalized according to your

actual body measurements. Salespeople enter the measurements into a computer, which selects from 500 design choices to find the best match. The order is then sent via modem to Levi's factory where the jeans are made by altering standard Levi's patterns. For about $65, the firm will deliver a pair of personalized jeans in about 3 weeks.[42]

Technology Rapid technological advances have enabled businesses to develop new capabilities for managing customer relationships. The ability to customize and rapidly deliver goods and services has become increasingly dependent on investments in technology like computer-aided design and manufacturing.

The Internet offers a way for businesses to connect with customers in a much more intimate manner than was previously available. Beneficial National Bank's mortgage division lets potential customers learn the details of mortgages by combining the Internet and telephone contact. Mortgage seekers dial into Beneficial's Web page and access a special area that automatically establishes a phone connection with a live customer service representative in the bank's mortgage department. The representative answers questions over the phone while simultaneously directing additional information to the customer's computer screen.[43]

Another communications tool helps businesses to communicate with their business customers. **Electronic data interchange (EDI)** is a quick and highly cost-efficient computer-to-computer exchange of invoices, orders, and other business documents. Later chapters on communications and technology revisit EDI.

Customer databases use information from company computers to identify and target specific groups of potential customers. This refinement allows a business to focus on marketing and management efforts that target its best customers. British Airways uses a customer database to enhance the traveling experiences of its most valued customers, members of the airline's Executive Club frequent-flier program. The database records details about the specific preferences of each club member. When a member makes a flight reservation, the information is available on the system so that ticketing representatives and flight attendants can make sure the member's preferences are met.[44]

Data warehouses are sophisticated customer databases that allow managers to combine data from several different organizational functions. Managers can then use the information to create a centralized, accurate profile of each customer's relationship with the firm as an aid to decision making. Kentucky Fried Chicken's data warehouse lets planners access up-to-the-minute data on exactly what food items customers are ordering in each of the company's 9,000 restaurants. KFC uses this information to improve menu selection and make adjustments to purchasing and staffing levels.[45]

Many supermarkets also track the purchases of their customers, storing the information in data warehouses. Using such a customer database, a supermarket can then send tar-geted promotions to customers based on their past preferences. For example, Food Lion supermarkets may send previous buyers of Dove brand soap a discount coupon for the product. This encourages customers to deepen their relationships with the store, because they believe that it recognizes and caters to their needs and preferences.[46]

Giant retailer Wal-Mart teamed with NCR to build a data warehouse capable of serving the needs of 3,000 Wal-Mart outlets worldwide. As Figure 7.12 explains, the system supplies buyers and vendors with information they need to make informed decisions on stock replenishment, buying trends, and pricing. Chapters 17 and 18 will look closer at these and other technological advances.

BUILDING AND MANAGING BUSINESS PARTNERSHIPS

Customer relationships aren't the only relationships that organizations form. To compete effectively in today's global marketplace, businesses must also manage their relationships with other businesses. Some business-to-business relationships revolve around buyer-seller connections. One firm provides materials or services that the other firm uses in serving its customers. Other business-to-business relationships link two or more firms to work together toward common goals. For example, two firms may use co-branding to boost the sales and market exposure of their individual products, or several firms may form a cooperative venture to jointly develop new technology. Increasingly, businesses are viewing their relationships with other businesses as partnerships.

A **partnership** is an affiliation between two or more companies that assist each other in achieving common goals. Partnerships can involve a single function or activity, such as product distribution, or all functions, such as the research and development, manufacturing, and marketing for a new product. Business partnerships help a firm to control its uncertainty and reduce its risk, in the process increasing profits. Organizations are motivated to form partnerships for

Figure 7.12 **The Wal-Mart Data Warehouse**

a variety of reasons. They may seek to protect or improve their positions in existing markets or gain access to new domestic or international markets. Other motives include sharing resources, reducing costs, warding off competitive threats, raising or creating barriers to entry, and learning new skills.

Types of Business Partnerships

Each business-to-business partnership can be classified as one of three types: buyer-seller, internal, or lateral partnerships.

Buyer-Seller Partnerships In a buyer-seller partnership, a firm purchases goods and services from one or more intimately related providers. For example, one firm may contract with an advertising agency to develop and place advertisements. Another company may depend on a partner to supply important components used in its manufacturing process. In a buyer-seller business partnership, however, the relationship may go much deeper than just supplying goods or services. Both parties may begin to rely on each other to provide additional value beyond exchanges of goods.

The mutually beneficial partnership between Levi Strauss and JCPenney is illustrated by their jointly sponsored promotion shown in Figure 7.13. Levi depends on retailers like JCPenney as the final link in its distribution channel to reach jeans buyers. To strengthen the bonds between partners, Levi ads feature JCPenney as a local source for the company's jeans. The firm also works closely with the retailer to provide specialized training for store employees, quick shipments of out-of-stock products, and special promotions. Both manufacturer and retailer benefit from this successful relationship.

Buyers, for example, may begin to expect special benefits such as price reductions, quick delivery, and high quality in return for directing their business to the seller. Department stores often demand that manufacturers guarantee specific profit margins as a condition of carrying their product lines. Retailers may also insist that sellers meet stringent requirements for packing and shipping or pay fines for failing to do so. Some retailers even specify that apparel manufacturers must ship merchandise on comparatively expensive hangers.[47]

Figure 7.13 **The Levi-JCPenney Business Partnership**

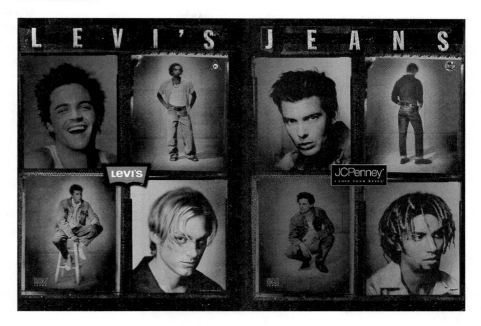

Why would a manufacturer agree to demands like these? The answer is a simple concept: Sellers have needs, too. Sellers depend on steady streams of cash to stabilize their finances, and they recognize potential opportunities to control marketing and even manufacturing costs by developing long-term relationships with buyers. The pressure to build and maintain buyer-seller partnerships is especially intense for small businesses. As a result, many sellers see the job of meeting buyer demands simply as part of their work of protecting their partnerships. "If your life is tied to these people, then you have to do business this way," explains the chief executive officer of one apparel company.[48]

A growing form of buyer-seller partnership is outsourcing. **Outsourcing** occurs when one business decides to hire another to perform tasks or functions previously handled by internal staff and systems. The benefits of outsourcing include reduced operating expenses, improved company focus on core strengths, and access to capabilities the firm lacks on its own. Businesses currently outsource a wide variety of functions such as data processing, telemarketing, accounting, manufacturing, and even human resource management. Altogether, U.S. businesses spend about $108 billion on outsourcing.[49]

Business Directory

outsourcing an arrangement in which one business hires another to perform tasks or functions previously handled by internal staff and systems.

Help future astronauts **take pictures**

further.

First Mark asked his buddy Joel to take his picture with the school's new Kodak digital camera and downloaded the image on to a computer.

Then he hopped on the World Wide Web and found a great interplanetary image of Saturn on the NASA Web site.

Mark drew a few aliens, scanned them into the computer using a Kodak photo scanner, and created his own take on space exploration.

He sent it out into cyberspace, where he met a future colleagues at, of all places, an astronomy class in Australia.

Kodak

To learn more about how Kodak products and solutions are bringing the classroom into the 21st century, visit our Web site: http://www.kodak.com/edu/. Or give us a call at 1-800-939-1630. Kodak is a trademark. ©Eastman Kodak Company 1997.

Kodak partnered with four of its main competitors—Canon, Fuji, Minolta, and Nikon—to develop the digital camera, which Mark (inside spacesuit) used to have his photo taken. Mark downloaded the image to a computer, added a Saturn image from the NASA World Wide Web site, drew some aliens and scanned them into the computer, and created the space exploration photo that was used in this ad.

The Southland Corp. operates 5,000 7Eleven stores in the United States, Canada, and Japan, all of them with heating and air conditioning requirements. Previously, each store handled maintenance of these systems. This arrangement proved costly and inefficient, however, so Southland decided to centralize maintenance by outsourc-ing it to a tight network of contractors. As a result, Southland has gained greater control over the cost of repairs and reduced downtime because preventive maintenance is scheduled from one central source.[50]

Even the U.S. Postal Service relies on outsourcing. When the USPS had trouble de-livering packages through its 2-day priority mail service, the agency turned to Emery Worldwide Airlines for help. To meet USPS needs, Emery will set up, staff, and manage ten priority mail processing plants on the east-ern seaboard.[51] Outsourcing is discussed in more detail in Chapter 9.

Internal Partnerships As outsourcing has in-creased in popularity, many businesses are also recognizing the importance of internal partnerships. The classic definition of the word *customer* as the buyer of a good or service is now more carefully applied to *external cus-tomers.* This change recognizes that customers within an organization also have their own needs. For example, in a company that manu-factures cellular phones, the team that assem-bles the phones is a customer of the firm's purchasing department. In essence, the manu-facturing plant buys cellular phone parts from the purchasing department, and the purchasing department acts as a supplier. In this partner-ship, the purchasing department must continue to fulfill the needs of manufacturing by select-ing vendors that provide the parts needed within price, quality, and time frame specifica-tions from manufacturing. Without recogniz-ing, building, and maintaining internal part-nerships, an organization will experience difficulties meeting the needs of its external partnerships.

Lateral Partnerships Lateral partnerships result from strategic relationships between separate businesses or organizations. Lateral partnerships involve no buyer or seller interactions; rather, the partners join to promote progress toward common aims by sharing resources, knowledge, or capabilities. Co-branding and co-marketing, discussed in the previous sec-tion, are two forms of lateral partnership. Another impor-tant form of lateral partnership is the strategic alliance.

Strategic Alliances

A **strategic alliance** is a partnership formed to create competitive advantage. Companies form strategic alliances when each believes that the other can offer an important benefit. Businesses of all sizes, all kinds, and in many locations have formed strategic alliances. One study found that American companies are entering strategic alliances 48 percent more often than they did just 3 years ago. Companies engaging in strategic alliances report greater growth in revenues and productivity than firms without alliances.[52]

Companies serving the same or different industries form many types of strategic alliances. Although alliances occur in all types of industries, they are particularly common among industrial manufacturers, electronics companies, and computer hardware and software firms. One study of leading U.S. and Canadian oil companies found that 84 percent expected future improvements in their performance to come mainly from alliances with other firms rather than from internal actions of their own.[53]

Strategic alliances can involve competition between a market leader and a follower or even between rivals. Most partnerships between competitors involve cooperative efforts to introduce new, industrywide standards or systems. Industrywide partnerships can help to build consumer confidence in such new products, which improves their chances of succeeding. Arch-rivals Eastman Kodak, Canon, Fuji, Minolta, and Nikon teamed up to develop and introduce the Advanced Photography System, which combines digital and conventional photography technologies. The four companies shared their research and development capabilities and patented technology to create a unique system that they hope will become a new standard in photography.[54]

The global marketplace offers additional opportunities for success through strategic alliances. By partnering with a firm already established in another country, a firm hoping to expand into that market can reduce its risk. In either arrangement, the partners agree in advance on the skills and resources that each will contribute to the alliance to achieve their mutual objectives and gain a competitive advantage. When Starbucks decided to expand into Japan, for example, the company joined forces with Japanese retailer Sazaby, Inc., to open five coffee shops. Sazaby helped Starbucks to identify retail sites and to understand Japanese consumer preferences.[55]

Ingredients of Successful Partnerships

Just as organizations must manage their relationships with customers, they must manage their relationships with other businesses, as well. Central to this process is a careful process for selecting appropriate partners. The first priority is to locate firms that can add value to the partnership, perhaps by supplying funding, extra manufacturing capacity, technical know-how, contacts, or distribution capabilities. The desirability of forming a partnership increases along with the value that partners can add. In many cases, the attributes of each partner complement each other.

The same elements that tie customers to a particular business—bonding, empathy, reciprocity, and trust—also play roles in the success of business partnerships. Long-term partnerships require bonds based on common values and goals. A highly ethical firm, for example, probably would not maintain a long-term relationship with a partner who suggested compromising product safety to boost short-term profits.

Both firms must feel that they receive adequate benefits from the partnership if it is to continue for the long term. Giant computer maker Digital Equipment Corp. has formed a strategic alliance with tiny Dragon Systems, a leading specialist in voice recognition systems for computers. Digital relies on Dragon to provide technological breakthroughs and enhancements that put Digital's products at the forefront of the market. Dragon, with only 200 employees, needs Digital to reach international markets and to gain credibility with other potential customers.[56]

Finally, trust is critical in business partnerships. Each party must trust that the other works to promote the interests of the partnership and not only its own concerns. Without trust, business partnerships crumble and relationships wither. Both parties must believe that each is fully committed to the other and that they share a desire to continue the relationship until mutual goals are satisfied.

SUMMARY OF LEARNING GOALS

1. Explain the role of vision in business success.

Vision is the ability to perceive the needs of the marketplace and develop methods for satisfying those needs. Vision helps new businesses to pinpoint the actions needed to take advantage of opportunities. In an existing firm, a clear vision of company purpose helps to unify the actions of far-flung divisions, keep customers satisfied, and sustain growth.

2. Describe the major benefits of planning.

The planning process identifies organizational goals and develops a road map of the actions necessary to reach them. Through realistic assessments of current and future conditions, planning helps a company to turn vision into action, take advantage of opportunities, and avoid costly mistakes.

3. Distinguish among strategic planning, tactical planning, and operational planning.

Strategic planning is a far-reaching process. It views the world through a wide-angle lens to determine the long-range focus and activities of the organization. Tactical planning focuses on the current and short-range activities required to implement the organization's strategies. Operational planning sets standards and work targets for functional areas such as production, human resources, and marketing.

4. Explain the six steps in the strategic planning process.

The first step of strategic planning is to translate the firm's vision into a mission statement that explains its overall intentions and aims. Next, planners must assess the firm's current competitive position by examining its strengths and weaknesses as well as probable future opportunities and threats. Based on this information, managers set specific objectives that elaborate what the organization hopes to accomplish. The next step is to develop strategies for reaching objectives that will differentiate the firm from its competitors. Managers then develop an action plan that specifies the specific methods for implementing the strategy. Finally, the results achieved by the plan are evaluated and the plan is refined as needed.

5. Identify the components of SWOT analysis. Explain its role in assessing a firm's competitive position.

SWOT analysis focuses on a firm's *s*trengths, *w*eaknesses, *o*pportunities, and *t*hreats. This organized procedure assesses a company's internal capabilities in order to avoid threats and take advantage of future market opportunities. SWOT analysis helps the firm to see its current situation in the competitive environment and the steps it must take to compete effectively in the future.

6. Describe the importance of relationships with customers, suppliers, employees, and others in achieving a company's objectives.

Effective management of relationships with customers helps a firm to protect itself against competitors and perhaps to increase profits. Forging relationships with employees helps to reduce turnover and, ultimately, to serve customer needs. Relationships with other businesses, such as partnerships and strategic alliances with suppliers, pay off by increasing the firm's capabilities and resources.

7. Explain the core elements of buyer-seller relationships.

A buyer-seller relationship is built around a network of promises that specify essential conditions for nurturing customer loyalty and trust. Emotional links with customers, such as bonding, empathy, reciprocity, and trust, knit together the interests and needs of both buyer and seller. Not all customers are equally committed to a relationship with a firm. Whenever possible, businesses should move customers toward greater commitment through mutually beneficial activities. Businesses can use methods based on marketing, production capabilities, human resources, and technology to develop strong links with customers.

8. Identify strategies and tactics for building and sustaining relationships with other organizations.

Businesses often seek to form partnerships with their suppliers and other organizations. This activity helps to control a firm's uncertainty and reduce its risk while increasing its profits. Partnerships with suppliers can be strengthened by working closely together to solve mutual problems and anticipate demand. Two or more businesses form strategic alliances when they believe they can achieve better results by joining forces than they can by competing as separate entities. Firms must manage their business-to-business relationships so that empathy, reciprocity, and trust bond the parties.

TEN BUSINESS TERMS YOU NEED TO KNOW

vision	competitive differentiation
planning	relationship management
mission statement	lifetime value of a customer
SWOT analysis	outsourcing
objectives	strategic alliance

Other Important Business Terms

business plan	affinity program
strategic planning	co-marketing
tactical planning	co-branding
operational planning	mass-customization
adaptive planning	electronic data interchange (EDI)
contingency planning	
forecasting	customer database
transaction management	data warehouse
frequency marketing	partnership

REVIEW QUESTIONS

1. Choose a well-known company and explain how vision has been important to its success or failure.
2. Distinguish between strategic, tactical, and operational planning. Review several magazine and newspaper business sections, and find examples of business planning at all three levels.
3. Why is contingency planning important? How large should a company grow before it begins to develop such plans?
4. What is a mission statement? How do objectives differ from mission statements? Write a mission statement for your school, church, team, or other organization.
5. Explain how the four elements of SWOT analysis help a business to focus on the future.

PARADIGM SIMULATION—
REALITY BITES IN THE VIRTUAL WORLD

In 1990, three young, unemployed software engineers—Mike Engledinger, Wes Hoffman, and Ron Toupal—followed their vision and formed Paradigm Simulation. "Originally, we all worked at the same company," says Mike Engledinger, Paradigm co-founder and vice-president of engineering. "That company did simulation and training applications, but they didn't see the computer graphics side as being all that important. They didn't think there was much of a future in it. As it turns out, there is, and we knew their was." Since it was founded, Paradigm has been blazing a trail in the simulation and virtual reality industries. The company has found success by making state-of-the-art technology more affordable and user-friendly to a broader consumer base. "Before Paradigm came along, 3-D simulation wasn't accessible to anybody," explains Wes Hoffman, co-founder and creative director. "It was too expensive."

At the core of their success has been a product called Vega—a software tool that enables programmers and non-programmers alike to quickly build interactive, 3-D visual simulations and virtual reality applications. "Our Vega product was revolutionary because it provided not only an application interface to engineers, but it also provided a graphical user interface—a point and click environment—that users could leverage off of," explains David Gatchel, executive vice-president of entertainment.

Paradigm's innovative software tools have attracted an impressive list of clients, including Chrysler, NASA, Silicon Graphics, BMW, and, most recently, the gaming giant Nintendo. "Nintendo was looking for a company that could help them bring 3-D games to the home market," says Gatchel. Nintendo selected Paradigm to create one of its most challenging games—Pilot Wings 64. Unveiled to glowing reviews, Pilot Wings 64 has proven to be one of Nintendo's best-selling games, giving Paradigm an impressive entrée into a lucrative new market. Soon, another Paradigm creation, an animated character named Egghead, will be an interactive star at Disney's Epcot Center.

Deals with Disney and Nintendo have sent Paradigm soaring. "Every year the company has doubled in size. And every year my biggest challenge is how I'm going to double it again. The business has to change dramatically," reveals Toupal, co-founder and president of Paradigm. While Paradigm's leaders look forward to the rewards of change and growth, there are concerns about the impact they will have on the relaxed corporate culture that has nurtured the company's success. "I think that's really been a challenge to maintain the small company atmosphere as the company grows," admits Hoffman. "A lot of the reason that we decided to start a company in the first place was because we all worked at large companies and were sick of the bureaucratic nonsense that didn't make any sense. But maintaining that kind of creative thinking in a large company where people start becoming kind of political and then develop some bureaucracy—it tends to start inhibiting really creative thinking."

"That's the number one challenge that we've had going from 10 to 70 people to 150 people—communicating the vision. Communicating and maintaining the culture. Attracting and retaining the great individuals that we've got," adds chief financial officer Ron Paige.

Despite its rapid growth, Paradigm's leaders are determined to preserve the relaxed, casual atmosphere they believe nurtures professional camaraderie, sparks creativity, and values the contributions of people above technology. "Technology is fleeting," says Toupal. "In the software business, the success of the business is directly attributed to the people."

Questions

1. Describe the importance of vision at Paradigm Simulations. How can the company maintain this vision as it grows?

2. How does Paradigm create a competitive differentiation? What are the sources of Paradigm's competitive advantage?

3. How is Paradigm using relationships to reach its goals?

PART II

Careers in Business

BUSINESS CAREER EXERCISES

Skills

At the end of Part I, you learned that your interests are very important in choosing a career. This exercise will help you discover your skills and talents, and you will be surprised at the number of skills you possess. In fact, it is not unusual for students to uncover 50 or more of their skills in this exercise. (By the way, this is not a time to be modest. If you think you have a skill, type it in. Your instructor can help you verify if you truly possess the skills you listed.)

This exercise will help you to:

▼ Identify many of your skills and talents.

▼ Discover you possess far more skills than you realize.

▼ Improve your awareness of your value to a potential employer.

How to Locate the Exercise Launch *Career Design* from the "Career Assistance" program group. Then select "Navigation" from the menu at the top of the screen, followed by "Career Sections" and then "Skills."

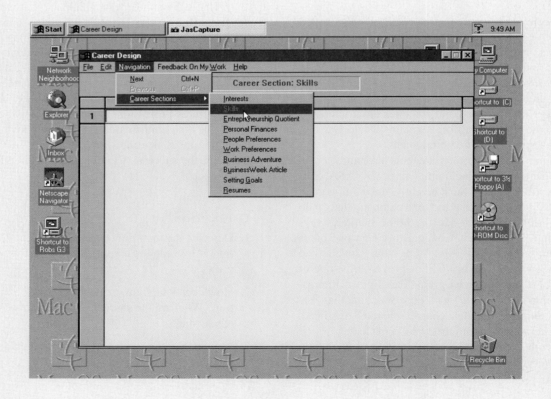

Entrepreneurship Quotient

Have you ever thought that you might want to start your own business some day? This exercise helps you determine whether you have what it takes to become an entrepreneur. Your instructor may also follow up with some important things to consider in deciding if a new business idea is worth pursuing.

This exercise will help you to:

▼ Develop a realistic picture of what it takes to become an entrepreneur.

▼ Gain some personal insights into whether you would enjoy starting your own business.

How to Locate the Exercise Launch *Career Design* from the "Career Assistance" program group. Then select "Navigation" from the menu at the top of the screen, followed by "Career Sections" and then "Entrepreneurship Quotient."

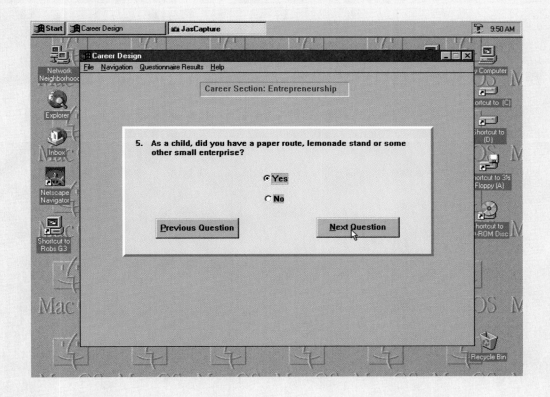

PART III | Management: Empowering People to Achieve Business Objectives

chapter 8

Management, Leadership, and the Internal Organization

LEARNING GOALS

1. Define management and describe the management pyramid.

2. Explain the three types of skills necessary for managerial success.

3. Discuss ways managers can efficiently and effectively allocate their time.

4. Distinguish between programmed and nonprogrammed decisions.

5. List the steps involved in the decision-making process.

6. Define leadership and identify different leadership styles.

7. Discuss the role of leaders in shaping an organization's culture.

8. Discuss the need for organization structure and list the steps in the organizing process.

9. Define departmentalization and identify five ways firms subdivide work activities.

10. Describe the different types of organization structures.

Fun in the Sun with Scott McNealy of Sun Microsystems

"Kick butt and have fun!" No, that's not any pregame prep talk for a professional hockey team. It's CEO Scott McNealy's version of the company culture at Sun Microsystems. Sun is the leading provider of network computing systems, including workstations (computers a cut above PCs), servers (computers that store data), and thin clients (basic computers that work with servers). And that's not all. Sun is also the creator of Java (the computer language that lets programmers write software for any system, including the Internet) and SPARC (the computer chip that McNealy predicts will be the alternative to Intel's). Sun Microsystems is well known for its aggressive marketing, just as McNealy him-

self is known for his belligerent, shoot-from-the-lip style of leadership.

Scott McNealy is one of the most outspoken CEOs around. Perhaps best known for his forceful, often colorful, one-line criticisms of Bill Gates and of Microsoft's stranglehold on the software industry, McNealy has been known to say things that make his colleagues cringe—he once assessed Microsoft's Windows and MS-DOS as "whipped cream on a road apple." His sarcasm can be rude, even vulgar. But his Gates-bashing

and colorful quotes have strengthened the company by keeping Sun in the spotlight. It is Scott McNealy who has single-handedly raised Sun's visibility.

McNealy is about more than quotes and tough talk. His technical and conceptual skills have been instrumental in shaping the company. For example, in his early days at Sun, the company grew so fast that its production lines nearly stopped. So McNealy moved his office from the executive suite to the factory floor and revamped the company's manufacturing. But he didn't stop there. He proceeded to trim the product line severely, focusing the company on computer networking above everything. And then he reorganized the entire company, increasing effectiveness by flattening the structure. Says McNealy, "We had a time when everything was a petition. We had a document that had like 36 signatures on it. And so we changed the rule. There'll be only two signatures on anything: Whoever's doing it, and whoever authorized it."

Energizing people has always been his special gift. "Energy comes right out of his pores," says Carol A. Bartz, CEO of Autodesk, another software firm. And that nonstop drive is matched only by his killer competitive instinct. He's an enthusiastic hockey player and golf player—and he's just as fervent about business. Whether on the ice, on the links, or at the conference table, McNealy is determined to win. It's just *not* in my nature *not* to be competitive," says McNealy. Oracle Corp's Lawrence J. Ellison praises McNealy for his passionate leadership and for his vigorous financial management. "Usually," says Ellison, "the financial guys aren't so outspokenly passionate, and all leaders are not detail-oriented."

www.sun.com

McNealy has changed Sun in three important ways. First, his vision has withstood the onslaught of such huge rivals as IBM, Hewlett-Packard, and Digital Equipment. So if the company seems a bit cocky at times, well, maybe it has a right to be. Some 35 percent of all Web servers around the globe are Sun machines. Plus, more and more companies are turning to Sun to satisfy their networking needs, including Federal Express, Gap, AT&T Universal Card Services, and Charles Schwab. And on top of that, with the company's UltraSPARC chip, Sun's workstations have grabbed the spotlight.

Second, McNealy's courage and commitment have molded a new image for his company. Sure, Sun's reputation is cocky and irreverent. But McNealy has also made Sun cool. Suddenly considered wise and competent, Sun has become the sage of the entire industry, the voice of reason, the leader of thought.

Third, McNealy has wisely made Sun fun, giving it a reputation for "cut-up" capers around headquarters. There was the time that company engineers constructed a golf course hole in McNealy's office (including a green and a water hazard). Then there was the time that McNealy was a general in an intramural squirt-gun war. Not to mention the conference where McNealy introduced his dog, Network, and set out cardboard fire hydrants bearing the names of Sun rivals. Humor permeates and binds the company, helping the people at Sun deal with their demanding jobs. In fact, when asked about McNealy, Dell Computer's vice president of finance said, "His humor and ability to raise a crowd to its feet is in many respects exactly what you need in CEOs and leaders of today's industry."

Sun Microsystems is a strong competitor and a constant innovator, not unlike its leader. The company has led its industry into network computing. In fact, Sun realized the importance of networking long before other major computers makers, including Microsoft. "The network is the computer," insists McNealy—an innovation in thinking that has helped the company grow and glow. Under McNealy's leadership, Sun maintains its offbeat edge, and judging by Sun's shining success, that edge has served the company well. With McNealy in charge, no one's looking for an eclipse anytime soon.[1]

CHAPTER OVERVIEW

The importance of effective managers like Scott McNealy cannot be overstated. When you look at any successful business such as Sun Microsystems, you'll see the skills of good managers behind that success. When companies fail, poor management usually is one of the leading causes.

A management career brings challenges that appeal to many students in introductory business courses. When asked about their professional objectives, many students say, "I want to be a manager." Perhaps you think that the role of a manager is basically being the boss. But in today's business world, companies are looking for much more than bosses. They want managers who understand technology, can adapt quickly to change, skillfully motivate subordinates, and realize the importance of satisfying customers. These types of managers will continue to be in great demand, as their performance strongly affects their firms' performance.

The last chapter discussed planning, the first of the four management functions. This chapter begins by describing the levels of management, the skills that managers at all levels in the organization need, and the types of decisions that managers make. It then discusses the importance of leadership and corporate culture. The second part of this chapter examines the second function of management—organizing.

THE DEFINITION OF MANAGEMENT

Management is the process of achieving organizational objectives through people and other resources. The manager's job is to combine human and technical resources in the best way possible to achieve the company's goals. Managers are not involved directly in production; that is, they do not themselves produce finished products. Instead, they direct the efforts of others to accomplish goals.

Management principles and concepts apply to not-for-profit organizations as well as profit-seeking firms. The local library director, the head of the Salvation Army, and a Boy Scout troop leader all perform the managerial functions of planning, organizing, directing, and controlling. Managers preside over organizations as diverse as Columbus State Community College, the New York Stock Exchange, and every Starbucks coffee shop.

DID YOU KNOW?

Managers are adopting very creative job titles. Yahoo's top executive, Jerry Yang, chose Chief Yahoo! as his title. Yang said the title helped him in his negotiations with Japanese billionaire Masayoshi Son. According to Yang, Son got a kick out of the title, which helped to "break the ice" in their meeting and resulted in Son agreeing to invest $106 million for a 31 percent stake in Yahoo!

The Management Pyramid

A local fast-food restaurant such as McDonald's typically works through a very simple organization that consists of an owner/manager and an assistant manager. By contrast, large organizations develop more complex management structures. Ford Motor Company, for example, manages its activities through a chairman of the board, 4 executive vice presidents, 5 group vice presidents, 28 vice presidents, and 7 staff officers, plus plant managers and supervisors. All of these people are managers, because they combine human and other resources to achieve company objectives. Their jobs differ, however, because they work at different levels of the organization.

In Chapter 5, you learned that a firm's management breaks down into three levels: top, middle, and supervisory management. These levels of management form a management pyramid, or hierarchy, as shown in Figure 8.1. The management pyramid is the traditional structure found in most organizations. Managers at each level of the pyramid perform different activities.

At the highest level of the management pyramid is **top management.** Top managers include such positions as chief executive officer, chief operating officer, and executive vice president. Top managers devote most of their time to developing long-range plans for their organizations. They make decisions such as whether to introduce new products, purchase other companies, or enter new geographic markets; they also develop strategic plans that guide the implementation of their decisions. As leaders, top managers are responsible for creating a vision for their organization and shaping their firms' corporate culture. Much of their time is also spent in outside activities involving governmental and community affairs.

Women and minorities may encounter more difficulty than white males in advancing to top management positions. According to the U.S. Labor Department, women hold 8 million of the country's 18 million managerial positions, but only 2.4 percent of top corporate positions are held by women. Part of the reason why few women have

---

Business Directory

management process of achieving organizational objectives through people and other resources.

top management jobs is the **glass ceiling,** an invisible barrier that resists the efforts of women in moving up the corporate hierarchy beyond a certain point. The arguments behind the glass ceiling are presented in Solving an Ethical Controversy.

Top managers in a growing number of firms—including JCPenney, Colgate-Palmolive, Dow Chemical, and

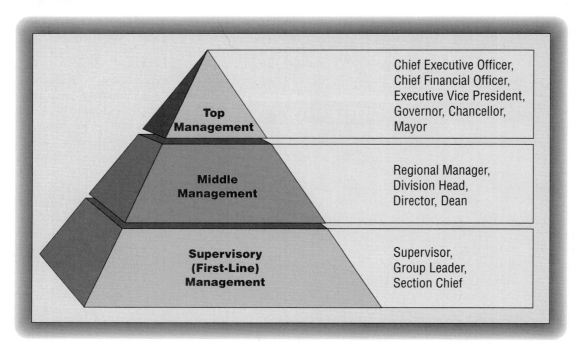

| Figure 8.1 | The Management Pyramid

Top Management — Chief Executive Officer, Chief Financial Officer, Executive Vice President, Governor, Chancellor, Mayor

Middle Management — Regional Manager, Division Head, Director, Dean

Supervisory (First-Line) Management — Supervisor, Group Leader, Section Chief

Hoechst Celanese—are establishing programs to help women break through the glass ceiling. Hoechst Celanese, a large chemical company, sets quotas that mandate the minimum number of women that must hold top management positions. It also maintains a formal mentoring program that creates opportunities for women and minorities to work alongside senior executives. The program gives women and minorities exposure to the firm's key decision makers and allows the mentors to learn how to be comfortable working outside an environment dominated by white males.

Colgate-Palmolive offers cross-training for women to help them gain experience in many functions such as marketing, manufacturing, and operations management. Colgate also pays a $3,000 fee for each woman it sends to Women's Organization for Mentoring, Education & Networking Unlimited, a training firm that teaches women how to succeed in a male-dominated environment. **Middle management,** the second tier in the management pyramid, includes positions such as general managers, plant managers, division managers, and branch managers. Middle managers' attention focuses on specific operations within the organization. They are responsible for developing de-

tailed plans and procedures to implement the strategic plans of top managers. For example, if top management decided to broaden the distribution of a product to a new region, a sales manager assigned to that region would be responsible for determining the number of salespeople assigned to that territory. If top management decided to institute a companywide total quality management program, a quality control manager in the customer service department might design a survey to gather feedback on customer satisfaction.

Supervisory management, or first-line management, includes positions such as supervisor, line manager, and group leader. These managers are directly responsible for assigning nonmanagerial employees to specific jobs and evaluating their performance every day. Managers at this first level of the pyramid work in direct and continuing contact with the employees who produce the firm's goods and services. They are responsible for implementing the plans developed by middle managers; they do this job by providing technical assistance to workers and motivating them to accomplish daily, weekly, and monthly goals.

SKILLS NEEDED FOR MANAGERIAL SUCCESS

Managers at every level in the management pyramid must exercise three basic types of skills: technical, human, and conceptual skills. All managers must acquire these skills in varying proportions, although the importance of each type of skill changes at different management levels. Figure 8.2 illustrates the varying importance of technical, human, and conceptual skills for top, middle, and first-line managers.

Technical skills are the manager's ability to understand and use techniques, knowledge, and tools and equipment of a specific discipline or department. Technical skills are particularly important for first-line managers, since they frequently interact with production employees who operate machinery, with salespeople who must explain the technical details of their firm's products, or with computer programmers who work on complicated software development assignments.

Jason Hoch, a project manager for TriNet Services, Inc., applies a variety of technical skills. TriNet is a 35-employee firm that provides a range of Internet and networking services. As a project manager, Hoch coordinates the work of employees, each of whom specializes in just one area such as graphics, multimedia, programming, and Web site development. "I need to know a lot about a lot of things," says Hoch. At a previous job as a Webmaster, Hoch developed his skills for creating and administering Web sites. At other jobs, he developed skills in graphics design, marketing, database integration, and programming languages and operating systems. Hoch would not be able to manage projects for customers if he lacked expertise in any of these technical skill areas.[2]

In general, as an organization member moves up the managerial hierarchy, technical skills lose relative importance. However, top executives in many firms often started out as technical experts. For example, the resume of a vice president of information systems probably lists experience as a computer analyst, while that of a vice president of marketing often shows a background in sales. As you learned in the opening vignette, Scott McNealy streamlined Sun Microsystem's manufacturing process so that it would be more efficient.

Human skills are interpersonal skills that enable a manager to work effectively with and through people. Human skills include the ability to communicate with, motivate, and lead employees to accomplish assigned activities. More generally, managers need human skills to interact with other people both inside and outside the organization. Globalization and increased workplace diversity have elevated the importance of human skills, as managers need to

relate to people from cultures and ethnic backgrounds different from their own. Recognizing the growing emphasis on human skills, many firms offer training in areas such as diversity, communication, and conflict resolution.

Mary Ann Byrnes knew that human skills would be essential to her success in managing a group of engineers who worked for ESL, a division of defense contractor TRW that handled top-secret work. When TRW spun off ESL as a separate firm to develop commercial applications for its military products, Byrnes was hired as CEO of the new company, Corsair Communications. Corsair had already attracted a customer that wanted a product its engineers had been developing, a device that tracks fraudulent use of cellular phones. Byrnes's challenge was to completely change the way the engineers worked so they would deliver the product ahead of competitors.

For government jobs, the engineers worked in strictest secrecy, and completed their separate assigned tasks by following established procedures for contracts that ran from 2 to 3 years. Their work involved no customer contact and no sense of urgency, cost control, or competition. One engineer described his work as a "10-percent-of-the-day kind of job. I'd go to meetings, and they'd decide I should change this to 4 watts instead of 3, and I'd write it down, and that was that." For Corsair, the engineers had to think and act like entrepreneurs to deliver products through quick and cost-effective methods. "We had some of the smartest scientists in the world," says Byrnes. "My job was to make them productive, to help them perfect in a short time what they had not been able to deliver before."

Byrnes used communication and motivation skills to encourage a sense of community and shared responsibility among the engineers and to instill a customer focus. Rather than working alone, the

---

| Figure 8.2 | **The Importance of Managerial Skills at Different Management Levels** |

Corsair CEO Mary Ann Byrnes used her human skills to motivate the company's highly talented engineers to adopt an entrepreneurial mindset allowing the company to develop products quickly that would satisfy customer needs.

SOLVING AN ETHICAL CONTROVERSY

Should Women Be Concerned about the Glass Ceiling?

The invisible career barrier that some say blocks women from top organizational jobs raises the question of gender inequity in the workplace. Some companies are working hard to right what some people perceive as unfair treatment of women that denies them opportunities to advance to top management positions.

But few employees—men and women included—make it to the top. Many employees have no aspirations to join the ranks of top management, and many lack the required emotional makeup or qualifications—usually an appropriate academic degree and at least 20 years of successful experience.

The controversy surrounding the glass ceiling issue often boils down to questioning why such a barrier would come to be and who is to blame. Some employees say working for a woman

boss can be a tough assignment. One woman who worked for three female bosses said they were "manipulative, extremely hard on female team members, but flirtatious with males." Another woman who worked for two female bosses agreed. "By contrast," she said, "I had two male bosses who mentored me, encouraged me to go back to school, and took pride in my achievements." Some women have even left the corporate world to start their own businesses motivated to avoid bad female bosses. One such entrepreneur says, "I can understand why bringing this out into the open may not be politically correct, but sometimes the truth hurts."

Pat Heim, author of a book called *Smashing the Glass Ceiling*, says that part of the reason why some employees dislike female bosses could relate to how they are raised as young girls. "Men grow up in hierarchies and understand how power is wielded. Girls grow up sharing power equally. There never was a 'boss doll player,'" says Heim.

Women who want to shatter the glass ceiling point to inequities in the workplace that prevent them from developing the skills they need to become good managers and candidates for top positions.

? *Are Organizations Responsible for Creating the Glass Ceiling?*

PRO

1. **The male-dominated workplace perpetuates negative preconceptions and stereotypes about women and their capabilities.**

2. **In the corporate world, an old-boys' network creates difficulties for women who want to succeed. Women with family responsibilities such as child care or elder care are limited in participating in informal networking functions, because many activities occur after work hours. Women who take maternity leave often are passed up for future promotions as a result.**

---

engineers joined together in teams that meet personally with each customer. Byrnes established pizza lunches during which she shared financial information about the company to help the engineers understand the importance of their work in achieving Corsair's goals. She empowered the engineers to make their own decisions, giving them a feeling of ownership. Through her human skills, Byrnes has inspired the engineers to revise the value they perceived in their work toward meeting their commitments to customers.[3]

www. **www.corsair.com**

Business Directory

time management effective allocation of available work time among different tasks.

Conceptual skills determine a manager's ability to see the organization as a unified whole and to understand how each part of the overall organization interacts with other parts. These skills confer an ability to see the big picture by acquiring, analyzing, and interpreting information. Conceptual skills are especially important for top-level managers, who must develop long-range plans for the future direction of their organization.

The conceptual skills of Eckhard Pfeiffer, the German-born CEO and president of Compaq Computer Corporation, have helped the company to triple its revenues and broaden its product base since he was named the top manager in 1991. To extend Compaq's reach beyond supplying personal computers for business customers, Pfeiffer introduced low-cost models for home use, one of the fastest-growing segments of the PC business. "What we realized before anyone is the unlimited potential of the PC," says Pfeiffer. To help Compaq achieve its goal of becoming one of the top three global in-

3. Women are channeled into staff positions such as manager of human resources or manager of corporate communications, positions that provide little visibility to key decision makers in the company. Few women are given line management responsibilities that give the responsibility for profits and losses and attract the attention of key executives.

4. Women need the commitment and good-faith efforts of organizations to support affirmative action programs that give them equal access and opportunities to compete based on their ability and merit.

CON

1. The glass ceiling is a concept that a small group of women—the feminists—use to advance their own economic interests. Affirmative action and special networking programs for women cost organizations money. Only a few women benefit at the expense of many, especially when people with weak qualifications are promoted simply to fill quotas.

2. To attain a top management position, one must commit oneself throughout a career and continuously work long hours. Many women decide to interrupt their careers to care for their children. Moving in and out of the workforce, they cannot meet the requirements of managerial experience needed for promotions to top positions.

3. Companies cannot find enough qualified women "in the pipeline" to be promoted. A shortage of women in the executive talent pool compared to the number of available men limits the numbers who rise to the top ranks.

SUMMARY

Some see good news for the future of women gaining promotions to top management. With many more women today earning college degrees than in the 1960s and 1970s, more women will be in the pipeline for promotions, because they will have the necessary academic qualifications.

Some also see bad news, though. Brenda Barnes shattered the glass ceil-

ing in a 20-year career that made her president and CEO of Pepsi-Cola North America. She recently quit that position after only 18 months, however. In announcing her resignation, Barnes said she wanted to be home to care for her three school-aged children. She said she hoped that her decision would not be interpreted as a signal that "women can't do it." But some people view Barnes's decision as a "disastrous loss for women" that will give new ammunition to critics of efforts to expand women's presence in top management.

Sources: Melanie Warner, "Is There a Gender Gap in Silicon Valley?" *Fortune*, March 24, 1999, accessed at www.pathfinder.com; Regina Fazio Maruca, "Workplace Equity," *Harvard Business Review*, November/December 1997, pp. 15–17; Jennifer Wells, "Stuck on the Ladder," *Maclean's*, October 20, 1997, pp. 60–64; Rosalie Osias, "A Disastrous Loss for Feminists," *New York Times*, October 19, 1997, p. L1; Anne Fisher, "Readers Sound Off: Women Bosses Really Can Be a Nightmare," *Fortune*, June 23, 1997, pp. 163–164; Linda Himelstein and Stephanie Anderson, "Breaking Through," *Business Week*, February 17, 1997, pp. 64–70; and Ida L. Castro and Diana Furchtgott-Roth, "Should Women Be Worried about the Glass Ceiling in the Workplace?" *Insight on the News*, February 10, 1997, pp. 24–27.

---

formation technology firms, Pfeiffer negotiated a merger with Digital Equipment Corp., the largest acquisition in the history of the computer industry. With the acquisition, Compaq can now enhance its offering to customers by including Digital's networked computing systems that help organizations compete in the global marketplace. Because of Pfeiffer's ability to think strategically, Compaq now offers products that span all areas of computing, from handheld computers that cost $649 to powerful, $2 million servers.[4]

www. www.compaq.com

DEVELOPING TIME MANAGEMENT SKILLS

Benjamin Franklin included the maxim "Time is money" in his *Poor Richard's Almanac* more than 250 years ago. It continues to apply in today's business environment as companies are searching with increasing intensity for ways

to cut costs and improve efficiency. **Time management** is the effective allocation of available work time among different tasks. Juggling priorities is an essential skill that all managers need to develop, because their work involves a variety of tasks carried on through frequent interruptions.

Guidelines for Effective Use of Time

Many guidelines for managing time have been suggested by experts who study time management. Some good practices include:

▼ Always leave at least one-quarter of your time unscheduled.

▼ Assign priorities to tasks.

▼ Break down big jobs into smaller ones.

▼ Learn to say *no*.

▼ When taking on something new, give up something old.

BUSINESS TOOL KIT

Developing Delegation Skills

Managers who are good delegators can reduce their stress, improve their organization's productivity, and enjoy the satisfaction of watching subordinates learn and grow. Effective delegation sometimes requires patience, trust, flexibility, and giving up activities that one loves to do, though.

▼ *Learn patience.* After Michael Merriman became CEO of Royal Appliance Manufacturing, Dirt Devil Inc., he set out on a mission to personally visit all the company's major retailers. One month later, he visited them again with his vice president of sales, who told Merriman, "You know, Mike, you can keep doing this if you want to, but if you see them too often, there is no role for me." Merriman realized the truth of the vice president's statement. "I was too gung ho," he admitted. "You can't undermine your people's authority. Nor can your business rely solely on my relationship with a couple key retailers."

▼ *Learn trust in others.* Tom Stendahl, CEO of Schwinn Cycling & Fitness, purchased the company out of bankruptcy. To rebuild it quickly, he split the business into units such as bikes, parts and accessories, and fitness. He then hired the best managers he could find. He told them, "Here it is guys, go out and reshape the world. You have total freedom." Stendahl views his job as a support role. "My job is to offer support whenever screwups happen—and you allow the screwups because you know that there will be more good coming out than bad."

▼ *Learn flexibility.* Jody Wright, founder and president of catalog retailer Motherwear, allows her employees to interview and hire new team members. Wright once took complete responsibility for hiring decisions, but she learned that some employees she hired were not compatible with current team members. Delegating the tasks of interviewing and hiring to her employees, Wright says, means that "integrating the person into the job takes less time. Everyone has already bought in."

▼ *Learn to give up activities you like to do.* "You don't always have to delegate something that you like to do, but you have no choice if the company is going to grow," says Joseph Leimandt, CEO of Trilogy Development Group. Being a software entrepreneur, Leimandt struggled to give up development and sales. "I don't get the personal satisfaction of writing code that runs on my machine and does cool stuff," says Leimandt. "There are times when I long to go down and stick my hands in it, but the upside is building the organization and getting to watch people grow."

Sources: Scott Bistayi, "Delegate—or Not?" *Forbes,* April 21, 1997, pp. 20-22; Bill Walsh, "Holy Macro," *Forbes,* April 24, 1996, p. 30; Roberta Maynard, "Do You Delegate as Much as You Can?" *Nation's Business,* July 1996, pp. 9–10; and Donna Fenn, "Employees Take Charge," *Inc.,* October 1995, p. 111.

The remaining paragraphs in this section discuss more detailed guidelines for wise time allocation developed by effective managers. Adapting these guidelines to your life as a student will help you to prepare for a job in the workplace.

Establish Goals and Set Priorities Make a list of long-term and short-term projects. Regularly review the list, and revise it as needed. Arrange the items in order of importance, and then divide them into specific tasks. Beginning at the top of the list, get to work. Do not get upset if your priorities change by the hour—just revise your list and get on with the work. Schedule your daily activities by recording them in an hour-by-hour appointment calendar.

Learn to Delegate Work In setting priorities, you must decide whether you really need to do a task yourself. One management professor lists only six activities appropriate for a top manager: plan, select the team, monitor their efforts, motivate, evaluate, and reward them. The manager should consider delegating other tasks, that is, assigning them to a subordinate.

Some questions should guide decisions about the tasks managers should delegate. One question is, would this project benefit a subordinate? In fact, an employee may eagerly welcome the opportunity to try something new and learn something valuable from the experience. Another question asks, is this task something that superiors believe the manager should be doing? If not, the task should be assigned to someone else. After deciding what work to delegate, the manager should follow a careful procedure to get desired results: Give clear instructions about what needs to be done; make sure workers understand instructions; set deadlines; and allow enough time to correct mistakes. The Business Tool Kit offers more tips on how to become a good delegator.

Concentrate on the Most Important Activities Learn the Pareto principle of time management: You can achieve 80 percent of your goals in only 20 percent of your time if you work on important tasks and avoid being distracted by those that contribute little toward accomplishing major goals. Chris Peters, a Microsoft vice president, says that people spend too much time worrying about unimportant little details that don't add much to satisfying customers. He explains, "Here's 100 things. Which 10 must I do and which 90 can I blow off?" To help him decide, Peters concentrates on customers. "Whenever I get confused, I think of my sister, walking into a computer store. What am I doing to make my sister happy?" he says.[5]

Do the Most Important Work at Your Most Alert Times
Effective time management calls for working on high-priority tasks during your most mentally alert periods of the day. Turn to low-priority tasks when your energy has ebbed.

Group Activities Together Set aside a period of time to read all of your mail and answer all of your phone calls. This technique will help you to make the most efficient use of your total time available. Timely recognition of employees who do good work is important to Steve Wittert, president of Paragon Steakhouse Restaurants in San Diego. During his hectic workdays, however, he seldom can take time to show appreciation to his staff. Wittert has set aside a time at the end of each day, when the work pace slows, to write personal notes of appreciation to staff members who made a difference that day.[6]

You can also combine routine tasks that do not require intense concentration, like filling out paperwork while talking on the phone, or making notes to yourself while waiting for a document to print. Time management also benefits if you make a weekly plan and stick to it instead of following daily to-do lists than can soon be filled with relatively unimportant tasks. The grander scale of a week-by-week plan helps with maintaining control of large or long-term projects.

Learn How to Handle Interruptions Incoming phone calls, unscheduled visitors, and even the mail can destroy your schedule. Control these interruptions by diverting all but essential calls to a secretary or assistant when you are working on an important task. You may also move to another office where no one will be able to find and interrupt you, set times when subordinates can talk to you and times when they cannot except for emergencies, and learn how to cut short long-winded callers.

Interrupting yourself also wastes time. Instead of getting yet another cup of coffee or leaving your desk to chat with a co-worker, try to finish the task at hand, even if it's a difficult or unpleasant one. Always look forward to the good feeling you have when you complete a task.

SPECIAL SKILLS FOR OVERSEAS MANAGERS

Many firms realize that growth requires expansion overseas.

Managers who accept assignments in international operations or foreign-based offices need special skills. They must learn local languages, cultural customs, and the practices and expectations of foreign business environments.

A firm incurs a huge cost when it places a manager in an overseas assignment. An international assignment in a European country usually costs a U.S. firm from two to three times the manager's annual salary. An assignment in an Asian country costs from three to five times the manager's compensation.[7]

Research by the Centre for International Briefing found that about 25 percent of American managers return home before completing their assignments—a failure rate three or four times higher than for European and Asian expatriates.[8] While U.S. managers bring proficient professional and technical skills to these assignments, culture shock and the stress of unfamiliar environments pose difficult challenges. The prevalence of two-income families also complicates matters, since transferred managers' spouses may not find comparable work in their new homes. Even if a spouse does not work, family members often struggle to adjust to living in a different culture.

To increase success rates for overseas assignments, some firms are implementing careful new methods for choosing foreign managers. AT&T hires psychologists to help select managers most suited to the challenges of working in different countries. Employees considered for these assignments must take a written test and go through management interviews. They must also complete the self-assessment checklist in Figure 8.3 to judge their own "cultural adaptability." Other firms assist overseas managers and families by providing training in local languages and cultures, finding jobs for spouses, and paying for private international schools for children.

MANAGERS AS DECISION MAKERS

Managers apply their conceptual, human, technical, and time management skills in their role as decision makers. Managers make decisions every day. **Decision making** is the process of recognizing a problem or opportunity and then finding a solution to it. The types of decisions that managers make can be classified as programmed and nonprogrammed decisions.

Business Directory

decision making process of recognizing a problem or opportunity, evaluating alternative solutions, selecting and implementing an alternative, and assessing the results.

| Figure 8.3 | **A Test of Cultural Adaptability** |

AT&T SELF-ASSESSMENT TEST OF CULTURAL ADAPTABILITY

	Yes	No
1. Would your spouse be interrupting a career to accompany you on an international assignment? If so, how do you think this will affect your spouse and your relationship with each other?	☐	☐
2. Do you enjoy the challenge of making your own way in new situations?	☐	☐
3. Is securing a job primarily your responsibility? Are you comfortable networking and being your own advocate?	☐	☐
4. Can you imagine living without television?	☐	☐
5. Is it important for you to spend significant amounts of time with people of your own ethnic, racial, religious, and national background?	☐	☐
6. As you look at your personal history, can you isolate any episodes that indicate a real interest in learning about other peoples and cultures? If so, briefly describe them.	☐	☐
7. Do you enjoy sampling foreign cuisines?	☐	☐

	Often	Sometimes	Rarely
8. Has it been your habit to vacation in foreign countries?	☐	☐	☐

	High	Average	Low
9. What is your tolerance for waiting for repairs?	☐	☐	☐

NOTE: Use back of form for detailed responses.

ating alternatives and making a new decision each time a situation occurs, they free managers to devote time to the more complex problems associated with nonprogrammed decisions.

A **nonprogrammed decision** involves a complex and unique problem or opportunity with important consequences for the organization. Examples of nonprogrammed decisions include entering a new geographic market, acquiring another company, or introducing a new product. Top managers at Kimberly-Clark Corp. made a nonprogrammed decision to redirect company resources away from their business of growing trees and converting them into pulp and paper and toward expanding their more profitable line of consumer products like Kleenex tissue. The company has sold most of its pulp and paper mills, and it continues to add new consumer products such as diapers, baby wipes, training and youth pants, and feminine and adult care products. "Today we are in the last stages of being a paper company on the way to being a full-fledged global consumer products company," says Wayne Sanders, Kimberly-Clark's chairman.[9] The Business Hall of Fame discusses several nonprogrammed decisions of German car maker Mercedes-Benz.

How Managers Make Decisions

Programmed and Nonprogrammed Decisions

Programmed and nonprogrammed decisions differ in their relative uniqueness. A **programmed decision** involves simple, common, and frequently occurring problems for which solutions have already been determined. Examples of programmed decisions include choosing the starting salary for a marketing assistant, reordering raw materials needed in the manufacturing process, and selecting the price discounts to offer customers who buy in large amounts. For these types of decisions, organizations develop rules, policies, and detailed procedures that managers apply to achieve consistent, quick, and inexpensive solutions to common problems. Since such solutions eliminate the time-consuming process of identifying and evalu-

Many managers rely on their intuition—or gut feelings—to decide how to solve problems or take advantage of opportunities. A survey of more than 600 managers conducted by consulting firm Kepner-Tregoe revealed that about one-third emphasize intuition in decision making.[10] Intuitive decision making works well when managers lack enough information to determine the probable outcome of a decision. They rely on their instincts and previous experience to solve problems and take advantage of opportunities.

Entrepreneurs often decide intuitively whether or not to launch new ventures. Ted Waitt relied on his intuition in deciding to launch Gateway 2000. Waitt worked at a computer store that ran a small, backroom operation selling computers over the phone. "People had these credit cards, and they could charge $3,000 on them. I didn't know such things existed," says Waitt. "I learned a lot about the industry and figured, 'If these guys can do it, I can do it.'"

Waitt is widely recognized for his success in intuitive decision making that has promoted strong growth. Gateway was the first computer firm to include color monitors, Windows software, Pentium chips, and CD-ROM drives as standard features of all systems. It was also the first computer firm to allow customers to custom-order and pay for new computers over the World Wide Web.[11]

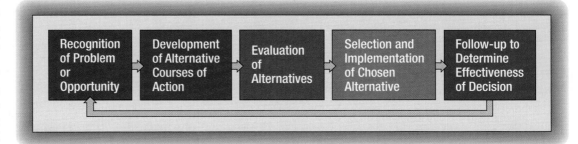

Figure 8.4 **Steps in the Decision-Making Process**

| Recognition of Problem or Opportunity | Development of Alternative Courses of Action | Evaluation of Alternatives | Selection and Implementation of Chosen Alternative | Follow-up to Determine Effectiveness of Decision |

www.gw2k.com

In a narrow sense, decision making involves choosing among two or more alternatives; the chosen alternative becomes the decision. In a broader sense, decision making involves a systematic, step-by-step process that helps managers make effective choices. This process begins when someone recognizes a problem or opportunity; it proceeds with developing different potential courses of action, evaluating the alternatives, selecting and implementing one of them, and assessing the outcome of the decision. The steps in the decision-making process are illustrated in Figure 8.4. This systematic approach can be applied to all decisions, with either programmed or nonprogrammed features.

Managers can follow the steps in this decision-making process as a rational way to reduce the risks associated with the outcomes of decisions. Making good decisions is never an easy task, however, because it involves taking risks that can influence a firm's success or failure. The Business Hall of Shame describes what can happen when management makes poor decisions.

MANAGERS AS LEADERS

The most visible component of a manager's responsibilities is **leadership,** directing or inspiring people to attain organizational goals. *Fortune* magazine's survey of the Best Companies to Work for in America has identified an important distinguishing charac-

teristic: a powerful, visionary leader. Leaders such as PeopleSoft's Dave Duffield, Mary Kay Ash of Mary Kay Cosmetics, Microsoft's Bill Gates, and Compaq Computer's Eckhard Pfeiffer are demanding managers, yet they inspire their employees to reach their full potential. These leaders not only inspire their subordinates to work hard; they also inspire others to model their own leadership behavior.

Because effective leadership is so important to organizational success, a great deal of related research has focused on the characteristics of a good leader. Great leaders do not all share the same qualities, but three traits are often mentioned: empathy (the ability to imagine oneself in another's position), self-awareness, and objectivity in dealing with others. Many great leaders share other traits, including courage, ability to inspire others, passion, commitment, flexibility, innovation, and willingness to experiment.

Leaders must challenge the status quo of how their organizations are managed and help others to face the adaptive challenges of today's workplace. Adaptive challenges are situations to which firms must adapt quickly to ensure their survival, such as when members of the marketing staff have difficulty working with operations personnel.[12]

Leadership involves the exercise of influence or power. This influence may derive from one or more sources. One source of power is the leader's position in the organization. For example, a manager of marketing has the authority to direct the activities of employees in that department. Another source of power comes from a leader's expertise and experience. A first-line supervisor with expert machinist skills will likely earn the respect of subordinates in the machining department. Some leaders derive power from their forceful personalities. Employees may admire a leader because they recognize an exceptionally kind and fair, humorous, energetic, or enthusiastic person.

Business Directory

leadership ability to direct or inspire people to attain organizational goals.

BUSINESS HALL OF FAME

Changing "Made in Germany" to "Made by Mercedes"

Mention the name *Mercedes*, and people immediately think of quality. German car maker Mercedes-Benz enjoys one of the most recognizable brand names in its industry. People associate the name with the precision engineering and craftsmanship of the German workers who build the cars for affluent buyers. Mercedes has always reinforced this image by emphasizing the origin of its cars with the proud label "Made in Ger-

many."' That label, however, doesn't apply to the company's new M-Class sport-utility vehicle, the company's first product made in a foreign plant.

To achieve their growth objectives, executives of Mercedes-Benz realized they had to broaden the firm's customer base. They decided to introduce new models that cost less than traditional ones in an effort to appeal to young people. One new model targeted at these young buyers is the M-Class sport-utility vehicle (SUV). With a base price of $35,000, the SUV is competitive with the Ford Explorer and Jeep Grand Cherokee.

To produce the relatively inexpensive vehicle, Mercedes managers had to decide where to make it. They decided to build their SUV outside Germany, where wages are among the highest in the world. German auto workers earn an average of $35.00 an hour, including benefits, compared to $21.50 in the United States and $15.50 in Italy. After considering 150 sites in 30 different U.S. states, Mercedes chose the small, rural town of Vance, Alabama to build its new plant and produce its new vehicle. "It was once sacrosanct to talk about our cars being 'Made in Germany,'" says

Herb Kelleher gains leadership power through his position as co-founder and chief executive officer of Southwest Airlines. But Kelleher's influence in motivating employees to outperform those at rival airlines comes from his dynamic personality, boundless energy, love of fun, and sincere concern for his employees. "My parents instilled in me the idea that everybody should be treated with dignity and respect," says Kelleher, "and that titles, traditions, status, and class didn't matter."

Kelleher leads by example, modeling the behavior that does matter—treating people nicely, having fun, and working hard. He's not above pitching in to help serve snacks to passengers and load luggage. Kelleher's personality inspires employees to follow his example. Southwest employees can unload and reload a plane in 20 minutes, while those at other airlines take almost an hour. "We've got exactly the same equipment," says Kelleher. "The difference is, when a plane pulls into a gate, our people run to meet it."[13]

www.iflyswa.com

The way in which a leader uses power to lead others determines his or her *leadership style*. Researchers have identified a continuum of leadership styles based on the amount of employee participation allowed or invited. At one end of the continuum, **autocratic leadership** is centered on the boss. Autocratic leaders make decisions on

their own without consulting employees. They reach decisions, communicate them to subordinates, and expect prompt implementation of instructions. An autocratic sales manager might assign quotas for individual salespeople.

Democratic leadership involves subordinates in making decisions. Located in the middle of the continuum, this leadership style centers on employees' contributions. Democratic leaders delegate assignments, ask employees for suggestions, and encourage participation. A democratic sales manager might allow sales personnel to participate in setting their sales quotas.

The most democratic style, at the other end of the continuum from autocratic leadership, is **free-rein leadership.** Free-rein leaders believe in minimal supervision and leave most decisions to their subordinates.

An important trend that has developed in business during the past decade is the concept of **empowerment,** a practice in which managers lead employees by sharing power, responsibility, and decision making with them. Shared leadership is the style of Guilio Mazzalupi, president and CEO of Sweden-based Atlas Copco AB. A global manufacturer of compressors, electric and pneumatic tools, and construction and mining equipment, Atlas Copco practices universal empowerment. Mazzalupi believes that each employee is "the center of the organization," whether the employee is a production worker or a manager. "We must get people to work together because it is people who solve problems, not managers," he says. "Managers have to create an environment so that people are in the best position to solve problems."

Jurgen E. Schrempp, chief executive of Mercedes' parent company Daimler Benz. "We have to change that to 'Made by Mercedes,' and never mind where they are assembled."

Although Mercedes managers made a concession in deciding where to produce their SUVs, they made no compromise in how they would complete this work. "The priority is quality, quality, quality," says Schrempp. Mercedes managers had to decide how to hire and train American factory workers to make cars that met the company's high quality standards, fearing that producing a poor-quality vehicle could tarnish the company's world-class reputation. Rather than trying to find people with automaking experi-

ence, they established hiring decision criteria on the basis of ability to work as a team member, to follow directions, and to understand the importance of continuous improvement and quality.

Of the 45,000 people who applied for the jobs, Mercedes hiring managers selected 1,500 workers. They decided that the best way to train American workers was giving them first-hand experience. Many new hires traveled to Germany for training that lasted from 1 month to 6 months. They worked side-by-side with German employees to learn the exacting way Mercedes builds its cars. After spending a month in Germany, one American worker said, "We are determined to build a quality vehicle."

QUESTIONS FOR CRITICAL THINKING

1. **Do you think Mercedes executives took a big gamble in relying on American workers to produce the company's new market entry?**

2. **Explain why the company's decisions to enter the sport-utility market and to build a foreign plant are nonprogrammed decisions.**

Sources: "Mercedes-Benz USA Opens New Vehicle Preparation Center in Carson, California," PR Newswire, April 19, 1999; David Woodruff, "Hot Wheels," *Business Week*, September 1997, pp. 56–57; Justin Martin, "Mercedes: Made in Alabama," *Fortune*, July 7, 1997, pp. 150–158; and Bill Vlasic, "In Alabama, the Soul of a New Mercedes?" *Business Week*, March 31, 1997, pp. 70–71.

Mazzalupi contends that managers will play different roles as business moves into the next century than they now practice. "Managers will have to be less concerned with supervision and control and be more concerned with development [of the business]," he says. "Our managers must perform the leadership role, be upfront, and be the leaders of the process and pull the 21,000 employees in the same direction." The empowering leader's role, according to Mazzalupi, is to support people, be fair, and provide the right example so all employees keep focused on the firm's customers. "The most important thing we all have to remember each day is that whatever we do must be to meet a customer need."[14]

Mazzalupi's view of empowerment is embraced by leaders of many companies including General Electric, Harley-Davidson, Ford, Chrysler, and Intel.

Chapter 10 discusses the many different ways in which organizations are empowering employees.

Southwest Airline employees love this man. Whether dressed up as Elvis or a chicken, Herb Kelleher energizes his troops through the power of his fun-loving and hard-working personality.

Which Leadership Style Is the Best One?

The most appropriate leadership style depends on the function of the leader, the subordinates, and the situation. Some leaders cannot work comfortably with high participation of subordinates in decision making. Some employees lack the ability or the desire to assume responsibility. Furthermore, the specific situation helps to determine the most effective style of interactions. Sometimes managers must handle problems that require immediate solutions without consulting employees. In different situations with less acute time pressure, participative decision making may work better for the same people.

BUSINESS HALL OF SHAME

From Admired to Acquired: The Five-Year Plan at Rubbermaid

Rubbermaid was among the top ten of *Fortune's* Most Admired companies, not just for a year, but for a decade. Making plastic housewares and commercial products, Rubbermaid was the picture of how to manage a company. But a few poor decisions and five years later, Rubbermaid was quietly acquired by Newell Company. What went wrong? CEO Wolfgang R. Schmidt said, "We hit a bump." But others, including former Rubbermaid managers, thought the problem went deeper.

The trouble started when the cost for Rubbermaid's raw material began to rise. Resin is used in almost all of the company's 5,000 products, and in 1994 the cost of resin shot up, eventually doubling. Rubbermaid's managers

had to decide to pass on the price hike to customers or lower their financial targets and absorb more of the cost. They decided to pass the price increase along. What they didn't see was how their decision would reveal the weaknesses in other decisions and the entire company.

When it passed along ballooning costs to customers, Rubbermaid ran into trouble quickly. Its salespeople had been trained in gentler times and weren't experienced in persuading buyers to accept sudden price jumps on familiar products. Important retailers got angry. They figured they couldn't pass higher prices on to consumers, so they refused to restock Rubbermaid goods and gave the shelf space to Rubbermaid's competitors. Of course, Rubbermaid's competitors were in the same cost crunch as Rubbermaid, but they held back on raising prices, which only convinced re-

tailers that Rubbermaid was being unreasonable.

The pricing decision sparked an outright feud with Wal-Mart, Rubbermaid's biggest customer. Already angered over chronically late deliveries, Wal-Mart's relations with Rubbermaid turned icy. In fact, Rubbermaid's managers may have overlooked an important change in customer relations. A decade before, retailers like Wal-Mart depended on Rubbermaid's brand name to get customers into their stores. But the balance of power had shifted from product makers to retailers: Wal-Mart could survive without Rubbermaid, but Rubbermaid needed Wal-Mart. Says one Rubbermaid executive, "We should have been helping customers increase their sales rather than fighting with them so long over prices."

To recover from the pricing bump, Rubbermaid had to make strong decisions in other areas. Yet, it was still slow to adjust to changes in its competition. Once considered junk peddlers, competing housewares makers had greatly improved over the years. In

---

Democratic leaders often ask for suggestions and advice from their employees but make the final decisions themselves. A manager who prefers the free-rein leadership style may be forced by circumstances to make a particular decision in an autocratic manner. For example, a manager may involve employees in interviewing and hiring decisions but take complete responsibility for firing any employee.

After years of research intended to determine the best types of leaders, experts agree that they cannot identify any single best style of leadership. Rather, they contend that the most effective style depends on the leader's base of power, the difficulty of the tasks involved, and the characteristics of the employees. Both extremely easy and extremely difficult situations are best-suited to leaders who emphasize the accomplishment of assigned tasks. Moderately difficult situations are best-suited to leaders who emphasize participation and good working relationships with subordinates.

CORPORATE CULTURE

The best leadership style to adopt often depends on the organization's **corporate culture,** its system of principles,

beliefs, and values. Managerial philosophies, communications networks, and workplace environments and practices all influence corporate culture.

The culture at GSD&M, an advertising agency, emphasizes a total focus on clients. To reinforce that culture, the agency has created "war rooms" painted in clients' company colors. The walls in a war room are covered with information about the client—earnings reports, stock prices, sales figures, competitive analyses, and press coverage. Employees spend time in their own offices, but they meet in the war rooms to conduct conference calls with clients, brainstorm ideas, and plan marketing campaigns. Roy Spence, the agency's president, says these special rooms help employees to keep their client-centered focus. "They remind us to keep our eye on the prize," says Spence, the prize being the client's success. Clients like the war rooms, too, because they show that employees working on their accounts are completely focused on them.[15]

A corporate culture is typically shaped by the leaders who founded and developed the company and by those who have succeeded them. One generation of employees passes on a corporate culture to newer employees. Sometimes, this transfer is part of formal training. New managers who attend sessions at McDonald's Hamburger Uni-

fact, Sterilite had raised its quality so much (and raised its prices so little) that Wal-Mart voted the company its most valued supplier. Consumers started noticing competitor's products early in the 1990s: As one consumer put it, "Rubbermaid's products are excellent but overpriced." Said another, "Five years ago, you were stuck with Rubbermaid, but now Sterilite is a good product." Even so, Rubbermaid decided to keep its premium pricing.

At the same time, operating expenses were high, yet Rubbermaid took its time deciding to update machinery, trim redundant jobs, and insure prompt delivery of goods. The company finally decided on a three-year program to save $335 million. Unfortunately, instead of saving that money to compensate for climbing resin prices, it decided to use those savings to offset startup costs in Europe.

To balance the loss of retailers, the growth of competitors, and the rising cost of resin, Rubbermaid decided to rely on international sales. But especially in Europe, its start was awkward.

The company had been selling abroad for more than 30 years, but its efforts were minimal. Building a global presence would take far longer than the five years originally specified.

Perhaps at the root of all its other problems was Rubbermaid's culture of growth. In the 1950s, the company vowed to double in size every six years. That meant setting yearly financial targets of 15 percent growth in revenues and profits. The culture succeeded for many years, but when the company began feeling pressures from several fronts, Rubbermaid stubbornly decided to stick with those stringent goals. Straining to feed its greed for growth proved most difficult. The company pushed its managers, only to have them quit or be forced out because they couldn't meet goals. Ultimately, the company fell short. And by the time Newell acquired it, Rubbermaid's net debt was $500 million.

Rubbermaid had excelled in product quality, creativity, and merchandizing. But management made some poor decisions about growth, customer relations, competition, operations, and international sales. As a result, Rubbermaid went from admired to acquired in five short years.

QUESTIONS FOR CRITICAL THINKING

1. Why didn't the weaknesses in Rubbermaid's culture, operations, and other areas show up before the increase in resin prices? Explain.

2. How will the increase in Net shopping affect the balance of power between manufacturers and retailers? Will the retailers keep the advantage? Or will manufacturers find enough buyers on the Web? Explain.

Sources: Jonathan R. Laing, "Riding into the Sunset," *Barron's*, February 15, 1999, accessed at www.wsj.com/archives; "Rubbermaid Reorganizes," *CNN Financial News*, January 21, 1998, accessed at www.cnnfn.com; and Lee Smith, "Rubbermaid Goes Thump," *Fortune*, October 2, 1995, accessed at www.pathfinder.com/fortune.

versity may learn skills in management, but they also acquire the basics of the organization's corporate culture. Employees can absorb corporate culture through informal contacts, as well as by talking with other workers and through their experiences on the job.

Managers use symbols, rituals, and ceremonies to reinforce corporate culture. Experimentation and inventiveness are part of the culture of AGI Inc., a firm that designs and prints unique packaging for cosmetics, compact discs, and multimedia software. Richard Block, AGI's CEO, performs a ritual at monthly companywide meetings. To encourage out-of-the-box thinking and open debate, Block gives prizes to employees who ask him the toughest questions and stands on his head while he answers them.[16]

Corporate culture can have a big impact on the success of an organization. Amy Miller, president of Amy's Ice Creams, uses the firm's corporate culture as a tool of competitive strategy. People who apply for jobs at her chain of 17 stores encounter the culture during the hiring process. Rather than filling out application forms, applicants receive white paper bags. Those who turn the bags into creative art are most likely to be hired. An applicant who produces "something unusual from a white paper bag tends to be an amusing person who would fit in with our environment," says Miller.

Amy Miller expects employees to create fun for customers. Like her competitors, she offers premium ice cream and good service. But her strategy seeks to differentiate her business from others by providing entertainment. Inventive employees wear costumes and bring props to work. They juggle ice cream scoops, dance on the freezer counter, and give free ice cream to customers who will sing or dance or recite poetry. Miller's culture of fun keeps customers coming back and keeps her company growing by 20 percent each year.[17]

In an organization with a strong culture, everyone knows and supports the same objectives. A company with a weak or constantly shifting culture lacks any clear sense

Business Directory

corporate culture organization's system of values, principles, and beliefs.

A culture of creativity differentiates Amy's Ice Creams shops from competitors. Amy hires only inventive people like these employees, who can create fun for customers.

of purpose. To achieve its goals, a business must also provide a framework that defines how employees should accomplish their tasks. This framework is the organization structure. The management function of organizing provides the framework within which employees perform their tasks.

STRUCTURE IN ORGANIZATIONS

The management function of **organizing** is the process of blending human and material resources through a formal structure of tasks and authority. It involves arranging work, dividing tasks among employees, and coordinating them to ensure implementation of plans and accomplishment of objectives. The result of the organizing process is an **organization,** which can be defined as a structured grouping of people working together to achieve common objectives. An organization features three key elements: human interaction, goal-directed activities, and structure. The organizing process should result in an overall structure that permits interactions among individuals and departments needed to achieve company goals.

The steps involved in the organizing process are shown in Figure 8.5. Managers must first determine the specific activities needed to implement plans and achieve goals. Next, they group these work activities into a logical structure. Then they assign work to specific employees and give the employees the resources they need to complete it. Managers must coordinate the work of different groups and employees within the business. Finally, they must evaluate the results of the organizing process to ensure effective and efficient progress toward planned goals. Evaluation often results in changes to the way work is organized.

Many factors influence the results of organizing. The list includes a firm's goals and competitive strategy, the type of goods or services it offers, the way it uses technology to accomplish work, and its size. Small firms typically create very simple structures. For example, the owner of a dry-cleaning business generally is the top manager, who hires several employees to process orders, launder the clothing, and make deliveries. The owner handles the functions of purchasing supplies such as detergents and hangers, hiring and training employees and coordinating their work, preparing advertisements for the local newspaper, and keeping books.

As a company grows, its structure increases in complexity. With increased size comes specialization and growing numbers of employees. A small firm may need only one salesperson. A larger firm may employ many salespeople along with a sales manager to direct and coordinate their work. While the owner of a small firm may serve as the bookkeeper, a larger firm may need to organize an accounting department and hire employees to work as cost clerks, payroll clerks, and accountants.

The organizing process should result in a well-defined structure so that employees know what expectations their jobs involve, to whom they report, and how their work contributes to the company's effort to meet its goals. To help employees understand how their work fits within the overall operation of the firm, managers prepare an **organization chart,** which is a

Business Directory

organizing management function of blending human and material resources through a formal structure of tasks and authority

organization structured grouping of people working together to achieve common goals

departmentalization process of dividing work activities into units within the organization.

visual representation of a firm's structure that illustrates job positions and functions. Figure 8.6 illustrates a sample organization chart. Each box in the chart shows the name of the person who holds the position. An organization chart depicts the division of a firm into departments that meet organizational needs.

Departmentalization

Departmentalization is the process of dividing work activities into units within the organization. This arrangement lets employees specialize in certain jobs in order to promote efficient performance. A marketing department may be headed by a marketing vice president, who directs the work of salespeople, marketing researchers, and advertising and public relations personnel. A human resources manager may head a department made up of people with special skills in the areas of recruiting and hiring, employee benefits administration, and labor relations. The five major forms of departmentalization subdivide work by product, geographic area, customer, function, and process.

Product Departmentalization This form organizes work units based on the goods and services a company offers. For example, the organization structure of Sony Corp. spans ten separate companies that define its different product groups such as semiconductors, home entertainment, recording media, broadcasting, and image and sound communications products.

Geographic Departmentalization This form organizes units by geographic region within a country or, for a multinational firm, by region throughout the world. Retailers like Dillard's are organized by divisions that serve different parts of the country. Railroads and gas and oil distributors also favor geographic departmentalization.

Customer Departmentalization A firm that offers a variety of goods and services targeted to different types of customers might structure itself based on customer depart-

mentalization. The Boeing Company, for example, has defined one operating unit that builds aircraft for commercial customers such as United Airlines and another that builds military airplanes, helicopters, and missile and space systems for government customers.

Functional Departmentalization Some firms organize work units according to business functions such as finance, marketing, human resources, and production. An advertising agency, for example, may create departments for artists, copywriters, media buyers, and marketing researchers.

Process Departmentalization Some goods and services require multiple work processes to complete their production. A manufacturer may set up separate departments for cutting material, heat-treating it, forming it into its final shape, and painting it.

As Figure 8.7 illustrates, a single company may implement several different departmentalization schemes. The departments initially are organized by functions, then subdivided by geographic areas, which are further organized according to customer types. In deciding on a form of departmentalization, managers take into account the type of good or service they produce, the size of their company, their customer base, and where their customers are located.

As organizations grow and change, they frequently restructure their operations. When software maker Intuit was a small, entrepreneurial firm with one product, it was organized by functional departments. All employees worked at one location in San Francisco, and it was easy to get people from different departments to work together. Top managers participated in product development and marketing decisions. When Intuit expanded its product line, acquired other companies, and opened facilities throughout the United States and in several international locations, however, functional departmentalization became a liability, because it slowed decision making. To enhance responsiveness to customer needs, Intuit restructured, creating separate business units that focused on individual products or markets. Each business unit has its own general manager and customer-focused mission. The unit's general managers and

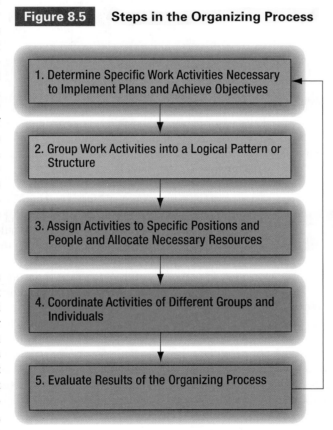

Figure 8.5 **Steps in the Organizing Process**

1. Determine Specific Work Activities Necessary to Implement Plans and Achieve Objectives

2. Group Work Activities into a Logical Pattern or Structure

3. Assign Activities to Specific Positions and People and Allocate Necessary Resources

4. Coordinate Activities of Different Groups and Individuals

5. Evaluate Results of the Organizing Process

| Figure 8.6 | **A Sample Organization Chart** |

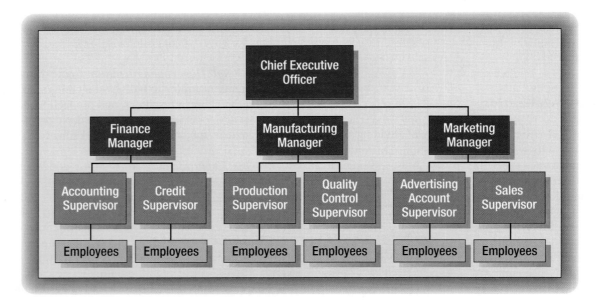

product teams enjoy complete decision-making responsibility for everything from product features to advertising plans.[18]

Delegating Work Assignments

After grouping activities into departments, managers assign this work to employees. The act of assigning activities to employees is called **delegation,** a concept introduced briefly in the time management section. Managers delegate work in order to free their own time for planning and decision making. Subordinates to whom managers assign tasks thus receive responsibility, or obligations to perform those tasks. Along with responsibilities, employees also receive authority, or the power to make decisions and to act on them so they can carry out their responsibilities. Delegation of responsibility and authority makes employees accountable to their supervisor or manager. *Accountability* means that employees are responsible for the results of the ways in which they perform their assignments; they must accept the consequences of their actions.

Authority and responsibility tend to move downward in organizations, as managers and supervisors delegate work to subordinates. However, accountability moves upward, as managers assume final accountability for performance by the employees they manage. Therefore,

managers carefully delegate tasks to the best-qualified people.

Span of Management The **span of management,** or *span of control,* is the number of subordinates a manager supervises. A top manager usually works within a narrow span of management, directing the work of the firm's top executives. First-line supervisors have wider spans of management, monitoring the work of many employees. The span of management varies considerably depending on many factors, including the type of work performed and employees' training. In recent years, a growing trend has brought ever wider spans of control, as companies have reduced their layers of management to flatten their organization structures, in the process increasing the decision-making responsibility they give to employees.

Information technology can also broaden the span of management. Firms like Owens-Corning, the building supplies manufacturer, have equipped their salespeople with laptop computers that provide instant access to product and customer information. This automation supports wide spans of control by regional managers, because the information allows salespeople to make decisions on their own.

Centralization and Decentralization How widely should managers disperse decision-making authority throughout an organization? A company that emphasizes **centralization** retains decision making at the top of the management hierarchy. A company that emphasizes **decentralization** locates decision making at lower levels. A trend toward decentralization has pushed decision making down to operating employees in many cases. Firms that have decentralized believe that the change can enhance their flexibility and responsiveness in serving customers.

TYPES OF ORGANIZATION STRUCTURES

Organizations can be classified under four main types according to the nature of their internal authority relationships. The four primary types are line, line-and-staff, committee, and matrix structures. These terms do not specify mutually exclusive categories, though. In fact, most contemporary organizations combine elements of one or more of these structures.

Line Organizations

A **line organization,** the oldest and simplest organizational structure, establishes a direct flow of authority from the chief executive to subordinates. The line organization defines a simple, clear **chain of command**—the set of relationships that indicates who gives direction to whom and who reports to whom. This arrangement helps to prevent buck-passing. Decisions can be made quickly because the manager has authority to control subordinates' actions.

A line organization brings an obvious defect, though. Each manager must accept complete responsibility for a number of activities and cannot possibly be an expert in all of them. This defect is apparent in medium-sized and large firms, where the pure line structure fails to take advantage of the specialized skills that are so vital to modern business. Managers become overburdened with administrative details and paperwork, leaving them little time for planning.

Thus, the line organization is an ineffective model in any but the smallest organizations. Hair salons, "mom-

and-pop" grocery stores, and small law firms can operate effectively with simple line structures. Ford, General Electric, and Boeing cannot.

Line-and-Staff Organizations

A **line-and-staff organization** combines the direct flow of authority of a line organization with staff departments that serve, advise, and support the line departments. Line de-

Figure 8.7 **Different Forms of Departmentalization within One Company**

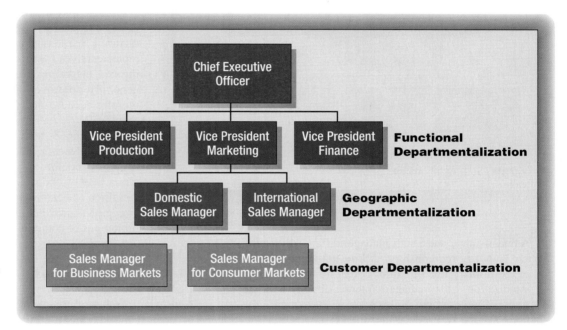

partments participate directly in decisions that affect the core operations of the organization. Staff departments lend specialized technical support. Examples of staff departments include labor relations, legal counsel, research and development, accounting, taxes, and information technology.

Figure 8.8 illustrates a line-and-staff organization. Accounting, engineering, and human resources are staff departments that support the line authority extending from the plant manager to the production manager and supervisors.

Business Directory

delegation act of assigning work activities to subordinates.

chain of command set of relationships that indicates who directs whose activities and who reports to whom.

| Figure 8.8 | **The Line-and-Staff Organization** |

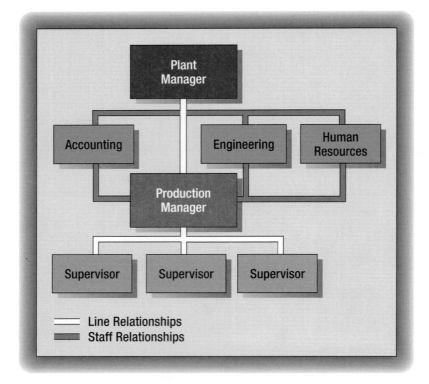

A line manager and a staff manager differ significantly in their authority relationships. A **line manager** forms a part of the primary line of authority that flows throughout the organization. Line managers interact directly with the functions of production, financing, or marketing—the functions needed to produce and market goods and services. A **staff manager** provides information, advice, or technical assistance to aid line managers. Staff managers do not have authority to give orders outside their own departments or to compel line managers to take action.

The line-and-staff organization is common in mid-sized and large organizations. It is an effective structure because it combines the line organization's capabilities for rapid decision making and direct communication with the expert knowledge of staff specialists.

Committee Organizations

A **committee organization** is a structure that places authority and responsibility jointly in the hands of a group of individuals rather than a single manager. This model typically appears as part of a regular line-and-staff structure. Examples of the committee structure emerge throughout organizations. PeopleSoft is managed by an operating committee of top executives. Some firms implement the concept of an office of the CEO, in which two or more executives share the duties of the chief executive officer, rather than designating a single individual for this role. At Rubbermaid, the Corporate Executive Committee consists of eight top management positions, including the chief executive officer, chief financial officer, chief operating officer, and the senior vice presidents of operations, information services, human resources, and business development and investor relations together with a general counsel.

Committees also work in other areas such as new-product development. A new-product committee may include managers from such areas as accounting, engineering, finance, manufacturing, marketing, and research. By including representatives from all areas involved in creating and marketing products, such a committee generally improves planning and employee morale, because decisions reflect diverse perspectives.

Committees tend to act slowly and conservatively, however, and they often make decisions by compromising conflicting interests rather than by choosing the best alternative. The definition of a camel as "a racehorse designed by committee" provides an apt description of some limitations of committee decisions.

Matrix Organizations

A growing number of organizations are using the **matrix, or project management, structure.** This structure links employees from different parts of the organization to work together on specific projects. Like the committee structure, the matrix structure typically defines a subform within the line-and-staff structure.

Figure 8.9 diagrams a matrix structure. For a specific project, a project manager assembles a group of employees from different functional areas. The employees retain their ties to the line-and-staff structure, as shown in the vertical white lines. As the horizontal gold lines indicate, however, employees are also members of project teams. Upon completion of a project, employees return to their "regular" jobs.

In the matrix structure, each employee reports to two managers—one line manager and one project manager. Employees who are selected to work on a special project, such as development of a new product, receive instructions from the project manager (horizontal authority), but they continue as employees in their permanent functional departments (vertical authority). The term *matrix* comes from the intersecting grid of horizontal and vertical lines of authority.

Figure 8.9 **The Matrix Organization**

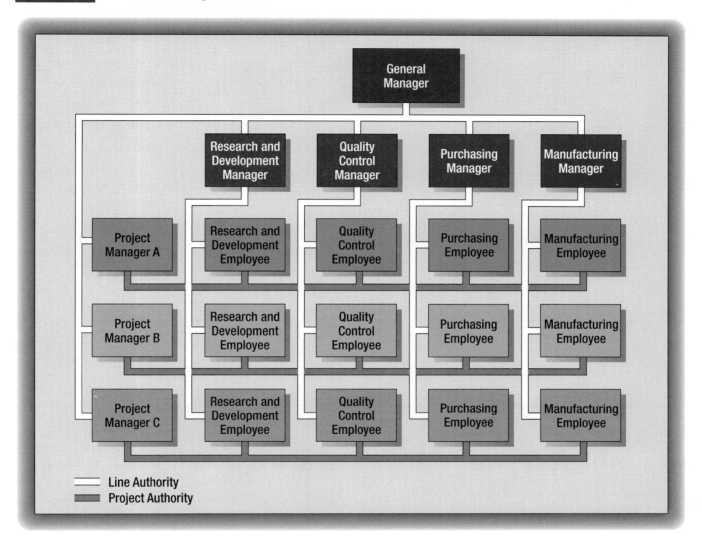

The matrix structure has become a popular organizational design widely used by high-technology and multinational firms as well as hospitals, consulting firms, and aerospace firms. Dow Chemical, Chase Manhattan Bank, Procter & Gamble, and the Harvard Business School have all established matrix structures. The National Aeronautics and Space Administration used the matrix structure for its Mercury and Apollo space missions.

The major benefits of the matrix structure come from its flexibility in adapting quickly to rapid changes in the environment and its capability for focusing resources on major problems or products. It also provides an outlet for employees' creativity and initiative, giving them opportunities that their functional jobs may deny them. However, it challenges the project manager to integrate the skills of specialists from many departments into a coordinated team.

For another disadvantage, employees may be confused and frustrated in reporting to two bosses.

Comparing the Four Types of Structure

Table 8.1 summarizes the advantages and disadvantages of each structure. Although most large companies are organized according to line-and-staff structures, the line organization is usually the best form for a small business. The committee form appears in limited applications in major corporations. The matrix approach is increasingly common in both medium-sized firms and large, multiproduct firms that need to focus diverse organizational resources on specific problems or projects.

Table 8.1	Comparing the Four Organizational Structures	
Form of Organization	**Advantages**	**Disadvantages**
Line	Simple and easy for both managers and subordinates to understand Clear delegation of authority and responsibility for each area	No specialization Overburdens top executives with administrative details
Line-and-staff	Specialists to advise top managers Employees reporting to one superior	Conflict between line and staff departments without clear relationships Staff managers limited to making recommendations to line managers
Committee	Combines judgment of several executives in diverse areas Improves morale through participation in decision making	Slow decisions Compromises rather than choices of the best alternatives
Matrix	Flexibility Strong focus on specific problems or unique technical issues Allows innovation without disrupting regular organization structure	Potential problems from accountability to more than one boss Potential difficulty in developing a cohesive team from diverse individuals recruited from various departments Potential for conflict between project managers and other department managers

SUMMARY OF LEARNING GOALS

1. Define management and describe the management pyramid.

Management is the process of achieving organizational objectives through people and other resources. The management pyramid depicts the hierarchical levels of management in organizations. At the highest level, top managers provide overall direction for company activities. Middle managers implement the strategies of top managers and direct the activities of supervisors. At the lowest level of the management hierarchy, supervisors, or first-line managers, interact directly with workers.

2. Explain the three types of skills necessary for managerial success.

The three basic managerial skills are technical, human, and conceptual skills. Technical skills, which are most important for first-line managers, involve capabilities to understand and use the techniques, tools, and knowledge of a specific discipline or department. All levels of managers need human skills, which involve working effectively with and through people. Conceptual skills are most important for top managers. They involve the capability to see the "big picture" of the organization as a whole and how each part contributes to its overall functioning.

3. Discuss ways managers can allocate their time efficiently and effectively.

Managers can learn to manage their time wisely by setting goals and priorities, learning to delegate work, focusing on important work, grouping activities together, and learning how to handle interruptions.

4. Distinguish between programmed and nonprogrammed decisions.

A programmed decision applies a company rule or policy to solve a frequently occurring problem. A nonprogrammed decision forms a response to a complex and unique problem with important consequences for the organization.

5. List the steps involved in the decision-making process.

The five-step approach to decision making includes recognizing a problem or opportunity, developing alternative courses of action, evaluating the alternatives, selecting and implementing an alternative, and following up the decision to determine its effectiveness.

6. Define leadership and identify different leadership styles.

Leadership is the act of motivating others or causing them to perform activities designed to achieve specific objectives. The basic styles are autocratic, democratic, and free-rein leadership. The best leadership style depends on three elements: the leader, the followers, and the situation. In contemporary business, leaders tend increasingly to involve employees in making decisions about their work.

7. Discuss the role of leaders in shaping an organization's culture.

Corporate culture refers to an organization's values, beliefs, and principles. It is typically shaped by a firm's founder and perpetuated through formal programs such as training, rituals, and ceremonies, as well as through informal discussions among employees. Corporate culture can powerfully influence a firm's success by giving it a competitive advantage.

8. Discuss the need for organizational structure and list the steps in the organizing process.

Organizations need structures through which to implement plans and accomplish objectives. The organizing process begins by determining the work to be done, then it groups those activities into a logical structure, assigns work to specific employees, and allocates the resources they need to accomplish their work. Managers must coordinate the work of different groups and evaluate the results of the organizing process.

9. Define departmentalization and identify five ways firms subdivide work activities.

Departmentalization is the subdivision of work activities into units within the organization. Firms subdivide work based on products, geographic locations, customers, functions, and processes.

10. Describe the different types of organizational structures.

Most firms implement one or more of four structures: line, line-and-staff, committee, and matrix structures. Each model has advantages and disadvantages.

TEN BUSINESS TERMS YOU NEED TO KNOW

management	organizing
time management	organization
decision making	departmentalization
leadership	delegation
corporate culture	chain of command

Other Important Business Terms

top management	empowerment
glass ceiling	organization chart
middle management	span of management
supervisory management	centralization
technical skills	decentralization
human skills	line organization
conceptual skills	line-and-staff organization
programmed decision	line manager
nonprogrammed decision	staff manager
autocratic leadership	committee organization
democratic leadership	matrix structure
free-rein leadership	

REVIEW QUESTIONS

1. Do you agree or disagree with this statement: "Management principles are universal"? Explain your answer.
2. What is the management pyramid? Why do you think businesspeople use a pyramid structure to portray the levels of management?
3. What types of skills must managers possess? Which type of skill is most important at each management level?
4. What are some of the techniques managers can apply to make the best use of their time?
5. Which is easier to make, a programmed or a nonprogrammed decision? How can managers reduce the risk of decision making?
6. Which of the three leadership styles would involve employees the most and the least in decision making? Can you identify a single, best leadership style? Why or why not?
7. What is a corporate culture? What actions of leaders contribute to creation of a corporate culture?
8. How do organizations subdivide work activities?
9. What are the four types of organization structures? Give an advantage and disadvantage of each.
10. What special skills does a manager need when he or she accepts an overseas assignment?

QUESTIONS FOR CRITICAL THINKING

1. Suppose that you are applying for a job at Amy's Ice Creams. Take a lunch-box-sized bag and produce the most creative application you can. Remember that the bag takes the place of the

application form, so include information about yourself that will land the job.

2. A *Fortune* magazine article about leadership said, "Great business leaders ought to reveal all the traits of a great lover—passion, commitment, ferocity. Nothing less will do." Do you think the analogy is a good one? Based on your work experiences and participation in school and community groups, what traits do you think are most important for a leader? What type of leader motivates you to do your best work?

3. PeopleSoft's CEO Dave Duffield can't stand internal squabbling, politicking, and backbiting among employees; he has fired employees for such behavior. Do you think that firing a employee for that reason is a good decision even though the employee is an excellent worker?

4. Napoleon always waited 6 months to reply to letters, because he believed that most of the problems raised in the correspondence would be either solved or forgotten in that time. Would Napoleon's approach to time management work in the business world?

5. When Mercedes-Benz opened its Alabama plant, it brought German managers and trainers to manage and monitor the work of American employees. Cultural differences emerged. The Germans criticized the Americans as lax, talkative, and superficial people who only wanted positive feedback. The CEO of the plant said that Americans always wanted to hear that they were doing a good job. The Americans said that the Germans were very blunt, didn't beat around the bush, and were perfectionists. They might phrase corrective feedback as, "That looks really bad, and you're going to redo it." How should the firm try to resolve these cultural differences?

Experiential Exercise

Directions: Rate each of the following questions according to this scale:
5 I always am like this.
4 I often am like this.
3 I sometimes am like this.
2 I rarely am like this.
1 I never am like this.

___ **1.** When I have a number of tasks or homework to do, I set priorities and organize the work around the deadlines. C

___ **2.** Most people would describe me as a good listener. H

___ **3.** When I am deciding on a particular course of action for myself (such as hobbies to pursue, languages to study, which job to take, special projects to be involved in), I typically consider the long-term (three years or more) implications of what I would choose to do. C

___ **4.** I prefer technical or quantitative courses rather than those involving literature, psychology, or sociology. T

___ **5.** When I have a serious disagreement with someone, I hang in there and talk it out until it is completely resolved. H.

___ **6.** When I have a project or assignment, I really get into the details rather than the "big picture" issues.* C

___ **7.** I would rather sit in front of my computer than spend a lot of time with people. T

___ **8.** I try to include others in activities or when there are discussions. H

___ **9.** When I take a course, I relate what I am learning to other courses I have taken or concepts I have learned elsewhere. C

___ **10.** When somebody makes a mistake, I want to correct the person and let her or him know the proper answer or approach.* H

___ **11.** I think it is better to be efficient with my time when talking with someone, rather than worry about the other person's needs, so that I can get on with my real work. T

___ **12.** I know my long-term vision for career, family, and other activities and have thought it over carefully. C

___ **13.** When solving problems, I would much rather analyze some data or statistics than meet with a group of people. T

___ **14.** When I am working on a group project and someone doesn't pull a full share of the load, I am more likely to complain to my friends rather than confront the slacker.* H

___ **15.** Talking about ideas or concepts can get me really enthused and excited. C

___ **16.** The type of management course for which this book is used is really a waste of time. T

___ **17.** I think it is better to be polite and not to hurt people's feelings.* H

___ **18.** Data or things interest me more than people. T

Scoring Key: Add the total points for the following sections. Note that starred(*) items are reverse scored:

1 I always am like this.
2 I often am like this.
3 I sometimes am like this.
4 I rarely am like this.
5 I never am like this.

1, 3, 6, 9, 12, 15   Conceptual skills total score _____
2, 5, 8, 10, 14, 17   Human skills total score _____
4, 7, 11, 13, 16, 18   Technical skills total score _____

The above skills are three abilities needed to be a good manager. Ideally, a manager should be strong (though not necessarily equal) in all three. Anyone noticeably weaker in any of the skills should take courses and read to build up that skill.

*reverse scoring item

Source: Dorothy Marcic, "Management Attitude Questionnaire," in Richard L. Daft, *Management,* fourth edition (Fort Worth: Dryden, 1997), p. 32.

Nothing but Net

1. **PDF Documents**. Many Web sites provide documents in Adobe's Acrobat (PDF) format. To view PDF documents, you must (1) have a copy of the Acrobat Reader program on your computer system and (2) use the Acrobat Reader program to open, view, and print the PDF file. Since you will need the Acrobat Reader to complete the next exercise, download a copy of the program at

   www.adobe.com/prodindex/acrobat/readstep.html

2. **Glass Ceiling.** To learn more about the glass ceiling and to use the Acrobat Reader you downloaded in the preceding exercise, visit

   www.ilr.cornell.edu/library/e_archive/glassceiling/

   Select the hyperlink to the Glass Ceiling Commission's final report and use your Acrobat Reader to skim the document, taking particular note of the "Recommendations" section.

3. **Leadership.** Test your leadership style with a questionnaire available at

   www.leaderx.com/

   After you complete the assessment, submit your responses. You will receive a customized report on your leadership style.

Note: Internet Web addresses change frequently. If you do not find the exact sites listed, you may need to access the organization's or company's home page and search from there.

HOLIGAN GROUP—
BUILDING A SOLID FOUNDATION

Founded in 1982 and based in Dallas, Texas, Holigan Companies have significant real estate operations. The family-owned company is managed by Chairman Harold Holigan and his son Michael, the president. The company has grown to be one of the largest home-building companies—operating in 5 states and across 23 communities—by bringing to the market affordable, comfortable, and efficient homes. The company's philosophy, Michael Hogan says, is "we help buyers understand the steps in buying a house and how easy it is to get into a Holigan home. We also allow customers a lot of flexibility with floor plans and input into how they want their home designed, at no additional expense." Michael has succeeded in being an individual that uses a hands-on approach and creativity in business.

Safety and energy efficiency are critically important at Holigan. The company steps ahead of its competitors by offering homes that have more efficient and cost-saving features to save consumers money in the long run. When building the homes, the company uses 2×6 studs and R-19 and R-38 insulation for sturdiness and heat savings, as well as extra measures that protect the houses during bad weather.

The Holigans have created a strong reputation for their company, which has allowed them to build brand recognition in the marketplace. Their quality and commitment of bringing consumers exactly what they want—low cost and additional benefits—has allowed them to be one of the top home building companies in the market. They are the first builder in the country with success in all three major areas: manufactured, modular, and conventional home building. Holigan has proven itself in the market as a top manufacturer and creator of homes.

The company's home-building success can partially be attributed to the creation of a television show called "Your New House," which airs on major network affiliates in many markets. The show started out as an infomercial, but became so popular that it spread to major networks. The show, with Michael Holigan as the host and "Super Handyman" Al Carrell, talks about issues related to building or fixing up a home. Ratings have continually risen. The two men demonstrate techniques and give advice on gardening, maintenance, landscaping, and remodeling, as well as advice on planning, finance, and efficiency within the home. Holigan has also diversified its media reach through the Internet and print.

Recently the company announced the formation of an exclusive home-building franchise division and formed a partnership with Olympus Real Estate Corporation to assist Holigan with equity capital for its extensive growth plans. Olympus was attracted to Holigan because of its reputation and quality and its media operations that support the company image and goals.

The company is planning to open retail stores to generate a friendly atmosphere while having one-stop shopping for items related to home building and maintenance. Holigan also plans to have individuals in the stores who can help with mortgage financing. Michael Holigan's goal is to open 100 stores nationwide within three years.

Questions

1. What managerial skills are evident in Michael Holigan's success? Provide examples.

2. Describe Holigan Group's organizational structure.

3. How would you describe Michael Holigan's leadership style?

Sources: Some research information for this case was accessed at the Holigan Group Web site at www.thisnewhouse.com, April 10, 1998.

chapter 9

Human Resource Management and Motivation

LEARNING GOALS

1. Explain the importance of human resource management and describe the responsibilities of human resource managers.

2. Explain the role of human resource planning in an organization's competitive strategy.

3. Discuss how firms recruit and select employees and the importance of compliance with employment-related legislation.

4. Describe how firms train and evaluate employees to develop effective workforces.

5. Explain the methods employers use to compensate employees through pay systems and benefit programs.

6. Discuss employee termination and the impact of downsizing and outsourcing.

7. Explain the concept of motivation in terms of satisfying employee needs.

8. Discuss how human resource managers apply theories of motivation in attracting, developing, and maintaining employees.

9. Identify the four categories of trends that will influence the work of human resource managers in the 21st century.

Giving People the Power to Prosper at Symantec

Why is Symantec one of the few software companies from the early eighties that's still around today? There is no one answer. Founded in 1982, Symantec Corporation leads the world in utility software for business and personal computing. It places 28th on *PC Magazine*'s list of "100 Most Influential Companies," it's the world's seventh largest PC software company, and it has more than 50 million customers around the globe. Symantec operates in 21 countries, with regional headquarters in The Netherlands, Australia, and Japan. And for all that, Symantec has one of the lowest profiles of any company its size. So why is it still around and still doing so well? CEO Gordon Eubanks splits the answer into two parts: "It isn't about making the most money. It's about creating jobs and creating value for customers."

Symantec has been creating value for its customers for years, concentrating on three product areas: (1) security and assistance software (such as Norton SystemWorks, a popular utility suite), (2) remote productivity solutions (such as WinFax PRO, a hassle-free way to send, receive, and manage faxes), and (3) Internet tools (such as Visual Café, a Java development tool). Unlike many companies that depended on one or two high-profile applications, Symantec has succeeded by pasting together a collection of products that lead the pack in a specific niche.

But focusing on customers is only half the answer. Symantec has been creating jobs (and doing much more than that) for its 2,400-plus employees. The company boasts that it has built a team of exceptional people, and it has done so by treating them exceptionally well. Symantec's focus on people is at the very heart of the company. Its mission statement talks about "creating extraordinary opportunities for employees," and employees are one of the six company values:

Australia	France	**SYMANTEC.**
Brasil	Italia	**The makers of**
Canada	日本 Japan	**Visual Page**
Deutschland	대한민국 Korea	
España	Nederland	Asia Pacific
	Россия Russia	
	Polska	Europe
	South Africa	
	Sverige	América Latina
	Schweiz	
	台灣 Taiwan	
	United Kingdom	
	United States	

Webmaster | Text Links

"We believe that employees desire to contribute to their fullest potential. We set expectations high and empower them to take ownership and stand accountable for their results. By providing extraordinary opportunities, we help them achieve career growth and a sense of personal fulfillment."

Symantec does its best to anticipate what employees might need. It helps them meet not only health and financial needs but personal and developmental needs as well. The company offers medical, dental, and vision plans. Employees are able to choose between HMO and PPO health care options, and they can get additional coverage for domestic partners and children. The company provides on-site fitness centers at some locations and subsidizes fitness memberships to local clubs. To help employees deal with diverse personal needs, the company offers a Personal Time Off Plan and a unique holiday schedule. Aside from salary and bonuses, Symantec offers financial benefits that include 401(k), *quarterly* profit sharing (most companies offer yearly bonuses, if at all), and employee stock purchase plans. The company has a Computer Purchase Program for its employees and even offers Symantec software at substantial discounts. Symantec also offers unmatched support programs to assist with both child adoption and education tuition needs. Plus, it even offers free soft drinks and munchies for all employees.

One industry observer casts Eubanks as a fanatic about the corny notion of giving good value. But corny or not, Eubanks leads his company in giving good value not only to customers but also to employees. What has enabled Symantec to stick around when so many other software companies haven't? It provides people with the power to prosper.[1]

www.symantec.com

CHAPTER OVERVIEW

The importance of people to the success of any organization is stressed in the very definition of *management:* the use of people and other resources to accomplish organizational objectives. Entertainment industry visionary Walt Disney expressed the value of employees this way: "You can dream, create, design, and build the most wonderful place in the world, but it requires people to make the dream a reality."

This chapter addresses the critical issues of human resource management and motivation. It begins with a discussion of the ways in which organizations attract, develop, and retain employees. Then it describes the concepts behind motivation and how human resource managers apply them to increase employee satisfaction and organizational effectiveness.

HUMAN RESOURCE MANAGEMENT: A VITAL MANAGERIAL FUNCTION

Most organizations devote considerable attention to **human resource management,** the function of attracting, developing, and retaining sufficient numbers of qualified employees to perform the activities necessary to accomplish organizational objectives. Human resource managers are responsible for developing specific programs and activities as well as creating a work environment that generates employee satisfaction and efficiency.

Relationships between employers and employees have changed enormously during the past century. At the beginning of the 20th century, firms hired employees by posting notices at their sites stating that workers were needed and would be hired the following day. Such a notice might list required skills, such as carpentry or welding, or simply list the number of employees the firm required. People looking for work would line up at the employer's shop or factory the next day—a small number in prosperous times and a larger number in less prosperous times. Someone in authority made hiring decisions after reviewing these candidates, often based on arbitrary criteria; sometimes the first people in line were hired, sometimes the healthiest and strongest were hired. After being hired, the new employees were expected to work under a precise set of rules, such as those listed in Figure 9.1.

Today, flexibility and complexity characterize the relationship between employers and employees. In Chapter 1, you learned that developing and sustaining a world-class workforce is an essential priority for effective competition by any firm. Human resource managers face challenges created by profound changes in the makeup of the labor force, a shortage of qualified job candidates, changes in the structure of the workplace, and employees' desires to balance their work and personal lives. These managers must meet their challenges by developing programs and policies that satisfy an increasingly diverse employee population while at the same time monitoring a growing number of employment-related laws that influence how they implement their firms' practices.

Large organizations created human resource departments that systematically handle the tasks of attracting, training, and retaining employees. Some human resource managers are called *generalists,* because they are responsible for several tasks. Others are called *specialists,* because they focus on individual areas of human resource management such as diversity training or employee benefits.

Entrepreneurs and small-business owners usually assume complete responsibility for human resource management. However, a growing number of small firms are outsourcing the function of human resource management to **professional employer organizations (PEOs).** A PEO is a company that helps small and mid-sized firms with a

| **Figure 9.1** | **Rules for Clerks, 1900** |

1. This store must be opened at sunrise. No mistake. Open at 6:00 A.M. summer and winter. Close about 8:30 or 9 P.M. the year round.
2. Store must be swept and dusted, doors and windows opened, lamps filled and trimmed, chimneys cleaned, counters, base shelves, and showcases dusted, pens made, a pail of water and the coal must be brought in before breakfast, if there is time to do it and attend to all the customers who call.
3. The store is not to be opened on the Sabbath day unless absolutely necessary and then only for a few minutes.
4. Should the store be opened on Sunday the clerks must go in alone and get tobacco for customers in need.
5. Clerks who are in the habit of smoking Spanish cigars, being shaved at the barber's, going to dancing parties and other places of amusement, and being out late at night will assuredly give the employer reason to be overly suspicious of employee integrity and honesty.
6. Clerks are allowed to smoke in the store provided they do not wait on women while smoking a "stogie."
7. Each store clerk must pay not less than $5.00 per year to the church and must attend Sunday school regularly.
8. Men clerks are given one evening a week off for courting and two if they go to the prayer meeting.
9. After the 14 hours in the store, leisure hours should be spent mostly in reading.

wide range of human resource services that include hiring and training employees, administering payroll and benefits programs, handling workers' compensation and unemployment insurance, and maintaining compliance with labor laws. PEOs work in partnership with employers in co-employer relationships. By handling a firm's human resource activities, a PEO enables a small firm to focus on producing the goods and services it sells.[2]

Businesspeople can view human resource management in two ways. In a narrow sense, it includes the functions of human resource professionals. But in a broader sense, it involves the entire organization, even when a special staff department assumes those responsibilities or when a firm outsources the functions. Supervisors and general managers also participate in hiring, training, evaluating performance, and motivating employees to ensure efficient work. Some firms even ask their employees to participate in hiring decisions and evaluating their co-workers' performance.

Business Directory

human resource management the function of attracting, developing, and retaining sufficient numbers of qualified employees to perform the activities necessary to accomplish organizational goals.

The core responsibilities of human resource management include planning for staffing needs, recruitment and selection, training and evaluating performance, compensation and benefits, and terminating employees. In accomplishing these tasks, human resource managers achieve their objectives of (1) providing qualified, well-trained employees for the organization, (2) maximizing employee effectiveness in the organization, and (3) satisfying individual employee needs through monetary compensation, benefits, opportunities to grow and advance, and job satisfaction.

HUMAN RESOURCE PLANNING

Human resource managers develop staffing plans based on their organization's competitive strategies. They forecast the number of employees their firm will need and determine the types of skills necessary to implement its plans. Human resource managers are responsible for adjusting their company's workforce to meet the requirements of expanding in new markets, reducing costs (which may require laying off employees), or adapting new technology. They formulate both long-term and short-term plans to provide the right number of qualified employees.

For example, Wal-Mart's human resource managers developed a special college internship program for international students to provide the retailer with managers for the new stores it plans to open in ten countries outside the United States, from Argentina to the People's Republic of China. "Many foreign nationals come to this country to study, then want to return to their native countries," says Mark Gunn, Wal-Mart's vice president of recruitment and placement. "We want to take advantage of this and align ourselves with that group." International students participating in the internship program receive on-the-job retailing experience and management training during their college years to prepare them for managing Wal-Mart stores in their native countries after they graduate.[3]

www. **www.wal-mart.com**

Ski resorts, catalog retailers, entertainment companies like Sea World and Disneyland, the Salvation Army, and many other organizations make short-term plans to recruit and train seasonal employees. Each year Whistler Mountain ski resort in British Columbia adds 800 employees during the ski season. Gord Ahrens, the resort's director of human resources, must recruit and train new hires who will commit to working the entire season and bring excellent customer service skills to their jobs. He posts his recruiting schedule and provides information about the resort on Whistler Mountain's Web site. In September, he begins screening the 5,000 applicants at a recruiting center. After conducting a series of job interviews, he selects new hires. "We have a set standard of quality," says Ahrens. "We won't settle for second-best." Ahrens motivates his seasonal workers by planning parties for them; giving them discounts on food, sports equipment, and ski lessons along with free ski passes worth $1,200; and rewarding top per-

Figure 9.2 **Steps in the Recruitment and Selection Process**

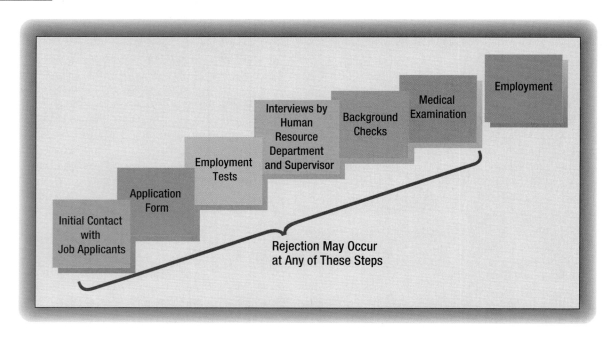

formers with prizes such as massages and heli-skiing. "We want them to have as much fun as our guests have," says Ahrens.[4]

RECRUITMENT AND SELECTION

In recruiting and selecting employees, human resource managers strive to match applicants' skills with those needed by the organization. To ensure that potential employees bring the necessary skills or the capacity to learn them, most firms implement the six-step approach to recruitment and selection shown in Figure 9.2.

Businesses access both internal and external sources to find qualified candidates for specific jobs. Policies of hiring from within emphasize internal sources, so that employers consider their own employees first for job openings. Internal recruiting is less expensive than external methods, and it helps to boost employee morale. But if recruiters can find no qualified internal candidate, they must look for people outside the organization. Recruitment from external sources involves advertising in newspapers and trade magazines, placing radio and TV ads, and working through employment agencies, college recruiting and internship offices, retiree job banks, jobs fairs, and state and private employment agencies.

One of the most effective external sources is employee referrals, in which employers ask current employees to recommend applicants from their networks of friends, rewarding them with bonuses or prizes for new hires. Cisco Systems, the computer networking firm, incorporates employee referrals into its recruiting efforts, as shown in Figure 9.3. Its so-called *friends* program rewards employees with generous cash bonuses, prizes, and lottery tickets for a free trip to Hawaii for referrals who are hired. The program targets top employees at other high-tech firms. "Cisco has an overall goal of getting the top 10 percent to 15 percent of people in our industry," says CEO John Chambers. "Our philosophy is very simple—if you get the best people in the industry to fit into your culture and you motivate them properly, then you're going to be an industry leader."[5]

Like Hewlett-Packard, many firms are using the Internet as a recruiting tool by posting jobs at their Web sites and listing positions at job banks such as Career Mosaic, Minorities' Job Bank, E-Span, and The Monster Board. Internet recruiting is a quick, efficient, inexpensive way for an employer to reach a large, global pool of job seekers. According to employers and career counselors, online recruiting will soon become the prevalent method of finding qualified job candidates.[6] The Business Tool Kit provides advice for tailoring your resume for online recruiters.

In hiring and recruiting employees, human resource managers must follow the requirements set out by federal and state laws. Chapter 2 described legislation that influences employers' hiring practices. Title VII of the Civil Rights Act of 1964 prohibits employers from discriminating against applicants based on their race, religion, color, sex, or national origin. The Americans with Disabilities Act of 1990 prohibits employers from discriminating against disabled applicants. The Civil Rights Act created the Equal Employment Opportunity Commission (EEOC) to investigate discrimination complaints. The EEOC also assists employers in setting up affirmative action programs to increase job opportunities for women, minorities, disabled people, and other protected groups. The Civil Rights Act of 1991 expanded the remedies available to victims of employment discrimination by including the right to a jury trial, punitive damages, and damages for emotional distress.

Failure to comply with equal employment opportunity legislation can expose an employer to risks like fines and penalties, bad publicity, and poor employee morale. The number of lawsuits against employers and the sizes of punitive damage awards have increased substantially since passage of the Civil Rights Act of 1991.[7] As a result, opponents have launched initiatives to reform employment law and affirmative action standards to protect employers against unwarranted litigation. For example, California

Figure 9.3 **Employee Referrals as a Recruitment Method**

Refer yourself to Hawaii.

A
REFER NEW EMPLOYEES TO CISCO.

LO
GET A CASH ($$$) BONUS AFTER THEY'VE BEEN HERE 30 DAYS.

HA
GET A CISCO LOTTO TICKET TO WIN VERY COOL NEW AWARDS. AND A CHANCE TO WIN FABULOUS DREAM VACATIONS!

CISCO SYSTEMS

PLEASE REFER TO THE EMPLOYEE REFERRAL POLICY FOR MORE DETAILS OR GO TO OUR WEB ADDRESS! HTTP://WWW.IN.CISCO.COM/HR/EMPLOYMENT/EMP_REF.HTML.

B U S I N E S S   T O O L   K I T

Tips for Crafting Your Electronic Resume

Job hunting in cyberspace requires an understanding of the differences between writing an electronic resume and writing a paper one. Both present basically the same content. You want to showcase your skills, abilities, and personal interests. But many human resource managers use electronic methods to process resumes they receive, so you need to follow a set of rules for preparing an online resume that pleases the computer. This year, millions of resumes mailed to more than 400 companies, government agencies, colleges, and universities will be scanned into computers that then use artificial intelligence software to search for keywords or codes, creating an electronic impression of the job candidate along the way. Here are some tips for tailoring your resume to the requirements of online recruiting:

▼ *Include keywords.* Insert as many nouns as possible that describe your ability and experiences. The scanning technology used to process online resumes searches for keywords specified in the computer programming to match applicants' qualifications with job requirements. For example, if you were applying for an accounting position, you might include *BS accounting, accounts payable, accounts receivable, IRS amendments,* and *CPA.* A good electronic resume presents a separate line of keywords related to your occupation at the bottom of the document because if 10 keywords are programmed and your resume includes five of them, you'll automatically be placed in the middle of the pack. Whether you know Lotus 1-2-3 is a side issue—if you don't include that word in your resume you may never get the chance to tell anyone about it. In writing a paper resume, you should avoid using acronyms, but you need to include them in your online resume. Use acronyms like TQM followed by the spelled out words or phrases—total quality management. Use business jargon as much as possible.

▼ *Avoid fancy touches.* Don't use bullets, boldfaced text, underlines, or other attention-getting touches in your online resume. According to one writer, "These flourishes often turn into gibberish when they are zapped through cyberspace."

▼ *Create the document in a plain-text format.* Because online resumes are often put in databases that may not read formatting codes, send your resume in a plain-text format like an ASCII text file.

▼ *Observe professional standards.* The recruiter will be impressed with your technical knowledge when you send your resume electronically, but don't get carried away. Use a formal writing style and avoid emoticons like a smiley face [:-)]. Fred Jandt, co-author of *Using the Internet and the World Wide Web in Your Job Search,* says he cringes when hearing of job seekers who attach electronic images of family members and pets to their online resumes.

▼ *Get help.* Many Web sites offer help in writing online resumes.

Job Smart Resume Guide:

www.jobsmart.org/tools/resume/index.htm

Job Bank USA Resume Resources:

www.interbiznet.co/hunt/tools.html

Resume Builder on the Monster Listing Service:

www.monster.com/

Resumix Creating Your Resume:

www.resumix.com/resume/resumeindex.html

Sources: Malcolm Fitch, "Cruise the Web to Land the Job of Your Dreams," *Money*, May 1997, pp. 29–30; Sherri Eng, "Tips for the Job Search," *Computerlink*, March 18, 1997, p. 19; and Audrey Arthur, "Take Your Job Search Online," *Black Enterprise*, March 1997, p. 56; Bob Fernandez, "Forget Those Fancy Resumes: They Simply Will Not Compute," *The Inquirer*, February 27, 1998, http://www.phillynews.com:80/inquirer/Feb/22/business/RESU22.html; Steven Ginsberg, "Selling Your Most Important Asset—You," *Washington Post*, February 23, 1998, http://www.washingtonpost.com:80

voters passed a proposition that prohibits the state from granting hiring preferences to minorities. The federal government is considering reforming laws that give preferential treatment to applicants based on their race, color, national origin, and sex. Other proposed legislation is aimed at protecting employees from discrimination because of their religious beliefs or sexual orientations.[8]

Increases in the number of protected employees and discrimination lawsuits have elevated the significance of human resource managers in the hiring process. Most discrimination lawsuits filed by disabled people result from violations of requirements for the interview process. To prevent violations, human resource managers must train line managers involved in the interviewing process to make them knowledgeable about employment law. For example, the law prohibits asking an applicant any questions relating to marital status, number of children, race, nationality, religion, or age.[9] Interviewers also cannot ask questions about applicants' criminal records, mental illness histories, or alcohol-related problems. For more information about employment-litigation issues, visit the Issues Management Program section on the home page of the Society for Human Resource Management.

www. www.shrm.org/issues.htm

Employers must also observe various other legal restrictions governing hiring practices. For example, some firms try to screen out high-risk employees by requiring drug testing for job applicants, particularly in industries where employees are responsible for public safety, such as airlines and other public transportation companies. Drug testing is a controversial practice, however, due to concerns about privacy. Also, positive test results may not accurately indicate drug use; traces of legal drugs, such as prescribed medications, may chemically resemble traces of illegal substances. Several states have passed laws restricting drug testing by employers.

The law prohibits the use of polygraph (lie detector) tests in almost all prehiring decisions, as well as in random testing of current employees. The only organizations exempt from this law are federal, state, and county governments; firms that do sensitive work under contract to the Defense Department, FBI, or CIA; pharmaceuticals firms that handle controlled substances; and security guard services.

Recruitment and selection is an expensive process, because a firm incurs costs for advertising job openings, interviewing applicants, and conducting background checks, employment tests, and medical exams. A bad hiring decision is an even more expensive mistake, though. The U.S. Department of Labor estimates that a bad hiring decision costs a firm almost one-third of an employee's first-year potential earnings. Other costs resulting from a bad hiring decision include potential lawsuits, unemployment compensation claims, recruiting and training a replacement, and reductions in productivity and employee morale.[10]

To avoid the costly results of a bad hiring decision, many employers require applicants to complete employment tests. These tests verify the skills that applicants list on their application forms or resumes and discuss during the interview. This precaution helps to ensure that candidates meet the requirements of the job. A variety of tests are available to gauge applicants' knowledge of mechanical, technical, language, and computer skills. For example, the QWIZ testing programs described in Figure 9.4 verify applicants' office and computer skills.

Lori Jacobson, manager of training and client service for Scott Levin, a pharmaceuticals consulting firm, started administering tests to avoid the problem of unsuccessful

Figure 9.4 **Testing Applicants to Verify Skills**

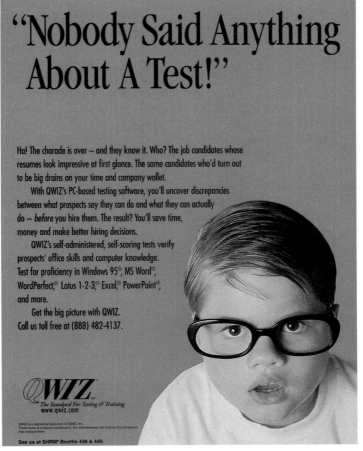

new hires. She says each bad hiring decision costs her company about $5,000 in recruiting and replacement expenses. Jacobson asks all applicants for marketing and administrative positions to take computerized tests to demonstrate their computing and clerical skills. Since implementing the tests, Jacobson has not had to replace one new hire. Most candidates applying for jobs at Scott Levin are not prepared to have their skills tested. "You should see the look on people's faces when I tell them they have to take a test," says Jacobson.[11]

ORIENTATION, TRAINING, AND EVALUATION

A newly hired employee usually completes an orientation program administered jointly by the human resource department and the department in which the employee will work. During orientation, employer representatives inform employees about company policies regarding employee rights and benefits. Many organizations give new hires copies of employee manuals that describe in detail benefits programs and working conditions and expectations.

To protect themselves from discrimination lawsuits, growing numbers of firms are including explicit employment-at-will policies in their employee manuals. **Employment at will** means that the employment relationship can be started or terminated at any time by either the employee or the employer for any reason. "Most people think they have some kind of right to their jobs," says attorney Jonathan L. Alpert. Fired employees frequently ask Alpert to help them sue their former employers. Alpert asks them, "For what?" They erroneously believe that the law prohibits employers from firing employees. In fact, however, successful lawsuits must cite specific illegal practices such as discrimination in hiring based on sex, race, age, or disability.[12]

Although most states' laws traditionally have recognized the practice of employment at will, court decisions in recent lawsuits have tended to favor employees in firing disputes when employers have failed to provide written proof of at-will policies and employees' acceptance of the policies. Some employers are also including provisions in their manuals that call for mandatory arbitration of employment disputes and waivers of the right to jury trials in such disputes.[13]

Employees are increasing their demands for training so they can build skills and knowledge that will prepare them for new job opportunities. A firm should view employee training as an ongoing process throughout each employee's tenure with the company. **On-the-job training,** one popular instructional method, trains employees for job duties by allowing them to perform the tasks under the guidance of experienced employees. A variation of on-the-job training is apprenticeship training, in which an employee learns a job by serving for a time as an assistant to a trained worker.

Apprenticeship programs are much more common in Europe than in the United States. While American apprenticeships usually focus on blue-collar trades, in Europe many new entrants to white-collar professions complete apprenticeships. German companies operate some 300 officially recognized apprenticeship programs, which prepare new workers for 30,000 to 40,000 jobs. One German company, Mannesmann, is trying to attract students to work there by combining business apprenticeships with university studies leading to a degree in economics. After earning the degree, an apprentice commits to work for Mannesmann for 3 years.[14]

Off-the-job training involves some form of classroom instruction such as lectures, conferences, audiovisual aids, programmed instruction, and special machines to teach employees everything from basic math and language skills to difficult, highly skilled tasks. Some firms are replacing classroom training with computer-based and online training programs. These programs offer many advantages: They can save an employer money by reducing travel costs and employee time away from work; they offer consistent presentations, because the training content does not vary with the quality of the instructor; audio and visual capabilities help these systems to simulate the work environment better than some classroom training could do. Employees also benefit from computer and online training; it allows them to learn at their own pace and convenience and gives them responsibility to take charge of their own learning processes.[15]

Professional Analysis Inc. (PAI), an environmental and safety consulting firm, replaced its classroom training

Business Directory

employment at will a practice that allows the employment relationship to begin or end at any time at the decision of either the employee or the employer for any reason.

on-the-job training a training method that teaches an employee to complete new tasks by performing them under the guidance of an experienced employee.

management development program training designed to improve the skills and broaden the knowledge of current and potential managers.

performance appraisal a method of evaluating an employee's job performance by comparing actual results to desired outcomes.

with a computerized system. The company would have encountered difficult obstacles in any effort to gather its 124 full-time and 200 part-time employees who work from eight different offices around the country at one location for training. PAI converted its in-house training programs, quality control classes, and OSHA training into software installed on its computer network. Jeff Ginsburg, PAI's human resource manager, says computerized training solved the firm's logistical problems. "It is a much better method of training," he says.[16]

Firms with operations in other countries often face new challenges in training employees. U.S. companies opening facilities in Russia, for example, discovered that employees there were not familiar with Western business practices, including telephone etiquette. Russian employees typically did not identify themselves or their companies when they answered the phone, and they resisted taking phone messages. To change this situation, FYI Information Resources, a U.S. market research and business planning firm, used role-playing exercises to teach the Russian employees at its offices how to answer the phone in a professional manner.[17]

When a firm decides to enter a foreign market, human resource managers must prepare employees who will work in overseas assignments by providing training in language skills, cultural practices, and adapting to the everyday living requirements abroad. While employees may begin an international assignment with the professional skills and job qualifications they need, most benefit from additional cultural and language training to help them make successful transitions.

A **management development program** provides training designed to improve the skills and broaden the knowledge of current and potential managers. Levi Strauss & Company mandates training for managers that includes required courses in leadership, diversity, and ethical decision making. Management training is often conducted off premises. General Motors, McDonald's, and Xerox are among the dozens of large firms that have established college-like institutes offering specific management development programs. Another type of off-premise training for managers covers benchmarking, or learning the best practices of the best companies. As Figure 9.5 illustrates, the Disney Institute offers seminars for managerial development at the Walt Disney World Resort. As part of their to-

tal quality management programs, many firms send their managers to the resort to learn about Disney's world-class practices in customer service.

Another important human resource management activity is **performance appraisal,** evaluation of an employee's job performance by comparing actual results to desired outcomes. Based on this evaluation, managers make objective decisions about compensation, promotions, additional training needs, transfers, or terminations. Rating employees' performance and communicating perceptions of their strengths and weaknesses are important elements in improving a firm's productivity and profits. Performance appraisals are not confined to business. Government agencies, not-for-profit organizations, and academic institutions also conduct them.

Figure 9.5 **Training Program for Management Development**

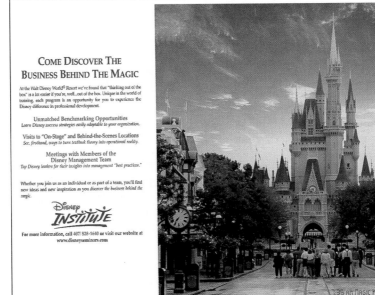

Some firms conduct peer reviews, in which employees assess the performance of co-workers, while other firms allow employees to review their supervisors and managers. A new trend in performance appraisal is the **360-degree performance review,** a process that gathers feedback from a review panel of several people, including co-workers, supervisors, managers, and sometimes customers.

PhotoDisc, a digital-stock-photography firm, combines 360-degree reviews with traditional appraisal methods in evaluating employees' performance. Designed to emphasize employee development, the 360-degree review is an optional session scheduled 6 months before the appraisal, which determines promotion and compensation decisions. An employee and supervisor select six to ten reviewers, who complete a three-page form to evaluate the employee's performance on criteria such as teamwork and follow-through. To ensure that the review arrives at an objective assessment, PhotoDisc hires an outside consultant to compile the results and prepare a summary, which is discussed by the employee and supervisor. The employee then prepares a plan addressing the issues raised in the review summary. Feedback from these reviews creates opportunities for PhotoDisc employees to improve their behavior and performance before their annual performance appraisals.[18]

COMPENSATION

Human resource managers work to develop an equitable compensation system spanning wages and salaries plus benefits. Because labor costs represent a sizable percentage of any firm's total product costs, excessive wage rates may make its goods and service too expensive to compete effectively in the marketplace. Inadequate wages, however, lead to high employee turnover, poor morale, and inefficient production.

The terms *wages* and *salary* are often used interchangeably, but they refer to different types of pay systems. *Wages* represent compensation based on an hourly pay rate or the amount of output produced. Firms generally pay wages to production employees, retail salespeople, and maintenance workers. *Salaries* represent compensation calculated on a weekly, monthly, or annual basis. Office personnel, executives, and professional employees usually receive salaries.

An effective compensation system should attract well-qualified workers, keep them satisfied in their jobs, and inspire them to produce. Most firms base their compensation policies on five factors: (1) salaries and wages paid by other companies that compete for the same people, (2) government legislation (including the federal minimum wage of $5.15 per hour), (3) the cost of living, (4) their own ability to pay, and (5) workers' productivity.

Many employers tie financial rewards to superior employee performance. They try to motivate employees to excel by offering some type of incentive compensation in addition to salaries or wages. Most implement four types of incentive compensation programs:

1. Profit sharing, which awards bonuses based on company profits

2. Gain sharing, which awards bonuses based on surpassing predetermined performance goals

3. Lump-sum bonuses, which award one-time cash payments based on performance

4. Pay for knowledge, which distributes wage or salary increases as employees learn new job tasks

Managers and top executives often earn incentive compensation based on their firms' profitability and stock performance. For example, Lawrence Coss, CEO and chairman of Green Tree Financial Corporation, earns compensation based on 2.5 percent of the firm's pretax income. Most top U.S. executives receive salaries plus long-term incentives such as stock options, which reward executives for increases in their firms' stock prices by giving them opportunities to buy stock at preset prices within certain time periods. Linking top executive pay to a company's stock price has resulted in huge compensation packages. In a recent year, Coss was paid $102 million in salary and bonus, and he also received 2 million stock options valued at $35 million as an incentive to continue increasing his firm's stock price.[19]

The compensation paid to top executives has prompted a wave of criticism from labor unions. They point out that the average CEO's salary is 200 times greater than the salary of a factory worker. Company shareholders and institutional investors are also scrutinizing pay-for-performance systems that have resulted in what they consider excessively high compensation for CEOs.

The high compensation of U.S. executives has also received attention from CEOs in other countries. The salaries of U.S. top managers compare to those of their counterparts in Brazil, France, Hong Kong, Germany, the United Kingdom, Japan, and Canada. But this similarity masks a huge difference in total compensation, mainly because of long-term incentives such as stock options, which are seldom given in other countries. Firms in Germany and Japan are prohibited by law from giving stock options to executives. However, many foreign firms are finding ways to boost the compensation of their CEOs. The globalization of business and international search for top executive talent are forcing foreign companies to increase their CEO compensation. "The U.S. has long used pay as a yardstick for a chief executive's talent and brains," says Charles Sweet, president

Business Directory

employee benefits employee rewards such as health insurance and retirement plans that employers give, entirely or in part, at their own expense.

flexible benefit plan a benefit system that offers employees a range of options from which they may choose the types of benefits they receive.

of the A. T. Kearney executive search firm. "Now that yardstick is used in lots of different parts of the world."[20]

www. www.atkearney.com

EMPLOYEE BENEFITS

In addition to wages and salaries, firms provide many benefits to employees and their families as part of the compensation they pay. **Employee benefits** are rewards such as retirement plans, insurance, sick leave, child care and elder care, and tuition reimbursement, provided entirely or in part at the company's expense. Some benefits are required by law. For example, firms are required to make social security contributions and payments to state employment insurance and workers' compensation programs that protect workers in case of job-related injuries or illnesses. The Family and Medical Leave Act of 1993 requires covered employers to offer up to 12 weeks of unpaid, job-protected leave to eligible employees.

Firms voluntarily provide other employee benefits, such as child care and health insurance, to help them attract and retain employees. Benefits represent a large component of an employee's total compensation. Wages account for 61 percent of the typical employee's earnings, while benefits determine the other 39 percent. The cost of all benefits that an employer pays for each full-time employee averages $14,086. Figure 9.6 illustrates the breakdown of employer-paid benefits.

The benefits packages offered by AT&T, Eli Lilly, Hallmark Cards, and many other large and small companies include "family friendly" benefits for working parents such as child-care provisions, seminars on parenting, and flexible work schedules. Research indicates that a work-family approach to benefits gives companies a strategic opportunity to improve productivity in the workplace and to boost employee satisfaction.[21]

While benefits emphasizing family needs are a top priority for working parents, such programs have drawn criticism from other members of the workforce, as described in Solving an Ethical Controversy.

In response to the increased diversity in the workplace, human resource managers are developing creative ways to tailor their benefit plans to the varying needs of employees. One approach sets up **flexible benefit plans,** also called *cafeteria plans.* Such a benefit system offers employees a range of options from which they can choose the types of benefits they receive. The most basic cafeteria plans allow employees to pay insurance premiums with pretax dollars. Under the most complex arrangements, employees may choose among several medical, dental, and vision plans, disability insurance, life insurance, and extra vacation days. Some plans also offer memberships in health clubs and child-care benefits. Typically, each employee receives a set allowance (called *flex dollars* or *credits)* to pay for purchases from this menu.[22]

Another way of increasing the flexibility of employee benefits involves time off from work. Instead of establishing set numbers of holidays, vacation days, and sick days, some employers give each employee a bank of *paid time off (PTO).* Employees use days from their PTO accounts without having to explain why they need the time. Trinity Communications, a marketing communications company based in Boston, offers a 6-week PTO bank each as part of its strategy for recognizing the diversity of its employees.

Figure 9.6   **Breakdown of Employer-Paid Benefits**

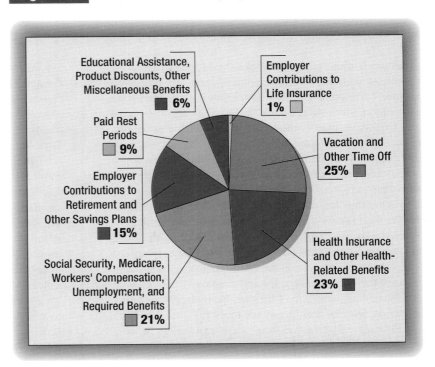

With such a plan, employees can take off days according to their needs such as the holidays they observe, the illnesses of family members, and their children's school schedules.[23]

In 1997, Congress permitted a trial of another creative employee benefit—the medical savings account (MSA). An MSA is basically a savings account that employees can

SOLVING AN ETHICAL CONTROVERSY

Are Family Friendly Benefits Unfair to Childless Employees?

Millions of working parents are struggling to balance the demands of their jobs and children. Employers have responded with a variety of programs such as flexible working hours, on-site child care, and paid parental leave. But at the same time that working parents are asking for more help from their employers, employees without children are protesting that family friendly programs discriminate against them.

"Programs and policies that exclude large groups of people are inherently unfair," says entrepreneur Ann Price. "If I don't have kids, family friendly

benefits, by definition, aren't very friendly to me."

Price is a member of The Childfree Network, an advocacy organization that is working to change what members perceive as inequities in the workplace resulting from benefits geared to working parents to help them balance their professional and personal lives. The group's agenda includes working to eliminate tax breaks and extra benefits for employees with dependent children. Members question, for example, why employer insurance programs pay for in-vitro fertilization procedures. "We find that appalling," says Leslie Lafayette, president of The Childfree Network. "Why am I subsidizing somebody who wants to have kids? Infertility is not a disease."

? Do Work-Family Benefits Discriminate against Childless Employees?

PRO

1. Flexible working hours are geared to employees with children. It's not fair that childless employees always have to cover on the job for parents who leave work early to watch their kids play soccer. Childless employees often have to work longer hours to complete assignments left by working parents.

2. Employees without children are subsidizing programs that benefit the families of working parents. "An on-site child-care center or a lactation room are icons of all the money that companies spend on

tap to pay health-care bills. MSAs are designed for use by businesses with 50 or fewer employees and self-employed people. They combine high-deductible health insurance with pretax savings accounts. Employees agree to have part of their pretax earnings deposited in the accounts, while the employer pays for the insurance policy and may contribute toward deductible charges. When an employee or self-employed person needs medical care, he or she pays with the funds in the savings account up to the amount of the deductible (as much as $2,250 for an individual or $4,000 for a family). An MSA balance may also fund non-covered expenses such as vision care, prescription drugs, and pregnancy-related coverage. MSAs can help small-business owners to save on their insurance costs. They also enhance the tax advantage for self-employed people, who can deduct only a portion of their health-plan premiums, by sheltering some of their insurance money.[24]

To help employees manage their expanding benefits options, some employers are putting their benefit plans online. Public Service Electric & Gas Company, a New Jer-

sey utility, allows its employees to access their benefit information and make changes using personal computers. Online benefit-management systems reduce employers' costs for administering the programs and give employees real-time information about their benefits, improving their ownership and control of their compensation packages.[25]

Another part of this trend toward responsiveness to employee needs is the option of flexible work plans. **Flexible work plans** are benefits that allow employees to adjust their working hours and places of work to accommodate their personal lives. Flexible work plan options include flextime, compressed workweeks, job sharing, and home-based work. By implementing these benefit programs, employers have reduced employee turnover and absenteeism and boosted productivity and job satisfaction.[26]

Flextime is a scheduling system that allows employees to set their own work hours within constraints specified by the firm. For example, an employer may require employees to be at work between the core hours of 10 a.m. and 3 p.m. rather than the regular workday hours of 9 to 5. Outside the core hours, employees can choose when to start and end their work days, opting either to arrive at work early, say at 7 a.m., and leave early, or to arrive later and work later than the standard day. Flextime is common in European coun-

Business Directory

flexible work plan a benefit system that allows employees to adjust their working hours and places of work to accommodate their personal lives.

employees with kids," says Price. "For childless workers they're a constant reminder of all the benefits dollars that aren't spent on us."

3. The decision to have or not to have children is a personal one. People who decide to have children should not expect employers and co-workers to accommodate their personal lives. Doing so diminishes the importance of work.

CON

1. Work is important, but so are families. Offering working parents child-care assistance is a way for employers to keep valued employees motivated and focused on their jobs. Employers who ignore the needs of working parents suffer from high absenteeism, turnover, and low morale.

2. Employers tend to publicize benefits targeted at working parents. But many high-cost benefits, such as wellness facilities and tuition reimbursement programs, are used primarily by employees without children. They get more than their fair share of the benefits pie.

3. As difficult as juggling family and career responsibilities are for married couples, many families are headed by single parents who may or may not have other family members around to help them. Benefits for single parents help them and their children survive.

SUMMARY

Aware of the complaints voiced by childless employees, some employers are changing the name of programs from "family friendly" to "work-life" to show that they value all employees.

Other firms are designing benefits programs with variable configurations to accommodate the needs of different workers. Ann Price, founder of the software firm Motek, Inc., asks her 20 employees to vote each year on the benefits they want. Because paid time off always tops the list, Price allows all employees to take a month off work to use as they wish—for a paternity leave or a vacation. Says Price, "It's the fairest system I can think of because everyone, regardless of their family status, gets the same amount of time to use as they please."

Sources: Nancy Winebarger, "Employee Benefits: What Single Parents Should Know," *Single Parent Magazine*, November 1998, accessed at www.singleparentmagazine.com; Kathleen Madigan, "'Family' Doesn't Always Mean Children," *Business Week*, September 15, 1997, p. 104; Diane Harris, "The Fairness Furor," *Working Mother*, September 1997, pp. 28–32; Joseph Nocera, "Oh, Quit Whining and Get Back to Work," *Fortune*, March 17, 1997, pp. 74–75; and Dan Fost, "Child Free with an Attitude," *American Demographics*, April 1996, p. 15.

tries; an estimated 40 percent of the Swiss workforce and 25 percent of German workers set flextime schedules. Growing numbers of U.S. firms are offering flextime, and increasing numbers of employees are taking advantage of this benefit. At a Xerox customer service center, 85 percent of 300 employees have chosen flextime, which resulted in a 30 percent reduction in absenteeism.

The **compressed workweek** is a scheduling option that allows employees to work the regular number of required hours in fewer than the typical 5 days. Employees at Hewlett-Packard's Financial Services Center in Colorado Springs, Colorado, asked their managers if they could work a compressed workweek of four 10-hour days rather than five 8-hour days. The employees, who handle financial transactions for the company's U.S. operations, cited two advantages: improved customer service because longer shifts would better cover the range of geographic time zones for customer calls, and improved employee morale. After agreeing to a trial of the compressed workweek proposal, managers discovered that productivity almost doubled among employees working 4

Family friendly flexible scheduling plans help Hewlett-Packard achieve its business goals. These employees work 10 hours for 4 days each week. The compressed workweek has boosted employee morale and productivity, cut overtime hours in half, and helped the firm attract and hire new employees.

days. According to Jerry Cashman, HP's work options program manager, the shortened workweek cut the number of overtime hours in half, resulting in a 50 percent cost savings to the salary budget. The program is also helping HP to attract and hire new employees.[27]

A **job sharing** program allows two or more employees to divide the tasks of one job. This plan appeals to a growing number of people who prefer to work part-time rather than full-time, such as older workers, students, working parents, and people who want to devote time to personal interests or leisure.

A **home-based work** program allows employees to perform their jobs from home instead of at the workplace. Home-based workers are sometimes called *telecommuters,* because many "commute" to work via personal computers, electronic mail, and fax. "Telecommuting is emerging as the hot new employee benefit as many companies exhaust their more traditional recruiting incentives in a tight labor market," says Adrienne Plotch, an executive with Olsten Corporation, a temporary-help agency. A survey by the agency revealed that additional firms plan to increase their use of telecommuting.[28] Working from home appeals especially powerfully to disabled workers, elderly people, and parents with small children. Because telecommuters work with minimal supervision, they need to be self-disciplined and reliable employees. They also need managers who are comfortable with setting goals and managing from afar.

TERMINATING EMPLOYEES

Either employer or employee can take the initiative to terminate employment. Employees decide to leave firms to start their own businesses, take jobs with other firms, or retire. Some firms ask employees who leave voluntarily to participate in **exit interviews** to find out why they decided to leave. These interviews give opportunities to learn about problems in the workplace, such as unreasonable supervisors or unfair work practices. Hallmark Cards conducts exit interviews, because "it is important for us at Hallmark to learn why someone wants to leave," says Dave Pylipow, director of employee relations. "In some cases, we have discovered people who were leaving who didn't really want to leave. They didn't know how well we thought of them. That's a learning tool for us to make sure we are paying attention to those folks and letting them know we have plans and opportunities for them."[29]

Employers sometimes terminate employees due to poor job performance, negative attitudes toward work and co-workers, and misconduct such as dishonesty or sexual harassment. Terminating poor performers is a necessary act, because they lower productivity and employee morale.

Co-workers resent employees who receive the same pay and benefits as themselves without contributing fairly to the company's work. Employers need to carefully document reasons for terminating employees. According to the Equal Employment Opportunity Commission, almost half of the cases it files against employers involve charges of wrongful dismissal.[30] In recent years, employers have terminated employees through downsizing and outsourcing.

Downsizing

During the 1980s and 1990s, employers terminated millions of employees through downsizing. **Downsizing** is the process of reducing the number of employees within a firm by eliminating jobs. Between 1991 and 1996, companies eliminated more than 3 million jobs, including many managerial positions. In 1997, AT&T announced plans to eliminate 17,000 positions during a 2-year period. Kodak, IBM, and Philip Morris also planned to reduce their workforces. In 1998, defense contractor Raytheon Systems reported that it would cut 8,700 jobs, about 10 percent of its workforce, and other defense contractors are expected to follow Raytheon as a result of cutbacks in government spending on weapons and defense systems.[31]

Companies downsize for many reasons. The two most common objectives of downsizing are to reduce costs by cutting overhead and streamlining the organizational structure and to increase customer satisfaction. Some firms report improvements in profits, market share, employee productivity, quality, and customer service after downsizing. According to recent studies, however, many large firms lost so many valuable, high-performing employees as they trimmed staff rolls, that their ability to compete declined.[32]

Eliminating jobs from downsizing has had devastating effects on employee morale. Workers who remained employed worried about their job security and became angry because they had to work harder for the same pay to keep the pace of earlier staffing levels, while their firms' top managers were rewarded with generous compensation for improving profits. As their feelings of commitment to their jobs waned, many employees voluntarily sought better employment. "It defies credibility to think people are going to do their best work if they are scared all the time and are looking for another job that will value their commitment more," says Barney Olsted, co-director of New Ways to Work, Inc. "Everyone understands economic realities, but they also understand that when the CEO's salary and management bonuses continue to go up, there is an inequity, and it has little to do with staying in business or tightening down or really running a lean organization."[33]

Business Directory

downsizing the process of reducing a firm's workforce to reduce costs and improve efficiency.

Many downsizing firms have reduced their workforces by offering early retirement plans, voluntary severance programs, and opportunities for internal reassignment to different jobs. Employers who valued their employees helped them to find jobs with other companies and set up job counseling centers. The Business Hall of Fame describes how one company showed genuine concern for its employees in the process of eliminating jobs.

The negative effects of downsizing on employees have led employers to reconsider the employment relationship. John Challenger of Challenger, Gray & Christmas, an outplacement firm that monitors companies' layoff plans, says: "In the second phase of downsizing, good companies can and are stepping forward to deal with some of the consequences and effects on the workforce."[34]

Employers have surveyed employees to determine what is important to them. Results have indicated that workers are less interested in job security than in career security. As a result of this shift, a typical employee wants opportunities for training to improve the skills needed for the next job. People are willing to work hard at their current jobs, but they also want to share in the success of their companies by receiving pay-for-performance compensation and stock options.

For human resource managers, the new employer-employee relationship requires developing continuous training and learning programs for employees. Unisys, an information management company, launched an intranet to give employees access to research tools that help them to improve their skills. Unisys also started an Internet career center for its 32,000 employees worldwide that lists job profiles and identifies career trends. "The career trends give them a vision for what's hot in the future, so they can set a course of development, plan, and get the skills necessary for the jobs of the future," says Pat Bradford, Unisys's vice president of resource productivity for the company's world-

wide human resources operation.[35] In the new employment relationship, firms are willing to provide resources for employees, but employees are expected to take responsibility for their work, training, and career development.

Outsourcing

Another important development has accompanied corporate downsizing. The trend toward outsourcing has led firms to rely on outside specialists to perform functions previously performed by company employees. Outsourcing began on a small scale, with firms contracting out services such as maintenance, cleaning, and delivery. Today, outsourcing has expanded to include outside contracting of many tasks once considered fundamental internal functions. For example, the early part of the chapter explained how many small firms outsource the entire human resource function by using the services of professional employer organizations. Large firms also outsource certain human resource tasks such as recruiting, training, and compensation. Some companies outsource such functions as information management, production of one or more elements of their product lines, accounting and legal services, and warehousing and delivery services.

The services most often outsourced include housekeeping; architectural design; grounds, building, utility, and furniture maintenance; food service; security; and relocation services. As shown in Figure 9.7, Argonaut offers a contract service that helps firms to meet the challenge of

Figure 9.7 **An Outsourcing Firm to Handle Increasing Workforce Mobility**

BUSINESS HALL OF FAME

Helping Employees Adjust to Change

NOVA Corporation is a Canadian company involved in worldwide natural gas services and petrochemicals with 6,000 employees in North America. Several years ago, NOVA reengineered its business processes with the goals of reducing costs and improving customer service. NOVA simplified its business processes to make its goods and services more accessible, reliable, and flexible than before. Reengineering resulted in improved customer satisfaction and cost reduction, but NOVA realized that the changes could seriously damage employee morale and commitment.

Reengineering eliminated many jobs, more than 25 percent of NOVA

employees experienced changes in their work assignments, and almost 33 percent took on new assignments. To help employees cope with these changes, NOVA created an Employee Transition & Continuity (ET&C) program. The program is based on NOVA's guiding principles that the company is responsible for the equitable treatment of everyone in the workplace and that employees are accountable for their performance through continuous learning. "The ET&C program assists people in gaining the skills they need to take control of the transition process," says Michael Lee, vice president of people for NOVA's chemical division.

The ET&C program was designed to respond to the varying needs of NOVA's diverse workforce. Its three main components create opportunities

for employees to start their own businesses, do volunteer work, and study for college degrees.

When her job was eliminated, Roberta Surro decided to take the Entrepreneurial Ventures option to open a coffeehouse. The company offered employees up to $25,000 to start their own firms and allowed them to use company resources for initial and ongoing business advice. While still working at her regular job, Surro got advice from NOVA colleagues on how to write a business plan. Surro says the financial and planning assistance "gave me the courage I needed to get started."

The Education Option gives employees up to $5,000 a year for tuition and book expenses while they attend college for a maximum of 4 years. NOVA continues to pay 50 percent of their salaries and gives them regular

---

an increasingly mobile workforce. Formerly the in-house relocation unit of General Motors, Argonaut is now an independent firm offering relocation services to companies that want to outsource the job of moving employees to different locations throughout the world.

Outsourcing complements downsizing in a variety of ways. It allows a firm to continue performing the functions it does best, while hiring other firms to do tasks that they can handle more competently and cost effectively than its own people can. Another benefit of outsourcing is the firm's ability to negotiate the best price among competing bidders and the chance to avoid the long-term resource costs associated with in-house operations. Firms that outsource also gain flexibility to change suppliers at the end of contract periods, if they desire. The key to successful outsourcing is a total commitment by both parties to form a partnership from which each derives benefits.

MOTIVATING EMPLOYEES

Effective human resource management makes important contributions to employee motivation. Flexible benefit programs, flexible work schedules, on-site child care, and bonus pay are all designed to motivate people to join a firm and become satisfied and productive workers. In his book

A Great Place to Work, author Robert Levering examined 20 top U.S. firms to discover what made them wonderful employers. He identified three factors, which he calls "the three *R*s". The first is expanding workers' responsibility for their jobs. The second involves sharing the rewards that the firm generates as equitably as possible. The third *R* calls for ensuring that employees have rights. These include some kind of grievance procedure, access to corporate records, and the right to confront those in authority without fearing reprisals.

Building the three *R*s into an organization should contribute to employee morale. **Morale** is the mental attitude of employees toward their employer and jobs. It involves a sense of common purpose among the members of work groups and throughout the organization as a whole. High morale is a sign of a well-managed organization, because workers' attitudes toward their jobs affect the quality of their work. One of the most obvious signs of poor manager-worker relations is poor morale. It lurks behind absenteeism, employee turnover, and strikes. It shows up in falling productivity and rising employee grievances. The Business Hall of Shame illustrates the causes and consequences of poor morale at one workplace.

What factors lead to high employee morale? A recent survey of 55,000 employees by the Gallup Organization revealed that high morale results when a firm gives employees

benefits such as health and dental coverage and profit sharing. This plan suited Wendy Zick, whose job was also eliminated. "I didn't have the chance to attend college when I was younger," says Zick. "Without this program paying part of my salary, I would have been working immediately."

The Community Support option allowed an employee to spend a year doing volunteer work while paying 50 percent of regular salary and continuing full benefits. When the departing employee finished such an assignment, NOVA gave a severance package. Tony Trojanowski took this option after his job was cut. He used his skills from working in human resources and materials management at NOVA to help teach disabled people how to operate a retail store at a not-for-profit training center. Trojanowski says his volunteer work helped the disabled to build transferable job skills and broadened his career. "I've gained valuable retail experience on top of my manu-

facturing background that has increased my ability to go out into the workforce and find something viable."

In addition to these options, NOVA offered employees other help. To help them "go where the jobs are," NOVA provided relocation assistance in the form of grants up to $5,000 to employees who moved at least 25 miles from their current addresses. The firm also allowed employees to take unpaid leaves of absence for up to 1 year. If the employee found no job available at NOVA when the leave expired, the firm offered a severance package and eligibility to participate in the ET&C program. Another option gave employees up to $5,000 to attend school part-time so they could upgrade their skills.

While the ET&C program was designed primarily for employees in transition, NOVA plans to offer it continually to give employees strategic career support. "It's not enough to tell people they must take control of their own

lives," says Sheila O'Brien, NOVA's senior vice president of people. "To adapt quickly in response to change, both the company and our employees require the ongoing network of support that the ET&C program provides."

QUESTIONS FOR CRITICAL THINKING

1. If you were a NOVA employee and your job was eliminated, which option would appeal most strongly to you?

2. Suppose that as a NOVA employee, you were asked for suggestions about how the company could expand its career support program. What suggestions would you offer?

Sources: "Working with Us," accessed at the NOVA Chemicals Web site, www.novachem.com, April 30, 1999; and "Balanced Scorecard," downloaded from http:/www.nova.ca/, January 24, 1998.

---

opportunities to do what they do best, and when workers believe that their opinions count, work in an environment where everyone is committed to quality, and believe their work supports achievement of their company's mission.[36]

| Figure 9.8 | The Process of Motivation |

Maintaining high employee morale results from an organization's understanding of human needs and its success at satisfying those needs in ways that reinforce organizational goals. Each person is motivated to take action designed to satisfy needs. A **need** is simply a felt lack of some useful benefit. It reflects a gap between an individual's actual state and his or her desired state. A **motive** is an inner state that directs a person toward the goal of satisfying a felt need. Once the need—the gap between where a person is now and where he or she wants to be—becomes important enough, it produces tension and the individual is moved (the root word for *motive*) to reduce this tension and return to a condition of equilibrium. Figure 9.8 depicts the principle behind this process. A need produces a motivation, which leads to goal-directed behavior, resulting in need satisfaction.

Maslow's Hierarchy of Needs Theory

Psychologist Abraham H. Maslow studied human needs to gain an understanding of how employers can motivate employees. He developed a widely accepted list of human needs based on these important assumptions:

▼ People are wanting animals whose needs depend on what they already possess.

▼ A satisfied need is not a motivator; only needs that remain unsatisfied can influence behavior.

▼ People's needs are arranged in a hierarchy of importance; once they satisfy one need, at least partially, another emerges and demands satisfaction.

BUSINESS HALL OF SHAME

Mitsubishi Tries to Boost Morale

Lots of companies today are pulling out all the stops in their efforts to please employees, but at Mitsubishi Motors' plant in Normal, Illinois, observers don't see much joy on the factory floor. Low morale and a long list of grievances plague the facility. Many employees say they work in an abusive environment. In 1994, 29 women filed a lawsuit against the Japanese firm, accusing management of fostering a climate of sexual harassment. In 1996, the Equal Employment Opportunity Commission filed a class-action suit against the company on behalf of some 330 women who claim they were targets of sexual harassment. The commission charged that harassment at the plant was "standard operating procedure."

Women workers on the assembly line contended that their jobs required them to put up with lewd comments and fondling by male employees. They also complained of exposure to crude graffiti and sexually explicit photos, coercion into sexual relations to win jobs, and threats of retaliatory abuse when they complained. Both men and women say that some of the plant's U.S. managers use sexually explicit language in ridiculing employees in front of other workers. Those who object to such treatment are assigned to undesirable work shifts and lose opportunities to earn overtime pay.

Under such conditions, it may appear puzzling why any employee wouldn't pack up his or her lunchbox and walk off the job. But few employees do. Employees stay because Mitsubishi pays the average worker $19 an hour, making the company one of the highest-paying employers in the area. One

woman suffers the abuse because she says that she can't afford to leave her $50,000-a-year assembly-line job.

After 3 years of fighting lawsuits, Mitsubishi has paid dearly in high settlement costs and bad publicity. While not agreeing that it was involved in any wrongdoing, Mitsubishi settled to the tune of $9.5 million with 27 of the 29 women who filed lawsuits. The EEOC's suit is expected to be the largest sexual harassment case ever brought.

In this age of enlightened management, few claim to understand why Mitsubishi did not take the responsibility to provide a harassment-free workplace. Some observers believe that, like other Japanese firms that set up plants in small U.S. communities in the 1980s, Mitsubishi's top managers were inexperienced in dealing with women and minorities in the workplace.

Other reasons surfaced in 1996 when the company hired Lynn Martin,

---

In his hierarchy of needs theory, Maslow proposed that all people feel basic needs that they must satisfy before they can consider higher-order needs. He identified five types of motivating needs.

1. *Physiological needs.* These most basic human needs include food, shelter, and clothing. In the workplace, employers satisfy these needs by paying salaries and wages and establishing comfortable working environments.

2. *Safety needs.* These needs refer to desires for physical and economic protection. Employers satisfy these needs by providing benefits such as retirement plans, job security, and workplaces that comply with OSHA requirements.

3. *Social (belongingness) needs.* People want to be accepted by family and other individuals and groups. At work, employees want to maintain good relationships with their co-workers and managers and to participate in group activities.

4. *Esteem needs.* People like to receive attention, recognition, and appreciation from others. Employees feel

good when they are recognized for good job performance and respected for their contributions.

5. *Self-actualization needs.* These needs drive people to seek fulfillment, realizing their own potential, fully using their talents and capabilities. Employers can satisfy these needs by offering challenging and creative work assignments and opportunities for advancement based on individual merit.

According to Maslow, people must satisfy the lower-order needs in the hierarchy (physiological and safety needs) before they are motivated to satisfy higher-order needs (social, esteem, and self-actualization needs). Figure 9.9 elaborates on employers' efforts to motivate employees by satisfying each level of needs.

The diversity of today's workforce challenges employers to satisfy the belongingness needs of people from many different cultures and ethnic backgrounds. Entrepreneur Mike Baldwin of Virtual Solutions, Inc., recognized that he had to devise special programs to satisfy the social needs of new hires. Unable to find skilled U.S. workers to design and write customized database software for his new company, Baldwin started recruiting in Taiwan, India,

former U.S. labor secretary, as a consultant to recommend reforms at the Mitsubishi plant. Martin discovered that the company completely focused on producing cars but paid little attention to the people who built them. She also noted that the company's human resource department was understaffed to serve 4,000 employees, the firm lacked any procedure for employees to report instances of abuse, it offered inadequate training in sexual harassment issues, and supervisors' training did not help them to develop interpersonal skills.

Based on her observations, Martin has launched 34 workplace reforms. Many are aimed at women. For example, women with children get pretax payroll deductions for child care to lower the cost burdens of this service on working mothers. Many incentives are intended to modify the behavior of supervisors. Martin established strict punishments for supervisors who harass employees, as well as financial rewards for supervisors who crack down on harassment. Supervisors must at-

tend 99 hours of training in conflict resolution and priorities for controlling their own misbehavior. Further, managers' raises are based in part on how effectively they deal with harassment problems.

The EEOC charges that these moves are merely paying lip service rather than solving problems. Many employees agree. "Where's the change?" asks a male employee, noting that many sexual harassment offenders are still on the job. A woman employee who continues to suffer abuse says that some male employees who completed harassment training say, "Now I know how to do it and not get caught!"

In 1997, Mitsubishi hired a new vice president and general manager of human resources. As a change agent known for his innovative personnel practices, he was expected to turn around the work environment. But after just 6 months on the job he resigned. Some workers who believe he is a man of integrity say that he left because the company wouldn't allow him to implement his innovative ideas.

QUESTIONS FOR CRITICAL THINKING

1. Would you be willing to sacrifice high pay for an employer with a better working environment?

2. If you were hired as the top human resource manager at Mitsubishi and were given authority to implement workplace changes, what innovations would you suggest to make the plant a model workplace?

Sources: Kathy McKinney, "Judge OKs Settlement on MMMA," *The Pantagraph*, June 24, 1998, accessed at www.pantagraph.com; Peter Annin and John McCormick, "More Than a Tune-up," *Newsweek*, November 24, 1997, pp. 50–52; "Work Week," *The Wall Street Journal*, November 4, 1997, p. A1; and De'Ann Weimer and Emily Thornton, "Slow Healing at Mitsubishi," *Business Week*, September 22, 1997, pp. 74–76.

Great Britain, and France. About 40 of the firm's 100 employees are foreigners. To give them a feeling of belongingness, Baldwin assigns a domestic mentor to each new employee. Mentors help in many ways, from teaching the foreigners American slang to getting drivers' licenses, opening bank accounts, and finding housing. Baldwin also plans social events like "international days" where ethnic food is served so all employees can learn about the different cultures represented in the workplace. Because soccer is a popular sport in the native countries of many foreign employees, Baldwin started sponsoring employee teams in the sport.[37]

www.vsol.com/home.html

Because most people in industrialized nations can afford to satisfy their lower-order needs, higher-order needs often play important roles in motivating employees there. Effective managers who understand higher-order needs can design programs that meet them. A management development program, for example, gives an employee the op-

portunity to grow by learning leadership skills. But how do firms satisfy higher-order needs like self-actualization for low-ranking employees such as factory workers? Some companies are experimenting with ways to add meaning to these workers' jobs through job enlargement and job enrichment.

Motivating Employees through Job Design

In their search for ways to improve employee productivity and morale, a growing number of firms are focusing on the motivation inherent in the job itself. Rather than simplifying the tasks involved in a job, employers are broadening tasks to add meaning and satisfaction to employees' work. Two ways employers are applying motivational theories to restructure jobs are job enlargement and job enrichment.

Job enlargement is a job design change that expands an employee's responsibilities by increasing the number and variety of tasks they entail. Some firms have successfully applied job enlargement by redesigning the production process. For example, at U.S. Shoe Company, factory

| Figure 9.9 | Maslow's Hierarchy of Needs |

Self-Actualization Needs
Accomplishment, opportunities for advancement, growth, and creativity

Example: Procter & Gamble's promotion-from-within policy gives employees chances to grow. Human resource manager Carol Tuttle has been promoted 7 times in 22 years. She's worked in brand management, advertising, and recruiting, and spent 6 years in Venezuela. "It's always challenging, always exciting. I don't think I've ever been bored for 5 minutes," she says.

Esteem Needs
Recognition and appreciation from others

Example: Entrepreneur Candace Bryan, chief executive of Kendle, a firm that designs clinical tests for drugs, keeps a photo gallery of her 288 employees posing with their favorite outside activities, from scuba diving to grandparenting.The recognition boosts employee morale and helps to make Bryan an inviting supervisor for prospective employees.

Social (Belongingness) Needs
Acceptance by other employees

Example: Valassis Communications, which prints coupon inserts for newspapers, sends employees memos introducing new hires. The employees, including the president of the company, then write "welcoming" notes to the new employee. "On your first day on the job, you're so nervous and you feel uncomfortable, and it just really makes a difference and makes you feel comfortable," says one new employee.

Safety Needs
Protection from harm, employee benefits

Example: Computer software maker SAS Institute believes that healthy employees make good employees. Two doctors and ten nurses staff its 7,500-square-foot on-site medical center, where employees and their dependents get free consultations, physical exams, emergency care, and many wellness programs.

Physiological Needs
Wages and working environment

Example: Granite Rock, an operator of rock, sand, and gravel quarries, pays entry-level employees $15.90 per hour and gives opportunities to move up to a "job owner" or "improvement champion" and earn base pay of $29.50 an hour.

workers each performed one task on the assembly line. U.S. Shoe has replaced the assembly line at most of its factories and created modular work areas where individual employees perform several shoe-making tasks rather than just one.

Job enrichment is a job design change that augments employees' authority in planning their work, deciding how it should be done, and learning new skills that help them grow. Many companies have developed job enrichment programs that empower employees to take responsibility for their work. The concept of worker empowerment will be discussed in the next chapter.

Through job enrichment, employers can motivate employees to satisfy higher-level needs than the limits of their previous jobs allowed. Consider factory worker Doreen Dickey, who took a $9-an-hour job at Foldcraft Corporation, a manufacturer of restaurant furniture. She expected her job of scraping and sanding excess sealants from seats to require boring and meaningless work. Then Foldcraft asked Dickey for her opinion on improving the sanding process and invited her to participate in an educational tour of factories in Central America. The tour included meetings with professors, managers, government officials, and union members. This opportunity completely changed Dickey's attitude toward her job. "I felt rejuvenated," she says. "My job may be mind-numbing, but I see more clearly where I fit in. The seat I work on reflects what I am and who I am." The job-enriching experience also improved Dickey's performance. "I'm discovering things about myself that I never realized," she says. "My head is spinning with ideas on how to make my job better."[38]

Motivating Employees through Managers' Attitudes

The attitudes that managers display toward employees also influence worker motivation. Managers' traditional view of workers as cogs in the production process—much like lathes, drill presses, and other equipment—led them to believe that money was the best way to motivate employees. Maslow's needs theory helped managers to understand that employees feel needs beyond those satisfied by monetary rewards. Psychologist Douglas McGregor, a student of Maslow, studied motivation from the perspective of how managers view employees.

After observing managers' interactions with employees, McGregor coined the terms *Theory X* and *Theory Y* as labels for the assumptions that different managers make about worker behavior and how these assumptions affect management styles.[39] Table 9.1 lists these assumptions.

Entrepreneur Mike Baldwin (center) helps to fulfill the belongingness needs of his diverse workforce. New hires shown here from India, Hong Kong, China, and Vietnam work with mentors who help them adjust to life in the United States. Baldwin plans special events to make these workers feel at home in their new environment.

DID YOU KNOW?

People really do like to work. *Adweek* conducted a nationwide survey asking Americans if they would quit their jobs if they won the big jackpot in a lottery. Almost 50 percent said no. More women than men said they would continue working. The age group with the highest percentage of "yes" answers was 18- to 24-year-olds.

Theory X assumes that employees dislike work and whenever possible try to avoid it. Thus, managers must coerce or control them or threaten punishment to achieve the organization's goals. Managers who accept this view feel that the average person prefers to receive direction, wishes to avoid responsibility, has relatively little ambition, and can be motivated only by money and job security. Managers who hold these assumptions are likely to keep their subordinates under close and constant observation, continually holding out the threat of disciplinary action, and demanding that they adhere closely to company policies and procedures.

Theory Y assumes that the typical person likes work and learns, under proper conditions, to accept and seek out responsibilities to fulfill social, esteem, and self-actualization needs. Theory Y managers consider the expenditure of physical and mental effort in work as an ordinary activity, as natural as play or rest. They assume that most people are capable of conceiving creative ways to solve work-related problems but that most organizations do not fully utilize the intelligence that most employees bring to their jobs. Unlike the traditional manage-

Table 9.1	Assumptions of Theory X and Theory Y
THEORY X ASSUMPTIONS	**THEORY Y ASSUMPTIONS**
1. Employees dislike work and will try to avoid it whenever possible.	1. Employees view work as a normal activity as natural as play or rest.
2. Employees must be coerced, controlled, or threatened to achieve organizational goals.	2. Employees will exercise self-direction when they are committed to achieving organizational objectives.
3. Employees try to avoid responsibility and want direction.	3. Employees typically accept and even want to take responsibility for their work.
4. Employees view job security as the most important factor associated with their work.	4. Employees have the intellectual potential to make decisions and find creative solutions to problems.

ment philosophy that relies on external control and constant supervision, Theory Y emphasizes self-control and self-direction.

Theory Y requires a different management approach that includes worker participation in decisions that Theory X would reserve for management. If people actually behave in the manner described by Theory X, they may do so because the organization satisfies only their lower-order needs. If the organization designs ways to satisfy their social, esteem, and self-actualization needs, as well, employees may be motivated to behave in different ways.

Another perspective on management was labeled **Theory Z** by William Ouchi. Theory Z organizations blend American and Japanese management practices, as shown in Figure 9.10. This approach views worker involvement as the key to increased productivity for the company and improved quality of work life for employees. Many U.S. firms have adopted the participative management style used in Japanese firms by asking workers for suggestions to improve their jobs and then giving them the authority to implement proposed changes.

A growing number of U.S. firms are showing holistic concern for employees and their families. Many employers are adjusting the workplace to satisfy the needs of employees. Some are going as far as allowing employees to bring their dogs to work. At Autodesk, a design software developer in San Rafael, California, 10 percent of the 2,300 employees take their dogs to work with them. "It would be real tough to change back to a job where I had to leave Pixel at home," says Ricki Brooke, manager of Autodesk's technical library. "She hates the weekends and looks forward to coming back to work."[40]

HUMAN RESOURCE CONCERNS FOR THE 21ST CENTURY

Four kinds of trends—demographic, workforce, economic, and work/life events—are shaping the responsibilities and practices of human resource managers.[41] They need to monitor these trends to prepare their organizations for recruiting, training, and retaining workforces motivated to direct their efforts toward achieving company goals.

Demographic Trends

The percentage of older workers in the workforce will grow, and these aging people will retain elder-care responsibilities for family members over the age of 85, one of the fast-growing segments of the population. Because of the rising education level of people with disabilities and the influence of the American with Disabilities Act, disabled people will be entering the workforce in increasing numbers. By 2005, workers from ethnic minorities will comprise about 28 percent of all employees. The composition of foreign-born employees continues to change, with continuing immigration from Asia and the Pacific Islands. In-

---

Figure 9.10 **Theory Z Management: A Blend of American and Japanese Methods**

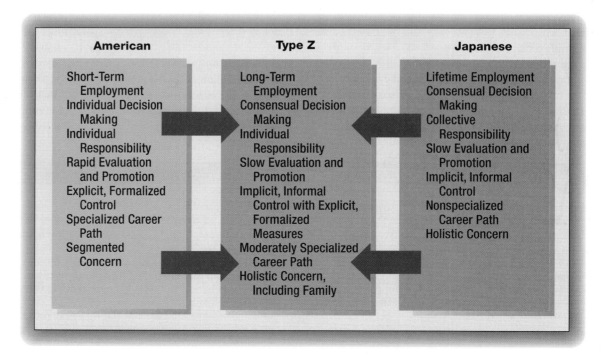

creasing numbers of employees will be single people and couples without children. The number of childless couples is expected to grow by almost 50 percent by 2010.

Workforce Trends

The use of contingent workers is expected to grow. **Contingent workers** are employees who work part-time, temporarily, or only to fulfill specific contracts. In general, these workers earn less pay than full-time employees, and they do not receive benefits or have access to employer-provided pension plans. The disparities in pay and benefits between contingent and regular employees may lead to legislation that protects part-time and temporary workers by requiring employers to provide benefits and retirement plans.

The demand for skilled workers is growing significantly, but employers are concerned with a potential shortage of educated and qualified workers, pointing to the poor quality of high school and college graduates. Adult illiteracy continues to be a problem. According to a Department of Education report, 90 million Americans are so poorly educated that they cannot "write a brief letter explaining an error on a credit card."

Employer surveys show some dissatisfaction with the work ethic of Generation Xers. In a survey of small-business owners, employers reported that those born between 1966 and 1978 are lazy, display short attention spans, give no loyalty to employers, feel no respect for authority, and show a poorer work ethic than previous generations.[42] Management experts disagree, noting that these young workers are ideally suited to the new workplace, because they are computer savvy, adapt quickly to change, are good team players, and find creative solutions to problems.

Because younger workers' values differ from those of the baby boom generation, they require different management and motivation techniques. Figure 9.11 shows what Generation Xers expect from their employers. "They are not interested in climbing the conventional job ladder. Offer them an extra $10,000 per year, and they won't necessarily hop jobs," says Pamela Hamilton, founder of Collab-

orative Communications, a public relations firm. Of Hamilton's 13 employees, 12 are Generation Xers. "What's critical to Gen Xers is feeling they have an impact on what the business is doing," says Hamilton. "Titles don't matter to them, but job responsibilities do. They really want to feel as though they are contributing. They will work very hard and very long hours if you manage them properly," she says.[43]

Work teams are expected to be the most important format for high-performance work, with employees from different functions such as marketing, purchasing, service delivery, and human resources collaborating on producing goods and services. Work teams will be discussed in detail in the next chapter.

Preventing lawsuits will remain a critical task for human resource managers, as the number of employment-related cases continues to rise. Current law allows "almost anyone not selected for a job to . . . maintain a court action," says federal judge Stanley Sporkin, who advocates reforms in the civil rights laws to reduce the number of lawsuits against employers.

Autodesk shows a holistic concern for its employees by offering an unusual benefit. It allows employees to bring four-legged "family members" to work, a practice that keeps employees motivated to stay with the software development firm.

Economic Trends

Changes in the economic environment will create new sets of human resource needs. With a significant portion of economic growth occurring in countries outside the United States and Europe, programs and practices of U.S. firms will show a growing influence from conditions and cultures of other countries. Employers will need to recruit global managers and employees with international skills and experience.

Companies will continue to focus on reducing costs, including the costs of labor. For human resource managers, this trend creates a challenge of finding ways to motivate employees to increase their productivity by making the workplace attractive while reducing employment costs. Employee discontent with executive compensation will grow, and workers will demand an increasing portion of

Business Directory

contingent worker an employee who works part-time, temporarily, or only to fulfill a specific contract.

firms' profits. Company shareholders and institutional investors will want stronger voices in determining the employment-related policies that influence a firm's economic performance. Proposals by the Securities and Exchange Commission would include investors in the decision-making process for employment-related issues such as affirmative action, sexual harassment, and sexual orientation.

Work/Life Trends

Employer-sponsored benefits and programs for elder care and child care will become increasingly common as employers recognize the need to accommodate aging workers, single parents with children, and two-income families. As a result of improved treatments for AIDS patients, many individuals with the condition will be returning to work. Employers will need to integrate these workers into their organizations and comply with laws that prohibit discrimination against them.

| Figure 9.11 | What Generation Xers Expect from Their Employers |

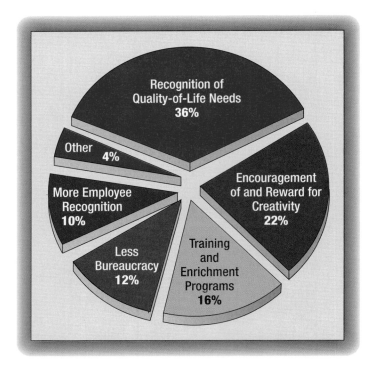

The physical work environment is also changing. Casual dress policies are spreading. To reduce the level of stress that employees feel, companies will be offering new nonmonetary benefits that add convenience to workers' daily lives. Employees at Wilton Connor Packaging Inc. in Charlotte, North Carolina, can bring their laundry to work and have it washed, dried, and folded at the company's expense. Additional firms will be providing concierge services. Insight, a direct marketing firm, has hired an on-site concierge to serve its 900 employees. This person arranges birthday and anniversary parties and coordinates film processing, dry cleaning, apparel alterations and auto detailing. Insight also opened a company store where employees can buy stamps and greeting cards.[44] Treating employees well by enriching the work environment will gain importance in efforts to recruit and retain a highly motivated workforce.

SUMMARY OF LEARNING GOALS

1. Explain the importance of human resource management and describe the responsibilities of human resource managers.

Organizations devote considerable attention to attracting, training, and retaining employees to help maintain their competitiveness. Human resource managers are responsible for recruiting, selecting, training, compensating, terminating, and motivating employees. They accomplish these tasks by developing specific programs and creating a work environment that generates employee satisfaction and efficiency.

2. Explain the role of human resource planning in an organization's competitive strategy.

A human resource plan is designed to implement a firm's competitive strategies by providing the right number of employees, training them to meet job requirements, and motivating them to be productive and satisfied workers.

3. Discuss how firms recruit and select employees and the importance of compliance with employment-related legislation.

Firms use internal and external methods to recruit and select qualified employees for specific jobs. Human resource managers must follow legal requirements in making hiring decisions. Failure to comply with employment laws can result in lawsuits and negative publicity.

4. Describe how firms train and evaluate employees to develop effective workforces.

Human resource managers use a variety of training techniques including on-the-job training, computerized training programs, and classroom methods. They conduct performance appraisals to assess employees' work and attitudes toward their jobs and co-workers.

5. Explain the methods employers use to compensate employees through pay systems and benefit programs.

Firms compensate employees with wages, salaries, and incentive pay systems such as profit sharing, gain sharing, bonuses, and pay-for-knowledge programs. Benefit programs vary among firms, but most companies offer health-care programs, insurance, retirement plans, paid holidays, and sick leave. A growing number of companies are offering flexible work plans such as flextime, compressed workweeks, job sharing, and home-based work.

6. Discuss employee termination and the impact of downsizing and outsourcing.

Either an employer or an employee can decide to terminate employment. Downsizing improves firms' competitive positions by reducing labor costs. Outsourcing helps companies to reduce costs and focus on the activities they do best.

7. Explain the concept of motivation in terms of satisfying employee needs.

All employees feel needs, and these needs differ among employees. Each person is motivated to take actions that satisfy his or her needs. Employers who recognize and understand differences in employee needs can develop programs that satisfy different needs and motivate workers to achieve organizational goals.

8. Discuss how human resource managers apply theories of motivation in attracting, developing, and maintaining employees.

Human resource managers develop benefits and other policies and programs to satisfy employees' physiological, safety, social, esteem, and self-actualization needs. Some motivational efforts, such as job enlargement and job enrichment, focus on the job duties themselves. Managers' attitudes toward employees also influence workers' motivation. Managers who display positive attitudes toward employees can motivate them by including them in decision making and problem solving.

9. Identify the four categories of trends that will influence the work of human resource managers in the 21st century.

Demographic, workforce, economic, and work/life trends will influence the tasks of human resource managers. These trends point to an increasingly diverse employee population with different needs that employers must satisfy in motivating employees to direct their work toward achieving organizational goals.

TEN BUSINESS TERMS YOU NEED TO KNOW

human resource management

employment at will

on-the-job training

management development program

performance appraisal

employee benefits

flexible benefit plan

flexible work plan

downsizing

contingent worker

Other Important Business Terms

professional employer organization (PEO)

360-degree performance review

flextime

compressed workweek

job sharing

home-based work

exit interview

morale

need

motive

job enlargement

job enrichment

Theory X

Theory Y

Theory Z

REVIEW QUESTIONS

1. What are the main responsibilities of human resource managers?
2. How are the plans of human resource managers influenced by corporate plans and competitive strategies?
3. What methods do firms use to recruit and train employees? How has technology influenced these tasks?
4. What techniques do firms use to train employees? Why is training gaining importance as a human resource concern?
5. What are performance appraisals? How does a regular performance appraisal differ from a 360-degree appraisal?
6. What major types of plans do employers implement to compensate employees that relate pay to employee performance?
7. Why are flexible benefit plans and flexible work plans becoming increasingly important aspects of employers' benefit programs?
8. How do downsizing and outsourcing affect employees, employers, and the jobs of human resource managers?
9. What employee needs do firms try to satisfy? Why are firms so concerned about satisfying employee needs?
10. How can managers' attitudes toward employees influence employee motivation?

QUESTIONS FOR CRITICAL THINKING

1. Do you think that firms pay CEOs too much money? In answering this question, consider the global shortage of top executive talent. Suppose you are a CEO of a large, multinational firm that rewards you with a multimillion-dollar compensation package. During your company's annual stockholder meeting, one stockholder asks you to justify the amount you earned. How would you respond?
2. If you worked for a company that offered a choice between a regular performance appraisal and a 360-degree appraisal, which would you choose? Which type of appraisal do you think is fairer to the employee?

3. Suppose you just started your own company and plan to hire four full-time and two part-time employees. You need to develop a benefit package that will motivate applicants to join you in your new venture. You are hoping to attract young workers in their early 20s. What benefits and work scheduling plans would you include in your package?

4. Suppose you are offered two jobs. One offer includes starting pay of $25,000 per year and a very basic benefit package of health insurance and a retirement plan. The other job offer includes starting pay of $20,000 and a comprehensive benefit package of health insurance, a retirement plan, flexible work hours, free employee lunches every day, and a state-of-the-art fitness center where you can get a free massage once a month. Which job offer would be more appealing to you? For the job paying $20,000, how would you try to negotiate a higher starting salary?

5. As a management development training specialist, you have been asked to conduct a training course for supervisors and managers at a manufacturing plant. The managers hold Theory X assumptions about workers. Your job is to train them so they will involve all plant workers in making decisions about their work. What training techniques would you use to help these managers move toward Theory Y and Theory Z approaches?

Experiential Exercise

Directions: To learn more about motivation, use yourself as a case study. List below three groups you've been a member of that you think would qualify as motivated groups (for example, civic groups, athletic teams, academic teams, employee groups, study groups, family groups, religious groups, political groups). The main requirement for a group to qualify as a motivated group is that the group accomplished what it set out to do and did an excellent job.

1.

2.

3.

Analyze each motivated group you listed and identify whether that group (a) gave its members responsibility for the group's performance, (b) shared the rewards of the group, and (c) ensured that each group member had rights.

Now list three groups you've belonged to that qualify as unmotivated groups—groups that did not perform well, accomplished none or only part of their goals, or did not produce high-quality work.

1.

2.

3.

Analyze each unmotivated group you listed and identify whether that group (a) gave its members responsibility for the group's performance, (b) shared the rewards of the group, and (c) ensured that each group member had rights.

What connections did you find between Robert Levering's three *R*s (responsibility, rewards, rights) and the two categories of groups you analyzed?

Nothing but Net

1. **Wired Human Resource Department.** Just as you get impressions about companies by how you are treated when you visit their human resource departments to inquire about job openings or to ask for job application forms, you also get impressions from how companies present themselves on the Internet. Go to several wired human resources departments, such as those listed here, and record your impressions—things you liked and didn't like—as you conduct your own online job search:

   General Electric: **199.35.160.14/**

   Microsoft: **www.microsoft.com/jobs/**

   Intel: **www.intel.com/intel/oppty/index.htm**

2. **Professional employer organizations.** To learn more about how organizations are out-sourcing the human resource management function to professional employer organizations, visit a site such as

   www.hrcentral.com/.

   List the basic human resource services available to organizations through sites you visit.

3. **Employee Benefits.** One benefit all employers are required to provide is social security. Find out more about this benefit by visiting the official site of the Social Security Administration at

   www.ssa.gov/

   Browse the services available at this site and record information regarding three services that you can tell a friend or relative approaching retirement age. The services should be those you consider most useful to someone planning for retirement.

Note: Internet Web addresses change frequently. If you do not find the exact sites listed, you may need to access the organization's or company's home page and search from there.

MANAGING CULTURAL DIVERSITY—JCPENNEY

In 1902, James Cash Penney opened his first store in Kemmerer, Wyoming, and named it "The Golden Rule." Penney's pledge to his customers was that they would find the best quality merchandise at the lowest possible prices. He insisted that customers always be served with courtesy and respect. Penney said, "If there is a secret of good management in the business of living, it lies in the partnerships we make, for no man is sufficient unto himself. I say partners because we believe that all our associates work together as partners."

Today, JCPenney is known not only as a major national department store retailer, but also for its mail-order catalog operations. Penney's operates over 1,246 stores in all 50 states and in Puerto Rico. These stores account for about 75 percent of sales. The catalog operation contributes 17 percent to overall corporate sales, and the company's Thrift Drug stores provide around 10 percent. JCPenney's primary competitive advantage is that it has 113 million square feet of prime retail space in malls.

In the 1990s, there are nearly 200,000 associates at JCPenney stores serving nearly 98 million customers each year. Mary Rostad, Vice President of Human Resources, states that "we really believe that our associates should have an opportunity to be part of the business strategies and the development of business opportunities." More than the increase in the size of the company, the changing demographics of the workforce and the marketplace have affected the JCPenney organization.

Charles Brown, Vice President and Director of Credit Operations, maintains that the JCPenney Company places a great emphasis on diversity by trying to understand it and by valuing the differences it brings to the workplace. "When you look at our associate population and our consumer base, you see mirrored what is happening in the U.S. as a whole. We understand that demographics are changing and that different types of people are entering the workplace. There are more women in the workplace, more minorities, more seniors. All these groups are part of our need to understand and value diversity. We see a connection

with the bottom line because they represent our customer, and the differences among our customers represent opportunities for us to fill their needs."

JCPenney associates participate in a one-and-a-half-day workshop, "Valuing Cultural Differences," designed to create an awareness of diversity. Management developed a position statement on diversity that is given to every associate so that they clearly understand the company's commitment to diversity. Part of this understanding is that it is everyone's responsibility to value diversity.

In 1989, the company backed its formal commitment to diversity with the formation of the minority advisory team and later, the women's advisory team. The charge to these teams was to explore and identify roadblocks to advancement for their constituents within JCPenney.

Recommendations from the minority and women's advisory teams resulted in the establishment of the company's mentoring programs. These programs were designed to increase the likelihood that minority associates would stay with the company and also to help them gain an understanding of the company's culture more quickly. The development of a career pathing program was the second major recommendation from the advisory teams. Making advancement opportunities more visible and providing assistance with career planning help not only to set realistic expectations, but to increase the speed of advancement. The third priority set by the advisory teams was to recruit top minority and female candidates.

Has JCPenney gained tangible benefits from its commitment to and investment in managing diversity? According to Charles Brown, because of the increasing awareness of diversity, the company is now targeting specific market segments. Minority and female associates are in leadership positions throughout the organization in increased numbers. But perhaps more important, Brown suggests, is that associates within the company now discuss sensitive issues that used to be avoided. Whether it's child care or race relations, the issues can be aired more openly and effectively.

Questions

1. How does JCPenney ensure that the company responds to the changing demographics of the workforce and the marketplace? How can it help the company's bottom line?

2. How does JCPenney empower its minority employees? What are some potential benefits and costs of such empowerment?

3. Explain the importance and responsibilities of JCPenney's human resource department in managing cultural diversity.

4. Would you classify the management style of JCPenney as fitting Theory X, Theory Y, or Theory Z? Explain.

chapter 10

Improving Performance through Empowerment, Teamwork, and Communication

LEARNING GOALS

1. Describe why organizations empower employees and methods of empowerment.

2. Distinguish between the two major types of teams in the workplace.

3. Identify the characteristics of an effective team and the roles played by team members.

4. Summarize the stages of team development.

5. Relate team cohesiveness and norms to effective team performance.

6. Describe the factors that can cause conflict in teams and how conflict can be resolved.

7. Explain the importance of effective communications skills in business.

8. Compare the different types of communication.

9. Identify and explain several important considerations in international business communication.

10. Discuss how advances in technology affect business communication.

"Team"-ing with Success: W. L. Gore Associates Have No Bosses—At All

Say you're working for a high-tech company, and you have a great idea for a blockbuster product. You think your idea can be a winner, so you talk with friends in the marketing and sales departments to get their feedback. They think your idea's great, so you all recruit more team members from engineering, production, and finance. Those members sign on, and everyone works together to fix problems, test prototypes, and set schedules. Eventually, your idea becomes a reality, and the product takes off and generates sales—and recognition for your team. Sound too good to be true? Not at W. L. Gore. Gore's employees are more than nurtured by bosses, more than independent from their bosses. They have no bosses—at all.

Headquartered in Newark, Delaware, Gore has 45 locations around the world and not one "employee." Instead, Gore has 7,300 associates. The $1.1 billion company is best

known for developing the high-tech fabric Gore-Tex. But Gore products are in hundreds of markets. Its wire and cables have landed on the moon, and the company has pioneered developments in work wear, active wear, tissue regeneration, printed circuit boards, fiber optics, and the detection and control of pollution. Founded in 1958 by Bill and Vieve Gore, the company is known for its innovative products and its unstructured organization.

From the beginning, Gore's flat lattice organization has operated on the belief that leaders should be chosen by the people who follow them. So Gore has no hierarchy, no chain of command, and no set channels of communication. The company states: "We encourage hands-on innovation and discourage bureaucracy, involving those closest to a project in decision making. Teams organize around opportunities and leaders emerge." Of course, for this bossless system to work, associates must commit to (1) being fair to each other; (2) encouraging and helping other associates to grow in knowledge, skill, and scope of responsibility; (3) making and keeping commitments; and (4) consulting other associates before taking any action that could hurt the company's reputation.

WWW. www.gore.com

Associates are hired for general work areas. For example, Terri Kelly works in the military-fabrics division. New associates receive guidance from sponsors. "People here should never wait around to be asked to join a team," says Kelly. "They have to volunteer." Sponsors help new associates commit to projects that match their skills and interests. But Kelly explains, "You won't get invited to join the hot teams until you've already contributed to projects that weren't so attractive. To get ahead, you must first demonstrate that you can take ownership of a project and stick with it."

Associates can quickly earn credibility. Leaders emerge naturally, earning followers by demonstrating special knowledge, skills, or experience. Says Kelly, "You cultivate followership by selling yourself, articulating your ideas, and developing a reputation for seeing things through." When Kelly gets an idea, she plans it out carefully. She might take an idea to someone in marketing to see whether a market exists for it. If not, she might abandon that idea. But if a market does exist, she would recruit the marketing person to join her team. In fact, Kelly would form her core team with people from other divisions. To get them involved and excited, she must help them think of her project as their own. "The project won't go anywhere if you don't let people run with it," explains Kelly.

Not only is this team-based environment keeping the company financially successful, but Gore continues to be listed on *Fortune* magazine's "100 Best Companies to Work For in America"—no easy feat. As companies try harder and harder to attract and keep good workers, those that empower their employees are having superior results. Gore believes that the traditional chain of command can block innovation and stifle creativity. With no bosses, Gore's people choose their own projects and assemble the resources they need to succeed, creating pride and camaraderie as well as products.[1]

CHAPTER OVERVIEW

In today's competitive business environment, W. L. Gore and thousands of other companies are trying to improve their performance. Like the company's innovative chief executives, Bill and Vieve Gore, top managers at most companies recognize that empowerment, teamwork, and communication are essential conditions for employee participation in improving organizational performance. Advances in information technology have powerfully influenced the ability of firms to give employees needed resources to make decisions, work in teams, and share information.

This chapter focuses on how organizations are involving employees by applying the concepts of empowerment, teamwork, and communication. It begins by discussing ways in which managers are expanding their employees' decision-making authority and responsibility. It then explains why firms are moving toward relying on teams of workers rather than individuals to make decisions. Finally, it discusses how effective communication allows workers to share information that improves decision making.

EMPOWERING EMPLOYEES

Organizations throughout the world are working to offer high-quality goods and services that create customer satisfaction. As part of this effort, many firms have adopted an approach to improving quality called **total quality management (TQM)**. This concept envisions a companywide commitment to quality based on achieving world-class performance and customer satisfaction as a crucial strategic objective.

A TQM organization involves all employees in determining customer requirements and what they need to do to meet those expectations. Marketers develop products that people want to buy; engineers design products to work the way customers want to use them; production workers build quality into every product they make; salespeople deliver what they promise to customers; information systems specialists use technology to ensure that the firm fills customer orders correctly and on time; financial managers help to determine prices that give value to customers.

The teachings of quality advocates such as W. Edwards Deming, Joseph Juran, Philip Crosby, and Armand Feigenbaum set guidelines for top managers in establishing quality programs. These pioneers have proposed that effective quality programs begin with the leadership of top managers, who build quality values into their organizations and communicate quality goals and benefits to employees, suppliers, and customers. Top management must also provide training for employees and the tools and resources they need to continuously improve products and work processes.

Empowerment of employees is an important component of quality programs. Top managers promote this goal by giving employees authority and responsibility to make decisions about their work without traditional managerial approval and control. Empowerment seeks to tap the brainpower of all employees to find improved ways of doing their jobs and executing their ideas. Empowering employees frees managers from hands-on control of subordinates. It also motivates workers by adding challenge to their jobs and giving them a feeling of ownership.

Managers empower employees by sharing company information, giving them decision-making authority, and rewarding employees based on company performance.

Sharing Information

Employers empower employees by keeping them informed about the company's financial performance. Companies like Springfield Remanufacturing Corporation report to employees financial information, such as profit and loss statements, as well as the salaries of top executives. They also provide training that helps employees to interpret financial statements and understand how their work contributes to bottom line results. Candy Smalley, a production team leader at Springfield Remanufacturing, says, "When I first came here and the CEO not only gave us the financials but expected us to learn them, I was astounded. We felt respected. And now we use those numbers to improve."[2]

 www.srcreman.com

In addition to sharing information about the company, an employer can empower employees by communicating information about industry trends, competitive performance, suppliers and customers, and external opportunities and threats.

Business Directory

total quality management (TQM) companywide program for improving the quality of goods and services by achieving world-class performance and customer satisfaction.

empowerment giving employees authority and responsibility to make decisions about their work without traditional managerial approval and control.

Employee empowerment has benefited from advances in information technology. Firms once needed layers of management to analyze information and communicate it up and down their organizational hierarchies. Now, however, the Internet, internal company networks and databases, and communication tools such as e-mail and videoconferencing allow operating employees to carry out many of these activities on their own.

To spur high-quality service, Wal-Mart empowers employees by giving them communication technology tools. The retailer spends half a billion dollars a year on information technology that informs store managers about top-selling products by number of units sold, total dollars, and profits. Department managers at Wal-Mart stores use this information in promoting top-selling merchandise and in making sure the items are in stock. Wal-Mart clerks use the information to check their prices against those of competitors. Without authorization from managers, clerks can lower a product's price, print out a new price on the store's laser printer, and alert Wal-Mart's home office of the lowered price. Through the company's satellite system, the home office sends the price change to stores throughout the country.[3]

While information technology helps to empower employees, many employers exercise close control over how employees use their information technology tools. The Solving an Ethical Controversy describes one such control technique.

Sharing Decision-Making Authority

Chapter 9 explained that employers are giving employees more authority and responsibility in choosing their benefits plans through cafeteria-style plans and in scheduling their workdays through flexible work programs. The concept of empowerment is truly implemented, however, when employees have the power to make decisions that influence

their work procedures in ways that are linked to a firm's vision and competitive strategy. This approach involves employees in suggesting improvements in their work and then allowing them to turn their ideas into actions.

Monarch Marking Systems hired a new top management team to turn around the long-languishing manufacturer of barcoding and price-marking equipment. The new management team discovered that most of the company's 500 employees had been working at the same assembly-line machines for decades. Convinced that they could use the brainpower of the employees to improve productivity, the managers formed problem-solving teams to tackle specific work problems, telling team members, "Go make it happen, then tell us about it." The teams were charged with generating their own ideas to solve the problems and making any changes needed to execute their ideas. They received authority to work out changes that involved other departments and suppliers.

The project to empower Monarch's workers produced impressive results. One team reduced the number of job categories from 120 to 32 by cross-training employees to handle multiple tasks. Another team decided to train machine operators to report their production figures online rather than delivering the reports on foot, a solution that saved the company 7,600 hours of work time.

Workers that assembled Monarch's top-selling product, a high-tech bar-code reader, completely reorganized their work process. Previously, they had assembled units traveling along a mechanical conveyor belt, with each worker doing part of the assembly. The team decided that workers could easily pass the 2-pound product from one to another. They eliminated the conveyor belt and designed a new workstation in a small area where workers faced each other and handed the products to co-workers. The new setup reduced the square footage of their assembly area by 70 percent, cut work-in-process inventory by $127,000, and reduced past-due shipments by 90 percent. The team members not only increased their productivity by 100 per-

Wal-Mart's computer and communication technology puts information in the hands of employees. Every employee knows the prices of products, their markups, and how many are sold. Sharing information results in high-quality communication among employees and between Wal-Mart and its customers.

cent, but they also enhanced their enjoyment of their work. Rather than remaining isolated at separate stations on the assembly line, employees could converse easily with co-workers, and employees ahead of their production goals could help others who fell behind goals.

Empowerment at Monarch has changed employee attitudes. Effie Winters, an employee who worked in an isolated job on the assembly line for 20 years, says, "We're not just pieces of equipment anymore. My input means something."[4]

www.monarch-marking.com

Firms are empowering employees in other ways, as well, including giving them tasks once handled by managers. At Cin-Made, a manufacturer of mailing tubes, hourly workers perform such traditional management tasks as purchasing supplies, hiring new employees, scheduling their own hours, overseeing the company's safety program, and administering its skill-based pay system.

Linking Rewards to Company Performance

Employers that empower workers should reward desirable ideas and actions. Compensation plans such as pay for performance, pay for knowledge, and gain sharing give employees a sense of ownership. Perhaps the ultimate step in convincing employees of their stake in the continuing prosperity of their firm is worker ownership, which makes employees financial participants in company performance.

According to the National Center for Employee Ownership (NCEO), about 11 million U.S. employees participate in **employee stock ownership plans (ESOPs).** These plans benefit employees by giving them ownership stakes in the companies for which they work, leading to potential profits when the value of their firm increases. Under ESOP plans, the employer buys company stock on behalf of the employees, whose accounts continue to grow in value tax-free until they retire.

To help employees understand the benefits of their ownership stakes, employers with ESOPs share financial information about company assets and performance, as well as the salaries of top managers. "Under an ESOP, you treat employees with the same respect you would accord a partner. Then they start behaving like owners," says Don Way, president of Thoits Insurance Service. Way says

that Thoits's ESOP has helped the company to recruit, retain, and motivate talented employees.[5]

 www.nceo.org

ESOPs are most popular in small firms, where they help to increase productivity and boost employee morale. Employees are motivated to work harder and smarter than they would without ESOPs, because as part owners, they share in their firm's financial success. "Everybody wants the company to do the best it possibly can," says Joe Cabral, president of Chatsworth Products, which makes support equipment for computer networks. The ESOP at Chatsworth "creates a vision for every employee and gets everybody pulling in the same direction," says Cabral.[6]

ESOPs have even helped to save failing businesses. Quincy Castings, for example, was a small firm losing money and about to be sold or closed. Management decided to initiate an ESOP and form all employees into quality-improvement teams, efforts that quickly boosted sales and profits. Gary Bardon, Quincy's president, attributes the firm's turnaround to its ESOP. Without the plan, Bardon says, employees "simply would not have appreciated the depths of our financial difficulties and the need to produce a much higher-quality product faster and at a more competitive price. That required people who were willing to work smarter and bring the best possible ideas to the table."[7]

Some large, well-known firms such as Avis and Publix Supermarkets also have ESOPs. One of the largest employee-owned firms is Science Applications International (SAIC). The Business Hall of Fame describes how employee ownership is just one of many ways in which SAIC empowers its employees.

TEAMWORK

Teamwork is the practice of organizing a group of workers to achieve a common objective. You have most likely experienced teamwork as a member of a sports team, a debate team, a band, or a school project work group. People commit to teamwork to perform certain functions or solve particular problems, both in business and in other areas. A

Business Directory

teamwork practice of organizing groups of people to work together to achieve a common objective.

SOLVING AN ETHICAL CONTROVERSY

Should Employers Monitor Employees' Activities on the Internet?

Employers empower employees to make decisions and perform their work without close supervision and control. Companies have equipped employees with computers and hooked them up to the World Wide Web to give wide access to information and support decision making.

Many firms risk controversy, however, by monitoring how employees use their information technology tools. The oversight is needed, they claim, because many employees abuse the tools provided to perform their work. Most firms that monitor their employees do so without disclosing the eavesdropping.

Employers estimate that employees who go online spend about one-third of their time on activities unrelated to their jobs. They use Internet links to send personal e-mail messages, chat on bulletin boards, shop online, play games, check sports scores, search for recipes, buy stocks, and conduct other personal financial transactions. A survey by the marketing research firm A. C. Nielsen found that in one month,

employees at IBM, Apple, and AT&T spent 13,048 hours—equal to 1,631 work days—at the *Penthouse* magazine site. A survey of 1,500 employees conducted by UCLA and consulting firm Arthur Andersen revealed that the primary use of e-mail is "to chat with other employees."

To combat the problem of cyberwaste, employers are monitoring employees' computer files and tracking their e-mail messages. They are hiring surveillance specialists and installing monitoring software to track and record everything employees do on their computers. A software program called "Little Brother" can track which Web sites employees visit. A report by the International Labor Organization concluded that "monitoring and surveillance techniques available as a result of advances in technology make methods of control more pervasive than ever before and raise serious questions of human rights."

 Is Computer Monitoring an Invasion of Employees' Privacy Rights?

PRO

1. Computer monitoring betrays the trusting relationship between the employer and the employee. Em-

ployers assign personal passwords to protect e-mail and the Internet, leading employees to believe that they have private and confidential access.

2. Employers should measure employees' performance by evaluating quality and productivity, not by counting the time they spend playing computer games or visiting chat rooms.

3. The concept of empowerment entails employee control of their work time. Computer monitoring defeats the idea of empowerment by retaining control in the hands of employers.

4. Taking breaks during the workday to send a personal e-mail or check a sports score are recreational activities that help reduce employee stress. These activities are no different from employees gathering around the water cooler to take short breaks from their work.

CON

1. Sending personal e-mail and recreational Web surfing undermine the productivity gains that personal computers are intended to bring to firms. "We're here for

---

team of workers cooperates to perform a certain function, such as developing a new car, or to solve a particular problem, such as improving methods for filling customer orders.

Teamwork is a growing trend in business, and in many other organizations such as hospitals, not-for-profits, and government agencies. The ability to work effectively as a team member rather than as an individual is a more important skill now than ever before. Teamwork is one of the most frequent topics of employee training programs, where individuals often learn team-building skills. Many firms emphasize the importance of teamwork during their hiring processes, asking job applicants about their previous experiences as team members. Companies want to hire people who can work well with other people in teams.

At Worthington Industries, an Ohio-based steel producer, job applicants are interviewed by teams of employ-

ees. After hiring, a new employee completes a 90-day probation period culminating in a vote by a team of about ten co-workers. Worthington's emphasis on team hiring helps to ensure that new members have the potential for teamwork, a priority that relates to the firm's compensation system. At Worthington, profit sharing accounts for about 40 percent of employees' pay. "Peers need an opportunity to weigh in on a candidate," says Eric Smolenski, a personnel manager. "They need a chance to ask whether they want to split the pie with a particular individual."[8]

Teamwork is an important consideration, because it encourages employees to pool their talents and ideas so they can achieve more together than they could achieve working as individuals. Lam Nguyen of Sun Microsystems used teamwork to boost employee efficiency. When Nguyen became the new manager of the company's failure analysis

business purposes, not for individual entertainment," says Jim Kinney, chief information officer at Kraft Foods. Kraft has installed software that prevents employees from visiting Web sites unrelated to their jobs.

2. Employers, not employees, own technology tools. These resources are company property. As such, employers have every right to know what employees are doing with these tools. Firms do not want to invest time and money for new technology that results in a waste of employees' time and employers' money. Kmart tells its employees that e-mail messages are written on company-owned "electronic stationery."

3. Employers need to monitor e-mail and Internet usage to protect themselves against possible lawsuits. Morgan Stanley, an investment banking firm, was sued for $70 million by several employees, who claimed that co-workers posted racist jokes on the company's e-mail system that created a hostile work environment. An employee lawsuit against R. R. Donnelley & Sons, a commercial printing firm, has cited 165 e-mail messages containing racial, ethnic, and sexual jokes to demonstrate a climate of employment discrimination and harassment.

Attorney Jay Waks, who represents firms in employment litigation, says that employers have no option but to protect themselves. "If they're going to be held liable, they'd better monitor," says Waks.

4. Employers have the legal right to monitor e-mail and Internet usage. The 1986 Electronic Communications Act allows companies to monitor employees' messages for "business purposes." Protecting themselves from lawsuits and time theft fall in the category of business purposes.

SUMMARY

Employers are addressing the privacy issues raised by employees. They have established written policies about e-mail and Internet usage and asked employees to sign them to indicate awareness. Such a policy likely states explicitly that e-mail and the Internet are services owned by the company, that the purpose of these services is strictly to conduct company business, and that the employer has the right to monitor any data in the firm's electronic communication system. They warn employees to visit only those sites "where you would want to leave your business card."

Other companies fire employees who irresponsibly use the Internet on company time. Compaq Computer, for example, dismissed a dozen employ-

ees for registering more than 1,000 visits to sex sites during work hours. AT&T has blocked employee access to the *Penthouse* page and other sex sites. But firing employees and blocking access to sites cost companies big money.

Advocates of employee rights are trying to protect workers from employer eavesdropping by encouraging the passage of laws ensuring workers' rights to privacy. The Electronic Privacy Information Center in Washington, D.C., was established to promote employee cyber-liberties. To learn more about the issue of employee monitoring, visit the center's Web site.

www.epic.com

Sources: "Worldtalk Launches Free Seminar Series Focused on Corporate Policies for Internet Usage," Business Wire, April 14, 1999; Amy Harmon, "On the Office PC, Bosses Opt for All Work, and No Play," *New York Times*, September 22, 1997, pp. A1, D11; Dana Hawkins, "Who's Watching Now?" *U.S. News & World Report*, September 15, 1997, pp. 56-58; Laurent Belsie, "Downloading Follies: More Companies Are Policing Workers' Use of the Internet," *San Diego Union-Tribune*, August 11, 1997, pp. C1, C2; Justin Martin, "Hunting Down the Porn Freaks," *Fortune*, July 21, 1997, p. 116; Michael Adams, "Mixed Messages," *Sales & Marketing Management*, June 1997, pp. 73–76; and Anne Fischer, "How Safe Is My E-Mail?" *Fortune*, October 14, 1996, p. 220.

department, he faced a difficult challenge. The 110 technicians in the department had fallen far behind in their work repairing defective printed circuit boards. They had a backlog of 5,000 circuit boards that needed repair. From conversations with the technicians, Nguyen learned that they resented having to meet a quota of fixing ten boards each day, so everyone fought over the easiest repair jobs.

Nguyen eliminated the quota system and organized the technicians into three teams based on their levels of technical skill and experience. He then assigned repair work to teams based on the complexity of the work that needed to be done. Within 6 months, the teams eliminated

the backlog. "If you work as a team, things will happen," says Nguyen.[9]

What Is a Team?

A **team** is a group of people with complementary skills who are committed to a common purpose, approach, and

Business Directory

team group of employees who are committed to a common purpose, approach, and set of performance goals.

The Right Way to Empower Employees

Dr. J. Robert Beyster never dreamed of becoming an entrepreneur. In fact, he considered entrepreneurship "somewhat distasteful." When Beyster worked as a physicist at Los Alamos National Laboratory during the 1950s, many of his co-workers left the laboratory to start their own companies. Beyster thought they should be focusing on scientific projects and wondered why they were "starting these crazy little companies."

Beyster later left the laboratory to work as a physicist for General Atomic, a defense contractor. When that firm was acquired by Gulf Oil, the new management team focused on manufacturing rather than on the small research projects Beyster loved. In 1969, he decided to start his own crazy little company, a research and engineering firm that today is called Science Applications International Corporation

(SAIC). The company was launched with two government contracts for nuclear power and weapons research.

From the beginning, Beyster decided that the employees would own the company. He wanted to manage his company differently from the way his previous employer was managed. There, managers were motivated more strongly by the financial interests of outside shareholders than by the research that he and other scientists were doing. At SAIC, Beyster determined, he would allow employees to purchase amounts of stock that reflected their contributions to building SAIC and providing quality service to customers. Beyster's ownership philosophy reflects three beliefs:

1. **Fairness suggests that those who contribute their energies to the company should own it and benefit from its success.**

2. **Employees with ownership interests are motivated to deliver excellent products to customers,**

participate in and positively influence the company's direction, insist on an ethical work environment, work together as teammates, and promote the company's financial growth.

3. **Employee-owned firms are driven by the broad, common interests of employees, shareholders, and managers rather than by the narrow, strictly financial interests of uninvolved outside owners.**

SAIC provides several ownership options to workers. An employee stock ownership plan covers all employees. Those who land new contracts for the firm can buy additional shares of stock in proportion to the values of the contracts. The company offers stock options and stock bonuses that reward employees for outstanding individual performance. Finally, each year SAIC identifies 200 employees as future leaders, awarding $25,000 in company stock to each one. SAIC maintains an internal stock market, where

---

set of performance goals. All team members hold themselves mutually responsible and accountable for accomplishing their objectives.

The trend in U.S. business toward developing teams started in the 1980s, when managers began to address quality concerns. They approached this goal in a variety of ways, including forming quality circles, in which workers meet weekly or monthly to discuss ways to improve quality. This concept spread as such teams demonstrated their ability to help companies reduce output of defective products and the time wasted in reworking those units. By 1987, two-thirds of America's 1,000 largest firms operated quality circles. By the mid-1990s, the percentage of major firms implementing quality circles to solve minor quality problems had declined, primarily because their focus on activities with limited scope typically produced only modest increases in productivity.

Companies continued to reduce layers of management through downsizing, and they became increasingly involved in international business. These trends encouraged formation of many different types of teams. Figure 10.1

shows that the list includes work teams, problem-solving teams, management teams, quality circles, and even virtual teams made up of geographically separated members who interact via computer. The current focus on teamwork centers on two basic types of teams: work teams and problem-solving teams.

Work Teams **Work teams,** which operate in about two-thirds of U.S. firms, are relatively permanent groups of employees. In this modern approach, small numbers of people with complementary skills perform the day-to-day work of the organization. General Motors Corporation creates work teams throughout the company. A permanent work team at one GM production facility is the Mutilation Coordination Team. Composed of several hourly workers, this team is responsible for improving quality by locating and fixing problems on the assembly line.[10]

When a work team is empowered with authority to make decisions about how the members complete their daily tasks, it is called a *self-managed team*. A self-managed team works most effectively when it combines

employees can trade shares with co-workers.

A fundamental part of SAIC's ownership system is employee empowerment. SAIC encompasses more than 400 independent operations, each with its own business plan. Beyster's strategy calls for hiring talented people, giving them seed money and their own profit and loss responsibility, and then letting them build their own businesses.

"What we've done is to build a company of entrepreneurs," says Beyster. "Not just one or two at the top. A company in which those who are motivated and capable can organize, manage, and assume the risk of different aspects of the company. In return they receive not only salary but ownership of the company."

All SAIC employees are given decision-making authority. "When I'm making a decision, I don't just make it as an information technology manager, I make it as an owner," says Narri Cooper, a director in SAIC's management information systems department. Beyster even extends employee empowerment to the overall direction of the company. Of the 22 members on

the board of directors, 9 are SAIC employees.

With 25,000 employees and revenues of $4 billion, SAIC is one of the nation's most successful employee-owned companies. Based in San Diego, the company helps to solve complex, technical problems in the areas of national and international security, information technology, environmental systems, energy, health systems and services, transportation, telecommunications, and space exploration. Beyster attributes SAIC's growth and success to his employee-owners. "I'm reluctant to take the credit," he says. "Employee ownership really did it."

www. **www.saic.com**

QUESTIONS FOR CRITICAL THINKING

1. Dr. Beyster formed the nonprofit Foundation for Enterprise Development to help entrepreneurs imple-

ment shared ownership and employee empowerment to help them compete effectively in the world marketplace. If you were to begin your own firm, would you seek advice from the foundation? Would you be willing to "share the wealth" with your employees? Why or why not?

2. The National Center for Employee Ownership points out a dramatic increase in recent years in stock options awarded by privately held companies like SAIC to employees. Why do you think these plans are on the rise?

Sources: "SAIC's Early Years: The Start-up of a High-Tech Leader" and "Why Is SAIC Employee-Owned?" accessed at http://www.saic.com, March 16, 1998; Carolyn T. Geer, "Turning Employees into Stakeholders," *Forbes*, December 1, 1997, pp. 154–157; and Larry Armstrong, "Happy Fallout Down at the Nuke Lab," *Business Week*, October 7, 1996, p. 42.

employees with a range of skills and functions. Members are cross-trained to perform each other's jobs as needed. As part of empowering these teams with the decision-making authority they need to perform their organizational roles, a firm usually must permit them to select fellow team members, spend money, solve problems, evaluate results, and plan future projects.[11] Distributing decision-making authority in this way can free members to concentrate on satisfying customers.

Problem-Solving Teams In contrast, a **problem-solving team** is a temporary combination of workers who gather to solve a specific problem and then disband. Like work teams, special-purpose problem-solving teams may self-manage their work. They differ from work teams in important ways, though. Whereas work teams are permanent units designed to handle any workplace problem that arises, problem-solving teams pursue specific missions. The missions can be broadly stated—such as finding out why customers aren't satisfied—or narrowly defined—such as solving the overheating problem in Generator 4.

Once the team completes its task by solving the problem, it usually disbands.

The Dutch brewer Heineken created a problem-solving team after management decided to close more than ten breweries throughout Europe. Because management did not have a clear idea of the best locations for future production plants, it formed a 13-member European Product Task Force with representatives from five countries. The team analyzed how many breweries Heineken would need, how much capacity each should have, and how the company could best take advantage of economies of scale while still remaining responsive to customers. The team took 18 months to formulate its findings and suggestions, most of which were quickly implemented, and then its members disbanded.[12]

When a team joins members from different functions within the company, such as production, marketing, and finance, it is called a *cross-functional team.* Most often cross-functional teams work on specific problems or projects, but they can also serve as permanent work-team arrangements. The value of cross-functional teams comes

Figure 10.1	Five Species of Teams

THE FIVE SPECIES OF TEAMS

The kingdom of teams can be confusing. Here's a rundown of the most common types.

Virtual Teams
A characteristic of this new type of work team: members talk by computer flying in and out as needed, and take turns as leader.

Management Teams
Consisting mainly of managers from various functions, like sales and production, this species coordinates work among teams.

Quality Circles
In danger of extinction, this type, typically made of workers and supervisors, meets intermittently to air work-place problems.

Problem-Solving Teams
This most popular of types comprises knowledge workers who gather to solve specific problems and then disband.

Work Teams
An increasingly popular species, work teams do just that—the daily work. When empowered, they are self-managed teams.

from their ability to bring many different perspectives to a work effort.

An advocate of cross-functional teams is Peter Neff, the CEO of Rhone-Poulenc, Inc., the U.S. subsidiary of France's leading chemical and pharmaceutical manufacturer. "You have to break down the boundaries between different parts of the organization," says Neff. "A lot of narrow silos will kill an organization. Companies that can't solve problems as teams won't last very long. Things are simply too complex to be done by specialists. You need to have people who know different parts of an issue get together to solve problems as a team."[13]

Certain types of teams work more effectively than others in particular circumstances, depending on their purposes. A cross-functional team can effectively develop an entirely new good or service. However, a vertical team with members from a single department, such as product engineering, may be a better choice to modify an existing product. Members of a cross-functional team take time to establish their roles and begin working together productively, and such a delay could be costly in a competitive marketplace.

One of the most innovative team approaches in business today involves vendor-client partnerships. Dana Corporation's Spicer Lighter Axle Division of Fort Wayne, Indiana, routinely supports one of its most important customers, Ford Motor Company, by placing its engineers on-site at the automaker's plants during the most critical phases of product design and manufacturing. Such inter-company product development teams iron out Ford's ob-

jectives, determine the limits of what Dana can provide, and radically reduce design errors as well as manufacturing waste and rework.[14]

TEAM CHARACTERISTICS

Effective teams share a number of characteristics. These include appropriate sizes, the roles played by members, and the diversity of members.

Team Size

Teams can range in size from as small as two people to as large as 150 people. In practice, however, most teams have fewer than 15 members. Although no ideal size limit applies to every team, many proponents of teamwork believe that they achieve maximum results with about 7 members. A group of this size is big enough to benefit from a variety of diverse skills, yet small enough to allow members to communicate easily and feel part of a close-knit group.

Certainly, groups smaller or larger than this general ideal size can do effective work, but they can create certain challenges for a team leader. Participants in small teams of two to four members often show a desire to get along with each other. They tend to favor informal interactions marked by discussions of personal topics, and they make only limited demands on team leaders. A large team with more than 12 members poses a different challenge for team leaders, because decision making may work slowly and participants may feel limited commitments to team goals. Large teams also tend to foster disagreements, absenteeism, and membership turnover. Subgroups may form, leading to possible conflicts among various factions. As a general rule, a team of more than 20 people should be divided into subteams, each with its own members and goals.

Team Roles

Team members tend to take on certain roles, as shown in Figure 10.2.[15] They can be classified as task specialist and socio-emotional roles. People who assume the task specialist role devote time and energy to helping the team accomplish its specific goals. These team members are the ones who actively propose new ideas and solutions to problems, evaluate the suggestions of others, ask for more information, and summarize group discussions.

Team members who play the socio-emotional role devote their time and energy to supporting the emotional needs of team members and to maintaining the team as a social unit. They encourage others to contribute ideas, try to reduce tensions that arise among team members, reconcile conflicts, and often change their own opinions in trying to maintain team harmony.

Some team members may assume dual roles by performing both task specialist and socio-emotional activities. Those who can assume dual roles often are chosen as team leaders, because they satisfy both types of needs. Finally, some members may fall into a nonparticipator role, in which they contribute little or nothing to accomplishing the task or satisfying social and emotional needs.

Managers work to form balanced teams with members capable of performing both task-oriented and social roles. Both roles are important, but too many members of either type can impair the team's ability to function. A team with too many task specialists may be productive in the short term but create an unsatisfying situation over a longer time period, because team members may become unsupportive of each other. Teams with too many socio-emotional types can be satisfying but unproductive, since participants may hesitate to disagree or to criticize each other.

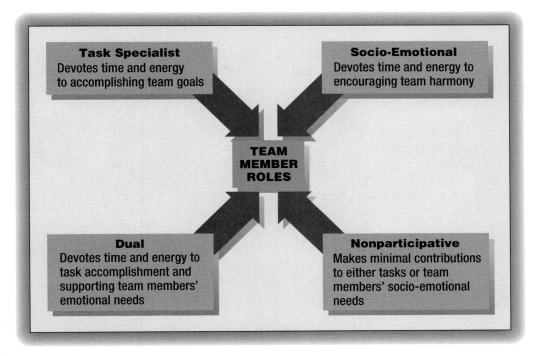

Figure 10.2 **Team Member Roles**

Team Diversity

Besides playing different roles, team members may bring to the team varied perspectives based on differences in their work experiences and age, gender, and cultural backgrounds. A cross-functional team establishes one type of diversity by bringing together the expertise of members from different functions in the organization. Another type of diversity defines a cross-cultural team.

Several research studies have supported the idea that diversity adds value to teamwork. At the University of North Texas, for example, the work of culturally diverse teams of business students was compared to that of all-white teams over a period of 17 weeks. By the end of the study, the teams that incorporated different cultures displayed a broader range of viewpoints and produced more innovative solutions to problems than did the homogeneous teams.

Many firms are realizing that diverse teams can help them to operate on a global scale. Intel, Maxus Energy, and other companies have set up international work teams to foster exchanges of insights about international markets and dissimilar business cultures.

International teamwork can be a challenge, though. When the Egyptian government planned a major construction project, it brought together employees from an Australian construction management firm, a Norwegian engineering company, and workers from several countries, including Egypt. To form these employees and outside contractors into teams, the project's managers had to settle on a common language. They chose English, although co-workers who shared a native language used it in discussions among themselves. Cultural differences also complicated work scheduling. Norwegian workers wanted to work Monday through Friday; Egyptians wanted to work Saturday through Wednesday. Management let each team work out its own solution and gained some unexpected benefits. These interactions led to creation of a schedule of overlapping shifts, resulting in increased contact between teams and 10 days of productivity from a 7-day work week.[16]

Teamwork in Small Organizations

Like large firms, small companies can benefit from teamwork. In fact, small firms themselves may function as teams. If a firm is limited to a small number of employees, say, between 10 and 15, the principles of managing teams may apply to the entire organization. Sometimes, small firms apply teamwork principles to their relationships with outside vendors or consultants.

The owner-manager of a small firm can cultivate the characteristics of successful teams. The manager can direct everyone's efforts toward the team's common purpose, empower team members, and ensure that the team includes a balance of task specialists and members comfortable playing a socio-emotional role. The manager also can recruit team members with diverse backgrounds and encourage everyone to contribute to the team.

Patricia Louko, founder and president of Books Plus, says she operates her bookstore as "a total team approach." Louko hires only part-time employees at Books Plus, an off-campus college bookstore in Lake Worth, Florida, that serves students from the four campuses of Palm Beach Community College. She cross-trains all employees, so they can perform every job in the store, including sales, customer service, ordering, receiving, and book buyback. Louko's employees also have genuine input into how the store is run. "Any employee is entitled to make any decision when working with customers [on matters such as

Bookstore owner Patricia Louko (right) takes a total team approach in operating her small business. She cross-trains all employees, so everyone can perform all the tasks involved in running the store.

price and trade-ins], and I usually go along with it," says Louko. "We have meetings about what will work and what will not work. I'm open to 'How do you think we can do this better?' If the group's in agreement, we switch."[17]

The concept of teamwork also applies to entrepreneurs. The key to success in managing the growth of a new venture often rests with the founder's ability to assemble a team of employees who bring skills and experiences that complement the founder's skills. When Susan and David Buchanan launched Aurum Software, they realized that their company could grow only if they hired someone with marketing expertise. To complement Susan's computer expertise and David's experience as an engineer, they hired Mary Coleman, a marketing professional, and named her chief executive officer.[18]

Perhaps the greatest challenge for an entrepreneur who wants to encourage teamwork is to sit back and let the team generate ideas. "It's not easy for an entrepreneur to take this role, but it is the way to get a productive team," says Lawrence Custis, a management consultant.[19]

The Process of Forming Teams

Teams can increase productivity, raise morale, and nurture innovation. However, these benefits result only if the type of team created matches the task to be accomplished. In addition to matching the type of team to the task, managers must select the right types of people to become team members. While many firms use teams, they often limit participation to certain groups of employees.

Since firms invest so much time and money creating and supporting teams, they must form these units carefully with several factors in mind. The first consideration must be the need for a team to accomplish a particular task. People often do work more productively as individuals rather than as team members. Before forming a team, management should analyze the work to be done, decide whether a team approach is preferable, and then select the best type of team.

"There are some organizations that set teams up because it's the flavor of the month," says Diane MacDonald of Mercer Management Consulting and co-author of a study on the effectiveness of teams. Only 13 percent of the teams studied, most of them in *Fortune* 1,000 companies, received high ratings for effectiveness.[20]

An organization must identify a purpose for forming a team, and that purpose must be clearly stated to team members. A study by another consulting firm, The Hay Group, revealed that the primary reason why teams fail is the lack of clear goals.[21]

When electronics manufacturer Texas Instruments decided to form teams, management grouped together employees from different functions such as sales and engineering. "We said, 'You're empowered; go do what you want to do,'" says J. D. Bryant, TI's senior organizational development consultant. "But that's not the gist of empowerment." The company's sales reps, traditionally highly individualistic workers, had no reason to embrace teamwork. That motivation changed when TI gave its teams specific goals tied to corporate objectives. One year, the goal was to reduce the cost of a wafer, a plate on which computer chips are built. United by that goal, sales reps and engineers worked as team members, frequently meeting to find ways to reduce costs. Sales reps also recognized incentives to reduce costs, such as travel and presentation expenses, because the company linked their compensation to their success at cutting costs.[22]

Managers can increase the likelihood of forming effective work teams by following the step-by-step approach outlined in Table 10.1. The process begins by studying successful teams in other organizations and ends by designing compensation plans for team members. When a firm's managers decide to form teams, they must accompany the move with a team-based pay plan that rewards members for achieving team goals. This priority can be a difficult one, since compensation must motivate individual team members while encouraging them to act together as a team. The most effective pay plans reward both team and individual performance. At Unisys Corporation, for example, each team member receives a team bonus and individual raises set by performance reviews conducted by a team coach plus three co-workers selected by the employee.[23]

Stages of Team Development

Teams typically progress through five stages of development, labeled forming, storming, norming, performing, and adjourning.[24] These stages are summarized in Figure 10.3.

Stage 1: Forming This first stage is an orientation period during which team members get to know each other and find out what behaviors are acceptable to the group. Team members begin with curiosity about expectations of them and whether they will fit in with the group. An effective team leader provides time for members to become acquainted.

Stage 2: Storming The personalities of team members begin to emerge at this stage as members clarify their roles and expectations. Conflicts may arise, as people disagree over the team's mission and jockey for position and control of the group. Subgroups may form based on common interests or concerns. At this stage, the team leader must encourage everyone to participate, allowing members to work through their uncertainties and conflicts. Teams must move beyond this stage in order to achieve real productivity.

Stage 3: Norming During this stage, members resolve differences between them, accept each other, and reach consensus about the roles of the team leaders and other participants. This stage is usually brief in duration, and the team leader should use it to emphasize the team's unity and the importance of its objectives.

Stage 4: Performing Team members focus on solving problems and accomplishing tasks at this stage. They interact frequently and handle conflicts in constructive ways. The team leader encourages contributions from all members.

Stage 5: Adjourning The team disbands at this stage after members have completed a task or solved a problem. During this phase, the focus is on wrapping up and summarizing the team's experiences and accomplishments. The team leader may recognize the team's accomplishments with a celebration, perhaps handing out plaques or awards.

Table 10.1	**A Step-by-Step Approach to Forming Effective Teams**

Step 1: Study other companies' teams.
Step 2: Involve appropriate people in planning and implementing teams.
Step 3: Seek and encourage feedback from team members.
Step 4: Set realistic goals, and distribute schedules.
Step 5: Be prepared to slow down when necessary.
Step 6: Regularly evaluate and adjust the original plan.
Step 7: Keep all team members informed.
Step 8: Be prepared to resolve conflict and confusion.
Step 9: Prepare a plan for team members' compensation.

Team Cohesiveness

Teams tend to maximize productivity when they form into highly cohesive units. **Team cohesiveness** is the extent to which team members are attracted to the team and motivated to remain a part of it. This cohesiveness typically increases when members interact frequently, share common

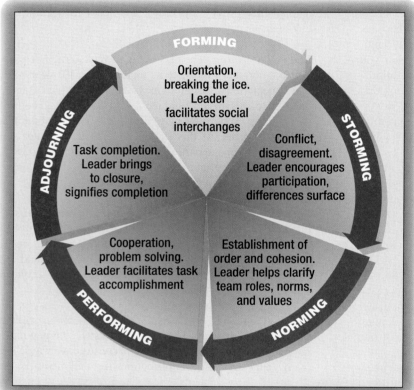

Figure 10.3   **Five Stages of Team Development**

attitudes and goals, and enjoy being together. When cohesiveness is low, morale suffers.

Some firms try to promote interaction among team members through the designs of work spaces. "It's tough to have an effective team if the vast majority of your floor plan is turned over to private offices grouped by job title," says Fritz Steele, an organizational consultant. Hewlett-Packard, Northern Telecom, and computer networking firm 3Com have all eliminated many private offices and adopted open office designs that encourage interaction among team members. They have built large, informal meeting areas and equipped them with computer workstations where teams of various sizes can work together on projects. "When people work in these areas, they get more involved in projects than anyplace else in the company," says Abe Darwish, vice president of real estate and site services at 3Com.[25]

Team Norms

A **team norm** is a standard of conduct shared by team members that guides their behavior. Norms are not formal, written guidelines; they are informal standards that identify key values and clarify team members' expectations.

For entrepreneur Richard Childress, a race-car team owner, effective team norms define the most critical condition for success in professional racing. The results of a race are often determined by teamwork, the ability of pit crew members to work quickly and seamlessly in refueling cars and sending them back on the track in seconds. All employees Childress hires for his racing teams, regardless of their previous experience, begin their work performing menial jobs like stacking tires and filling water bottles, a practice that allows Childress and other team members to judge from the beginning how well new employees are willing to cooperate with other team members. "Attitude is more important than expertise—you've got to have people who won't let you down," says one team member. Childress dismisses anyone with a large ego and a lack of humility who cannot learn to conform to the norm of working selflessly together as a single, unified whole.[26]

Team Conflict

Among all of a team leader's skills, none is more important than the ability to manage conflict. **Conflict** is an antagonistic interaction in which one party attempts to thwart the intentions or goals of another. A certain amount of conflict is inevitable in teams, but too much can impair the ability of team members to exchange ideas, cooperate with each other, and produce results.

Conflict can stem from many sources. It frequently results from competition for scarce resources, such as information, money, or supplies. In addition, team members may experience personality clashes or differ in their ideas about what the team should accomplish. Poor communication also can cause misunderstandings and resentment. Finally, conflict can result in the absence of clear job responsibilities or team roles.

The introduction of teams at Chrysler Corp. brought personality clashes and squabbling over turf and functional responsibilities. Some members insisted on remaining focused on their previous areas of expertise, even though this limitation detracted from the team's collective output. The company dealt with such conflicts by urging employees who resisted change to attend behavior-modification classes. Team members who were not able to adapt left the company.[27]

Styles of Conflict Resolution

No one best method determines measures to manage all conflicts. The most effective reaction depends on the particular situation. Conflict resolution styles represent a continuum ranging from assertive to cooperative responses.

▼ *The Competing Style.* This decisive, assertive approach might be summarized in the expression, "We'll do this task my way." While it does not build team rapport, the competing style can be useful for unpopular decisions or emergencies. This approach also helps to end conflict that escalates beyond hope of any other form of resolution.

▼ *The Avoiding Style.* Neither assertive nor cooperative, avoiding conflict is an effective response when the problem results from some trivial cause or creates a no-win situation, when more information is needed, or when open conflict would cause harm.

▼ *The Compromising Style.* This style blends both assertiveness and cooperation. It works well when conflict arises between two opposing and equally important goals, when combatants are equally powerful, or when the situation brings pressure to achieve an immediate solution.

▼ *The Accommodating Style.* Marked by active cooperation, this style can help to maintain team harmony. A team member may choose to back down in a disagreement on an issue that seems more important to others in the group than to himself or herself.

▼ *The Collaborating Style.* This style combines active assertiveness and cooperation. While it can require lengthy, time-consuming negotiations, it can achieve a win-win situation. It is useful when consensus from all parties is an important goal, or when the viewpoints

of all participants must be merged into a single, mutually acceptable solution.

Northern Telecom encourages teamwork by designing open office spaces that encourage easy interactions between team members.

A team leader can limit the disruptive impact of conflict by focusing team members on broad goals bigger than the immediate sources of disagreement. A team leader can handle conflict that results from ambiguous or overlapping responsibilities by clarifying participants' respective tasks and areas of authority. The leader may encourage the opponents to negotiate an agreement between themselves. This method works well if the individuals deal with the situation in a businesslike, unemotional way. A stubborn disagreement may be turned over to a mediator, an outside party who will discuss the situation with both sides and bring the parties to a mutual decision.

Perhaps the team leader's most important contribution to conflict resolution is to facilitate good communication. Ongoing, effective communication ensures that team members perceive each other accurately, understand what is expected of them, and obtain the information they need. Improved communication increases the chances of working

Business Directory

team cohesiveness extent to which team members feel attracted to the team and motivated to remain a part of it.

team norm informal standard of conduct shared by team members that guides their behavior

cooperatively as a team. The remainder of this chapter discusses the importance of effective communication and the development of good communication skills.

THE IMPORTANCE OF EFFECTIVE COMMUNICATION

Communication can be defined as a meaningful exchange of information through messages. Effective communication is essential to business. Managers spend about 80 percent of their time in direct communications with others, whether on the phone, in meetings, or in individual conversations. The other 20 percent is spent on desk work, much of which also involves communication in the form of writing and reading.

Communication skills are important throughout an organization. Communication with the marketplace in the form of marketing research helps a company to learn what products people want and what changes they would like in existing offerings. Communication among engineers, marketers, and production employees enables a company to create products that provide customer satisfaction. Communication through advertising and personal sales presentations creates a favorable image for the company and persuades customers to buy.

The Process of Communication

Every communication follows a step-by-step process that involves interactions among six elements: sender, message, channel, audience, feedback, and context. This process is illustrated in Figure 10.4.

In the first step, the *sender* composes the message and sends it through a communication carrier, or *channel*. *Encoding* a message means that the sender translates its meaning into understandable terms and a form that allows transmission through a chosen channel. The sender can communicate a particular message through many different channels, including written messages, face-to-face conversations, and electronic mail. The *audience* consists of the person or persons who receive the message. In *decoding*, the receiver of the message interprets its meaning. *Feedback* from the audience—a response to the sender's communication—helps the sender to determine whether the audience has correctly interpreted the intended meaning of the message.

Every communication takes place in some sort of situational and cultural context. The *context* can exert a powerful influence on how well the process works. A conversation between two people in a quiet room, for example, may be a very different experience from the same conversation held in a crowded and noisy room.

Senders need to pay attention to audience feedback, even solicit it if none is forthcoming, since this response clarifies whether the communication has conveyed the intended message. Even with the best of intentions, sender and audience can misunderstand each other. A major manufacturer once announced a 10 percent pay reduction by sending individual letters signed by the president to employees. The immediate effect was the opposite of what was expected. Employees greeted the message with amusement rather than disappointment: It had arrived at each employee's desk on April Fool's Day! Unfortunately, the company had to provide official verification to establish the reality of the pay cut.

Verifying that employees understand messages is especially important in firms that practice total quality management. This practice demands strong employee commitment to customer satisfaction and a full understanding of each person's contribution. Quality-driven companies often seek out and reward employee ideas. For example, the Ritz-Carlton hotel chain maintains an extensive employee feedback program that includes a system for reviewing quality problems reported by employees.

Figure 10.4   **The Communication Process**

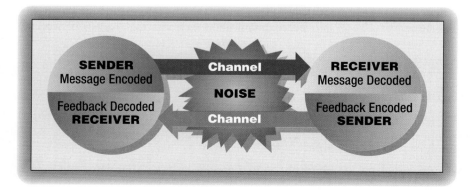

Table 10.2	Forms of Communication	
Form	**Description**	**Example**
Oral communication	Communication transmitted through speech	Personal conversations, speeches, meetings, voice mail, telephone conversations, videoconferences
Written communication	Communication transmitted through writing	Letters, memos, formal reports, news releases, e-mail, faxes
Formal communication	Communication transmitted through the chain of command within an organization to other members or to people outside the organization	Internal—memos, reports, meetings, written proposals, oral presentations, meeting minutes; external—letters, written proposals, oral presentations, speeches, news releases, press conferences
Informal communication	Communication transmitted outside formally authorized channels without regard for the organization's hierarchy of authority	Rumors spread through the grapevine
Verbal communication	Transmission of messages in the form of words	Meetings, telephone calls, voice mail, videoconferences
Nonverbal communication	Communication transmitted through actions and behaviors rather than through words	Gestures, facial expressions, posture, body language, dress, makeup

www.

www.ritz-carlton.com

Customers are also a key source of feedback for companies that practice TQM. Many companies measure customer satisfaction through formal research, such as analysis of purchasing patterns and regular surveys of customers. Buehler Food Markets of Wooster, Ohio, uses customer feedback collected every day to fine-tune its ready-to-heat home meals. This firm, the creator of "dinner for two" double entrees and side-dish combinations, caters to its customers by implementing suggestions that many of them have offered. Buehler food-service manager Gary Stadden says the company receives about 150 responses per week from the preaddressed cards that it includes with each meal. The input from customers has resulted in changes from adding gravy to side dishes of mashed potatoes to alterations in packaging.[28]

Noise during the communication process is some type of interference that influences the transmission of messages and feedback. Noise can result from simple physical factors such as poor reception of a radio commercial. It can also be caused by more complex differences in people's attitudes and perceptions. A message communicated by a

They said it

"If I went back to college again, I'd concentrate on two areas: learning to write and to speak before an audience. Nothing in life is more important than the ability to communicate effectively."

Gerald R. Ford (1913–)
Former president of the United States

manager may be interpreted differently by co-workers with different ethnic and cultural backgrounds.

Basic Forms of Communication

People communicate in many different ways. Some obvious methods include calling a meeting of team members or writing a formal mission statement. Other, much less obvious methods include gestures and facial expressions during a conversation or leaning forward when speaking to someone. These subtle variations can significantly influence the reception of the message. Different communications can assume various forms: oral and written, formal and informal, and verbal and nonverbal communications, as summarized in Table 10.2.

Oral Communication Managers spend a great deal of their time in oral communications, both in person and on the phone. Some people prefer to communicate this way, believing that oral channels accurately carry messages. Face-to-face oral communication allows people

Business Directory

communication meaningful exchange of information through messages.

BUSINESS HALL OF SHAME

Wanted: Managers with Big Ears

Employees are brimming with ideas, but few employers seem to be listening to them. In a nationwide survey of employees conducted by IN TOUCH, a voice messaging firm, 90 percent of respondents said they believe they have good ideas to offer, and 80 percent felt confident in expressing their ideas. But their suggestions aren't being heard. Why? Respondents said managers simply aren't interested in listening and don't take the time to listen.

Peter Lilienthal, founder and president of IN TOUCH, says, "It's our belief that the most underutilized and underdeveloped resource in American business remains the ideas, creativity, and commitment of our workers." The problem can be fixed, however, if managers learn how to become active listeners. Consider the experience of Marc Brownstein.

Brownstein had built a successful career in advertising. He had worked for a New York agency on large accounts such as American Express, AT&T, and Hallmark Cards. At 30, he decided to leave the big-time ad world and return to Philadelphia to run the family business, the Brownstein Group, a small advertising and public relations firm. The business was very successful, as measured by billings and awards won.

Brownstein enrolled in a management development course 5 years after joining the company. The course required him to ask his department managers to fill out a survey evaluating his performance. On the first day of training, class members were told to open the sealed envelopes that contained the evaluations and to read them.

"I was blown away," says Brownstein, after reading managers' opinions. They evaluated Brownstein as a poor boss, complaining that he didn't listen well, seldom gave feedback, and never shared any information about the firm's financial health. "We were winning, winning, winning," says Brownstein, "and I was losing."

One way the agency was losing was low employee morale. Employee turnover in the 20-person agency was extremely high at 30 percent a year. Based on the survey comments, Brownstein realized he was in danger of losing additional talented workers.

---

to combine words with such cues as facial expressions and tones of voice. Oral communication over the telephone lacks visual cues, but it offers some advantages of face-to-face oral communication, such as opportunities to hear tone of voice and provide immediate feedback.

To add visual cues for listeners far away from senders, companies like British Petroleum use videoconferencing, which combines cameras, computers, and sometimes satellite systems to transmit images as well as voice messages. Technological advances are making videoconferencing available to a growing number of businesses. A desktop system costing less than $3,000 can use a personal computer to display an image of the person sending the message along with data, charts, and text.

In any medium, a vital component of oral communication is **listening,** the skill of receiving a message and interpreting its genuine meaning by accurately grasping the facts and feelings conveyed. While listening is the first communication skill that people learn and the one they use most often, it is also the one in which they receive the least formal training.

Listening may seem easy, since the listener makes no obvious effort. This apparent passivity creates a deceptive picture, however. While the average person talks at a rate of roughly 150 words per minute, the brain can handle up to 400 words per minute. This discrepancy can lead to boredom, inattention, and misinterpretation. In fact, immediately after listening to a message, the average person can recall only half of it. After several days, the proportion of a message that a listener can recall falls to 25 percent or less.

Certain types of listening behaviors are common in both business and personal interactions:

▼ *Cynical listening.* This defensive type of listening occurs when the receiver of a message feels that the sender seeks to gain some advantage from the communication.

▼ *Offensive listening.* In this type of listening, the receiver tries to catch the speaker in a mistake or contradiction.

Business Directory

listening skill of receiving a message and interpreting its intended meaning by grasping the facts and feelings it conveys.

He discussed the problems the managers cited in their surveys with his father Berny, the founder of the agency, who still served as its chief executive. Brownstein's father advised him to allow the employees "to get more involved with the business."

Because many of the managers' complaints focused on poor communication, Brownstein set up biweekly meetings for department managers and monthly meetings for all employees. During the meetings, he encouraged everyone to voice their concerns, interests, and complaints, and he discussed the firm's financial health and addressed employee worries about rumors of clients leaving.

Brownstein and his father also decided to give up their sole authority over decisions about which accounts the firm should solicit and accept. They included department managers in these decisions by taking votes on new accounts. One time, the agency had an opportunity to take on a new account to make a film for a marketing research firm that would bring the agency $1.5 million in revenues; the Brownsteins wanted to accept the project, but managers voted against it. One manager said, "I think it shows a lot that Marc and Berny are willing to turn down income to keep their people here."

By improving his listening skills, Marc Brownstein has improved employee relations and the agency's bottom line. Employee turnover has been cut in half, and the agency's billings are higher than they have ever been.

QUESTIONS FOR CRITICAL THINKING

1. Do you think Brownstein's decision to allow employees to vote on new business accounts is a wise business decision? Why or why not?

2. **With such high employee turnover, how could Brownstein have gathered employee feedback about why so many people were leaving the firm? Do you think exit interviews would have alerted Brownstein to the communication problems within his firm?**

Sources: "TBG Wins Big at ADDY Awards," The Brownstein Group press release, March 5, 1999, accessed at www.brownsteingroup.com; Hilary Stout, "Self-Evaluation Brings Change to a Family's Ad Agency," *The Wall Street Journal*, January 6, 1998, p. B2; "Lend Them an Ear," *HR Focus*, December 1997, p. 7; and Alexander Lucia, "Leaders Know How to Listen," *HR Focus*, April 1997, p. 25.

▼ *Polite listening.* In this mechanical type of listening, the receiver of the message listens to be polite rather than to communicate. Polite listeners are usually inattentive and spend their time rehearsing what they want to say when the speaker finishes. Chicago White Sox announcer Tom Paciorek was referring to polite listening when he defined *boredom* as "having to listen to someone talk about himself when I want to talk about me."[29]

▼ *Active listening.* This form of listening requires involvement with the information and empathy with the speaker's situation. In both business and personal life, active listening is the basis for effective communication.

Learning how to be an active listener is an especially important goal for business managers. One exercise in a workshop on leadership asks managers and employees to identify important leadership traits by drawing a figure that depicts the characteristics of an effective leader. In 90 percent of the drawings, workshop participants illustrate effective leaders by drawing them with large ears, big hearts, or both. The people who participate in the exercise believe that listening to employees and empathizing with their concerns are critical to achieving desired results such as increased quality and productivity. Active listening shows that managers really care about what employees have to say. Active listeners build trust and improve employer-employee relationships.[30] The Business Hall of Shame illustrates how poor listening can lead to low employee morale.

Written Communication Effective written communication reflects its audience, the channel carrying the message, and the appropriate degree of formality. When writing a formal business document, such as a complex report, a manager must plan in advance and carefully construct the document. The process of writing a formal document can be divided into five stages: planning, research, organization, composition and design, and revision.[31]

Written communication via electronic mail and computer networks may call for a less formal writing style, including short sentences, phrases, and lists. Writers for electronic media often communicate through combinations of words, acronyms, and emoticons, which are symbols constructed with punctuation marks and letters. Figure 10.5 illustrates several emoticons, which resemble faces when you look at them sideways. By adding emoticons to e-mail, writers can convey some of a message's emotional content. Despite the informality of e-mail messages, writing skills such as clear and concise wording remain important considerations. Some guidelines on writing e-mail messages are presented in the Business Tool Kit.

Formal Communication A **formal communication channel** carries messages that flow within the chain of command or task responsibility structure defined by an organization. The most familiar channel, downward communication, carries messages from someone who holds a senior position in the organization to subordinates. Managers, for example, may communicate downward by sending employees e-mail messages, presiding at departmental meetings, giving employees policy manuals, posting notices on bulletin boards, and reporting news in company newsletters.

Many firms also define formal channels for upward communications. These channels encourage communication from employees to supervisors and upward to top management levels. Employee surveys, suggestion boxes, and systems that allow employees to voice complaints are examples of upward communication channels.

Informal Communication In**formal communication channels** carry messages outside formally authorized channels within the organization's hierarchy of authority. A familiar example of an informal channel is the **grapevine,** an internal information channel that passes information from unofficial sources. Research shows that many employees cite the grapevine as their most frequent source of information. Grapevines rapidly disseminate information. While a message sent through formal channels may take days to reach its audience, messages that travel via grapevines can arrive within hours. Grapevines also are surprisingly reliable links. They pass on accurate information 75 to 96 percent of the time. However, even a tiny inaccuracy can distort an entire message.

The spontaneity of informal communication may diminish when a company's employees are spread among many locations. For example, employees who telecommute or travel may miss out on opportunities to build smooth working relationships or exchange ideas. In those situations, communication technology can help firms to promote informal communication. Some companies establish online chat areas for employees, so they can visit each other during breaks. Some also encourage employees to

create home pages that describe their interests and hobbies. Caroline Davis, president of the Worth Collection, a women's clothing company based in New York City, actively communicates with her management team of four vice presidents located in four different states. She sometimes arranges group telephone conversations to discuss books or magazine articles.[32]

Verbal and Nonverbal Communication So far, this section has considered different forms of verbal communication, or communication that conveys meaning through words. Perhaps equally important is **nonverbal communication,** which transmits messages through actions and behaviors. Gestures, posture, eye contact, tone of voice, even clothing choices—all of these nonverbal actions become communication cues. Nonverbal cues can strongly influence oral communication by altering or distorting intended meanings.

Nonverbal cues can have a far greater impact on communications than people realize. One study, for example, divided face-to-face conversations into three sources of communication cues: verbal cues (the actual words spoken), vocal cues (pitch, tone, and timbre of a person's voice), and facial expressions. The researchers found some surprising relative weights of these factors in message interpretation: verbal cues (7 percent), vocal cues (38 percent), and facial expressions (55 percent).[33]

Even personal space—the physical distance between people who are engaging in communication—can convey powerful messages. Figure 10.6 shows a continuum of personal space and social interaction with four zones: intimate, personal, social, and public zones. In the United States, most business conversations occur within the social zone, roughly between 4 and 12 feet apart. If one person tries to approach closer than that, the other will likely feel discomfort or even a threat.

Interpreting nonverbal cues can be especially challenging for people with different cultural backgrounds. Concepts of appropriate personal space, for example, differ dramatically throughout the world. Latin Americans conduct business discussions in positions that most Americans and northern Europeans find uncomfortably close. Americans often back away to preserve their personal space, a gesture that Latin Americans perceive as a sign of cold and

Figure 10.5 **Emoticons to Add Emotional Content to E-Mail Communications**

Emoticon	Meaning
:-)	Happy face
:-(	Depressed or upset by a remark
:-I	Indifferent
;-)	Winking
:-/	Skeptical
:-P	Sticking out tongue
:-D	Laughing at someone
:-@	Screaming
8-)	Wearing sunglasses
::-)	Wearing regular glasses
(-:	Left-handed

E-Mail Etiquette

An e-mail message may express its meaning in a less formal way than a traditional letter, but the message is still a business communication. As such, it should convey a professional image. Here are a few pointers to keep in mind when composing e-mail correspondence:

▼ *Proofread your work.* Carefully check your message to avoid sending e-mail with misspelled words or grammatical errors. Even though the content of your message may be understood by the recipient, spelling and grammar errors may project a negative image of carelessness or incompetence in writing. If your e-mail software has a spell-checking feature, use it. If it doesn't, use your dictionary to check spellings.

▼ *Type in both uppercase and lowercase letters.* Some e-mail writers risk offending others by writing messages in all capital letters. A message written in all capital letters is not only difficult to read, but it also gives the impression of the written equivalent of shouting.

▼ *Learn common online acronyms.* E-mail is intended to boost employees' efficiency and productivity. You can save time in writing e-mail by becoming familiar with acronyms frequently used in online messages. These include FYI (for your information), ASAP (as soon as possible), BTW (by the way), and IM(H)O (in my [humble] opinion).

▼ *Use emoticons to convey nonverbal intent.* The symbols shown in Figure 10.5 can help message receivers interpret the meaning of your message, but make judicious use of them. Some experts advise that humor and sarcasm should be avoided in e-mail messages, because nuances generally don't travel well in this electronic medium.

▼ *Be prudent about the content of your message.* Before sending your message, edit it to make sure that it communicates positive content. Delete any statements that may show racial, ethnic, or sexual bias. Also delete any negative comments about your boss or co-workers and expressions of anger or frustration. Companies have fired employees for insulting comments they included about their bosses in e-mail messages. Some of these employees have filed lawsuits against the employers, claiming that such a reason for dismissal amounts to an invasion of their privacy; these claimants have lost their cases in court.

unfriendly relations. To protect themselves from such personal "threats," experienced Americans separate themselves across desks or tables from their Latin American counterparts. "The result," explains cultural anthropologist Edward T. Hall, "is that the Latin American may even climb over the obstacles until he has achieved a distance at which he can comfortably talk."[34]

People send nonverbal messages even when they consciously try to avoid doing so. Sometimes, nonverbal cues convey a person's true attitudes and thoughts, which may differ from spoken meanings. A discrepancy between verbal and nonverbal messages may indicate an untruthful message. Generally, when verbal and nonverbal cues conflict, receivers of the communication tend to believe the nonverbal content.

Such a conflict seems inevitable when a company tries to marry two incompatible trends such as downsizing and treating employees as the company's most valuable asset. A company may try to disguise the conflict with euphemisms such as "career-transition program" (a phrase used at General Motors), "reshaping" (National Semiconductor), or "elimination of employment security policy"

(Pacific Bell), but employees still have to reconcile the verbal message about the importance of employees with the nonverbal message of layoffs.

COMMUNICATION WITHIN THE ORGANIZATION

Internal communication sends messages through channels within an organization. Examples include memos, meetings, speeches, phone conversations, even a simple chat over lunch. Internal communication may be relatively simple in a small organization, since it often involves face-to-face interactions. Unclear interpretations can be remedied by further conversation.

Synergex, a software company in Gold River, California, fosters internal communication through many channels.

Business Directory

internal communication system that sends messages through channels within an organization.

| Figure 10.6 | The Influence of Personal Space in Nonverbal Communication |

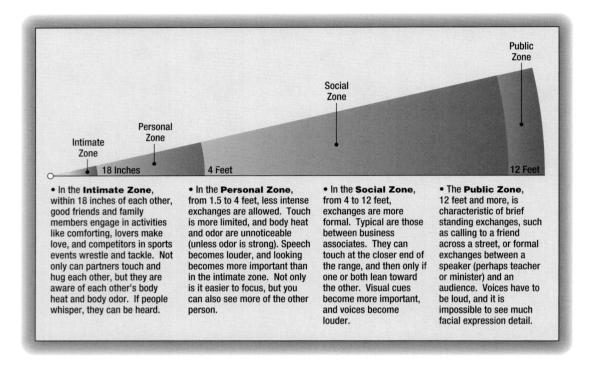

• In the **Intimate Zone**, within 18 inches of each other, good friends and family members engage in activities like comforting, lovers make love, and competitors in sports events wrestle and tackle. Not only can partners touch and hug each other, but they are aware of each other's body heat and body odor. If people whisper, they can be heard.

• In the **Personal Zone**, from 1.5 to 4 feet, less intense exchanges are allowed. Touch is more limited, and body heat and odor are unnoticeable (unless odor is strong). Speech becomes louder, and looking becomes more important than in the intimate zone. Not only is it easier to focus, but you can also see more of the other person.

• In the **Social Zone**, from 4 to 12 feet, exchanges are more formal. Typical are those between business associates. They can touch at the closer end of the range, and then only if one or both lean toward the other. Visual cues become more important, and voices become louder.

• The **Public Zone**, 12 feet and more, is characteristic of brief standing exchanges, such as calling to a friend across a street, or formal exchanges between a speaker (perhaps teacher or minister) and an audience. Voices have to be loud, and it is impossible to see much facial expression detail.

The company holds biweekly open forums, during which employees are encouraged to inform, thank, and question each other. During biweekly team meetings, members discuss their individual and team goals and give status reports on their activities. Synergex also sponsors learning-at-lunch programs, during which employees from different departments explain their jobs to one another so everyone understands each other's work. The company publishes a biweekly newsletter on its internal network that presents news about the company, its products, and meetings. A shared computer database enables employees to ask and answer technical questions. Each employee receives monthly financial statements for the firm provided by the chief financial officer.

Synergex derives many benefits from its channels of internal communication. They help to reduce duplication of work efforts among the firm's 100 employees while encouraging teamwork and improving employee morale. But the most significant benefit, according to Michele C. Wong, president of Synergex, is enhanced customer service. "The company's management is convinced that when employees—especially the sales and product-support staffs—are kept up-to-date on Synergex's overall direction and product news, they can be more articulate and forthcoming with customers," she says. "Having quick access to accurate information enables them to satisfy customers a higher percentage of the time. And in the competitive soft-

ware industry, where time is often the most critical factor, that's no small thing."[35]

www.synergex.com/dischome.htm

Internal communication becomes increasingly difficult as the organization grows and adds employees. Messages, many transmitted in writing, often pass through several hierarchical layers in a formal organization. The distortion of the original message as it flows through several intermediaries is illustrated by the following sequence:

Memo from Colonel to Executive Officer
Tomorrow evening at approximately 2000 hours, Halley's Comet will be visible in this area, an event which occurs only once every 76 years. Have the troops fall out in the battalion area in fatigues, and I will explain this rare phenomenon to them. In case of rain, we will not be able to see anything, so assemble them in the theater and I will show them films of the comet.

Executive Officer to Company Commander
By order of the colonel, tomorrow at 2000 hours, Halley's Comet will appear above the battalion area. If it rains, fall the troops out in fatigues, then

march to the theater where this rare phenomenon will take place, something which occurs only once every 76 years.

Company Commander to Lieutenant
By order of the colonel, be in fatigues at 2000 hours tomorrow. The phenomenal Halley's Comet will appear in the theater. In case of rain, in the battalion area, the colonel will give another order, something which occurs once every 76 years.

Lieutenant to Sergeant
Tomorrow at 2000 hours, the colonel will appear in the theater with Halley's Comet, something which happens every 76 years. If it rains, the colonel will order the comet into the battalion area.

Sergeant to Squad
When it rains tomorrow at 2000 hours, the phenomenal 76-year-old General Halley, accompanied by the colonel, will drive his comet through the battalion area in fatigues.

The sender of a message must continually make certain that it is both clearly communicated in writing or verbally and likely to be interpreted correctly.

To facilitate internal communication, many firms are relying heavily on e-mail. "E-mail has become a fundamental part of corporate communications," says Mark Johnson, CEO of software publisher MFJ International.[36] It removes time and geography constraints and improves the accuracy and speed of information exchanges. The Yankee Group, a technology research firm, predicts that by 2000, about 100 million people will use e-mail for business communications.[37]

At Texaco, managers and employees use e-mail not only to transmit information but to manage the flow of information throughout the company. Rather than calling a meeting to check the status of a project or conduct a feasibility study, managers poll project team members via e-mail. According to Betty Zimmerman, Texaco's manager of messaging, e-mail is more efficient than in-person meetings and trying to reach employees in different time zones by telephone.[38]

www.texaco.com

Face-to-face meetings form part of the many internal communication channels Michele Wong (right) uses to promote teamwork and keep employees at Synergex informed about the company's products and people.

Communicating in Teams

Communications among team members can be divided into two broad categories: centralized and decentralized communications. In a **centralized communication network,** team members exchange messages through a single person to solve problems or make decisions. In a **decentralized communication network,** members communicate freely with other team members and arrive at decisions together.

Which type of network supports more effective communications? The answer depends on the nature of the team's problem or decision. Research has shown that centralized networks usually solve simple problems more quickly and accurately than decentralized ones. Members simply pass information along to the central decision maker, who acts. However, for complex problems, a decentralized network actually works faster and comes up with more accurate answers. Team members pool their data, provide wide-ranging input into decisions, and emerge with high-quality solutions.

This research indicates that organizations should establish centralized team networks to deal with simple problems, but they should set up decentralized teams to handle complex issues. Members of decentralized teams should be encouraged to share information with each other and to generate as much input as possible to the solution.[39]

Decentralized teams work well for the complex process of new-product development. Two important keys to success in this process are allowing all members of the team to voice concerns and getting all of the members involved early in the project. These priorities are especially important for firms that need to create well-designed products that meet customer needs and allow efficient production.

COMMUNICATION OUTSIDE THE ORGANIZATION

External communication is a meaningful exchange of information through messages transmitted between an organization and its major audiences, such as customers, suppliers, other firms, the general public, and government officials. Businesses use external communication to keep their operations functioning, to maintain their positions in the marketplace, and to build customer relationships by supplying information about topics such as product modifications and price changes.

External communications move messages through many different channels, but fax machines are quickly joining telephones as the methods of choice. A Gallup/Pitney Bowes poll of large and mid-sized firms revealed that the telephone call is the most common means of external communication, followed by the fax. Faxing ranked first for international messages and documents.[40]

The central focus of a company's external communication, of course, is the customer, since creating goods and services that provide customer satisfaction is the ultimate purpose of business. Every communication with customers—including sales presentations, order fulfillment documents, and advertisements—should create goodwill and contribute to customer satisfaction. Figure 10.7 illustrates an external communication from United Airlines. By promising to give customers the "plane truth" about delayed flights, United attempts to create goodwill and customer satisfaction. This message eases discomfort during

times when the airline cannot avoid the unpleasant traveling experience of sitting on a plane and wondering why it has not taken off.

Iris Harrell, owner of Harrell Remodeling in Menlo Park, California, focuses her firm's external communications on building customer satisfaction. When the company remodels a kitchen, she sends customers a note when the project reaches two-thirds completion. The note apologizes for the inconvenience of a torn-up kitchen and includes a gift certificate for dinner at a nearby restaurant. Harrell also sends notes to her customers' neighbors in which she encourages them to call her if they have trouble with noise, trash, or parking resulting from the remodeling project. According to Harrell, these communications benefit the company, as about 75 percent of the firm's revenues come from repeat customers and referrals.[41]

COMMUNICATION TECHNOLOGY

Whether managers are communicating with employees, customers, or suppliers on the other side of the world or across the country, they rely increasingly on the latest technology such as computers, videoconferencing, fax, cellular phones, and e-mail. Technological developments provide four major benefits for organizations. First, they speed up business operations by letting people exchange information and make decisions much more quickly than they could without the new tools. Second, technologies bypass functional boundaries, so people in different departments can communicate directly rather than through formal channels. Third, they may allow people with diverse skills, such as employees in different departments, to work together. Finally, by improving internal processes and easing external communication, they may enhance customer service. Chapters 17 and 18 explain in detail how new technologies are enhancing communications within firms and with customers, vendors, and others outside the firm.

| Figure 10.7 | **External Communication to Promote Customer Satisfaction** |

INTERNATIONAL BUSINESS COMMUNICATION

Communication can be a special challenge in the international business arena. An international message's appropriateness depends in part on an accurate translation that conveys the intended nuances of meaning. When PepsiCo marketers wanted to build sales in China, they created a promotional campaign based on the theme "Come Alive with Pepsi." Poor sales surprised them, until they discovered that the direct Chinese translation of their slogan was "Bring your ancestors back from the dead." Managers ordered a hasty rewrite of the theme.

As this example shows, businesspeople who want to succeed in the global marketplace must ensure that they send only linguistically and culturally appropriate messages. Airlines, for example, should avoid signs like one that ABC correspondent John Ford once saw above a ticket counter in Copenhagen: "We take your bags and send them in all directions."[42] Of course, the airline really meant that it would send passengers' luggage anywhere the owners requested they should go.

Communication snafus occur even among English-speaking countries. The British, for example, call trucks *lorries,* and the hood of a car is a *bonnet* to them. A car's windshield is a *windscreen,* and an elevator is a *lift.* Little wonder that playwright George Bernard Shaw referred to the United States and Great Britain as "two countries separated by a common language."

Communication improves when parties understand the cultural contexts that surround and influence every attempt at sending an international message. Anthropologists divide cultures by low context and high context. Communication in **low-context cultures** tends to rely on explicit written and verbal messages. Examples include Switzerland, Germany, the Scandinavian countries, and the United States.

Communication in **high-context cultures,** however, likely depends not only on the message itself, but also on the conditions that surround it, such as nonverbal cues and personal relationships between the parties. Westerners must carefully temper their low-context style to the expectations of colleagues and clients from high-context countries. While Americans tend to favor direct interactions and want to "get down to business" soon after shaking hands or sitting down to a business dinner, businesspeople in Mexico and Asian and Near Eastern countries prefer to become acquainted before discussing details. When conducting business in these cultures, wise visitors allow time for relaxed meals during which business-related topics are avoided and individuals engage in small talk and discuss their families, countries, and leisure activities. They may get together for several meetings before actually transacting any business.

Differences among countries in workplace environments also influence the process of communication. For example, the open communication style in U.S. firms is foreign to workers in Russia, where employees have long expected specific directions about what to do and where asking questions was an invitation to trouble. Managers of foreign firms operating in Russia often encounter difficulties communicating with Russian employees, who are reluctant to ask for help and avoid giving feedback to messages.

"Expat managers think if they tell someone to do something, it should get done," says Kim Balaschak, a former general director of Pure Sunshine, a Russian-U.S. orange juice producer. "In other words, they 'send' a message and consider it received. Russian employees 'receive' the message but rarely give feedback." Without feedback, messages are subject to misinterpretation, because employees often do not ask for clarification when they do not understand the messages. "The result," says Balaschak, "is that the Russian does something usually not exactly what the manager had in mind, and then feels insecure—and the manager starts mumbling about the incompetence of Russian employees."

Expatriate managers need to understand the previous working environment in Russia and employees' lack of experience in the communication process typical of Western firms. "Patience and respect are crucial," says Elaine Sullivan, human resource manager at Deloitte & Touche, a U.S. investment banking firm that has been operating in Moscow since 1991. "It takes time for a two-way communication to evolve. You've got to explain your reasons for doing or asking certain things and make it clear that the Western way isn't necessarily the only or 'right' way. It's a real achievement when an employee finally starts offering his or her own suggestions for how to make things happen," says Sullivan.[43]

Despite the communication challenges associated with international business, most U.S. managers, and many from other countries as well, have not yet developed adequate global perspectives. One survey of international managers revealed that only one in ten rated language as one of the seven most important aspects of global business. Only one in five regarded cultural differences as particularly noteworthy considerations.[44]

Business Directory

external communication   meaningful exchange of information through messages transmitted between an organization and its major audiences.

SUMMARY OF LEARNING GOALS

1. Describe why organizations empower employees and methods of empowerment.

By empowering employees, a firm finds better ways to perform jobs, motivates employees by enhancing the challenges and satisfaction in their work, and frees managers from hands-on control so they can focus on other tasks. Employers empower workers by sharing information, distributing decision-making authority and responsibility, and linking rewards to company performance.

2. Distinguish between the two major types of teams in the workplace.

The two major types of teams are work teams and problem-solving teams. Work teams are permanent groups of co-workers who perform the day-to-day tasks necessary to operate the organization. Problem-solving teams are temporary groups of employees who gather to solve specific problems and then disband.

3. Identify the characteristics of an effective team and the roles played by team members.

Three important characteristics of a team are its size, member roles, and diversity. Effective teams typically combine between 5 and 12 members, with about 7 members being the ideal size. Team members can play task specialist, socio-emotional, dual, or nonparticipator roles. Effective teams balance the first three roles. Research indicates that diverse teams tend to display broader ranges of viewpoints and produce more innovative solutions to problems than do homogeneous teams.

4. Summarize the stages of team development.

A team passes through five stages of development: (1) forming, an orientation period during which members get to know each other and find out what behaviors are acceptable to the group; (2) storming, during which members' individual personalities emerge as they clarify their roles and expectations; (3) norming, when differences are resolved, members accept each other, and consensus emerges about the roles of the team leader and other participants; (4) performing, characterized by problem solving and a focus on task accomplishment; and (5) adjourning, with a focus on wrapping up and summarizing the team's experiences and accomplishments.

5. Relate team cohesiveness and norms to effective team performance.

Team cohesiveness is the extent to which team members are attracted to the team and motivated to remain in it. Team norms are standards of conduct shared by team members that guide their behavior. Generally, highly cohesive teams whose members share certain standards of conduct tend to achieve strong productivity and effectiveness.

6. Describe the factors that can cause conflict in teams and how conflict can be resolved.

Conflict can stem from many sources: competition for scarce resources, personality clashes, conflicting goals, poor communication, unclear job responsibilities, or team role assignments. Conflict resolution styles range from assertive to cooperative measures. The most effective resolution style varies according to the situation. Resolution styles include the competing style, the avoiding style, the compromising style, the accommodating style, and the collaborating style. A team leader can limit conflict by focusing team members on broad goals, clarifying participants' respective tasks and areas of authority, acting as mediator, and facilitating effective communication.

7. Explain the importance of effective communications skills in business.

Managers and employees spend much of their time exchanging information through messages. Communication helps all employees to understand the company's goals and values and the parts they play in achieving those goals.

8. Compare the different types of communication.

People exchange messages in many ways: oral and written, formal and informal, verbal and nonverbal communication. While some people prefer oral channels because they accurately convey messages, nonverbal cues can distort meaning. Effective written communication reflects its audience, its channel, and the appropriate degree of formality. Formal communication channels carry messages within the chain of command or task responsibility relationships defined by an organization. Informal communication channels, such as the grapevine, carry messages outside the formal chain of command. Nonverbal communication plays a larger role than most people realize. Generally, when verbal and nonverbal cues conflict, the receiver of a message tends to believe the meaning conveyed by nonverbal elements.

9. Identify and explain several important considerations in international business communication.

Differences in workplace environments, language translation, and the cultural contexts of messages create challenges to communication in the international business arena. Communication in low-context cultures tends to rely on explicit written and verbal messages. In high-context cultures, communication depends not only on explicitly stated messages but also on nonverbal cues and personal relationships between parties.

10. Discuss how advances in technology affect business communication.

Information technology tools such as computers, videoconferencing, and e-mail can improve the efficiency and speed of communications by helping businesspeople to create, organize, and distribute messages among employees in different time zones and geographic locations.

TEN BUSINESS TERMS YOU NEED TO KNOW

total quality management (TQM)	team norm
empowerment	communication
teamwork	listening
team	internal communication
team cohesiveness	external communication

Other Important Business Terms

employee stock ownership plan (ESOP)	grapevine
work team	nonverbal communication
problem-solving team	centralized communication network
task-specialist role	decentralized communication network
socio-emotional role	low-context culture
conflict	high-context culture
formal communication channel	
informal communication channel	

REVIEW QUESTIONS

1. What are three ways in which employers can empower employees?
2. What is the difference between a work team and a problem-solving team?
3. How does a task-specialist team role differ from a socio-emotional role?
4. What happens during each stage of team development?
5. What are some of the reasons for conflict among team members? What steps can team leaders take to resolve conflicts?
6. What are the six elements involved in the communication process? How does noise interfere with the communication process?
7. What is the difference between verbal and nonverbal communication?
8. What role does listening play in the communication process?
9. How does information technology influence communication in business today?
10. What factors should businesspeople consider in carrying out international communications?

QUESTIONS FOR CRITICAL THINKING

1. Suppose that you have just started your own company and have begun hiring new employees. The people you are interviewing are all aware of the possibilities of employee empowerment and ask you during their job interviews how you plan to empower them, should they decide to work for you. How would you respond? Would you be willing to give your employees an ownership stake in the company? Why or why not?
2. Are you a good listener? Ask a friend or classmate to draw a figure of you that shows what type of listener you are. Then draw a figure of yourself depicting the type of listener you believe you are. Compare the two drawings.
3. Suppose that you have accepted a position as an assistant manager of a juice bar. After reading in *Entrepreneur* magazine about the importance of teamwork, the owner wants you to build a team in her small company. How would you explain to the employees why teamwork is an important priority? What would you do to develop a team at the juice bar?
4. Ask a friend or classmate to evaluate the nonverbal aspects of the way you communicate. Based on this evaluation, do you think that your nonverbal communication adds to or detracts from the messages you intend to communicate?
5. Sarah Ahn, director of marketing at American Express, says, "I don't think we need to use all the different channels of communication that we have. I warn people that I am not an E-mail person, so they know not to send me urgent stuff on E-mail. . . . To me E-mail is an impersonal way to communicate. Sometimes you feel like people E-mail because they don't want to talk to you. If someone has a quick question, I'd rather have them just stop by and talk to me, because then you interact with your people a lot more." Do you agree or disagree with Sarah Ahn's evaluation of e-mail as a communication channel?

Experiential Exercise

Directions: Think about a student group with which you have worked. Answer the questions below as they pertain to the functioning of that group. Answers will tell you how cohesive your team is.

	Disagree Strongly				Agree Strongly
1. Group meetings were held regularly and everyone attended.	1	2	3	4	5
2. We talked about and shared the same goals for group work and grade.	1	2	3	4	5
3. We spent most of our meeting time talking business, but discussions were open-ended and active.	1	2	3	4	5
4. We talked through any conflicts and disagreements until they were resolved.	1	2	3	4	5
5. Group members listened carefully to one another.	1	2	3	4	5
6. We really trusted each other, speaking personally about what we really felt.	1	2	3	4	5
7. Leadership roles were rotated and shared, with people taking initiative at appropriate times for the good of the group.	1	2	3	4	5
8. Each member found a way to contribute to the final work product.	1	2	3	4	5
9. I was really satisfied being a member of the group.	1	2	3	4	5
10. We freely gave each other credit for jobs well done.	1	2	3	4	5
11. Group members gave and received feedback to help the group do even better.	1	2	3	4	5
12. We held each other accountable; each member was accountable to the group.	1	2	3	4	5
13. Group members really liked and respected each other.	1	2	3	4	5

Total Score _____

The questions here are about team cohesion. If you scored 52 or greater, your group experienced authentic teamwork. Congratulations. If you scored between 39 and 51, there was a positive group identity that might have been developed even further. If you scored between 26 and 38, group identity was weak and probably not very satisfying. If you scored below 26, it was hardly a group at all, resembling a loose collection of individuals.

Remember, teamwork doesn't happen by itself. Individuals like you have to understand what a team is and then work to make it happen. What can you do to make a student group more like a team? Do you have the courage to take the initiative?

Source: Richard L. Daft and Dorothy Marcic, "Manager's Workbook: Is Your Group a Cohesive Team?" in *Understanding Management,* second edition (Fort Worth: Dryden, 1998), pp. 531–532.

Nothing but Net

1. **Team Building.** Use your search engine to find a site such as

   www.oeg.net/tmb.html

   that will provide information on the team-building process. Find three ideas to help improve the performance of a team of which you are currently a member—an athletic team, an employee group, a campus or community organization, etc. Report back to your class the ideas you implemented and what impact they had on your team's performance.

2. **Communication.** The communication process starts with the sender composing a message. When you have prepared a formal communication such as a speech or written report, research was vital to your communication's success. That is why you should become familiar with LibrarySpot, a virtual library resource center for students or anyone exploring the Web for research information. Visit LibrarySpot and find several resources that might be helpful to you in preparing a communication—either one you're working on now or one for the future.

   www.libraryspot.com

3. **E-Mail.** The Internet provides advice on how to use e-mail effectively. Visit one of the sites listed and prepare a two- to three-paragraph summary of the ideas you found most helpful to improve your e-mail skill.

   www.webfoot.com/advice/email.top.html

   www.cappyscove.com/bobf/e-mail/index.html

   www.ucc.ie/info/net/acronyms/acro.html

Note: Internet Web addresses change frequently. If you do not find the exact sites listed, you may need to access the organization's or company's home page and search from there.

LEADING THROUGH EMPOWERMENT AT SOUTHWEST AIRLINES

Southwest Airlines has achieved its success by choosing to follow a radically different strategy from its competitors. Begun in the late 1960s as a low-fare, low-frills, high-frequency, short-haul, point-to-point, single-class, irreverent airline, it has grown and increased its astounding success by doing the same thing at each new airport to which it expands. While many airline industry analysts would give Herb Kelleher, the founder and CEO of Southwest, the primary credit for this, Kelleher himself would be more likely to give credit to his employees, whom he describes as people who thrive on competition and who marshal their vigor to prevail.

Southwest Airlines has built its business and corporate cultures around three key tenets: focus on the customer, empower and involve all employees in decision-making and innovation, and make improvements at every opportunity. These are not just slogans on posters. Take for example the Southwest customer service agent who was approached by a near-panicked customer who was desperately trying to check his dog onto his flight to California. Because Southwest does not fly animals, he very well might have missed connecting with his vacationing family. The service agent volunteered to take the dog home, care for it, and bring the dog back two weeks later, upon the man's return! A torn-up back lawn along with a very appreciative customer were the outcomes.

How does an organization instill in its employees willingness to make decisions, to take risks, and in essence, to be leaders? Libby Sartain, Vice-President of People, describes the culture at Southwest as one ". . . designed to avoid complacency, to encourage high spirits." Bureaucracy and rules tend to be kept to a minimum, with employees encouraged "to do what they think is the right thing to do when it comes to servicing our customers."

With little emphasis on hierarchy and lots of emphasis on breaking the rules when it makes sense, employees at Southwest Airlines are carefully selected and trained to be successful in such an organizational culture. "Southwest Airlines does a lot of things to foster pride and a sense of ownership among our employees," claims VP Sartain. Southwest starts by selecting people who show the ability to develop a high degree of commitment to a team.

From the day employees join the company, they take part in a continuous learning process, from orientation to the company to leadership training for all employees. "Leadership begins at Southwest Airlines from the minute you walk in the door as an employee. We don't just view leaders as being the top leadership, and, in fact, our culture allows no elitism at all. Since we work as one big team," Sartain states, "we start employees from the moment they are hired training them to be good leaders. Since we promote from within that's always worked well for us because leadership develops as the person progresses in his or her career."

The corporate culture at Southwest consistently fosters ownership, pride, and involvement of its employees in their jobs, in Southwest Airlines and even in the community. Employees are given many opportunities to get involved at Southwest, even beyond their job descriptions. Sherry Phelps claims that "you make your job what you want it to be." In order to make the feeling and reality of ownership even higher, Southwest Airlines implemented a profit-sharing and employee stock ownership program from its earliest days.

"We tell our people that we value inconsistency," Kelleher explains. Employees have to be trained and ready to make decisions. As Kelleher says, "What we tell our people is, 'Hey, we can't anticipate all of these things; you handle them the best way possible. You make a judgment and use your discretion; we trust you'll do the right thing. If we think you've done something erroneous, we'll let you know—without criticism, without backbiting.'"

Questions

1. What is teamwork and how is it applied at Southwest Airlines? Explain.

2. What is employee empowerment? How does Southwest instill in its employees willingness to make decisions and take risks?

3. Describe the importance of good communication skills within an organization. Give examples from Southwest Airlines.

4. Think about the places you have worked. How were teamwork and empowerment practiced in those organizations? How did they compare with what has been described about Southwest Airlines? What impact have those differences had on your workplace(s)?

chapter 11

Labor-Management Relations

LEARNING GOALS

1. Summarize the history of labor unions, and list their primary goals.

2. Describe the structure of organized labor.

3. Identify the major federal laws that affect labor unions, and explain the key provisions of each law.

4. Explain how unions are formed, how they achieve their goals through collective bargaining, and the issues addressed in their contracts.

5. Describe the roles played by mediators and arbitrators in labor negotiations.

6. Identify the steps in the union grievance process.

7. Outline the tactics or "weapons" of labor and management in conflicts between them.

8. Describe how unions and employers are developing partner relationships.

9. Discuss employee-employer relationships in nonunion firms.

10. Explain the challenges facing labor unions and unions' strategies to rebuild their membership.

Workers of America Can Even Unite Online

It's been a long match, and some tough rounds still remain. Organized labor has been struggling to rebuild its shrinking membership, but the effort has been gradual. In the 1950s, 35 percent of U.S. workers belonged to labor unions; today that number is closer to 14 percent. Yet although the share of the workforce that belongs to unions is still declining slightly, the number of union members has increased (from 16.1 million to 16.2 million). The improvement is largely due to labor's aggressive organizing efforts, but it's also a result of changing focus. The AFL-CIO is a good example of how unions are broadening their appeal and establishing a presence online.

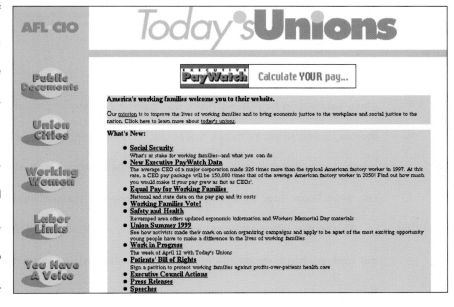

As president of the AFL-CIO, John J. Sweeney is energetic and imaginative. His mission is urgent, and to accomplish it, he's willing to change both himself and his organization. Since Sweeney took over, unions have stood up to companies such as UPS, GM, and US West. And labor has scored some impressive points in the political ring as well: increasing the minimum wage, fighting to ensure all workers at home and abroad have basic work standards and protections, and protecting its clout by defeating California's Proposition 226, which would have forced unions to get member approval before pledging dues money to political campaigns. Sweeney has redefined labor issues, broadening the focus from contracts to issues that affect all working families, such as health care, job protection, Social Security, and the gap between rich and poor.

The AFL-CIO is one of many organizations that are moving their organizing efforts to the Web. They can reach more people online and meet different needs. The first thing you see is a mission statement: to improve the lives of working families—to bring economic justice to the workplace and social justice to our nation. The AFL-CIO seeks a stronger voice for workers at work, in politics, in the economy, and in our communities. The site links AFL-CIO interests with government regulation, trade issues, and community concerns. As one example, an entire page is devoted to equal pay.

www.aflcio.org

Says executive vice president Linda Chavez-Thomson, "Greater public exposure can be a powerful weapon in fighting for equal pay." So the site tells visitors exactly how much the pay gap between men and women will cost them. The AFL-CIO represents over 5.6 million women, making it the largest organization of working women in the country.

Many other features are included on the AFL-CIO site: information on Social Security, workplace safety and health, worker's compensation, and ergonomic injuries. The site offers weekly news stories, union press releases, speeches, and the congressional voting record. Browsers can track corporate executives' salaries, bonuses, and stock options and compare them with worker wages. They can even learn how to form a union or become a trained union organizer.

Organized labor faces tough challenges, yet President Sweeney is encouraged. "We're reaching out and growing, especially in the communities where working families most benefit from unionization," he says. "Our commitment and dedication to organizing . . . is beginning to bear fruit—but we still have a long way to go." Labor is fighting on, and willing to change—even taking its fight online.[1]

CHAPTER OVERVIEW

Every society and culture develops some system of industrial relations. The people who head the organizations that provide necessary goods and services, the people who do the work, and the government organizations that maintain the society define the various industrial relationships. This chapter focuses on the relationships between labor and management.

The chapter begins by exploring reasons for the emergence of labor unions and a brief history of their operations in the United States. Next it focuses on legislation that af-

fects labor-management relations. The process of collective bargaining is then discussed, along with an examination of union and management weapons. The chapter concludes with a look at the future of labor-management relations.

EMERGENCE OF LABOR UNIONS

Organized labor did not originate in the United States. For hundreds of years, organizations of craft workers have operated in Europe and Asia. Over the years, they have developed into powerful workers' organizations. Today, with the growing interdependence among nations around the world and the increasing number of multinational corporations, an understanding of labor-management relations becomes imperative for business students.

A report by the International Labor Organization (ILO) on unions in 92 countries indicates significant reductions in membership in the United States, Great Britain, France, Germany, and most other industrial nations. Reasons cited include the shift away from manufacturing and the resulting loss of many traditionally unionized jobs, corporate downsizing, outsourcing, and increased employment of temporary and part-time workers. Union membership has also dropped substantially in central and eastern European countries following the end of compulsory unionism.

However, union membership has grown considerably in some industrialized and developing nations. Between 1985 and 1995, membership increased by 127 percent in South Africa, 92 percent in Spain, 90 percent in Chile, and 61 percent in South Korea. Even though membership declined in 70 of the 92 countries covered in the ILO survey, "the numbers by no means tell the whole story," says Duncan Campbell, one of the report's authors. "If anything, the significance and importance of unions and of industrial relations have been maintained or even increased in a majority of these countries," says Campbell. [2] The basic, underlying purpose of unions—to protect and provide for workers—is a consistent characteristic of every organized labor union throughout the world.

The Need for Labor Unions

The industrial revolution brought efficiency improvements through specialization and division of labor. These changes increased efficiency, because each worker could specialize in some aspect of the production process and become proficient at it. Bringing together numerous workers also increased output as compared to traditional handicraft methods of production. The factory system converted the jack-of-all-trades into a specialist.

The industrial revolution also produced a more sinister impact on the lives of workers in the 19th and early 20th centuries, though. Specialization made them dependent on the factory for their livelihoods. In prosperous times, they could count on employment, but periodic depressions threw them out of work. Unemployment insurance was a subject for dreamers, and the image of the poorhouse represented reality for unemployed workers.

Bad working conditions often prevailed. Jobs in many factories required long workdays with no protective safety

standards. At the beginning of the 19th century, young children worked for a few pennies a day to help their families. In Boston in 1830, children comprised two-fifths of the labor force. The labor of young women drove the entire cotton and woolen industries. Work hours lasted from daybreak to dark, all for low wages. In the spinning and weaving mills of New Jersey, children's earnings averaged a little more than $1 a week.

By the end of the 19th century, the typical workweek ran to 60 hours, but in some industries, such as steel, 72 or even 84 hours was a common standard. That breaks down to seven 12-hour days a week. Working conditions were frequently unsafe, and child labor continued.

Workers gradually learned that bargaining as a unified group could bring them improvements in job security, wages, and working conditions. The organized efforts of Philadelphia printers in 1786 resulted in the first U.S. minimum wage—$1 a day. After 100 more years, New York City streetcar conductors banded together in successful negotiations that reduced their workday from 17 to 12 hours.

The sweeping changes in labor-management relations over the past century produced profound changes in wages, hours of work, and working conditions for employees in most industrialized nations. In today's global economy, however, child labor has reemerged as a worldwide labor issue, as discussed in the Solving an Ethical Controversy box.

THE HISTORY OF U.S. LABOR UNIONS

Although the history of trade unionism in the United States began before the Declaration of Independence, early unions were loose-knit, local organizations that served primarily as friendship groups or benevolent societies to help fellow workers in need. Such unions were typically short-lived, growing during prosperous times and suffering severely during depressions.

Early Labor Organizations

For more than 200 years, individual workers have sought methods of improving their living standards, working conditions, and job security. Over time, as workers began to unite, they realized that collectively they often grew sufficiently strong to elicit responses to their demands. This inspired the birth of labor unions. A **labor union** is a group

Business Directory

labor union a group of workers who have banded together to achieve common goals in the key areas of wages, hours, and working conditions.

SOLVING AN ETHICAL CONTROVERSY

Should the Public Tolerate Child Labor?

Consumers were shocked to learn that the McKids clothing they bought from Wal-Mart for their children was produced by other children forced to toil for long hours, receiving poor pay and no benefits. In Bangladesh, youngsters between 9 and 12 years old make 5 cents an hour sewing shirts. They work past midnight and have been beaten for their mistakes. In Guatemala 13-year-olds make 31 cents an hour sewing Wal-Mart clothing. They are forced to work seven days a week and are disciplined if they work too slowly. In Honduras, 13-, 14-, and 15-year-olds earn 25 cents for each $19.96 pair of Kathie Lee Gifford pants they make. They must work 13-hour shifts, and they are allowed to use the bathrooms only twice a day.

Nike's track record overseas hasn't been any better. The company has come under harsh criticism and heavy media coverage for poor factory working conditions, forced overtime, use of child labor, and low wages. Nike has vowed to reform.

Many people believed that child labor was a thing of the past. But around the world today, some 250 million children between 5 and 15 are being exploited—deprived of human rights and even a living wage. Most are working in third-world nations, but even in industrialized countries such as the United States, hundreds of thousands of children work in fields, in sweatshops, and elsewhere. Some people want to abolish child labor for the sake of the children; others believe child labor must be tolerated as necessary to support families and economies in developing nations.

? *Should Business, Government, Consumer, and Labor Groups Work Together to Ban Child Labor?*

PRO

1. Nations progress economically when adults work and children study in school. The workplace does not teach children the academic and social skills they will need to succeed when they become adults. Most children work because they are victims of poverty, but working early rather than attending school simply perpetuates the cycle of poverty.

2. Exploiting children for economic gain is a moral offense. Manufacturers and retailers benefit financially at the expense of children who work for low wages.

3. Children who work take jobs away from unemployed adults.

---

of workers who have banded together to achieve common goals in the important areas of wages, hours, and working conditions.

Two types of labor unions operate in the United States: craft unions and industrial unions. A *craft union* unites skilled workers in a specific craft or trade, such as carpenters, painters, printers, and heavy-equipment operators. An *industrial union* combines all workers in a given industry, regardless of their occupations or skill levels. Industrial unions include the United Steelworkers, the United Auto Workers, the Amalgamated Clothing Workers, and the United Transportation Union.

The first truly national union was the Knights of Labor, founded in 1869. By 1886, its membership exceeded 700,000 workers, but it soon split into factions. One faction promoted revolutionary aims, wanting the government to take over production. The second faction wanted the union to continue focusing on the economic well-being of union members and opposed the socialist tendencies of some members. This faction merged

They said it

"To be free, the workers must have choice. To have choice, they must retain in their own hands the right to determine under what conditions they will work."

Samuel Gompers, 1850–1924

with a group of unaffiliated craft unions in 1886 to form the **American Federation of Labor (AFL),** which became a national union of affiliated, individual craft unions.

The AFL's first president was Samuel Gompers, a dynamic man who believed that labor unions should operate within the framework of the existing economic system and who vehemently opposed socialism. Gompers' bread-and-butter concept of unionism kept the labor movement focused on the critical objectives of wages, hours, and working conditions. The AFL grew rapidly, and by 1920, three out of four organized workers were AFL members.

Unions grew slowly between 1920 and 1935, though. The philosophy of organizing labor along craft lines had spurred the AFL's 40-year growth record, but it encountered difficulties as few nonunion, skilled craft workers remained for it to organize. Several unions in the AFL began to organize workers in the mass-production automobile and steel industries. Successes in organizing the communications, mining, newspaper, steel, rubber, and automobile industries resulted in the for-

4. Children are vulnerable workers. They have no voice in the workplace and are less likely than adults to complain about low wages, abusive treatment, and unsafe working conditions.

CON

1. Most child labor occurs in developing nations in Africa, Asia, and Latin America. Employing children in these countries is part of the economic development process that all nations go through during industrialized growth. Wages and standards of living in these countries may seem very low to people living in economically advantaged nations with higher wages and standards of living. But cheap labor is one thing developing countries can offer to attract foreign investment and move along the road to further development.

2. Children who work contribute to the economic welfare of their families. Their parents cannot afford to

send them to school. They are grateful to find opportunities for their children to work and contribute to family income. They view opportunities to work as blessings, not curses.

3. The movement to ban child labor is driven by people who want to protect domestic jobs by restricting imports and stopping companies from contracting out work to lower-wage nations.

SUMMARY

Many people believe that businesses around the world must respect human rights, preserve human dignity, and pay a living wage. These people are actively campaigning against products and companies that support child labor. They are also supporting and working with organizations such as the U.S. Department of Labor to fight against abusive child labor.

Since 1992 the International Program for the Elimination of Child Labor (IPEC) has been working to eliminate child labor—especially when children

must work under forced conditions, in hazardous occupations, or in dangerous conditions. The IPEC also works to eliminate the employment of particularly vulnerable workers such as girls and boys under the age of 12.

UNICEF's fight against child labor includes building schools for former child laborers, providing credit to poor families, advocating compulsory education, and persuading corporations not to employ children under any conditions that violate the *Convention on the Rights of the Child.* And celebrities, such as Kathie Lee Gifford, once made aware of the workers' situations, are campaigning for increased worker safety and human rights.

Source: Eyal Press, "A Nike Sneak," selected editorial to *The Nation,* April 5, 1999, accessed at www.thenation.com; UNICEF Web site, accessed at www.unicefusa.org, March 18, 1999; "The People's Right to Know Campaign," *National Labor Committee,* accessed at www.nlcnet.org, March 12, 1999; "Clinton Announces Funds to Combat International Child Labor," *US Newswire,* March 10, 1999, accessed at www.usnewswire.com.

mation of a new group, the **Congress of Industrial Organizations (CIO)**—a national union of affiliated, individual industrial unions. This new technique of organizing entire industries rather than individual crafts was so successful that the CIO soon rivaled the AFL in size.

By 1945, total union membership had passed 14 million workers, 35.5 percent of the U.S. labor force. In 1955, the AFL and CIO united under the presidency of George Meany. Today, almost all major national unions in the United States are affiliated with the AFL–CIO. With 77 member unions and 12.9 million union members, the AFL–CIO represents about 80 percent of organized American workers.[3]

www.aflcio.org

Currently, 16.3 million U.S. workers—14.5 percent of the nation's labor force—belong to labor unions. Of these, 9.4 million union members work in private industry, accounting for 10.2 percent of the private sector workforce. The other 6.9 million union members are employed in federal, state, and local governments; they account for 37.7 percent of government workers.[4] These numbers represent the lowest level of union membership since the Great Depression of the 1930s. Union membership has been declining steadily since the 1940s and 1950s, when about one-third of the U.S. workforce belonged to unions.

According to the U.S. Bureau of Labor Statistics, the highest proportion of union membership is in the government transportation, public utilities, construction, and manufacturing industries, as shown in Figure 11.1. Although blue-collar workers represent the traditional strength of unions, organized labor has gained an increasingly white-collar and female profile, as the U.S. economy has evolved from a manufacturing basis to a service-based system.

In recent years, unions have been most successful in their efforts to recruit government workers and employees in service industries such as health care. The fastest-growing national union in the United States is the Service Employees International Union (SEIU), whose membership has doubled to 1.1 million workers during the past 15 years.[5] Many new SEIU members are women who work as nurse's aides, cooks, and launderers in nursing homes.

Other new SEIU recruits are registered nurses who work in hospitals and medical centers. [6]

LOCAL, NATIONAL, AND INTERNATIONAL UNIONS

Like the formal structure of a large organization, labor unions typically forge links to form a hierarchy. A **national union** joins together many local unions, which make up the entire union organizational structure. The **local union** operates as a branch of a national union, representing union members in a given geographic area. For example, Local 4321 is a union that represents postal workers in Salisbury, Maryland. Local 4321 is a branch of a large national union, the American Postal Workers Union.

Local craft unions represent workers such as carpenters and plumbers in a particular area. The local union receives its charter from the national union and operates under the national union's constitution, bylaws, and rules. Most organized workers identify closely with their local unions and are acquainted with local union officers, even though they seldom attend regular union meetings except for those that deal with important issues such as contract negotiations, strike votes, or union elections. An estimated 5 to 10 percent of unionized workers regularly attend local union meetings.

Large national and international unions in the United States include the National Education Association, Teamsters, International Brotherhood of Electrical Workers, International Association of Machinists and Aerospace Workers, United Steelworkers of America, and the American Federation of Teachers. Almost half of U.S. union members belong to one of these giant organizations.

| **Figure 11.1** | **The Percentage of Workers in U.S. Unions by Industry** |

- Agriculture **1.9**
- Real Estate **2.4**
- Wholesale/Retail **5.6**
- Finance/Insurance/Services **5.7**
- Mining **14.0**
- Manufacturing **17.2**
- Construction **18.5**
- Public Utilities **25.9**
- Transportation **27.0**
- Government **37.7**
- All Workers **14.5**

In such industries as automobiles, steel, and electrical products, collective bargaining over major issues occurs at the national level with participation by representatives of various local unions. An **international union** is a union with members outside the United States, usually in Canada. Some such unions choose names to reflect their international status, such as the International Union of Operating Engineers and the Seafarers International Union.

While local unions form the base of the union structure, federations such as the AFL–CIO occupy the top. A **federation** brings together many national and international unions to serve mediation and political functions. Public Services International is an international trade union federation that represents 20 million public-sector workers in 130 countries. As one major function, a federation mediates disputes between affiliated unions. In addition, it performs a political function, representing organized labor in world affairs and in contacts with unions in other nations. Federation representatives frequently speak before Congress and other branches of government, and they assist in coordinating efforts to organize nonunion workers.

However, some unions, such as the National Education Association, do not belong to the major U.S. federation, the AFL–CIO. In 1989, the AFL–CIO readmitted the nation's second-largest union, the Teamsters, 30 years after expelling it for refusing to answer charges of corruption.

Just as many corporations have restructured to improve their competitiveness, unions are trying to reinvigorate the labor movement by creating leaner organizational structures. The Business Hall of Fame box illustrates some union restructuring efforts.

LABOR LEGISLATION

Government attitudes toward unions have varied considerably during the past century. These shifting attitudes appear clearly in Table 11.1, which summarizes major pieces of legislation enacted during this period.

Business Directory

closed shop an employment policy, illegal in the United States, requiring a firm to hire only current union members.

Union Security Provisions

Since unions focus their efforts on improving the incomes and working conditions of all workers, their belief that every employee should join a union should not seem surprising. A **closed shop** is a business with an employment agreement that prohibits management from hiring nonunion workers. To get a job at such a firm, a worker must join the union, and remaining a union member is a condition of continued employment. Unions have considered the closed shop an essential ingredient of security, giving them unquestioned power in demands for wages and working conditions. Unions argue in favor of the

closed shop, because all employees enjoy the benefits of union contracts, they claim, so all should support the union.

Employers have argued, however, that forcing people to join an organization as a condition of employment violates a fundamental principle of freedom. Moreover, if an employer can hire only union members, it might have to pass over the best, most qualified workers. Finally, employers have claimed that a guaranteed membership may make union leaders irresponsible and lead them to deal dishonestly with their members. The U.S. Congress showed its support for these arguments by passing the Taft-Hartley Act, which prohibits the closed shop.

Table 11.1	Labor Legislation

1932 Norris-La Guardia Act

Early federal legislation that protects unions by greatly reducing management's ability to obtain court injunctions to halt union activities. Before this act, employers could easily obtain court decrees forbidding strikes, peaceful picketing, and even membership drives. Such an injunction automatically made the union a wrongdoer in the eyes of the law if it continued the activities.

1935 National Labor Relations Act (Wagner Act)

Legislation that legalized collective bargaining and required employers to negotiate with elected representatives of their employees. It established the National Labor Relations Board (NLRB) to supervise union elections and prohibit unfair labor practices such as firing workers for joining unions, refusing to hire union sympathizers, threatening to close if workers unionize, interfering with or dominating the administration of a union, and refusing to bargain with a union.

1938 Fair Labor Standards Act

Continuing the wave of pro-union legislation, it set a federal minimum wage and maximum basic workweek for workers employed in industries engaged in interstate commerce. It also outlawed child labor. The first minimum wage was set at $0.25 an hour, with exceptions for farm workers and retail employees.

1947 Taft-Hartley Act (Labor-Management Relations Act or LMRA)

As unions continued to grow, legislation began focusing on unfair practices of unions as well as employers. The Taft-Hartley Act limited unions' power by prohibiting such practices as coercing employees to join unions; coercing employers to discriminate against employees who are not union members, except for failure to pay union dues under union shop agreements; discrimination against nonunion employees; picketing or conducting secondary boycotts or strikes for illegal purposes; featherbedding; and excessive initiation fees under union shop agreements.

1959 Landrum-Griffin Act (Labor-Management Reporting and Disclosure Act)

Legislation that amended the Taft-Hartley Act to promote honesty and democracy in running unions' internal affairs. It required a union to set a constitution and bylaws and to hold regularly scheduled elections of union officers by secret ballot, and it set forth a bill of rights for members. The act also requires unions to submit certain financial reports to the U.S. secretary of labor.

1988 Plant-Closing Notification Act

Legislation that required employers with more than 100 employees to give workers and local elected officials 60 days' warning of a shutdown or mass layoff. It also created the Worker Readjustment Program to assist displaced workers.

Working toward a Leaner Labor Organization

When John Sweeney became president of the AFL–CIO in 1995, he outlined a plan to save the labor unions. One part of his strategy focused on restructuring. "We have to change every level of our structure," says Sweeney. "If we do, labor unions will grow again."

Some union members don't agree with Sweeney's growth strategy, which includes downsizing. After all, unions have criticized corporate America for downsizing, because it has eliminated union workers' jobs. Sweeney trimmed

the federation's 450 staffers by one-fifth. He eliminated some departments, restructured others to focus on organizing campaigns, and established new ones to encourage union member ownership. He encouraged other national union leaders to follow his example.

One of a new breed of labor union leaders who is backing Sweeney's plan is Douglas McCarron, the new president of the 500,000-member United Brotherhood of Carpenters. Shortly after accepting his new position, McCarron fired or retired more than one-third of the union's 225 headquarters staff members. To save money, he also outsourced some functions such as printing. In explaining his

actions, McCarron said, "We have a product to deliver, and we have to do it more efficiently. Who says you're entitled to a lifetime job just because you work at a union?"

McCarron's next step in trimming his union's structure was eliminating 110 of its councils and local unions, actions that reduced costs and resulted in larger groups that covered broader geographic areas. Labor councils consist of representatives of all the unions in a major metropolitan area. These changes have boosted the effectiveness of organizing campaigns. The downsizing saved money, which the union spends to pay members to act as full-time organizers. Reducing the

Under a modification of the closed shop, the **union shop,** all current employees must join the union as soon as an election certifies it as their legitimate bargaining agent. New employees must join the union within a specified period, normally 30 days, after hiring. The majority of all union contracts specify union shop requirements.

An **agency shop** is a business with an employment agreement that allows it to hire all qualified employees, but nonunion workers must pay the union a fee equal to union dues. This agreement eliminates what the unions have labeled *free riders*, nonmembers who might benefit from union negotiations without financially supporting the union.

The **open shop,** the opposite of the closed shop, makes union membership voluntary for all existing and new employees. Individuals who choose not to join a union are not required to pay union dues or fees.

The Taft-Hartley Act permits states to pass **right-to-work laws** that prohibit union shops and outlaw compulsory union membership. Located mainly in the South, West, and Great Plains areas, the 21 right-to-work states are identified in Figure 11.2.

Unfair Labor Practices

The Taft-Hartley Act outlaws unfair practices of unions, as well as employers, such as refusal to bargain with the employer, striking without 60 days' notice, most secondary boycotts, and featherbedding, or demanding pay for workers who do no work. In one classic example, the British civil service created a job in 1803 for a worker to stand on the Cliffs of Dover with a spyglass and ring a bell if Napoleon approached. The job was abolished in 1945.

One of a union's most powerful weapons is a **boycott,** an attempt to prevent people from purchasing a firm's goods or services. The law identifies two kinds of boycotts: primary and secondary boycotts. In a *primary boycott*, union members urge people not to patronize a firm directly in-

Business Directory

union shop an employment policy requiring nonunion workers to join a union that represents a firm's workers within a specified period.

agency shop an employment policy allowing workers to reject union membership but requiring them to pay fees equal to union dues.

open shop an employment policy making union membership and dues voluntary for all workers.

number of unions and councils also simplified the process for contractors to hire union members for jobs.

The changes angered local union leaders who lost their jobs, but Henry Zieger, a program director at the Association for Union Democracy, applauds McCarron's moves. He says, "There was a lot of cronyism and Mob guys before, which McCarron has changed." A top AFL–CIO official agrees that unions need to downsize, saying that "many unions are filled with patronage and people who are lazy or incompetent. That has to change."

Other unions are following McCarron's lead. The Union of Needletrades, Industrial, and Textile Employees has cut its 150-member organizing staff by 25 percent. Those who lost their jobs were poor performers. "We've set per-formance standards, and when people don't meet them, they will go," says Bruce Raynor, the union's organizing director.

Another goal of unions' downsizing efforts is to empower rank-and-file union members and increase their involvement in decision making. Most members simply pay their dues and attend meetings only to vote for new officers. The important tasks of processing union members' complaints, bargaining for contracts, and staging organizing campaigns are done by professional staff members, but that's starting to change. Successful unions like the Service Employees International Union are training members to process complaints and handle on-the-job problems themselves. Tom Woodruff, the union's organizing director, says, "A union has to be something you do, not something you pay someone else to do for you."

Sources: Bert Durand, "Carpenters Union Gets New Leader in New England," press release April 7, 1997, www.carpenters.org/bergeron.htm; Aaron Bernstein, "Sweeney's Blitz," *Business Week*, February 17, 1997, pp. 56–62; and Aaron Bernstein, "Meet the Al Dunlap of the Union Hall," *Business Week*, February 17, 1997, p. 62.

QUESTIONS FOR CRITICAL THINKING

1. **In what ways can downsizing strengthen unions?**

2. **What benefits do unions gain by empowering local members?**

---

volved in a labor dispute. In contrast, a *secondary boycott* is intended to force an employer to stop dealing with another firm involved in a labor dispute. The union pressures an otherwise uninvolved party in order to force its real adversary into capitulating. The Taft-Hartley Act outlaws secondary boycotts deemed coercive by the courts. The Business Tool Kit box explains how you can view a master list of national boycotts sanctioned by the AFL–CIO.

Taft-Hartley also allows employers to sue unions for breach of contract and to engage in antiunion activities as long as they do not stoop to coercive tactics. Unions must make financial reports to their members and disclose their officers' salaries; they cannot use dues to fund political contributions or charge excessive initiation fees. The act also provides for a cooling-off period—an 80-day suspension of threatened strikes that the president of the United States and the courts find "imperil the national health and safety." During this period, employees must return to work or continue working. At the end of the 80 days, union members must vote by secret ballot on the latest company offer.

Figure 11.2   **States with Right-to-Work Laws**

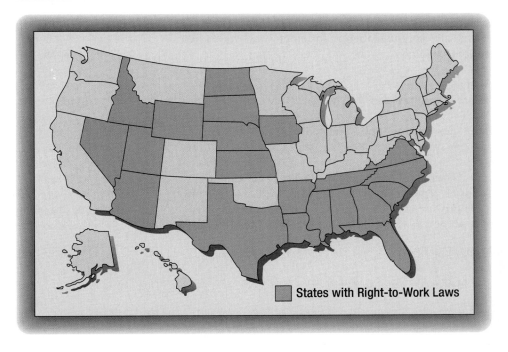

States with Right-to-Work Laws

BUSINESS TOOL KIT

To Buy or Not to Buy

Whether you're planning a trip or buying a new car, labor unions give you easy ways to support businesses that promote their causes and boycott those that don't. For example, the Union Label & Service Trades Department of the AFL–CIO maintains Web sites that list goods and services on "Do Buy" and "Do Not Buy" rosters.

Products on the Do Not Buy site are those made by firms against which the federation has sanctioned a boycott. In visiting the site you'll find product categories such as apparel and accessories, building materials and tools, food and beverages, furniture, and transportation and travel. For each company or product listed, you can click to receive further background information on the boycott to learn which union initiated it and why the union doesn't want you to purchase the products. Some sites include the e-mail and postal addresses and phone numbers of the boycotted firms so you can call or write them and voice your support of the union boycott.

www. **www.unionlabel.org/donotbuy**

One company on the Do Not Buy list is Alitalia Airlines, which is owned and subsidized by the Italian government. The boycott against it was initiated by the International Association of Machinists and Aerospace Workers, which represents 285 Alitalia employees in six U.S. cities. These employees are on strike to protest Alitalia's demands for wage cuts of up to 40 percent, increases in medical-insurance deductibles, the unlimited right to contract out work once performed by union members, and the right to increase hiring of part-time employees. The information at this site gives you alternative direct-flight carriers backed by the union, such as United Airlines and Delta.

The Do Buy site allows you to search a database of union-made goods and services ranging from cars to hotels and restaurants. If you want to patronize a hotel with union workers, visit the Union Hotel Guide. It lists lodging facilities by state and also includes properties in Canada, the Virgin Islands, and Puerto Rico. To help you make a lodging decision, the site has direct links to many of the listed hotels.

www. **www.unionlabel.org/dobuy**

THE COLLECTIVE BARGAINING PROCESS

As its primary objective, a labor union seeks to improve wages, hours, and working conditions for its members. It works to achieve this goal primarily through **collective bargaining,** a process of negotiation between management and union representatives for the purpose of arriving at mutually acceptable terms for employees' wages and working conditions.

How Employees Form a Union

Before workers can form a union, they must conduct an organizing drive to collect the signatures of at least 30 percent of their fellow employees on special authorization cards. These cards designate the union as the employees' exclusive representative in bargaining with management. If the drive secures the required signatures, the union can then petition the National Labor Relations Board (NLRB)

for an election. As Figure 11.3 describes, if more than 50 percent of the employees vote in favor of union representation, the union achieves certification.

Once a majority of a firm's workers accept a union as their representative, the National Labor Relations Board certifies the union, and the firm's management must recognize it as the legal collective bargaining agent for all employees. This move sets the stage for union representatives and management to meet formally at the bargaining table to work out a collective bargaining agreement.

Bargaining Patterns

Bargaining patterns and the number of unions and employers involved vary for different industries and occupational categories. Most collective bargaining involves *single-plant, single-employer agreements*. On the other hand, a *multiplant, single-employer agreement* applies to all plants operated by an employer.

Coalition bargaining involves negotiations between a coalition of several unions that represent the employees of one company. For example, the Coordinated Bargaining Committee is a group of 14 unions that negotiate for 46,000 workers at General

Business Directory

collective bargaining negotiation between management and union representatives concerning wages and working conditions for an entire group of workers.

Electric plants. The coalition represents a diverse group of unions, including the Communications Workers of America, the American Flint Glass Workers Union, the International Federation of Professional and Technical Engineers, and the Sheet Metal Workers International Association.

In *industrywide bargaining,* a single, national union engages in collective bargaining with several employers in a particular industry. The United Auto Workers union, for example, negotiates a 3-year labor contract that covers 400,000 workers at Ford Motor Company, General Motors, and Chrysler Corporation.[7]

| **Figure 11.3** | **Steps in Starting a Union** |

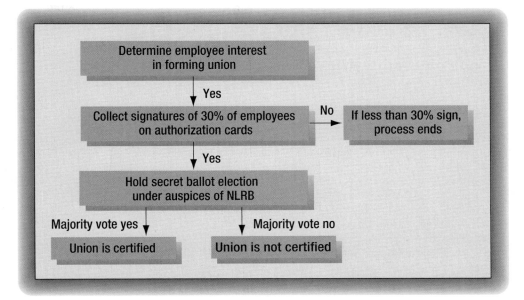

WWW.
www.uaw.org

In general, employers prefer to bargain with individual, local unions rather than dealing with coalitions of several unions. Small, separate unions are likely to exert less influence and power than a coalition would wield.

Bargaining Zone

Issues covered in bargaining agreements include wages, work hours, benefits, union activities and responsibilities, grievance procedures and arbitration, and employee rights and seniority. As in all types of negotiations, the collective bargaining process features volleys of demands, proposals, and counterproposals that ultimately result in compromise and agreement.

Negotiations begin with lists of initial demands by the union and management. These demands are simply starting points in the negotiations, and they rarely, if ever, become final agreements. Each party also identifies a final offer beyond which it will not bargain. If the union does not accept management's final offer, its members may strike. If management rejects the union's final offer, it may close the plant, move its operations, or bring new employees into its existing facility rather than

agree to a settlement that would prevent profitable operation.

Between the union's and management's initial and final offers is the **bargaining zone,** an area within which both parties will likely come to agreement. Sometimes, however, bargaining doesn't succeed. Unfortunately, the two parties may not be the only ones affected as the Business Hall of Shame illustrates. The final agreement depends on the negotiating skills and relative power of management and union representatives.

Alexander Trotman, Ford's chairman, and Stephen Yokich, president of the United Auto Workers union, worked within the bargaining zone to settle on a contract agreement acceptable to both parties. Major contract issues included job security, wages and pension benefits, and outsourcing. Trotman agreed to keep Ford's employment at no less than 95 percent of its then-current level of 105,000 employees. Yokich conceded, however, that the employment guarantee would not apply if the economy goes into a recession, allowing Ford to reduce its workforce during a slow economy. Trotman also agreed to give workers improved pension benefits, $2,000 bonuses during the first year of the contract, and 3 percent annual wage increases during the second and third years.

During the bargaining process, Yokich dropped his initial demand for a contract provision that would have allowed UAW members to strike over outsourcing issues. He

Business Directory

bargaining zone range of collective bargaining between conditions that induce a union to strike and those that induce management to close the plant.

BUSINESS HALL OF SHAME

Losing Points at the NBA

No deal! When NBA commissioner David Stern faced NBA Players Association executive director Billy Hunter over the bargaining table, both sides knew that high-end player salaries would not remain unchecked. Even so, the amounts being discussed were astronomical—the owners insisting on a maximum of $12.5 million and the players holding out for $15 million. Ultimately, the numbers weren't as important as who would be in charge—the players' union or the league commissioner. Add a clash of egos to this power struggle, and a standoff was pretty much unavoidable.

By the time an agreement was reached, the losses had mounted: $500 million in salaries, three months of the 1998–1999 season, and the 1999 NBA All-Star game in Philadelphia. But those weren't the only losses suffered because of the basketball lockout. Countless businesses, millions of dollars, and thousands of jobs depend on the NBA playing ball, and yet, those folks had no say in how (or whether) the game would be played.

Duke's restaurant and bar is just a couple of blocks from Seattle's Key Arena. "Every time there's a home game, it's like New Year's Eve," says manager Norris Bacho. "Those games drive our sales." And not just Duke's sales. Waiters, chefs, parking-lot attendants, and even the vendors who deliver food and restaurant supplies—all of them depend on Duke's brisk sales for their livelihood.

Across the country, the manager of a sports souvenir shop in New York's Madison Square Garden noted how slow business was on the nights the Knicks games were canceled. Keeping the ball rolling during the lockout was difficult for retailers. Many were left holding NBA-related merchandise with slim hope it would sell soon.

One observer predicted the lockout would injure sneaker companies—not only because basketball shoes account for such a large part of the market but also because the televised games boost sales by showcasing famous players performing in the companies' shoes. Indeed, Nike scores a major part of its profits from professional basketball, and the company blames a 51 percent drop in earnings on the NBA lockout.

---

also dropped a demand for a provision that would have forced Ford and the other automakers to pressure their suppliers to unionize. Yokich set a precedent by allowing Ford to add jobs for workers making auto parts within company plants and pay the workers a permanently lower wage than those of current assembly-line workers and outside suppliers. This was the first time the UAW had agreed to such a two-tier wage system.

Both Trotman and Yokich expressed satisfaction with their negotiations. Trotman said, "We think we have a good deal." Yokich believed the agreement was one that both companies could live with.[8]

Union Contracts

A union contract typically covers a 2-year or 3-year period. Such an agreement often represents days and even weeks of discussion, disagreement, compromise, and eventual agreement. Once the negotiators reach agreement, union members must vote to accept or reject the contract. If they reject it, union representatives may resume the bargaining process with management representatives, or the union members may strike to try to fulfill their demands.

Once ratified by the union membership, the contract becomes a legally binding agreement that governs all labor-management rela-

Ford and the UAW both made concessions in negotiating a new 3-year labor contract. Ford's Trotman (at left) and the UAW's Yokich shake hands to clinch the deal.

The arenas themselves suffered some of the worst losses during the lockout. Finding a 41-night substitute is next to impossible. Moreover, in some cities, taxpayers were left holding the ball since nearly half of the NBA arenas are municipally owned. In Seattle, for example, the Key Arena is owned and operated by the city, and since it opened in 1995, the home of the Supersonics has generated some $1 million in profits for the city each year. But during the lockout, Seattle lost more than $2 million in revenues while still paying overhead. Another example is Charlotte, where profits from the NBA arena run a smaller auditorium, keep a convention center open, and keep hundreds of people working.

In fact, it's the employees who were hit the hardest—from concession workers to janitors, from ushers to parking-lot attendants. These workers depend on the NBA for their income—not millions of dollars, but $5.15 an hour in many cases. And yet, with millions of dollars in the game, no one considered the hourly workers or their troubles.

QUESTIONS FOR CRITICAL THINKING

1. **When bargaining agents are considering strikes or lockouts, how much consideration do they owe to businesses that depend on them? Explain your answer.**

2. **Do fans play any role in sports industry decisions to strike or lockout players? Why or why not?**

Sources: Bill Brewster, "You've Got Game," *ABC-News.com*, January 7, 1999, accessed at abcnews.go.com; Mike Kahn, "All-Night Bargaining Session Saves NBA Season," *CBS SportsLine*, January 6, 1999, accessed at www.sportsline.com; Bill Brewster, "NBA Lockout Slams Arenas," *ABC-News.com*, December 21, 1998, accessed at abc-news.go.com; "Nike Blames Lockout for Loss," *ABCNews.com*, December 18, 1998, accessed at abc-news.go.com.

tions during the period specified. Union contracts typically cover such areas as wages and benefits, industrial relations, and the methods for settlement of labor-management disputes.

Some industries or occupations call for specific contract provisions. A local teacher union's contract, for example, included a guarantee of equipment and materials to successfully include special-needs students in regular classrooms. A United Farm Workers contract for lettuce pickers employed by Bruce Church Inc. in California included a housing allowance of $1 per hour worked, the formation of a labor-management safety committee, and limitations on the use of pesticides. Some contracts are only a few pages long, while others run more than 200 pages. Figure 11.4 indicates topics typically included in a standard union contract.

Wage Adjustments in Labor Contracts

In addition to setting wages during contract negotiations, labor and management representatives often agree to provisions for wage adjustments during the life of the contract. Some adjustments, such as cost-of-living adjustments (COLAs) and wage reopeners, can benefit employees; others, such as givebacks, can benefit the organization.

During periods of rising prices, unions support rising wage demands by arguing that an increase in the cost of living without an offsetting wage increase amounts to a cut in real wages and a drop in purchasing power. Consequently, unions and management must agree on an indicator for the cost of living. Usually, they settle on the *Consumer Price Index (CPI)* as determined by the Bureau of Labor Statistics. The CPI tracks the costs of such expenses as housing, clothing, food, and automobiles. The union and management must negotiate the base period, the starting date, and the CPI configuration most appropriate for the contract's calculations. Management receives nothing in return for this wage increase, since it does not reflect a change in employees' productivity.

Approximately 30 percent of all organized workers are covered by contracts with **cost-of-living-adjustment (COLA) clauses,** also called *escalator clauses*. Such clauses are designed to protect the real incomes of workers during periods of inflation by increasing wages in proportion to increases in the CPI. A low inflation rate during the past few years has diminished the importance of COLA clauses in labor contracts. Still, COLA provisions are becoming more common, not only in labor agreements, but also outside the collective bargaining arena. For example, benefits for social security recipients and military and civil service retirees now rise automatically with inflation. An estimated 50 million U.S. citizens now have their incomes adjusted by some automatic COLA.

Wage reopener clauses, another method of achieving wage adjustments, allow contract parties to renegotiate

| Figure 11.4 | Typical Provisions in a Union Contract |

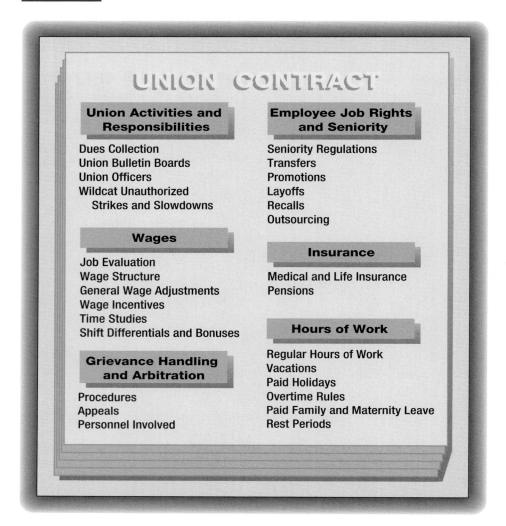

German workers the highest-paid employees in the world. But in recent years, German workers have been making concessions to help improve their employers' productivity and global competitiveness and to stem the tide of job loss to lower-wage countries. "The German worker is making a sacrifice," says Hubertus von Grunberg, CEO of Continental, a tire manufacturer. At Continental, workers agreed to increase their workweek by 75 minutes and made other concessions worth about $20 million.

Givebacks in Germany began in small and mid-sized firms in the mid-1990s. Since 1994, the 40 employees at Gustav Selter Ltd., a knitting needle manufacturer, have agreed to work flexible hours and take pay cuts totaling 16 percent in exchange for receiving a share of company profits. Owner Thomas Selter says, "At the grass roots, major change is under way." The givebacks have helped Selter to increase company revenues and profits.

The giveback trend has spread to large firms such as Bayer, Volkswagen, and Daimler Benz. In negotiations with Volkswagen, IG Metall, Germany's largest labor union, has agreed to a two-tier wage system, with temporary workers earning 10 percent less than current employees. The chemical workers' union representing Bayer employees has conceded to reduce employee bonuses and discontinue an employee stock-purchase program. Workers who assemble jets at the Hamburg plant of Daimler Benz Aerospace agreed to increase their workweek from 35 to 40 hours and work up to 100 hours of overtime each year, without receiving extra financial compensation; instead, the company offered time off during periods of slack workload. The givebacks are great benefits to employers, because Germany imposes difficult and expensive burdens when firms lay off employees.[9]

SETTLING UNION-MANAGEMENT DISPUTES

Although strikes make newspaper headlines, 95 percent of all union-management negotiations result in signed agreements without work stoppages. Approximately 140,000

wages at a predetermined date during the life of the contract. Reopener clauses are written into almost 10 percent of all labor contracts.

Attention of both union and nonunion employees in recent years has focused sharply on the nation's balance of trade deficit and how well U.S. companies compete in world markets. As one tangible response, unions in many major industries have allowed **givebacks**—wage and benefit concessions to help employers remain competitive and continue to provide jobs for union members.

Givebacks may happen in industries fighting off competition from abroad including autos, rubber manufacturing, steel mills, cement, agricultural and construction equipment, and meatpacking. They have also occurred in such industries as airlines, trucking, and telecommunications, where deregulation forced firms to become more cost-conscious to remain competitive.

Wage adjustments and givebacks raise controversies in other countries, too. Through the years, Germany's powerful unions have negotiated generous wage increases, making

union contracts are currently in force in the United States. Of these, 133,000 emerged from successful negotiations with no work stoppages. The courts are the most visible and familiar vehicles for dispute settlement, but negotiation settles most labor disputes. Both sides feel real motivation to make a negotiation work, since each invests so much time, money, and personnel costs in a court settlement. Other dispute resolution mechanisms such as mediation, fact-finding, and arbitration are quicker, cheaper, less procedurally complicated options that generate less publicity.

Mediation

When negotiations between union and management representatives break down, they sometimes resort to a voluntary process to settle disputes. This **mediation** process brings in a third party, called a *mediator,* to make recommendations for settling differences.

The Taft-Hartley Act requires union and management representatives to notify each other of desired changes in a union contract 60 days before it expires. They must also notify a special agency, the Federal Mediation and Conciliation Service, within 30 days after that time if workers have not accepted a new contract. The agency's staff of several hundred mediators assists in settling the union-management disagreements that affect interstate commerce. In addition, some states, among them New York, Pennsylvania, and California, operate their own labor mediation agencies.

Although the mediator does not serve as a decision maker, he or she can assist union and management representatives in reaching an agreement by offering suggestions, advice, and compromise solutions. Because both sides must give their confidence and trust to the mediator, that person's impartiality is essential to the process. Community social or political leaders, attorneys, professors, and distinguished national figures often serve as mediators.

In 1997, President Clinton created a special group of mediators to investigate and help resolve a dispute between Amtrak and workers represented by the Brotherhood of Maintenance of Way Employees. The union members who maintain tracks, bridges, and electrical power systems in the Amtrak system planned to strike over a contract dispute involving salaries, benefits, and work rules. The mediators were successful in helping Amtrak and the union reach an agreement, averting a

Historically, Germany's powerful unions have won huge wage increases for members. Today, German workers are agreeing to givebacks. To avoid job cuts, the workers shown here at DaimlerChrysler Aerospace gave up overtime pay and agreed to increase their workweek.

strike that threatened to cause major disruption of passenger and freight rail service.[10]

Arbitration

When parties cannot resolve disputes voluntarily through mediation, they begin the process of **arbitration**—bringing in an impartial third party called an *arbitrator* to render a binding decision in the dispute. Both union members and management must approve the impartial third party, and he or she renders a legally enforceable decision. In essence, the arbitrator acts as a judge, making a decision after listening to both sides of the argument. In *voluntary arbitration,* both union and management representatives decide to present their unresolved issues to an impartial third party. Arbitration provisions appear in 90 percent of all union contracts to resolve issues on which union and management representatives fail to agree.

Occasionally, a third party, usually the federal government, will require management and labor to submit to *compulsory arbitration.* Although it remains rare in the United States, considerable interest focuses on compulsory arbitration as a means of eliminating prolonged strikes in major industries that threaten to disrupt the economy.

Arbitrators settled a 2-year wage dispute between police officers and New York City. The 29,000 members of the Patrolmen's Benevolent Association rejected a 13.3

> ## They said it
>
> "The collective bargaining system will operate satisfactorily only if bargaining is intelligent and if considerable restraint is exercised in the actual use of industrial warfare."
>
> George W. Taylor,
> called "the father of
> American arbitration"
> 1901–1972

| Figure 11.5 | **Steps in the Grievance Procedure** |

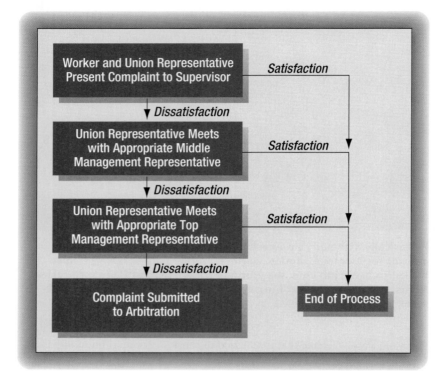

doubtedly would follow. This would severely damage the city's financial stability."[11]

GRIEVANCE PROCEDURES

A union contract guides relations between the firm's management and its employees and states the rights of each party. No contract, regardless of how detailed it is, can eliminate the possibility of later disagreement, though.

Differences of opinion may arise, for example, on how to interpret a particular clause in the contract. Management may interpret a contract's layoff policy as based on seniority for each work shift. The union may see it as based on the seniority of all employees. Over half of the contract disagreements that occur each year involve employee suspensions, transfers, and terminations; seniority; and vacation and work schedules.

Such a difference can generate a **griev-ance,** a complaint, by a single worker or the entire union, that management is violating some provision of the union contract. Because grievance handling is the primary source of contact between union officials and management during periods between contract negotiations, the resolution of grievances plays a major role in the parties' relationship.

Since grievances are likely to arise over such matters as transfers, work assignments, and seniority, almost all union contracts require that workers submit these complaints to formal grievance procedures. Figure 11.5 shows the five steps in a typical grievance procedure. The employee first submits the grievance to the immediate supervisor through the shop steward, the union's representative in the organization. If the supervisor solves the problem, it goes no further. If this first step produces no satisfactory agreement, however, a higher union official may take the grievance to a higher manager. If the highest company officer cannot settle the grievance, an outside arbitrator makes a final, binding decision.

percent salary increase over 5 years offered by Mayor Guiliani. The union also wanted productivity bonuses of several thousand dollars for each officer, explaining that the police deserved bonuses, because they were responsible for the sharp decline in the city's crime rate.

The city's Office of Collective Bargaining, an independent group governed by a board with representatives from unions and the city government, formed a three-member arbitration panel to handle the dispute. The arbitrators rejected the union's demand for bonuses and upheld the mayor's salary offer, explaining that the increase was in line with pay increases of other municipal workers. In their ruling, the arbitrators said that granting the police more money would result in other municipal workers demanding salary increases. "It would create chaos," the arbitrators wrote. "Whipsawing efforts by every municipal union un-

WEAPONS OF UNIONS AND MANAGEMENT

Although labor and management settle most differences through the collective bargaining process or through formal grievance procedures, both unions and management

Business Directory

grievance employee or union complaint that management is violating some provision of the union contract.

strike employees' temporary work stoppage until a dispute is settled or a contract signed.

picketing workers' marching at a plant entrance to protest some management practice.

occasionally resort to weapons of power to make their demands known.

Union Weapons

The chief weapons of unions are strikes, picketing, and boycotts. In a **strike** or *walkout*, one of the most effective tools of the labor union, employees precipitate a temporary work stoppage until a dispute has been settled or a contract signed. Since a company does not pay striking workers, the union generally establishes a fund to provide workers' wages, allowing them to continue striking without financial hardship.

Although the power to strike represents unions' ultimate weapon, they do not lightly decide to wield it. The number of strikes has diminished significantly over recent decades, from 3,055 in 1975 to 385 in 1995. One of the largest and longest strikes in recent years was the Teamsters union's 15-day strike against United Parcel Service in 1997. The strike, the first nationwide walkout in the company's 90-year history, involved 180,000 UPS workers who demanded wage increases, improved pension benefits, job upgrades from part-time to full-time, and the assurance that no UPS driver would be replaced or eliminated through subcontracting. The union won its demands in the settlement, resulting in a 5-year contract that ended the strike. The strike was an expensive battle for UPS, costing the company an estimated $600,000 in profits. James Kelly, chairman and CEO of UPS, said the strike "caused a lot of damage and hardship both to UPS people and our customers." He said that "the reality is that the customers are not all coming back, and we will have fewer jobs."[12]

Not all union members can resort to strikes or threats of strikes. Even though federal employees have been permitted to join unions and bargain collectively since 1962, they are not allowed to strike. Each federal civilian employee takes a no-strike pledge when hired. In 1981, when the Professional Air Traffic Controllers union went on strike to reinforce its contract demands, President Ronald Reagan fired more than 11,000 federal workers and replaced them with nonunion employees. His decision was based on the argument that strikes by public employees are not in the public's best interest.

In some instances, laws prohibit strikes by state and municipal employees. In these cases, workers such as police officers and firefighters, sanitation workers, hospital employees, and even prison guards may still go on strike by calling in sick. Hence, police strikes have come to be known as the *blue flu*.

Picketing—workers' marching at the entrances of the employer's plant as a public protest against some management practice—gives unions another effective way to apply pressure. As long as picketing does not involve violence or intimidation, it is protected under the U.S. Constitution as free speech. Picketing may accompany a strike, or it may protest alleged unfair labor practices. For example, when French automaker Renault announced plans to close a plant in Belgium that employed 3,100 workers, labor union members in France and Belgium staged massive rallies to protest the loss of jobs as an unfair labor practice. In spite of the protests, Renault closed its plant in Vilvoorde, leaving thousands of its assembly-line workers without jobs. Renault's downsizing decision was intended to improve the company's profitability.[13]

Some 60,000 union members marched in Brussels to protest the closing of Renault's assembly plant in Belgium. Growing numbers of European firms are downsizing in efforts to improve their global competitiveness.

 www.renault.com

Because union workers usually refuse to cross picket lines maintained by other union members, the picketed firm may be unable to obtain deliveries and other services. When management at Air France announced plans to reduce the airline's workforce and cut some workers' wages, for example, thousands of Air France employees picketed airports in Paris. The government was forced to back down when the picketing disrupted flights and airport operations.

As defined earlier, a boycott is an organized attempt to keep the public from purchasing the goods or services of a firm. Some unions have organized remarkably successful boycotts, and some unions even fine members who defy primary boycotts.

Although the Taft-Hartley Act outlaws coercive secondary boycotts, Supreme Court rulings have significantly expanded the rights of unions to use this weapon. Although they cannot picket a firm to force it to stop dealing with another company involved in a labor dispute, the court protected other forms of expression, such as distributing handbills at the site of the first firm.

Management Weapons

Management has its own weapons for dealing with organized labor. In the past, firms have used the **lockout**—in effect, a management strike to bring pressure on union members by closing the firm. Firms rarely lock out workers today unless a union strike has partially shut down a plant. Ron LaBow, chairman of WHX Corporation, closed down several plants of its Wheeling-Pittsburgh Steel subsidiary when 4,500 members of the United Steelworkers of America went on strike over pensions in 1996. LaBow even threatened to liquidate the subsidiary, the ninth largest U.S. steel company. The union retaliated by using a new tactic—a letter-writing campaign to the parent company's major stockholders—informing them that the strike had cut WHX's stock price in half. The investors encouraged LaBow to resolve the dispute, which he did. The strike lasted 10 months, after which LaBow reopened the plants and recalled workers following successful negotiations for a new contract.[14]

In the past, managers at organizations ranging from International Paper Company to the National Football League have resorted to replacing striking workers with **strikebreakers,** nonunion workers who cross picket lines to fill the jobs of striking workers. Firms can relatively easily recruit strikebreakers in high-status fields such as professional football and in high-paying industries located in areas of high unemployment. Nevertheless, even in favorable conditions, management frequently encounters difficulties in securing sufficient numbers of replacement workers with required skills. Some employers have resorted to reassigning supervisory personnel and other nonunion employees to continue operations during strikes.

Management sometimes obtains an **injunction**—a court order prohibiting some practice—to prevent excessive picketing or certain unfair union practices. Before passage of the Norris-La Guardia Act, firms frequently used injunctions to prohibit all types of strikes. Since then, court orders have been limited to restraining violence, restricting picketing, and preventing damage to company property.

Gannett Company and Knight-Ridder Inc. obtained an injunction that ordered picketers away from the gates of their *Detroit Free Press* and *The Detroit News* newspaper plants. Gannett and Knight-Ridder, co-owners of the papers, sought the injunction after strikers surrounded the papers' printing plants. To make deliveries, management had to airlift the papers out by helicopter.

About 2,500 of the papers' distribution, editorial, and production workers represented by six unions walked off their jobs in 1995, after contract negotiations collapsed. The workers refused management demands to change union work rules in ways that would help the papers to cut costs. Management replaced the strikers with permanent employees, never missing a day of publication, and eliminated the union work rules. The striking journalists kept union members informed of the strike activities by publishing an online newspaper.

After a 19-month strike, the strikers offered to return to work on management's terms. Management accepted the unions' offer but offered positions to only 200 staffers. It refused to displace the strikebreakers. In 1997, the National Labor Relations Board sought an injunction against the papers, alleging that management had committed several illegal labor practices, including setting a new pay scale. A district court judge denied the request for an injunction, but the NLRB planned to appeal the decision, which could take several years. If higher courts deny the appeal, management will have succeeded in busting the union.[15]

> ### DID YOU KNOW?
>
> The highest-ranking woman and minority in the American labor movement is Linda Chavez-Thompson. The daughter of Mexican immigrants, she was picking cotton at the age of 10. One of eight children, she grew up with a dad who believed that boys needed education but girls didn't. She was forced to drop out of high school at 15 to help support her family. Determined to learn, she became an avid reader. Her grandfather taught her public speaking and bopped her on the head each time she mispronounced a word. From a bilingual secretary at a local union, Chavez-Thompson worked her way up to become executive vice president of the AFL–CIO.

www. **www.rust.net/workers/strike.html**

Some employers have formed **employers' associations** to cooperate in their efforts and present a united front in dealing with labor unions. Employers' associations may even act as negotiators for individual employers that want to reach agreements with labor unions. An industry characterized by many, small firms and a single, large union may follow an increasing tendency for industrywide bargaining between the union and a single representative of the industry's employers. Building contractors may bargain as a group with construction unions, for example. Although they do not negotiate contracts, the National Association of Manufacturers and the United States Chamber of Commerce are examples of employers' associations. Both groups promote the views of their members on key issues.

THE TREND TOWARD UNION-MANAGEMENT COOPERATION

The hostile and antagonistic attitudes that often characterize labor-management relationships are beginning to change. Some unions and employers are developing partner relationships that benefit union members by giving them job security while helping employers to maintain competitiveness. For example, US West and the Communications Workers of America included a provision in their labor contract that establishes an apprenticeship program for training existing employees so they can compete for future telecommunications jobs the company will need to fill. The needle trades union and Levi Strauss formed a partnership to reduce costs and keep production in the United States.[16]

www. www3.cwa-union.org/home/

A growing number of local teachers' unions are teaming with school management in an effort to satisfy the public's demands for quality improvements in schools. With a focus on raising academic standards, restructuring schools, and improving quality in education, teachers and administrators are transforming collective bargaining into collaborative negotiations. One union replaced the traditional labor contract with a joint labor-management "constitution" that allows teachers to comanage the school district.[17]

The International Association of Machinists is marketing itself as a resource for employers. The union has set up a school that teaches plant managers and local union leaders how to establish a labor-management partnership and create high-performance work teams to increase productivity. Following the 1-week training period, the union sends a consultant, free of charge, to the employer's plant to help managers and union leaders from all functions—marketing to manufacturing—create team systems and joint decision-making councils.[18]

Another union/management partnership acts as an employment agency. The Laborers International Union of North America set up a foundation with building contractors to provide bid specifications on construction jobs throughout the nation. It also supplies trained workers for both union and nonunion firms. The service helps contrac-

Job protection and a bigger voice in the way their companies are run are reasons why labor unions are forming partnerships with employers. At the machinists' union school shown here, union leaders and members of management learn how to work together to create high-performance work teams.

tors who have a difficult time finding qualified personnel. For example, Radian International, an environmental cleanup firm, used the foundation's service when it couldn't find properly trained workers it needed for a new contract to clean up an EPA Superfund site. "We can't always find qualified people in this field, so the union acts like a temp service," says Timothy Mains, a Radian attorney.[19]

EMPLOYEE-MANAGEMENT RELATIONS IN NONUNION ORGANIZATIONS

Although unionization is an implicit assumption in almost any discussion of labor-management relations, unions represent less than one in ten U.S. workers in the private sector. A very small business may employ only a handful of nonunion workers. Another portion of the nonunionized segment of the U.S. labor force consists of managerial employees. Other nonunion employees work in industries where unions have never developed strength. Still other nonunion employees have simply rejected attempts to establish unions in their workplaces.

Management often chooses to offer a compensation and benefit structure comparable to those of unionized firms in the area. Willingness to offer comparable wages and working conditions coupled with effective communications, emphasis on promotions from within, employee empowerment, and employee participation in goal setting and grievance handling may help an employer to avert unionization by convincing workers that they would receive few additional benefits for the union dues they would have to pay. In fact, many argue that the threat of joining a union gives nonunion employees an effective tool in securing desired wages, benefits, and working conditions.

Grievance Programs for Nonunion Employees

Employees who believe they have suffered discrimination, sexual harassment, dismissal without cause, or inadequate promotion opportunities can file lawsuits against their firms or file charges with the U.S. Equal Employment Opportunity Commission or a state human rights commission. These actions, however, can lead to expensive and lengthy proceedings.

At a growing number of firms, employers are giving employees other options for resolving their grievances by instituting **alternative dispute resolution (ADR) programs.** These programs vary among companies, but most include open-door policies, employee hot lines, peer review councils, mediation, and arbitration.[20]

An *open-door policy* ensures employees that they can discuss issues with supervisors or other managers or human resource representatives. An *employee hot line* gives employees the opportunity to call a phone number and air a complaint or get advice on how to file a formal complaint. Some firms, like publisher McGraw-Hill, provide employees with a phone number so they can talk confidentially to someone outside the firm about the grievance process. *Mediation* and *arbitration* work in much the same way as they do in unionized organizations, with mediation resulting in a nonbinding solution and arbitration in a binding solution. At TRW Inc., however, if an employee is not satisfied with an arbitrator's solution, he or she has the right to file a lawsuit against the company.

Firms such as Citicorp have established **peer-review boards** to handle disputes. These boards typically consist of three employee peers and several management representatives. Peer review can be a valuable tool for building an open, trusting atmosphere. It can help managers to deter union organizing and, perhaps most importantly, stem the rising number of costly legal claims for wrongful discharge, discrimination, and harassment.

The need for worker protection provided by labor unions diminishes considerably in firms that encourage employees to communicate their complaints through programs designed to resolve grievances. Federal Express, a nonunion company, has one of the best grievance programs. Its Guaranteed Fair Treatment program is one of many reasons employees feel they do not need a union. The program allows all employees to appeal any manager's decision, including those of CEO Fred Smith, who spends more than 4 hours each week reviewing employee complaints. [21]

An effective grievance procedure generally includes the following elements:

▼ The grievance procedure should follow written policies and procedures, and every employee should receive a copy.

▼ Grievances should be settled at the lowest possible organizational level, preferably between the dissatisfied employee and the supervisor.

▼ The grievance procedure should follow a series of distinct steps; each stage should exhaust all possible solutions before progressing to the next step.

Job Security in Nonunion Companies

Job security has always been a primary motivation for workers to form labor unions. Today, however, even unions cannot guarantee their members lifetime job security. For example, the Korean government passed a new labor law that allows companies to fire and lay off workers, overriding the lifetime employment guarantees given to union members. The law was passed to decrease labor costs, which have threatened the competitiveness of Korean companies by rising faster than productivity gains. Passage of the law outraged Korean workers, who staged massive protest rallies, some of which resulted in violence and the arrests of union leaders. [22]

Recognizing the importance of job security, many nonunion firms, including large companies such as Federal Express and Amgen, have implemented no-layoff policies. The century-old Lincoln Electric Co. in Euclid, Ohio, provides each of its employees with a guarantee of continuous employment as part of the firm's incentive plan. The employment guarantee and a policy of promoting from within enable Lincoln to invest heavily in employee training. When a sales slump idles workers, the firm trains them to perform other jobs within the company rather than laying them off. With job security and one of the best pay packages in the United States, Lincoln's employees have never wanted a union. [23]

www. www.lincolnelectric.com

Instead of no-layoff guarantees, firms may offer incentives for early retirement and resignation to reduce staffing levels. These workforce reductions have separated hundreds of thousands of workers over the past few years, allowing companies to cut staff without resorting to layoffs. Although such a program may cost the employer some of its most highly qualified and experienced workers, the change often replaces older workers with younger employees who receive lower wages. At the same time, rewarding senior employees with early retirement bonuses is likely to enhance overall employee morale, in contrast to the destructive effects of a decision to lay off workers.

CHALLENGES FACING ORGANIZED LABOR

Despite their valuable contributions to business, uncertainty clouds the future role of labor unions. Throughout the world, unions are representing fewer employees than they have for decades. The reasons for declining membership vary from country to country, but several factors have contributed to the decline in union membership in industrialized nations: downsizing by large, unionized firms to improve global competitiveness, a shift in favor of free-market ideologies, and labor legislation. In Israel, membership in the country's labor federation, Histadrut, dropped 76 percent after the government passed a law barring the federation from offering members health-care coverage.[24]

One broad economic trend in the United States that has hurt unions is the shift from a manufacturing economy to a service economy. Manufacturing workers have made unions strong in the past. Although unions retain this strength in the automotive, steel, and aerospace industries, they have not been able to organize employees in fast-growing, high-tech industries such as computers and electronics and in service industries such as financial services.[25]

With global competition forcing companies to improve their efficiency and productivity, many union jobs have been replaced by technology such as automated production facilities. Although unions benefit their members by raising wages and improving benefits, employers are now aggressively trying to minimize their labor costs. To do so, they are turning to low-cost alternatives such as temporary, part-time, and contract workers and outsourcing work to nonunion suppliers.

Outsourcing has also made inroads in the public sector. Many school systems have lost union jobs to private companies that supply services ranging from food service, transportation, and maintenance to accounting and tax work. The National Education Association is trying to protect union jobs in school systems by offering a video—"Contracting Out: Strategies for Fighting Back"—as shown in Figure 11.6.

Today's workplace is very different from the workplaces in which early unions emerged. Unions grew by giving industrial workers a voice in decisions about their wages and working conditions. Today, many employers value their employees as their most important assets, train them to boost productivity, involve them in decision making, and motivate them with good wages, benefits, and flexible work hours. "The heart of the unions is in the right place; job protection is how they rose to a position of influence in society," says William Bridges, a consultant who helps firms in transition. According to Bridges, unions need to shift their focus from wage increases and job protection to making union workers valuable assets to employers. He says, "The future of unions has to shift to worker development and worker support. That is the business unions need to be in and the area that is crying out for union help."[26]

INITIATIVES TO REBUILD UNIONS

AFL–CIO president John Sweeney is leading the drive to rebuild unions to achieve goals of increasing the organizations' membership and political power. According to Sweeney, "There are two keys to our success or failure in rebuilding this movement . . . and in restoring the voice of American workers in our society—one is organizing and the other is politics. We can't succeed at rebuilding our membership base without winning in politics, and we can't win in politics without substantially increasing our numbers."[27]

To achieve these goals, the AFL–CIO has committed one-third of its budget, $30 million, to organizing campaigns to recruit new members. The federation has encouraged its member unions to increase their organizing budgets, which typically amount to only 3 percent of their

Figure 11.6 **Union Efforts to Combat Outsourcing**

The United Farm Workers' effort to unionize 20,000 strawberry workers is backed by other unions and not-for-profit groups. Shown here is a rally in Watsonville, California, attended by the strawberry pickers, AFL–CIO president John Sweeney, Reverend Jesse Jackson, and leaders of religious, environmental, and women's groups.

ployers, asking them not to threaten or fire any union supporters.[30]

Recently, the AFL–CIO launched a $35 million advertising campaign to convince nonunion workers of the value of labor unions, to change the public's negative attitude toward unions, and to support political candidates that favor the labor movement's agenda. The federation is encouraging local union members to become politically active in their communities and to educate their co-workers on the benefits of unions. "In the past, union members didn't want to talk to nonunion workers. I tell them that's wrong," says Jim Rudicil, campaign director of the Las Vegas unionizing campaign. "Organizing is most effective when it starts at the grassroots level."[31]

In addition to the structural changes described earlier in the Business Hall of Fame box, the AFL–CIO has formed a separate department for organizing. It has also established several programs targeted at involving students and retired workers in organizing activities. In Union Summer, the federation recruits college students to work as union organizers in campaigns throughout the country. In Senior Summer, retired union workers assist union organizers in their local communities. To achieve economies of scale and increase their organizing resources and influence, three of the largest U.S. unions are merging. The consolidation of the United Steelworkers of America, the United Auto Workers, and the International Association of Machinists will result in the largest U.S. union, with 2 million members.

To increase their membership, unions are focusing their organizing efforts on unskilled, low-wage service workers in the health-care and lodging industries and on agricultural workers. Instead of simply passing out organizing literature, they are using new tactics in targeting these groups, visiting workers at their homes and in the fields to discuss forming unions. Organizers are also targeting professional occupations such as doctors and the growing number of skilled contingency workers. About 45,000 of the 640,000 U.S. doctors now belong to unions. The number continues to grow, as doctors turn to unions to protect their interests from the powerful health maintenance organizations that the doctors claim restrict them in caring for patients.[32]

annual expenditures compared to the 50 percent that was designated for organizing in the 1930s.[28]

Another of Sweeney's strategies to strengthen labor unions is coordinating multiunion membership drives. In the past, individual unions have organized their own campaigns. Today, different unions are joining forces to stage recruitment drives targeted at workers in specific cities or industries. For example, in Las Vegas, 15 unions representing workers in the building and construction trades have formed the Building Trades Organizing Project to organize workers for the companies participating in the city's building boom.[29]

In another joint organizing effort, the AFL–CIO, the Teamsters union, and the United Farm Workers are trying to organize 20,000 workers in northern California's strawberry industry. To build public support for their campaign, the unions have formed alliances with some 80 religious, social, women's, minority, and environmental groups to pressure the strawberry growers to allow union elections. The League of United Latin American Citizens is helping to raise money for strawberry pickers, and the Sierra Club, an environmental group, has filed a lawsuit against the growers.

Such alliances are also promoting organizing campaigns in the poultry processing and nursing home industries. To help poultry workers, 40 religious leaders formed the Interfaith Committee for Worker Justice. The group developed a code of ethics directed at poultry processing em-

On yet another front, unions are using so-called *corporate campaigns* to pressure employers to accept unions. In such a campaign, a union contacts an employer's suppliers, customers, creditors, stockholders, and board members to rally support for its cause. Through their pension fund investments, unions are stockholders in many corporations. The AFL–CIO formed an investments department to monitor union assets, giving unions the opportunity to suggest corporate board members and prepare shareholder resolutions that benefit their members.[33]

SUMMARY OF LEARNING GOALS

1. Summarize the history of labor unions, and list their primary goals.

Attempts to form labor unions began in the 19th century when workers united to improve their pay and working conditions. Two types of unions emerged: Craft unions joined skilled workers in crafts or trades; industrial unions joined workers from different occupations in the same industry. Unions grew slowly until 1935. From 1935 to 1955, they experienced their greatest period of growth. Since then union membership has steadily declined.

2. Describe the structure of organized labor.

Unions have a hierarchical structure. At the base is the local union that operates in a given geographic area. Many local unions comprise a national union. An international union joins members from multiple countries. At the top of the hierarchy is the federation, an association consisting of many national and international unions.

3. Identify the major federal laws that affect labor unions, and explain the key provisions of each law.

The Norris-La Guardia Act of 1932 protects unions by reducing management's ability to stop union activities. The National Labor Relations Act (Wagner Act) of 1935 requires management to bargain collectively with elected employee representatives and outlaws a number of unfair management practices. The Fair Labor Standards Act of 1938 set a federal minimum wage and outlawed child labor. In efforts to balance power between labor and management, the Taft-Hartley Act of 1947 and the Landrum-Griffin Act of 1959 were passed to outlaw a number of unfair labor practices of unions and employers. The Plant-Closing Notification Act of 1988 requires any employer with more than 100 employees to give 60 days' notice before a plant shutdown or mass layoff.

4. Explain how unions are formed, how they achieve their goals through collective bargaining, and the issues addressed in their contracts.

Employees form a union by initiating an organizing drive, collecting signatures of 30 percent or more of their fellow workers, and petitioning the National Labor Relations Board for an election. The union is certified if it receives more than 50 percent of the employee vote. Union representatives and employers negotiate their demands during collective bargaining sessions. The agreement they reach is set forth in a contract that is accepted or rejected by a vote of union members. Contracts cover wages and benefits, working conditions, grievance handling and arbitration, union activities and responsibilities, and employee rights and seniority.

5. Describe the roles played by mediators and arbitrators in labor negotiations.

Mediators and arbitrators assist negotiations. A mediator offers advice and makes recommendations. An arbitrator listens to both sides and then makes a decision that becomes binding for both parties.

6. Identify the steps in the union grievance process.

An employee with a complaint and a union representative (the shop steward) present the grievance to a supervisor. If this contact doesn't resolve the dispute, union representatives meet with higher-level managers. If no satisfactory agreement is reached, the grievance is submitted to an arbitrator.

7. Outline the tactics or "weapons" of labor and management.

Although most differences between labor and management are settled through the collective bargaining or grievance processes, both unions and management have other ways to make their demands known. The chief weapons of unions are the strike, picketing, and the boycott. Management's weapons are hiring strikebreakers, petitioning courts for injunctions, locking out workers, and forming employers' associations.

8. Describe how unions and employers are developing partner relationships.

Some unions and employers are teaming up to develop cooperative partnerships such as training programs. The partnerships give workers job security and help to improve employers' competitiveness.

9. Discuss employee-employer relationships in nonunion firms.

Employees in many small firms and many occupational groups including managers are not union members. Employers in nonunion settings try to prevent unionization by satisfying employees by offering them competitive wages and benefits. Employers help employees to resolve grievances through a number of resolution practices including open-door policies, employee hot lines, peer-review boards, mediation, and arbitration. Some employers establish no-layoff guarantees. Some employers that reduce their workforces offer employees early retirement and resignation incentives.

10. Explain the challenges facing labor unions and unions' strategies to rebuild their membership.

A number of factors have contributed to the decline in union membership, including labor legislation, the loss of traditionally unionized jobs in the manufacturing sector, and employers' increasing use of temporary and contract workers. Unions' growth strategies include changing the structure of unions to improve their efficiency and empower local union members, committing increasing financial resources to organizing and advertising campaigns, combining the efforts of several unions to cooperate in organizing activities, and forming alliances with different organizations. Unions are trying to rebuild their membership base by organizing both professional and unskilled workers in service industries as well as agricultural workers.

TEN BUSINESS TERMS YOU NEED TO KNOW

labor union

closed shop

union shop

agency shop

open shop

collective bargaining

bargaining zone

grievance

strike

picketing

Other Important Business Terms

American Federation of Labor (AFL)

Congress of Industrial Organizations (CIO)

national union

local union

international union

federation

right-to-work law

boycott

cost-of-living-adjustment (COLA) clause

giveback

mediation

arbitration

lockout

strikebreaker

injunction

employers' association

alternative dispute resolution (ADR) program

peer-review board

REVIEW QUESTIONS

1. Why did labor unions emerge?
2. What differences distinguish local, national, and international unions? What is a labor federation?
3. What major laws have influenced labor-management relations in the United States?
4. How do state right-to-work laws affect employees and employers?
5. What are bargaining zones? What part do they play in the collective bargaining process?
6. How does a closed shop differ from a union shop, an agency shop, and an open shop? Which of these arrangements is directly affected by the Taft-Hartley Act?
7. What is the difference between a mediator and an arbitrator?
8. What role does the shop steward play in the union grievance process? Compare and contrast the ways grievances are handled in union and nonunion workplaces.
9. What are the major tactics or weapons of union and management?
10. What major challenges are unions facing in their efforts to rebuild their membership? Which union strategies do you think will be most effective in gaining new members?

QUESTIONS FOR CRITICAL THINKING

1. If you had a choice between working in a union or nonunion workplace, which would you choose? Give several reasons to support your answer.
2. Suppose that you have realized your dream of starting your own company, Fantastic Fashions. During the early years, you designed and sewed your own clothing. As your company grew, you began hiring employees to sew your garments. You paid them well, gave them good benefits, and included them in profit-sharing. You established an open-door policy in which any dissatisfied employee could discuss a grievance with you. One day you learned that several employees were trying to organize a union in your workplace. Would you encourage your employees to unionize? If not, what would you do to discourage them from forming a union?
3. Many teachers in public schools belong to unions. Some critics of teachers' unions blame them for the decline in student achievement levels, arguing that unions support poor teachers who are more interested in wage increases and protecting their jobs than in helping students to learn. Based on your experiences, do you agree or disagree with the critics of teachers' unions?
4. Federal Express, a nonunion company, sponsors "driver appreciation" events in which drivers are treated to barbeque parties. One driver who is trying to organize a union at FedEx calls these parties "another dirty, low-down trick." But FedEx managers say the parties are just a way to show appreciation to workers. In your opinion, is FedEx justified in keeping its workers happy by saying thank you with an appreciation party, or do you

think that the gesture is merely an attempt to keep out unions?

5. In the past, a strike was one of the union's most effective weapons. Critics of unions say that one of the reasons strikes have lost effectiveness is that the public has little sympathy for workers who

earn good salaries and enjoy health-care benefits and pensions but still walk off their jobs wanting more money. Since unions want to improve their public image, do you think they should abolish strikes altogether and work harder at the negotiating table?

Experiential Exercise

Directions: Interview two individuals—one pro-union and the other anti-union. Sample questions that could be useful for your interview follow. Be prepared to share your findings in a class discussion about the reasons people support or do not support union representation. You may add to or delete from the list of questions provided. Because interviewees could answer many of the following questions with an "it depends" response, encourage them to give concrete responses based on their personal experiences or opinions.

1. What is the main reason for classifying yourself as pro- or anti-union?
2. In what way(s) do you believe unions have influenced our society?
3. Overall, have unions had a neutral, positive, or negative impact on productivity?
4. To what degree is today's standard of living a result of the efforts of the labor movement?
5. In general, do you believe managers treat their employees more fairly in a unionized or a nonunionized setting?
6. Is labor-management communication better in a unionized or nonunionized setting?
7. What impact does unionization have on an organization's disciplinary process?
8. Are unions necessary to balance the power and authority of management?
9. Are decisions about pay increases and promotions more likely to be fair in a unionized or nonunionized setting?
10. Are union dues too low, too high, or just right when you consider what the members get through collective bargaining?

Nothing but Net

1. **Union Affiliation's Impact on Pay.** The U.S. Bureau of Labor Statistics provides the median weekly earnings of full-time wage and salary workers by occupation and industry. The data are presented in three categories: union members, those represented by unions, and nonunion workers. Identify the occupations and/or industries with the largest wage or salary gap based on union affiliation.

   stats.bls.gov/news.release/union2.t04.htm

2. **Union Web Sites.** Visit a union Web site (sample addresses are listed). Assume you are an employee who is seeking information to help you decide whether to vote in favor of union representation at your company. List the information at the Web site that most persuaded you to vote for union representation.

   Communication Workers of America:

   www.cwa-6450.org/index.htm

United Auto Workers:

www.uaw.org/

Service Employees International Union:

www.seiu.org/seiutop.html

3. **Child Labor.** Use your search engine to find information on child labor. One example is the report on child labor abuses in the apparel industry at

www.dol.gov/dol/ilab/public/media/reports/apparel/main.htm

Summarize in a one- to two-page paper your findings concerning the nature and extent of the problem and actions of those who are trying to abolish child labor.

Note: Internet Web addresses change frequently. If you do not find the exact sites listed, you may need to access the organization's or company's home page and search from there.

TREATING EMPLOYEES RIGHT

Herb Kelleher, chairman, president, and CEO of Southwest Airlines, recently told attendees at a leadership conference, "I think that in business there is a new wave of leadership that is perhaps more enlightened, more fair, more humane, more participative, and more family oriented rather than turf conscious and adversarial." A growing number of companies demonstrate this new leadership wave and are enjoying success as a result. Following are four such companies.

SOUTHWEST AIRLINES

Southwest Airlines is consistently named one of the top ten best companies to work for in America. CEO Herb Kelleher is legendary for his unconventional managerial style, which has left an indelible mark on the airline's corporate culture. Kelleher has said that the men and women of Southwest Airlines possess "psychic ownership" of the company. Southwest's success is a testament to its employees.

Kelleher says, "I would much rather have a company that was bound by love than bound by fear." Libby Sartain, vice president of people adds, "Southwest's culture is designed to promote high spirit and avoid complacency. We have little hierarchy here. Our employees are

encouraged to be creative and innovative, to break the rules when they need to in order to provide good service to our customers."

NORTH TEXAS PUBLIC BROADCASTING

Many employers, like the executives at nonprofit public broadcasting station KERA Channel 13, are discovering that employees are motivated by more than monetary rewards. Sylvia Komatsu, vice president of programming, says, "I think those of us who work for public broadcasting really see it as a calling. We feel strongly and care very deeply about the work we do, and we realize that it is within public broadcasting that we have the most freedom to work on projects that we think are important and help make a difference in the world. We have limited resources compared to the commercial stations, but we work at a place which has a mission."

FOSSIL

The chance to make a difference is a key motivator among the men and women—many of them very young—who work at Fossil. According to Senior VP International Sales and Marketing, Gary Bolinger, "We have a culture that we've developed, an environment where creative people can flourish. We sharpen that environment by giving them some discipline and focus, and then probably most important, we turn them loose to do their jobs. We do have a lot of young people around the building. They have a lot of responsibility that they're able to perform their jobs at a pretty early age compared to the other companies that I've been associated with."

LA MADELEINE

The food-service industry is notorious for high employee turnover. But at La Madeleine French Bakery & Cafes, founder Patrick Esquerré has successfully created a sense of family among his growing staff. It is La Madeleine's family of associates who are responsible for making the chain of neighborhood cafes an unqualified success in a growing number of U.S. cities.

Patrick Esquerré says, "I think they perceive me as the father of the family. And I'm very glad to be that because that means we are very close to each other. We take care of each other." Similarly, Bill Buchanan, regional director adds, "Many times you end up working 70, 75, 80 hour work weeks with other firms. Here at La Madeleine, we really focus on the quality of life for all our managers. We feel it's important that they enjoy their life and their families and their friends. Because it makes them a healthier individual and they're happier when they're at work. And they will be more successful."

Questions

1. If an organization has union members as employees, management-employee relations cannot be cooperative and productive. Do you agree with this statement? Explain using the case information.

2. Why should organizations treat employees right? Could organizations like Fossil, Southwest, and La Madeleine have succeeded without treating employees right?

3. Employees and unions are only interested in monetary motivation. True or false? Explain.

chapter 12

Creating and Producing World-Class Goods and Services

LEARNING GOALS

1. Outline the importance of production and operations management to a firm.

2. Discuss the role of computers and related technologies in production.

3. Identify the factors involved in a plant location decision.

4. Describe the major tasks of production and operations managers.

5. Compare alternative layouts for production facilities.

6. List the steps in the purchasing process.

7. Compare the advantages and disadvantages of maintaining large inventories.

8. Identify the steps in the production-control process.

9. Discuss the benefits of quality control.

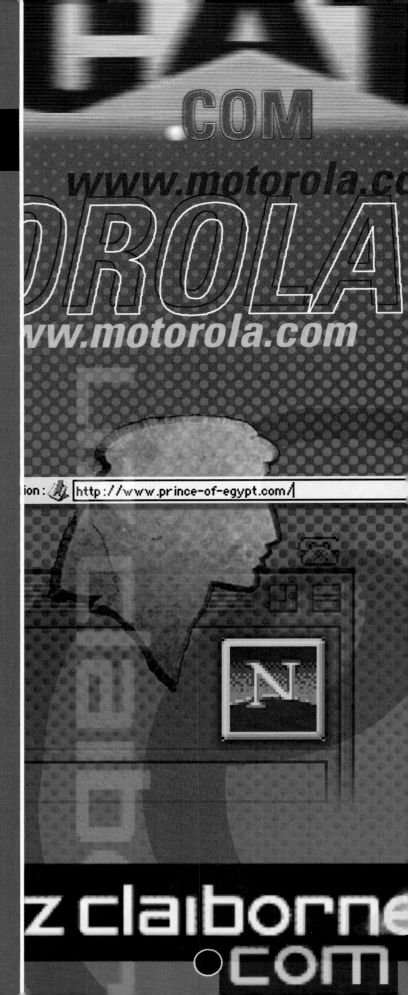

Fine-"Tooning" Production at DreamWorks SKG

How could it not succeed? DreamWorks SKG was the talk of Hollywood when the studio was formed back in 1994. Created by movie producer Steven Spielberg, former Disney studio chief Jeffrey Katzenberg, and music industry magician David Geffen, DreamWorks was expected to produce ground-breaking films, TV programming, interactive software, and records. The company's performance was less than energetic for the first several years, but DreamWorks recently lived up to expectations with films such as *Deep Impact, Saving Private Ryan, Antz,* and *The Prince of Egypt.* With just 6 films, Dream-Works garnered nearly 7 percent of 1998 movie-industry revenues, which ranked it seventh, ahead of Miramax's 33 pictures and of Universal's and MGM's 14 pictures each.

Yet even with this long-awaited success, DreamWorks can't afford to rest on its recent laurels. Only three out of ten movies make a profit, and even doing well at the box office doesn't guarantee prosperity. Production costs for the average live-action movie exceed $80 million. Of course, animated films can be a bit cheaper to produce; there are no huge celebrity salaries to pay, for example. Moreover, returns on animated films can be much higher (from licensing agreements for toys, fast-food  deals, and other tie-ins), and these returns can continue to pay off for years after the movie has left theaters. *The Lion King,* which Katzenberg oversaw at Disney, has blossomed into a $1 billion franchise. With *Antz* and *The Prince of Egypt* doing so well, David Geffen says, "We think we have carved a place out for ourselves in the marketplace for quality animation."

Still, producing a feature-length cartoon is far from child's play. *The Prince of Egypt* cost $70 million and took four years to make—all for 90 minutes of entertainment. And the film's production involved a lot more than crayons and paper. To begin with, DreamWorks needed people to produce the film, so it hired 800 employees. Just for *The Prince of Egypt,* the studio needed directors, producers, a song writer, a composer, and 350 artists, animators, and technicians, who were hired from more than 35 countries. The studio also hired top-notch voices for the film, including Val Kilmer, Ralph Fiennes, Sandra Bullock, Danny Glover, Jeff Goldblum, Steve Martin, Helen Mirren, Michelle Pfeiffer, Martin Short, and Patrick Stewart. Of course, all these people needed somewhere to work, so Dream-Works located, designed, and built a whole new animation studio—even though DreamWorks itself hadn't yet started work on its own new home.

www.prince-of-egypt.com

Production planning for *The Prince of Egypt* was no flight of fancy—although some flying was involved. The entire creative team journeyed to Egypt and the Sinai peninsula to learn about the area, experience the culture, and seek inspiration. "There's an intangible connection that comes from being on the actual spot," says songwriter Stephen Schwartz, "seeing the locations and breathing the air." To make sure the quality of the film would not be hindered by inaccuracy or assumption, the studio planned the movie around the advice of 335 Egyptologists, archaeologists, historians, and hieroglyphics experts. The film was even screened before 75 cardinals at the Vatican. In fact, more than 350 religious leaders attended hundreds of meetings to advise DreamWorks about *The Prince of Egypt.* The studio made dozens of changes based on their recommendations, including using different skin colors for slaves (to show that Jews weren't the only people enslaved by the Egyptian pharaoh), changing the name of a camel, removing some Arab stereotypes, and even changing some dialogue (which required Val Kilmer to re-record a small section of the soundtrack).

In addition to the production issues such as story line, setting, and historical and cultural accuracy, DreamWorks had to contend with the animation process itself. Rather than pencil and paper or paint and brush, today's animation relies more and more on technology. For character and production design, DreamWorks invented new approaches as it went. Animators used some commercial software, refined other software, created their own new software, and tweaked traditional animation processes—giving the film a distinctive new look. Of its 1,800 shots, 1,180 have special effects, which are made even more special by the live-action-effects artists who worked alongside the traditional animation artists.

The Prince of Egypt reached new heights in animation by seamlessly blending two-dimensional (traditional) and three-dimensional (computerized) animation with unique "camera" positions to give a sense of movement that is more realistic. The coordination of these high-tech elements was amazing. Just to complete the parting of the Red Sea, twelve artists took three years, and computers took 30,000 hours in rendering time. The hieroglyphic nightmare sequence lasted two minutes on screen and took 10 months to create. For DreamWorks, as for any company producing any product, successfully managing production makes the difference between a nightmare and a dream come true.[1]

CHAPTER OVERVIEW

Society allows businesses to operate only as long as they contribute to public well-being. By producing and marketing desired goods and services, businesses satisfy this commitment. They create what economists call *utility*—the want satisfying power of a good or service. Businesses can create or enhance four basic kinds of utility: time, place, ownership, and form utility. A firm's marketing operation generates time, place, and ownership utility by offering goods and services to consumers when they want to buy at convenient locations where title to the products can be transferred.

Firms create form utility by converting raw materials and other inputs into finished products. For example, Liz Claiborne converts fabric, thread, zippers, and other materials and components into women's apparel. In other words, the firm's production function creates form utility.

www. **www.lizclaiborne.com**

Production applies resources like people and machinery to convert materials into finished goods or services. The task of **production and operations management** is to manage the application of people and machinery in converting materials and resources into finished goods and services. Figure 12.1 illustrates the production process.

People sometimes use the terms *production* and *manufacturing* interchangeably, but they ignore an important difference. *Production* is a broader term that spans both manufacturing and nonmanufacturing industries. For instance, companies in extractive industries such as fishing, lumber, and mining engage in production, as do creators of services. Services are intangible outputs of production systems. They include outputs as diverse as trash hauling, education, haircuts, tax accounting, health-care delivery, mail delivery, transportation, and lodging. Figure 12.2 lists five examples of production systems for a variety of goods and services.

Whether the production process results in a tangible good or an intangible service, it always converts inputs into

outputs. This conversion process may make major changes in raw materials or combine finished parts. A butcher performs a production function by reducing a side of beef to ground beef, steaks, and roasts. A subway system combines

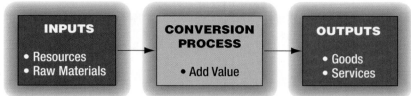

Figure 12.1 **The Production Process: Converting Inputs to Outputs**

rails, trains, and employees to create its output: passenger transportation services. Both of these processes create form utility.

This chapter describes the process of producing goods and services. It looks at the importance of production and operations management to a business and discusses new technologies that are transforming the production function. It then discusses the tasks of the production and operations manager, the importance of quality, and the impact of production on the environment.

STRATEGIC IMPORTANCE OF THE PRODUCTION FUNCTION

Along with marketing, accounting, and human resource management, production is a vital business activity. Indeed, without production, none of the other functions would operate. Without a good or service to sell, a company cannot generate profits. Without profits, the firm quickly fails. The production process is just as crucial in a not-for-profit organization, since the good or service it offers justifies the organization's existence. In short, the production function adds value to a company's inputs by converting them into marketable outputs.

DID YOU KNOW?

Xerox invented both the personal computer and laser printer but failed to bring either product to market.

Business Directory

production application of resources like people and machinery to convert materials into finished goods or services.

production and operations management managing people and machinery in converting materials and resources into finished goods and services.

This added value comes from features of the outputs for which customers will pay money.

Clearly, effective production and operations management can lower a firm's costs of production, boost the quality of its goods and services, and allow it to respond dependably to customers' demands. Skillful management of production can also promote flexibility, so a company can respond quickly when customers' demands change. Consider that Hewlett-Packard spent 4 years developing the K-jet printer in the 1980s. Today, a comparable project would take 40 percent less time due to improved production management techniques.[2]

Mass Production

The United States began as a colonial supplier of raw materials to Europe and evolved into an industrial giant. Much of this remarkable change resulted from **mass production,** a system for manufacturing products in large amounts through effective combinations of specialized labor, mechanization, and standardization. Mass production makes outputs available in large quantities at lower prices than individually crafted items would have to carry.

Mass production begins with specialization of labor, dividing work into its simplest components so that each worker can concentrate on performing one task. By separating jobs into small tasks, managers create conditions for high productivity through mechanization, in which machines perform work previously done by people.

The third component of mass production—standardization—involves producing uniform, interchangeable goods and parts. Standardized parts simplify the process of replacing defective or worn-out components. If your car's windshield wiper blades wear out, for instance, you can buy replacements at AutoZone. Just think how long you would wait—and how much more you would spend—if you had to hire someone to individually craft the replacements!

A logical extension of these principles of specialization, mechanization, and standardization led to development of the **assembly line.** This manufacturing technique moves the product along a conveyor belt past a number of work stations, where workers perform specialized tasks such as welding, painting, installing individual parts, and tightening bolts. Henry Ford generated phenomenal results by applying this concept, in the process revolutionizing the auto assembly process. Before implementing the assembly line, Ford's workers assembled Model T cars at the rate of one per worker for each 12-hour workday. The assembly-line technique slashed the number of work hours per car to 1.5. Not surprisingly, dozens of other industries built on assembling complex products quickly adopted the assembly-line technique.

| Figure 12.2 | Typical Production Systems |

Example	Primary Inputs	Transformation	Outputs
Pet Food Factory	Grain, water, fish meal, personnel, tools, machines, paper bags, cans, buildings, utilities	Converts raw materials into finished goods	Pet food products
Trucking Firm	Trucks, personnel, buildings, fuel, goods to be shipped, packaging supplies, truck parts, utilities	Packages and transports goods from sources to destinations	Delivered goods
Department Store	Buildings, displays, shopping carts, machines, stock goods, personnel, supplies, utilities	Attracts customers, stores goods, sells products	Marketed goods
Automobile Body Shop	Damaged autos, paints, supplies, machines, tools, buildings, personnel, utilities	Transforms damaged auto bodies into facsimiles of the originals	Repaired automobile bodies
County Sheriff's Department	Supplies, personnel, equipment, automobiles, office furniture, buildings, utilities	Detects crimes, brings criminals to justice, keeps the peace	Acceptable crime rates and peaceful communities

Although mass production brings advantages for a firm, it imposes limitations, too. It is a highly efficient method of producing large numbers of similar products. However, mass production loses its efficiency advantage when production requires small batches of different items. To avoid this reduction, companies may focus on efficient production methods rather than on making what customers really want. Furthermore, specialization can lead to boring jobs, since each worker must repeat the same task all day. To improve their competitive capabilities, many firms are adopting new, increasingly flexible production systems, such as flexible production, customer-driven production, and the team concept. Mass production and these new techniques are not mutually exclusive choices, however. Many firms retain their mass-production systems, but improve them by combining new approaches with the traditional methods.

Flexible Production

Flexible production is an important goal at Caterpillar, which has spent $1.8 billion over the past 10 years to modernize and automate its factories. In many of the company's plants, sophisticated new tools allow fewer workers to perform production work faster than in the past. At the company's Montgomery, Illinois, factory, 39 riderless vehicles slide quietly down factory aisles guided by lasers to carry parts to the assembly line as needed.[3]

 www.cat.com

Like Caterpillar, many companies now recognize the advantages of flexible, *lean* production methods that reduce requirements for workers and inventory. While mass production efficiently creates large batches of similar items, flexible production can cost-effectively produce smaller batches. Flexible production methods also require new arrangements for customer contact, inventory, design, and engineering.

Manufacturers throughout the world use assembly lines to mass produce standardized goods. At Toshiba's factory in Ome, Japan, each worker performs a specialized task that contributes to production of notebook computers.

Customer-Driven Production

A customer-driven production system evaluates customers' demands to link what a manufacturer makes with what customers want to buy. Japanese firms have implemented this approach in many of their factories with notable success. Many U.S. companies have established computer links between their factories and retailers' systems that allow them to base production directly on retail sales.

Team Concept

Some production methods challenge the emphasis in mass production on specialized workers performing repetitive tasks. The team concept combines employees from various departments and functions such as design, manufacturing, finance, and maintenance to work together in designing and building products. Work teams may also include members from outside the firm, such as suppliers and customers. This kind of teamwork is sometimes called *concurrent engineering*, since the team completes engineering concurrently with design, production, and other functions.

Raytheon Aircraft once purchased metals from 83 suppliers; now A. M. Castle & Co. is its sole-source vendor. The Raytheon-Castle partnership operates a joint material/production review team charged with finding opportunities to trim costs. End producers also participate on this team. According to Castle's Allen Winfrey: "We involve metallurgists, engineers, and supply management. Their job is to analyze new technology, grades of materials, and market trends to make sure that Raytheon Aircraft's dollars are wisely spent. In just one instance, the team determined that changing to a different size sheet would result in an instant 25 percent saving in scrap metal."[4]

Business Directory

assembly line manufacturing technique that carries the product on a conveyor system past several work stations, where workers perform specialized tasks.

PRODUCTION PROCESSES

Classification can divide the methods by which firms produce goods and services according to their means of operating and time requirements. A good or service results from either an analytic or a synthetic system involving either a continuous or an intermittent process. An analytic production system reduces a raw material to its component parts in order to extract one or more marketable products. Petroleum refining breaks down crude oil into gasoline, wax, fuel oil, kerosene, tar, and other products. A meat-packing plant slaughters cattle to produce various cuts of meat, glue from the horns and hooves, and leather from the hides.

A synthetic production system reverses the method of an analytic system. It combines a number of raw materials or parts or transforms raw materials to produce finished products. A Ford assembly line produces an automobile by combining thousands of individual parts. Other synthetic production systems make drugs, chemicals, and stainless steel.

A continuous production process generates finished products over a period of days, months, or even years in long production runs. The steel industry provides a classic example. Its blast furnaces never completely shut down except for malfunctions. Petroleum refineries, chemical plants, and nuclear power facilities also practice continuous production. A shutdown can ruin such equipment, with extremely costly results.

An intermittent production process generates products in short production runs, shutting down machines frequently or changing their configurations in order to produce different products. Most services result from intermittent production systems. Accountants, plumbers, electricians, and dentists traditionally have not attempted to standardize their services, because each service provider confronts different problems that require individual approaches or production systems. This thinking has encountered challenges in recent years, however, as service

Campbell Soup Company uses a synthetic system in producing its soups, snacks, and other food products. The company makes its top-selling Goldfish brand snack crackers by combining ingredients, forming the dough into fish shapes, and baking it to produce the finished crackers.

providers have sought to enhance productivity. The move to industrialize the service sector is illustrated by the production systems at Jiffy Lube auto service, giant vision-products retailers such as Lens Crafter, the Olive Garden restaurant chain, Terminix pest control services, home-cleaning services such as Merry Maids, and the growing number of dental chains located in regional shopping centers. Movement toward continuous production processes, once thought impossible for services, is revolutionizing the service sector.

TECHNOLOGY AND THE PRODUCTION PROCESS

Like other business functions, production has changed dramatically as computers and related technologies have developed. In addition to boosting efficiency in the production process, automation allows companies to redesign their current methods to enhance flexibility. This change allows a company to design and create new products faster, modify them more rapidly, and meet customers' changing needs more effectively than it could achieve with traditional methods. Important production technologies today include robots, computer-aided design, computer-aided manufacturing, flexible manufacturing systems, and computer-integrated manufacturing.

Robots

Many companies have freed people from boring, sometimes dangerous assignments by replacing blue-collar workers with steel-collar workers: robots. A **robot** is a reprogrammable machine capable of performing a variety of tasks that require programmed manipulations of materials and tools. Robots can repeat the same tasks over and over without varying their movements.

Initially, robots were most common in automotive and electronics production, but growing numbers of industries are adding them to production lines, as improvements in technology bring progressively less expensive and more flexible alternatives. Firms operate many different types of robots. The simplest kind, a pick-and-place robot, moves in only two or three directions as it picks up something from one spot and places it in another. So-called *field robots* assist human workers in nonmanufacturing, often hazardous, environments such as nuclear power plants, space stations, and even battlefields.

Computer-Aided Design and Computer-Aided Manufacturing

A process called **computer-aided design (CAD)** enables engineers to design parts and buildings on computer screens faster and with fewer mistakes than they could achieve working with traditional drafting systems. Using an electronic pen, an engineer can sketch three-dimensional designs on an electronic drafting board or directly on the screen. The computer then provides tools to make major and minor design changes and to analyze the design for certain characteristics or problems. Engineers can now put a new car design through a simulated road test to project its real-world performance. If they find a problem with weight distribution, for example, they can make the necessary changes on a computer terminal. Only when they satisfy themselves with all of the structural characteristics of their design will they manufacture an actual car model. In a similar manner, Boeing's aircraft designers analyzed the shape and strength of proposed aircraft fuselage and wing configurations under various conditions. The Business Hall of Fame describes another successful application of CAD technology at Chrysler.

The process of **computer-aided manufacturing (CAM)** picks up where the CAD system leaves off. Computer tools enable a manufacturer to analyze the steps that a machine must take to produce a needed product or part. Electronic signals transmitted to processing equipment provide instructions for performing the appropriate production steps in the correct order. CAD and CAM technologies are now used in conjunction at most modern production facilities. Even small companies can afford these software tools, as the Business Tool Kit on page 393 explains.

deliver materials. All components are linked by electronic controls that dictate activities at each stage of the manufacturing sequence, even automatically replacing broken or worn-out drill bits and other implements.

General Motors is reorganizing its global operations based on flexible manufacturing systems that can customize cars for different markets. According to Lou Hughes, who heads GM's Opel and Vauxhall divisions in Europe, "We're learning to take a car platform and wrap stuff around it that lets us be very responsive to individual markets without going through all the reengineering of heating systems and body structure." The FMS approach will allow GM to adapt the basic platform of its new Opel Astra model, a popular subcompact in Europe, to make new versions of its Chevy Cavalier and Saturn cars for the North American market. Another result of this system is increased product quality. GM's goal for the new Astra is to deliver a problem-free car.[5]

www.gm.com

Computer-Integrated Manufacturing

Companies integrate robots, CAD/CAM, FMS, computers, and other technologies to implement **computer-integrated manufacturing (CIM),** a production system in which computers help workers to design products, control machines, handle materials, and control the production function in an integrated fashion. CIM does not necessarily imply more automation and fewer people than other alternatives. It does involve a new type of automation organized around the computer. The key to CIM is a centralized computer system that integrates and controls separate processes and functions.

Flexible Manufacturing Systems

A **flexible manufacturing system (FMS)** is a facility that workers can quickly modify to manufacture different products. The typical system consists of computer-controlled machining centers to produce metal parts, robots to handle the parts, and remote-controlled carts to

Business Directory

robot reprogrammable machine capable of performing numerous tasks that require programmed manipulations of materials and tools.

computer-aided design (CAD) system for interactions between a designer and a computer to conceive a product, facility, or part that meets predetermined specifications.

computer-aided manufacturing (CAM) electronic tools to analyze CAD output and determine necessary steps to implement the design, followed by electronic transmission of instructions to guide the activities of production equipment.

computer-integrated manufacturing (CIM) production system that integrates computer tools and human workers to design products, handle materials, and control production.

Chrysler's Cyber Cars

When Chrysler Corp. unveiled its new line of full-sized cars—the Dodge Intrepid and Chrysler Concorde (known as *LH cars*)—their dramatic styling made an immediate hit with consumers and the automotive press. Unfortunately, quality problems such as water leaks, inadequate headlights, and mysterious rattles soon soured the public, and sales slumped. While Chrysler is a major producer of trucks, minivans, and sport-utility vehicles—with about one-quarter of the U.S. market—it is only a minor player in the passenger car market, holding less than a 10 percent market share. When the company undertook a redesign of the LH cars, Chrysler managers decided to follow a very different process.

The 1998 Dodge Intrepid and Chrysler Concorde models were introduced with bold new styling, added interior room, and more powerful engines than previous models had offered. In addition, the Intrepid and Concorde represented the world's first paperless

cars. The LH cars were primarily designed and tested in a virtual world, not a physical one. Digital model assembly —DMA as it is known at Chrysler—allowed the company to save months of design time and millions of dollars, while significantly improving product quality.

In traditional automobile manufacturing, designers and engineers create paper drawings of new models. Clay models are then constructed to assess such factors as styling appeal and aerodynamics. Next, actual prototypes are built and tested. Only after all the details are ironed out, problems solved, conflicts resolved, and changes made, does the model enter production. This traditional approach to design required an expensive and time-consuming process.

By contrast, Chrysler used powerful Silicon Graphics computer work stations, along with commercially available and proprietary software, to design the 1998 Dodge Intrepid and Chrysler Concorde. Designers and engineers applied the tools to visualize and analyze such activities as model

reduction, fits, assembly processing, and vehicle configurations on the computer. Over 5,500 digital images of parts were created and analyzed. Everyone involved in the LH project was able to review design changes and issues in real time.

www.sgi.com

Digital prototyping eliminated the need for awkward, inefficient paper drawings and greatly reduced the number of expensive clay models that the company had to produce. This change saved both time and money. Art Anderson, manager of large-car platform advanced vehicle engineering at Chrysler, states that "the DMA process was a major contributor in reducing the design and engineering cycle time from 39 to 31 months." Speeding new models to market is a very important capability in today's fickle and highly competitive auto market. In addition, the DMA process reduced the cost of designing the new Intrepid

---

To succeed in a highly competitive apparel market, century-old Russell Corporation has spent over $500 million in the last few years to install computer-integrated manufacturing systems that have turned it into the nation's largest supplier of athletic uniforms. In its textile mills, seeing-eye computers sort fabrics by color, lasers cut the fabrics, robots sew seams, and automated, remotely guided vehicles carry materials from one section of the plant to another.[6]

THE LOCATION DECISION

One of a firm's major decisions focuses on choosing the right place to build a production facility. As Table 12.1 shows, the best locations provide advantages in three categories: transportation, physical, and human factors.

Transportation factors include proximity to markets and raw materials along with availability of alternative modes for transporting both inputs and outputs. Physical

variables involve such issues as water supplies, available energy, and options for disposing of hazardous wastes. Human factors include an area's labor supply, local regulations, and living conditions.

A firm that wants to locate in a community often must prepare an **environmental impact study** that analyzes how a proposed plant would affect the quality of life in the surrounding area. Regulatory agencies typically require such studies to cover topics like the impact on transportation facilities; energy requirements; water and sewage treatment needs; natural plant life and wildlife; and water, air, and noise pollution.

Labor costs, and perhaps even the availability of any workers with needed qualifications, also raise important issues. Some labor-intensive industries have relocated plants to rural areas with readily available labor pools and limited high-wage alternatives. Still other firms have moved production offshore in search of low labor costs. The Solving an Ethical Controversy on pages 396 and 397 explains one aspect of the decision to base a location choice on labor costs.

and Concorde models by an estimated $80 million, and it dramatically improved product quality. Designers exorcised noisy, underpowered engines and annoying road noise.

The DMA process allowed Chrysler designers and engineers to visualize and test thousands of different engines, suspension systems, and interior configurations, looking for the optimal package. The new engines, for example, are lighter and smaller than earlier ones, but they offer 25 percent more horsepower, burn 10 percent less fuel, and emit less pollution.

During the DMA process, over 1,500 fit and design issues were resolved before the first physical prototypes of the Intrepid and Concorde were even built. For example, engineers verified the assembly processes required to attach the power train and body panels onto the chassis prior to actual installation. For comparison, while building the prototype for the 1993 Dodge Intrepid model, engineers spent 3 weeks to complete these operations because they encountered so many interferences. With the 1998 Intrepid and Concorde, components fit the first time.

According to Chrysler's Anderson, "the key enabler of the DMA process is being able to efficiently and quickly communicate via interactive visualization of the issues at hand." Pictures, Anderson believes, convey much more than words can convey on their own. The computer-based system allows real-time reviews of design changes and issues, with interactive images projected during coordination meetings. "These images allow us to clearly communicate what the real issues are and then resolve them in minutes, versus the old 12-week physical mock-up process. This technology will be applied to every future project at Chrysler Corporation," Anderson stated.

The end result of Chrysler's digital prototyping system are cars that one automobile writer has described as "stunning," writing that the new aluminum engines—produced by the DMA process—"may be the best power trains Chrysler has ever built." Concludes Chrysler's Anderson, "we never could have done what we've done without the [new computer] systems."

www.chrysler.com

QUESTIONS FOR CRITICAL THINKING

1. What advantages does computerized design offer for both the manufacturer and the consumer? Do you think computers will ever totally eliminate the need to build prototypes?

2. After reading about Chrysler's new LH cars, would you consider buying a Dodge Intrepid or Chrysler Concorde if you were in the market for a new car? Why or why not?

Sources: "DaimlerChrysler Places First in Three Segments of the 1999 Total Quality Award™ Survey," DaimlerChrysler press release, PR Newswire, April 27, 1999; Bill Vlasic, "Chrysler Learns from Its Mistakes," *Business Week*, October 20, 1997, p. 166; Thomas Hoffman, "Visual Tools Key to Chrysler Cost-Cutting," *Computerworld*, August 18, 1997, p. 4; Gerry Kobe, "98 Chrysler LH Program," *Automotive Industries*, May 1997, pp. 34–37; Jack Keebler, "Chrysler Designers Blast a Home Run Out of the Styling Park," *Motor Trend*, March 1997, pp. 58–61; Bill Vlasic, "Trucks? Sure. But Can Chrysler Build a Hot Car?" *Business Week*, January 20, 1997, p. 27; and Chrysler Corp. press releases.

Availability of qualified employees is a factor in a location decision. Software makers and high-tech firms concentrate in areas with the technical talent they need, including Silicon Valley; Seattle; Boston; Portland, Oregon; Austin, Texas; and North Carolina's Research Triangle.

TASKS OF PRODUCTION MANAGERS

Production and operations managers oversee the work of people and machinery to convert inputs (materials and resources) into finished goods and services. As Figure 12.3 shows, these managers perform four major tasks. First, they plan the overall production process. Next, they determine the best layout for the firm's production facilities and implement the production plan. Finally, they control the production process to maintain the highest possible quality. Part of the control process involves continuous evaluation of results. If problems occur, managers return to the first step and adjust the process.

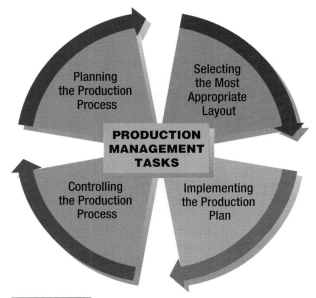

Figure 12.3 **Tasks of Production Managers**

Table 12.1	Factors in the Location Decision
Location Factor	**Examples of Affected Businesses**
TRANSPORTATION	
Proximity to markets	Baking companies and manufacturers of other perishable products, dry cleaners, hotels, other services
Proximity to raw materials	Mining companies
Availability of transportation alternatives	Brick manufacturers, retail stores
HUMAN FACTORS	
Labor supply	Auto manufacturers, hotels
Local regulations	Explosives manufacturers, welding shops
Community living conditions	All businesses
PHYSICAL FACTORS	
Water supply	Paper mills
Energy	Aluminum, chemical, and fertilizer manufacturers
Hazardous wastes	All businesses

PLANNING THE PRODUCTION PROCESS

A firm's production planning begins with its choice of the goods or services to offer its customers. This decision is the essence of the firm's reason for operating. Other decisions such as machinery purchases, pricing decisions, and selection of retail outlets all grow out of product planning.

Marketing research studies elicit consumer reactions to proposed products, test prototypes of new items, and estimate their potential sales and profitability levels. The production department concerns itself primarily with (1) converting original product concepts into final specifications and (2) designing the most efficient possible facilities to produce the new product. The new good or service must not only win acceptance from consumers; it must also achieve economical production to assure an acceptable return on company funds invested in the project.

Motorola's Mansfield, Massachusetts, plant had to gear up to produce cable modems in just 6 weeks. Brian McMichen, the facility's manager of production technologies, knew that he faced a tough challenge to get all the needed assembly instruction paperwork ready for the complex new item. He decided to use the Web to get the instructions to the factory floor.

Assembly line workers readily adopted the new pro-duction approach. In fact, they even suggested some useful changes. For example, they asked McMichen to add specifications on each screen to reduce time they would spend moving from section to section. Motorola was delighted with the results. The assembly line instructions were ready on time, and the new system cost only $5,000.[7]

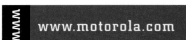

www.motorola.com

DETERMINING THE FACILITY LAYOUT

Once managers have established the activities needed in their firm's production process, they can determine the best layout for the facility. This decision requires them to consider all phases of production and the necessary inputs at each step. Figure 12.4 on page 394 shows three common layout designs: process, product, and fixed-position layouts. It also shows a customer-oriented layout typical of service providers' production systems.

A process layout groups machinery and equipment according to their functions. The work in process moves around the plant to reach work stations. A process layout

Affordable CAD

Few can question that computer-aided design (CAD) has revolutionized the processes of designing and manufacturing many products. The stories of Boeing and Chrysler told in this chapter are good illustrations of the advantages of CAD. Products can be designed faster and cheaper, but with higher quality, using CAD tools. Many small businesses and entrepreneurs who want benefit from computer-aided design quickly discover, however, the high cost of the CAD systems used by major companies. Boeing invests millions of dollars in CAD hardware and software.

Happily, anyone can find a number of good, relatively inexpensive CAD software programs available today, many of them based on larger, more expensive programs. What's more, these affordable CAD programs will easily run on any Windows 95/NT based personal computer. While the low-cost CAD programs couldn't handle the computerized design of a commercial jetliner, they are well-suited for many professional uses, though some may be better at certain tasks than others. Clearly, CAD power is now a very affordable resource.

According to *PC Magazine*, someone looking for an affordable CAD program should consider the following packages. (Prices are approximate, and newer versions of each may be available.)

▼ AutoCAD LT (Autodesk, $490, www.autodesk.com/autocadlt)

▼ Imagineer Technical 2.0 (Intergraph, $495, www.intergraph.com/imagine)

▼ Turbo CAD (Microcomputer Software, $300, www.imsisoft.com)

▼ Vdraft (Softsource, $450, www.vdraft.com)

PC Magazine reports that all four programs take full advantage of Windows 95/NT 32-bit program code. All offer features familiar to most personal computer users, such as ToolTips, wizards, and Microsoft Office compatible toolbars. Each has unique and attractive features. For example, *PC Magazine*'s review noted that Imagineer Technical's user interface stood out as more modern and intuitive than other packages. The review praised Turbo CAD's capability to drag and drop symbols from the symbol library palette. Vdraft can open multiple drawings at the same time.

Of the four, however, the reviewers at *PC Magazine* gave their highest rating to AutoCAD LT, citing compatibility, power, functionality, and ease of use. They preferred this program, even though it allows the user to open only one drawing at a time. This ranking is no surprise, since Autodesk's AutoCAD is considered to set the standard for CAD software. However, AutoCAD LT has about 80 percent of the features of its bigger sibling at less than 10 percent of the price.

Source: David Cohn, "A Whole New Side to CAD," *PC Magazine*, December 2, 1997.

---

often facilitates production of a variety of nonstandard items in relatively small batches.

A product layout sets up production equipment along a product-flow line, and the work in process moves along this line past work stations. This type of layout efficiently produces large numbers of similar products, but it may prove inflexible and able to accommodate only a few product variations.

A fixed-position layout places the product in one spot, and workers, materials, and equipment come to it. This approach suits production of a very large, bulky, heavy, or fragile product. Examples include building a bridge or assembling an airplane.

A service organization must also decide on an appropriate layout for its production process. The firm should arrange its facilities to enhance the interactions between customers and its services. A hospital, for instance,

arranges various departments, each specializing in a different function such as radiology, intensive care, and surgery. Patients move to different departments depending on their needs. If you think of patients as the inputs, the hospital implements a form of the process layout.

IMPLEMENTING THE PRODUCTION PLAN

After planning the production process and determining the best layout, a firm's production managers begin to implement the production plan. This activity involves (1) deciding whether to make, buy, or lease components; (2) selecting the best suppliers for materials; and (3) controlling inventory to keep enough, but not too much, on hand.

Figure 12.4   **Basic Facility Layouts**

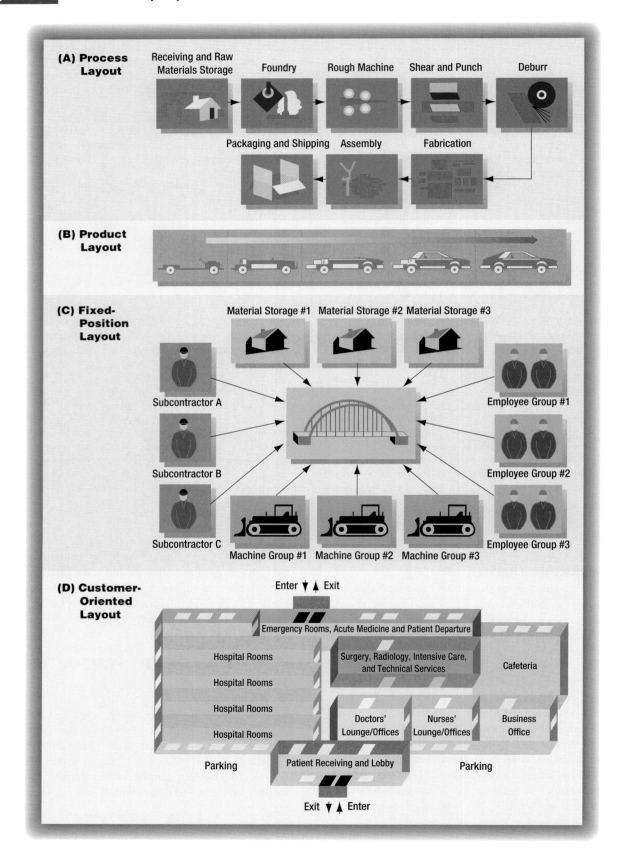

Make, Buy, or Lease Decision

One of the fundamental issues facing every producer is the **make, buy, or lease decision**—choosing whether to manufacture a needed product or component in house, purchase it from an outside supplier, or lease it. This decision is a critical one for many organizations. For instance, IBM long resisted subcontracting for outside production of its commercial PC line, despite extensive competitive pressure from Dell Computer. (See Chapter 7.)

Omaha-based Inacom Corp., IBM's biggest distributor, argued that it could significantly cut production time and inventory costs if the computer giant would allow it to assemble the PCs (rather than just storing IBM-produced units). Inacom's management even built a $20 million assembly plant in Ontario, California, in anticipation of IBM's approval. Eventually, an agreement allowed Inacom and other selected distributors to handle final assembly of 60 percent of IBM's commercial PC line. As a result, IBM units are now ready in 4 hours from receipt of an order. Order fulfillment once required 2 days. In addition, total manufacturing costs have also declined by an estimated 10 percent.[8]

Several factors affect the make, buy, or lease decision, including the costs of leasing or purchasing parts from outside suppliers compared to the costs of producing them in house. The decision sometimes hinges on the availability of outside suppliers that can dependably meet standards for quality and quantity. The need for confidentiality sometimes affects the decision, as does the short-term or long-term duration of the firm's need for supplies. Because airlines often experience equipment shortages, for example, they may arrange for short-term leases of engines and other aircraft components to meet immediate operating needs.

Even when the firm decides to purchase from outside suppliers, production managers should maintain access to multiple supply sources. An alternative supplier assures that the firm can obtain needed materials despite strikes, quality assurance problems, or other situations that may affect inputs.

Selecting the Right Supplier

Once a company decides what inputs to purchase, it must choose the best vendors for its needs. To make this choice, production managers compare the quality, prices, availability, and services offered by competing companies. Different suppliers may offer virtually identical quality levels and prices, so choices often depend on factors such as the firm's previous experience with each supplier, speed of delivery, warranties on purchases, and other services.

For a major purchase, negotiations between the purchaser and potential vendors may stretch over several weeks or even months, and the buying decision may rest with a number of colleagues. The choice of a supplier for an industrial drill press, for example, may require a joint decision by the production, engineering, purchasing, and maintenance departments. These departments often must reconcile their different views to settle on a purchasing decision.

Firms often purchase raw materials and component parts on long-term contracts. If a manufacturer requires a continuous supply of materials, a 1-year or 2-year contract with a supplier helps to ensure availability.

Today, many firms are building long-term relationships with vendors and slashing the number of suppliers with whom they do business. At the same time, they call upon vendors to expand their roles in the production process. When Motorola reduced its vendors, Craftsman Custom Metal fabricators of Schiller Park, Illinois, made the cut. However, Craftsman's management worried that the 275-person firm sold half of its volume to Motorola. Price pressure and the loss of trade secrets via this partnership topped the list of their concerns.

Events revealed no need to worry. Craftsman's partnership with Motorola has worked so well that it has gone on to forge similar links with other customers and vendors. Craftsman's CEO, Bruce Bendoff, put it this way: "Motorola's program was a little scary for us, but it was also a huge opportunity."[9]

In order to meet the strict demands of today's production managers, suppliers must raise their own quality standards. Part of this task involves ensuring that parts meet manufacturers' specifications before they leave a supplier's factory.

They said it

"Production is the goose that lays the golden egg. Payrolls make consumers."

George Humphrey (1890–1970)
American industrialist and U.S.
Secretary of the Treasury

Inventory Control

Production managers' responsibility for **inventory control** requires them to balance the need to keep stocks on hand to meet demand against the costs of carrying the inventory. Among the expenses involved in storing inventory are warehousing costs, taxes, insurance, and maintenance. A firm wastes money if it holds more inventory than it needs, but a shortage of raw materials, parts, or goods for sale often results in delays and unhappy customers. Firms lose business when they consistently fail to meet promised delivery dates or when they offer only empty shelves to patrons. Production managers must balance this threat against the cost of holding inventory to set acceptable stocking levels.

Effective inventory control can save a great deal of money. In one common technique, many firms maintain **perpetual inventory** systems to continuously monitor the amounts and locations of their stocks. Such inventory control systems typically rely on computers, and many automatically generate orders and print necessary documents at

SOLVING AN ETHICAL CONTROVERSY

Are Celebrities Responsible for the Products They Endorse?

Star defensive end Reggie White of the Green Bay Packers recently joined the ranks of human rights and labor activists by attacking Nike for alleged sweatshop conditions in the factories that produce its shoes. Nike, with something like 40 percent of the athletic shoe market in the United States, contracts with overseas factories, mostly located in Asia, to produce all of its shoes. Human rights and labor activists have alleged poor treatment of workers at many of these plants, including low pay, long working hours, and dangerous working conditions. An internal report prepared on behalf of Nike by the accounting firm of Ernst & Young found that workers in Nike's plants in Vietnam work 65 hours a week for less than $10. The report also found that the air is so bad in the factories that over 75 percent of the workers suffer from respiratory problems and that

workers are generally treated like recruits in a military boot camp.

When told of investigators' findings, White said "The reason they [Nike] have these sweatshops is for cheap labor. They'd rather hire the cheap labor than hire the kid in the neighborhood who is buying their shoes. There are people who need jobs here." White added, "I'm not going to lie to you. I've been disappointed by them." White's comments seemed unusual because he earns somewhere between $200,000 and $250,000 per year endorsing Nike's shoes. In the same interview when he blasted Nike's labor practices, however, White indicated that he had no plans to end his relationship with the company. "Nike still makes the best shoes," he said.

In contrast to Reggie White, Nike's best-known celebrity endorser, Michael Jordan, took a somewhat different approach when asked about conditions in Nike's Asian factories. Jordan said "I think that's Nike's decision to do what it can to make sure everything is correctly done. I don't know the complete situation. Why should I? I'm trying to do

my job. Hopefully, Nike will do the right thing." Nike pays Jordan an estimated $20 million a year—more, some critics claim, than the entire amount paid Vietnamese workers to make Nike shoes in a year.

Celebrities endorsing Nike products aren't the only ones who have been caught up in the sweatshop issue. Well-known talk show hostess Kathie Lee Gifford was confronted with evidence of human rights and labor abuses in sweatshops producing a line of clothing bearing her name, Kathie Lee Plus, and sold by retail giant Wal-Mart. Gifford almost immediately became a crusader against sweatshops. She vowed to "shine a light on the cockroaches." Gifford helped persuade Wal-Mart to adopt a strict new code of conduct and monitoring system for all of its contractors and subcontractors.

 Should celebrities publicly prod companies to improve working conditions and establish monitoring systems at the plants that make the products the celebrities endorse?

---

the appropriate times. Many supermarkets link their scanning devices to perpetual inventory systems that reorder needed merchandise. As the system records a shopper's purchase, it reduces an inventory count stored in the computer. Once inventory on hand drops to a predetermined level, the system automatically reorders the merchandise.

Some companies go further and hand over their inventory control functions to suppliers. This concept is known as **vendor managed inventory.** Bose Corporation—the

audio equipment maker—has set up arrangements with some vendors that effectively transfer control of its inventory to the sellers. Such a vendor's on-site representative is responsible for monitoring Bose's inventory and placing orders when needed without Bose's approval.

Just-in-Time Systems

A **just-in-time (JIT) system** implements a broad management philosophy that reaches beyond the narrow activity of inventory control to influence the entire system of production and operations management. A JIT system seeks to eliminate all sources

Business Directory

just-in-time (JIT) system management philosophy aimed at improving profits and return on investment by involving workers in the operations process and eliminating waste through cost reductions, inventory reductions, and quality improvements.

PRO

1. Because of their name recognition, celebrities can powerfully influence public opinion. Companies are more likely to respond when criticized by celebrities than by labor or human rights activists. Celebrities have achieved some success in improving working conditions, eliminating sweatshops, and getting companies to adopt stronger codes of conduct and monitoring systems for contractors.

2. Sweatshop conditions are moral offenses. Celebrities have an ethical responsibility to speak out against poor working conditions, regardless of whether or not they have been paid by the companies involved.

CON

1. Celebrities do not fully understand the situation at the factories, nor do they understand why companies such as Nike produce products overseas. While wages may seem low and working conditions poor by American standards, these factories are among the few sources of decent jobs in places such as China and Vietnam. These workers would actually be worse off if the plants were to close.

2. Celebrities may react to manipulation by groups with hidden anti-business agendas. Many of the groups confronting celebrities over alleged sweatshop conditions want to restrict imports, protect domestic jobs, and stop companies from outsourcing production to foreign subcontractors.

SUMMARY

The debate over the role of celebrity endorsements in eliminating sweatshops raises some difficult and complex questions, many of which are similar to the questions concerning child labor discussed in Chapter 11. On one hand, celebrities do seem to have accepted some responsibility that extends beyond merely endorsing products and, of course, collecting their fees. Even if sweatshop jobs—such as those in Nike's Asian plants—are good jobs, working conditions and wages could certainly be improved.

On the other hand, companies such as Nike use foreign outsourcing for reasons much more complicated than most celebrities probably understand.

Wading into the debate over sweatshops without fully understanding all of these issues may be a mistake. Many people may also see hypocrisy if celebrities criticize companies for their labor practices and yet continue to endorse their merchandise and collect their fees. Some might view these celebrities as mere followers of trends, resulting in increased public cynicism and harm to all involved.

Sources: Jodie Morse, "Campus Awakening: The Sweatshop Issue Has Galvanized College Activists. But Are Students Being Used by Big Labor?" *Time*, April 12, 1999, accessed at www.pathfinder.com; Luc Lampriere, "Nike's PR Blitz on Overseas Labor," *World Press Review*, January 1998, pp. 32–33; Bill Mesler, "No-sweat Holidays?" *The Nation*, January 26, 1998, p. 8; Bernard Sanders, "Just Do It, Nike," *The Nation*, December 8, 1997, p. 6; "A Potent Weapon in the War against Sweatshops," *Business Week*, December 1, 1997, p. 40; "Packers' White Condemns Nike Labor Practices, but Still Likes the Shoes," Associated Press Newswire, November 14, 1997; Alan Attwood, "Will Tiger Mend Nike's Image?" *World Press Review*, July 1997, pp. 30–31; and Julie Polter, "M-I-C-K-E-Y, Kathie Lee, and Me," *Sojourners*, March/April 1997, pp. 12–13.

of waste—anything that does not add value—in operations activities by providing the right part at the right place at the right time. Compared with traditional production, this program reduces inventory and costs as it improves the quality of goods and services.

The inventory control function in a JIT system supplies parts to a production line or a company as needed. This action lowers factory inventory levels and inventory control costs. The JIT system also lets firms respond quickly to changes in the market, retaining only the most essential personnel to maintain inventory.

JIT production shifts much of the responsibility for carrying inventory to vendors, which operate on forecasts and keep stocks on hand to respond to manufacturers' needs. Suppliers that cannot keep enough high-quality parts on hand often lose customers to suppliers who can.

Bose Corp. uses a just-in-time system called *JIT II*. Doranco, a family owned supplier of metal products, is part of Bose's JIT II program. As a result, Doranco's Joe Doran spends a lot of time in Bose's Framington, Massachusetts, headquarters.

One day, Doran heard that a Bose customer had just bought out the firm's inventory of a certain loudspeaker. Doran quickly checked with Bose's engineering department and offered a JIT-style solution to the potential out-of-stock problem. As Doran tells the story: "We were able to call our manufacturing facility, intercept second-shift production, realign production, and deliver finished product to the Bose distribution warehouse by noon the next day." Bose was back in stock, and Duranco recorded a major sale.[10]

Reengineering

Reducing cycle times has become a major goal of production and operations management. Many firms are reengineering their processes to accomplish this objective. **Reengineering** is the process of mapping out delivery-chain processes in detail to identify potential reductions in cycle times or process errors through applications of technology to those key steps. When a company reengineers a process, it carefully evaluates and then modifies management systems, job designs, and work flows in an effort to improve efficiency and reduce cycle time. Ford Motor Co. offers a classic illustration. At one time, the Ford vendor-payment system kept 400 accounting department employees awash in a sea of paperwork. When top managers learned that rival Mazda performed the same work with only five workers in its accounts payable division, they recognized a need for reengineering. Computers now match receipt records, purchase orders, and invoices and then automatically prepare checks. Today, only 100 Ford employees handle the same work, and company vendors receive payments immediately upon receipt of shipments.[11]

Under Bose Corp.'s JIT II program, suppliers' employees work on site, including Joe Doran of Doranco. By working together closely as partners, both suppliers and customers benefit from improvements in the efficiency of inventory control.

Materials Requirement Planning

Clearly, effective inventory control requires careful planning to make sure the firm has all the inputs it needs to make its products. How do production and operations managers coordinate all of this information? They rely on **materials requirement planning (MRP)**, a computer-based production planning system that allows a firm to ensure that it has all parts and materials it needs to produce its goods and services at the right time and place and in the right amounts.

Production managers use special computer programs to create schedules that identify the specific parts and materials required to produce an item. These schedules specify the exact quantities required of each and the dates on which to release orders to suppliers so deliveries will support the best timing within the production cycle. A small company might get by without an MRP system. If a firm makes a simple product with few components, a telephone call may ensure overnight delivery of crucial parts. For a complex product, however, such as a car or an F-15 fighter jet, MRP becomes an invaluable tool.

CONTROLLING THE PRODUCTION PROCESS

So far, this chapter has discussed three basic tasks of production and operations managers: planning the overall production process, determining the plant layout, and implementing the production plan. Their final task, and perhaps the most important one of all, remains: controlling the production process to maintain the highest possible quality. **Production control** creates a well-defined set of procedures for coordinating people, materials, and machinery to provide maximum production efficiency. Suppose that a watch factory must produce 80,000 watches during October. Production-control executives break down this total into a daily production assignment of 4,000 watches for each of the month's 20 working days. Next, they determine the number of workers, raw materials, parts, and machines the plant needs to meet the production schedule.

Similarly, a manager in a service business such as a restaurant must estimate how many meals the outlet will serve each day and then determine the number of people needed to prepare and serve the food, as well as how much food to purchase and how often. For example, the restaurant manager may need to buy meat, fish, and fresh vegetables every day or every other day to ensure freshness, while buying canned and frozen foods less often, depending on storage space.

production systems, such systems tend to depend more on people than on materials.

Manufacturing Resource Planning

While an MRP system controls inventory, a more advanced computer-based system controls all of a firm's production resources. Called **manufacturing resource planning (MRP II)**, the system integrates planning data from individual departments—marketing, production, engineering, and finance—to produce a master business plan for the entire organization. MRP II then translates the business plan into various forecasts, setting requirements for inventory, materials handling, personnel, and the production schedule. All managers have access to this information. MRP II automatically responds to a change in a sales forecast by adjusting production scheduling. Some MRP II software can even advise managers on solutions to manufacturing and other production problems.

Five Steps in Production Control

Figure 12.5 illustrates production control as a five-step process composed of planning, routing, scheduling, dispatching, and follow-up. These steps are part of the firm's overall emphasis on total quality management.

Production Planning The phase of production control called **production planning** determines the amount of resources (including raw materials and other components) a firm needs to produce a certain output. The production planning process develops a bill of materials that lists all needed parts and materials. By comparing information about needed parts and materials with the firm's perpetual inventory data, purchasing personnel can identify necessary purchases. The MRP system establishes delivery schedules to ensure that needed parts and materials arrive at regular intervals as required during the production process. Production planning also ensures the availability of needed machines and workers. Although material inputs contribute to service-

Routing Another phase of production control called **routing** determines the sequence of work throughout the facility and specifies who will perform each aspect of production at what location. Routing choices depend on two factors: the nature of the good or service and the facility layouts discussed earlier in the chapter—product, process, or fixed-position layouts.

Scheduling In the **scheduling** phase of production control, production managers develop timetables that specify how long each operation in the production process takes and when workers should perform it. Efficient scheduling ensures that production will meet delivery schedules and make efficient use of resources.

Scheduling is an extremely important activity for a manufacturer of a complex product with many parts or production stages. Think of all the component parts needed to make a Toyota Camry. Scheduling must make each one available in the right place, at the right time, and in the right amounts to ensure a smooth production process.

Scheduling practices vary considerably in service-related organizations. Local delivery companies or doctors' offices may use relatively unsophisticated scheduling systems, resorting to such devices as "first come, first served" rules, appointment schedules, or take-a-number systems. They may call in part-time workers and use standby equipment to handle demand fluctuations. On the other hand, hospitals typically implement sophisticated scheduling systems similar to those of manufacturers.

Production managers look to a number of analytical methods for help with scheduling. One of the oldest methods, the Gantt chart, tracks projected and actual work progress over time. Gantt charts like the one in Figure 12.6 remain popular because they show at a glance the status of a particular project. However, they are most effective for scheduling relatively simple projects.

A complex project might require a **PERT (Program Evaluation and Review Technique)** chart, which seeks to minimize delays by coordinating all aspects of the production process. First developed for the military, PERT has been modified for industry. For example, the simplified

Figure 12.5 Five Steps in Production Control

Figure 12.6	Gantt Chart

Invoice Number	Quantity Desired	September					October				November				December			
		2	9	16	23	30	7	14	21	28	6	13	20	27	4	11	18	25
C18952	6,250																	
C19033	4,800																	
C19147	3,850																	
C19186	5,250																	
C19203	3,700																	

PERT diagram in Figure 12.7 summarizes the schedule for construction of a house. The red line indicates the **critical path**—the sequence of operations that requires the longest time for completion. Operations outside the critical path allow some slack time and can be performed earlier or delayed until later in the production process. Managers can assign some workers and machinery to critical-path tasks early in the process, then reassign them to noncritical operations as needed.

In practice, a PERT network may consist of thousands of events and cover months of time. Complex computer programs help production managers to develop such a network and find the critical path among the maze of events and activities.

Dispatching The phase of production control in which the manager instructs each department on what work to do and the time allowed for its completion is called **dispatching.** The dispatcher authorizes performance, provides instructions, and lists job priorities.

Follow-Up Because even the best plans sometimes go awry, production managers need tools to keep them aware of problems that arise. **Follow-up** is the phase of production control in which supervisors spot problems in the production process and determine needed adjustments. Problems take many forms; machinery malfunctions, delayed shipments, and employee absenteeism can all affect production. The production-control system must report these delays to managers so they can adjust schedules.

IMPORTANCE OF QUALITY

As discussed throughout the text, quality is just as vital in the product development and production functions as in other areas of business. Growing numbers of companies are realizing that they can build quality products most effectively by incorporating it into product designs from the very beginning. Investing money up front in quality design and development ultimately decreases the cost of quality, measured by costs that result from failure to make the good or service right the first time. These costs average at least 20 percent of sales revenue for most companies. Some typical costs of quality include downtime, repair costs, rework, and employee turnover. Production and operations managers must set up systems to track and reduce such costs. If managers concentrate on producing a quality product that satisfies the needs of customers, they will reduce costs of quality as a byproduct. The Business Hall of Shame box illustrates the full potential cost of quality.

Quality control is an important aspect of CEO John F. Welch's strategy for General Electric. GE's quality control program is based on training some 10,000 managers as so-called *black belts*. After spending 4 months learning various statistical and quality control techniques, the black belts then work full-time setting up quality control projects. GE believes the program could save the firm $7 to $10 billion over the next decade. Welch also sees marketing advantages in the black belt program: "Your customers are happy with you, you are not fire-fighting, you are not running in a reactive mode."[12]

| **Figure 12.7** | **PERT Diagram for Building a House** |

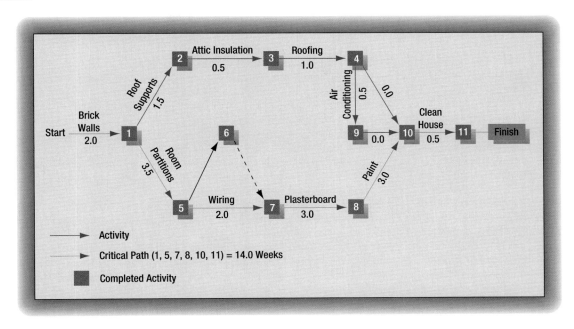

Quality Control

Quality control involves measuring goods and services against established quality standards. Firms need such checks to spot defective products and to avoid delivering inferior shipments to customers. Devices for monitoring quality levels of a firm's output include visual inspections, electronic sensors, robots, and X-rays. A high rejection rate on a product or component sends a danger signal that production is not achieving quality standards.

Of course, a company cannot rely solely on inspections to achieve its quality goals. A typical American factory spends up to half of its operating budget identifying and fixing mistakes, a costly and time-consuming process. Instead, quality-driven production managers identify all processes involved in producing goods and services and work to maximize their efficiency. The causes of problems in the processes must be found and eliminated. If a company concentrates its efforts on improving processes, a quality product will result.

ISO Certification

The **International Standards Organization (ISO)** was established in Europe to ensure consistent quality among products manufactured and sold throughout the member nations of the European Union. ISO standards have now become a widely recognized quality model throughout the world.

In fact, ISO certification is now a condition of doing business with many major European firms. To receive ISO certification, a company must undergo an on-site audit to ensure that documented quality procedures are in place and that all employees understand and follow these procedures. Production managers meet ISO requirements through an ongoing process involving periodic recertification. Approximately one-fourth of all corporations worldwide now require that suppliers and vendors fully meet ISO 9000 standards.

> **DID YOU KNOW?**
>
> Due to increased quality, the average American household keeps a new car twice as long today compared with 1980.

BUSINESS HALL OF SHAME

McDonald's Quality Problem

McDonald's has recently experienced some tough times. The world's largest fast-food chain has seen sluggish sales growth, several new-product flops, and mediocre profits. One of the greatest brand names in the world has been tarnished. Many people have begun to ask: "What has gone wrong with McDonald's?"

Even though McDonald's is in little immediate danger of losing its throne as king of the fast-food chains, danger signs abound. Over the past 10 years the share of U.S. fast-food dollars spent at McDonald's has fallen by more than 2 points to around 16 percent. The firm has suffered this erosion in spite of the fact that it has added 50 percent more restaurants over the same period, far more than competitors. Domestic sales have risen by less than 20 percent since 1990, while overall operating profits have failed to keep pace with inflation. Same-store sales—sales at

restaurants open at least 1 year—fell or just barely increased during some recent years. Operating profits per restaurant have dropped by 40 percent, adjusted for inflation, over the past 10 years.

Even more astonishing, these trends have occurred with Americans eating out more than ever before. The percentage of household food budgets spent at restaurants is now close to 40 percent, a record. While McDonald's remains hugely popular with preschool children, older kids and adults appear to be abandoning the golden arches in droves. One mother in Austin, Texas, commented that she rarely eats McDonald's food even though her young children still like it.

Most outside observers point to the company's failure to adapt to changing consumer tastes as one source of the recent problems at McDonald's. Both Burger King and Wendy's—the company's chief rivals in the fast-food business—have offered far more innovative menus in recent years. For example, Wendy's same-store sales have

risen for almost 24 consecutive months, success that industry experts credit to new menu items.

 **www.burgerking.com
www.wendys.com**

McDonald's has tried to change its menu. Over the past few years, the company has tried pasta, fried chicken, fajitas, and even carrot sticks. But, the changes failed to impress consumers, and McDonald's soon abandoned them and went back to its core menu. In addition, the firm has suffered several well-publicized marketing disasters, including the Arch Deluxe. McDonald's spent an estimated $100 million introducing the Arch Deluxe line; hundreds of restaurants have now axed it because of poor sales.

A more fundamental problem facing McDonald's, however, can be summed up in two words: poor quality. McDonald's has long stressed con-

SUMMARY OF LEARNING GOALS

1. Outline the importance of production and operations management to a firm.

Like marketing, accounting, and human resource management, production and operations management is a vital business function. Without a marketable good or service, a company cannot create profits, and it soon fails. The production process is also crucial in a not-for-profit organization, since the good or service it produces justifies the organization's existence. Production and operations management plays an important strategic role by lowering the costs of production, boosting output quality, and allowing the firm to respond flexibly and dependably to customers' demands.

2. Discuss the role of computers and related technologies in production.

Computer-driven automation allows companies to design, create, and modify products rapidly and produce them in ways that effectively meet customers' changing needs. Important design

and/or production technologies include robots, computer-aided design (CAD), computer-aided manufacturing (CAM), and computer-integrated manufacturing (CIM).

3. Identify the factors involved in a plant location decision.

Criteria for choosing the best site for a production facility fall into three categories: transportation, human, and physical factors. Transportation factors include proximity to markets and raw materials along with availability of transportation alternatives. Physical variables involve such issues as water supply, available energy, and options for disposing of hazardous wastes. Human factors include the area's labor supply, local regulations, and living conditions.

4. Describe the major tasks of production and operations managers.

Production and operations managers use people and machinery to convert inputs (materials and resources) into finished goods and

venience and speed. Yet 90 percent of consumers rank taste and quality as "very important" factors when choosing a place to eat. On the other hand, less than half listed speed and location as even moderately important factors. McDonald's quality doesn't fare well in comparisons. According to a recent survey, consumers said both Burger King and Wendy's offered better food than McDonald's by wide margins. Another survey put McDonald's 87th out of 91 restaurant chains in food quality, right behind Hooters. Even loyal McDonald's customers have complained that the food doesn't seem to taste as good as it once did.

Competitors poke fun at McDonald's quality problems, pointing out that their food is never precooked, and it doesn't sit under heat lamps, two techniques on which McDonald's has long relied. Wendy's constantly pushes themes such as "hot and juicy" and "fresh" in all of its advertisements and even on its Web site. Burger King recently launched a $70 million ad campaign claiming that consumers in a major survey thought Burger King French fries tasted better than McDonald's fries.

After a long period of denial, McDonald's has finally decided to do something about the quality of its food. The company is rapidly developing and testing new equipment to improve food quality. New toasters will heat buns in less than 10 seconds, rather than the 25 seconds that current equipment takes. High-tech holding cabinets will keep beef and chicken patties hot for up to 20 minutes without drying them out. Also, new computer software will help to project, within a very short period of time, what items will be needed. McDonald's has set a goal of hot food, served faster, with freshly toasted buns. Say you don't want mustard on your hamburger? That request will be no problem with the new system, McDonald's claims. Now, customers grumble, asking for something different on a food item often means a long wait.

These changes will carry expensive prices. Estimates project that the new equipment will cost close to $500 million, or over $25,000 per restaurant. Experts differ about whether or not these changes will restore some of McDonald's luster. According to Ron Paul, president of a major consulting firm, "It's the food. If McDonald's has finally figured this out, it would be a very, very big deal." On the other hand, Dean Haskell,

an industry analyst, commented that "McDonald's is playing catch-up. They will remain behind the competition and continue to struggle."

 www.mcdonalds.com

QUESTIONS FOR CRITICAL THINKING

1. Do you agree with the conclusion that McDonald's has a quality problem with its food? If so, why did the company let quality deteriorate?

2. Will the changes in McDonald's food-production process really improve product quality in the long run? Will a quality improvement fix what's wrong with McDonald's?

Sources: "McDonald's First Quarter Net Rises 11 Percent," Reuters Limited, April 23, 1999; Bruce Horovitz, "My Job Is Always on the Line," *USA Today*, March 16, 1998, p. 8B; David Leohardt, "McDonald's: Can It Regain Its Golden Touch?" *Business Week*, March 9, 1998, pp. 70–77; and Dottie Enrico, "Burger King Ads Fire Salvo in Fast-Food French Fry War," *USA Today*, March 9, 1998, p. 8B.

---

services. Four major tasks are involved. First, the managers must plan the overall production process. Next, they must pick the best layout for production facilities and implement their production plans. Finally, they are responsible for controlling the production process and evaluating results in order to maintain the highest possible quality.

5. Compare alternative layouts for production facilities.

Process layouts effectively produce nonstandard products in relatively small batches. Product layouts facilitate production of designs with limited variations in relatively large quantities. Fixed-position layouts are common when production involves very large, heavy, or fragile products. Customer-oriented layouts are typical for service facilities where success depends on interaction between customers and service facilities.

6. List the steps in the purchasing process.

In the make, buy, or lease decision, production and operations

managers determine whether to manufacture needed inputs in-house, purchase them, or lease them from an outside supplier. Managers responsible for purchasing determine the correct materials to purchase, select appropriate suppliers, and develop an efficient ordering system. The objective is to buy the right materials in the right amounts at the right time and in the right place.

7. Compare the advantages and disadvantages of maintaining large inventories.

The task of inventory control is to balance the need to maintain adequate supplies against the need to minimize funds invested in inventory. Excessive inventory results in unnecessary expenditures for warehousing, taxes, insurance, and maintenance. Inadequate inventory may mean production delays, lost sales, and inefficient operations.

8. Identify the steps in the production-control process.

The production-control process consists of five steps: planning, routing, scheduling, dispatching, and follow-up. Quality control is an important consideration throughout this process. Coordination of each of these phases should result in high production efficiency and low production costs.

9. Discuss the benefits of quality control.

Quality control involves evaluating goods and services against established quality standards. Such checks are necessary to spot defective products and to see that they are not shipped to customers. Devices for monitoring quality levels of the firm's output include visual inspection, electronic sensors, robots, and X-rays. Quality is just as vital in product development; investing money up front in quality design and development ultimately decreases the costs of quality.

TEN BUSINESS TERMS YOU NEED TO KNOW

production

production and operations management

assembly line

robot

computer-aided design (CAD)

computer-aided manufacturing (CAM)

computer-integrated manufacturing (CIM)

just-in-time (JIT) system

materials requirement planning (MRP)

manufacturing resource planning (MRP II)

Other Important Business Terms

mass production

flexible manufacturing system (FMS)

environmental impact study

make, buy, or lease decision

inventory control

perpetual inventory

vendor-managed inventory

reengineering

production control

production planning

routing

scheduling

PERT (Program Evaluation and Review Technique)

critical path

dispatching

follow-up

quality control

International Standards Organization (ISO)

REVIEW QUESTIONS

1. Give an example of production facilities in your vicinity that use each of the following manufacturing methods:
   a. analytic process
   b. synthetic process
   c. continuous process
   d. intermittent process
2. Suggest types of form utility that the following firms might produce:
   a. lawn-care service
   b. oil refinery
   c. commercial bus line
   d. software producer
3. Explain why effective production and operations management can provide a strategic advantage for a firm. Cite an example.
4. Distinguish between MRP and MRP II. What business purpose does each technique serve?
5. Explain the concept of a flexible manufacturing system.
6. Pick a facility layout for each type of business:
   a. watch repair shop
   b. medical examination room
   c. 1-hour dry cleaner
   d. retail gift shop
7. Describe the technological improvements transforming the production function.
8. What factors are likely to be most important in the make, buy, or lease decision? List instances when make, buy, or lease decisions might be made for the following types of firms:
   a. tropical plant store
   b. concrete company
   c. wedding planner
   d. antique furniture refinishing shop
9. Relate the tasks of production and operations managers to each of the following businesses. Give specific examples of each component.
   a. major league baseball stadium
   b. locally owned pharmacy
   c. commercial laundry
   d. VCR assembly line
10. Distinguish among CAD, CAM, and CIM.

QUESTIONS FOR CRITICAL THINKING

1. Compare the production processes used at McDonald's, Burger King, Taco Bell, and Red Lobster. What similarities and differences do you see? Why do you think the firms selected their particular approaches to the production process?
2. Read accounts of early production efforts. For instance, you might look at Henry Ford's or Eli Whitney's philosophy of production.
3. A successful production plan provides sufficient manufactured, purchased, or leased materials; efficient production schedules; and a controlled inventory. Develop a proposed production plan—including make, buy, or lease decisions—for a small business in your area. Present the plan to your class for comment and critique.

4. Evaluate your locality as a prospective industrial site. What are the area's strengths and weaknesses? Suggest businesses that might be a good match to your location.

5. Suggest ways in which each of the following organizations could practice effective quality control:

a. exporter of electrical equipment
b. packing house for farm produce
c. municipal golf course
d. pharmaceuticals manufacturer

Experiential Exercise

Directions: a plant tour of a local manufacturing operation for those in your class who are interested in learning more about the manufacturing process. Here are some ideas to help you in your planning efforts:

1. When you contact the plant's public relations department or whichever department coordinates the plant tours, identify yourself as a student from your school. Explain that you are coordinating a plant tour for your class and give the estimated number of students in the tour group. Let the person know that the purpose of the tour is to enhance your classroom and textbook study of the manufacturing process.

2. Be careful to find out all the conditions the company sets forth for its group tours and make sure to communicate those conditions to the members of your tour group.

3. To increase the meaningfulness of the tour experience, students taking the tour should have (a) attended the class session(s) in which this chapter was covered and (b) read Chapter 12 in its entirety. Meeting these requirements will help group members know what to look for and what questions to ask along the way.

4. Designate one to two students from the tour group to give a brief report to the entire class about what they learned on the tour. These students should be different from the tour coordinator, if possible.

5. Write a thank-you note to express your appreciation for the tour to the individual(s) at the company who helped coordinate and/or conduct the tour.

Nothing but Net

1. **Manufacturing.** Go on a virtual tour of Nissan's Smyrna, Tennessee, plant by visiting the Web site listed. Write a brief description of what you learned about the manufacturing process at each of the main plant areas: (a) stamping, (b) body assembly, (c) component assembly, (d) paint, and (e) trim and chassis.

   www.nissan-na.com/smyrna/index.html

2. **Inventory Control and MRP.** Use your search engine to find Web sites, such as the one listed, that provide information on inventory control and scheduling systems:

   http://cadlab.mit.edu/~krish/15.566/home.html

   Another site that contains more than 50 inventory-related links is found at

   www.cris.com/~kthill/sites.htm

   Present your findings during class discussion on inventory.

3. **Quality.** Write a one- to two-page summary about the Malcolm Baldrige National Quality Award by visiting one of these Web sites:

   www.asqc.org/abtquality/awards/baldrige.html

   www.quality.nist.gov/

   At a minimum, your report should describe the award, give a brief overview of the application process and the criteria by which the companies are evaluated, and list the most recent winners of the award.

   Note: Internet Web addresses change frequently. If you do not find the exact sites listed, you may need to access the organization's or company's home page and search from there.

FOSSIL—A WATCH FOR EVERY WRIST

When Fossil recently opened the doors on its chain of specialty stores, it created the perfect place to showcase its ever-growing product line. "This is Fossil in a box. Really, for us to be able to communicate the essence of the brand, we had to be in a retail setting where it was all together in one place—where you could walk into this environment and it's very readily communicated what our brand image was from a product perspective," says vice president of Image Tim Hale.

At the retail stores surrounded by Fossil's trademark salute to 1950s' nostalgia, shoppers can choose from hundreds of different Fossil products. Although Fossil is best known for its fashion-savvy watches, the company's trendy eye wear, leather goods, sports caps, and even boxer shorts are becoming hot fashion accessories around the world. While the majority of its products are manufactured in Hong Kong, Fossil designs its products at its corporate headquarters in Richardson, Texas.

Stephanie Thatcher, director of marketing, says, "For each product division that we have—watches, sunglasses, leather goods—we have a design team. That design team spends a lot of time overseas researching trends and seeing what's new and happening. Spending a lot of time in Europe and in Hong Kong, and really finding out what's going on in those markets and then adapting them to our market and to our customers."

Whether it's a Fossil kiosk in Hong Kong or the flagship Fossil store in Dallas, Fossil employs a universal product strategy. "We have a business system that works, and that system is that you buy at least 85 percent of your product from a core assortment that we have identified as our best-selling product. We still do realize there are some cultural differences. Some parts of the world like a little more gold than silver, some areas sell more blue dials than yellow dials, and we allow a 15 percent tweak factor for regional differences in taste levels," says Gary Bolinger, senior vice president of international sales and marketing.

Market research helps Fossil determine which items will compose its core assortment of products. Based on this sales analysis, Fossil has organized its watch division into distinct product lines, such as women's dress bracelet business, Fossil blue sports watches for active people, and multifunctional business (the chronograph watch and multifunction watches). Fossil's fourth line is a recent addition to its core of watch products.

Competitive pricing has always been an important part of Fossil's product plan. Fossil uses a bottom-down philosophy in pricing. Its annual sales continues to rise because of the company's keen ability to anticipate fashion trends, fashion-forward designs, and a relatively short product-development cycle. "We work on a cycle that is about nine months from concept to actual launch at retail," says senior VP of watch product, Dermott Bland. "We have an international concept meeting where all our international subsidiary partners come to Dallas, and we hold a brainstorming session where we present new concept ideas. They give us their feedback on those ideas." Some of Fossil's new product ideas include lucrative licensing agreements with other companies.

Finding new ways to tap into consumer needs and wants has the company well on the way to putting a Fossil watch on every wrist. One thing Fossil will be doing for a long time is creating innovative and well-made products for consumers around the world.

Questions

1. What factors might have influenced Fossil's decision to locate manufacturing facilities in Hong Kong?

2. What different inventory management systems could Fossil consider?

3. Because of its unique product image of Americana, Fossil can sell its product worldwide without cultural or societal limitations. Do you agree with this statement? Why or why not?

Careers in Business

BUSINESS CAREER EXERCISES

Setting Goals

You have read about the importance of planning—such as establishing clear goals—in building and maintaining a successful business. It is just as valuable to set personal and professional goals to achieve what you want in your life.

This exercise will help you to:

▼ Clarify the areas of life that are important to you.

▼ Take important steps towards making your desires a reality.

How to Locate the Exercise Launch *Career Design* from the "Career Assistance" program group. Then select "Navigation" from the menu at the top of the screen, followed by "Career Sections" and then "Setting Goals."

big part, but there are many other factors. In fact, you may have heard someone say, "I don't really like what I'm doing, but this is such a great place to work I don't want to quit." In this exercise, you will find out what kind of working conditions you want on the job.

This exercise will help you to:

▼ Develop a clear picture of exactly what working conditions are important to you.

▼ Learn that your work environment can be just as important to job satisfaction as the work itself.

How to Locate the Exercise Launch *Career Design* from the "Career Assistance" program group. Then select "Navigation" from the menu at the top of the screen, followed by "Career Sections" and then "Work Preferences."

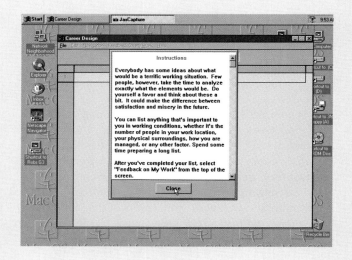

Work Preferences

Have you ever thought about what makes a job appealing or unappealing? Obviously, the actual work you do plays a

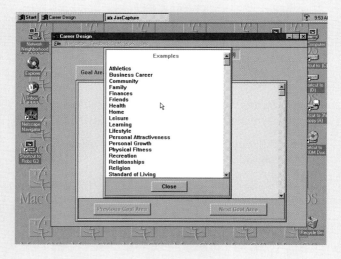

People Preferences

Have you ever thought about how you enjoyed a certain job—or disliked one—because of the people at work? This exercise will probably bring out some strong feelings. In this exercise, you list all the things you like and dislike about people you have encountered in the workplace. You even decide which of those characteristics are so important in future co-workers that the next job you take has to have employees who possess them.

This exercise will help you to:

▼ Develop a clear picture of the types of people you prefer in your work setting.

▼ Learn that the people with whom you work can have a significant impact on job satisfaction.

How to Locate the Exercise   Launch *Career Design* from the "Career Assistance" program group. Then select "Navigation" from the menu at the top of the screen, followed by "Career Sections" and then "People Preferences."

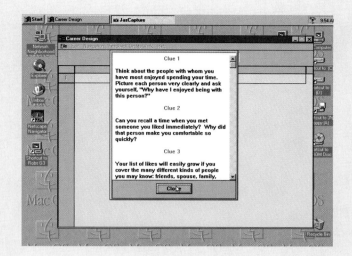

PART IV | Marketing Management

chapter 13

Customer-Driven Marketing

LEARNING GOALS

1. Explain how marketing creates utility, and list the major functions of marketing.

2. Explain the marketing concept and relate how customer satisfaction and total quality management contribute to added value.

3. Identify the components of a market.

4. Outline the basic steps in developing a marketing strategy.

5. Identify the components of the marketing environment.

6. Describe the marketing research function.

7. Identify the methods for segmenting consumer and business markets.

8. Define and contrast buyer behavior and consumer behavior.

9. Describe relationship marketing and explain its importance in strategic planning.

Going Once, Going Twice . . . Sold! Online at eBay Auctions

What would you pay for a refurbished Toshiba laptop computer? How about a Tinkerbell teacup or tickets to the original Woodstock rock music festival? The Internet offers thousands of auction-related Web sites, where you can bid on anything from live cattle to Elvis memorabilia. Some sites offer virtual swaps in the world's biggest garage sales; others hawk excess inventory through the new distribution channel. Sites like FairMarket help you create auctions for your own business Web site, while OpenSite Technologies offers easy-to-customize tools for do-it-yourself auctions. Onsale Inc. specializes in high-tech equipment, and uBid.com takes possession of all merchandise it offers on its auction site. Surplus Auction offers brand-name hardware and software, and even fine-arts auction giant Sotheby's is jumping online, featuring art items from $300 to $10,000.

Auctions have always represented marketing at its most basic—bringing buyers and sellers together where the buyer can inspect the item before bidding. But the Internet has taken this interaction to heights undreamed of.

eBay is a good example. As the world's largest online auction site, eBay (www.ebay.com) offers nearly 2 million items in a thousand different categories, ranging from antiques and automobiles to computers and sports memorabilia. Each month, people log on and view 600 million pages. With this stripped-down customer-driven approach, eBay never handles the merchandise or the money transactions between buyers and sellers. Its revenues come from Web posting fees and sales commissions, and it has been profitable since it first appeared on the Web back in 1995.

One happy eBay client is Ron Tipton, owner of Tipton's Coins and Jewelry in Salem, Oregon. Tipton has been remarkably successful in selling slow-moving items to eBay bidders, so successful that

he has seriously considered closing his store and going totally virtual. "It's particularly effective for unusual items," he reports, perhaps because eBay is so effective reaching buyers with very narrow interests. Andrew Malin, another eBay seller, has sold over 2,000 items there. "It's an unbelievable opportunity to market merchandise," he says. "Instead of putting it in the antiques mall where 200 people see, or a live auction with 300 people, you have 70 million on the Internet."

.WWW

www.ebay.com

Online auctions follow two basic formats. The *Yankee format* is used by most auction houses, including eBay. Bidding starts at a baseline price and stays open for a predetermined time (a few minutes to a few weeks). Each item usually has its own page, including a description, photo, and a starting price. In many cases, bidders are notified by e-mail when higher bids are received, so they have a chance to bid higher. The *Dutch format* is a bottom-up approach used by a few online auctions, including Klik-klok. A certain quantity of an item is made available for a specified time—two minutes on Klik-klok. When bidding starts, the item is available at its stated price. Then the price drops—usually a few dollars every 20 seconds or so. The object is to hold out for the lowest price until just before all the items are gone. The longer you wait, the more the price goes down.

The greatest advantage of online auctions is gaining access to hard-to-find items (such as a 1996 New York Yankees World Series trophy) or to items not available in stores (such as overstocked inventory or last year's models). Also, sellers have quick access to potential buyers, since they can list items on the Internet in less than an hour, instead of days or weeks with print ads.

But Web auctions do have disadvantages. For one thing, they won't necessarily save money. "Sometimes I put in a bid for 50 percent of the value of a product, just to see if I get it—but I never do," explains Kurt Jenkins, an information systems manager from Tennessee. That is because "an auction is not a negotiation between buyer and seller," says Jay Walker, founder of Priceline.com. "It's a competition among buyers." Online auctions also entail some risks: Auction houses don't usually guarantee the items they list, some items that were purchased were never delivered, and some companies may be driving up bids. Last year, the National Consumers League's Internet Fraud Watch received more complaints about Web auctions than anything else. On eBay, buyers and sellers rank each other using a point system. Then these rankings are posted so that everyone can check them before doing business.

Online auctions are clearly a hit with private individuals, and they are becoming a popular way for small businesses to buy or sell on the Internet. Since 1995, business-to-business online auction revenues have grown to more than 1 billion dollars. Some observers see online auctions as a sign of the future. "It's going to basically eliminate the middleman and create a whole new level of competition," says investment newsletter editor James Dines. But it's already clear that individuals and businesses are finding online auctions both fun and profitable.[1]

CHAPTER OVERVIEW

Business success in the 21st century is directly tied to a company's ability to identify and serve its target markets. Although online customers may seem to be a massive, formless market, marketers see huge untapped potential in the Web. From Web surfers to shoppers in the grocery aisles, companies are gathering mountains of data on every aspect of consumer lifestyles and buying behaviors. Marketers use this data to understand the needs and wants of consumers as preparation for satisfying them.

All organizations—profit-oriented and not-for-profit, manufacturing and retailing—*must* serve consumer needs to succeed. Marketing is the link between the organization and the consumer. It is the way in which buyer needs are determined and the means by which consumers are informed that the organization can meet those needs.

This chapter begins with an examination of the marketing concept and how businesspeople develop a marketing strategy. The marketing environment is discussed with a focus on technology's impact on marketing. The chapter then turns to marketing research techniques, leading to in-depth coverage of market segmentation and buyer behavior. The chapter closes with a detailed look at the important role played by customer relationships in today's highly competitive business world.

| Figure 13.1 | **Marketing: Determining Wants and Needs of Sports Fans** |

In addition to selling goods and services, marketing techniques also help people to advocate ideas or viewpoints and to educate others. For example, the American Diabetes Association mails out questionnaires that ask, "Are you at risk for diabetes?" The documents list risk factors and common symptoms of the disease and describe the work of the association. **Marketing** is the process of determining customer wants and needs and then providing the goods and services that meet or exceed expectations.

Marshall Field, founder of the giant department store chain, explained marketing quite clearly when he advised one employee to "Give the lady what she wants." The phrase became the company motto, and it remains a business truism that reflects the importance of a customer orientation to an organization. Marketers for *The Sporting News* determined that their readers were more interested in sports reporting than the swimsuits modeled in an annual issue of rival magazine *Sports Illustrated*. The humorous ad in Figure 13.1 emphasizes the importance of satisfying the needs and wants of the magazine's target market.

Marketing is more than just selling. It is a process that begins with discovering unmet consumer needs and continues with researching the potential market; producing a good or service that satisfies the targeted consumers; and promoting, pricing, and distributing that good or service. Throughout the entire marketing process, a successful company focuses on building customer relationships.

When two or more parties benefit from trading things of value, they have entered into an **exchange process.**

WHAT IS MARKETING?

All organizations—profit-oriented and not-for-profit—must serve consumer needs to succeed. Perhaps J. C. Penney best expressed this priority when he told his store managers, "Either you or your replacement will greet the customer within the first 60 seconds."

Business Directory

marketing process of planning and executing the conception, pricing, promotion, and distribution of ideas, goods, services, organizations, and events to create and maintain relationships that satisfy individual and organizational objectives.

Consider a hypothetical island society consisting of two groups, each producing its own food and clothing. One group is particularly skilled in textiles and pottery; the other group consists of farmers and ranchers. The exchange process allows each group to concentrate on what it does best by trading excess goods for scarce ones. This specialization and division of work increases total production and raises the standards of living of both groups. The exchange process could not occur, however, if each group did not market its products. This example shows that marketing is a prime determinant of society's overall standard of living.

How Marketing Creates Utility

Marketing is a complex activity that affects many aspects of an organization and its dealings with consumers. The ability of a good or service to satisfy the wants and needs of consumers is called **utility**. A company's production function creates *form utility* by converting raw materials and other inputs into finished goods and services. The marketing function, however, creates time, place, and ownership utility. *Time utility* is created by making a good or service available when consumers want to purchase it. *Place utility* is created by making a product available in a location convenient for consumers. *Ownership utility* is the arrangement of an orderly transfer of goods and services from the seller to the buyer. The Business Hall of Shame discusses NordicTrack's failure to provide utility to its customers.

Figure 13.2 Marketing to Create Time, Place, and Ownership Utility

AT HYUNDAI EVERYTHING FITS TOGETHER TO PUT OUR CUSTOMER FIRST

Campaign FA (Full Speed Ahead) 2000 is Hyundai Merchant Marine's total commitment to delivering the highest quality service to you as we move together into the next century. "Customer First", a vital element of our Campaign FA 2000, is our company-wide effort to make sure that everything we do fits together to put your needs first. In 1996 we'll introduce five swift new 5,046 TEU vessels into our transpacific service to satisfy your space, equipment and scheduling specifications. Our advanced state of the art EDI communications network enables us to constantly monitor your cargo from point of origin to final destination. For your convenience, we provide a growing inventory of large capacity 45' containers. Campaign FA 2000 means that Hyundai Merchant Marine is well-equipped to always put you first and to meet all of your shipping requirements – now and in the future. Contact us today to discover the many advantages that Campaign FA 2000 will surely deliver for you.

HYUNDAI MERCHANT MARINE CO., LTD.
Moving Toward The Future

International shipping company Hyundai Merchant Marine provides all three types of marketing utility for its customers. As Figure 13.2 emphasizes, Hyundai's primary commitment to customer needs is the cornerstone of its efforts to deliver high-quality transport services.

Functions of Marketing

In creating time, place, and ownership utility, marketing performs the eight basic functions shown in Figure 13.3: buying, selling, transporting, storing, standardizing and grading, financing, risk taking, and securing market information.

Buying and selling are the exchange functions of marketing. Marketers must study why consumers buy certain goods and services. Indeed, this study of consumer behavior is critical to the firm's overall success.

Transporting involves physical movement of a product from the seller to the buyer, and storing involves warehousing goods until they are needed for sale. Standardizing and grading ensures that product offerings meet established quality and quantity criteria for size, weight, and other product variables. Products in many industries, such as agricultural products and car tires, must meet specific grading standards. The financing function involves extending credit to consumers, wholesalers, and retailers.

In the last marketing function, a firm collects and analyzes market information to determine what will sell and who will buy it. This risk-taking function stems from uncertainty about how consumers will react to products designed for future sale. Marketers must act as entrepreneurial risk takers in many instances. For example, Toyota has spent millions to develop the Prius model, a car that runs on both electricity and gasoline. Currently, the hybrid auto shown in Figure

Business Directory

utility want-satisfying power of a good or service.

marketing concept companywide consumer orientation to promote long-run success.

customer satisfaction result of a good or service meeting or exceeding the buyer's needs and expectations.

13.4 is only available in Japan, where the $18,000 price is only slightly higher than that of a new Corolla. Although development costs and tiny production runs mean that Toyota is not recouping even one-third of the Prius's total cost, the Japanese automaker is betting that the environmentally friendly auto will attract a steadily growing number of buyers and eventually generate profits.

www.toyota.co.jp/Lighthouse/

EVOLUTION OF THE MARKETING CONCEPT

Marketing has always been a part of business, from the earliest village traders to large, contemporary organizations producing and selling complex goods and services. Over time, however, marketing activities evolved through the four eras listed in Figure 13.5: the production, sales, and marketing eras, and now the relationship era.

For centuries, organizations of the *production era* stressed efficiency in producing quality products. They shared an attitude toward marketing summed up in a paraphrase of the story line to the award-winning motion picture *Field of Dreams:* "If you build it, they will come." Although this production orientation continued into the 20th century, it gradually gave way to a *sales orientation,* in which businesses assumed that consumers would buy only as a result of energetic sales efforts. Organizations didn't fully recognize the importance of their customers until the *marketing era* of the 1950s, when they began to adopt a consumer orientation. This focus has intensified in recent years, leading to the emergence of the *relationship era* in the 1990s. The emphasis on customer satisfaction characteristic of this era is discussed in further detail later in the chapter.

Emergence of the Marketing Concept

The term **marketing concept** refers to a companywide consumer orientation with the objective of achieving long-run success. It repudiates the assumption of customer loyalty in the production orientation, summarized in the statement, "Build a better mousetrap and the world will beat a path to your door." Instead, the marketing concept implies that marketplace success begins with the customer; a firm should analyze his or her needs and then work backward to produce products that fulfill them. The emergence of the marketing concept can be explained best by the shift from a *seller's market*—one with a shortage of goods and services—to a *buyer's market*—one with an abundance of goods and services. During the 1950s, the United States became a strong buyer's market, forcing companies to satisfy customers rather than just producing and selling goods and services.

Delivering Added Value through Customer Satisfaction and Quality

What is the most important sale for a company? Some assume the first, but many marketers argue that the second sale is the most important one, since repeat purchases are concrete evidence of **customer satisfaction**. The con-

Figure 13.3 **The Basic Functions of Marketing**

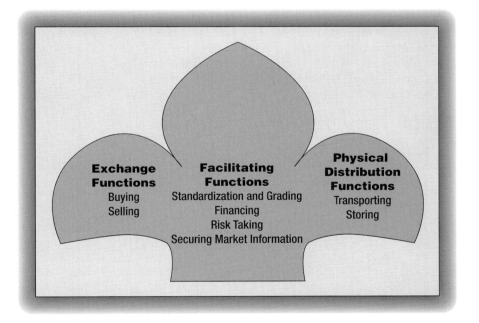

Exchange Functions
Buying
Selling

Facilitating Functions
Standardization and Grading
Financing
Risk Taking
Securing Market Information

Physical Distribution Functions
Transporting
Storing

cept of a good or service pleasing buyers because it has met or exceeded their needs and expectations is crucial to an organization's continued operation; a company that fails to match the customer satisfaction that its competitors provide will not stay in business for very long. The Business Tool Kit provides an overview of some steps to promote good customer service.

Figure 13.4   **Toyota: Taking Risks with the World's First Hybrid Automobile**

Increasing customer loyalty by just 5 percent translates into significant increases in lifetime profits per customer. The best way to keep a customer is to offer more than just goods and services. Customers today want *value,* their perceptions of the balance between the quality of goods or services and the prices. When a company exceeds value expectations by adding features, lowering its price, enhancing customer service, or making other improvements that increase customer satisfaction, it provides a **value-added** good or service. As long as customers feel that they have received value, that is, good quality for a fair price, they are likely to remain satisfied with the company and continue their relationships. Providing superior customer service can generate long-term success.

The emergence of the relationship era has changed the way salespeople view customers. They have modified the attitude "I'm here to sell you" to emphasize a mindset of "I'm here to serve you." Firms build relationships with customers by listening to them and responding to their special needs and wants. In today's high-tech environment, customer service is often the factor that gives one firm a competitive advantage.[2]

Quality—the degree of excellence or superiority of an organization's goods and services—is another way firms enhance customer satisfaction. Quality can encompass both the tangible and

Figure 13.5   **Four Eras in the History of Marketing**

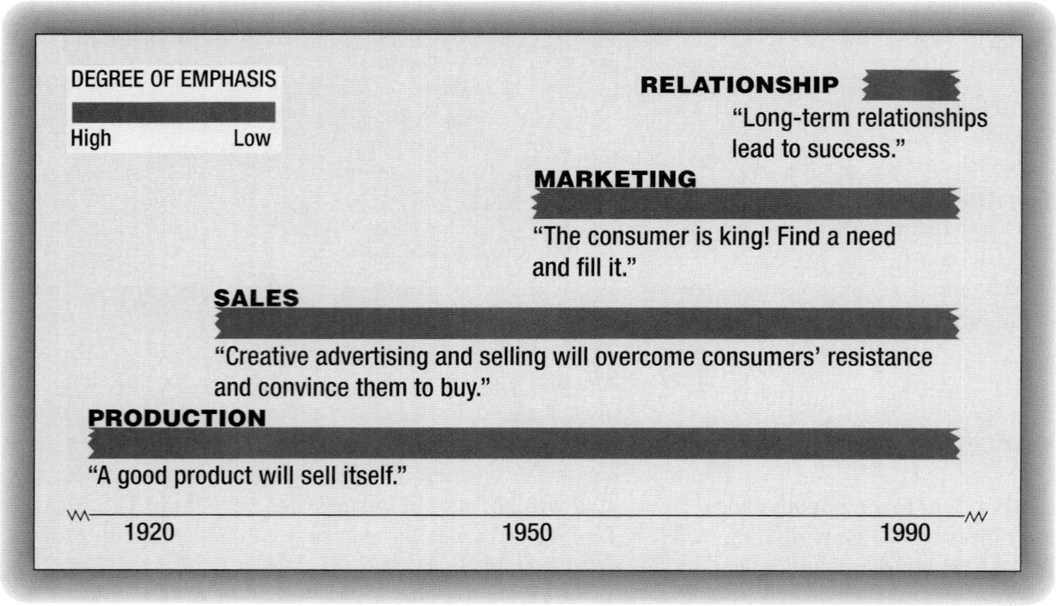

DEGREE OF EMPHASIS

High   Low

RELATIONSHIP
"Long-term relationships lead to success."

MARKETING
"The consumer is king! Find a need and fill it."

SALES
"Creative advertising and selling will overcome consumers' resistance and convince them to buy."

PRODUCTION
"A good product will sell itself."

1920   1950   1990

Basic Steps to Superior Customer Service

No matter what you are selling, it isn't worth anything if you don't have one thing: customers. Once you have attracted them, do whatever you must to keep them. The following tips are not new—they are tried-and-true principles, as WinterSilks vice president John Reindl will attest. The $35 million Middleton, Wisconsin catalog retailer of silk apparel ties its success directly to employee involvement in its commitment to providing superior service.

▼ *Talk to your customers.* All salaried employees at WinterSilks, including top management, are required to take a minimum of 50 phone orders each year.

▼ *Check out your competitors.* Employees actually become customers of WinterSilks' rivals. First, they call in catalog orders with competitors. After receiving their orders and evaluating the products, they then return them. Finally, a group discussion is held where everyone talks about their experiences with competitors and grades them on product quality and customer service.

▼ *Share customer feedback.* Every month, WinterSilks gives every staff member a list of the top ten customer comments—both good and bad. This way, employees can see the whole picture and recognize areas where they have excelled and where they need improvement.

All of these efforts to involve employees in developing superior service have helped WinterSilks to build strong, loyal customer relationships.

Source: Christopher Caggiano, "How Do I Improve Our Customer Service?" *Inc.*, August 1997, p. 92.

intangible characteristics of a good or service. In its technical meaning, it relates to physical product traits, such as durability and reliability. However, it also includes customer service. As author and quality management consultant A. V. Feigenbaum notes, "Quality is what your customer says it is—not what you say it is. To find out about your quality, ask your customer."[3]

The Importance of Customer Satisfaction

Successful companies all share one important characteristic: They make every effort to ensure the satisfaction of their customers. Customer satisfaction is a critical condition for building long-lasting relationships. The fundamental premise of the marketing concept is to focus all organizational efforts on providing superior customer service in order to retain existing customers and attract new ones. The following paragraphs discuss criteria for customer satisfaction both within and outside of the organization, how to obtain and use customer feedback, and how to measure customer satisfaction.

Internal Marketing So far, the text has discussed customers as people or other organizations that buy or use a firm's goods or services, that is, **external customers.** However, marketing in an organization concerned with quality must also serve **internal customers**—employees or other

departments within the organization whose job performance affects the firm's ability to deliver superior products and customer service to external customers.

Internal marketing involves managerial actions that help all members of an organization to understand, accept, and fulfill their respective roles in implementing its marketing strategy. An internal marketing program shows employees how their work activities affect the firm's marketing programs and contribute to customer satisfaction. Employee knowledge and involvement are important goals of internal marketing.

Companies that excel at satisfying customers actively keep their employees informed about organizational goals and strategies as well as external customer needs. To aid communication flows between departments and functional areas, many organizations have set up *intranets,* computer-based employee information systems. In the oil and gas industry, monitoring production and costs versus operating budgets is a critical function. Gulf Canada needed a faster way than it had to collect and analyze information from its field locations around the world, so it installed an intranet-based decision support system. Analysts can now retrieve data in less than 10 minutes, create reports, and evaluate the impact of regional decisions on the company's mission.[4] Communicating timely information to employees helps them to boost the effectiveness of their job performance, thereby increasing overall company productivity. Employee satisfaction is a critical objective of internal marketing. Dissatisfied employees often spread negative

BUSINESS HALL OF SHAME

Falling Off the Track at NordicTrack

The 1980s witnessed an explosion in fitness awareness and commitment. Sidewalks, streets, and parks were filled with people pursuing health by running, jogging, and walking. Fitness club memberships soared, with such lures as aerobics classes, Stairmasters, and other workout machines. But today's fight for fitness is more likely to be staged at home. It is more private and much more convenient, especially if you have to squeeze in your workouts between classes, or taking the kids to soccer practice.

The decision to make fitness an in-home challenge turned the home-exercise industry into a $4 billion business. A huge chunk of this total was claimed by NordicTrack, the machine that simulates cross-country skiing. Exercise fanatics loved it, labeling NordicTrack the essence of what a fitness machine should be. But today the company is bankrupt. So why did people stop buying the product? "We weren't as nimble as we should have been," said company president William E. Shepard.

The first NordicTrack dates to 1976, when inventor Ed Pauls created it in his Minnesota basement. It proved an immediate success. Ten years later, Pauls decided to cash in, selling his company to CML for $22 million. By 1993, NordicTrack sales hit $500 million. But by 1999, the company had fallen off the track and the firm filed for bankruptcy protection.

Managers looking for an explanation of this failure could not blame the product itself. NordicTrack always received superior ratings for quality. The machine was built well and performed as promised. In fact, it was so durable that it actually cost the firm money in terms of possible replacement sales. Once you had one, you never needed another.

A sizable part of the fitness market consists of impulse buyers who never stop looking for newer and better solutions. Enticed by the latest infomercial, they try new contraptions ranging from stomach flatteners to thigh hardeners. NordicTrack marketers didn't worry about what fitness customers were looking for. They knew they already had the answer.

With more customer feedback they

---

word-of-mouth messages to people outside the organization that can affect purchasing behavior.

The internal marketing process can also affect suppliers. By enlisting their participation, a firm can ensure that suppliers help to add value for its end customers.

Obtaining Customer Feedback Knowledge of customers' needs, wants, and expectations is a critical resource in a firm's customer satisfaction efforts. One of the best ways to find out how buyers perceive a company or its products is to obtain *customer feedback* through such means as toll-free hot lines, customer satisfaction surveys, Web site message boards, and written correspondence. Some firms find out how well they have satisfied their customers by calling them or making personal visits to their businesses or residences. Customer complaints generate excellent customer feedback, since they present the company with an opportunity to overcome problems and improve its service. Customers often feel greater loyalty to a company after a conflict has been resolved than if they had never complained at all. Complaints can also allow firms to gather innovative ideas for improvement.

Marketers at Stouffer's Foods use customer feedback in developing ideas for new Lean Cuisine frozen dishes. As Figure 13.6 points out, requests for traditional foods led to the addition of oven-roasted beef to Lean Cuisine's product line.

Measuring Customer Satisfaction After gathering feedback about customer satisfaction, a firm should initiate a

Figure 13.6	**Using Customer Feedback for New-Product Ideas**

might have learned that the Nordic-Track machine asked more of customers than the typical treadmill. The company might have been more successful appealing to a narrower audience (one that relishes a strenuous workout) and then designing a new machine for the less intrepid exercisers.

As sales began to decline, Nordic-Track decided to abandon its direct-to-customers distribution approach using direct mail, 800-order numbers, and infomercials. Dozens of small Nordic-Track stores were opened in suburban malls, but results were disappointing. The stores only stocked NordicTracks and were so small that little or no room was available for customers to test the machines before buying. Would-be buyers were also annoyed when they could not take the equipment home with them. They had to wait for it to be shipped.

NordicTrack's fate is now in the hands of ICON Health & Fitness, the world's largest manufacturer and marketer of home-fitness equipment. ICON has acquired some of Nordic-Track's assets and is trying a new approach. Rather than depending on direct marketing, it is teaming with Sears, Roebuck to sell the machine in Sears retail outlets. ICON marketers believe they have a better idea of how to satisfy NordicTrack customers. Clearly, the old product-centered approach proved disastrous when it ignored customer service.

QUESTIONS FOR CRITICAL THINKING

1. NordicTrack's president summed up its need this way. "We need what Volkswagen did. We need our own new Beetle." What part of

the marketing concept does Shepard appear to be overlooking? Explain.

2. Now that ICON is selling Nordic-Track equipment, it is not assuming responsibility for warranties on products previously sold by NordicTrack; it's offering service for a price. How will such a policy affect customer satisfaction? Explain.

Sources: "ICON Acquires Certain Assets of Nordic-Track," NordicTrack press release, accessed at www.nordictrack.com, March 12, 1999; "Sears to Be the Exclusive National Retailer of NordicTrack Home Fitness Equipment," Sears press release, January 18, 1999, accessed at www.prnewswire.com; and Jay Weiner, "How NordicTrack Lost Its Footing," *Business Week*, December 14, 1998, p. 138.

customer satisfaction measurement (CSM) program—a set of ongoing procedures for measuring input against customer satisfaction goals and developing an action plan for improvement. A CSM program helps to track customer satisfaction and dissatisfaction over time by identifying changes in customer attitudes and then guiding efforts to improve them.

CSM programs vary widely, but most include the following steps:

1. Determine what activities are critical to a business's success and what measurement systems it currently uses.

2. Survey a representative group of customers to identify important attributes in their use of a good or service.

3. Conduct research to determine the company's performance on the selected attributes.

4. Analyze results to develop action plans.

The American Customer Satisfaction Index (ACSI) is another method for measuring customer satisfaction across industries. Developed by the University of Michigan and the American Society of Quality Control, the annual report is based on a massive survey of how U.S. consumers rate a wide range of goods and services. The 1998 satisfaction index revealed some surprising facts. While the decline in the overall index has recently slowed, only one industry group showed continued improvement over the life of the

measurement: the police. The losers were computer makers, who have continued to fail to meet customer service demands in spite of fantastic new innovations, and the broadcast media, who fell a full 20 percent in their customer satisfaction ratings.[5]

www.asqc.org/abtquality/awards/acsi.html

As increasing numbers of managers recognize the importance of customer satisfaction to business success, they are taking the concept one step further than surveys. As American Express research director Doug Filak explains, "What really matters is how we improve the bottom line. You have to look beyond satisfaction to what is happening in your business overall. A focus on improving customer satisfaction is critical, but by focusing on satisfaction, we learned more about our products' other dimensions." Filak recognized that satisfying internal customers—employees and shareholders—was just as critical to success as pleasing external customers. Satisfied employees improved business results, which satisfied shareholders.

Satisfying external customers involved identifying benefits and drawbacks of the company's products. Both card members and service establishments disliked the original card's fees. In response, customers were offered the Delta Sky Miles Optima card, which rewards frequent users with free air travel. The Optima card was later extended for retail use, as well. "We've really been able to prove the linkage between improving customer satisfaction and business results," Filak explains. "We've also shown that there are many components of a business that drive satisfaction of a product."[6]

Cybercompanies also are developing Internet marketing strategies that focus on improving customer satisfaction. Several general guidelines have been established. One of the most important states that a Web-based firm should

for success in any profit-seeking firm as well as any not-for-profit organization.

Judgments of quality can reflect tangible factors, such as reliability and durability, as well as intangible factors, such as whether a customer enjoys the purchasing experience. In fact, the level of customer satisfaction could represent a report card for quality performance. Figure 13.7 shows the steps a firm must take to become a total quality organization.

Figure 13.7 **How a Total Quality Organization Provides Superior Customer Service**

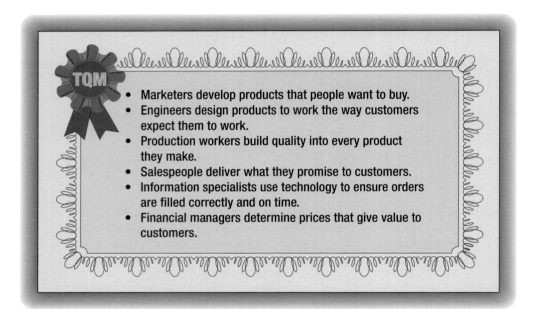

- Marketers develop products that people want to buy.
- Engineers design products to work the way customers expect them to work.
- Production workers build quality into every product they make.
- Salespeople deliver what they promise to customers.
- Information specialists use technology to ensure orders are filled correctly and on time.
- Financial managers determine prices that give value to customers.

Does quality pay? Absolutely! Studies show that quality programs can boost company revenues by as much as 40 percent while cutting production costs 20 to 50 percent. TQM can save 40 percent on space and inventory and cut production time by as much as 70 percent, building strong customer loyalty. As increasing numbers of firms have realized the direct impact of TQM programs on profitability and competitiveness, quality has become an essential factor in contemporary business. A company that fails to provide the same level of quality as its competitors will not stay in business very long.

dedicate staff members to answer customers' questions, resolve complaints, and offer additional information. Web sites can be ideal tools for increasing customer satisfaction when they provide two-way communication opportunities 24 hours a day.[7]

Measuring customer satisfaction typically involves marketing research, discussed in detail later in this chapter. The next section highlights the importance of quality in customer satisfaction.

Total Quality Management and Customer Satisfaction

As Chapter 12 explained, *total quality management (TQM)* is an effort to involve all employees in a firm to continually improve products and work processes with the goal of achieving customer satisfaction and world-class performance. Quality can be a key factor in a firm's competitive advantage over its rivals. This broad concept encompasses every aspect of business, making it an imperative condition

EXPANDING MARKETING'S TRADITIONAL BOUNDARIES

The marketing concept has traditionally been associated with product offerings of profit-seeking organizations. However, the current trend toward consumer orientation has expanded applications of the marketing concept to not-for-profit sectors and other nontraditional areas ranging from religious organizations to political campaigns. This section examines the evolution of nontraditional marketing applications.

Not-for-Profit Marketing

Today, over 1.1 million not-for-profit organizations are benefiting by applying many of the same strategies and principles used by profit-seeking firms. In an effort to reach historically undercounted populations, including Hispanics, Asians, and Native Americans, the Department of

Commerce hired Young & Rubicam to handle advertising for the U.S. census in 2000.[8] This and other not-for-profits can market tangible or intangible goods, services, or both.

Not-for-profit organizations operate in both public and private sectors. Public groups include federal, state, and local government units as well as agencies that receive tax funding. A state's department of natural resources, for instance, regulates land conservation and environmental programs; the local animal-control office enforces ordinances that protect both people and animals; a city's public health board ensures safe drinking water for its citizens.

The private not-for-profit sector includes many different types of organizations, including labor unions, hospitals, Notre Dame University's football team, art museums, and local youth organizations. Although some private not-for-profits generate surplus revenue, they work toward primary goals other than earning profits. Any excess funds are plowed back into their organizational missions.

Many not-for-profits apply marketing tools to reach their audiences, secure funding, improve their images, and accomplish their overall missions, including the American Museum of Natural History, YMCAs, the Audubon Zoo in New Orleans, and art museums like the New York Museum of Modern Art. One art industry spokesperson summed up these changes as follows: "Many years ago, *marketing* was a word that museum people reacted to with some distaste. No one feels that way today, especially as the need for fund-raising grows and the number of charitable philanthropic dollars available hasn't grown."[9] Even smaller, regional museums, such as the Fleischer Museum in Scottsdale, Arizona, actively publicize their exhibitions, such as the Russian Impressionists exhibit described in Figure 13.8, to serve current and prospective members and increase cultural activities in their communities.

A not-for-profit organization may adopt the marketing concept by forming a partnership with a profit-seeking company to promote the firm's message or image. Companies spend millions of dollars vying for Olympic sponsorships. The Olympic Games receive needed funds, and the sponsors associate their goods and services with the world's best-known not-for-profit sports organization.

Nontraditional Marketing

Growth in the number of not-for-profit organizations has forced their executives to adopt business-like strategies and tactics to reach diverse audiences and successfully compete with other nontraditional organizations. The five major categories of nontraditional marketing are shown in Figure 13.9. Although most involve not-for-profit organizations, profit-seeking organizations conduct special events like FanFests linked with major sporting events as well as person marketing involving celebrities.

Figure 13.8 **Marketing Activities by a Not-for-Profit Organization**

▼ **Person marketing** refers to efforts designed to attract the attention, interest, and preference of a target market toward a person. Campaign managers for a political candidate, for instance, conduct marketing research, identify groups of voters and financial supporters, and then design advertising campaigns, fund-raising events, and political rallies to reach them. Celebrities also engage in person marketing as a means of expanding their audiences; improving sales of concert tickets, books, and CDs; and enhancing their images among fans. To promote the sale of his recent *Pilgrim* CD, pop star Eric Clapton made numerous appearances on radio and television shows and headlined a U.S. concert tour. As Figure 13.10 describes, he also formed a sponsorship alliance with Lexus to promote himself and the tour.

www. **www.lexus.com/clapton**

▼ **Place marketing** attempts to attract people to a particular area, such as a city, state, or nation. The photo of San Antonio's famed River Walk in Figure 13.10 is designed to attract family and business visitors to one of America's most historic, romantic cities. In addition to describing San Antonio as an alluring destination for vacationers, the figure also informs convention planners of a major expansion in exhibit space and the proximity of the convention center to the Alamo and other local attractions.

▼ **Cause marketing** promotes a cause or social issue, such as gun control, child-abuse prevention, and antismoking campaigns. Special fundraising programs for charities and causes range from the annual Jerry Lewis Labor Day Telethon for the Muscular Dystrophy Association to the American Red Cross's "Fit for Life" relay races. In some cases, promotional products help organizations to secure consumer goodwill—and donations. Elton John's re-recording of his song "Candle in the Wind" brought in $33 million for the Diana, Princess of Wales, Memorial Fund in only 5 weeks. Profit-seeking companies attempting to enhance their public images often join forces with charities and causes, providing financial, marketing, and human resources. A $42,500 new-home sponsorship entitles a profit-seeking company to use the Habitat for Humanity name and logo in promotions and to display its name on signs at construction sites.[10] The Solving an Ethical Controversy reports on a disagreement over such a link between a profit-seeking company and a not-for-profit organization.

The classic approach to a cause-related promotion ties a donation to a consumer purchase, such as when a company promises to donate $1 for each item it sells. Other firms establish programs of contributions to not-for-profit organizations. Nike, for example, funded a 5-year program to help over 2,000 Boys & Girls Clubs of America. Says Boys & Girls Clubs marketing

vice president Kurt Aschermann, "We don't create a program and then get it funded. We create partnerships, then build programs based on [Nike's] market strategy. We get great programming that Nike pays for, and Nike gets to say they help 2.85 million kids."[11]

▼ **Event marketing** involves marketing or sponsoring short-term events such as athletic competitions and cultural and charitable performances. Like cause marketing, event marketing often forges partnerships between not-for-profit and profit-seeking organizations. One event that helps to support U.S. farmers is singer Willie Nelson's annual Farm Aid concert.

▼ **Organization marketing** attempts to influence consumers to accept the goals of, receive the services of, or contribute in some way to an organization. Many groups employ this practice, including mutual-benefit organizations such as political groups, churches, and labor unions; service organizations like colleges and universities, museums, and hospitals; and government organizations such as police and fire departments, military services, and the U.S. National Park Service. Many charitable organizations mail greeting cards with donation requests enclosed to raise awareness of their groups and explain their objectives.

Figure 13.9 **Categories of Nontraditional Marketing**

DEVELOPING A MARKETING STRATEGY

Decision makers in any successful organization, profit oriented or not for profit, follow a two-step process to develop a *marketing strategy*. First, they study and analyze potential target markets and then choose among them. Second, they create a marketing mix to satisfy the chosen market. Figure 13.11 shows the relationship among the target market, the marketing mix variables, and the marketing environment. Later discussions will refer back to this figure as they cover each topic. This section describes the development of a marketing strategy, and the next discusses marketing's environmental framework.

Figure 13.10 Person Marketing and Place Marketing

A written marketing plan often becomes a key component of a firm's overall business plan. The marketing plan outlines its marketing strategy and includes information about the target market, sales and revenue goals, the marketing budget, and the timing for implementing the elements of the marketing mix.

Selecting a Target Market

The expression "find a need and fill it" is perhaps the simplest explanation of the two elements of a marketing strategy. A firm's marketers find a need through careful and continuing study of the individuals and business decision makers in its potential market. A *market* consists of people with purchasing power, willingness to buy, and authority to make purchase decisions.

Markets can be classified by type of product. **Consumer products** are goods and services purchased by end users, such as CDs, shampoo, and eyeglasses. **Business products**—sometimes called *industrial* or *organiza-* *tional products*—are goods and services purchased to be used, either directly or indirectly, in the production of other goods for resale. A product can fit in either classification, depending on who buys it and why. A computer, for example, can be either a consumer or business product.

An organization's **target market** is the group of consumers toward whom it directs its marketing efforts. Consumer needs and wants vary considerably, and no single organization has the resources to satisfy everyone.

Eli Lilly, the global leader in insulin products, spent $7 million last year on direct marketing communications with diabetics, who comprise its target market. Lilly marketers saw a threat from copy-cat products if they relied solely on the traditional method of depending on doctors to educate their patients and then prescribe medication. "The traditional way of pushing the message through doctors just doesn't work. It's almost impossible to break through the

Business Directory

target market group of people toward whom an organization markets its goods, services, or ideas with a strategy designed to satisfy their specific needs and preferences.

SOLVING AN ETHICAL CONTROVERSY

Should a Not-for-Profit Sell the Right to Display Its Logo?

Almost every U.S. adult has heard of the AMA—the American Medical Association. Nightly news reports frequently relay its endorsements, recommendations, or condemnations. The AMA logo—a serpent twined around the staff of Aesculapius, the ancient Greek father of medicine—is a widely recognized seal of approval. Indeed, this 300,000-physician organization wields a powerful sword in matters that affect U.S. consumers, companies, and health issues, in general.

The 150-year-old not-for-profit organization evaluates doctor performance, encourages continuing med-

ical education, supports cost controls, and monitors patient outcomes. However, the AMA's mission—to speak for all doctors on matters of public health and their professional interests—has proved a difficult task to achieve in recent years.

Once representing 80 percent of all doctors, AMA membership has dropped dramatically to less than half that proportion today. Increasing specialization among physicians over the past 20 years—and the resulting growth in associations for those specialties—has been a major factor in this decline. In addition, the AMA is spending large sums to support a growing number of current health issues, including campaigns against underage smoking, late-term abortions, and domestic violence. With a dwin-

dling membership and increased spending, the AMA has been seeking new sources of revenue—and raising some members' blood pressure in the process.

One flap began in 1997 when a small group of AMA board members and managers conceived a brilliant plan to raise money to support education and research. Although the plan identified an admirable end objective, it employed questionable means, calling for the AMA to grant permission for Sunbeam to use the AMA logo on a variety of the company's health-care products in exchange for royalties.

Within a week, outraged member physicians and medical experts forced AMA leaders to perform surgery on the Sunbeam deal, cutting out royalty provisions, an exclusivity agreement, and

---

clutter, especially in the diabetes market," says a Lilly spokesperson. Print ads market Lilly's insulin products directly to consumers. Since these products are sold only by prescription, Lilly marketers are counting on diabetics to request the new products from their doctors.[12]

In an attempt to reach increasingly diverse segments of the population, some firms are forming alliances with others. For instance, Citibank recently agreed to sponsor recording artist Elton John's "Big Picture" world tour. Citibank is targeting upscale baby boomers with this latest promotional campaign. For an estimated $5 million, Elton John will appear in Citibank television ads and has agreed not to sign any other endorsement deals for the year.[13]

Figure 13.11 Relationship between a Target Market, the Marketing Mix, and the Marketing Environment Framework

the venerable logo—the organization's seal of approval. The AMA now accepts only enough money to cover the cost of printing educational materials to accompany the products.

 Should Not-for-Profits Sell Their Seals of Approval?

PRO

1. The AMA is not doing anything that hasn't been done before many times. For example, Florida orange juice producers pay $1 million to the American Cancer Society for its endorsement of their product.

2. Products that carry the AMA endorsement are beneficial goods and services. The public benefits from assurance of these products' safety.

3. Royalties received by the AMA would have been put to good use in support of education, research, and lobbying.

CON

1. When a not-for-profit organization as powerful as the AMA endorses a good or service, it unfairly influences consumer purchases.

2. If all not-for-profits were to endorse goods and services throughout the market, they would lower consumers' perceptions of the value of any seal of approval.

3. In effect, the practice of receiving royalties commercializes not-for-profit activities, perhaps swaying the balance of power in the political lobbying arena.

SUMMARY

For years, not-for-profits have been selling their logos as endorsements of commercial products. Perhaps the best-known case is the American Dental Association's endorsement of Crest toothpaste in 1960. Within 2 years fol-

lowing the endorsement, the failing Crest brand had become the best-selling toothpaste in America. However, over 65 different brands of toothpaste now carry the ADA's seal of approval. Although the controversy has recently erupted, the practice has been going on for too many years to stop overnight. Most likely, receiving payment for use of a seal of approval or logo will continue, but it will be closely watched, if not highly regulated.

Sources: "In the Post-Sunbeam Era, AMA Works to Reinvent Itself," American Academy of Family Physicians Director's Newsletter, December 10, 1998, accessed at www.aafp.org; Phillip J. Longman, "Endorsements for Sale," *U.S. News & World Report*, September 1, 1997, p. 11; and Richard A. Melcher, "The AMA Isn't Feeling So Hot," *Business Week*, September 1, 1997, p. 33.

Developing a Marketing Mix

Marketing decision making can be divided into four strategies: product, pricing, place (or distribution), and promotion strategies. A firm's **marketing mix** blends the four strategies to fit the needs and preferences of a specific target market. Marketing success depends, not on the four individual strategies, but on their unique combination.

Product strategy involves more than just designing a good or service with needed attributes. It also includes decisions about package design, brand name, trademarks, warranties, product image, new-product development, and customer service. Think, for instance, about your favorite soft drink. Do you like it for its taste alone, or do other attributes, such as clever ads, attractive packaging, and overall image, also contribute to your brand preference?

One of the most difficult areas of marketing decision making, *pricing strategy*, deals with the methods of setting profitable and justifiable prices. Such actions are closely regulated and subject to considerable public scrutiny. Research shows that consumers' perceptions of product quality relate closely to price: A high price correlates to high perceived quality. Most marketers believe that this perceived price-quality relationship spans a

relatively wide range of prices, although extreme prices may contribute to an overly expensive or cheap image. Chapter 14 discusses pricing in depth.

Place (or distribution) *strategy* ensures that customers receive their purchases in the proper quantities at the right times and locations. Chapter 15 focuses on the various modes of transportation and the roles played by retailers and wholesalers in distribution channels.

Promotional strategy, the final marketing mix element, involves informing, persuading, and influencing consumer purchase decisions. Chapter 16 examines the many aspects of promotion, including personal selling, advertising, sales promotion, and public relations.

Even though Figure 13.11 depicts the marketing mix variables as four separate elements, they actually represent interdependent decisions. They function as related components in an overall system designed to produce customer satisfaction rather than independent sets of decisions. For example, the Life Stride shoes shown in Figure 13.12 are distributed through a limited number of upscale retail

Business Directory

marketing mix blending the four elements of marketing strategy—product, price, place, and promotion—to satisfy chosen consumer segments.

stores to maintain the product's image. Promotional techniques and themes must also enhance this image. Pricing and the use of discounts are based on such factors as markups needed to motivate retailers to effectively display, promote, and sell the product, product image, and the firm's production and marketing costs.

As every chapter of *Contemporary Business* has emphasized, the Internet is bringing rapid changes in traditional business procedures and operations. E-commerce requires innovative marketing tactics and strategies, since cyberfirms often have little or no inventory (product), immense Web capabilities for promotion, direct distribution systems, and competitive pricing capabilities. Even so, virtual companies also must design their own marketing mixes to serve their target markets.

Marketing Products Abroad: Standardization versus Adaptation

Marketing a good or service in foreign markets means deciding whether to offer the same product supported by the same marketing mix in every market—*standardization*—or to develop a unique mix to fit each market—*adaptation*.

The advantages of standardizing the marketing mix include reliable marketing performance and low costs. This approach works best with business goods, such as steel, chemicals, and aircraft, with little sensitivity to a nation's culture.

Adaptation, on the other hand, lets marketers vary their strategy mix to suit local competitive conditions, consumer preferences, and government regulations. Consumer products generally require adaptation, because they tend to be more culture-dependent than business products are. Moscow's oldest and largest confectionery, the Red October Chocolate Factory, has become the most successful candy

Figure 13.12 **Coordinating All Four Marketing Mix Variables to Satisfy the Life Stride Target Market**

company in Russia by recognizing the unique taste preferences of Russian consumers. "Russian chocolate has a different taste and feel. It's grittier because they use more cocoa. It's not as sweet," says one international chocolate expert. Foreign candy-makers, such as Mars and Hershey's, failed to recognize the cultural preferences in this market, and their Russian ventures struggled. Of the top ten chocolate bars in Russia, only one is foreign made—Mars's Dove bar in sixth place.[14]

Increasingly, companies are trying to build adaptability into the designs of standardized goods and services. *Mass customization* allows a company to mass produce goods and services while adding unique features to individual orders. This technique seeks to retain enough flexibility to satisfy a wide segment of the population without losing a product's identity and brand awareness. The Internet is playing a major role in mass customization strategies for both domestic and international sales.

The Custom Foot is the first retailer to dedicate an entire store without inventory to mass-customized products. The shoes are manufactured only after a computer scanner at the store records a customer's precise measurements. The Westport, Connecticut-based, shoe store chain sends data via computer to factories in Italy, where the leather shoes are custom made. Every style is available in all sizes for both men and women.[15]

www. **www.thecustomfoot.com**

In contrast, Reebok International is attempting to send a cohesive, worldwide message. Spending $100 million on a global ad campaign, the giant sports-shoe manufacturer plans to boost sponsorship and endorsement contracts. "We want to be the most respected brand by 2000," says Reebok global sports market-

Business Directory

environmental scanning process of collecting information about the external marketing environment in order to identify and interpret potential trends.

ing vice president John Boulter. "That means there will be a more unified approach to international marketing. We want to become an absolutely global company."[16]

THE MARKETING ENVIRONMENT

Earlier chapters have introduced many of the components that make up a firm's marketing environment. Chapter 1 began with an overview of today's rapidly changing and highly competitive world of business. This competitive environment is influenced by a collage of social-cultural factors, as discussed in Chapter 2, and economic factors, the subject of Chapter 3. Political and legal factors, such as those presented in Chapter 4, also define what marketers can and cannot do in certain places. Throughout the text, examples have highlighted the impact of technology on every aspect of business, showing how real firms trade goods, services, and information. Chapters 17 and 18 will focus on technology in even greater detail. Figure 13.11 brought all these factors together in one big picture, illustrating the importance of the five environmental elements on marketing activities.

A target market is the central focus of any organization—profit-seeking or not-for-profit, large or small. To reach its target market, a firm must first develop a marketing mix directly tied to its customers' needs and wants. Decisions about the target market and marketing mix must fit within the surrounding framework of the environment, which is divided into five components: competitive, political/legal, economic, technological, and social/cultural forces. These forces influence conditions in every society; however, the most influential force in one market may have little impact on other markets.

Although external forces frequently operate outside managers' control, they still must consider the impact of environmental factors together with the variables of the marketing mix in developing their firm's marketing plans and strategies. Marketers must continually identify, ana-

ACCESS THE WORLD.
THE MODEM THAT WORKS EVERYWHERE.

The Xircom CreditCard Modem 56-GlobalACCESS™
Now you can send and receive data across town or across the hemisphere at the fastest available 56Kbps¹ speeds.
Our durable MiniDock™ connector system provides the kind of connection you can count on. Add Xircom's unique GlobalACCESS™ features and versatile GSM/PCS 1900 digital cellular capabilities, and you get the maximum mobility for anytime, anywhere communications. Best of all, you can enjoy the benefits of this

high-speed modem now and in the future. All of Xircom's 56K PC Card modems are easily software-upgradable to the future ITU standard at no charge.
Look for the Xircom CreditCard Modem 56-GlobalACCESS at your local computer retailer. Or learn more about Xircom's family of modems, including the CreditCard Modem 56™ and CreditCard Modem 33.6-Upgradable™ (to 56K) at www.xircom.com.
With Xircom, you've got the power, speed and flexibility to communicate around the globe.

Xircom
The Mobile Networking Experts.

The Xircom CreditCard Modem 56 allows globetrotting business users to send and receive data from virtually any city at the fastest available downloading speeds.

lyze, and monitor these factors; assess their impact on goods, services, and marketing activities; and make appropriate adjustments to their marketing mixes.

Environmental Scanning and Environmental Management

Marketers must carefully and continually monitor crucial trends and developments in the business environment. **Environmental scanning** is the process of collecting information about the external marketing environment to identify and interpret potential trends. This activity continues with analysis of the collected information to determine whether identified trends represent opportunities or threats to the company. This judgment, in turn, allows decision makers to determine their firm's best response to a particular environmental change.

Environmental scanning is a critical management responsibility in the rapidly changing computer industry. As the Internet continues to bring the world closer together, new barriers to entry reflect the impact of these changes. Incompatibility among software and hardware systems is a new barrier characteristic of cyberbusiness. Xircom, a mobile networking company, recognized the need for compatibility among network systems and introduced CreditCard Modem 56—a universal communications connector with GlobalACCESS features. Early detection of a future need gives firms such as Xircom a competitive advantage.

Environmental scanning is a vital component of effective *environmental management*—the effort to attain organizational objectives by predicting and influencing the firm's competitive, political/legal, economic, technological, and social/cultural environments. This influence can result from a number of activities by the firm's management. For example, they may exercise political power by joining political action committees (PACs) to lobby legislators and contribute to the campaigns of sympathetic candidates. In this way, many businesspeople hope to achieve the desired modifications in regulations, laws, and tariff restrictions.

The development of a global marketplace has complicated environmental scanning and environmental management. These processes may now track political developments, economic trends, and cultural influences throughout the world. The drive to compete globally has led many firms to form alliances with foreign companies that can provide this intelligence. Industries that once operated entirely within national borders now compete against global rivals. Telecommunications and electric utility companies are opening up new worldwide markets through alliances. Electric utilities are also looking overseas for markets with higher earnings potential than they find in domestic markets.

Through successful research and development efforts, firms may influence changes in their own technological environments. A research breakthrough may reduce production costs or give a product superior features. While the marketing environment may exceed the confines of the firm and its marketing mix components, effective marketers continually seek to predict its impact on marketing decisions and to modify its conditions whenever they can.

In addition to its effect on current marketing decisions, the dynamic marketing environment compels managers at every level to continually reevaluate marketing decisions in response to changing conditions. Even modest environmental shifts can alter the results of marketing decisions.

Elements of the Marketing Environment

In selecting a target market and developing a marketing mix, marketers must consider the five environmental forces: competitive, political/legal, economic, technological, and social/cultural forces. These external forces provide the framework for planning product, pricing, place, and promotion strategies aimed at the target market.

To some extent, all organizations are affected by the external forces in the marketing environment over which they have little or no control. Marketers must monitor these factors and assess their likely impact on goods, services,

Figure 13.13 Tobacco Advertising—Heavily Regulated by Government

Keep it Basic

SURGEON GENERAL'S WARNING: Smoking Causes Lung Cancer, Heart Disease, Emphysema, And May Complicate Pregnancy.

and marketing practices, leading to appropriate adjustments in marketing strategy.

Competitive Environment Marketers must continually monitor the activities of their firm's competitors in order to devise a strategy that will give them a marketing edge. This effort often proves a difficult task, since the competitive environment may change day by day. Few companies are as fortunate as Whole Foods, a mom-and-pop organic food store that has become the nation's largest natural-food supermarket chain primarily due to a lack of competition in the market.

Whole Foods opened in 1980 in Austin, Texas, serving a tiny market of natural-food dieters who wanted organically grown foods and natural supplements. The $4-billion-a-year chain grew 900 percent in the 1990s, largely due to a 3-year acquisition campaign. Buying out competitors has put Whole Foods at the top of its market, and co-founder and chairman John Mackey hopes to stay there. "We're trying to make it as difficult and as costly as possible for competitors to enter markets where we dominate," he explains.[17]

Political and Legal Environment Federal, state, and local laws regulate many marketing activities, ranging from package labeling to product features related to safety. These laws are designed to maintain a competitive environment and protect consumers; noncompliance can result in fines, embarrassing negative publicity, and possibly expensive judgments in civil lawsuits. Furthermore, the legal environment can change enormously from year to year. The tobacco industry, for example, has fought against a barrage of political and legal battles for several decades. In 1998, it settled health claims by agreeing to pay nearly $250 billion over a 25-year period. Tobacco marketers also agreed to give up billboard advertising and the use of cartoon characters such as Joe Camel. Print ads, such as the one shown in Figure 13.13, are still permitted, but merchandise emblazoned with tobacco brands cannot be sold. Critics have long argued that such ads and merchandise make smoking more appealing to children.[18]

Regulations enacted at the federal, state, and local levels affect marketing practices, as do the actions of independent regulatory agencies. These requirements and prohibitions touch on all aspects of marketing decision making—designing, labeling, packaging, distributing, advertising, and promoting goods and services.

International marketers also must recognize the major regulations that affect their activities. UniLever's $2 billion Indian operation recently hit legal snares with an ad campaign for its New Pepsodent brand that claimed the product was "102 percent better than the leading toothpaste." Although Colgate was not actually mentioned in the ads, Indian judges ruled that UniLever was "trying to mislead and misinform consumers," and ordered the claim removed from its ads.[19]

Economic Environment Economic forces such as inflation, unemployment, and business cycles influence how much money consumers are willing and able to spend as well as what they buy. Since all marketing activity is directed toward satisfying consumer wants and needs, marketers must understand how economic conditions influence buying decisions.

As Chapter 3 pointed out, consumer buying differs in each stage of the *business cycle*—the alternating economic sequence of prosperity and recession. During a recession, for example, consumers tend to buy basic products with low prices. Marketers might respond by lowering prices and increasing promotional spending to stimulate demand. Different strategies succeed during prosperous times, when consumers are more willing to purchase expensive goods and services. During such times, marketers might consider raising prices, expanding distribution, and extending product lines.

Technological Environment As we enter the new century, we are learning how the new era's communication technologies significantly affect how marketers design, produce, price, distribute, and promote their firms' goods and services. In one of the biggest-ever online ad campaigns from Ford Motor Co., the 1999 Mercury Cougar coupe is cruising the information highway hoping to pick up drivers 25 to 40 years old, about 60 percent of them women. Whereas car sales typically involve one-on-one personalized promotional interactions, the Web will soon become an accepted medium for the Big Three automakers, as more and more consumers bypass dealers and go straight to "factory showrooms."[20]

www.1999cougar.com

As earlier chapters have explained, *technology* is an application of knowledge to business based on scientific discoveries, inventions, and innovations. New technology generates new goods and services for consumers; it also improves existing products, strengthens customer service, and often reduces prices through new, cost-efficient production and distribution methods. However, it can make a product obsolete—remember vinyl records, 8-track tapes, and diaper services?

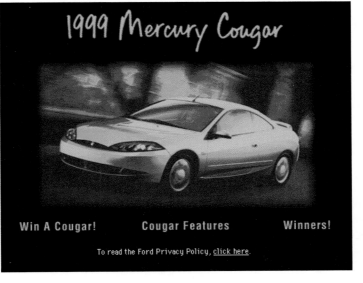

From its Web site, the Ford Motor Company advertises the features of the new Cougar as well as giving site visitors the opportunity to "bag yourself a Cougar and one for a friend."

As an example of the effect of the technological revolution on marketing, consider two key developments: the Internet and interactive marketing. Marketing writer Don Peppers has identified three important capabilities for conducting business on the Internet. "One," he explains, "is the ability to remember our customers and identify them individually in our database. Another is the ability to interact with our customers one at a time . . . And third, the computer allows us to tailor our reproduction and service delivery process to mass customize."[21] Chapters 17 and 18 further emphasize the impact of technology on contemporary business.

Social and Cultural Environment The dynamics of the social and cultural environment are powerful forces affecting marketing decisions. In recent years, concerns about recycling, pollution, and waste disposal have increased the number of ecologically friendly goods and services on the market. Population trends also play important roles in marketing mix decisions. The U.S. population, for example, is growing older and increasingly diversified. Many products are now packaged especially for senior citizens; others now carry multilingual labels. Chapter 2 discussed a number of ways in which the social and cultural environment affects the marketing mix.

MARKETING RESEARCH FOR IMPROVED MARKETING DECISIONS

Marketing research involves more than just collecting information. Researchers must decide how to collect the information, interpret the results, and communicate those results to managers in a way that supports decision making. **Marketing research** is the process of collecting and evaluating information to help marketers make effective decisions. It links marketers to the marketplace by providing data about potential target markets that helps them to design effective marketing mixes. The Business Hall of Fame describes one firm's successful application of research data to a business decision.

Marketers conduct research for five basic reasons:

1. Identify marketing problems and opportunities

2. Analyze competitors' strategies

3. Evaluate and predict consumer behavior

4. Gauge the performance of existing products and package designs, and assess the potential of new ones

5. Develop price, promotion, and distribution plans.

Obtaining Marketing Research Data

Marketing researchers are concerned with both internal and external data. They generate *internal data* within their organizations. Financial records provide a tremendous amount of useful information, such as changes in accounts receivable, inventory levels, sales generated by different categories of customers or product lines, profitability of particular divisions, or comparisons of sales by territories, salespeople, customers, or product lines.

Researchers gather *external data* from sources outside their firms, including previously published data. Trade associations, for example, publish reports on activities in particular industries. Advertising agencies collect information on the audiences reached by various media. National marketing research firms offer information through subscription services.

Low cost and quick, easy access cause marketing researchers to begin searching for needed information by exhausting all possible sources of *secondary,* or previously collected, *data* before investing the time and money required to collect firsthand data. Federal, state, and local government publications are among the marketing researcher's most important data sources. The most frequently used government statistics include census data, containing such population characteristics as age, gender, race, education level, household size and composition, occupation, employment status, and income. Such information helps marketers to assess the buying behavior of certain segments of the population, anticipate changes in the marketplace, and identify markets with above-average growth potential. Most government data can now be accessed over the Internet. Chapter 5 contains many Web addresses where business owners can surf for needed data. The Internet has revolutionized the marketing research process by providing access to immense amounts of information at any time, anywhere. Computer-based research methods are discussed later in the chapter.

Even though secondary data represent a quick and inexpensive resource, marketing researchers often discover that previously published information gives insufficient insight into some marketing problems. In some cases, the secondary data may be too old for current purposes. Census data will be collected again in 2000; until then much of the data currently available is obsolete for fast-growing areas such as Las Vegas and Orlando. Previously collected data may also be assembled in an inappropriate format for a current marketing research investigation. For example, the researcher may need data divided by city blocks that is available only aggregated for the city as a whole. Other data—particularly data about consumer attitudes or intentions—may be impossible to find. Researchers in these situations may be forced to collect *primary data*—data collected for the first time through observation or surveys.

Marketing researchers commonly collect primary data through *observational studies,* in which they view the actions of selected subjects, either directly or through mechanical devices. Traffic counts and people meters help in making decisions about location, hours of operation, or usage patterns. Internet sites measure traffic, but researchers must recognize that people on the Net are not a mass market; they are members of diverse target markets. Although the Internet can be a boon to marketing research, a product can easily be lost in the midst of all the clutter.

Some information cannot be obtained through simple observation. When researchers need information about attitudes, opinions, and motives, they must ask questions by conducting *surveys.* Survey methods include telephone in-

Business Directory

marketing research   collection and use of information to support marketing decision making.

terviews; mail, fax, and online questionnaires; personal interviews; and focus groups. A focus group brings together 8 to 12 people to discuss a particular topic. Ideas generated during focus group interviews are especially helpful to marketers in developing new products, improving existing products, and creating effective advertising campaigns.

The Internet is proving to be a valuable tool in managing online focus groups. Today, online focus groups test new products, evaluate the performance of existing ones, brainstorm hot ideas, and enhance traditional marketing research.[22]

Applying Marketing Research Data

The information collected by researchers is valuable only when it supports decisions within the framework of the organization's strategic plan. As the accuracy of information collected by researchers increases, so does the effectiveness of resulting marketing strategies.

Sometimes, marketing research can become the focal point of a firm's marketing efforts. Juno Online Services, shown in Figure 13.14, attracted more than 2 million users in 12 months for its free e-mail service. The service makes money by selling advertising presented to users. To convince would-be advertisers that they can target their ads to match consumer interests and demographics, Juno sales representatives can tell them exactly how many people visited a site and the demographic characteristics of these prospects, helping to measure the advertiser's success in reaching its target audience.

www.juno.com

Computer-Based Marketing Research Systems

A growing number of businesses are attempting to harness the power of computers to create strategic advantage for

| Figure 13.14 | **Using Marketing Research to Attract Business Customers** |

Do you really want to try to sell her hairspray?

She's not buying it. Period. So before she tells you what to do with your product, allow us. Advertise it on Juno, the advertiser-supported free e-mail service. We've signed up more than two million members in just twelve months, making us one of the fastest growing media vehicles around. Juno targets your ads to match subscribers' interests and demographics, so you don't have to buy impressions you don't want. We can tell you exactly how many people you've reached and who they are, in more detail than any other medium, online or off. That makes us 100% targetable and measurable. What a radical idea.

Free to read.   Free to write.   Free to everyone.

JUNO
Free Internet E·mail
www.advertise@juno.com
www.juno.com
or call 1-800-267-JUNO

themselves. Few products lack *universal product code (UPC)* symbols somewhere on their packaging. After scanning the information carried in the fine lines of the bar code, a computer identifies the product, where it was made, and its price. Managers use this data to schedule inventory, ordering, and delivery; track sales; and test the effectiveness of promotions and new-product introductions.

Marketing research firms, such as A. C. Nielsen and Data General, store consumer data in commercially available databases. Companies subscribe to these databases because they would spend more time and money doing the research in-house. Using information from massive data warehouses, consulting firms such as Inter-Act Systems, Retail Systems Consulting, and Stratmar Systems work with companies to develop programs that reward their best customers. In the process, these programs try to cement loyal relationships between the firms and their customers.[23] Three important contributions of computer systems to marketing research are marketing information systems, marketing decision support systems, and data mining.

www.dg.com

Marketing Information Systems A **marketing information system (MIS)** is a planned, computer-based system designed to provide managers with a continuous flow of information relevant to their specific decisions and areas of responsibility. An MIS can help marketing researchers to manage an overwhelming flood of information by applying computer tools to organize data in a logical and accessible manner. Through the MIS, a company can monitor its marketing strategies and identify problems.

A properly designed marketing information system can serve as a company's nerve center, continually monitoring the marketplace and providing instantaneous information. As Figure 13.15 shows, an MIS gathers data from

Figure 13.15 Computer-Based Marketing Research Systems: MIS and MDSS

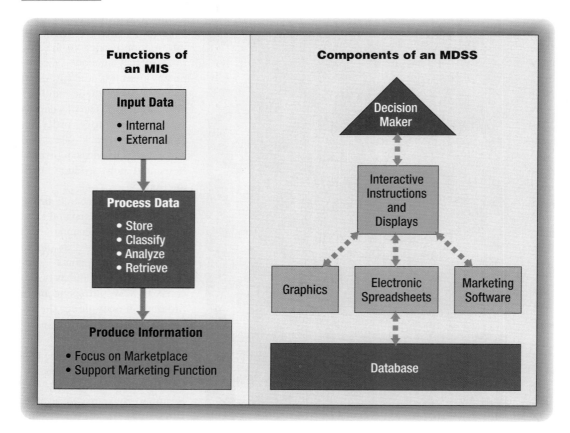

mental changes. An MDSS can create simulations or models to illustrate the likely results of changes in marketing strategies or market conditions.

Figure 13.15 shows the components of a typical MDSS, including a database, graphics functions, an electronic spreadsheet, and modeling software. In general, an MIS provides raw data, and the MDSS develops this data into business intelligence—information useful for decision making.

Data Mining **Data mining** is the process of searching through customer files to detect patterns. These patterns in masses of computer data suggest predictive models of real-world business activities. Accurate data mining can help businesspeople to forecast recessions, weed out credit-card fraud, and pinpoint sales prospects. Inaccurate data mining can produce false correlations that range from useless to dangerous in their effects.

Data warehouses store massive amounts of information. By identifying patterns and connections, marketers can increase the accuracy of their predictions about the likely effectiveness of strategy options. This new information industry has established standard techniques to enhance decision-support systems with accurate information. Says one systems architect, "The warehouse provides a common ground for data. It should be unbiased." Just as important is the applicability of the data retrieved. Explains Harvard Business School's database marketing manager Todd Greenwood, "When we built the data warehouse, everybody wanted everything. We now realize that all of that was not needed."[24]

both inside and outside the organization; it then processes that data to produce information that is relevant to marketing issues and supports the marketing function. Processing steps could involve storing data for later use, classifying and analyzing it, and retrieving it easily when needed.

An MIS permits a continuous, systematic, comprehensive study of any deviations from marketing goals. It also allows managers to adjust actions as conditions change.

Marketing Decision Support Systems A **marketing decision support system (MDSS)** consists of computer software that helps researchers quickly obtain information and apply it in a way that supports marketing decisions. An MDSS takes the MIS design one step further by allowing managers to explore and make connections between varying information about the state of the market, consumer behavior, sales forecasts, competitors' actions, and environ-

As computer technologies continue to transform the business landscape, companies will find new ways of using data mining in marketing deci-

Business Directory

sion making. Desktop computers now are powerful enough to serve as data-mining tools.[25]

MARKET SEGMENTATION

The information collected by researchers is valuable only when it helps managers to understand their decisions. Boosting the accuracy of the information that a company collects also increases the effectiveness of resulting marketing strategies. Marketing research can cover a broad range, perhaps an entire industry or nation, or it can focus on very specific details, such as individual purchase patterns. Identifying the characteristics of a target market is a crucial step toward a successful marketing strategy. **Market segmentation** is the process of dividing a total market into several relatively homogeneous groups. Both profit-seeking and not-for-profit organizations use market segmentation to help them reach desirable target markets.

The broadcast industry provides an excellent example of market segmentation. During the 1960s, most American

Data General's data warehouse provides cost-effective assistance for clients in developing customer profiles and analyzing buying patterns.

viewers watched programming from the major television networks—ABC, CBS, and NBC—and few tuned in to the UHF stations. During the 1970s, however, the fledgling cable industry added such drawing cards as HBO and Turner Broadcasting's TBS Superstation. Then came new cable networks like CNN and MTV during the 1980s, coupled with the introduction of the VCR, which let viewers watch recorded programs whenever they wanted. The direct-broadcast satellites of the 1990s made the notion of narrowcasting a reality, giving viewers access to hundreds of channels, each specializing in topics from golf to gardening to food—all vying for an audience. Yet to come are digital broadcasting services and Internet channels, which are expected to offer more than 1,000 channels or "content windows."[26]

Market segmentation attempts to isolate the traits that distinguish a certain group of consumers from the overall market. However, segmentation does not always promote marketing success. Table 13.1 lists several criteria that

Table 13.1	Criteria for Market Segmentation	
Criterion	**Example**
A segment must be a measurable group.	Disposable income data are available for such segments as senior citizens, teens, and gays.
A segment must be accessible for communications.	The growing Hispanic American market can be reached through national Spanish-language TV stations, 375 radio stations, and 1,000-plus print publications.
A segment must be large enough to offer profit potential.	Some retail stores specialize in products designed especially for left-handed consumers. Although dwarfs represent a market for small autos and other products, their numbers are insufficient to attract firms willing to specialize in these products.

BUSINESS HALL OF FAME

Harley-Davidson: Rolling Thunder on the Road

Once you experience the low, warm, vibrating song that a Harley-Davidson motorcycle sings as it motors down the road, the melody becomes a sweet, familiar sound. Nothing sounds like a Harley.

Nothing looks like a Harley. Others try to imitate the classic "Hog," Harley's biggest bike, but none compare. Also, no other bike comes equipped with its reputation and a cult-like appeal. Owning a Harley is a one-of-a-kind experience, "like owning a piece of art," says Bob Brihn of Carmichael Lynch, Harley's long-time ad agency.

Harley is the king of the biker world with more than 20 percent of all U.S. motorcycle sales and over half the $1.3 billion market for heavyweight cycles, like the 1,200 cc Hog. But the company didn't make a steady uphill ride to the top. During the 1970s, Harley's then parent company, sporting-goods conglomerate AMF, pushed to expand manufacturing capacity. Quality dropped, sales fell, and inventory piled up. In 1981, Harley staged the biggest leveraged buyout ever recorded at that time.

For 2 years following the takeover, the company fought bankruptcy. A new engine design and Softail suspension accompanied customer service innovations. Harley was the first in the industry to offer test rides, and the company guaranteed trade-in allowances for new owners. Harley's reputation rose higher than ever, and sales rapidly grew. Production jumped from 30,000 in 1985 to 44,000 in 1989. A new era in Harley-Davidson history began in 1990. More Hogs were on the road around the world than ever before. Today, over 125,000 bikes roll off the company's assembly line each year.

Behind all this success are Harley's highly brand-loyal customers, reinforced by a new breed of Hog riders. Still, management remained hesitant to speed up production. With strong memories of unsalable inventory, they wanted some validation that the market would continue to grow. As CEO Richard F. Teerlink explains, "We've been blessed with a heritage. But we can't simply rely on the mystique."

What Teerlink did rely on was strategy based on research. He clearly saw that the company sold many of its new bikes to white-collar motorcyclists dubbed "Rubbies" (Rich Urban Bikers). The growing roster of Harley owners included names like Jay Leno, Malcolm Forbes, and Elizabeth Taylor. Flattered by all the free, high-society press coverage, Harley's director of business planning Frank Cimermancic still needed reassurance that the company had found a new band of long-time customers and not followers of a fad who would eventually turn in their two-wheelers, flooding the used-bike

---

should be considered before segmenting a market. The effectiveness of a segmentation strategy depends on how well the market meets these criteria. Once marketers identify a target market segment, they can create an appropriate marketing strategy.

How Market Segmentation Works

An initial distinction separates consumer and business markets based on the types of products they handle. Marketers segment their target markets in different ways, depending on whether their firms offer consumer or business products. The four common bases for segmenting consumer markets are geographic segmentation, demographic segmentation, psychographic segmentation, and product-related segmentation.

Business markets, however, are segmented on only three criteria: customer-based segmentation, end-use segmentation, and geographic segmentation. Figure 13.16 illustrates the segmentation methods for these two types of markets.

Segmenting Consumer Markets

Businesspeople have practiced consumer market segmentation for centuries in countries around the world. History is full of tales of merchants traveling by land and sea to bring exotic spices and fabrics thousands of miles to distant markets. In addition to geographic segmentation, today's marketers also define customer groups based on demographic and psychographic criteria as well as product-related distinctions.

Geographic Segmentation Perhaps the oldest segmentation method is **geographic segmentation**—dividing an overall market into homogeneous groups on the basis of population locations. While geographic location does not ensure homogeneity of consumer buying decisions, this segmentation approach is useful when consumer preferences and purchase patterns for a good or service differ between regions. For example, suburbanites predictably purchase more lawn-care products than do their urban counterparts. Also, residents of northern states purchase snowblowers and auto windshield ice scrapers, products considered oddities in warm climates.

market with low-priced castoffs. He recalls, "If we got the answer right, we could become a force in the industry. If we got it wrong, we would go right back to the early 1980s. Nobody wanted to make the wrong decision and watch 20 percent of our employees walk away with their possessions in a cardboard box."

Another question remained: Should Harley market its product differently to its new audiences? Traditional bikers had loyally supported the company in its worst years. Management knew their needs and satisfied them. They didn't figure these Hog riders would forsake them now. They worried about this new market, though.

To answer their questions, the company's marketers held focus groups with current owners, would-be owners, and owners of other brands. Participants created cut-and-paste pictures that represented how they felt about Harley-Davidson. Overwhelmingly, the responses expressed fun, the great outdoors, and freedom. Next, the company mailed out 16,000 questionnaires with, as Cimermancic says, "a battery

of psychological, sociological, and demographic questions you typically see in studies."

One common thread united the more than 5,000 responses. As Cimermancic recalls, "Independence, freedom, and power were universal Harley appeals." Harley identified seven core customer groups:

▼ Adventure-Loving Traditionalists

▼ Sensitive Pragmatists

▼ Stylish Status-Seekers

▼ Laid-Back Campers

▼ Classy Capitalists

▼ Cool-Headed Loners

▼ Cocky Misfits

Based on research, and the growing length of the company's 2-year waiting list, Harley has decided to push up production numbers. The Hogs are on an uphill grade that Harley plans to ride for a couple of years. Don't expect the market to be glutted anytime soon,

though. Harley still barely meets half of the demand for Hogs.

QUESTIONS FOR CRITICAL THINKING

1. Do you think Harley-Davidson should boost production to meet its current demand? Why do you think the company lets customers languish so long on a waiting list?

2. What other marketing research could Harley management conduct to find out who its customers are and the reasons they buy?

3. Harley has diversified into other licensed products sold in dealer showrooms that target died-in-the-wool Harley riders. How important is Harley's cult reputation to sales of these products? Do they benefit motorcycle sales? How?

Sources: Stuart F. Brown, "Gearing Up for the Cruiser Wars," *Fortune*, August 3, 1998, accessed at www.pathfinder.com; and Richard A. Melcher, "Tune-Up Time for Harley," *Business Week*, April 8, 1996, pp. 90, 94.

BMW motorcycle marketers target urbanites in their marketing campaigns, like the one illustrated in Figure 13.17. Harried residents of congested urban centers face continuing battles for convenient parking, and navigating their neighborhood streets can be a major challenge. BMW ads offer a solution and encourage these people to test drive the new F650 motorcycle.

www.bmwusa.com

Sometimes geographic segmentation succeeds, not by catering to the habits or preferences of the people of a certain region, but rather because a product, or a way of marketing it, is new to that region. Cornbread, for example, is considered an exotic foreign food in Great Britain, where cornmeal is available mainly through health-food stores. Similarly, sushi has become a popular cuisine in the United States.

Population size, a common geographic segmentation factor, helps to define target markets as urban, suburban,

and rural markets. However, businesses also need to consider a wide variety of other variables, such as job growth and migration patterns, before deciding to expand into new areas. Some businesses may decide to combine areas or even entire countries that share similar population and product-use patterns instead of treating each as an independent segment.

Demographic Segmentation By far the most common method of market segmentation, **demographic segmentation** distinguishes markets on the basis of such demographic or socioeconomic characteristics as income, age, occupation, household size, stage in the family life cycle, education, ethnic group, and gender. The U.S. Census Bureau is one of the best sources of demographic information for the domestic market.

Women have become attractive prospects for marketers in the 1990s. At the same time, however, they have changed from one of the easiest-reached demographic segments for package-goods manufacturers to one of the hardest to reach. Procter & Gamble launched a new Web site, ParentTime at Work, targeting women who work outside

Figure 13.16   Methods of Segmenting Consumer and Business Markets

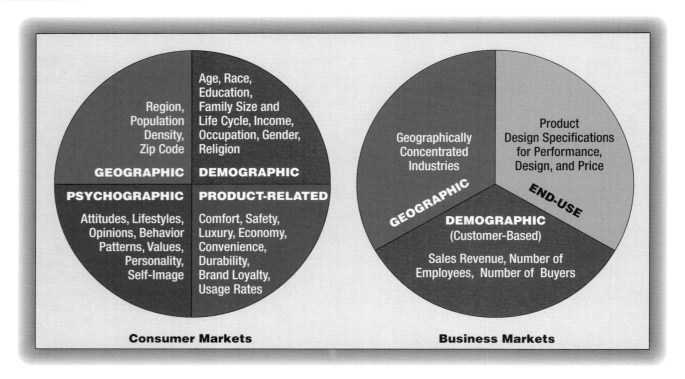

the home. Says one project developer, "We offer P&G access to women in a time period when marketers have not been able to get them."[27]

Gender is a fairly simple way to define markets for certain products—perfume and cosmetics for women and hammers and drills for men. However, some products have spread beyond such gender stereotypes. Sporting goods and exercise equipment, for example, are now popular consumer purchases for both men and women. Men dominated purchase decisions for automobiles. Now, however, automobile manufacturers are straddling gender barriers by designing products and promotions to attract women.

Age is perhaps the most volatile factor in demographic segmentation in the United States, with its rapidly aging population. By 2020, one of every three Americans will be over 50 years old, and companies are now increasingly focusing attention on reaching this growing part of the market.

DID YOU KNOW?

Despite heavy post-World War II migration northward, the majority of African Americans (55 percent) still live in the South. Nearly 19 million strong, they constitute more than 20 percent of the region's total population.

Ethnic minority groups in the United States hold combined purchasing power of $750 billion a year—an amount that has not been overlooked by marketers. The three largest minority groups in the United States are African Americans, Hispanic Americans, and Asian Americans. Asian Americans are the wealthiest of America's growing ethnic groups; in fact, they have a higher average household income ($46,695) than their Anglo counterparts ($40,646). Both Citibank and Bank of America are trying to capture part of this 11 million person market. Bank of America launched three commercials on 12 Asian-language television stations in California. The ads aired in Cantonese, Mandarin, Korean, and Vietnamese. Citibank is also trying to reach this target group with premium incentives. New and existing customers who deposit $150,000 or more are presented with a collector's edition crystal dragon designed by Swarovski; $30,000 depositors receive 3.2-gram 24-karat gold dragon pendants; those who deposit $80,000 get 8.6-gram pendants.[28]

Demographic segmentation is somewhat more difficult in foreign markets than in domestic ones. Many countries do not regularly conduct census studies of their popu-

Figure 13.17 **Geographic Segmentation to Target Motorcycle Buyers**

Be not afraid.

The F650 ST is $7,490 and the best way to get around the city. To find out why, see your retailer for a test ride. For more information, please call 1-800-345-4BMW, or contact http://www.bmwusa.com

The Ultimate Riding Machine

graphic segments composed of individuals who had never before considered used-car purchases because of dependability concerns. The GM program was intended to ease these fears by including a 3-day/150-mile money-back guarantee and a 1-year warranty. The ad shown in Figure 13.18 invites vacationers to travel across the United States in a used car that passes GM's 110-step certification process.[29]

Psychographic studies have evaluated motivations for purchases of hundreds of goods and services, ranging from soft drinks to health-care services. The resulting data has helped firms to tailor their marketing strategies to carefully chosen market segments. Two frequently used methods of developing psychographic profiles of different buyer groups are AIO statements and the VALS 2 grouping system.

AIO statements are verbal descriptions of various activities, interests, and opinions. Researchers ask consumers in a sample whether they agree or disagree with each statement. The answers are then tabulated and analyzed by computer for use in identifying various lifestyle categories.

VALS 2 (for *values and lifestyles*) is a psychographic segmentation system developed by research and consulting firm SRI International. Its categories are based on two concepts:

▼ Resources (income, education, self-confidence, health, eagerness to buy, and energy level)

▼ Self-orientation (principle-oriented, status-oriented, and action-oriented)

Analysis of these two concepts allows researchers to categorize each respondent in one of the eight groupings shown in Figure 13.19. People categorized as fulfillers tend to be mature, home-oriented, well-educated professionals who like value and welcome new ideas. By contrast, makers are self-sufficient individuals with little interest in material possessions.

To learn which VALS 2 psychographic category you most closely resemble, visit SRI's Web site, complete the questionnaire, and receive immediate feedback.

www.future.sri.com/

lations, and others, such as Great Britain, Japan, Spain, France, and Italy, do not collect income data. One online source of global demographic information is the International Programs Center (IPC), which provides a searchable database of population statistics for many countries. A link appears on the Web page for the U.S. Bureau of the Census.

www.census.gov

Psychographic Segmentation In recent years, marketing researchers have tried to formulate lifelike portraits of consumers. This effort has led to another strategy for segmenting target markets, **psychographic segmentation,** which divides consumer markets into groups with similar psychological characteristics, values, and lifestyles. *Lifestyle* is the summation of a person's needs, preferences, motives, attitudes, social habits, and cultural background.

In a proactive move to reduce the glut of used cars created by the growing popularity of auto leasing, General Motors Corp. devised a special marketing program for "Certified Used Vehicles." Promotions focused on psycho-

Product-Related Segmentation Using **product-related segmentation,** marketers can divide a consumer market into groups based on buyers' relationships to the good or service. The three most popular approaches to product-related segmentation are based on benefits sought, usage rates, and brand loyalty.

Segmenting by *benefits sought* focuses on the attributes that people seek in a good or service and the benefits they expect to receive from it. Whirlpool tells customers

Figure 13.18 **Psychographic Segmentation in the Used-Car Market**

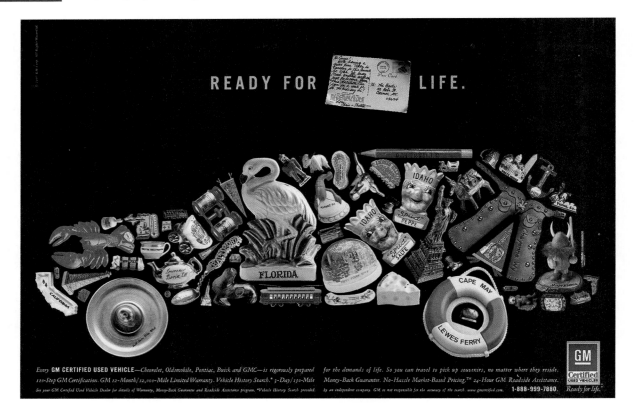

when they wash their clothes in its newest machine, they should follow all directions except "hand wash only." The giant home-appliance manufacturer promises that its new washer's gentle agitating cycle eliminates the need for hand washing.

Even if a business offers only one product line, marketers must remember to consider product benefits. Two people may buy the same product for very different reasons. A can of WD40 lubricant may help users to quiet a squeaking door hinge, clean an electrical contact point, or loosen a bolt on a lawn-mower engine.

A consumer market can also be segmented according to the amounts of a product that different consumers buy and use. Segmentation by *product usage rate* usually defines such categories as heavy users, medium users, and light users. The *80/20 principle* states that roughly 80 percent of a product's revenues come from only 20 percent of its buyers. Managers at Sheboygan, Wisconsin-based Schultz Sav-O Stores, operator of that area's Piggly Wiggly outlets, found that approximately 25 percent of its customer base supplies 70 percent of its revenues. Retailers such as American Stores and Grand Union are mining their frequent-shopper databases for information that can power customer-specific loyalty marketing programs. Says one industry expert, "Now that retailers can identify the 20 per-

cent of their customers that produce 80 percent of their sales volume and profit, through frequent-shopper cards and point-of-sale data, the question is, how do they establish a quality dialog with those customers on an ongoing basis?"[30]

The third technique for product-related segmentation divides customers by *brand loyalty.* Marketers define groups of consumers with similar degrees of brand loyalty. They then attempt to tie loyal customers to a good or service by giving away logo-emblazoned premiums, such as T-shirts, nylon sports bags, or foam-rubber drink holders.

Segmenting Business Markets

In many ways, the segmentation process for business markets resembles that for consumer markets. However, some specific methods differ. Marketers divide business markets through geographic segmentation; demographic, or customer-based, segmentation; and end-use segmentation.

Geographic segmentation methods for business markets resemble those for consumer markets. Many business-to-business marketers target geographically concentrated industries, such as aircraft manufacturing, automobiles, and oil-field equipment.

Demographic, or customer-based, segmentation begins with a good or service design intended to suit a specific organizational market. Costume makers, for example, might target the theater and performing arts market. To simplify the process of focusing on a particular type of business customer, the federal government has established the *Standard Industrial Classification (SIC)* system. The system assigns 7-digit SIC codes that divide firms into broad industry segments and then further subdivides them. In addition, firms can be grouped by size based on their sales revenues or numbers of employees.

End-use segmentation focuses on the precise way in which a business purchaser will use a product. Resembling benefits-sought segmentation for consumer markets, this method helps small and medium-sized companies to target specific end-user markets rather than competing directly with large firms for wider customer groups. For example, Goodyear tires are included as critical components of new Lexus automobiles. The tire manufacturer also distributes its tires to Goodyear retail outlets, which resell them in small quantities to business buyers and final consumers. Other end-users include auto- and truck-rental firms and large taxi companies that purchase replacement tires.

| **Figure 13.19** | **VALS 2 Psychographic Groupings** |

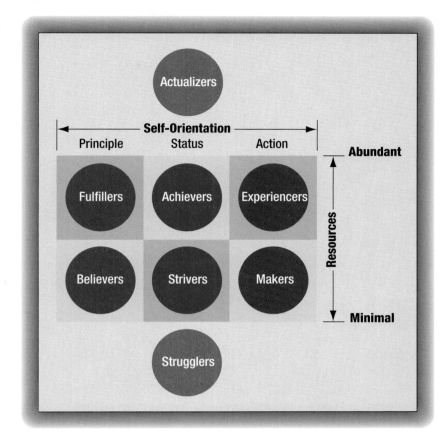

BUYER BEHAVIOR: DETERMINING WHAT CUSTOMERS WANT

A fundamental marketing task is to find out why people buy one product and not another. The answer requires an understanding of **buyer behavior,** the purchase processes of individual consumers who buy goods and services for their own use and organizational buyers who purchase business products. In contrast, **consumer behavior** refers to the actions of ultimate consumers directly involved in obtaining, consuming, and disposing of products, and the decision processes that precede and follow these actions.

Determinants of Consumer Behavior

By studying people's purchasing behavior, marketers can identify consumers' attitudes toward and uses of their company's products. This investigation also helps to improve the effectiveness of marketing strategies for reaching these people. Both personal and interpersonal factors influence the behavior of an ultimate consumer. Personal influences on consumer behavior include individual needs and motives, perceptions, attitudes, learned experiences, and self-concept. Marketers frequently apply psychological techniques to understand what motivates people to buy and to study consumers' emotional reactions to goods and services.

The interpersonal determinants of consumer behavior include cultural, social, and family influences. For example, retailers of ethnically oriented lines of clothing have found that carrying these goods enhances the loyalty of customers from the appropriate groups. Such factors, however, vary in different countries—even countries with a common language, such as Great Britain and Ireland.

Determinants of Business Buying Behavior

Because a number of people can influence typical business product purchases, business buyers face a variety of organizational influences in addition to their own preferences. A design engineer may help to set the specifications that potential vendors must satisfy. A procurement

Figure 13.20   **Steps in the Buyer Behavior Process**

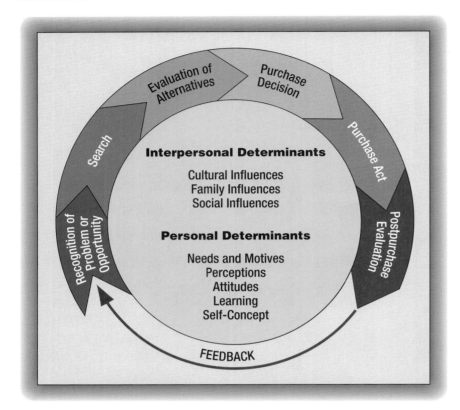

that change becomes an opportunity to enjoy.

To solve the problem or take advantage of the opportunity, the consumer seeks out information about the intended purchase and evaluates alternatives, such as available brands. The goal of this activity is to find the best response to the perceived problem or opportunity.

Eventually, the consumer reaches a decision and completes the transaction (the purchase act). Later, he or she evaluates the experience with the purchase (postpurchase evaluation). Feelings about the experience will influence future purchase decisions (feedback). The various steps in the sequence are affected by both interpersonal and personal factors.

CREATING, MAINTAINING, AND STRENGTHENING MARKETING RELATIONSHIPS

Chapter 7 discussed how businesses have moved from transaction management to relationship management in developing strategic plans intended to gain competitive advantage. **Relationship marketing** is the application of the same principles to a specific area of business—marketing. The Business Tool Kit cites important advice from sales managers about establishing and maintaining solid relationships.

Relationship marketing goes beyond an effort for making the sale to a drive for making the sale again and again. To keep particular customers coming back, firms must exceed their needs and wants so they will make repeat purchases. As its ultimate goal, relationship marketing seeks to achieve customer satisfaction, as discussed earlier in this chapter.

Good relationships with customers can be vital strategic weapons for a firm. By identifying current purchasers and maintaining positive relationships with them, organizations can efficiently target their best customers. Studying current customers' buying habits and preferences can help marketers to identify potential new customers and establish ongoing contact with them, as well.

Information technologies, such as computer databases, provide strong support for ef-

manager may invite selected companies to bid on a purchase. A production supervisor may evaluate the operational aspects of the proposals that the firm receives, and the vice president of manufacturing may head a committee making the final decision.

Steps in the Buyer Behavior Process

Consumer decision making follows the sequential process outlined in Figure 13.20, with interpersonal and personal influences affecting every step. The process begins when the consumer recognizes a problem or opportunity. If someone needs a new pair of shoes, that need becomes a problem to solve. If someone receives a promotion and a $5-an-hour raise,

Business Directory

relationship marketing developing and maintaining long-term, cost-effective exchange relationships with individual customers, suppliers, employees, and other partners for mutual benefit.

Figure 13.21 **Profiting from Customer Retention**

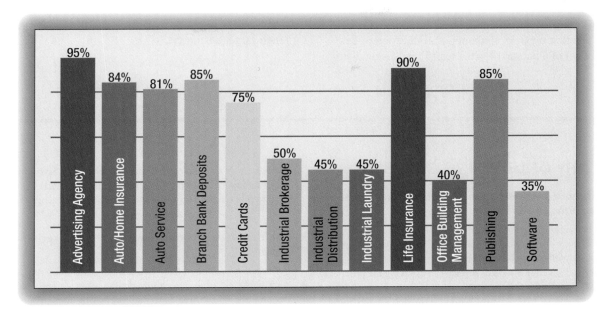

fective relationship marketing. Marketers can maintain databases on current customers' tastes, price range preferences, and lifestyles, and they can quickly obtain names and other information about good prospects. The Internet, with its capabilities for interactive electronic commerce, creates additional opportunities for firms to build close customer relationships. Service industries, such as airlines, have been in the forefront of relationship marketing, since their staff members often personally meet and interact with customers.

Retaining customers is the primary benefit of relationship marketing. Figure 13.21 shows how a 5 percent increase in customer retention increases the net profits of companies in various industries. Says business consultant and author Frederick Reichheld, "The only strategy for sustained growth is high [customer] retention. If you're serious about fostering loyalty . . . find out how to deliver far better value to your most important accounts."[31]

BUSINESS TOOL KIT

Building Loyal Customer Relationships

Customer retention is a primary concern of many executives today. The following ten tips compile brainstorming ideas offered by sales managers to help marketers build and maintain strong relationships with customers:

1. Send salespeople to work out of your best customers' offices, so they can gain firsthand knowledge of each firm's needs.

2. Reward salespeople for holding onto customer accounts beyond the first or second sale.

3. Learn about the customers' marketplace by interviewing their customers, suppliers, and competitors.

4. Hold a retreat with a major customer, and share information about best practices.

5. Invite customers to hold seminars to educate your salespeople about their companies or industries.

6. Set up a customer council in which major accounts offer advice on improving goods and services.

7. Develop a preferred-customer pricing strategy and frequent-buyer reward program.

8. Reward customers for referring new business.

9. Develop business and marketing plans with customers.

10. Partner with customers to work on a major project.

Source: Tom McDonald, "How to Build Loyalty," *Sales & Marketing Management*, March 1998, p. 34.

WHAT'S AHEAD

The following three chapters examine each of the elements of the marketing mix by which firms satisfy selected target markets. The first two mix elements—product and price—are the subject of Chapter 14. Chapter 15 focuses on distri-bution and examines channel design and physical distribu-tion of products from producer to consumer or business user. The final chapter in this section covers promotion and the various methods marketers use to communicate with their target customers.

SUMMARY OF LEARNING GOALS

1. Explain how marketing creates utility, and list the major functions of marketing.

Exchange is the process by which two or more parties give some-thing of value to one another to satisfy felt needs. Marketing is closely linked with the exchange process. It creates utility—the want-satisfying power of a good or service—by making the product available when and where consumers want to buy and by arranging for orderly transfers of ownership. While production creates form utility, marketing creates time, place, and ownership utility.

The eight basic functions of marketing are buying, selling, transporting, storing, standardizing and grading, financing, risk taking, and acquiring market information.

2. Explain the marketing concept and relate how cus-tomer satisfaction and total quality management con-tribute to added value.

The marketing concept refers to a companywide consumer orien-tation with the objective of achieving long-run success. It can be explained best by the shift from a seller's market—one with a shortage of goods and services—to a buyer's market—one with an abundance of goods and services.

Customer satisfaction and total quality management reflect the relative excellence or superiority of an organization's goods and services. Customers seek more than just a fair price; they want added value. A good or service provides added value by delivering more than buyers expect in the form of added features, a reduced price, enhanced customer service, a strengthened warranty, or other marketing mix improvements that increase customer satisfaction.

3. Identify the components of a market.

A market consists of people with purchasing power and willing-ness and authority to buy. Markets can be classified by the types of products they handle. Consumer products are goods and ser-vices purchased by ultimate users. Business products are goods and services purchased to be used, directly or indirectly, in the production of other products for resale.

4. Outline the basic steps in developing a marketing strategy.

All organizations, profit-oriented and not-for-profit, need to develop marketing strategies to effectively reach customers. This process in-volves analyzing the overall market, selecting a target market, and developing a marketing mix. Often, company marketers develop a marketing plan that expresses their marketing strategy.

5. Identify the components of the marketing environ-ment.

Marketers operate in five environments: the competitive, political and legal, economic, technological, and social and cultural envi-ronments. These five external forces provide a framework for planning product, pricing, place (or distribution), and promo-tional strategies aimed at a target market.

6. Describe the marketing research function.

Marketing research is the information-gathering function that links marketers to the marketplace. It provides the information about po-tential target markets that planners need to design effective mar-keting mixes. Marketers conduct research for five basic reasons:

1. Identify marketing problems and opportunities
2. Analyze competitors' strategies
3. Evaluate and predict consumer behavior
4. Gauge the performance of existing products and package de-signs, and assess the potential of new ones
5. Develop pricing, promotion, and distribution plans.

Marketing research involves more than just collecting infor-mation; researchers must also decide how to collect the informa-tion, and then they interpret and communicate the results.

7. Identify the methods for segmenting consumer and business markets.

Consumer markets can be divided according to demographic characteristics, such as age and family size; geographic factors; psychographic variables, which involve behavioral and lifestyle profiles; and product-related variables, such as the benefits con-sumers seek when buying a product or the degree of brand loyalty they feel toward it.

Business markets are segmented according to three criteria: geographic characteristics, customer-based specifications for products, and end-user applications.

8. Define and contrast buyer behavior and consumer behavior.

Buyer behavior refers to the purchase processes of *both* individual consumers who buy goods and services for their own use and organizational buyers who purchase business products. Because a number of people may participate in business purchase decisions, business buyers encounter a variety of organizational influences in addition to their own preferences.

Consumer behavior, on the other hand, refers to the actions of ultimate consumers with direct effects on obtaining, consuming, and disposing of products, as well as the decision processes that precede and follow these actions. Personal influences on consumer behavior include an individual's needs and motives, perceptions, attitudes, learned experiences, and self-concept. The interpersonal determinants include cultural influences, social influences, and family influences.

9. Describe relationship marketing and explain its importance in strategic planning.

Relationship marketing is an organization's attempt to develop long-term, cost-effective links with individual customers for mutual benefit. Good relationships with customers can be a vital strategic weapon for a firm. By identifying current purchasers and maintaining a positive relationship with them, an organization can efficiently target its best customers. Information technologies, such as computers, databases, and spreadsheets, support effective relationship marketing.

TEN BUSINESS TERMS YOU NEED TO KNOW

marketing	marketing mix
utility	environmental scanning
marketing concept	marketing research
customer satisfaction	market segmentation
target market	relationship marketing

Other Important Business Terms

exchange process	marketing decision support system (MDSS)
value-added	data mining
external customer	geographic segmentation
internal customer	demographic segmentation
person marketing	psychographic segmentation
place marketing	product-related segmentation
cause marketing	end-use segmentation
event marketing	buyer behavior
organization marketing	consumer behavior
consumer product	
business product	
market information system (MIS)	

REVIEW QUESTIONS

1. Define and differentiate between the four types of utility. Explain marketing's role in the creation of utility.
2. For each of the eight marketing functions, identify a business that performs one or more of these functions. What does this list suggest?
3. Briefly describe the evolution of marketing and the importance of the marketing concept in developing customer relationships.
4. Explain how firms can provide added value to their goods and services. What impact do customer satisfaction and total quality management have on adding value to a product?
5. What constitutes a market? Distinguish between a consumer market and a business market.
6. Explain the three basic steps in developing a marketing strategy. What is a target market?
7. Explain how marketing environments influence marketing strategy. Cite an example of each of these environments.
8. Describe the marketing research function and explain how computer-based technologies are enhancing research.
9. List and explain the bases used to segment consumer and business markets.
10. Compare the characteristics of consumer and business buyer behavior.

QUESTIONS FOR CRITICAL THINKING

1. C-It B-It is an interactive video shopping service that offers viewers over 250,000 products. C-It B-It customers can comparison shop, via interactive video on TV screens, for numerous models of the same item and compare prices against those of competitors. Manufacturers ship purchases directly to buyers. Relate C-It B-It's operation to the chapter's discussion of utility. What types of utility are being created?
2. Suppose you are an executive for a Japanese firm that is considering marketing a line of canned fish products in the United States. What type of market information would you want to have about the U.S. market? Discuss how environmental factors would impact your decision to enter this market.
3. Cadillac recently introduced its new compact car, the Catera. Describe the target market for this new car in your area and develop an effective marketing strategy to reach these consumers.
4. Linkman's is a sporting goods manufacturer that just developed a new life-preserver that conforms to fit any wearer. Assume you are given the task of marketing this new product. Define your target market. Would you target consumer or business markets? Explain your reasons.
5. Littering is a problem on campuses across the United States. Most, in fact, hire groundskeepers to

do nothing but pick up litter discarded by careless students. Conduct interviews to determine how students feel about litter on campus. Then perform an observational study to determine if the littering problem would be reduced if more trash recepta-cles were available. First, observe an area without a trash can that is heavily littered. Then place a trash can nearby and record any changes in students' disposal habits. What do your findings indicate?

Experiential Exercise

Directions: Focus groups are one source discussed in the chapter for obtaining marketing research data. In this exercise, you will coordinate and conduct an informal focus group interview.

1. Identify a service on campus, such as the library, bookstore, computer labs, or food court that you believe could be improved. Your assignment is to interview those who use the service to get ideas for improvements.
2. Develop a list of five to seven questions to generate ideas from focus group participants on how to improve the service. Consider meeting with the manager of the campus service you select to determine whether he or she would like to participate in your market research project.
3. Ask 8 to 12 students from class, the residence halls, or another student-gathering place on campus to be members of the focus group.
4. Throughout the interview, record the ideas generated by the focus group as members respond to your prepared questions.
5. Summarize your findings in a one- to two-page report, and submit it to your instructor for his or her review.
6. **Optional**: If you have included the manager of the service in your focus group (step 2 above), you should submit a copy of your report to that individual as well.

Nothing but Net

1. **Measuring Customer Satisfaction.** Visit the Web site of a company you are interested in to see how it uses its site to measure customer satisfaction. One such example can be found by clicking on "Customer Survey" on Polaroid's home page at

   www.polaroid.com/

   Summarize the reaction customers might have to this means of obtaining customer input. What are the advantages and disadvantages for companies who include a customer survey on their home pages?
2. **Not-for-Profit Marketing.** Identify and evaluate the impact on you personally (positive, neutral, or negative) of the Web site marketing strategies used by a not-for-profit organization, such as the American Red Cross, the Olympic Games, or the National Air and Space Museum:

   www.redcross.org/

   www.olympic.org/

   www.nasm.edu/NASMpage.html

   What elements of the site made you react the way you did?
3. **Marketing Research.** J. D. Power and Associates is an international marketing information firm that collects consumer opinions and customer satisfaction data in the automotive, financial, telecommunications, and travel industries.

   www.jdpower.com/award.html

   Select an award category, identify the award winners, and summarize the criteria used to determine the rankings.

ROGAINE—MARKETING AN ACCIDENTAL MIRACLE

For baby boomers struggling to grow old gracefully in a society that places a major emphasis on appearance, hair loss is a nightmare. "Back in the early '70s, Upjohn was testing a product in the laboratories to see if it was effective, and one of the side effects we found in a high percentage of people who were using it was excessive hair growth all over their body," remembers Tim Thieme, Upjohn's director of product management. "We were very disappointed at first because this was a drug for hypertension."

Follow-up research confirmed that the product dubbed Rogaine did indeed grow hair. Upjohn submitted its data to the federal Food and Drug Administration and waited for approval to begin marketing Rogaine. Approval was granted, and suddenly, Upjohn had the first legitimate hair-growth product in history.

Although Rogaine is now available as an over-the-counter treatment in millions of grocery and drug stores, the FDA first restricted its sale as a prescription treatment that could only be obtained from physicians. "We knew this was going to be a consumer-driven product," admits Thieme. "We had to determine internally whether we would advertise to the consumer. Once that decision was made, we had other hurdles we had to overcome before we could reach the consumer, and that dealt with the Food and Drug Administration and what they were going to let us say or not say about the product."

In the beginning, the FDA allowed Upjohn to say very little about Rogaine. Its first television commercials for the product were soft-sell spots that simply encouraged consumers to consult their physicians about hair loss and treatment options. Later, as the FDA became more comfortable with Rogaine, Upjohn was able to launch a more aggressive campaign with more specific television commercials and newspaper and magazine ads. Each message provided toll-free numbers consumers could call for more information. Callers were then sent an informational video, along with a brochure listing doctors who offered Rogaine, and a $10 gift certificate redeemable with their first prescription.

Early on, Upjohn's research revealed that a significant number of women suffer from hair loss, and they have an even harder time accepting hair loss than their male counterparts. "We understood that there was a different segment here that we had to address, and we had to get to them in the most efficient way," says Eldon Eby, director of consumer promotion. "Women wanted more information, in many cases, than men, and different kinds of information." Upjohn established toll-free numbers specifically for women. Female callers receive a free information video featuring testimonials from women who had experienced success with Rogaine, and a list of area doctors offering it to their patients.

More than 20 years after its discovery, diligent consumer analysis and strategic target marketing have enabled Upjohn not only to transform a failed treatment for hypertension into one of the company's most lucrative products but to be a pioneer in cosmopseudical treatments.

Questions

1. What was Rogaine's original marketing strategy? How was it developed?

2. Describe how Rogaine reaches its target market. What segmentation bases are used?

3. How did Rogaine deal with the Food and Drug Administration's restrictions on its consumer advertising? Give examples.

chapter **14**

Developing and Pricing Goods and Services

LEARNING GOALS

1. Define *product* and list the elements of a product strategy.

2. Describe the classifications of consumer goods, business goods, and services.

3. Discuss the product mix and product lines.

4. Describe the four stages of the product life cycle.

5. List the stages of new-product development.

6. Explain how firms identify their products.

7. Outline the different types of pricing objectives.

8. Discuss how firms set prices in the marketplace.

9. Explain how to use breakeven analysis in pricing strategy.

10. Differentiate between skimming and penetration pricing strategies.

Revealing All With PriceSCAN

Before you buy a camera, you want to know what company has the best price. How can you find out? Jump onto the Internet. To save you money and help take the hassle out of shopping, David Cost and Jeffrey Trester started PriceSCAN. The company provides unbiased pricing and product information on books, computers, CDs, electronic equipment, movies, and video games. It maintains current data on other companies' prices and offers that data to you on its Web site for free. With a few mouse clicks, you can get up-to-date information about who has the best price for the type of camera you want. And you can do so in minutes—saving days or even weeks of phoning, faxing, and traveling around town to contact individual companies.

In fact, more shopping-guide Web sites are appearing all the time. You can compare prices on cars and cell phones, among other products. For example, Esmarts.com highlights the lowest prices for products, ranging from long-distance calling plans to toys. Wireless Dimension compares wireless-phone plans across the country. Even Internet biggies like the *Washington Post* sites are comparing prices for you. Generally shopping-guide companies earn revenues by selling ad space on their sites.

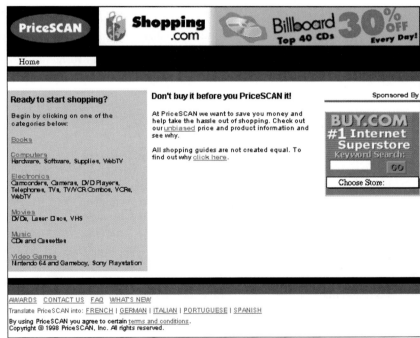

Some also collect a cut of the sales that result from referring customers. For example, from some companies Esmarts gets between 5 and 8 percent of the sales resulting from its referrals.

This means that shopping guides aren't necessarily the same. For example, the *Washington Post* sites use price-comparison software from a company called Junglee (an acquisition of Amazon.com). For its price comparisons, Junglee searches *only* those sites that pay it a commission on any resulting sales. But some of the cheapest prices are from sites that can't afford to pay the referral fee and are therefore not listed. So the question of bias arises as some wonder whether seller-sponsored sites are truly listing the cheapest prices. "People shopping on the Internet tend not to be idiots," says

PriceSCAN co-founder Jeffrey Trester. "They will recognize that more objective comparisons exist elsewhere." For example, PriceSCAN accepts no money from vendors, deriving revenue from advertising and from selling its pricing information.

The new price-revealing trend is pretty unpopular with marketers, both online and off. "Big vendors can't get away with charging higher prices just because customers don't know any better," says PriceSCAN co-founder David Cost. Some Marketers worry about a future in which shoppers consider absolutely nothing but price. Once customers are no longer influenced by service, product quality, or brand identity, vendors fear the marketing mix will become skewed and unmanageable. But Cost believes that the main reason marketers dislike pricing services is their guilt over the prices they charge. "People on the high end were embarrassed," says Cost. "They'd call us and ask us to take their prices down." But PriceSCAN did not comply. When some vendors tried to counter by withholding access to their databases, PriceSCAN simply turned to companies' printed catalogs and typed the prices in. In the end, vendors realized that PriceSCAN would refer buyers to them when their pricing was right, so however reluctantly, they began furnishing PriceSCAN with their pricing data.[1]

WWW.

www.pricescan.com

CHAPTER OVERVIEW

To prepare a successful plan for satisfying a firm's target market, managers must conceive a unique marketing mix. In a very real sense, creating products designed to fill customer needs is the reason for a firm's existence. Society permits businesses to operate as long as they serve its members by providing want-satisfying products at competitive prices. Pricing strategy is a second major determinant of consumer acceptance and a critical factor in ensuring that a profit-seeking firm earns adequate profit and that a not-for-profit organization generates sufficient revenues to meet its expenses. As we saw in the opening vignette, online shopping services such as PriceSCAN are altering consumers' perceptions of pricing. And businesses are having to adjust to this newfound customer power. Pricing strategies will be increasingly scrutinized in the interconnected world of cybershopping and e-commerce.

This chapter begins by describing the classifications of goods and services, the product mix, and the product life cycle. It then discusses how firms develop, identify, and package products. The chapter next describes pricing strategy for those products: how firms set pricing objectives and determine the best prices for their goods and services. The chapter concludes with a look at consumer perceptions of prices.

WHAT IS A PRODUCT?

Engineers and other production specialists tend to think of products as collections of physical characteristics. A Honda is a combination of rubber tires, plastic components, sheet metal panels, glass windows, an engine, and seats. However, marketers know better than that. The marketing definition describes a **product** as a bundle of physical, service, and symbolic attributes designed to provide customer satisfaction. Included in this broader definition are considerations of package design, brand names, warranties, and product image.

Focusing on Benefits

The CEO of a major appliance manufacturer once startled his stockholders with this statement: "Last year our customers bought over 1 million quarter-inch drill bits, and none of them wanted to buy the product. They all wanted quarter-inch holes." Successful marketers recognize the need to focus their firm's product-design, packaging, and promotional decisions on giving consumers the bundle of benefits they seek from the product.

Tommy Hilfiger isn't selling just clothing and fragrances. His apparel company offers buyers the elements of a youthful, fun-filled lifestyle; for one benefit, coordinated apparel ends worries about which shirt goes with which slacks. Hilfiger clothing lets the wearer feel good

Figure 14.1 Emphasizing Benefits for Clothing and Computers

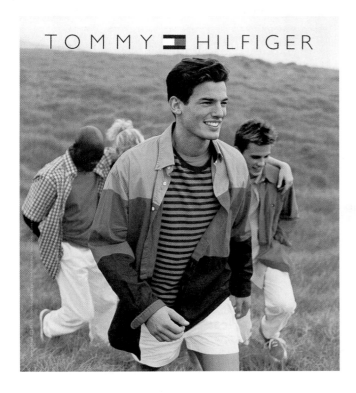

about being an American without projecting an overbearing attitude.

The need to focus on buyer solutions and product benefits is illustrated by the two examples shown in Figure 14.1. The Hilfiger ad depicts young friends enjoying each other's company; their casual, yet stylish, attire blends with their lifestyles. In the second example, NetSchools Corp. alleviates parent concerns by emphasizing the durability of its StudyPro laptop computer, which can withstand abuse by young children.

Services Are Products, Too

A considerable portion of people's budgets pays for "products" with no tangible features. A haircut, an oil change, a cellular phone call, and a weekend at the beach are all included in a broad category of products called *services*. Businesses buy services such as training programs, marketing research, delivery, building maintenance, and security. **Services** are intangible tasks that satisfy needs of final consumers or business users.

Most products that people buy combine both tangible goods and intangible services. A special dinner in a good restaurant is expected to include excellent food and a similar level of service. Purchase a new set of tires, and you may discover that such services as mounting, balancing, and periodic rotation are also included.

Without services, people would not receive mail, cash checks, attend college, or even watch movies. The service sector is becoming an increasingly significant force leading up to the 21st century, as satellite broadcasting and Internet usage continue to grow in economic importance.

Customer Service as a Product Every organization—profit-seeking and not-for-profit, large corporations and sole proprietorships, manufacturers and service providers—must recognize the importance of customer service and include it as a key ingredient in all product offerings. Every employee must demonstrate a commitment to making a happy customer. Paying attention to every detail in the process of delivering satisfaction is the key to success in contemporary business. Organizations with such a focus want to give customers experiences that exceed any they had with competitors.

Warranties Are Important, Too A warranty or guarantee is an added benefit that accompanies a tangible good or service. A **warranty** is a legal guarantee that a good or service will serve the purpose for which it is intended. Warranties make integral contributions to customer service in that they protect consumers from dissatisfaction. Even when a company states no such protections, certain rights are always guaranteed to consumers by law. In addition to these implied rights, sellers may offer explicit product warranties or guarantees. A major factor in the quality image of Zippo lighters and Cross pens is the lifetime warranty each product carries. No proof of purchase is needed; simply return a defective lighter or pen to the manufacturer, and it will be repaired or replaced free of charge.

Cable television marketers have begun to offer warranties to set their services apart in this increasingly competitive industry. In recent years, cable companies have faced erosion of their earlier monopoly positions as well as new competitors like satellite-dish communications and wireless microwave services. To combat these rivals and to counter widespread perceptions of weak concern for customer service, a number of major cable TV suppliers have agreed to industrywide service guarantees. A customer typically receives a month of free service if the company fails to fulfill its service pledges.

CLASSIFYING CONSUMER AND BUSINESS PRODUCTS

Following the distinction between consumer markets and business markets, products can be broadly categorized as either consumer products or business products, depending on who purchases them for what reasons. A sweater purchased by someone who wants an addition to her personal wardrobe is a consumer product. A group of sweaters purchased by a clothing buyer at Dillard's department stores will be added to the store's inventory and eventually resold. Both the consumer products and business products categories can be further subdivided. By determining the category into which each product falls, marketers gain extensive information regarding the ap-

propriate distribution, promotion, and pricing strategies to use in marketing it.

www.dillards.com

Categories of Consumer Products

Marketers focus on consumer buying habits to classify consumer products by type. They seek answers to several questions regarding purchases: Who? What? When? Where? How? The answers place a purchase in one of three categories—convenience, shopping, and specialty products.

Convenience products are items that consumers purchase frequently, immediately, and with little effort. Vending machines, Circle K stores, and local magazine stands usually stock convenience products. Examples include newspapers, chewing gum, magazines, milk, beer, bread, and snack foods.

Shopping products are typically purchased only after comparisons between products in competing stores to evaluate such characteristics as price, quality, style, and color. Someone looking for carpet may visit several flooring showrooms, examine dozens of patterns and colors, and spend days making the final decision.

Specialty products are those that purchasers are willing to make special efforts to obtain. Purchasers of specialty products are already familiar with the items and see no reasonable substitutes for them. Specialty products tend to carry expensive price tags and well-known brand names. Often, they are distributed through limited numbers of exclusive dealers in specific geographic areas. Examples include Louis Vuitton luggage, Porsche autos, designer clothing, and flights to Europe on the Concorde.

Remember that the good or service itself does not determine its classification. Rather, classification depends on predominant purchasing patterns. A convenience item for one person may be a shopping good for someone else, but if the product is purchased most often on the basis of convenience, then it will be classified as such. The Timex watch in Figure 14.2 fits the classification of a shopping product; however, the diamond-encrusted Gucci model is a specialty good.

Categories of Business Goods and Services

Business products (also known as *industrial* or *organizational products)* fall into five main categories: installations, accessory equipment, component parts and materials, raw

> **They said it**
>
> "In our factory, we make lipstick. In our advertising, we sell hope."
>
> Charles Revson (1906–1975)
> Chairman, Revlon, Inc.

Figure 14.2 **Differentiating between a Shopping Product and a Specialty Product**

materials, and supplies. While marketers classify consumer products according to buying patterns, business product classifications are based on how customers use them as well as their basic characteristics. Long-lived products whose sales usually involve large sums of money are called *capital items*. Less costly products that are consumed within a year are referred to as *expense items*.

Installations are pieces or collections of major capital equipment such as new factory systems, heavy machinery, and custom-made equipment. Business buyers use installations in producing goods and services for sale to their own customers. New locomotives represent installations for the Burlington Northern Railroad. A newly constructed bottling plant in Hungary is an installation for Coca-Cola's international operations.

Accessory equipment includes capital items that are usually less expensive and shorter-lived than installations. Examples are hand tools, scanners, and fax machines. Buyers use some accessory equipment, such as portable drills, to produce other goods and services. Other equipment, such as a personal computer, helps them to perform important administrative and operating functions.

Component parts and materials are business products that are included as part of other firms' final products. Some component parts become visible in finished goods, such as the BFGoodrich T/A tires shown in Figure 14.3. BFGoodrich supplies the tires as standard equipment on every Callaway Speedster.

Raw materials are similar to component parts and materials, because they become inputs in the production of other firms' final products. The list includes farm products such as cotton, wheat, fertilizer, cattle, and milk as well as natural materials, like iron ore, turquoise, lumber, and coal. Standardized grading assures buyers of most raw materials that they receive products of uniform quality.

Supplies are expense items used in a firm's daily operations that do not become part of final products. They can

include paper, pens, paper clips, light bulbs, and cleaning supplies.

Categories of Services

Both ultimate consumers and business purchasers represent markets for services. Child-care centers and shoe-repair shops provide services for consumers, while Manpower's temporary personnel and Andersen Consulting's business advisors offer business services. Like tangible goods, services can be distinguished on the basis of their buyers and how they use the products. When Terminix sprays an apartment to eradicate pests, it is performing a consumer service. Performing a similar service for an office complex, it sells a business service.

Like tangible goods, services can also be categorized as convenience, shopping, or specialty products, depending on the buying patterns of customers. However, six characteristics distinguish them from goods:

▼ Services, unlike goods, are intangible products.

▼ From a buyer's perspective, the service provider

Figure 14.3 **Component Parts: Critical Elements of the Finished Product**

is the service; the two are inseparable in the buyer's mind.

▼ Services are perishable, because firms cannot stockpile them in inventory.

▼ Services cannot easily be standardized, since they must suit individual customers' needs.

▼ The customer often plays a major role in marketing, producing, and distributing a service.

▼ Service quality shows wide variations, some of them tied directly to price.

Marketing Strategy Implications for Consumer and Business Products

A classification scheme for consumer and business products is a useful tool in developing marketing strategies. For example, after classifying an item as a shopping product,

marketers gain an immediate idea of its promotion, pricing, and distribution needs. Figure 14.4 details the impact of the consumer product classifications on various aspects of a marketing strategy.

Business products require different marketing strategies. Because manufacturers market most installations and many component parts directly to relatively small numbers of buyers, their promotional efforts emphasize personal selling rather than advertising. By contrast, marketers of supplies and accessory equipment rely more heavily on advertising, since they distribute their products through intermediaries, such as the wholesalers discussed in Chapter 15. Additionally, producers of installations and component parts may involve their customers in new-product development, especially for custom-made business products. Finally, firms that market supplies and accessory equipment place greater emphasis on competitive pricing strategies than do other business products marketers, who tend to concentrate on product quality and service.

Figure 14.4 **Marketing Impacts of Consumer Product Classifications**

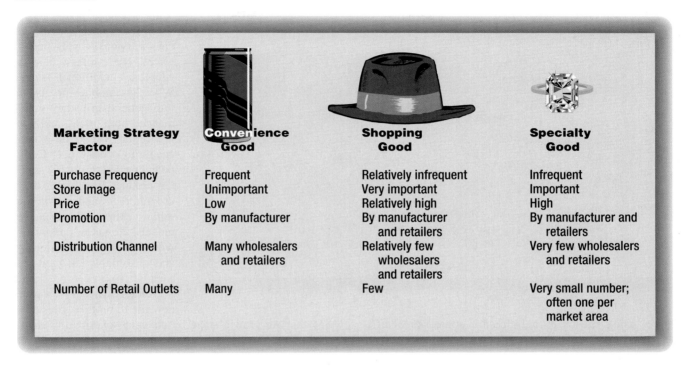

Marketing Strategy Factor	Convenience Good	Shopping Good	Specialty Good
Purchase Frequency	Frequent	Relatively infrequent	Infrequent
Store Image	Unimportant	Very important	Important
Price	Low	Relatively high	High
Promotion	By manufacturer	By manufacturer and retailers	By manufacturer and retailers
Distribution Channel	Many wholesalers and retailers	Relatively few wholesalers and retailers	Very few wholesalers and retailers
Number of Retail Outlets	Many	Few	Very small number; often one per market area

THE PRODUCT LIFE CYCLE

Successful products pass through several stages from initial introduction to ultimate sales decline and departure from the marketplace. The **product life cycle** spans four stages: introduction, growth, maturity, and decline. Figure 14.5 shows typical industry sales and profits over such a period and cites current examples of products in each life-cycle stage.

Products take widely varying amounts of time to pass through each life-cycle stage. A new fad item may have a total life span of 2 or 3 years or even less, with an introductory stage of only 90 days. By contrast, refrigerators have held in the maturity stage for over 50 years. Increasing competition and rapid improvements in technology compress many products' life cycles and force some products to extinction.

Promotional emphasis shifts from providing product information in the early stages to heavy brand promotion in the highly competitive later ones. Profits assume a similarly predictable pattern through the stages. Understanding the characteristics of all four stages of the product life cycle helps marketers to adapt their marketing strategies to fit each life-cycle stage.

Introduction

In the early stages of the product life cycle, the firm attempts to build demand for its new offering. Because neither consumers nor distributors may be aware of the product, promotional programs inform the market about the item and explain its features, uses, and benefits.

The fast-paced information technology industry launches so many new products that even the most technology-oriented customer must struggle to keep up with progress. Mention one of its latest innovations, voice-recognition software, and it may conjure up images of HAL, the renegade computer in the classic movie *2001: A Space Odyssey.* But marketers who introduced this product in 1997 recognized that their immediate task was to gain consumer awareness and find ways to entice early users to try out the innovation. Once people become acquainted with the system's ease of use and other advantages, orders will begin to grow. According to one industry expert, "By 2001, we'll see around 30 percent

Business Directory

product life cycle four basic stages through which a successful product progresses—introduction, growth, maturity, and decline.

| Figure 14.5 | **Stages in the Product Life Cycle** |

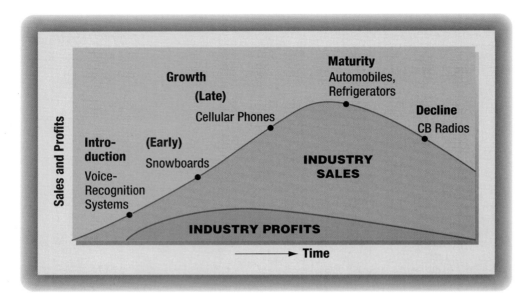

To expand its share of a growing market, a firm may begin to change styles, target specific segments with different versions, and lower prices. These efforts help to stimulate additional sales. When automobiles first came into general use, they commanded high prices, and you just about had to be a mechanic to operate one. Computers passed through a similar product life cycle; only programmers understood the initial, extremely expensive models. However, computers will soon be as user-friendly and affordable as today's cars.[3]

of users using speech recognition for some aspect of their daily work."[2]

A firm incurs financial losses during the introduction stage of the life cycle due to low initial sales, expenses involved in developing the new product, and the promotional outlays needed to inform prospective buyers about it. Although a firm like Procter & Gamble or Lever Bros. may spend over $20 million launching a new detergent, such expenditures create the possibility that the marketer will benefit from the profits associated with later life-cycle stages.

Growth

Sales climb quickly during a product's growth stage, as new customers join the early users, who are now repurchasing the item. Person-to-person referrals and continued promotion by the firm induce others to make trial purchases. The climbing sales volume begins to generate profits.

During the early part of the growth stage, marketing efforts continue to focus on establishing a product in the market and building brand awareness. Seeing opportunities for high profits, competitors begin to enter the field with similar offerings.

Later in the growth stage, the strategy shifts to building loyalty among consumers and intermediaries. Industry sales continue to grow, but at a slowing rate, since most potential buyers have purchased the product.

Other firms try to give new life to product sales during the late growth stage by changing distribution channels. Amy Nye has made a career by establishing a direct route to CD buyers. She opened her first AltiTUNES outlets in three New York-area airport terminals. Says Nye, "I prefer a kiosk because you can do the same or better business, but it costs half as much to build. Operating out of 12 kiosks in six airports, AltiTUNES now generates sales over $2 million."[4]

Maturity

Industry sales continue increasing early in the maturity stage, but eventually they reach a saturation level that limits further expansion. Marketers emphasize market segmentation during this time, frequently adding new product variations aimed at different customer groups. Often, this activity results in an oversupply of the product in an already saturated marketplace. Competition intensifies, as firms realize that market share growth usually requires them to take away sales from competitors. Some marketers reduce prices to enhance their own products' appeal.

Extending the Product Life Cycle During the maturity stage, firms spend heavily on promotion to protect their market shares and to distinguish their products from those of competitors. They also try hard to extend the product life cycle. Marketers use several methods to promote continued growth, including increasing frequency of use; seeking new customers and untapped market segments; finding new product uses; and changing package sizes and labels and product designs. Service companies focus on improving or adding new service features and promote guarantees of satisfaction. Most companies also try to add new prod-

Figure 14.6 **Extending the Product Life Cycle of Cereal by Targeting Adults for Promotions**

Who crunches 1/3 of the adult cereal? 50+!

You'll be bowled over by the billions of bowls of flakes, fibers, crisps, oats, and oatmeal that 50+ consumes. To get a place at the breakfast table, call Steve Alexander at 212-599-1880. It's a new face. A new voice. A new market.

Modern Maturity
A new market.

ucts regularly so that their offerings occupy all stages of the product life cycle.

After a series of price wars in the mid-1990s, breakfast-cereal marketers looked for new ways to change the image of their product as more than just a morning meal for kids. Kellogg's launched a spin-off of its highly popular Corn Flakes cereal, Honey Crunch Corn Flakes, targeting the adult population, who eat cereal morning, noon, and night. Why are adults so attracted to cereal these days? Many regard it as a quick, nutritious food. In fact, some claim that cereal is the ultimate fast food, especially if eaten straight from the box. Says one marketing consultant, "Consumers want food no more than 5 minutes from their right arm. Cereal makes that deadline." After just 1 year of adult-oriented promotions, ready-to-eat cereal doubled in sales.[5] As Figure 14.6 points out, people aged 50 and older consume one-third of all Cheerios, Kellogg's Corn Flakes, Grape-Nuts Flakes, and other adult cereals.

Decline

Industry sales fall steadily during the decline stage, as changing consumer preferences or the introduction of a

significant product innovation causes purchasing patterns to shift toward new alternatives. Sales of station wagons nose-dived in the wake of expanding demand for sport-utility vehicles. Cassette tape sales have also slowed as music lovers have converted to CDs.

Although the industry as a whole does not generate profits during the decline stage, some producers can prosper as a growing number of their competitors exit the industry. Prices tend to hold steady if a loyal market segment continues to buy the product. Because they expect a continuing sales decline, marketers are reluctant to invest in significant changes in a product's style, design, or other features during this stage.

Marketing Strategies for Stages in the Product Life Cycle

The product life cycle concept is an invaluable management tool. Table 14.1 shows appropriate adaptations to marketing strategies to match the characteristics of each stage. Each element of the marketing mix may require adjustment as the product moves from one stage to the next.

Table 14.1	Marketing Strategies for Stages in the Product Life Cycle				

Objective	Competition	Product	Price	Place (Distribution)	Promotion
INTRODUCTION					
Build consumer awareness Encourage trial purchases	Few direct competitors	Highly standardized product Few variations in features	Either skimming (high price) or penetration (low price)	Set up a distribution network	Heavy expenditures on informative promotion and advertising
GROWTH					
Build brand loyalty and market share Practice market segmentation	Competition intensifies as high profits attract new entries	Differentiated products for different market segments	Different prices for different segments	Expand distribution coverage	Focus on building demand and strengthening brand preference
MATURITY					
Seek new product uses—and users Encourage increasing purchase frequency	Intense competition as marketers practice market segmentation	Emphasis on quality and cost reductions	Pricing to maintain market share and meet competition	Emphasize relationship marketing to build dealer loyalty	Promotion to wholesalers and retailers Consumer promotions focus on persuasive and reminder advertising
DECLINE					
Consider leaving the industry if declining sales result in losses	Competitors begin to leave the industry	Few changes in product features	Stable prices Resistance to price cutting	Begin to phase out marginal dealers	Minimal promotion

The product life cycle concept is a useful tool for designing a marketing strategy flexible enough to match the varying marketplace characteristics at different life-cycle stages. For instance, marketers know that advertising emphasis will change from informative to persuasive messages as the product faces new competitors during the growth stage; this understanding permits them to anticipate competitors' actions and make necessary adjustments. These competitive moves may include product and package variations and changes in pricing and distribution.

Examples of *product variations* might include Plymouth's introduction of its Prowler, a racy roadster, to compete with Mercedes-Benz and BMW models in the United

States. In the Philippines, Jollibee Foods, a local fast-food franchiser, has bested global giant McDonald's by adjusting its product seasonings and menu offerings to cater to local tastes. As the firm's international manager, Manola Tingzon, puts it, "We have come up with dishes that are popular in the country we're in, and we make the burgers suitable to their palate." In addition to fries and burgers, Jollibee offers chicken curry in its Indonesian stores and a spicy chicken dish in China. These efforts to tailor its food to local tastes have given Jollibee a 56 percent market share in Asia, far surpassing McDonald's 19 percent share.[6]

Package variations have been particularly effective strategic adaptations in the late 1990s, as marketers have targeted the aging segment of the U.S. population. Brands asleep for decades are back. From Cracker Jack to Burma Shave, companies are pulling nostalgic packaging out of the closet or linking today's product to remembered glories. Volkswagen is a perfect example of such a back-to-the-future strategy. The company reintroduced the Beetle with Flower Power advertisements targeting the 1960s hippie generation, many of whom fondly remember painting Bugs with bright, day-glo flowers. The German car maker quickly explains, however, that the "groovy" new Beetle is definitely not short on comforts. Such a strategy gives a sense of familiarity and credibility to the product. As one Generation X consumer puts it, "I see it more as rediscovering than retro." Marketers also know that the nostalgia fad is not simply about Americans reliving a Golden Age; it is about remembering the best parts of the past and giving them new life in a new age.[7]

www www3.vw.com/index1.htm

Price changes, such as the breakfast-cereal price wars of the late 1990s, force industrywide adaptation. In addition, *changes in distribution* contribute to marketing efforts for many firms entering foreign markets or facing fierce competition.

PRODUCT LINES AND THE PRODUCT MIX

The product life cycle concept is a helpful tool for making product decisions. However, companies usually sell more than just a single product. Rather, they offer several different, complementary products or develop new products to replace those finishing out their life cycles. A company's **product line** is a group of related products marked by physical similarities or intended for a similar market. Figure 14.7 highlights various product lines that make up Procter & Gamble's **product mix,** the combination of goods and services that a firm offers to consumers and business users. P&G's product mix consists of several product lines: soap, detergents, toothpastes, shampoos, and paper tissue products. Service

Figure 14.7 Product Mix and Product Lines for Procter & Gamble

Product Lines	Product Mix
Bar soap	Camay, Coast, Safeguard, Zest
Cleaners and cleansers	Comet, Mr. Clean, Spic & Span, Top Job
Cooking oils	Crisco, Puritan
Dishwasher detergents	Cascade, Dawn, Ivory Liquid, Joy
Disposable diapers	Luvs, Pampers
Paper products	Banner, Charmin, Puffs, White Cloud
Shampoos	Head & Shoulders, Ivory, Pert Plus, Prell
Toothpastes	Crest, Gleem

providers also define product lines and product mixes. A beauty salon may offer hair-cutting, coloring, and styling services as well as manicures and facials.

Marketers must continually assess their firm's product mix to ensure company growth, to satisfy changing consumer needs and wants, and to respond to competing offerings. Consumer concerns about health, for instance, have led to the introduction of reduced-fat versions of many food items.

Clearly, successful product mixes and product lines undergo constant change. To remain competitive, marketers look for gaps in their firm's assortment and fill them with new products or modified versions of current ones. The firm may also gain by canceling a particular product line. DaimlerChrysler recently pulled the plug on its line of Eagle cars. Says one dealer, "Getting rid of it won't amount to a hill of beans. I have one Eagle Talon on the lot—and it's been sitting there for 6 months." The company can redirect the resources devoted to the line to other product lines. General Motors is also dropping marginal models. With more than 30 nameplates, it recently stopped production of the Buick Skylark and Roadmaster and the Chevrolet Caprice.[8]

NEW-PRODUCT DEVELOPMENT

New products are the lifeblood of any organization. Few products remain economically viable for extended periods,

Business Directory

product line group of related products that are physically similar or are intended for a similar market.

product mix company's assortment of product lines and individual offerings.

so a firm must periodically add new ones to assure continued prosperity. Some new products may result from major technological breakthroughs; others simply extend current product lines.

At each stage of new-product development, the potential for failure increases. In fact, estimates suggest that firms work on 50 new-product ideas for every product that finally reaches the marketplace. An estimated 20,000 new household, grocery, and drugstore items are introduced in a typical year, but only one in ten ever sits on retailers' shelves.

Product Development Strategies

A firm's product development strategy depends on its existing product mix, the match between current offerings and overall marketing objectives, and the current market positions of products early in their life cycles. The product development strategy matrix in Figure 14.8 illustrates the interactive roles of product and market characteristics.

A *market development strategy* concentrates on finding new markets for current products. Market segmentation, discussed earlier in Chapter 13, is a useful tool for implementing such a strategy. A *product development strategy* seeks to introduce new products into identifiable or established markets. Firms often try to increase market share by introducing new products into markets where they already have established positions. General Electric pursued this strategy when it decided to invest $10 million to back the wind-up flashlight manufactured by South African company BayGen. The $60 flashlights produce only 4 to 5 minutes of light per winding, which limits their usefulness except in emergencies, but for GE, they represent a new addition to its product line. BayGen is also working on crank-type cellular phones and personal computers.[9]

Figure 14.8 **Alternative Product Development Strategies**

	Old Product	New Product
Old Market	Market Penetration	Product Development
New Market	Market Development	Product Diversification

A *market penetration strategy* seeks to increase sales of current products in familiar markets. Firms using this strategy may modify products, improve quality, or promote new uses and benefits. The fourth alternative, a *product diversification strategy,* focuses on developing entirely new products for new markets. Some firms look for new target markets that complement their existing markets; others look in completely new directions.

Stages in New-Product Development

The most successful new products are significant innovations that deliver unique benefits. Getting a new product to market involves an orderly process of overlapping steps. Throughout this effort, teamwork among experts across divisional boundaries often allows a firm to strengthen its new-product development process. Figure 14.9 shows the path that new-product development follows.

Firms aim most newly developed products at satisfying specific customer needs or wants. New-product development is becoming an increasingly efficient and cost-effective practice, because marketers use the systematic methods discussed in the following paragraphs.

Generating New-Product Ideas
The process starts by generating ideas for new offerings. Ideas come from many sources, including customers, suppliers, employees, research scientists, marketing researchers, inventors outside the firm, and competing products. The most successful ideas work directly to satisfy customer needs or resolve consumer complaints.

Screening In screening ideas, marketers evaluate their commercial potential. Some organizations maintain checklists of development standards that guide judgments about whether an idea should be

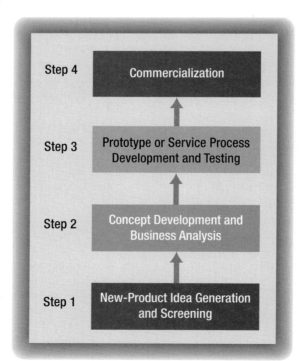

Figure 14.9 **Process for Developing New Goods and Services**

Step 4 — Commercialization

Step 3 — Prototype or Service Process Development and Testing

Step 2 — Concept Development and Business Analysis

Step 1 — New-Product Idea Generation and Screening

Internet Help for Inventors

Lots of people conceive innovative ideas, but only a few convert those "Wouldn't it be great if . . ." ideas into successful products. Most lack any experience in taking a product to market and don't know where to begin. If you're one of them, help is on the way via the Internet.

The Net now allows inventors to gather all kinds of information anonymously and without having to reveal their product ideas to others. These Web sites offer some of the best online sources for the various aspects of turning an idea into a profitable business venture.

▼ **www.ibm.com/patent:** In addition to the U.S. Patent and Trademark Office, inventors can visit this IBM-sponsored site to perform patent searches.

▼ **www.invent.org:** The National Inventors' Hall of Fame manages this site, which contains information about inventor competitions and contests. It also suggests many related Web sites.

▼ **www.inventing.com:** This Boston-based Web site maintained by Impulse Communications will display information about your idea for a monthly fee ($20). The site also lists firms willing to help inventors.

▼ **www.inventnet.com:** This site provides independent inventors with up-to-the-minute information and assistance in developing and marketing their inventions.

▼ **www.thomasregister.com:** The *Thomas Register* is a traditional, multivolume library resource listing manufacturers of all kinds of products. It is now online with listings for more than 155,000 U.S. and Canadian manufacturers.

▼ **www.tscentral.com:** This Trade Show Central site offers details on more than 30,000 trade shows, and some allow online registration.

Source: Tomima Edmark, "At Your Fingertips," *Entrepreneur*, March 1998, pp. 100–103.

abandoned or considered further. The screening stage may also allow for open discussions of new-product ideas among representatives of different functional areas in an organization.

Business Analysis Further evaluations determine whether ideas that survive the screening stage fit with the company's product, distribution, and promotional resources. Marketers also assess potential sales, profits, growth rate, and competitive strengths. This stage includes concept testing, or marketing research designed to solicit initial consumer reactions to new-product ideas before proceeding with product development. The Business Tool Kit suggests some Internet-based resources to help with evaluation of a product idea.

Prototype or Service Process Development Financial outlays increase substantially as a firm first converts a product idea into a physical product. At this stage, it creates a functioning prototype or a detailed description of the services to be provided. The conversion process is the joint responsibility of the firm's development engineers and its marketers, who provide feedback on consumer reactions to the proposed product design, package, color, and other physical features.

An innovation may commonly take 15 or 20 years to become a marketable product. However, some products never get off the ground, their development hampered by government regulations, lack of capital resources, or simply failure to create a working model. Alliant Techsystems Inc. has overcome many of these challenges, but, after nearly 20 years and $3 billion in research and development, its unmanned aerial vehicle (UAV) still sits in the hangar. Meanwhile, Israel Aircraft Industries refined the existing technology and began selling UAVs in the 1970s. IAI generates $160 million a year from its pilotless planes, which offer far fewer capabilities than the Alliant prototype.[10]

A prototype may go through numerous modifications before the original mock-up reaches the stage of a final product. Many firms implement computer-aided design systems to reduce the number of prototypes that developers must build. Tests measure the product's actual features and benefits as well as consumer perceptions of it. Inadequate testing during this stage can doom a product introduction, and even a company, to failure.

Nissan recently tried to capitalize on consumer acceptance of its Infiniti QX4 model by extending that luxury product line to include a sport-utility vehicle. Infiniti designers worked up five different designs, while marketers surveyed 200 Infiniti and non-Infiniti customers throughout the United States. Three criteria guided selection of the survey participants: age (35-64), income (more than $125,000 annually), and willingness to buy a luxury car. Based on the winning design, clay and fiberglass models were constructed. About 100 customers and a 10-member advisory board provided input at each phase of development. Only 6 months after the prototype was built, the new QX4 sport utility was in dealer showrooms across the nation.[11]

Test Marketing To gauge consumer acceptance of a product, many firms test market their new offerings. Up to this point, the product development team has obtained consumer feedback by submitting free products to consumers, who then give their reactions. Test marketing is the first stage at which the product must perform in a real-life business environment.

Test marketing introduces a trial version of a new product, supported by a complete marketing campaign, to a selected city or media coverage area with a population reasonably similar to that of the total market. Test market results help managers to determine the product's likely performance in a full-scale introduction.

Some firms choose to skip test marketing and move directly from product development to commercialization. These companies cite four main problems with using test marketing:

1. Test marketing is an expensive project.

2. Competitors who learn about a test marketing project may try to skew results by lowering their prices, distributing coupons, or running special promotions in the area.

3. Long-lived durable goods (like refrigerators and televisions) are seldom test marketed due to the major financial investments required to develop and launch them.

4. Test marketing can alert competitors to future plans prior to full-scale introduction.

In general, marketers should omit test marketing only for a product that is highly likely to succeed. Companies deciding to skip test marketing can choose several other options for predicting market acceptance. A firm may simulate a test marketing campaign through computer modeling software. A second approach is actually a compromise between a small-scale test market and a full-scale market launch. Marketers using this approach may offer the item in a single geographic region and use feedback from this partial launch to adjust prices, vary options or warranty terms, change promotional appeals, or modify channels for distributing the product. Another option is to limit a product's introduction to just one retail chain, which allows marketers to control and evaluate promotions and results. In still another method, a firm may try out a new product in another country before marketing it in the United States or the entire world.

Commercialization In this stage, sometimes referred to as a *product launch,* the firm offers its new product in the general marketplace. Although a company invests considerable time and money in devising pricing, distribution, and promotion strategies to support the new product offering, success is not guaranteed until consumer acceptance is achieved. Gerber baby-food marketers recently learned this lesson when they tried to market the company's Singles line of meals-in-a-jar for adults. Most consumers regarded the concept of "Gerber for Adults" as an oxymoron. Since the name Gerber has become synonymous with nutrition for babies and pureed food products, the brand never found a responsive adult market.

A firm must establish marketing programs, fund outlays for production facilities, and acquaint its sales force, marketing intermediaries, and potential customers with the new product. A firm today can expect to spend $20 million to $50 million to complete a successful new-product launch. However, of some 25,000 new items that appear each year, fewer than 20 percent succeed.[12] The Business Hall of Fame on pages 466 and 467 relates the story of C. J. Walter who in 1906 turned an investment of $1.50 into a fortune.

PRODUCT IDENTIFICATION

Organizations identify their products in several ways, including distinctive brands, packages, and labels. This section's discussion of product identification begins with a look at brands, brand names, and trademarks. Almost every product design incorporates some way for consumers to distinguish it from others. A **brand** is a name, term, sign, symbol, design, or some combination of these elements that helps to identify a firm's products and differentiate them from competitors' offerings. Diet Coke, Dr Pepper, and Surge are all made by the Coca-Cola Company, but a unique combination of name, symbol, and package design distinguishes each brand from the others.

Business Directory

test marketing trial introduction of a new product, supported by a complete marketing campaign, to a selected area with a population typical of the total market.

brand name, term, sign, symbol, design, or some combination that identifies the products of a firm.

BUSINESS TOOL KIT

How to Register Your Trademark

A trademark is "any mark in any form that serves to identify a company's products and distinguish them from the offerings of competitors." For this reason, firms cannot secure exclusive rights to use descriptive, generic words like *cola, aspirin, bicycle,* or *elevator*. Also, they must overcome extremely difficult obstacles to register colors. (Owens Corning did manage to acquire exclusive use of the color pink for its fiberglass insulation by convincing the court that its extensive use of the Pink Panther cartoon character in its promotions had conditioned the buying public to identify its product by the color.) You stand a much better chance of successfully registering your brand if you use a letter, word, phrase, number, picture, design, or a combination than if you seek to protect a less specific characteristic.

You don't need a lawyer to secure trademark protection. Simply follow this four-step process.

1. **Obtain a written application by calling the U.S. Patent and Trademark Office at 800–786–9199, or visit the agency's Web site:**

www.uspto.gov

Complete the application, including your name, citizenship status, address, verification that you own the mark and that it is not currently in use by another legal entity, and proof of either the first date you used the mark, its first use in commerce, or when you intend to use it. You must also specify the class of merchandise under which your trademark falls.

2. **Provide an accurate drawing of the mark. If you are seeking protection for a letter, number, or combination, you can simply type the trademark on a clean sheet of paper.**

3. **Submit three examples of the actual trademark as it is or will be used.**

4. **Enclose a check or money order to cover the registration fee, currently $245 for each class of merchandise under which you want your trademark registered.**

Once you have a registered trademark, you should insert ™ beside it. Trademark registrations limit access by others for 20 years, but if you don't use it, you lose it.

Source: Adapted from "Registering Your Trademark," *Entrepreneur*, April 1997, p. 96.

A **brand name** is the part of a brand consisting of words or letters that form a name that identifies and distinguishes the firm's offering from those of competitors. A brand name is the part of a brand that can be vocalized; a *brand mark* is a symbol or pictorial design that cannot be vocalized. Many brand names, such as McDonald's, Ford, American Express, and IBM, are famous around the world.

Brands are important elements of product images. If consumers are aware of a particular brand, its appearance anywhere becomes advertising for the firm. Nike's trademark swoosh, for example, provides instant advertising to anyone who sees it. Successful branding also helps a firm to escape some price competition, since well-known brands often sell at considerable price premiums over their competitors.

A **trademark** is a brand with legal protection against another company's use, not only of the brand name, but also of pictorial designs, slogans, packaging elements, and product features such as color and shape. Harley-Davidson has established trademark protection for its name, slogan,

and emblem. The Business Tool Kit explains how to register a trademark.

Mercedes recently launched an advertising campaign linking its trademark to an image of glamour and sex appeal. Look closely at the ad in Figure 14.10 and you will see the Mercedes Benz three-pronged trademark substituted for film-star Marilyn Monroe's beauty mark.

Brand Categories

Some firms market their goods and services without any efforts at branding. Such items are called **generic products** or *generic brands*. They are characterized by plain packaging, minimal labeling, and little or no advertising; generally, they meet only minimal quality standards. Generic brands are typically priced considerably lower than comparable manufacturers' and private brands.

Most products carry distinctive brand names. Even standardized grocery items like fruit, vegetables, and prepared salads carry small labels identifying them as Dole grapes, Sunkist lemons, or Chiquita bananas. Companies that practice branding classify brands in several ways: manufacturer's (national) brands, private (store) brands, family brands, and individual brands. In making branding decisions, marketers must weigh the benefits and shortcomings of each type of brand.

Family and Individual Brands A **family brand** is a single brand name that identifies several related products. For example, Sears markets a complete line of appliances under the Kenmore brand name, and Nike's famous brand includes athletic shoes, apparel, and accessories. Figure 14.11 promotes the Land O' Lakes line of dairy products with the tag line, "The good things in life never really change."

When a firm that practices family branding introduces a new product, both customers and retailers recognize the familiar brand name. Promoting individual products in the line benefits all products within the well-known family brand.

Other firms create **individual brands** by giving a different brand name to each product within a line. For example, Lever Bros. markets its different bath soaps (Caress, Dove, Lifebuoy, and Lux) and toothpastes (Aim, Close Up, and Pepsodent) under individual brand names. Each brand targets a unique market segment. Lever Bros. hopes that toothpaste purchasers who dislike Pepsodent will buy another of its own brands like Close Up instead of a competitor's brand. Individual branding builds competition within a firm and enables the company to increase overall sales.

Manufacturer's Brand versus Private Brand A brand offered and promoted by a manufacturer or producer is known as a **manufacturer's brand** (or *national brand*). Examples include Chanel, Swatch, Bic, Crest, and Dr Pepper. Clorox Co., which controls over 70 percent of its market, has recently tried to distance itself from private-label products and competition from giants like Procter & Gamble by assuming the role of leader in quality bleach

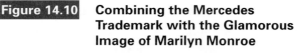

Figure 14.10 **Combining the Mercedes Trademark with the Glamorous Image of Marilyn Monroe**

products. Betting on the value of its brand, the Clorox product carries a price 30 percent higher than store label products.[13]

However, not all brand names belong to producers. Some are the property of wholesalers or retailers. A **private brand** (or *store brand*) identifies a product that is not linked to the manufacturer, but instead carries the label of a retailer or wholesaler. Private label products control 25 percent of the apparel industry. JCPenney's Arizona label and Sears's Canyon River Blues line of jeans are private brands. Sears has been a leader in private brands for years with Diehard batteries, Craftsman tools, and Kenmore appliances.

The growth of private brands parallels that of chain stores in the United States. These retailers define their own brands to maintain control over the images, quality levels, and prices of products they sell. Moreover, private brands usually carry lower prices, sometimes up to 35 percent less, than manufacturer's brands. Many manufacturers boost their business with retail giants by producing products to their specifications and adding the retailers' private brands. To these producers, private brands represent additional sales. Other producers mount aggressive responses to threats from private brands in the belief that such low-priced offerings siphon off sales of their own brands.

Characteristics of an Effective Brand Name

Brand names promote buyers' awareness of the nature and quality of competing products. To accomplish this goal, they should communicate product images to consumers. One effective technique is to create a name that links the product with the positioning concept. For example, the name *Dial* reinforces the concept of 24-hour protection, and *Taster's Choice* instant coffee supports the promotional claim, "Tastes and smells like ground roast coffee."

An effective brand name must be easy to pronounce, recognize, and remember. Short names such as *Sony* and *Tide* meet this requirement, as do nicknames like *Bud* and *Coke*. Effective brand names must also attract attention. Top brand

Figure 14.11 **Promotion Based on a Family Brand**

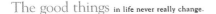

The good things in life never really change.

We just

continue

to offer your family

a lot more of them.

Made with tradition. Made for today.

names for attention-getting value are Intensive Care lotion, Cheerios, and "I Can't Believe It's Not Butter" margarine.

Some brand names identify products too effectively for the producers' own good. When a class of products becomes generally known by the original brand name of a specific offering, the brand name may legally become a *generic name*. In such cases, the original owner loses exclusive claim to the brand name. Generic names that at one time were brand names include nylon, aspirin, escalator, kerosene, and zipper.

DID YOU KNOW?

Trademark filings are hitting all-time highs, primarily due to trendy online names. In 1997, 879,300 Web sites were using a form of the word *web* in their domain names. Other popular names added to the list since then are *cyber, link, power,* and *net,* which is the most popular incorporated word-part.

Most companies take precautions to protect their brand names, though. Trademark law states that brand names cannot contain words in general use, such as *television* or *automobile*. No organization can claim exclusive use of generic words—words that describe types of products.

Marketers are increasingly hard-pressed to coin effective brand names, as multitudes of competitors rush to stake out identities for their own products. The Internet also presents new challenges for marketers searching for effective brand names, since they must now regard any Web site as a worldwide presence. An excellent brand name in one country may prove disastrous in another. Sometimes, a brand name must accommodate universal promotions or those in specific countries or regions.

To find effective names, some firms rely on computer software or databases to spew out options. Others prefer brainstorming. One brand consultant remembers coming up with a name for a communications company, Telemon. "It was wonderful," he recalls, "until we went to Thailand, where it means 'intercourse with your mother.'"[14] One helpful tool in selecting a name is to remember that every language has short *a*, long *o*, and *k* sounds; thus, Coca-Cola, Kodak, and Texaco work as effective brand names in any country.

BUSINESS HALL OF FAME

Setting the Style with Madam C. J. Walker

The black woman would not be ignored, and she shouted over the gathering: "I am a woman who came from the cotton fields of the South. I was promoted from there to the washtub. Then I was promoted to the cook kitchen. And from there I promoted myself into the business of manufacturing hair goods and preparations... I have built my own factory on my own ground." And with that, Madam C. J. Walker got the attention of everyone attending Booker T. Washington's National Negro Business League Convention in 1912. Nearly a hundred years later, she continues to get our attention.

Born Sarah Breedlove in 1867, Walker was orphaned at 7, married at 14, and widowed at 20. While working as a washerwoman around 1904, she began losing her hair, as did many black women of her time from stress, diet, and hygiene-related scalp diseases. She tried various hair products and worked for Annie Malone, founder of Poro's "Wonderful Hair Grower."

Walker was impressed by the potential of these products. She took her daughter and $1.50 in savings, moved to Denver, and married her third husband—Charles Joseph Walker, a newspaper sales agent. By 1906, Walker and her husband were in business selling Madam C. J. Walker's Wonderful Hair Grower. She claimed she got the formula for her scalp condi-

tioner from a "big African man" in a dream. But her marketing sense didn't come from a dream.

She understood that her product was more than the physical scalp conditioner. It encompassed service also. She traveled throughout the South and Southeast, selling her products to black women door to door and demonstrating her treatments in churches and lodges. She developed the Walker System, expanding her Hair Grower to a line of products, including Madam C. J. Walker's Vegetable Shampoo. She attracted clients and agents she called *hair culturists, scalp specialists,* and *beauty culturists.*

Walker understood her product's image was important—from its dream-inspired beginnings to its packaging in

BUILDING BRAND LOYALTY AND BRAND EQUITY

Brands achieve widely varying consumer familiarity and acceptance. The marketer's task is to generate the maximum possible consumer loyalty to a brand. While a racing enthusiast may insist on a Callaway Speedster when buying a car, a purchase of a loaf of bread might involve little preference for any one brand. Increasing consumer loyalty to a particular brand increases the value of that brand to the firm. Thus, brand loyalty is at the heart of brand equity. The value of a brand is its good name, which it earns as consumers become loyal to it over a period of time and through repeat purchases.[15]

However, a presence on the market for 50 years or longer still doesn't make a product a best seller for the firm. Take Vlasic pickles, a brand that creates sales of $250 million a year. Still, Campbell Soup Co. sees the products as a slow-growing, second-tier category with little room for innovation. Companies such as Campbell often sell off these second-tier brands.[16]

For years, brand-building marketing strategies remained limited to the consumer realm—products sold to retail customers, not corporate purchasing departments. Says one marketing communications director, "Business-to-business has traditionally spent a lot less on marketing communications. But the principles of good brand building apply wherever you go." Not many business-to-business

brands have become famous, although the short list includes Intel, Marriott, Xerox, and IBM, along with service providers such as Manpower and ServiceMaster. The focus on building brand equity for business brands has increased in recent years.[17]

Brand Loyalty

Marketers measure brand loyalty in three stages: brand recognition, brand preference, and brand insistence. **Brand recognition** is brand acceptance strong enough that the consumer is aware of a brand, but not enough to cause a preference over competing brands. Advertising and distributing free samples are the most common ways to increase brand recognition. Once consumers have used a product, seen it advertised, or noticed it in stores, it moves from the unknown to the known category, increasing the probability that they will purchase it. Other strategies include offering discount coupons for purchases.

Measuring the effectiveness of these methods has been a marketing task for decades. New York-based Target Marketing & Research surveyed 2,000 people attending state fairs and other special events in eight cities to gauge the influence of samples on brand trial, brand loyalty, and brand switching. Most respondents said they evaluated products based on samples. This method was followed in order of effectiveness by word-of-mouth reports, coupons, adver-

decorative tin canisters and its name. Even her "Walker agents" supported the product image, making house calls in white shirtwaists tucked into long black skirts and carrying black satchels with the preparations. Basically, Walker understood that she was in business to satisfy customers.

www.madamcjwalker.com

In 1908 she opened Lelia College to train her agents in how to use, demonstrate, and sell her hair-care products. She also advertised with impressive before-and-after ads, which appeared in newspapers and magazines popular with African-American readers. In 1910 she built a factory in Indianapolis, a hair and manicure salon, and another training school. In 1913 Walker expanded her business into Central America and the Caribbean. As her business grew, Walker organized her agents into local and state clubs. And in 1917, she held a convention in Philadelphia for her Madam C. J. Walker Hair Culturists Union of America—one of the first national meetings of U.S. businesswomen.

By the time of her death in 1919, Madam C. J. Walker had become not only a millionaire but also one of the most successful business executives in the early 20th century, a philanthropist (supporting causes such as the Indianapolis YMCA), and a social activist (taking special interest in the NAACP's anti-lynching movement).

QUESTIONS FOR CRITICAL THINKING

1. Madam C. J. Walker Enterprises Inc. is still operating in Indianapolis, making its six original products. Would selling the products door to door still work today? Explain.

2. Would Madam C. J. Walker's hair-care products be considered convenience goods, shopping goods, or specialty goods? Explain.

Sources: "Madam C. J. Walker," accessed at www.madamcjwalker.com, March 19, 1999; "Faces of Science: African Americans in the Sciences," accessed at www.lib.lsu.edu, March 19, 1999; Lawrence Otis Graham, "Living in a Class Apart," *U.S. News & World Report*, February 15, 1999, pp. 48–52; Henry Louis Gates Jr., "Madam's Crusade," *Time*, December 7, 1998, p. 165; and "Maiden Voyage," *Entrepreneur*, September 1998, p. 45.

tising, and, lastly, games and contests. Sampling at special events was the least effective way to enhance brand recognition, increase brand trials, or encourage consumers to switch brands, however; worst of all, the handouts did little for brand loyalty.[18]

More likely than not, a consumer who is satisfied with a purchase will buy that brand again. **Brand preference** occurs when a consumer chooses one firm's brand, when it is available, over a competitor's. At this stage, consumers rely on previous experience when selecting a product. Automobiles and apparel fall into this category.

Brand insistence is the ultimate degree of brand loyalty in which the consumer will accept no substitute for a preferred brand. If the desired product is not readily available, the consumer will look for another outlet, special order it from a factory, or turn to mail-order or telephone buying. A product at this stage has achieved a monopoly position with its consumers. Few firms can achieve brand insistence for their products. Cosmetics are one example of a product that might inspire this degree of brand loyalty.

Music retailer N2K has created strong brand loyalty for its niche market with its popular Web site, Music Boulevard, as Figure 14.12 shows. The firm has worked to increase brand loyalty by offering cybermusic fans easy access to their favorite artists. For example, not only do rock and roll enthusiasts have their own site, Roctropolis, but N2K has narrowed the customer focus even further with its David Bowie Web site.[19]

www.musicblvd.com
www.rocktropolis.com
www.davidbowie.com

Brand Equity

Brand equity refers to the added value that a widely respected, highly successful name gives to a product in the marketplace. This value results from a combination of factors including awareness, loyalty, and perceived quality, as well as any feelings or images the customer associates with the brand. *Brand awareness* means that the product is the

Business Directory

brand equity added value that a certain brand name gives to a product.

first one that comes to mind when a product category is mentioned. *Brand association* is a link between a brand and other favorable images. Marketers create brand awareness and association with tie-ins to other product users, a popular celebrity, a particular geographic area, or even competitors.

High brand equity offers financial advantages to a firm, since the product commands a comparatively large market share. Because brand loyalty often reduces the price sensitivity of consumers, high-equity brands generate high profits and stock returns. The Business Tool Kit on page 471 gives some suggestions for reinforcing a brand's strength.

The Value of Brand Equity
How can a business evaluate brand equity? The global advertising agency Young & Rubicam (Y&R) has developed the *Brand Asset Valuator* system that examines the brand-equity positions of over 8,000 brands around the world. According to Y&R, a firm builds brand equity around four dimensions of brand personality. As shown in Figure 14.13, they are differentiation, relevance, esteem, and knowledge. Based on these criteria, the ten global brands with the highest equity include Coca-Cola, Nescafé, Kodak, Budweiser, Kellogg's, Nike, Marlboro, Motorola, Gillette, and Bacardi.[20]

Differentiation refers to a brand's ability to stand apart from competitors. *Relevance* refers to the real and perceived importance of the brand to a large consumer segment. *Esteem* is a combination of perceived quality and consumer perceptions about the growing or declining popularity of a brand. The final brand equity dimension is *knowledge,* the extent of customers' awareness of the brand and understanding of its identity.

A typical large company assigns the task of managing a brand's marketing strategies to a *brand manager.* This marketing professional plans and implements the balance of promotional, pricing, distribution, and product arrange-

ments that leads to strong brand equity. Procter & Gamble first implemented a brand manager system in 1931.[21]

While brand managers' roles have changed in many ways since then, the functions are still critical to brand success. General Motors Europe and Ford of Europe no longer maintain centralized brand management systems. Instead, the giant automakers plan their brand management around regional needs.[22]

PACKAGES AND LABELS

The original purpose of packaging was to protect products against damage, spoilage, and theft. Labels functioned primarily to identify products and communicate usage information. Over the years, however, packaging has played an increasingly important role in product strategy. In addition to these traditional functions, both packaging and labeling support branding strategies and contribute to advertising efforts.

Only a Falcon can fly in and out of a short, 3000 ft airport today— then cross the Pacific tomorrow.

Short strips, long trips. It's a family tradition.

Engineered with passion.

A large business jet with agility? Only Dassault can deliver this—by drawing upon decades of fighter aircraft expertise. Your Falcon flies into—and out of—thousands of small airports around the globe. This legendary versatility is just one reason why Falcons are known as the best designed, best built, *best flying* business jets at the top of the market. For information about all four of the Falcon models, contact John Rosanvallon in the U.S. at (201) 541-4600 or Jean-Claude Bouxin in Paris at (331) 40-83-93-09.

DASSAULT FALCON JET
www.falconjet.com

French business jet manufacturer Dassault has launched a brand-building marketing campaign for its highly regarded Falcon model. The firm credits decades of experience making fighter aircraft for its ability to build a well-designed, comfortable line of long-distance business planes.

Packaging

A product's package can powerfully influence buyers' purchase decisions. In addition to protecting products, many manufacturers upgrade packages to convey high-quality images. Others design packages to improve product usage, and still others to reduce waste. A package serves several objectives that fit loosely under three general goals:

1. Protection against damage, spoilage, and pilferage

2. Assistance in marketing the product

3. Cost effectiveness

Packaging also offers a means for marketers to differentiate their product from competitors. Innovative packaging plays a key role in the success of global brands like Coca-Cola, Absolut vodka, and Perrier. Figure 14.14

illustrates how the French bottler of sparkling mineral water distinguishes its product from literally hundreds of competitors by featuring its shape and colorful design in print ads.

Packaging represents one of the biggest elements of production costs for many consumer products. Although it performs a number of functions for the producer, marketers, and consumers, it must do so at a reasonable cost. Some changes can make packages both cheaper and safer for the environment. Others can encourage consumer use. This second objective has guided the U.S. Census Bureau's new packaging changes for instruments to complete the 2000 population count. In addition to new type fonts and clarified wording, the bureau is also changing distribution channels for the surveys to allow responses via the Internet and toll-free phone calls. Marketers tested two envelopes. One bore a warning in bold, black letters: "YOUR RESPONSE IS REQUIRED BY LAW." The other (which the agency actually chose) shows a bright yellow circle with white letters that read, "Count me in!"[23]

Marketers today are repackaging goods at an unprecedented pace—as often as every 2 years for some products. Says one advertising agent, "You used to find you would redesign a package and it was there for 5 years minimum; maybe it's half that now."[24]

Choosing the right package is an especially crucial decision in international marketing, since worldwide sales introduce many

Figure 14.12 **Creating Brand Preference among Internet Music Lovers**

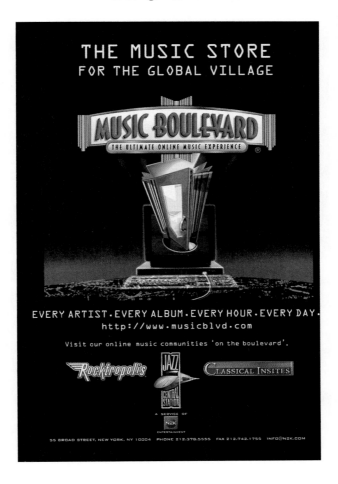

variables. According to one package design company president, "Color is the most important issue in packaging. Red is a pretty positive color worldwide, gold usually signifies quality." While green has a healthy, low-fat connotation in the United States, however, it may not convey the same message in other cultures. Package size also varies according to each country's purchasing patterns and market conditions. In Japan, Europe, and Latin America, consumers don't have much storage or refrigerator space and prefer to buy smaller packages than U.S. buyers favor. Beverages are typically sold by individual containers instead of in six-packs. Package weight is another important issue, since the cost of shipping is usually based on weight. In some areas, customs duties are also assessed according to gross shipment weights, including the packaging.[25]

Labeling

Coke and Pepsi have recently renewed their ongoing product-design battle. This time the challenge is to create the hottest new graphics for their labels—The Red or The Blue. Coca-Cola held onto existing design elements, including its script logo and curvy glass bottle, but changes added oversized water droplets and additional depth to the script type. Pepsi celebrated its 100th anniversary with updated graphics on a new, blue, crushed-ice background. Both companies plan global marketing initiatives for their new labels.[26]

Figure 14.13 **Dimensions of Brand Equity**

Differentiation → Relevance → Esteem → Knowledge → BRAND EQUITY

Effective labeling serves several functions:

▼ It attracts the buyer's attention.

▼ It describes the package contents.

▼ It conveys the benefits of the product inside.

▼ It provides information on warranties, warnings, and other consumer matters.

▼ It gives an indication of price, value, and uses.

The **label** is the descriptive part of a product's package that lists the brand name or symbol, name and address of the manufacturer or distributor, product composition and size, nutritional information for food products, and recommended uses. It also plays an important role in attracting consumer attention and encouraging a purchase at this critical point.

Green labeling, which is a product-related extension of green marketing (discussed in Chapter 2), involves placing approval seals and environmental claims on packages. For instance, a label may tell the consumer that a package is made entirely from recycled materials. A growing number of consumers have complained recently about problems in understanding the meanings of some green labels. The term *organic* became so popular that it appeared on labels for products from frozen dinners and bottled wine to fresh fruit and fertilizers. The U.S. Department of Agriculture stepped in, as it has for other product labeling issues, and replaced a plethora of state and private regulations with a consistent standard for labeling packages as *organic* products.[27]

www.usda.gov

Labeling requirements differ from one country to another. In the United States, the Food and Drug Administration regulates product labeling. In Canada, labels must give information in both French and English. Several

Figure 14.14 **Creating Product Differentiation with Unique Package Designs**

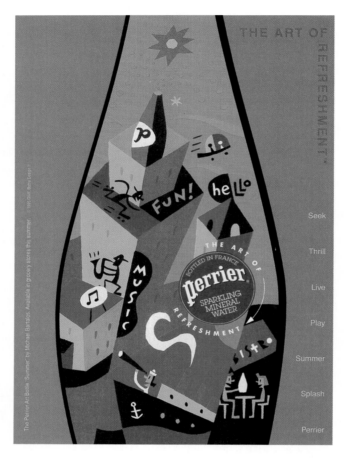

nations in Europe have developed their own standards for labels, as well. The European Union's ecolabel program specifies a standard symbol for products that are manufactured with low energy, water, and detergent consumption.

Today, labels perform important administrative functions, as well as marketing ones, by carrying universal product code (UPC) symbols, commonly referred to as *bar codes,* as discussed in Chapter 13. First introduced in 1974, the UPC system is a labor-saving innovation that has improved inventory control, reduced checkout time, and cut pricing errors. One thing it does not provide is information that a consumer can read and understand. Few people can look at a UPC symbol and tell where the product was made or its price. This limitation has led many consumer groups to push for individual item-pricing. Retailers, however, complain of added costs involved in placing prices on every item. Currently, Michigan enforces the most stringent requirements for item pricing, imposing a hefty fine up to $25,000 for each violation.[28]

PRICE IN THE MARKETING MIX

Every successful product offers some utility, or want-satisfying power. However, individual preferences determine how much *value* a particular consumer associates with a particular good or service. One person may value leisure-time pursuits while another assigns a higher priority to acquiring property and automobiles. However, all consumers have limited amounts of money and a variety of possible uses for it. Therefore, the **price**—the exchange value of a good or service—becomes a major factor in consumer buying decisions.

As Chapter 3 discussed, prices also help to direct activities throughout the overall economic system. A firm uses various factors of production, such as natural resources, labor, and capital, based on their relative prices. High wage rates may cause a firm to install labor-saving

How to Create Strong Brands

One of the academics best-known among professional marketers is University of California-Berkeley professor David A. Aaker. The brand-building guru has developed a formula that ties brand equity to stock performance, attracting followers in companies such as Saturn, General Electric, and Harley-Davidson.

A key to successful brand building is to understand how to develop brand identity—to know what the brand stands for and how to most effectively express that identity. Here are some basic tips Aaker suggests for building, preserving, and maintaining a strong brand:

▼ *Brand Identity.* The identity of a brand reflects more than the product itself. Marketers should consider the brand as a person, as the organization, and as a symbol.

▼ *Brand Position.* Each brand must occupy a position that provides clear guidance for marketing and promotional efforts.

▼ *Brand Communication.* The brand must be communicated in an enduring way that enhances its identity and position over time.

▼ *Brand Consistency and Compatibility.* Marketers must consistently maintain the brand's identity, position, and execution over time. The brands in a firm's portfolio must complement each other.

▼ *Brand Equity.* Track brand equity over time, including awareness, perceived quality, brand loyalty, and brand associations.

▼ *Brand Management.* Assign a person to manage the brand by coordinating execution in different media and markets. Continue investing in brands.

Source: Based on David A. Aaker, *Building Strong Brands* (New York: Simon & Schuster, 1995).

---

machinery, just as high interest rates may lead management to postpone a new capital expenditure. Prices and volumes sold determine the revenue and profits a firm receives.

PRICING OBJECTIVES

Marketers attempt to accomplish certain objectives through their pricing decisions. Research has shown that pricing objectives vary from firm to firm, and many companies pursue multiple pricing objectives. Some try to improve profits by setting high prices, while others set low prices to attract new business. The four basic categories of pricing objectives are (1) profitability, (2) volume, (3) meeting competition, and (4) prestige.

Profitability Objectives

Most firms pursue some type of profitability objectives in their pricing strategies. Marketers know that:

$$\text{Profit} = \text{Revenue} - \text{Expenses}$$

Also, revenue is a result of the selling price times the quantity sold:

$$\text{Total Revenue} = \text{Price} \times \text{Quantity Sold}$$

Some firms try to maximize profits by increasing prices until sales volumes decline. This approach may or may not work. A 10 percent price hike that reduces volume by only 8 percent increases profitability, but a 5 percent hike that reduces volume by 6 percent reduces overall profits. In fact, a small reduction in price can result in a major reduction in profits, as illustrated in Figure 14.15.

Business Directory

price exchange value of a good or service.

Some marketers seem to believe that price conscious-ness is a personality trait—that some people are "stingy" and others are "big-spenders." In fact, however, price consciousness is the result of how much spending money (discretionary income) a consumer has and how much the consumer thinks the product is worth (value). Research suggests that price is the primary consideration for only 15 percent to 35 percent of buyers in most cate-

Figure 14.15 **Perils of a Price Cut**

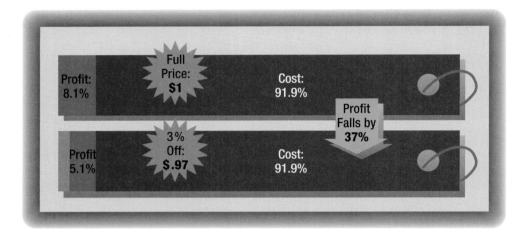

gories. But marketers are increasingly treating price as if it were the only consideration in consumer buying behavior. Far too often, low-price strategies compromise long-term plans.

Since price is an easily observed characteristic of competing products, it represents a powerful marketing weapon. However, it is also one of the easiest product traits to match by competitors. In marketplace confrontations based on price cutting, the reduced prices must generate enough added sales to offset the reduction in per-unit revenues, or they will leave all firms worse off than before the changes. Credit-card companies are learning this lesson the hard way as they seek to entice cardholders to switch companies by offering below-average interest rates. They gain customers, all right, but as soon as the introductory rate period ends, savvy borrowers surf the financial Web for another deal. In this promotion, credit-card marketers have succeeded only in creating a new, highly disloyal consumer group—card surfers.[29]

The principle of **profit maximization** forms the basis of much of economic theory, yet its application often creates difficult problems in practice. Many firms have turned to a simpler profitability objective—the *target-return goal.* Most target-return pricing goals state desired profitability levels as financial returns on either sales or investment. For example, a company might specify a goal of a 9 percent return on sales or a 20 percent return on investment.

Volume Objectives

In another approach to pricing strategy called **sales maximization,** managers set an acceptable minimum level of profitability and then set prices that will generate the highest possible sales volume without driving profits below that level. This strategy views sales expansion as a more important priority than short-run profits to the firm's long-term competitive position. In order to attract customers, stores may advertise certain products called *loss leaders* at or below costs.

Home PCs priced under $1,000 now account for 30 percent of all retail PC sales. Personal computer marketers have recently offered low prices to attract new buyers, but the growth in the number of PCs sold has not increased revenues. Sony Corp., Acer America Corp., and IBM have all suffered recent losses in the home-PC market. These low-priced PCs also cannibalize sales of more expensive products with higher profit margins.[30]

A second volume objective bases pricing decisions on **market share**—the percentage of a market controlled by a certain company or product. One firm may seek to achieve a 25 percent market share in a certain industry. Another may want to maintain or expand its market share for particular products or product lines.

Pricing objectives based on market share have become popular for several reasons. One of the most important is the ease of applying market share statistics as yardsticks for measuring managerial and corporate performance. Another is that increased sales may reduce per-unit production costs and boost profits. A firm can produce 100,000 pens for a lower per-unit cost than it would pay to make just a few dozen. The Business Hall of Shame presents a story of one firm's miscalculation in a pricing decision intended to reinforce market share.

Pricing to Meet Competition

A third set of pricing objectives seeks simply to meet competitors' prices. In many lines of business, firms set their own prices to match those of established industry price leaders.

These types of objectives de-emphasize the price element of the marketing mix and focus competitive efforts on nonprice variables. Price is a highly visible component of a

BUSINESS HALL OF SHAME

Flying the Predatory Skies

The late 1990s were memorable years for the airline industry as the major competitors, including American, United, Delta, and Northwest, enjoyed record earnings. Not only has passenger traffic increased significantly in the past year, but the airlines added to their revenues by boosting airfares 9 percent. But the industry has been plagued by accusations of unfair competition and price-gouging and Congress is threatening to impose fines to stop predatory behavior by big airlines.

Critics say the megacarriers are taking advantage of Congress' 1978 deregulation of the industry by charging high airfares in isolated markets and slashing them only when they are trying to drive out low-cost competitors. This penalizes people living in cities like Des Moines, Iowa, and Rochester and Buffalo, New York, as well as firms conducting business over those routes.

Take the experience of Pro Air Inc., a tiny start-up whose entire fleet consists of a pair of brand-new Boeing 737s. When the new carrier decided to use price as its primary competitive weapon in attracting air travelers, it offered a $69 one-way fare between Milwaukee and Detroit. But its giant competitor, Northwest, retaliated by matching the fare. After a few months, Pro Air discontinued service to Milwaukee. Northwest then tripled most of its fares on the route to more than $200.

Mobile, Alabama, air travelers watched a replay of the Pro Air–Northwest battle recently when Air-Tran's predecessor, ValuJet, discontinued air service, leaving Delta as the sole major jet carrier serving the market. Within 24 hours after ValuJet's pullout, Delta raised fares by 600 percent on some tickets.

In addition to the higher prices paid by travelers in the less competitive markets, the moves by major airlines to match price cuts by discount airlines have driven many of them out of business. Among the casualties are Pan Am, Sun Jet, and Air South. Even the survivors like Frontier Airlines and Reno Air have posted significant losses recently.

The major carriers blame the failures on inadequate capital and poor management. They also point to the limited routes offered by the smaller air carriers and their lack of frequent-flyer incentive programs. But most industry analysts disagree. As Secretary of Transportation Rodney Slater put it, "There is growing concern that the major carriers are willing to lose money—lots of it—in the short run to drive off competition." Both the Transportation and Justice departments have begun looking into possible anti-competitive practices in the industry.

QUESTIONS FOR CRITICAL THINKING

1. The major air carriers argue that the practice of matching price cuts in certain markets is not predatory pricing, but simply a basic business decision to remain competitive. Do you agree?

2. Opponents of deregulation point to such industries as cable TV service and air transportation as examples of price-gouging that occurs in the absence of control over pricing decisions. Summarize the advantages of deregulation in these industries. What disadvantages are present?

Sources: Karen Kerrigan, "Ticket Regulation Could Send Airfares Up, Up and Away," *The Business Journal*, June 15, 1998, accessed at www.amcity.com; Glen Johnson, "Congress Gives Airfare Warning," *Mobile Register*, April 24, 1998, p. 6B; and Adam Zagorin, "Hunting the Predators," *Time*, April 20, 1998, p. 48.

firm's marketing mix and an easily used and effective tool for obtaining an advantage over competitors. The ease of duplicating prices leads many marketers to try to avoid price wars by favoring nonprice strategies, such as adding value, improving quality, educating consumers, and establishing relationships. The airline industry's recent experience exemplifies competitors' actions and reactions to price cuts.[31]

In markets characterized by competitive pricing, other marketing mix elements gain importance in purchase decisions. In such instances, overall product value, not just price, determines product choice. In recent years, **value pricing** has emerged to emphasize benefits a product provides in comparison to the price and quality levels of competing offerings. Many marketers follow value-pricing principles to attract consumers who want more quality for their money. While value-priced products generally cost less than premium brands, marketers point out that *value* doesn't necessarily mean a cheap price.

Prestige Objectives

Another category of objectives, unrelated to either profitability or sales volume, encompasses the effect of prices on prestige. Prestige pricing establishes a rela-

SOLVING AN ETHICAL CONTROVERSY

Is Ticket Scalping as Bad as Some Say?

When tickets went on sale in San Jose, California, for the upcoming concert by The Artist Formerly Known as Prince, the show sold out in only 7 minutes. Shortly after hearing of the sellout, The Artist canceled the show. Why cancel a sold out performance? Ticket scalping. His manager Billy Sparks explained, "We weren't trying to come here and sell out in 10 minutes, and then have the fans shut out. To have people tack 300, 400 percent on the ticket price—that's not right."

Ticket scalping is a $30 billion industry in the United States alone. To control traffic, the White House gives visitors free tickets; they are not sold to generate revenue. The presidential residence is supported by tax dollars; in effect, it belongs to the people. But ticket scalpers (or *ticket brokers,* as they prefer to be called) often are the first in line for the free tickets, which they later sell to tourists for as much as $50.

Another group opposed to scalpers are owners of major league sports franchises. Jerry Colangelo, president of the Arizona Diamondbacks and Phoenix Suns, complains that scalpers

"made money off me without my permission and that was not right." In general, this group feels that by selling tickets at exorbitant prices, scalpers steal from the teams.

Consumers are divided in their opinions of ticket scalping. Some believe the practice prevents average families from attending sporting and cultural events. Others say, "Let the market work and everyone wins." So far efforts to regulate scalping have foundered on difficult if not impossible obstacles. Although about half the states and most major cities have established laws intended to protect consumers, loosely written provisions and

tively high price to develop and maintain an image of quality and exclusiveness. Marketers set such objectives because they recognize the role of price in communicating an overall image for the firm and its products. To many people, experiencing a Cirque du Soleil performance is worth the $40 ticket price. The Solving an Ethical Controversy discusses one unintended result of prestige pricing.

Russell Klein, president and owner of New York City-based distributor Easton International, has successfully introduced American women to five prestigious lines of imported hosiery. Why do these products carry so much prestige? Partly because they are designer brands imported from Austria, France, Germany, and Italy, and partly because their prices average $40 a pair. To create and maintain an image of exclusivity and designer quality, Klein has set up eye-catching displays in swanky shops like Saks Fifth Avenue and Bergdorf Goodman. He has also hired sales specialists to assist department store staff in delivering superior, personalized service.[32]

HOW PRICES ARE DETERMINED

While pricing is usually regarded as a function of marketing, it also requires considerable input from other areas of the company. Accounting and financial managers have al-

ways played major roles in pricing by providing sales and cost data necessary for sound decision making. Production and industrial engineering personnel play similarly important roles. Computer analysts, for example, ensure that the firm's information system provides up-to-date information needed in pricing. Managers at all levels must realize the importance of pricing and the contributions of different departments in choosing the right price.

Prices are determined in two basic ways—by applying the theoretical concepts of supply and demand and by completing cost-oriented analyses. While economic theory provides an overall viewpoint, cost-based pricing considers the decision as a practical, hands-on task.

Price Determination in Economic Theory

Economic theory, as discussed in Chapter 3, assumes all participants emphasize profit maximization. This concept dictates that managers set a market price at the point where the amount of a product desired at a given price equals the amount that suppliers will provide at that price. In other words, this price occurs at the point where the amount demanded and the amount supplied are in equilibrium. The demand curve is a schedule of amounts that consumers demand at different price levels.

To better understand the concept of demand-supply pricing, consider how a ticket to a baseball game gets its

weak enforcement limit their effectiveness. One man was arrested for trying to sell a ticket below cost!

 Should Governments Legalize Ticket Scalping?

PRO

1. The ticket purchaser is the owner of the product, and no one can deny that person the right to resell it.

2. The free market should determine price. After all, the buyer has the option of refusing to pay the asking price.

3. Sports franchise owners can charge any price they want. Ticket brokers should not be penalized for doing the same thing.

CON

1. Everyone has a right to affordable tickets. Ticket scalpers prevent consumers from gaining equal opportunities to obtain tickets at fair prices.

2. When ticket scalpers can't sell their high-priced tickets, revenues are lost for parking, concessions, and memorabilia—and empty stadium seats are not good press.

3. Since most stadiums are tax-supported facilities, ticket scalping privatizes revenue for public facilities.

4. Ticket scalping raises prices, since nothing stops owners from raising prices in an effort to get the same profit return themselves.

SUMMARY

People will continue to debate whether ticket scalping is free enterprise at work or a criminal activity. Until then, this centuries-old practice will remain entrenched in capitalist societies.

Sources: Robert Mihalek, "The Scalping Game," *OhioOnline,* accessed at www.ohioonline.net/v01/iof/scalped.html, April 2, 1998; Pete du Pont, "In Praise of Ticket Scalping," *Intellectual Capital,* December 4, 1997; and Gina Arnold, "Princely Sums," *Metroactive,* April 17, 1997.

price. Figure 14.16 shows that as the price rises, the quantity of tickets demanded falls. The demand curve reflects decreases in the quantity demanded at successively higher prices; the supply curve reflects sellers' willingness to offer different quantities of tickets for sale at different prices. According to economic theory, in the long run, the market price always settles where the demand and supply curves intersect—the equilibrium price.

Price Determination in Practice

Although economic theory leads to optimal decisions regarding the overall market for a product, marketers must set the prices of individual brands based on limited information about supply and demand. Anticipating how much of a product they will sell at a certain price requires difficult analysis, so businesses tend to adopt **cost-** **based pricing** formulas that calculate base-cost figures per unit and then add markups to cover unassigned costs and to provide profits.

These approaches to price determination are simpler and easier to use than economic theory; however, mar-

Figure 14.16 **Demand and Supply Curves for Baseball Tickets**

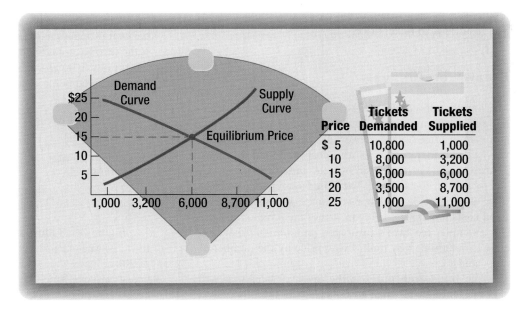

Price	Tickets Demanded	Tickets Supplied
$ 5	10,800	1,000
10	8,000	3,200
15	6,000	6,000
20	3,500	8,700
25	1,000	11,000

Figure 14.17 The Markup Chain

NOW SHOWING

STAR WARS:
The Phantom Menace

Production and Marketing Expenses		Distribution Expenses	Theater Fees		Ticket Price:
Studio expenses	$1.38	$1.44	Expenses	$ 0.60	
Advertising	1.20		Profits	0.54	
Actors' share of gross	0.48				
Misc. expenses	0.36				

$$\$3.42 \ + \ \$1.44 \ + \ \$1.14 \ =$$

Star Wars $6.00

keters must apply them flexibly in particular situations. Cost-based pricing totals all costs associated with offering a product in the market, including production, transportation, and marketing expenses. An added amount, the *markup,* then covers any unexpected or overlooked expenses and ensures a profit. The total becomes the price. Wholesalers and retailers typically practice markup pricing. For example, in Figure 14.17, the wholesaler responsible for distributing prints of the new *Star Wars* movie adds a markup of $1.44 to cover costs and generate a profit. The retailer (the theater owner, in this case) adds another $1.14. The result is a $6 ticket price.

Breakeven Analysis

Marketers often conduct **breakeven analysis** to determine the minimum sales volume a product must generate at a certain price level to cover all costs. This method involves a consideration of various costs and total revenues. Total cost (*TC*) is composed of total variable costs (*TVC*) and total fixed costs (*TFC*). **Variable costs** change with the level of production (as labor and raw materials do), while **fixed costs** remain stable regardless of the production level (for example, the firm's insurance premiums). Total revenue is determined by multiplying price by the number of units sold.

The **breakeven point** is the level of sales that will generate enough revenue to cover all of the company's fixed and variable costs. It is the point at which total revenue just equals total costs. Sales beyond the breakeven point will generate profits; sales volume below the breakeven point will result in losses. The following formulas give the breakeven point in units and dollars:

$$\text{Breakeven point (in units)} = \frac{\text{Total fixed cost}}{\text{Contribution to fixed costs per unit}}$$

$$\text{Breakeven point (in dollars)} = \frac{\text{Total fixed cost}}{1 - \text{Variable cost per unit/Price}}$$

A product selling for $20 with a variable cost of $14 per unit produces a $6 per-unit contribution to fixed costs. If the firm has total fixed costs of $42,000, then it must sell 7,000 units to break even on the product. The calculation of the breakeven point in units and dollars is:

$$\text{Breakeven point (in units)} = \frac{\$42,000}{\$20 - \$14} = \frac{\$42,000}{\$6} = 7,000 \text{ units}$$

$$\text{Breakeven point (in dollars)} = \frac{\$42,000}{1 - \$14/\$20} = \frac{\$42,000}{1 - 0.7}$$

$$= \frac{\$42,000}{0.3} = \$140,000$$

Figure 14.18 illustrates this breakeven point in graphic form. Marketers use breakeven analysis to determine the profits or losses that would result from several different proposed prices. Since different prices produce different breakeven points, marketers could compare their calculations of required sales to break even with sales estimates from marketing research studies. This comparison can identify the best price, one that would attract enough customers to exceed the breakeven point and earn profits for the firm.

Including Consumer Demand in Breakeven Analysis

Breakeven analysis considers only costs; it does not indicate whether enough customers will buy the number of units the firm must sell at a particular price in order to break even on the product. Most firms develop estimates of consumer demand through surveys of likely customers, interviews with retailers who would be handling the product, and assessments of prices charged by competitors. Then the breakeven points for several possible prices are calculated and compared with sales estimates for each price. This practice is referred to as *modified breakeven analysis*. Marketers narrow down price alternatives in this way until they identify only those that appear capable of achieving at least breakeven sales.

Alternative Pricing Strategies

The specific strategies that firms use to price their goods and services grow out of the marketing strategies they formulate to accomplish overall organizational objectives. One firm's marketers may price products to attract customers across a wide range; another group of marketers may set prices to appeal to a small segment of a larger market; still another group may simply try to match competitors' price tags. In general, firms can choose from three alternative pricing strategies: skimming, penetration, and competitive pricing.

Skimming Pricing Strategy
A **skimming pricing strategy** sets an intentionally high price relative to the prices of

competing products. The name comes from the expression "skimming the cream." This pricing strategy often works for introduction of a distinctive good or service with little or no competition, although it can be used throughout most stages of the product life cycle. A skimming strategy helps marketers to set a price that distinguishes a firm's high-end product from those of competitors.

A skimming strategy also allows a manufacturer to quickly recover its research and development costs, and it

Figure 14.18 Breakeven Analysis

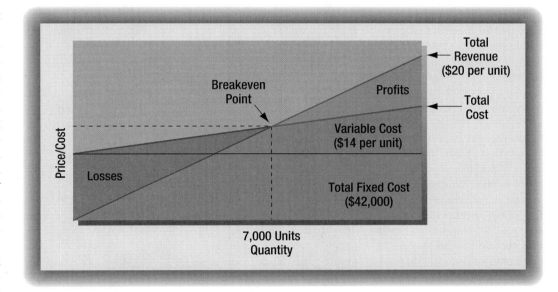

lets a firm maximize revenue from a new product before competitors enter the field. Marketers often use skimming strategies to segment a product's overall market by price. Another advantage is that it permits marketers to control demand in the introductory stages of a product's life cycle and then adjust production to match demand. The one big problem with a skimming strategy is that it attracts competition.

Exclusive perfumes such as Chloé Narcisse shown in Figure 14.19 typically employ skimming pricing strategies. The costs of the perfume ingredients are almost insignificant when compared to the retail price; in fact, the most expensive component of such a product is typically the unique container.

Business Directory

breakeven analysis pricing technique that determines the sales volume that a firm must achieve at a specified price in order to generate enough revenue to cover its total cost.

Penetration Pricing By contrast, a **penetration pricing strategy** sets a low price as a major marketing weapon. Marketers often price new products noticeably lower than competing offerings when they enter new industries characterized by dozens of competing brands. Once the new product achieves some market recognition through consumer trial purchases stimulated by its low price, marketers may increase the price to the level of competing products.

Penetration pricing assumes that a below-market price will attract buyers and move a brand from an unknown newcomer at least to the brand-recognition stage or even the brand-preference stage. Since many firms begin penetration pricing with the intention of increasing prices in the future, success depends on generating many consumer trial purchases. This strategy is particularly effective when introduction of a new product will likely attract strong competition. Such a strategy may allow a new product to reach the mass market quickly and capture a large share prior to entry by competitors. Research shows that about 25 percent of companies frequently use penetration pricing strategies.

Everyday low pricing (EDLP) is a strategy devoted to maintaining continuous low prices rather than relying on short-term price-cutting tactics such as cents-off coupons, rebates, and special sales. EDLP is used by retailers that consistently offer low prices to consumers; manufacturers also use EDLP to set stable prices for retailers.

Competitive Pricing Although many organizations rely heavily on price as a competitive weapon, even more implement **competitive pricing strategies.** They try to reduce the emphasis on price competition by matching other firms' prices and concentrating their own marketing efforts on the product, distribution, and promotional elements of the marketing mix. In fact, in industries with relatively homogeneous products, competitors must match one another's price reductions in order to maintain

| Figure 14.19 | **Use of Skimming Pricing Strategy in Marketing Perfume** |

market share and remain competitive.

By pricing their products at the general levels of competing offerings, marketers largely negate the price variable in their marketing strategies.

CONSUMER PERCEPTIONS OF PRICES

In addition to costs, marketers must also consider how consumers perceive prices. If a buyer views a price as too high or too low, the marketer must correct the situation. Price-quality relationships and psychological pricing are important considerations.

Price-Quality Relationships

Research shows that a consumer's perception of product quality is related closely to an item's price; a high price raises perceptions of quality. Most marketers believe that this perceived price-quality relationship holds over a relatively wide range of prices, although consumers may view extreme prices as either too expensive or too cheap to consider paying. Marketing managers need to study and experiment with prices, because the price-quality relationship can critically affect a firm's pricing strategy. The Chevy ad shown in Figure 14.20 claims car buyers get more features than they pay for when they choose the Cavalier.

The world's auto giants expect to place high sticker prices on the electric cars they are mandated to sell in California by the late 1990s. However, Renaissance Cars, Inc. of Florida sees a different outcome. The firm is betting that consumers will buy more cars if it offers high quality at the right price. The firm is introducing its Tropica, a two-seat electric vehicle with a maximum speed of 62 mph that meets all freeway safety requirements, in California and Florida. The convertible is targeted to commuters, retirees, and college-age consumers who want dependable, affordable transportation. Renaissance has priced the Tropica at least $10,000 below the preliminary guesstimates for comparable models from the big automakers.[33]

Psychological Pricing

Many marketers believe that consumers find certain prices more psychologically appealing than others. The image-pricing goals mentioned earlier are an example of psychological pricing, an approach used throughout the world.

Have you ever wondered why retailers set prices like $39.95, $19.98, or $9.99 instead of $40.00, $20.00, or $10.00? Before the age of cash registers and sales taxes, retailers followed this practice of *odd pricing* to force clerks to make correct change as part of cash control efforts. It is now a common practice in retail pricing, because many store managers believe that consumers favor uneven amounts. In fact, some stores use prices ending in 1, 2, 3, 4, 6, or 7 to avoid the look of more common prices like $5.95, $10.98, and $19.99. Their prices are more likely to be $1.11, $3.22, $3.86, $4.53, $5.74, or $9.97.

WHAT'S AHEAD

This chapter has introduced the key marketing tasks of developing, marketing, packaging, and pricing goods and services. The next chapter focuses on three major components of an organization's distribution strategy: distribution channels, wholesalers and retailers who make up many distribution channels, and logistics and physical distribution.

Figure 14.20 **Chevrolet: Emphasizing Price-Quality Relationships**

SUMMARY OF LEARNING GOALS

1. Define *product* and list the elements of a product strategy.

A product is a bundle of physical, service, and symbolic attributes designed to satisfy consumer wants. The marketing conception of a product includes the brand, product image, warranty, service attributes, packaging, and labeling, in addition to the physical or functional characteristics of the good or service.

2. Describe the classifications of consumer goods, business goods, and services.

Goods and services can be classified as consumer or business products. Consumer products are those purchased by ultimate consumers for their own use. They can be either convenience products, shopping products, or specialty products, depending on consumer habits in buying them. Business products are those purchased for use either directly or indirectly in the production of other goods and services for resale. They can be classified as installations, accessory equipment, component parts and materials, raw materials, and supplies. This classification is based on how the items are used and product characteristics. Services can be classified as either consumer or business services.

3. Discuss the product mix and product lines.

The product mix is the assortment of goods and services a firm offers to consumers and industrial users. A product line is a series of related products. The product mix is a combination of product lines and individual offerings.

4. Describe the four stages of the product life cycle.

All products pass through four stages in their product life cycles: introduction, growth, maturity, and decline. In the introduction stage, the firm attempts to elicit demand for the new product. In the product's growth stage, sales climb, and the company earns its first profits on the product. In the maturity stage, sales reach a saturation level. In the decline stage, both sales and profits decline. Marketers sometimes employ strategies to extend the product life cycle, including increasing frequency of use, adding new users, finding new uses for the product, and changing package size, labeling, or product quality.

5. List the stages of new-product development.

The stages of the new-product development process are (1) idea generation and screening, (2) concept development and business analysis, (3) prototype or service process development and testing, and (4) commercialization. At each stage, marketers face "go/no go" decisions about whether to continue to the next stage, modify the new product, or discontinue the development process.

6. Explain how firms identify their products.

Products are identified by brands, brand names, and trademarks, which are important elements of product images. Effective brand names are easy to pronounce, recognize, and remember, and they project the right images to buyers. Brand names cannot contain generic words. Under certain circumstances, companies lose exclusive rights to their brand names if common use makes them generic terms for product categories. Some brand names belong to retailers or distributors rather than to manufacturers. Many retailers now offer a third option: no-brand generic products. Brand loyalty is measured in three degrees: brand recognition, brand preference, and brand insistence. Some marketers use family brands to identify several related items in a product line. Others employ individual branding strategies by giving each product within a line a different brand name.

7. Outline the different types of pricing objectives.

Pricing objectives can be classified as profitability, volume, meeting competition, and prestige objectives. Profitability objectives seek profit maximization; management requires increasing levels of profitability and sets target-return goals in the form of rates of return on either investment or sales. Volume objectives include sales maximization, a strategy in which management sets an acceptable minimum level of profitability and then tries to maximize sales, and market-share goals, which are specified as percentages of certain markets. Some prices are set simply to meet competitors' prices in the marketplace. Prestige pricing maintains a high price to create an image of exclusivity for a product.

8. Discuss how firms set prices in the marketplace.

Pricing is an important function of marketing. Price determination can be viewed from two perspectives. Economists explain prices by describing the interaction of demand and supply. A more practical, less theoretical approach to price strategy, called *cost-based pricing,* totals fixed and variable costs and then adds an amount to cover any unexpected or unconsidered expenses and ensure a profit.

9. Explain how to use breakeven analysis in pricing strategy.

Breakeven analysis supports pricing decisions by comparing total costs and total revenues to determine a breakeven point in units. It does this by dividing total fixed costs by the per-unit contribution to fixed costs. Sales beyond the breakeven point result in profits. Breakeven points can be calculated for various prices. The resulting breakeven volumes can then be compared to marketing research estimates of likely sales volume in determining a final price based on both consumer demand and the firm's need to recover its costs and generate a satisfactory return on investment.

10. Differentiate between skimming and penetration pricing strategies.

A skimming strategy sets a relatively high price compared to similar products and then gradually lowers it. Penetration pricing sets a price lower than similar products and eventually raises it after the product gains wide market acceptance.

TEN BUSINESS TERMS YOU NEED TO KNOW

product	test marketing
service	brand
product life cycle	brand equity
product line	price
product mix	breakeven analysis

Other Important Business Terms

warranty	profit maximization
brand name	sales maximization
trademark	market share
generic product	value pricing
family brand	cost-based pricing
individual brand	variable cost
manufacturer's (national) brand	fixed cost
private brand	breakeven point
brand recognition	skimming pricing strategy
brand preference	penetration pricing strategy
brand insistence	competitive pricing strategy
label	

REVIEW QUESTIONS

1. How do marketers define *product?* What is included in a marketer's concept of product?
2. Differentiate among the following categories of consumer goods, business goods, and services:
   a. Convenience, shopping, and specialty products
   b. Installations, accessory equipment, component parts and materials, raw materials, and supplies
   c. Consumer and business services
3. Identify a product that is both a consumer and business product, and explain why it can have a dual classification.
4. What is meant by the term *product mix?* Identify the primary components of a product mix.
5. Identify products in each category of the product life cycle. Why did you classify these products as you did?
6. Identify the stages in new-product development and illustrate each stage with a hypothetical example. What is the chief purpose of test marketing?
7. Differentiate among brands, brand names, and trademarks. Choose four or five brand names and list the characteristics that make each of them effective.
8. Explain the relationship between brand loyalty and brand equity. What functions do packaging and labeling perform?
9. Identify the major pricing objectives used by different companies. Which ones do you think are most important to marketers? Why?
10. Contrast skimming and penetration pricing strategies. What types of products or market situations best suit each strategy?

QUESTIONS FOR CRITICAL THINKING

1. Every year, Testing 1-2-3 distributes over a million free Campus Pacs to students at 400 colleges and universities. In addition, 100,000 Pacs are delivered through the top 50 schools with large minority enrollments. Describe how a marketer with a new product can use this information in the introduction and commercialization phases of the development process.
2. Dannon recently moved beyond its highly successful yogurt products into the bottled-water market. Explain the advantages and challenges marketers face in promoting Dannon's new product.
3. Suggest a brand name for each of the following new products and explain why you chose each name:
   a. a development of exclusive homesites
   b. a low-price term life insurance policy sold by mail
   c. an extra-durable, single-edged razor blade
   d. a portable drill that is considerably faster than its competition
4. Levi Strauss is a brand name; it is also listed in several dictionaries as a synonym for blue denim jeans. What implications for product strategy decisions does this pose for Levi marketers?
5. Assume you are the marketing manager for a new hockey franchise. Your team will be using an arena with 3,000 first-class seats, 5,000 regular seats, and 2,000 seats behind the nets. How will you go about setting ticket prices?

Experiential Exercise

DIRECTIONS: Use breakeven analysis to answer the following questions related to Palomino Inc. (PI): PI's product sells for $250. The variable cost per unit is $200. PI estimates its fixed costs for the coming year will be $200,000.

1. How many product units must PI sell to break even? _____
2. What is PI's breakeven point in dollars? _____
3. If market research studies indicate that PI will sell 5,000 units in the coming year, will PI realize a profit or a loss? _____ How much? _____

Check your work against the answers provided at the end of the exercise section.

Nothing but Net

1. **Warranties.** Conduct a search using the words "warranties" and a product category in which you are interested, such as "cars" or "computers." Select several links to analyze how various companies are using warranties as a means of marketing their products. Another interesting site to visit that will provide you with more information on the importance of warranties is

www.warrantynet.com

2. **New-Product Development.** "Internet Help for Investors," the Business Tool Kit on page 461, lists six Internet resources useful to individuals and organizations attempting to convert a promising idea into a successful new product. Visit each of the six sites listed and identify the two you consider most important to someone interested in launching a new product.

3. **Price in the Marketing Mix.** A full-page ad appearing in the April 10, 1998, *USA Today* states in part:

> Welcome to pricelineSM. We're a powerful new buying service that lets you name your own price for leisure airline tickets (and, coming soon . . . new cars). Here's how it works. Simply call us toll-free or visit our Web site at priceline.com. You decide where and when you want to travel and the price you want to pay. At priceline, we work with the major airlines to help them fill the more than 500,000 seats that fly empty every day. In just one hour, you'll know if we can get you your tickets—at your price. The airlines fill their planes . . . and you get your price. . . . You can use priceline to travel anywhere on the planet and you can try it free.

> Visit www.priceline.com to see how this company has applied pricing concepts you learned in this chapter.

Note: Internet Web addresses change frequently. If you do not find the exact sites listed, you may need to access the organization's or company's home page and search from there.

Answers to Experiential Exercise:

1. $\dfrac{\$200,000}{250 - 200} = \dfrac{\$200,000}{50} = 4,000$ units

2. $\dfrac{\$200,000}{1 - 200/250} = \dfrac{\$200,000}{.2} = \$1,000,000$

3. 5,000 units $\times$ \$250 = \$1,250,000 - \$1,000,000 = profit of \$250,000

DREW PEARSON COMPANIES:
Super Bowl Champ Puts a Cap on Success

When the Dallas Cowboys' wide receiver Drew Pearson played in his third Super Bowl, he had no idea he'd become the CEO of one of the nation's top designers and manufacturers of sports caps. "When I left professional football, it was hard to imagine that my earning power off the field would ever eclipse my earning power on the field," reveals Pearson. Drew Pearson Companies (DPC) is one of only six companies to have scored licenses with the NFL, NBA, Major League Baseball, and the National Hockey League. Equally impressive is the fact that DPC is the only company to have exclusive worldwide rights with the Walt Disney Company.

Nicknamed "The Clutch" during his Cowboy days, Pearson was accustomed to making spectacular plays. But DPC's superstar rise in the headwear industry hasn't been without a few fumbles along the way. "Of course, being a former NFL player, I thought the natural thing would be to approach the NFL first," says Pearson. "Roger Stauback, who was an initial investor, and I went to New York to meet with NFL Properties. The meeting lasted maybe 35 minutes. They just told us no."

In time, Pearson proved that DPC had the financial resources and capabilities to produce quality products, and it became the first minority-owned business to secure a licensing agreement with the NFL. But more importantly, DPC discovered its competitive edge. "What's really set us apart from our competitors is our innovative designs," admits Pearson. Colorful, intricately stitched hats with names like "the Jagged Edge" are DPC's trademark. Early on, the firm embraced technology to create fashion-forward caps. "We were able to bring together in our creative services area the first computer-generated art that could show three-dimensional variations in designs—forward looks, backward looks—things that our competition had no clue as to how we were generating."

In 1995, DPC shipped 30 million trend-setting caps to 7,500 retailers throughout the United States, making it the industry's fastest growing headwear company. The company's aggressive growth has been the payoff for Pearson's winning vision. "We knew that the sports licensing industry, especially in the headwear category, is very competitive. We had to do something to set ourselves apart." To reduce its reliance on sports licensing, DPC began courting the entertainment industry and was rewarded with lucrative licensing rights to feature Mickey Mouse, Looney Tunes characters, the Flintstones, Barney, Garfield, and other pop-culture icons on its headwear. "Our number one selling hat is Mickey Mouse," says Pearson. "It outsells the NFL, it outsells Major League Baseball, it even outsold the Chicago Bulls."

Impressive sales in the domestic market have served as a catalyst for the firm's expansion worldwide. "Drew Pearson Companies is a global company. We made that decision to focus on the international market worldwide approximately three years ago," says Mike Russell, executive vice president of marketing. "From the standpoint of developing products to sell internationally, we're somewhat unique in our industry since Mickey Mouse doesn't change whether he's sold in the Far East or Central America. We have a definitive line of products that transcend international markets, and the demand for American logo products is continually growing internationally."

With new products and new markets on the horizon, DPC is poised to extend its winning streak well into the new century. "No matter what level of success we reach, we know there's more to attain. There's more to garner. We're not the number one headwear company in the world, and that's a goal of ours."

Questions

1. How does DPC extend its product life cycle?

2. How do the stages for new product development apply to high-quality sports caps? Explain.

3. How does the firm differentiate its headwear from that of other manufacturers?

chapter 15

Distributing Goods and Services

LEARNING GOALS

1. Explain how distribution creates value for customers and competitive advantage for businesses.

2. Describe the various categories of distribution channels, and identify the factors that influence channel selection.

3. Explain the roles marketing intermediaries play in distribution channels.

4. Describe how retailers effectively use pricing, promotion, location, and merchandise selection in order to compete.

5. Identify the major components of an effective distribution strategy.

6. List the different types of conflict that can occur in a distribution channel and the methods firms use to reduce channel conflict.

7. Describe the importance of logistics and physical distribution in controlling the supply chain.

8. Explain how the components of a physical distribution system work together to reduce costs and meet customer service standards.

9. Compare the alternative transportation modes on the bases of flexibility, dependability, and cost.

Streamline Offers a Lifestyle Solution

Short on time? Who isn't today? A company called Streamline may offer some help for overbooked executives and overstressed households. For just $30 a month, busy families can visit Streamline's Web site to order groceries from more than 10,000 items—and that's not all. They can order bottled water, pet food, meats, and fresh baked goods. They can take care of dry cleaning needs, video rentals, and film for processing. Families can also order freshly prepared meals, ship UPS packages, and buy stamps. Streamline even collects returnable bottles and clothing donations for the homeless. And customers don't even have to be home to take delivery. In each customer's garage, the company sets up

a storage unit with three compartments: refrigerator, freezer, and room-temperature storage shelves along with keypad access to the garage. Streamline takes care of its customers' weekly shopping and errands so that they can use those precious hours in other ways.

Streamline is about more than high-tech distribution—it's more than a delivery service, and it offers more than groceries. "We are not in the grocery business," says founder and CEO Tim DeMello. "We are in the lifestyle-solutions business." True, Streamline works to smooth the distribution process. But it does more than acquire, store, and transport the products consumers need. "I want to simplify people's lives," says DeMello. "Time away from work has become precious, and the last way people want to spend it is driving from errand to errand with children in tow."

So how does Streamline know which families will be interested? The company is very specific about the customers it wants. Streamline's ideal is the "busy suburban family": young and middle-aged couples making at least $65,000 a year and having at least one child. "It's easy to get customers," says DeMello. "It's harder to get the right customers." The company wants customers who value time over cost—the ones who will regularly count on Streamline for a significant amount of business and who will be so satisfied that they refer new people to Streamline. In fact, Streamline helps a prospect decide if Streamline best suits their lifestyle needs.

www.streamline.com

Once the right customers sign on, the company goes out of its way to keep them satisfied—right from the beginning. A Streamline field agent visits each customer's home and uses a bar-code scanner to list the items that are already in the pantry, the refrigerator, and the medicine cabinet. From this inventory, the agent creates the customer's first "personal shopping list," which is posted on Streamline's Web site so that the customer can edit it and place orders from it as often as once a week. Customers can run side-by-side onscreen comparisons of products, and they can even specify their preference for size and ripeness of fresh fruit and vegetables. One of Streamline's most popular services is called Don't Run Out℠. Families assign an automatic replenish cycle to specific items that are guaranteed to be delivered whether you get online and order or not (such as coffee, dish soap, milk, diapers). "It's extraordinary," says Gina Wilcox, director of strategic relations for Streamline. "The consumer makes a purchase decision once, and we fill the order throughout the year. It redefines brand loyalty. It redefines marketing." And to make sure the company keeps on doing a good job, Streamline constantly measures customer satisfaction, encouraging families to rate each interaction.

By satisfying customers' needs, Streamline has earned remarkable customer loyalty. In fact, competitors will have a hard time charming Streamline customers into trying a new service. They can't compete with the incredible amount of time Streamline has already invested and the strong bonds of trust they have already established. The lifestyle solutions offered by Streamline are much needed and much appreciated. "I absolutely love it," says Sandra Charton, a lawyer who is married to another lawyer. Not only doesn't she have to be home, says Charton, but with the refrigerated storage unit, she doesn't even feel pressured to unpack. "It's like having a wife, actually."[1]

CHAPTER OVERVIEW

As earlier chapters have discussed, business involves an exchange between producers and customers. Good product design and creative promotion may convince customers that they want to buy a firm's goods and services, but if those would-be purchasers cannot actually buy the product, the exchange cannot be completed. The items that people wish to buy are often manufactured thousands of miles away, even in other countries. Yet they still want to com-

plete quick, convenient transactions that require minimal efforts. To meet these expectations, firms must strategically manage distribution.

Distribution—the element of the marketing mix responsible for moving goods and services from producers to buyers—is a vital marketing concern. The marketing functions and specialized intermediaries in a distribution channel build a bridge that links buyers with the organizations that create the products they want. In fact, distribution contributes to three of the four types of utility—time, place, and ownership utility. This activity adds value to a product by getting it to the right place at the time when the consumer wants to buy it.

This chapter examines the basic distribution strategies and marketing intermediaries that help to move goods and services from producers to buyers. It discusses criteria for decisions about where to sell products and contributions of successful distribution to a firm's competitiveness. Finally, the chapter looks at logistics, the process of physically moving information, goods, and services.

DISTRIBUTION STRATEGY

In the highly competitive soft drink industry, getting a product on grocery store shelves can be a tough challenge. First choice for prime shelf space goes to powerful giants like Coke and Pepsi. Brands with smaller market shares—Dr Pepper, Seven-Up, Hires Root Beer, and RC Cola—struggle for their places on the remaining shelf space.

Urban Juice & Soda takes a very different approach. The tiny Canadian firm markets soda flavors like bubble gum and strawberry-lime under the Jones Soda Co. and Wazu Water brand names. Company founder Peter Van Solk targets his drinks at consumers 14 to 24 years old—teenagers and young adults who don't spend much time in grocery stores. Instead of battling for shelf space in supermarkets, Van Solk distributes his drinks in surf shops, music stores, and tattoo parlors. "First of all, people are spending more time in those stores, and secondly, I'm not competing against any other beverages," he says. As a result, Urban Juice & Soda has developed strong brand awareness for its product line that small beverage marketers don't usually enjoy.[2]

Urban Juice & Soda provides a good example of the importance of distribution strategy to a firm's marketing efforts. Marketers must carefully choose how and where their goods will reach their target markets by selecting the right distribution channels. **Distribution channels** are the paths through which products—and legal

In addition to its innovative distribution system, Urban Juice & Soda Co. takes a fresh approach to packaging and labeling. Images on Jones Soda labels vary from flavor to flavor, reflecting the drink marketer's philosophy of change and fun. They stand out on retail shelves, and no one will confuse them with Coke or Pepsi products.

ownership of them—flow from producer to consumer. Ideally, the choice of a distribution channel should support a firm's overall marketing strategy by providing consumers with convenient ways to obtain the goods and services they desire.

Types of Distribution Channels

In their first decision for distribution channel selection, marketers choose which type of channel will best meet both their firm's marketing objectives and the needs of its customers.

As shown in Figure 15.1, marketers can choose either a **direct distribution channel,** which carries goods directly from producer to consumer or business user, or

Figure 15.1 **Alternative Distribution Channels**

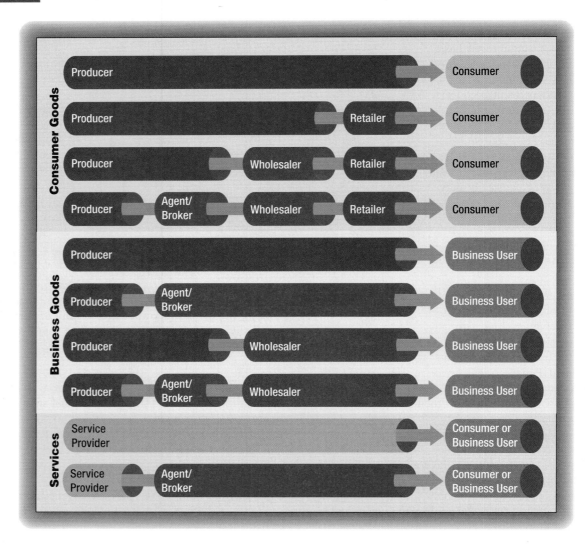

distribution channels that involve several different marketing intermediaries. A **marketing intermediary,** or *middleman,* is a business firm that moves goods between producers and consumers or business users. Retailers and wholesalers are both marketing intermediaries.

No one channel suits every product. The best choice depends on the circumstances of the market and on consumer needs. The choice of a distribution channel may also change over time as marketers strive to maintain their competitiveness. This section takes a closer look at how both direct and indirect distribution channels can support marketing strategies.

Direct Distribution The shortest and simplest means of connecting producers and customers is a direct channel. Goods and services that travel through direct distribution channels move directly from their production points to business buyers or ultimate consumers. This approach is most common in the business-to-business market. It also serves consumers who buy fresh fruits and vegetables at rural, roadside stands. Service purchases ranging from banking

Business Directory

marketing intermediary channel member, either wholesaler or retailer, that moves goods between producer and consumer or business user.

wholesaling intermediary channel member that sells goods primarily to retailers, other wholesalers, or business users.

and 10-minute oil changes to ear-piercing employ direct distribution, as does Mary Kay cosmetics, which sends company sales associates to customers' homes or apartments.

Direct distribution offers advantages in marketing relatively expensive, complex products that might require demonstrations. These strengths are especially valuable in the business-to-business market. Most major industrial installations, accessory equipment, component parts, business services, and even raw materials are typically marketed through direct contacts between producers and business buyers. For this reason, marketers of business products depend on highly trained sales personnel to sell their products and provide ongoing services to their customers, dealing with postsales problems their clients may encounter.

ChemStation, a $25 million manufacturer of industrial detergents, is one such business-to-business marketer. The firm's customers range from food-processing plants to truck-cleaning facilities, each with unique cleaning needs. ChemStation's salespeople visit customers to determine their special cleaning problems. The salespeople then confer with the company's engineering department to develop a customized detergent for each customer. Salespeople also help to train their customers' employees on safe use of the detergents they supply for each cleaning task. They also closely monitor customer inventories to ensure adequate supplies at all times.[3]

The Internet is making direct distribution an attractive option for many companies. As most of the earlier examples of electronic commerce have shown, a sizable percentage of Internet sales are generated, not by producers, but by firms with novel approaches to retailing. However, Dell Computer and Gateway 2000 market computer systems directly to both ultimate consumers and business buyers over the Internet. Distribution strategy in electronic commerce is dis-

Figure 15.2 **Using Intermediaries in a Distribution Channel for Furniture**

FURNITURE THAT MATCHES YOUR PERSONALITY.
NOT YOUR DRAPES.

Eclectic. Funky. Even traditional. Whatever your personal style, Thomasville's got you covered. With hundreds of styles to choose from, we have furniture to match any personality, even your more colorful ones. And with Thomasville, not only will you find furniture that fits your personality, you'll also find furniture that fits your budget. For a free catalog or for the Thomasville retailer nearest you, call us at 1-800-050-1058. For information about our entire line of Thomasville furniture, check us out on the web at www.thomasville.com

Thomasville
MAKE YOURSELF AT HOME™

cussed in more detail later in the chapter.

Distribution Channels Using Marketing Intermediaries Although direct channels allow simple and straightforward connections between producers and their customers, the list of channel alternatives in Figure 15.1 suggests that direct distribution is not the best choice in every instance. Some products sell in small quantities for relatively low prices to thousands of buyers scattered throughout the nation. Producers of such products cannot cost-effectively contact each of these customers directly, so they distribute products through specialized intermediaries called *retail stores*.

Since its founding in 1904, Thomasville Furniture Industries has grown from a tiny chair maker to a major producer of bedroom, dining room, and living room furniture. Its 7,000 employees work at 27 Thomasville plants in Mississippi, North Carolina, Tennessee, and Virginia. The company relies on an international network of retail stores to distribute its furniture to buyers. Its new Web site facilitates contacts between customers and retail outlets by identifying the store nearest to each cybershopper's ZIP code. Figure 15.2 illustrates another way Thomasville assists its retail partners through promotions aimed at enhancing perceptions of the quality and style of its furniture lines.

Along with retail stores, the second category of marketing institutions found in many distribution channels are **wholesaling intermediaries**. These marketing organizations consist of individuals or firms that sell to retailers, other wholesalers, and business buyers ranging from manufacturers to government agencies and not-for-profit organizations. Unlike retailers, they do not sell directly to ultimate consumers. Instead, they function as pipelines for goods moving from producers to retail stores, business users, or other wholesaling intermediaries.

Fleming Cos., the nation's largest grocery wholesaler, operates 33 warehouses across the country. The warehouses are stocked with thousands of products that Fleming purchases from many different U.S. and foreign manufacturers. Fleming then resells these goods to independent grocery stores and supermarket chains. In other words, Fleming acts as an intermediary between the grocery stores and food producers.[4]

In addition, Fleming's customers serve as marketing intermediaries between thousands of manufacturers and final consumers. **Retailers,** like the grocery stores that buy from Fleming, are marketing intermediaries that sell goods and services to final consumers. Since people frequently come in contact with retailers, the so-called "last 3 feet of the distribution channel," they are much more familiar with them than with wholesaling intermediaries. Consumers purchase food, clothing, furniture, appliances, and a host of other products from retailers. Retailers need not operate from physical storefronts, though. Some, like J. Crew, sell merchandise produced by other firms through catalogs; others, like Streamline, sell their goods and services over the Internet.

Moving Goods through Marketing Intermediaries Producers can move goods through a distribution channel over many paths, most of which involve one or more marketing intermediaries. A brief list summarizes some of the most common distribution channels using intermediaries:

▼ *Producer to Retailer to Consumer* Some manufacturers distribute their products directly to retailers. In the clothing industry, for example, many producers employ salespeople who deal with retailers.

▼ *Producer to Wholesaler to Retailer to Consumer* Thousands of manufacturers rely on this traditional channel to distribute consumer goods. They can often distribute more efficiently through wholesalers than they could by selling directly to thousands of separate retailers. Many large manufacturers of food products do not want the burden of keeping small grocery stores stocked with their goods. They prefer to deal directly with larger buyers, such as Fleming Co. By selling in bulk to Fleming, suppliers avoid hiring large corps of salespeople, yet they still get their products into stores throughout the nation.

▼ *Producer to Wholesaler to Wholesaler to Retailer to Consumer* In some industries, distribution channels include multiple wholesaling intermediaries. Two such industries are agricultural products such as canned and frozen foods and petroleum products like gasoline and heating oil. In these industries, intermediaries at an extra wholesaling level divide, sort, and distribute bulky items.

▼ *Producer to Wholesaler to Business User* Some business-to-business products flow through indirect channels from producer to wholesaler to user. Wal-Mart's Sam's Club outlets open early on Tuesdays and Thursdays to serve business-card holders, the firm's commercial accounts, opening to retail customers later in the day.

A later section of this chapter takes a closer look at the roles that wholesalers and retailers play in the distribution chain. The next section discusses reasons why producers choose to involve marketing intermediaries in their distribution networks.

Functions of Marketing Intermediaries

If a firm could work through the shortest and simplest distribution channel by selling directly to consumers, why would its managers choose to involve marketing intermediaries? You might think that adding intermediaries to the distribution process must add to the final cost of products, but more often than not, this choice actually lowers consumer prices. Most intermediaries perform functions essential to efficient marketing. Without them, many of the products people want and need would never reach end users. Marketing intermediaries, like wholesalers and retailers, often add significant value to a good or service as it moves through the distribution channel by creating utility, providing services, and reducing costs.

Creating Utility Marketing intermediaries add utility to the distribution chain by smoothing the distribution process. They help to ensure that products are available for sale when and where consumers want to purchase them. They also simplify exchanges of ownership required to complete transactions.

For example, if you want something warm to eat on a cold winter night, you don't call up the Campbell Soup Co. and ask them to sell you a can of chicken noodle soup. Instead, you go to the nearest grocery store, where you find

Business Directory

retailer channel member that sells goods and services to individuals for their own use rather than for resale.

not only chicken noodle, but also a wide variety of other soups from both Campbell's and other soup makers. Planning ahead, you decide to get some spaghetti and tomato sauce for tomorrow night's dinner, as well.

The grocery store has created utility for you in several ways. First, it makes the soup you want available in a convenient location. Second, it saves you from individually contacting the soup, spaghetti, and sauce manufacturers. The store has already arranged to offer a wide choice of products on its shelves. Finally, you can pay for all your purchases at once at the checkout counter rather than exchanging money several times with the various manufacturers.

Providing Services Marketing intermediaries often specialize in certain functions, so they can perform these activities more efficiently than producers or consumers could on their own. As Figure 15.3 shows, intermediaries provide services such as buying, selling, storing, and transporting products.

Most of the small, independent grocery stores that buy inventory from wholesalers like Fleming cannot afford to own and operate their own warehouses. However, they can create demand only if they place the right items on their shelves. Fleming performs an important function for its customers by handling their transportation and storage needs.

Marketing intermediaries also provide useful information to other channel members. Since wholesalers cover larger geographic territories than typical retailers, they can often supply retail customers with information regarding consumer acceptance of new products, successful promotions by retailers in other cities, and

details about new-product introductions. Today, 60 percent of the nation's supermarkets encourage customers to carry and present frequent-shopper cards as a way to build shopper loyalty and to learn about customer buying patterns. This information helps to guide product reorders and distribution of store coupons that match buying patterns. For example, cardholders with infants may receive discount coupons for Huggies diapers, Gerber food products, and baby bottles.

Marketing intermediaries often perform another value-added function by transforming products to increase their usefulness to buyers. Retail meat markets purchase sides of beef and convert them into different cuts of steak, roasts, and ground meat. MicroAge buys computers from manufacturers like Compaq, Hewlett-Packard, and IBM, then modifies them before reselling them to computer stores and large corporate customers.

Figure 15.3   **Services Performed by Marketing Intermediaries**

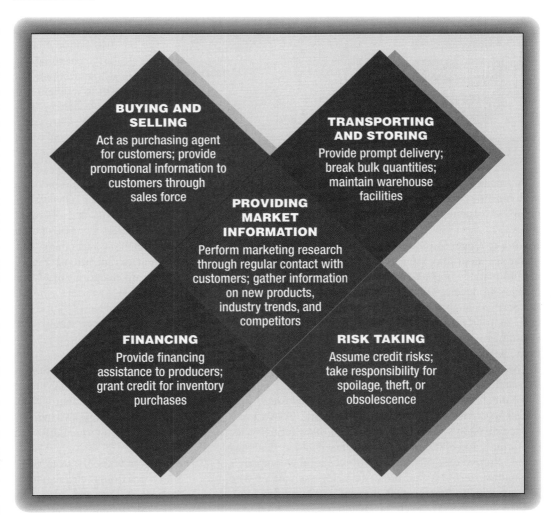

BUYING AND SELLING
Act as purchasing agent for customers; provide promotional information to customers through sales force

TRANSPORTING AND STORING
Provide prompt delivery; break bulk quantities; maintain warehouse facilities

PROVIDING MARKET INFORMATION
Perform marketing research through regular contact with customers; gather information on new products, industry trends, and competitors

FINANCING
Provide financing assistance to producers; grant credit for inventory purchases

RISK TAKING
Assume credit risks; take responsibility for spoilage, theft, or obsolescence

MicroAge stocks more than 30,000 computer components in its 300,000-square-foot warehouse, allowing the firm's employees to install the specific components and software requested by each customer prior to shipment. For

| Figure 15.4 | **Reducing Transactions through Marketing Intermediaries** |

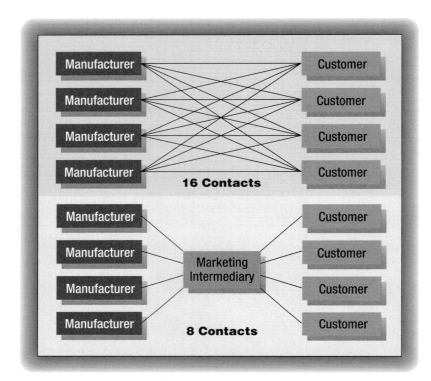

some manufacturers, MicroAge even manages their support hot lines, helping customers to set up and run new computer systems.[5]

Reducing Costs Although the costs that marketing intermediaries incur may seem likely to add to the cost of a final product, the opposite often results. By representing numerous producers, a marketing intermediary actually cuts the costs of buying and selling. As Figure 15.4 shows, if each of four manufacturers were to sell directly to four consumers, it would have to complete 16 separate transactions. Adding a marketing intermediary, such as a retailer, to the exchange process cuts the number of necessary transactions to 8.

Sometimes, marketing intermediaries can help producers to downsize their workforces. Nestlé USA's food-service division sells to restaurants and other food-service operations. Recently, Nestlé managers decided that they could improve cost-efficiency by replacing the company's 14 southwestern regional direct sales representatives with independent brokers specializing in supplying the food-service industry. "To reach the customers we wanted to in

that region, we couldn't afford a direct sales effort," explains Mike Mitchell, a Nestlé senior vice president.[6]

Often, marketing intermediaries reduce the costs of products that their customers buy from them. Buying in large quantities, they may qualify for quantity discounts, allowing them to pass along these savings to their customers. Many small retailers discover that manufacturers are unwilling to sell the quantities they want directly to them. By contrast, large wholesalers place sizable orders and receive good service and low prices.

In the health-care industry, Cardinal Health provides drugs and medical supplies to hospitals, HMOs, and individual pharmacies. Since Cardinal buys in bulk from manufacturers, the wholesaler can secure considerably lower costs than each of its customers would pay to purchase the same goods directly from the manufacturers.[7]

WHOLESALING

Obviously, wholesalers play crucial roles in the distribution channels for many goods, particularly consumer goods. As defined earlier, wholesalers are marketing intermediaries that sell to retailers, business purchasers, and other wholesalers—but not directly to ultimate consumers. This section of the chapter focuses on the different types of wholesaling intermediaries and their role in moving goods from producer to consumer.

Wholesaling intermediaries can be classified on the basis of ownership. *Ownership* refers to the person or company that owns and operates the wholesaling function. Manufacturers own or operate some wholesaling operations, retailers own others, and still others operate as independent organizations. Figure 15.5 outlines the various ownership categories of wholesaling intermediaries.

Manufacturer-Owned Wholesaling Intermediaries

A manufacturer's marketing managers may decide to distribute goods directly through company-owned facilities in order to maintain control of distribution or customer service. Firms operate two main types of manufacturer-owned wholesaling intermediaries: sales branches and sales offices.

Sales branches stock the products they distribute and fill orders from their inventories. In addition, they can also provide storage and serve as offices for sales representatives. Sales branches are common in the chemical, petroleum products, motor vehicle, and machine and equipment industries.

A *sales office* is exactly what the name implies, an office for a producer's salespeople, who represent its products in a particular territory. Manufacturers set up sales offices in various regions in order to support local selling efforts and improve customer service. For example, some manufacturers of kitchen and bathroom fixtures maintain showrooms to display their products. Builders and decorators can visit these showrooms to see how the items would look in place. Unlike sales branches, however, sales offices do not perform storage functions or warehouse any inventory. When a customer orders a product at a showroom or other sales office, the merchandise is delivered from a separate warehouse.

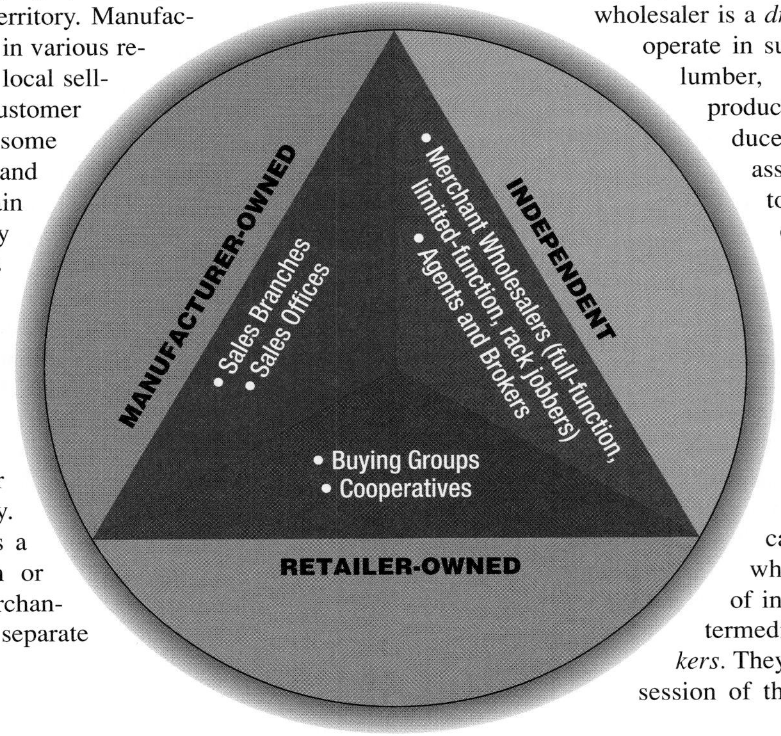

Independent Wholesaling Intermediaries

Figure 15.5   **Categories of Wholesaling Intermediaries**

This type of intermediary is a profit-seeking business that represents a number of different manufacturers when they make sales calls to retailers, manufacturers, and other business accounts. These intermediaries account for about two-thirds of all wholesale trade. Independent wholesalers are classified as either merchant wholesalers or agents and brokers, depending on whether they take title to the products they handle.

Merchant wholesalers are independently-owned wholesaling intermediaries that take title to the goods they handle. Within this category, a *full-function merchant wholesaler* provides a complete assortment of services for retailers or industrial buyers. Both Cardinal Health and Fleming Co. are full-function merchant wholesalers.

A subtype of full-function merchant wholesaler is a *rack jobber*. A rack jobber stocks, displays, and services particular retail products, such as paperback books or greeting cards in a drugstore or supermarket. Usually the retailer receives a commission based on actual sales as payment for providing merchandise space to a rack jobber.

A *limited-function merchant wholesaler* also takes legal title to the products it handles, but it provides fewer services to the retailers to which it sells. Some limited-

function merchant wholesalers only warehouse products without offering delivery service. Others warehouse and deliver products but provide no financing.

One example of a limited-function merchant wholesaler is a *drop shipper*. Drop shippers operate in such industries as coal and lumber, characterized by bulky products for which no single producer can provide a complete assortment. They give access to many related goods by contacting numerous producers and negotiating the best possible prices. Due to the burden of shipping and handling such products, cost considerations call for producers to ship them directly to the drop shipper's customers.

Along with these categories of merchant wholesalers, a second group of independent wholesaling intermediaries are *agents and brokers*. They may or may not take possession of the goods they handle, but they never take title. They normally perform fewer services than merchant wholesalers offer, working mainly to bring together buyers and sellers. Two similar intermediaries familiar to many people are stockbrokers and real estate agents. Since they represent ultimate consumers, both are considered retailers. However, they perform functions similar to those of agents and brokers at the wholesale level, since they do not take possession or title to sellers' property. They create time and ownership utility for both buyer and seller by helping to carry out transactions.

International Commerce Exchange System (ICES) is a broker that uses the Internet to connect sellers with buyers. A manufacturer with products to sell contacts ICES. The company then adds the manufacturer's goods to its electronic catalog, which it distributes to potential buyers, usually retailers or other wholesalers, via the Internet. ICES has brokered deals in products from excess inventories of sports coats to T-squares. "We're a global matchmaker," says ICES president Ross Glatzer. "We bring buyers and sellers together."[8]

www.icesinc.com

Manufacturers' agents are another important type of wholesaling intermediary. Also known as *manufacturers' reps* or *independent reps,* they act as independent sales forces by representing manufacturers of related, but non-competing, products. They receive commissions based on percentages of the sales they make.

Jerry Whitlock is a manufacturers' agent who sells seals and gaskets to factories. His office is filled with hundreds of catalogs, brochures, and other sales literature from the manufacturers he represents. Whitlock calls on factory purchasing agents throughout his assigned territory and supplies them with needed seals and gaskets. Last year, his home-based business generated $1 million in sales.[9] The Business Tool Kit suggests some tips for selecting a manufacturers' agent.

Other agent wholesaling intermediaries include sales agents, who typically represent larger territories than those of manufacturers' agents, and commission merchants, who sell agricultural products for farmers. A final type, auction houses, allow potential buyers to inspect merchandise prior to bidding on it. Figure 15.6 describes an auction of antiques and fine art conducted by Neal Auction Co. of New Orleans. Art galleries and antique dealers place bids on items of interest, and the auction company earns compensation based on the sales prices.

Retailer-Owned Cooperatives and Buying Offices

Retailers sometimes band together to form their own wholesaling organizations. Such an organization can take the form of either a buying group or a cooperative. The participating retailers set up the new operation to reduce costs or to provide some special service that is not readily available in the marketplace. To achieve cost savings through quantity purchases, independent retailers may form a buying group that negotiates bulk sales with manufacturers. In a cooperative, an independent group of retailers may decide to band together to share functions like shipping or warehousing.

Each of the 10,500 True Value hardware stores is an independent retailer. To compete against such corporate giants as Home Depot, Lowe's, and Builder's Square, these small retailers have banded together under the name *True Value* and formed a cooperative buying group, TruServ. By combining their orders from hardware manufacturers, the True Value owners can negotiate better prices than they would pay individually, which, in turn, helps them to offer competitive prices to consumers. Additionally, TruServ operates distribution and warehousing centers that support the True Value stores, providing additional savings.[10]

RETAILING

Retailers are the final elements of the distribution channel. Not including automobiles, approximately $1.8 trillion worth of goods are sold through retailers in the United States each year.[11] Each of the five largest U.S.-based retailers—Wal-Mart, Sears, Kmart, Dayton Hudson, and JCPenney—generates more than $25 billion in sales every year. Since retailers are often the only channel members that deal directly with final customers, they must remain constantly alert to consumer needs. They must also keep pace with the developments in the fast-changing business environment. As Chapter 4 explained, some retailers are also expanding internationally, opening vast new opportunities. This section takes a closer look at retailing and the critical roles that retailers play in the distribution channel.

Wheel of Retailing

Retailers never operate in a static environment. Over time, competitive strategies change, new types of retailers emerge, and marketing institutions unable or unwilling to respond to changing markets and new cus-

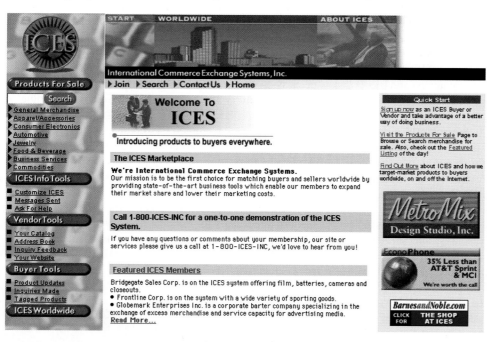

Cyberspace broker ICES is a global matchmaker, assisting buyers and sellers by offering substantial discounts on surplus products ranging from toys to lamps.

tomer expectations go out of business. The **wheel of retailing** is a theory intended to explain how and why these changes occur.

According to this theory, new types of retailers enter the market and gain a competitive foothold by offering low prices and limited services. Once they become established, these companies gradually add more services, causing them to raise prices and making them vulnerable to newer retailing models with appeals based on low prices.

As Figure 15.7 shows, most major developments over time in retailing appear to fit the wheel pattern. The low-price/limited-service position has characterized early department stores, catalog retailers, supermarkets, discount stores, and—most recently—Internet retailers and giant "big-box stores," such as PetsMart, Barnes & Noble, and Staples. Most of these retailers raise price levels gradually as they add new services.

For a recent example, consider how book selling has changed in the past decade. In the late 1980s, independent bookstores began to lose business to giant chains like Barnes & Noble and Borders Books. These chains generated sales volumes that allowed them to buy in bulk and offer discount prices to customers. Initially, they lacked many of the personalized services that small, local bookstores provided. Eventually, however, they began to add services to compete with each other. Some now offer comfortable reading areas, designer coffees, poetry-reading sessions, and book-signing engagements by authors.

Then Amazon.com entered the market in a totally new way—book selling on the Internet. Customers found cut-rate pricing for books ordered through an electronic system. Amazon.com minimized costs by maintaining no stocks of books. Rather, it relied on book wholesalers to fill its orders. Soon, Barnes & Noble also set up a Web site. To remain competitive, Amazon.com increased its inventory to stretch the selection it offered. This change will ultimately force its prices to rise in order to cover expenses involved in cataloging, promoting, and shipping the extra selections on its Web site. Thus, the wheel of retailing

Figure 15.6   Auctioneers—Agent Wholesaling Intermediaries

Neal Auction Company

Spring Estates Auction
April 3, 4 & 5

Featuring fine American, English & French furniture, decorative arts and paintings, including property deaccessioned by the Hermann - Grima/ Gallier Historic Houses, New Orleans

Auctioneers & Appraisers of Antiques & Fine Art
4038 Magazine Street • New Orleans, LA • 504-899-5329
fax 504-897-3808 • 800-467-5329 • www.nealauction.com

may turn again, forcing Amazon.com to look for more innovative ways to meet competition.[12]

The wheel of retailing shows how the principle of survival of the fittest determines success in the retail industry. As the Business Hall of Shame illustrates, retailers that fail to change fail to survive. "You have to keep challenging and reinventing yourself," explains Bruce Shamper, CEO of General Nutrition Co., which runs the GNC chain of nutritional supplement stores. "If not, someone else will beat you to it."[13]

Types of Retailers

The wheel of retailing suggests a range of many different types of retailers. One way to look at retailers is to group them into two broad categories: nonstore retailers and store retailers. Nonstore retailers do not sell through physical storefronts; instead, they contact customers and resell goods through other methods. Examples include catalog houses and Internet retailers. Store retailers maintain traditional, physical storefronts. This category includes convenience stores, department stores, factory outlets, and warehouse clubs. Today, however, many retailers span both categories. JCPenney sells merchandise in its stores, through its catalog, and also over its Internet site. Some manufacturers also are retailers. For example, both Levi Strauss and Nike operate their own retail outlets in addition to selling through independent outlets.

www.   **www.jcpenney.com**

The following sections take a closer look at these two categories of retailers and some of the challenges they face.

Business Directory

wheel of retailing   theory explaining changes in retailing as a process in which new retailers gain a competitive foothold by offering low prices and limited services, then add services and raise prices, creating opportunities for new low-price competitors.

Figure 15.7   The Wheel of Retailing

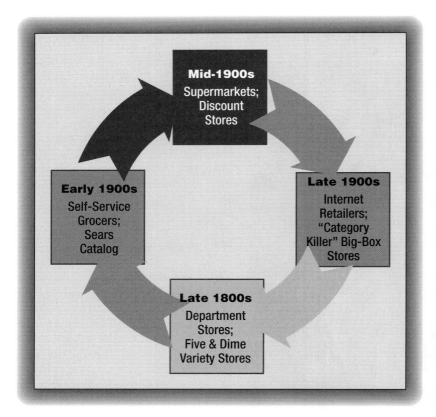

Nonstore Retailers

Although most retail transactions occur in stores, nonstore retailing serves as an important marketing outlet for many products. In fact, nonstore retailers currently account for $72 billion in sales, and that number is expected to grow to $93 billion a year through 2001.[14] Nonstore retailing includes direct-response retailing, Internet retailing, automatic merchandising, and direct selling.

Direct-Response Retailing   Direct-response retailing takes many forms. Retailers reach prospective customers through catalogs, telemarketing, and even magazine, newspaper, and television ads. Every year, over 13 billion catalogs are mailed to consumers and businesses, and some $80 million in merchandise is sold through these outlets.[15] Home-shopping networks are another direct-selling vehicle.

Direct-response customers can order merchandise by mail, telephone, computer, and fax machine, as well as by visiting the mail-order desk in a retail store. After the customer places an order, the retailer ships the merchandise to the customer's home or to a local store for pick-up.

One of the most important reasons customers choose direct-response retailers is convenience. Research about shoppers who buy from catalogs, for example, has shown that they want to save time and avoid the hassles associated with retail stores.[16]

Customer service is another important motivation for shoppers to buy through direct-response retailers. These retailers may provide toll-free numbers and liberal return policies in order to satisfy customer expectations.

Internet Retailing   A growing number of Internet-based retailers sell directly to customers via sites on the World Wide Web and online services such as America Online. These firms operate from virtual storefronts, usually maintaining little or no inventory. Instead, they order directly from vendors to fill customer orders received via electronic communications.

Internet retailing is a rapidly growing phenomenon. In 1997, online retail sales more than doubled to $2.6 billion.[17] As Table 15.1 shows, five product categories will each ring up at least $500 million on the Internet in 2000: travel services; personal computer hardware; entertainment products; books and music; and gifts, flowers, and greetings. Online sales for these merchandise categories will increase five-fold between 1997 and the beginning of the new century.[18]

Many traditional retailers are experimenting with Internet retailing. Store retailers that have set up virtual storefronts include Bloomingdale's, The Gap, Sears, and Office Depot. When Wal-Mart launched its online shopping site, 1 million shoppers visited the site on the first day it opened.[19] Today, shoppers visiting this virtual Wal-Mart can choose from a wide variety of merchandise including apparel, books, housewares, and even gardening equipment and supplies. Shoppers can also hunt bargains in the Wal-Mart Web site's clearance section.

Both Service Merchandise and Macy's have launched gift registries on their Web sites. As Figure 15.8 illustrates, visitors to the sites can register, browse, or make online

Table 15.1   Internet Merchandise Sales Estimates for 2000

Product Category	Estimated Sales (in billions)
Travel services	$4.7
Personal computer hardware	2.9
Entertainment	1.9
Books and music	0.8
Gifts, flowers, and greetings	0.6
Apparel and footwear	0.4
Food and beverages	0.4
Jewelry	0.1
Consumer electronics (except computers)	0.1
Sporting goods	0.1

BUSINESS TOOL KIT

How to Find the Right Independent Sales Rep for Your Product

Manufacturers' agents have proven an outstanding channel choice for thousands of businesses. Since they are paid on commission, they don't require the training and human resource expenses associated with creating and maintaining a regular sales force. For a manufacturer considering expanding operations into a new state or international market, these intermediaries offer an inexpensive market-entry alternative. Little-known manufacturers may discover that independent agents with established customer bases and strong relationships in their territories can generate sales that might not have been possible otherwise. But where do you find these problem solvers? Experts suggest four ideas for finding qualified independent sales reps:

▼ Decide what you want the manufacturers' agent to accomplish. What industry are you trying to reach? What types of customers do you want the sales rep to handle: retailers, other businesses, or wholesale distributors? What territory will the rep cover?

▼ Usually independent sales reps deal in more than one type of product line. Identify other products that your target customers are buying. Contact the store buyers, purchasing executives, or manufacturers for those products, and ask whether the manufacturer sells directly or through independent sales reps. If they use sales reps, ask for referrals.

▼ Ask other manufacturers' agents for referrals. Most will be pleased to recommend someone that suits your product line or target market.

▼ Ask your local, regional, or national industry trade association for referrals. Many list manufacturers' agents in their member newsletters.

Source: Based on "Early Starts," *Business Start-Ups*, December 1997, p. 6.

---

purchases. Although some retailers fear cannibalizing instore sales, these services also attract customers from areas without the retailers' outlets.[20]

Internet commerce is discussed in further detail in Chapter 17.

Automatic Merchandising Automatic merchandising through vending machines is another retailing method for various types of consumer goods. Candy, soft drinks, ice, chewing gum, sandwiches, and soup are typical vending machine items. Soft drinks account for 40 percent of all

Figure 15.8   **Promoting Customer Convenience with Online Gift Registries**

BUSINESS HALL OF SHAME

Good-Bye to Good Buys at Woolworth

By the time you were born, once-common variety stores had already begun to disappear, seemingly falling victim to the wheel of retailing. At one time, however, the so-called "five & dimes" were retail stars—and Woolworth shone the brightest of all.

The birth of this retailing institution can be traced to 1879, when 27-year-old Frank Woolworth had an idea. He opened a store in Utica, New York, that carried a wide variety of merchandise, most of it priced at 5 cents or less per item.

Woolworth's concept was an instantaneous success. By the turn of the century, the world's first variety store had also grown to become the first giant retail chain. Woolworth stores could be found on thousands of Main Streets, selling products from goldfish to laundry detergent at some of the lowest prices around. The company even expanded overseas, growing to over 2,100 stores in its heyday. Although other retailers tried to copy Woolworth, none executed the concept with so much success.

Over the last 20 years, however, Woolworth stores faced new challenges. Consumers abandoned downtown shopping areas in favor of suburban shopping centers and giant regional malls. Fast-food retailers like McDonald's made nostalgic relics of Woolworth lunch counters. Huge discounters like Wal-Mart and Kmart attracted Woolworth's customers with larger stores, wider varieties of merchandise, and lower prices. "Everybody—the supermarkets, Toys R Us, department stores, and large discounters—have been chipping away at parts of their business for years," says one retail analyst.

---

vending-machine sales, more than double the amount generated by the second-highest category, snack foods and candy.

The ability of these machines to accept paper currency greatly expanded automatic merchandising sales. Some movie theaters now place vending machines selling movie-inspired CDs and T-shirts in their lobbies. An estimated 5 million vending machines in the United States annually sell approximately $28 billion in goods. The majority of vending machine retailers, however, are small, entrepreneurial firms. In fact, 75 percent of them earn less than $1 million a year.[21]

Direct Selling In the final type of nonstore retailing, some manufacturers sell their products directly to consumers, bypassing independent wholesalers and retailers. Well-known firms using the direct-selling approach include Fuller Brush Co., Kirby and Electrolux vacuum cleaners, Avon cosmetics, and Amway household products. Party-plan selling methods of companies like Tupperware, Mary Kay Cosmetics, and Home Interior are also forms of direct selling.

Store Retailers

Although nonstore retailing methods—especially direct-response retailing and Internet selling—are rapidly growing, 90 percent of all retail sales take place in retail stores. Store retailers range in size from tiny newsstands to multi-story department stores. As Table 15.2 shows, they com-

pete by varying the product lines they carry and the services they offer to their customers.

Specialty retailers like Just for Feet, which sells athletic footwear, compete by offering thousands of products in a single product line. In contrast, new 170,000-square-foot Super Kmart stores stock the chain's typical lines of clothing and housewares along with a full-service grocery line including butchers and bakers, hair salons, florists, bank branches, and even UPS shipping services.

 www.kmart.com

Another retail competitive strategy involves developing unique bundles of services desired by target customers. Full-service retailers such as Bloomingdale's and Nordstrom have built global reputations for outstanding service. By contrast, limited-service retailers such as supermarkets, discount houses, and off-price retailers charge lower prices by eliminating the costs of such traditional services as credit, extensive salesperson assistance, and delivery.[22] The Business Hall of Fame discusses one firm's efforts to find the right combination of products, services, and image.

How Retailers Compete

Retailers compete with each other in many ways. Nonstore retailers focus on making the shopping experience as convenient as possible for consumers. Chili retailer Hot! Hot!

Although Woolworth executives were all too familiar with the wheel of retailing, they were unable to compete with the powerful forces that reshaped their industry. By 1990, the retail chain was losing money. It closed 1,900 unprofitable stores over the next 3 years and redirected its efforts toward highly profitable specialty chains like Foot Locker and Lady Foot Locker stores and its Champs Sports chain of sporting goods outlets. Also profitable was its Northern Reflections chain of clothing stores.

Even though profits from these new retail ventures propped up Woolworth stores, the inevitable occurred in 1998. Company executives announced that all Woolworth stores would be closed by 1999. "The consumer has changed towards shopping at large 'big-box' discount retailers. That has left the Woolworth division without a clear niche," said CEO Roger Farah. Even the Woolworth corporate name will be changed, cutting the company's links to its 19th-century roots.

QUESTIONS FOR CRITICAL THINKING

1. Relate the history of Woolworth stores to the wheel of retailing theory. What type of retail format do you think will replace today's successful large discounters?

2. Discuss the retail strategies the F. W. Woolworth Co. might have implemented to help its stores compete. Which of these strategies do you think would have had the greatest chance of success? Why?

3. Evaluate the company's decision to focus on its specialty retail outlets, Foot Locker, Champs Sports, and Northern Reflections. What challenges might these retail outlets face in the next decade?

Sources: "Woolworth Sports New Name," CNN Financial News, April 2, 1998, accessed at www2.cn-nfn.com; Yumiko Ono, "What's in a Name? Woolworth Seeks to Shed Dime Store Image," *The Wall Street Journal*, March 20, 1998, p. B6; William Kates, "Goodbuy, Woolworth," *The Columbian*, October 20, 1997, p. B9; and Paul Schrieber, "Life after Woolworth," *Newsday*, September 15, 1997, p. C10.

Hot! reaches customers far beyond its San Francisco location by offering Internet retailing to fans of spicy condiments around the world. Specialty retailers like The Nature Company offer customers maximum atmosphere in the form of soothing background music and hands-on access to such environmentally-oriented products as telescopes, globes, minerals, and books.

Like manufacturers, every retailer must develop a marketing strategy based on solid goals and strategic plans. Successful retailers convey images that alert consumers to the stores' identities and the shopping experiences they provide. Nordstrom, for example, has established a retail image very different from that of Family Dollar. A customer willing to pay premium prices for new fashions and

Table 15.2 Types of Retail Stores

Store Type	Description	Example
Specialty store	Offers complete selection in a narrow line of merchandise	Shoe stores, jewelry stores, camera shops
Convenience store	Offers staple convenience goods, easily accessible locations, long store hours, and rapid checkouts	7-Eleven, Circle K, gasoline stations
Discount store	Offers wide selection of merchandise at low prices; off-price discounters offer designer or brand-name merchandise	Kmart, Target, Wal-Mart, T. J. Maxx, Marshall's
Warehouse club	Large, warehouse-style store selling food and general merchandise at discount prices to membership cardholders	Costco, Sam's Club
Factory outlet	Manufacturer-owned store selling seconds, production overruns, or discontinued lines	Nike, Reebok, Dooney & Bourke, Liz Claiborne, Eddie Bauer
Supermarket	Large, self-service retailer offering a wide selection of food and nonfood merchandise	Safeway, Winn-Dixie, Kroger, Lucky
Supercenter	Giant store offering food and general merchandise at discount prices	Super Kmart
Department store	Offers a wide variety of merchandise selections (furniture, cosmetics, housewares) and many customer services	Bloomingdale's, Dillard's, Marshall Field's, JCPenney, Sears

BUSINESS HALL OF FAME

Bath & Body Works Cleans Up

Beth Pritchard is a woman with a mission. She plans to turn the chain of specialty stores she heads into "the McDonald's of toiletries." If Bath & Body Works' performance over the last few years is any indication of future success, Pritchard is well on her way toward reaching that goal.

Launched in 1990 by parent company The Limited, Bath & Body Works

(B&BW) has grown into the nation's leading bath-shop chain. Although B&BW sales represent just 9 percent of sales for The Limited, B&BW's $192 million in operating profits contribute almost 30 percent of the parent company's total earnings.

From scented soap to herbal shampoo, the chain's line of personal-care products attracts customers in search of affordable luxury. Innovation is a key factor in Pritchard's growth strategy. She describes the firm as "passionately committed to finding what's

next." About 30 percent of the company's inventory at any specific time is composed of new products.

Pritchard recognizes that merchandise alone doesn't guarantee retailing success, though. "Because you don't desperately need our products, we must entertain you," she explains. "It's a Disney mentality." Step into any Bath & Body Works outlet, and suddenly the mall seems very far behind you. Each store is designed to project an image that reflects "American Midwest values: appreciation for nature, healthy

---

personalized service might choose Nordstrom. A customer looking for low-priced bargains and little or no service would visit a local Family Dollar store.

In order to create the desired retail image, all components of a retailer's strategy must complement each other. After identifying target markets to serve, retailers must choose merchandising, customer service, pricing, and location strategies that will attract customers in those market segments.

Figure 15.9   Clothing for the Baby Gap Target Market

Identifying a Target Market The first step in developing a competitive retailing strategy is to select a target market. This choice requires careful evaluation of the size and profit potential of the chosen market segment and the current level of competition for the segment's business.

Customer research by marketers at The Gap revealed that a substantial percentage of the chain's regular customers had children and sufficient purchasing power to dress them in fashionable, high-quality garments. Separate sections within Gap outlets were created to feature Baby Gap and Gap Kids clothing lines. Figure 15.9 shows a sample of the Baby Gap product line.

Product Strategy After identifying a target market, the retailer must develop a product strategy to determine the best mix of merchandise to carry in its effort to satisfy that market. Retail strategists must decide on the general product categories, product lines, and level of variety to offer. A retailer's product strategy should determine consistent choices of pricing, promotional, and customer service strategies to attract and retain target customers.

Talbots has forged a successful product strategy that in-

environment, and family values." Farm-house style wooden furniture in warm colors evokes rural America. Bath products are displayed in old barrels. The stores work hard for this homey and welcoming feel.

When Pritchard became CEO in 1991, the B&BW chain consisted of 95 stores. Since then, she's expanded the number of outlets to 750 and hopes to boost market coverage to 1,700 stores, far surpassing her nearest competitor. Bath & Body Works outlets are located in upscale shopping malls across the United States, and Pritchard is now looking abroad for new markets. Five stores are currently being tested in Great Britain, and plans call for expan-

sion to other European countries in the next 2 years.

Just as McDonald's is the best-known brand in hamburgers, Pritchard sees Bath & Body Works as becoming the standard retailer for toiletries. "We're a brand that happens to have stores that distribute our product," she explains. The strategy seems to be working.

QUESTIONS FOR CRITICAL THINKING

1. Identify the strategies that Bath & Body Works has used to create a competitive retail image.
2. Do you agree with Pritchard's assessment that she's creating a

brand, not just a retail chain? Give specific examples to defend your answer.
3. What dangers are involved in Pritchard's strategy of rapid expansion into European markets? How can they be avoided or minimized?

Sources: "Intimate Brands' April Same Store Sales Rise 7 Percent," Reuters Limited, May 3, 1999; Lori Bongiorno, "The McDonald's of Toiletries," *Business Week*, August 4, 1997, pp. 79–80; and "Intimate Brands to Close Some Stores," *Reuters News Service*, accessed at www.pathfinder.com, January 28, 1998.

cludes a sophisticated mix of classic-styled women's clothing aimed at high-income professionals shopping for suits, dresses, tailored pants, and preppie-style accessories. A management decision to try to attract younger, less conservative shoppers than Talbots' 600 outlets had traditionally served resulted in the addition of short skirts, tight-fitting slacks, and other trendy, casual items in bright colors like tangerine and aqua. The strategy change backfired. The attempt to attract younger shoppers failed, and the merchandise changes alienated Talbots' core shoppers, causing sales to plummet and the previous years' profits to turn into an $11.5 million loss. "We moved too far," admits CEO Arnold B. Zetcher. Talbots quickly returned to its traditional mix of classic clothes in a vigorous effort to woo former customers back to its stores.[23]

Many retailers try to increase sales by diversifying their product lines, a practice known as **scrambled merchandising.** Originally, drugstores just sold medicines. Then they added soda fountains and newspapers. Now, they sell cameras, small appliances, greeting cards, cosmetics, toys, and even clothing.

Supermarkets are changing, as well, offering varied goods and services well beyond traditional grocery products. Kroger supermarkets have perfume counters, and Fred Meyer stores sell jewelry and apparel in addition to food. HyVee, an Iowa-based supermarket chain, offers high-priced gift items such as $210 decorative clocks and $270 cigar humidors. During the holiday season, HyVee even offers to gift-wrap these purchases for customers. Part of the motivation for this drive toward diversification stems from competitive pressure. Wal-Mart, Kmart, and Target stores all have opened supercenters with grocery sections.[24]

Customer Service Strategy A retailer's customer service strategy focuses on attracting and retaining target customers in order to maximize sales and profits. Some stores provide wide varieties of customer services for shoppers, such as gift wrapping, alterations, return privileges, interior design services, and delivery. Less obvious customer service strategy decisions include devising ways to make shopping easy, fast, and convenient for shoppers. Other stores offer only "bare bones" customer service, stressing low prices instead.

Contrast the customer service strategies of two different retailers selling computers and other electronics equipment—CompUSA and Fry's Electronics. CompUSA's 134 stores offer a wide variety of extra services along with computer-related equipment. Each store has a repair shop, classrooms where customer training sessions are held, and a delivery van with a crew of installers. CompUSA even custom-builds computers for customers with unique computing needs. Computer purchasers choose CompUSA because they want personal service and technical advice about computers.[25]

Fry's Electronics, on the other hand, takes a vastly different approach to customer service. Its 16 megastores are enormous, some as large as 184,000 square feet, and stock over 30,000 items. Supplies and inventory are stacked everywhere in the aisles. Security guards patrol the store looking for potential shoplifters. Customers typically cannot get help from employees and must be willing to serve themselves. The store hires minimum-wage employees without technical knowledge and offers bonuses for talking customers into taking store credit instead of cash for returned purchases. If customers complain, Fry's rarely responds to their complaints.

Yet, Fry's has achieved enviable success. Customers tolerate the infuriating service because they know the San

Talbots' ill-fated attempt to lure young shoppers into its stores with a more casual merchandise line turned off its core target market of high-income professionals. This year's selections return the apparel chain to its profitable niche in the retail market.

Jose, California-based chain offers one-stop electronics shopping with terrific selection and low prices.[26]

Pricing Strategy As Fry's illustrates, pricing can play a major role in consumers' perceptions of a retailer. Therefore, a retailer's pricing strategy must support its overall marketing objectives and policies.

Retailers are the channel members that determine the prices consumers pay for goods and services. They base their pricing decisions on the costs of purchasing products from other channel members and offering services to customers. Discount retailers, for example, usually buy in large volumes so they can offer merchandise at low prices.

Ross Stores learned the importance of pricing strategy when the discount clothing chain attempted to move away from its successful pricing structure. Much of its success had come selling "packaway" goods—end-of-season, name-brand merchandise that had failed to sell during a particular time period. Ross bought these goods from producers like Ralph Lauren and sold them at big discounts.

Hoping to expand sales, however, Ross started selling current styles of merchandise at higher prices alongside its bargain-priced goods. Instead of boosting sales, the plan sank the company's volume. Customers stopped

shopping at Ross, because the higher-priced goods contradicted its image as a discount retailer. Once management discovered the problem, they changed their retail strategy, eliminating the higher-priced goods. Sales rebounded, as customers again began to perceive Ross as a store that offered great deals on clothing. "Customers are coming in for a bargain, if not necessarily for a blouse," says CEO Michael Balmuth.[27]

Location Strategy A good location often makes the difference between success and failure in retailing. The location decision depends on the retailer's size, financial resources, product offerings, competition, and, of course, target market. In addition to deciding whether to locate in a downtown business district, an outlying area, or a neighborhood shopping center, a retailer must also consider factors like the side of the street to choose to take advantage of traffic patterns. The visibility of a store's signage, parking availability, and complementary stores located nearby should also influence the choice of a retail location.

Retail stores quickly followed the country's shifting population from urban to suburban areas beginning in the 1950s. Department stores began to augment their traditional downtown sites by opening branches in suburban

They said it

"Location, location, location."

William Dillard (1914–)
Founder, Dillard's department stores

shopping centers. Other retailers focused exclusively on suburbanites for their business. A **planned shopping center** is a group of retail stores planned, coordinated, and marketed as a unit to shoppers in a geographic trade area. By providing single, convenient locations with free parking facilities, shopping centers have largely replaced downtown shopping in many urban areas. Each month, over 185 million adults visit one or more of the nation's 42,000 shopping centers.[28]

Although the Mad Hatter beckons customers to this Fry's megastore, customers endure minimal service under rows of security cameras in return for outstanding selection and rock-bottom prices.

However, several trends have begun to erode the popularity of shopping-center retailing. First, many time-pressed consumers are reducing the time they spend shopping. The growth in catalog purchasing and Internet retailing is at least partially explained by the speed and convenience these outlets offer. It also explains some of the appeal of one-stop shopping at large, free-standing stores like Wal-Mart.

Another factor depressing growth prospects of major regional shopping malls is the popularity of small centers with specialty appeals. More than half of the shopping centers currently operating cover less than 100,000 square-feet each.[29] In contrast to a shopping mall, which offers a wide variety of stores selling products in varying categories, a specialty center targets a more narrowly defined market segment by offering an assortment of similar stores. For example, a specialty center might attract value-conscious consumers by gathering together factory outlets and discount stores. Another specialty center may target upscale shoppers by placing several high-fashion clothing and accessory stores together.

A small but growing number of national retailers are locating away from shopping centers. The Gap, for example, has located one-third of its stores in metropolitan locations like mid-town Manhattan. The company dubs these locations "neighborhood" stores and believes they attract customers by offering the ambiance and convenience of an old-fashioned city neighborhood. "A significant portion of our future sites will be off the mall," says one Gap executive.[30]

Saks Fifth Avenue has opened stores in nonmall locations. Saks Main Street units typically serve affluent suburban areas, offering merchandise carefully chosen to reflect the styles and needs of customers in the surrounding communities. The company currently runs three Main Street units and plans to open two more in the next year.[31]

Promotional Strategy A retailer designs advertisements and develops other promotions both to stimulate demand and to provide information, such as the store's location, merchandise offerings, prices, and hours. Retailers set up in-store displays to attract customer attention to various merchandise. Store personnel also play a key role in a retailer's promotional strategy. Retail salespeople communicate the store's image and persuade shoppers to buy. They serve as sources of information about the store's goods and services. Many retailers have intensified their efforts to train and motivate salespeople in order to keep customers satisfied and increase the likelihood of repeat purchases.

A retailer's promotion also projects a certain image designed to attract its target market. Sears, Roebuck had developed a strong image as a retailer of hardware and appliances. When the chain's sales flattened, however, company executives knew they needed to broaden the stores' image with customers. In response, they introduced a highly successful series of advertisements, illustrated in Figure 15.10, that invited female consumers to "come see the softer side of Sears." Small retailers have developed their own strategies for attracting attention without spending huge sums on promotion, as the Business Tool Kit explains.

Store Atmosphere A successful retailer closely aligns its merchandising, pricing, and promotion strategies with *store atmospherics,* the physical characteristics of a store and its amenities, to influence consumer perceptions. Atmospherics begin with the store's exterior, which should help to draw customers inside. Many retailers use eye-catching architectural designs to gain customer attention and interest. Interior atmospheric elements include store layout, merchandise presentation, lighting, color, sounds, and cleanliness. These elements should support overall

Figure 15.10 **Using Promotion to Enhance the Image of Sears as a Fashion Retailer**

"He got something to strengthen his legs."

"I got something to weaken his knees."

Come see the softer side of **SEARS**

strategy by complementing the retailer's image, responding to customer interests, and encouraging shoppers to buy.

Sporting-goods retailer REI uses atmospherics to maximum advantage in its flagship store in downtown Seattle. REI's target customers are outdoor enthusiasts who enjoy active sports like rock climbing, mountain biking, and wilderness camping. The store facility gives potential customers the opportunity to try out its products be-fore they commit to buying them. Built at a cost of $30 million, the store features the world's tallest free-standing, indoor climbing structure and a mountain biking trail on which customers can test equipment and outerwear. Recognizing the environmental consciousness of most of its customers, REI uses solar energy and natural light extensively throughout the store, and countertops are made from recycled newspaper and soybeans.[32]

Global Retailing

Fiercely competitive retailing in the United States features saturated markets that limit opportunities to increase sales and market share. This competitive environment has spurred a growing number of retailers to look abroad for growth opportunities in new markets.

Toys R Us, Wal-Mart, Pier 1 Imports, and Bath & Body Works are among the thousands of retailers opening outlets in Asian and European countries. U.S. catalog retailers are also going global for new business. Europe's relatively affluent, well-developed markets have attracted such catalogers as Eddie Bauer, Lillian Vernon, and L. L.

BUSINESS TOOL KIT

Attracting Customers on a Shoestring Promotion Budget

Small retailers often face a disadvantage in competing with the large retailing chains and their large advertising and promotion budgets. They have found some low-cost ways to bring customers to their stores, though:

▼ Ask customers to recommend your store to their friends and relatives.

▼ Mail a "welcome to the neighborhood" flyer to new residents. Many local newspapers list the new owners of houses that have recently sold.

▼ Team up with other small, noncompeting retailers in your area. Split the cost to send area residents a direct mail flyer or newsletter that promotes all of your stores.

▼ Get involved in your community. Sponsor community improvement projects, join local business associations, support your local schools and sports teams.

▼ Start a customer database. Keep track of individual customer preferences, needs, and buying habits. Invite listed customers to visit the store to see new merchandise that you think they'd like.

▼ Sponsor special events that tie in with your retail concept. A bookstore might form a monthly reading group. A children's clothing store might invite a local pediatrician to speak about child-care issues.

Bean. German consumers purchase 5.8 percent of all products by mail order, almost double the 3.0 percent mail-order purchase rate of U.S. shoppers.[33]

Foreign retailers are also joining the competitive battles in the U.S. market with their own local stores. IKEA, Benetton, and Food Lion are all foreign companies with outlets in the United States.

As Chapter 4 discussed, global retailing offers growing opportunities, but it also presents challenges to firms entering the international arena. While many products travel easily among different countries and cultures, others require significant modifications in their original marketing strategies to attract and meet the needs and wants of international shoppers.

Climbers at REI's indoor climbing facility experience atmospherics at the downtown Seattle store.

the level of distribution intensity. Additionally, businesses need to pinpoint strategies for successfully managing their distribution channels to limit conflict between channel members.

Selecting a Distribution Channel

Firms can distribute goods and services through a wide variety of channels. In deciding which distribution channel offers the best efficiency, business managers need to consider the factors shown in Figure 15.11: the market, the product, the producer, and the competition. These factors are often interrelated and may change over time.

Lands' End, for example, has targeted customers in the large and growing professional classes in Europe and such Asian markets as Japan, Hong Kong, and Singapore. These countries' well-established infrastructures and efficient postal services help the Wisconsin marketer to distribute its catalogs.

In each market, however, Lands' End marketers were forced to adjust their domestic strategies. High-quality, American-style clothing proved popular with Germans, but the company's lifetime warranty produced lawsuits from German mail-order competitors, which typically require customers to return merchandise within 2 weeks. In Asia, the company's classically tailored clothing styles appealed only weakly to local shoppers, who prefer flashier apparel such as short skirts. Lands' End also adjusted pattern sizes to fit Asian customers.[34]

DISTRIBUTION STRATEGY DECISIONS

Every firm faces several strategic decisions in choosing how to distribute its goods and services. The most basic among them are the selection of a specific distribution channel and

Market Factors A firm's most important consideration in choosing a distribution channel is the market segment it will serve. Ideally, a channel decision should reflect the needs and desires of the company's target customers. Who are the company's customers and where are they located? How often will they need to purchase the firm's products? To reach a target market with a small number of buyers or buyers concentrated in one geographic area, a direct channel may be the most feasible alternative. On the other hand, if the firm must reach geographically dispersed customers or those who need to make frequent purchases of small amounts of goods, then the channel may need to incorporate marketing intermediaries to ensure that goods are available when and where customers want them.

Product Factors Product characteristics also affect a distribution channel strategy. In general, complex, expensive, custom-made, or perishable products require short distribution channels involving few intermediaries. On the other hand, standardized products or products with low unit values usually pass through relatively long distribution channels.

DID YOU KNOW?

▼ Many Japanese food stores are resupplied three times a day to ensure product freshness.

▼ Federal Express has encountered great trouble getting Russian drivers to wash their trucks with company-supplied soap. The drivers prefer to take the soap—so much higher quality than the local version—home to their families.

▼ In a Japanese department store, the "bargain basement" is located on an upper floor.

Product factors also influence choices of intermediaries in the distribution channels. Hill's Science Diet pet food products, for example, offer higher nutritional value than other pet food brands. They also cost more money. To convince customers that the nutritional quality justifies the prices, Hill's has crafted a careful distribution channel strategy. First, Science Diet products are not available in supermarkets. While they are sold through selected pet stores, even more vital links in the distribution chain are veterinary clinics. Hill's sales representatives, many of whom are veterinarians themselves, visit clinics and encourage veterinarians to recommend the Science Diet brand to pet owners. Many animal clinics are also Science Diet retailers, selling the pet food products directly to customers.[35]

Producer Factors A firm's management, financial, and marketing resources also influence its choice of distribution channels. Financially strong manufacturers with broad product lines typically establish their own sales representatives, warehouses, and credit departments to serve both retailers and consumers. Small firms usually depend on marketing intermediaries to perform these functions. Businesses without adequate financial resources may also have difficulty satisfying bulk orders from large wholesalers or retailers.

Securing financial backing is one of the greatest challenges facing a new business, as Glory Foods owners learned when they first started out in business. Glory Foods fills a market niche for traditional soul-food items like black-eyed peas, peppered vinegar, and canned sweet potatoes. The company's three partners each chipped in $20,000 to launch the company. They distributed their products to large supermarket chains like Kroger and Food Lion but ran into trou-

Figure 15.11	Factors Affecting Channel Choice

MARKET FACTORS
Market Size
Business Buyers or
    Ultimate Consumers
Order Size
Frequency

PRODUCT FACTORS
Perishability
Product Complexity
Product Costs
Product-Service
    Purchase
    Requirements

PRODUCER FACTORS
Management, Financial,
    and Marketing
    Resources
Size of Current Product
    Line
Need for Channel Control

COMPETITIVE FACTORS
Availability of Independent
    Intermediaries with
    ability and willingness
    to perform required
    marketing functions

South Carolina vegetable grower Joseph Frison, Jr. supplies Glory Foods with ingredients for its line of farm-fresh black-eyed peas, grits, and peppered vinegar.

ble when these large retailers placed orders that Glory Foods couldn't fill from its funds on hand. Until the company arranged a line of credit, it had to negotiate with retailers for smaller orders.[36]

Competitive Factors Competitive performance is a key consideration when choosing a distribution channel. A producer loses customers when an intermediary fails to achieve effective promotion or delivery of its products. Apple Computers, for example, has long struggled to get computer wholesalers to devote adequate attention to its line. Recently, Apple announced it would no longer distribute computers through three of its five major wholesalers due to its dissatisfaction with their efforts to promote and market its product line.[37]

When entering a new market, any strategy requires managers to identify the most efficient distribution channel. For most of its history, eyewear manufacturer Randolph Engineering sold its aviator sunglasses directly to its primary customer, the U.S. armed forces. However, military cutbacks in the early 1990s forced Randolph to seek new markets. One option was to sell its sunglasses directly to American consumers. However, this choice would entail head-to-head competition with two deeply entrenched brands, Oakley and Ray-Ban. Both of these potential competitors had long-standing relationships with key U.S. wholesalers that limited Randolph's ability to get its products into stores.

Instead, Randolph decided to sell its eyewear in European markets, with fewer well-established competitors and lower barriers to entry. The venture succeeded because European customers perceived Randolph's eyewear as a status symbol. Eventually, Randolph set up distributorships in 72 countries. The company is now trying to move into the American market by distributing through manufacturers' representatives who sell the Randolph line to optical stores. Randolph is also distributing its shades through its Web site and upscale catalogs like J. Peterman.[38]

www.randolphusa.com

Selecting Distribution Intensity

Another important strategic distribution decision sets the level of distribution intensity. *Distribution intensity* refers to the number of intermediaries or outlets through which a manufacturer distributes its goods. For example, only one Mercedes-Benz dealership may be operating in your immediate area, but you can find Coca-Cola everywhere—in supermarkets, convenience stores, gas stations, vending machines, and restaurants. Obviously, Mercedes-Benz has chosen a different level of distribution intensity than Coca-Cola. In general, market coverage varies along a continuum with three different intensity levels: intensive distribution, selective distribution, and exclusive distribution.

▼ **Intensive distribution** involves placing a firm's products in nearly every available outlet. Generally, intensive distribution suits low-priced, convenience goods such as chewing gum, newspapers, and soft drinks. This kind of market saturation requires cooperation by many intermediaries, including wholesalers and retailers, in order to achieve maximum market coverage.

▼ **Selective distribution** is a market-coverage strategy in which a manufacturer selects only a limited number of retailers to distribute its prod-

uct lines. Selective distribution can reduce total marketing costs and establish strong working relationships within the distribution channel.

▼ **Exclusive distribution,** at the other end of the continuum from intensive distribution, involves limited market coverage by a single retailer or wholesaler in a specific geographic territory. The approach suits relatively expensive specialty products, such as the Kawasaki Jet Ski shown in Figure 15.12. Retailers are carefully selected to enhance the product's image in the market and to make certain that well-trained sales and service personnel will contribute to customer satisfaction. Although manufacturers may sacrifice some market coverage by granting an exclusive territory to a single intermediary, the decision usually pays off in developing and maintaining an image of quality and prestige.

During the past two decades, Vans has experimented with various degrees of distribution intensity for its shoes. Initially, company-owned stores brought the products to the company's teenage customers. When a character in the 1982 hit movie *Fast Times at Ridgemont High* wore a pair, their popularity soared. Vans decided to intensify its market coverage to include independent surf and skateboard shops. By the early 1990s, major outlets were also carrying the Vans brand, and management decided to expand into international markets. Somewhere along the way, though, Vans executives overlooked the main reason teenagers wanted the shoes: They were hard to find. Vans, like Nike in recent years, was hurt by its own success. As Vans vice president Steve Van Doren put it, "The kids didn't want to see what they wear in every store in every mall."

Vans decided to return to its early distribution strategy in order to regain its status as a cult favorite. Two new lines of shoes designed specifically for skateboarders were

Figure 15.12 **Exclusive Distribution—Manufacturer-Retailer Partnerships Created to Market Specialty Products**

Without water, there is no life.

Kawasaki JET SKI

The three-passenger 1100 STX is just one of seven genuine JET SKI® watercraft models to choose from. To find out more, or for directions to the nearest body of water, visit your Kawasaki dealer. Call 1-800-661-RIDE or visit us at www.kawasaki.com

developed and distributed through extremely selective channels. "We don't even sell them in our own 90 stores," says Van Doren. "The product is dedicated. It's made for skaters, and it's only going into those stores."[39]

Managing Distribution Channels

After selecting the most appropriate distribution strategy and the degree of intensity, attention then turns to channel management. Manufacturers must develop and maintain relationships with wholesalers and retailers in their distribution channels to ensure that these intermediaries devote sufficient time and resources to selling and marketing their products.

Several concerns arise in the course of distribution channel management. First, producers must carefully identify incentives needed to induce channel members to promote their products. Decisions about pricing, training, packaging, and other support efforts must complement a firm's overall distribution strategy in order to build positive relationships with channel members.

Power within the channel is also another factor. Not all channel members exert equal influence in the distribution chain. The **channel captain** is the dominant channel member, that is, the producer, wholesaler, or retailer with the most power in the distribution channel. The channel captain often controls many decisions about operations throughout the channel and the role each channel member plays in the distribution process. Traditionally, channel captains have been producers of the products distributed by other firms or wholesalers with power over small manufacturers and tiny, localized retailers. While these relationships remain common in some distribution networks, the growth of large retailers like Wal-Mart has increasingly moved power away from producers and wholesalers.

Consider, for example, the power wielded by Costco. With $22 billion in annual sales, its warehouse stores have enormous buying power with producers. Costco carries fewer products but much larger quantities than supermarkets. To place their products on Costco shelves, producers must meet the company's high standards for quality and pricing economies. Costco engineers values for its members by participating directly in decisions about production and distribution of the goods it sells. For example, in order to minimize shoplifting of razor blades, Costco asked Gillette to develop special theft-resistant packaging for goods it supplied to the chain. Costco also pressed Canadian and Chilean suppliers of salmon fillets to change the way they processed their fish so that Costco could satisfy its customers with low prices for a high-quality, boneless product.[40]

A distribution network functions smoothly only when all members cooperate in a well-organized effort to achieve maximum operating efficiencies. Because of the imbalance of power within many distribution channels, however, conflict often occurs between channel members. Finding ways to resolve channel conflict is an important distribution management task, one that usually falls to the channel captain.

Horizontal or vertical conflict can interfere with a distribution channel's effectiveness. In **horizontal channel conflict,** disagreements erupt among members at the same level in the distribution chain or among marketing intermediaries of the same type.

Vertical channel conflict occurs between members at different levels in the distribution chain. Such problems may arise if retailers develop their own private brands to compete with producers' brands, or if producers establish their own retail stores or create mail-order operations that compete with retailers. Levi Strauss, for example, has seen its sales drop, as retailers like JCPenney and Sears have introduced and promoted their own private-label jeans.[41]

The owners of Subway's 13,136 franchised stores—a number second only to McDonald's—complained bitterly about too many competing stores opening in their neighborhoods. Most franchises grant exclusive territories of a few miles to minimize cannibalization, but not Subway. Founder Fred DeLuca believes that clustering Subway outlets together boosts awareness and increases revenues. Consequently, he has moved to add Subway outlets in gas stations, often located within a few blocks of existing restaurants. Meanwhile, average revenues per store have dropped 8 percent from their 1994 high of $280,000, and 160 lawsuits have been filed—five times more than the total for McDonald's, Hardee's, KFC, or Burger King. DeLuca's reaction to the vertical channel conflict: "It bothers me that people lose money, but I don't lose sleep over it. This is America."[42]

Preventing vertical conflict is an even trickier challenge than before in the age of electronic commerce. Maytag, for example, allowed its Web site visitors to order its new Neptune washing machines before they reached retailers. Well-aware of its dependence on retailers,

Business Directory

channel captain dominant company that exerts the most power in a distribution channel.

supply chain complete sequence of suppliers that contribute to creating and delivering a good or service.

however, Maytag did not cut its retail partners out of the distribution loop. Instead, when the new machines arrived at nearby retailers, Maytag alerted them to customer orders booked over the Web. The retailer then contacted the customers and completed the sales. However, the success of Maytag's presale program has encouraged the company to consider the possibility of completing online orders itself, entirely bypassing retailers.[43]

Other manufacturers are involving channel members in their Internet marketing efforts. Fruit of the Loom, for instance, distributes its T-shirts to small screen-printing retailers through wholesalers. The retailers print designs on the T-shirts and sell them at concerts, sporting events, and souvenir shops. Not only has Fruit of the Loom set up a special intranet just so its wholesalers can place orders electronically, but it also helps them to build their own retail Web sites.[44] Solving an Ethical Controversy reviews another current source of channel conflict.

Vertical Marketing Systems Thousands of marketers have developed **vertical marketing systems (VMSs),** planned distribution networks designed to improve channel efficiency and prevent conflict among channel members along with other distribution problems. In the past, most distribution channels developed, not in planned sequences, but simply as momentarily convenient arrangements to meet consumer needs. Three types of vertical marketing systems—corporate, administered, and contractual—establish better planned channel networks.

▼ In a *corporate vertical marketing system,* one enterprise owns all of the channel members. Standard Brands, for example, manufactures home-improvement products and paints. It then sells its merchandise through company-owned retail outlets.

▼ An *administered vertical marketing system* is a distribution system dominated by the channel captain. A manufacturer, wholesaler, or retailer can fill this role. For example, The Gap has eliminated wholesalers. Instead, the chain places orders directly with apparel factories for products to be produced according to the firm's specifications.[45]

▼ *Contractual vertical marketing systems* have the greatest impact of all three options on a distribution strategy. Such a system binds channel members through a contractual agreement. The chapter has already discussed one type of contractual VMS—the retail cooperative—in which retailers set up their own wholesaling operation. A second type of contractual VMS is a *franchising* system, discussed in detail in Chapter 5. A final type of contractual VMS is a wholesaler-

sponsored voluntary chain of retail stores. Under this kind of agreement, a wholesaler provides marketing programs, merchandise selection, and other services to independent retailers that agree to purchase its products. A contractual VMS such as IGA Food Stores helps independent retailers to compete with mass merchandisers and retail chains.

LOGISTICS AND PHYSICAL DISTRIBUTION

A firm's choice of distribution channels creates the final link in the **supply chain,** the complete sequence of suppliers that contribute to creating and delivering a good or service to business users and final consumers. The supply chain begins when the raw materials used in production are delivered to the producer and continues with the actual production activities that create finished goods. Finally, the finished goods move through the producer's distribution channels to end customers.

Consider how Mickey Mouse ears make their way from the factory to the Magic Kingdom. The ear-hats are manufactured in Taiwan and shipped in various quantities, depending on the season. The ears then spend 7 days on an ocean-going cargo ship bound for Los Angeles. When they arrive, they wait about 2 days longer for completion of required customs forms and clearance for entry into the United States. Next, they are unloaded off the cargo ship and trucked to a warehouse where the order is consolidated. This step takes another 2 days.

Once again, Mickey's ears are loaded into trucks. They spend about 5 days traveling over the road before arriving at Disney World's distribution center in Orlando. There, the ears are sorted, weighed, logged in, and finally put into temporary storage. This processing takes about 2 days.

Soon, one of Disney World's many retail stores notices low stocks of Mickey Mouse ears. A store staff member alerts the distribution center, which packs the requested number and readies them for delivery the next day. Finally, after 24 days in transit, the Mickey Mouse ears are moved to the retail store. The store's employees then put the Mickey ears on display, and they are ready for sale.[46]

The supply chain can also be viewed as a *value chain.* Each link of the chain adds benefits for consumers, as raw materials and component parts move through manufacturing where they are converted into finished products for customers. The value chain includes all of the activities that add value to the finished good: design, quality manufacturing, customer service, and delivery. In order to maximize value for customers, businesses search for opportunities to add benefits in each activity they perform.

SOLVING AN ETHICAL CONTROVERSY

Should Large Retail Chains Try to Censor the Music They Sell?

Don't try to find Sheryl Crow's second album at your local Wal-Mart. When Crow refused to change a song line about children buying guns at Wal-Mart stores, the retailer told Crow it wouldn't be selling the album. Wal-Mart's decision probably cost the Grammy winner at least 400,000 lost sales.

As the largest single retailer of pop music in the country, Wal-Mart wields enormous power in the industry. The chain demands that recording artists meet rigid standards that avoid lyrics and album covers that offend its sensibilities.

Unlike Crow, many recording artists are willing to meet Wal-Mart's terms in order to increase the distribution of

their albums. The group White Zombie reluctantly agreed to airbrush a bikini onto a naked woman on the cover of *Supersexy Swingin' Sounds*. The band made the decision after realizing that fans in rural areas might not be able to buy the record anywhere but Wal-Mart. Local H agreed to rewrite the lyrics of two songs and remix a third in order to comply with Wal-Mart's content standards. The sanitized versions appear in Wal-Mart racks with small stickers that read "edited."

"Selling a record implying behavior that is against all we stand for is something we just could not profit from," says Dale Ingram, Wal-Mart's director of public relations. Other retail chains, like Kmart and Target, also monitor the content of the CDs they sell, but Wal-Mart's clout is much greater than theirs, giving the chain influence over the way records are produced

throughout this country.

 Should Large Retail Chains Try to Control the Content of the Music They Sell?

PRO

1. Wal-Mart's policy is simply a merchandising decision. Asking a record company to change a CD's cover art is no different from asking an apparel manufacturer to supply a certain amount of green women's blouses.

2. Retailers must satisfy the desires of their target markets. Wal-Mart's target market is family-oriented middle America. By insisting on lyrics that do not risk offending its target market, Wal-Mart is using good business sense and protecting its retail image. The company says it has received thousands of

---

The process of actually coordinating the flow of goods, services, and information among members of the supply chain is called **logistics.** The term originally referred to strategic movements of military troops and supplies. Today, however, it describes all of the business activities involved in actually managing movements through the supply chain with the ultimate goal of getting finished goods to customers.

Businesses spend more than $250 billion a year on logistics management, a figure that continues to grow as marketers look for ways to add value throughout their supply chains.[47] Logistics and supply chain management also gain importance as increasing numbers of firms enter global markets, expanding the need for efficient movement of goods not just across the country but around the world.

Physical Distribution

Physical distribution, the activities aimed at efficiently moving finished goods from the production line to the consumer, is a major focus of logistics management.

Although some marketers use the terms *physical distribution* and *transportation* interchangeably, their meanings differ. As Figure 15.13 shows, physical distribution is a broader concept that includes transportation and numerous other elements that help to link buyers and sellers. An effectively managed physical distribution system can increase customers' satisfaction by ensuring reliable movements of products through the supply chain.

A firm's physical distribution system begins by establishing guidelines for customer service. **Customer service standards** are the quantitative guidelines set by a firm to specify the quality of service it intends to provide for its customers. For example, a firm's managers may decide that all customer orders will be processed within 24 hours after receipt in the company's telemarketing center.

Business Directory

logistics all business activities involved in managing movements of goods through the supply chain.

letters from consumers supporting the policy.

3. Requesting changes in lyrics or cover art is not censorship, because all parties involved—the artists, the record companies, and the stores—must approve the revisions. Artists have the right to refuse and find other places to distribute their albums.

4. Wal-Mart provides vital services for the music distribution channel by selling more than 50 million CDs each year. The most powerful member in a distribution channel should have the right to influence what is produced.

CON

1. Wal-Mart's policy misleads consumers. Many do not even realize they are buying sanitized versions of the original album. The stickers that label an album as "edited" measure only one-sixteenth inch.

2. Consumers who actually buy and

listen to pop music are the ones driving Wal-Mart's record sales. Wal-Mart should satisfy their desire to hear unedited, uncensored music.

3. The policies of Wal-Mart and other retailers amount to censorship. Wal-Mart is crushing musical freedom.

4. Wal-Mart's lack of clear guidelines could lead to favoritism. The company might carry only albums produced by certain companies. "I don't know who the judge and jury is over there," says Val Azzoli, CEO of Atlantic Group. "Do they put records through the Wal-Mart standards machine, and if Sam Walton's face doesn't appear, they're no good?"

SUMMARY

Some record labels and artists complain about Wal-Mart's policies. Part of the problem, they say, is that Wal-Mart doesn't articulate clear guidelines for

offensive or expletive material. Instead, company executives review each album individually and decide on a case-by-case basis whether to accept or reject it. The company points out that it usually invites artists to make changes in order to get the albums into Wal-Mart stores. "Artists and labels decide if they want to change it or not," says Ingram. "That's free-market enterprise at work."

Sources: Eric Boehlert, "Meet the New Boss: Wal-Mart," *Rolling Stone*, July 10–24, 1997, p. 30; and Tom Long, "Does Anybody Care If Wal-Mart Crushes Musical Freedom?" *Detroit News*, January 17, 1997, accessed at www.detnews.com, January 1998.

Volvo is working hard to improve its customer service standards for U.S. buyers. Buyers in the western United States typically must wait 5 to 6 weeks for delivery from Volvo's Swedish assembly plants. By improving distribution procedures and switching transport carriers, the company expects to cut delivery time in half. By improving the delivery schedule, Volvo marketers hope to reverse the tendency of many customers to simply switch to competing brands that offer immediate delivery.[48]

After setting customer service standards, managers continue to assemble and coordinate the other five elements of physical distribution in ways that achieve these service goals at the lowest possible cost. Considerations include transportation, warehousing, materials handling, inventory control, and order processing.

Transporting Goods The choice among transporta-

tion options to ship products depends on several factors. Some products, such as perishable items, require relatively quick transportation in order to ensure satisfactory customer service. Cost is another important consideration, as transportation expenses account for between 40 and 60 percent of the distribution costs incurred by many businesses.[49]

Physical distribution managers can choose among several different types of transportation companies and transportation modes: common carriers, contract carriers, private

Figure 15.13 **Elements of a Physical Distribution System**

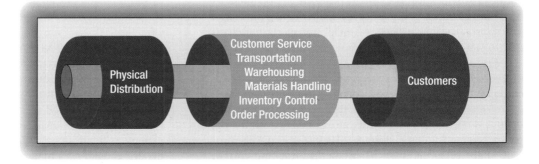

Physical Distribution → Customer Service / Transportation / Warehousing / Materials Handling / Inventory Control / Order Processing → Customers

carriers, and freight forwarders. *Common carriers* such as United Airlines and Consolidated Freightways use various modes of transportation to provide for-hire shipping services to the general public. A truck line like Averitt Express transports general merchandise for any individual party willing to pay its fee. Figure 15.14 highlights the services provided by this common carrier for shipments within a 13-state region between Virginia and Texas—including a 90 percent next—day delivery standard.

Figure 15.14 **Common Carriers—For-Hire Transporters Serving Firms that Outsource Their Transportation Functions**

Contract carriers are hired to transport goods under contracts or agreements with individual customers. They do not offer transportation services to the general public. They usually offer specialized services to meet the individual transportation needs of particular customers. Some contract carriers serve certain industries exclusively or solicit large shipments from particular shippers.

Private carriers are just that: private companies that transport their own property in their own vehicles and do not offer services for hire. Shell, for example, operates its own fleet of ocean-going crude-oil tanker ships. Similarly, Wal-Mart's extensive fleet of trucks transports merchandise to stores.

Freight forwarders differ in that they do not own any of the equipment for transporting freight. Instead, they are common carriers that lease or contract for bulk purchases of transportation services from other carriers, such as airlines and railroads. Freight forwarders then resell this capacity to small-volume shippers. They also typically provide other services, such as invoicing, tracking freight

shipments, and preparing customs documents. Freight forwarders are important intermediaries in the transportation industry. They save carriers the trouble of handling and billing for many small shipments and help shippers to obtain the least expensive possible transportation services.

Modes of Transportation The five major transportation modes are railroads, trucking carriers, water carriers, air freight carriers, and pipelines. Table 15.3 compares them according to the criteria of speed, reliability, shipment frequency, availability, and cost.

Railroads—The Nation's Transportation Backbone Although trucks overshadow all other transport modes based on dollar expenditures by users, railroads carry the heaviest burden as measured by ton-miles. A ton-mile indicates the shipping activity required to move 1 ton of freight 1 mile. Railroads carry over 1 trillion ton-miles of freight a year, in part because they offer the most efficient way to move bulky commodities over long distances.[50] Industries that rely heavily on this transportation mode include manufacturers of coal, chemicals, grain, and wood products. For example, 75 percent of all the resin used to produce plastic in the United States is shipped by rail.[51]

A recent industry trend has brought extensive consolidation through mergers and acquisitions. These mergers have combined large railroad companies such as Burlington Northern and the Santa Fe line. As a result, the number of large, cross-country railroads has dropped dramatically in recent years. While this change has created operating efficiencies for rail companies, shippers complain that the reduced competition has weakened rail service and eroded their power to negotiate rates. For example, shippers with access to only one rail carrier typically pay 60 percent more than shippers that can choose between two competing carriers.[52]

Motor Carriers—The Flexible Giant The trucking industry has grown dramatically in recent decades. Today, four-fifths of the nation's transportation expenditures pay to move freight over the highway system. Trucking offers a relatively fast method of shipment and consistent service for both large and small volumes. Another significant advantage is flexibility. A truck carrier can operate wherever the driver can find a road, while trains depend on rails, and

| Table 15.3 | Comparison of Transportation Modes | | | | | |

Type of Carrier	Total Transportation Expenditures (%)	Domestic Intercity Volume (%)	Factor				
			Speed	Dependability in Meeting Schedules	Frequency of Shipments	Availability in Different Locations	Cost
Truck	81%	28%	Fast	High	High	Very high	High
Rail	8	37	Average	Average	Low	High	Medium
Water	5	15	Very slow	Average	Very low	Low	Very low
Air	4	<1	Very fast	High	Average	Average	Very high
Pipeline	2	19	Slow	High	High	Very low	Low

planes require airports. Although a number of transcontinental highway carriers move goods from coast to coast, motor carriers are most efficient for shorter distances of 300 to 400 miles. Products most often transported by truck include clothing, furniture, fixtures, food, leather products, and machinery.

Air Freight—Fast but Expensive Air carriers are handling an expanding volume of freight, as shippers seek to satisfy increased customer demand for fast delivery. The growth of international business operations is also contributing to increased use of air transport. By 2013, air carriers will deliver twice as much cargo as they do now, especially on routes between European and Asian countries.[53] The cost of air transportation usually limits it to perishable and valuable products, such as flowers and furs, as well as time-critical shipments of industrial equipment components.

Most U.S. airlines also operate as common carriers and handle air freight. Some of them engage in charter work, a form of contract carriage. Other air carriers, known as *supplemental carriers,* may operate air fleets specifically for cargo transport. Some business organizations own or lease their own aircraft to transport freight.

Water Carriers—Cheap but Slow Water transportation, although slow, is one of the least expensive modes of transportation. Loading freight into standardized, modular shipping containers maximizes the savings of water transportation by limiting costs for loading, unloading, and other handling of goods. Water transportation lends itself mainly to hauling bulk commodities like fuel, petroleum products, coal, chemicals, minerals, and farm products.

Water carriers may operate on inland waterways or across oceans. *Inland water carriers* move cargo on rivers such as the Mississippi, Arkansas, Ohio, and the Tennessee-Tombigbee waterways. Much of this freight travels on barges pushed by mammoth tugs. *Ocean-going freighters* operate on the Great Lakes, between U.S. port cities, and in international commerce. Technology is expected to lead to new ship designs for ocean-going vessels that will expedite shipping times. On the horizon is the FastShip, which is capable of crossing the Atlantic in just 3.5 days, about half the time needed by conventional ships. The FastShip is expected to be in regular service by 2000. Although FastShip rates will be higher than current costs, many shippers believe the benefits of time saved in transit will offset the extra cost.[54]

Pipelines—Specialized Conveyance More than 214,000 miles of pipelines crisscross the United States, forming an extremely efficient network for transporting natural gas, petroleum products, and coal. Some commodities are ground into small pieces and mixed with water to form a slurry that is then pumped through the pipelines. Pipelines rank third after railroads and motor carriers in ton-miles transported, but they move suitable products more cheaply and rapidly than other modes of transportation do.

Intermodal Transportation Increasingly, shippers are choosing to combine transportation methods to move products. Intermodal transportation allows shippers to gain the service and cost advantages of various transportation modes. For instance, a company might ship goods in highway trailers that ride part way on railroad flatcars. This system combines the long-haul capacity of rail transport with the door-to-door flexibility of trucking. Shippers spent more than $82 billion on intermodal truck-rail shipments in 1997. Other intermodal methods combine truck and air modes or water and truck modes.

Warehousing Warehousing is the physical distribution element that involves storing products as they move through the distribution channel. Goods flow through two

Conrail Helped Sunkist Develop A Fresh Approach.

Hear Sunkist Director of Transportation Laurence Stern tell how Conrail made the right connections for Sunkist. Call, toll-free, 800-553-4284.

Sunkist's goal was a more efficient system of rushing fresh Western citrus to Eastern supermarkets.
But making that system work meant meeting an exacting schedule of intermodal connections. So they called Conrail.
And today, 8 years later, Conrail is still making those timely connections. Picking up shipments of Sunkist fruit from Western

railroads in Chicago, and speeding them on to markets throughout the Northeast. Consistently on time and fresh.
Maybe you didn't think Conrail could move that fast. But our network of connections with truck, rail and overseas shipping lines enables us to offer direct service to 6 of the 10 largest consumer markets in America: more than 42 million people in

the Northeast and Midwest.
To learn how Conrail can solve your transportation problem, or to hear Laurence Stern, director of transportation for Sunkist, tell how we helped him, call us at 800-553-4284.
Because if you're shipping to or through Conrail territory, we can show you a fresh approach, too. Tell us your story. Then watch how fast we can move.

Conrail. We've Made The Right Connections.

Intermodal transportation rushed fresh Sunkist citrus to eastern supermarkets. Conrail combined rail and truck shipments in a piggyback system to speed these perishable products across the United States.

types of warehouses: storage and distribution warehouses. *Storage warehouses* hold goods for moderate to long periods to balance supply and demand between producers and purchasers. *Distribution warehouses* are temporary storage facilities, often holding goods for 24 hours or less, that collect shipments and redistribute goods to other channel members.

Disney operates both storage and distribution warehouses throughout central Florida. Its eight warehouses supply the Magic Kingdom, Epcot Center, Disney/MGM Studios, and 15 hotels with over 400,000 items. These goods are distributed to 262 retail stores, 450 food-service locations, and 2,000 other locations on Disney property as needed. "Walt Disney World is basically a city of 160,000 people," says Tom Nabbe, Disney World's distribution services manager. "From a distribution standpoint, we're supplying that city with everything from Mickey plush toys to watermelon, 7 days a week, 24 hours a day. And that's a lot of hard work."

To expedite shipments, individual warehouses specialize in handling retail merchandise, food-service items, or general supply items. Some items—like Mickey Mouse ears—sit in the warehouses for only short periods of time. They are tagged, weighed, and repacked and then sent to retail stores. Other items—like office supplies and props for exhibits—are stored for longer terms so they are ready when needed. To manage the entire operation, Disney relies on a computerized warehouse management system that tracks every item from its arrival at one of the warehouses until it leaves.[55]

Materials Handling **Materials handling** is the physical distribution activity that moves items within plants, warehouses, transportation terminals, and stores. Firms handle goods with equipment such as forklifts, conveyor belts, and trucks. Costs rise every time an item is handled during its flow through the supply chain. Therefore, one important goal of modern materials handling is to eliminate steps that do not add value for final customers.

Unitization and containerization are two techniques that help firms to accomplish this goal. *Unitization* involves combining as many packages as possible into one load to be handled by a single truck or forklift. *Containerization* collects packages, usually from several unitized loads, into a compact form that is relatively easy to transfer. Both containerization and unitization have significantly reduced transportation costs for many products by cutting materials handling time, theft, insurance costs, damage, and scheduling problems.

Lennox Industries, a manufacturer of heating and air conditioning systems, cut costs significantly by redesigning several of its materials-handling methods. The company found that, on average, an air conditioner or hot water heater in its warehouse was handled 36 times from the time it left the assembly line until it was installed in a home. This handling frequently resulted in damage by forklift operators, who had difficulty picking up individual units.

To solve these problems, Lennox designed special corrugated cartons and added new forklift equipment. Both changes allow equipment to pick up individual units from the top, rather than the bottom, which has reduced damage. Lennox also began moving some products through the warehouse along conveyor belts. All containers are now bar coded as they leave the factory, further reducing warehouse handling. Lennox estimates it will save nearly $900,000 a year through these new materials handling methods.[56]

Inventory Control *Inventory* is the amount of finished goods a firm has ready for distribution. It is also an expensive resource. Holding $1,000 worth of inventory for just 1 year can cost a company $250 for storage, insurance, taxes, and handling. At the same time, however, businesses need to keep enough inventory on hand to meet customer demand. **Inventory control** attempts to balance the priority of limiting costs of holding stocks with that of meeting customer demand through a variety of management methods.

The Gap carefully controls inventories for its worldwide network of 1,900 stores. More than 500 factories produce apparel and other products for the retail chain, many of them with short life spans due to changing consumer tastes. Inventory must also reach stores in time for different seasons. To keep tabs on its inventory, the firm uses a variety of methods. First, each store enters sales information into the company computer system. Gap planners use this information to alert suppliers about what products need replenishment. After the merchandise is made, it is shipped to regional distribution centers and on to stores. In order to keep inventory levels low, stores have very little storage space, raising the importance of timing deliveries.[57]

The Gap's inventory management system makes use of the just-in-time (JIT) methods described in Chapter 12. By entering materials and inventory into the supply chain only as required, the firm minimizes the costs of holding unnecessary inventory.

Order Processing **Order processing** includes all of the tasks required to prepare customer orders for shipment. It also involves the steps involved in receiving shipments that arrive. Like the other components of physical distribution, order processing directly affects a firm's ability to meet its customer-service standards. Inefficient order-processing procedures also add to costs. In order to satisfy customers, firms may have to compensate for order processing inefficiencies by shipping products via costly transportation modes or by maintaining large inventories.

Managers at personal-care products maker Alberto-Culver recognized a need to solve inefficiencies in the firm's order-processing system in order to keep customers satisfied. Wal-Mart and other large retailers began demanding special labeling on Alberto-Culver shipments. They also wanted a closer link between Alberto-Culver's warehouses and their own inventory databases. They were increasingly dissatisfied with the 12 to 14 days the supplier needed to fill orders, especially because warehouses often ended up shipping incomplete orders due to poor inventory record keeping. The company responded by redesigning its warehouse and installing a computerized inventory management system.

New procedures for processing orders were also instituted. As a result, the firm's inventory turns over faster than before. Retailers' orders are filled 91 percent complete and arrive in 8 to 10 days. If necessary, orders can even be shipped within 2 hours. Alberto-Culver now has the flexibility necessary to handle orders in ways that meet customer expectations.[58]

WHAT'S AHEAD

This chapter has discussed how businesses ensure that customers receive the right products at the right times and places. Of course, it has assumed that customers want the goods and services being offered. The next chapter looks at how businesses use advertising, selling, and other promotional methods to inform, persuade, and remind customers to buy their product offerings.

SUMMARY OF LEARNING GOALS

1. Explain how distribution creates value for customers and competitive advantage for businesses.

Distribution creates value by providing place, time, and ownership utility. It helps customers to purchase goods conveniently, quickly, and with a minimum of effort. By strategically managing distribution, firms can gain competitive advantage. Not only does effective distribution support the consumer demand created by superior product design and promotion, but it also satisfies customer expectations. A well-chosen distribution strategy also helps to cut costs and boost profits by eliminating unnecessary steps in the supply chain.

2. Describe the various categories of distribution channels, and identify the factors that influence channel selection.

Marketers can choose either a direct distribution channel, which

moves goods directly from the producer to the consumer, or indirect distribution channels, which involve marketing intermediaries in the paths through which products—and legal ownership of them—flow from producer to consumer. Ideally, the choice of a distribution channel should support a firm's overall marketing strategy by providing consumers with convenient ways to obtain the goods and services they desire. The distribution channel should support a firm's overall marketing strategy. Firms must consider their target markets, the types of good being distributed, their own internal systems and concerns, and competitive factors before selecting distribution channels.

3. Explain the roles marketing intermediaries play in distribution channels.

Marketing intermediaries, or middlemen, include wholesalers and retailers. They help to smooth the distribution paths for goods by creating utility, performing marketing functions, and cutting costs. They save producers from dealing directly with large numbers of end-users. Instead, marketing intermediaries handle these tasks. They often specialize in certain functions and can perform these activities more efficiently than producers can. By representing numerous producers, marketing intermediaries cut the costs of buying and selling. Because they can consolidate orders, they may also negotiate better prices than individual consumers could attain.

4. Describe how retailers use pricing, promotion, location, and merchandise selection in order to compete effectively.

After identifying a target market, a retailer must plan pricing, promotion, product, and location strategies for attracting and satisfying that market. These activities help to create a retail image that sets the store apart from its competitors. In developing product strategy, retailers must decide on the general product categories, product lines, and selections to offer. Pricing can play a major role in consumers' perceptions of a retailer. Retailers are the channel members that determine the prices consumers pay for goods and services, and they base their prices on the costs of their own purchases from other channel members and the services they offer customers. Their location decisions depend on size, financial resources, product offerings, and, of course, the target market. Retailers use promotion to project an image that will attract target market customers. Promotional activities also provide information about a store's location, prices, and merchandise in order to entice consumers. Store atmospherics, the physical characteristics of a retail outlet and its amenities, also encourage customers to shop there.

5. Identify the major components of an effective distribution strategy.

A firm must consider whether to move products through direct or indirect distribution. Once the decision is made, the company needs to identify the types of marketing intermediaries, if any, through which it will distribute its goods and services. Another component is market intensity. The business must decide on the amount of market coverage—intensive, selective, or exclusive—needed to achieve its marketing strategies. Finally, attention must be paid to managing the distribution channel. An especially important goal is minimizing conflict between channel members.

6. List the different types of conflict that can occur in a distribution channel and the methods firms use to reduce channel conflict.

Power is not distributed evenly in most distribution channels. Imbalances often lead to conflicts between channel members. Conflict can be either *horizontal,* involving disagreements between channel members at the same level in the distribution chain, or *vertical,* occurring between channel members at different levels. Many companies have developed vertical marketing systems (VMSs), planned networks of distribution channels designed to avoid conflict among channel members and resolve other distribution problems.

7. Describe the importance of logistics and physical distribution in controlling the supply chain.

A firm's choice of distribution channels creates the final link in its supply chain, the complete sequence of suppliers that contribute to creating and delivering its good or service. The process of coordinating the flow of goods, services, and information among members of the supply chain is called *logistics.* Ideally, value is added to goods along each step of the supply chain through activities like superior product design, quality manufacturing, customer service, and efficient delivery.

A major focus of logistics is physical distribution, the activities aimed at physically moving finished goods from the production line to the consumer. Effective management of physical distribution can increase customer satisfaction by ensuring reliable, cost-efficient movement of goods through the supply chain.

8. Explain how the components of a physical distribution system work together to reduce costs and meet customer service standards.

A firm's physical distribution system begins by establishing guidelines for customer service. The firm must also identify the most cost-effective and reliable mode of transporting goods through the distribution channel. Other components of a physical distribution system include warehousing, materials handling, inventory control, and order processing. Each of these components also contributes to the firm's ability to get goods to consumers on time and in a reliable, cost-efficient manner.

9. Compare the alternative transportation modes on the bases of flexibility, dependability, and cost.

Rail transportation is the most efficient way to move bulk shipments over long distances. Rail is a relatively dependable and cost-effective option, but it is not always a flexible one. Trucking offers a fast way to ship and consistent service for both large and small shippers. Trucking is a very flexible alternative, because trucks can haul goods wherever drivers can find roads. Air carriers are the fastest way to move shipments, but air transport is more expensive than other transportation modes. Water transportation, although slow, is one of the least expensive modes of transportation. It lends itself mainly to hauling bulk commodities that are easily containerized. The nation's pipelines form an extremely efficient, rapid, and inexpensive transportation network for products like natural gas and petroleum. Many shippers combine transportation methods in a technique called *intermodal transportation* to move shipments as needed. This approach allows shippers to gain the service and cost advantages of various transportation modes.

TEN BUSINESS TERMS YOU NEED TO KNOW

distribution	retailer
distribution channel	wheel of retailing
direct distribution channel	channel captain
marketing intermediary	supply chain
wholesaling intermediary	logistics

Other Important Business Terms

scrambled merchandising	physical distribution
planned shopping center	customer service standards
intensive distribution	warehousing
selective distribution	materials handling
exclusive distribution	inventory control
horizontal channel conflict	order processing
vertical channel conflict	
vertical marketing system (VMS)	

REVIEW QUESTIONS

1. Outline the major categories of distribution channels and explain the factors marketers consider in choosing a specific distribution channel.
2. How do marketing intermediaries create value for customers? What specific functions do marketing intermediaries perform? Why would a producer prefer to utilize marketing intermediaries rather than perform these functions itself?
3. What are the most important decisions a business needs to make in developing an effective distribution strategy? Which do you think is the most critical one? Why?
4. Differentiate among intensive, exclusive, and selective distribution strategies. Give examples of firms that have successfully used each strategy.
5. What is a vertical marketing system? What role does it play in distribution strategy? Outline the major types of vertical marketing systems.
6. What is the wheel of retailing? Give an example that illustrates this concept.
7. Identify the various steps a retailer takes in developing a retail image. How does a retailer's target market influence each of these steps?
8. Explain the role of logistics in a firm's distribution strategy. Why is logistics an important consideration?
9. Outline the strengths and weaknesses of the various modes of transportation.
10. Explain how firms can improve their competitiveness through effective physical distribution. Outline the various components of physical distribution.

QUESTIONS FOR CRITICAL THINKING

1. Bio-Safe Enterprises, a small Oregon firm, has created an amazing hand lotion that prevents the spread of germs. The company has identified the following target market as possible customers:
   a. parents of newborns
   b. owners and managers of restaurants
   c. hospital purchasing offices
   d. individual consumers who are concerned with staying healthy

   Help Bio-Safe decide on the best distribution strategy for reaching each group. Suggest whether the firm should use direct or indirect channels and outline the marketing intermediaries the company might need to involve.
2. Make a list of all the items you bought in a recent visit to the supermarket. Suppose that no supermarket were available in your local area. Describe the steps you would need to go through to locate and buy each of these products. Relate this to the value added by marketing intermediaries.
3. Visit a local retail store. Based on your observations, describe the customer segment the store seems to be targeting. How is the store using promotion, pricing, location, and merchandise strategies to reach that target market? What recommendations would you make to improve the store's ability to compete with other retailers targeting the same customer segment?
4. Which type of distribution intensity would best suit the following products?
   a. Rolls-Royce automobiles
   b. Microsoft Windows '99 software
   c. Tissue paper
   d. Bulldozers and other large earth-moving equipment
   e. Levi's jeans
5. Suggest the most appropriate method for transporting each of the following goods. Explain your choices.
   a. gasoline
   b. canned soup
   c. watermelon
   d. teak furniture from Thailand
   e. oak furniture from North Carolina
   f. industrial parts that a business customer needs to repair a critical piece of machinery

Experiential Exercise

Background: Payless Shoe Source is the leading retailer of shoes in the $3 to $25 price range. The chain's 4,265 stores stock an average of 10,000 pairs of shoes in a retail space of 3,000 square feet. Payless's target customers are women who buy shoes not only for themselves but also for their children. Payless is facing new competition from Wal-Mart, the second-biggest seller of low-priced shoes.

Directions

1. If both Payless and Wal-Mart stores are located in your community, visit both stores to compare their shoe selections. If either of these chains do not have an outlet nearby, visit a shoe store catering to a similar target market.
2. Compare the promotional, merchandise, location, and pricing strategies of both locations.
3. Suggest strategies that might help Payless prevent Wal-Mart from gaining any further market share.
4. Identify additional information about Payless's target customers that its managers should collect to help them develop an effective marketing strategy.
5. Should Payless consider expanding into higher-priced shoe lines or stay with its current merchandise? Provide supporting arguments for the advice you suggest.

Source: Adapted from Louis E. Boone and David L. Kurtz, *Contemporary Marketing,* 1999 (Dryden Press, 1999), p. 524.

Nothing but Net

1. **Independent Wholesaling Intermediaries.** Assume the role of a home buyer, and visit one of the many Web sites on the Internet that will connect you with home-buying information. One such site is

   www.coldwellbanker.com/

   Prepare a list of the categories of information available at the Web site that could help you meet your information needs as a home buyer.
2. **Internet Retailing.** Here's an opportunity to try out the search engine of search engines:

   www.dogpile.com

   Visit this site to search for Internet retailing sites where you can shop for any of the products listed in Table 15.1. For example, key in the search words "jewelry sales" and examine the search results from each of the search engines provided, such as Yahoo!, GoTo.com, PlanetSearch, Thunderstone, What U Seek, Magellan, Lycos, WebCrawler, InfoSeek, Excite, and AltaVista. Compare the results generated from the different search engines, and discuss the growth of Internet retailing.
3. **Location Strategy.** Visit the Web site for the 400-plus store Mall of America, located in Minneapolis. List three factors that make this mall's location a desirable one.

   www.mallofamerica.com/

Note: Internet Web addresses change frequently. If you do not find the exact sites listed, you may need to access the organization's or company's home page and search from there.

LEVERAGING THE LINKS OF LOGISTICS

With revenues of more than $20 billion, Dow Chemical company is the fifth largest chemical producer in the world. Dow manufactures and supplies more than 2,500 product families, including chemicals, plastics, agricultural products, and environmental services. Most of Dow's products become raw material inputs by business customers. Dow produces chemicals at 40 processing plants in more than 30 countries.

Dow's logistics system links the processing plants to business customers worldwide. From its storage tanks, Dow delivers products to buyers via many transportation modes. Oceangoing vessels move products between continents, and barges transport them along rivers and seacoasts. On land, tanker trucks move small shipments short distances, while railroads move large shipments long distances in tanker and hopper cars.

Transporting hazardous chemicals is just one of many challenges Dow faces in continually improving its logistics system. "The real key to logistics is meeting all customers' needs by having the right product at the right place at the right time," says Bill Fillmore, supply chain project leader. In North America, Dow spends over $1 billion a year on logistics activities. Improving logistics provides critical help in maintaining Dow's ability to compete, because improvements enhance customer service, reduce costs, and increase company profits.

In the past, customers bought chemicals on price alone. Today, customers want just-in-time delivery service to reduce their inventory levels and their costs. Logistics efficiency is also a major source of cost reduction at Dow. "We're working to improve the materials management processes at Dow to improve the value of the company and to contribute to shareholder value," says Richard Gerardo, vice president of materials management, North America.

Dow is using information technology, quality management techniques, and supply chain management to boost the efficiency and effectiveness of its logistics system. Computer systems at processing plants monitor and control movement and storage of products. An electronic data interchange system transmits customer orders from computers at headquarters in Midland, Michigan, to processing plants. Computerized systems track a customer's shipment from the time it leaves the processing plant until it arrives at its destination. Using laptop computers, account managers can instantly communicate shipment status information to customer via e-mail.

Dow and its channel partners practice quality management techniques such as employee empowerment and preventive maintenance to improve chemical logistics safety, quality, and reliability. Employees responsible for transporting hazardous materials in the field are empowered to make necessary decisions on the spot. Through preventive maintenance of logistics equipment, Dow works to ensure safety and reliable deliveries. For example, Dow uses detector cars equipped with ultrasonic devices plus twice weekly visual inspections to monitor the rail carrier's tracks.

Dow conducts phone surveys with customers, asking them to evaluate its products and service performance, and compares this performance with that of Dow's best competitors. According to Dick Sosville, vice president of sales and marketing for Dow, North America, the customer satisfaction surveys move Dow toward the goal of becoming a more market-driven company.

Dow and its channel partners apply supply chain management techniques to improve logistics. For example, one cross-functional team assembled members from Dow, a rail carrier, and a customer to tackle the customer's problem with excess inventory. The team mapped the current logistics process and uncovered various problems. After studying the current process and discussing optional routes and interchange points, the team members mapped out a new logistics process. Implementation of the new logistics system resulted in cost savings of more than $200,000 a year.

Questions

1. What role does logistics play in Dow Chemical's competitive advantage?

2. What value-added services does Dow's logistics system provide to customers?

3. Describe how Dow uses the supply chain management techniques to improve logistics.

Sources: Some of the research material for this case was downloaded from http://www.dow.com/, April 18, 1997; William Miller, "Making Pollution Prevention Pay," *Industry Week,* May 20, 1996, p. 136–L; William Keenan, Jr., "Plugging into Your Customer Needs," *Sales and Marketing Management,* January 1996, pp. 62–66.

chapter 16

Promoting Goods and Services Using Integrated Marketing Communications

LEARNING GOALS

1. Relate the concept of integrated marketing communications to the development of a firm's promotional strategy.

2. Explain the concept of a promotional mix and list the objectives of promotion.

3. Summarize the different types of advertising and advertising media.

4. Explain the roles of sales promotion and public relations in promotional strategy.

5. Identify the various personal selling tasks and the steps in the sales process.

6. Discuss the role of sponsorships and cross promotions in integrated marketing communications planning.

7. Explain how public relations supports other elements of the promotional mix.

8. Identify the factors that influence the selection of a promotional mix.

9. Contrast pushing and pulling promotional strategies.

10. Identify the major ethical issues involved in promotion.

Joe Boxer Sells Skivvies with "Guerrilla" Marketing

Nicholas Graham's promotional philosophy can be summed up as "follow the crowd and you will never be followed by the crowd." Graham is CUO (chief underpants officer) of Joe Boxer Corp., one of apparel's fastest-growing firms and a major player in the underwear market. But to turn his product into a house-hold name, Graham knew he had to go up against such dominant names as Calvin Klein and Ralph Lauren. Both competitors have been praised—and condemned—for using sex to sell their underwear so, Joe Boxer decided to simply make people laugh. At 30,000 feet, Graham once impersonated a flight attendant on Virgin Atlantic Airways and persuaded 400 passengers to change their underwear mid-

flight. He even launched his underwear into orbit by arranging to have one pair of Joe Boxer and a Russian-made pair transported to the Mir spacecraft.

Mention the word promotion to the typical shopper and you produce images of advertising—on television and radio; in magazines and newspapers; and on billboards, buses, and taxicabs. But advertising is only one component in a firm's promotional mix. Joe Boxer's Graham grabs the spotlight with gusto, using humor, irreverence, and the old-

fashioned stunt. If superior promotion is measured by its ability to stretch the funds available (in promotion lingo, "to get more bang for the buck"), then Graham has all the right ideas. "The brand is the amusement park," he says. "The product is the souvenir."

"Somehow, being an underwear company gave us license to be funny," says Joe Boxer creative director Denise Slattery. "We knew that if we could extend ourselves through fun uses of the media, we could get the word out that Joe Boxer was a fun brand to buy." In fact, the product's birth was surrounded with humor. In 1985, Graham was in business for himself, designing and selling a line of neckties to department stores and specialty retailers. As a wedding gift to a store buyer, he concocted a pair of X-rated boxers. When the gift's recipient encouraged him to make more, Graham attached a raccoon tail to a pair of red-plaid boxers. The novelty skivvies sold like wildfire, and Joe Boxer was born. That same year, the company got its first big shot of publicity when a thousand pairs of Joe Boxer shorts were confiscated by the U.S. Secret Service. The briefs had been silk-screened with images of $100 bills, each so realistic that they violated counterfeiting laws. The story was picked up in newspapers, magazines, and on television—and Joe Boxer's promotional strategy was born.

Marketers refer to this approach as guerrilla marketing, a fast-hitting, spectacle-centered, and irreverent method of informing and persuading customers to buy your brand. Through this approach, Joe Boxer generated "77 percent awareness on a shoestring budget and guerrilla stunts," according

www. www.joeboxer.com

to marketing director Luanne Calvert. At first, the company stuck to novelty wear—including inflatable underwear, 3-D underwear, briefs that quack, and unmentionables that read "no, no,

no" in daylight, and "yes, yes, yes" at night. But today, 75 percent of company sales are made up of solid-color underwear. At half of the department stores selling Graham's briefs, Joe Boxer is the number-one brand. Graham's wacky humor has played a major role in building a unique pair of underpants into a multimillion-dollar phenomenon.

But just because Graham is now a very rich man doesn't mean the fun is going to stop anytime soon. A quick peek at the company's 14,000-foot New York showroom reveals that it's anything but sedate. Visitors come face-to-face with an eight-foot tall revolving banana and a bank of funhouse mirrors. They can also get an eyeful of Graham's favorite piece—the bright white conference room table covered with bold black letters spelling out "blah... blah... blah." And even though the company has expanded its promotional mix to include print advertising, Graham hasn't forgotten the value of unique products in grabbing our attention—just consider his canned underwear.

Joe Boxer products can now be found in vending machines in airports, train stations, health clubs, and amusement parks. Operated with a credit card, the dispensers spit out pop-top cans of boxer shorts and tees. But that's not all. These panty peddlers are wisecrackers; their motion-activated voices toss out such advice as, "Looks like you need some underwear" to passersby. A novel approach to retailing. But what did you expect from a man who has already sent his skivvies into space?[1]

CHAPTER OVERVIEW

Wacky stunts like those of Joe Boxer's CEO are one form of promotion, the final element in the marketing mix. This chapter completes the book's discussion of marketing strategy by focusing on the different types of promotional activities. In the process, it introduces the concept of integrated marketing communications.

Promotion is the function of informing, persuading, and influencing a purchase decision. This activity is as important to not-for-profit organizations such as the YMCA and New York Philharmonic Orchestra as to profit-seeking companies like Nike and Titleist.

Some promotional strategies try to develop *primary demand,* or consumer desire for a general product category. The objective of such a campaign is to stimulate sales for an entire industry, so that individual firms benefit from this market growth. A popular recent example is the "Got Milk?" campaign. Real-life and cartoon celebrities ranging from Spike Lee to Bart Simpson are featured in the print and television messages to capture audience attention. Figure 16.1 shows Denver Bronco quarterback John Elway in a typical ad sponsored by the California Milk Processors Board.

Most promotional strategies, however, seek to stimulate *selective demand*—desire for a specific brand. By promoting Tiger Woods's endorsement of their company's golf apparel, Nike marketers want to encourage customers to purchase their clothes, not Reebok's. Sales promotions that distribute cents-off coupons also encourage shoppers to purchase specific brands.

Clearly, marketers choose among many promotional options to communicate with potential customers. Each marketing message a buyer receives, in a television or magazine ad, Web site, direct-mail ad, event sponsorship, or sales call, reflects on the product, place, person, cause, or organization promoted in the content. In a process of **integrated marketing communications (IMC)**, marketers coordinate all promotional activities—advertising, sales promotion, sponsorships, personal sales presentations, and public relations—to execute a unified, customer-focused promotional strategy. This coordination avoids confusing the consumer and focuses positive attention on the promotional message.

The chapter opens by explaining the role of IMC and then discusses the objectives of promotion and the importance of promotional planning. Next, it examines the components of the promotional mix—advertising, sales promotion, personal selling, and public relations. The section on sponsorships and cross promotions demonstrates how marketers incorporate several elements into an IMC plan. Then the chapter examines promotional strategies

| Figure 16.1 | Celebrity Promotion Designed to Stimulate Primary Demand |

The Only Thing That Tastes Better Is Victory.

BRONCOS 7

MILK
Where's *your* mustache?

and techniques for selecting a promotional mix and measuring effectiveness. It concludes with brief discussions of international promotion and promotional ethics.

INTEGRATED MARKETING COMMUNICATIONS

Readership of the *Los Angeles Times* was sagging due to changing lifestyles that left people little time to read. In response, marketers at the 110-year old newspaper launched an integrated marketing program with the unifying theme, "Get the Story. Get the *Times.*" The campaign's messages featured real news stories to show consumers what they would miss by not reading the *Times*. A series of "cliffhanger" broadcast, print, and outdoor ads teased viewers by cutting off before communicating critical information. Billboards left big holes instead of completing sentences. Similarly, TV ads went blank at critical moments, radio ads stopped in mid-sentence, and print ads resembled an article ripped in half. These ads accompanied telemarketing appeals and price incentives. By emphasizing the relevance of the *Times* to potential readers' lives, the IMC campaign raised circulation almost 5 percent, the largest increase for a U.S. newspaper.[2]

Los Angeles Times marketers successfully applied the marketing concept and relationship marketing techniques to develop customer-oriented marketing programs. Their integrated marketing communications strategy demonstrates how IMC focuses on customer needs to create a unified promotional message. The *Times* and its advertising agency began working together to identify consumer needs; they then moved backward to develop messages showing how their product met those needs. Finally, they selected the best marketing channels through which to reach consumers.

To gain a competitive advantage marketers who implement IMC must broaden their view of promotion. As media options continue to multiply, they can no longer simply rely on traditional broadcast and print media and direct mail; plans must include all forms of customer contact. Packaging, store displays, sales promotions, event sponsorships, sales presentations, and online and interactive media also communicate information about a brand, company, or organization. Unless marketers develop an integrated approach and present a consistent message from all sources, they may confuse consumers with conflicting messages. With IMC, marketers create a unified personality for the good, brand, or service they promote. Coordinated activity also enhances the effectiveness of efforts to reach and serve target markets.

Fruit of the Loom took a unique IMC approach by featuring a specialty promotion item. Figure 16.2 is part of a 4-page insert in *Rolling Stone* magazine that featured a miniature version of its new Comfort briefs. Over one million pairs of these mini-underpants were included for the magazine's readers to inspect. "Everything about our new briefs is more comfortable, and you get a sense of that by touching the mini-version," says Dirk Herrman, vice president of brand marketing. "We hope it inspires people to try a pair of our real briefs." The insert also included a special "Seven for Six" pack offer. The company repeated the campaign's theme, "Take the Comfort Challenge," in a sweepstakes with Comfort Cruiser luxury vans as top prizes. To enter, customers had to match style numbers on the special underwear packages with game pieces from Sunday newspaper magazines. Print and broadcast ads supported the sweepstakes promotion.[3]

Designing Effective IMC Programs

Today's complex marketing environment incorporates both opportunities and challenges from multiple markets

 Combining Print Ads and Product Samples in the Fruit of the Loom IMC Program

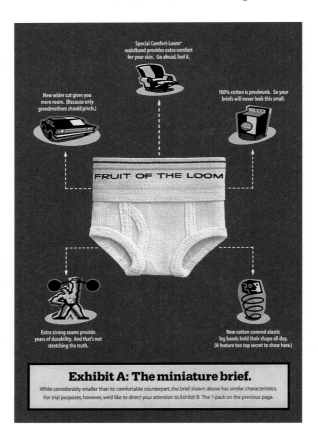

and expanding media options. IMC provides a framework within which an organization can develop promotional strategies to reach many different market segments. Two important elements of IMC programs are teamwork and databases.

Marketing managers set the goals and objectives for the firm's promotional strategy in accordance with overall organizational objectives and the goals of the marketing organization. Based on these objectives, marketers weave the various elements of the strategy—personal selling, advertising, sales promotion, sponsorships, publicity, and public relations—into an integrated communications plan. This document becomes a central part of the firm's total marketing strategy to reach its selected market segments. The feedback mechanism, including marketing research and field reports, completes the system by identifying any deviations from the plan and suggesting improvements.

IMC's big-picture approach involves teamwork between the marketing department and other departments like customer service, billing, and order processing that interact with consumers. The teamwork also extends to outside vendors. Prudential Insurance Co. and its advertising agency, Fallon McElligott, used a team approach to change consumer perceptions of the insurer. Prudential had established a strong brand identity through its "rock" logo, which conveyed stability. To many people, however, the rock also conveyed the image of a stodgy company that served people full of anxiety about the future. Working with Prudential marketing executives, ad agency personnel conducted surveys to determine the types of messages that produced the best consumer responses. Using this feedback, they created a series of promotions that showed how Prudential's many units, from insurance to securities and real estate, could help people take control of financial planning. The ads presented real people—not models—telling how they had started planning for their future financial needs as young adults and how well they were currently living as retirees. The old "Get a piece of the rock" slogan was replaced with the more empowering, "Live well. Make a plan. Be your own rock."[4]

As discussed in Chapter 13, database technology is an important marketing research tool, and it plays a criti-

Table 16.1	Comparing the Components of the Promotional Mix	
Component	**Advantages**	**Disadvantages**
Advertising	Reaches large consumer audience at low cost per contact Allows strong control of the message Message can be modified to match different audiences	Difficult to measure effectiveness Limited value for closing sales
Personal selling	Message can be tailored for each customer Produces immediate buyer response Effectiveness is easily measured	High cost per contact High expense and difficulty of attracting and retaining effective salespeople
Sales promotion	Attracts attention and creates awareness Effectiveness is easily measured Produces short-term sales increases	Difficult to differentiate from similar programs of competitors Nonpersonal appeal
Public relations	Enhances product or company credibility Creates a positive attitude about the product or company	Difficult to measure effectiveness Often devoted to nonmarketing activities

cal role in IMC programs, as well. Databases containing basic customer information like names and addresses, demographic information, lifestyle considerations, brand preferences, and purchasing patterns allow organizations to develop detailed consumer profiles. Companies may also benefit from data on the wholesalers and retailers with which they have channel partnerships. This information helps marketers to identify trends in buying patterns and create the right promotional strategies to maximize sales and profits. Cosner Comtech, a Montana cellular communications company, analyzed and segmented its customers based on sales data. After discovering that only 12 percent of its customers generated more than half of its sales, Cosner designed special promotions for these customers.[5]

As other examples throughout this chapter will show, companies are implementing IMC for many different types of promotional programs.

THE PROMOTIONAL MIX

Just as every organization creates a marketing mix combining product, pricing, place (distribution), and promotion strategies, each also requires a similar mix that blends the many facets of promotion into a cohesive plan. The **promotional mix** consists of two components—personal selling and nonpersonal selling activities—that marketers combine to meet the needs of their firm's target customers and effectively and efficiently communicate its message to them. *Personal selling* is the most basic form of promotion: a direct person-to-person promotional presentation

to a potential buyer. The buyer-seller communication can take place during a face-to-face meeting or via telephone, videoconference, or interactive computer link.

Nonpersonal selling consists of advertising, sales promotion, direct marketing, and public relations. While advertising is the best-known form of nonpersonal selling, sales promotion accounts for about two-thirds of marketing expenditures in this category.

Each component in the promotional mix offers its own advantages and disadvantages, as Table 16.1 demonstrates. By selecting the appropriate combination of promotional mix elements, marketers attempt to achieve their firm's promotional objectives. Typical allocations of promotional funds within the promotional mix vary by industry. Industrial manufacturers typically spend more on personal selling than on advertising, while consumer-goods producers focus on advertising. Subsequent sections of this chapter discuss how the individual parts of the mix contribute to an effective promotional strategy.

Objectives of Promotional Strategy

Promotional strategy objectives vary among organizations. Some use promotion to expand their markets, others to defend their current positions, still others to present corporate viewpoints on public issues. Promotional strategies can also help firms to reach selected markets. As Figure 16.3

Business Directory

promotional mix combination of personal and nonpersonal selling techniques designed to achieve promotional objectives.

illustrates, common objectives include providing information, differentiating a product, increasing sales, stabilizing sales, and accentuating a product's value.

Marketers often pursue multiple promotional objectives at the same time. AT&T developed the theme, "It's all within your reach," for a television campaign to increase sales, retain market share, and expand into new markets, including high-technology services like Internet access. AT&T marketers grew concerned about customer complaints about confusing, overly aggressive long-distance phone company promotions, leading people simply to ignore promotions for the services. The old "Reach Out and Touch Someone" ads were replaced with humor and drama—emotional snapshots depicting life in the high-tech 1990s. One memorable TV ad shows a working mother who takes a day off to be with her children. Another shows a teenage couple flirting via e-mail. The goal of this campaign is to get customers to view AT&T as more than a high-tech phone company. As company vice president Stephen Graham puts it, "This campaign shows how our products can help improve their lives."[6]

Providing Information
A major portion of U.S. advertising primarily distributes information. Large sections in Wednesday and Thursday editions of daily newspapers consist of ads and inserts that tell shoppers about specially featured products at grocery stores. Health insurance advertisements in Sunday newspaper supplements emphasize information about rising hospital costs. Field salespeople keep buyers aware of the latest technological advances in a particular field. Fashion retailers advertise to keep consumers abreast of current styles.

Promotional campaigns are often geared to specific market segments. The Arizona Department of Commerce promotion shown in Figure 16.4 targets businesses looking for sites to expand or relocate operations. It tells why the Cactus State is the Southwest's leader in attracting new businesses by describing the advantages for companies that locate there.

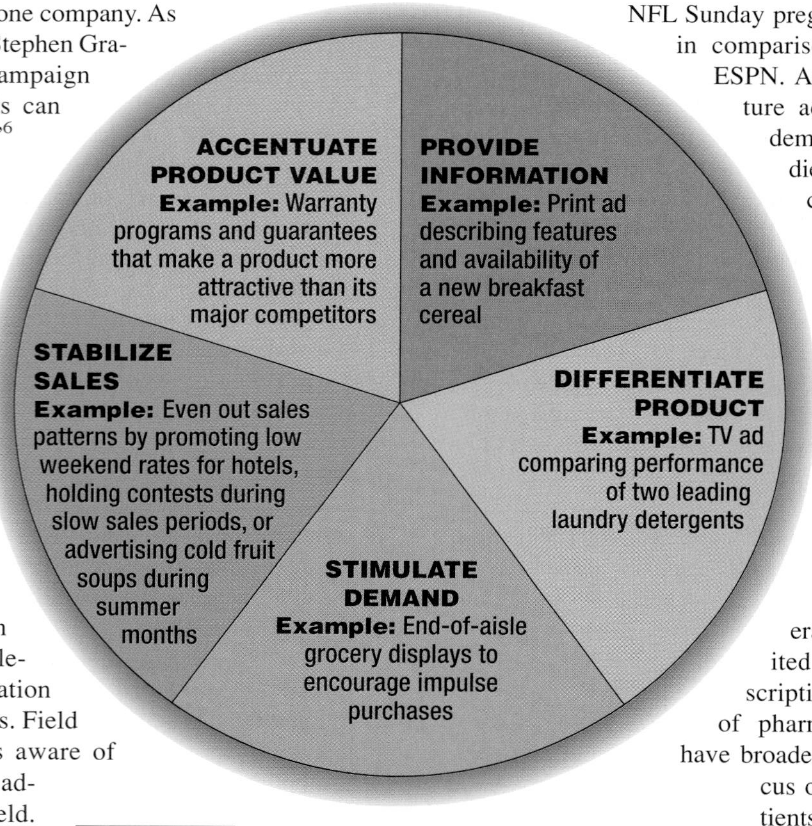

Differentiating a Product Marketers often develop promotional strategies to differentiate their firms' goods and services from those of competitors. Applying a concept called **positioning,** they attempt to establish their own places in the minds of consumers. The idea is to communicate to prospective purchasers meaningful distinctions about the attributes, price, quality, or use of a good or service. Examples include:

▼ Attributes: Scope mouthwash tastes better than Listerine.

▼ Price/quality: The Whopper tastes better and costs less than the Big Mac.

▼ Competitors: Avis is No. 2 in auto rentals, so its people try harder.

Among increasing competition between TV sports programs, the Fox network has positioned its NFL Sunday pregame show as the leader in comparison to rivals NBC and ESPN. Ads for the program feature actual viewer ratings to demonstrate the show's audience leadership over its competitors.

Increasing Sales Increasing sales volume is the most common objective of a promotional strategy. As noted earlier, some strategies concentrate on stimulating primary demand, although most focus on selective demand. Recent changes in federal regulations have limited advertising for prescription drugs, so a number of pharmaceuticals companies have broadened their traditional focus on physicians to the patients themselves. As the Allegra ad in Figure 16.5 illustrates, these promotions are designed to encourage patients to ask their physicians to prescribe the promoted medicines.

Despite the expense of consumer ads, the results are paying off for the drug makers. Sales jumped after Bristol-Myers Squibb launched an aggressive print and television ad campaign for Pravachol, an anticholesterol drug. Merck marketers have reported a dramatic market-share increase from 31 percent to 71 percent for the company's Fosamax

Figure 16.3 **Five Major Promotional Objectives**

ACCENTUATE PRODUCT VALUE
Example: Warranty programs and guarantees that make a product more attractive than its major competitors

PROVIDE INFORMATION
Example: Print ad describing features and availability of a new breakfast cereal

STABILIZE SALES
Example: Even out sales patterns by promoting low weekend rates for hotels, holding contests during slow sales periods, or advertising cold fruit soups during summer months

DIFFERENTIATE PRODUCT
Example: TV ad comparing performance of two leading laundry detergents

STIMULATE DEMAND
Example: End-of-aisle grocery displays to encourage impulse purchases

anti-osteoporosis drug following a direct-to-consumer promotion. In addition, drug marketers are eager to build brand equity for their products to protect against loss of sales to generic versions once their patents expire.[7]

Stabilizing Sales Sales stabilization is another goal of promotional strategy. Firms often promote sales contests during slack periods, motivating sales personnel by offering prizes such as vacation trips, televisions, and scholarships to those who meet certain goals. Companies distribute sales promotion materials—calendars, pens, and the like—to customers to stimulate sales during off-seasons. A stable sales pattern brings several advantages. It evens out the production cycle, reduces some management and production costs, and simplifies financial, purchasing, and marketing planning. An effective promotional strategy can contribute to accomplishing these goals.

Advertising is another tool for stabilizing sales. A common problem in the hotel industry occurs when hotels crowded on weekdays with business travelers sit relatively empty on weekends. These hotels often advertise weekend packages to attract tourists by offering low rates and including some meals. To boost ice cream sales during winter months in cold climates, Ben & Jerry's ran special promotions such as reduced prices based on daily temperatures or "white sales" that offered 10 percent off whipped cream and vanilla ice cream.[8]

Accentuating the Product's Value Some promotional strategies enhance product values by explaining unrecognized ownership utility benefits to buyers. For example, car makers offer long-

| Figure 16.4 | **Informative Advertising to Encourage Businesses to Relocate to Arizona** |

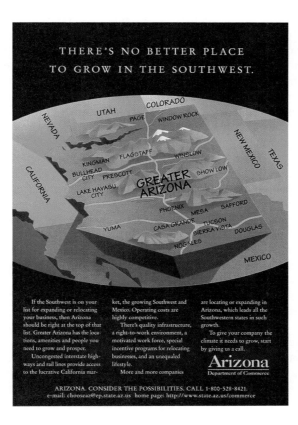

term warranty programs and promote the excellence of their repair services.

The creation of brand equity, as discussed in Chapter 14, also enhances a product's image and increases its desirability. Boston Market developed a promotional campaign targeting mothers who want to provide home-style meals but cannot fit cooking into their busy schedules. The chain promoted its combination of quality, home-style food, and fast-food convenience to make Boston Market seem like an ally in mothers' efforts to bring families together at dinner time. The ads promote a positive association between Boston Market and family values.[9]

Promotional Planning

Today's marketers can promote their products in many more ways than ever before, and the lines between the different elements of the promotional mix are blurring.

| Figure 16.5 | **Promotion Designed to Increase Demand for a Prescription Drug** |

For example, a growing number of marketers pay placement fees to gain appearances of their products in movies and television shows. Sales of Reese's Pieces soared after the candy was featured in the movie *E.T.* BMW used a James Bond movie to introduce its new sports model. Some product-program linkages are quite subtle, as when medical drama *Chicago Hope* introduced a new character, Lisa Catera—and Cadillac ran an ad during that episode encouraging viewers to "Lease a Catera."

The increasing complexity and sophistication of marketing communications requires careful promotional planning to coordinate IMC strategies. Table 16.2 shows the basic steps in the promotional planning process.

To develop the first unified marketing plan for bowling products, major companies in the industry financed an IMC program designed to enhance the sport's image. Even though millions of people bowl, few participate on a regular basis. League play, long a staple base for most bowling centers, has slipped considerably over the past decade.

Planners for the IMC program set an objective to increase bowling's appeal with both amateurs and professional players. The program began with research aimed at profiling the typical bowler. The data dispelled the stereotype of bowlers as low-income, beer-swilling men. Although the market is largely made up of 18- to 34-year-old men, they command an impressive median income of $45,000. Planners decided to focus on an additional market segment made up of children and teens who might become lifelong bowlers. Television, which improves the sport's visibility and communicates its competitive excitement, is a key component of the IMC plan. The plan also calls for efforts at licensing and corporate sponsorships as bowling's popularity rises.[10]

Within this background of integrated marketing communications, the following sections fill in details about the major components of the promotional mix: advertising, sales promotion, personal selling, and public relations.

ADVERTISING

As mentioned earlier in the chapter, the components of nonpersonal selling are advertising, sales promotion, and public relations. Of these, advertising is the most visible form of nonpersonal promotion, and the most effective for many firms.

Advertising refers to paid, nonpersonal sales communications usually directed at large numbers of potential buyers. While people in the United States often think of advertising as a typically American function, it is now a global activity. In fact, five of the world's top ten advertising organizations are headquartered outside the United States. The 100 leading U.S. advertisers spend over $50 billion a year. Procter & Gamble, with a total ad spending of $2.6 billion, ranks first, closely followed by General Motors ($2.4 billion), and Philip Morris ($2.3 billion). Rounding out the top five are Chrysler and Time Warner, with $1.4 billion each.[11]

Advertising expenditures can vary considerably from industry to industry and company to company. As Table 16.3 shows, the automotive industry is the top spender measured in aggregate dollars. Other industries allocate larger percentages of sales to advertising. For example, the retail mail-order industry spends 14 percent of sales on advertising. At the other extreme, the nonresidential general contracting industry spends only two-tenths of 1 percent of total sales on advertising.

Often marketers combine advertising with other types of promotional activities. For example, companies no longer view Super Bowl commercials as end products in

Table 16.2	The Promotional Planning Process	

Step	Description
Review firm's marketing strategy	Review products to evaluate their strengths and weaknesses, current market positions, and the roles of the promotional mix elements in the overall marketing plan
Conduct environmental assessment	Evaluate internal and external factors, including the organization and capabilities of the firm's promotional specialists, results of previous programs, market characteristics, consumer preferences, competition, and general business and economic environments
Establish promotional objectives	Set objectives for each promotional area—advertising, sales promotion, direct marketing, personal selling, and public relations—based on overall marketing objectives
Develop budget	Devise a budget capable of providing the financial resources needed to achieve promotional objectives
Develop IMC program content	Coordinate all promotional components to ensure a consistent IMC program
Implement program	Assign in-house and outside specialists to create ads, direct-mail pieces, and sales messages that make up the IMC campaign and to communicate them via appropriate promotional channels
Assess promotional effectiveness	Gather feedback about promotional effectiveness to determine the success of the IMC program in achieving its objectives and make any needed adjustments

themselves. They want to get maximum mileage for the high cost of those ads—$2 million for a 30-second spot—so they use the time to seize viewers' attention and hold it beyond the 30-second limit. Intel ran two ads during the 1998 game. The first showed a burglar stealing something from Intel labs. The ad invited viewers to the company's Web site to vote on who the criminal is. Their votes determined the second ad, which ran near the end of the game. Intel's goal for the ad was to build Web traffic. M&M's used its Super Bowl commercial to promote a contest that lasted through the spring.[12]

Types of Advertising

The two basic types of ads are product and institutional advertisements. **Product advertising** consists of messages designed to sell a particular good or service. Advertisements for the Toyota Camry, an American Airlines flight, or a retail purchase at Macy's would be classified as product advertising. **Institutional advertising** involves messages that promote concepts, ideas, or philosophies or goodwill for industries, companies, organizations, or government entities. Figure 16.6 shows two attention-grabbing ads: a product ad for Merrill Lynch financial services and institutional advertising from the U.S. Army. In the Merrill Lynch message, the dangling rock climber conveys the idea of taking investment risk, while the text promotes a product that combines earnings potential with protection when stock prices fall. The Army ad uses a computer mouse designed in a camouflage pattern to remind the reader of a uniform. The message directs readers to the Web for more information.

A form of institutional advertising that is growing in importance, **advocacy advertising,** promotes a specific viewpoint on a public issue as a way to influence public opinion and the legislative process. Both not-for-profit organizations and businesses use advocacy advertising (sometimes called *cause advertising*). For example, the Office of National Drug Control Policy jointly sponsors antidrug campaigns with the Partnership for a Drug-Free America and its state affiliates. One recent newspaper ad asked parents, "Are you waiting for your kids to talk to *you* about pot?" The ad offered a free booklet titled, "Marijuana: Facts Parents Need to Know" and listed local and national resources for additional help and information. A companion radio commercial warned of the risk of death from sniffing toxic inhalants.

Table 16.3	Top Ten Advertising Spenders by Industry	
Industry		**Total U.S. Spending ($ billions)**
1. Automobile		$11.6
2. Retailing		9.4
3. Business and consumer services		8.4
4. Entertainment and amusements		5.4
5. Food products		4.0
6. Drugs and remedies		3.6
7. Toiletries and cosmetics		3.3
8. Travel services, hotels, and resorts		2.6
9. Computers, office equipment, and stationery		2.0
10. Confectionery, snacks, and soft drinks		1.7

Advertising and the Product Life Cycle

Both product and institutional advertising fall into one of three categories, based on whether the ads intend to inform, persuade, or remind. A firm uses *informative advertising* to build initial demand for a product in the introductory phase of the product life cycle. The advertising campaign for Biore's Pore Perfect, a new product to remove dirt from nose pores, took a forthright approach to demonstrating product benefits rather than the beautiful-skin pitch typical of such products. To demonstrate the product's effectiveness, the print ads showed just how the product, an adhesive strip, removed pore-clogging dirt. Consumers responded positively to seeing the actual results and snapped up boxes of Biore, despite a cost of $6 for a box of six. Ponds followed quickly with a rival product.[13]

Persuasive advertising attempts to improve the competitive status of a product, institution, or concept, usually in the growth and maturity stages of the product life cycle. Burger King featured its reformulated French fries in a promotional campaign to improve its competitive position against McDonald's, whose fries had long been considered the best-tasting of any fast-food outlet.

> ## They said it
>
> "Doing business without advertising is like winking at a girl in the dark. You know what you are doing, but nobody else does."
>
> **Stuart Henderson Britt (1907–1979) American educator**

Business Directory

advertising paid, nonpersonal communication delivered through various media and designed to inform or persuade members of a particular audience.

Figure 16.6   **Product and Institutional Advertising**

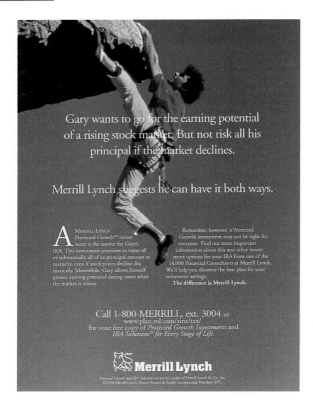

One of the most popular types of persuasive product advertising, **comparative advertising,** compares products directly to their competitors. Comparative advertising is especially effective for promoting new products. Many companies have used such appeals in recent years. American Express and Visa use this form of advertising for their credit cards. Visa touts the wider acceptance of its card with commercials that tell consumers to bring along their Visa cards to specific locations, like the Olympic games, where merchants do not accept American Express. American Express has launched its own campaign that shows a Visa customer stranded in Paris unable to get help with his Visa card.[14]

Reminder-oriented advertising often appears in the late maturity or decline stages of the product life cycle to maintain awareness of the importance and usefulness of a product, concept, or institution. Convenience store chain AM/PM Mini Markets has focused ads on what consumers already liked about the stores in its "Too Much Good Stuff" campaign. In focus groups, the company's advertising agency learned that customers visited the stores for the selection of snack foods they carried. The television ads sought to strengthen this emotional bond with customers by showing what really happens: People enter the store for one item and then make impulse purchases of several oth-

ers. Because these customers felt good about treating themselves to impulse purchases, the ads not only reinforced the positive image of AM/PM as a fun place to visit but also resulted in increased sales.[15]

Advertising Media

All marketers must choose how to allocate their advertising budgets among various media. As Table 16.4 demonstrates, all media offer advantages and disadvantages. Cost is another important consideration in media selection, but marketers must give equal emphasis to choosing the media best-suited for communicating their message. Television and newspapers are the two leading advertising media, in large part because of their flexibility. Interactive media, which now receive less than 1 percent of total advertising spending, are expected to grow the most in the next 3 years, with cable television predicted to rank second in relative growth.[16]

Newspapers Although television has moved from being a minor player in the world of advertising back in 1950 to its current ranking as co-leader with newspapers, daily and weekly newspapers continue to be the media favorites for thousands of advertisers. Marketers can easily tailor newspaper advertising for individual communities and reach nearly everyone in an area. In addition, readers can refer back to these ads, and advertisers can coordinate their messages with other promotional efforts. In fact, readers rank advertising as the third most useful feature in newspapers, after national and local news. A disadvantage comes from the relatively short life span; people usually discard their papers after reading.

The sheer volume of advertising in a typical newspaper produces intense competition for reader attention. Successful newspaper advertisers make newsworthy announcements in their ads, such as sales, new stores opening, or new products launched. Retailers rank first among newspaper advertisers, followed by automobile firms.

Although newspapers initially worried that the Web would erode their traditional role of providing news, advertising, and entertainment guides, they have experienced the opposite result. Most newspapers now

Introducing the new National Champion. People are already talking dynasty.

In the biggest upset this season, our delicious new fries defeated McDonald's® fries in a nationwide taste test to become the new champs—and it wasn't even close. With a powerful combination of hot and crispy, new Burger King® fries are sure to be a fan favorite for a long time to come, and have firmly established themselves as the fries to beat—and eat.

The taste that beat McDonald's® fries.

©1997 Burger King Corporation. Burger King Corporation is the exclusive licensee of the registered Burger King and Bun Halves Logo trademarks. McDonald's is a registered trademark of McDonald's Corp.

Persuasive ads must do more than simply claim superiority over marketplace rivals—they need to prove it. Burger King cited the results of a blind-sampling comparison to claim that its crispy new fries tasted better than McDonald's in a nationwide taste test.

maintain Web sites to complement their print editions, some of which offer separate material and features. For example, the *Los Angeles Times* personalizes its Web page with "Hunter," a free news-retrieval service that delivers a customized electronic newspaper based on a list of topics that the visitor selects. Newspaper sites are popular Web destinations, helping to build customer loyalty for the publications.[17]

Television Television advertising can be classified as network, national, local, and cable ads. The major national networks (ABC, CBS, NBC, Fox, Warner Brothers, and United Paramount Network) represent about 35 percent of all television ads. Despite a decline in audience share and growing competition from cable, network television remains the easiest way for advertisers to reach large numbers of viewers—10 million to 20 million with a single commercial. Among the heavy users of network television are auto manufacturers, financial services companies, and fast-food chains.

Table 16.4 Comparison of Advertising Media Alternatives

Media Outlet	Percentage of Total[a]	Advantages	Disadvantages
Newspapers	26%	Tailored to individual communities; ability to refer back to ads	Short life span
Television	22	Mass coverage; repetition; flexibility; prestige	High cost; temporary message; public distrust; lack of selectivity
Direct mail	18	Selectivity; intense coverage; speed; flexibility; opportunity to convey complete information; personalization	High cost; consumer resistance; dependence on effective mailing list
Radio	7	Immediacy; low cost; flexibility; targeted audience; mobility	Short life span; highly fragmented audience
Magazines	5	Selectivity; quality image reproduction; long life; prestige	Lack of flexibility
Outdoor	1	Quick, visual communication of simple ideas; link to local goods and services; repetition	Brief exposure; environmental concerns
Interactive	<1	Two-way communications; flexibility; link to self-directed entertainment	Poor image reproduction; limited scheduling options; difficult to measure effectiveness

[a]An additional 25 percent is spent on a variety of miscellaneous media, including Yellow Pages listings, business papers, transit displays, point-of-purchase displays, cinema advertising, and regional farm papers.

Each major network conveys a "personality" that attracts certain types of advertisers. For example, NBC sees itself as the true mass medium network, appealing to a wide range of viewers. ABC is positioning itself as the family network, while Fox has a solid hold on young adult viewers.[18]

Cable services continue to make inroads into the television sector, with ad revenues expected to grow about three times faster than those of traditional broadcast television. Viewers are responding positively to cable's diversity of programming. Record numbers have recently watched prime-time cable shows, giving the medium almost a one-third share of the market; at the same time, audience share of the three major networks—ABC, CBS, and NBC—fell below 50 percent. However, the cost for cable advertising is still well below broadcast rates: an average of $7.50 per thousand homes, versus $11.00 for broadcast television.

Choosing among over 50 cable networks, advertisers can narrowly target specialized markets and reach selected demographic groups, often very small ones. This selectivity is a major selling point for cable television as opposed to the mass-market reach of network broadcasts. As prime-time ratings climb at large cable networks such as TNT, Nickelodeon, Lifetime, A&E, and the Discovery Channel, ad revenues are also rising about 15 percent a year. Smaller cable channels are also seeing audiences grow, often at the expense of more established cable networks like CNN and ESPN.[19] Active advertising campaigns in trade publications, such as the ad for Animal Planet in Figure 16.7, highlight the types of audiences that advertisers can reach with promotions on specific cable channels.

| **Figure 16.7** | **Cable Television Networks: Targeting Specific Audiences** |

Irresistible **TV**

WELCOME TO ANIMAL PLANET—the only place on television where you always come face-to-face with the most fascinating creatures on Earth. You'll be captivated by the world's best wildlife documentaries, dramas, pet care programs, shows for kids and gripping real-life adventures. For unique entertainment about the extraordinary animals who share our planet, come to Animal Planet. A new network from the people who bring you the Discovery Channel. CALL YOUR CABLE OR SATELLITE COMPANY AND ASK FOR ANIMAL PLANET.

Animal Planet™

All Animals. All The Time.
www.animaldiscovery.com

The tremendous growth in television advertising is easy to understand. Television combines the sound of radio with dynamic visual depictions of products and associated images. It can also emulate one-on-one sales presentations by demonstrating product usage and benefits. Mass coverage, repetition, flexibility, and prestige are other positive features. Marketers can now beam their TV commercials to grocery store checkout lines, health clubs, and even schools.

On the other hand, television is an expensive advertising medium. A 30-second spot on the final episode of *Seinfeld* cost $1.5 million, whereas the same ad on a new network TV comedy or drama ranges from $55,000 to $400,000. Because of the high cost, advertisers demand guarantees of audience size and receive compensation if a show fails to deliver the promised number of viewers.[20]

Other disadvantages include the temporary nature of the message, some public distrust, and lack of selectivity, that is, the ability to reach a specific target market without a lot of wasted coverage. Advertisers are also unhappy with the number of ads that networks run, causing clutter that reduces a particular ad's impact on viewers. The recently implemented program ratings system may present another problem for placement of television ads. Sponsors may avoid programs with violent or sexual content that might offend their target markets.

Radio The average U.S. household owns five radios, a market penetration that makes radio an important advertising medium. Advertisers like the opportunity to reach listeners as they commute to and from work, and morning and evening "drive time" shows command top ad rates.

DID YOU KNOW?

▼ In Chile, billboards cannot be designed to "distract" drivers.

▼ French law prohibits foreign words in ads and on product labels.

▼ In Germany, direct-mail pieces may not be mailed to named individuals.

▼ Indonesian law forbids the use of foreign models or locations in consumer product advertising.

▼ In Venezuela, kids in TV ads must "speak" with dubbed-in adult voices.

Advantages of radio include immediacy, low cost, targeted audience selection, flexibility, and mobility. Stations can adjust their formats to adapt to changing local audience preferences. Advertisers can place commercials on stations that are popular with the groups they wish to target. Disadvantages include the short life span of a radio message and its highly fragmented audience.

Clean Shower is one company that believes in the benefits of radio advertising. With only a $1 million

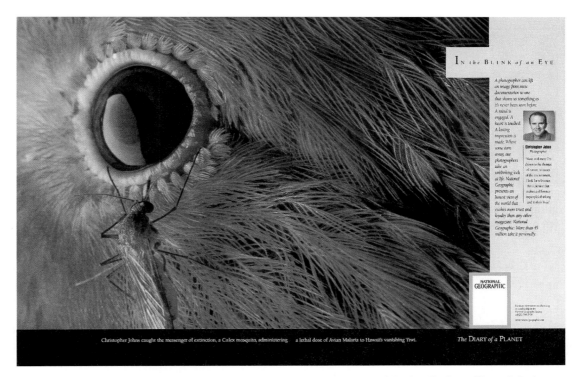

Christopher Johns caught the messenger of extinction, a Culex mosquito, administering a lethal dose of Avian Malaria to Hawaii's vanishing 'Iiwi.

The DIARY of a PLANET

***National Geographic* sales representatives provide advertisers with detailed profiles of their readers, citing demographic, geographic, and lifestyle characteristics. Reader research data demonstrate the venerable magazine's ability to deliver an upscale audience for advertisers' promotional messages.**

advertising budget—a fraction of what a large company spends to launch a new product—the startup company developed a clever radio ad campaign for its new shower cleaner. Clean Shower shipped samples of the new product to 1,000 local and national radio disc jockeys and talk-show hosts and asked them to try it. Radio ads were then purchased on their stations using the local personalities to describe their own experiences with Clean Shower. The personal touch was a huge success with listeners, and supermarkets were swamped with shopper requests for the new product. Within 6 months following the first radio testimonials, the number of stores carrying Clean Shower doubled.[21]

Magazines Magazines include consumer publications and trade journals that serve as business-to-business links. *Time, GQ,* and *Sports Illustrated* are consumer magazines, while *Advertising Age, HR Focus, Biotech Business,* and the *Journal of Environmental Health* fall into the trade category. About 40 percent of magazine advertising appears in weekly magazines. *Modern Maturity,* with about 23 million subscribers, is the nation's largest magazine measured by paid subscriptions. Automotive firms spend the most on consumer magazine advertising. Computers and office equipment and drugs and remedies are two fast-growing areas. Business and consumer services and the travel industry are also heavy users of consumer magazine adver-

tising. Computer, automotive, and health-care companies advertise heavily in trade magazines.

www. **www.adage.com**

Advantages of magazines include selectivity, high-quality image reproduction, long message life, and prestige. A magazine ad can provide more information than a 30-second television spot. The main disadvantage of magazines is less flexibility than newspapers and broadcast media.

However, magazines are taking steps to customize their publications and target advertising messages to different regions of the country. One method places local advertising in regional editions of the magazine. *Sunset* magazine, which specializes in coverage of Western living, includes articles about gardening and other topics tailored to individual regions. An advertiser wanting to reach San Diego readers can place ads in that edition. Other magazines attach wraparounds (half-size covers on top of full-size covers) to highlight articles inside that relate to particular areas; different wraparounds appear in different parts of the country.

Magazines are a natural choice for targeted advertising. Media buyers study demographics of subscribers and select magazines that attract the desired readers. For example, a company with a product geared to young women

Figure 16.8	Branded Architecture: Coca Cola's 3-D Outdoor Ads

would advertise in *Glamour* and *Cosmopolitan;* one with a product that appeals to entrepreneurs might choose *Inc., Success,* or *Entrepreneur.*

Direct Mail The average American household receives about 550 pieces of direct mail each year, including 100 catalogs. The huge growth in the variety of direct-mail offerings combined with the convenience offered to the busy, time-pressed shoppers of the late 1990s has made direct mail a $350 billion business.[22]

Direct mail's advantages include selectivity, intense coverage, speed, flexibility, complete information, and personalization. Also sellers quickly learn what types of ads bring the best results. On the negative side, direct mail is a very expensive medium dependent on effective mailing lists. Some campaigns meet with consumer resistance. However, a campaign doesn't require a very high response rate to make the mailing a worthwhile investment. One study showed that every dollar spent on direct-mail advertising generates $10 in sales, over twice the effectiveness of television advertising.

Address lists are at the heart of direct-mail advertising. Using data-mining techniques to develop models for market segmentation, direct-mail marketers develop customer profiles that show the traits of consumers who are likely to buy their products or donate to their organizations. Catalog retailers sometimes experiment by mailing direct-mail pieces at random to people who subscribe to particular magazines. Next, they analyze the orders received from the mailings and develop profiles of purchasers. Finally, they rent additional subscriber names that match the profiles they have developed.

As paper and postage costs rise, catalog firms and other direct-mail marketers are working to improve response rates. "The goal for our industry is to mail smarter. The goal isn't always to mail more," says David Hochberg, a Lillian Vernon vice president. L. L. Bean mails fewer catalogs than it once sent, but sales have risen. With narrowly targeted lists, Lillian Vernon can send its Lilly's Kids catalog to parents and grandparents, while In the Company of Dogs can target animal lovers who spend money on their pets.[23]

Certain techniques improve response rates: personalized letters, especially from celebrities; phrases that include the word *free,* like "free gift" and "buy one, get one free"; premiums accompanying appeals from charities; postscripts that highlight the benefits of responding to offers.

The design of the direct-mail piece itself is also carefully chosen to boost readership and avoid winding up unopened in the trash. Envelopes may resemble invoices or government mailings. Some shout "Rush/Priority" but contain only cents-off coupons. Even the right stamp, rather than metered postage, improves response rates.

Outdoor Advertising Outdoor advertising, like billboards and illuminated or animated signs or displays, accounts for about 1 percent of total advertising expenditures. Advertisers are exploring new forms of outdoor media, as well, many of which involve technology: computerized paintings, video billboards, trivision (which displays three revolving images on one billboard), moving billboards mounted on trucks, and interactive video kiosks in subway stations. The strength of this medium lies in its capability for quick communication of simple ideas. Other advantages are repetition and ability to promote goods and services available for sale near the locations of the ads.

Outdoor advertising suffers from several disadvantages, however. The medium requires brief messages, and mounting concern for aesthetic and environmental issues is raising opposition. The Highway Beautification Act of 1965 regulates placement of outdoor advertising near interstate highways.

Outdoor advertising companies have been reducing their reliance on tobacco companies in anticipation of proposed bans on tobacco advertising. Companies like Procter & Gamble, which had a positive experience with billboards in a campaign promoting Pantene shampoo, are filling tobacco's place. Delta Airlines introduced its business class service with a "living billboard" in New York's Times Square, where real people occupied a set with airline seats.[24]

"Branded architecture" is the newest form of outdoor advertising. Figure 16.8 shows how Coca-Cola capitalized on the well-known shape of its bottle. Instead of continuing its traditional concession arrangement with the Atlanta Braves baseball team, it created Sky Field, an experiential exhibit featuring the soft drink, at Atlanta's Turner Field. A 42-foot-high Coke bottle made of baseball bats, mitts, and balls sends forth fireworks every time a member of the Braves hits a home run. Visitors can rest in large chairs with backs in the shape of Coke bottles, and kids can run down model base paths or sit in a dugout. In Las Vegas, a Coca-Cola store features a huge, see-through Coke bottle with an inside elevator that takes visitors to a tasting room several levels above the floor. Unlike print, broadcast, or online ads that consumers can quickly bypass, these 3-D outdoor ads are essentially zap-proof displays.[25]

BUSINESS TOOL KIT

Web Ads that Work

The best beginning for creating effective Web ads is to understand what to avoid. Here are some of the major *don'ts:*

▼ Multimedia ads should not slow Web page downloads.

▼ No ad should appear in the middle of a Web page; instead, place it as a banner at the top or bottom.

▼ Ads should not appear embedded in general site content.

The *do's* can be summarized in one word: *Personalize.*

▼ *Know your audience.* Target specialized audiences so that you reach the consumers most interested in your product. Although sites like Yahoo! and Netscape produce millions of daily hits, much of the coverage is wasted.

▼ *Match the product to the site.* Ads for financial services get lost on most sports sites.

▼ *Make careful use of technology.* Top executives want information in a clear and quick format. Some special audio and video features may enhance your appeal; others slow downloads and annoy the audience.

▼ *Frequently change banner ads.* Rotate banners and remove poor performers.

Sources: Annette Hamilton, "What You Don't Know about Web Ads Will Cost You," *ZDNet AnchorDesk*, November 10, 1997, accessed at www.zdnet.com/anchordesk; and "NetTips," *NETMarketing*, March 27, 1998, accessed at netb2b.com.

Interactive Media Ranging from Web sites to video displays on shopping carts and information kiosks in malls and financial institutions, interactive media are changing the nature of advertising. Although it currently commands only a tiny portion of media spending, interactive advertising is the fastest-growing media segment. Online advertising, the largest component of this category, more than tripled last year, with annual revenues soaring to $940 million. Global Internet advertising revenues reached $5 billion in 2000.[26]

These optimistic projections reflect several trends. Rising numbers of Web surfers are spending more time browsing the Web, and new online advertising forms are expanding the impact of banner ads, the first form of Internet promotion. Half of online ad expenditures by 2002 will come from sponsorships, such as commitments by Kellogg and Sears to the Sony Play Station entertainment site, and interstitials—full-screen ads that appear between screens.

Interactive advertising directly involves the audience, creating two-way communications between marketers and consumers. Unlike the traditional role of advertising—providing brief, entertaining, attention-catching messages—interactive media provide information to help consumers throughout the purchase and consumption processes. Consumers choose how much they wish to learn about products, and they provide information about themselves to advertis-ers. After actively participating, they are more likely to notice and remember online ads than television ads.

No longer are technology companies the only Web advertisers. Large automotive, consumer products, and financial services advertisers—General Motors, Procter & Gamble, American Express, and Fidelity Investments, for example—are turning to online media in increasing numbers.

"What we found is that at least 10 percent of consumer leads generated from the Internet converted into car buyers within 3 months," says Jon Bucci, Toyota's U.S. marketing manager for interactive communications. "That's a far higher rate than any other lead-generation device we have found." The company's banner ads at other sites drive traffic to the Toyota Web site, where prospective buyers are linked with local dealers to learn the latest financing offers.[27] Current Toyota owners even get coupons to save on their next oil changes. The Business Tool Kit gives some tips for maximizing the effectiveness of online ads.

www. www.toyota.com

Successful interactive advertising adds value by offering the audience more than just product-related information.

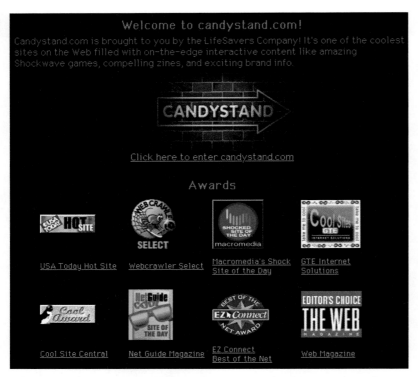

LifeSavers' CandyStand Web site is an example of interactive advertising that ties all of the company's promotions to its Web site.

World Wide Web ads can also include company store features, customer service lines, and other content, promoting brand loyalty and building relationships with consumers. Sharon Fordham, president of Nabisco's LifeSavers unit, took a long-range approach to Web site development. She focused not on one-time hits or information but on making the LifeSavers Web site, Candystand, a destination site. Her marketing team's goals included building brand equity for individual brands, cross-selling LifeSavers products, and making the site fun for the whole family.

At highly interactive brand home pages, visitors play games like the Bubble Yum Foul Shot Shoot-Out and Ice Breakers Slap-Shot Shoot-Out. Some sites invite users to solve puzzles and enter sweepstakes and contests. Free screensavers, Internet greeting cards, magazines, and lots of video games keep visitors busy and eager to return. The Care*Free gum site offers promotions like disposable cameras for proofs of purchase. The company even displays the best photos of Shiny Smiles, the gum's tag line, on the Web site. Now LifeSavers is tying all its promotions to the Web site.[28]

www.candystand.com

The many kid-oriented Web sites like Candystand raise an important issue for marketers and parents. They present advertising messages in entertainment form, including games using brand logos, and children often register, giving out personal information, in order to participate. The Solving an Ethical Controversy feature discusses whether the government should take the lead in regulating online advertising to children. The subject of online promotion will arise again in this chapter's discussions of technology, sponsorships, and cross promotion, and in the following chapter.

Other Media Options As consumers filter out traditional advertising messages, marketers look for new ways to catch their attention. In addition to the major media, firms promote through many other vehicles such as infomercials and specialized media. **Infomercials** are a form of broadcast direct marketing. These 30-minute programs resemble regular television programs devoted to selling goods or services. The long format allows an advertiser to thoroughly present product benefits, increase awareness, and make an impact on consumers. Advertisers also receive immediate responses in the form of sales or inquiries, because most infomercials feature toll-free phone numbers.

In the past, infomercials sold mainly "miracle" products like beauty aids, exercise products, and kitchen gadgets. Today, they are gaining popularity with Fortune 500 marketers. Companies like Sears, Braun, Warner Music, GTE, and SmithKline Beecham have experienced success with infomercials.

Other specialized media used for product promotions include advertising in movie theaters and on airline movie screens. Movie theaters screen commercials for soft drinks like Coca-Cola, Pepsi, and Dr Pepper before beginning feature presentations. Many firms display advertising messages on trucks, while others use transit advertising, posting their ads in and on public transportation like buses, commuter trains, bus shelters, and taxicabs.

The sky makes space for several other advertising vehicles. Airplanes trail promotional messages over sporting events. Maxwell House and Eastman Kodak have used hot-air balloons to promote their brands. Brands like Budweiser, Fuji Film, Gulf Oil, Met Life, and Blockbuster each pay up to $350,000 per month to advertise their brand images on blimps. These alternative media can be employed separately or in conjunction with more traditional approaches.

Ads appear in printed programs of live-theater productions, and firms such as PepsiCo and Chrysler advertise on movie videocassettes. Directory advertising includes the familiar Yellow Pages listings in telephone books and thousands of other types of directories, most presenting business-related promotions. About 10 percent of total advertising revenue goes to Yellow Pages ads.

SALES PROMOTION

Traditionally viewed as a supplement to a firm's sales or advertising efforts, sales promotion has emerged as an integral part of the promotional mix and now accounts for more marketing dollars than advertising. **Sales promotion** consists of forms of promotion other than advertising, personal selling, and public relations that enhance consumer purchasing and dealer effectiveness.

Both retailers and manufacturers use sales promotions to offer consumers extra incentives to buy. Beyond the short-term advantage of increased sales, sales promotions can also help marketers to build brand equity and enhance customer relationships. Companies now spend over $250 billion each year on sales promotion activities targeted at consumers and business buyers. Examples include samples, coupons, contests, displays, trade shows, and dealer incentives.

Sales promotions complement advertising, and marketers get the best results when they combine the two. Advertising and in-store displays may highlight sweepstakes and contests. Ads create awareness, while sales promotions lead directly to trial or purchase. Promotions encourage immediate action, because they impose time limits. For example, cents-off coupons and rebates carry expiration dates. Also, sales promotions generate measurable results, allowing companies to evaluate their effectiveness without much difficulty.

Consumer-Oriented Promotions

The goal of a customer-oriented sales promotion is to get new and existing customers to try or buy products. In addition, marketers want to encourage repeat purchases by rewarding current users, increase sales of complementary products, and boost impulse purchases. Table 16.5 shows the consumer promotions most popular among packaged goods manufacturers.

Coupons, Rebates, Samples, and Premiums Coupons, advertising clippings, and cards included in packages are the

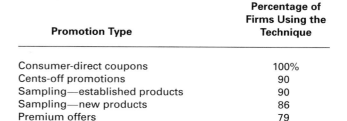

Table 16.5	Popular Consumer Promotions

Promotion Type	Percentage of Firms Using the Technique
Consumer-direct coupons	100%
Cents-off promotions	90
Sampling—established products	90
Sampling—new products	86
Premium offers	79
In-store coupons	76
Coupons in retailers' ads	76
Electronic retail promotions	72
Sweepstakes	69
Contests	52

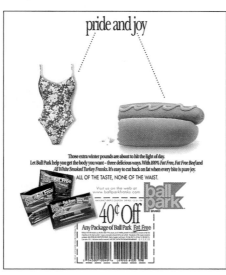

Coupons are among the most widely used forms of promotion.

most widely used sales promotion techniques. Customers redeem the coupons for small price discounts when they purchase the promoted products. Such an offer may persuade a customer to try a new or different product. Many retailers, including southern supermarket giant Winn-Dixie and West Coast competitors Ralph's and Von's, double the face values of manufacturers' coupons.

Consumers typically redeem only about 2 percent of the 6 billion coupons that producers annually distribute. They love coupons, however, and many protested when Procter & Gamble tried to eliminate them in three upstate New York cities in 1996. "We look at couponing as a wasteful practice," says Linda Ulrey, P&G spokeswoman. "There is nothing from our point of view that is efficient about a practice that fails 90 percent of the time." Yet consumers noticed the missing coupons, not lower prices on the company's products, and P&G was forced to reinstate coupons.[29]

Current trends emphasize in-store distribution of coupons and register receipt machines that offer coupons targeted to consumers' actual purchases. Many supermarkets now use clipless coupons that give discounts when special cards are scanned at checkout. Coupons are even

SOLVING AN ETHICAL CONTROVERSY

Can Internet Marketers Ethically Solicit Business from Children?

On any given day, millions of children log on to the Internet, spending hours roaming from site to site playing games, exchanging messages, and reading on-line magazines. This pastime sounds innocent, but most of these kid-oriented sites are created by advertisers who are targeting their messages to the fastest-growing segment of Internet users.

Marketers see an irresistible combination: 10 million cybertots—children between the ages of 4 and 12 with a huge, direct influence on sales of $170 billion in goods and services. Businesses like Kellogg, Disney, and Toys "R" Us have discovered a way to make advertising seem like entertainment instead of an interruption.

The interactive nature of the Internet makes it an even more powerful way to reach children than television

advertising. Most sites offer all sorts of alluring games or premiums. But to use them, the kids have to register by providing their names, e-mail addresses, locations, dates of birth, genders, and other information. Children's advo-

cates like the Center for Media Education have been fighting hard to protect unsuspecting youngsters from loss of privacy and aggressive marketing practices. Consensus has not yet emerged about how far government

available online at sites like HotCoupons, Supermarkets Online, and CoolSavings.com.

Rebates offer cash back to consumers who mail in required proofs of purchase. Refunds help packaged goods manufacturers to increase purchase rates, promote multiple purchases, and reward product users. Other types of companies also offer rebates, especially for electronics and computer-related products. For example, Visoneer offered a $50 rebate on its PaperPort scanners.

A sample is a free gift of a product distributed by mail, door-to-door, in a demonstration, or inside packages of another product. Although sampling is an expensive form of sales promotion, it generates a higher response rate than most other techniques. About three-quarters of consumers who receive samples try them. Sampling allows marketers to target potential customers and be sure that the product reaches them.

can or should go to regulate online advertising to children.

 Should the Government Regulate Online Advertising to Children?

PRO

1. The number of children on the Internet, already in the millions, is continuing astronomical growth. "There's probably no other good or service that we can think of that is like it in terms of kids' interest," says an advertising director for Saatchi & Saatchi. With so much at stake, people cannot depend on self-regulation by advertisers.

2. Most children are not sophisticated enough to resist the intrusions of this medium. They freely provide extensive personal information in order to qualify for site offerings. Without some potential punitive action from agencies like the Federal Trade Commission, companies will continue to gather personal data to benefit their own marketing.

3. Guidelines being developed by the Direct Marketing Association, Internet Services Association, Center for Media Education, and Consumer Federation of America may state useful requirements, but they would not set legally binding standards as FTC rules would.

CON

1. Children may need some protection, but advertisers have a right to freely target that market. "The children's protection rationale has brought forth proposals for draconian advertising restrictions in every area," says Dan Jaffe of the Association of National Advertisers (ANA). "The ANA's position is that children need special protection. But they should be able to be reached by advertisers."

2. Industry guidelines provide sufficient safety. Federal regulations would impede free speech, as guaranteed by the Constitution. "Congress is undermining our First Amendment protection by using children as the battering ram," says the ANA's Jaffe.

3. Internet technology is still evolving. Effective legislation and regulation must wait. Some proposals set unreasonable standards, such as requiring sites to obtain original written signatures from parents before children can provide information, as the Center for Media Education has proposed.

SUMMARY

Cyberlibertarians fear that too much regulation would destroy the free exchange of ideas that makes the Internet such a unique medium. However, as the number of children going online continues to grow, both parents and children's advocates are concerned that this market is too tantalizing to advertisers. While few question the need to protect children from aggressive marketing, debate continues about whether the protection should take the form of government legislation and how it should work.

Sources: Ted Bridis, "Government Details Kid's Online Privacy," The Associated Press, April 21, 1999; "45 Million Kids Could be Online by 2002, Study Says," *Advertising Age,* October 1997; and Catherine Yang, "Is www.sleaze.com about to Be Flamed?" *Business Week,* December 8, 1997, p. 44.

Firms also distribute samples over the Internet. In a clever tax-season promotion for Excedrin, Bristol-Myers Squibb developed targeted banner ads that allowed customers to request samples to relieve their tax-time headaches. The pharmaceuticals company linked its promotion with that for Intuit's TurboTax, a leading tax software package, allowing customers to register for a demonstration version of TurboTax at the same site. "We more than doubled our expected numbers, and demographically the names proved younger than TV," says Peggy Kelly, vice president of advertising services at Bristol-Myers Squibb.[30]

A premium is an item given free or at a reduced price with the purchase of another product. For example, cosmetics companies like Estée Lauder and Clinique offer gifts with purchases of special cosmetics and perfume sets. Fast-food restaurants are big users of premiums. McDonald's capitalized on the Beanie Baby craze by offering special Teenie Beanie Babies in Happy Meals. The toys were so popular that McDonald's ran out in 10 days. Sellers find that consumers also like in-pack items like stickers, trading cards, and other small collectibles. Phone cards are also gaining popularity as premiums.

Contests and Sweepstakes Contests, sweepstakes, and games offer cash or merchandise as prizes to participating winners. Firms often sponsor these activities to introduce new goods and services and to attract additional customers. Contests require entrants to solve problems or write essays, sometimes with proofs of purchase. Sweepstakes choose winners by chance and require no product purchase. Consumers prefer them since contests require more effort to enter. Companies like sweepstakes, too, because they are inexpensive to run and determine the number of winners from the beginning. With contests, the company cannot predict the number of people who will correctly complete the puzzle or gather the right number of symbols from scratch-off cards. Sweepstakes and contests can reinforce a company's image and advertising message, but consumer attention may focus on the promotion rather than the product.

Contests, games, and sweepstakes are also popular elements of many Web sites, helping them to attract visitors. Making reservations at Travelocity's one-stop travel site during a certain period automatically enters customers into the site's second birthday sweepstakes with a prize of a Hawaiian vacation. Candystand runs a variety of contests with prizes that appeal to kids like Sony PlayStation video game systems, autographed sports memorabilia, and snowboards.

In recent years, a number of court rulings and legal restrictions have limited the use of contests. Companies must proceed carefully in advertising their contests and prizes. The Business Hall of Shame describes how American Family Publishers and Publishers Clearing House, two large magazine subscription services, ran afoul of the law with promotional sweepstakes criticized for deceptive tactics.

Specialty Advertising Take a look around your home. Do you have items such as pens, T-shirts, calendars, or a calculator imprinted with the name of the businesses that gave them to you? These offers are examples of **specialty advertising,** in which a company gives away useful merchandise carrying its name, logo, or business slogan. Because those products are useful and often personalized with the recipient's names, people tend to keep and use them, giving the advertisers repeated exposure. Originally designed to identify and create goodwill for advertisers, specialty advertising now generates sales leads and develops traffic for stores and trade show exhibitors.

Wearables like T-shirts and baseball caps account for about one-fourth of ad specialties, followed by pens and pencils, glassware/ceramics, and calendars. The healthcare, financial services, and computer industries are among the top users of specialty items.[31]

Polo Sport gifts that travel from Ralph Lauren

Ralph Lauren marketers designed a successful sales promotion by offering Polo Sport fitness bags with a Polo fragrance purchase.

trade promotions include point-of-purchase advertising and trade shows.

Point-of-purchase (POP) advertising consists of displays or demonstrations that promote products when and where consumers buy them, such as in retail stores. Video advertising on supermarket shopping carts and end-of-aisle displays in supermarkets are two types of POP advertising.

This on-site sales promotion takes advantage of many shoppers' tendencies to make purchase decisions in the store. POP ads can very effectively continue a theme developed by some other aspect of the firm's promotional strategy, as in-store displays supplement themes developed in ads or other promotional mix elements.

Manufacturers and importers often host or exhibit at **trade shows** to promote goods or services to members of their distribution channels. These shows are often organized by industry trade associations, perhaps as part of annual meetings or conventions. Each year, over 4,300 different shows are held in the United States and Canada, attracting more than 1.3 million exhibitors and 895 million attendees. Such shows are particularly important in the computer, toy, furniture, and fashion industries. They are especially effective methods for new-product introductions and for generating sales leads. Some trade shows attempt to reach ultimate consumers. Home, recreation, and automobile shows, for instance, allow businesses to display and demonstrate home-care, recreation, and other consumer products to entire communities.

Trade-Oriented Promotions

Sales promotion techniques can also contribute to campaigns directed to retailers and wholesalers. *Trade promotion* is sales promotion geared to marketing intermediaries rather than to consumers. Marketers use trade promotion to encourage retailers to stock new products, continue carrying existing ones, and promote both effectively to consumers. Successful trade promotions offer financial incentives. They require careful timing, attention to costs, and easy implementation for intermediaries. These promotions should bring quick results and improve retail sales. Major

PERSONAL SELLING

Selling, one of the oldest business activities, has been around for thousands of years. Many companies consider **personal selling**—a person-to-person promotional presentation to a potential buyer—as the key to marketing effectiveness. Unless a seller matches a firm's goods or services to the needs of a particular client or customer, none of the firm's other departments produces any benefits. Today, sales and sales-related jobs employ about 15 million Americans. Average selling expenses represent 10 to 15 percent of a typical company's total sales, compared to 1 to 3 percent for advertising. This cost often is the firm's single largest marketing expense.

How do marketers decide whether to make personal selling the primary component of their firm's marketing mix? In general, firms are likely to emphasize personal selling rather than advertising or sales promotion under four conditions:

▼ *Customers* are relatively few in number and geographically concentrated

▼ The *product* is technically complex, involves trade-ins, and requires special handling.

▼ The product carries a relatively high *price*.

▼ It moves through relatively short *distribution channels*.

The sales functions of most companies are experiencing rapid change. Some changes have been only cosmetic, such as changing the job title from salesperson to account representative or associate, while its duties stay the same. Many firms are making more significant changes in their sales forces, though. Sales duties have been expanded, and in some companies, the job itself has changed. Today's salespeople are more concerned than those of past years with establishing long-term buyer-seller relationships and acting as consultants to their customers. They focus not just on closing sales, but on helping customers to decide what they need and working with them to ensure the most efficient possible product use.

Personal selling can occur in several environments, each of which can involve business-to-business or business-to-consumer selling. Sales representatives who make sales calls on prospective customers at their homes or businesses are involved in *field selling*. Companies that sell major industrial equipment typically rely heavily on field selling. *Over-the-counter selling* describes sales activities in retail and some wholesale locations. Customers visit the seller's lo-

cation to purchase the desired items. *Telemarketing* sales representatives make their presentations over the phone. A later discussion in this section reviews telemarketing in more detail.

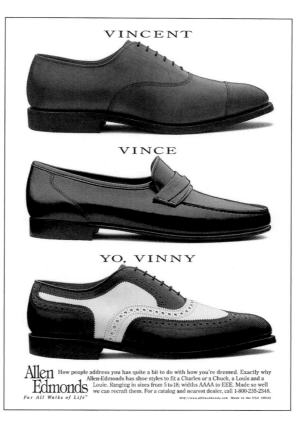

Figure 16.9 **Order Processing: Major Sales Task for Over-the-Counter Selling**

Sales Tasks

All sales activities involve assisting customers in some manner. Although a salesperson's work can vary significantly from one company or situation to another, it usually includes three basic tasks: order processing, creative selling, and missionary selling.

Most sales personnel perform all three tasks to some extent. A sales representative promoting a highly technical product may do 55 percent missionary selling, 40 percent creative selling, and 5 percent order processing. By contrast, a salesperson at a retail store carrying the Allen Edmonds line of shoes shown in Figure 16.9 may do 70 percent order processing, 15 percent creative selling, and 15 percent missionary selling. Marketers often classify sales jobs based on these three sales tasks to evaluate a salesperson's primary task.

Order Processing Although both field selling and telemarketing involve this activity, **order processing** is most often related to over-the-counter selling in retail and wholesale firms. The salesperson identifies customer needs, points out products to meet them, and processes the order. Efficient and accurate order handling is critical to satisfying customers' needs. Effective salespeople check the quality of the products their customers receive, know their customers' markets, and ensure that their firms can supply products when needed.

Route sales personnel process orders for such consumer goods as bread, milk, soft drinks, and snack foods.

They check each store's stock, report inventory needs to the store manager, and complete the sale. Most sales positions include at least minor order processing functions. These activities become the primary duty in cases where customers can readily identify and acknowledge their needs. The later discussion of sales force automation will explain how many companies now use technology to simplify order processing.

Creative Selling Sales representatives for most business products and some consumer items perform **creative selling,** a persuasive type of promotional presentation. Creative selling promotes a good or service whose benefits are not readily apparent and/or whose purchase decision requires a careful analysis of alternatives. Sales of intangible products such as the insurance policy described in Figure 16.10 rely heavily on creative selling. The message focuses on methods of reducing risk from accidents, asking interested readers to contact the insurance company to learn more about its business insurance coverage.

Creative selling is the key to success at Watlow Electric Manufacturing, a mid-sized manufacturer of industrial heaters. Its products are customized to the individual customer's specifications, and no two installations implement the same standards. Watlow's sales force is highly trained to create engineered solutions. They must build customer relationships over repeated calls. Because Watlow requires a high level of expertise from its salespeople, it makes a substantial investment in them. The company spends between $300 and $350 for travel, salesperson compensation, and entertainment for each sales call—double the amount spent by competitors. This expenditure also includes the cost of computers installed to free up sales representatives' time to make more sales calls.[32]

Missionary Selling Sales work also includes an indirect form of selling in which the representative promotes goodwill for a company and/or provides technical or operational assistance to the customer; this practice is called **missionary selling.** Many businesses that sell technical equipment, such as IBM and Xerox, provide systems specialists who act as consultants to customers. These salespeople work to solve problems and sometimes to help their clients with questions not directly related to their employers' products. Other industries also use missionary selling techniques. Pharmaceuticals company representatives call on physicians to persuade them, as indirect customers, to prescribe the company's medications. The actual sales, however, are handled through wholesalers that sell to pharmacies that fill the prescriptions.

The Sales Process

The events of the sales process typically follow the seven-step sequence shown in Figure 16.11: prospecting and qualifying, the approach, the presentation, the demonstration, handling objections, the closing, and the follow-up. Remember the importance of flexibility, though; a good salesperson is not afraid to vary the sales process based on a customer's responses and needs. The process of selling to a potential customer who is unfamiliar with the company's products must differ from the process for serving a long-time customer.

Prospecting and Qualifying At the prospecting stage, salespeople identify potential customers. They may seek leads for prospective sales from such sources as previous customers, friends, business associates, neighbors, other sales personnel, and other employees in the firm.

The qualifying process identifies potential customers who have financial ability and authority to buy. Those who lack the necessary financial resources or who cannot make purchase decisions are not qualified prospects. Companies use different tactics to identify and qualify prospects. Some companies, like Cleveland software company Tribute Inc., rely on business development teams to do this legwork. They send direct mail and then provide leads to sales reps based on responses. Other companies believe in the paramount importance of personal visits from sales representatives.[33]

Approach Successful salespeople make careful preparations, analyzing all available data about a prospective cus-

Figure 16.10 Creative Selling in Insurance Marketing

Figure 16.11   **Steps in the Sales Process**

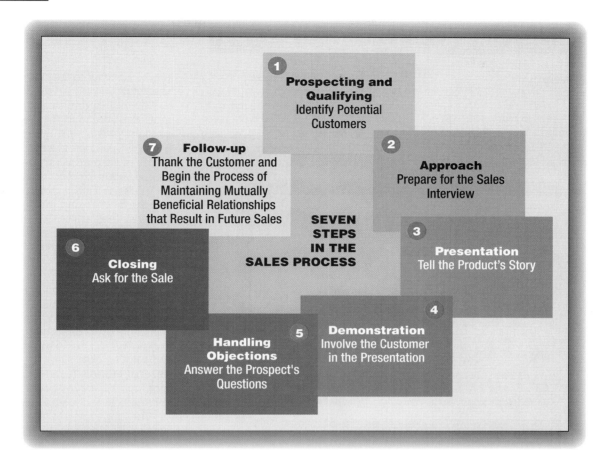

tomer's product lines and other pertinent information before making the initial contact. They realize the importance of a first impression in influencing a customer's future attitudes toward the selling company and its products.

Successful salespeople learn to "read" their customers. Wilson Learning Corp., a sales training firm, teaches sales representatives how to identify different customer styles and adapt their approaches in response. Customers with warm, folksy attitudes respond best when salespeople take the time to chat and build rapport. The same approach can turn off buyers that Wilson Learning labels "cool customers," since they want salespeople to get to the point. An analytical customer—Wilson's third category—responds to a slow and cautious approach that provides a thorough explanation of how the company's products can solve the customer's problems.[34]

Presentation At the presentation stage, salespeople communicate promotional messages. Usually, they describe the major features of their products, highlight advantages, and cite examples of consumer satisfaction.

Dormont Manufacturing Co. sales managers decided to assist their sales representatives by changing consumer perceptions about the company. The Pittsburgh-area maker of gas appliance connectors and related products prepared a virtual factory tour on CD/ROM, complete with animated characters like Monty the Gas Hose that showed how the company could help buyers solve unique problems. Sales representatives began to include this element as part of their presentations to current and prospective customers. Customers who had previously only ordered gas hoses began expanding their orders to include such additional products as coupling devices and valves.[35]

Demonstration A demonstration involves the prospect in the sales presentation, reinforcing the message that the salesperson has been communicating. This activity often represents a critical step in the sales process. Paper manufacturers, for example, produce elaborate booklets to help their salespeople demonstrate different types of paper, finishes, and graphic techniques. Such demonstrations allow salespeople to show printed samples of different paper

BUSINESS HALL OF SHAME

Swept Away

The message seems to carry a straight-forward meaning. You get a thick, gray envelope in the mail with the smiling faces of Ed McMahon and Dick Clark on the front. Inside, among sheets of magazine coupons and forms to complete, is a letter with the message: "YOUR NAME, You've Finally Made It—You're Set for Life with $11,075,000.00. Guaranteed!" The only hitch, apparently, is that you have to return the letter to the company's processing office before a stated deadline.

You trust Ed and Dick and the letter that says you're a winner. So why wouldn't you rush to buy those subscriptions and perhaps even fly to the city whose mailing address was on the envelope, ready to collect your winnings?

That's what more than a dozen people did in 1997 and 1998 when they received their envelopes from American Family Publishers. All of them showed up in Tampa to be the first to return claim numbers only to find they weren't winners.

Both American Family and its rival, Publishers Clearing House, have been blamed for misleading entrants into thinking they've already won and that buying the magazine subscriptions enhances their chances of winning. Connecticut officials found that some senior citizens even bought multiple subscriptions to the same magazine.

"The language is confusing and the type on the disclaimers is often difficult

OPEN IMMEDIATELY: SECURITY-SEALED WINNER IDENTIFICATION DOCUMENT ENCLOSED

specimens to art directors, designers, printers, and other potential customers. A demonstration ride in a new automobile gives the salesperson an opportunity to point out special features and strengths, while the customer experiences the performance of the vehicle. Although the striking advertisement in Figure 16.12 may bring prospects into the BMW dealer's showroom, placing the driver behind the wheel of the new M roadster demonstrates the model's qualities in a manner not possible through other promotional alternatives.

Some products are too large to carry to prospective buyers or require special installation to demonstrate. Using laptop computers and multimedia presentations, sales representatives can demonstrate these products for customers.

Handling Objections Some salespeople fear prospects' objections, because they view the questions as criticism. Instead, salespeople should try to view objections as opportunities to extend presentations and answer questions. Proper handling of objections allows sales personnel to remove obstacles and complete sales. This step can turn into a positive stage of the sales process by allowing the sales-person to present additional information and offer a unique solution as a way to clarify a point. The key is to sell benefits, not features: How will this product help the customer?

Closing The critical point in a selling relationship—the time at which the salesperson actually asks the prospect to buy—is the closing. If the presentation effectively matches product features to customer needs, the closing should be a natural conclusion. However, a surprising number of sales personnel struggle to actually ask for customers' orders.

Salespeople have developed a variety of successful closing techniques over the years. Some of the more popular ones include:

▼ The technique "If I can show you . . . " first identifies the prospect's major concern in purchasing the good or service and then offers convincing evidence of the offering's ability to resolve it. ("If I can show you how the new heating system will reduce your energy costs by 25 percent, would you be willing to let us install it?")

to see because it's so tiny," says Bridget Small of the American Association of Retired Persons, whose members have been recruited by state attorneys general to help with investigations of the sweepstakes. "Also, sometimes it's not clear that consumers don't need to pay, or buy magazines, to win."

As a result of such allegations of deceptive direct-marketing practices, states have investigated American Family and Publishers Clearing House. Florida, Indiana, and Connecticut filed lawsuits against American Family and its celebrity spokesmen, and more than 30 states reached a settlement with the company in March 1998. It agreed to stop using the slogan "You're our newest winner!" Additional requirements include prominently displaying the words "no purchase necessary" and telling consumers how to get off the company's mailing lists.

Both companies make money by selling magazines to sweepstakes entrants. The take is high—between 75 and 90 percent, with the rest going to the magazines, which profit from renewals. Of the $7 billion Americans spend annually on magazine subscrip-

tions, about 12 percent comes from the "stamp sheet" sales dominated by American Family and Publishers Clearing House.

With such fierce competition between the two companies, their tricky techniques often mirror each other's. In 1994, a Publishers Clearing House mailing told all recipients that they were "finalists" for the sweepstakes jackpot. American Family Publishers did the same. Not long after, 14 state attorneys general started investigating the companies. Publishers Clearing House eventually dropped the term *finalists* and paid $490,000 in fines. American Family also dropped the practice.

Because of legal troubles, as well as competition from state lotteries and legalized gambling, both companies are considering new directions—perhaps more but smaller cash prizes or family vacations.

"There is no question the industry needs a shake-up and some new ideas," says Susan Kaughman, American Family's chief executive officer. "Maybe the answer is to make the prizes more real and tangible."

QUESTIONS FOR CRITICAL THINKING

1. Henry Cowen, the sweepstakes industry's elder statesman, says of mailing recipients, "People aren't very smart, you know. So you have to be careful." What is the connection between an industry's perception of its customers and the business practices it uses?

2. How do other businesses manipulate their messages in ways that could stimulate accusations of deception? How could they design appealing but not deceptive pitches?

Sources: Adam Zagorin, "Sweepstakes under Scrutiny," *Time*, March 22, 1999, accessed at www.pathfinder.com; Adapted from Susan Abram, "Sweepstakes Firm's Slogan Not a Winner," *Los Angeles Times*, March 17, 1998, p. D1, D9; Greg Jaffe, "Sweepstakes Industry May Not Be a WINNER!" *The Wall Street Journal*, February 18, 1998, p. B1; Richard Jerome, Don Sider, and John Hannah, "Pushing the Envelope," *People*, March 15, 1998, p. 131; and Tom Lowry, "Settlement Won't End American Family Woes," *USA Today*, March 20, 1998, pp. B1–B2.

▼ The alternative-decision technique poses choices for the prospect, either of which favors the seller. ("Will you take this sweater or that one?")

▼ In the SRO (standing room only) technique, the seller warns the prospect to conclude a sales agreement immediately because the product may not be available later, or an important feature, such as its price, will soon change.

▼ A seller can use silence as a closing technique, since discontinuing the sales presentation forces the prospect to take some type of action, making either a positive or negative decision.

▼ An extra-inducement close offers special incentives designed to motivate a favorable buyer response. Extra inducements may include quantity discounts, special servicing arrangements, or layaway options.

The term *close* actually portrays an inaccurate picture. The sales process should emphasize relationship management, not special closing techniques. As one sales manager

puts it, "You shouldn't think of it as closing a sale but as opening a customer relationship. We understand the things that are important to them, we've presented in that manner, we've demonstrated in that manner. Sure, it takes a little longer to go through the process, but if it means trading a 30 percent closing ratio for a 70 percent ratio, I'll spend the time any day."[36]

Follow-up In the same way, the salesperson's actions after the sale continue the relationship and may well determine whether the customer will make another purchase. After closing, the seller should process the order quickly and efficiently and reassure the customer about the purchase decision. Follow-up is a vital activity for building a long-term working relationship with customers, ensuring that products satisfy them, and delivering needed service. By calling soon after a purchase, the salesperson provides psychological reinforcement for the customer's decision to buy. It also gives the seller a chance to correct any problems with the purchase.

Follow-up strengthens the bond between salespeople and customers. Car dealers implement extensive follow-up

Figure 16.12 **Demonstration—Critical Stage in the Sales Process**

programs, including calls soon after purchase decisions, thank you notes from salespeople, customer satisfaction surveys from both dealerships and car manufacturers, and calls from service managers inviting customers to use the dealer's service department.

Proper follow-up is a logical part of the sales process. It involves not only continuing contact with customers but a review of the sales process. Salespeople should ask themselves, "Why did I lose or close that sale? What could I have done differently to improve the outcome?" The Business Tool Kit lists some additional tips for successful personal selling.

Recent Trends in Personal Selling

As noted earlier, personal selling requires different strategies in today's competitive business environment than salespeople implemented in the past. Rather than making face-to-face presentations to potential customers, firms may rely on telemarketing to solicit business and/or to fill orders placed directly by buyers. Salespeople also sell to teams of corporate representatives called *decision-making units.* Especially in business-to-business situations involving technical products, customers expect sales reps to answer technical questions, understand technical jargon, and communicate using sophisticated technological tools—or they must bring along someone who can. Patience is also required, because the sales cycle, from initial contact to closing, may take years, especially for large, expensive equipment. To address these concerns, companies are turning to relationship selling, consultative selling, team selling, and

sales force automation—major personal selling trends that are changing the sales forces of companies of all sizes.

Telemarketing **Telemarketing,** personal selling conducted entirely by telephone, is also one of the most common forms of direct marketing. It provides a firm's marketers with a high return on their expenditures, an immediate response, and an opportunity for personalized, two-way conversation. It's also an effective method: Telemarketing results in over $175 billion in consumer sales each year.[37]

Many firms use this method because expense or other obstacles prevent salespeople from meeting all potential customers in person. Telemarketers use databases to target prospects based on demographic data. A company may use telemarketing at every stage of the sales process, or it may rely on telephone contacts only for certain stages such as prospecting or follow-up.

Telemarketing takes two forms. A sales representative who calls you during dinner to sell magazine subscriptions or insurance is practicing *outbound telemarketing. Inbound telemarketing* occurs when the customer calls a toll-free phone number to get information or place an order. Print ads for catalog companies like Lands' End and The Sharper Image encourage customers to call and request catalogs or place orders.

Fraud and invasion of privacy are the two biggest areas of concern in telemarketing. According to Federal Trade Commission (FTC) estimates, consumers lose $40 billion a year through telephone fraud. To crack down on abusive and annoying telemarketing practices, the FTC passed a Telemarketing Sales Rule in 1996. Telemarketers must disclose that they are selling something and on whose behalf they call before they make their presentations. The rule also limits calls to between 8 a.m. and 9 p.m., requires sellers to disclose details on exchange policies, and requires them to keep lists of people who do not want to receive calls.

Special Selling Strategies As competitive pressures mount, a widening universe of firms are emphasizing **relationship selling,** in which a salesperson builds a mutually beneficial relationship with a customer through regular contacts over an extended period. To create strong, lasting relationships with customers, salespeople must meet buyer's expectations. Such buyer-seller bonds become in-

BUSINESS TOOL KIT

Do's and Don'ts for Sales Success

The way sales representatives present themselves during sales calls sets the stage for what follows. While they must bring thorough knowledge of the products and the benefits they offer to customers, salespeople can ruin promising sales within the first few minutes if they show poor manners. To increase your chances of success, avoid common etiquette blunders in any interaction with clients. Never make these mistakes:

- ▼ Using vulgar language.
- ▼ Arriving late for meetings.
- ▼ Dressing in unprofessional or inappropriate clothing.
- ▼ Failing to remember customer names, and addressing a customer by a nickname during a first meeting.
- ▼ Keeping customers on hold.
- ▼ Interrupting others frequently or showing a condescending attitude.
- ▼ Failing to shake hands, or offering a limp handshake.
- ▼ Demonstrating poor table manners.

But the process of developing long-term customer relationships only starts with the sales call. It continues long after the customer places an initial order. Here are several "do's" to help you follow up with customers:

- ▼ Call customers to express your thanks and make sure that they are satisfied with your goods and services.
- ▼ Take responsibility for any problems that arise, instead of blaming another department. Don't argue; solve them.
- ▼ Be upfront about what you can and cannot do. Customers won't appreciate finding out later that you promised something you can't deliver.
- ▼ Use the personal touch, not just electronic communications. Send hand-written notes to long-term customers from time to time. Gifts also keep your name in their minds.

Source: Danielle Kennedy, "Second Time Around," *Entrepreneur,* May 1997, pp. 96–99.

creasingly important as companies reduce the number of suppliers from which they buy and look for companies that provide excellent customer service and satisfaction. Salespeople must also find ways to distinguish themselves from others offering similar products.

Because a few large accounts make up a major share of its business, relationships are critical for toy manufacturer Ohio Art Co., famed for its Etch-a-Sketch toy. Ohio Art builds customer relationships by involving its retailers, which include Wal-Mart and Toys "R" Us, in the toy-development process. Feedback travels in two directions. The retailers get toys that sell, and Ohio Art gets advice to improve its business.[38]

The Ohio Art approach is also an example of consultative selling, which works hand-in-hand with relationship selling to build customer loyalty. Salespeople can no longer rely on the once-popular "good old boy" sales style—getting chummy with customers, buying them meals or drinks, giving the standard sales pitch, applying pressure, and expecting to get the sale. Instead, **consulta-**

tive selling calls for meeting customers' needs by listening to them, understanding and caring about their problems, paying attention to details, and following through after the sale.

Team selling joins salespeople with specialists from other functional areas of the firm to complete the selling process. In this way, it complements relationship and consultative selling strategies. Teams can be formally assigned units or assembled for specific, temporary selling situations. Ohio Art sends teams with account representatives, marketing people, and high-level managers on all its sales calls.

In sales situations that call for detailed knowledge of new, complex, and ever-changing technologies, team selling has enhanced competitive strength for many companies to help them meet customers' needs. Many customers prefer the team approach, which makes them feel like they receive exceptional service. Another advantage is the formation of relationships between companies rather than individuals. MCI used team selling to win a $100 million,

5-year contract from the U.S. Postal Service to develop and manage a telecommunications network connecting 34,000 locations. A large staff from several MCI locations and divisions—data marketing, engineering, and operations—developed the proposal. Such teamwork is a very important aspect of selling to the federal government. The Postal Service wanted company engineers, rather than salespeople, to make the presentation, requiring the sales representatives to step back from their normal roles.[39]

Sales Force Automation
Several earlier examples have shown how salespeople are applying new technologies to the sales process, a trend called **sales force automation (SFA)**. This trend incorporates a broad range of tools, from e-mail, mobile communications devices like pagers and cellular phones, and laptop computers to increasingly sophisticated software systems that automate the sales process. Currently available SFA software packages help sales managers to develop account territories, plan sales campaigns, perform detailed analyses of sales trends, and forecast future sales. Sales personnel can use the system to analyze customer databases to develop leads, schedule sales campaigns, automatically file orders and expense reports, and tap into company databases for instant updates on prices, policies, and products.

Among its many benefits, SFA improves the consistency of the sales approach, speeds response times, and reduces sales cycles. Salespeople can design product packages and close deals on the spot, instead of collecting information from customers and returning to their offices to prepare proposals.

Sales representatives at Gulf Industries, a Torrance, California, signmaker, carry laptop computers that store designs for over 400 pieces of preapproved artwork. They combine these designs into signs that fit customer needs, price the signs, and print out contracts—all in less than an hour without leaving the customer's location. Instead of taking 3 hours to develop a design and then returning to the office to check with designers and engineers before issuing

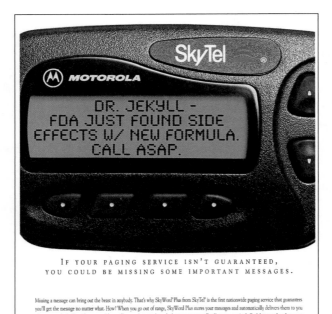

IF YOUR PAGING SERVICE ISN'T GUARANTEED, YOU COULD BE MISSING SOME IMPORTANT MESSAGES.

Missing a message can bring out the beast in anybody. That's why SkyWord! Plus from SkyTel! is the first nationwide paging service that guarantees you'll get the message no matter what. How? When you go out of range, SkyWord Plus stores your messages and automatically delivers them to you when you get back. Even if your pager's been off or your batteries have died, your messages will still get to you. And all of this costs less than most ordinary paging. So get SkyTel. And get the message, guaranteed. Limited-time offer: Call now and get a personal 800/888 number for free.

FEATURE	SKYWORD PLUS SERVICE	OTHER NATIONWIDE SERVICES
Guaranteed Delivery	Yes	No
E-Mail On Your Pager	Yes	Maybe
Protection Against Garbled Messages	Yes	No
Monthly Cost	$24.95	$35 - $99

SkyTel features advanced messaging pagers by Motorola.

SkyWord Plus price includes 800 10-character messages. Equipment and enhanced services available at an additional charge. ©1998 SkyTel. SkyTel is a subsidiary of MCI, a WorldCom company.

SkyTel Call 1-800-395-6277 or visit www.skytel.com

Sales force automation innovations like the SkyTel advanced messaging pager keep mobile sales professionals in touch with customers and the office. The Motorola system also includes e-mail delivery via the pager and message storage if the pager is turned off.

a proposal, they complete the entire process on the spot. Gulf's sales increased almost 30 percent since launching the SFA program after 5 years of flat revenues. Salespeople who used the technology approach averaged 25 percent more sales than others who followed traditional methods.[40]

IMC IN ACTION: SPONSORSHIPS AND CROSS PROMOTIONS

With so many promotions in so many different forms competing for consumer attention, marketers continually search out new opportunities to promote products using IMC programs. An increasingly common choice—commercial sponsorship of an event or activity—integrates several elements of the promotional mix. **Sponsorship** occurs when an organization provides cash or in-kind resources to an event or activity in exchange for a direct association with it. Marketers in different companies are also combining their promotional efforts for related products using a technique called **cross promotion**.

Sponsorships

Currently a $17 billion business worldwide and almost $7 billion in the United States alone, sponsorships are growing over 10 percent a year. Sports sponsorships attract two-thirds of total sponsorship dollars, with entertainment, festivals, causes, and the arts dividing up the rest.[41]

Sponsors receive two primary benefits: exposure to the event's audience and the image associated with the activity by its audience. Sponsors typically gain the rights to use the name of the person or event in their promotions, advertise during media coverage of the event, post promotional signs at the venue, set up sales promotions, and engage in personal selling to clients invited to attend the event. Event sponsors frequently establish hospitality tents where they entertain channel members and potential customers. Sponsorships play an important role in relationship marketing, bringing together the event, its participants, and the sponsoring firms. This unique promotional opportunity allows participating marketers to reach a narrow but highly desirable audience.

Companies choose events to sponsor based on the target audiences they want to reach and the images of the sports or events. Successful sponsorship requires a product that matches the demographics of the audience and also fits with the selling season. For example, a beer company sponsorship fits a professional football game, while suntan lotion at an ice-skating competition does not. Image also counts. Rolex and Porsche would be appropriate sponsors of yachting races or polo matches but not of rodeos.

Sporting event sponsorships range from the Olympic games and national sports leagues to golf tournaments and local sporting events. The Business Hall of Fame may surprise some, however, when it reveals that the largest single category of sporting event sponsorships—$1 billion a year—is neither football nor basketball but motor sports.

Anheuser-Busch, Philip Morris, Coca-Cola, General Motors, and PepsiCo are the top spenders among U.S. sports sponsors. GM's Buick and Cadillac divisions sponsor PGA golf tours to forge bonds with the sport's affluent, well-educated players and fans. Sponsorship is also an international promotional activity; the U.S. Postal Service, Italian car manufacturer Fiat, and Credit Lyonnais, a major French bank, sponsor the annual Tour de France bicycle race.

Sports are not the only events that interest sponsors. Citibank recently invested $5 billion in an exclusive sponsorship of singer Elton John's "Big Picture" world concert tour. To emphasize that relationship, the singer appeared in the bank's television ads. Through its tour sponsorship, Citibank conveyed a distinctive, internationally recognized image and used music to reach customers around the world. "We needed a citizen of the world," explained Brian Ruder, Citibank executive vice president for global marketing. Elton John fit the bill perfectly, as a global celebrity and humanitarian.[42]

Arts sponsorships offer companies a different way to promote themselves and reach specific target markets. These deals have bypassed former limits such as placing signs at exhibit entrances or small print on commemorative posters. As public funding for the arts declines, museums are delighted to receive rising support from the private sector. Museum sponsorships are comparative bargains for self-promoting companies.

For example, Subaru sponsors a traveling science exhibit at Philadelphia's Franklin Institute Science Museum. The car manufacturer donated four Legacy station wagons to carry the show's resources to schools. Student visitors to the exhibit receive bags that include invitations for their parents to test drive Subaru cars. For a minimal investment, Subaru gains increased brand recognition with the parents of 500,000 local school children a year. The company's marketing director Timothy Mahoney considers this program a better return on investment than the $2 million it spent advertising during a recent Super Bowl.[43]

Intel, Discover Card, MCI, and Trans-World Airlines each paid $10 million to sponsor the Smithsonian Institution's traveling 150th anniversary exhibit. In addition to being mentioned in the Smithsonian's television ads, the sponsors set up their own exhibits at tour sites. TWA also sponsored an Italian art and history exhibit at the St. Louis Art Museum. The airline then advertised its travel packages to Italy in museum newsletters and articles.

DID YOU KNOW?

The 1996 Summer Olympic Games in Atlanta attracted more members of the media (15,000) than athletes (10,800).

WWW. **www.si.edu/newstart.htm**

Cross Promotions

Remember how popular BMW's Z3 roadster became after its introduction in the James Bond film, *Goldeneye*? Have you racked up frequent flyer mileage by charging purchases on a Citibank/American Airlines AAdvantage Program Visa or MasterCard? These product tie-ins are just two examples of *cross promotions,* in which marketers join forces to promote products. The marketing partners share the cost of the campaign—an important benefit as media costs rise. These partnership efforts between established

Business Directory

sales force automation (SFA) applying computers and other technologies to improve the efficiency and competitiveness of the sales function.

sponsorship providing cash or other resources to an event or activity in exchange for a direct association with it.

cross promotion promotional strategy in which marketing partners share the cost of a campaign that meets their mutual needs.

BUSINESS HALL OF FAME

NASCAR Drives Home Sales for Sponsors

The good ol' boys who started stock-car racing 50 years ago must be turning in their graves. NASCAR's gone to the yuppies.

Need proof? Check out the four-wheeled billboards that zip around tracks in races like the Daytona 500 and the Winston Cup series. Joining ads for traditional tobacco, motor oil, and beer sponsors on the cars' hoods, trunk lids, and other body panels are logos for the Cartoon Network, Burger King, McDonald's, Lowe's home improvement centers, Cheerios, Procter & Gamble, and DuPont. You can pay with a NASCAR MasterCard for jackets or artwork at the NASCAR Thunder retail store in Atlanta or a meal at one of the NASCAR Cafés in Nashville or Myrtle Beach, South Carolina.

NASCAR's even gone online. Its Web site, NASCAR Online, generated over 3 million hits when it was launched in 1996. The following year,

a licensing agreement with interactive entertainment software company Electronic Arts led to the development of a series of interactive racing games. The racing organization also signed with Total Entertainment Network to de-

---

brands enhance the benefit a company gains from its investments of time and money.

The movie industry is one of the most prominent users of cross promotion. Movie studios partner with fast-food chains to create public awareness of their films. Placing toys with characters from current movies in kids' meals increases the chances that the children will ask to see the movies. Figure 16.13 shows Taco Bell's tie-in with Warner Brothers' *Batman and Robin* movie. Customers played a game that offered them a chance to win the Batmobile.

Kraft's Country Tour concert combines sponsorship and cross promotion. The Kraft Country Tour Cookhouse accompanied country music star Vince Gill to 21 of the 80 cities on a concert tour. The traveling kitchen was a mobile sampling festival, complete with contests, sweepstakes, broadcast sound stage, and food. The fun included demonstrations of easy-to-prepare dishes using Kraft brands, a recipe booklet, and giveaways of an exclusive Gill CD. The Cookhouse entertained consumers while promoting Kraft brands.[44]

PUBLIC RELATIONS

Two more elements, public relations (PR) and publicity, support other elements in the promotional mix. They usually pursue objectives broader in scope than those of advertising and sales promotion. Through PR, companies attempt to improve their prestige and image with the public by distributing specific messages or ideas to target audiences. Cause-related promotional activities are often supported by PR and publicity campaigns. As such, PR is an important part of a company's promotional plan.

Public relations refers to an organization's non-paid communications with its various public audiences, such as customers, vendors, news media, employees, stockholders, the government, and the general public. Many of these communication efforts serve marketing purposes. Public relations is an efficient, indirect communications channel for promoting products. It can publicize products and help to create and maintain a positive image of the company.

velop the NASCAR Racing Online Series, which allows anyone with Internet access to experience NASCAR competition online.

www.nascar.com

What is powering this new marriage between sophisticated companies and a sport long considered entertainment for rural Southerners?

Stock-car racing has a new audience. The old demographic of working-class Southern males is history. Today's stock-car fanatics cut across income and education levels. They like popular drivers such as Jeff Gordon and Dale Earnhardt, who don't carry the same troublesome reputations often found among basketball, football, and baseball players.

"The public is fed up with controversies and hold-outs by pro athletes in other sports," says Mark Dyer, president of NASCAR Café. "Compared to them, NASCAR drivers have images that are courageous and competitive."

Women now make up 40 percent of NASCAR event attendees, up from 15 percent in 1975. Almost one-third of to-

day's fans have household incomes over $50,000, and more than one-quarter are managers or professionals. "Not even the Olympics have grown as fast as NASCAR," says Lesa Ukman, editor of IEG Sponsorship Report. "They've done the best marketing job of any sport in America."

Upgraded facilities, air-conditioned VIP boxes, and gourmet food have helped to draw this new crowd. As a result, indicated by the flashy logos that cover the cars, big businesses once uninterested in stock-car racing are spending upwards of $4 million to sponsor teams.

They gain big payoffs for their investments. Performance Research data shows that 72 percent of NASCAR fans buy sponsors' products, compared to 36 percent of NFL fans and 38 percent of NBA fans. Another reassuring statistic for sponsors is brand recognition. In a survey of 1,000 racing fans, respondents identified more than 200 companies and brands associated with NASCAR.

If the sport has outgrown its traditional fans—and sponsors like Hooters of America—no one is considering the change a crisis. On the contrary, this fast-growing sport expects revenues to

hit $4 billion by 2000. "We're not just about car racing any more," says France, "we're an entertainment company."

QUESTIONS FOR CRITICAL THINKING

1. What other industries or forms of entertainment are gaining interest from consumers outside their traditional fan populations? What techniques are they using to make this transition?

2. The Cartoon Network, MCI, and other sophisticated brand names are untraditional sponsors of stock-car racing. What risks do these new sponsors take when they support an unconventional—for them—form of entertainment? Would wise marketers get involved early or wait until the market proves itself?

Sources: Roy S. Johnson, "Speed Sells!" *Fortune*, April 12, 1999, accessed at www.pathfinder.com; "Cheerios Zooms into NASCAR," *Business Wire*, January 12, 1998; Ed Hinton, "Inside Motor Sports," *Sports Illustrated*, February 23, 1998, p. 98; and Bruce Horovitz, "New Breed of Sponsors Race to NASCAR," *USA Today*, April 5, 1996, p. 1B.

Public relations has recently grown substantially as a result of increased public pressure on industry regarding ethical business conduct, environmentalism, and internationalism. Many top executives are increasing their involvement in public relations. The public expects top managers to take responsibility for company actions. Those who do not are widely criticized.

The PR department links a firm with the media. It provides press releases and holds news conferences to announce new products, formation of strategic alliances, management changes, financial results, and similar developments. Publications issued by the PR department include newsletters, brochures, and reports.

General Mills is one company that's using PR to generate publicity for its products. Its promotional strategy aims to reduce its reliance on television ads, citing their rising cost and con-

tinuing fragmentation of audiences. A company campaign distributes a free Betty Crocker question-and-answer food column to newspapers. It has also sponsored a Bisquick pancake breakfast for candidates at the 1996 New Hampshire presidential primary.[45] During the week prior to the 1998 Masters golf tournament, Wheaties public relations specialists distributed media releases and cereal boxes featuring the likeness of reigning champion Tiger Woods.

Public relations can sometimes achieve more valuable promotional messages than paid advertisements. Viewers may ignore television commercials, but not the sports announcer who shows the Wheaties box during the show.

Business Directory

public relations organization's nonpaid communications and relationships with public audiences.

General Mills won market share from Post and Kellogg with its PR focus—even though it cut marketing spending.

Publicity

The type of public relations that most closely approaches promoting a company's products is **publicity,** nonpersonal stimulation of demand for a good, service, place, idea, event, person, or organization by unpaid placement of significant news in print or broadcast media. The chess contest between champion Gary Kasparov and IBM's Big Blue computer showed how companies can use publicity to great benefit. "It was brilliant. How else do you communicate that you've got the smartest computer in the world?" says Allen Adamson, a corporate identity expert.[46] Other notable publicity campaigns include:

▼ Oscar Mayer's 1996 audition of 65,000 kids to select one who would sing the company jingle in a commercial. For only $3 million, Oscar Mayer increased brand awareness and posted a large increase in sales.

▼ Taco Bell's tongue-in-cheek ads touting its purchase of the Liberty Bell. This $400,000 campaign was actually an April Fool's Day promotion, but it sparked over 400 stories in newspapers and on television.

Sometimes PR departments have to defuse negative publicity that occurs through no fault of their own. Ryder trucks, for example, were mentioned during news stories about the Oklahoma City bombings. Who can forget O. J. Simpson's Bruno Magli shoes? Ironically, the detailed description of the shoes during the trial gave the company an estimated $100 million in free publicity that pushed sales up 50 percent![47]

PROMOTIONAL STRATEGIES

Many of this chapter's examples have demonstrated considerable overlap between the elements of the promotional mix. Clear boundaries no longer distinguish advertising from sales promotion or sponsorships. The Internet and other in-

Figure 16.13 **Taco Bell–Warner Bros. Cross Promotion**

teractive media also change how marketers promote products. By blending advertising, sales promotion, personal selling, and public relations, marketers create an integrated promotional mix that takes into account the market, product type, stage in the product life cycle, price, and promotional budget. Then they implement one of two promotional alternatives: pulling or pushing strategies. Finally, marketers must measure the effectiveness of their promotional strategies.

Selecting a Promotional Mix

Choosing the most appropriate promotional mix is one of the toughest tasks confronting a company's marketers. The following questions provide some general guidelines for allocating promotional efforts and expenditures among personal selling, advertising, sales promotion, sponsorships, and public relations:

▼ *What is your target market?* A drill-press manufacturer that markets to business buyers is likely to emphasize personal selling in its promotional mix. By contrast, marketers of Scope mouthwash depend more on effective advertising campaigns.

▼ *What is the value of the product?* Most companies cannot afford to market low-priced goods like toothpaste, cosmetics, soft drinks, and candy through extensive personal selling to end users, so they choose advertising instead. High-priced products in both business and consumer markets, however, require promotional mixes based on personal selling. Examples include time-share vacation condominiums and Boeing aircraft.

▼ *What time frame is involved?* Marketers usually rely on advertising before actual sales. An effective and consistent advertising theme may favorably influence a person's reaction to an approaching salesperson. Except for self-service situations, however, a salesperson is typically involved in completing an actual transaction. Marketers often expose customers to advertising again after the sale to assure them that they made the right choices and to precondition them for repeat purchases.

Pushing and Pulling Strategies

Marketers can choose between two general promotional strategies: a pushing strategy or a pulling strategy. A **pushing strategy** relies on personal selling to market a product to wholesalers and retailers in a company's distribution channels. Marketers promote the product to members of the marketing channel, not end users. Sales personnel explain to marketing intermediaries why they should carry a particular good or service, usually supported by offers of special discounts and promotional materials. Marketers also provide **cooperative advertising** allowances in which they share the cost of local advertising of their firm's product or line with channel partners. All of these strategies are designed to motivate wholesalers and retailers to push the good or service to their own customers.

The Wheaties "Breakfast of Champions" box design combines PR, advertising, and celebrity endorsements to generate maximum consumer exposure.

A **pulling strategy** attempts to promote a product by generating consumer demand for it, primarily through advertising and sales promotion appeals. Most advertising targets ultimate consumers, who then ask retailers for the good or service, inducing them to demand the product from the supplier. Marketers hope that strong consumer demand will pull the product through the marketing channel by forcing marketing intermediaries to carry it.

Most marketing situations require combinations of pushing and pulling strategies, although the emphasis can vary. Consumer products usually depend more heavily on pulling strategies than do business products, which favor pushing strategies. Nintendo of America watched its sales fall with the release of Sony's 32-bit PlayStation, then it responded by launching an IMC campaign with push and pull strategies to introduce the N64, the first 64-bit video game system. Initially, the company kept consumers in suspense to build demand. Several months prior to release of the product, the company showed the game set to the trade and then started advertising in game magazines. Tie-ins with Nickelodeon and Kellogg also sparked interest in the soon-to-be-released prod-

uct. Perhaps the most important campaign element was a unique sampling program. Nintendo teamed with Blockbuster Entertainment to let kids rent the N64 game units before they went on sale at retail stores. "We were able to show kids and their parents that N64 wasn't just another video game system," says Peter Main, Nintendo vice president of sales and marketing. "Promotions helped spread the word, and by the time we advertised it, every man, woman, and child knew about it."[48]

Increasing Promotional Effectiveness

Because promotion represents a major expenditure for many firms, marketers need some means of determining how well a campaign is accomplishing its promotional objectives. Companies want their advertising agencies and in-house marketing personnel to demonstrate how their promotional programs contribute to improved brand awareness, increased sales, and growing profits. Marketers are well-aware that customers encounter hundreds of advertising messages and sales promotions every day, leading to an ability to practice selective perception and simply screen out much of this stimulus.

Specialized research firms such as A. C. Nielsen provide advertisers with data about audience size and characteristics for media options like magazines, newspapers, and radio and TV programs. Advertisers have been lining up to pay $70,000 per spot to run ads during "South Park," the Comedy Central animated hit featuring four foul-mouthed third-graders. As Figure 16.14 points out, the program is watched by some 5 million people every week, even though the cable channel is available in only about half of the nation's homes. Even more attractive than this audience's size is its composition: The program is particularly strong among the 18- to 24-year-olds coveted by advertisers. Research also reveals that it is one of television's top "destination" shows—a program for which busy viewers turn on the set, then sit down and watch.[49]

They said it

"Half the money I spend on advertising is wasted, and the trouble is, I don't know which half."

John Wanamaker (1838–1922)
American merchant

Novel forms of advertising and sales promotion, such as ads on videocassettes and before features at movie theaters, animated billboards, and new types of sales promotions, are aimed at increasing the likelihood that messages will be seen and heard. The Internet and other interactive media also provide different ways to reach target audiences. Coordinated methods move a company toward the objective of delivering promotional messages that potential customers receive and remember. By measuring promotional effectiveness, organizations can examine different strategies, prevent mistakes before spending money on specific programs, and improve promotions in the future.

Determining whether an advertising message has achieved its intended objective is one of the most difficult undertakings in marketing. Sales promotions and direct marketing are somewhat easier to evaluate, because they involve measurable consumer responses. Like advertising, public relations is also difficult to assess in purely objective terms.

Figure 16.14 **Using Audience Research to Match Advertising with TV Program Audiences**

20s, advertisers make ads as unalike as possible, designing messages that seem like entertainment.

Companies also have to carefully consider the line between advertising and entertainment. "Advertorials" in magazines (special advertising sections with articles on a topic) present sponsors' products in article format, and television infomercials mimic regular programming. Web site content also challenges audience members to separate advertising appeals from editorial or entertainment elements, as the CandyStand site illustrates.

Puffery and Deception

Advertisers must exercise caution when promoting products. A statement such as "The most advanced system ever developed" is an example of *puffery,* exaggerated claims of a product's superiority or use of doubtful, subjective, or vague statements. While consumers seem to accept some flexibility with the truth in advertising to distinguish a product and get people to buy, puffery raises ethical questions. Where is the line between claims that attract attention and those that state implied guarantees? To what degree are advertisers deliberately making misleading statements?

The Uniform Commercial Code standardizes sales and business practices throughout the United States. It makes a distinction between puffery and specific or quantifiable statements about product quality or performance that amount to an "express warranty," for which the company must stand behind its claim. General boasts of product superiority and vague claims are considered puffery, not warranties. They are considered so self-praising or exaggerated that the average consumer would not rely on them to make a buying decision. If a marketer makes a quantifiable statement, on the other hand, it implies a certain level of performance. Tests can establish the validity of a claim that one brand of batteries outlasts a rival brand.

ETHICS IN PROMOTION

Of the four elements in the marketing mix, promotion is the one that raises the most ethical questions. Many people share a negative view of advertising, labeling it as propaganda rather than information. They criticize its influence on consumers, potential to create unnecessary needs and wants, overemphasis on sex and beauty, and delivery of inappropriate messages to children. Ads with sexual, ethnically stereotyping, sexist, or ageist themes are also under attack.

Although the law allows certain types of advertising, they involve ethical issues. For example, many people favor curtailing or eliminating advertising to children. To woo young consumers, especially teens and those in their

They said it

"The most powerful element in advertising is the truth."

William Bernbach (1911–1982)
Founder, Doyle Dane Bernbach
advertising agency

Recall the Business Hall of Shame, which reported on customers deceived by promotional materials into thinking they had won sweepstakes. These examples show how sales promotions provide opportunities for unscrupulous companies to take advantage of consumers. For example, some companies may not fulfill rebate and premium offers or mislead consumers by inaccurately stating the odds of winning sweepstakes or contests.

Personal selling also raises its share of ethical dilemmas. Salespeople have used company cars for personal purposes, practiced deceptive tactics such as shipping unordered merchandise to win sales contests, or padded expense reports. Bribing customers with large gifts or cash kickbacks to increase sales is another example of unethical conduct. Many firms have adopted company codes of ethics to promote ethical awareness and prevent lapses.

WHAT'S AHEAD

As this chapter demonstrates, technology is playing an increasingly important role in promotional strategy. Interactive media, largely unknown a decade ago, now enable two-way communications with consumers. Other areas of business operations, from management to production to marketing research, use different forms of technology to improve efficiency and increase profitability. Chapter 17 discusses how technology and the Internet change the business environment and help businesses succeed.

SUMMARY OF LEARNING GOALS

1. Relate the concept of integrated marketing communications to the development of a firm's promotional strategy.

In practicing integrated marketing communications, a firm coordinates all promotional activities to produce a unified, customer-focused message. IMC begins by identifying consumer needs and then moves backward to show how a company's products meet those needs. Then marketers select the promotional media that best target and reach customers. Teamwork, database marketing, and careful promotional planning to coordinate IMC strategy components are important elements of these programs. Increasing complexity and sophistication in marketing communications requires careful promotional planning to coordinate IMC strategies.

2. Explain the concept of a promotional mix and list the objectives of promotion.

A company's promotional mix integrates two components: personal selling and nonpersonal selling, which includes advertising, sales promotion, and public relations. By selecting the appropriate combination of promotional mix elements, marketers attempt to achieve the firm's five major promotional objectives: provide information, differentiate a product, increase demand, stabilize sales, and accentuate the product's value.

3. Summarize the different types of advertising and advertising media.

Advertising, the most visible form of nonpersonal promotion, is designed to inform, persuade, or remind. Product advertising places a message to promote a good or service, while institutional advertising promotes a concept, idea, or philosophy. Newspapers and television represent the largest advertising media categories, along with magazines, radio, direct mail, and outdoor advertising. Interactive media such as the World Wide Web represent the fastest growing type of media. Interactive advertising directly involves the viewer, who controls the flow of information.

4. Explain the roles of sales promotion and public relations in promotional strategy.

Consumer-oriented sales promotions like coupons, rebates, samples, premiums, contests, sweepstakes, and specialty advertising offer an extra incentive to buy a product. Point-of-purchase advertising displays and trade shows are sales promotions directed to the trade markets.

5. Identify the various personal selling tasks and the steps in the sales process.

Personal selling involves face-to-face interactions between seller and buyer. The primary sales tasks are order processing, creative selling, and missionary selling. The seven-step sales process includes prospecting and qualifying, approach, presentation, demonstration, handling objections, closing, and follow-up.

6. Discuss the role of sponsorships and cross promotions in integrated marketing communications planning.

Sponsorships and cross promotions are two IMC strategies for increasing product awareness and building relationships. Organizations use sponsorships to gain exposure to the event audiences and to link their products to the images associated with the sponsored events or activities. Marketers select events to sponsor based on their target audiences. With cross promotions, like product tie-ins between fast-food chains and movies, marketers jointly promote products and share promotional costs.

7. Explain how public relations supports other elements of the promotional mix.

Pubic relations (PR) is an efficient, indirect promotional alternative. It improves a company's prestige and image with the public. PR uses a variety of marketing communications such as media releases, news conferences, and article placements and story ideas in other media to generate publicity for a company.

8. Identify the factors that influence the selection of a promotional mix.

Marketers begin by focusing on their company's target market, product value, time frame, and budget. By analyzing these factors, they develop a promotional mix and allocate resources and expenditures among personal selling, advertising, sales promotion, sponsorships, and public relations.

9. Contrast pushing and pulling promotional strategies.

With pushing strategies, marketers use personal selling to promote their company's product to retailers and wholesalers, not end users. Practices include special incentives such as discounts, promotional materials, and cooperative advertising. Advertising and sales promotions are part of pulling strategies, which build consumer awareness so that consumers will ask retailers to carry the product. The strategies are not exclusive choices; in fact, most companies combine them to increase promotional effectiveness.

10. Identify the major ethical issues involved in promotion.

Promotion is the element of the marketing mix that raises the most ethical questions. Many consumers believe that advertising exerts too much influence on buyers and that it deceives customers by exaggerating product claims and consciously blurring the line between promotion and entertainment. Contests that don't disclose the odds of winning and bribes to customer representatives to increase sales are other examples of unethical behavior.

TEN BUSINESS TERMS YOU NEED TO KNOW

promotion

integrated marketing communications (IMC)

promotional mix

advertising

sales promotion

personal selling

sales force automation (SFA)

sponsorship

cross promotion

public relations

Other Important Business Terms

positioning

product advertising

institutional advertising

advocacy (cause) advertising

comparative advertising

infomercial

specialty advertising

point-of-purchase (POP) advertising

trade show

order processing

creative selling

missionary selling

telemarketing

relationship selling

consultative selling

team selling

publicity

pushing strategy

cooperative advertising

pulling strategy

REVIEW QUESTIONS

1. Explain why marketers use integrated marketing communications (IMC) to develop promotional strategies. What goals can promotion accomplish?
2. Relate the concept of the promotional mix to the marketing mix. What promotional mix would be appropriate for each of the following products?
   a. New breakfast cereal
   b. Compaq personal computer
   c. Specialty steel products sold to manufacturers
   d. Advertising agency
3. Differentiate among product advertising, institutional advertising, and advocacy (or cause) advertising. Also explain the differences among informative, persuasive, comparative, and reminder-oriented advertising.
4. Which is the most popular advertising medium measured in total advertising volume? How do other media rank in order of promotional expenditures?
5. Distinguish between advertising and sales promotion. Describe the principal methods of sales promotion, citing examples of each.
6. Explain each of the steps in the sales process. Cite examples of each step. What is the primary sales task in each of the following occupations?
   a. Office supply salesperson selling to local business firms
   b. Counter help at Burger King
   c. Representative for an outdoor advertising firm
   d. Salesperson representing Dow Chemical
7. How can companies use sponsorships and cross promotion in their promotional strategies?
8. What variables should marketers consider when selecting a promotional mix? Explain how each variable influences promotional strategy.

9. Differentiate between pushing and pulling strategies. Under what circumstances should each be employed?
10. Why does promotion raise more ethical concerns than other elements of the marketing mix?

QUESTIONS FOR CRITICAL THINKING

1. Choose a product that you purchased recently which is sold nationally. Identify the various media used to promote the product and analyze the promotional mix. Do you agree with the company's marketing strategies, or would you recommend changes to the mix?
2. Describe the best television commercial and magazine ad you've seen in the past 6 months. What made them memorable? Compare and contrast the use of the two advertising media for promoting the products.
3. What type of sales promotion techniques would you recommend for the following businesses, and why?

   a. Independent insurance agency
   b. BMW dealership
   c. Neighborhood restaurant
   d. Hardware wholesaler

4. Should a small company with limited advertising funds consider sponsorship as a viable means of promoting its products? Explain the benefits and drawbacks of sponsorships, and suggest a likely pairing of a sponsor with an event.
5. School Marketing Partners develops advertiser-supported lunch fliers for school cafeterias. A recent example was a school lunch menu with a scene from Fox's animated feature movie *Anastasia*. The company encourages school food-service directors to create menu items using character names, like Rasputin's Rib-B-Cue. Some school lunch program managers say that the colorful menus encourage kids to eat more nutritious foods. But many parents and educators criticize such promotional efforts, saying that marketing messages don't belong on the school sites and may imply endorsement from teachers. Do you think this type of brand-oriented promotion to school children is ethical? Defend your answer.

Experiential Exercise

Directions: To learn more about the objectives of promotional strategy, visit three or four different types of stores—such as a clothing store, an office supply store, a discount retailer, and a music/video store—to evaluate and compare their promotions. Without repeating the examples given in Figure 16.3, write the store name and one example of a product display or other promotional strategy you observed that is designed to:

1. Stimulate demand _____

   _____

   _____

2. Differentiate the product _____

   _____

   _____

3. Provide information _____

   _____

   _____

4. Accentuate product value _____
_____
_____

5. Stabilize sales _____
_____
_____

Nothing but Net

1. **Integrated Marketing Communications.** The winter 1998 issue of *Fortune's Technology Buyer's Guide* states that corporations spend between $200,000 and $1 million to create their Web sites. Identify companies that have particularly effective magazine ads, television commercials, or event sponsorships. Analyze how well the Web site ties in with the other marketing messages to contribute to a unified customer-focused promotional strategy. Possible sites include

   www.revlon.com
   www.ragu.com
   www.pampers.com
   www.mci.com
   www.nike.com

2. **Contests and Sweepstakes.** Many companies use contests and sweepstakes to keep visitors coming back to their Web sites or to generate excitement about a new product release. For example, Disney had a virtual grand opening of its Animal Kingdom at

   www.disney.com

   which included the Animal Kingdom Adventure Sweepstakes. Disney's Web site generated a great deal of excitement about the opening of Disney's newest theme park and gave away a lot of valuable prizes. Find a contest or sweepstakes you can enter by using your search engine or try these sites:

   www.sweepstakesonline.com
   www.net-quest.com/contests

3. **Increasing Promotional Effectiveness.** Some companies look to outside organizations to provide feedback on the effectiveness of their Web advertising and promotions. For example, at

   www.cybergold.com

   you can find opportunities to earn money by visiting Web sites and joining Internet services. Visit CyberGold's Web site and briefly explain how it works and the types of marketers who advertise there. Evaluate this method of getting attention directed toward an organization's message.

Note: Internet Web addresses change frequently. If you do not find the exact sites listed, you may need to access the organization's or company's home page and search from there.

LAUNCHING TOMMY: The New American Fragrance

Designer Tommy Hilfiger is no novice when it comes to relationship marketing. In need of financing to expand his line of designer menswear, Hilfiger formed a partnership with Silas Chou, owner of Hong Kong's oldest textile and apparel firm. The move turned out to be brilliant. Drawing on Chou's long experience in textiles and manufacturing, Hilfiger found that he could produce and position quality clothing for less than half the cost of competing designer lines such as Ralph Lauren. In 1989, the first year of their partnership, Hilfiger and Chou generated sales of $25 million. By 1997, Tommy Hilfiger USA was generating over $400 million in sales.

To market his fragrance, Hilfiger again decided to practice relationship marketing, and once again through an unusual arrangement. He signed a licensing agreement with Aramis Inc., an Estee Lauder subsidiary. For the previous half-century, Estee Lauder had avoided partnerships with outside designers, choosing instead to develop its own fragrance brands. But the Lauder family saw the alliance with Hilfiger as an ideal means of competing in the designer men's fragrance market. "The whole Lauder family is behind this," says Aramis Executive Creative Director Jeanne Chinard. "We were all waiting for him. He is the perfect match for us."

Aramis, which once controlled 50 percent of men's fragrance sales in department stores, had seen its market share drop to about 13 percent. Company executives were counting on Tommy to put Aramis back in the race with Calvin Klein and Ralph Lauren.

The first-year marketing plan for the new fragrance included plans to distribute 750,000 free samples at department stores, supported by magazine and TV advertising, and outdoor ads promoting the theme "a new American fragrance." Hilfiger planned to promote Tommy by tying the fragrance imagery into his clothing ads.

Realizing the importance of distribution to the success of a new fragrance, Aramis marketers proceeded to launch the product—dubbed Tommy: The New American Fragrance—by contacting a number of department store chains, including Hudson's Department Stores, with which Aramis had enjoyed a long-standing supplier-customer partnership. Hudson's marketers saw benefits from the co-marketing plan with Aramis. The co-marketing agreement gave Hudson's exclusive rights to launch and stock the new Tommy fragrance in its geographic area. For its part, Hudson's developed a marketing plan for promoting Tommy in each market through TV ads and visuals within the stores. In-store display designs coordinated with the national Tommy advertising campaign.

Preparing and training Hudson's sales associates for product launch was another key component in the marketing plan for Tommy. It included working closely with the salespeople, motivating them, and focusing on product knowledge, clientele building, advertising, and individual store sales goals.

Because Hudson's customers were heavy purchasers of Tommy Hilfiger clothing, they were likely to be receptive to the new fragrance carrying the Tommy name and marketed using similar imagery. Sales associates learned how to use Hudson's database to obtain lists of customers who had purchased Tommy Hilfiger clothing. These customers received invitations to receptions introducing the new fragrance along with offers of a free gift and the opportunity to be among the first purchasers of the new product. The co-marketing alliance between Hudson's and Aramis proved highly successful for both partners.

Questions

1. Describe the marketing strategy used to launch the fragrance Tommy.

2. What advertising media were used in promoting Tommy? What other methods or media could have been used to reach the target audience?

3. Does the launch of Tommy use a push or pull promotional strategy? Explain.

Careers in Business

BUSINESS CAREER EXERCISES

Sales Career

Discovering Your Business Career provides extensive information about seven business careers, one of which is sales. Literally millions of people selling goods and services every day. To succeed as a salesperson, you must not only convince prospects that you will meet their needs but do it better or cheaper than your competitors. Some of your job activities include calling on prospects, making sales presentations, preparing written proposals, and following up with customers after a sale.

    This exercise will help you to:

▼ Identify your level of interest in sales as a business career.

▼ Find out details about the skills required, job activities, career advancement, and earnings potential for this occupation.

How to Locate the Exercise

1. Launch *Discovering Your Business Career* from the "Career Assistance" program group.

2. If you have not already completed the questionnaire, select "Questionnaire" in the upper right corner of the main menu. Your responses to the questionnaire will be applied to all other exercises that you complete in *Discovering Your Business Career.* After completing the questionnaire, return to the main menu.

3. At the main menu, click on the red "play" button for "Sales" to see a presentation summarizing this career.

4. Next, click on the word "Sales" to enter the career profile section on this career.

5. Click on the red button below the word "Compatibility."

6. Select "Sales" from the menu of seven business careers.

7. Watch the video that summarizes your degree of compatibility with a career in sales.

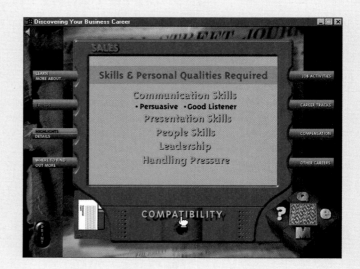

8. Read the detailed compatibility report on the left side of the screen. You can obtain a printout of this report by clicking on "Print" in the lower left corner of the screen.

9. Click on the word "Return" to go back to the "Compatibility" menu of business careers.

10. Click on the red triangular arrow to the left of the word "Sales" to return to the career profile on sales.

11. Review the sections about this career that interest you. You can get a complete printout of all the sections on sales by clicking on "Print" in the lower left corner of the screen.

Store Operations Career

The largest retailers employ thousands of employees, so a career in store operations represents a major job opportunity. You may eventually get promoted to store manager overseeing hundreds of employees and millions of dollars in annual sales. As you progress in your career, you'll spend most of your time training and motivating employees, handling customers, tracking inventory, and ensuring that products are attractively displayed.

This exercise will help you to:

▼ Identify your level of interest in store operations as a business career.

▼ Find out details about the skills required, job activities, career advancement and earnings potential for this occupation.

How to Locate the Exercise

1. Launch *Discovering Your Business Career* from the "Career Assistance" program group.

2. At the main menu, click on the red "play" button for "Store Operations" to see a presentation summarizing this career.

3. Next, click on the words "Store Operations" to enter the career profile on this career.

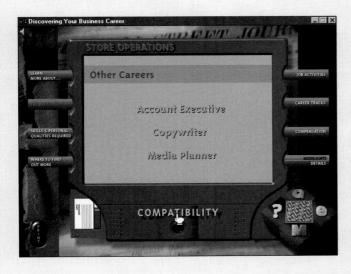

4. Click on the red button below the word "Compatibility."

5. Select "Store Operations" from the menu of seven business careers.

6. Watch the video that summarizes your degree of compatibility with a career in store operations.

7. Read the detailed compatibility report on the left side of the screen. You can obtain a printout of this report by clicking on "Print" in the lower left corner of the screen.

8. Click on the word "Return" to go back to the "Compatibility" menu of business careers.

9. Click on the red triangular arrow to the left of the words "Store Operations" to return to the career profile on store operations.

10. Review the sections about the career that interest you. You can get a complete printout of all the sections on store operations by clicking on "Print" in the lower left corner of the screen.

BusinessWeek Article

It is 20 years in the future. As a result of your successful business career, one of the most prominent business magazines in the world has decided to feature a story about you! Even better, they will allow you to write the story.

This is your chance to imagine what you want to accomplish in the years ahead. This article is excellent publicity for you, and it has two distinct advantages over advertising: Readers will probably find it more believable than an ad, and it is free!

This exercise will help you to:

▼ Clarify how you want to contribute to the world of business.

▼ Create a picture of your career direction.

How to Locate the Exercise Launch *Career Design* from the "Career Assistance" program group. Then select "Navigation" from the menu at the top of the screen, followed by "Career Sections" and then "*BusinessWeek* Article."

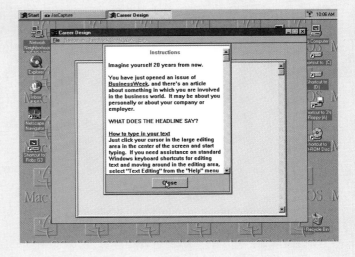

PART V | Managing Technology and Information

chapter **17**

Using Technology and the Internet to Succeed in Business

LEARNING GOALS

1. List the ways in which technology helps companies to create and maintain competitive advantage.

2. Explain the impact of technology on the general business environment and selected industries.

3. Identify the key issues involved in managing technology.

4. Compare the benefits and costs of implementing new technology.

5. Discuss how the Internet provides new routes to business success.

6. List the major forms of electronic commerce and the problems associated with Internet selling.

7. Describe how companies develop and manage successful Web sites.

8. Explain how global opportunities result from technological advances.

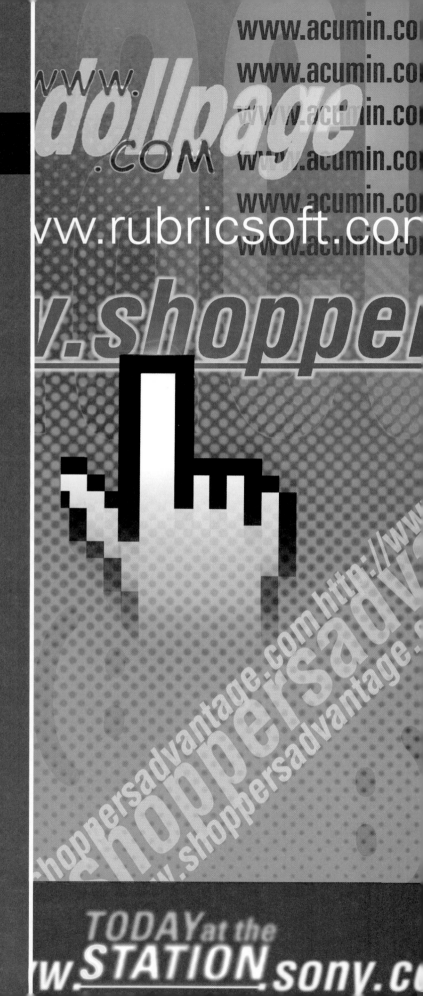

Upgrading Technology with New Tools from Rubric, Inc.

Rubric is one company that helps businesses succeed through technology. Business has changed dramatically in recent years. Companies are abandoning traditional one-way tactics and strategies associated with market share, mass production, and mass marketing. No longer do firms make one product for all and promote it with a single advertising campaign. Today's bidirectional strategies rely on specific information about individual customers to tailor products so that they will suit particular needs. Business must now focus on customer share, mass customization, and continuous relationship marketing. By collecting more and better information, businesses are cultivating and developing strong customer relationships.

Companies use the Internet to communicate with prospective customers, in a targeted, personalized, immediate, and economical way. They are flooding the Internet with marketing efforts, and their need for new tools is growing. To compete effectively, react quickly to the ever-changing environment, encompass the efforts of all departments involved, be as productive as possible, and measure the progress of every effort, businesses need tools that are automated, comprehensive, and easy to use—they need the Enterprise Marketing Automation (EMA) software tools that Rubric is offering.

EMA automates such marketing responsibilities as planning, direct-mail management, order fulfillment, telemarketing, and Web-based marketing, combining them into an integrated process. Companies not only create marketing processes but also can change them as rapidly as the market requires. If a particular strategy doesn't appear to be working within three or four days, marketers "can dump it and start again," says Rubric CEO Anu Shukla.

With Rubric's software tools automating the work flow of people in marketing and sales, computers keep track of all the details and salespeople focus on selling. But Rubric doesn't stop there. Its EMA tools do more than help find and create highly qualified leads and opportunities. Once potential customers are located, Rubric's software never lets anyone fall through the cracks. It makes sure that customers are contacted in the most appropriate ways. For example, when a customer buys a software product, Rubric's EMA program automatically tracks software upgrades and reminds the salesperson to visit, call, or contact the customer when an upgrade is available.

At Hewlett-Packard, Rubric's software creates an "if–then" scenario. As HP's David Welch explains, the program might say, "If company X bought a printer six months ago, it's about time for more toner." So it automatically sends a message via e-mail, fax, or voice mail to remind the supplier. "Say we have a customer who's bought a certain printer," says Welch. "We may want to send a note offering a deal on an upgrade," so the program automatically follows up.

Even though Rubric provides cutting-edge technology, one of its major selling points is that its products were designed for average people. Marketers can set the software up without having to wait for the information technology department to install, calibrate, or run it. By automating marketing campaigns, Rubric EMA encourages e-commerce. By letting companies conduct more targeted and personalized campaigns, it cuts costs, increases marketing effectiveness, and streamlines global campaign management. By generating more qualified prospects and verifying revenue increases that result from marketing efforts, Rubric EMA optimizes continuous relationship marketing programs and justifies marketing expenditures. In short, Rubric provides the tools that today's companies need to plan, execute, and measure Web-based and traditional marketing campaigns.[1]

CHAPTER OVERVIEW

Like Rubric and other businesses worldwide, firms in every industry are integrating the Internet and other forms of technology into their business operations. Successful companies, whether they provide technology for others or apply it in their own businesses, recognize that it is a central strategic element for growth and profitability. Managers must ask themselves: What does the new technology mean to me and my business? **Technology,** as Chapter 1 explained, involves the application to business of knowledge based on discoveries in science, inventions, and innovations. Throughout this book, examples have shown how technology affects all areas of business operations, from management to production to promotion.

Technological developments, such as Intel Corp.'s 1971 introduction of the microprocessor chip, represent revolutionary changes in business, education, government, and in people's personal lives. Creation of a tiny silicon square that processes instructions and data made development of the personal computer a feasible project. But as Figure 17.1 illustrates, the microchip has changed industries in ways far beyond its desktop computer origins.

This chapter starts by considering the importance of technology as a tool to help a company to maintain a competitive edge in the global marketplace. To understand technology's impact on businesses more fully, it explores how technological advances change the players, dynamics, and rules in selected industries. Managing technology may require new approaches, such as incorporating it into the planning process, evaluating its costs and benefits, and dealing with regulatory and ethical issues.

The next section of the chapter focuses on the Internet, one of today's dominant technological change

Figure 17.1 **Applying Microchip Technology to Agriculture, Automobiles, Consumer Appliances, and Medicine**

agents. The text describes how individuals and businesses use the Internet. Later discussions review electronic commerce and its implications for both businesses and consumers, including how companies use Web sites to further their objectives.

Technology also drives the globalization of business, and this chapter investigates its role in helping companies to take advantage of new opportunities around the world. The chapter ends with a look ahead to see what technology holds for the future.

TECHNOLOGY FOR A COMPETITIVE EDGE

As the new century approaches, we are living in the midst of a revolution unlike any that has come before. Technology is transforming not only individual businesses but underlying economic and organizational structures, as well.

For decades, steel, oil, and other heavy industries dominated big business. Today, the emphasis is on computers, software, telecommunications, semiconductors, pharmaceuticals, and other knowledge-based products. Technology is the driving force behind the growth of these industries, many of them barely 25 years old.

Technological innovation has never set a faster pace. Automakers waited 55 years for their product to be adopted by 25 percent of potential drivers; PC makers

reached the same market penetration goal in only 15 years. The first computer chip operated at a speed of about 60,000 instructions per second. This rate has doubled every 18 months, and by 1999, the Pentium II chip could process 500 million instructions every second at a fraction of the cost of the earlier, less capable model.[2] The speed of acceptance for other technologies is also increasing, as each new technology creates greater demand for still more improvements.

To remain competitive in a technology-driven economy, successful companies must respond to and master changes in the technological environment. If they fail to do so, they risk falling behind. Before businesses can achieve this mastery, however, they must become comfortable with new technologies. Typically, they start by using technology to automate existing processes. While this step improves productivity, it does not significantly change the status quo. As employees begin to understand the technology, however, they can apply it to completely alter business processes. The speed and eagerness with which a company embraces technology throughout the organization directly affect its ability to compete in the future.

Consider the impact of technology on the process of buying and selling securities. Discount stock brokerage

Business Directory

technology application to business of knowledge based on discoveries in science, inventions, and innovations.

Charles Schwab & Co. was an early adopter of computer technology, giving it a significant advantage over its competitors. From basic record keeping using customer databases, it expanded into electronic trading. Its e.Schwab program was one of the first **online services,** in which sales and purchases were completed by computers communicating through telecommunications or network links. Customers' computers are connected directly to the Schwab computer system, bypassing the need to place transactions with a broker. Today, Schwab leads the market in online trading services, with about 35 percent of electronic brokerage customers. However, new companies like E*Trade, which pioneered Internet-based trading, are nipping at Schwab's heels.[3]

www.schwab.com

Creating Competitive Advantage through Technology

Like Charles Schwab & Co., businesses must view technology as an indispensable strategic tool and a competitive necessity. Gone are the days when technology could be dismissed as too complex or expensive. As outlined in Table 17.1, technology creates opportunities to forge competitive advantage in everything from product develop-

ment and customer service to access to the global marketplace.

If the use of technology to achieve competitive advantage is symbolic of life in the 21st century, then sports fans are likely to point to it as further evidence of how businesslike sports have become. Nowhere is this change more evident than in the National Football League. Nearly 500,000 homes expand their football-watching schedules by subscribing to the NFL Sunday Ticket package on DirecTV and C-Band, paying $159 a season. On the field, players and coaches turn to state-of-the-art technology such as wireless radio transmitters that send scrambled messages between coach and quarterback and portable electronic stimulators for pain relief. As Denver Broncos head coach Mike Shanahan explains, "In every business, people are trying to get the edge with technology. Football is no different."[4]

Examples throughout the chapter discuss other ways technology helps companies to achieve competitive advantage.

Who Uses Technology?

In today's technology-hungry culture, almost everyone uses its innovations. From cellular phones to bioengineered vegetables to genetic research, technology changes lifestyles through new developments at work, home, school, and play. Consumer acceptance of technology is

Table 17.1 How Technology Creates Competitive Advantage

Contribution	Example
Speeds product development	The massive Boeing 777 aircraft development project accomplished design and testing entirely by computer using 5,000 design workstations and 10,000 PCs. The paperless approach shaved a year from development time and saved $100 million in manufacturing costs.
Tightens customer relationships	Pioneer online book seller Amazon.com creates a sense of community by including online author interviews, reviews, and live discussions. Its database tracks customer interests, suggests other books that a site visitor may like, and alerts customers of newly released books that match their interests.
Encourages new strategic directions	Microsoft has adopted an "embrace and extend" strategy by modifying its consumer and business products to make them compatible with the Internet. It has acquired over 50 Internet-related companies and launched such Web sites as Expedia, one of the largest online travel services; CarPoint, a car-buying service; and Sidewalk, listings of entertainment and activities for selected cities.
Improves work force efficiency	Mobile technologies like pagers, cellular phones, and laptop computers with modems allow employees to stay in touch with their offices while traveling. National Starch & Chemical sales reps use laptops to call up current price lists, place orders, and track customer orders, allowing almost instantaneous access.
Levels the playing field for small businesses	Monitor Medical competes in the cost-conscious health-care field with giants like Baxter International by using computer networks that let customers check inventories and order products directly on the company information system. The streamlined order-processing system has boosted sales, cut phone bills 10 percent, and permitted growth without adding personnel.
Improves access to the global marketplace	Lehigh Valley Safety Supply, a maker of steel-toed work boots, uses a Web site to offer 24-hour service and expand its customer base beyond its six-state market area to places as far away as Indonesia.

growing dramatically with improved ease of use. Almost all U.S. households have televisions and phones, 90 percent own VCRs, 41 percent have PCs, and 40 percent own cellular phones.[5]

From kindergarten to college classrooms, teachers and students use technology to facilitate learning, add fun to instruction in basic skills, and access worldwide resources. At the college level, students submit assignments on computer disks or over the Internet. They can collaborate on group projects via computer, buy textbooks on CD-ROM, and download lectures, assignments, and other course information from Web pages. In addition to classroom applications, colleges and universities use technology to streamline administrative functions. At Virginia Tech, for example, students use the campus online network to apply for financial aid, check their transcripts, see class schedules, and find work-study jobs.

Recognizing a growing business opportunity, Portland, Oregon, software developer Universal Algorithms developed CollegeNET. This Web-based application service allows students to apply to subscriber institutions online and search for scholarship availability. The paperless, online application process saves time for both schools and students, who can check the status of their applications online.[6]

In the top photo, the field at Philadelphia's Veterans Stadium is displayed on the video monitor. Eagles' Mike Dougherty videotapes game action (bottom left), while Eagles' assistant coach Bill Callahan reviews taped images with players (bottom right).

www.collegenet.com

Technology is even more pervasive in business. It contributes to both large and small firms in all industries as well as the not-for-profit sector. One of the most obvious applications is information management through databases, electronic data interchange (EDI), the Internet, and similar tools. Senior managers use these and other types of information technology to track their companies' current performance and learn about competitors' products, pricing, and financial condition. As described in the marketing chapters, technology helps with market research, identification and targeting of specific cus-

tomers, gathering competitive data on rivals, promoting and selling products, distributing information, and offering superior customer service. Retailers combine electronic data interchange and scanner technology to track sales data and automatically place restocking orders directly with manufacturers.

As Figure 17.2 describes, Data General marketers can now track customer shopping patterns and create a realistic, three-dimensional portrait of their firm's typical customer. By improving knowledge of customers, retailers can refine targeting for their marketing efforts and reduce costs.

Technology also gives sales representatives the critical information they need to win new accounts and

Business Directory

online service method of completing sales and purchases using computers connected through telecommunications or network links.

retain current customers. Cadence Design Systems, which specializes in software and services for computer chip design, recently replaced bulky manuals with an easy-to-update, integrated database system. Salespeople have immediate access to customer purchase histories, current specifications on more than 3,000 complex products, and technical resources. With this up-to-the-minute data, a representative can prepare a customized sales proposal and negotiate and close the transaction without any need to return to the office. The system also makes information on all transactions available to Cadence's worldwide sales force. Armed with this data, Cadence representatives know how to address customer needs. "Our customer relationships couldn't be stronger," says Cory Lei-bow, vice president of worldwide sales operations.[7]

Technology also improves communications with employees, customers, and suppliers. For example, human resource managers can reach out through e-mail and intranets to inform employees of policy changes. Job applicants can now submit electronic resumés. Improved communications between companies, vendors, and customers can shorten product development cycles. LSI Logic Corp., a Milpitas, California, designer of microprocessor chips, uses a restricted Web site to aid distribution of design information to subcontractors. LSI's ability to cut design time for the Sony Playstation video game helped Sony to bring its product to market about 6 weeks faster than its rivals could achieve.[8]

As Chapter 12 explained, production managers use technology to automate factory operations, track inventories, and order materials from vendors. At Lexington's Kentucky-American Water Co., operations manager Sam Stockton and his staff work with a complex system of computers and sensors that automate water treatment and flow to the company's 250,000 customers. The sensor system uses a special software program to track usage trends, tank levels, and potential trouble spots such as

| **Figure 17.2** | **Using Technology to Identify Target Markets** |

overflows and drops in pressure. Operators can quickly make adjustments from a monitoring station. If distribution changes and water pressure drops below a certain point, they can direct the system to automatically activate booster pumps.[9]

These applications of technology are just the tip of the iceberg. Later sections of this chapter take a more detailed look at the Internet and extranets in electronic commerce. Chapter 18 discusses corporate information systems, including intranets.

NEW TECHNOLOGIES, CHANGING INDUSTRIES

As many examples in *Contemporary Business* demonstrate, technology changes business processes, helps companies to develop and market products, and affects how managers structure and operate their organizations. Technology also blurs the boundaries between industries, bringing in new players. Companies in every industry must reevaluate their strategies and objectives in light of changing players and industry dynamics. This change in conditions may require them to form partnerships with or acquire companies that possess the technology they need.

In addition, technology creates new markets and even new industries. With the increasing dependence on information technology, companies are offering goods and services to help firms manage technology. The interactive multimedia industry, for example, emerged from the convergence of computer, communications media, and knowledge industries.

The discussion so far has pointed out technology's impact on management, production, and marketing. Later chapters will look at the financial services industry. This section explores how companies in five sectors—telecommunications, media, entertainment, health care, and agribusiness—are reinventing themselves in response to technological advances in their industries.

Telecommunications

Technology is the basis of the telecommunications industry, which includes providers of traditional telephone, cellular, wireless, satellite, and cable television services. Telecommunications companies today face increased competition from other types of information providers, such as **Internet service providers (ISPs)**, organizations that provide access to the Internet through their own local networks.

A major trend shaping the future of telecommunications is the widespread acceptance of **digital technology,** which represents data as easily storable and reproducible strings of "bits," designated by zeros and ones. Converting information, including words, pictures, and audio clips, to a digital format dramatically improves efficiency of storage and transmission. Huge amounts of information can be compressed and sent almost instantaneously, with higher quality than nondigital (analog) transmissions can offer.[10]

Digital technology enables communications using the Internet, direct broadcast satellite systems, cordless phones, and similar devices. Electronic links allow people to work from virtual offices and shop in virtual stores at any time of day, almost any place in the world. Information need no longer take physical form such as paper documents like reports, checks, or photographs. Digitizing has also been responsible for the convergence of computer, communications, and information technologies.[11]

What does digitizing mean for the telecommunications industry? GTE is a good example of how the new breed of telecommunications companies react to changing technologies. Once primarily a local phone service provider, it owned widely scattered systems around the country, mostly in rural areas. Deregulation and new technologies dropped barriers to expansion, permitting GTE to move into both long-distance and local phone service. Software connects its separate systems, changing fragmented markets into a national network. GTE also began selling phone services in new areas, and it is acquiring cellular phone franchises around the country.

GTE is betting that a large part of the telecommu-

Figure 17.3 Achieving Competitive Advantage by Offering Internet Security for Telecommunications

Of course we can **protect** your information on the Internet.

After all, this was one of our test sites.

GTE
INTERNETWORKING

nications business will shift from voice to data such as e-mail and facsimile machines. The Internet, with its increased demand for data communications, plays a major part in the company's expansion strategy. In addition to building its own private data network, GTE acquired BBN, the company that developed the Internet for the Department of Defense, and it bought part ownership of a fiber optic network. Figure 17.3 highlights one of the many reasons GTE purchased BBN: to acquire its experience and expertise in ensuring privacy for Internet users.

Special software allows PC-to-PC phone calls over the Internet, slashing costs of traditional phone rates, since customers pay only for local connections at either end. Recent improvements in voice quality have encouraged customer acceptance of this technology. Medium-sized and large corporations already use the Internet for about 20 percent of their voice communications, and demand among individual consumers also pleases providers. An estimated one in every five phone calls will travel over data networks by 2002. These trends present significant opportunities for telecommunications services and equipment companies.[12]

Satellite communications systems also compete in the data and voice traffic markets. Motorola's Iridium system provides voice, fax, and paging services. Other

Business Directory

Internet service provider (ISP) organization that provides access to the Internet, usually via the public telephone network.

companies use satellites to provide Internet access, and consumer acceptance is driving growth in satellite television services such as DirecTV and United States Satellite Broadcasting.

Print and Broadcast Media

One of the most visible technology transformations involves print and broadcast media. Consumers once bought magazines and newspapers or turned on the television to find the latest news and leisure activities. Today, they can also turn to their computers and the World Wide Web.

In response to these developments, most media companies include Web sites as important components of their product offerings. Readers can browse current editions or search online archives for specific articles. The sites often include special features, such as audio clips, that are not available in print editions.

Charles Martin of CMP Media, a publisher of computer magazines, has described changes brought by the Internet in the role of the publisher. Readers are no longer passive recipients but can decide what information they want and when. "Publishers must look at the Internet as much more than a place to just distribute an electronic version of their print publications," he says. "Readers will be able to regularly and repeatedly select various sources and create their own publications."[13]

Some publishers are now putting electronic versions of their books online. The National Academy Press (NAP), for example, offers 1,700 volumes. Contrary to expectations that electronic editions would steal sales from traditional books, NAP has found that in some cases offering the online version caused sales of the print version to double or even triple.[14]

From Broadcasting to Webcasting

As broadcasting shifts toward a digital format, the television and Internet move closer together, and radios and tele-

Businesses are using the World Wide Web to reach more customers and serve their needs. JAMTV Music Network is an Internet Web Site that provides Webcasting of concerts, backstage interviews with band members, artist photographs, and sample songs. You can even order a CD from its online store.

visions become interactive devices. **Webcasting,** the process of broadcasting audio-visual transmissions across the Internet, makes full use of the multimedia capabilities of the Internet. JAMTV's live concerts are examples of Webcasting in action.

As with print media, the formerly passive viewer/listener becomes an active user who decides what to see and when. Already satellite-direct television and cable pay-per-view offer some of these on-demand services. The mass media format—one program to many viewers—is beginning to give way to a variety of narrowcasting channels, where many consumers can access multitudes of smaller information units targeted to specific interest groups, on demand.

Further evidence of the convergence between television and computers comes from the *set-top box* that brings the Internet to the viewer's television. These easy-to-use computing devices allow consumers to surf the Web on their television sets at a cost well below that of the cheapest PC. Microsoft has positioned itself to become a major supplier of software for digital programming devices with its acquisition of WebTV, a startup firm with innovative technology. Interactive, networked televisions will offer enhanced features that integrate programs and Web sites. For example, a viewer watching a music awards show could link to a Web page with more information on the winning performer and then click to order the artist's latest CD.[15]

Clearly, these trends present major challenges for established media companies. They face an increasingly difficult task in conducting market research and creating publications and programs in an ever-changing environment where consumers act as their own publishers and programmers.

Click Here for Entertainment

In addition to its impact on publishing and broadcasting, other leisure activities are shifting to the Internet. People now watch concerts on JAMTV's Music Network, check football scores at the ESPNSportsZone, play online games at Total Entertainment Network (TEN), and search out appealing recipes at Epicurious. Through sites like these, the Web offers users endless ways to pursue hobbies or special interests. Web surfing is beginning to upstage television as a form of entertainment. In a recent survey, more than three-quarters of PC users said that using their computers was now taking time away from watching television.[16]

www.
www.epicurious.com
www.ten.net
ESPN.SportsZone.com

As a result, established entertainment companies must now incorporate Internet strategies to capture market share. They see the Web as a way to leverage their brands, increase their overall entertainment value, and capitalize on the trend toward increased Web use. The Disney Company's Daily Blast Web site is a subscription service for children 3 to 12 years old featuring familiar Disney characters and stories. Disney's Family Web site offers advice columns, games and activities, and electronic greeting cards. Nickelodeon is another company using the Web for cross-promotion. Its free Web site features television program listings, games, trivia, jokes, and information encouraging kids to volunteer to help community organizations.[17]

Electronics and entertainment conglomerate Sony Corp. of America offers several types of Internet-related products. At its premier interactive entertainment site, The Station, the entire family can play music and games and enter contests. Figure 17.4 shows The Station's Web page, with entertainment options such as SIREN, a music channel; single player online versions of television game shows Jeopardy! and Wheel of Fortune; Soap City, a community for fans of Sony's popular daytime soap operas; and Wonderland, a family area with interactive games, stories, and learning activities. The Station was an immediate hit, recording a very high growth rate for registered accounts on the Web, including a large female audience. "Our goal is to make The Station the primary online entertainment destination for fun and games," says Sony Online Ventures president Mitchell Cannold.[18]

www.
www.station.sony.com

Technology in the Health-Care Industry

Technology is revolutionizing health care. Already it is improving delivery of patient care, boosting the efficiency of administrative procedures, and speeding medical research. Telemedicine connects PCs, networks, and special multimedia software to allow health-care providers to consult with colleagues and patients regardless of location. Benefits include enhanced access to health care for patients living outside metropolitan areas, reductions in clinic and hospital visits, opportunities to discuss treatment options with growing networks of specialists, and expansion of patient interactions.

At Minneapolis-based Allina Health Systems, a videoconferencing system links 28 facilities around Minnesota. Primary-care physicians at outlying clinics consult with specialists at other locations, who can watch their online colleagues' examinations and recommend treatments without forcing patients to travel to distant facilities.[19]

Genetic research is another cutting edge technology. By combining computers and biotechnology, researchers have improved their ability to decipher the genetic codes of organisms and to separate individual genes to learn what each does. At Darwin Molecular Corp. in Bothell, Washington, researchers use a special technique to arrange DNA on silicon chips, a process that helps them to identify 500 genes that change when certain cells turn cancerous. This information provides important clues that could result in early diagnoses and new strategies for preventing cancer.

Some forms of genetic research generate heated controversy, however. Recent reports of projects to clone farm animals, for example, have raised ethical issues about

Figure 17.4 **Entertainment Alternatives on the Sony Station**

SOLVING AN ETHICAL CONTROVERSY

Cloning: Future Cure or Curse?

The 21st century is bringing to real life ideas once known only in science fiction stories like H. G. Wells' *The Island of Dr. Moreau.* Although the stories were popular among readers of all ages in many countries, the reality now presents an issue of major controversy throughout the world.

Recent announcements of the birth of a cloned sheep, Dolly, in England and a calf in Wisconsin brought fearful responses. A Chicago scientist then threatened to attempt human cloning, sparking further intense debate. President Clinton called for a 5-year ban on the cloning of humans. The National Bioethics Advisory Commission has recommended that human cloning be made a criminal offense.

Many people today worry that if sheep and cattle can be cloned, so can humans. Scientists claim that these fears lack foundation.

 Should Cloning Be Allowed?

PRO

1. Cloning technology can be an invaluable tool for biotechnology

firms. They can develop everything from dietary supplement products to what scientists call *xenotransplantation*—raising animals with genetically engineered organs or tissues for transplantation to human recipients.

2. Research on human embryos could lead to an understanding of how individual genes turn off and on. This breakthrough could uncover the origins of many hereditary diseases, with promise for developing genes that could produce new tissue like skin for burn patients and bone marrow for cancer patients.

3. Gene manipulation can assist livestock breeders to develop farm animals with desired traits, like the ability to increase production of milk, meat, or wool.

appropriate uses of this technology and its possible application to humans, as the nearby box illustrates.

Agribusiness in the New Century

Technology has recently been blazing new trails in rural areas as well as in offices and factories. A recent Farm Bureau study revealed that 83 percent of all farmers use computers, 73 percent use cellular phones, and 33 percent surf the Internet.[20] Agricultural researchers and farmers apply technology to boost crop yields and improve produce. Through genetic engineering, researchers are developing strains of plants resistant to drought, disease, and rot while growing faster and offering better nutrition than previous versions. For example, Monsanto's genetically engineered soybean seeds resist the herbicide Roundup, so that farmers can kill weeds but not the plants. The company claims that the seeds also produce two bushels more per acre than comparable rivals.

Satellite technology makes a number of contributions in efforts to protect crops and increase productivity. Figure 17.5 shows one beneficiary of information provided by satellite. Increasingly sophisticated weather satellites provide grow-

ers like Floridian Steve Young with advance notice of forthcoming freezes. Armed with this information, Young sprays his citrus trees with a fine mist of water that will freeze, actually protecting the plants from the cold weather.

Using technology to aid decisions about crop management is the goal of a growing trend called *precision agriculture.* Crop-yield monitors, global positioning satellites (GPS), and computer mapping technology help farmers to pinpoint exactly how much their fields produce, section by section. The yield monitor collects data on how much each section of a field produces. GPS provides permanent points of reference that allow year-to-year comparisons of the fields. Farmers convert this data into crop-yield maps with color-coded sections based on productivity. This information helps them to customize their applications of fertilizer, pesticide, or herbicide for individual planting areas, based on those sectors' specific needs.

MANAGING TECHNOLOGY

Technology provides a way for managers to differentiate their company from competitors, whether through improved products, reduced costs, accelerated delivery, or en-

CON

1. No consensus currently establishes the line between acceptable and unacceptable cloning research. Even President Clinton, who has called for a ban on cloning human embryos, has said, "I want to make clear that there is nothing inherently wrong with these new techniques—used for proper purposes. In fact, they hold the promise of revolutionary new medical treatments and life-saving cures."

2. Many people, such as members of the American Life League and the National Right to Life Committee, believe that life begins at conception. They argue that destruction of an embryo, a necessary stage in cloning, is destroying a life.

3. If animals can be cloned for distinctive traits, that same technique can be applied to humans. Critics fear that cloning could create duplicate humans for use as sources of spare parts for organ transplants. These concerns are not limited to the United States. In 1998, 19 European nations agreed to prohibit human cloning.

SUMMARY

Many scientists, ecstatic over the leap in technology for genetic manipulation, maintain that the ethical concerns over cloning are misplaced. Cloning technology offers rich potential to aid humans in the areas of cancer and hereditary disease research, creation of medicines, and tissue creation. They feel that the public's worries are based on erroneous information about both genes and the cloning process, a complicated and frequently unsuccessful undertaking. Researchers made more than 275 attempts before deriving a sheep clone.

Pro-life groups, politicians, and others who believe that life begins at conception have long opposed cloning human embryos that may later be destroyed. Others worry that people will seek cloning technology for spare parts or "designer" children. But geneticists are eager to explore the process in the hopes of discovering how genes work, as they search for clues about the origins of cancer and hereditary diseases.

Sources: "Geron Aims to Clone Human Tissue for Transplants," Reuters Limited, May 5, 1999; "Cloning May Cause Long-term Health Problems," Reuters Limited, April 30, 1999; "Canada Firm Clones Goat Triplets to Make Spider Silk," Reuters Limited, April 28, 1999; "Europe to Sign Ban on Human Cloning," *USA Today,* January 12, 1998, p. A1; "Clinton Wants Ban on Human Cloning," *Mobile Register,* January 11, 1998, p. A6; Gina Kolata, *Clone: The Road to Dolly, and the Path Ahead.* New York: Morrow, 1998; and Lee M. Silver, *Remaking Eden.* New York: Avon, 1998.

hanced customer service. To achieve this objective, decision makers must incorporate technology planning into the firm's overall planning process. As part of the decision to acquire technology, managers must also balance the costs of purchasing and operating technology resources with the benefits they bring. Firms in every industry are integrating the Internet and other forms of technology into their business operations. Successful companies, whether they provide technology for others or apply it in their own businesses, recognize it as a central strategic element for growth and profitability.

Technology Planning

The growing rate of technological change coupled with compressed product life cycles make technology planning a critical management responsibility. The media hype that accompanies each technological innovation further complicates the process. First, managers must assess those "latest and greatest" product claims to decide which technologies have merit for application in their firm. A company's philosophy toward technology, whether it pursues state-of-the-art innovations or a more conservative approach, is an-

other consideration. Timing also comes into play. Adopting new technology too early may be risky, since the innovation may not yet be fully tested and perfected. However, waiting too long may reduce any competitive advantage that the innovation confers.[21]

To evaluate technology in light of business needs and directions, managers seek to determine whether the proposed technology will:

▼ Improve the design or production of the firm's goods and services

▼ Expand its ability to attract new customers

▼ Broaden and deepen customer relationships

▼ Develop new distribution channels

▼ Secure new information to help the firm satisfy customer needs

▼ Use the electronic marketplace to advantage

Technology planning also involves deciding which new technologies a company should incorporate into

Figure 17.5 **Using Satellite Data to Prevent Crop Loss**

agers and operating employees encourage adoption of the latest technology as a means of increasing productivity. To find the right balance between cost control and productivity improvements, decision makers must analyze the benefits and costs of implementing new technology, as Figure 17.7 indicates.

Planners cannot always easily assign a dollar value to a particular technology proposal. A straightforward computation gives the cost savings from distributing electronic rather than printed versions of company newslet-

its product mix. Technology giant Hewlett-Packard Corp. (HP), known for its computers and printers, recently changed its strategic direction to stay at technology's cutting edge. As Figure 17.6 shows, HP is challenging such long-time industry giants as Eastman Kodak, Nikon, Canon, and Fuji in the digital imaging marketplace.

For HP, digital photography is a logical extension of its existing technology expertise. Its systems use computer chips, not film, to record images. To view them, users need a computer and screen or printer. Industry experts believe that digital cameras will eventually replace traditional film cameras. While consumers are not flocking to change right now, HP is betting that they will like the speed and convenience of printing out high-quality photos at home. "It will fundamentally change the way people think about photography," predicts CEO Lewis E. Platt.[22]

Benefits and Costs of Technology

Before committing to an investment in new technology, top managers usually require tangible evidence that the firm will recover the proposed expenditures through cost savings or increased sales and that company profitability and growth will be enhanced. At the same time, many man-

ters and employee manuals. To evaluate production machinery, companies can measure the additional units produced by new technology or similar benchmarks. Other types of benefits, however, may not lend themselves to such precise financial analysis. Assigning a value to improved communication between employees and customers or measuring the productivity gains received by a financial analyst from a faster PC may not be so clear cut a judgment.

Technology Benefits With careful planning and implementation, the entire organization can benefit from adopting new technology. Advantages range from cost savings to an improved work environment:

▼ Cost savings. Technology can reduce costs by speeding up production cycles, streamlining administration and ordering processes, and facilitating communications. New Jersey Steel's $50 million investment in state-of-the-art plant equipment was directly responsible for a 20 percent reduction in costs. For service companies like Alltel Mortgage Service of Jacksonville, Florida, automating clerical procedures means big savings. The company handles payment processing and similar tasks for mortgage companies. When Alltel replaced its manual mortgage-

Figure 17.6 **Hewlett-Packard's Application of Its Technology Expertise to Digital Photography**

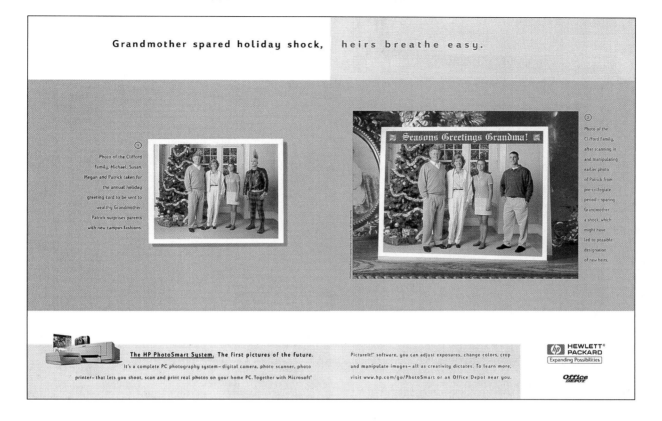

tracking processes with Mortgage Electronic Registration Systems (MERS), tracking and transfer costs were cut as much as 75 percent.

▼ *Improved productivity.* At New Jersey Steel, productivity rose 25 percent after installing the new machinery. Alltel's automated MERS project improved mortgage-processing speed and accuracy, while also reducing the potential for human error.[23]

▼ *Enhanced customer service.* Customers of Gallatin Steel, a high-tech steel minimill located in Ghent, Kentucky, achieve fast delivery on customized orders, even in tiny quantities. "We can take almost any order from scrap to coil in 2 hours," says president John Holditch. A fiber-optic network integrates manufacturing systems with ordering, financial, and scheduling systems. If a customer has a complaint, Gallatin can track it back to see where the problem originated.[24] Pink Jeep Tours, featured in this chapter's Business Hall of Fame, improved both customer ser-

vice and productivity with a new reservations system.

▼ *Companywide knowledge base.* Information technology encourages employees to share their expertise across an entire enterprise, making effective use of their collective knowledge—a valuable company resource. Such an innovation can yield substantial benefits. At Andersen Consulting, a project team saved 6 weeks and about $200,000 in repair work by posting a perplexing problem on the company's Knowledge Xchange intranet and finding a solution from another group.[25]

▼ *Increased employee involvement in decision making.* Technology tends to consolidate organizations and reduce management levels. This change increases employee access to information and shifts decision making to new people. The typical result is a gain in employee satisfaction.

Figure 17.7   **Weighing the Costs and Benefits of Adopting New Technology**

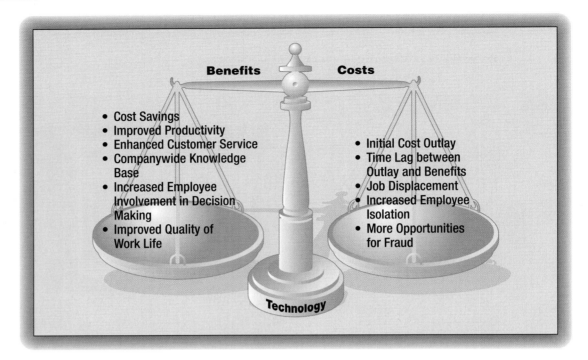

▼ *Improved quality of work life.* Technologies such as computer networks, the Internet, and various forms of messaging software allow telecommuting and other flexible work arrangements. Over 11 million U.S. workers now telecommute for at least part of the workweek. Companies that offer a telecommuting option find that it helps them to attract and retain key employees, and they save money in the process. IBM, for example, saves about $75 million a year by reducing its need for sales force offices through telecommuting.[26]

Technology Costs   Technology also has a downside. Implementing a new project usually creates important costs, some of which go beyond just financial considerations.

▼ *Initial cost outlay.* Dollar outlays for new technology include not only the prices of equipment, software, and installation, but firms may also incur expenses for consultants who design customized systems and for building renovations to accommodate new equipment. Buying new PCs for a department may also require software upgrades, printers, scanners, and modems.

▼ *Time lag between outlay and benefits.* Innovators must wait patiently for technology to take hold and for people to learn to use it. A technology in-

vestment may not pay off for several years. For example, the savings from New Jersey Steel's project were not realized for over 2 years.[27]

▼ *Job displacement.* Often, automating clerical or manufacturing tasks results in workforce cutbacks. When steel mills were giant facilities with huge blast furnaces, they required thousands of workers. Technological advances resulted in minimills with electric rather than coal furnaces—and only a few hundred employees. Today, a visitor to Gallatin Steel's minimill must look hard to see employees in the factory. Only 38 workers per shift operate the facility. Computers, laser beams, and other devices control the manufacturing process.[28]

▼ *Increased employee isolation.* While employees like the flexibility that telecommuting offers, many discover that working alone creates a feeling of isolation. They also miss out on opportunities to meet personally with their managers and to network with peers. Working at the office for at least part of the week helps to overcome this problem.

▼ *Opportunities for fraud and other criminal activities.* As a growing share of communications traffic moves onto electronic networks, the potential rises for unauthorized access to corporate and individual information. Someone hacking into a company's files could discover details of a new product and reveal them to competitors. Technology might also allow unauthorized access to databases with confidential information on credit-card purchases, tax payments, and medical records. In the wrong hands, this data could result in an "electronic mugging" that opens the door to credit-card fraud or other abuse.

Other Issues

Managers face additional issues related to technology management. For instance, they must address human concerns such as employee resistance to new technology. This adjustment problem goes beyond the purely technical aspects of learning to use the technology; such a change may also require a cultural shift in employee attitudes toward work. Typically, employees view knowledge as power, and they tend to guard rather than share it. Today, many companies emphasize collaborative efforts. To take full advantage of this initiative, managers must revise employee job objectives to emphasize contributing to the corporate knowledge base.

Ethical concerns also accompany applications of technology. Genetic testing is one such controversial area. Precise interpretation of genetic testing data remains a difficult problem. Insurance companies could use such tests to refuse health or life insurance to people whose tests showed greater risk, or they might charge higher premiums for coverage based on such information. Employers could use the information to hire workers without genetic tendencies to serious diseases. In Britain, Stephen Frost discovered how genetic test-

This Sales Meeting Is Saving Nick $18,420.

CU@Work™
Video Chat Sales for the Net

That's what Nick would have spent flying everyone in. Instead, Nick uses the CU@Work Video Chat software bundle to keep his sales force up-to-date. It connects Nick with his team using their PCs and the Internet. They CU@Work every Monday morning to get product updates, new pricing, the latest success stories, service info and more. Nick also uses it to Video Chat with key clients and improve service and face time. The whole system cost Nick far less than flying in a few sales people. Now Nick's team is always up-to-date with the latest info at a fraction of the cost of travel.

Got a sales force? Get in their face with CU@Work. Use the competitive advantage of CU@Work for your company. Visit our web site or call for more info.

www.cuseeme.com/pub/cu-sales.html

Call 800-241-7463

WHITE PINE SOFTWARE
US 603-886-9050 • Europe +33 4.93.59.43.43
NASDAQ: WPNE

White Pine
Keeping You Connected

Cost savings prompted this sales manager to purchase CU@Work video chat software for his sales force. He and his sales team conduct a virtual sales meeting at the beginning of each week, exchanging information on product updates, new pricing, service information, and other pertinent developments.

ing changes an employer's attitudes. His test revealed that he had a 50-50 chance of eventually getting Huntington's chorea, a serious disease. His employer, an insurance company, made his work situation so unpleasant after learning about the test that he had to leave his job.[29]

The discussion so far has taken a broad view of technology, from biotechnology to manufacturing automation. The next section focuses on a major contributor to the changing business technology environment: the Internet.

THE INTERNET: KEY TO SUCCESS

Want to find the cheapest price for a new car, computer, hotel room, or insurance? How about movie reviews and a schedule of what's playing in your neighborhood? Suppose you want to sell a product to Mexico but don't know the size of the market or the relevant export regulations. Just go online. With a few clicks of your computer's mouse, you can find the answer to just about any question using the Internet and World Wide Web.

While many people think of the Internet as a fairly recent development, it began in 1969 as a Department of Defense experiment networking four computers to facilitate communications in the event of a nuclear war. Until about 1993, the **Internet** (or *Net*) was an obscure computer **network** with few commercial applications. Today, however, this all-purpose, global network of networks allows computer users anywhere to send and receive data, sound, and video data. Its growth has been phenomenal, with host computers doubling annually to over 25 million in 1998;

Business Directory

Internet (or Net) worldwide network of interconnected computers that, within limits, lets anyone with access to a personal computer send and receive images and data anywhere.

BUSINESS HALL OF FAME

Small Business Takes a Big Byte of Technology

Businesspeople sometimes feel like they're struggling without the very latest computer equipment or software. But imagine having your whole scheduling system literally come tumbling down in pieces on the floor when someone bumps into it.

For years that's what would happen at world headquarters of Pink Jeep Tours. The Sedona, Arizona-based company offers guided jeep tours through the famous sandstone formations in the area. Agents booked tours by manually entering basic information and then posting the tour party

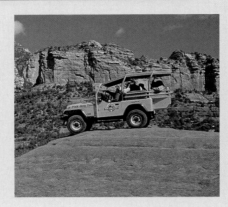

schedules on magnetic boards. One quick brush against the boards and the entire schedule would become alphabet soup.

To say that Pink Jeep needed to improve its handling of reservation information is a gross understatement. In 1995, CEO Shawn Wendell decided to replace this inefficient system with a $200,000 state-of-the-art reservations system. He hired Software Innovations in Flagstaff, Arizona, to create customized software.

Wendell couldn't be happier with the results, even though the investment in the new system exceeded the project budget. "We had to rebudget our long-term expenses and really tighten our belts," he says. It was worth it, however. Overnight, the Pentium-based workstations, high-speed modems, and user-friendly, interlinked software reduced the speed of taking

---

about 88 million people around the world use the Internet and online services like America Online.[30]

A major factor in the Internet's growth was the introduction of browser technology that provided point-and-click access to the **World Wide Web** (*WWW* or *Web*). The Web is actually an interlinked collection of graphically rich information sources within the larger Internet. Web documents are organized into **Web sites** composed of web pages that integrate text, graphics, audio, and video elements. The pages include **hypertext** links, or cross-references, to other documents. Browser software helps users to locate, retrieve, and display the requested information. By simply clicking on highlighted words, phrases, or image areas, they can explore the Web. Netscape Navigator and Microsoft Internet Explorer are two of the most widely used Web browsers.

Today the Web is the most popular Internet resource. The number of Web sites grew from just over 100 in 1993 to over 700,000 by 1998. This activity continues to double about every 6 months. Of this number, about two-thirds are commercial sites.

Although the Internet has only been considered an industry for about 5 years, it already generates over $10 billion in revenues and involves many different types of companies. For example, telecommunications companies provide local and long-distance network transmission lines, while computer and electronics manufacturers supply hardware, software, and other system resources that help to complete the Internet's infrastructure. Software developers create programs for a host of Internet applications such as multimedia transmissions and Web page design. Entertainment and media companies develop the content that Web surfers see, and service businesses offer Web site design and specialized software for electronic commerce. Also included are companies that sell goods and services to business and individual customers via banner ads on their Web pages.

Business Directory

World Wide Web (WWW or Web) collection of resources on the Internet that offers easy access to text, graphics, sound, and other multimedia resources.

Web site integrated document composed of Web pages that integrate text, graphics, audio, and video elements, as well as hypertext links to other documents.

Traveling the Information Superhighway

The Internet is a remarkable system of cooperating net-

reservations from up to 10 minutes to less than 60 seconds. Because the system alerts employees if a tour is overbooked, they can suggest other options to customers. "With that huge increase in productivity, we were able to cut the reservation staff in half, while we increased sales by about 50 percent. Our fill rate on tours used to be about 72 percent; now it's 94 percent," says Wendell.

The new technology has also given the company a cutting-edge marketing tool: a Web page. The site features a virtual brochure complete with photos, prices, contact information, and an online information request form.

www. www.pinkjeep.com

All in all, the system has created a powerful tool for Pink Jeep Tours. It operates virtually error-free, Wendell says; it supports improved financial management, and it allows Pink Jeep to generate comprehensive reports that have even enhanced the company's valued relationship with the U.S. Forest Service, which issues its special tour permits.

QUESTIONS FOR CRITICAL THINKING

1. Do you deal regularly with businesses that still rely too much on low-tech systems? In what ways could investing in new technology make them more efficient, boost customer relations, or in other ways improve their competitiveness?

2. What mistakes might a company make when deciding to invest in technology? How does increased efficiency in the form of voice mail or portable communications affect employees and customers?

Sources: "What Is Pink Jeep Tours?" Pink Jeep Tours Web site, May 5, 1999, accessed at www. pinkjeep.com; Heather Page, "Wired for Success," *Entrepreneur*, May 1997, pp. 132–140; and Herman Mehling, "VAR Helps Pink Jeep Stand Out," *Computer Reseller News*, July 21, 1997, pp. 47, 50.

---

works. In seconds, you can send e-mail from Montana to Hong Kong, search the archives of newspapers from around the world, plan your next vacation, gather product information, or buy a best-selling novel.

To understand how this complex system of networks operates, follow the journey of an e-mail message that you send to a friend in a different state. As shown in Figure 17.8, your message begins its Internet journey at your PC, from which it travels through regular phone lines or higher-speed connections; modems convert digital data into analog form compatible with

phone lines. The data arrives at the modems of your Internet service provider (ISP), defined earlier in the chapter as a

Figure 17.8 **How Information Travels on the Internet**

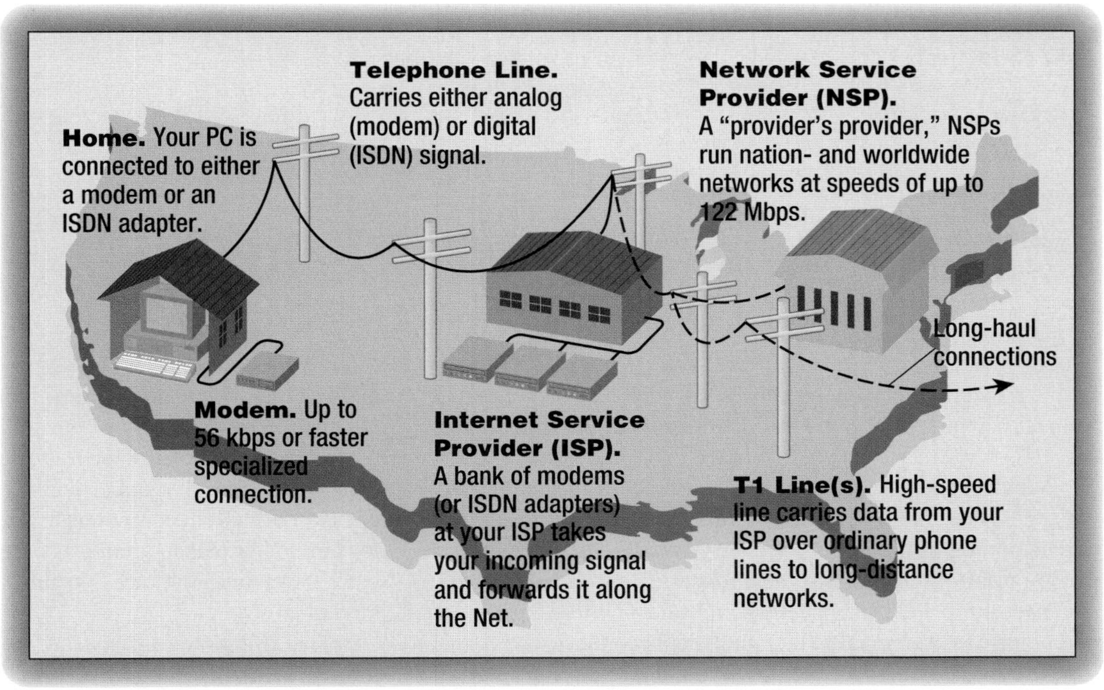

Home. Your PC is connected to either a modem or an ISDN adapter.

Telephone Line. Carries either analog (modem) or digital (ISDN) signal.

Network Service Provider (NSP). A "provider's provider," NSPs run nation- and worldwide networks at speeds of up to 122 Mbps.

Modem. Up to 56 kbps or faster specialized connection.

Internet Service Provider (ISP). A bank of modems (or ISDN adapters) at your ISP takes your incoming signal and forwards it along the Net.

Long-haul connections

T1 Line(s). High-speed line carries data from your ISP over ordinary phone lines to long-distance networks.

Choosing the Right ISP

Your Internet service provider (ISP) is your link to the online world. Its high-speed connection lets you visit chat rooms and Web sites, read electronic versions of newspapers and magazines, play games, post messages in special discussion areas, send e-mail, and download files.

With over 4,000 ISPs available, how can you choose the best one? First, consider how you plan to use the Internet. Will it be for personal or business use? What types of content do you want to access? Do you want to be able to sign on when you're away from home? Also, you need to choose an ISP that is compatible with your computer and modem setup.

Online services like America Online (AOL), CompuServe (CS), and Microsoft Network (MSN) offer original content (chat rooms, discussion boards for special interests, special databases) in addition to Internet access. Using them requires only a relatively simple process, making them ideal for novice Net surfers.

However, don't overlook regional and local ISPs. Although their access numbers serve only specific regions, they may offer more services than national competitors at lower prices. Some offer toll-free phone numbers you can call from out of town. In some communities, cable companies now provide high-speed Internet service, as well as specialized local content. If you have access to the Internet at school or through a friend, check the Computer Currents Web site (www.currents.net) for a list of ISPs serving your area.

Now you are ready to check out specific ISPs. The following guidelines are adapted from the *Computer Currents* checklist:

▼ *Pricing:* What pricing options does the ISP offer? Does it charge a flat monthly rate for unlimited access, hourly rates for light users, or both? Does it charge a setup fee or surcharges for peak-hour usage or "premium" services such as specialized databases?

▼ *Access:* Is the call local? What computer types and modem speeds does the provider support? Check out the ease of access during peak hours such as at noon and during the evening.

▼ *Content:* Do you want original content or just the Internet/Web? Do the ISP's own offerings meet your interests and needs? Does it limit the number of e-mail messages or provide multiple e-mail addresses per account?

▼ *Software:* What software does the ISP supply, and does it charge for software? Can you use a different browser than the one it provides? How easily can you set up your system and connect?

▼ *Web page hosting:* Does the service provider offer storage space for a personal or business Web page on its server? How much storage is included in the basic package?

▼ *Technical support:* During what hours can you access tech support available, and how easily can you get through to a rep? Can you also get help via e-mail or online documentation?

▼ *Special concerns:* Does the ISP provide secure service for online commerce?

Once you've narrowed your choices, get referrals from friends and colleagues. Use the free trial period that most ISPs offer to check one out, making sure that you can access it during peak hours and reach tech support.

Source: Adapted from "Choosing an ISP," *Computer Currents*, downloaded from www.currents.net, October 1, 1997; Caron Golden, "Searching, Searching," *Santa Monica Daily Breeze*, September 25, 1997, p. F-1; and Rebecca Rohan, "The ABCs of ISPs," *Black Enterprise*, May 1997, p. 36.

business that provides Internet access through its own series of local networks. Over 4,000 ISPs offer local Internet access to North American cybernauts.

What happens when the message reaches the recipient's ISP network? The answer to this question requires an understanding of the notion of client/server systems. Such a computing system splits the processing workload between desktop PCs (the clients) and one or more larger computers (the server) to which the clients connect.

The message you sent is stored in the distribution side of the client/server system. Technically, a **server** is a spe-

cial computer that holds information, then provides it to clients on request. A **client** is another computer that relies on the resources of one or more servers for help with its own processing. Servers efficiently distribute resources to a network of client computers as needed. When your friend logs on to her ISP and requests e-mail, the message travels back through phone or cable lines and to her computer's modem.

The ISP functions as the intermediary for its customers. Monthly or hourly user fees cover the cost of equipment such as ISP modems, servers, related software, proprietary and leased networks, and in some cases, original content. The Business Tool Kit reviews some criteria for selecting an Internet service provider to perform this function.

Who's on the Net?

People in almost 200 countries throughout the world currently use the Internet. As Figure 17.9 shows, about two-thirds of all Net users live in the United States, Canada, and Mexico.

Recent studies of Internet users in the United States reveal some major trends:

▼ The gender gap is narrowing, and women now represent over 40 percent of Internet users. This change is an important development for businesspeople, given women's role as key purchasing decision makers.

▼ The average age of users is rising. The average age of Net users is now in the mid-30s, and almost half are over 40. The arrival of more mainstream users, not just young, tech-savvy Web surfers, will change the future product mixes of online services.

▼ Net users tend to be more affluent and tend to attain higher levels of education than the general population.

▼ Time spent online is rising, taking away from television, magazines, and newspapers.[31]

Using the Net

What do these Netizens do online? Despite advances in multimedia resources, the Internet remains primarily a communications and information service. E-mail, the most popular use, and chat rooms are rapidly replacing postal and telephone service for many users' personal correspondence. Between 1992 and 1997, e-mail users grew from 2 percent to 15 percent of the population, and this proportion could reach 50 percent by 2001. E-mail volume is already huge—over 100 million messages each day. In fact, consumers re-

Figure 17.9 **Worldwide Internet Users**

| How Many People Are Online? ||
Region	People Online (thousands)
Africa	1,000
Asia/Pacific	14,000
Europe	18,000
Middle East	750
North America	54,000
South America	1,250
World Total	89,000

sponding to a recent survey said that they spend at least one-third of their online time on e-mail.

Beyond that correspondence function, the top four reasons people use the Internet or an online service are research, education, news, and entertainment. Online shopping remains low on the list. Only about 10 percent of Net surfers consider themselves online shoppers, although about one-quarter have bought something online.[32] Cybershopping is increasing, however, with development of methods to reduce online security problems. The most popular site categories are shown in Figure 17.10.

Businesses use the Internet and Web in more specific ways than consumers. Executives turn to the Web to gather information about their rivals or to assess industry trends. The Business Tool Kit titled "Navigating the Net" relates some tips for navigation techniques. For example, executives can visit competitors' Web sites to learn about new-product announcements and check financial reports. Company Web sites help marketing managers to collect valuable data about potential customers by asking visitors for personal information through registration or sweepstakes entry forms. Figure 17.11 shows a sweepstakes run by music store CDnow offering free compact discs. To enter, visitors to this site provided their names and e-mail addresses along with other information. With demographic data, marketers can develop personalized content, services, and advertising geared to their typical Web site users.

 www.cdnow.com

As earlier chapters have shown, the Web plays an increasing role in businesses' marketing and distribution strategies. Promotion, through either an individual Web site or a banner ad placed on someone else's site, is one of the top uses of the WWW. Because a company can instantly become a direct marketer through a Web site, it offers an ideal medium for one-to-one marketing and sales of customized products. For example, Philadelphia-based Acumin Corp. manufactures personalized vitamins. At its

Figure 17.10   **Most Popular Web Site Content**

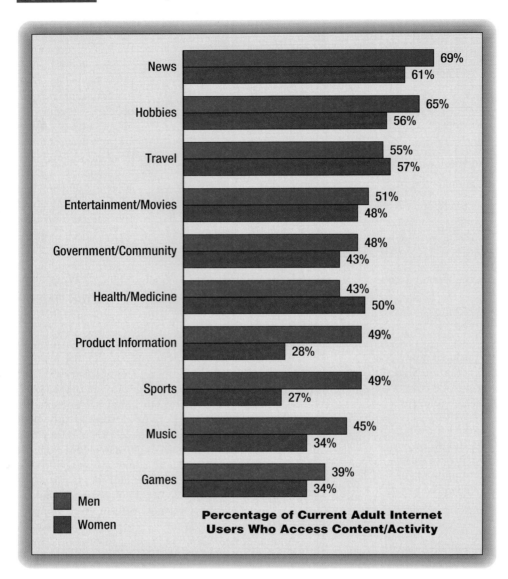

	Men	Women
News	69%	61%
Hobbies	65%	56%
Travel	55%	57%
Entertainment/Movies	51%	48%
Government/Community	48%	43%
Health/Medicine	43%	50%
Product Information	49%	28%
Sports	49%	27%
Music	45%	34%
Games	39%	34%

**Percentage of Current Adult Internet
Users Who Access Content/Activity**

As growing numbers of companies use direct marketing to sell their products on the Web, electronic commerce is becoming increasingly important. As the following section explains, succeeding with e-commerce depends on understanding the Web's advantages as well as its limitations and incorporating its resources into the firm's business plans and strategies.

ELECTRONIC COMMERCE

When buyers for Fujitsu Business Communications in Anaheim, California, need office supplies, they simply log on to Boise Cascade Office Products' extranet—a secure, specialized network linking the firm and its customers. The electronic system automates the entire ordering process, obtaining necessary internal approvals for orders and providing overnight delivery, eliminating previous delays of 3 to 5 days. The system benefits both customers and vendor. The reduced handling and paperwork from Internet orders save Boise Cascade about 45 cents per product.[33]

Like Fujitsu and Boise Cascade, companies around the world are discovering the advantages of **electronic commerce (e-commerce)**— marketing goods and services through computers by exchanging information between buyers and sellers, in the process minimizing paperwork and simplifying payment procedures. Like other types of buyer-seller interaction, e-commerce involves a chain of events for customer and seller. It starts with product information; moves through the order, invoicing, and payment processes; and ends with customer service.

The first wave of e-commerce brought techniques such as charge-card approval systems, point-of-sale terminals, scanners, and even early Internet selling—

Web site, a visitor completes a questionnaire that Acumin uses to develop a "personal formula" and create multivitamins based on individual needs.

www.acumin.com

Business Directory

electronic commerce (e-commerce)   process for online marketing of goods and services—including product information; ordering, invoicing, and payment processes; and customer service.

BUSINESS TOOL KIT

Navigating the Net

With more than 200,000 Web sites to choose from, how do you find the information you need? Whether you want a company profile to prepare for a job interview or economic statistics for a report, the Web has it. Some basic search strategies can simplify the process of navigating through this maze of resources.

With a little practice, you will learn the best ways to search online information sources. One method is to browse through an area of general interest, clicking to narrow the field as something catches your attention. Another is to hunt for specific information. Internet **search engines**—directories and indexes of Web sites—are ideal tools for either technique. Popular search engines include Alta Vista, Excite, InfoSeek, and Yahoo! Each organizes information differently, so try them to find the one you like best. Entering key words brings up links to the sites that relate to your inquiry. As you narrow the meanings of your key words, you find results closer to your topic. The online help manuals at each search site offer suggestions to improve your searches.

You might begin at one of the hundreds of databases and other sources of online information, available both through the Internet and through commercial online services such as CompuServe and America Online. For example, America Online's company research area includes several types of reports on firms with publicly traded stock. Most major newspapers and magazines maintain their own Web sites where you can search for articles on specific topics. CompuServe gives access to several periodical databases such as Knowledge Index and Business Database Plus, available for a surcharge, where you can search many publications to find articles on a specific topic.

An invaluable source of online information is the *Directory of Online Databases*, published quarterly by Cuadra Associates.

Sources: Adapted from Michael H. Martin, "Digging Data out of Cyberspace," *Fortune*, April 1, 1996, pp. 147–148; and Margot Williams, "Tips for Scaling the Mountain of Information on the Web," *Washington Post*, September 22, 1997, p. F21.

all activities focused mainly on lowering sellers' costs. As expanding groups of businesses discover the benefits of e-commerce, and as the Internet offers progressively more affordable services for almost any business, power begins to shift toward buyers, who gain access to wide ranges of vendors. "It's not about the vendor offering and the customer buying anymore," says Internet consultant Esther Dyson. "It's about the customer specifying and the vendor fulfilling." The result is a fiercely competitive environment where innovative companies have important advantages.[34]

A number of e-commerce innovations promote both business-to-business and business-to-consumer marketing.

For example, New York's Chase Manhattan Bank uses computerized video kiosks to explain different types of financial products to customers. In many cities, residents can pay taxes and fines, get applications for permits and licenses, and access other government information at kiosks similar to automated teller machines.[35]

The growth of e-commerce has attracted an army of specialized software firms and other service suppliers who provide expertise for firms making their first steps into this new competitive arena. As Figure 17.12 describes, global computer giant IBM offers its business customers both software and services designed to build virtual stores that go far beyond traditional Web sites.

Figure 17.11 **Web Page Sweepstakes Designed to Generate Database Information**

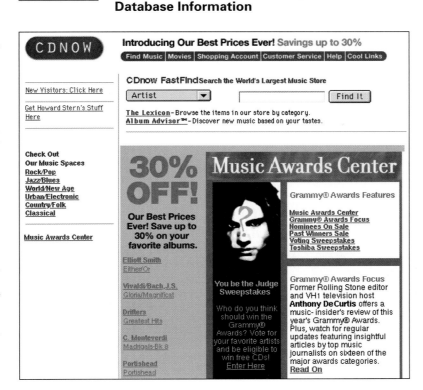

The Acumin Web site is an important complement to the firm's promotional activities, offering visitors answers to frequently asked questions plus useful information on designing a personalized vitamin program.

Profiting from E-Commerce

While much of the hype about e-commerce centers on sales of goods and services over the World Wide Web, online product sales represent only one of several ways to generate revenue online. In fact, although most companies have found only limited Web retailing profits,

everyday business-to-business transactions account for most e-commerce revenues.

Although most people associate e-commerce with selling, Web advertising currently generates the most business-to-consumer revenues—over $1 billion each year. This number will reach $5 billion by 2000.[36] Internet product sales rank second in importance as a WWW revenue producer.

So far, however, only a very small percentage of companies report profits from their Web sites. Microsoft closed many of its Web sites, revamped its Network site, and dropped plans to charge for an online political journal. Time Warner's Pathfinder site, which features online versions of magazines like *Time, Fortune, People,* and *Money,* has been a money-loser since birth, but management knows the importance of establishing its presence early in the race for cyberbusiness.

But e-commerce is not just about revenue generation. Equally important benefits include expanded marketplace reach, cost savings, and improved customer relationships. Putting massive industrial catalogs on the Web, for example, saves publishing and postage costs. With a few keystrokes, customers can send orders and service requests directly from their computers to the seller's computer—cutting out the need for intermediaries, including telephone order takers, and customer service representatives.

Figure 17.12   **IBM's Big Push into Electronic Commerce**

Business-to-Business Exchanges Lead the Way

Transactions between businesses are driving e-commerce growth three times faster than transactions between businesses and ultimate consumers. The business-to-business online sector is expected to account for over $325 billion in sales by 2002. Boeing, Boise Cascade, and Cisco Systems each generate well over $1 billion a year in Internet sales. In addition to generating revenues from product sales, interbusiness e-commerce also increases availability of product descriptions and greatly reduces the $250 billion that U.S. corporations spend each year on order processing.[37] The principal forms of business-to-business e-commerce include electronic data interchange and Internet-based commerce, including extranets.

Electronic Data Interchange One of the oldest forms of e-commerce is **electronic data interchange (EDI),** computer-to-computer exchanges of invoices, purchase orders, price quotations, and other business documents between buyers and sellers. Ordering supplies and materials through EDI cuts paper flow and speeds the order cycle. In addition, by receiving daily inventory status reports from vendors, companies can set production schedules to match demand.

Wal-Mart was one of the first major corporations to adopt EDI. In fact, the retailer refuses to do business with distributors and manufacturers that do not use compatible EDI standards. "You can help suppliers manage their inventory and smooth out peaks and valleys in the product cycle with EDI," explains Wal-Mart vice president Monique Hines.[38]

Internet Commerce Internet-based commerce is still in its early stages, even for business-to-business transactions. Thus far, most activity has focused on delivering product information and customer service. The Internet, as most companies discover, gives more help for saving money than for making it.

Internet commerce is well-suited for business-to-business transactions, which typically involve more steps than consumer purchases require. Orders placed over the Internet typically contain fewer errors than handwritten ones, and, when mistakes occur, the technology helps to quickly locate them. Giant clothing manufacturer Fruit of the Loom uses a central Web site to help customers locate needed merchandise. For example, when T-shirt printer Dave Schlez needs shirts in a certain color and fabric for his shop, Shine-On Shirts in San Jose, California, he can enter his request at Fruit of the Loom's Web site and find out which nearby wholesalers have the needed products in stock. He may even be able to place his order from the central Web site or the wholesaler's site.

Fruit of the Loom executives believe that the company's Web site is a valuable

competitive tool, even though they spent several million dollars to establish it. "If we help our distributors gain sales, we sell more product, and they'll be more likely to rely on us as a business partner than our competition. The goodwill generated by it has more than paid for it," says senior vice president and CIO Bob Heise.[39]

Extranets Internet commerce also offers an efficient way for businesses to collaborate with suppliers, partners, and customers through **extranets,** secure networks used for electronic commerce and accessible through the firm's Web site by external customers or other authorized users. Extranets go beyond the ordering and fulfillment processes in EDI by giving selected outsiders access to internal information. As with other forms of e-commerce, extranets provide additional benefits such as close relationships with business partners.

Security and access authorization remain critical issues, and most companies create *virtual private networks* that protect communications traveling through the public networks. These networks control who uses their resources and what users can access. Also, they cost considerably less than leasing dedicated lines.

A simple extranet might cost about $50,000, but this basic system would usually offer access only to inventory and price lists. A more complex version might provide search features, and the cost rises as capabilities expand, perhaps up to $10 million. At Boeing's PART Page, customers can get information on over 410,000 types of spare jetliner parts. They can check Boeing's inventory database, get price quotes, place orders, and check order status. The extranet also streamlines order processing. Within a year of its launch, about half of Boeing's customers used the PART Page, ordering products worth $40 million online.[40]

Business Directory

electronic data interchange (EDI) computer-to-computer exchanges of invoices, orders, and other business documents.

extranet secure network accessible through a Web site by external customers or organizations for electronic commerce. It provides more customer-specific information than a public site.

Business-to-Consumer Internet Retailing

In addition to helping firms to reach international customers, the Internet offers an inexpensive way to market products to consumers. Driven by convenience and improved security for transmitting credit-card numbers and other financial information, online retail sales will exceed $7 billion within the next two years.

Major retailers are staking their claims in cyberspace. Wal-Mart received such a positive response to its Web site that it expanded online product offerings from 2,500 to 40,000 items. Macy's and Bloomingdale's department stores have put their bridal registry, personal shopping, and interior-decorating services online.

CUC International, a leading direct marketer with a variety of membership buying clubs, was one of the first consumer-goods marketers to successfully apply its direct marketing, database management, membership fulfillment, and cross-selling expertise to Internet commerce. By 1997, while other companies were still waiting to see if cyber-shopping would catch on, CUC members ordered about $100 million a month from its various club Web sites such as Shoppers Advantage.

www.shoppersadvantage.com

Microsoft's Expedia online travel service represents a popular Internet business application. In addition to providing information and booking flights, hotel reservations, and auto rentals, the Web site supplies "insider" tips designed to resemble conversations with travelers who have recently visited the chosen destinations.

Online retail selling works best for nontechnical products like flowers, books, CDs, and travel and financial services. Even the sale of somewhat technical items, such as personal computers, has proven enormously successful through the combination of low prices, user-friendly Web sites, and 24-hour customer support offered by firms like Dell Computer and Gateway 2000. In general though, cybershoppers like familiar goods that they can safely purchase without touching them or trying them out first. Unique products are also well-suited for Internet commerce. For example, Tri-State Antique Center in Canonsburg, Pennsylvania, now attracts shoppers seeking unusual items from around the country instead of just local sources.

Security for Internet Payment Systems In response to consumer concerns about sending credit-card numbers over the Internet, companies have developed secure payment systems for e-commerce. Netscape Communications is one of several organizations that encrypt any sensitive information. **Encryption** is the process of encoding data for security purposes. When such a system is active, users see a special icon that indicates that they are at a protected Web site.

To increase consumer security, a consortium of companies, including Visa, MasterCard, and various technology suppliers, created Secure Electronic Transaction (SET), an industrywide standard for secure Internet payment transactions. SET buyers register with a bank and pay for purchases with digital certificates that verify their identities. Adopting a standard technology provides consistency

The ad for Microsoft's Expedia is an appropriate place to ask, "Where do you want to go today?" The travel-related Web site lets Web surfers book trips and compare air fares, hotel rates, and car-rental offers.

among merchants, card companies, software developers, and financial institutions. For example, CyberCash, a company that specializes in providing secure online payment systems, incorporates SET into its encryption system.

Because **smart cards**—plastic cards that store information on embedded computer chips rather than magnetic strips—are convenient and easily carried, they are among the most popular methods of Internet payment. In addition to storing e-cash, they can store data from several credit-card companies, a driver's license number, and even health information. The biggest problem Internet retailers currently face is agreeing on a standard card reader. Figure 17.13 shows several different types of smart cards.

Problems Facing Internet Marketers

As noted earlier, e-commerce is not without its problems. In the business-to-business sector, reliability issues and distribution channel conflicts affect the rate of acceptance. In business-to-consumer markets, the key issues include transaction security, consumer attitudes, and difficulty in measuring the effectiveness of Internet-based promotion.

Reliability When the stock market plummeted more than 500 points in a single day in 1997, online investors rushed to their computers to trade stocks. They quickly found themselves stuck in Internet traffic jams. The Internet's increasing popularity has also increased the likelihood of delays and service outages—even as more users depend on their links. Overloaded ISP servers and network lines, rising network costs, and expanding customer needs tax an already strained system. Until technology catches up with demand, many companies are limiting their online commercial ventures to activities that are not time sensitive. Users can postpone retail purchases, banking, and information transactions for a few hours if they cannot access the Internet—or make a telephone call, instead. However, Internet-only companies can't afford to lose a day's revenues if their links to the Net crash.

Solutions to these problems are on the way. ISPs are adding capacity, and networking equipment manufacturers have recently introduced new models capable of handling higher volumes of Internet traffic than older devices could manage. To offset reliability concerns, many businesses operate backup systems to ensure availability of Internet connections to customers. Others, such as online retailer 1World Mall, maintain accounts with multiple ISPs in different locations. As the California firm's Web site operator puts it, "The only way we'd be affected is if the entire West Coast fell off the map."[41]

Figure 17.13 **Smart Cards: Popular Internet Payment System**

Channel Conflicts The Internet adds another channel through which businesses can distribute their products. In many instances, a direct route from buyer to seller creates conflicts with current distribution channel partners. At great time and expense, companies nurture their distributor relationships, and they don't want to damage them when sales shift to the Web.

The success of direct PC marketers like Dell Computer and Gateway 2000 has captured the attention of other PC manufacturers, now considering direct sales over the Internet themselves. Retailers, for the most part, do not approve of suppliers competing with them by selling directly to customers.

Business Directory

smart card multipurpose card with an embedded computer chip that stores electronic cash and other information, such as credit-card data, health records, and driver's license number.

BUSINESS HALL OF SHAME

Big Blue's E-Mall Is a Bust

When computer giant IBM decided to enter online retailing in 1996, the natural choice seemed to be to create its own cybermall, World Avenue, with virtual storefronts and sales clerks.

Promoted as "the world's leading Internet mall," the site had 16 tenants, including department store chains like Gottschalks and Hudson Bay Stores. World Avenue also offered several technical features that set it apart from competing services. When shoppers made online purchases, they were offered suggestions on complementary merchandise. A second benefit came from the ability to create a database of information about a consumer's shopping and buying habits.

Although the virtual stores benefited from IBM's prestigious name and huge promotional effort, the Achilles heel of the project proved to be IBM's lack of expertise in online business-to-consumer retailing. As one mall merchant explained, "They had a lot of resources they could have used to promote that site, but there was not a mention of World Avenue." Within a year, suffering from dismal shopper traffic—only four customers visited the home page on its busiest days—and generating minimal revenues, IBM quietly closed down the mall site.

World Avenue is not, unfortunately, the only online mall failure. In just 6 months, imall's 1,600 online storefronts lost a combined $1 million. Says one e-commerce analyst, "Online malls are dead. You can't sell location, an unlimited resource on the Web, the way you can in the physical world. People don't stroll by your shop on the way to a department store. On the Internet, everything is next door."

Since closing World Avenue, IBM has moved on to a new sector of e-commerce, launching a global advertising and marketing campaign promoting the Internet as the place to do big business. As IBM's ad for e-business illustrates, the company's goal is to be the technical force behind e-commerce or, as one industry expert put it, "to be the construction company instead of the mall manager."

Internet Security Online security poses a major roadblock to the acceptance of consumer-oriented e-commerce in three areas: payment, privacy, and credibility. As the earlier discussion explained, many companies now offer secure payment systems to Web consumers. However, online merchants still battle against relatively low credibility, since the Internet is fairly new to most consumers. Established brand names and companies that are familiar to online shoppers have greater credibility than do newcomers to the Internet.

Consumers also want to know that they can browse the Web without leaving trails of personal information about buying and viewing habits. They want assurances that any information they provide won't be sold to others without their permission. In response to these concerns, online merchants are taking steps to protect consumer information. Internet companies that display the TRUSTe logo must disclose how they collect personal data and what they do with it; they also agree to TRUSTe audits of their compliance with the stated policy.[42]

Consumer Attitudes Although Web-watchers disagree about how quickly e-commerce will gain acceptance among consumers, a generally accepted conclusion holds that cybershopping and online retail purchases will grow sharply as e-commerce becomes a safer and more familiar process.

Companies still must overcome one major stumbling block to increasing Web purchases, though. Many consumers consider the shopping experience more important than increased convenience. The Business Hall of Shame profiles one company's struggle with buyers' preference for walking around a store, touching the merchandise, and talking to salespeople. To enhance consumer interactions, net retailers are now focusing on developing relationship-oriented consumerism. Consumers expect the Internet to help them find quality products at the best price. While e-commerce won't replace traditional retailing, it has already taken a place alongside mail-order catalogs.

> **They said it**
>
> "The Net is a 10.5 on the Richter scale of economic change."
>
> Nicholas Negroponte (1945–)
> American writer and director of
> the MIT Media Laboratory

SETTING UP A WEB SITE: DOING BUSINESS ON THE INTERNET

Business Web sites serve many purposes. They broaden customer bases, provide immediate accessibility to current catalogs, take and process orders, and offer personalized customer service. As Figure 17.14 shows, small companies are big users of the Web, representing about 60 percent of all commercial Web sites. For them, the Web offers a rela-

WHAT'S THE DIFFERENCE BETWEEN A LITTLE KID WITH A WEB SITE AND A MAJOR CORPORATION WITH ONE? NOTHING. THAT'S THE PROBLEM.

Building a publishing-only Web site is the first step to becoming an e-business. A step that most businesses (and a lot of little kids) have already taken. That's fine as far as it goes – it's a very cost-efficient way to distribute basic information.

But the real payoff (for businesses, at least) comes with steps two and three. Step two is moving to "self-service" Web sites – where customers can do things like check the status of an account or trace a package online.

Step three is moving to transaction-based Web sites – not just buying and selling, but all processes that require a dynamic and interactive flow of information.

IBM has already helped thousands of companies use the Web to make the leap from being a business with a Web site to being an e-business – putting their core processes online to improve service, cut costs or to actually sell things.

For example, we helped Charles Schwab Web-enable their brokerage systems for online trading and customer service. Since opening, Schwab's Web service has generated over one million online accounts totaling over $68 billion in assets.

e-business economics are compelling. According to a recent Booz-Allen & Hamilton study, a traditional bank transaction costs $1.07; the same transaction over the Web costs about 1c. A traditional airline ticket costs $8 to process; an e-ticket costs just $1. Customers love the convenience; management loves the lower costs.

IBM solutions have already helped thousands of businesses become e-businesses. To find out how IBM can help you do the same, bookmark www.ibm.com/e-business or call us today at 1 800 IBM 7080, extension NC32.

IBM.
Solutions for a small planet™

tively inexpensive way to reach vast numbers of potential customers.

As technology becomes increasingly easy to use, anyone with a computer equipped with a modem can open an Internet access account and place a Web site on the Internet. How people or organizations use their sites to achieve their goals determines whether or not their sites succeed.

Developing Successful Web Sites

When judging Web sites, success means different things to different businesses. One firm might feel satisfied by maintaining a popular site that conveys information or reinforces name recognition—just as a billboard or magazine ad does—without requiring any

Figure 17.14 **Who's on the Web?**

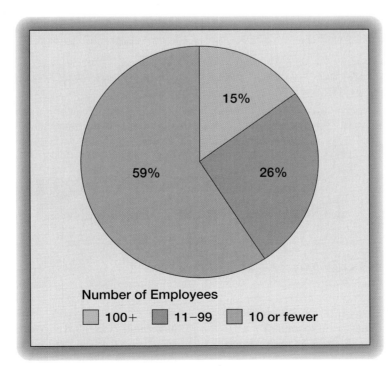

Number of Employees: 100+ 11–99 10 or fewer

15% 26% 59%

immediate sales activity. For example, Web sites like those of *The New York Times* and *USA Today* draw many visitors who want the latest news. The Web sites of Yahoo!, Netscape, C|Net, and ESPNSportsZone are successful, because they attract millions of visitors. High-traffic sites like these add another dimension to their success by selling advertising space to other businesses.

Internet merchants need to attract customers who transact business on the spot. Some companies find success by hosting Web sites that offer some value-added service to create goodwill for potential customers. Organizations like the Mayo Clinic and accounting giant Ernst & Young provide useful information or links to related sites that people frequently visit.

Tips for Creating a Successful Web Site

Web sites serve as online storefronts for companies, whether they provide information or sell products. A site's **home page,** the first screenful of information that users see when they visit a Web site, is the front door that welcomes visitors into a business and links them to the rest of the site's content. As with a traditional retail store or office, sites should be well-organized, easy to navigate, and full of resources that users want.

How do you go about building a compelling Web site for your company or yourself? If you have some computer experience and enjoy using technology in creative ways, you may want to design the site yourself using specialized software like Adobe's PageMill. The alternative is to hire a specialized designer. Even if you choose to hire someone, work closely with the designer to get the results you want.

Here are some guidelines to follow in Web site construction:

▼ *Develop content that will bring people back again and again.* If your site sells gourmet foods, include recipes for your products and links to other food-related sites.

▼ *Keep the site updated with fresh content.* Change the recipes at frequent intervals; add new coupon offerings with expiration dates; give cybershoppers a reason to keep coming back to your site.

▼ *Looks matter.* Set up the pages in a clean, simple, and elegant design. Display graphics to add interest, but don't let them overwhelm the site—or take too much time to download.

▼ *Take advantage of the Internet's potential for interactivity.* Avoid brochure-like text; create bulletin boards and chat rooms for consumer reactions; hold surveys or contests to gauge consumer attitudes.

▼ *Make it easy and quick to use, with a good table of contents.* A page should load quickly, present readable displays, and allow easy navigation. Follow the "three-click rule": Ensure that visitors can get needed information in three clicks or less.

▼ *Don't forget the obvious.* Make sure that contact information such as addresses, telephone and fax numbers, and e-mail addresses are easy to find.

▼ *Promote the site.* Include your Web address on business cards, on company stationery, and in ads. List your site with search engines such as Yahoo! and Alta Vista, which funnel 85 percent of search activity.

A do-it-yourself designer should also make use of such resources as *How to Put Information on the Web.* Visit:

WWW.   www.w3.org/pub/WWW/Provider

Sources: See Sandra E. Eddy, "A Lasting Impression," *Business Start Ups*, May 1997, p. 14; Frank Hertz, "Web Presence," *Success*, March 1997, pp. 58–60; and David Noack, "Choosing the Right Path to the Net," *Nation's Business*, March 1997, p. 16.

Planning and Preparation What is the company's goal for its Web site? Answering this question is the first and most important step in the Web site development process. "For many, the tendency in designing a Web site is to jump right in and start creating snazzy images, animation, and other goodies," says Jeff Carlson, editor of Internet newsletter *TidBITS*. That can be the worst way to begin. Instead, says Carlson, "It's important to build a solid foundation of ideas, goals, schedules, and budgets."[43]

That's what Barry Gainer did when he set out to expand the sales of Indian River Gift Fruit Co., his family's Titusville, Florida business. He set a goal of using the Internet to reach millions of new customers at a relatively low cost. Before launching the site, Gainer researched the most economical ways of getting a company on the Web and sought advice from experts. His advance planning paid off. He found the right company to host his site and hired experts to design and update the Web pages. In its first year, the tempting pictures of fruits and convenient options for ordering online or by phone or fax generated 25 percent of his firm's $1 million revenues.[44]

Other key decisions include whether to create and maintain a site in-house or to contract with outside experts. Some companies may prefer to retain control over content and design by producing their own sites. However, since acquiring the expertise to develop Web sites can require some very time-consuming study, hiring specialists may prove a more cost-effective option.

Naming the Web site is another important early step in the planning process. A Web address should reflect the company and/or its products and be easy to remember. The part of the name that follows the site name is called the **domain name.** Examples include ".com" and ".org" and ".edu." Nearly 90 percent of names are in the .com domain.

Cost and Maintenance

As with any technological investment, Web site costs are an important consideration. The highly variable cost of a Web site includes not only development expenses but also

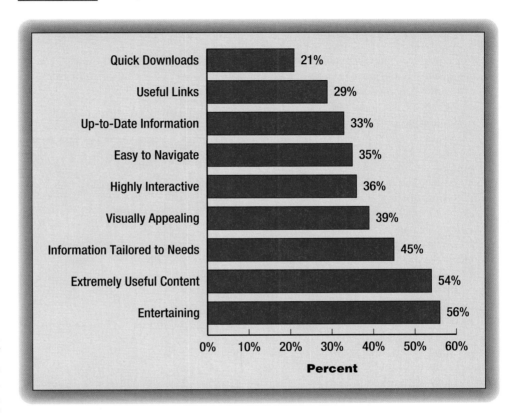

Figure 17.15   Why Visitors Return to Web Sites

Quick Downloads — 21%
Useful Links — 29%
Up-to-Date Information — 33%
Easy to Navigate — 35%
Highly Interactive — 36%
Visually Appealing — 39%
Information Tailored to Needs — 45%
Extremely Useful Content — 54%
Entertaining — 56%

Percent

Content and Connections   Content is the most important factor in planning a Web site. As Figure 17.15 shows, content-related reasons are the most important factors in determining whether visitors return to a site. Standards for good content vary for every site, but available resources should be relevant to viewers, easy to access and understand, updated regularly, and written or displayed in a compelling, entertaining way.

After making content decisions and designing the site, the next step is connecting to the Internet by placing the required computer files on a server. Companies can have their own dedicated Web servers or contract to place their Web sites on servers at ISPs or other host companies.

Connections to related Web sites through hyperlinks increase exposure and traffic. However, hyperlinks can also lure visitors away to other sites.

the cost of placing the site on a Web server, maintaining and updating it, and promoting it. Although developing a commercial Web site typically costs between $30,000 and $100,000, it can cost as little as $19.95 for a monthly subscription to a Web server such as America Online.[45]

The cost of putting a site on a server also varies in a wide range. ISPs like America Online, CompuServe, and NetCom host many commercial sites for basic monthly charges depending on the number of Web pages. MCI Internet offers an entry-level server package for $15,000 plus $1,000 a month for a special phone line. In addition, most small businesses lack the necessary expertise to set up and run their own servers; they are better off outsourcing to meet their hosting and maintenance needs.[46]

In addition to installation and connection fees, managers must ensure that their company's Web site stays current over time. Visitors don't return to a site if they know the information never changes. Consequently, updating design and content is another major expense.

Measuring Effectiveness

How does management gauge the return from investing in a Web site? Measuring the effectiveness of a Web site is a tricky process, and one site's answer depends on the major purpose that it serves. Profitability is relatively easy to measure in companies that generate revenues directly from online product orders, advertising, or subscription sales. However, a telephone order resulting from an ad on a Web site still shows the sale as a phone sale—not a Web site sale—even though the order originated at the site.

For many companies, revenue is not a major Web site objective. Only about 15 percent of large companies use their Web sites to generate revenue; the rest use them to showcase their products and to offer information about their organizations.

Some standards guide efforts to collect and analyze traditional consumer purchase data, such as how many Ohio residents bought new Accords last year, watched the Comedy Channel's *South Park,* or tried Burger King's new French fries. Still, the Internet presents several challenges for market analysts. It is difficult to be sure how many people use the Internet, how often, and what they actually do online. Some Web pages display counters that measure the number of visits. However, the counters can't tell whether someone has spent time on the page or skipped over it on the way to another site, or whether that person is a first time or repeat viewer.

As the Internet gains popularity, new models for measuring its effectiveness will be developed. ABVS Interactive now provides independent evaluation and verification of Web site activity, but it can only audit the number of times a Web page is viewed and the number of times a reader visits an advertiser's site.

Other companies, such as PC-Meter LP and Relevant Knowledge, recruit panels of computer users to track Internet site performance and evaluate Web activity; this service works in much the same way that ACNielsen monitors television audiences. The WebTrends service, described in Figure 17.16, provides information on Web site visitors, including where they come from, what they see, and the number of "hits" during different times of the day.

Figure 17.16 **Measuring Web Site Traffic**

USING TECHNOLOGY TO CREATE GLOBAL OPPORTUNITIES

For many companies, future growth is directly linked to a global strategy that incorporates the latest technology. The United States leads the world in technology and communications infrastructure, and in ownership of PCs and other consumer technology products, creating a huge international growth opportunity.

One-fifth of the world's population—some 1.2 billion people—live in China, but only 3 million PCs were sold there last year. U.S. companies are well-aware that the Chinese PC market is growing at more than 50 percent a year. Intel wasted no time in creating brand recognition for its Pentium processor there. It launched an ad campaign to reach both computer-literate Chinese and the millions of others who have never seen a PC. Intel has also granted licenses to Great Wall Computer Group, the largest memory chip manufacturer in China, and collaborates with the government on product-development projects.[47]

Similarly, Hewlett-Packard and Microsoft joined forces with a group of European retailers to bring e-commerce to continental Christmas shoppers. Using HP computers and Microsoft software, they created a holiday season Web site that featured products from 50 merchants in nine countries. Cybershoppers could buy Irish crystal, Swiss chocolates, and English plum pudding. The project offered a chance for HP and Microsoft to build an Internet infrastructure in a new market with virtually no competition.[48]

Telecommunications companies are also joining forces to provide worldwide networks for global communications. Ameritech, a regional Bell operating company, became the largest U.S. investor in Europe's telecommunications industry when it acquired a controlling interest in Tele Danmark, Denmark's national telecommunications utility. With stakes in state telephone companies in Belgium, Norway, and Hungary, Ameritech was well-positioned to expand after the 1998 deregulation of the $176 billion European phone market.[49]

Satellite technology has also brought entertainment to viewers around the world. MTV, for example, reaches an audience of 70 million in Latin America and Asia. Its programming and other U.S.-produced shows give brand recognition to Western products from McDonald's burgers to Levi's jeans.

Today, over 85 percent of major British corporations and 74 percent of those in Ireland have Internet connections, and eastern European countries are catching up to the leaders. About two-thirds of the companies listed on the Hungarian, Polish, Slovenian, and Czech Republic stock exchanges have Net hook-ups.[50]

Computer networks enable companies to coordinate global workforces in new ways. For example, computer programmers in Beijing write software for IBM. Every day they transmit their work over the Internet to an IBM office in Seattle. Programmers there add to it and send it on to two groups in Belarus and Latvia. It then moves on to India, arriving back in China by the next morning. Work on such projects no longer stops when programmers in one country go home for the day. This team approach speeds up product development. "We call it Java around the clock," says John Patrick, IBM's vice president for Internet technology. "It's like we've created a 48-hour day through the Internet."[51]

With an estimated 88 million users around the world, the Internet creates an enormous pool of potential customers. Companies can market their goods and services internationally and locate distribution sources and trading partners. Customers can search for products at their convenience, browsing through online catalogs that always show current information.

The Internet is especially valuable for small businesses that would otherwise have difficulty finding customers overseas. The Doll Collection served only its local Louisville, Kentucky, clientele until it opened a Web site. Now customers from around the world can order dolls such as Madame Alexander and Barbie using e-commerce. In its first year on the Internet, The Doll Collection has more than quadrupled its sales.[52]

www.dollpage.com

Technology can also heighten competition. In the virtual global marketplace, rivals can cross the oceans to enter your market. Many industrial companies use the Internet to search through online catalogs for the lowest-priced parts. No longer can local suppliers assume that they have locked up the business of neighboring firms. General Electric uses its Total Purchasing Network to acquire over $1 billion in materials each year. GE simply posts its part needs, and suppliers anywhere can place electronic bids.

The computer age is transforming the world as we know it, as more countries develop telecommunications and computer networks. The following section takes a look at some future technologies that soon may become commonplace in the new century.

TOMORROW'S TECHNOLOGIES

The remarkable changes in people's lives today can be traced to technological breakthroughs that were the stuff of dreams just a century ago. The advances of the 20th century—from an age of automation to an era built out of zeros and ones—are outlined in Table 17.2.

What promise does the new century hold? Computer technology will be designed around the human body and link to networks through wireless technologies. Miniature wearable computers will build screens into eyeglasses or

Table 17.2 A Century of Technology

Decade	Movement	Inventors	Invention	Communication
1900s	Automation	Wright brothers; Marconi	Diesel engine	Wireless; telephone
1910s	Electricalization	Thomas Edison; Henry Ford	Refrigeration	Phonograph
1920s	Modernization	RCA; Walt Disney	Electric shaver	Radio; talkies
1930s	Futurization	Albert Einstein	Nylon	Radar; FM radio
1940s	Fission	Manhattan Project; Edwin Land	Atom bomb	Television; LP albums
1950s	Americanization	GM; GE	UNIVAC	Stereo; transistor radio
1960s	Exploration	NASA; AT&T	Felt-tip pen	Color TV; Princess phone
1970s	Japanization	Sony; Panasonic	Calculator	CB; personal stereo
1980s	Information	Steve Jobs; Paul Allen	Macintosh	PC; CD; VCR; cable TV
1990s	Digitization	Bill Gates; Dreamworks	CD-ROM	Internet; fax; cellular phone

watches and store the processors and batteries somewhere else, perhaps in the user's shoes. Personal area networks (PANs) will use the electrical current in the human body to turn people into data transmitters and allow them to automatically exchange digital information. Already IBM has demonstrated a prototype PAN allowing businesspeople equipped with card-size transmitters and receivers to exchange information.

Homes will also be wired. A video doorbell with voice messaging capabilities will greet visitors and link to a PC and a security system. PCs will act as control centers to monitor and operate lighting, heating/air conditioning systems, and appliances at scheduled times. Multiple display screens with touch-screen or voice-activated interfaces will be located throughout these cyberhomes. In the kitchen, a PC with bar code scanner will keep track of the food on the shelves and in the refrigerator, suggest recipes using what's on hand, and automatically prepare orders for the online grocery service.[53]

People will enjoy improvements in health. Monitoring equipment in the home will send information to medical care providers. For example, a respirator could be hooked into a phone line so that it would automatically call 911 if sensors detected a problem.[54] By 2010, scientists will introduce genetic therapy to treat cancer and other genetic diseases. Artificial skin and blood will also aid in medical treatment.

As smart-card technology spreads, cash will become an obsolete relic. The federal government is leading the way toward a paperless and cashless society. By 2001, the Pentagon will be totally paperless, with all documents available on the Internet and electronic systems for purchasing and payments.[55] The rest of the government will follow within a few years. Soon thereafter, individuals will be able to pay all their bills using smart cards that consolidate all their financial and personal data into single master accounts.

Cars will change, as well. Instead of gasoline engines, by 2020 cars will run on hydrogen fuel cells that last for thousands of miles. These environmentally friendly vehicles won't pollute; their only waste product will be water.

As the power of computer chips continues to climb, complex tasks like handwriting recognition, text-to-speech and speech-to-text capabilities, and instantaneous language translation will become routine functions. Virtual reality will be widely available, supporting sophisticated simulations for training and market research. Doctors will be able to practice surgery before actually performing it, while businesses can analyze customer shopping patterns in virtual stores. By 2010, chips will have 1 billion transistors—100 times more than those common in 1998—giving them the potential to handle the most complex multimedia simulations with lightning speed.

Nanotechnology, submicroscopic systems for constructing materials and objects one atom at a time, crosses over from science fiction to reality in 2015. Among its first applications are tiny nanomachines with sensors that can travel through a person's body to transmit information about its composition and perform basic cell repair. Nanotechnology will also transform traditional manufacturing; by 2025, desktop factories will produce simple products.[56]

Telecommuting will evolve further as improvements in remote access computing allow users to interact with their companies' servers from anywhere in the world. Today's wireless cellular phone networks are just a taste of what's ahead, as wireless modems and satellite projects reach completion and create worldwide communications networks. Research findings to date provide indications of vast potential for genetic research.

WHAT'S AHEAD

This chapter has examined how technology creates new market opportunities, both domestically and abroad, for companies whose managers respond to and master its applications. The following chapter extends this discussion by considering how companies' internal management information systems help personnel to meet their information technology objectives.

SUMMARY OF LEARNING GOALS

1. List the ways in which technology helps companies to create and maintain competitive advantage.

Technology is an indispensable strategic ally and competitive necessity for today's companies. It benefits all areas by improving worker efficiency and lowering product and administrative costs. Technology also encourages companies to move in new strategic directions and to reinforce customer relationships. It speeds product develop-

ment cycles. For small businesses, technology creates a level playing field on which they can compete with larger corporations.

2. Explain the impact of technology on the general business environment and selected industries.

Technology changes competitive conditions by bringing new players with cutting-edge applications into an industry. It also blurs the lines between industries, allowing companies to enter new areas.

Technology creates new markets and even new industries, such as the Internet and interactive multimedia industries. The Internet's interactive nature and multimedia capabilities have forced media companies to rethink how they publish or broadcast their products.

3. Identify the key issues involved in managing technology.

Because technology is becoming a central strategic element for growth and profitability, companies must incorporate technology planning into their overall planning processes. When evaluating potential technology acquisitions, managers must ask how the technologies will affect internal operations, production methods, costs, and distribution channels. They also must determine whether the innovations will open up new markets. Other issues to consider include employee resistance to new technology and standards for using technology in ethical and socially responsible ways.

4. Compare the benefits and costs of implementing new technology.

Technology brings both benefits and costs to a company. On the benefits side, it can reduce costs and improve productivity by speeding up production cycles, streamlining administration and ordering processes, automating clerical procedures, and improving communications. Technology can also improve the quality of work life by supporting flexible work arrangements like telecommuting. However, these benefits carry associated costs. In addition to initial financial outlays, ongoing costs such as administration, supplies, training, repairs, maintenance, and upgrades can add substantially to overall costs. Firms may not realize payoffs from technology investments for several years.

5. Discuss how the Internet provides new routes to business success.

The Internet, a worldwide network of interconnected computers, removes limitations of time and place so that transactions can occur 24 hours a day between people in different countries. It creates opportunities for companies that provide Internet infrastructure, access, and content, as well as for firms that use its resources in their business operations. The Internet offers a cost-effective way for managers to gather competitive intelligence; perform market research; showcase, sell, and in some cases distribute products; and offer customer service and technical support.

6. List the major forms of electronic commerce and the problems associated with Internet selling.

Electronic commerce is the process of selling goods and services through computer-based exchanges of data. It spans the entire supply chain, including product information; ordering, invoicing, and payment processes; and customer service. Companies generate revenues from product sales, subscription fees, and advertising sales. Businesses use electronic data interchange (EDI), the Internet, and extranets to process transactions with other businesses. The growth of Internet retailing is currently limited by capacity constraints, reliability problems, and channel conflicts. Online security for payment systems and confidentiality of data is a major obstacle to consumer-oriented Internet commerce. Also, many consumers are not yet comfortable with the idea of cyber-shopping.

7. Describe how companies develop and manage successful Web sites.

Businesses establish Web sites to expand their customer bases, increase consumer awareness of their products, improve customer communications, and provide customer service. Before designing a Web site, a company's decision makers must first determine what they want to achieve with the site. Other important decisions include who should create, host, and manage the site; how to promote it; and how much funding to allocate. Successful Web sites contain informative, up-to-date, and visually appealing content. Sites should also download quickly and allow easy navigation. Finally, management must develop ways of measuring how well a site accomplishes its objectives.

8. Explain how global opportunities result from technological advances.

Technology allows companies to compete in the global market and workplace. Even the smallest firms can sell products and find new sources of supply in international markets. Through its own Web site, a company can immediately reach customers all over the world. Improved communications among employees in different locations create new ways of collaborating on projects.

TEN BUSINESS TERMS YOU NEED TO KNOW

technology	Web site
online service	electronic commerce (e-commerce)
Internet service provider (ISP)	electronic data interchange (EDI)
Internet	
World Wide Web (WWW or Web)	extranet
	smart card

Other Important Business Terms

digital technology	client
Webcasting	search engine
network	encryption
hypertext	home page
server	domain name

REVIEW QUESTIONS

1. Identify three ways in which technology gives a company a competitive edge, including an example for each. How can technology increase productivity for marketing, sales, human resource management, and operations personnel?

2. Select an industry and discuss how specific forms of technology change the operations of companies in the sector.
3. List the key questions that a manager should ask when evaluating a possible acquisition of new technology.
4. Compare the benefits and costs of adopting new technology.
5. Explain how managers can use the Internet to facilitate business operations. Which industries are most likely to profit from the Internet? Which might suffer financial setbacks?
6. Discuss the differences in electronic commerce between a business selling to other businesses and one focusing on consumer markets. Identify a company in each category, and describe the form of e-commerce it practices and how it generates revenue.
7. What major problems hamper the growth of Internet commerce? Suggest some possible solutions.
8. Discuss the characteristics of a successful Web site. What steps can companies take to create successful sites?
9. What conditions complicate attempts to measure the effectiveness of Web sites?
10. Explain how technology opens global market opportunities.

QUESTIONS FOR CRITICAL THINKING

1. Publisher Bill Henderson, the owner of the Pushcart Press, is a cofounder of the Lead Pencil Club, whose 3,000 members oppose the way the electronic revolution is taking over society. "It's a phony revolution, and I'm sick of it," he says. "All they're doing is speeding things up, getting there faster and faster, making people work faster, and jamming their brains like encyclopedias and making them feel they don't know anything. . . . I don't need any more information. I want less."

   a. Do you agree or disagree with Henderson? Why or why not?
   b. Make a ten-item list of both the positive and negative impacts of technological innovation on society in the last 25 years. Do the benefits to society of new technology outweigh the costs?
2. Paula Brown, president of JB Chemical Co. Inc. in North Las Vegas, has just received bad news. A major client is closing its Nevada plant and moving to Tennessee, where it will purchase needed chemicals from local suppliers. As a result, JB Chemical will lose some $15,000 to $20,000 in sales a month, nearly one-third of its $2 million annual sales. Discuss how technology can help Brown with this problem. Outline a technology plan for JB Chemical that will allow the company to either keep most of the client's business despite the move or attract new customers. What specific types of technology should JB Chemical choose for its limited investment? How could your suggestions help to bring in business?
3. Do you agree or disagree that technology has helped small businesses to compete with larger companies? Explain.
4. Evaluate how technology affects your relationships with the following organizations. Make recommendations for how these organizations could use technology more effectively to strengthen customer ties.
   a. Your bank
   b. Your college or university
   c. Your doctor
   d. Your supermarket
   e. Your favorite clothing store
5. A recent poll revealed that only 19 percent of Web surfing respondents had purchased a good or service after seeing an online ad for it. Almost 75 percent indicated that they were less likely to purchase something advertised online than a comparable product promoted in television and print ads. What can businesses do to change consumer attitudes toward Internet retailing?

Experiential Exercise

Directions: This chapter includes a discussion on developing Web sites. Many colleges and universities allow students to place home pages on the school's system. If your school provides you with that service or if you have access to the Internet through a local Internet service provider or a commercial source such as America Online, then create your personal Web site.

One source of assistance in developing your Web page is located at

homepager.tripod.com/

If you're interested in getting more deeply involved in home page development, you may wish to explore other commercial software packages, shareware, or free Web-page editors. Some of the following Web sites include demonstrations that will allow you to try out a program before making your decision.

Commercial Software

FrontPage: www.microsoft.com/msoffice/frontpage/default.htm

Claris Home Page: www.claris.com/

HTML Assistant: www.brooknorth.com/

Free Shareware

Hypertext Master: www.soton.ac.uk/~mjt495/anarchy/htmled31.html

Easy HTML: ox.ncsa.uiuc.edu/easyhtml/easy.html

Nothing but Net

1. **From Broadcasting to Webcasting.** Visit the Web site for AudioNet—The Broadcast Network on the Internet

   www.audionet.com

   and complete the following:
   (a) List the minimum system requirements and software necessary in order to enjoy the programming at this site.
   (b) Check out the various broadcasts under such headings as Featured Programming, Sports, Business, Music, Special Interest, Politics, Live Radio, Television, CD Jukebox, and AudioBooks.
2. **Entertainment.** Identify a Web site that provides links to the top entertainment sites on the Internet. One such site is

   www.zdnet.com/pcmag/special/web100/_entertainment.htm

   Locate two entertainment sites that you like, learn enough about the sites so you can tell a friend about them, and recommend them to someone else to try out.
3. **Internet Retailing.** Assume the role of a consumer who wishes to purchase a product over the Internet. Use a search engine to find two electronic commerce Web sites that sell the product you wish to purchase. For example, if you decided you want to order flowers to send to your mother for Mother's Day, you could visit

   www.1800flowers.com/

   or

   www.virtualflowers.com.

   After visiting and comparing your two selected sites, write a two- to three-paragraph paper in which you identify
   (a) the product you wish to purchase
   (b) the two sites you visited
   (c) the site you would buy from if you were really going to do so
   (d) the reasons you chose one Internet retailer over the other.

Note: *Internet Web addresses change frequently. If you do not find the exact sites listed, you may need to access the organization's or company's home page and search from there.*

A SEARCH ENGINE NAMED YAHOO!

Yahoo! creators Jerry Yang and David Filo trace the beginnings of their company to 1994 when, as Ph.D. students at Stanford, they started compiling lists of their favorite Web pages. This activity led to the creation of a free directory called *David's Guide to the World Wide Web.* The enthusiastically positive response from people who used the directory convinced Yang and Filo to turn their hobby into a business. They conducted market research by asking other Internet surfers for suggestions, and they developed customized software to locate, identify, and edit material stored on the Internet. Then they launched Yahoo! "My dad used to call us yahoos," says Filo, "which is fitting since the Internet is a wild frontier." On a typical day, 2 million visitors access the Yahoo! site.

The explosive growth of the Internet, coupled with corresponding increases in the number of users, created a need for a search engine like Yahoo! "Somebody could create a great Web page about soccer," explains Filo, "but nobody would know it was there. What we did was organize the Web for people."

Yang and Filo's marketing plan specified sources of revenues that would ensure profitability. To encourage use of this site, Yahoo! does not charge users for the service itself. Instead, the firm generates revenues from advertising and licensing fees paid by the online services. A Yahoo! advertiser pays a fee for each impression, that is, every time a computer loads a Web page with its ad.

A major milestone in Yahoo's success occurred when Netscape chose to replace Netscape Destinations with Netscape Guide by Yahoo! This move made Yahoo! the default Web browser directory. When Navigator users click on the Guide button they are automatically routed to Yahoo! and offered a choice of eight of the most popular categories on the Web.

Even though they pioneered search engine technology, Yang and Filo realized that others could easily duplicate their services. They decided to create brand loyalty by transforming Yahoo! into a media company. First, they formed an alliance with the Japanese media conglomerate Softbank and launched two brand extensions: a print and online magazine called *Yahoo! Internet Life* and a personal computer information center on the Web called Yahoo! Computing. In partnership with such publishers such as Fodor's and the Village Voice, Yahoo! is also creating online city guides for New York, Chicago, Los Angeles, Boston, San Francisco, and Dallas/Fort Worth.

Another Yahoo! alliance aimed at strengthening the company's drive to become a media company involves MTV Music Television. Yang and Filo recently launched a co-branded venture called *MTV Yahoo! Unfurled,* a combination of music-related editorials and an online guide to other music sites on the Web. "We're partnering with Yahoo! because it's the search engine that's really built a brand name for itself," says MTV executive Matt Farber. "We both understand the importance of branding, and that's essential to our partnership."

The list of Yahoo! online services continues to grow. *Yahooligans* is an online directory for children, and *Beatrice's Web Guide* is targeted at women. The company has also moved into narrowcasting, an electronic delivery service for customized information, launching *My Yahoo!* This service delivers updates from a user's favorite Web sites and information about new sites that relate to the user's personal interests.

With $8.6 million in annual revenues, Yahoo! continues to adapt to the Internet's ever-changing environment. By sponsoring and participating in a variety of community programs, Yang and Filo help to promote the development of Internet education and programming. Yahoo! is also connecting classrooms to the Internet, providing free educational seminars, and offering promotional exposure for not-for-profit organizations on its Web sites.

Questions

1. What strategies is Yahoo! implementing to remain competitive in the technology-driven economy?

2. What types of benefits does Yahoo! provide through its Internet search engine for its customers?

3. Since Yahoo! does not charge users for the service it provides, how does it make money and stay in business?

chapter 18

Using Technology to Manage Information

LEARNING GOALS

1. Discuss the purpose of a management information system.

2. Explain how information systems are evolving in response to trends in information technology.

3. Identify basic types of computer hardware and software.

4. Summarize important contributions and limitations of computers.

5. Define the major business applications of computers.

6. Describe the areas in which businesses need to protect their information systems.

Digital Xerox—Not Just For Copying Anymore!

Businesses everywhere are realizing that knowledge is the most important asset they own. But with speedy new information technology, most offices are drowning in information while starving for knowledge. To expand knowledge and maximize its use, businesses must find the most effective ways of sharing their knowledge among employees. Throughout history—from the manuscripts that monks copied by hand to late-breaking news stories on the Web—documents have been the way humans share what they know with each other. The photocopier was a huge leap in business information sharing. But they've now gone high tech. Today' documents and the critical knowledge they carry can be managed and exchanged most effectively by smart tools that help employees work easily and efficiently and help them move seamlessly between paper and digital documents.

With tools such as Xerox's digital copier and DocuShare software, companies can get the right information to the right people at the right time. Of course, the solution to sharing knowl-

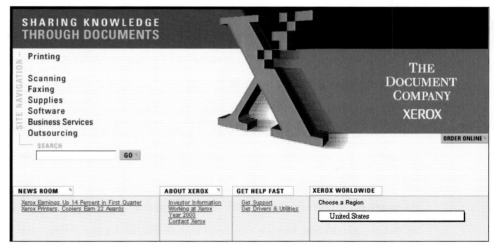

edge doesn't rest with technology alone. Corporate knowledge resides not only in paper and electronic documents but also in employee's brains. Xerox Chairman Paul Allaire explains the company "not only looks at the technologies behind copying, printing, scanning, faxing, and mailing but also looks at the processes people use to accomplish their work." Digitizing documents and using networks to connect everybody to everything enables businesses to scan, copy, and print on a network from a desktop—and at speeds never before possible in an office. With these products, a company can develop a catalog or a financial report in its Albuquerque headquarters and, in moments, print out a few thousand copies in its London office.

Xerox's digital technology is already at work around the world. People in Germany are getting books published on demand. They send an electronic order to a publisher, who pulls a file off the network and sends it to the Document Technology Center. Called The Xerox Book in Time, this technology may someday mean that no book will ever be out of print. At the University of Miami, Xerox systems are being used to archive the world"s largest collection of Cuban historical artifacts and to place these documents on the Internet. In Sweden, Xerox implemented a worldwide digital document management system that is being used by engineering teams whose members are located all around the globe. With the Xerox system, team members can easily capture, share, and reuse critical information, so their collaboration is both dynamic and streamlined.

Xerox is also working on future developments that are just as exciting. For example, using special DataGlyph marks, a 25-page document will be scanned and reduced to a one-page, two-sided document. One side will offer a text summary of the entire 25 pages. On the other side, DataGlyph marks will encode the original 25-page document, which can be read by machines and restored to its original form. Another innovation, called "askOnce," will allow users to search for information both on the Internet and in multiple databases in one step. In addition, the knowledge broker will remember every search, providing updates when new information becomes available. And specialized "knowledge robots" will reside on your network, study what you search for and read, and learn about the people you communicate with most frequently. These "knowbots" will then go out on the network, track down the information that will most likely interest you, and deliver it to your computer.

WWW.
www.xerox.com/go/xrx/hm.jsp

Determined to create and deliver technologies that help office workers share knowledge, Xerox transformed its products from analog to digital and transformed its focus from offering customers a product in a box to offering them service and solutions. The company makes its solutions easy to use by applying the expertise it gained from years of making copiers easy to use. Moreover, it makes sure its products integrate easily with operating systems such as Microsoft Windows and applications such as Oracle databases. People can now transform hard copy into digital documents, transfer that knowledge to the Internet, and send it either to computers or to other copiers. As Xerox president and CEO Rick Thoman explains, "The copier is now embedded with intelligence and becomes a sort of smart digital portal."[1]

CHAPTER OVERVIEW

Xerox's management knows that access to the right information is vital to business success. In fact, someone once gave the recipe for an effective decision as "90 percent information and 10 percent inspiration." Information relevant to business decisions is a key resource of companies in every industry.

This chapter explores how businesses successfully manage that resource. It looks at how they use information systems to organize and locate information. Because most of these systems rely on computers and related technologies, the chapter also discusses computers and their applications in business settings.

MANAGEMENT INFORMATION SYSTEMS

▼ What is the sales potential for our brand in Indonesia compared with its prospects in Malaysia and Thailand?

▼ If we raise the price for the brand by 2 percent, how will the change affect sales in each country?

▼ How do our wage rates compare with those of similar firms in Philadelphia?

▼ What are the per-unit storage costs for Model 401?

Every day, businesspeople ask questions such as these. An effective information system helps them to find answers. A **management information system (MIS)** is an organized method for providing past, present, and projected information on internal operations as well as external intelligence to support decision making.

A large organization typically assigns responsibility for directing its MIS and related computer operations to an executive called the **chief information officer (CIO).** Generally, the CIO reports directly to the firm's CEO.

A company needs information from a variety of sources to carry out almost every activity—internal and external—that it performs. Information can make the difference between staying in business or going broke. Keeping on top of changing consumer demands, competitors' actions, and the latest government regulations will help a firm to fine-tune existing products, develop new winners, and maintain effective marketing. The Business Hall of Fame tells how Clarklift/FIT developed an information system that gave the company a competitive advantage.

Commercial online databases provide instant information.

Databases

The heart of a management information system is its **database**—a centralized, integrated collection of data resources. Firms design their databases to meet particular information processing and retrieval requirements that their decision makers encounter. A database serves as an electronic file cabinet, capable of storing massive amounts of data and retrieving it within seconds. A database also helps a firm to target its direct marketing efforts by providing details about prospective customers.

Online Databases Whether or not they create and maintain their own databases, many firms look up online data. Online systems give access to enormous amounts of government data, ranging from census data to many agency regulations. Another source of free information is company Web sites. Businesses can visit home pages to look for information about customers, suppliers, and competitors. Trade associations and universities also maintain Web sites with information on topics of interest. A handy source of addresses for company Web sites is ComFind, which lists addresses for company names entered by users.

www. **www.comfind.com**

Some companies subscribe to commercial services that provide fee-for-service databases on particular topics. In addition to broad-based databases available through such services as Prodigy, CompuServe, and America Online, firms can access specialized databases geared to particular industries and functions. Many professional groups have set up bulletin board systems on the Internet where experts trade information. For example, HRCOMM, a bulletin board service based in Pleasant Hill, California,

Business Directory

management information system (MIS) organized method for providing past, present, and projected information on internal operations as well as external intelligence to support decision making.

database centralized, integrated collection of data resources.

Information System Drives Clarklift/FIT to Business Success

Lenders seldom give prizes to companies for being great customers, but that's what happened to Clarklift/FIT, which runs three forklift dealerships in Florida. Clarklift's major source of financing is Citicorp, and the bank recently gave Clarklift its Distinguished Dealer Award.

Clarklift was "distinguished" by its success at learning to manage information and to use it to improve efficiency

and provide superior service. The push that started Clarklift along that learning curve came from Citicorp itself. It was a push Clarklift badly needed.

The company had approached Citicorp because its monthly bills and the cost of inventory were eating up all Clarklift's cash. As a condition of backing Clarklift, Citicorp arranged for an audit of the company's information systems to verify that it could keep the bank supplied with the kind of financial data it needed. The audit team found a less-than-impressive system. An IBM minicomputer ran an inventory and accounting program that was

full of data but not set up to answer such basic questions as which accounts were 60 days past due.

Fortunately, the system also included a program called Monarch. This "report mining" tool from Datawatch extracts data from existing reports, lets users manipulate it, and inserts it into commonly used programs like Excel spreadsheets. Ken Daley, Clarklift's chief financial officer, taught himself how to use Monarch so that he could start preparing the reports Citicorp demanded.

A surprise was in store for Daley and dealership owner Wayne Reece.

allows its members—hundreds of human resource professionals—to discuss topics, research its library of surveys, and look for consultants.

Anyone can now easily publish and retrieve information via the Internet. This wide access is certainly a benefit for information seekers, but it poses a challenge, as well. People gathering information online must verify the reliability of their sources. In case of doubt, they should try to confirm their information with other reliable sources.

Information System Programs

With so much information available online and through other sources, the challenge has shifted from acquiring data toward sorting through it to find the most useful elements. Of the information filling corporate databases, IBM estimates that only about 7 percent is ever used.[2] The key to a useful information system is the program that links users to data.

Information system programs range from general tools that help users to look up data by letting them type in topics to specialized systems that keep track of costs, sales, inventory levels, and other data. For example, the Benefits Management Network provides a system for tracking each employee's benefits. Entering information about the employee triggers the system's automatic functions to provide coverage and start billing for the benefits.[3]

Decision Support Systems A **decision support system (DSS)** is an information system that quickly provides relevant data to help businesspeople choose courses of action.

It includes software tools that help decision makers to generate the information they need. DSS tools may vary from company to company, but they typically include retrieval features that help users to obtain needed information from a database, simulation elements that let employees create computer models to evaluate future company performance under different conditions, and presentation tools that let them create graphs and charts.

A decision support system called *DSS On-Line* has enabled Snap-on Tools Company to build sales, cut costs, and satisfy customers all at the same time. Snap-on markets hand and power tools through a network of independent dealers, who drive trucks full of inventory from customer to customer. It introduced the information system as a way to reduce errors in order entry. In the past, dealers scribbled orders on scraps of paper and mailed or faxed them to headquarters, where employees entered them in the company's files. Now, with DSS On-Line, each dealer takes a computer on the road. During a customer visit, the dealer can use the computer to look up product information including special promotions, download flyers, enter orders, get quick credit approval, and automatically update inventory records. Back at Snap-on headquarters, employees receive daily downloads of data and use the system to process orders and manage the company's inventory. Dealers report that they spend far less time hunting for information and filling out paperwork, and far more meeting customer needs, than before the innovation.[4]

www.snapon.com

In preparing reports for Citicorp, they started learning about their business as they never had before. A check of parts inventory showed Daley and Reece that they were carrying unused parts they could return for $127,500 in cash. They also found easy ways to keep track of such useful information as which forklifts were rented most often and which sales reps' quotes were resulting in sales.

Impressed, Reece continued to upgrade Clarklift's information system. He added personal computers and gave his entire staff access to the company's databases and the Internet. He automated the process of preparing quotes for customers and started generating lists of customers with particular types of needs, so that the com-pany could target them with related communications.

Best of all, Clarklift's information system has given its management a way to keep on top of activities. Is a particular dealership focusing on the most profitable models? If not, Reece gets his employees refocused. Not surprisingly, sales are growing, inventory costs are down, and profits are rising, all because Reece enabled himself and his employees to find the information they already had.

QUESTIONS FOR CRITICAL THINKING

1. **Not every lender conducts a formal evaluation of a prospective borrower's information system.**

Why do you think Citicorp audited Clarklift/FIT's information system? Do you think such audits adequately explore company operations? Explain.

2. **What kinds of data in Clarklift's information system does this story mention? What other kinds of information would you want if you were a manager at Clarklift?**

Sources: Datawatch white paper, accessed at http://www.datawatch.com/index.html, February 18, 1998; Joshua Macht, "The Accidental Automator," *Inc. Technology*, June 17, 1997, pp. 66–71; "Report Mining: A New Way to Access Corporate Information."

Executive Information Systems Sometimes firms create specialized information systems to address the needs of employees at specific levels. An **executive information system (EIS)** allows top managers to access the firm's primary databases, often by touching the computer screen or pointing with a mouse. EIS software typically produces easy-to-read, full-color graphics and charts. A typical EIS allows users to choose between many kinds of data, such as

Information overload—gathering data is not the same as using it.

| Figure 18.1 | **Partial Expert System for Auto Engine Repair** |

IF the engine is misfiring **AND**
IF the plug wires are worn,

THEN turn off the engine, replace the plug wires, turn on the engine, listen again for misfiring cylinders.

IF the engine fires properly, **QUIT.**

IF the engine is misfiring **AND**
IF the distributor cap is cracked,

THEN turn off the engine, replace the distributor cap, turn on the engine, listen again for misfiring cylinders.

IF the engine fires properly, **QUIT.**

IF the engine is misfiring **AND**
IF any spark plug tests faulty,

THEN turn off the engine, replace all spark plugs, turn on the engine, listen again for misfiring cylinders.

IF the engine fires properly, **QUIT.**

IF the engine is misfiring **AND**
IF the fuel filter is clogged,

THEN turn off the engine, replace the filter element, turn on the engine, listen again for misfiring cylinders.

IF the engine fires properly, **QUIT.**

in a specific subject area in order to solve problems.

Figure 18.1 illustrates an expert system based on relevant facts and information regarding misfiring in an auto engine. If you take your car to a repair shop with such a complaint, the mechanic will generally follow certain rules to diagnose the problem. The process usually begins by listening to the engine. If the mechanic detects misfiring, the process continues by checking the spark plug wires, distributor, and spark plugs one by one. The step-by-step expert system approach solves problems based on "If x, then y" relationships developed from a knowledge base accumulated over years of experience, classes, reports from other mechanics, and books and repair manuals.

Trends in Information Systems

Until recently, limited processing speeds and storage capacities required companies to devote entire systems to individual tasks, such as tracking accounts payable, production, or payroll. These isolated systems divided up access to information. For instance, salespeople might know sales levels, but not order status

the firm's financial statements and sales figures as well as stock market trends for the company and industry. Managers can start by looking at summaries and then proceed to request more detailed information if they wish.

Top management at Kmart can retrieve detailed, daily information on sales of any of the 100,000 items carried in the firm's outlets, thanks to the firm's Retail Automation System. Satellite dishes mounted on all store buildings transmit daily sales reports to a mainframe at company headquarters. If a company official wants to determine yesterday's sales of the popular Timex Indiglo watch, the information is available within a matter of seconds. Want to compare per-store sales of the watch in Oregon with those in Maryland? A simple query will display the data in a full-color chart on the screen.

Expert Systems An **expert system** is a computer program that imitates human thinking through complicated sets of "if . . . then" rules. The system applies human knowledge

or product return data. Today, computers have broken down the barriers between functions and shrunk the geography of business. Modern computer networks help people to obtain and share information, even to collaborate in real time, across departments and locations.

Many companies connect their offices and buildings by creating **local area networks (LANs),** computer networks that connect machines within limited areas (such as one building or several buildings near each other). LANs are useful tools, because they link personal computers and allow them to share printers, documents, and information.

A LAN or some other computer network within an organization supports teamwork and information sharing. A network patterned after the Internet has transformed the bureaucracy at the U.S. military's largest joint command, the U.S. Atlantic Command (ACOM). ACOM personnel can look up the command's home page to learn the schedules of admirals and generals, search for messages by key words, and check reference materials such as weapons guides and a glossary of acronyms. Army Major Bill Robinson used the network to collaborate with dozens of experts when he wrote a research report. "By blending technology with expertise," said Robinson, "I was able to do in 90 days what otherwise would have taken 2 years."[5]

Computer networks have their disadvantages, too. Organizations must carefully plan and control them. Otherwise, each division might develop its own system that does not effectively link up with other divisions' systems. Issues of privacy and security also arise. Should everyone in the company be able to access all of the company's data? What about confidential human resource files or the corporation's payroll system? A later section of the chapter will examine several of these issues.

DID YOU KNOW?

The *Computer Industry Almanac* forecasts that by the end of this century, two-thirds of computing power and more than two-thirds of all personal computers will be located outside the United States.

COMPUTER HARDWARE AND SOFTWARE

English mathematician William Shanks spent one-third of his life computing the mathematical constant pi to 707 decimal places, only to discover that he had made a mistake at the 528th place! A modern computer can duplicate Shanks's work without error in less than 5 seconds.

A computer is a programmable electronic device that can store, retrieve, and process data. Just a few decades ago, these machines were considered exotic curiosities. Today, they have become so indispensable to business that few managers can imagine running their businesses without computers.

Types of Computer Hardware

Hardware consists of all the tangible elements of a computer system—the input devices, the machines that store and process data and perform the required calculations, and the output devices that present the results to information users. Input devices allow users to enter data and commands for processing, storage, and output. Common input devices are the keyboard, mouse, scanner, modem, microphone, and touch screen. Output devices are the hardware elements that transmit or display documents and other results of a computer system's work. Examples include the monitor (screen), printer, fax machine, modem, and speakers. Notice that some devices, such as the screen and modem, can serve both input and output functions.

Computer processing units incorporate widely varying memory capacities and processing speeds. As shown in Figure 18.2, these differences define three broad classifications of computers: mainframes, minicomputers, and personal computers. A **mainframe** computer is the largest type of computer system with the most extensive storage capacity and the fastest processing speeds. Some observers have argued that mainframes are the dinosaurs of the 21st-century computer industry. However, these giant computers are not destined for early extinction, primarily because they can handle dinosaur-sized tasks. In fact, they continue to evolve as people discover new applications for them. Especially powerful mainframes called **supercomputers** can handle extremely rapid, complex calculations involving thousands of variables, most commonly in scientific research settings.

A **minicomputer** is an intermediate-sized computer—more compact and less expensive than a mainframe, but also slower and with less memory. These intermediate computers often toil in universities, factories, and research labs. Minicomputers such as IBM's AS/400 also appeal to many small businesses that need more power than personal computers can offer to handle specialized tasks.[6]

Personal computers (PCs) are common today in schools and homes, as well as in businesses. They have earned increasing popularity due to their ever-expanding capabilities to handle many of the functions that mainframes performed just a few decades ago. These advances were made possible by the development of powerful chips—thin silicon wafers that carry integrated circuits (networks of transistors and electronic circuits). In particular, a microprocessor is a fingernail-sized chip that contains an entire central processing unit. Intelligent functions of today's new cars, toys, and watches also rely on microprocessors. Additional chips provide instructions and memory to convert a microprocessor into a personal computer.

As technology continues to improve, computers continue to diminish in size. Laptop computers are PCs lightweight enough to be easily portable and small enough to rest on a person's lap. Notebook computers like the IBM Thinkpad are small enough to slip into a briefcase, yet more powerful than many 2- or 3-year-old desktop units.

Business Directory

hardware all the tangible elements of a computer system—the input devices, processing unit, and output devices.

| Figure 18.2 | **Types of Computers** |

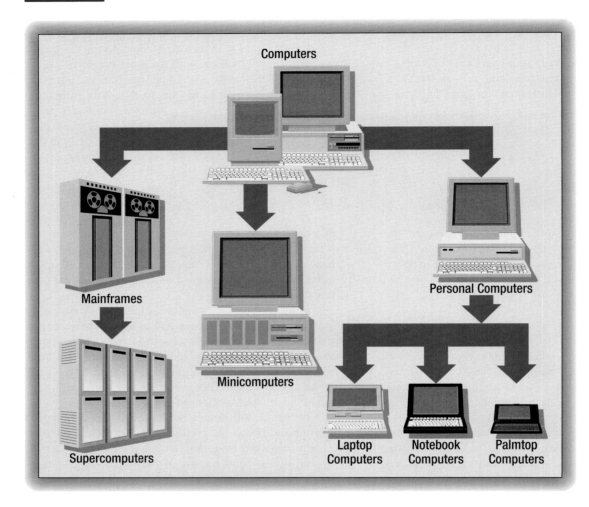

numbers and appointments. The early models from Franklin Electronic Publishers (called Rex PC companion) do not directly accept input. Rather, the user slides the Rex into a slot on a laptop or a docking station on a desktop computer.[7] Timex is developing the DataLink personal information manager. Worn like a wristwatch, it provides access to data about appointments and phone numbers.[8] These new technologies have limitations, such as tiny keyboards and the need to recharge batteries, but technological improvements may soon overcome these hurdles. Other observers predict that the next hot trend is network computers, which are essentially desktop terminals that download applications from network servers.

Many notebook models have "docking" capabilities that allow them to plug into a desktop to share data. Palmtop models, such as the PalmPilot, fit in a shirt pocket and run on ordinary AA batteries. The latest palmtop computers can run common applications like word processing and database software, as well as store documents and graphics created on a desktop computer. Many models have color screens and can link up through wireless modems to bigger, stationary systems.

The future will bring even smaller PCs. Industry technologists have been developing a credit-card-sized computer for storing and retrieving information such as phone

Types of Software

Software refers to the sets of instructions that tell the computer hardware what to do. These instructions, written in various computer languages, may take the form of custom-designed packages uniquely created to fulfill a business's specialized needs or off-the-shelf, commercial packages that provide commonly desired capabilities.

The software that controls the basic workings of a computer system is its **operating system.** Today, most business PCs use a version of

Business Directory

software   sets of instructions that tell computer hardware what to do.

Microsoft's popular Windows operating system (or its ancestor, MS-DOS). Other widely used operating systems include UNIX and the Apple Macintosh operating system.

Operating-system designers have faced important challenges as businesses have shifted from standalone computers to networks, since computers running different operating systems may have difficulty sharing data. For example, if one employee writes a report on an older Windows computer, another employee with an older Macintosh may have to overcome limitations to display and edit the report. That problem may lose significance in the future, thanks to a new programming language called *Java*. Programs written in Java can run on any type of computer or operating system, so companies are increasingly snapping up Java applications to develop their databases and computer networks. For example, American Airlines' Sabre Group reservations unit is rewriting its reservations system in Java.[9]

A program that performs the specific tasks that the user wants to carry out—like writing a letter or looking up data—is called **applications software.** Leading off-the-shelf software packages include Microsoft Word, Lotus Notes, and Netscape Navigator. The Business Tool Kit describes some modern resources to help you choose among the many available software packages.

A later section of this chapter discusses major categories of applications used by businesses.

Contributions and Limitations of Computers

Computers offer fast, accurate processing and capabilities for storing large quantities of information in small spaces. They can quickly gather and display volumes of data and perform the mechanical, often boring, work of recording and maintaining incoming information. The tremendous speed of computers can save time when correcting problems, implementing solutions, and taking advantage of business opportunities. These machines can perform repetitive tasks, such as adding endless strings of numbers or

Palmtop computers: many functions in small packages

comparing collected data against established standards, that would soon wear out human beings.

Like any time-saving or labor-saving device, the computer's advantages also bring a number of potential problems. A firm may need costly, custom-designed computer equipment and software to meet its particular needs. In addition, computers can make disastrous mistakes when programmed incorrectly, as when a computerized defense system almost tried to shoot down the moon. At about the same time, an amazed magazine subscriber received 700 copies of the same issue in the mail. Computers can also become crutches rather than decision-making tools when people rely too heavily on them.

Finally, computers can alienate customers if firms use them so extensively that they eliminate human contact with customers. To overcome consumer resentment toward depersonalized, computer-generated letters, a Charleston, West Virginia, hospital uses this message:

> Hello there. I am the hospital's computer. As yet, no one but me knows that you have not been making regular payments on this account. However, if I have not processed a payment from you within 10 days, I will tell a human, who will resort to other means of collection.

HOW COMPUTERS HELP BUSINESSPEOPLE

Computers and related technologies are revolutionizing the techniques by which businesses manage information. These new technologies affect contemporary business in three primary ways. First, the enhanced timeliness and quantity of information improve the speed and effectiveness of decision making. Second, computers make accurate, unbiased data available to all interested parties. Finally, their information-sharing capabilities support team decision making at low levels of an organization's hierarchy. Every industry has felt some impact as computers and information systems have spread. (Unfortunately, not

---

BUSINESS TOOL KIT

Choosing Software

The Internet is lowering the risks of choosing and using software. When you want to buy a new program or get the most out of one that you own, log on to the Net to see what you can learn:

▼ *Read the reviews.* Use your Web browser to find press releases about new products and reviews of the software's performance.

▼ *Look for "trialware."* Visit the Web sites of software manufacturers whose products interest you. Many companies offer trial versions that you can download for free and use for limited periods. If you like the programs, you can then pay for unlimited use.

▼ *Look for promotional materials.* The Web sites of software manufacturers may also give details about products you're considering. After you buy, go back to the site periodically to check for bug fixes and patches to correct the glitches that always seem to pop up in new software.

▼ *Check out discussion groups.* Informal and company-sponsored groups have formed to share ideas for using many popular software titles. Reading the questions in such a forum may teach you about problems before you experience them. You also may find a great source of support—and even camaraderie—after you buy.

Source: Some of these tips are based on Robert McGarvey, "Test Drive," *Entrepreneur,* January 1997, p. 22.

---

every business helped by computers is a legitimate commercial operation; criminals have also reaped the benefits of information technology, as have crime fighters.)

Some of the most widely used business applications of computers include word processing, desktop publishing, spreadsheets, electronic mail, presentation graphics, multimedia and interactive media, and groupware and intranets. Users once acquired applications such as these as individual software packages. Today, however, they normally buy **integrated software,** which combines several applications into a single package that can share modules for data handling and processing (such as storing files on disk and printing). For example, Microsoft's popular Office 97 suite brings together word processing, presentation graphics, database management, spreadsheets, and an information manager, all on a personal computer. (Office 97 also comes in a Small Business Edition with a slightly different set of components geared to the needs of small businesses.) Besides such off-the-shelf packages, businesses also may buy integrated software tailored to their specific needs. Maid-Pro, a cleaning service, uses ServiceWorks, integrated software that combines accounting, scheduling, and contact management (for keeping track of clients).[10]

 www.microsoft.com

Word Processing

One of the most popular business applications, **word processing,** uses computers to type, store, retrieve, edit, and print various types of documents. If you have ever used a typewriter to write a paper, you know the advantages of a personal computer in revising sentences, checking spelling, and correcting mistakes.

Word processing helps a company to handle huge volumes of correspondence, process numerous documents, and personalize form letters. Some firms use special-purpose computers, called *dedicated word processors,* designed exclusively for this purpose. However, most word processing involves general-purpose computers running such word-processing software packages as Word, WordPerfect, MacWrite, or WordStar. The newest versions of these programs enable users to include graphics and spreadsheets from other programs in word-processing documents and to create Web sites by translating documents into hypertext markup language (HTML), the language of the World Wide Web.

As word-processing capabilities have grown, a growing number of business-people have strived to create "paperless offices." They

Business Directory

word processing business application that uses computers to type, store, retrieve, edit, and print various types of documents.

spreadsheet software package that creates the computerized equivalent of an accountant's worksheet, allowing the user to manipulate variables and see the impact of possible scenarios on operating results.

| Figure 18.3 | How a Spreadsheet Works |

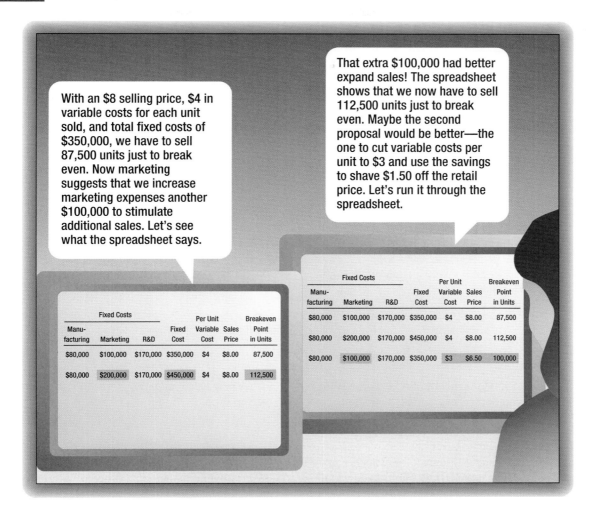

want to set achievable goals for electronically creating, transmitting, storing, and retrieving documents, eliminating any need to print them. Although the idea appeals to both efficiency and environmentalist priorities, it can be very difficult to achieve, as the Business Hall of Shame illustrates.

Desktop Publishing

Many business systems extend word processing capabilities to create sophisticated documents. **Desktop publishing** employs computer technology to allow users to design and produce attractively formatted printed material themselves rather than hiring professionals. Desktop publishing software combines high-quality type, graphics, and layout tools to create output that may look as attractive as documents produced by professional publishers and printers. Advanced equipment can scan photos and drawings and duplicate them on the printed page.

Many firms use desktop publishing systems to print newsletters, reports, and form letters. Advertising and graphic arts departments often use desktop publishing systems to create brochures and marketing materials. A good desktop publishing system can save a company money by allowing staff members to produce such documents.

Spreadsheets

An electronic **spreadsheet** is the computerized equivalent of an accountant's worksheet. This software package permits businesspeople to manipulate decision variables and determine their impacts on such outcomes as profits or sales. Popular spreadsheet software packages include Lotus 1-2-3, Excel, and Quattro Pro.

Figure 18.3 demonstrates how a manager uses a spreadsheet to set a price for a proposed product. Assume that the firm plans to sell a new product at $8 per unit. It can produce the product with variable costs of $4 per unit.

BUSINESS HALL OF SHAME

Hire Quality Goes to War against Paper

At his Chicago job-placement firm, Hire Quality, founder Dan Caulfield made sure everyone recognized paper as Public Enemy Number One. In a highly competitive industry with thin profit margins, Caulfield was convinced that his business's survival required a paperless office. This vision helped Caulfield to attract a number of large clients, including Brinks Home Security, NYNEX (of the regional U.S. phone companies), and United Parcel Service.

Certainly, the necessary technology was available for purchase. The move didn't even require exotic equipment. Caulfield developed a system by which job candidates would register with Hire Quality via e-mail or on disk. Data about them would be entered into a database that allowed searches for specific job experience or characteristics. The database could also store resumes as word-processing documents attached to the candidates' records. When an employer asked for candidates to fill a position, a Hire Quality employee searched the database, called applicants with the right characteristics, and asked a series of questions. Candidates who passed this screening completed more detailed interviews. Hire Quality faxed the resumes of those who survived the interviews to the client without ever using a printer. Most employees also had scanners on their desks, just in case a piece of paper should sneak into the company.

The components of the system made sense, at least to Caulfield, who knew that his staff could not possibly search on paper for the tens of thousands of candidates his clients wanted every month. However, the path to a paperless office has been a thorny one, indeed. First, the technology has gobbled up profits. In the company's startup years, Caulfield spent almost 40 percent of revenues on information technology. On the bright side, that investment has dramatically cut the costs of running the business day to

Total fixed costs of $350,000 include $80,000 for such manufacturing overhead outlays as salaries, general office expenses, rent, utilities, and interest charges; $100,000 for marketing expenditures; and $170,000 for research and development on the product. The spreadsheet calculation, using the basic breakeven model introduced in Chapter 14, reveals that the company must sell 87,500 units to cover all costs and break even at the $8 price.

What if the firm's marketing director persuades other members of the group to increase marketing expenditures to $200,000? As the first computer screen shows, the $100,000 increase in marketing expenditures boosts total fixed costs to $450,000, raising the newly calculated breakeven point to 112,500 units. As soon as the analyst changes figures in one or more cells of the spreadsheet, the computer recalculates all figures. This feature eliminates the tedious chore of recalculating and revising figures by hand.

The second computer screen demonstrates the impact of a reduction in variable costs to $3.00 by switching to lower-cost materials coupled with a $1.50 reduction in the product's selling price. The new breakeven point is 100,000 units.

This relatively simple example demonstrates how easily a manager can analyze alternative decisions using a spreadsheet. A more complex spreadsheet may stretch across 50 columns, or even wider, but the software still makes new calculations as fast as the manager can change the variables.

Electronic Mail

Besides manipulating spreadsheets and generating documents, businesspeople need to communicate directly with company colleagues and others outside their organizations. Increasingly, they turn to their computers for this function and send messages via electronic mail (e-mail). By a recent count, about 37 million workers in the United States had access to e-mail, and the number is rapidly rising.[11]

Besides linking businesses with their customers and suppliers, as described in Chapter 17, e-mail is a fast and easy means of internal communication. It is especially useful in organizations with employees in several countries. For the cost of dialing a local access number, employees can send and receive messages with their co-workers around the world, each logging on at whatever time suits her or his schedule.

E-mail supports active teamwork at VeriFone Inc. Once a customer in Greece questioned whether VeriFone could really handle the big job that a sales representative was proposing. The rep knew the company had handled similar jobs, but he needed details. As soon as he left the meeting, he plugged a phone into his laptop and beamed a distress call to the company's worldwide

They said it

"What the Web does is create more conversations. That reveals knowledge gaps faster and allows people to act on it."

Sherman Woo
Director, Global Village Labs,
U S West

day, so Caulfield forecasts a prosperous future based on the investment in technology.

The next big challenge was getting people to use the system. Many candidates faxed rather than e-mailed their applications, generating paper instead of electronic files. Scanning the faxes produced disappointing results, and employees eventually gave up on reformatting the scrambled documents. They preferred to re-fax the faxes to clients. Employees also complained of eye strain caused by staring at a computer screen all day. Sometimes, they would print out documents just to give their eyes a rest from the monitors.

Caulfield did as much as he could think of to motivate employees to achieve a paperless office. He set up penalties. He placed a jar by the

printer to remind employees that they should pay $1 for using the fax machine and $0.25 per page for printing a resume. But the piles of paper continued to grow, and so did Caulfield's frustration. One day he swept through Hire Quality's office with a waste barrel and snatched up every bit of paper he could get his hands on. He dragged the barrel to the fire escape and started a bonfire.

That experience was a turning point for both Caulfield and his employees. The employees became convinced of his seriousness, and they are now trying hard to avoid paper. As for Caulfield, he has come to terms with the difficulty of achieving a paperless office. He removed the penalty jar from the printer and is concentrating on more specific innovations, such as encouraging electronic data interchange with his firm's biggest clients.

Sources: "About Hire Quality," Hire Quality Web site, www.hire-quality.com, accessed May 10, 1999; and Joshua Macht, "Pulp Addiction," *Inc. Technology*, March 18, 1997, pp. 43–46.

QUESTIONS FOR CRITICAL THINKING

1. Why do you think Hire Quality's employees hesitated to give up paper? Would you expect a similar response at other companies? Why?

2. Do you think the paperless office is a realistic goal for an organization? If so, how could an organization implement the concept more effectively than Hire Quality did? If not, what changes (such as new technology) would be necessary to make a practical, working paperless office?

---

sales and support staff. A VeriFone employee in San Francisco was monitoring e-mail for such messages, and he quickly set up a conference call with marketing personnel in Hong Kong and Atlanta. They planned a procedure for gathering data, and before long they had assembled detailed accounts of VeriFone's successes around the world. The next day, the Greek sales rep retrieved their presentation on his computer, returned to the customer, and closed the sale.[12]

www.verifone.com

Certainly, e-mail can help companies reduce paperwork, time wasted in playing telephone tag, and similar inefficiencies. However, like any means of communication, it has limits. E-mail is most suitable for short, unemotional messages. To send long documents, businesspeople often prefer to attach them to electronic messages as separate files or to mail or fax them. Also, senders should be aware that e-mail to a colleague is not a private exchange.

Presentation Graphics

Analyzing columns and rows of numbers can be a dull and difficult task. When people see data displayed as charts or graphs, however, they can of-

ten identify patterns and relationships that raw data did not reveal. Such tools can improve decisions. Businesspeople once had to labor to create those charts and graphs or send them to artists and wait. Those practices have changed with the widespread availability of **presentation software** such as Microsoft's PowerPoint and Corel's Presentations. Such a program includes graphics and tools for manipulating them to create a variety of charts, graphs, and pictures, like those shown in Figure 18.4. By combining these elements in ways that are easy to read, a user can prepare slides, handouts, or transparency masters for effective reports and proposals. For example, to persuade management to fund a new project, an employee might create a series of graphs to illustrate how the project will benefit the organization over time.

Multimedia and Interactive Media

Modern computers, even personal computers, have moved beyond numbers, text, and graphs to encompass multimedia and interactive media capabilities. **Multimedia computing** refers to technologies that integrate two or

Business Directory

multimedia computing technologies that integrate two or more types of media, such as text, voice, sound, video, graphics, and/or animation, into a computer-based application.

| Figure 18.4 | **Examples of Visuals Created with Presentation Software** |

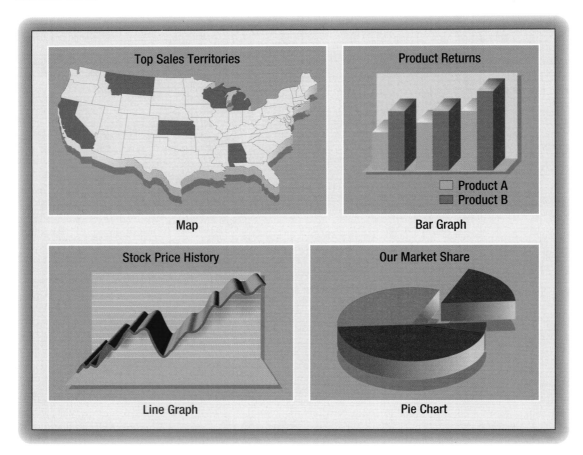

Map

Bar Graph
- Product A
- Product B

Line Graph

Pie Chart

Among the most promising business applications for multimedia computing are employee training and business presentations. Multimedia systems helped Duracell to implement a worldwide training program. The company produced CD-ROMs incorporating video, animation, and graphics, but little text and no audio. That combination helped the company to overcome language barriers in training Chinese equipment operators.[13] Dormont Manufacturing Company used multimedia marketing presentations to correct misperceptions that its facility, which makes gas appliance connectors, is a low-tech operation. The company produced a brief multimedia tour incorporating animation, still photos, and videos. Customers who view the presentation not only get a clear picture of the company, but they also see how it can meet additional needs.[14]

more types of media, such as text, voice, sound, full-motion video, still video, graphics, and/or animation, into computer-based applications. Many multimedia applications are stored on CD-ROMs, because their spiral-type storage patterns effectively support retrieval of continuous blocks of data, such as converted music or animation sequences. CD-ROMs are also useful because of their durability and large capacity. A single CD-ROM can store 680 megabytes of data, enough for an entire encyclopedia.

Many applications of multimedia computing use **interactive media**—programs that allow users to interact with computer displays. For example, when Chrysler developed multimedia training courses for its quality-assurance program, it included interactive features along with graphics, photographs, animation, audio, video, and text. Users of the program don't just sit back and watch; they choose course modules, engage in role playing, move objects around the screen, and complete test forms at the ends of the modules. The system keeps track of

Business Directory

groupware software that combines information sharing through a common database with communication via e-mail so that employees can collaborate on projects.

intranet company network that links employees via Internet tools like e-mail, hypertext links, database searches using Web browsers, and so on, limiting access to organization members.

firewall software that prevents entry to an intranet from an unauthorized location or by an unauthorized person.

how long learners spend on each module and how well they score on each test.[15]

The Chattanooga Group, which produces machines for physical therapy, avoided language barriers in its training materials by combining interactive technology with a multimedia program that sticks to text and pictures. The equipment comes with a disk that stores training-manual text in four languages: English, Japanese, Spanish, and German. With a computer mounted on the equipment, the user looks at pictures and touches the screen to call up the part of the manual that applies to a situation, such as how to work on an injured knee.[16]

Groupware and Intranets

An especially useful interactive medium is **groupware,** computer software that combines information sharing through a common database with communication via e-mail. Using groupware, employees can work together on a single document at the same time, viewing one another's changes. They can also discuss ideas and check one another's calendars to schedule meetings or other group efforts.

Groupware packages include Lotus Notes, Exchange, GroupWise, Collabra Share, and GroupSystems. The editors of *CIO* magazine use Lotus Notes to brainstorm story ideas and develop articles with writers from coast to coast. However, the publication's staff has encountered difficulties learning groupware that the basics of e-mail did not entail; using the full potential of such a system often requires some prodding.[17]

A broader approach to sharing information in an organization is to establish a company network patterned after the Internet. Such a network, called an **intranet,** links employees through Internet tools like e-mail, hypertext links, database searches using the major Web browsers, and so on, but it limits access only to organization members. The intranet excludes nonemployees and others without valid passwords by incorporating software known as a **firewall**. Firewalls are available as off-the-shelf packages such as FireWall/Plus, On Guard, and SmartWall. They limit data transfers to certain locations and log system use so managers can identify attempts to log on with invalid passwords and other threats to system security. Especially so-

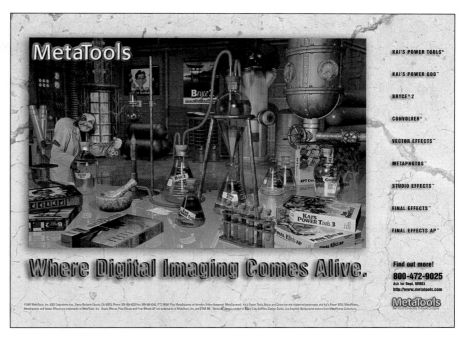

Multimedia computer tools combine many special effects.

phisticated packages immediately alert system administrators about suspicious activities and let authorized personnel use smart cards to log on from remote terminals.[18]

Intranets offer important advantages over more familiar, and now rather old-fashioned, computer networks. Perhaps most importantly, they solve problems of linking different kinds of computers. Like the Internet, intranets can integrate computers running all kinds of operating systems. In addition, intranets are relatively easy and inexpensive to set up; most businesses already have some of the required tools, such as PCs and Web browser software. Intranets also support teamwork among employees who travel or work from home. Any intranet member with the right identification, a PC, and a modem can dial up the intranet, check messages, and search for information in the company's database.

Among the large U.S. industrial companies known as the *Fortune 1000,* more than two-thirds have already developed or begun developing intranets.[19] AT&T's intranet includes news highlights, the latest data on the company's stock and financial performance, and links to sites maintained by the training and human resources departments.[20] An intranet is an essential part of the information system for Schlumberger, whose 50,000 employees develop oil fields in over 90 countries, often in remote locations. The intranet lets employees collaborate with scientists and engineers around the globe. Engineers can use their computers to download design tools and advice. No electrical outlet nearby in the desert? No problem. Engineers at such locations communicate through satellite dishes mounted on their trucks.[21]

PROTECTING INFORMATION SYSTEMS

As information systems become increasingly important business assets, they also become progressively harder to replace. When computers are connected to a network, a problem at any location can affect the entire network. While many computer security issues go beyond the scope of this textbook, this section will discuss three important security threats: computer crime, viruses, and natural disasters that may damage information systems. Solving an Ethical Controversy takes a look at security issues surrounding databases.

Computer Crime

Computers provide efficient ways for employees to share information. But they may also allow flows of information to people with more malicious intentions. Common computer crimes involve stealing or altering data in several ways:

▼ Employees or outsiders may change or invent data to produce inaccurate information.

▼ They may change computer programs to create false information or illegal transactions.

As computers diminish in size, chances for theft increase.

▼ Unauthorized people can access computer systems for their own illicit benefit.

Computer crime is on the rise. Recently, the Pentagon suffered a widely publicized series of break-ins to its computers. Hackers entered unclassified networks and installed "trapdoors" through which they could later obtain information. The FBI is investigating the problem and so far reports limited damage.[22] This example illustrates the need for organizations of all types to be aware of and take steps to prevent such breaches.

System administrators implement two basic protections against computer crime. They try to prevent access to their systems by unauthorized users and to prevent viewing of data by unauthorized system users.

Intranets: the newest way to link employees.

To prevent access, the simplest method requires authorized users to enter passwords. The company may also install firewalls, described in an earlier section. To prevent system users from reading sensitive information, the company may use encryption software, such as Pretty Good Privacy, PCCrypto, or SecurPC. In general, these programs require that the sender and receiver of a message each enter a key, or string of characters, to encode and decode messages. The most secure of these programs are impossible to crack without supercomputer resources, but their use for international messages may be prohibited.[23] Hackers are continually breaking through existing defenses, so software developers continue to invent new and more elaborate protective measures. The U.S. government has set up a Web site to help businesses and other computer users learn about security issues.

| Figure 18.5 | Online Resource for Protection against Computer Crime: Computer Security Resource Clearinghouse |

Figure 18.5 shows the home page of the Computer Security Resource Clearinghouse, where you can obtain information, link up to professional and government sites, and order publications about computer security.

Another form of computer crime is as old as crime itself: theft of equipment. As the size of computer hardware diminishes, it becomes increasingly vulnerable to theft. In particular, laptops are big enough to be easily visible to thieves, yet small enough for them to pick up quickly and disappear. The best protection is to avoid leaving laptops and other electronic gear unattended or out of reach. For example, in an airport, wait until the last possible moment to put equipment on the x-ray conveyor belt along with any other metal items so someone cannot grab your computer while you wait for possessions to pass through the machine.[24]

Every year, businesses lose enormous sums to computer crime. Often they are reluctant to admit these losses publicly, fearing negative images. Fortunately, basic precautions will go a long way toward preventing such crime.

Computer Viruses

Rather than directly tampering with a company's data or computers, computer criminals may create "viruses" to infect computers at random. **Computer viruses** are programs that secretly attach themselves to other programs or files and change them or destroy data. Viruses can be programmed to remain dormant for a long time, after which the infections suddenly activate themselves and cause problems.

A virus can reproduce by copying itself to other programs stored on the same diskette or disk drive. It spreads as users install infected software on their systems or exchange files with others, usually by e-mail, electronic bulletin boards, trading disks, or downloading programs or data from unknown sources on the Internet. With widespread data sharing in networks, including intranets and the Internet, viruses can do more damage today than ever before. According to a survey by the National Computer Security Association, 70 percent of corporate computer networks have been infected by viruses.[25]

Some viruses result from pranks that get out of hand. One German student sent a Christmas greeting over a computer network that ended up spreading into IBM's international network and within hours attached itself to every mailing list it encountered.

Other viruses involve deliberate crimes. The Michelangelo virus, for example, erases data in computers that are used on March 6, the Italian artist's birthday. In a single year, over one-sixth of major U.S. companies reported infections by this virus. It also infected computers in England, the Netherlands, Austria, and South Africa.

SOLVING AN ETHICAL CONTROVERSY

Should the Government Limit Applications of Police Databases?

Modern computer technology enables users to create databases that contain more than numbers and words; they can also collect sounds, images, and videos. This ability gives police departments a new tool for catching suspects: databases of digitized photos.

The technology combines two activities: creating a composite image and finding a match within a database of photos. To create the composite image, software such as Image-Ware uses a database of photos containing thousands of facial features. Guided by a witness, the police

artist selects features and adjusts their placement. Often, the resulting composites give more accurate portrayals than traditional sketches could provide.

Furthermore, the computer stores these images in digitized form. Image-Ware can then search a database of digitized photos and find a match. In Los Angeles County, a detective used the system to find a carjacker. The victim described the perpetrator, and the detective prepared a digitized composite photo. The computer then searched the county's database of mug shots and found an almost perfect match. The police arrested the suspect, and he confessed to the crime. Since the software has been on the market, Image-Ware, the company, has sold or leased

the program to about 600 U.S. police departments.

The possibility of collecting photo databases beyond the traditional mug shots has raised an ethical question, though. Systems like ImageWare can also search files of driver's license photos, a procedure that violates civil liberties, according to critics. Image-Ware's CEO says that the program only makes a positive match between two images; it does not assign guilt.

 Should the Government Limit Police Access to Photo Databases?

PRO

1. Including driver's license photos in a search amounts to treating every

---

The simplest way to protect against computer viruses is to install one or more of the many available virus protection software packages. The list includes Norton Anti-Virus, VirusScan Deluxe, and PC-cillin II, all priced well under $100. These programs continuously monitor systems for viruses and automatically eliminate any they spot. Users must regularly update them, however, by going online to download the latest virus descriptions. This essential precaution helps to maintain protection, since hackers constantly create new viruses. Users should also carefully choose the files they load onto their systems; when possible, avoid buying software that appears to have been previously opened or viewing e-mail messages from mysterious sources.

Disaster Recovery and Backup

Natural disasters, power failures, equipment malfunctions, and human error can disrupt even the most sophisticated information systems. In addition, some experts are predicting an unprecedented problem at the turn of

The year 2000 problem could mean trouble for businesses and customers.

driver as a potential suspect. That technique would increase the likelihood of an innocent person being arrested and charged with a crime.

2. Witnesses do not always accurately recollect details. The system overemphasizes their ability to recall details. Jurors might be so wowed by the technology that a case of mistaken identity would be almost impossible to demonstrate.

3. Someone who applies for a driver's license will not realize that the police may include his or her photo in a search for crime suspects. This fact makes the technique an unfair invasion of privacy.

CON

1. Police have long used sketches to help them find suspects. Searching

digitized images is a more accurate version of the same process, so it may reduce the likelihood of arresting innocent people.

2. Most law-abiding people would be willing to let police search their driver's license photos to help reduce crime.

3. Criminals are adopting modern technology, from spreadsheets and e-mail to electronic ordering and encryption software, to help them carry out and hide their crimes. To keep up, police also need broad access to modern technology. Without it, they will be hampered in their fight against crime—especially high-tech crime.

SUMMARY

Those who appreciate the consequences of mistaken criminal charges worry when a police department

widens its net, as with a database of digitized photos. A law-abiding citizen whose driver's license photo is on file may bear a physical resemblance to some criminals. On the other hand, those who appreciate the pain of a crime victim want the police to have at their disposal any legitimate crime-fighting tool. They point out that systems like ImageWare only help in identifying suspects; the justice system still determines guilt.

Protection of privacy and protection from crime have often seemed at odds in the U.S. criminal justice system. Both are desirable goals, so the challenge is to strike an acceptable balance.

Sources: "Local Police Department Goes High Tech," ImageWare Software, Inc., Web site, March 4, 1998, accessed at www.iwsinc.com; and Bill Richards, "Cops Nab Perps with Digitized Drawings and Databases," *The Wall Street Journal*, January 28, 1998, pp. B1–B2.

---

the millennium. Until recently, computer systems were programmed to represent years as two digits (for example, in the date 2/22/99, "99" represents the year 1999). Those computer systems can interpret data stating the year as 2000 only as an error or a reference to a century-old date. In a problem known as the *millenium bug* or the *Y2K problem,* a system that is not set up to handle dates after 1999 will stall or crash when it comes across a 21st-century date. For these and other possible problems, an organization needs to engage in **disaster recovery planning**—deciding how it can prevent system failures and continue operating if its computer system fails. To check whether you have adequately prepared for the year 2000 problem, see the Business Tool Kit, "Are You Ready for 2000?"

Prevention can avoid many costly problems. The most basic precaution is routinely backing up software and data. Whenever a company buys software, someone should immediately make a copy and store it in a safe place. System administrators should regularly back up data, as well, perhaps at the end of each workday. Companies that do not want to pay for such options as tape drives or removable hard disks can back up their data to an online storage service such as Connected Corporation or Network Associates. In addition, individuals must back up their own work. Many programs include easy functions to back up the contents of a document every few minutes—a short procedure that can pre-

vent the need to recreate hours of work following a power surge.

www.connected.com
www.networkassociate.com

Besides backing up data, technology planners should consider how an organization will respond in the event of a natural disaster, such as a flood or electrical failure. A large company with sensitive information may be willing to pay for an extra hardware installation in a secure location, but even a small company can be prepared for trouble with a backup tape of data and a source of rental PCs. Palay Display, whose 16 employees sell retail fixtures and displays from its headquarters in Grand Forks, North Dakota, was ready with a disaster recovery plan when the Red River flooded the town. When company owner Howard Palay realized that Grand Forks would be evacuated, he loaded the computer holding the company's records into his minivan and drove to the company's branch office in Minneapolis. With help from the computer vendor, Palay was able to hook up his computer to the network in Minneapolis and keep his company operating.[26]

Are You Ready for 2000?

As the 1990s drew to a close, the horror stories began: Payment terminals that won't accept a credit card with an expiration date in 2000. Information systems that don't know how to handle project deadlines after December 31, 1999. Experts predict widespread computer crashes by January 1, 2000.

Will your system be one of the casualties? Are you ready for 2000? To find out, answer the following questions for the computer system you use at school, at home, or at work:

1. If you use a personal computer, does it have a Windows 95 or later operating system? If so, your system will probably survive. By the mid-1990s, programmers had begun preparing for the turn of the millennium.

2. Are you using a PC that runs on a version of MS-DOS or Windows 3.1? If so, get ready for it to choke on those dates.

3. Is your system hooked up to a mainframe or minicomputer purchased before the mid-1990s? A positive answer is bad news. Find out whether your school or employer is updating its software and expects to have the patch ready in time for the millennium.

4. Even if your hardware and operating system are just a couple of years old, is your applications software ready for Y2K? Often, organizations use customized software, tweaking the code as necessary as they upgrade their systems. If the company starts out with something that is not Y2K compliant, even an updated version may suffer problems.

5. Whatever the age of your system, have you tested it with dates from the 21st century? If not, you should. If possible, have the test done by a professional who can help you recover if the system crashes.

If, in spite of your best efforts, you do have a run-in with the millennium bug, you won't be the only one. In a widely cited prediction, Y2K consultants at Gartner Group warn that 30 percent of companies' critical functions will crash because of the bug, and 10 percent of businesses will fail.

Source: Bronwyn Fryer, "Millennium Bug Busting," *Inside Technology Training,* February 1998, pp. 28-29; Leigh Buchanan, "Zero Zero Hour," *Inc. Technology,* November 15, 1997, p. 38; and Leigh Buchanan, "Uneasy Rider," *Inc. Technology,* November 15, 1997, pp. 45-46.

SUMMARY OF LEARNING GOALS

1. Discuss the purpose of a management information system.

A management information system (MIS) is an organized method for supporting decision making by providing data about internal and external activities, including forecasts. It supports decision making by gathering this information, organizing it, and making it readily available to decision makers. At the heart of an MIS, a database typically stores data as electronic files. Many databases are available online; others are produced by individual companies and stored on their own computer systems. An MIS provides access to such data through some type of information system program, such as those used in a decision support system, expert system, or executive information system.

2. Explain how information systems are evolving in response to trends in information technology.

Limits on information technology once required separate information systems devoted to particular tasks, such as accounting, inventory control, or production. Enhanced processing power and superior communications technology now allow contemporary information systems to link users and data throughout organizations via local area networks or the Internet. Users may simultaneously look up documents, discuss them, and collaborate on decisions. This capability supports teamwork and breaks down barriers between departments and locations.

3. Identify basic types of computer hardware and software.

Computer hardware consists of the tangible elements of a computer system—its input devices, output devices, and processors. Input devices include the keyboard, mouse, scanner, modem, microphone, and touch screen. Output devices include the monitor, printer, fax machine, modem, and speakers. Computer processing units differ widely in processing power and capacity. Based on these differences, computers may be categorized from largest to smallest as mainframes, minicomputers, and personal computers. Computer software provides the sets of instructions that tell the hardware what to do. The software that controls the basic workings of the computer is its operating system. Other programs, called *applications software,* perform the specific tasks that users want to complete.

4. Summarize important contributions and limitations of computers.

Computers are fast, accurate systems capable of storing large quantities of information in small spaces. They can quickly record and organize data and then sort through it to find specific facts needed by the user. On the down side, some computer systems are expensive investments. Programming errors or other problems can allow these speedy, efficient machines to multiply small problems into business disasters. People who are overly impressed with a computer system's abilities may mistakenly rely on its output as a substitute for good judgment. Also, computers should never replace personal contact with customers.

5. Define the major business applications of computers.

Word processing uses computers to type, store, retrieve, edit, and print documents. Desktop publishing takes word processing a step further, generating high-quality type, graphics, and layouts to create output that resembles professionally published materials. Electronic spreadsheets permit businesspeople to manipulate decision variables on worksheets and determine the impact of potential events on operating outcomes and decisions. Electronic mail connects employees without regard to their geographic locations. Presentation software includes tools and graphics files for creating a variety of charts, graphs, and pictures to support presentations and proposals. Multimedia computing brings together two or more types of media, such as text, voice, sound, video, graphics, and/or animation. Interactive media consists of program applications that allow users to interact with computer displays. Groupware is software that combines information sharing through a database with communication via e-mail, enabling two or more people to collaborate on a document or other project in real time. An intranet links employees through the tools of the Internet, such as e-mail, hypertext links, and Web browsers; firewalls limit access to authorized intranet users.

6. Describe the areas in which businesses need to protect their information systems.

Businesses need to protect their systems against computer crime, such as unauthorized access and theft of computer hardware. Protections against access include passwords, firewalls, and encryption software. Businesses also need protection from computer viruses. The simplest solution is to install virus protection software. Finally, businesses need to engage in disaster recovery planning to prepare for natural disasters, power failures, equipment malfunctions, and such human-generated errors as the so-called millennium bug. A cornerstone of disaster recovery planning is to set up and enforce policies for frequently backing up data.

TEN BUSINESS TERMS YOU NEED TO KNOW

management information system (MIS)	spreadsheet
database	multimedia computing
hardware	groupware
software	intranet
word processing	firewall

Other Important Business Terms

chief information officer (CIO)	personal computer (PC)
decision support system (DSS)	operating system
	applications software
executive information system	integrated software
expert system	desktop publishing
local area network (LAN)	presentation software
mainframe	interactive media
supercomputers	computer virus
minicomputer	disaster recovery planning

REVIEW QUESTIONS

1. Explain the purpose of a management information system and its functions in an organization.
2. What are the components of a typical MIS today? How have information systems evolved to support the modern emphasis on teamwork?
3. What specific characteristics are responsible for the popularity of computers today?
4. Describe the difference between operating systems and applications software. Give an example of each.
5. Summarize the major contributions of computers to business activities. What potential problems do they bring? Suggest steps to minimize each of these problems.
6. What is integrated software? List some pros and cons of using this type of software.
7. The chapter described major types of applications software, such as word processing and multimedia packages. For each of the following functions within a business, identify at least two applications that would make useful contributions. Briefly describe how the business might use the application.
   a. Human resources
   b. Marketing
   c. Physical distribution
   d. Production and inventory control

e. Customer service
f. Legal
g. Finance and accounting

8. What is an intranet? Summarize some benefits and challenges it delivers.
9. How can businesses protect themselves from computer crime and computer viruses?
10. What is a disaster recovery plan? List some information system "disasters" that an organization might encounter.

QUESTIONS FOR CRITICAL THINKING

1. What databases contain information about you? Work with a partner or small group (or discuss this question in class) to see how many databases you can identify. How do you benefit from appearing in these databases? What potential problems can arise from your inclusion?
2. If you could ask a software developer to provide you with an information system to help you in your role as a student, what elements would the system include? Consider the components of an information system (database plus hardware and software), as well as the types of technology introduced in this chapter. Do you currently have access to any of these components?
3. Do you think that mainframes and minicomputers will continue to play a significant role in businesses in the future? Explain.
4. Groupware and intranets provide technological links through which employees can collaborate on projects, but often employees do not really apply that technology. Why? What conclusions can you draw about the process of introducing information technology into an organization?
5. Consider the computer(s) you use for school or work. From what risks does your computer system need protection? How are you or others providing that protection? Can you think of additional security you should be providing? Why do companies often fail to provide adequate protection for their information systems?

Experiential Exercise

Directions: This chapter's Business Tool Kit familiarized you with the prediction that computer systems around the world will crash on January 1, 2000. To help you understand this problem more thoroughly, research the topic and prepare a three- to five-minute speech to present to your classmates. Use the outline below or set one up yourself.

I. Identifying Year 2000 problems for
  A. Health care organizations
  B. Financial institutions
  C. Government

II. Making computer systems Year 2000 compliant
  A. What are companies doing?
  B. What is the U.S. government doing?

III. Predicting what is most likely to happen in the year 2000

Information on this topic is readily available in computer-related magazines, newspapers, and journals as well as on the Internet. If you are doing this project after the year 2000, use the following outline:

I. Reviewing the pre–January 1, 2000, hype about the Year 2000 problems

II. Examining what companies and the U.S. government did to make their computer systems Year 2000 compliant

III. Analyzing actual Year 2000 problems that occurred

Nothing but Net

1. **Application Software.** Software companies frequently use the Internet to pass along hints or tips on how to get the most from their products. Some vendors also allow you to download free add-ons that will enhance your use of their products. Use your Web browser to locate information on how you can make more effective use of a program you use regularly. Include at least one hint, tip, or download that you can share with someone who also uses the program. Some possible Web sites follow:

   www.microsoft.com/office/enhoffice.asp
   www.quark.com/
   www.corel.com/

2. **Protecting Information Systems.** Select a security threat discussed in the chapter that you are interested in learning more about: computer crime, viruses, or natural disasters that may damage information systems. Use your Web browser to locate sites that will allow you to learn more about your area of interest. Two possibilities are:

   www.lsli.com/
   www.norton.com/

3. **Decision Support Systems.** Visit the Web site of a company, such as the one listed, that creates software to aid in decision making. If the site you visit provides information about client companies that have successfully used its software products, then provide a brief summary of what the company used the product for and how it helped improve the decision-making process. If no examples are provided, then briefly describe one of the DSS products listed on the Web site—its function and examples of who might use the product.

   www.sas.com/

Note: Internet Web addresses change frequently. If you do not find the exact sites listed, you may need to access the organization's or company's home page and search from there.

HUMAN GENOME SCIENCES

Founded in 1992, Maryland-based Human Genome Sciences (HGS) and its founder, chairman, and CEO William A. Haseltine have defied the naysayers. In its relatively short history, the company has already identified more than 1 million partial gene sequences, representing an estimated 90 percent of the genes in the human body. HGS's mission is to develop products to predict, prevent, treat, and cure disease based on its leadership in the discovery and understanding of human and microbial genes.

HGS uses its extensive knowledge of genes to determine which human proteins may be used as new pharmaceutical products. To create these new pharmaceutical products, HGS is working in partnership with other biotechnical and pharmaceutical companies. HGS has secured more than 200 patent applications with the U.S. Patent and Trademark Office and has attained more than 170 collaborative research engagements at various universities around the world.

Computer technology has advanced HGS's mission by improving and automating the procedure of identifying and characterizing genes. The procedure requires the use of information systems to analyze information on the samples collected every day. From that information are drawn gene characteristics. To clarify the importance of information systems, Chief Information Officer Mike Fannon says, "The thing that HGS really brought to the

party in terms of gene discovery is our ability to go from large numbers of experimental results—on the order of several million over the last five years—and to be able to make inferences about those experimental results using computational methods."

Computerized computation and data management have helped the company grow and integrate on a scale that would not have been possible ten years ago. The individuals who work at HGS can't imagine how operations would run without computers because of the overwhelming amount of information and data the company processes and tracks every day. HGS currently has more computers than employees, and it is investing in end-user and server-based equipment to handle its future needs.

HGS has always focused very hard on the issue of security and has implemented a variety of procedures to maintain it. These procedures include (1) having connection between the company and its partners wired with encryption devices so no outsiders can attain unauthorized information, (2) using Internet firewalls to decrease and monitor the number of connections into HGS, (3) creating rules that no information can be seen across the net, and (4) using cryptographic and authentication devices.

The company values the talent and abilities of its employees. Mike Fannon states, "We view automation as a way to enhance the way people do work rather than to replace the way people do work." In an environment that deals with research, HGS's biggest asset is its scientists' intuition and their inferences about the outcomes of the experiments.

What is coming on the high-tech frontier? HGS would like to see technological advances dealing with research and satellite imaging, the availability of video sequencing, and the ability to predict the three-dimensional structure of a protein.

Questions

1. Describe the importance of computer technology at HGS.

2. How does HGS go about protecting its data?

3. New technology and automation always results in employee layoffs. Do you agree with this statement? Why or why not?

chapter 19

Understanding Accounting and Financial Statements

LEARNING GOALS

1. Explain the functions of accounting and its importance to the firm's management and to outside parties, such as investors, creditors, and government agencies.

2. Identify the three basic business activities involving accounting.

3. Describe the roles played by public, management, government, and not-for-profit accountants.

4. Outline the steps in the accounting process.

5. Explain the functions of the balance sheet, the income statement, and the statement of cash flows, and identify the major components of these financial statements.

6. Discuss how financial ratios are used in analyzing a firm's financial strengths and weaknesses.

7. Describe the role of budgets in a business.

8. Explain how exchange rates influence international accounting practices and the importance of uniform financial statements for global business.

Finding Financial Figures for Johnson & Johnson Online

Congratulations! You're about to graduate, and you've landed an interview with Johnson & Johnson—a company you've admired for a long time. To prepare for your interview, you want to get as much current information about the company as you can. Of course, you want to work for a financially sound company, so you're especially interested in finding financial figures. You could contact the company directly and request a copy of its annual report. Each year publicly owned companies publish annual reports that present important financial information prepared by accountants. The reports reveal profitability or losses and how firms spend and invest their funds. But to be in time for your interview, you need information fast, so turn on your computer and visit the company's Web site. You'll find everything you need—not only the company's annual report but other financial data.

In growing numbers, businesses are using the Internet to publish their financial information. Some companies have been placing their bottom line online for years—companies such as Microsoft, Intel, Exxon Mobil, 3Com, IBM, and Medtronics. The Internet offers a fast and effective way to communicate with employees, investors, financial analysts, and people like you.

Johnson & Johnson provides a wealth of financial information on the Web. You can find quarterly or midyear reports for the current year. You can read Johnson & Johnson's entire current annual report, which begins with the letter to shareowners from Chairman and CEO Ralph S. Larsen and Vice Chair Robert N. Wilson. It has a section on company news such as advances in surgical instruments for bypass surgery, new products from genetic engineering, and current areas of research. Of course, the report contains all financial statements and has an independent auditor's report.

Johnson & Johnson offers online publications that abbreviate financial statements and supplement information that appears in the annual report. For example, you can read reports on the company's subsidiaries, including Five-Year Selected Financial Data, a Consolidated Balance Sheet, Sales Growth Rates, Share Repurchase Information, and much more. Johnson & Johnson provides facts to investors that summarize company performance in terms of worldwide sales, worldwide market leadership, new product development, and future growth. You can even read a financial history of the company that dates back to 1887.

www.

www.jnj.com/home.html

Putting financial information online allows Johnson & Johnson to give interested users much more information than it can on printed reports. Moreover, publishing figures on the Web helps the company reach many more people than it could with a printed report. The Web also offers companies a variety of ways to make the information more interesting. Companies can add audio and visual clips to give pizzazz to their financial data, including speeches given by company executives and slide presentations from financial meetings.

Accounting experts envision an increase in electronic trolling for financial information as more firms display their income statements and balance sheets on their Web sites. "I think eventually most SEC-mandated public company financial statements will be online," says Michael G. Edwards, an internal auditor for BB&T Bank in Winston-Salem, North Carolina. Edwards helps to review his bank's financial statements before they are communicated to the public. "I think the push toward real-time information will continue…. Like it or not, I think all auditors eventually will be information systems auditors."[1]

CHAPTER OVERVIEW

Accounting professionals are responsible for preparing the financial information that organizations present in their annual reports. Whether you begin your career by working for a company or by starting your own firm, you need to understand what accountants do and why their work is so important in contemporary business.

Accounting is the process of measuring, interpreting, and communicating financial information to enable people inside and outside the firm to make informed decisions. Like statistics, accounting is a language of business. Accountants gather, record,

DID YOU KNOW?

More than half of America's accounting and auditing professionals are women. According to the latest statistics published by the Department of Labor, 56 percent of accountants and auditors are women.

report, and interpret financial information in a way that describes the status and operation of an organization and aids in decision making.

Millions of men and women throughout the world list their occupations as accountant. In the United States alone, about 1.5 million accountants carry out these critical tasks.[2] The availability of jobs and relatively high starting salaries for talented graduates have made accounting one of the most popular business majors on college campuses.

This chapter begins by describing who uses accounting information. It also discusses the three basic categories of business activities in which all organizations participate or by which they are influenced: financing, investing, and operating. It explains the accounting process and then discusses the development of accounting statements from information about financial transactions. It presents the methods of interpreting these statements and examines the role of budgets in planning and controlling for a business.

USERS OF ACCOUNTING INFORMATION

People both inside and outside an organization rely on accounting information about it to help them make business decisions. Figure 19.1 lists the users of accounting information and the applications they find for it.

Managers within a business, government agency, or not-for-profit organization are the major users of accounting information, since it helps them to plan and control daily and long-range operations. Business owners and boards of trustees of not-for-profit groups also rely on accounting data to determine how well managers are operating the businesses or organizations. Union officials use accounting data in contract negotiations, and employees refer to it as they monitor their firms' productivity and profitability performance. The Solving an Ethical Controversy box debates the conflicting roles of auditors in supplying financial information to different parties.

To help employees understand how their work affects the bottom line, many companies share sensitive financial information with their employees and teach them how to understand and use financial statements. Furniture maker Herman Miller gives videos to employees that detail and explain all of the company's financial information. Manco, a distributor of tape and other consumer products to Wal-Mart and other large retailers, posts the company's revenues, profits, and expenses on large charts in its employee lunchroom. At Monsanto Canada, a life-sciences company, employees learn the basics of accounting at a 1-day seminar by playing The Finance Game, which gives them training in how to analyze the financial statements in Monsanto's annual report.[3] Not all companies, however, like the idea of sharing financial data with employees.

Figure 19.1 **Users of Accounting Information**

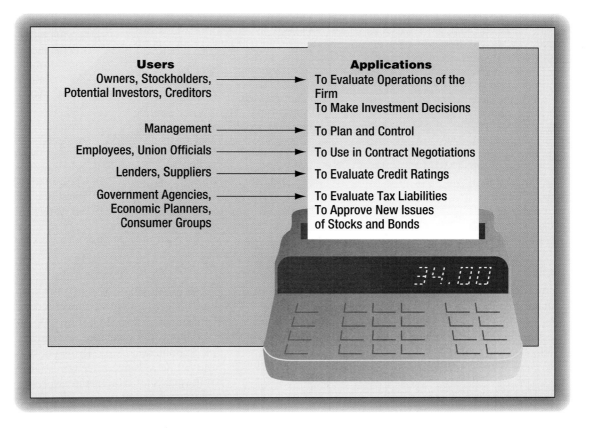

Users	Applications
Owners, Stockholders, Potential Investors, Creditors	To Evaluate Operations of the Firm / To Make Investment Decisions
Management	To Plan and Control
Employees, Union Officials	To Use in Contract Negotiations
Lenders, Suppliers	To Evaluate Credit Ratings
Government Agencies, Economic Planners, Consumer Groups	To Evaluate Tax Liabilities / To Approve New Issues of Stocks and Bonds

Outside the firm, potential investors evaluate accounting information to help them decide whether to buy its securities. Bankers and other lenders use accounting information to evaluate a potential client's financial soundness. The

Business Directory

accounting the practice of measuring, interpreting, and communicating financial information to support internal and external business decision making.

SOLVING AN ETHICAL CONTROVERSY

Should Company Auditors Act as Bean Counters or Gumshoes?

It was a miracle—or so everybody thought when Sunbeam achieved its remarkable 1997 turnaround with $123.1 million in earnings. But that dramatic turnaround never really happened. A three-month internal audit later revealed that the company's inflated statement resulted from improper accounting moves. For example, Sunbeam recognized revenue in improper periods by billing customers for products and then holding the goods for delivery later. It recorded some sales in 1997 that should have been recorded in 1998. It booked a number of sales with terms so flexible that the transactions were more like consignments than bona fide sales, especially when customers never finalized many of these transactions. Sunbeam also incorrectly assigned $337.6 million in costs to its recent restructuring—far more than allowed by generally accepted accounting principles. Once all these "missteps" were corrected, Sunbeam's financial reports showed a small loss for 1997 rather than a spectacular turnaround.

But how could this have happened? Auditors work inside and outside the company to guarantee that only proper procedures are used to prepare financial statements and reports, right? Well, there seems to be some question about an auditor's loyalties, duties, and responsibilities—even among auditors themselves.

On one hand, companies and accountants characterize their relationship with auditors as one of trust, one in which auditors offer advice but do not investigate company fraud. On the other hand, SEC chairman Arthur Levitt has called that relationship "a game of nods and winks" played to achieve the earnings that are forecast on Wall Street. SEC chief accountant Lynn Turner says, "Recent high-profile financial frauds raise questions about the efficiency of the audit process."

 Should Auditors Be Responsible for Uncovering Financial Fraud?

PRO

1. Auditors should consider as their clients those people in the general public who invest in companies, not the managers of the companies that hire them.

2. The Statement on Auditing Standards (SAS) Number 82 explicitly asserts that misstatements can be caused by either error or fraud—and that the auditor has the responsibility to detect misstatements caused by both error and fraud.

Internal Revenue Service and state tax officials use it to evaluate a company's tax payments for the year. Citizens' groups and government agencies use such information in assessing the efficiency of operations like a charitable organization, a local school system, or a city museum or zoo.

Accounting and the Environments of Business

Accountants play fundamental roles not only in business but also in other aspects of society. Their work influences each of the business environments discussed earlier in this book. They clearly contribute important information to help managers deal with the competitive and economic environments. Less obvious contributions help others to understand, predict, and react to the technological, regulatory, and social and cultural environments.

For example, Karen Stevenson Brown, a certified public accountant, provides consulting services to help health-care providers compete. Brown also contributes to the understanding of a significant social concern: the care of the elderly. She has combined her interest in computers and her concern for the welfare of older people in a Web site for consumers who need information related to eldercare. Recognizing that eldercare is growing in importance as the U.S. population ages, Brown designed the Eldercare Web, an online resource directory of articles and links to useful information that covers all aspects of the subject. Brown's site offers guidance to the families of elderly patients and other caregivers in finding information about laws, goods and services, living arrangements, and the social, physical, spiritual, and financial needs of elderly people.[4]

 www.eldercare.com

BUSINESS ACTIVITIES INVOLVING ACCOUNTING

The natural progression of a business begins with financing. Subsequent steps, including investing, lead to operat-

3. SAS 82 requires that any evidence of fraud, even if considered clearly inconsequential, be reported to an appropriate level of management.

CON

1. Auditors who investigate company fraud would lose the trust of their clients, making for a poor working relationship. Auditors tend to do all in their power to cooperate with and stay loyal to the companies that select and pay them.

2. Management conspiracy could prevent normal audit procedures from uncovering fraud. Even proper sampling procedures may not uncover fraudulent transactions.

3. Detection of fraud may be beyond normal auditor training; for example, an auditor may examine a forged document but may not be a handwriting expert.

4. Auditors may lack the practical business experience necessary to perform such high-level assessments.

5. Auditors, as well as management, face increased pressure to meet investors' earnings expectations.

SUMMARY

The American Institute of Certified Public Accountants (AICPA) is a professional organization that offers guidance for interpreting auditing rules, and it maintains a strict code of conduct. The organization continues to address problems such as revenue recognition, which were found to be involved in more than half of 200 fraud cases reviewed in the past ten years. Also, the AICPA has recently created a task force to issue recommendations for auditing merger acquisitions—another problem area.

The auditing profession is moving in several directions at once, including accounting, consulting, and giving investment advice, as well as serving the public interest with typical auditing procedures. As head of the AICPA, Olivia Kirtley believes the auditing code of conduct provides adequate protection against the potential for conflict of interest that may develop when an auditing firm serves as both auditor and consultant to the same company.

Some in the industry believe that what's needed is a stronger emphasis on training—both for fraud awareness and ethics. Kirtley notes that auditors are only one leg in "the three-legged stool to make sure statements are accurate." The other two legs are management and the company's audit committees. To help educate audit committees and keep them abreast of their duties, the AICPA is developing an informative newsletter just for them.

Sources: "The Auditor's Fraud Detection Responsibilities," Cotton & Company, LLP, accessed at www.cottoncpa.com, April 2, 1999; Robin G. Blumenthal, "Fully Accountable: Auditors Scrutinized after Spate of Frauds," *Barron's*, March 29, 1999, p. 21, accessed at www.djnr.com; The Associated Press, "Audit: 'Chainsaw Al' Turnaround a Myth," *Seattle Times*, October 21, 1998, accessed at www.seattle-times.com; Martha Brannigan, "Sunbeam Audit to Repudiate '97 Turnaround," *The Wall Street Journal*, October 20, 1998, pp. A3, A10; Ernst & Young, "Training, Technology Lacking in Fight against Corporate Fraud," *Canada NewsWire*, July 8, 1998, accessed at www.newswire.ca.

ing the business. All organizations, profit-oriented and not-for-profit, perform these three basic activities, and accounting plays a key role in each one:

1. *Financing activities* provide necessary funds to start a business and to expand it after it begins operating.

2. *Investing activities* provide valuable assets required to run a business.

3. *Operating activities* focus on selling goods and services, but they also consider expenses as important elements of sound financial management.

Thomas First and Thomas Scott performed these three activities during the start-up and growth of Nantucket Nectars, a producer of all-natural fruit juices. They financed their new venture from personal savings and money contributed by family members. They invested these funds in production equipment (a bottle-cap handpress), supplies (recycled bottles), and raw materials (cane sugar and canned and fresh fruit). First and Scott's operating activities involved promoting their juice through radio ads, hir-

ing recent college graduates to pass out free samples at college sporting events, and hiring distributors to deliver their juice drinks to retailers. The role of accounting has increased considerably since Nantucket Nectars began operating, driven by the firm's rapid growth. Since 1990, it has become one of the fastest-growing private companies in the United States with revenues reaching $30 million. First and Scott have now invested funds to expand their product line and to market their juice drinks in several foreign countries.[5]

 www.juiceguys.com

ACCOUNTING PROFESSIONALS

Accounting professionals work in a variety of areas in and for business firms, government agencies, and not-for-profit organizations. They can be classified as public, management, government, and not-for-profit accountants.

Figure 19.2	Accounting to Help Clients Improve Performance

YOUR HOUSE. YOUR COMPETITOR'S. HOW COME?

You may not care very much about acreage, square footage, or a driveway that doubles the length of your commute.

On the other hand, if you have the sense that your company isn't as profitable as it could be, maybe it's time to do something about it.

At Ernst & Young, we can help maximize the profitability of virtually every facet of your business.

Is your tax strategy optimal? Should you consider outsourcing? Can you get your products to market faster? How do your health-care costs compare with industry benchmarks? Is your information technology ready for the year 2000? Would a strategic acquisition make sense for you? How much rent should you pay in Kuala Lumpur?

We address these kinds of issues for our clients every day. And it sometimes takes only a single idea to make a multimillion-dollar difference in corporate profits.

So if you'd like to discuss anything related to your business, we hope you'll call.

Because even if you're perfectly happy with your house, you may still want to give some thought to an expansion.

Of your bottom line.

THERE ISN'T A BUSINESS WE CAN'T IMPROVE

EJ ERNST & YOUNG

Public Accountants

A **public accountant** provides accounting services to individuals or business firms for a fee. Most public accounting firms provide three basic services to clients: (1) auditing, or examining, financial records; (2) tax preparation, planning, and related services; and (3) management consulting. Since they are not employees of a client firm, public accountants are in a position to provide unbiased advice about the firm's financial condition.[6]

The four largest U.S. public accounting firms, the so-called "Big Four," are Arthur Andersen, Deloitte & Touche, Ernst & Young-KPMG Peat Marwick, and Price Waterhouse-Coopers & Lybrand. Together, the Big Four firms represent almost half of accounting's total revenues of $40 billion in the United States. An increasing proportion of Big Four revenues comes from management consulting services.[7] Ernst & Young, for example, employs 10,500 management consultants worldwide in the areas of information technology and performance improvement. The ad in Figure 19.2 suggests some of the ways they can help clients to improve operations and profitability.

Management Accountants

An accountant employed by a business other than a public accounting firm is called a **management accountant.** Such a person is responsible for collecting and recording financial transactions and preparing financial statements used by the firm's managers in decision making. Management accountants provide timely, relevant, accurate, and concise information that managers can use to operate their firms more effectively and more profitably than they could without this input.[8] In addition to preparing financial statements, a management accountant plays a major role in interpreting them. In presenting financial information to managers, a management accountant should provide answers to many important questions: Where is the company going? What advantageous opportunities await it? Do certain situations expose the company to excessive risk? Does the firm's information system provide detailed and timely information to all levels of management?[9] **Certified public accountants (CPAs)** demonstrate their accounting knowledge by meeting state requirements for education and experience and successfully completing a number of rigorous tests in accounting theory and practice, auditing, and law. Other accountants who meet specified educational and experience requirements and pass certification exams carry the titles *certified management accountant (CMA)* or *certified internal auditor (CIA).*

Management accountants frequently specialize in different aspects of accounting. A *cost accountant,* for example, determines the cost of goods and services and helps to set their prices. A *tax accountant* works to minimize a firm's tax bill and assumes responsibility for its federal, state, county, and city tax returns. An *internal auditor* examines the firm's financial practices to ensure that records include accurate data and that its operations comply with federal, state, and local laws and regulations.

Government and Not-for-Profit Accountants

Federal, state, and local governments also require accounting services. **Government accountants** and those who work for not-for-profit organizations perform professional services similar to those of management accountants. Instead of the business firm's reporting emphasis on measuring profit or loss, however, accountants in these situations concern themselves with determining how efficiently the organizations accomplish their objectives. Among the many government agencies that employ accountants are the Environmental Protection Agency, the FBI, the IRS, and state and local governments. Not-for-profit organizations, such as churches, labor unions, political parties, charities,

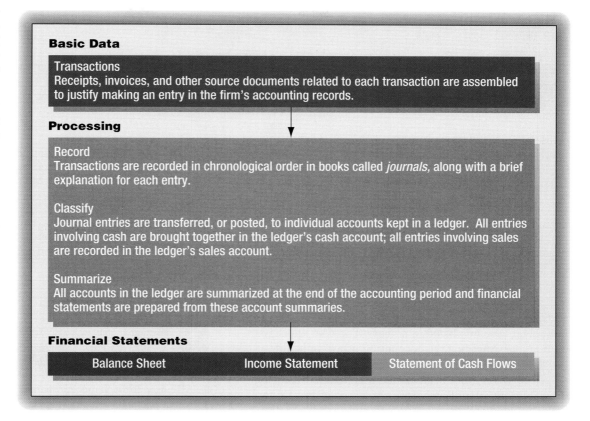

Figure 19.3 **The Accounting Process**

Basic Data

Transactions
Receipts, invoices, and other source documents related to each transaction are assembled to justify making an entry in the firm's accounting records.

Processing

Record
Transactions are recorded in chronological order in books called *journals,* along with a brief explanation for each entry.

Classify
Journal entries are transferred, or posted, to individual accounts kept in a ledger. All entries involving cash are brought together in the ledger's cash account; all entries involving sales are recorded in the ledger's sales account.

Summarize
All accounts in the ledger are summarized at the end of the accounting period and financial statements are prepared from these account summaries.

Financial Statements

Balance Sheet	Income Statement	Statement of Cash Flows

schools, hospitals, and universities, also hire accountants. In fact, the not-for-profit sector is one of the fastest-growing segments of accounting practice. An increasing number of not-for-profits are publishing financial information, because contributors want to know how the groups spend the money that they donate.

WWW. www.irs.ustreas.gov/prod/cover.html

THE ACCOUNTING PROCESS

Accounting deals with financial transactions between a firm and its employees, customers, suppliers, owners, bankers, and various government agencies. For example, weekly payroll checks result in cash outflows to compensate employees. A payment to a vender results in receipt of needed materials for the production process. Cash, check, and credit purchases by customers generate funds to cover the costs of operations and to earn a profit. Prompt payment of bills preserves the firm's credit rating and its future ability to obtain loans. The procedural cycle in which accountants convert data about individual transactions to financial statements is called the **accounting process**. Figure 19.3 illustrates the activities involved in the accounting process: recording, classifying, and summarizing transactions in order to produce financial statements for the firm's management and other interested parties.

The Impact of Computer Technology on the Accounting Process

For hundreds of years, recordkeepers have recorded, or *posted,* transactions through manual entries in *journals.* They then transferred the information, or posted it, to

Business Directory

accounting process the set of activities involved in converting information about individual transactions into financial statements.

BUSINESS HALL OF FAME

Need an Accountant? Consider a Virtual One

Owners of start-ups and small businesses need accounting expertise, but they often can't afford to hire management accountants or pay the high fees of big accounting firms. Entrepreneur Stephen King, a former CPA with Ernst & Young, saw an opportunity in this dilemma and started his own company, Virtual Growth Inc., to serve the needs of entrepreneurs and small firms.

"We're attempting to redefine accounting services for small businesses by putting together a network of small local accountants who together are part of a big data center," says King. "We supplement their technology with our own."

Virtual Growth's network of specialists offers clients all the accounting services they need from tax preparation and planning to accounting-system design and strategic business planning. The service works like this: A client contacts a local accountant

within the Virtual Growth network. As the client's business outgrows the services offered by the local accountant, he or she contacts other accountants in the network who provide the needed services.

According to King, computer technology enables Virtual Growth to function as a virtual chief financial officer and virtual accounting department for small firms. Clients transmit their financial information, such as new sales and invoices, by weekly or biweekly e-mail messages to Virtual Growth's

---

individual accounts listed in *ledgers*. The computer revolution has simplified the accounting process, making it faster and easier that the former manual method. Computerized accounting systems have eliminated most of the recording, classifying, and summarizing tasks once done by hand. As *point-of-sale terminals* replace cash registers, computer systems perform a number of functions each time they record sales. These terminals not only recall prices from computer system memory and maintain perpetual inventory counts of individual items in stock, but they also automatically perform accounting data-entry functions.

Accounting software programs are used widely in both large and small businesses today. They allow a do-it-once approach, in which a single input leads to automatic conversion of each sale into a journal entry, which then is stored until needed. Up-to-date financial statements and financial ratios then can be requested when needed by decision makers. Improvements in accounting software continue to make the process even faster and easier than it is now. Another benefit of automated accounting systems is their ability to produce financial reports that convert numbers into easily understood graphs.

Because the accounting needs of entrepreneurs and small businesses differ from those of large firms, accounting software makers have designed programs that meet specific user needs. Programs for entrepreneurial and small firms, referred to as *low-end accounting software,* include QuickBooks Pro, One-Write Plus Accounting, ACTPlus Accounting, DacEasy Accounting & Payroll, Great Plains Profit, Peachtree Complete Accounting, and M.Y.O.B. Accounting.[10]

www.myob.com

Designed for large companies, *high-end accounting software* packages include CODA Financials, Computron Financials, CA Masterpiece, SmartStream, System 21, Oracle Financials, PeopleSoft Financials, Tamaris, R/3, OneWorld, Open Enterprise Financial System, and Financial Management 2000.[11]

www.oracle.com

For firms that conduct business worldwide, software producers have introduced new accounting programs that handle all of a company's accounting information for every country in which it operates. This change represents an improvement over systems that require different programs for individual countries. The software handles different languages and currencies as well as the financial, legal, and tax requirements of each nation in which a firm conducts business.[12]

The Internet is also influencing the accounting process. As described in the opening vignette, Web sites have given Microsoft and other firms new options for presenting their financial information to interested users. Accounting firms are using the Internet to market their services and to communicate with their clients. Using e-mail, they can quickly and inexpensively send information to customers and receive input from them. The Business Hall of Fame box describes how one entrepreneur created a new accounting service via the Internet.

headquarters in New York. "Then they can download anything they want from within their data file anytime, which means they have access to financial information 24 hours a day," says King, "which is much more than most growing companies can say now."

During its first year in business, Virtual Growth formed electronic relationships with 80 small firms. One satisfied customer is AdOne Classified Network, a New York City provider of Internet-based classified ads. Brendan Burns of AdOne describes the firm's relationship with Virtual Growth as an ideal one, because the company gets the accounting expertise it

needs at a time when it can't afford and doesn't need a management accountant.

"Weekly, we send a package to Virtual Growth, our CPA firm, which inputs the data into a QuickBooks computer file," says Burns. "It then transfers the information to us electronically, all properly classified. We update it ourselves internally and produce accurate, timely financials each month."

QUESTIONS FOR CRITICAL THINKING

1. How does Stephen King exemplify the classic entrepreneur?

2. If you started your own company, would you feel comfortable with a virtual accounting relationship, or would you prefer a personal relationship with the person or persons handling your important financial information?

Sources: American Institute of Certified Public Accountants, "Pathfinder Profile—Stephen King: The Virtual World of Outsourcing," accessed May 13, 1999, at www.cpavision.org; Jill Andresky Fraser, "Our Business Is Small. How Can We Afford Top-Quality Accounting Expertise?" *Inc.*, June 1997, p. 96; Jill Andresky Fraser, "How Many Accountants Does It Take to Change an Industry?" *Inc.*, April 1997, pp. 63–69; and "The New Accountants," *Inc.*, April 1997, p. 68.

THE FOUNDATION OF THE ACCOUNTING SYSTEM

In order to provide reliable, consistent, and unbiased information to decision makers, accountants follow guidelines, or standards, known as *generally accepted accounting principles (GAAP)*. These principles encompass the conventions, rules, and procedures for determining acceptable accounting practices at a particular time. Accountants adhere to GAAP to create uniform financial statements for comparison between firms. GAAP ensure a solid basis for sound business decision making.

Two accounting statements form the foundation of the entire accounting system: the balance sheet and the income statement. The information found in these statements is calculated using the accounting equation and the double-entry system. A third statement, the statement of cash flows, is frequently prepared to focus specifically on the sources and uses of cash for a firm from its operating, investing, and financing activities.

The Accounting Equation

Four fundamental terms appear in the accounting equation: assets, equities, liabilities, and owners' equity. An **asset** is anything of value owned or leased by a business. Assets include land, buildings, supplies, cash, accounts receivable and notes

receivable (amounts owed to the business as payment for credit sales), and marketable securities.

Although most assets are tangible objects such as equipment, buildings, and inventories, intangible possessions such as patents and trademarks are often some of a firm's most important assets. This kind of asset is especially essential for computer software firms and biotechnology companies. Thomas First and Thomas Scott consider their brand name, All-Natural Nantucket Nectars, and their company slogan, "We're juice guys," as two of their most valuable assets, because these labels convey the natural goodness of the products and distinguish them from those of other drink producers. First and Scott promote their trademarked brand name and slogan in product advertising and at their Web site, as shown in Figure 19.4.

Equity is a claim against the assets of a business. Two major classifications of individuals hold equity in a firm: *creditors* (liability holders) and *owners*. A **liability** of a business is anything owed to creditors—that is, the claims of the firm's creditors. When the firm purchases inventory, land, or machinery on credit, the claims of creditors are

Business Directory

asset anything of value owned or leased by a business.

equity a claim against the assets of a business.

liability a claim against a firm's assets by a creditor.

| **Figure 19.4** | **Trademarks: Important Assets of Nantucket Nectars** |

shown as accounts payable or notes payable. Wages and salaries owed to employees also represent liabilities (known as *wages* payable).

Owners' equity represents the owners' initial investment in the business plus retained earnings that were not paid out over time in dividends. A strong owners' equity position often is used as evidence of a firm's financial strength and stability.

The basic **accounting equation** states that assets equal liabilities plus owners' equity. This equality reflects the financial position of a firm at any point in time:

$$Assets = Liabilities + Owners'\ equity$$

Since financing comes from either creditors or owners, the right side of the accounting equation also represents the business's financial structure.

The relationship expressed by the accounting equation underlies development of the balance sheet and the income statement. These two statements reflect the firm's current financial position and the most recent analysis of its income, expenses, and profits for interested parties inside and outside the firm. They provide a fundamental ba-

sis for planning activities and help staff members to attract new investors, secure borrowed funds, and complete tax returns.

FINANCIAL STATEMENTS

Financial statements provide managers with essential information they need to evaluate the *liquidity* position of an organization—its ability to meet current obligations and needs by converting assets into cash; the firm's profitability; and its overall financial health. The balance sheet, income statement, and statement of cash flows provide a foundation on which managers can base their decisions. By interpreting the data provided in these financial statements, the appropriate information can be communicated to internal decision makers and to interested parties outside the organization.

The Balance Sheet

A firm's **balance sheet** shows its financial position on a particular date. It is similar to a photograph of the firm's assets together with its liabilities and owners' equity at a specific moment in time. Balance sheets must be prepared at regular intervals, since a firm's managers and other internal parties often request this information every day, week, or at least every month. On the other hand, external users, such as stockholders or industry analysts, may use this information less frequently, perhaps every quarter or once a year.

The accounting equation provides an important aid to understanding as a diagram that is explained by the balance sheet. Listing the various assets on the balance sheet indicates sources of the firm's strengths—where it gets money. These assets, shown in descending order of liquidity (convertibility to cash), represent the *uses* that management has made of available funds. On the other side of the equation, liabilities and owners' equity indicate the *sources* of the firm's assets. Liabilities reflect the claims of creditors—financial institutions or bondholders that have made loans to the firm, suppliers that have provided goods and services on credit, and others to be

Business Directory

owners' equity all claims of the proprietor, partners, or stockholders against the assets of a firm, equal to the excess of assets over liabilities.

accounting equation the basic concept that assets equal liabilities plus owners' equity.

balance sheet a statement of a firm's financial position on a particular date.

paid, such as federal, state, and local tax authorities. Owners' equity represents the owners' claims (those of stockholders, in the case of a corporation) against the firm's assets. It amounts to the excess of all assets over liabilities.

Figure 19.5 shows the balance sheet for Rocky Mountain

Ski Patrol, a Pueblo, Colorado, retailer of ski equipment, clothing, group tours, and instruction. The basic accounting equation is illustrated by the three classifications of assets, liabilities, and owners' equity on the company's balance sheet. Total assets must equal the total of liabilities and owners' equity.

Figure 19.5   Balance Sheet for Rocky Mountain Ski Patrol

① Current Assets
Cash and other liquid assets that can or will be converted to cash or used within 1 year

② Fixed Assets
Relatively permanent plant, property, and equipment expected to be used for periods longer than 1 year

③ Current Liabilities
Claims of creditors that are to be repaid within 1 year

④ Long-Term Liabilities
Debts that come due 1 year or more after the date of the balance sheet

⑤ Owners' Equity
Claims of the proprietor, partners, or stockholders against the assets of a firm; the excess of assets over liabilities

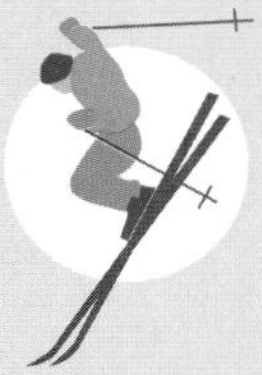

ROCKY MOUNTAIN SKI PATROL
Balance Sheet
as of December 31, 199X

ASSETS

① *Current Assets*
Cash	$ 8,000	
Marketable Securities	30,000	
Accounts Receivable	194,000	
Inventory	124,000	
Total Current Assets		$ 356,000

② *Fixed Assets*
Store Equipment	$ 112,000	
Furniture and Fixtures	40,000	
Total Fixed Assets		$ 152,000
Total Assets		$ 508,000

LIABILITIES AND OWNERS' EQUITY

③ *Current Liabilities*
Accounts Payable	$ 82,000	
Current Installments of Long-Term Debt	30,000	
Accrued Expenses	14,000	
Income Taxes Payable	$ 12,000	
Total Current Liabilities		$ 138,000

④ *Long-Term Liabilities*
Long-Term Notes Payable	$ 60,000	
Total Long-Term Liabilities		$ 60,000
Total Liabilities		$ 198,000

⑤ *Owners' Equity*
Common Stock (160,000 shares @ $1)	$ 160,000	
Retained Earnings	150,000	
Total Owners' Equity		$ 310,000
Total Liabilities and Owners' Equity		$ 508,000

The Income Statement

While the balance sheet reflects a firm's financial situation at a specific point in time, the income statement represents the *flow* of resources that reveals the performance of the organization over a specific time period. Resembling a motion picture rather than a photograph, the **income statement** is a financial record summarizing a firm's financial performance in terms of revenues, expenses, and profits over a given time period.

In addition to reporting the firm's ultimate profit or loss results, the income statement helps decision makers to focus on overall revenues and the costs involved in generating these revenues. Managers of a not-for-profit organization use this statement to determine whether its revenues from contributions and other sources will cover its operating costs. Finally, the income statement provides much of the basic data needed to calculate the financial ratios managers use in planning and controlling activities. Figure 19.6 shows an income statement for Rocky Mountain Ski Patrol.

An income statement (sometimes called a *profit and loss* or *P&L statement)* begins with total sales or revenues generated during a year, quarter, or month. Subsequent lines then deduct all of the costs related to producing the revenues. Typical categories of costs include administrative and marketing expenses, costs involved in producing the firm's good or service, interest, and taxes; after all of them have been subtracted, the remaining net income may be distributed to the firm's owners (stockholders, proprietors, or partners) or reinvested in the company as retained earnings. The final figure on the income statement—net income after taxes—is the well-known **bottom line.**

The Statement of Cash Flows

In addition to the income statement and the balance sheet, many firms require accountants to prepare a third accounting statement—the statement of cash flows. Every company listed on an organized stock exchange must prepare a statement of cash flows and submit it as part of the annual package of registration information. In addition, commercial lenders often require that a borrower submit a statement of cash flows. The **statement of cash flows** provides investors and creditors with relevant information about a firm's cash receipts and cash payments for its operations, investments, and financing during an accounting period. Figure 19.7 shows the statement of cash flows for Rocky Mountain Ski Patrol.

The fact that cash flow is the lifeblood of every organization is evidenced by the business failure rate. Many owners of firms that fail put the blame on inadequate cash flow. The Business Tool Kit box offers ways in which self-employed professionals can improve cash flow. Proponents of the statement of cash flows hope that its preparation and scrutiny by affected parties will prevent financial disaster for otherwise profitable firms, too many of which are forced into bankruptcy due to a lack of funds needed to continue day-to-day operations.

FINANCIAL RATIO ANALYSIS

Accounting professionals fulfill important responsibilities beyond preparing financial statements. In a more critical role, they help managers to interpret the statements by comparing data about the firm's current activities to that for previous periods and to results posted by other companies in the industry. **Ratio analysis** is one of the most commonly used tools for measuring the firm's liquidity, profitability, and reliance on debt financing, as well as the effectiveness of management's use of its resources. This analysis also allows comparisons with other firms and with the firm's own past performance.

Ratios assist managers by interpreting actual performance and making comparisons with what should have happened. Comparisons with ratios of similar companies help managers to understand their firm's performance relative to competitors' results. These industry standards serve as important yardsticks and help to pinpoint problem areas as well as areas of excellence. Ratios for the current accounting period also may be compared with similar calculations for previous periods to spot developing trends. Ratios can be classified according to their specific purposes. The four major categories of financial ratios are summarized in Table 19.1.

Liquidity Ratios

A firm's ability to meet its short-term obligations when they must be paid is measured by **liquidity ratios.** Increasing liquidity reduces the likelihood that a firm will face emergencies caused by the need to raise

Business Directory

income statement a financial record of a company's revenues, expenses, and profits over a period of time.

statement of cash flows a statement of a firm's cash receipts and cash payments that presents information on its sources and uses of cash.

funds to repay loans. On the other hand, firms with low liquidity may be forced to choose between default or borrowing from high-cost lending sources to meet their maturing obligations.

Two commonly used liquidity ratios are the current ratio and the acid-test ratio. The *current ratio* compares current assets to current liabilities, giving managers information about the firm's ability to pay its current debts as they

Figure 19.6 **Income Statement for Rocky Mountain Ski Patrol**

① Revenues
Funds received from sales of goods and services and from interest payments, dividends, royalties, and rents (grants and contributions can be revenue sources for not-for-profit firms)

② Cost of Goods Sold
Cost of merchandise or services that generate the firm's revenue, including a *Purchases* section for retailers and *Cost of Goods Manufactured* for producers

③ Selling Expenses
Advertising, selling, and other expenses incurred in marketing and distributing the firm's output

④ General and Administrative Expenses
Office salaries and supplies, rent, and other operational expenses not directly related to the acquisition, production, or sale of the firm's output

⑤ Net Income
Profit or loss incurred over a specific period, determined by subtracting all expenses from revenues

ROCKY MOUNTAIN SKI PATROL
Income Statement
Year Ending December 31, 199X

① Revenues
Gross Sales — $ 600,000
Less: Sales Returns and Allowances — 16,000
Net Sales — $ 584,000

② Cost of Goods Sold
Beginning Inventory — $ 130,000
Purchases during Year — 246,000
Cost of Goods Available for Sale — 376,000
Less: Ending Inventory — 112,000
Cost of Goods Sold — $ 264,000

Gross Profit — $ 320,000

Operating Expenses
③ Selling Expenses — $ 150,000
④ General and Administrative Expenses — 96,000
Total Operating Expenses — $ 246,000

Net Income before Taxes — 74,000
Less: Income Taxes — 14,000

⑤ Net Income — $ 60,000

| Figure 19.7 | Statement of Cash Flows for Rocky Mountain Ski Patrol |

① Operating Activities
The nuts & bolts, day-to-day activities of a company carrying on its regular business.

② Investing Activities
Transactions by a company to accumulate or use cash in ways that will affect operating activities in the future.

③ Financing Activities
Ways to transfer cash to/from outsiders and/or owners.

④ Net Change in Cash for the Year
A reconcilement of cash from the beginning to the end of an accounting period.

ROCKY MOUNTAIN SKI PATROL
Statement of Cash Flows
Year Ending December 31, 199X

① Cash flows from operating activities:

Cash received from customers	$ 608,000	
Cash paid to suppliers and employees	(521,000)	
Interest paid	(12,000)	
Income taxes paid	(8,000)	
Interest and dividends received	5,000	
Net cash provided by operating activities		$ 72,000

② Cash flows from investing activities:

Proceeds from sale of marketable securities	$ 9,000	
Payments for purchase of equipment	(11,000)	
Net cash provided by investing activities		$ (2,000)

③ Cash flows from financing activities:

Repayment of short-term notes	$ (64,000)	
Proceeds from issuance of long-term debt	40,000	
Payment of dividends	(60,000)	
		$ (84,000)

④ Net change in cash for the year — (14,000)

Cash balance, beginning of year — 22,000

Cash balance, end of year — $ 8,000

mature. The current ratio of Rocky Mountain Ski Patrol can be computed as follows:

$$\text{Current ratio} = \frac{\text{Current assets}}{\text{Current liabilities}} = \frac{\$356{,}000}{\$138{,}000} = 2.6 \text{ to } 1$$

In other words, Rocky Mountain Ski Patrol has $2.60 of current assets for every $1.00 of current liabilities. In general, a current ratio of 2 to 1 is considered to indicate satisfactory financial condition. This rule of thumb must be considered along with other factors, such

Remedies for the Cash-Flow Blues

The increase in outsourcing by America's businesses has created self-employment opportunities for many people. But while they often find plentiful work, many independent contractors from writers to Web designers are finding themselves in a cash-flow crunch. Their problem stems from slow-paying clients. It's not unusual for a self-employed person to wait several months to receive payment for completed work. Experts suggest the following measures to help maintain positive cash flow:

▼ Ask for one-third to one-half of your contract fee upfront. This initial payment will help you to pay your expenses as they fall due.

▼ Specify payment terms in writing in the job contract, specifying the dates you expect to receive payment. This provision will often shorten your wait for payment.

▼ Include a late-fee penalty in your contract, charging your client 2 percent when your payment is 30 days overdue. This extra cost will encourage your client to pay on time.

▼ When a client doesn't make good on a promise that your check is in the mail, quit in the middle of the project. It's not worth your time or frustration to continue the battle of getting paid.

Sources: Joann S. Lublin, "Waiting for Payment Vexes Self-Employed," *The Wall Street Journal*, September 3, 1997, pp. B1, B2; Deidra Ann Parrish, "Getting the Cash to Flow Your Way," *Black Enterprise*, July 1997, pp. 80–88; and Sally-Jo Bowman, "How to Weigh Your Options: Freelancing Full-Time," *Writer's Digest*, November 1996, pp. 22–24.

as the nature of the business, the season of the year, and the quality of the company's management. Rocky Mountain Ski Patrol management and other interested parties are likely to evaluate this ratio of 2.6 to 1 by comparing it to ratios for previous operating periods and to industry averages.

The *acid-test* (or *quick)* ratio measures the ability of a firm to meet its debt payments on short notice. This ratio compares *quick assets*—highly liquid current assets—against current liabilities. It excludes inventory or prepaid expenses, considering only cash, marketable securities, and accounts receivable.

Table 19.1	Financial Ratios and What They Measure
Ratio	**What It Measures**
LIQUIDITY RATIOS	
Current ratio Acid-test ratio	The firm's ability to meet its short-term obligations when they must be paid.
PROFITABILITY RATIOS	
Earnings per share Return on sales Return on equity	The firm's ability to generate revenues in excess of its operating costs and other expenses.
LEVERAGE RATIO	
Debt to owners' equity	The extent to which the firm relies on debt financing.
ACTIVITY RATIO	
Inventory turnover	The effectiveness of uses of the firm's resources.

Rocky Mountain Ski Patrol's current balance sheet lists the following quick assets: cash ($8,000), marketable securities ($30,000), and accounts receivable ($194,000). The firm's acid-test ratio is computed as:

$$\text{Acid-test ratio} = \frac{\text{Quick assets}}{\text{Current liabilities}} = \frac{\$232,000}{\$138,000} = 1.7 \text{ to } 1$$

Because the traditional rule of thumb for an adequate acid-test ratio is 1 to 1, Rocky Mountain Ski Patrol appears to be in a good short-term credit position. However, the same cautions apply here as for the current ratio. The ratio should be compared with industry averages and data from previous operating periods in determining its appropriateness for the firm.

Profitability Ratios

Some ratios measure the organization's overall financial performance by evaluating its ability to generate revenues in excess of operating costs and other expenses. These measures are called **profitability ratios.** To compute these ratios, accountants compare the firm's earnings with total sales or investments. Over a period of time, profitability ratios may reveal the effectiveness of management in operating the business. Three important profitability ratios are *earnings per share, return on sales,* and *return on equity.*

$$\text{Earnings per share} = \frac{\text{Net income after taxes}}{\text{Common shares outstanding}}$$

$$= \frac{\$60,000}{160,000} = \$0.375$$

$$\text{Return on sales} = \frac{\text{Net income}}{\text{Net sales}} = \frac{\$60,000}{\$584,000}$$

$$= 10.3 \text{ percent}$$

$$\text{Return on equity} = \frac{\text{Net income}}{\text{Total owners' equity}}$$

$$= \frac{\$60,000}{\$310,000} = 19.4 \text{ percent}$$

All of these ratios support positive evaluations of the current operations of Rocky Mountain Ski Patrol. For example, the return on sales ratio indicates that the firm realized a profit of 10.3 cents for every dollar of sales. Although this ratio varies widely among business firms, Rocky Mountain Ski Patrol compares favorably with retailers in general, which average about 5 percent return on sales. However, this ratio, like the other profitability ratios, should be evaluated in relation to profit forecasts, past performance, or more specific industry averages to enhance the interpretation of results. Similarly, while the firm's re-

turn on equity of almost 20 percent appears to reflect satisfactory performance, the degree of risk in the industry also must be considered.

Profitability ratios are widely used indicators of business success. For example, Cisco Systems of San Jose, California, earned one of the highest rankings in the nation for growth companies when its earnings per share ratio reflected a 72 percent increase over 5 years. Cisco, a technology firm that supplies many of the products needed to make the Internet work, plans to continue its high earnings growth. It recently formed a strategic alliance with Microsoft to create industry standards for secure networks. Cisco is also the primary contractor in MCI's $3 billion contract to rewire and replace the U.S. Postal Service computer system.[13]

www.cisco.com

Leverage Ratios

Leverage ratios measure the extent to which a firm relies on debt financing. They provide particularly interesting information to potential investors and lenders. If management has assumed too much debt in financing the firm's operations, problems may arise in meeting future interest payments and repaying outstanding loans. Relying too heavily on debt financing can lead to bankruptcy, as described in the Business Hall of Shame box. More generally, both investors and lenders may prefer to deal with firms whose owners have invested enough of their own money in their companies to avoid overreliance on borrowing. The *debt to owners' equity ratio* helps analysts to evaluate these concerns.

$$\text{Debt to owners' equity ratio} = \frac{\text{Total liabilities}}{\text{Owners' equity}}$$

$$= \frac{\$198,000}{\$310,000} = 64 \text{ percent}$$

A debt to equity ratio greater than 1 indicates that a firm is relying more on debt financing than owners' equity. Clearly, Rocky Mountain Ski Patrol's owners have invested considerably more than the total amount of liabilities shown on the firm's balance sheet.

Activity Ratios

Activity ratios measure the effectiveness of management's use of the firm's resources. The most frequently used activity ratio, the *inventory turnover ratio,* indicates the number of times merchandise moves through a business.

BUSINESS HALL OF SHAME

The Perils of Taking on Too Much Debt

Some South Korean companies are in trouble. Saddled with mountains of debt and unable to repay their bank loans, companies large and small are going bankrupt. "How many companies will go bust is hard to say," says Lee Keun Mo, research director at ING Barings Securities Ltd. in Seoul, the country's capital. "But firms with poor cash flow and with debt-equity ratios in excess of 10 will suffer."

One company that suffered was Woosung Construction, which collapsed beneath the weight of a perilously high debt to equity ratio of 17.2 and a total debt burden of $1.9 billion. Other casualties include firms owned by some of Korea's largest *chaebols*, or conglomerates. Hanbo Steel & General Construction, Korea's second-largest steel producer, owned by its 14th largest conglomerate, went bankrupt after its debt grew to 20 times its equity capital. Another conglomerate, Sammi Steel, folded under debt of $2.2 billion and a debt to equity ratio of 6.4.

To prevent the bankruptcy of other debt-ridden firms—including Kia Motors, the nation's second-largest car maker, Oriental Brewery, and Jinro, a rice-wine maker—the South Korean government and the country's financial institutions have placed near-bankrupt firms under bankruptcy protection. Creditors are lowering interest rates on existing loans, extending repayment periods, and issuing emergency loans.

"These incidents have given companies a good lesson that there's a great risk in borrowing too much," says Han Seung Soo, South Korea's former finance minister. Many of South Korea's industrial giants sowed the seeds of financial problems when they borrowed too much money to finance rapid growth. The South Korean government encouraged banks to extend credit to fast-growing firms to fuel the nation's economic growth. But when the once-booming economy started to slow, the borrowers' revenues decreased and they couldn't repay their bank loans.

Unpaid loans have posed serious threats to some South Korean banks,

giving them liquidity problems of their own. When Hanbo Steel went bankrupt, it owed 1.1 trillion won to Korea First Bank, a sum that amounted to 60 percent of the bank's capital. As a result, banks have tightened their lending policies. "Bankers are now dead set against making loans under political pressure," says Kim Hun Soo, head of research at Merrill Lynch & Company in Seoul. "They can resist by saying, 'We almost went kaput because of you guys.'"

QUESTIONS FOR CRITICAL THINKING

1. **Who do you think is most responsible for the financial crisis in South Korea?**

2. **What lessons can other businesspeople learn from the bankruptcies of South Korean companies?**

Sources: Donald Macintyre, "Korea Thinks Small," *Time*, April 19, 1999, accessed at www.pathfinder.com; Namju Cho, "Payment Delay Indicates Bailouts Need Shoring Up in South Korea," *The Wall Street Journal*, July 30, 1997, p. A10; and Andrew Pollack, "Koreans Place Kia Motors under Bankruptcy Shield," *New York Times*, July 16, 1997, p. C6.

$$\text{Inventory turnover ratio} = \frac{\text{Cost of goods sold}}{\text{Average inventory}}$$

$$= \frac{\$264,000}{\$121,000} = 2.2 \text{ times}$$

Average inventory for Rocky Mountain Ski Patrol is determined by adding the January 1 beginning inventory of $130,000 and the December 31 ending inventory of $112,000, as shown on the income statement, and dividing by 2. Comparing the 2.2 inventory turnover ratio with industry standards gives a measure of efficiency. Furniture and jewelry retailers average an annual turnover of 1.5 times. A supermarket's turnover rate can be as high as once every 2 weeks.

The four categories of financial ratios relate balance sheet and income statement data to one another and assist management in pinpointing a firm's strengths and weak-

nesses. Large, multiproduct firms that operate in diverse markets use sophisticated information systems to update their financial ratios every day or even every hour. Each company's management must decide on an appropriate review schedule to avoid the costly and time-consuming mistake of overmonitoring.

BUDGETING

Although the financial statements discussed in this chapter focus on past business activities, they also provide the basis for planning in the future. A **budget** is a planning and controlling tool that reflects the firm's expected sales revenues, operating expenses, and cash receipts and outlays. It quantifies the firm's plans for a specified future period. Since it reflects management estimates of expected sales, cash inflows and outflows, and costs, the budget serves as a financial blueprint. It becomes the standard for comparison against actual performance.

Budget preparation is frequently a time-consuming task that involves many people from various departments within the firm. The complexity of the budgeting process varies with the size and complexity of the organization. Large corporations such as Sony, Intel, and Boeing maintain complex and sophisticated budgeting systems. Their budgets help managers to integrate their numerous divisions in addition to serving as planning and controlling tools. But budgeting in both large and small firms is similar to household budgeting in its purpose: to match income and expenses in a way that accomplishes objectives and correctly times cash inflows and outflows.

Since the accounting department is an organization's financial nerve center, it provides much of the data for budget development. The overall master, or operating, budget is actually a composite of many individual budgets for separate units of the firm. These typically include the production budget, cash budget, capital expenditures budget, advertising budget, and sales budget.

At the HON Company, a maker of office furniture in the United States and Canada, accountants develop a master budget as a composite of individual function budgets such as the sales budget. The sales budget, in turn, is composed of data from a territory budget and a marketing budget. Budgets are usually prepared annually, but some firms prepare them monthly or quarterly for control purposes. HON managers, for example, prepare budgets four times a year, because the office furniture industry is highly cyclical and its variations generally reflect the state of the economy as a whole. Department managers work together to produce an updated four-quarter budget at the start of each quarter. This continuous updating helps managers to react quickly to unexpected changes in the industry and economy.[14]

Figure 19.8 illustrates a sample cash budget for Rocky Mountain Ski Patrol. Management has set a $6,000 minimum cash balance. The cash budget indicates months in which the firm will invest excess funds to earn interest rather than leaving them idle in a bank account. The document also indicates periods in which the firm will need temporary loans to finance operations. Finally, the cash budget produces a tangible standard against which to compare actual cash inflows and outflows.

INTERNATIONAL ACCOUNTING

Today, accounting procedures and practices must be adapted to accommodate an international business envi-

> ## They said it
>
> "I gave him an unlimited budget and he exceeded it."
>
> Edward Bennett Williams
> (1920–1988)
> Former owner, Washington
> Redskins football club
> (referring to former
> Head Coach George Allen)

ronment. Nestlé, the giant chocolate and food products multinational, operates throughout the world. It derives 98 percent of its revenues from outside Switzerland, its headquarters country. International accounting practices for global firms must reliably translate the financial statements of the firm's international affiliates, branches, and subsidiaries and convert data about foreign-currency transactions to dollars. Also, the euro, Europe's new single currency, will influence the accounting and financial reporting processes of firms operating in European countries.[15]

Exchange Rates

As defined in Chapter 3, an *exchange rate* is the ratio at which a country's currency can be exchanged for other currencies or gold. Currencies can be treated as goods to be bought and sold. Like the price of any good or service, currency prices change daily according to supply and demand. Exchange rate fluctuations affect accounting entries in ways that complicate accounting practices for single-currency transactions.

Accountants who deal with international transactions must appropriately record their firms' foreign sales and purchases. As mentioned earlier, however, new, high-end accounting software helps firms to handle all of their international transactions within a single program. An international firm's consolidated financial statements must reflect any gains or losses due to fluctuations in exchange rates during specific periods of time. Financial statements that cover operations in two or more countries also need to treat fluctuations consistently to allow for comparison.

International Accounting Standards

The International Accounting Standards Committee (IASC) was established in 1973 to promote worldwide consistency in financial reporting practices. The IASC is recognized worldwide as the body with sole responsibility and authority to issue pronouncements on international accounting standards. The International Federation of Accountants supports the work of the IASC and develops international guidelines for auditing, ethics, education, and management accounting. Every 5 years, an international congress is held to judge progress in achieving consistency in standards. This meeting works toward the objective of enchancing comparability between financial data in varying nations and currencies.

Figure 19.8 **Six-Month Cash Budget for Rocky Mountain Ski Patrol**

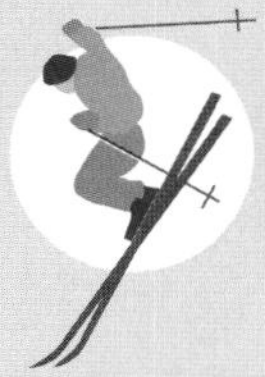

ROCKY MOUNTAIN SKI PATROL
P.O. Box 2646
Pueblo, Colorado

Sample Cash Budget
January–June 199X

	January	February	March	April	May	June
Beginning Monthly Balance	$ 6,000	$ 6,000	$ 6,000	$ 6,000	$ 6,000	$ 6,000
Add: Cash Receipts (collections from customers, interest receipts, and other cash inflows)	4,000	14,000	12,000	10,000	8,000	18,000
Cash Available for Firm's Use	$10,000	$ 20,000	$ 18,000	$ 16,000	$ 14,000	$ 24,000
Deduct: Cash Disbursements (for payroll, materials, income taxes, utilities, interest payments, etc.)	10,000	8,000	10,000	12,000	6,000	14,000
Preliminary Monthly Balance	$ - 0 -	$ 12,000	$ 8,000	$ 4,000	$ 8,000	$ 10,000
Minimum Required Cash Balance	6,000	6,000	6,000	6,000	6,000	6,000
Excess (or Deficiency)	(6,000)	6,000	2,000	(2,000)	2,000	4,000
Short-Term Investment of Excess			2,000		2,000	4,000
Liquidation of Short-Term Investment				2,000		
Short-Term Loan to Cover Deficiency	6,000					
Repayment of Short-Term Loan		6,000				
Ending Monthly Balance	$ 6,000	$ 6,000	$ 6,000	$ 6,000	$ 6,000	$ 6,000

www. **www.iasc.org.uk/frame/index.html**

The formation of a single European market and NAFTA have led to wide recognition of the necessity for comparability and uniformity of international accounting standards. An increasing number of institutional investors are buying shares in foreign multinational corporations. In response to global investors' needs, more and more firms are beginning to report their financial information according to International Accounting Standards (IAS). This practice helps investors to compare the financial results of firms in different countries.[16]

SUMMARY OF LEARNING GOALS

1. Explain the functions of accounting and its importance to the firm's management and to outside parties, such as investors, creditors, and government agencies.

Accountants measure, interpret, and communicate financial information to parties inside and outside the firm to support effective decision making. Accountants are responsible for gathering, recording, and interpreting financial information to management. They also provide financial information on the status and operations of the firm for evaluation by such outside parties as government agencies, stockholders, potential investors, and lenders.

2. Identify the three basic business activities involving accounting.

Accounting plays key roles in financing activities, which help to start and expand an organization; investing activities, which provide the assets it needs to continue operating; and operating activities, which focus on selling goods and services and paying expenses incurred in regular operations.

3. Describe the roles played by public, management, government, and not-for-profit accountants.

Public accountants are independent organizations of individual providers of accounting services, such as tax statement preparation, management consulting, and accounting system design, to other firms or individuals for a fee. Management accountants are responsible for collecting and recording financial transactions, preparing financial statements, and interpreting them for managers in their own firms. Government and not-for-profit accountants perform many of the same functions as management accountants, but their analysis emphasizes how effectively the organization or agency is operating rather than its profits and losses.

4. Outline the steps in the accounting process.

The accounting process involves recording, classifying, and summarizing data about transactions and then using this information to produce financial statements for the firm's managers and other interested parties. Transactions are recorded chronologically in journals, posted in ledgers, and then summarized in accounting statements.

5. Explain the functions of the balance sheet, the income statement, and the statement of cash flows, and identify the major components of these financial statements.

The balance sheet shows the financial position of a company on a particular date. The three major classifications of balance sheet data represent the components of the accounting equation: assets, liabilities, and owners' equity. The income statement shows the results of a firm's operations over a specific period. It focuses on the firm's activities—its revenues and expenditures—and the resulting profit or loss during the period. The major components of the income statement are revenues, cost of goods sold, expenses, and profit or loss. The statement of cash flows indicates a firm's cash receipts and cash payments during an accounting period. It shows the sources and uses of cash in the three basic business activities of financing, investing, and operating.

6. Discuss how financial ratios are used in analyzing a firm's financial strengths and weaknesses.

Liquidity ratios measure a firm's ability to meet short-term obligations. Examples are the current ratio and acid-test ratio.

Profitability ratios assess the overall financial performance of the business. Earnings per share, return on sales, and return on owners' equity are examples. Leverage ratios, such as the debt to equity ratio, measure the extent to which the firm relies on debt to finance its operations. Activity ratios, such as the inventory turnover ratio, measure how effectively a firm uses its resources. Financial ratios assist managers and outside evaluators in comparing a firm's current financial information with that of previous years and with results for other firms in the same industry.

7. Describe the role of budgets in a business.

Budgets are financial guidelines for future periods reflecting expected sales revenues, operating expenses, and/or cash receipts and outlays. They represent management expectations for future occurrences based on plans that have been made. Budgets serve as important planning and controlling tools by providing standards against which actual performance can be measured.

8. Explain how exchange rates influence international accounting practices and the importance of uniform financial statements for global business.

An exchange rate is the ratio at which a country's currency can be exchanged for other currencies or gold. Daily changes in exchange rates affect the accounting entries for sales and purchases of firms involved in international markets. These fluctuations create either losses or gains for particular companies. Data about international financial transactions must be translated into the currency of the country in which the parent company resides. The International Accounting Standards Committee was established to provide worldwide consistency in financial reporting practices and comparability and uniformity of international accounting standards.

TEN BUSINESS TERMS YOU NEED TO KNOW

accounting	owners' equity
accounting process	accounting equation
asset	balance sheet
equity	income statement
liability	statement of cash flows

Other Important Business Terms

public accountant	ratio analysis
management accountant	liquidity ratios
certified public accountant (CPA)	profitability ratios
	leverage ratios
government accountant	activity ratios
bottom line	budget

REVIEW QUESTIONS

1. Who are the major users of accounting information, and how do they use this data?
2. In which three major business activities do accountants play major roles?
3. How does a public accountant differ from a management accountant?
4. What are the steps in the accounting process? How does the use of computers influence the accounting process?
5. Explain the following statement: "The balance sheet is a detailed expression of the accounting equation."
6. What are the primary purposes of the balance sheet, the income statement, and the statement of cash flows?
7. How do the four categories of financial ratios discussed in the chapter help managers and people outside the firm to evaluate its financial position?
8. List the similarities and differences between budgeting and the process of developing financial statements.
9. Why do firms prepare budgets?
10. What financial statements are affected by exchange rates in international accounting? What are the benefits of uniform international financial standards?

QUESTIONS FOR CRITICAL THINKING

1. You've just received a letter from a not-for-profit organization asking you to make a donation to the group. You would like to support the group, but before writing a check, you want to know how the organization spends the funds it receives from donors. You write to the not-for-profit and ask for some financial information. Which financial statement would you evaluate most closely in determining whether you would make a donation?
2. Your grandfather sends you a large check for your birthday, asking that you use the money to buy stock in a company. He recommends that you check out firms' financial ratios before you invest. Which ratios would be most helpful to you in deciding where to invest your grandfather's gift?
3. Suppose that you are a management accountant for a firm that operates in 12 European countries. You need to unify many accounting and financial reporting processes by restating data from individual country currencies such as the peso and lira to Europe's new single currency, the euro. Which financial statements and which components of these statements will be affected by the adoption of the new single currency?
4. In the past, accountants were often called *bean counters.* Today, accountants are taking on increasing responsibility for helping their firms to succeed in the fast-changing business environment. One writer has suggested that an accountant must assume the roles of artist, educator, and visionary. Describe how accountants can fulfill these roles.
5. Suppose that you are offered a job with a small, private company that doesn't publish its financial information. Before you accept the position, you ask the owner if you can look over the firm's financial statements to determine its condition. The owner laughs and tells you that she doesn't let *anybody* other than her accountant see that financial information. What could you tell your prospective employer that might convince her to share financial data with her employees and train them to understand how their work affects the bottom line?

Experiential Exercise

Directions: Adapting the format of Figure 19.8, Six-Month Cash Budget for Rocky Mountain Ski Patrol, prepare on a separate sheet of paper your personal one-month cash budget for next month. Keep in mind the following suggestions as you prepare your budget:

1. Beginning Monthly Balance. This amount could be based on a minimum cash balance you keep in your checking account and should include only the cash available for your use. Money such as that invested in a 401(k) retirement plan should not be included.
2. Cash Receipts. In addition to income from your salary or wages, include other cash sources such as cash gifts you anticipate receiving, as well as income from part-time or self-employment work, dividends and interest, or tax refunds.
3. Cash Disbursements. When estimating next month's disbursements, include any of the following that apply to your situation:

▼ Household expenses (mortgage/rent, utilities, maintenance, home furnishings, telephone, cable TV, household supplies, groceries)

▼ Education (tuition, fees, textbooks, supplies)

▼ Work (transportation, meals)

▼ Clothing (purchases, cleaning, laundry)

▼ Automobile (auto payments, fuel, repairs)

▼ Insurance (life, auto, homeowner's, renter's, health and dental)

▼ Taxes (income, property, social security)

▼ Savings and investments

▼ Entertainment/recreation (health club, vacation/travel, dining, movies)

▼ Debt repayment (credit cards, installment loans)

▼ Miscellaneous (charitable contributions, child care, gifts, medical expenses)

Nothing but Net

1. **The Big Four.** Compare the Web sites for two of the Big Four accounting firms; the Web addresses for Price Waterhouse and Arthur Andersen are two possibilities:

   www.pw.com
   www.arthurandersen.com/homepage.htm

   Answer these questions about the two firms you're comparing:
   (a) Which firm has been in existence longer?
   (b) Which firm does a better job of attracting potential employees through its Web site?
   (c) Which firm is better at integrating technology into the services it provides its customers?
   Provide reasons for each of your answers.

2. **Financial statements.** EDGAR, the Electronic Data Gathering, Analysis, and Retrieval system, is a well-known source of financial statement information available from the U.S. Securities and Exchange Commission (SEC). EDGAR performs automated collection, validation, indexing, acceptance, and forwarding of submissions by companies and others who are required by law to file forms with the SEC.

   Visit the EDGAR Web site at

   www.sec.gov/edaux/formlynx.htm

   and select the 10-Q form for any company of your choosing. Identify the financial statements contained in the 10-Q that were also discussed in the chapter.

3. **Exchange rates.** Visit a Web site that provides currency exchange rates, such as the CNN Financial Network at

   cnnfn.com/markets/currencies.html

   List the exchange rate per U.S. dollar for each of the following currencies:

   ▼ Japanese yen

   ▼ South African rand

   ▼ Canadian dollar

Note: Internet Web addresses change frequently. If you do not find the exact sites listed, you may need to access the organization's or company's home page and search from there.

NORTH TEXAS PUBLIC BROADCASTING:
CAREFUL FINANCIAL PLANNING

North Texas Public Broadcasting, a Dallas-based non-profit organization, holds the licenses to three vital public broadcasting stations: television stations KERA 13 and KDTN Channel 2 and radio station KERA 90.1. NTPB is committed to serving its communities by excelling in production, presentation, and distribution of programming that educates, inspires, enriches, informs, and entertains millions of television viewers and radio listeners. This goal is a tall order for a nonprofit organization that depends on the generosity of its viewers and other PBS contributors. Yet, as the operator of the most-watched PBS station in the nation, not only is NTPB delighting viewers with daily doses of "Sesame Street" and "The NewsHour with Jim Lehrer," it is currently producing an ambitious national documentary series on the Mexican-American War and recently completed construction of a new state-of-the-art broadcast center.

"How could we operate a $12 to $14 million-a-year annual budget plus build an $8.6 million facility and not owe any money?" asks Dr. Richard Meyer, president and CEO. "The answer is fiscal stability and operating in the black year after year—developing a cash reserve and having the ability to raise money from a variety of sources, such as foundations, businesses, and the general public."

Despite the uncertain nature of charitable giving and declining government support, careful financial planning and control systems have allowed NTPB to enjoy healthy growth. "Every year, each department looks at its budget in terms of what we spent the previous years and also what we're expecting to do," says Sylvia Komatsu, vice president of national programming. "We work together as a team because we have to know the big picture of the entire station in order to do our individual departmental budgets. How much revenue do we think we can raise next year from a number of different sources, whether it's through pledge, whether it's through corporate underwriting or our productions, whether it's through grants we may receive from the federal government or from corporations of foundations. We all submit our projections to the business office, which then works with each of us to make sure we arrive at an overall budget that we think meets the needs of each of the departments."

Susan Harmon, vice president of finance, believes NTPB has been successful because it has always operated on a "pay as you go" basis. "Every month we get financials, and we look at where all of our income streams are and how expenses are going," she explains, "If we've had a pledge drive that was off, we might look at what the projection is for a couple of months after the drive and how we can make up the shortfall."

Because pledge drive minutes translate directly into dollars, managing this valuable on-air commodity is a near science. Says Michael Seymour, vice president of broadcasting, "When a pledge drive falls short of its goal, it doesn't mean we have to do another pledge drive. We can use that message in direct mail pieces to say to people that we need your support because we didn't make our goal. But obviously, the pledge drives continue to provide a barometer as to whether people feel public television is important in their life."

Every year, millions of viewers in Dallas, Fort Worth, Denton, and other areas of north, east, and west Texas demonstrate that public broadcasting is indeed important to their lives by donating over 50 percent of NTPB's operating budget. More than 1,600 foundations and corporate and individual donors contributed to a capital campaign that raised complete funding for the new broadcast center—a lasting testament to the significance of public broadcasting in the viewers' collective lives.

Questions

1. Describe the role of budgets in the financial functioning of North Texas Public Broadcasting.

2. Like most for-profit companies, NTPB has to estimate the amount of additional funds it needs to balance its budget. Since NTPB doesn't borrow money or have any stock to sell, how does it raise additional capital?

3. Since NTPB is a nonprofit organization, it does not have to worry about financial statements. Do you agree with this statement? Why or why not?

PART V

Careers in Business

BUSINESS CAREER EXERCISES

Information Systems Career

More than ever, employers want graduates who are capable of understanding and applying both business and computer knowledge to business problems and opportunities. Systems analysts and other information systems professionals help employees in departments such as marketing, production, and human resources to work more efficiently and effectively. For example, they might design a computerized system for keeping more accurate and up-to-date inventory records or a database for tracking customers and their activities.

This exercise will help you to:

▼ Identify your level of interest in information systems as a business career.

▼ Find out details about the skills required, job activities, career advancement, and earnings potential for this occupation.

How to Locate the Exercise

1. Launch *Discovering Your Business Career* from the "Career Assistance" program group.

2. At the main menu, click on the red "play" button for "Information Systems" to see a presentation summarizing this career.

3. Next, click on the words "Information Systems" to enter the career profile on this career.

4. Click on the red button below the word "Compatibility."

5. Select "Information Systems" from the menu of seven business careers.

6. Watch the video that summarizes your degree of compatibility with a career in information systems.

7. Read the detailed compatibility report on the left side of the screen. You can obtain a printout of this report by clicking on "Print" in the lower left corner of the screen.

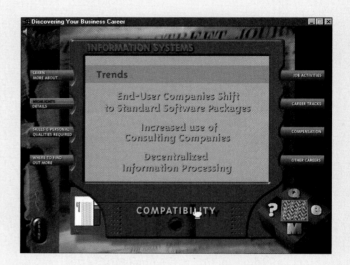

8. Click on the word "Return" to go back to the "Compatibility" menu of business careers.

9. Click on the red triangular arrow to the left of the words "Information Systems" to return to the career profile on information systems.

10. Review the sections about this career that interest you. You can get a complete printout of all the sections on information systems by clicking on "Print" in the lower left corner of the screen.

Accounting Career

It is difficult to imagine a career more basic to business than accounting. Someone needs to keep track of company finances and report on its financial status. Job opportunities within the broad field of accounting are varied, such as auditing a company's accounting practices for accuracy and efficiency, tracking a company's production and administrative costs, preparing financial reports, and handling tax issues.

This exercise will help you to:

▼ Identify your level of interest in accounting as a business career.

▼ Find out details about the skills required, job activities, career advancement, and earnings potential for this occupation.

How to Locate the Exercise

1. Launch *Discovering Your Business Career* from the "Career Assistance" program group.

2. At the main menu, click on the red "play" button for "Accounting" to see a presentation summarizing this career.

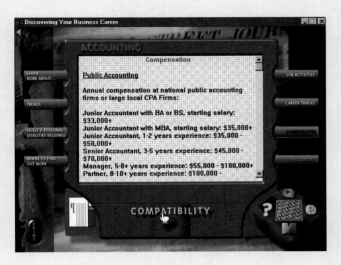

3. Next, click on the word "Accounting" to enter the career profile on this career.

4. Click on the red button below the word "Compatibility."

5. Select "Accounting" from the menu of seven business careers.

6. Watch the video that summarizes your degree of compatibility with a career in accounting.

7. Read the detailed compatibility report on the left side of the screen. You can obtain a printout of this report by clicking on "Print" in the lower left corner of the screen.

8. Click on the word "Return" to go back to the "Compatibility" menu of business careers.

9. Click on the red triangular arrow to the left of the word "Accounting" to return to the career profile on accounting.

10. Review the sections about this career that interest you. You can get a complete printout of all the sections on accounting by clicking on "Print" in the lower left corner of the screen.

PART VI | Managing Financial Resources

Chapter 20

Financial Management and Institutions

Chapter 21

Financing and Investing through Securities Markets

chapter 20

Financial Management and Institutions

LEARNING GOALS

1. Identify the functions performed by a firm's financial managers.

2. Describe the characteristics a form of money should have, and list the functions of money.

3. Distinguish between money (M1) and near-money (M2).

4. Explain how a firm uses funds.

5. Compare the two major sources of funds for a business.

6. Identify likely sources of short-term and long-term funds.

7. Describe the major categories of financial institutions and the sources and uses of their funds.

8. Explain the functions of the Federal Reserve System and the tools it uses to increase or decrease the money supply.

9. Describe the institutions and practices for regulating bank safety.

Uncle Sam Levels the Playing Field with EDGAR

Uncle Sam likes us all to play fair and goes a long way to make sure we do. For example, by regulating all transactions involving stocks and bonds, the federal government protects investors and ensures that securities markets operate fairly. The Securities and Exchange Commission (SEC) is the federal agency responsible for regulating firms that buy or sell securities and people who give investment advice. The SEC also makes sure that investors have access to all information concerning publicly traded securities. It requires all companies and others selling a new stock or bond issue to the general public to file relevant financial information with the government, and these documents must be submitted electronically.

To increase efficiency and fairness, most SEC filings are stored with EDGAR, the Electronic Data Gathering, Analysis, and Retrieval system. EDGAR accelerates the receipt and dissemination of these files by automatically collecting, validating, indexing, accepting, and forwarding each submission. A huge benefit for individual investors, EDGAR "levels the playing field" by making it possible for the small investor to get the same information

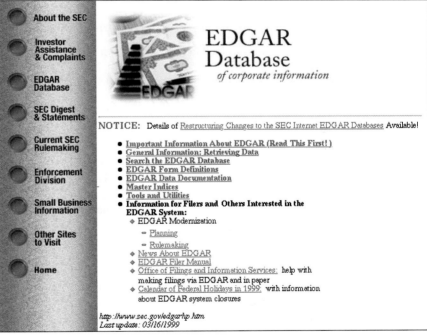

that large institutions and analysts obtain through professional "data miners." But for all its technology and good intentions, EDGAR isn't perfect. A filing can take a full business day to appear on EDGAR's site, and not every filing appears there. Plus, even though EDGAR offers downloadable information, it uses an old-fashioned DOS conversion program, which takes a long, long time.

Luckily, users can get help from several commercial firms, including FreeEDGAR, Edgar Online, and LIVEDGAR. These companies offer easier access to SEC information, quicker download times, and even e-mail alerts for target companies. In fact, FreeEDGAR and Edgar Online can put EDGAR data into PC databases or word-processing programs for their users. All of these companies are constantly looking for better ways to handle EDGAR's 40 gigabytes of information—and so is the SEC.

The commission is revamping EDGAR to include more company details and graphics. And to make filings easier—both for companies to submit and for viewers to read—EDGAR will allow documents in Hypertext Markup Language (HTML), the language used in most Web pages. Filings in plain text format, or ASCII, are readable, but they're harder to work with and not attractive.

www.

www.sec.gov/edgarhp.html

Carl Malamud may have the most impact on EDGAR's future format. Working with the non-profit Internet Multicasting Service and New York University, Malamud was the first to put the SEC company filings online in 1994. Together with Marshall Rose, another Internet pioneer, Malamud now wants to help people see EDGAR's data in a new and better way. Using a new technology called XML, or Extensible Markup Language, Malamud can apply identification tags to individual pieces of information so that EDGAR users can search within multiple documents to find, say, all annual reports from financial-services companies or only the balance sheets from each firm. Users will also be able to see results in the form of a map showing connections between various financial tables. Uncle Sam wants to provide us information that's easy to get, and Carl Malamud is determined to help out.[1]

CHAPTER OVERVIEW

Previous chapters have discussed two essential functions that a business must perform. First, the firm must produce a good or service or contract with suppliers to produce it. Second, the firm must market its good or service to prospective customers. This chapter introduces a third, equally important function: A company's managers must ensure that it has enough money to perform its other tasks successfully, both now and in the future. Adequate funds must be available to buy materials and equipment, pay bills, purchase additional facilities, and compensate employees. This third business function is **finance**—planning, obtaining, and managing the company's funds in order to accomplish its objectives in the most effective possible way.

Handling money is an expensive activity for both financial institutions and businesses. As a result, firms are developing cashless ways to complete financial transactions. Electronic commerce is playing a growing role in the financial management strategies of many firms, including filing statements with the SEC.

An organization's financial objectives include not only meeting expenses but also maximizing its overall value, often determined by the value of its common stock. Financial managers are responsible for both meeting expenses and increasing profits for stockholders.

This chapter focuses on the role of financial managers, why businesses need funds, and the various types and sources of funds in businesses. It discusses how the Federal Reserve System regulates the institutions that make up the U.S. financial system, and it examines the role of that system in the global business environment.

THE ROLE OF THE FINANCIAL MANAGER

Organizations are placing greater emphasis on measuring and reducing the costs of conducting business as well as increasing revenues and profits. As a result, **financial managers**—staff members responsible for developing and implementing their firm's financial plan and for determining the most appropriate sources and uses of funds—are among the most vital people on the corporate payroll.

The growing importance of financial managers is reflected in an expanding number of CEOs promoted from financial management positions. A recent study of major corporations has revealed that nearly one in three chief executives has a finance or banking background.[2] For example, M. Douglas Ivestor, the chairman and CEO of The Coca-Cola Company, joined the firm as a member of its internal auditing staff, leading to promotions through the financial ranks to become chief financial officer, president, and chief operating officer. Ivestor is credited with helping Coca-Cola use its strong credit standing and assets to build up cash to finance global expansion.[3]

Job titles for top financial management positions include vice president of finance and chief financial officer (CFO). Effective management of money can reduce the number of times that a company will need to raise additional capital. It also helps the firm to attract financing in times of need, because investors and lenders recognize and prefer companies with well-managed finances.

In performing their jobs, financial managers continually seek to balance risks with expected financial returns. *Risk* is the uncertainty of gain or loss; *return* is the gain or loss that results from an investment over a specified period. A heavy reliance on borrowed funds may raise the return on the owners' or stockholders' investment. Financial managers strive to maximize the wealth of their firm's stockholders by striking a balance between the risk of available investments and their potential returns. This balance is called the **risk-return trade-off.** An increase in a firm's cash on hand, for example, reduces the risk of meeting unexpected cash needs. However, because cash does not generate income, failure to invest surplus funds in an earning asset (such as in marketable securities) can reduce a firm's potential return or profitability.

Every financial manager must perform this risk-return balancing act. When Douglas Becker and Christopher Hoehn-Saric bought Sylvan Learning Systems in 1991, the company earned annual revenues of $10 million by franchising 400 basic-skills tutoring centers throughout North America. "For us," says Becker, "it wasn't a question of how to make tutoring grow 15 percent or 20 percent each year, but how to create a multinational, multibillion-dollar company around education." To realize their ambitious goals, Becker and Hoehn-Saric looked for ways to utilize their tutoring

Douglas Becker, president of Sylvan Learning Systems, visits students at one of the firm's tutoring centers. By making a risky investment in computer technology, Becker grew his little, kid-centered company into a worldwide, multibillion-dollar firm.

centers during the hours when children weren't receiving instruction. They recognized an opportunity to fill their space by offering computer-based testing for professional certification and licensing programs and for graduate-school admissions. By presenting these tests on personal computers, they hoped to replace paper-and-pencil tests and give immediate feedback about results.

But setting up a computerized testing system involved an enormous investment. Becker and Hoehn-Saric needed $6 million—more than half of their revenues—to buy 750 computers, furniture, and software and to hire new employees. They raised the capital by persuading some franchisees to invest in the new venture and by investing every spare penny from the parent company's funds. Also, rather than spending a lot up front to buy computer equipment, they leased it from IBM Credit Corp. "We took a huge risk," says Becker. "It was make or break for us." The risk paid off with handsome returns. The $6 million investment has resulted in about $130 million in testing revenue, making Sylvan the global leader in providing educational services to families, schools, and industry. Today, Sylvan operates 1,500 testing centers in more than 80 countries. [4]

www. **www.educate.com**

Business Directory

finance the business function of planning, obtaining, and managing a company's funds in order to accomplish its objectives in the most effective possible way.

financial manager an organizational staff member responsible for developing and implementing the firm's financial plan and for determining the most appropriate sources and uses of funds.

The Financial Plan

Financial managers develop their organization's **financial plan,** a document that specifies the funds needed by a firm for a period of time, the timing of inflows and outflows, and the most appropriate sources and uses of funds. The financial plan is based on forecasts of production costs, purchasing needs, and expected sales activities for the period covered. Financial managers use forecasts to determine the specific amounts and timing of expenditures and receipts. They build a financial plan on answers to three questions:

1. What funds will the firm require during the appropriate period of operations?

2. How will it obtain the necessary funds?

3. When will it need more funds?

Some funds flow into the firm when it sells its goods or services, but funding needs vary, specifying different amounts at different times. The financial plan must reflect both the amounts and timing of inflows and outflows of funds. Even a profitable firm may well face a financial squeeze as a result of its need for funds when sales lag, when the volume of its credit sales increases, or when customers are slow in making payments.

Security First Network Bank, the first Internet-based bank, experienced a cash-flow crunch in marketing its software to other financial institutions. SFNB miscalculated the timing of the inflow of funds, expecting immediate payment of about $2 million from the banks that bought its Internet software for their own operations. Most software customers wanted SFNB to do the processing work, however, for which they paid only a few hundred thousand dollars each up front. Typically, SFNB takes 4 to 6 months to link a bank customer to its data processing system. After that, it must wait for the banks to introduce Internet banking to their own customers before receiving substantial revenues. According to Robert Stockwell, Security First's chief financial officer, the unanticipated delay in incoming funds resulted in a short-term cash-flow problem.[5]

The cash inflows and outflows of a business are similar to those of a household. The members of a household may depend on weekly or monthly paychecks for funds, but their expenditures vary greatly from one pay period to the next. The financial plan should indicate when the flows of funds entering and leaving the organization will occur and in what amounts.

A good financial plan also involves **financial control,** a process of checking actual revenues, costs, and expenses and comparing them against forecasts. If this process reveals significant differences between projected and actual figures, it is important to discover them early in order to take timely corrective action.

At Allen Systems Group, a software developer in Naples, Florida, an effective financial manager makes a critical contribution to efficient global operations. Frederick Roberts, the firm's chief financial officer, is responsible for building and monitoring the company's international banking relationships. At one point, Roberts noticed that international customers often paid their bills weeks or months later than customers in the United States. In response, he set up bank accounts in key European and Asian cities where most of the firm's customers were located, a move that eliminated the problem with late-paying accounts. Roberts also closely watches the market to assess the services and fees of different international banks, especially those that affect cross-border transactions. Keeping a close eye on bank service fees puts Roberts in a good position to negotiate his own firm's fees and to control its expenses.[6]

CHARACTERISTICS AND FUNCTIONS OF MONEY

Playwright George Bernard Shaw once said that the *lack* of money is the root of all evil. Many businesspeople would agree, for money is the lubricant of contemporary business. Firms require adequate funds to finance their operations and carry out management plans.

Characteristics of Money

Money is anything generally accepted as payment for goods and services. Most early forms of money imposed a number of serious disadvantages on users. For example, a cow is a poor form of money for an owner who wants only a loaf of bread and some cheese. Exchanges based on money permit economic specialization and provide a general basis for purchasing power, provided that the money has certain characteristics. It must be divisible, portable, durable, and difficult to counterfeit, and it should have a stable value.

Divisibility A U.S. dollar can be converted into pennies, nickels, dimes, and quarters. The Canadian dollar is divided similarly, except that Canada has 1- and 2-dollar coins, nicknamed the *loonie* and *toonie*. Mexico's nuevo peso is broken down into centavos. People can easily exchange these forms of money for products ranging from chewing gum to cars. Today, most economic activity is concerned with making and spending money.

Portability The light weight of modern, paper currency facilitates the exchange process. Portability is an important characteristic, since a typical dollar bill changes hands 400 times during its lifetime, staying in the average person's pocket or purse less than 2 days.

Durability U.S. dollar bills survive an average of 12 to 18 months, and they can survive folding some 4,000 times without tearing. Although coins and paper currency wear out over time, they are replaced easily with new money.

Difficulty in Counterfeiting Widespread distribution of counterfeit money could undermine a nation's monetary system by ruining the value of legitimate money. For this reason, governments define counterfeiting as a serious crime and take elaborate steps to prevent it. U.S. currency accounts for 80 percent of all counterfeit money intercepted by Interpol, the international police agency. To increase the difficulty of counterfeiting U.S. currency, the Treasury Department is in the process of redesigning it. The new currency adds a letter to each bill's serial number along with the seal of the Federal Reserve, larger portraits, and polymer threads that run vertically through the bills and glow under ultraviolet light.[7]

Stability A good form of money should maintain a stable value. If the value of

---

DID YOU KNOW?

A continuing debate centers on phasing out the penny. Imagine never finding a lucky penny! Half of the population wants to keep pennies in circulation, while the other half would be happy to leave them to history and simply round transactions to the nearest nickel. Producing pennies costs taxpayers about $8 million a year. Rounding prices to the nearest nickel, by one estimate, would cost $600 million in overcharges. Let's keep the penny.

---

money fluctuates, people hesitate to trade goods and services for it. Inflation, therefore, creates a serious concern for governments. When people fear that money will lose much of its value, they begin to abandon it and look for safer means of storing their wealth. Runaway inflation, when the value of money may decrease 20 percent or more in a single year, often spurs people to move toward barter systems, exchanging the output of their work directly for the output produced by others.

Russia had to cope with near total erosion of value of the ruble after the fall of the Berlin Wall in 1989. Inflation there became so severe that virtually all sectors of the economy began relying on a barter system. Many businesses lacked sufficient rubles to pay their employees, so workers often took home the products that their companies made, accepting tires, paint, or pots and pans as payments. One firm in Siberia still pays its workers in coffins. The cash shortage has forced Russian employees to function without money. A movie theater in Altai, Siberia, accepts two eggs from patrons in exchange for tickets. Russian tax officials report that only 20 percent of financial transactions in the fuel and energy industries involve cash. Even the federal and local governments allow manufacturing firms to pay their taxes with cans of paint or other products.[8]

Functions of Money

Money performs three basic functions. First, it serves primarily as a *medium of exchange*—a means of facilitating economic transactions and eliminating the need for a barter system. Second, it functions as a *unit of account*—a common standard for measuring the value of all goods and services. Third, money acts as a *temporary store of value*—a way of keeping accumulated wealth until the owner needs it to make new purchases. Money offers one big

Many countries have incorporated new features into their currency to increase the difficulty of counterfeiting. Canadian currency incorporates a thin square that changes color when viewed at different angles, making it difficult to reproduce with a color copier.

| Figure 20.1 | The Financial Planning Process |

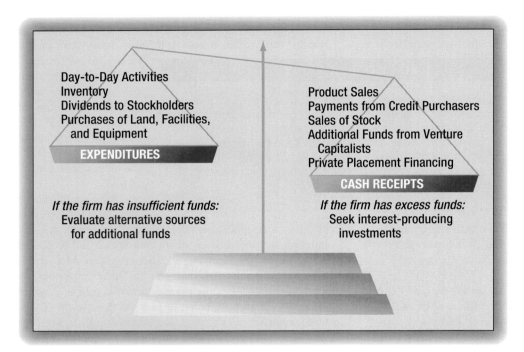

EXPENDITURES
- Day-to-Day Activities
- Inventory
- Dividends to Stockholders
- Purchases of Land, Facilities, and Equipment

If the firm has insufficient funds:
Evaluate alternative sources for additional funds

CASH RECEIPTS
- Product Sales
- Payments from Credit Purchasers
- Sales of Stock
- Additional Funds from Venture Capitalists
- Private Placement Financing

If the firm has excess funds:
Seek interest-producing investments

advantage as a store of value. Its high *liquidity* allows people to obtain and dispose of it in quick and easy transactions. The chief advantage of money is its immediate availability for purchasing products or paying debts.

THE MONEY SUPPLY AND NEAR-MONEY

The U.S. money supply spans several categories of assets: coins, paper money, traveler's checks, demand deposits (checking accounts), interest-bearing NOW (negotiable order of withdrawal) accounts, and credit union share draft accounts. Government reports and business publications often use the term *M1* to refer to the total of these categories of money.

In addition to these types of money, a number of other assets, known as **near-money** are almost as liquid as cash or checking accounts but do not serve directly as a medium of exchange. Users must complete some transaction before these assets can fulfill all the functions of money. Time deposits (savings accounts), government bonds, money mar-

ket mutual funds, and credit cards are considered near-money. The total of near-money and money (M1) is commonly designated *M2*.

In recent years, the use of credit cards—so-called *plastic money*—has significantly increased. Many entrepreneurs rely on this type of near-money, as mentioned in Chapter 6, to provide seed capital in financing their new ventures. Lisa Conte charged $40,000 on credit cards to finance her new company, Shaman Pharmaceuticals Inc., which produces drugs made from plants found in South American rain forests.[9]

Businesses from manufacturers like General Motors to catalog and specialty retailers have joined banks in offering their own credit cards. With annual interest rates on cards averaging about 15 percent, it's easy to understand why such diverse organizations want a piece of the credit card market. As the Solving an Ethical Controversy box indicates, however, credit card issuers are taking some blame for rising consumer debt, which is contributing to an alarming increase in personal bankruptcy filings.

WHY ORGANIZATIONS NEED FUNDS

Organizations require funds for many reasons. They need money to run day-to-day operations, compensate current employees and hire new ones, pay for inventory, make interest payments on loans, pay dividends to stockholders, and purchase land, facilities, and equipment. A firm's financial plan identifies the amounts and timing of its specific cash needs.

By comparing these needs with expenditures and expected cash receipts (from sales, payments made by credit purchasers, and other sources), financial managers determine precisely what additional funds they must obtain at any given time. If inflows exceed cash needs, financial managers invest the surplus to earn interest. On the other hand, if inflows do not meet cash needs, they seek additional sources of funds. Figure 20.1 illustrates this process.

Business Directory

near-money an asset almost as liquid as cash or a checking account but that cannot serve directly as a medium of exchange.

Generating Funds from Excess Cash

Many financial managers choose to invest the majority of their firms' excess cash balances in marketable securities. These financial instruments are often considered near-money because they are, by definition, marketable and easy to convert into cash. Three of the most common types of marketable securities are U.S. Treasury bills, commercial paper, and certificates of deposit.

Treasury bills are among the most popular marketable securities because, as issues of the U.S. government, they are considered virtually risk-free and easy to resell. *Commercial paper* is a short-term note issued by a major corporation with a very high credit standing and backed solely by the reputation of the issuing firm. Commercial paper is riskier than a Treasury bill and lacks a well-developed market for resale prior to maturity, but it pays the purchaser a higher rate of interest.

A *certificate of deposit (CD)* is a short-term note issued by a financial institution such as a commercial bank, savings and loan association, or credit union. The sizes and maturity dates of CDs vary considerably and can be tailored to meet the needs of the purchasers. Large CDs in denominations of $100,000 can be purchased for periods as short as 24 hours. At the other extreme, 10-year CDs are available in denominations as low as $100 to $250.

SOURCES OF FUNDS

To this point, the discussion has focused on half of the definition of finance—the reasons why organizations need funds and how they use them. A firm's financial plan must give equal importance, however, to the choice of the best sources of needed funds. Sources of funds fall into two major categories: debt capital and equity capital.

Debt capital represents funds obtained through borrowing (referred to as *debt financing* in Chapter 6). **Equity capital** consists of funds provided by the firm's owners when they reinvest earnings, make additional contributions, liquidate assets, issue stock to the general public, or raise contributions from venture capitalists and other investors (referred to as *equity financing* in Chapter 6). A firm also obtains equity capital by saving revenues from day-to-day operations. These sources are shown in Figure 20.2.

A company's cash needs vary from one time period to the next, and even an established firm may not generate sufficient funds from operations to cover all costs of a major expansion or a significant investment in new equipment. In these instances, financial managers must evaluate the potential benefits and drawbacks of seeking funds by borrowing. As an alternative to borrowing, the firm may raise equity capital in several ways. A financial manager's job includes determining the most

---

Figure 20.2 **Debt and Equity Capital: Two Basic Sources of Funds**

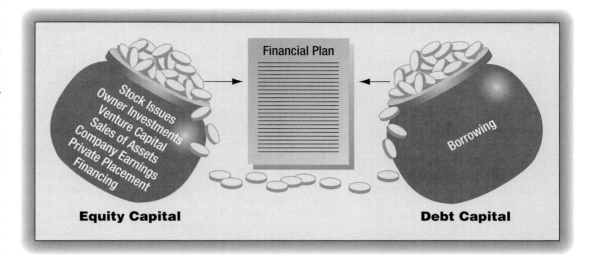

Financial Plan

Stock Issues
Owner Investments
Venture Capital
Sales of Assets
Company Earnings
Private Placement
Financing

Borrowing

Equity Capital   **Debt Capital**

They said it

"You must spend money if you wish to make money."

Plautus, 254–184 B.C.

Business Directory

debt capital funds obtained through borrowing.

equity capital funds provided by the firm's owners when they reinvest earnings, liquidate assets, make additional contributions, issue stock to the general public, or raise contributions from investors.

SOLVING AN ETHICAL CONTROVERSY

Are Credit Card Issuers Responsible for Rising Consumer Debt?

In a recent year, Americans charged more than $1 trillion on credit cards. In the same year, a record 1.1 million Americans declared personal bankruptcy, up 29 percent over the previous year. Why are so many Americans going bankrupt? The increase in bankruptcies is a function of rising consumer debt, and many people blame banks and other lenders for issuing credit cards and extending too much credit to people who cannot repay the debts they pile up. Stephen Brobeck, head of the Consumer Federation of America, says that if credit card issuers would "extend credit more prudently and responsibly, you would see a dramatic fall in bankruptcies."

Credit card issuers annually mail more than 2 billion credit card solicitations, an average of 20 to each U.S. household. Almost 60 percent of households with incomes less than $20,000 received offers of credit cards. One-fourth of families with annual incomes under $10,000 have credit cards. A study of bankruptcy petitions conducted by the Credit Research Center at Purdue University revealed that people who file

Chapter 7 bankruptcy have an average after-tax income of $19,800 and total credit card debts of $17,544.

In response to a USA Today/CNN/Gallup poll, bankruptcy filers cited credit card debt as a major cause of their financial trouble. Burdened with credit card debt, many respondents said that an unexpected event—a job loss, divorce, or medical expense—left them unable to repay their debts. Grace and Bernie Herbert filed for bankruptcy following a job loss and a large medical expense for their child's surgery. The couple had no health insurance, and they owed $23,000 on their credit cards. "The credit card companies were very gracious by continuously extending these unbelievable lines of credit," says Grace. "We had $100,000 of credit available to us on cards, and our income was around $45,000. I'm sorry, but that's crazy." Even after they filed for bankruptcy, the Herberts continued to receive offers for credit cards.

 Are credit card issuers irresponsible in giving consumers too much credit?

PRO

1. Credit card issuers make it too easy for people to get into debt. Their aggressive marketing strate-

gies encourage credit card use by inappropriately extending credit limits. The average credit line available on bank cards doubled from $750 to $1,500 over a recent 5-year period. Issuers have the power to reduce consumer debt by limiting credit lines to 20 percent of cardholders' incomes.

2. Credit card issuers allow consumers to carry large balances and make only small, minimum payments each month. Issuers profit when people do not pay off their bills. Those who pay only the minimum monthly requirements incur high interest rate charges on their balances.

3. Credit card issuers should act responsibly by informing credit card users of the costs involved in using credit cards and the financial consequences of taking on too much debt.

CON

1. People who charge too much on their credit cards and cannot repay their charges are simply living beyond their means. Individuals must take responsibility for taking on too much debt. They are to blame for putting them-

---

cost-effective balance between equity and borrowed funds and the proper blend of short-term and long-term funds. Table 20.1 compares debt capital and equity capital on four criteria.

William Gordon, the chief financial officer of BET Holdings Inc., had to evaluate sources of funds when the company decided to expand beyond its core business of cable TV programming for an African American audience. BET invested more than $20 million in new ventures to achieve its goals of increasing shareholder value and becoming a multimedia entertainment conglomerate. The company has relied on equity capital, using the cash flow generated by its profitable cable network to finance some of its capital-intensive expansion projects. "Diversification

is never easy, and one of the hardest challenges of management is to reinvest the company's revenues," says Dob Bennett, president of Liberty Media Corp., which owns 22 percent of BET Holdings. One of the company's most promising new ventures is BET SoundStage, a restaurant chain with an entertainment theme. BET plans to build 20 SoundStage restaurants throughout the United States within 5 years. BET is also planning to build a SoundStage-style casino in Las Vegas.

For some new ventures, BET has formed strategic partnerships with other firms to reduce its capital expenditures and to gain expertise in areas where it lacks previous experience. BET shares a 50/50 equity investment with its partners. An example is the online service MSBET, a joint

selves in positions that threaten their financial stability. After all, issuers do not force people to accept or use credit cards.

2. Credit card issuers do not want to give cards to people who cannot repay their debts, because resulting losses diminish the lenders' profits. Issuers check applicants' credit reports and apply sophisticated credit-scoring systems to help them identify bad risks. "They don't send out solicitations with the idea that they're not going to get repaid," says Thomas Layman, chief economist of Visa.

3. Credit cards offer many benefits that checks or cash cannot match. They are a safe, convenient, and efficient way to pay for goods and services. Many new business startups use personal credit cards to finance their ventures, providing them with credit they might not be able to get in other ways. Payment by credit cards simplifies many transactions, such as making airline and hotel reservations.

4. A lax bankruptcy code makes it too easy for people to erase their debt. People who file under Chapter 13 of the U.S. Bankruptcy Code repay their debt from future earnings, but the vast majority, about 70 percent, file under Chapter 7, a

lenient category in which the courts discharge the debts. In a recent year, courts discharged $30 billion in household debt. "Bankruptcy has become the latest entitlement in this country," says Lawrence Chimerine, a consulting economist for MasterCard. "The normal rules of behavior aren't followed by borrowers."

SUMMARY

The government and credit card issuers are taking measures to combat misuse of credit. Congress has created a special commission to recommend reforms to the Bankruptcy Code with the intention of discouraging debtors from erasing their debts.

To limit their losses, Visa and MasterCard are lobbying the courts to evaluate a bankruptcy applicant's financial condition to determine whether the debtor should file under Chapter 13 and repay the debts or under Chapter 7. The companies are also challenging the credit card purchases that debtors make before they file for bankruptcy. Some consumers continue to buy on credit even after deciding to file for bankruptcy.

Recent research has revealed warning signs that often precede bankruptcy. These include making a major purchase (such as a car), carrying a high credit card balance ($8,000 or more), exceeding credit limits, and

living in an area with high bankruptcy rates. Based on these and other warning signs, issuers have designed a bankruptcy predictor score that rates the likelihood of a person going bankrupt. A high score may prompt the lender to take preventative action by freezing an account, denying increases in credit lines, advising the user to seek credit counseling, or closing the account.

Sources: Mitchell Schnurman, "Consumer Advocates, Banks Debate Teen Credit Cards," *San Jose Mercury News*, May 11, 1999, accessed at www7.mercurycenter.com; CBS News, "Hooked on Plastic," CBS MarketWatch, May 10, 1999, accessed at cbs.marketwatch.com; Damon Darlin, "The Newest American Entitlement," *Forbes*, September 8, 1997, pp. 113, 116; Kim Clark, "Why So Many Americans Are Going Bankrupt," *Fortune*, August 4, 1997, pp. 24–25; Mary Kane, "Lenders Look for Bankruptcy Warning Signals," *Mobile Register*, July 6, 1997, pp. 1F–2F; Christine Dugas, "Bankruptcy Stigma Lessens," *USA Today*, June 10, 1997, pp. 1A–2A; Joshua Wolf Shenk, "In Debt All the Way up to Their Nose Rings," *U.S. News & World Report*, June 9, 1997, pp. 38–39; Daniel McGinn, "Deadbeat Nation," *Newsweek*, April 14, 1997, p. 50; and "Have Credit Card Issuers Been Irresponsible in Giving Consumers Too Much Debt?" *At Home with Consumers* 18, no. 1 (1994), pp. 1–8.

Table 20.1	Comparison of Debt and Equity Capital		
Criterion	**Debt**		**Equity**
Maturity	A contract specifies a date by which the borrower must repay the loan.		Securities specify no maturity dates.
Claim on assets	Lenders have prior claims on assets.		Stockholders have claims only after the firm satisfies the claims of lenders.
Claim on income	Lenders have prior claim on fixed interest payments, which must be paid before dividends can be paid to stockholders. Interest payments are a contractual obligation of the borrowing firm.		Stockholders have a residual claim after all creditors have been paid. Dividends are paid at the discretion of the board of directors; they are not a contractual obligation of the firm.
Right to a voice in management	Lenders are creditors, not owners. They have no voice in company affairs unless they do not receive interest payments.		Stockholders are the owners of the company, and most can voice preferences for its operation.

BET is betting that its online service with equity partner Microsoft will be the cyberspace site of choice for African Americans.

stances, financial managers evaluate short-term sources of needed funds. By definition, these sources must be repaid within 1 year.

The major short-term source of funds is *trade credit,* extended by suppliers when a firm makes open-account purchases from them. A second source is *unsecured bank loans,* for which the business does not pledge any assets as collateral. Another option is *secured short-term loans,* for which the firm pledges specific collateral such as inventory. Large firms with unquestioned financial stability can raise money from a fourth source—by selling *commercial paper.* Commercial paper typically is sold in denominations of $100,000 with maturity terms of 30 to 90 days. Issuing commercial paper to raise funds usually reduces interest costs by 1 or 2 percent compared to borrowing short-term funds from a bank.

venture with Microsoft. "We want to be the great aggregate of African American content on the Web," says Barry Johnson, MSBET's president. Plans for the venture also include production of CD-ROMs and other multimedia entertainment products.[10]

www.betnetworks.com
www.msbet.com

Short-Term Sources of Funds

Many times throughout a year, an organization may discover that its cash needs exceed its available funds. For example, retailers generate surplus cash for most of the year, but they need to build up inventory just before the Christmas season, so they need to acquire additional funds to finance merchandise purchases until holiday sales generate revenue. As they collect on sales during the Christmas season, they use the incoming funds to repay the suppliers of the borrowed funds. In these in-

Long-Term Sources of Funds

Funds from short-term sources can help a firm to meet current needs for cash or inventory. A larger need, however, like acquiring another company or making a major purchase such as land or new equipment, requires funds for a much longer period. Unlike short-term sources, long-term sources can be repaid over a period of 1 year or longer.

Organizations acquire funds from three long-term financing sources. One is long-term loans issued by financial institutions such as banks, insurance companies, and pension funds. For example, in Figure 20.3, Bank of America explains that it arranged long-term loans for a client that needed financing to build a power plant in Asia. A second source is **bonds**—certificates of indebtedness sold to raise long-term funds for corporations or government agencies. A third source is *equity financing* acquired by selling stock in the company, selling company assets, reinvesting company earnings, or raising additional contributions from venture capitalists, private investors, or owners.

Public Sale of Stocks and Bonds Sales of stocks and bonds represent a major source of funds for business corporations. Such a sale provides cash inflows for the issuing firm and either a share in its ownership (for a stock purchaser) or a specified rate of interest and repayment at a stated time (for a bond purchaser). Because stock and

Business Directory

bond a certificate of indebtedness sold to raise long-term funds for a corporation or government agency.

bond issues of many corporations are traded on organized securities exchanges, stockholders and bondholders can easily sell these assets. The decision whether to issue stock or bonds to finance a corporation's plans is an important decision discussed in more detail in the next chapter.

Venture Capital A typical business begins operations with an investment of about $25,000. As Chapter 6 explained, entrepreneurs often finance their start-ups with money from their personal savings, from contributions by friends and family members, and from loan programs offered by the Small Business Administration. Those that need large amounts of money, however, often look to venture capital funds.

Venture capital usually is provided by outside investors in exchange for an ownership share in the business. Larger investments usually require bigger management roles for the venture capitalists. For example, when Dennis Gabrick went to a venture capital group to help fund Nature Preserved, his commercial interior landscaping business, he was in for a surprise. The group put up a two-thirds stake amounting to $750,000, but the investors demoted Gabrick to vice president and installed their own president and chief financial officer.[11]

The venture capitalist may be a corporation, a wealthy individual, a pension fund, or a major endowment fund. In exchange for funds, the venture capitalist receives shares of the corporation's stock at relatively low prices and becomes a part-owner of the corporation. Frequently venture capitalists provide management consulting advice as well as funds. Some also want to be represented on the firm's board of directors and often expect to take an active role in managing the business.[12]

In return for their risky investments in struggling firms, venture capitalists may earn substantial profits should the firms succeed and issue shares of stock to the general public. Hundreds of venture capitalists take such risks in the United States today. According to Venture Economics, venture capitalists invested more than $9.4 billion in 1,625 firms during a recent year.[13]

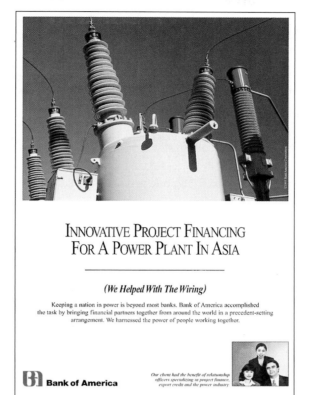

Figure 20.3 **Banks: A Source of Long-Term Financing**

INNOVATIVE PROJECT FINANCING FOR A POWER PLANT IN ASIA

(We Helped With The Wiring)

Bank of America

> "Creditors have better memories than debtors."
>
> Benjamin Franklin, 1706–1790

Venture capitalists typically receive dozens of proposals every month from businesses seeking funds. These investors reject most applications, looking with favor only on soundly managed firms with unique goods or services in rapidly growing industries. The Business Tool Kit box gives an idea of the type of entrepreneur and company in which venture capitalists are likely to invest.

High-tech industries attract a large share of venture capital investments. When Lounette Dyer needed financing to back her new venture, Cogit Corp., she called Ruthann Quindlen of Institutional Venture Partners for funds. "When she called, it took me about a nanosecond to decide to back her," says Quindlen. The firm gave Dyer $1 million in exchange for an equity stake in Cogit, which writes data-mining software that uses complex algorithms to uncover patterns in large corporate databases. Dyer received an additional $1 million from a second venture capital firm, New Enterprise Associates.[14] Other fast-growing industries that generate venture capital interest include health care and telecommunications.

Private Placement Financing Many entrepreneurs and growth-oriented firms focus on venture capitalists for funding, but substantially more money is available from private placement investors, who typically supply cash in the form of loans. However, some private placement deals combine debt and equity financing. More than $203 billion worth of private placements were completed in a recent year, according to Securities Data Co., a research firm. Companies seeking financing through private placements have a better chance of succeeding when they work with investment banking firms.[15]

Private placements offer several advantages over financing options limited only to equity. First, a financial manager can draw from a large base of potential investors, including insurance companies, banks, pension funds, private investment pools, and so-called *angel* investors. Second, private placement investors do not require the detailed management control that venture capitalists do.

BUSINESS TOOL KIT

Tips from Two Venture Capitalists

Many entrepreneurs waste a lot of time and effort trying to attract venture capital. The truth is, most have only a slim chance of persuading institutional venture capitalists to invest in their companies. Based on 30 years of experience as a venture capitalist, Frederick J. Beste III of Mid-Atlantic Venture Funds, L.P., says that venture capitalists "have to get used to disappointing 99 entrepreneurs for every one they please." According to Beste, venture capitalists are "risk reducers—they prospect in the land of the commercially unfinanceable, and try to differentiate the superstars from the merely enthusiastic."

In evaluating entrepreneurial prospects, Beste looks for a set of characteristics and practices that separate exceptional entrepreneurs from others:

▼ Sound knowledge of their marketplaces, their competitors, and the financial dynamics of their companies (Exceptional candidates understand the importance of cash flow and the factors that drive cash flow and profitability in their businesses.)

▼ Internal locus of control, inner confidence, and strong achievement orientation

▼ Ability to make plans and to work hard in executing them

▼ Ability to recognize the risks associated with their ventures and take steps to minimize the impact of those risks. "They rent space, buy used furniture and equipment, and draw a pittance of a salary," says Beste. "They are quite content to delay civilized living and celebrations until they can be paid for out of earnings."

▼ Ability to hire smart people and give them an equity stake in the firm

Venture capitalist John Martinson, managing partner of Edison Venture Fund, suggests that an entrepreneur should answer the following questions before contacting an institutional venture capitalist:

▼ Are you a technology company? "In general," Martinson says, "eighty percent of a venture capitalist's portfolio is in technology."

▼ Is your product capable of becoming a market leader?

▼ Can your company be built at low expense? "Venture capitalists like to build companies on the cheap," says Martinson, "to limit the downside risk and because they don't want to have to rely on other sources of capital to pitch in to help the company reach its goal."

▼ Can you identify a clear distribution channel for your product?

▼ Can your product be marketed without significant customer support or service?

▼ Can your product generate growth margins of more than 50 percent?

▼ Can your company grow to sales of $5 million in 5 years, with further prospects of reaching $50 million to $100 million?

If you can answer yes to Martinson's questions and you fit Beste's profile, a venture capital firm just might consider investing in your business.

Sources: Frederick J. Beste III, "The Twelve (Almost) Sure-Fire Secrets to Entrepreneurial Success," Venture Capital Institute Bookstore, envista.com/vci/surefire.html, downloaded July 8, 1997; and David R. Evanson, "Capital Questions," *Entrepreneur*, March 1997, pp. 62–65.

Third, private placements support a wide range of small firms that need funding to grow. Gary Russell, founder and CEO of North American Sports Camps, used private placement financing to raise capital for a project to expand his tiny soccer camp into a $3.5 million firm with 600 camps nationwide. The funding also enabled Russell to branch out into other sports such as golf and football.[16]

Leverage Raising needed cash by borrowing allows a firm to benefit from the principle of **leverage,** a technique of increasing the rate of return on funds invested through the use of borrowed funds. Like the fulcrum on which a lever rests, the interest payments on borrowed funds are fixed. The key to managing leverage is ensuring that a company's earnings remain larger than its interest payments, which increases the leverage on the rate of return on stockholders'

Table 20.2 How Leverage Works

Leverage Corp.		Equity Corp.	
Common stock	$ 10,000	Common stock	$100,000
Bonds (at 10% interest)	90,000	Bonds	0
	100,000		100,000
Earnings	30,000	Earnings	30,000
Less bond interest	9,000	Less bond interest	0
Net income/profit	21,000	Net income/profit	30,000
Return to stockholders	21,000 = 210%	Return to stockholders	30,000 = 30%
	$ 10,000		$100,000

investment. Of course, if the company earns less than its interest payments, stockholders lose money on their original investments.

Table 20.2 shows two identical firms that choose to raise funds in different ways. Leverage Corp. obtains 90 percent of its funds from lenders who purchase company bonds. Equity Corp. raises all of its funds through sales of company stock. Each company earns $30,000. Leverage Corp. pays $9,000 in interest to bondholders and earns a 210 percent return for its owners' $10,000 investment. Equity Corp. provides only a 30 percent return on its stockholders' investment of $100,000.

As long as earnings exceed interest payments on borrowed funds, financial leverage allows a firm to increase the rate of return on its stockholders' investment. However, leverage also works in reverse. If, for example, Equity Corp. earnings drop to $5,000, stockholders earn a 5 percent return on their investment. Because Leverage Corp. must pay its bondholders $9,000 in interest, however, the $5,000 gain actually becomes a $4,000 loss for stockholders. For a second problem, overreliance on borrowed funds reduces management's flexibility in future decisions.

THE U.S. FINANCIAL SYSTEM

Traditionally, the U.S. financial system has been divided into two categories: deposit institutions (which accept deposits from customers or members and provide some form of checking accounts) and nondeposit institutions. Deposit institutions include commercial banks, thrifts (savings and loan associations and savings banks), and credit unions. Nondeposit financial institutions include insurance companies, pension funds, and consumer and commercial finance companies.

The fundamental ele-

ments of the U.S. financial system are approximately 9,500 **commercial banks.** These profit-making businesses hold deposits of individuals, business firms, and not-for-profit organizations in the form of checking or savings accounts. They generate additional funds by selling certificates of deposit and borrowing from the Federal Reserve System. Banks then loan these funds to individuals, business firms, and not-for-profit organizations. By charging higher interest rates to borrowers than they pay to depositors and others who provide funds, the banks generate revenue to cover their operating expenses and earn profits. Figure 20.4 shows how a commercial bank performs its functions.

Banks generate additional revenue by charging fees for some services. Because fees vary considerably from bank to bank, businesses and consumers should compare them before choosing a bank. Customers are voicing increasing dissatisfaction with rising bank fees.

Types and Services of Commercial Banks

Most U.S. commercial banks are *state banks*—commercial banks chartered by individual state governments. About one-fourth of all commercial banks are chartered by the federal government and are referred to as *national banks*. These comparatively large institutions hold about 60 percent of total commercial bank deposits. While the regulations affecting state and national banks vary slightly, they differ little in their services to individual depositors or borrowers. The five largest U.S. banks are Chase Manhattan, Citicorp., BankAmerica Corp., NationsBank, and J. P. Morgan.[17]

Business Directory

leverage the technique of increasing the rate of return on an investment by financing it with borrowed funds.

| Figure 20.4 | Operations of a Commercial Bank |

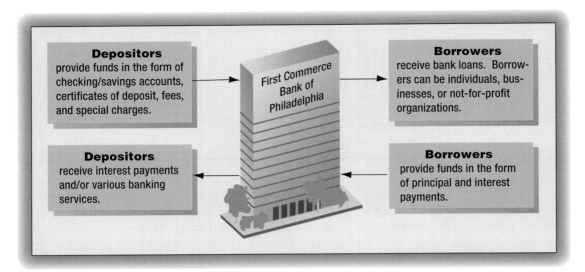

Depositors
provide funds in the form of checking/savings accounts, certificates of deposit, fees, and special charges.

Depositors
receive interest payments and/or various banking services.

First Commerce Bank of Philadelphia

Borrowers
receive bank loans. Borrowers can be individuals, businesses, or not-for-profit organizations.

Borrowers
provide funds in the form of principal and interest payments.

count brokerage services, wire transfers (which permit immediate movement of funds by electronic transfers to distant banks), and financial counseling. Most banks provide low-cost traveler's checks and overdraft protection for checking accounts, which automatically provides small loans at relatively low interest rates for de-

The term *full-service bank* accurately describes the typical commercial bank, which provides a wide variety of services to its depositors. In addition to checking and savings accounts and personal and business loans, commercial banks typically offer bank credit cards, safe deposit boxes, tax-deferred individual retirement accounts (IRAs), dis-

positors who write checks exceeding their account balances.

Check processing begins when an account holder writes a check—a document addressed to a bank or other financial institution that gives written, legal authorization to withdraw a specified amount of money from an account and to pay that amount to a specified person or business. In

BUSINESS HALL OF SHAME

ATM Fees—Making People Pay to Use Their Own Money

At one time, banks paid customers for their trust and for the privilege of using their money. Today, people who want to use their own money must pay the banks a fee... sometimes two fees. And to add insult to injury, trying to avoid the fees is getting more and more difficult.

Automatic Teller Machines (ATMs) were introduced by banks to give their customers more choices and offer them greater convenience. If consumers used ATMs, banks would save money and then pass these savings on to their customers. At least that's what it said in the information brochures when ATMs

were first introduced. But bank profits are at record highs, and the only thing being passed on to customers is more fees.

When one bank's customers use another bank's ATM, they pay one fee to their own bank—called an "off-us" fee—and a surcharge to the other bank, apparently for the convenience of using its ATM. Some 93 percent of all banks impose this surcharge; therefore, most people are paying two fees at any ATM not owned by their bank.

So why not just go to your own bank? Sales consultant Christa Eberhart explains, "You try really hard to avoid the fees, but it's kind of tough when you're out of town and something comes up." In addition, people on a lunch break from work or out late at night don't have the time to hunt

down a free ATM when they need cash, especially when those free ATMs are becoming so few and far between.

Banks have encouraged us to use ATMs because an ATM transaction costs only around 25 cents—far cheaper than a teller transaction, which costs well over a dollar. So when people try to avoid ATM fees by using tellers for any transaction that could have been completed at an ATM, some banks charge their customers yet another fee, apparently for the bank's additional trouble to give them their own money.

Bankers maintain that the surcharges have paid for the spread of ATMs to places like theaters, hospitals, and neighborhood markets. The surcharges are needed, explain bankers, to make the machines profitable—cov-

Figure 20.5, a purchasing agent for the Sea View Apartments buys a $150 carpet shampoo machine from Sears. The check that pays for the machine authorizes the Georgia National Bank of Savannah, where Sea View has a checking account, to reduce Sea View's balance by $150. The bank pays this sum to Sears to cover the cost of the machine. If both parties have checking accounts at the same bank, check processing is an easy chore; the bank simply increases Sears's balance by $150 and reduces Sea View's balance by the same amount.

However, if this purchase involved the retailer's Chicago checking account, the Federal Reserve System (the U.S. central bank) would act as a collector, as it does for most such intercity transactions. It handles a large number of the 180 million checks written every business day. You can trace the route a check has taken by examining the endorsement stamps on the reverse side.

Banks have increased their accessibility to customers by setting up *automated teller machines (ATMs)*. ATMs are electronic machines that permit customers to make banking transactions 24 hours a day by entering personal identification numbers (PINs). Networked systems enable ATM users to access their bank accounts from distant states and

They said it

"Banking is a risk industry. Unless bankers take risks, they cannot support their communities nor the industries and businesses making up those communities."

Philip E. Coldwell, 1922 –
Federal Reserve
former Board member

countries. Citibank has programmed its ATMs in 31 countries to give instructions for transactions in 11 different languages. Technological advances are expanding the capabilities of ATMs. For example, some new machines can accept applications for unsecured loans and home mortgages.[18]

The growing popularity of ATMs has led many owners to charge fees ranging from $0.50 to $2.00 per transaction, along with an additional charge by the customer's own bank. The Business Hall of Shame discusses increasing ATM fees. Some consumers are paying as much as $4.00 for the convenience. Income from these access fees is used to install more ATMs in more locations. For example, Banc One Corp. plans to extend its ATM network from 2,000 machines to 20,000 over 3 years. Consumers throughout the world are willing to pay a premium price for the convenience of ATMs. Hong Kong has the largest concentration of ATMs in the world. An ATM installed at a subway station in Kowloon handles 500 transactions each day, twice the number handled at a typical ATM in the United States. The demand for ATMs is especially high in developing nations such as China, Russia, and India, where people must contend with cash shortages although most financial transactions still involve exchanges of cash.[19]

---

ering expenses such as maintenance, telecommunications services, installation, rent, and security costs. Besides, most banks charge their own customers nothing for using their own ATMs.

Chase Manhattan began imposing ATM surcharges "to ensure that non-customers who use Chase's network contribute to the significant cost of operation," says bank spokesperson Ken Herz. And Citibank imposed the fees to save its own customers from standing in long lines, said spokesperson Mark Rodgers. Before that, Citibank's ATMs had been "magnets" for other banks' customers wishing to avoid the fees.

The fact is that income from ATM surcharges has been rising steadily, now around $2.1 billion—up from $1 billion just a year ago—and it continues to rise. The average transaction fee has also risen. For an ATM transaction conducted at a "foreign" machine, consumers are paying an average of $2.57, with an average surcharge of

$1.37—all for a transaction estimated to cost between 25 and 27 cents. Consumers are angry and frustrated because these fees come on top of other bank fees that are rising and continually being added, such as the fees to use tellers and higher fees for money orders and reordering checks.

With some planning, consumers can avoid ATM fees. They can take out more money each time they make a withdrawal, and they can get cash back when they use their debit cards at the supermarket. Studies show that consumers are already using their own bank's ATM more often than ever before. But sometimes, when planning ahead isn't possible, people simply get stuck paying the fees.

QUESTIONS FOR CRITICAL THINKING

1. Consumer groups criticize ATM fees as unjustified and excessive.

Why would banks risk customer anger by charging such fees if they truly don't need them? Please explain your answer.

2. Connecticut and Iowa have prohibited ATM surcharges. Should other states follow their example? Should the federal government step in and regulate this aspect of banking, or should the market determine what banks can and cannot charge? Please explain.

Sources: Jeff McKinney, "Banks Making Money from Convenience," Gannet News Service, April 12, 1999, accessed at nrstg1s.djnr.com; "ATM/Debit Card Use Rises," CNN Financial News, April 5, 1999, accessed at www.cnnfn.com; Andrew Clark, "Report: Most Banks Impose ATM Surcharges," Reuters Limited, April 2, 1999; Marcy Gordon, "Most Banks Impose ATM Surcharges," the Associated Press, April 1, 1999; Steven Syre and Charlie Stein, "The Boston Globe Boston Capital Column," Knight-Ridder Business News, February 18, 1999, accessed at nrstg1s.djnr.com.

| Figure 20.5 | A Check's Journey through the Federal Reserve System |

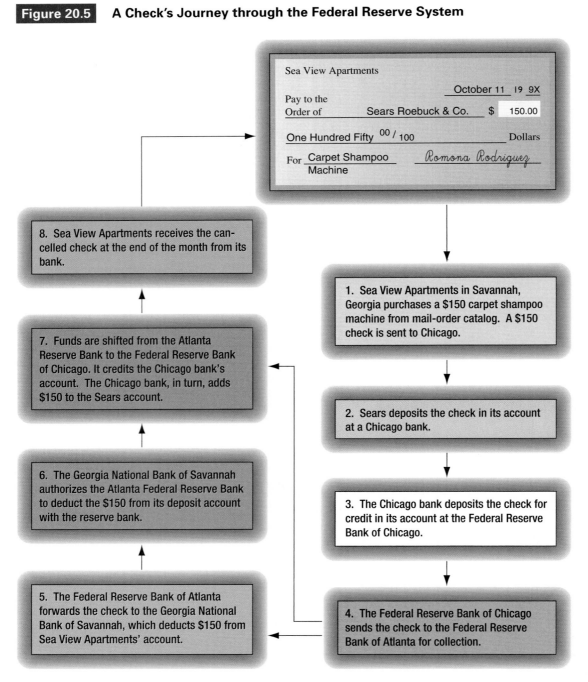

Sea View Apartments

October 11 19 9X

Pay to the
Order of   Sears Roebuck & Co. $ 150.00

One Hundred Fifty 00 / 100   Dollars

For Carpet Shampoo   Romona Rodriguez
        Machine

8. Sea View Apartments receives the cancelled check at the end of the month from its bank.

1. Sea View Apartments in Savannah, Georgia purchases a $150 carpet shampoo machine from mail-order catalog. A $150 check is sent to Chicago.

7. Funds are shifted from the Atlanta Reserve Bank to the Federal Reserve Bank of Chicago. It credits the Chicago bank's account. The Chicago bank, in turn, adds $150 to the Sears account.

2. Sears deposits the check in its account at a Chicago bank.

6. The Georgia National Bank of Savannah authorizes the Atlanta Federal Reserve Bank to deduct the $150 from its deposit account with the reserve bank.

3. The Chicago bank deposits the check for credit in its account at the Federal Reserve Bank of Chicago.

5. The Federal Reserve Bank of Atlanta forwards the check to the Georgia National Bank of Savannah, which deducts $150 from Sea View Apartments' account.

4. The Federal Reserve Bank of Chicago sends the check to the Federal Reserve Bank of Atlanta for collection.

ing, mailing, and clearing paper checks as high as $70 billion a year.[20] Another benefit of EFTS is the wealth of data that can accompany electronic payments, including invoice numbers, whether discounts were taken, and which dividends are to be paid.

The U.S. government plans to make the switch to electronic funds transfers by January 1, 1999. After that date, nearly all Social Security checks and other federal payments made each year will arrive as electronic data rather than paper documents. Recipients who do not have bank accounts will be given electronic benefit transfer cards that they can use to withdraw benefits at automated machines or spend them at point-of-sale terminals. Congress estimates that the switch to a checkless system will save the government $423 million over 5 years.[21]

Growing numbers of financial institutions are offering additional electronic banking services through **electronic funds transfer systems (EFTSs),** computerized systems for conducting financial transactions over electronic links. Only about 10 percent of large and mid-sized U.S. firms now rely on EFTS technology as their primary means of billing and payment distribution, but that percentage is expected to grow significantly in coming years. One reason is that EFTS saves money; estimates place the cost of print-

Another bank product is the debit card (also called a *check card),* which consumers can use to make purchases that are deducted directly from their checking or savings accounts. A debit card looks like a credit card, but it acts like a check. Unlike credit cards, debit cards can help consumers to live within their means, because payments for purchases are deducted from their bank accounts rather than accumulating as debt. Many banks are issuing debit cards as replacements for ATM cards, and many consumers are using them instead of cash and checks. Options include two types of debit cards: on-line and off-line cards. On-line debit cards require users to enter personal identification numbers when they make purchases. After punching in the correct number, the amount of a user's purchase is immediately deducted from her or his account. An off-line card, such as Visa's check card and MasterCard's Master Money, does not require a PIN, just a signature at the time of purchase.[22]

Recently, several large U.S. banks—First Union, NationsBank, and Wachovia Bank—have started testing so-called *smart cards,* which have been tested extensively in European and Asian countries for several years. A smart card looks like a credit card, but an embedded microchip stores monetary value and other information such as transaction data. Smart cards can replace cash, leading some observers to describe them as the biggest card innovation in more than two decades. At special bank dispensers, consumers can buy cards that store values of $20, $50, and $100 for use in paying for purchases at retail stores, restaurants, and other locations that have installed special reading machines. Some experts predict that a consumer's credit, ATM, and debit cards will soon be combined into a single smart card.[23]

In addition to providing a host of new services for customers, full-service commercial banks are trying to boost revenues by designing products targeted at certain market segments. The Business Hall of Fame box describes how Whitney National Bank is developing programs for entrepreneurs and small businesses.

Thrift Institutions

The term *thrift institutions* refers to savings and loan associations and savings banks. These financial institutions offer a variety of banking services such as home mortgages, loans, passbook accounts, time deposits, traveler's checks, consumer leasing, trust services, and credit cards—all at rates competitive with those of commercial banks. A **savings and loan association (S&L)** is a thrift institution that offers both savings and checking accounts; it uses most of its funds to make home mortgage loans. S&Ls now compete directly with banks in the commercial real estate lending business. **Savings banks,** also known as *mutual savings banks,* are state-chartered institutions with operations similar to those of S&Ls. Although savings banks once were concentrated in the New England states, they increasingly are expanding to other parts of the country.

Thrifts, most of them locally owned and managed, continue to play a critical role in mortgage and community lending. Congress recently enacted legislation designed to assist these institutions in meeting the lending needs of their communities.[24]

Credit Unions

A third type of deposit institution, a **credit union,** is a member-owned financial cooperative that pays interest to depositors, offers share draft (checking) accounts, and makes short-term loans and some home mortgage loans. It is typically sponsored by a company, union, or professional or religious group. The nation's 11,500 federally insured credit unions provide consumer loans at competitive rates for their members. They also offer interest-bearing checking accounts, life insurance, and financial counseling services. While credit unions tend to be relatively small (only 35 percent have assets of $10 million or more), they operate in every state and serve over 68 million members. Credit unions have loans outstanding totaling almost $200 billion.[25]

Nondeposit Financial Institutions

Other suppliers of funds and financial services for businesses include insurance companies, pension funds, and consumer and commercial finance companies. An *insurance company* provides financial protection against unforeseen costs for policyholders in return for premium payments. These firms use the funds generated by premiums to make long-term loans to corporations; they also make commercial and real estate mortgage loans and purchase government bonds.

A *pension fund* holds and invests a large pool of money accumulated by a company, union, or not-for-profit organization to provide retirement income for employees or members. Participants in the pension fund may begin to collect monthly payments upon retiring or upon reaching a certain age. Like insurance companies, pension funds invest in long-term mortgages on commercial property, business loans, and government bonds along with common stock in major firms. More than 80 percent of large companies still operate pension funds despite the growing popularity of 401(k) retirement plans. Under the 401(k) plans, employees make their own investment decisions and have access to all accumulated funds upon retirement.[26]

Consumer and commercial finance companies offer short-term loans to borrowers, who pledge tangible items such as inventory, machinery, property, or accounts receivable as security against nonpayment. A *commercial finance company* such as Commercial Credit or CIT supplies short-term funds to businesses that pledge tangible assets such as inventory, machinery, or property as collateral. A *consumer finance company,* such as Household Financial, plays a similar role for personal loans. GE Capital Services is a combined consumer and commercial finance company. GE Capital's advertising message in Figure 20.6 is targeted at commercial lenders, listing the different financial products it provides for businesses. Consumer and commercial finance companies obtain funds by selling bonds and arranging their own short-term loans from other firms.

Financial Supermarkets Today, some nondeposit institutions are doing just about everything that commercial banks do. The term *financial supermarket* describes a growing number of nonbank companies that offer a wide range of financial services, including investments, loans, real estate, banking, brokerage, financial planning, and insurance. Examples of financial supermarkets include American Express and brokerage firms such as Merrill Lynch and Smith Barney.[27]

Table 20.3 summarizes the sources and uses of funds for deposit and nondeposit institutions.

THE FEDERAL RESERVE SYSTEM

Since 1913, a growing number of U.S. financial institutions have been regulated by the **Federal Reserve System,** commonly referred to as the Fed. The Federal Reserve System consists of 12 regional Federal Reserve Banks and a seven-person Board of Governors, headed by a chairman. The Fed identifies each region by number and Reserve Bank city, as shown in Figure 20.7. In practice, the Federal Reserve acts as a clearinghouse for checks and regulates activities in the commercial banking system.

While all national banks are required to be members of the Federal Reserve System, membership is optional for state-chartered banks. In all, about 3,750 banks hold memberships. The Fed's regulatory powers cover all deposit institutions, whether or not they are members.

In addition to banking regulation, the Federal Reserve is responsible for ensuring that the U.S. money supply grows at an appropriate rate that allows the economy to expand without excessive price increases that could lead to inflation. When the available total of money and credit grows too slowly, consumers and businesses cannot afford to pay high interest rates on loans to buy homes and automobiles or invest in new equipment and facilities to fund business expansion. The Fed uses three major monetary policy tools—open market operations, reserve requirements, and discount rates—to influence the cost and availability of money and credit in the U.S. economy.[28]

The Fed's most important monetary policy tool is *open market operations,* the technique of controlling the money supply by buying and selling U.S. government securities (bonds). When the Fed buys bonds from securities dealers, the money it pays them enters circulation, increasing the money supply and making more money available to member banks. The extra money available for lending induces banks to reduce interest rates on loans. Low-rate loans stimulate consumer and business purchases. In contrast, when the Fed sells government securities, the money generated from these transactions is taken out of circulation, reducing the money supply and raising interest rates. By selling securities, the Fed tries to counter the threat of inflation, which slows economic growth by discouraging business investment and inhibiting consumer buying, as incomes do not increase as rapidly as the prices for goods and services. Over the years, open market operations have been used increasingly as a flexible means of expanding and contracting the money supply.

The Federal Reserve requires that all deposit institutions maintain reserves based on the balances they hold in checking accounts, NOW accounts, and share draft accounts. *Reserve requirements* are the portions of a bank's checking and savings deposits that it must hold in cash on its premises or on deposit at its regional Federal

| Figure 20.6 | **A Nondeposit Financial Institution as a Source of Funds** |

Business Directory

Federal Reserve System the U.S. central bank, consisting of 12 regional banks overseen by a Board of Governors, that regulates the U.S. banking system and acts as a clearinghouse for checks.

Table 20.3 Sources and Uses of Funds for Financial Institutions

Institution Type	Typical Investments	Types of Accounts Offered to Depositors	Primary Sources of Funds
DEPOSIT INSTITUTIONS			
Commercial bank	Personal loans Business loans Increasingly involved in real estate construction and home mortgage loans	Checking accounts NOW accounts Savings accounts Time deposits Money market deposit accounts	Customer deposits Interest earned on loans
Savings and loan association	Bond purchases Home mortgages Construction loans	Savings accounts NOW accounts Time deposits Money market deposit accounts	Customer deposits Interest earned on loans
Savings bank	Bond purchases Home mortgages Construction loans	Savings accounts NOW accounts Time deposits Money market deposit accounts	Customer deposits Interest earned on loans
Credit union	Short-term consumer loans Increasingly involved in longer-term lending, including mortgage loans	Share draft accounts Savings accounts Money market deposit accounts	Deposits by members Interest earned on loans
NONDEPOSIT INSTITUTIONS			
Insurance company	Corporate, long-term loans Mortgages for commercial real estate—major buildings/shopping centers		Premiums paid by policyholders Earnings on investments
Pension fund	Some long-term mortgages on commercial property and business loans		Contributions by member employees and employers Earnings on investments
Commercial and/or consumer finance company	Short-term loans to businesses (commercial finance company) Individual consumer loans (consumer finance company)		Interest earned on loans Bond sales Short-term borrowing from other firms

Reserve bank. For example, if the Fed sets the reserve requirement at 10 percent, a bank that receives a $500 deposit must reserve $50, so its officers can lend only $450. By changing the percentage of required reserves, the Fed can affect the amount of money available for making loans. A higher reserve requirement reduces the amount of money that banks can extend as credit to consumers and businesses. When the Fed lowers the reserve requirement, banks can distribute more of their funds as loans, thus stimulating the economy through expanded business investment and consumer purchases. However, changing the reserve requirement is a drastic action, since even a 1 percent variation in the reserve requirement means a potential fluctuation of billions of dollars in the money supply. It also

creates an expensive and complex burden for banks. For these reasons, the Fed only rarely uses this tool.

A third monetary-control tool of the Fed, the *discount rate,* is the interest rate at which Federal Reserve Banks make short-term loans to deposit institutions. A bank or credit union might need a short-term loan from the Fed if an unexpected increase in withdrawals leaves it temporarily unable to meet its reserve requirements. The law requires that each Federal Reserve Bank revise its discount rate every 2 weeks, subject to approval by the Board of Governors. In practice, the discount rate is the same at all Reserve Banks, because the credit market is national in scope.

When the Fed wants to slow the pace of economic activity to prevent inflation, it increases the discount rate,

| Figure 20.7 | The Federal Reserve System: Regional Banks and Their Districts |

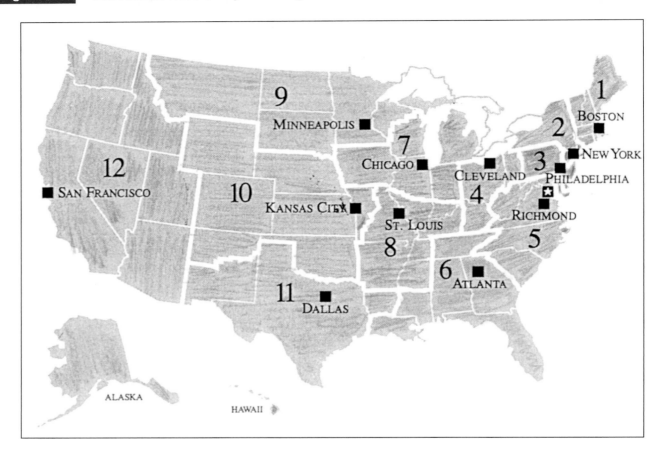

motivating bankers to tighten access to new loans. This response results in a decrease in the money supply. In contrast, the Fed decreases the discount rate when it wants to boost a slow-growing economy. A drop in this rate encourages member banks to increase their borrowing from the Fed, giving them more money available to make loans to consumers and businesses. The Fed has adjusted the discount rate often in recent years to control the money supply. For example, during a period of slow economic growth between December 1990 and July 1992, the Fed lowered the discount rate seven times from 7 percent at the beginning of the period to 3 percent, the lowest rate in 30 years. It has raised the discount rate several times since 1994. Even small changes in the discount rate can have large effects on the economy.

The Federal Reserve also has the authority to exercise *selective credit controls*. This set of tools includes the power to set *margin requirements*—the percentage of the purchase price of a security that an investor must pay in cash on credit purchases of stocks and bonds. Table 20.4 illustrates how the tools of the Federal Reserve stimulate or slow the economy.

Transactions in international markets also affect the U.S. money supply. On the **foreign exchange market**, purchases and sales exchange one nation's currency for that of another country. Billions of U.S. dollars are traded this way every day. The Fed can lower the exchange value of the dollar by selling dollars and buying foreign currencies, and it can raise the dollar's exchange value by doing the opposite—buying dollars and selling foreign currencies. When the Fed buys a foreign currency, the effect is

Business Directory

foreign exchange market the market where traders exchange one nation's currency for that of another nation.

Table 20.4 Federal Reserve Tools

General Tool	Action	Effect on Money Supply	Short-Term Effect on the Economy
Reserve requirement change	Increase reserve requirements	Reduces money supply	Boosts interest rates and slows economic activity
	Decrease reserve requirements	Increases money supply	Reduces interest rates and accelerates economic activity
Discount rate change	Increase discount rate	Reduces money supply	Boosts interest rates and slows economic activity
	Decrease discount rate	Increases money supply	Reduces interest rates and accelerates economic activity
Open market operation	Buy government securities	Increases money supply	Reduces interest rates and accelerates economic activity
	Sell government securities	Reduces money supply	Boosts interest rates and slows economic activity

SELECTIVE CREDIT CONTROLS

Margin requirement change	Increase margin requirements		Reduces credit purchases of securities with a negative impact on prices and trading activity on securities exchanges
	Reduce margin requirements		Increases credit purchases of securities with a positive impact on prices and trading activity on securities exchanges

the same as buying securities because it increases the U.S. banking system's reserves. Selling foreign currencies, on the other hand, is like selling securities, in that it depletes bank reserves.

 www.bog.frb.fed.us

Bank Safety

Many family histories include stories of money lost due to bank failures. To increase public confidence in the security of financial institutions and to prevent so-called *runs* on banks by panicked depositors seeking to withdraw their account balances in times of economic crisis, specialized federal insurance programs have been created that cover most commercial banks, thrifts, and credit unions. For example, deposits at all commercial banks that are members of the Federal Reserve System are insured by the **Federal Deposit Insurance Corporation (FDIC).** The FDIC insures depositors' accounts up to a maximum of $100,000 per account and sets requirements for sound banking practices. Deposits at federally insured thrift institutions are covered by a subsidiary of the FDIC. In addition, 88 percent of U.S. credit unions are federally insured by the National Credit Union Share Insurance Fund (NCUSIF).

The FDIC's primary technique for ensuring the safety and soundness of commercial banks and thrifts is its unannounced inspections. Individual institutions must open their books at least once a year for detailed reviews by bank examiners. A **bank examiner** is a trained financial analyst who inspects the financial records and management practices of a federally insured financial institution. Other commercial banks are inspected by examiners from the federal Comptroller of the Currency, the Federal Reserve System, or state banking commissions or other regulatory authorities. Such an examination, which may take from 1 week to several months, evaluates the bank in the following areas: ability of management, levels and sources of

BUSINESS HALL OF FAME

Small Firms Can Bank on New Services

Entrepreneurs and small businesses constantly struggle to find bank loans and lines of credit to keep their businesses afloat. To increase their chances of getting financing, they need to work hard at creating good relationships with their bankers. Says one entrepreneur, "Your banker is not just your banker, he's your partner."

But the partnership between banks and their small-business customers is beginning to change. It's the banks, rather than their customers, that are working harder to build partner relationships. Once reluctant to make rela-

tively risky small-business loans, banks are expanding their willingness to loan money to small firms, and several banks are streamlining their loan application procedures. Some banks are even creating new convenience services and programs targeted at entrepreneurs and small-business owners.

Whitney National Bank in New Orleans recently launched a new Business Edge Banking program for start-ups and small firms. As part of the program, Whitney created a no-fee checking account for any firm that writes fewer than 150 checks a month and keeps a $2,500 minimum balance. "We found there was a real need for a business checking account that is as easy [to use] as a personal checking

account," says Rebecca Dey, Whitney's vice president.

Another part of the program is Whitney's Business Owners ATM card, which provides 24-hour account access. "I know what small businesses' hours are," says Dey. "They're doing banking at 9 p.m. and on weekends." Whitney is also helping small-business customers manage their cash more efficiently by offering them consolidated monthly statements that report all account and loan activity. Customers can also receive daily fax transmissions that detail the previous day's activity on their accounts.

Whitney's Business Edge Banking services are a direct result of feedback from small-business customers, a mar-

earnings, adequacy of properties pledged to secure loans, capital, and current liquidity.

If bank examiners find serious problems in one or more of these areas, they include the bank on a problem list. Regulators view such a bank as a candidate for failure unless management takes corrective actions immediately, such as arranging for emergency loans or enlisting management assistance. Sometimes, the government may even replace the bank's directors. A written examination report typically discusses needed improvements, and regulators express concerns in meetings with the bank's top management and board members. Bank problem lists remain confidential documents, and few depositors ever become aware of such actions. More frequent examinations also evaluate efforts to correct problems.

Should problems uncovered during an examination require immediate action, more drastic measures can be taken. If the government cannot locate a satisfactory merger partner or buyer, it may close the institution. In such a case, regulators secure control of the financial records and physical facilities and freeze accounts, typically in an abrupt move after business hours on a Friday. By the following Monday, they have either allowed another bank to assume control or have paid off depositors up to the $100,000 deposit insurance limit. Any assets held by the failed institution are sold, and the proceeds are divided among creditors and holders of accounts exceeding the $100,000 insurance maximum.

THE U.S. FINANCIAL SYSTEM: A GLOBAL PERSPECTIVE

Financial services have become a global industry, and any review should consider the U.S. financial system in its international context. Citibank serves millions of banking customers around the globe with the world's largest branch network. Citicorp, J.P. Morgan, and Bankers Trust all hold more than 45 percent of their assets abroad. Chase Manhattan, the nation's largest bank, holds more than half of its assets in foreign countries.[29]

While most Americans recognize large U.S. banks such as BankAmerica and Citibank among the global financial giants, only three of the world's top 30 banks (measured by revenues) are U.S. institutions—Citicorp, Chase Manhattan, and BankAmerica. The Bank of Tokyo-Mitsubishi of Japan is the world's largest bank. The second largest is Deutsche Bank of Germany, and the third largest is Credit Agricole of France. Seven of the world's 30 largest banks are based in Japan, six are based in France, and five are German banks. Credit Suisse of Switzerland, the world's tenth largest bank, advertises its financial products throughout the world, as shown in Figure 20.8. It maintains operations in London, Tokyo, Hong Kong, and Sydney.[30]

ket segment that the bank defines as firms with fewer than 20 employees and less than $5 million in annual sales. Whitney's focus on this market segment represents part of a new trend in banking. A growing number of banks throughout the country are reaching out to small businesses by designing special programs and services for them.

Banks are beginning to pay more attention to the financial needs of entrepreneurs and small-business owners for several reasons. First, the market segment is growing, and banks want to capitalize on this growth. Second, many large firms that banks have traditionally served are increasingly turning to securities markets as lower-cost financing alternatives.

Another reason for the change is offered by Ann Grochala, director of bank operations at the Independent Bankers Association of America. According to Grochala, banks are experiencing increased competition from nonbank financial institutions, including insurance companies and commercial finance companies, that are helping entrepreneurs and small businesses to finance equipment and inventory. By offering cash management, business checking accounts, electronic banking, and other special services, Grochala believes that banks boost their chances of competing with nonbanking institutions.

QUESTIONS FOR CRITICAL THINKING

1. **Considering the high failure rate of start-ups and small businesses, do you think that banks should target this business segment? Why or why not?**

2. **Suppose that you work for a bank that is interested in designing special programs for entrepreneurs and small-business customers. Which marketing research tool or tools would you use to find out what types of services this market segment wants and needs?**

Sources: Ron Ence, "Community Banker Says Regulatory Burden Gap Hurts Local Lending," Independent Community Bankers of America press release, May 12, 1999, accessed at www.ibaa.org; Stephanie Barlow, "Buddy System," *Entrepreneur*, March 1997, pp. 121–127; Michael Selz, "Struggling Entrepreneurs Find Bankers More Willing to Lend," *The Wall Street Journal*, January 13, 1997, pp. B1–B2; and "Getting a Bank to Stick with You," *Nation's Business*, September 1996, pp. 24–25.

Like the Federal Reserve in the United States, most nations define their own central banking authorities that control their money supplies. For example, the central bank in Germany is the Bundesbank, and in the United Kingdom, the Bank of England performs this function. Policymakers at other nations' central banks often respond to changes in the U.S. financial system by making similar changes in their own systems. When the Fed raises U.S. interest rates, for example, central banks in Japan and Germany may also raise their rates. These changes can influence events in countries around the world. Higher U.S. or German interest rates not only increase the cost of borrowing for American and German firms, but they also reduce the amount of money available for loans to borrowers in Asia and Latin America.

International banks and other providers of financial services play important roles in global business. They help to transfer purchasing power from buyers to sellers and from lenders to borrowers. They also provide credit to importers and reduce the risks associated with exchange rates. Even small and mid-sized banks are entering the global financial community. New Orleans-based Hibernia Corp. recently began advising the central bank of Belize on how to find and obtain financing for major infrastructure projects. Among the projects Belize is considering are privatization of its port, expansion of its airport, and the development of an off-shore banking industry.[31]

Figure 20.8 **Credit Suisse: One of the World's Largest Banks**

SUMMARY OF LEARNING GOALS

1. Identify the functions performed by a firm's financial managers.

The major responsibility of financial managers is to develop and implement a financial plan for their organization. The firm's financial plan is based on forecasts of expenditures and receipts for a specified period and reflects the timing of cash inflows and outflows. The planners systematically determine their company's need for funds during the period and the most appropriate sources from which it can obtain them. In short, the financial manager is responsible for both raising and spending money.

2. Describe the characteristics a form of money should have, and list the functions of money.

Money should be divisible, portable, durable, stable in value, and difficult to counterfeit.

3. Distinguish between money (M1) and near-money (M2).

Money (M1) is defined as anything generally accepted in payment for goods and services, such as coins, paper money, and checks. Near-money, or M2, consists of assets that are almost as liquid as money but that do not function directly as a medium of exchange, such as time deposits, government bonds, and money market funds.

4. Explain how a firm uses funds.

Organizations use funds to run their day-to-day operations, pay for inventory, make interest payments on loans, pay dividends to stockholders, and purchase land, facilities, and equipment. Most financial managers choose to invest excess cash in marketable securities.

5. Compare the two major sources of funds for a business.

Debt capital and equity capital are the two major sources from which businesses acquire funds. Debt capital represents funds obtained through borrowing. Equity capital comes from several sources, including stock issues, additional investments by the firm's owners, previous earnings reinvested in the firm, contributions from venture capitalists and other investors, and cash obtained by liquidating assets.

6. Identify likely sources of short-term and long-term funds.

Sources of short-term funds include trade credit (generated automatically through open-account purchases from suppliers), unsecured loans, secured loans (for which the firm must pledge collateral), and sales of commercial paper by large firms with unquestioned financial stability. Sources of long-term financing include long-term loans repaid over 1 year or longer, bonds, and equity funds (ownership funds obtained from selling stock in the company, selling assets, reinvesting company earnings, or accu-

mulating additional contributions by owners, venture capitalists, or other investors).

7. Describe the major categories of financial institutions and the sources and uses of their funds.

The U.S. financial system consists of deposit and nondeposit institutions. Deposit institutions, such as commercial banks, thrifts, and credit unions, accept deposits from customers or members and offer some form of checking account. Nondeposit financial institutions include insurance companies, pension funds, and finance companies. They offer funding for businesses and serve as mortgage lenders to finance commercial real estate deals.

8. Explain the functions of the Federal Reserve System and the tools it uses to increase or decrease the money supply.

The Federal Reserve System is the U.S. central bank; it controls the supply of credit and money in the economy in order to promote growth with price stability. Its tools include reserve requirements, open market operations, and the discount rate. The Fed's governors increase the reserve requirement or the discount rate to reduce the money supply, and they decrease the reserve requirement or the discount rate to increase the money supply. Open market operations increase the money supply when the Fed purchases government bonds, and they decrease the money supply when it sells bonds. Selective credit controls and purchases and sales of foreign currencies also help the Fed to influence the economy.

9. Describe the institutions and practices for regulating bank safety.

Many commercial banks are members of the Federal Reserve System, and their deposits are insured by the Federal Deposit Insurance Corporation (FDIC). The FDIC insures depositors' accounts up to a maximum of $100,000 per account and sets requirements for sound banking practices. Deposits at federally insured thrift institutions are covered by a subsidiary of the FDIC. Most credit unions are insured by the National Credit Union Share Insurance Fund (NCUSIF). Government efforts to guarantee the safety and soundness of banks and thrifts rely primarily on unannounced inspections of the books at individual institutions at least once a year by bank examiners.

TEN BUSINESS TERMS YOU NEED TO KNOW

finance	equity capital
financial manager	bond
financial plan	leverage
money and near-money	Federal Reserve System
debt capital	foreign exchange market

Other Business Terms

risk-return trade-off

financial control

commercial bank

electronic funds transfer
  system (EFTS)

savings and loan association
  (S&L)

savings bank

credit union

Federal Deposit Insurance
  Corporation (FDIC)

bank examiner

REVIEW QUESTIONS

1. What functions does a financial manager perform? What role does forecasting play in these functions?
2. How do organizations use money? Cite specific examples.
3. What primary uses might a firm define for short-term financing? What is the difference between secured and unsecured loans?
4. What is the difference between debt capital and equity capital? Name several sources of equity capital.
5. List the sources for long-term financing. How do borrowed funds produce leverage? How does borrowing affect a firm's financial performance?
6. What are the basic functions of money?
7. How does M1 differ from M2?
8. What categories describe financial institutions in the United States? What are the primary sources and uses of funds available in each institution?
9. What is the role of the Federal Reserve System? How does the Fed use open market operations, reserve requirements, and discount rates to influence the money supply?
10. In what ways are financial institutions using technology to provide services to their customers?

QUESTIONS FOR CRITICAL THINKING

1. The chairman of the Federal Reserve Board plays a critical role in the U.S. financial system. William McChesney Martin, chairman from 1951 to 1970, has described the job as "the chaperone who takes away the punch bowl when the party gets going good." Relate Martin's job description to the monetary tools the Fed uses. What does the "punch bowl" represent in Martin's statement?
2. Consumers today can choose between many options for banking services and financial institutions. In selecting a banking method and institution, which criteria would be most important to you? For example, would convenience outweigh costs?
3. You decide to start a business with a friend. Your friend is the creative type and would like to focus on the marketing strategy while you act as the financial manager. How would you get start-up funds? Would you prefer debt or equity financing?
4. Why was the Federal Deposit Insurance Corporation created? How does it protect the soundness of the banking system? What does it do when a bank fails?
5. Suppose that your start-up company needs a huge infusion of capital. A venture capitalist has agreed to give you the money you need to grow, but she tells you that you will own only 20 percent of the company after the deal, and you'll be replaced by a new chief executive. Would you be willing to take the money but lose control of your firm?

Experiential Exercise

Directions: This exercise focuses on financial controls and is a continuation of the Experiential Exercise in Chapter 19 in which you prepared a personal one-month cash budget.

1. Copy your work from Chapter 19 in the table that follows, in the column labeled "Budgeted."
2. Track your expenses for the month and record your actual expenses in the column labeled "Actual."
3. Compare your budgeted amounts with the actual amounts you spent and record the difference in the last column.
4. Answer the questions following the table.

Category	Budgeted	Actual	Difference
Household expenses			
Education			
Work			
Clothing			
Automobile			
Insurance			
Taxes			
Savings and investments			
Entertainment/recreation			
Debt			
Miscellaneous			

Questions:
1. Which expense category or categories had a significant difference between the budgeted figures and actual expenses?
2. What are causes for the difference?
3. What correction, if any, is necessary to control this expense in future months?

Nothing but Net

1. **Banking by Browser.** Find a Web site that provides a listing of Internet banks, such as

   www.onlinebankingreport.com/fullserv.html

   Answer the following questions:
   a. How many U.S. banks are listed?
   b. Which state has the most Internet bank headquarters?
   c. How many world banks are listed?
   d. Which country has the highest representation of Internet bank headquarters?
   e. Which Internet bank has the earliest date for being added to the list?
   f. Which Internet bank was most recently added to the list?
   g. Randomly select a world Internet bank to visit. What languages, if any, are offered at the site?

2. **The Role of the Financial Manager.** One responsibility financial managers have is to maximize the wealth of the firm's stockholders by balancing the risk of an investment and its potential gain. To experience this balancing act personally, imagine that you have $10,000 to invest in a mutual fund. Your job is to explore your options and find the fund or funds that you believe will provide the highest return with a comfortable level of risk. Remember that the high-growth funds come with greater risk than do the low-growth funds. The Quicken Financial Network at

   www.quicken.com/investments/mutualfunds/top25

   is one Web site that allows investors to identify types of funds and then see a list of the 25 top-performing funds in that category. Explore your options, and write a short report on which fund(s) you selected to invest your $10,000 and the criteria you used to make that decision. Be sure to include the balance between risk and potential gain that you chose.

3. **The Federal Reserve System.** Write a short report on the seven-person Board of Governors, including how appointments to the board are made, what the length of a term is, who the current members are, and how long each has been a member. Also include brief biographical data about the chairman and vice chairman of the board. One Web site that provides such information is

   www.bog.frb.fed.us/

Note: Internet Web addresses change frequently. If you do not find the exact sites listed, you may need to access the organization's or company's home page and search from there.

FIRSTBANK CORPORATION

Mergers, acquisitions, and the creation of megabanks characterize the banking industry of the late 1990s. As laws prohibiting interstate banking crumble, commercial banking in the United States is beginning to resemble banking in other nations, where a relatively few international banks provide financial services for the entire country. A few banking institutions have turned this trend into a competitive advantage both by their orientation to the local community and by offering services that the giants are eliminating. That is exactly what Firstbank Corporation has done.

The Michigan-based corporation owns and operates three commercial banks: the Bank of Alma, Firstbank, and 1st Bank. With branches spread over the entire state, Firstbank is able to offer the traditional banking services of checking, savings, and time deposits; trust services; and installment and consumer loans that meet customers' needs for commercial, agricultural, real estate, home improvement, automobile, and personal loans.

Firstbank is not unlike other banks in that it depends on deposits and interest payments on loans to generate revenues. However, in recent years, income received in the form of loans increased by only 7 percent. During the same period, interest on investment securities actually fell 6 percent. Management knew these figures would not spell success in the long run and took decisive measures to increase revenue.

Firstbank management had to decide on a strategy that would allow a small regional bank to compete successfully with the banking giants. Large banks have resources such as large marketing departments, the ability to handle huge sums of capital, and an international presence that gives them access to customers throughout the world. However, the current trend is for large banks to cut back on services—critical items that local banks can provide their customers. Firstbank management identified several opportunities to retain their loyal customers and, at the same time, attract new ones. Firstbank managers operated on the basic premise that they provide their customers with greater levels of service.

Advantages a local bank has are its ability to react more quickly to customers' needs by designing special deposit and loan product offerings, quicker decision making, and the ability to build and maintain close relationships with its customers.

Firstbank President and CEO John A. McCormack has pointed out that the one constant in banking is change through consolidation and opportunity to expand market share and income through acquisition. However, expansion means the responsibilities of the bank's financial manager are increased. It becomes critical for forecasts of cash inflows and outflows to be accurate. This is particularly true during times of expansion since the financial manager must ensure that funds will be readily available when needed, while making sure that none of the bank's assets are sitting idle.

Faced with expansion opportunities in local markets, Firstbank managers recognized the need for additional funds. In 1993 they made a public offering of 334,958 shares of common stock, which generated $5.5 million in equity capital. Of these funds, $3.2 million was used to repay all outstanding notes payable, $1 million was used to make a capital infusion at its 1st Bank subsidiary, and the remaining $1.3 million was used to acquire additional bank branches.

The stock offering and the focus on customer service at each of the subsidiary banks have allowed Firstbank to grow faster than would have been possible through internal deposit and loan generation alone. In fact, over the past 10 years, assets have grown from $127.3 million to $325 million, and the future looks bright for Firstbank's small local bank network.

Questions

1. Describe the responsibilities of a financial manager. How do they apply to Firstbank Corporation?

2. What is the difference between financing with debt capital and equity capital? Why would Firstbank choose to finance with equity capital? Explain.

3. How can small-town banks like Firstbank compete with banking giants that also have a presence in their marketplace?

chapter 21

Financing and Investing through Securities Markets

LEARNING GOALS

1. Distinguish between the primary market for securities and the secondary market.

2. Compare common stock, preferred stock, and bonds, and explain why particular investors might prefer each type of security.

3. Identify the four basic objectives of investors and the types of securities most likely to reach each objective.

4. Explain the process of selling or purchasing a security listed on an organized securities exchange.

5. Describe the information included in stock, bond, and mutual fund quotations.

6. Explain the role of mutual funds in securities markets.

7. Evaluate the major features of state and federal laws designed to protect investors.

Online Trading—Just a Keystroke Away with Ameritrade

People who buy and sell shares of stocks and mutual funds are getting tired. They're not tired of trading but waiting to place orders with their brick-and-mortar brokerage houses. And they're tired of paying high brokerage commissions. But if they can get on the Internet, they can establish an account with an online deep-discount broker. Then all the trading they want is only a keystroke away. Cyberbrokers like Ameritrade offer online transactions that are fast. They provide research and market information that is up-to-the-minute. And they charge commissions that are extremely low. No wonder they have already lured more than 6 million investors to trade on the Net. About one in every seven equity trades is now placed on the Web. With the tally already past 5 million online accounts, observers expect online

trading accounts to double within a year. In fact, Ameritrade aims to double its brokerage accounts every year. It is well on its way, with a record 82,000 new accounts opened during a recent quarter.

Having launched the company in 1975 with $10,500 in borrowed money, Chairman and Co-CEO J. Joe Ricketts became the first U.S. broker to offer touch-tone phone trading in 1988. Ameritrade has been online since 1994, and with his family, Ricketts controls 63 percent of the company's shares—that's more than $5 billion worth. It looks like online brokers are here to stay. And Ameritrade isn't the only one around.

Facing rivals such as Charles Schwab, E*Trade, Datek, SureTrade, and Waterhouse Securities, Ameritrade must compete not only on prices but also on service. At $8 per trade on the Internet, Ameritrade offers one of the lowest minimum commissions around, and convenience tops the company's list of customer services. You can conduct transactions over your touch-tone phone 24 hours a day for just $12 a trade. The system leads you through the quote and order process and prompts you for entries using your phone keypad. For $18 a trade, you can get assistance from a professional broker. Or if you prefer, you can place orders, get quotes, and view positions and balances with a

Sharp Zaurus Personal Digital Assistant—a lightweight device that lets you trade from anywhere using a simple modem connection.

Through alliances with Internet giants Yahoo! and America Online, Ameritrade expands its convenience by making it easy for clients to find and use its services.

www.ameritrade.com

Perhaps best of all, the site provides access to Market Guide research, which provides reports on more than 10,000 publicly traded companies. From quick facts such as snapshots of a company's key financial ratios, pricing data, and recent earnings statements and company profiles—including quarterly and annual income statements, balance sheet, key officers, and industry comparisons—Ameritrade gives you the information you need. Plus, with StockQuest, users have a powerful, easy-to-use tool that offers 50 predefined variables to screen the firms clients are interested in. You can even create your own variables, portfolios, and reports.

Ameritrade is transforming itself from a small Midwestern firm to a high-volume cyber powerhouse. Of course, as with almost every trader on the Net, Ameritrade has experienced Web site slowdowns and even downright outages. But the company's technology is improving. Co-CEO Tom Lewis is supervising the computer system upgrade and the improvement of phone-based customer service. Lewis says that he and his team are "really getting a handle on this thing." Additional technology spending is pegged at $100 million over the next two years. Ameritrade is working hard to help its clients get news, track companies' performances, and trade shares—all with just the stroke of a computer key.[1]

CHAPTER OVERVIEW

The previous chapter discussed two sources of funding for long-term financial needs: debt capital and equity capital. Long-term debt capital takes the form of corporate bonds, U.S. government bonds, and municipal bonds. Equity cap-

ital takes the form of stocks—shares of ownership in the corporation. Stocks and bonds are commonly called **securities,** because both represent obligations on the part of issuers to provide purchasers with expected or stated returns on the funds invested or loaned.

This chapter explains how stocks and bonds are bought and sold in two marketplaces, the primary market and the secondary market. It discusses the different types of stocks and bonds and the characteristics of each that lead investors to choose specific securities that help them to achieve their investment objectives. The chapter also

Business Directory

security a stock or bond that represents an obligation of the issuer to provide the purchaser an expected or stated return on the investment.

primary market exchanges in which firms sell new issues of securities publicly for the first time.

examines the information included in reports of securities transactions, and it describes the laws that regulate the securities market and protect investors.

THE PRIMARY MARKET

In the **primary market,** firms issue securities and sell them initially to the public. When a company needs capital to expand a plant, develop products, acquire another firm, or pursue other business goals, it may make a stock or bond offering.

A stock offering gives investors the opportunity to purchase ownership shares in the firm and to take part in its future growth in exchange for providing current capital. A stock offering in the primary market is called an *initial public offering (IPO).* Recent years have brought a significant increase in IPOs, up from 172 in 1990 to 870 in 1996, when IPOs generated $49.8 billion (1997 saw just over 600 IPOs, with $43.1 billion generated).[2]

The growth in IPOs has reflected the rise in public security sales by entrepreneurial firms, such as Netscape Communications and Yahoo!, to raise the money they need to grow their businesses. The trend has relied on the strong support of investors willing to buy shares in these high-risk, high-reward investments. Well-established private companies like Revlon, Dominick's Supermarkets, Gulfstream Aerospace, and Steinway Musical Instruments use IPOs to revitalize their firms with infusions of new capital. Foreign start-ups and privatized organizations have also contributed to the growth in IPOs. For example, Vimpel Communications in Moscow completed an IPO 2 years after it began providing cellular telecommunications services in Russia. The stock offering is helping Vimpel to build the infrastructure needed to expand its services and market them to a larger subscriber base.[3]

Companies and government agencies also use primary markets to raise funds by issuing bonds. For example, the federal government sells U.S. Treasury bonds to finance part of the budget deficit. State and local governments typically issue municipal bonds to finance long-term capital projects such as the construction of new schools or municipal buildings.

Announcements of stock and bond offerings appear daily in business newspapers such as *The Wall Street Journal.* These announcements take the form of simple, black-

and-white ads called *tombstones.* The tombstone ads in Figure 21.1 inform the public that Audio Book Club offers approximately 2.4 million shares of common stock at $10 per share, and System Software Associates, Inc. desires to acquire $138 million in debt capital by selling bonds paying 7 percent annual interest with repayment of principal in 2002.

Although some companies market stock and bond issues directly to the public, most large offerings are handled

Russian start-up Vimpel Communications employed folk dancers to promote its initial public offering that it listed on the New York Stock Exchange. Representing 3,930,000 shares of common stock, the IPO is helping Vimpel to expand its cellular phone network in Moscow.

by financial specialists called **investment bankers,** or *underwriters.* An investment banker is a financial intermediary who specializes in selling new stock and bond issues for business firms and government agencies. An investment banker acquires the newly issued securities from the company or agency and then resells them to other investors. The underwriters for the Audio Book Club and System Software Associates issues are listed at the bottom of the tombstones shown in Figure 21.1.

Investment bankers underwrite stock and bond issues at a discount, keeping the difference between the issue prices and the selling prices as compensation for services rendered (including the risk they incur and related expenses). Although underwriting fees are negotiable, they usually range from 6 percent to 8 percent of the public offering price. An underwriter also receives an expense allowance that generally amounts to 2 percent of the offering price of the shares.

In addition to locating buyers for the issue, the underwriter typically advises the issuer on such details as general

Figure 21.1   **Tombstones Announcing Stock and Bond Offerings**

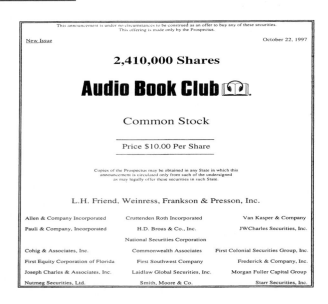

characteristics of the issue, its pricing, and the timing of the offering. Several investment bankers commonly participate in the underwriting process. Often the primary, or lead, underwriter does not take complete responsibility for the public issue. Instead, it may form a syndicate by selling either all or part of the shares to other underwriters who, in turn, sell them to the public.

When Multicom Publishing Inc. of Seattle needed money to expand its line of CD-ROMs, the company raised $7.2 million in an initial public offering. Laidlaw Equities Inc. was the lead underwriter in Multicom's IPO. Laidlaw priced the securities at $6.50 a share. It bought 345,000 of the 1.1 million shares offered in the sale and paid Multicom $5.98 per share. The underwriting fee Laidlaw earned, $179,400, was the difference between the offering price of $6.50 at which it sold the stock to the public and the $5.98 it paid Multicom for each share. Laidlaw formed a syndicate of 25 other investment banks to sell the remaining 755,000 shares.[4]

www.multicom.com

THE SECONDARY MARKET

Daily news reports of stock and bond trading refer to transactions in the **secondary market,** a collection of places where previously issued shares of stock and bonds are traded among owners other than the issuing firms. Compo- nents of this market offer convenient locations for buyers and sellers to make exchanges. The issuing corporations do not receive the proceeds from such transactions, and gains and losses affect only the current and future owners of the securities. The various elements of the secondary market are discussed later in the chapter.

STOCK

Shares of stock are units of ownership in a corporation. Although many corporations issue only one type of stock, the markets trade two types: common stock and preferred stock.

Common Stock

The basic form of corporate ownership is embodied in **common stock.** Purchasers of common stock are the true owners of a corporation. In return for the money they invest, they expect to receive payments in the form of dividends and/or capital gains resulting from increases in the value of their stock holdings.

Holders of common stock vote on major company decisions, such as purchasing another company or electing a board of directors. They benefit from company success, and they risk the loss of their investments if the company fails. Because creditors and preferred stockholders receive their returns before common stockholders, holders of common stock are said to have a *residual claim* on company assets.

Common stock is sold on either a par value or no-par value basis. *Par value* is an arbitrary value for stock designated by the company. It is usually under $1 per share. In some states, par value forms the basis for state incorporation taxes. Because par value is highly arbitrary, most corporations issue no-par value stock. In either case, the total number of shares outstanding represents the total ownership of the firm, and the value of an individual stockholder's investment is based on the number of shares owned and their market price rather than on an arbitrary par value.

Sometimes confusion arises over two other types of stock value: market value and book value. *Market value* is the price at which a stock issue is currently selling. It is easily determined by referring to the financial section of daily newspapers. Market value usually varies from day to day, depending on company earnings and investor expectations about future prospects for the firm. *Book value* is determined by subtracting the company's liabilities, including the value of any preferred stock it has issued, from its assets. When this net figure is divided by the number of shares of common stock, the book value of each share is known.

Preferred Stock

In addition to common stock, many corporations issue **preferred stock**—stock whose owners receive preference in the payment of dividends. Also, if the company is dissolved, holders of preferred stock have claims on the firm's assets that require payment before payment of any claim by common stockholders.

In return for this privileged position, preferred stockholders usually sacrifice voting rights. When preferred stockholders do hold voting rights, they typically are limited to such important proposals as mergers, sales of company property, and dissolution of the company itself. Although preferred stockholders are granted certain privileges over common stockholders, they still are considered owners of the firm, and their dividends, therefore, are not guaranteed.

Preferred stock often is issued with a conversion privilege. This *convertible preferred stock* gives stockholders the option of exchanging their preferred shares for common stock at a stated price. James River convertible preferred stock currently pays an annual dividend of $3.50 per share and is convertible into 1.25 shares of James River's common stock.

Preferred stock usually is issued to attract conservative investors who want the margin of safety in the security's preference over common stock. Although preferred stock represents equity capital, many people consider it a compromise between bonds and common stock.

BONDS

Bondholders are creditors, not owners, of a corporation. By selling bonds, a firm obtains long-term debt capital. Municipal, state, and federal government units also acquire funds in this way. Bonds are issued in various denominations, usually between $1,000 and $25,000. Each issue indicates a definite rate of interest to be paid to the bondholder and a maturity date on which the issuer will repay the borrowed funds. Because bondholders are creditors of the corporation, they have a claim on the firm's assets that must be satisfied before any claims of preferred and common stockholders in the event of the firm's dissolution.

Types of Bonds

A prospective bondholder can choose among a variety of bonds. Six major types of bonds are summarized in

---

DID YOU KNOW?

▼ More than 75 percent of stockholders have graduated from college. The average shareholder has 15 years of formal schooling; fewer than 6 percent have not received high school diplomas.

▼ As many women own stock as do men. Adult males comprise 48 percent of all stockholders, and adult females also comprise 48 percent. The remaining 4 percent is held by children.

▼ More than 60 million people own shares in publicly traded corporations. This total represents more than one of every four U.S. households.

Business Directory

secondary market the collection of places where subsequent owners trade previously issued shares of stocks and bonds.

common stock a security that provides the owner voting rights in major company decisions but only a residual claim on company assets.

preferred stock a security that provides the owner preferential dividend payments and first claim on company assets after satisfaction of all debts; it seldom confers voting rights.

Table 21.1 Major Types of Bonds and Their Distinguishing Characteristics

Type of Bond	Distinguishing Characteristics
Secured	Backed by specific pledges of company or government assets
Unsecured (debenture)	Backed by the financial reputation of the issuing corporation or government unit
Convertible	Can be converted into common stock at the bondholder's option
Serial	Parts of a large issue that mature on different dates
Sinking fund	Issuer makes yearly deposits of funds sufficient to redeem the bonds when they mature
Callable (redeemable)	Gives the issuing corporation or government agency the option of redeeming the bonds before the issue's maturity date

Table 21.1. A **secured bond** is backed by a specific pledge of company assets. For example, mortgage bonds are backed by real and personal property owned by the firm, such as machinery or furniture, and collateral trust bonds are backed by stocks and bonds of other companies owned by the borrowing firm. In the event of default, bondholders may receive the proceeds from selling these assets.

Because bond purchasers want to balance their financial returns with their risks, bonds backed by pledges of specific assets are less risky than those without such collateral. Consequently, a firm can issue secured bonds at lower interest rates than it would have to pay for comparable unsecured bonds.

However, a number of firms do issue unsecured bonds, called **debentures**. These bonds are backed only by the reputations of the issuing corporations or government units. Only governments and major corporations with extremely sound financial reputations can find buyers for their debentures.

A *government bond* represents funds borrowed by the U.S. federal government. Because such an issue is backed by the full faith and credit of the U.S. government, these bonds are considered the least risky of all debt obligations. A *municipal bond* is a debt issue of a state or political subdivision, such as a county or city. An important feature of municipal bonds is the exemption of interest payments from federal income tax; most also pay interest exempt from taxes in the states and localities in which they are issued. Because of this attractive feature, these bonds can carry significantly lower interest rates than comparable issues.

In order to entice speculative purchasers to buy their debt securities, corporations sometimes issue *convertible bonds*. A convertible bond gives its holder the option of converting it into a specific number of shares of common stock. The number of shares of stock exchanged for each bond is specified in the bond indenture—the legal contract that specifies all provisions of the bond issue. A $1,000 bond might be convertible into 50 shares of common stock. If the common stock is selling at $18 when the bonds are issued, the conversion privilege has no value. But if the stock price rises to $30, this conversion privilege has a value of $1,500. Convertible bonds offer lower interest rates than those lacking conversion privileges, helping to reduce the interest expenses of the issuing firms. Some bond purchasers prefer such bonds, even at lower interest rates, since they value the potential for additional gains if the price of the firm's stock increases.

Quality Ratings for Bonds

When most people think of investing, they immediately think of the stock market. But it is not the only investment arena available. Investors seeking safe havens for their money often choose the bond market.

Two factors determine the price of a bond: its riskiness and its interest rate. Because the bondholder is a creditor of the company, he or she has first claim on the firm's assets if it is liquidated. For this reason, bonds generally expose owners to less risk than stocks, although this relationship does not always hold. To judge the degree of risk in a bond, investors should ask the following questions:

▼ Will the company or government agency issuing the bond be able to pay the principal when due?

▼ Will it likely make the interest payments?

▼ Is the bond already in default?

In general, the risk of a bond issue is reflected in its

Business Directory

secured bond a debt security backed by a specific pledge of company assets.

debenture a bond backed only by the reputation of the issuer.

ratings provided by the two bond-rating services—Standard & Poor's (S&P) and Moody's. The most risk-free bonds are rated AAA by Standard & Poor's and Aaa by Moody's. The ratings descend to the level of so-called *junk bonds,* and then down to the most speculative issues, usually those already in default. Table 21.2 illustrates S&P's and Moody's bond ratings.

Junk bonds attract investors by offering high yields in exchange for elevated risk. Today, junk bonds generally earn between 3 and 5 percent higher interest rates than AAA bonds.

The second factor affecting the price of a bond is its interest rate. Other things being equal, a higher interest rate raises the price at which a bond will be bought and sold. But everything else usually is not equal; the bonds may not be equally risky, or one may tie up money for a longer period of time than the other. Consequently, investors must evaluate the trade-offs involved.

Another important influence on bond prices is the market interest rate. When interest rates go up, bond prices go down, because bondholders are locked into interest rates lower than purchasers could gain with newly issued securities.

Retiring Bonds

Because bonds in an issue mature on a specific date, the issuing corporation must have the necessary funds available to repay the principal at that time. The two most common methods of repayment distinguish serial bonds from sinking fund bonds.

In the case of a *serial bond,* a corporation simply issues a large number of bonds that mature at different dates. For example, if a corporation decides to issue $4.5 million in serial bonds for a 30-year period, the maturity dates may

determine that no bonds mature for the first 15 years. Beginning with the 16th year, $300,000 in bonds may mature each year until the bonds are repaid at the end of the 30 years. Serial bonds are often issued by city governments.

A variation of the concept of serial bonds is the sinking fund bond. Under this plan, the issuer makes annual deposits to accumulate funds for use in redeeming the bonds when they mature. These deposits are made with a bond trustee, usually a major bank with the responsibility of representing bondholders. The deposits must be large enough that their total plus accrued interest will be sufficient to redeem the bonds at maturity.

A *callable bond* has a provision that allows the issuing corporation to redeem it before its maturity date after paying a premium. For instance, a 20-year bond may not be callable for the first 10 years. Between 11 and 15 years, it might be callable at a premium of $50, and between 16 and 20 years it might be callable at its face value.

Why issue callable bonds? If a corporation issues 30-year bonds paying 10 percent annual interest, and interest rates decline to 8 percent, it could pay less interest on the same principal by issuing new securities. It may decide to call the 10 percent bonds, repaying the principal from the proceeds of newly issued bonds that pay a lower rate of interest. Such actions may be financially sound, even though the firm would incur additional costs in retiring the old bonds and issuing new ones.

SMALL BUSINESS AND THE SECURITIES MARKET

Many small businesses have long complained that Wall Street investment banks deny them the level of service reserved for larger clients. This difference is reflected in the size of the **underwriting spread**—the difference between

Table 21.2 Moody's and Standard & Poor's Bond Ratings

Moody's	Interpretation	Standard & Poor's	Interpretation
Aaa	Prime quality	AAA	Bank investment quality
Aa	High grade	AA	
A	Upper medium grade	A	
Baa	Medium grade	BBB	
		BB	
Ba	Lower medium grade or speculative	B	Speculative
B	Speculative	CCC	
		CC	
Caa	From very speculative to near or in default	C	
Ca			
C		DDD	In default (with a rating based on the issuer's relative salvage value)
		DD	
		D	

the price paid to the issuer and the price charged to investors. Generally, underwriting spreads tend to grow as the size of a security issue shrinks.

Consequently, some small companies are trying different approaches in selling their securities to the public. One approach is the direct public offering (DPO), in which small firms sell shares directly to individual investors, bypassing investment bankers. In DPOs, firms target customers, employees, suppliers, distributors, and friends as investors. DPOs tend to attract conservative investors who have natural affinities for the companies in which they invest.[5] The Business Hall of Fame describes how an entrepreneurial firm raised equity capital through a direct public offering.

Other entrepreneurs are raising money through public offerings on the Internet. In February 1996, Spring Street Brewing Company, a New York-based microbrewery, initiated the first electronic public offering (EPO) on the Internet. The company needed cash but was unable to attract an investment banker willing to underwrite a stock issue for an underwriting spread that its managers could tolerate. Spring Street posted a note on its home page offering its stock to customers. Some 3,500 investors bought $1.6 million in stock via Spring Street's Web site. At the same time, the company created a virtual exchange—dubbed Wit-Trade—where investors can post buy or sell offers for Spring Street stock.[6]

plaza.interport.net/witbeer/

Electronic public offerings provide small firms with an inexpensive way to reach large groups of potential investors. They eliminate the costs involved in printing and sending out prospectuses—booklets full of company financial information that the Securities and Exchange Commission requires firms to send to stock purchasers. In an EPO, a small company posts its prospectus on a Web site. "The Internet cuts the fat out of reaching the public, opening whole new pools of funds for these companies," says Julio Gomez, a consultant to firms that do business on the Internet.[7]

SECURITIES PURCHASERS

Two general types of investors buy securities: institutional and individual purchasers. An **institutional investor** is an organization that invests its own funds or those it holds in trust for others. Included in this definition are insurance companies, retirement funds, mutual funds, commercial banks, and thrift institutions, as well as other investors such as not-for-profit organizations and foundations. Figure 21.2 shows the breakdown of institutional investors according to these categories.

Institutional investors buy and sell large quantities, often in blocks of 10,000 or more shares per transaction. Such block trading accounts for more than half of the total daily volume on organized securities exchanges, and institutional investors account for about two-thirds of all trading volume. The number of investors who own shares through mutual funds or employers' pension plans is steadily rising, and the firms that manage their funds now control more than half of all U.S. equities.

Institutional investors have become the most important force in today's securities markets. In fact, mutual funds now provide most of the new money that goes into stocks. Despite the importance of institutional investors,

BUSINESS HALL OF FAME

Turning Customers into Investors

When Ann Withey and Andrew Martin launched Annie's Homegrown Inc. in 1989, they decided to create a special bond with their customers. Annie's markets all-natural macaroni and cheese dinners and other pasta entree mixes. By 1996 the company earned $6 million in revenues, and its products were distributed to supermarkets and natural-food stores in all 50 states.

People who buy Annie's products get more than high-quality, preservative-free pasta. Annie's uses its product packaging to inform customers about the company's commitment to support ethical, socially responsible, and environmentally conscious business practices. Messages on the package invite customers to write Annie's to receive free "Be Green" bumper stickers. Other messages encourage them to visit Annie's Web site, where they can read the company's *Be Green* online magazine.

The package also includes a letter from Ann Withey, who explains why

the firm's 14 employees started a program called S.A.V.E., for Support American Volunteer Efforts. The package copy offers a free S.A.V.E. booklet containing ideas for community volunteering. Withey encourages customer feedback by including her home phone number and company address.

By responding to customer letters and phone calls, Annie's has built a database of loyal customers. One customer letter said, "Thank you for producing a wonderful, high quality product that is everything it should be . . . while keeping green issues in

however, individual investors still play a vital role. Some 60 million Americans own stocks, either directly or by investing in stock mutual funds. Furthermore, many institutional investments reflect the demands of individual investors. For instance, many mutual fund families have added international stock funds in recent years.

Investment Motivations

Why do individuals and institutions invest? For some, the motivation is **speculation**—the hope of making a large profit on stocks within a short time. Speculation may take the form of acting on a corporate merger rumor or simply purchasing high-risk stocks, such as low-priced *penny* stocks (so called because they sell for less than $5 per share).

A second motivation is long-term growth in stock value. Investors who chose growth as a primary goal invest

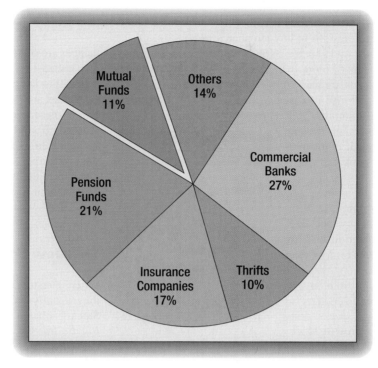

Figure 21.2 **Category Breakdown of Institutional Investors**

in fast-growing firms like Nike, Microsoft, Amgen, Home Depot, Harley-Davidson, Intel, United Healthcare, Oracle, and Compaq Computers—all of which increased stockholder return by 35 percent or more each year during the past decade. From 1986 to 1996, Amgen, a pharmaceuticals company, has posted an annual return rate of 67.8 percent to investors while company revenues have grown at an annual rate of 108 percent.[8]

Growth-oriented investors are also likely to benefit from stock splits, which typically occur in fast-growing companies. A stock split changes the capital structure of a firm by dividing each single share into multiple shares at correspondingly lower prices. This reduction in the price of the stock makes it easier for new investors to buy.

In still another investment motivation, some securities owners use stocks and bonds to supplement income. The income received from securities investments is called the investor's *return*, or **yield.** Yield is calculated by dividing

---

mind." According to Withey, customers "take pleasure in supporting us. . . . Their encouragement is the basis of our success."

When Annie's needed to raise money to expand the distribution of its products, it turned to its customers for help. In 1995, Annie's launched a year-long direct public offering by inserting an announcement inside each pasta package, sending 40,000 letters to customers, running an ad in *Mother Jones* magazine, and posting a notice along with the entire prospectus on its Web site. "Our whole thinking was to make our customers our owners, and to enlist them as a marketing team because they care about our company," says Deborah Churchill, vice chairman of Annie's.

In the DPO, Annie's offered 600,000 shares of common stock at $6 per share. The offering generated more than $1.5 million from 2,435 investors (more than 30 percent generated from the Web site), whom the company refers to as "Annie's Army." Annie's used the funds to branch out into about 1,000 supermarkets throughout the country. The infusion of capital helped Annie's to increase its revenues by $1 million.

QUESTIONS FOR CRITICAL THINKING

1. What role did Annie's packaging play in the success of the company's direct public offering?

2. Would you enlist in "Annie's Army"? Why, or why not?

www. **www.annies.com**

Sources: Mary Scott, "Annie's Homegrown Courts Buyer," Natural Foods Merchandiser stock update, November 1998, accessed at www.nfm-online.com; "Welcome! by Annie," downloaded from www.annies.com on November 18,1997; Carol Steinberg, "The DPO Revolution," *Success*, March 1997, p. 14; Andrew Serwer, "Bunny Wabbit Wanna Go Pubwick?" *Fortune*, December 23, 1996; and Stephanie Gruner, "Let Your Packaging Do the Talking," *Inc.*, July 1996, p. 88.

dividends or interest income by market price. The yield from any particular security varies with the market price and the dividend or other income payments.

Investors motivated primarily by income concentrate on the dividends of companies in which they consider investing. Someone with enough foresight to buy ten shares of General Motors Corp. stock in 1940 for $468 would have received dividend payments of more than $8,000 by the mid-1990s. Because dividends are paid from company earnings, investors consider a company's past record for paying dividends, its current profitability, and its prospects for future earnings. Purchasers of income stocks are likely to own shares of companies in stable industries such as banking, insurance, and public utilities.

Investors who seek safety as their primary objective are likely to purchase high-quality bonds and preferred stocks. These securities offer substantial protection and are likely to continue paying good returns over the long term.

Most investors pursue multiple investment goals. Those who emphasize safety of principal may buy some growth stocks along with bonds. Those who buy growth stocks may choose to diversify by adding comparatively safe investments to their portfolios. Table 21.3 provides a useful guide for evaluating stocks and bonds based on the three general long-term investment objectives.

Liquidity and Taxes In addition to the three primary investment goals, investors must consider two other factors: liquidity and taxes. Because the prices of securities vary widely, investors cannot count on making profits whenever they decide to sell. Liquidity is a measure of the speed at which assets can be converted to cash; if this consideration is important, investors should choose securities that tend to remain stable in price.

Taxes can also influence investment decisions. The tax that has the greatest impact on investments is the federal income tax, which is levied on investment income and on capital gains (increases in the value of assets such as stocks and bonds). Taxes on wealth, such as the federal estate tax or property taxes, can also affect decisions about specific types of investments. Some investments, purchases of gold or antiques, also may be subject to sales taxes.

SECURITIES EXCHANGES

Securities exchanges are centralized marketplaces for stocks and bonds. Often called **stock exchanges,** these institutions handle transactions in both stocks and bonds. Although corporations' securities are traded, the corporations are not involved directly in these transactions, and they receive no proceeds from the sales. The securities traded at organized exchanges already have been issued by corporations, which received the proceeds from the issues at the time of underwriting. Sales in a stock exchange occur between individual and corporate investors.

The New York Stock Exchange

When investors talk about "the stock market," they usually are referring to the New York Stock Exchange, or NYSE. Referred to as the *Big Board,* the NYSE is arguably the best-known stock exchange in the world. It is also one of the world's oldest and largest. The shares of more than 2,900 of the world's best-known firms trade on the NYSE, including those of 320 foreign firms from 42 countries. To allow its stock to trade on the NYSE, a firm must apply to the exchange for listing.

To transact business on the NYSE, an investment firm must be a member, meaning it must own at least one of the 1,366 *seats* on the exchange. Seats are bought and sold. In 1817, when the NYSE was founded, a seat sold for $25. In 1997, one of the seats sold for $1.5 million.[9]

To reach its goal of becoming the first truly global stock exchange, the NYSE is investing in new technology that will allow it to handle trades of 3 billion shares a day compared to the 500 million shares it currently trades in a normal day. It is trying to attract more firms and retain current listings by providing customers with advertising support, as shown in Figure 21.3. The NYSE is increasing its visibility by allowing more TV stations to set up broadcast

> They said it
>
> There are two times in a man's life when he should not speculate: when he can't afford it, and when he can."
>
> Mark Twain (1835–1910)
> American author

	Investment Objective		
Table 21.3 Long-Term Investment Objectives of Securities			
Type of Security	Safety	Income	Growth
Bond	Best	Very steady	Usually none
Preferred stock	Good	Steady	Variable
Common stock	Least	Variable	Best

Figure 21.3 Promoting Firms Listed on the New York Stock Exchange

booths on its trading floor and making real-time stock prices available to stations such as CNBC and CNNFN.[10]

www.nyse.com

The American Stock Exchange and Regional Exchanges

Another U.S. national exchange is the American Stock Exchange, or AMEX. The AMEX, also located in New York, is much smaller than the NYSE, handling some 22 million shares a day, and it focuses on listing smaller firms with national followings.[11]

To be listed on the NYSE or AMEX, a firm must meet a number of requirements, including number of shares held by the general public, pretax income for latest fiscal year, and net tangible assets. The less strict requirements for listing on the AMEX make it an attractive seasoning board for firms not ready to be listed on the Big Board. In fact, many of the firms now listed

on the NYSE originally were part of the AMEX but transferred to the Big Board after they achieved sufficient earnings and asset values.

www.amex.com

In addition to the NYSE and AMEX, several regional exchanges operate in the United States. These include the Midwest (in Chicago), Pacific (in San Francisco), Boston, Cincinnati, and Philadelphia Stock Exchanges. Originally established to trade the shares of relatively small firms operating in limited geographic areas, the regional exchanges now list securities of many major corporations, as well. The largest regional exchange, the Midwest, handles about 8 percent of all trades in NYSE-listed stocks. About half of the companies listed on the NYSE also are listed on one or more regional boards.

stock exchange a location at which traders buy and sell stocks and bonds.

Trading activity is flourishing in new stock exchanges being launched in emerging markets, such as the Muscat Securities Market in Oman shown here. From a gallery above the trading floor, observers use binoculars to monitor brokers' trading transactions, which are posted on blackboards.

Even though they are regional rather than national, the Midwest and Pacific exchanges actually handle trades with larger total market values than the AMEX handles. They still are dwarfed, however, by the NYSE and the Tokyo Stock Exchange.

Foreign Stock Exchanges

Stock exchanges are not unique to the United States. In fact, the world's oldest board, the Amsterdam Stock Exchange, began operations in 1611. The London Stock Exchange, which lists more than 7,000 securities, traces its beginnings to pre-American Revolution times. Foreign exchanges are significant securities markets. During the last 10 years, more shares were traded on the Tokyo Stock Exchange than were traded on the New York Stock Exchange.

Foreign exchanges are gaining market share in global trading, actively trading shares from many companies around the world. Of the more than 2,500 securities traded on the Geneva, Switzerland exchange, about 250 stocks and 900 bonds are issued by non-Swiss firms. Some U.S. firms list their securities both at home and abroad. In fact, the London Stock Exchange trades more than 20 million shares daily of NYSE-listed stocks—over 10 percent of the NYSE's volume. Other American companies prefer to list with foreign exchanges to avoid the Big Board's strict listing requirements.

Stock exchanges in developing European, Asian, and South American countries are growing rapidly to handle the explosive growth in global investing. For example, the Brazilian exchange now lists 560 stocks, China has 640 listings, and South Korea has 765 listings. The International Finance Corporation reports that the number of exchanges in emerging markets has tripled since 1985 to about 85. In Africa and eastern Europe alone, it is estimated that about 12 new exchanges will be built within the next 10 years.[12]

Global Securities Trading

International stock exchanges are becoming a reality. GLOBEX, an international 24-hour trading system, links traders from around the world to exchanges. GLOBEX recently received permission to add terminals in Japan. The 12 major exchanges in the European Union are working toward forming one unified exchange. In the process, they will have to overcome significant differences between different nations' business methods. For instance, the stock market in Paris reveals volume and price information within seconds of a trade, while investors in Milan may have to wait until the following day.

A big step toward unifying the different markets is Eurolist, a cross-listing of securities issued by over 250 major European companies. While some European firms already list their stock on more than one exchange, they find it a costly activity. One company with securities trading on six different markets estimates that its annual listing fees total almost $60,000, and the cost of meeting all the different disclosure requirements comes to nearly $1 million a year. Eurolist reduces listing charges to a single fee and allows firms to qualify for listing just by meeting their home countries' requirements.[13]

The NASDAQ System

In addition to both domestic and foreign stock exchanges, investors can also trade in the over-the-counter (OTC) market, an informal method for trading securities through

Individual investors can get up-to-the-minute information about stocks listed on NASDAQ by visiting its Market Site via the company's Web site.

market makers who fill customers' buy and sell orders. Unlike traditional stock exchanges, the OTC market has no trading floor on which securities are bought and sold. Instead, brokers bring together buyers and sellers by computer and telephone.

Dealers involved in OTC transactions keep in regular contact with one another, and the prices of the securities they trade are established by supply and demand. A dealer "makes a market" in a stock by quoting a bid price (what it will pay for a security) and an asked price, or selling price. An investor who decides to purchase an OTC stock or bond issue contacts a broker, who contacts the dealers handling the security in search of the best price. When the investor and dealer agree on a price, a market is made. The OTC market includes more than 500 market-maker firms, including such well-known brokerage firms as Merrill Lynch and Goldman Sachs.

At the heart of the OTC market is the **National Association of Securities Dealers Automated Quotation (NASDAQ) system,** a nationwide electronic trading network. About 4,800 companies list their securities with NASDAQ. In a typical year, it trades over 100 billion shares with a total market value in excess of $2,400 billion. In number of shares traded, NASDAQ is larger than the NYSE today.

Many firms whose stocks are traded on OTC markets have too few shares outstanding to be listed on the NYSE or AMEX. Others have too few stockholders, and still others lack sufficient earnings to qualify for listing. The OTC market includes the shares of most insurance companies and banks and the bonds issued by many city and state government units. A number of major corporations have chosen not to list their stocks and bonds on the national and regional exchanges, opting instead for NASDAQ listings. Many of the leading U.S. technology companies—including Microsoft, Sun Microsystems, Intel, Cisco Systems, and Amgen—are listed on the NASDAQ system.

In 1997, NASDAQ unveiled its high-tech Market Site, a

room with 100 video monitors at its New York headquarters building. Designed as an information resource for individual investors, Market Site displays stock information and news broadcasts and can be accessed via NASDAQ's Web site.

www.nasdaq.com

BUYING AND SELLING SECURITIES

A typical securities transaction involves a stockbroker, a financial intermediary who buys and sells securities for individual and institutional investors. The Business Tool Kit presents some practical tips on selecting a stockbroker.

Placing an Order

An investor who wants to purchase Boeing common stock would typically initiate the transaction by contacting a stockbroker. Local staff members would convey the order to the firm's member at the NYSE, who would go directly to the location on the floor of the exchange where Boeing is traded and attempt to make the purchase.

An investor request to buy or sell stock at the current market price is a *market order.* The NYSE representative would carry the order for Boeing on a best-price basis. On the other hand, an investor request to buy or sell stock at a specified price is a *limit order.* To carry out such an order, the representative would enter a notation of the limit order at the post that handles Boeing stock. If the price reaches the specified price, the order is carried out.

Stock trading is normally conducted in quantities of 100 shares, called *round lots.* Investors can purchase fewer than 100 shares, however, by buying odd lots; purchases or

Selecting a Stockbroker

One of the most important decisions an investor makes is choosing a stockbroker. Before making this decision, investors should take the following steps:

▼ Determine what financial objectives you want to emphasize, and prepare a personal financial profile.

▼ Interview several stockbrokers at different firms, asking them about their investment experience, professional backgrounds, and education.

▼ Call your state securities regulator and ask if prospective stockbrokers are licensed to do business in your state. The federal Securities and Exchange Commission maintains an online directory of state securities regulators.

▼ Check to see if securities regulators or criminal authorities have ever taken any disciplinary action against the stockbrokers. You can find this information by calling 1-800-289-9999, a toll-free hot line operated by the National Association of Securities Dealers, Inc.

▼ Ask each stockbroker to send you a copy of his or her commission schedule and a list of other investment fees. Find out what you are required to pay when opening, maintaining, and closing an account.

▼ Resist the pressure of stockbrokers who want you to open an account with them immediately. Take your time in doing the necessary background investigation so you will select a broker that best meets your personal financial needs and investment objectives.

Like many other businesspeople, stockbrokers often reach potential customers by calling them on the phone, a practice known as *cold calling*. Although cold calling is a legitimate way to get new clients, it's used by some dishonest stockbrokers to pressure people into buying stocks in small, unknown firms that are highly risky or part of an investment scam.

If you receive a phone call from a broker using high-pressure sales tactics to promote a once-in-a-lifetime investment opportunity, it's especially important that you investigate the background of the broker by following the steps listed above. Wise investors never buy an investment based only on a telephone solicitation. If the stock offer seems appealing to you, ask the broker to send you written information about the company and make sure the investment is registered with the Securities and Exchange Commission and your state securities agency. Then get a second opinion about the stock offer by contacting another broker or your financial advisor.

Sources: "Invest Wisely: Advice from Your Securities Industry Regulators," and "Cold Calling," Office of Investor Education and Assistance, U.S. Securities and Exchange Commission, 450 5th Street NW, Washington, DC, 20549.

sales of fewer than 100 shares of stock are then grouped together to make up one or more round lots, and the shares of stock or sales proceeds are then distributed to the investors who entered the odd-lot orders.

Two frequently mentioned stock market terms refer to investor attitudes. A **bull** is an investor who expects stock prices to rise. Based on that assumption, bulls buy securities when prices are low and plan to resell them later when prices are higher to earn a profit. When stock market prices continue to rise, market observers speak of a *bull market,* which encourages buying and forward thinking.

A **bear** is an investor who expects stock prices to decline. Based on that assumption, bears are likely to sell their securities in anticipation of falling market prices. When stock market prices continue to fall, market observers speak of a *bear market.*

Costs of Trading

When you buy or sell securities through a stockbroker, you pay fees for the related services. These costs vary among brokerage firms but generally range from 1 to 2 percent of the total value of a stock transaction.

Business Directory

bull an investor who expects stock prices to rise as part of a general upward market trend.

bear an investor who expects stock prices to decline as part of a general downward market trend.

Discount brokerage firms compete with traditional, full-service brokers by offering fewer services and charging lower commissions. For instance, while full-service broker Merrill Lynch might collect a $95 commission for selling 100 shares, a discount broker such as Charles Schwab might charge $30 for the same trade. As the amount of a transaction rises, so does the savings on commissions with a discount broker, since the commission as a percentage of the amount invested declines as the cost of the investment rises.

Online brokerage firms such as Ameritrade, featured in the opening story of this chapter, charge even lower commission fees than those of discount brokers. By charging low fees and offering a wealth of investment information, online firms are attracting a growing number of individual investors. One investor who left his full-service brokerage firm to become an online customer of Lombard Institutional Brokerage Inc. said, "My broker was so nice, but boy, they were robbing me. All he ever did was place my trades. I can do that for myself."[14]

One research firm predicts that by 2001, online investing will account for about 9 percent of the total value of all stock and mutual fund investments. More than 30 firms offer online services, including full-service securities firms such as Donaldson, Lufkin & Jenrette, whose low-cost service is described in Figure 21.4. Discount broker Charles Schwab even offers its customers a 20 percent discount when they cybertrade using the firm's e.Schwab online service.[15]

Since the introduction of discount brokerages and online services, the commission practices of full-service brokers have come under attack, as investors examine fee structures.

Computerized Trading

The securities trading staff at NationsBanc Corp. do not even need to speak when placing a buy or sell order, which may range from $15 million to $500 million in any given day. Instead, they log their orders directly onto computers, which execute the trades. Perhaps the most useful feature of this ap-

proach, according to Mary Primm, senior vice president of NationsBanc, is the direct electronic communication between the computerized trading system and other computer systems at the bank. "The portfolio manager now has the ability to execute a trade electronically by entering it into the system and is assured that the system automatically will update the information to the accounting and custodial systems," she explains.[16]

More and more of today's stock trading is done through computer networks like NationsBanc's, and that percentage is certain to rise. Electronic systems have revolutionized securities trading by creating vast networks that deliver lightning speed, low overhead, and anonymity. Commissions charged for using such systems average about 2 cents per share, less than half the typical rate that large institutions pay on traditional trades through stockbrokers. About 40 percent of the dollar volume of trading at the New York Stock Exchange comes through the exchange's automated order-handling system.[17]

The Fourth Market

The so-called *fourth market* systems match buyers directly with sellers, bypassing both NASDAQ and the stock exchanges. Alternative trading systems include electronic

Figure 21.4 **Offering Investors Low-Cost Trading Online**

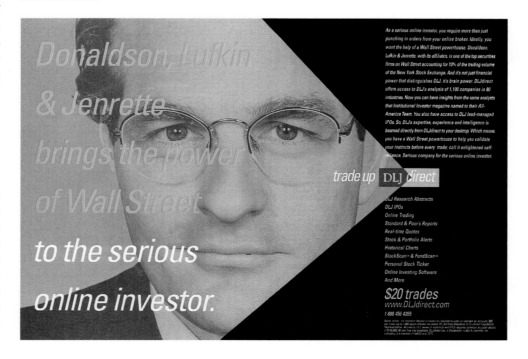

SOLVING AN ETHICAL CONTROVERSY

Should Hedge Funds Expect to Be Rescued from Their Greed?

Long-Term Capital Management (LTCM) is a hedge fund, an investment vehicle for wealthy investors who use mostly borrowed money to get awe-inspiring returns. In the broadest sense, a hedge fund tries to neutralize the risks of market trading (or hedging its plays) by buying and selling at the same time. These funds achieve their goals in many ways: Some hedge funds never actually borrow to invest; others leverage assets, keeping the ratio around 2 to 1.

Former vice chairman of Salomon Brothers and now fund manager at LTCM, John Meriwether had a strategy that was supposed to be foolproof: Find investments that couldn't go wrong and bet on them with borrowed money. The result would be large profits without risk. LTCM's strategy involved Treasury bond futures—borrowing to buy securities and selling them, hoping to buy them back later at a lower price. The fund also invested in higher-yield, higher-risk securities, backed by mortgage or corporate debt. As long as Treasury bond prices

dropped or remained stable, the strategy would generate enormous profits. But, the market didn't cooperate.

When stocks plunged, bond prices shot up, and LTCM was left with a huge debt ratio that was greater than 50 to 1. It began having trouble meeting its minimum capital requirements—making its "margin call"—and the fund nearly defaulted. Estimated losses were in the hundreds of billions of dollars. The collapse of LTCM would bring chaos to the world financial system, and the Federal Reserve worried about the large banks that had loaned money to the fund. So the Fed convinced some of the largest firms on Wall Street to bail out LTCM with $3.6 billion. Oversight Partner I, LLC, was formed of fourteen financial institutions, including Chase Manhattan, Goldman Sachs, Merrill Lynch, and Salomon Smith Barney.

But the bailout is viewed by some as unfair. People are outraged that investors who are rich enough and greedy enough to endanger world markets will be saved from ruin simply because they are too big to let fail.

 Should Top Banks Lend Billions to Save Hedge Funds?

PRO

1. Bailing out LTCM was unavoidable

because the Fed believed that the collapse of such a huge fund would put too much stress on the world markets. So it avoided a global market meltdown, which would have hurt smaller investors much worse than the bailout.

2. The bailout doesn't threaten small investors or even involve their money. Smaller investors are protected by the Securities Investors Protection Corporation, which insures up to $500,000 invested with a brokerage, and by the Federal Deposit Insurance Corporation, which insures up to $100,000 of funds in banks.

3. Bailing out LTCM doesn't threaten the country's banks. In fact, most banks have lost very little to hedge funds—partly because few hedge funds have ever defaulted.

4. Bailing out the fund is better than trying to regulate it because some things simply cannot be regulated. Federal Reserve Chairman Alan Greenspan says, "I know of no legislation to help us prevent [humans] from making dumb mistakes." Besides, any direct oversight would simply prompt hedge funds to move their operations offshore.

---

communications networks such as Instinet and Bloomberg TradeBook, which allow institutions to trade among themselves. The computerized systems are becoming increasingly popular among institutional traders, who view them as low-cost alternatives to NASDAQ and the stock exchanges. These systems handle about 20 percent of the orders in over-the-counter stocks and almost 4 percent of orders in securities listed on the NYSE.[18]

A growing number of major corporations offer even more direct ways to purchase securities. Individual investors who would like to acquire common stock in Exxon, Disney, American Ex-

They said it

"Never invest in anything that eats or needs repainting."

Billy Rose (1899–1966)
American theatrical impresario

press, Ford, IBM, Merck, and McDonald's can purchase shares directly from the companies. Almost half of the 330 firms that offer such direct purchase plans are foreign firms such as Sony, Benetton, and British Airways, that list their stocks on U.S. exchanges.[19]

The share price for a direct purchase is set at the closing price on the day of purchase. Buying directly usually costs less than using a discount broker or online service. Companies typically charge one-time enrollment fees ranging from $5 to $15 and small fees for individual transactions. Most firms set minimum purchase requirements starting as low as $50. As

5. Bailing out hedge funds protects the nation's banks, which can be severely damaged by hedge fund losses. Chase Manhattan Corporation, the nation's largest bank, has exposed $3.2 billion of its portfolio to hedge funds.

6. The bailout of LTCM has taught the market an important lesson. "The market has clearly learned from the LTCM incident," says Federal Reserve Governor Laurence Meyer. "Our supervisory staff has seen significant tightening of credit standards on hedge funds as well as improvements in the risk management processes at major banking institutions." Meyer points out that "currently, no national bank's exposure exceeds 3 percent of its total equity capital."

CON

1. The bailout of LTCM was wrong because it merely saved super-rich investors from going broke.

2. Bailing out hedge funds is wrong because it invites banks to support these funds while denying them access to meaningful information. Hedge funds are extremely secretive; they don't want to reveal anything that would let outsiders in on their strategies.

3. Hedge fund bailouts are wrong because they encourage investors to gamble with borrowed money and the outcome is not guaranteed. "When you're leveraged, you have to make margin calls," says Stan Jones, of FIMAT USA. "So it's not enough to be right. You have to be right at the right time."

4. Bailing out funds such as LTCM invites people to invest in ideas that are ultimately unprofitable. In two years, the people who invested in hedge funds would actually have done better to put their money into indexed mutual funds.

5. Bailing out LTCM is wrong because it will only lead to bailing out other hedge funds. Even though LTCM's debt ratio was unusual, its shortcomings in risk management are found in other funds, says Fed Governor Meyer.

SUMMARY

When LTCM nearly collapsed, observers believed it was the end of hedge funds. Either the remaining hedge funds would crumble under the weight of enormous debt or they would be abandoned by investors seeking safer funds. But the doomsayers were proven wrong when the funds made a comeback.

This reversal happened for several reasons. First, the LTCM episode was not followed by a series of hedge fund disasters. Second, many hedge funds have a clause that prevents investors from withdrawing their funds for up to 180 days—time for everything to quiet down. Third, and most important in the eyes of the Federal Reserve, financial advisors adopted the right strategy to avoid future problems. Banks have assumed the responsibility for evaluating the risks involved in lending to hedge funds, says Governor Meyer. "The real key to effective market discipline lies in the players themselves—the private sector."

However, the New York Federal Reserve president emphasized that "it is important that supervisors ensure progress continues. Memories tend to be short, and we want to make sure that as markets calm down . . . banks do not return to the old ways of doing business." After all, the lesson learned from LTCM's near collapse is not that it's risky to leverage. Investors already know that. The lesson is that even the safest looking, dead sure, open-and-shut bet can sometimes go wrong.

Sources: "Hedge Fund Bailout Shows Need for Transparency—S&P," Reuters Limited, April 5, 1999; Alan Kohler, "Hedging: Long and Short of It," *AFR (Australian Financial Review) Net Services*, April 1–5, 1999, accessed at www.afr.com; Andrew Clark, "U.S. Regulators: Banks Learned from LTCM," Reuters Limited, March 24, 1999; Peter Viles, "1998: LTCM Collapses," CNN Financial News, December 8, 1998, accessed at www.cnnfn.com; Martine Costello, "When Wall St. Takes Risks," CNN Financial News, September 30, 1998, accessed at www.cnnfn.com; "Hedge Fund Gets Help," CNN Financial News, September 23, 1998, accessed at www.cnnfn.com.

with mutual funds, investors in direct purchase programs buy in dollar amounts rather than specific numbers of shares.

Companies offer direct purchase programs to attract long-term individual investors and to raise capital inexpensively by eliminating the expenses for the services of investment banks. The programs benefit investors because they allow individuals to avoid paying high commissions on initial purchases. "These are for people willing to do their own research and hold on to the shares for at least 3 years," says stock expert Charles Carlson.[20]

To buy stock directly, investors simply call a company and ask for an enrollment form, fill it out, and return it with a check to the program's administrator. The Netstock Direct Web site lists firms offering direct stock programs and information on minimum purchase requirements and fees.

www.netstockdirect.com

READING THE FINANCIAL NEWS

At least two or three pages of most major daily newspapers are devoted to reporting current financial news. This coverage typically focuses on the previous day's securities transactions. Stocks and bonds traded on the NYSE and AMEX are listed alphabetically in the newspaper. Information is provided on the volume of sales and the price of each security.

Since 1792, the NYSE has quoted stock prices as fractions, in eighths of a dollar or 12.5 cents. In 1997, it started quoting prices in sixteenths of a dollar, or increments of 6.25 cents. By 2000, it plans to switch completely to a decimal system, quoting prices in dollars and cents. The use of decimals will simplify individual investors' efforts to understand price quotes. According to several studies, trading in decimals should also result in savings for investors of between $1.5 billion and $4.0 billion a year in trading costs. The decimal system will reduce the amount of stock-brokers' spreads—the difference between what they pay to buy stocks and what they charge customers for them. The AMEX, NASDAQ, and regional exchanges also plan to switch to the decimal system. Converting to the decimal system will make U.S. exchanges more compatible with world stock markets, as the United States is the only major nation that does not quote stock prices in decimals.[21]

Stock Quotations

To understand how to read the stock tables found in newspapers, you need to understand how to interpret the symbols in the various columns. As Figure 21.5 explains, the

Figure 21.5 **How to Read Stock Quote Tables**

	52-Weeks					Yld		Vol.				Net
	High	Low	Stock	Sym	Div	%	PE	(100s)	High	Low	Close	Chg
	$76^{15}/_{16}$	$37^{7}/_8$	BarnettBks	BBI	1.24	1.8	23	4303	$69^1/_8$	$67^3/_8$	$67^5/_8$	$-1^5/_{16}$
	$46^7/_8$	$24^5/_8$	BarretRes	BRR		...	34	808	34	$33^1/_2$	$33^5/_8$	$-^1/_8$
↓	$30^1/_2$	$18^{15}/_{16}$	BarckGld	ABX	.16f	.9	dd	15968	$19^1/_{16}$	$17^5/_8$	$17^3/_4$	$-1^1/_2$
	$14^5/_8$	$9^1/_2$	BarryRG	RGB		...	15	156	$12^3/_{16}$	12	$12^1/_{16}$	$-^1/_{16}$
	$29^5/_{16}$	$24^3/_8$	Bass	BAS	1.07e	3.8	...	16	29	$28^1/_2$	$28^1/_2$	$-^1/_2$
	$8^1/_2$	5	BattleMtn	BMG	.05	1.0	dd	2525	$5^3/_8$	$5^3/_{16}$	$5^1/_4$	$-^1/_{16}$
	$52^3/_8$	$46^3/_4$	BattleMtn pf		3.25	6.9	...	20	$47^7/_{16}$	$46^{15}/_{16}$	$46^{15}/_{16}$	$-^1/_{16}$
	$47^7/_8$	$32^1/_2$	BauschLomb	BOL	1.04	2.7	38	627	$39^5/_{16}$	$38^7/_8$	39	$-^9/_{16}$

1 **52-WEEK INDICATORS:** ↑ = Hit 52-week high during the day. ↓ = Hit 52-week low.

2 **52-WEEK HIGH/LOW:** Highest and lowest trading prices in the past 52 weeks, adjusted for splits. New issues begin at the date of issue.

3 **STOCK and FOOTNOTES:** The company's name abbreviated. A capital letter usually means a new word. BarnettBks, for example, is Barnett Banks. The stock ticker symbol is expressed in capital letters. For Barnett Banks it is BBI. Stock footnotes include: **n** - new. **pf** - preferred. **rt.** - rights. **s** - stock split, or dividend of more than 20 percent in past 52 weeks. **un** - stock sales in multiple-share units. **v** - trading halted on primary market. **vi** - in bankruptcy or receivership or being reorganized under the Bankruptcy Act, or securities assumed by such companies. **wi** - when issued. **x** - ex-dividend. **xdis** - ex-distribution, paid after stock dividend or split.

4 **DIVIDEND:** Dividends are usually annual payments based on the last quarterly or semiannual declaration. Special or extra dividends or payments are identified in footnotes: **a** - also extra or extras. **b** - annual rate plus stock dividend. **e** - irregular cash dividend. **g** - dividend paid in Canadian money; stock prices in U. S. dollars. **i** - declared or paid after stock dividend or split. **j** - paid this year, dividends omitted, deferred or no action taken at last dividend meeting. **k** - declared or paid this year, an accumulative issue with dividends in arrears. **r** - declared or paid in preceding 12 months plus stock dividend. **t** - paid stock in preceding 12 months, estimated cash value on ex-dividend or ex-distribution date.

5 **YIELD:** Percentage return from a dividend based on the stock's closing price.

6 **PE:** Price-to-earnings ratio, calculated by taking the last closing price of the stock and dividing it by the earnings per share for the latest four quarters.

7 **VOLUME:** Trading volume in 100-share lots. A listing of 4,303 means 430,300 shares traded during the day. A figure preceded by a "z" is the actual number of shares traded.

8 **HIGH/LOW:** High and low for the day.

9 **CLOSE:** Closing price.

10 **NET CHG:** Change in price from the close of the previous trading day.

symbol in Column 1 is the 52-week indicator. An arrow pointing up means that a stock hit its 52-week high during the day, and an arrow pointing down means that a stock hit its 52-week low. Column 2 gives the stock's highest and lowest trading prices during the past 52 weeks. Column 3 contains the abbreviation for the company's name, footnotes that provide information about the stock (*pf*, for example, refers to preferred stock), and the stock ticker symbol. Column 4 lists the dividend, usually an annual payment based on the last quarterly or semiannual declaration. Column 5 presents the yield, the percentage return from dividends based on the stock's closing price.

Column 6 lists the stock's **price-earnings (P/E) ratio,** the current market price divided by the annual earnings per share. The stock's trading volume in 100-share lots is in Column 7, and its highest and lowest prices for the day appear in Column 8. Column 9 gives the closing price for the day, and Column 10 summarizes the stock's net change in price from the close of the previous trading day.

line with the market interest rate. Bonds with the notation *cv* are convertible bonds.

Figure 21.6   **How to Read Bond Quote Tables**

1 BOND: Abbreviation of company name.

2 ANNUAL INTEREST RATE: Annual percentage rate of interest specified on the bond certificate.

3 MATURITY DATE: Year in which the bond issuer will repay bondholders the face value of each bond.

4 YIELD: Percentage return from interest payment calculated on the basis of the bond's closing price; **cv** indicates a bond that is convertible into shares of common stock at a specified price.

5 VOLUME: Number of bonds traded during the day.

6 CLOSE: Closing price.

7 NET CHANGE: Change in the price from the close of the previous trading day.

Bonds	Cur Yld	Vol	Close	Net Chg
ATT $8^1/_8 24$	7.8	15	$104^3/_4$	$-1^1/_8$
ATT $8^5/_8 31$	7.9	5	$109^1/_2$	...
Alza 5s06	cv	17	$97^3/_4$	$-^3/_4$
AMedia $11^5/_8 04$	10.7	10	109	-1
Amoco $8^5/_8 16$	8.1	13	$106^1/_4$	$+1^1/_4$
Amresco $8^3/_4 99$	8.7	5	101	...
Argosy 12s01	cv	60	85	$+^1/_2$
Argosy $13^1/_4 04$	13.0	20	102	$+^1/_4$
BellsoT $6^3/_8 04$	6.3	50	$100^3/_4$	$-^1/_8$
BethSt 8.45s05	8.4	5	$100^3/_8$	$-^5/_8$
Bevrly 9s06	8.7	20	103	...

Bond Quotations

To learn how to read corporate bond quotations, pick a bond listed in Figure 21.6 and examine the adjacent columns of information. Most bonds are issued in denominations of $1,000; thus, bond prices must be read differently from stock prices. The closing price of the first AT&T bond reads $104\frac{3}{4}$, but this does not mean $104.75. Because bond prices are quoted as a percentage of the $1,000 price stated on the face of the bond, the $104\frac{3}{4}$ means $1,047.50.

The notation following the bond name (such as "9s06" after the Beverly bond) indicates the interest rate stated on the bond certificate, 9 percent, and the maturity date of 2006. The first figure is the interest rate, the second is the maturity date. The current yield for the Beverly bond is 8.7 percent, slightly less than the 9.0 percent stated interest rate. The price of the bond will rise to keep the yield in

The next column indicates the total trading volume for the day. The volume of 20 listed for Beverly means that $20,000 worth of bonds were traded. The closing bond price is listed next, followed by the percentage of net change in this price since the previous day's closing.

STOCK INDEXES

A feature of most daily television and radio newscasts is the report of current stock indexes or averages. The most familiar are the **Dow Jones averages** (known collectively as the *Dow*). The Standard & Poor's Index is another familiar measure. Both indexes (and many others) have been developed to reflect general activity of the stock market.

The Dow is actually three different indexes based on the market prices of 30 industrial, 20 transportation, and 15

Business Directory

Dow Jones averages   indexes of stock market activity based on the market prices of 30 industrial, 20 transportation, and 15 utility stocks.

utility stocks. The more broadly based Standard & Poor's Index is developed from the market performance of 400 industrial, 40 financial, 40 utility, and 20 transportation stocks.

The Dow Jones Industrial Average (DJIA) has served as a general measure of changes in overall stock prices and a reflection of the U.S. economy since it was developed in 1884 by Charles H. Dow, the original editor of *The Wall Street Journal*. The term *industrial* is a misnomer today, because the index now combines industrial corporations like General Motors, Union Carbide, and Boeing with such nonindustrial firms as American Express, McDonald's, and Sears Roebuck. Table 21.4 lists the 30 stocks included in the DJIA.

Periodic changes in the DJIA stocks reflect changes in the U.S. economy. The most recent change occurred in 1997, when the index added Hewlett-Packard, Johnson & Johnson, Travelers Group, and Wal-Mart Stores and dropped Westinghouse Electric, Texaco, Bethlehem Steel, and Woolworth Corporation. The changes were made to increase the representation of firms in the technology, finance, and health-care industries so that the index better reflects the overall stock market and the U.S. economy.[22] The Dow remains the most widely reported barometer of stock market activity.

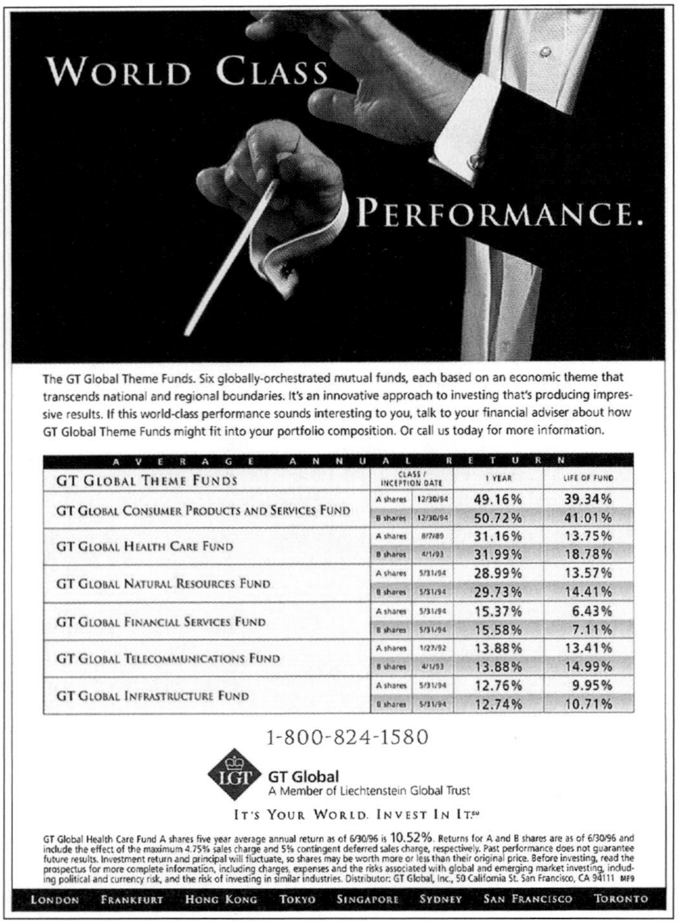

MUTUAL FUNDS

Many investors choose another investment option called **mutual funds,** financial organizations that pool investment money from purchasers of their securities and use the money to acquire diversified portfolios of securities. Investors who buy shares of a mutual fund become part owners of a large number of companies, thereby lessening their individual risk. Mutual funds are managed by experienced professionals whose careers are based on success in analyzing the securities markets and specific industries and companies.

The percentage of household equity assets held by mutual funds has risen sharply since 1981, from about 5 percent to over 40 percent. Approximately 50 million people in the United States currently own shares in mutual funds. They maintain almost 100 million accounts, which hold close to $3 trillion in total assets.

Today's mutual fund investors choose among more than 6,500 mutual funds in the United States. Some mutual funds invest only in stocks, some invest only in bonds, others invest in short-term money market securities, and some funds combine the three categories. Many specific funds pursue limited goals within these broad categories. Some funds invest only in

Figure 21.7 **Mutual Funds Based on Global Economic Themes**

Table 21.4 The 30 Stocks in the Dow Jones Industrial Average

Allied-Signal	Eastman Kodak	Merck
Aluminum Company of America	Exxon	3M
American Express	General Electric	J.P. Morgan
AT&T	General Motors	Philip Morris
Boeing	Goodyear	Procter & Gamble
Caterpillar	Hewlett-Packard	Sears Roebuck
Chevron	IBM	Travelers Group
Coca-Cola	International Paper	Union Carbide
Walt Disney	Johnson & Johnson	United Technologies
DuPont	McDonald's	Wal-Mart Stores

firms in certain industries, some only in large firms or small firms, and others in firms all over the world or in certain parts of the world. The mutual funds of GT Global highlighted in Figure 21.7 are based on economic themes such as natural resources and infrastructure. A number of mutual funds have been developed for socially responsible investors. The Domini Social Equity Fund, for example, invests in companies that have good records in areas such as employee relations, community involvement, environmental awareness, and the treatment of women and minorities. The fund avoids investing in firms whose revenue comes from gambling, alcohol, and tobacco.[23]

Reading mutual fund tables is a relatively simple task. The first two columns in Figure 21.8 list the organization issuing and managing the fund, the different types of

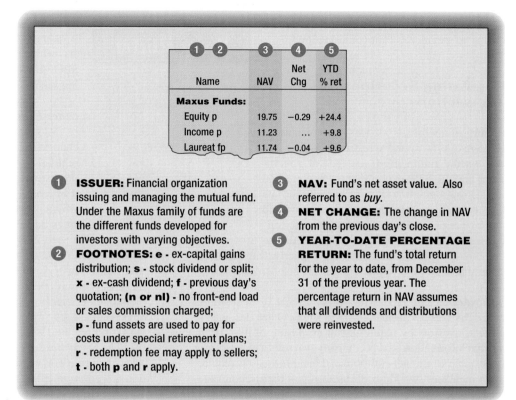

Figure 21.8 **How to Read Mutual Fund Tables**

			Net	YTD
Name	NAV		Chg	% ret
Maxus Funds:				
Equity p	19.75		−0.29	+24.4
Income p	11.23		...	+9.8
Laureat fp	11.74		−0.04	+9.6

① ISSUER: Financial organization issuing and managing the mutual fund. Under the Maxus family of funds are the different funds developed for investors with varying objectives.

② FOOTNOTES: e - ex-capital gains distribution; **s** - stock dividend or split; **x** - ex-cash dividend; **f** - previous day's quotation; **(n or nl)** - no front-end load or sales commission charged; **p** - fund assets are used to pay for costs under special retirement plans; **r** - redemption fee may apply to sellers; **t** - both **p** and **r** apply.

③ NAV: Fund's net asset value. Also referred to as *buy*.

④ NET CHANGE: The change in NAV from the previous day's close.

⑤ YEAR-TO-DATE PERCENTAGE RETURN: The fund's total return for the year to date, from December 31 of the previous year. The percentage return in NAV assumes that all dividends and distributions were reinvested.

funds offered for investors with different objectives, and footnotes. The NAV column lists the fund's net asset value, the price at which investors can buy its shares. The Net Change column shows gains or losses in NAV from the previous day's close. The figures in the last column, the Year-to-Date Percentage Return, indicate each fund's total return from December 31 of the previous year, assuming that all dividends and distributions were reinvested.

LEGAL AND ETHICAL ISSUES IN SECURITIES TRADING

The long-running bull market that began in 1991 has attracted millions of new investors, but it has also brought an increase in securities fraud and illegal trading practices. Examples include broker theft from a client's portfolio, unauthorized trading of a customer's stock to generate commissions, and giving false information to investors. The law requires that someone selling securities must tell investors the truth about all aspects of any investment opportunity.[24]

Ethical issues in securities trading include program trading and insider trading. **Program trading** is a controversial practice in which computer systems are programmed to buy or sell securities if certain conditions

arise. Program trading started as a type of portfolio insurance that allowed market players to hedge their bets with automatic buy or sell orders whenever their stock prices reached certain levels. The practice has become controversial, however, because many people blamed it for the 1987 stock market crash, when the market value of the nation's leading stocks dropped 23 percent in a single day. In fact, program trading accounted for only 15 percent of that day's trades. However, it can result in significant price swings in individual stocks when the same set of conditions triggers many buy and sell orders. For this reason, many people have suggested that the practice be banned.

Insider trading refers to illegal securities trading by people who profit from their access to nonpublic information about a company, such as a pending merger or a major oil discovery. While this practice is prohibited by the Securities Exchange Act of 1934, Securities and Exchange Commission (SEC) analysis of stock trading patterns before major announcements has uncovered many cases of insider trading. The Insider Trading Act of 1984 expanded the authority of the SEC to investigate unethical use of inside information.

The SEC's definition of insider trading goes beyond corporate insiders—people such as officers or directors of a company whose stock they trade. It includes lawyers, accountants, investment bankers, and reporters—anyone who uses confidential company information to profit in the stock market at the expense of regular investors. According to the SEC, any outsider who uses a position of trust to gain access to market-sensitive information and then trades on that information is guilty of insider trading.[25]

Regulating Securities Transactions

Reports of unethical practices often lead to the passage of laws aimed at restricting such practices in the future. Both the federal government and all state governments have enacted legislation regulating sales of securities. State laws typically require that most securities sold there be registered with appropriate state officials, usually the secretary of state, and that securities dealers and salespeople annually renew licenses. In addition, several federal laws regulate interstate sales of securities.

Securities Act of 1933 The *Securities Act of 1933,* often called the *Truth in Securities Act,* is a federal law designed to protect investors by requiring full disclosure of relevant financial information by any company that sells a new stock or bond issue to the general public. This information requirement mandates two kinds of disclosure: a registration statement containing detailed company information filed with the Securities and Exchange Commission and a prospectus, a condensed version of the registration statement printed in booklet form that must be furnished to each purchaser.

Securities Exchange Act of 1934 The *Securities Exchange Act of 1934* created the Securities and Exchange

They said it

"It is not the return on my investment that I am concerned about; it is the return of my investment."

Will Rogers (1879–1935)
American actor and humorist

Commission (SEC) to regulate the national stock exchanges, and it established strict rules for trading on organized exchanges. A 1964 amendment extended the authority of the SEC to the over-the-counter market. Brokerage firms, individual brokers, and dealers selling OTC stocks are regulated by the SEC. Any broker engaged in buying and selling securities must pass an examination.

Other Federal Legislation The *Maloney Act of 1938,* an amendment to the Securities Exchange Act of 1934, authorized the self-regulation of OTC securities operations. This provision led to the creation of the *National Association of Securities Dealers (NASD),* which is responsible for regulating OTC securities businesses. All new brokers and dealers who sell OTC securities must pass written examinations.

The *Investment Company Act of 1940* brought the mutual fund industry under SEC jurisdiction. Mutual funds must register with the SEC. Also, the state and federal laws mentioned earlier protect investors from securities trading abuses and stock price manipulations like those that occurred before the 1930s.

The *Securities Investor Protection Act of 1970* created a not-for-profit corporation, the Securities Investor Protection Corporation (SIPC), that insures the accounts of brokerage firm clients against loss due to broker insolvency for up to cash values of $100,000. Losses of securities are insured up to $500,000. SIPC protection works like the protection that the FDIC provides to bank depositors, but it differs in one important respect: The FDIC is a federal agency, while the SIPC is a membership organization composed of all national securities exchanges and registered

BUSINESS HALL OF SHAME

A Web of Deception

Penny stock fraud is a big and profitable business. Promoters of penny stocks can make a fortune by driving up the prices of low-priced issues while selling shares to investors. Although it is difficult to prosecute, penny stock fraud is getting increased attention from securities regulators and law enforcement officials, partly because of the increasing role of technology in investing.

The SEC is closely watching the trading of penny stocks on the Internet. It has formed the Cyberforce, a group of volunteers who patrol the Internet and report suspicious activity. Through its enforcement division, the SEC is bringing charges against firms that make fraudulent stock offerings on their Web sites.

In the first criminal case involving Internet stock fraud, a federal judge sentenced Theodore Melcher, a stock advisor, to a year in prison and fined him $20,000. Melcher, owner of SGA

Goldstar Research Inc., published a daily Internet stock newsletter called *SGA Goldstar Whisper Stocks* in which he advised subscribers to buy stock in Systems of Excellence, a maker of video teleconferencing equipment. Melcher told subscribers the stock was "a once in a lifetime opportunity" and that the company was a rumored takeover candidate. The stock price increased from 27 cents per share to almost $5 before regulators discovered the fraud. Then the price dropped to a penny a share, and Sys-

brokers. Funding comes through assessments on member firms. Although the SIPC protects investors against financial disasters resulting from a brokerage's bankruptcy, it does not provide protection against market losses caused by price declines.

The *Securities Enforcement Remedies and Penny Stock Reform Act of 1990* expanded the SEC's role in dealing with securities violations. The law resulted from an epidemic of penny stock fraud during the 1980s in which brokers used high-pressure sales tactics to push up stock prices and then sold their own shares, which quickly decreased share prices. Regulators estimate that abuses in the penny stock market have increased threefold since the passage of the law, defrauding investors of $6 billion each year.[26] The law created three tiers of fines, based on the severity of violations, that range from $5,000 to $500,000. The Business Hall of Shame describes a stock fraud case involving the sale of penny stocks.

In addition to creating and enforcing laws that protect investors, the SEC operates an Investor Education and Assistance Office that publishes information on how to choose investments wisely and how to file complaints. Through its EDGAR (Electronic Data Gathering, Analysis, and Retrieval) database of corporate filings, the SEC provides an online resource tool for investors. The agency requires all publicly traded U.S. companies to submit their SEC filings in electronic form to aid in investor access. These documents, along with company annual reports and other financial information, are made available to the public through the SEC's Web site.

www.sec.gov

DEVELOPING A PERSONAL FINANCIAL PLAN

Now that you have studied various types of investment options, you need to apply what you have learned to manage your own money. Here are some tips from the pros for developing a contemporary financial plan.

▼ *Set up a regular savings plan.* Experts advise that you save enough money to live for 6 to 9 months without a salary, if necessary. They also suggest that you save and invest at least 20 percent of your pretax annual salary. This saving can take the form of a retirement plan, savings account, or other investments.

▼ *Pay off your debt.* As you learned in Chapter 20, Americans are carrying more debt on their credit cards than ever, and a growing number of Americans are ending up in bankruptcy court. You don't want to be one of them. Carrying charges on credit cards can cost an average of 19 percent each year in interest. To avoid interest charges, pay off your credit card balance each month.

▼ *Consider investing in stocks.* Despite the ups and downs of the stock market, many experts still believe that stocks deliver the highest profits of all investment alternatives over the long run. Through the years, stocks have averaged an annual return of 11 percent, better than the average return on bonds and many other investments. Consider reinvesting your stock dividends rather than taking cash payments. The compounding of your reinvested dividends can make a huge differ-

tems of Excellence filed for bankruptcy protection.

Melcher failed to tell subscribers that he had received 250,000 shares of stock in the company in exchange for giving it favorable reports. He sold his shares at the same time he was telling people to buy and hold them, earning $515,802 in trading profits. During his trial, he admitted to making up the rumor that the company was a takeover candidate.

"This important case should be a clear signal to those who use the remarkable technology of the Internet to snare vulnerable citizens in a worldwide web of deception," said Helen Fahey, U.S. Attorney for eastern Virginia.

The web of deception also resulted in a 46-month prison sentence for Charles Huttoe, the former president of Systems of Excellence, who pleaded guilty to charges of conspiring to commit securities fraud and money laundering. Merle Finkel, an accountant, also pleaded guilty to charges of conspiracy to commit stock and bank fraud for creating false financial documents for Systems of Excellence and other companies.

QUESTIONS FOR CRITICAL THINKING

1. **Would you buy stocks based on information provided by an Internet stock advisor?**

2. **What could investors have done to protect themselves against this stock fraud?**

Sources: "SEC Targets Outrageous Claims in Its Third Sweep of Net Fraud," *The Wall Street Journal*, May 12, 1999, accessed at www.msnbc.com; Michael Schroeder, "SGA Goldstar's President Is Sentenced to Prison in Internet Stock-Fraud Case," *The Wall Street Journal*, September 15, 1997, p. B12; Leslie Eaton, "Fraud Case Focuses on Internet," *New York Times*, September 14, 1997, p. BU5; and J. Schulz, "Offerings Online," *Worth*, July 1997, pp. 75–79.

ence over time. For example, someone who had invested $10,000 in the stock market in 1966 and taken all dividends in cash would have received $27,361 in dividends and had an investment worth $92,212 at the end of 1996. But someone who had invested the same $10,000 and reinvested all dividends would have ended up with stock worth $285,422 over the same period.[27]

▼ *Add bonds to your portfolio.* If you decide to buy bonds, financial advisors suggest devoting 20 to 30 percent of your investment balance to these securities.

▼ *Shop around.* Do research to identify the best mutual funds and the money managers with the lowest fees.

▼ *Diversify!* Spread your money around to lower your risk. Develop a balanced portfolio that in-cludes stocks, bonds, and mutual funds. Divide your money among international equity funds and large, medium-sized, and small companies.

▼ *Look abroad.* Investment strategists advise that you diversify your portfolio geographically by investing in markets around the globe. International investing offers new opportunities, since two-thirds of the world's stocks originate and trade outside the United States. The gross domestic products of emerging markets such as Poland and Hungary are growing twice as fast as the U.S. GDP, resulting in better stock returns there. But since emerging markets expose investors to high risk, strategists advise that they account for a small portion—5 to 10 percent—of your portfolio. Foreign stocks, they predict, will continue to generate annual returns of about 12 percent.

SUMMARY OF LEARNING GOALS

1. Distinguish between the primary market for securities and the secondary market.

The primary market serves businesses and government units that want to sell new issues of securities. The secondary market handles transactions of previously issued securities.

2. Compare common stock, preferred stock, and bonds, and explain why particular investors might prefer each type of security.

Owners of common stock have voting rights, but they have only residual claims on the firm's assets. Preferred stockholders receive preference in the payment of dividends and have first claim on the firm's assets after debts have been paid, but they usually do not have voting rights. Bondholders are creditors, not owners, of a corporation, not-for-profit organization, or government unit.

3. Identify the four basic objectives of investors and the types of securities most likely to reach each objective.

The four basic objectives of investors are speculation, growth in the value of the investment, income, and safety. Common stocks are the most risky of the primary investment alternatives, but they offer potential for investment growth. Preferred stocks have limited growth opportunities, but they are reasonably safe and offer steady income. Bonds typically are purchased to achieve safety and income objectives.

4. Explain the process of selling or purchasing a security listed on an organized securities exchange.

Securities purchases and sales are handled by stockbrokers. After a broker receives a customer's order, it is conveyed to the stock exchange through a communications terminal. The firm's floor broker executes the transaction and communicates a confirmation to the broker, who notifies the customer that the transaction has been completed. In online trading, individuals buy and sell securities without dealing with stockbrokers.

5. Describe the information included in stock, bond, and mutual fund quotations.

Information in a NYSE or AMEX stock quotation includes the 52-week indicator, the highest and lowest trading prices during the previous 52 weeks, the company's abbreviated name, footnotes, dividend, yield, price-earnings (P/E) ratio, volume, the stock's highest and lowest prices for the day, the closing price for that day, and the stock's change in price from the close of the previous trading day.

A bond quotation includes the maturity date and interest rate, the current yield, the volume of bonds traded on the day, the high and low prices of the bond on the day, and a comparison of the day's closing price with that of the previous day. Tables of mutual funds list each fund's net asset value (NAV), the change in NAV from the previous day, and the year-to-date total return.

6. Explain the role of mutual funds in securities markets.

Mutual funds are professionally managed investment companies that own shares in many different companies. Investors purchase shares of the mutual fund, which make them part owners of a large, diversified investment portfolio.

7. Evaluate the major features of state and federal laws designed to protect investors.

The Securities Act of 1933, the Securities Exchange Act of 1934, and individual state securities laws regulate organized securities exchanges and over-the-counter markets. These laws also protect investors by requiring disclosure of financial information from companies issuing securities. The Securities and Exchange Commission (SEC) enforces federal legislation and regulates brokers, brokerage firms, and mutual fund transactions. The Securities Investor Protection Corporation (SIPC) insures brokerage firm accounts against loss due to dealer or broker insolvency. The Insider Trading Act of 1984 expanded the authority of the SEC to investigate insider trading. The Securities Enforcement Remedies and Penny Stock Reform Act of 1990 expanded the SEC's role in dealing with securities violations and created three tiers of fines based on the severity of the violation.

TEN BUSINESS TERMS YOU NEED TO KNOW

security	secured bond
primary market	debenture
secondary market	stock exchange
common stock	bull
preferred stock	bear

Other Important Business Terms

investment banker	price-earnings (P/E) ratio
underwriting spread	Dow Jones averages
institutional investor	mutual fund
speculation	program trading
yield	insider trading
National Association of Securities Dealers Automated Quotation (NASDAQ) system	

REVIEW QUESTIONS

1. In what ways is the secondary market different from the primary market? With which market are investment bankers involved? What role do investment bankers play in their clients' financial decisions?
2. What is common stock? Explain the different methods used for evaluating common stock.
3. What are the major types of bonds issued by corporations and government units? What primary methods do firms use to retire bonds?
4. What are the major goals of investors? Which type of security is most appropriate to achieve each general goal?
5. How do market orders differ from limit orders, round lots from odd lots, and bull investors from bear investors?
6. How does the New York Stock Exchange operate? Compare the operations of the NYSE with those of the NASDAQ system.
7. How do stock indexes affect securities trading? Why does the DJIA add and drop companies from its index?
8. How does an investor place an order for common stock? Explain how computerized and online trading have revolutionized the securities industry.
9. What are the benefits of investing in mutual funds?
10. What major laws affect securities transactions? In what ways does the Securities and Exchange Commission protect individual investors?

QUESTIONS FOR CRITICAL THINKING

1. Assume that you are a psychiatrist. During a counseling session your patient tells you of an impending takeover of the company that employs her. You act on the information by buying stock in the company. Based on the SEC's definition of insider trading, would you be guilty of committing securities fraud? What if you were a bartender and heard the same information from one of your patrons and then invested? Would you be crossing the legal line?
2. Assume that you just inherited $20,000 from your uncle and his will stipulates that you must invest all the money until you complete your education. Prepare an investment plan for your inheritance.
3. Would you feel comfortable investing the $20,000 you inherited in Question 2 using an online service, or would you enlist the services of a stockbroker? Give reasons for your choice.
4. Assume that you are an entrepreneur and need money to expand your business. You own a juice bar in one city but would like to open outlets throughout your state. How could you raise money through a direct public offering?
5. Scott Schumer spent 17 years working as a trader at a conventional stock exchange. Now he trades using the GLOBEX electronic system. Schumer believes that trading on the floor of stock exchanges—called *pit trading*—is an archaic relic and that some day pit trading will also be a computerized process. Do you agree with Schumer's assessment of pit trading? Why or why not?

Experiential Exercise

In this exercise, you apply the seven guidelines in the final section of the chapter, "Developing a Personal Financial Plan," to your own financial situation.

Directions: For each guideline listed,

▼ check the "Yes" column if you already include the item in your current financial plan.

▼ check "Will Use" if you plan to follow through and include the item in your financial plan.

▼ check "No" if you don't intend to include the item in your current financial plan.

In the section "Explanation" following each guideline,

▼ for each "Yes" selected, summarize how you are currently applying the guideline.

▼ for each "Will Use" selected, summarize what specifically you intend to do to make the guideline part of your financial plan.

▼ for each "No" selected, give the reason(s) against using the guideline in your situation.

	Yes	Will Use	No
1. Set up a regular savings plan. Explanation:	_____	_____	_____
2. Pay off your debt. Explanation:	_____	_____	_____
3. Consider investing in stocks. Explanation:	_____	_____	_____
4. Add bonds to your portfolio. Explanation:	_____	_____	_____
5. Shop around. Explanation:	_____	_____	_____
6. Diversify. Explanation:	_____	_____	_____
7. Look abroad. Explanation:	_____	_____	_____

Nothing but Net

1. **Foreign Stock Exchanges.** Conduct a Web search to find various stock exchanges around the world. For example,

   www.euroyellowpages.com/wldstock.html

   provides links to stock exchanges worldwide in such places as Africa, Asia, Australia, the Caribbean, Europe, the Middle East, North America, and South America. Visit at least one stock exchange Web site in each part of the world to determine similarities and differences among the stock exchanges.

2. **Online Investing.** Visit a Web site, such as Charles Schwab & Co., to try a demonstration and learn more about online investing. Use the demonstration to see how you can get quotes, place trades, check account balances, and access company news.

   www.schwab.com/trading/demo/html/start.html

3. **Stock Averages.** Visit the Dow Jones Web site to learn more about the Dow Jones averages. Write a one-page report including information on the averages that is not already in the chapter's discussion of the Dow Jones averages. With your report, submit printouts of Industrial Average timeline charts for any two decades you choose.

   averages.dowjones.com/frameset.html

Note: Internet Web addresses change frequently. If you do not find the exact sites listed, you may need to access the organization's or company's home page and search from there.

RONEY & COMPANY

Unless you live in the Midwest, chances are good that you have never heard of Roney & Company. But the firm's name is synonymous with quality service and customer satisfaction to its 70,000 clients. Headquartered in Detroit and operating 27 branches throughout Indiana, Michigan, and Ohio, Roney's commitment to building and maintaining strong customer relationships has resulted in its position as Michigan's oldest and largest investment securities firm. Roney & Company is organized as a partnership consisting of more than 100 partners and a staff of 575 professionals.

The cornerstone of any business is its ability to build and maintain relationships based on a solid foundation of trust. Since its founding in 1925, Roney's central focus has been on continually evaluating and improving customer service in every department. Many of the firm's clients have conducted their brokerage business with Roney for years. In fact, long-time clients are an important source of new business through referrals. In addition, Roney & Company has improved its service to current clients and added new ones by expanding its services beyond simply buying and selling stocks and bonds.

Like other brokerage firms, Roney & Company is actively involved in the secondary market for securities through the purchase and sale of stocks and bonds for its clientele. Roney's bond department and mutual funds department provide expertise for clients interested in these investment vehicles. The firm's securities analysts prepare lists of recommended stocks, bonds, and mutual funds based on different investment criteria, and they work with account executives to determine which are most appropriate for individual clients.

Another service provided to Roney clients involves the primary market for securities. Even though the firm is dwarfed in size by giant competitors like Merrill Lynch,

First Boston, and Prudential Securities, it is large enough to offer extensive access to financial markets. At the same time, it provides clients with the personalized attention that is the hallmark of successful regional brokerage firms.

Business clients turn to Roney & Company for a variety of financing needs such as "going public" by making an offering of common stock, or making a "private placement" of stock with a small group of investors, or secure debt financing. In all of these situations, Roney has the expertise to compile the needed financial projections, decide on the structure and placement of a stock or bond offering, and prepare all of the documents required for such offerings. In addition, Roney & Company senior executives counsel clients throughout the entire process.

Roney & Company also provides specialized services for its clients in the area of mergers and acquisitions, and the firm has responded to the aging American population by strengthening its services in retirement and estate planning. It offers clients a full range of investment alternatives to meet their unique needs and objectives.

The foundation of a mutually satisfactory customer relationship lies with each employee in every department—from research, corporate finance, and investment planning to mergers and acquisitions. Roney's competitive advantage results from a combination of its size, the personalized attention it provides for each client, and the comprehensive services each account executive is able to offer its clients. Instead of simply selling products, the firm views itself as part of a large, comprehensive financial relationship in which it can offer the appropriate combination of investment services needed by its clients. Given the number of years most Roney clients have been Roney clients, this relationship is continuing to meet their needs.

Questions

1. What financial products and services does Roney & Company deal with in the primary and secondary markets?

2. How can a small regional firm like Roney & Company compete with giants like Merrill Lynch and First Boston?

3. If a small business owner needs capital to expand her business, how can Roney & Company help her?

Careers in Business

BUSINESS CAREER EXERCISES

Corporate Financial Management Career

Corporate financial managers provide information to other managers for decision making, and they encourage change and improvements that can lead to greater company profitability. As part of your job, you will probably collaborate with one or more departments, such as research and development, production, or marketing. Specific job activities include preparing budgets, forecasts, and business plans, as well as reviewing internal operations to identify ways of increasing revenues, reducing costs, and improving product quality.

This exercise will help you to:

▼ Identify your level of interest in corporate financial management as a business career.

▼ Find out details about the skills required, job activities, career advancement, and earnings potential for this occupation.

How to Locate the Exercise

1. Launch *Discovering Your Business Career* from the "Career Assistance" program group.

2. At the main menu, click on the red "play" button for "Corporate Financial Management" to see a presentation summarizing this career.

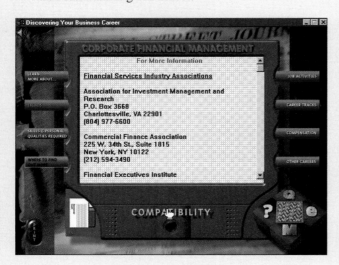

3. Next, click on the words "Corporate Financial Management" to enter the career profile on this career.

4. Click on the red button below the word "Compatibility."

5. Select "Corporate Financial Management" from the menu of seven business careers.

6. Watch the video that summarizes your degree of compatibility with a career in corporate financial management.

7. Read the detailed compatibility report on the left side of the screen. You can obtain a printout of this report by clicking on "Print" in the lower left corner of the screen.

8. Click on the word "Return" to go back to the "Compatibility" menu of business careers.

9. Click on the red triangular arrow to the left of the words "Corporate Financial Management" to return to the career profile on corporate financial management.

10. Review the sections about this career that interest you. You can get a complete printout of all the sections on corporate financial management by clicking on "Print" in the lower left corner of the screen.

Retail Bank Management Career

Retail banking is the most visible and familiar aspect of banking. A retail bank manager oversees a local bank or branch bank providing a range of financial services to both consumers and commercial customers. Services include checking and savings accounts, loans (personal, business, automobile, and home mortgage), bank credit cards, safe deposit boxes, wire transfers (moving funds from one bank to another via electronic transfer), tax-advantaged individual retirement accounts (IRAs), and financial counseling.

This exercise will help you to:

▼ Identify your level of interest in retail bank management as a business career.

▼ Find out details about the skills required, job activities, career advancement, and earnings potential for this occupation.

How to Locate the Exercise

1. Launch *Discovering Your Business Career* from the "Career Assistance" program group.

2. At the main menu, click on the red "play" button for "Retail Bank Management" to see a presentation summarizing this career.

3. Next, click on the words "Retail Bank Management" to enter the career profile on this career.

4. Click on the red button below the word "Compatibility."

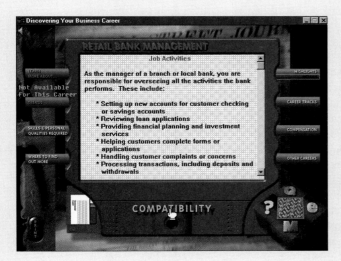

5. Select "Retail Bank Management" from the menu of seven business careers.

6. Watch the video that summarizes your degree of compatibility with a career in retail bank management.

7. Read the detailed compatibility report on the left side of the screen. You can obtain a printout of this report by clicking on "Print" in the lower left corner of the screen.

8. Click on the word "Return" to go back to the "Compatibility" menu of business careers.

9. Click on the red triangular arrow to the left of the words "Retail Bank Management" to return to the career profile on retail bank management.

10. Review the sections about this career that interest you. You can get a complete printout of all the sec-

tions on retail bank management by clicking on "Print" in the lower left corner of the screen.

Personal Finances

As you learned in Chapter 20, one of the responsibilities of a financial manager is to assist a business in determining the amount of money it needs to pursue its goals and then help it raise any needed funds. You experience some of these same responsibilities on a smaller scale with your own finances. First, you determine how much money you need for your education, housing, food, and miscellaneous expenses. Second, you raise the money you need through employment or other resources.

When you graduate, your goals will certainly change. You will probably have much higher expectations about your standard of living than you do now as a student. It is important to determine exactly what your expectations are and what is required, both financially and professionally, to meet them.

This exercise will help you to:

▼ Determine what level of compensation you need when you graduate to sustain the lifestyle you want.

▼ Determine whether a given career direction will meet those financial expectations.

How to Locate the Exercise Launch *Career Design* from the "Career Assistance" program group. Then select "Navigation" from the menu at the top of the screen, followed by "Career Sections" and then "Personal Finances."

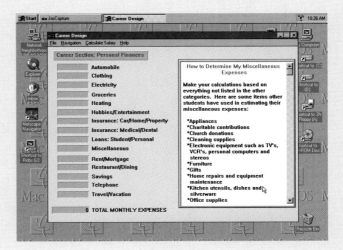

Continuing Video Case

Part I   Hard Candy—Blue Toenails Turn to Green

When Dineh Mohajer decided to paint her toenails baby blue with a polish she custom-blended in her bathroom, she didn't know she was about to become a fashion icon. She didn't know she would become the creative force behind a multimillion-dollar company. And she didn't know she'd spark a frenzied copycat craze in the fiercely competitive cosmetics industry. She just knew she wanted baby blue nail polish. When she couldn't find it, she made it herself. When the saleswomen at a trendy Los Angeles shoe salon admired her pastel toes, Mohajer's sister Pooneh said, "We should go into business. This is crazy. Everyone's dying for this product." The sisters became partners, each investing $200. They brought in Dineh's boyfriend, Ben Einstein, as a third partner, and Hard Candy was born.

Hard Candy's first sale came as a surprise during a presentation of the polishes at Los Angeles's Fred Segal. A young girl spotted the samples and begged her mother to buy all four bottles. The store immediately ordered 200 more bottles of Sky, Sunshine, Lime, and Violet. Family and friends worked day and night to fill orders. Hard Candy took off.

Hard Candy's main advantage in the marketplace is its ability to serve a niche in the cosmetics market. "We have developed a direct line to the consumer," explains Einstein, vice president and cofounder. "We know exactly what's happening because we are young. I guess we have our ears to the street, and we know when something is changing. I don't think if you're 60 years old, living in New York City, and you're on the 58th floor you're going to have your fingers on anything. It's not the same thing as just seeing the trends on Melrose or Beverly Hills. We know as fast as they come. That's our advantage."

Hard Candy understands that every product has an intrinsic value that sets it apart from competitors. Mohajer contends that her products have a value that is futuristic. But the company has set its sights on the global market as well as the future. It has been particularly successful in the United States, Japan, and London, plans to expand to South America, and will increase its distribution in Japan and Asia.

Hard Candy is famous for its trendy makeup colors and offbeat product names. Baby Doll shown here, is the company's newest blusher.

Although Hard Candy is still a young company, social responsibility is an important issue. "One hundred percent of the profits from our new color, Love, will be donated to the American Foundation for AIDS Research (AMFAR)," says Mohajer. "I think Hard Candy has been blessed in a way, so it's only right that we do something that's charitable—something that we believe helps our customers." Hard Candy strongly believes that it is important to raise awareness about AIDS, particularly among young people.

When Mohajer started Hard Candy, she was just 22 years old. She found out quickly that it was hard to get people to take her seriously. "In the very beginning I'd have to say Dineh was extremely resourceful," says Pooneh. "She does not take no for an answer." Mohajer's drive and persistence eventually paid off, and she continues to be the driving force behind Hard Candy. She is extremely focused on creativity, product development, and public relations. Einstein is in charge of big-picture issues and competitive strategies. Pooneh Mohajer is interested in the bottom line—that is, with business dealings and contracts. "It is nice because we all kind of balance each other out," she explains.

The three contend they don't worry about competition that much. Staying focused on their goals is a major concern. "You have to stay focused on what you are doing, or you lose sight of your goal and eventually get caught up in things that are not going to help you accomplish what you're trying to accomplish," says Mohajer. Staying focused has enabled Hard Candy to surpass its founder's wildest expectations. Famous for the provocative names of its one-of-a-kind colors, Hard Candy's best-selling products include Ecstasy nail polish, Lovechild lipstick, Hippie Chick lip liner, and Techno and Cyber eye shadows. Other products include eye gliders, glitter eyes, mascara, and lip pencils.

From its Beverly Hills headquarters, Hard Candy has captured the attention of fashion originals including Dennis Rodman, Madonna, Drew Barrymore, and Smashing Pumpkins. It has also attracted the attention of cosmetics giants Revlon, L'Oréal, and Cover Girl. With such publicity and attention, everyone will be keeping a "glitter eye" focused on Hard Candy's future.

Questions

1. What skills do managers need to lead businesses in the 21st century? List the skills you think are most important. How do these skills relate to Hard Candy?

2. What is meant by the term *social responsibility*? How does it relate to Hard Candy? Why is it important for a business to be socially responsible?

3. How do the forces of supply and demand affect Hard Candy? What are some ways the company can help predict demand for its products? Increase demand?

4. Since Hard Candy wants to expand globally, what different levels of involvement can it use? What alternative strategies for international business can it employ?

Part II   From Chaos to Cosmetic Structure

Founded by accident in 1995, Hard Candy has come a long way from its early days. "Hard Candy started like the typical entrepreneurial American dream story where you sit around writing on napkins because you don't have any paper," says Pooneh Mohajer, vice president and cofounder. According to Ben Einstein, "The idea started as a way to make a little bit of extra money over the summer." In the beginning running the company was very easy, but it quickly became unbearable. Hard Candy couldn't keep products in stock because the demand among young girls was so overwhelming. But despite the early production glitches, Hard Candy has always been innovative. When the company began manufacturing its revolutionary powder-based glitter eye pencil, the Food and Drug Administration (FDA) and the Cosmetic, Toiletry, and Fragrance Association (CTFA) didn't even have a category for the ingredients. "To sell this product we had to do human testing and then get approval from the FDA and the CTFA to release this product because it was so innovative. Nothing had been on the market similar to this before," says Einstein.

Hard Candy's innovation propelled the start-up company to overnight success, but it left its founders with little time to deal with many of the nuts and bolts issues of organizing a business. Einstein contacted the consulting firm of Ernst & Young for help, and with a $50,000 loan from Dineh Mohajer's parents, Hard Candy retained the firm. "Ernst & Young provides an entrepreneurial support division that specializes in taking young companies—like Hard Candy—helping them grow, and establishing a nurturing relationship," explains Mohajer.

Ernst & Young also conducted a search to find an ad hoc CEO to help the company organize and implement business systems. "It was basically a temporary thing," says Dineh Mohajer. "For a given term, a CEO comes in and helps companies that need short-term direction and integration of systems—basically cleaning house and setting up of procedures." A new executive in charge of financial information inventory systems was brought on board, as well as a vice president of sales. "Some of the first steps we took in strategic planning were hiring departments heads. We hired marketing, production, and sales managers throughout the country and overseas," says Geannie Chavez, vice president of sales. "Hard Candy started to grow so quickly that if it didn't have some kind of formal structure implemented in the organization, the company wouldn't be able to take its success to the next level. Hard Candy needed the guidance that the seasoned CEO brought to the company."

"When you're in the middle of running and putting out fires left and right, it's like crisis management," says Pooneh Mohajer. "It's very difficult to take a step back, take a deep breath, and say, 'Okay, what's our strategy here?' With the expertise of the new CEO, we were able to implement accounting systems, inventory tracking systems, and basically put together a management team, a controller, which are all crucial management positions that Hard Candy needed to take the company to the next level."

Although Hard Candy is growing at an astonishing rate, its fairly loose structure has kept the corporate grind at bay. "We are doing better about conducting meetings and making sure we accomplish goals on a regular basis," admits Einstein. Because Hard Candy is still a small business, making decisions is still relatively easy. In the near future, the firm plans to expand its sales, marketing, public relations, and other departments, including accounting and operations.

With more than three years under their belts and some business systems in place, the three founders are confident enough to run the business themselves. The temporary CEO is gone. "Collectively the three owners are the CEOs," explains Dineh Mohajer, "but individually, we don't have the track record as being CEOs." Remarkably, this team approach has fueled Hard Candy's success. Although the company's structure may be as unconventional as its product colors and names, it works. Today, Hard Candy offers seasonal cosmetic lines, and plans to expand its distribution into South America and Asia and introduce a line of Hard Candy clothing and accessories. There are still issues and challenges that can't be glossed over, but as Dineh Mohajer explains, "I am a business owner; my heart is in the business."

Questions

1. What advantages and disadvantages of a small business apply to Hard Candy? Explain.

2. What characteristics of entrepreneurs apply to Hard Candy's founders?

3. How can strategic planning help Hard Candy?

4. In your opinion, what form of business ownership may be appropriate for Hard Candy? Why?

Part III   Candy Culture with Gen-X Flavor

Starting her company at the age of 22, Dineh Mohajer personifies the attitudes and preferences of her generation. "Dineh and other employees live the life-style that our customers want," reveals Geannie Chavez, vice president of sales, "which makes it easier for our company to understand the needs and demographics of our customers without having to form focus groups. The company is moving into different cosmetic areas from where it started," Chavez explains, "which includes developing an eye liner that has outdone the other lines Hard Candy produced before. This shows that customers are willing to purchase whatever we offer." In addition to this advantage, Hard Candy's employees are knowledgeable about issues that are happening around the world. Managers travel to see how the company is performing in different countries.

Hard Candy is evolving and growing. "The company is in a state of continual change and transition," says Pooneh Mohajer. "I am glad that the company is not in a state where it is steady because it inhibits the creativity aspect in terms of product development and corporate culture." The management style of the three founders is also continuing to evolve because the company is still young. Hard Candy is definitely not the typical corporate environment. It is free flowing. Pooneh Mohajer explains, "It's kind of a collaborative brainstorming. Everybody's input is valuable, not only with the creativity but also in terms of management and improving overall operations."

Ben Einstein has a different style with regard to how he manages at Hard Candy. "I am more like a one-minute manager. I like to let people do what they want and have to do and self-police their actions; then I follow up," says Ben. "I am not on top of anybody in the company." This view is shared by others at Hard Candy. According to Dineh Mohajer, "If you have good people who know what needs to be done, then there is no reason to hold their hand." She believes in creating and maintaining an open, exciting, and creative environment for her employees. "My motto is not to rule with fear, but to rule with empowerment—to bring people in who are capable and whom you can empower and they can empower you."

For Dineh Mohajer and Hard Candy, hiring the right people is a crucial step to success. "I have been hasty in the past. When you are pressed for time and 3,000 orders behind, you don't necessarily make the right moves. You are only as good as your team—the people you have empowered and delegated the responsibilities to." Mohajer believes in treating people right and in developing strong relationships but not accepting any undesirable behavior. "If you allow it to be a good environment and allow people to flourish in their jobs, you are facilitating and motivating," she explains. From a 22-year-old starting a company, in just three years Mohajer has already come a long way in matching her management style to today's employees.

Questions

1. Describe the leadership style of Hard Candy's founders. How does this style shape the corporate culture?

2. Would you describe Dineh Mohajer as a Theory X or Theory Y manager? What needs, according to Maslow's hierarchy, motivate her?

3. Mohajer talks about teams and empowerment at Hard Candy. What steps can she take to increase the likelihood of forming effective teams?

Part IV   Painting the World

Since its beginning, Hard Candy has introduced many different product lines. Its first line consisted of nail polishes in light pastel colors. Later the company introduced brighter and darker colors to appeal to a wider range of people. Now the company is targeting men because of the interest it found through mailing lists and telemarketing campaigns. "When we designed the line of nail polish for men, we took into account the colors that we felt were best-selling to men in our original line, as well as a bit of focus studies in groups to see which colors would work best," says Ben Einstein. "We sold Candy Man in retail spots across the United States, but in the urban areas like San Francisco, Los Angeles, and New York, I think there's a higher concentration of men who are buying it."

"The competitive advantage that we have is what we really are about—being innovative and doing things in terms of what's next, what's cool, what do people want, what can we supply the industry or the customer within the industry that they don't already have," explains Dineh Mohajer. "Every line has an intrinsic value to it by having its identity very clearly defined. Hard Candy's value is that it's futuristic. It's got a very specific young, cutting edge sort of . . . it's very Hard Candy. That, in fact, is our competitive advantage because we have been leaders and setting standards of new products. We developed the colors and everybody knocked us off. We developed Glitter Eye, which was a very unique eyeliner—a very soft powder formula with glitter in it. That was something that we had to pioneer categories for, in terms of regulation with the CTFA."

When Hard Candy comes out with a new product, it is on a smaller scale than most of the cosmetics giants. "Once we come out with something that we've innovated or gotten the CTFA and FDA approval for, it's very quick for these larger companies to copy what we do and put it out in mass scale," explains Einstein. "Our strategy for remaining in the front seat as far as innovations in cosmetics is concerned is just to keep our eyes focused forward, and when we finish a product to make sure it gets the right type of support."

Hard Candy markets to upscale retailers "because I identify with that customer because I am that customer, so it was only natural for me to go and sell it there," explains Dineh Mohajer.

Keeping up with information technology, Hard Candy has established its own Web site. "In the first 24 hours, we had 48,000 hits. We get requests daily, and we have to respond to it. It's a huge area of opportunity for us, and we're presently hiring in-house people to take care of it. People were just exclaiming like, 'You finally have your Web page,' and 'We're so excited,' and 'This is my favorite color.' So, it's about the life-styles and about the interaction that we have with our customer," says vice president of sales Geannie Chavez.

www.hardcandy.com

Hard Candy plans to expand its products into more international markets. The company is already doing well in London and Japan. According to Mohajer, "Expansion has to do with

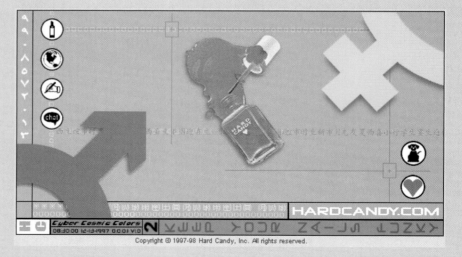

Hard Candy has expanded by offering its cosmetics on the Web. The site received 48,000 hits in its first 24 hours.

consumer research. It has to do with competitive analysis, but mainly I would say it's driven from expanding the line, but doing so such that the integrity of our vision is never compromised."

Questions

1. How does Hard Candy obtain customer preferences and feedback? How would you apply market segmentation for Hard Candy?

2. How can the process for developing new products work at Hard Candy?

3. Describe Hard Candy's distribution strategy to reach its target market.

4. How does Hard Candy go about promoting its products?

Appendixes

appendix A

Your Career in Business

Searching Cyberspace for a Career

Virtual job fairs, video conference job interviews, on-line résumés, computerized skill tests. Even the traditional one-to-one human contact of filling job openings has become wired. The reason? Companies spend a lot of time and money finding, selecting, and hiring new employees. Anything that can help them streamline the process and locate better candidates is welcome. Computers make the search faster and more cost effective, so companies are plugging in for their recruiting at a steadily growing rate.

To give you a sample of what's available in the virtual job market and help you digitize your career search, here are a few of the newest twists on high-tech job searches.

Virtual Job Fairs. These nationwide recruiting events take place over computer networks. Typically a dozen or more corporations and a similar number of universities participate in the fairs. Once a fair has been scheduled, corporate participants list job descriptions, and students post profiles that recruiters can review online. Once interview candidates are selected, potential job candidates are notified via e-mail. Students then contact the host of the job fair to schedule their interview, usually held over the Internet.

Videoconference Interviews. Campus career centers now routinely offer virtual interviews in which candidates can see, hear, and speak to company recruiters. The only thing lacking is a firm handshake to start the interview. Recruiters like the process because they are able to interview many more candidates, sometimes thousands of miles away, without time spent in the air, on the road, and in motels and restaurants. Companies like it because they often do not have large human resource departments or travel budgets and they can recruit from a worldwide pool of candidates, if they want. Job seekers like it because they can interview

.WWW

www.monster.com
www.careermosaic.com
www.collegegrad.com

with companies that were not coming on campus for interviews, and they still are able to speak with recruiters "face to face." Participants in the interviews typically see themselves, the other person, and copies of résumés on screen.

Online Job Postings. Job seekers are increasingly turning to online Web sites to search for job openings and post résumés. Three of the best-known general job sites are The Monster Board, CareerMosaic, and College Grad Job Hunter. Growth in these sites has been phenomenal; the number of job postings on The Monster Board alone leapt from 16,000 to 50,000 in only a year. In fact, you could get more responses than you want by using a general on-

Online job postings have helped companies and job candidates hook up. Once mainly for people seeking careers in high-tech fields, online job sites are now expanding to more career fields.

line site, depending on your career skills. People with high-tech skills often generate the most interest from online sites, but the sites are expanding for all careers.

Computer Skills Tests. Use of computers to test applicants' skills during an interview is a new, if somewhat disturbing, trend. In addition to the traditional interview with a human resource professional and possibly a manager, candidates may have their job skills and poise tested during an interview. Imagine this scenario: You arrive for a job interview with a major bank. In addition to the traditional employee data and questionnaires you fill out, you are tested on your skills for a bank teller position. You have to make change using certain bills and coins. You also deal with an angry customer who repeatedly changes her mind on the amount of cash she wants. Meanwhile, the interviewer records your every move and comment, as well as the time you took to complete the transaction. How? The interviewer is a computer, and you are interacting with the customer on screen. This happened to one job applicant, whose response to the test was mixed even though she received high marks.

Does the digitized world hold the key to job search success? Perhaps. Can it help? Definitely.[1]

IMPORTANCE OF YOUR CAREER DECISION

Selecting a career may be the most important decision you will ever make. This appendix will begin by discussing the best way to approach career decisions and how to prepare for your first **entry-level job,** that is, your first permanent employment after leaving school. It will then look at a range of business careers and discuss employment opportunities in fields that are related to each major part of the text. In many cases, Bureau of Labor Statistics employment projections to 2000 are also included. You can use these sections as starting points in evaluating your career plans.

To make those plans, you need to become aware of employment projections and trends. According to the Bureau of Labor Statistics, over the next decade the number of new jobs in every major occupational category will grow. During the same period, the number of American workers ages 25 to 34 will fall by 2.9 million men and almost 1.0 million women. These trends translate into exciting opportunities for those entering the work force. As Alan Reynolds, director of economic research at the Hudson Institute, comments, "Young Americans will be in a strong position to enjoy rapid increases in real incomes over the next 2 decades."[2]

Education will improve your prospects of finding and keeping the right job. Figure A.1 shows employment and total job openings from 1996 to 2006 and 1996 median weekly earnings by education and training. As you can see, with more education, you are likely to earn more. This trend holds true throughout a person's working life. In 1979, only 47 percent of the nation's best-paid workers (those in the top 10 percent income bracket) had college degrees; today 64 percent of them do.[3]

In addition to taking classes, try to gain related experience, either through a job or participation in campus organizations. Cooperative education programs, internships, or work-study programs can also give you hands-on experience while you pursue your education.

SELF-ASSESSMENT FOR CAREER DEVELOPMENT

You are going to spend a lot of time during your life working, so why not find a job that you enjoy? In order to choose the line of work that suits you best, you must first understand yourself. Self-assessment can be difficult, because it involves answering some tough questions. Remember, however, it does pay off by helping you find a career that will be enjoyable and rewarding.

Not surprisingly, different people have different work-related values. Figure A.2 lists the results of one study that asked U.S. employees to rank the aspects of a job that were most important to them. Most respondents ranked as most important the chance to do something that made them feel good about themselves; other valued job characteristics included the chance to accomplish something worthwhile and the opportunity to learn. These workers ranked the physical environment of a job and its promotional opportunities among the least important aspects.[4]

Take a moment to rank the job factors listed in Figure A.2 as they affect your own job satisfaction. Which are most and least important to you? Be honest with yourself and rank these aspects according to how you really feel, as opposed to how other people might rank them. You can use this self-assessment exercise as a starting point for exploring careers that best meet the needs you identify as important.

A lot of resources offer help in choosing and planning your career. They include school libraries, career guidance

---

Figure A.1	Employment and Job Openings (1996–2006) and 1996 Median Weekly Earnings by Education and Training Category

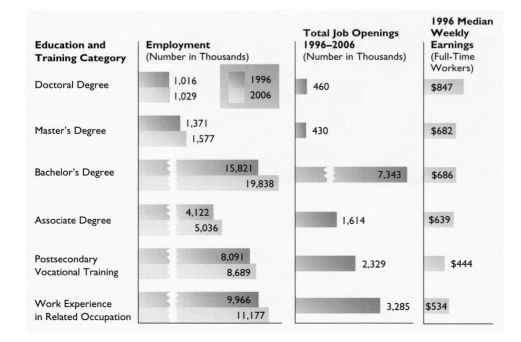

Education and Training Category	Employment (Number in Thousands)	Total Job Openings 1996–2006 (Number in Thousands)	1996 Median Weekly Earnings (Full-Time Workers)
Doctoral Degree	1,016 (1996) / 1,029 (2006)	460	$847
Master's Degree	1,371 / 1,577	430	$682
Bachelor's Degree	15,821 / 19,838	7,343	$686
Associate Degree	4,122 / 5,036	1,614	$639
Postsecondary Vocational Training	8,091 / 8,689	2,329	$444
Work Experience in Related Occupation	9,966 / 11,177	3,285	$534

and placement offices, counseling centers, and online job search services. You may also wish to talk with graduates from your school who are working in fields that interest you.

As another option, you might arrange an **informational interview,** a session with a company representative designed to gather more information about a company or an occupation, rather than to apply for a job. If you are interested in a particular firm, for example, perhaps you could arrange an informational interview with someone who works there to find out what it is really like. If you are curious about a profession, but are not sure it is for you, arrange an informational interview with someone who does that job. Find out what it really involves.

JOB SEARCH GUIDELINES

Once you have chosen a career that seems right for you, get your job search under way. Many others want good, entry-level positions, and you must expect competition. The best first step is to locate available positions that interest you, then be resourceful! Your success depends on gathering as much information as possible. Register at your school's placement office. Establish a placement or credentials file, including letters of recommendation and supporting personal information. Most placement offices send out periodic lists of new job vacancies, so be sure to get your name and address on the mailing list. Become familiar with the process by which your placement office allocates limited interview slots with attractive employers.

Preparing Job Placement Materials

Most placement or credentials files include the following information: (1) letters of recommendation from people who know you—instructors, employers, and others; (2)

| Figure A.2 | **Most Important Aspects of a Job** |

ASPECT OF JOB	RANKED IMPORTANCE	RANKED SATISFACTION
Chances to do something that makes you feel good about yourself	1	8
Chances to accomplish something worthwhile	2	6
Chances to learn new things	3	10
Opportunity to develop your skills and abilities	4	12
Amount of freedom you have on your job	5	2
Chances you have to do things you do best	6	11
Resources you have to do your job	7	9
Respect you receive from co-workers	8	3
Amount of information you get about your job performance	9	17
Your chances for taking part in making decisions	10	14
Amount of job security you have	11	5
Amount of pay you get	12	16
Way you are treated by co-workers	13	4
Friendliness of co-workers	14	1
Amount of praise you get for a job well done	15	15
Amount of fringe benefits you get	16	7
Chances for promotion	17	18
Physical surroundings of your job	18	13

Note: Data comes from a systematic random sample drawn from 23,008 questionnaires that readers returned.

transcripts of academic work to date; (3) a personal data form to report factual information; and (4) a statement of career goals. The placement office will provide special forms to help you to develop your placement file. Complete these forms neatly and accurately, since employers are extremely interested in your ability to communicate in writing. Keep a copy of the final file for later use in preparing similar information for other employment sources. Check back with the placement office to make sure your file is in order.

Letters of reference are very important. Secure recommendations selectively, and try to include a business instructor in your list of references. Always ask people personally if they will write a letter of recommendation for you. Be prepared to give them brief outlines of your

Business Directory

entry-level job   first permanent employment after leaving school.

informational interview   session with a company representative designed to get information about a job or occupation.

academic preparation along with information concerning your job preferences and career objectives. This will help them to prepare letters and may enable them to respond quickly. Remember, however, that these people are usually busy. Allow them enough time to prepare their reference letters, then follow up on missing ones.

Finding Employment through the Internet

The Internet is playing an increasingly important role for both employers and job seekers. Companies of all sizes are posting their job opportunities on the Web, both on their own sites and on specialized job sites, such as *CareerMosaic*® (www.careermosaic.com) and *The Monster Board*® (www.monster.com). The largest job sites may receive hundreds of thousands of visits each day. Newspapers, the source for traditional classified want ads, also post these same ads on the Web. Job seekers can even visit sites that merge ads from many different newspapers into one searchable database, such as *CareerPath.com* (www.careerpath.com). Some sites go a step further and create separate sections for each career area. For example, there are entire sections devoted exclusively to accounting, marketing, and other business professions. Searches are narrowed according to geographic location, entry-level, company name, job title, job description, and other categories.

Job seekers also connect with employers by posting their résumés on job sites. As an added service, many sites offer guidance in the preparation of a résumé. Employers search the résumé database for prospects with the right qualifications. In one common approach, the employer lists one or more keywords, such as "public relations," "network architecture," or "auditing," and then browses the résumés that contain all the required keywords. However, if job seekers want to enter new careers or jobs where technical terms are not used to describe their education and previous work experience, employers may not find their résumés.

Some job sites offer sections devoted exclusively to college students. *College Grad Job Hunter* (www.collegegrad.com) is a good example of an entire site focusing on entry-level opportunities. Job sites may list employers who are interested in hiring recent college graduates, internship opportunities, and provide general career resources covering areas such as wage and salary information, interviewing, résumés, and financial aid. There are Web sites that post job opportunities by employers seeking graduates from specific colleges and universities and work in coordination with college placement offices, such as *JobTrak* (www.jobtrak.com). *Career Magazine* (www.careermag.com) offers a wide range of career resources, as well as articles on job trends, work issues, and other topics.

The *Contemporary Business* Web site at www.contemporarybusiness.com hosts a comprehensive job and career assistance section. The site is updated frequently to include the best job and career sites for identifying and landing the career you want, as well as current strategies for getting the best results from your Web-based career activities.

Finding Employment through Other Sources

The next step—identifying specific job openings—involves seeking out additional sources of information on available jobs, such as educational placement offices and private and public employment services.

Educational Placement Offices Your school placement office is a good place to begin this search, as well. If you have completed formal academic coursework with more than one school, check with placement offices at each school about setting up a placement file. Some colleges have reciprocity agreements that permit students who have completed course work at several schools to establish files with each school's placement office.

Private Employment Agencies Other useful sources to consider are private employment agencies. These firms often specialize in certain types of jobs, performing several services for both employers and job candidates that are not available elsewhere. For example, some private agencies interview, test, and screen job applicants.

A private employment agency usually charges the prospective employer a fee for finding a suitable employee. In some cases, the job seeker is expected to pay a fee. Be sure that you understand the terms of any agreement you sign with a private employment agency.

State Employment Offices For still another source of job leads, check the employment offices of your state government. However, in many states, these public agencies process unemployment compensation along with other related work. Because of the mix of duties, some people view state employment agencies as providing services for semiskilled or unskilled workers. These agencies do list jobs in many professional categories, though.

Business Directory

résumé written summary of personal, educational, and professional achievements.

Other Sources A variety of other sources can help you to identify job openings. Newspaper employment advertisements, especially Sunday editions of metropolitan newspapers, often prove to be rich sources of job leads. Trade journals or magazines may report this information. College instructors and administrators, community organizations such as the local chamber of commerce, and family and friends can often give direction.

Another approach is to identify all the organizations where you think you might like to work. Mail a letter of inquiry and your résumé to those companies. If possible, direct your mailings to a specific person who has the authority to hire new employees. The letter should ask briefly about employment opportunities in a particular line of work. It should also ask for a personal interview.

Writing a Résumé

Regardless of how you identify job openings, you must learn how to develop and use a **résumé,** a written summary of your personal, educational, and professional achievements. The résumé is a very personal document covering your educational background, work experience, career preferences, major interests, and other personal information. It should also include such basic information as your address and telephone number.

The primary purpose of a résumé is to highlight your qualifications for a job, usually on a single page. An attractive layout facilitates the employer's review of your qualifications. Figures A.3, A.4, and A.5 illustrate traditional résumés in chronological, functional, and results-oriented formats.

A job seeker can prepare a résumé in several ways. Some use narrative sentences to explain job duties and career goals; others present information in outline form. A résumé to accompany a placement office credentials file can be quite short. Remember, too, to design it around your own needs and objectives.

Figure A.3	**Chronological Résumé**

Beatrice Conner
4256 Pinebluff Lane
Cleveland, Ohio 44120
216–555–3296

OBJECTIVE

Challenging office management position in a results-oriented company where my organizing people skills can be applied; leading to an operations management position.

WORK EXPERIENCE

1997–Present ADM Distribution Enterprises, Cleveland, Ohio

Office Manager of leading regional soft-drink bottler. Coordinating all bookkeeping, correspondence, scheduling of 12-truck fleet to serve 300 customers, promotional mailings and personnel records, including payroll. Installing computerized systems.

1995–1997 Merriweather, Hicks & Bradshaw Attorneys, Columbus, Ohio

Office Supervisor and Executive Secretary for Douglas H. Bradshaw, Managing Partner. Supervising four clerical workers and two paraprofessionals, automating legal research and correspondence functions, improving filing and dictation systems, and assisting in coordinating outside services and relations with other firms and agencies. Promoted three times in 1 year from Secretary to Office Supervisor.

1990–1995 Conner & Sons Custom Coverings, Cleveland, Ohio

Secretary in father's upholstery and awning company. Performing all office functions over the years, running the office when the manager was on vacation.

EDUCATION

Mill Valley High School, Honors, Certificate 1995

McBundy Community College, Office Management, Automated Office Systems, Associate Degree 1996

Telecom Systems, Word Processing Seminar Series, Certificate 1997

PERSONAL

Member of various professional associations; avid reader; enjoy sports such as camping, cycling, scuba diving, skiing; enjoy volunteering in community projects.

Increasing numbers of organizations are moving toward automated (paperless) résumé processing and applicant tracking systems. Thus, if you write and design a technology-compatible résumé and cover letter, you'll enjoy an edge over an applicant whose résumé and cover letter can't be added to a data base. Figure A.6 lists tips for creating a "scanner friendly" résumé.

Here's the typical route that résumé/cover letters take at Systems and Computer Technology Corporation (SCT) and other organizations using automated systems:

Cover letters and résumés are assigned a source code or a position code (connected to a particular job opening). They are scanned using optical character recognition

Figure A.4 **Functional Résumé**

Timothy M. Richards
Two Seaside Drive
Los Angeles, CA 90026
213–555–7092

OBJECTIVE
Joining a cohesive team effort in county government that has a positive impact on the quality of life in constituent communities, particularly in terms of traffic management and control.

EXPERIENCE
Administration
Coordinating multilevel projects within fixed time frames and budget restrictions; maintaining smooth and frequent communications under adverse conditions of competing political party interference; sustaining loyalty throughout.

Planning
Preparing strategic, long-range, and intermediate-range plans using latest computer models; gaining participation and commitment of all key groups in planning processes; establishing reporting points and methods for all milestones in statewide political campaign; integrating planning for financial, strategic actions, capital items, and breaking issues on an ongoing basis.

Problem Solving
Writing position papers for contingencies and for direct appeal in state representative campaign; facilitating 50 discussion groups to reach consensus; contributing to strategy sessions on three campaigns; four months of coordinating community traffic-pattern hearings.

Leadership
Acting as a spokesperson with print and broadcast media and grassroots elements; establishing focus on common issues bringing differing factions together; setting standards and models for operating in various environments.

Traffic Management
Establishing computer-based modeling capability for 10,000 residents in a community traffic control project; assisting in implementing a three-tiered measuring system for tracking in-bound traffic volume in a high-risk neighborhood; submitting three proposals, now under consideration, for traffic reform in targeted communities.

WORK HISTORY	Valley Systems Research Co.
1996–Present	Whittier Community Traffic Study Project
1996	Federal Traffic Studies Grant
1995–1996	Part-time staff of four political campaigns
1990–1995	U. S. Navy Lieutenant

EDUCATION	UCLA mid-program, M.S. Communications
Currently enrolled	University of Oregon, B.S. Political Science
1994	Loma Linda Junior College, A.S. Journalism

PERSONAL
Held various leadership positions in school and in community action groups. Special recognition for 5 years' work on city and college task forces. U.S. Navy Reservist.

(OCR). OCR converts graphic images into text. The information from the résumé/cover letter resides in a data base until the organization purges it. (Sometimes the data base also holds images of the résumé and cover letter.) Companies' purge policies vary.

Next, the computer uses artificial intelligence to read the recognized text and pulls out key words from each section (objective, education, experience). Typically, says Frances Moscoe, director of SCT Academy, a training division of SCT, the computer looks for standard résumé sections (for example, "Word Experience" or "Education") so it's vital to stick to standard headings. After the computer has scanned the résumé and cover letter, it assigns one or more job categories to the applicant's record and builds a skills inventory from the information it has read. The more skills the computer finds on the résumé and cover letter, the better the chances that the résumé will be picked from the data base for a job opening.

Those involved in the hiring process can query the data base using criteria or key words that they hope will find candidates whose skills and/or experiences fit the job opening. Résumés matching the job opening's criteria are typically forwarded electronically to the person with hiring authority, who then selects candidates for interviews.[5]

Studying Employment Opportunities

You should carefully study the various employment opportunities you have identified. Obviously, you will like some more than others, but you should consider a variety of factors when assessing each job possibility: (1) the actual job responsibilities, (2) industry characteristics, (3) the nature of the company, (4) the geographic location, (5) salary and advancement opportunities, and (6) the job's contribution to your long-run career objectives.

Too many graduates consider only the most striking features of a job, perhaps the location or the salary. However, a comprehensive review of job openings should provide a balanced perspective of the overall employment opportunity, including both long-run and short-run factors.

Job Interviews

The first objective of your job search is to obtain an appointment for an interview with a prospective employer. Whether you initially interview with a computer, as in the opening story to this appendix, or with a human being, it is important to plan and prepare. You want to enter the interview equipped with a good understanding of the company, its industry, and its competitors. Prepare yourself by researching the following essential information about the company:

1. How was the company founded?

2. What is its current position in the industry?

3. What is its financial status?

4. In which markets does it compete?

5. How is the firm organized?

6. Who are its competitors?

7. How many people does it employ?

8. Where are its plants and offices located?

This information is useful in several ways. First, it helps to give you a feeling of confidence during the interview. Second, it can keep you from making an unwise employment decision. Third, it can impress an interviewer, who may well try to determine how much an applicant knows about the company as a way of evaluating that person's interest level. A candidate who fails to make the effort to obtain such information often risks elimination from further consideration.

Where do you get this pre-interview information? First, your school placement office or employment agency should have information on prospective employers. Business instructors at your school may also provide tips. Your school or community library should have various references to help you investigate a firm, or you can write directly to a company. Many firms publish career brochures as well as annual reports. Finally, ask friends and relatives for input. They or someone they know may have had experience with the company.

Interviewers report two main reasons for poor performance in job interviews. Many job seekers fail due to ineffective communication, either because of inadequate preparation for their interviews or because they lack confidence. Remember that the interviewer will first determine whether

| Figure A.5 | **Results-Oriented Résumé** |

T. L. Chambers
3609 N.W. 57th Street
St. Louis, MO 63166
314–555–2394

OBJECTIVE

To apply my expertise as a construction foreman to a management role in an organization seeking improvements in overall production, long-term employee relationships, and the ability to attract top talent from the construction field.

EXPERIENCE

DAL Construction Company, St. Louis, Missouri, 1995–Present
Established automated, on-site recordkeeping system improving communications and morale between field and office, saving 400 work hours per year, and reducing the number of accounting errors by 20 percent. As foreman, developed a crew selected as "first choice crew" by most workers wanting transfers. Completed five housing projects ahead of deadline and under budget.

St. Louis County Housing Authority, St. Louis, Missouri, 1993–1994, Summers
Created friendly, productive atmosphere among workers enabling first on-time job completion in 4 years and one-half of usual materials waste. Initiated pilot materials delivery program with potential savings of 3.5 percent of yearly maintenance budget.

Jackson County Housing Authority, Kansas City, Missouri, 1992
Produced information pamphlet increasing applications for county housing by 22 percent. Introduced labor-management discussion techniques saving jobs and over $21,000 in lost time.

Carnegie Brothers Construction Company, West Palm Beach, Florida, 1990–1991
Introduced expediting methods saving 5 percent of overhead cost on all jobs and attracting a new $1.6 million client. Cut new-worker orientation time in half and on-site accidents by one-fourth through training and modeling desired behavior.

Payton, Durnbell & Associates Architects, Kansas City, Kansas, 1989
Developed and monitored productivity improvements saving 60 percent on information transfer costs for firm's 12 largest jobs.

EDUCATION
1994–1995   Washington University, B.S. English
1992–1993   Central Missouri State University, English

PERSONAL
Highly self-motivated manager. Single and willing to relocate. Avid reader and writer.

you can communicate effectively. You should be specific in answering and asking questions, and you should clearly and positively express your concerns. The questions that interviewers ask most often include the following:

Why do you want this job?
Where do you see yourself 10 years from now?
What are your strengths?
What are your weaknesses?
Why should I hire you?

It is important to know who is doing the interviewing and who will make the final hiring decision. Most people who conduct initial job interviews work in their firms'

Figure A.6 **Tips for Creating a "Scanner Friendly" Résumé**

1. Send originals; photocopies or faxed copies cause degraded text when scanned.

2. Use light-colored 8½" × 11" paper printed on one side only.

3. Do not use 11" × 17" paper folded to create pamphlet-like résumés.

4. Use popular sans serif fonts (e.g., Helvetica or Arial) in sizes from 10 to 14 points.

5. Avoid tabs.

6. Avoid graphics, shading, script fonts, italics, underlining, and boldfaced text.

7. Avoid horizontal and vertical lines.

8. Avoid parentheses and brackets.

9. Avoid compressed lines of text.

10. Use wide margins around the text.

11. Do not fold résumé when mailed.

12. Avoid dot matrix printers.

13. Avoid stapling the résumé.

human resources divisions. These staff workers can make recommendations to line managers about which individuals to employ. Line managers get involved in interviewing later in the hiring process. Some decisions come from human resources personnel together with the immediate supervisor of the prospective employee. More often, immediate supervisors make the decisions alone. Rarely does the human resources department have sole hiring authority.

In a typical format, the interviewer talks little during the interview. This type of **open-ended interview** forces you to talk about yourself and your goals. If you appear unorganized, the interviewer may eliminate you on that basis alone. When faced with this type of situation, be sure to express your thoughts clearly and keep the conversation on target. Talk for about 10 minutes, then ask some specific questions of the interviewer. (Come prepared with questions to ask!) Listen carefully to the responses. Remember that if you prepare for a job interview, it will become a mutual exchange of information.

A successful first interview will probably lead to an invitation to come back for another interview. Sometimes this will include a request to take a battery of tests. Most students do very well on these tests because they have had plenty of practice in college!

Employment Decision

By this time, the employer knows a lot about you from your placement file, résumé, and first interview. You should also know a lot about the company. The primary purpose of further interviews is to determine whether you can work effectively within the organization.

If you create a positive impression during your second or later interviews, you may be offered a job. Again, your decision to accept the offer should depend on how well the career opportunity matches your career objectives. Make the best entry-level job decision you can, and learn from it. Learn your job responsibilities as quickly and thoroughly as possible, then start looking for other ways to improve your performance and that of your employer.

NONTRADITIONAL STUDENTS

At one time, colleges and universities seemed to serve a market of mostly 18- to 22-year-olds. This was the primary age group that sought to break into the job market. Times have certainly changed.

More people are returning to school to complete degrees, and more people who already have college degrees are returning for more education. These students are often referred to as **nontraditional students**. Although the term covers any student who does not fit into the 18- to 22-year-old age group (the "traditional" clients of higher education), it is actually inaccurate, since older students have become the norm on many campuses. In any case, nontraditional students have two other characteristics: they work, either full-time or part-time, and college is often only one of their daily responsibilities. Many are married, and many, regardless of marital status, have children.

Most nontraditional students come from one of the following groups:

1. **Displaced homemakers** Full-time homemakers often return to school or join the work force because of divorce or widowhood or for economic reasons.

2. *Military service veterans* Another major segment of nontraditional students enters school after discharge from the military. Many of them lack practical job skills.

3. **Technologically displaced workers** Someone who lost a job to automation or industry cutbacks may return to school. Recently, middle-level and upper-level managers have joined the ranks of displaced workers as their companies have cut costs by eliminating their jobs.[6]

4. *Older, full-time employees*   These workers may enter school to seek additional education to enhance career prospects or for personal satisfaction.

Challenges Faced by Nontraditional Students

Nontraditional students often face different challenges than younger students. One is scheduling; often older students must juggle the responsibilities of work, school, and family. They may have to study at odd times: during meals, while commuting, or after putting the kids to bed. For another challenge, nontraditional students may be trying to change careers, so they must both learn skills in a different field and work toward breaking into that field with a new job.

Take heart, though. Nontraditional students also have a very important advantage: experience. Even experience in an unrelated field is a plus. Older students know how businesses operate. Often they have developed useful skills in human relations, management, budgeting, and communications. Also, through observing other people's mistakes and living through their own, they have often learned what not to do.

Like other students, nontraditional students need to assess their accomplishments, skills, likes, and dislikes. The same exercises and resources suggested earlier can help both traditional and older students to assess their strengths and determine their career goals.

YOUR CAREER: A LONG-RANGE VIEW

Throughout your career, it is important to stay flexible and continue learning. Challenging new skills will be required of managers and other businesspeople during the next decade. Remain open to unexpected changes and opportunities that can help you to learn and develop new skills. "Don't get into this 1950s 'I am going to stay here forever' mindset," advises executive recruiter Kenneth Kelley. "In the next 20 or 30 years, you may have three different positions." Since it has been well documented that typical graduates will have five or more different jobs during their lifetime, skills that transfer will be highly desirable for a career path.

Jonathan Webb, for example, earned a bachelor's degree in banking and finance at Morehouse University and obtained an entry-level position as a securities analyst. He wanted to move into a sales position, however, so he took classes in investment banking and began selling securities to institutional investors such as banks and insurance companies. Today Webb is a vice president of regional institutional sales at Shearson Lehman's Chicago division. He appreciates the importance of learning a wide variety of work skills. "At Lehman Bros., if you work as a lending officer, you have to prepare a lot of numbers and sell it internally first so your client outside is not misled," he explains. "You need strong communication and sales skills."[7]

The most important skill to learn may be just that: the ability to learn. James Challenger, an outplacement consultant in Chicago, notes that employers want workers who can collect and analyze both verbal and numerical information. His advice to students is, "Study what you like, and learn to think." Lew Shumaker, manager of college relations for DuPont, emphasizes the importance of flexibility and the talent to function well in a culturally diverse workplace. "Over the past few years 60 percent of our new hires have been women or members of minority groups," says Shumaker. "So we are looking for graduates who have shown that they value those who are different from themselves."[8]

FINAL NOTE—THE AUTHORS' VIEW

We believe that choosing a career is one of the most important decisions you will ever make. Choosing wisely and staying open to new opportunities can help to make it a happy decision, too. Just imagine the satisfaction of getting paid to do something you enjoy!

Do not procrastinate or trust others to make this decision for you. Follow the steps outlined here and in other sources, and make your own decision. Your instructors, parents, friends, and advisors will offer to help in a multitude of ways, but in the end, it is your own decision.

We hope that this textbook has presented a panorama of career options for you. Whatever you decide, be sure it is right for you. As the old saying goes, "You pass this way only once." Enjoy!

Business Directory

open-ended interview   interview designed to force an applicant to talk about personal qualifications and goals.

nontraditional student   any student who does not fall into the 18- to 22-year-old age group.

displaced homemaker   homemaker who returns to school or takes a job because of divorce or widowhood or for economic reasons.

technologically displaced worker   worker who loses a job due to automation or industrial cutbacks.

IMPORTANT BUSINESS TERMS YOU NEED TO KNOW

entry-level job

informational interview

résumé

open-ended interview

nontraditional student

displaced homemaker

technologically displaced worker

ASSIGNMENTS

1. Construct your own résumé following the procedures outlined in this appendix. Ask your instructors, friends, relatives, and associates to criticize it. What did you learn from this exercise?
2. Conduct an informational interview with someone in your community who is working in a profession that interests you. (Remember that this person is busy. Call first to request an appointment. The interview should take no more than 15 to 20 minutes; come prepared with questions to ask.) Discuss with the class what you learned from the interview.
3. Discuss how you would answer each of the questions that interviewers most often ask.
4. Choose a partner and take turns interviewing each other for a job in front of the class. (Use the interview questions mentioned in this chapter.) After the interview, ask the class to give you feedback on how you looked and acted during your interview. Would they advise you to do or say anything differently?
5. Discuss what you can do to prepare yourself to become a successful businessperson who possesses the skills necessary to succeed in the next decade.
6. Access the Career Center at the College View Web site:

   www.collegeview.com/careers

   Search the site to explore your interests, do self-assessments, learn about career training and internships, and other career information. Write a short summary of what you found and areas that interest you.

BUSINESS CAREER EXERCISE

Résumés

Whether you are applying for a part-time or summer job before graduation or a full-time position after graduation, you need a well-prepared résumé. Effective résumés communicate what you can offer a prospective employer, and the process of preparing a résumé helps you clarify your best assets.

This exercise will help you to:

▼ Select the résumé format (chronological, functional, or results oriented) that best represents your education, skills, and experience.

▼ Prepare both general résumés and custom résumés for specific employers.

How to Locate the Exercise Launch *Career Design* from the "Career Assistance" program group. Then select "Navigation" from the menu at the top of the screen, followed by "Career Sections" and then "Résumés."

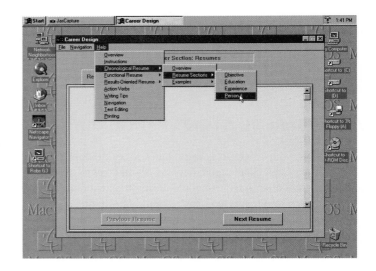

appendix B

Risk Management and Insurance

Victories in the War on AIDS

Life is filled with risks, none of which has been more frightening during the last 20 years than the threat of AIDS. More than half a million people in the United States have contracted AIDS, including nearly 8,000 children under the age of thirteen. Nearly 400,000 adults and 4,600 children have died. Worldwide, 30 million people are living with AIDS, and nearly 12 million have died, 400,000 of whom were children.

Insurance claims paid to AIDS victims have soared, causing experts to predict that AIDS would soon account for 20 percent of all life insurance claims. Treatment for AIDS—when it was available at all—was, it seemed, inhumanely expensive. A single drug dose might cost $200; a year of treatment could cost nearly $400,000. Some insurance companies responded by requiring all life insurance applicants to take a screening test for the presence of HIV or the AIDS virus. Others tried to deny AIDS benefits outright. Of course, all of these numbers hardly begin to reflect the emotional cost of the disease.

As research has progressed over the last decade or so and treatments become more refined, HIV and AIDS patients have begun to live longer; some are now essentially symptom free. There have been huge strides in the war against AIDS. Still, there's no magic cure, no vaccine. "The situation is neither black nor white," cautions leading researcher Dr. David Ho of the Aaron Diamond AIDS Research Center. "We must paint it in the proper shade of gray." Although many patients respond well to medication, their immune systems appear to be permanently damaged, leaving them susceptible to other illnesses. And many patients cannot be weaned off medication, even though symp-

www.goldenrule.com

toms seem to disappear. "So far, everyone who has gone off medication has [experienced the virus coming] back," observes Warner C. Greene, director of the Gladstone Institute of Virology and Immunology. Finally, just because the AIDS virus recedes enough so that it is undetectable, doesn't mean it isn't there.

So, the good news is that AIDS is no longer an automatic death sentence. The bad news is that the long-term effects of AIDS are still very damaging—and costly. This means that insurance companies, treatment facilities, legislators, employers, and others must find a humane way to calculate and manage the many risks of AIDS. Dr. David Ho and his partner, Alan Perelson of the Los Alamos National Laboratory, are using mathematical models to show how combinations of certain drugs can be used to shorten the time of treat-

ment required for patients. The State of California, which has the second-highest number of AIDS cases (New York has the highest), has prohibited health insurance companies from using antibody tests to screen health insurance applicants. However, life insurance companies may still use the tests. Consider the responses of insurance companies to the AIDS crisis. New York Life Insurance company has funded $8.5 million in AIDS research. By contrast, Guardian Life dropped coverage for hair stylists. Golden Rule Insurance, whose policy reflects its name, offers full coverage without AIDS testing but requires that the policy buyer remain free of AIDS for one year after purchasing the policy. Impaired Risk Specialists offers insurance to individuals such as AIDS patients who previously have been unable to obtain insurance.

Making predictions about the course AIDS will take is a difficult, complex process, and it is one of the risks that businesses and individuals will face in the 21st century. As you read this appendix, think about other types of uncertainty that employers and employees face together, and focus on ways to deal with these risks.[1]

Risk is a daily fact of life for both individuals and businesses. Sometimes the risk appears in the form of serious illnesses. Sometimes it appears in the form of property loss, such as the luxury homes that slid down muddy hillsides in California as a result of El Niño rains during early 1998. Sometimes risk occurs as a result of the actions of others—such as the devastating bomb attack that took the lives of men, women, and children at the Oklahoma City Federal building. Sometimes risk occurs as a result of our own actions—we fail to wear a seatbelt while driving or decline an extended warranty on the new VCR.

Companies face various forms of risk each day. In 1995, a devastating fire destroyed two manufacturing plants owned by Malden Mills of Lawrence, Massachu-

setts. Malden Mills makes Polartec and Polarfleece, a synthetic fleece used to make all kinds of outdoor wear. Instead of closing the company's doors and sending workers home, CEO Aaron Feuerstein used the insurance money to put as many back to work as he could—and kept the rest on the payroll, with health benefits. It cost Malden Mills, a family-owned business, about $10 million to pay 1,400 workers for 90 days plus full health-care benefits for 180 days.

Feuerstein began to rebuild immediately. Some employees occupied temporary quarters during construction. "After the fire we relocated in temporary buildings with broken windows and freezing cold," recalls Jose Melo, an executive board member. "We had to put on our overcoats, but we got the work out!" Everyone struggled together to keep the company in business. Malden Mills received federal and state assistance, as well as a UNITE $100,000 special assistance fund for its union members. Just ten months after the fire, the first new Malden Mills plant opened. Later, the U.S. Department of Labor made a $1 million grant to the company to pay for a two-year Incumbent Worker Pilot Project to help retrain Malden Mills workers to use the equipment in its new facilities. Aaron Feuerstein was touted as an American hero. "There was no way that I was going to take 3,000 people and throw them into the street," he said emphatically. "And there was no way I was going to condemn Lawrence to economic oblivion."[2]

To fulfill their responsibilities of achieving organizational objectives, managers must understand the types of risks they face and develop methods for dealing with them. One important method of dealing with risk is to shift it to specialized firms called *insurance companies.* This appendix discusses the concept of insurance in an individual firm. It begins by defining the meaning of *risk.*

CONCEPT OF RISK

Risk is uncertainty about loss or injury. The business firm's list of risk-filled decisions is long. A factory or warehouse faces the risk of fire, burglary, water damage, and physical deterioration. Accidents, judgments due to lawsuits, and nonpayment of bills by customers are other risks. Analysts divide risk into two major types: speculative risk and pure risk.

Speculative risk gives the firm or individual the chance of either a profit or a loss. Purchasing shares of stock on the basis of the latest hot tip can result in profits or losses. Expanding operations into a new market may result in higher profits or the loss of invested funds.

Pure risk, on the other hand, involves only the chance of loss. Automobile drivers, for example, always face the risk of accidents. Should they occur, the drivers and others may suffer financial and physical loss. If they do not occur, however, the insurance company gains. Insurance often helps people to protect against financial loss resulting from pure risk.

RISK MANAGEMENT

Because risk is an unavoidable part of business, managers must find ways of deal-

DID YOU KNOW?

Some HMOs pay bonuses to member primary care physicians for limiting the number of referrals they make to specialists each month.

ing with it. Recognizing it is an important first step. After that, the manager has four methods available for dealing with risk: avoiding it, reducing its frequency or severity, self-insuring against it, or shifting the risk to insurance companies.

The manager must consider many factors when evaluating the risk of conducting business at home and abroad. These include a nation's economic stability, social and cultural factors such as language, available technologies, distribution systems, and government regulations. Firms find lower risk in countries with stable economic, social/cultural, technological, and political/legal environments.

Avoiding Risk

Some firms are willing to take high risks for potentially high rewards, while others are unwilling to risk the potential losses involved in developing new and untried products. Although avoiding risk may ensure profitability, it stifles innovation. As a result, risk-averse companies are rarely leaders in their industries.

Reducing Risk

Managers can reduce or even eliminate many types of risk by removing hazards or taking preventive measures. Many companies develop safety programs to educate employees about potential hazards and the proper methods of performing certain dangerous tasks. For instance, any employee who works at a hazardous waste site is required to have training and medical monitoring that meet the federal Office of Health and Safety (OSHA) standards. The training and monitoring not only reduces risk, it pays off on the bottom line. Foster Wheeler Environmental Corp. is one company affected by these regulations. The firm has a strong, proactive health and safety training program that has resulted in a reduced number of workers' compensation claims. In addition, by reducing OSHA-recorded injuries and illnesses, Foster Wheeler has been able to obtain reduced insurance rates.[3]

Business Directory

risk uncertainty about loss or injury.

All of these actions can reduce the risk involved in business operations, but they cannot eliminate risk entirely. Most major business insurers assist their clients in avoiding or minimizing risk by offering the services of loss-prevention experts to conduct thorough reviews of operations. These safety and health professionals evaluate customers' work environments and recommend procedures and equipment to help firms minimize worker injuries and property losses.

Is your retained risk safe from the great unknown?

Some companies set up funds to cover possible losses. AM-RE Managers helps self-insured companies manage their risk through consulting services.

Self-Insuring Against Risk

Instead of purchasing insurance against certain kinds of pure risk, some multiplant, geographically scattered firms accumulate funds to cover possible losses. Such a **self-insurance fund** is a special fund created by setting aside cash reserves periodically that the firm can draw upon in the event of a financial loss resulting from a pure risk. The firm makes regular payments to the fund, and it charges losses to the fund. Such a fund typically accompanies a risk-reduction program aimed at minimizing losses. Self-insurance is most useful in cases where a company faces similar risks and the risks are spread over a broad geographic area.

Shifting Risk to an Insurance Company

Although a firm can take steps to avoid or reduce risk, the most common method of dealing with it is to shift it to others in the form of **insurance**—the process by which a firm, for a fee, agrees to pay another firm or individual a sum of money stated in a written contract when a loss occurs. The insured party's fee to the insurance company for coverage against losses is called a *premium*. Insurance substitutes a small, known loss—the insurance premium—for a larger, unknown loss that may or may not occur. In the case of life insurance, the loss—death—is a certainty; the main uncertainty is the date when it will occur.

It is important for the insurer to understand the customer's business, risk exposure, and insurance needs. Many firms that engage in production and marketing activities in several countries choose to do business with insurance companies that maintain global networks of offices and agents.

BASIC INSURANCE CONCEPTS

Insurance companies accumulate premiums to cover eventual losses. The returns from insurance company investments may allow them to reduce premiums, generate profits, or both. By investing accumulated funds, insurance companies represent a major source of long-term financing for other businesses.

An insurance company is a professional risk taker. For a fee, it accepts risks of loss or damage to businesses and individuals. Three basic principles underlie insurance: the concept of insurable interest, the concept of insurable risks, and the law of large numbers.

Insurable Interest

To purchase insurance, an applicant must demonstrate an **insurable interest** in the property or life of the insured. The policyholder must stand to suffer a loss, financial or otherwise, due to fire, accident, death, or lawsuit. For life insurance, a friend or rel-

Business Directory

self-insurance fund account set up to cover losses due to pure risks.

insurance process by which an insurer, in exchange for a fee, agrees to reimburse a firm or individual for losses up to specified limits.

mortality table table with data that predicts the number of persons in each age category who will die in a given year.

ative may have an insurable interest despite facing no prospect of financial loss in the event of the insured's death.

Because top managers are important assets to a firm, it can purchase key executive insurance on their lives. A businessperson cannot collect on insurance to cover damage to the property of competitors in which that person has no insurable interest, nor can an individual citizen purchase an insurance policy on the life of the president of the United States, since he or she lacks an insurable interest.

Insurable Risk

Insurable risk refers to the requirements that a risk must meet in order for the insurer to provide protection. Insurers impose five basic requirements on insurable risk:

1. The likelihood of loss should be predictable.

2. The loss should be financially measurable.

3. The loss should be fortuitous or accidental.

4. The risk should be spread over a wide geographic area.

5. The insurance company has the right to set standards for accepting risks.

Law of Large Numbers

Insurance is based on the law of averages, or statistical probability. Insurance companies have studied the chances of occurrences of deaths, injuries, lawsuits, and all types of hazards. From their investigations, they have developed the **law of large numbers,** a probability calculation of the likelihood of the occurrence of perils, on which they base their premiums. They also use actuarial tables to predict the number of fires, automobile accidents, plane crashes, and deaths that will occur in a given year.

An example can demonstrate how insurers can use the law of large numbers to calculate premiums. Previously collected statistical data on a small city with 50,000 homes indicates that the city will experience an average of 500 fires a year, with damages totaling an average of $30,000 per occurrence. What is the minimum annual premium an insurance company would charge to insure a house against fire?

To simplify the calculations, assume that the premiums would not produce profits or cover any of the insurance company's operating expenses. In total, fires in the city would generate claims of $15 million (500 homes damaged × $30,000). If these losses were spread over all 50,000 homes, each homeowner would be charged an annual premium of $300 ($15 million divided by 50,000 homes). In reality, though, the insurance company would set the premium at a higher figure to cover its operating expenses and to earn a reasonable return.

An insurer uses a **mortality table** like the one in Table B.1 to predict the number of people in each age category who will die in a given year. The data come from past experiences with large numbers of male and female policyholders of different ages. After determining the

| | | Expectation of Life in Years | | | | Expected Deaths per 1,000 Alive at Specified Age | | | | |
| | | White | | African American | | | White | | African American | |
Age	Total	Male	Female	Male	Female	Total	Male	Female	Male	Female
At Birth	74.9	72.3	78.9	64.9	73.4	9.99	9.55	7.47	19.19	16.26
1	74.7	72.0	78.5	65.2	73.6	0.70	0.73	0.55	1.17	0.88
5	70.8	68.1	74.6	61.4	69.8	0.30	0.30	0.23	0.54	0.40
10	65.9	63.2	69.7	56.5	64.9	0.17	0.17	0.13	0.24	0.25
15	61.0	58.3	64.8	51.6	60.0	0.64	0.85	0.38	1.07	0.38
20	56.3	53.6	59.9	47.0	55.1	1.09	1.51	0.51	2.47	0.72
25	51.6	49.0	55.0	42.7	50.4	1.19	1.57	0.52	3.22	1.13
30	46.9	44.4	50.2	38.4	45.7	1.35	1.69	0.61	4.14	1.58
35	42.2	39.8	45.4	34.3	41.1	1.73	2.05	0.82	5.91	2.30
40	37.6	35.2	40.6	30.3	36.6	2.22	2.60	1.21	7.49	3.22
45	33.0	30.7	35.8	26.5	32.2	3.17	3.65	1.95	9.54	4.39
50	28.6	26.3	31.2	22.8	28.0	4.98	5.74	3.26	13.16	6.48
55	24.4	22.2	26.8	19.4	24.0	7.96	9.57	5.37	17.62	9.77
60	20.5	18.4	22.6	16.2	20.3	12.61	15.64	8.63	25.31	15.19
65	16.9	14.9	18.7	13.4	16.9	18.72	23.60	13.17	35.26	21.26

Table B.1 Mortality Tables and Insurance Premiums

policyholder's expected death rate, the insurer can calculate the premium for a life insurance policy to provide sufficient income to pay death benefits and to cover its own operating expenses. For example, a 30-year-old African-American male would usually pay higher insurance premiums than a 20-year-old African-American male because the number of deaths per thousand increases to 4.14 from 2.47 over the 10-year difference in ages. As the age of the insured increases, the length of expected life decreases and the life insurance premium rises. The same type of calculation sets the premium for an automobile or fire insurance policy. The law of large numbers is the basis of all insurance premium calculations.

SOURCES OF INSURANCE

The term **insurance company** includes both private companies, such as Prudential, John Hancock, State Farm, and Travelers, and a number of public agencies that provide insurance coverage for business firms, not-for-profit organizations, and individuals.

Public Insurance Companies

A *public insurance company* is a state or federal government agency established to provide specialized insurance protection for individuals and organizations. It provides protection in such areas as job loss (unemployment insurance), work-related injuries (workers' compensation), and retirement and disability (Social Security). Public insurance companies also sponsor specialized programs, such as deposit, flood, and crop insurance.

Unemployment Insurance Every state has an *unemployment insurance* program that assists unemployed workers by providing financial benefits, job counseling, and placement services. Compensation amounts vary depending on workers' previous incomes and the states in which they file claims. These insurance programs are funded by payroll taxes paid by employers.

Workers' Compensation Under state laws, employers must provide *workers' compensation insurance* to guaran-

tee payment of wages and salaries, medical care costs, and such rehabilitation services as retraining, job placement, and vocational rehabilitation to employees who are injured on the job. Workers' compensation protects employees in all 50 states and Puerto Rico. In addition, workers' compensation provides benefits in the form of weekly payments or single, lump-sum payments to survivors of workers who die as a result of work-related injuries. Premiums are based on the company's payroll, the on-the-job hazards to which it exposes workers, and its safety record.[4]

Social Security The federal government is the largest insurer in the United States. Its Social Security program, officially titled *Old-Age, Survivors, Disability, and Health Insurance (OASDHI)*, grew out of the Social Security Act of 1935. *Medicare* was added to the OASDHI program to provide health insurance for persons 65 years or older and certain other Social Security recipients. More than nine out of ten U.S. employees and their dependents are eligible for Social Security program benefits.

 www.ssa.gov

Private Insurance Companies

Much of the insurance in force is provided by private insurance companies. These companies are typically categorized by ownership as stock companies and mutual companies. Insurance companies, whether they operate as stock or mutual companies, share the objective of minimizing the premiums necessary to cover operating expenses and to pay for personal or property losses.

Stock Companies A *stock insurance company* operates to earn a profit. Stockholders do not have to be policyholders; they invest funds in the firm by purchasing its stock in order to receive dividends from earnings or to benefit from increases in stock prices. The company earns profits from two sources: (1) insurance premiums in excess of claims and operating costs, and (2) earnings from company investments in mortgages, stocks, bonds, and real estate. Stock companies dominate the insurance industry, with the exception of life insurance, which is controlled by mutual insurance companies.

Mutual Companies A *mutual insurance company* is a type of insurance cooperative owned by its policyholders. The mutual company is chartered by the state and governed by a board of directors elected by the policyholders. Prudential Insurance Company of America, the nation's largest insurer, is a mutual company.

Unlike a stock company, a mutual company earns no profits for its owners. As a not-for-profit organization, it returns any surplus funds that remain after it covers operating expenses and claims and establishes necessary reserves to policyholders in the form of dividends or premium reductions.

TYPES OF INSURANCE

Although insurers offer hundreds of policies to individuals and businesses, they fall conveniently into three broad categories: (1) property and liability insurance, (2) health insurance, and (3) life insurance.

Property and Liability Insurance

As Figure B.1 shows, property and liability insurance defines a general category of insurance that provides protection against a number of perils. **Property losses** are financial losses resulting from interruption of business operations or physical damage to property as a result of

fires, accidents, theft, or other destructive events. The destruction caused by El Niño serves as an example. The cyclical trend of ocean warming that brought severe storms, floods, tornadoes, and ice storms across the United States during the winter of 1997–1998 left some people dead, others homeless and wondering whether to rebuild. A month or so before severe storms hit California, the Federal Emergency Management Agency aired an urgent radio announcement encouraging homeowners to buy flood insurance—which only costs about $350 for a year's coverage. "Without flood insurance, many people could lose everything," warned the announcement. "Don't wait for El Niño's rains to start." Although requests for information about flood insurance increased from 15 per day to 40, the number was pitifully low compared with the number of homeowners—and of those 40 who requested flood insurance, not many actually purchased the insurance.

"A lot of people [were] in denial, saying, that won't happen to me," notes State Farm insurance agent Lonnie Haskins. In San Francisco, CAL Insurance & Assoc. sent a letter about El Niño to approximately 1,500 customers; only two purchased flood insurance. Typically, people don't worry about disaster insurance until after the disaster—or right before a predicted disaster. But FEMA policies don't become active until 30 days after they are issued.

Figure B.1   **Solving the Property and Liability Insurance Puzzle**

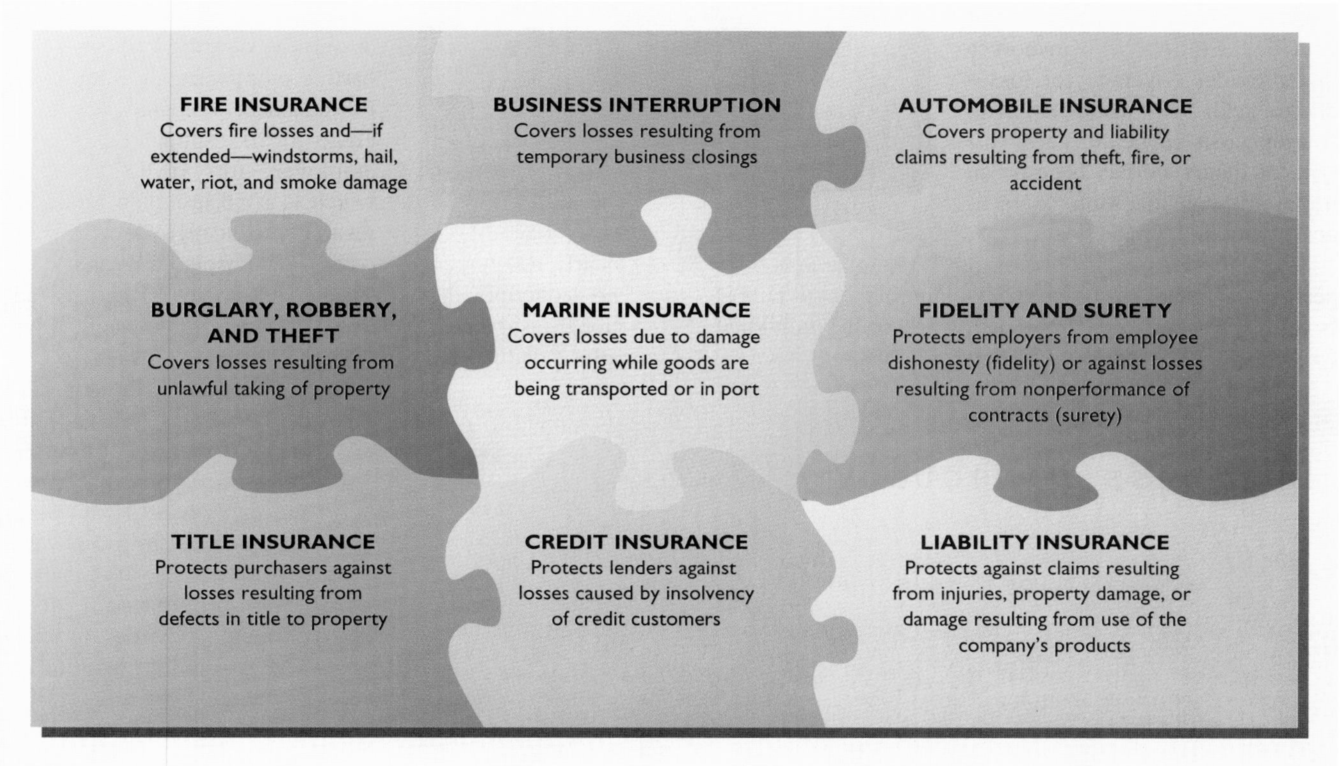

FIRE INSURANCE Covers fire losses and—if extended—windstorms, hail, water, riot, and smoke damage

BUSINESS INTERRUPTION Covers losses resulting from temporary business closings

AUTOMOBILE INSURANCE Covers property and liability claims resulting from theft, fire, or accident

BURGLARY, ROBBERY, AND THEFT Covers losses resulting from unlawful taking of property

MARINE INSURANCE Covers losses due to damage occurring while goods are being transported or in port

FIDELITY AND SURETY Protects employers from employee dishonesty (fidelity) or against losses resulting from nonperformance of contracts (surety)

TITLE INSURANCE Protects purchasers against losses resulting from defects in title to property

CREDIT INSURANCE Protects lenders against losses caused by insolvency of credit customers

LIABILITY INSURANCE Protects against claims resulting from injuries, property damage, or damage resulting from use of the company's products

Most people don't bother with flood insurance because the risk seems low. It's also true that many insurance agents overlook flood insurance because the commission for these premiums is so low—about $35. In addition to encouraging homeowners to buy flood insurance, FEMA warned that individuals should not count on the federal government to bail them out financially if their homes were flooded.

Liability losses are financial losses suffered by business firms or individuals held responsible for property damage or injuries suffered by others. In the past decade alone, courts have decided in favor of plaintiffs in a variety of new types of liability charges, including invasion of privacy, defamation, fraud, intentional infliction of emotional stress, and sexual harassment. Some experts now recommend that companies protect themselves from such disputes by purchasing a separate employment practices liability insurance (EPLI) policy. Illinois-based Shand Morahan & Company, is one insurer that now offers this type of policy.[5]

Health Insurance

Everyone faces the risk of getting sick or being injured in some way. To guard against this risk, most Americans have some form of **health insurance**—insurance that provides coverage for losses due to sickness or accidents. With soaring costs in health care, this type of insurance has become an important consideration of businesses and individuals.[6]

Most businesses and not-for-profit organizations offer health and accident insurance for their employees as part of benefit packages. These *group policies* resemble individual coverage, but are offered at lower premiums.

Private insurance companies, such as Cigna, Nationwide, and Provident Insurance, offer group health packages to employees. The not-for-profit Blue Cross/Blue Shield plans are locally-organized organizations that contract with hospitals, physicians, and other providers for their services at negotiated rates. This alternative to private insurance companies currently insures about 68 million people. Figure B.2 illustrates the coverage included in such group plans.

A **health maintenance organization (HMO)** is a prepaid medical expense plan that provides a comprehensive set of health services and benefits to policyholders, who pay monthly fees. It employs its own physicians and health care specialists and often owns hospitals and clinical facilities. Among the largest HMOs are Kaiser Permanente, the Health Insurance Plan of New York, and the Group Health Cooperative of Seattle. Federal law requires employers to offer such plans to employees as alternatives to group insurance plans in areas where HMOs are available.

Today, 85 percent of employees at companies with ten or more workers are enrolled in HMOs. Adding employees and their families together, roughly 160 million Americans are enrolled in these plans. One reason for this dramatic increase in HMO membership is the desire for controlled costs—on the part of employers and employees. For instance, companies pay an average $3,165 annually per active employee for HMO coverage, which is $356 less than traditional insurance. Since HMOs usually pay nearly 100 percent of doctors' and hospital bills and charge no deductible, they are attractive to many workers. (Traditional insurance typically pays 80 percent of medical bills after a deductible is met.)[7]

However, the effort to contain costs has caused a backlash because of restrictions placed on both doctors and patients by HMO plans. For instance, in recent years several states have passed laws prohibiting "drive-through" deliveries, in which HMOs required hospitals to discharge new mothers and babies within 24 to 48 hours after delivery. Similarly, patients with serious or unusual

| Figure B.2 | **Blue Cross/Blue Shield Provides Health Insurance Coverage** |

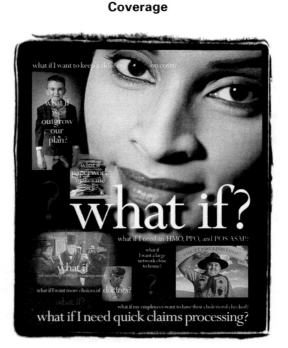

Business Directory

liability loss financial loss suffered by a business firm or individual held responsible for property damage or injuries suffered by others.

health insurance insurance that covers losses due to sickness or accidents.

health maintenance organization (HMO) prepaid medical expense plan that provides a comprehensive set of health services and benefits to policyholders, who pay monthly fees.

key executive insurance life insurance designed to reimburse an organization for loss of the services of an important executive.

conditions have charged that they have been denied proper treatment because of cost. HMO patients may have to get their prescriptions filled at certain participating pharmacies, regardless of price or location. Furthermore, many HMOs hire pharmacy benefits managers (PBMs) to control drug prescription costs. If a PBM promises to sell more of a manufacturer's pharmaceuticals, the PBM will get them at a better price. However, this doesn't mean that the patient is getting the best formula for his or her problem.[8]

In what has been called a major revolt against HMO restrictions and near-monopolies, 26 large corporations in the Minneapolis area—including 3M, Honeywell, Dayton Hudson, and Pillsbury—have banded together to circumvent HMOs altogether, instead directly hiring doctors and other medical services. These health-care professionals are free to organize and charge whatever they want to, but if they overcharge or deliver poor service, the consortium of companies will get word out fast—and business for the poor performers is likely to suffer a fatal blow.[9]

www.honeywell.com

A *preferred provider organization (PPO)* negotiates reduced prices from hospitals and physicians and then offers their services in packages to employers. Employees typically enjoy lower premiums under PPOs than under conventional plans. In addition, PPOs are less restrictive than traditional HMOs. Under a PPO, members can choose among a list of doctors, hospitals, and other care providers who have agreed to discounted fees. As a result, people have become increasingly attracted to PPOs.[10]

Table B.2 shows five major types of health insurance: hospitalization, surgical and medical payments, major medical, dental, and disability income insurance.

Life Insurance

Life insurance differs from all other types of insurance discussed so far because it deals with the risk of a certain event—death. Life insurance is a common employee benefit in most firms because its purchase provides financial protection for the family of the policyholder. Because most households need financial security, two of every three U.S. citizens are covered by life insurance.

Table B.3 outlines the provisions of the major types of life insurance. A company can choose to offer one type or a combination of them as part of its total benefit package for its employees. In addition, consumers may opt to purchase life insurance on their own, either through a traditional life insurance agent or online. Websure SM is the first Web site to offer life insurance directly to consumers. Visitors to the site can gather information about different plans before making a purchase.[11]

www.websure.com

Table B.2	Types of Health Insurance
Hospitalization insurance	Health insurance designed to pay for most hospital costs
Surgical and medical payments insurance	Health insurance designed to pay the costs of surgery, medical specialists, and physicians' care in the hospital during the patient's recovery
Major medical insurance	Health insurance that protects the insured against catastrophic financial losses by covering expenses that exceed the coverage limits of basic policies
Dental insurance	Health insurance designed to pay specified percentages of dental expenses
Disability income insurance	Health insurance designed to protect against loss of income while the insured is disabled as a result of an accident or illness

Table B.3	Types of Life Insurance
Term insurance	Life insurance that pays a death benefit if the policyholder dies within a specified period of time. (It has no value at the end of that period.)
Credit life insurance	Term life insurance that repays the balance owed on a house or other major credit purchase if the policyholder dies.
Whole life insurance	Life insurance that combines protection and savings for the individual who pays premiums throughout a lifetime. A cash surrender value represents the savings portion of the policy.
Endowment insurance	Life insurance that provides coverage for a specified period, after which the face value is refunded to the policyholder.
Variable life insurance	Hybrid form of whole life insurance in which the policyholder can decide how to invest the cash surrender value.
Universal life insurance	Hybrid form of life insurance combining term insurance with a tax-deferred savings account.

How Much Life Insurance Should You Have?

People can purchase individual life insurance policies for almost any amount. Unlike property and liability insurance, the life insurance purchases are limited only by the amount of premiums that people can afford to pay, provided that the purchasers meet medical qualifications.

Although many experts agree that the average family has too little insurance, few agree on exactly how much is enough. Some recommend that the average adult who is supporting a family should carry enough life insurance to equal four or five times his or her annual salary. However, if you are single, with no dependents, just starting your career, you might not need life insurance at all. Also, be sure to educate yourself about different types of life insurance before purchasing a plan.

Businesses, as well as individuals, buy life insurance. The death of a sole proprietor, partner, or a key executive is likely to result in financial losses to an organization. **Key executive insurance** is life insurance designed to reimburse the organization for the loss of the services of an important executive and to cover the expenses of securing a qualified replacement.

TEN BUSINESS TERMS YOU NEED TO KNOW

risk

self-insurance fund

insurance

mortality table

insurance company

property loss

liability loss

health insurance

health maintenance organization (HMO)

key executive insurance

Other Important Business Terms

speculative risk

pure risk

insurable interest

insurable risk

law of large numbers

ASSIGNMENTS

1. Malden Mills, manufacturer of Polartec and Polarfleece outerwear, responded to a devastating fire by keeping employees on the payroll, maintaining their health insurance, and rebuilding the manufacturing facilities. What steps might CEO Aaron Feuerstein take to reduce risk in the future?

2. Using your computer, access the Internet to find information on the various lawsuits against tobacco companies. Try keywords such as: tobacco lawsuits; tobacco settlements; Brown & Williamson; R.J. Reynolds; Phillip Morris. What is the current status of these lawsuits and the proposed national settlement? Discuss your findings with the class.

3. What type of health insurance do you (or your family) have—traditional or HMO? As a consumer, what do you consider to be the pros and cons of your type of plan?

4. Describe one aspect of health care in the United States that *you* think needs to be reformed. Justify your answer.

BUSINESS CAREER EXERCISE

Insurance Claims Adjuster

Both individuals and businesses seek protection from potential losses by taking out insurance policies, including health, vehicle, property, and liability coverage. The insurance claims adjuster handles the claims submitted to an insurance company, such as automobile collision damages, losses to property (damages from theft, fire, and wind), and medical expenses. The adjuster not only determines whether the claim is covered under the customer's insurance policy but also attempts to handle the claim fairly for all parties.

This exercise will help you to:

▼   Identify your level of interest in a business career as an insurance claims adjuster.

▼   Find out details about the skills required, job activities, career advancement, and earnings potential for this occupation.

How to Locate the Exercise

1. Launch *Discovering Your Business Career* from the "Career Assistance" program group.

2. At the main menu, click on the red "play" button for "Insurance" to see a presentation summarizing insurance claims adjusting.

3. Next, click on the word "Insurance" to enter the career profile on this career.

4. Then, click on the red button below the word "Compatibility."

5. Select "Insurance" from the menu of seven business careers.

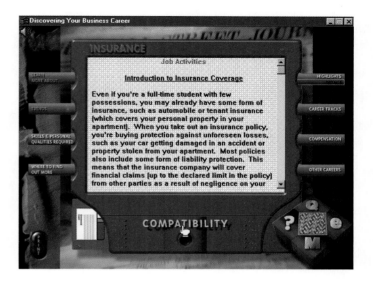

6. Watch the video that summarizes your degree of compatibility with a career in insurance claims adjusting.

7. Read the detailed compatibility report on the left side of the screen. You can obtain a printout of this report by clicking on "Print" in the lower left corner of the screen.

8. Click on the word "Return" to go back to the "Compatibility" menu of business careers.

9. Click on the red triangular arrow to the left of the word "Insurance" to return to the career profile on insurance claims adjusting.

10. Review the sections about this career that interest you. You can get a complete printout of all the sections on insurance by clicking on "Print" in the lower left corner of the screen.

appendix C

Business Law

The Beef Industry's Beef with Oprah

It was a defining moment, one that brought together two unlikely businesses in a manner that members of each probably would have preferred to avoid. Talk show mega-host Oprah Winfrey was airing a program entitled "Dangerous Food," about a month after a reported outbreak of "mad cow disease" (bovine spongiform encephalopathy) in Great Britain. Victims were thought to have contracted the brain-wasting disease from eating contaminated beef, which in turn was tainted through the practice of including portions of slaughtered cattle in the feed of livestock. Howard Lyman, a former rancher who is now a beef industry critic, appeared on Winfrey's program as a guest, where he described the practice of feeding cattle to cattle. (The U.S. Food and Drug Administration banned the practice in the United States a year after the program aired.) Lyman claimed that the possibility that beef cattle might ingest contaminated feed "could make AIDS look like the common cold" if people ate the tainted beef. Oprah then uttered her now-famous statement: "It has just stopped me cold from eating another burger!"

What does this scenario have to do with business law? A lot. After the program aired, American beef prices, which were already dropping, immediately plunged from 62 cents per pound to 55 cents per pound. Texas rancher Paul Engler, who claims he lost $6 million in sales because of the plummeting prices, decided to sue Winfrey and her company, Harpo Productions, under a Texas law that forbids the defamation of food—in this case, beef. Thus, the entertainment industry and the beef industry became locked in legal combat, each claiming to be on the right side of the law, for different reasons.

Texas is not the only state with a food-libel law on the books; in fact, thirteen states that rely heavily on agriculture for income have passed similar laws, and several others are now considering them. Food disparagement laws originated when the CBS program "60 Minutes" aired a report that linked the pesticide Alar—sprayed over commercial apple orchards—to cancer in children. Washington State apple growers, whose livelihoods were adversely affected, sued CBS and lost. So the agriculture industry campaigned hard for laws prohibiting defamation of food products. Critics of the laws claim that foods don't have civil rights. But Steve Kopperud of the American Feed Industry Association explains the laws this way: "The states are reacting to the deep frustration of the food industry. Farmers and ranchers are not faceless corporations—there is a human element to this."

Then there's the other side of the argument: civil rights protected by the First Amendment. Winfrey sees this as the central issue of the trial: the "right to ask questions and hold a public debate on issues that impact the general public and my audience." David Bederman, an Emory University law professor, is equally concerned that the food libel laws infringe on First Amendment rights. "The statutes at first were regarded as quirky and weird, but they are an area where First Amendment rights are bumping up against commercial interests," he says. Bederman has tried unsuccessfully to challenge the food disparagement law in Georgia, where Emory University is located.

So each side of the beef trial had a different view of what the central issue itself was. Shortly after the trial began, U.S. District Judge Mary Lou Robinson, who presided over the case, surprised both sides with her ruling that the original basis for the case—violation of the food disparagement law—was not valid. Robinson reduced the suit to a basic business defamation case, which meant that the cattle ranchers had to prove that Winfrey and Lyman deliberately made false statements about the beef industry in general and the plaintiffs in particular.

The jury of eight women and four men decided in favor of Winfrey and Harpo Productions. Presiding juror Christy Sams explained the verdict. "There were valid points on both sides, and we just took the facts as we were presented them and made our decision. . . . I think we based it mainly on the facts." Christy allowed that the jury agreed with the cattle ranchers' assertion that free speech must be accompanied by responsibility but did not believe that Winfrey broke the law. Juror Pat Gowdy observed, "We felt that many rights have eroded in this country. Freedom of speech may be the only one left to help us get back what we've lost." After the verdict, cattleman Engler claimed a practical victory in that, "We did accomplish that main objective to convince the U.S. people, the consumers, that U.S. beef is safe. I want to see responsible reporting and responsible talk show hosts." Winfrey exclaimed, "Free speech not only lives, it rocks!" Have we seen the end of this issue? Hardly. Some of the cattlemen have now filed a libel suit in a Texas district court, and they have appealed the federal verdict.[1]

This appendix on business law will give you a greater understanding of the ways in which law influences all types of business activities, not just those involving celebrities and beef. A basic understanding of business law gives managers a competitive edge in both the domestic and global marketplaces.

All management decisions must take into account business law. Some require in-depth planning and review of the law; others involve only simple checks of the legality of proposed actions. Executives learn how to apply legal standards to their decisions in much the same way they develop any other business skill: through constant practice and ongoing study. If they lack the experience and judgment to determine the legality of a matter, they should consult attorneys.

Law consists of the standards set by government and society in the form of either legislation or custom. The broad body of principles, regulations, rules, and customs that govern the actions of all members of society, including businesspeople, is derived from several sources. **Common law** refers to the body of law arising out of judicial decisions related to the unwritten law the United States inherited from England. This unwritten law is based on customs and court decisions beginning in early England.

Statutory law, or written law, includes state and federal constitutions, legislative enactments, treaties of the federal government, and ordinances of local governments. Statutes must be drawn precisely and reasonably to be constitutional (and thus enforceable), but courts must frequently interpret their intentions and meanings. The court rulings often result in statutory laws being changed or even discarded.

With the growth of the global economy, a knowledge of international law becomes crucial. **International law** refers to the numerous regulations that govern international commerce. Companies must be aware of the domestic laws of trading partners, the rules set by the international trading community, and the guidelines established by regional and international organizations.

One resource for companies going global is an international agency called the International Institute for the Unification of Private Law, known as UNIDROIT (French for "one law"). It has been working to develop uniform law

guidelines on a global basis. One of the most recent efforts of UNIDROIT is setting up an online database called UNILAW. This database could be accessed for information on international sales and trade, international dispute resolution, and cultural property. UNILAW will be set up in stages as time and funds allow.[2]

NATURE OF BUSINESS LAW

In a broad sense, all law is business law because all firms are subject to the entire body of law, just as individuals are. In a narrower sense, however, **business law** consists of those aspects of law that most directly influence and regulate the management of various types of business activity. Specific laws vary widely in their effects from business to business and from industry to industry. Different laws affect small companies and large corporations. The legal interests of the automobile industry, for example, differ from those of real estate developers.

State and local statutes also have varying applications. Some state laws affect all businesses that operate in a particular state. Workers' compensation laws, which govern payments to workers for injuries incurred on the job, are an example. Other state laws apply only to certain firms or business activities. For example, states have specific licensing requirements for businesses like law firms, funeral directors, and hair salons. Many local ordinances also deal with specific business activities. For example, regulation of the sizes and types of business signs is commonplace.

COURT SYSTEM

The **judiciary,** or court system, is the branch of government charged with deciding disputes among parties by applying laws. The judiciary consists of several types or levels of courts, each with a specific jurisdiction. Court systems are organized at the federal, state, and local levels. Administrative agencies also perform some limited judicial functions, but these agencies are more properly regarded as belonging to the executive or legislative branches of government.

Business Directory

law standards set by government and society in the form of either legislation or custom.

business law the aspects of law that most directly influence and regulate the management of various types of business activity.

judiciary the branch of government charged with deciding disputes among parties through the application of laws.

Trial Courts

At both the federal and state levels, **trial courts**—courts of general jurisdiction—hear wide ranges of cases. Unless a case is assigned by law to another court or to an administrative agency, a court of general jurisdiction will hear it. The majority of cases, both criminal and civil, pass through these courts. Within the federal system, trial courts are known as *U.S. district courts,* and at least one such court operates in each state. In the state court systems, the general jurisdiction courts are usually called *circuit courts,* and most states provide one for each county. Some states call their general jurisdiction courts by other names, such as *superior courts, common pleas courts,* or *district courts.*

State judiciary systems also include a wide range of courts with lower or more specific jurisdictions. These courts have limited jurisdictions in that they hear only certain sizes or types of cases, as set forth by statute or constitution. In most states, parties can appeal the decisions of the lower courts to the general jurisdiction courts. Examples of lower courts are probate courts (which settle deceased persons' estates) and small claims courts (where people can represent themselves in suits involving limited amounts of damages).

Appellate Courts

Appeals of decisions of general trial courts are heard by **appellate courts.** Both the federal and state systems have appellate courts. An appeal usually is filed when the losing party feels that the case was wrongly decided by the judge or jury. The appeals process allows a higher court to review the case and correct any lower court error complained of by the appellant, the party making the appeal.

The federal court's appeals system, together with those of most states, consists of two tiers of courts. The federal courts at the intermediate level, called *U.S. circuit courts of appeal,* hear appeals of decisions from the U.S. district courts.

In an ongoing antitrust case involving Microsoft's Windows 95 operating system and its Internet browser, Microsoft recently filed a written argument with a federal appeals court—the Court of Appeals for the District of Columbia in Washington. The 19-page brief disputed an order issued in December 1997 that the company must offer Windows 95 without its Internet Explorer browser. The outcome of the case will have a profound effect on Microsoft's business, both now and in the future.[3]

The intermediate level of a state's appellate courts, if any exists, is known as the *court of appeals* or the *district court of appeals* in most states.

Appeals from decisions of the U.S. circuit courts of appeal can go to the nation's highest court, the U.S. Supreme Court. Appeals from state courts of appeal are heard by the highest court in each state, usually called the *state supreme court.* In a state without intermediate appellate courts, the state supreme court hears appeals directly from the trial courts. Parties not satisfied by the verdict of a state supreme court can appeal to the U.S. Supreme Court and may be granted a hearing if they can cite grounds for such an appeal and if the Supreme Court considers the case significant enough to be heard. It is unusual for a case to go all the way to the U.S. Supreme Court; in an average year, the court may hear less than 150 of the thousands of cases that people file with it.

While the great majority of cases are resolved by the system of courts described here, certain highly specialized cases require particular expertise. Such cases are assigned to special courts by constitutional provisions or statutes. Examples of specialized federal courts are the U.S. Tax Court (for tax cases) and the U.S. Court of Claims (which hears claims against the U.S. government itself). Similar specialized courts operate at the state level.

For example, Delaware's Chancery Court is a 200-year-old institution specializing in corporate governance. Its five chancellors hear about 1,000 cases annually. This tiny court, located in Wilmington's Rodney Square, is important because almost 50 percent of the companies listed on the New York Stock Exchange are incorporated in Delaware. As early as 1913, many firms, attracted by Delaware's low corporate taxes, began relocating from New Jersey. As another draw, Delaware updates its corporate laws regularly. A Corporate Law Council, with members drawn from many of the state's largest law firms, periodically reviews trends in corporate law and recommends changes.

Yet another plus is Delaware's Division of Corporations, which has been quick to adopt new technologies and add extra services. For instance, the division uses a computerized imaging system to store pictures of all documents, even envelopes; it also maintains a 4 P.M.-to-midnight shift to process documents and to assist West Coast companies that need help after the close of business hours on the East Coast.

Perhaps the main reason why many firms choose to incorporate in Delaware, however, is the Chancery Court itself. "The Delaware Chancery Court is a well-respected court," says attorney David King. "The judges are especially conversant in business. . . . A judge is not hearing a divorce or custody case in the morning before moving on to a big takeover case in the afternoon."

A growing trend has seen Chancery Court decisions favor the rights of corporate shareholders. This approach to business law emphasizes a company's obligation to get the best deal possible for those who own stock in it. In some cases, for example, the court has forced company directors to accept the highest bidder in a takeover war, even if they would prefer to sell to another. Several takeover verdicts have mandated that managers must choose the most profitable option if it best serves the shareholders' interests.

> ## They said it
>
> "First, there is the law. It must be obeyed. But the law is the minimum. You must act ethically."
>
> **IBM employee guidelines**

In other cases, the Chancery Court has mandated that companies must reimburse shareholders who did not receive full value for their money. One case involved Home Shopping Network, which placed a notice on shares warning that their value could decrease, depending on the outcome of pending litigation. As a result, share prices plummeted, and the company repurchased them at a cheaper rate. Bondholders complained, and the court ruled against the company. Another time, Enserch Corporation shareholders claimed that the company had failed to compensate those who exchanged Enserch Exploration Partners stock for Enserch shares; the court ordered Enserch Corporation to pay an extra $3.42 per share.[4] An index of recent Delaware Chancery Court opinions is available on the Internet.

www.justice.widener.edu/~Lic/ de_opinions/chance.97.htm

Administrative Agencies

Administrative agencies, also known as *bureaus, commissions,* or *boards,* decide a variety of cases at all levels of government. They sometimes derive powers and responsibilities from constitutional provisions, but usually state or federal statutes make this determination. Technically, they conduct hearings or inquiries rather than trials. The parties are often represented by attorneys, evidence and testimony are included, and the agency issues legally binding decisions based on government regulations.

Examples of federal administrative agencies are the Federal Trade Commission, the National Labor Relations Board, and the Federal Energy Regulatory Commission. Examples at the state level include public utility commissions and boards that govern the licensing of various trades and professions. Zoning boards, planning commissions, and boards of appeal operate at the city or county level.

The FTC has the broadest powers of any of the federal regulatory agencies. It enforces laws regulating unfair business practices, and it can stop false and deceptive advertising practices. Mergers of companies that result in large conglomerates have drawn much of the FTC's recent attention. For example, the FTC is investigating the proposed merger of Compaq Computer and Digital Equipment Corp.—the largest merger to date in the computer industry—valued at $9.6 billion. In another case, the FTC ruled against Toys 'R' Us for anticompetitive practices. The FTC ruled that the toy store used its leverage in the retail industry to pressure toy makers to stop selling their full product lines to warehouse clubs, thus giving Toys 'R' Us unfair advantage in the marketplace and keeping prices unnaturally high.[5]

MAJOR COMPONENTS OF BUSINESS LAW

The cornerstones of U.S. business law are contract law; sales law; the Uniform Commercial Code; negotiable instruments law; property law; the law of bailment; agency law; tort law; bankruptcy law; patent, trademark, and copyright law; and tax law. The sections that follow set out the key provisions of each of these legal concepts.

CONTRACT LAW

Contract law is important because it affects most aspects of a business operation. It is the legal foundation on which business dealings are conducted. A **contract** is a legally enforceable agreement between two or more parties regarding a specified act or thing.

Contract Requirements

The four elements of an enforceable contract are agreement, consideration, legal and serious purpose, and capacity. The parties must reach agreement about the act or thing specified. For such an agreement, or contract, to be valid and legally enforceable, each party must furnish consideration—the value or benefit that a party provides to the others with whom the contract is made. Legal consideration for a contract exists when, for example, A agrees to work for B and B agrees to pay A a specified salary. The contract is just as valid if B actually pays A at the time A agrees to work. Similarly, valid consideration exists even if no promises are exchanged but A works for B and B pays A for the work.

In addition to consideration, an enforceable contract must involve a legal and serious purpose. Agreements made in a joking manner, related to purely social matters, or involving the commission of crimes are not enforceable

Business Directory

contract a legally enforceable agreement between two or more parties regarding a specified act or thing.

sales law law governing the sale of goods or services for money or on credit.

negotiable instruments commercial paper that is transferable among individuals and businesses.

as legal contracts. An agreement between two competitors to fix the prices for their products is not enforceable as a contract because the subject matter is illegal and carrying out the agreement would violate the law.

The last element of a legally enforceable contract is capacity, the legal ability of a party to enter into agreements. The law does not permit certain persons, such as those judged to be insane, to enter into legally enforceable contracts.

Contracts govern almost all types of business activities. Examples of valid contracts are purchase agreements with suppliers, labor contracts, group insurance policies for employees, franchise agreements, and sales contracts.

Breach of Contract

A violation of a valid contract is called a **breach of contract.** The injured party can go to court to enforce the contract provisions and, in some cases, collect **damages**—financial payments to compensate for a loss and related suffering.

For instance, Sun Microsystems sued Microsoft for what it saw as a breach of contract involving its Java software. (Java is a major component of Internet Web sites and is used by 116 licensing companies.) In its licensing agreements, Sun requires companies that use Java to be sure that any of their modifications pass Java compatibility tests—in effect, ensuring that anyone can access and use any Java applications. Two of Microsoft's Java applications—the Internet Explorer 4.0 browser and Software Development Kit for Java—failed Sun's tests for compatibility. This means that applications written with those programs may not run on computer operating systems or Internet browsers not developed by Microsoft. After attempts to reach an agreement failed, Sun sued Microsoft in October 1997 for breach of the licensing contract. The case is now working its way through the legal system.[6]

SALES LAW

Sales law governs sales of goods or services for money or on credit. The law of sales derives from contract law, since a sales agreement or sales transaction is a special kind of contract that people enter into millions of times each day. As economic transactions, sales can exchange services or real estate as well as products, but the law of sales is concerned only with transfers of tangible personal property. The law involved with intangible personal property and real estate will be examined later.

Sales law has evolved in a distinct manner. It goes back to ancient English law based largely on the customs of merchants and including a system of merchant courts to resolve disputes. Many of these customs and practices were adopted in the United States as part of common law.

Later, the Uniform Commercial Code provided uniformity in all commercial laws, including sales law.

UNIFORM COMMERCIAL CODE (UCC)

The Uniform Commercial Code (UCC) is the basis for commercial law in the United States. It has been adopted by all states except Louisiana, which adopted only part of it.[7] The UCC covers the law of sales as well as other specific areas of commercial law.

Article 2 of the UCC specifies the circumstances under which a buyer and a seller enter into a sales contract. Ordinarily such agreements are based on the express conduct of the parties. The UCC generally requires written agreements for enforceable sales contracts for products worth more than $500. The formation of a sales contract is quite flexible because certain missing terms in a written contract or other ambiguities do not keep the contract from being legally enforceable. A court will look to past dealings, commercial customs, and other standards of reasonableness to evaluate whether a legal contract exists.

A court will also consider these variables when either the buyer or the seller seeks to enforce his or her rights when the other party fails to perform as specified in the contract, performs only partially, or performs in a defective or unsatisfactory way. The UCC's remedies in such cases consist largely of monetary damages awarded to injured parties. The UCC defines the rights of the parties to have the contract specifically performed, to have it terminated, and to reclaim the goods or place a lien—a legal claim—against them.

Warranties

Article 2 of the UCC also sets forth the law of warranties for sales transactions. Products carry two basic types of warranties. An express warranty is a specific representation made by the seller regarding the product, while an implied warranty is one legally imposed on the seller. Generally, unless implied warranties are disclaimed by the seller in writing, they are automatically effective. Other provisions of Article 2 govern the rights of acceptance, rejection, and inspection of products by the buyer; the rights of the parties during manufacture, shipment, delivery, and passing of title to products; the legal significance of sales documents; and the placement of the risk of loss in the event of destruction or damage to the products during manufacture, shipment, or delivery.

Negotiable Instruments

The term **negotiable instrument** refers to commercial paper that is transferable among individuals and busi-

Figure C.1   **Four Kinds of Endorsements**

check payable to the bearer. A blank endorsement should not be used for an instrument that moves through the mail.

2. A special endorsement specifies the person to whom the instrument is payable. With this kind of endorsement, only the person whose name appears after "Pay to the order of . . ." can profit from the instrument.

3. A qualified endorsement contains words stating that the endorser is not guaranteeing payment of the instrument. The qualified endorsement of "Without Recourse (signed)" limits the endorser's liability if the instrument is not backed by sufficient funds.

4. A restrictive endorsement limits the negotiability of the instrument. One of the most common restrictive endorsements, "For Deposit Only," is useful if an instrument (usually a check) is lost or stolen, because it means that the instrument can only be deposited to the indicated account; it cannot be cashed.

nesses. The most common example of a negotiable instrument is a check; drafts, certificates of deposit, and notes are also sometimes considered negotiable instruments.

Article 3 of the UCC specifies that a negotiable instrument must be written and must meet several additional conditions:

1. It must be signed by the maker or drawer.

2. It must contain an unconditional promise or order to pay a certain sum of money.

3. It must be payable on demand or at a definite time.

4. It must be payable to order or to bearer.

Checks and other forms of commercial paper are transferred when the payee signs the back of the instrument, a procedure known as *endorsement*. The four kinds of endorsements described by Article 3 of the UCC, shown in Figure C.1, include the following:

1. A blank endorsement consists only of the name of the payee. To make a blank endorsement, the payee need only sign the back of the instrument, which makes the

PROPERTY LAW

Property law is a key feature of the private enterprise system. Property is something for which a person or firm has the unrestricted right of possession or use. Property rights are guaranteed and protected by the U.S. Constitution.

Property can be divided into several categories. Tangible personal property consists of physical things such as equipment, supplies, and delivery vehicles. Intangible personal property is nonphysical property that is most often represented by a document or other written instrument, although it may be as vague and remote as a computer entry. You are probably familiar with certain types of intangible personal property such as checks and money orders. Other, less well-known examples are important to the businesses or individuals who own and use them. Examples are stocks, bonds, Treasury bills, notes, letters of credit, and warehouse receipts. Mortgages are also intangible personal property.

A third category of property is real property, or real estate. Some customs surrounding real property have been formalized in statutes.

Business Directory

agency a legal relationship whereby one party, called a principal, appoints another party, called the agent, to enter into contracts with third parties in the principal's behalf.

Case law helps to guide real property owners in their transactions and conduct. All firms have some concern with real estate law because of the need to own or occupy the space or building where they conduct business. Some companies are created to serve these real estate needs. Real estate developers, builders, contractors, brokers, appraisers, mortgage companies, escrow companies, title companies, and architects all deal with various aspects of real property law.

LAW OF BAILMENT

The law of bailment deals with the surrender of personal property by one person to another when the property is to be returned at a later date. The person delivering the property is known as the *bailor,* and the person receiving the property is the *bailee.* Some bailments benefit bailees, others benefit bailors, and still others provide mutual benefits. Most courts now require that all parties practice reasonable care in all bailment situations. The degree of benefit received from the bailment is a factor in court decisions about whether or not parties have met the reasonable care standard.[8]

Rules govern settlement of bailment disputes, which commonly arise in business settings such as hotels, restaurants, banks, and parking lots. The law focuses on actual delivery of an item. For example, a patron in a restaurant who hangs a coat on a hook has made no actual delivery to the restaurant's proprietor. Therefore, the proprietor is not liable for theft or damage. On the other hand, if the restaurant has a coat checking room and the patron receives a claim check, the coat has been delivered and the proprietor is liable for theft of or damage to the coat.

LAW OF AGENCY

An **agency** relationship exists when one party, called a *principal,* appoints another party, called the *agent,* to enter into contracts with third parties on the principal's behalf.[9] While the agency relationship can be as simple as one family member acting on behalf of another, the legal concept is most closely identified with commercial activities. All types of firms conduct business affairs through a variety of agents, such as partners, directors, corporate officers, and sales personnel.

The law of agency is based on common law principles and case law decisions of state and federal courts. Relatively little agency law has been enacted into statute. The law of agency is important because the principal is generally bound by the actions of the agent.

The legal basis for holding the principal liable for acts of the agent is the Latin maxim of *respondent superior* ("let the master answer"). In a case involving agency law, the court must decide the rights and obligations of the various parties. Generally, the principal is held liable if an agency relationship existed and the agent had some type of authority to do the wrongful act. The agent in such cases is liable to the principal for any damages.

LAW OF TORTS

A **tort** (French for "wrong") refers to a civil wrong inflicted on another person or the person's property.[10] The law of torts is closely related to the law of agency because a business entity, or principal, can be held liable for torts committed by its agents in the course of business dealings. Tort law differs from both criminal and contract law. While criminal law is concerned with crimes against the state or society, tort law deals with compensation for injured persons who are the victims of noncriminal wrongs.

Tort cases can result in considerable judgments. For instance, in recent years, a jury awarded an 81-year-old Albuquerque woman $2.7 million in punitive damages from McDonald's. The woman received third-degree burns when a cup of coffee spilled on her. The judge later reduced the damages to $480,000 in a decision upheld by the New Mexico Supreme Court.[11]

Types of Torts

A tort may be intentional, or it may be caused by negligence. Assault, slander, libel, and fraud are examples of intentional torts. Businesses can become involved in such cases through the actions of both owners and employees. A security guard who roughly handles a suspected shoplifter and holds the suspect in the manager's office for questioning may be committing a tort if his or her conduct does excessive or otherwise unjustified harm. Under agency law, the store owner can be held liable for any damages or injury caused by the security guard.

The other major group of torts result from negligence. This type of tort is based on carelessness rather than intentional behavior that causes injury to another person. Under agency law, businesses are held liable for the negligence of their employees or agents. The delivery truck driver who kills a pedestrian while delivering goods creates a tort liability for his or her employer if the accident results from negligence.

DID YOU KNOW?

For many Arabs, their signature on a contract is much less meaningful than the fact that they have given their word.

When U.S. negotiators table a proposal they intend to delay a decision. In Britain, *tabling* means that immediate action is to be taken.

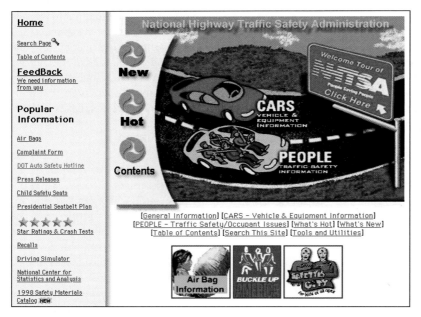

The National Highway Traffic Safety Administration is responsible for reducing death and injuries caused by traffic accidents. One of its functions is to set and monitor automobile safety standards. The NHTSA maintains this Web site to inform the public about safety issues and to gather information.

Product Liability An area of tort law known as **product liability** has been developed by both statutory and case law to hold businesses liable for negligence in the design, manufacture, sale, and/or use of products. Some states have extended the theory of tort law to cover injuries caused by products, regardless of whether the manufacturer is proven negligent. This legal concept is known as *strict product liability.*[12]

The business response to product liability has been mixed. To avoid lawsuits and fines, some recall defective products voluntarily; others decide to fight recall mandates for certain products. Automobile safety is one area in which product safety is closely monitored. The National Highway Traffic Safety Administration (NHTSA) orders recalls of cars that it considers unsafe so that they can be repaired. In June 1996, it ordered the recall of 91,000 1995 Chrysler Cirrus and Dodge Stratus cars because it found the seatbelt anchors were not strong enough. In a highly unusual move, Chrysler fought the court-ordered recall and fine, which could add up to $1.6 million. But when a U.S. court of appeals ruled against Chrysler a year and a half later, the company decided to comply with the recall.[13]

BANKRUPTCY LAW

Bankruptcy, the legal nonpayment of financial obligations, is a common occurrence in contemporary society. The term *bankruptcy* is derived from "banca rotta," or "broken bench," since creditors in medieval Italy would break up the benches of merchants who did not pay their bills.[14]

Federal legislation passed in 1918 and revised several times since provides for orderly handling of bankruptcies by the federal court system. The legal process of bankruptcy has two purposes. One is to protect creditors by providing a way to seize and distribute debtors' assets. The second goal, which is almost unique to the United States, is to protect debtors, too, allowing them to start fresh and thus benefiting society in general.[15]

Federal law recognizes two types of bankruptcies. Under voluntary bankruptcy, a person or firm asks to be judged bankrupt because of inability to pay off creditors. Under involuntary bankruptcy, creditors may request that a party be judged bankrupt.

Personal Bankruptcies

Bankruptcy law offers individuals two primary options.[16] Chapter 13 of the bankruptcy law—the wage earner plan—allows a person to set up a 3-year debt repayment plan. (The bankruptcy judge can extend the time to 5 years.) Debtors often end up repaying only a portion of what they owe under Chapter 13. The court considers the bankrupt party's current income in determining the repayment schedule. Chapter 13 is available only if unsecured debts do not exceed $100,000 and secured debts do not exceed $350,000, although Congress may pass legislation to raise these limits.

About 70 percent of all bankruptcies, however, are resolved by the other alternative. Chapter 7 sets out a liquidation plan under which a trustee sells the bankrupt person's assets and divides the proceeds among creditors. Judges can deny the use of Chapter 7, but the initial choice of Chapter 13 does not preclude a later switch to Chapter 7.

Chapter 7 exempts certain property from the claims of creditors:

1. Home equity up to $7,500

2. Motor vehicle equity up to $1,200

3. Amount of $200 on each personal item such as household furnishings, clothes, and books, up to a maximum of $4,000

4. Amount of $500 on personal property

5. Another $400 on any other property

6. Tools of one's trade or prescribed health needs up to $750

Husbands and wives filing jointly can double these amounts. Some states set different allowances than those specified in Chapter 7. Missouri, for example, exempts only $8,000. Florida offers the most liberal exemptions; its homestead law exempts up to 160 acres in rural areas and half an acre in a city. The Sunshine State also exempts all wages, annuities, partnership profits, pension plans, and property owned jointly with a spouse.[17]

A third personal bankruptcy option, Chapter 12, allows farmers with debts up to $1.5 million to set up repayment plans. This supersedes the debt limit set by Chapter 13.

At the beginning of 1998, Americans owed more than $1.2 trillion in credit. In a recent year, a record 1.1 million Americans declared personal bankruptcy—up 29 percent from the previous year. Consumer debt is a major factor contributing to personal bankruptcy, and with lenders mailing out credit applications, even to college students without steady jobs, the upward trend is likely to continue.[18]

Business Bankruptcies

Businesses can also go bankrupt. The specific provision under which they do this, Chapter 11, allows a firm to reorganize and develop a plan to repay its debts. Chapter 11 also permits prepackaged bankruptcies, in which companies enter bankruptcy proceedings after obtaining approval of most (as opposed to all) of their creditors. The terms are then imposed on all creditors. Often companies can emerge from prepackaged bankruptcies sooner than those that opt for conventional Chapter 11 bankruptcy proceedings.

Ironically, declaring bankruptcy under Chapter 11 may keep a bankrupt company in business. Consider the Federated chain of department stores, which filed for bankruptcy after taking on too much debt. The chain's 45,000 creditors were grouped into 77 classes of debt. In 26 months, the company was reorganized into 14 units; 24 of the creditor groups received full payment, and Federated's 80,000 employees kept their jobs.[19]

TRADEMARKS, PATENTS, AND COPYRIGHTS

Trademarks, patents, and copyrights provide legal protection for key business assets by giving a firm the ex-clusive right to use those assets. A **trademark** consists of words, symbols, or other designations used by firms to identify their products. The Lanham Act (1946) provides for federal registration of trademarks. McDonald's, for example, is protective of its trademark golden arches logo and the prefix "Mc-" it attaches to its products. The company has tried to restrict their use by other people or businesses, sometimes to its harm. In a widely publicized case, the company may actually have hurt its corporate image overseas. The case involved a small sandwich shop in the United Kingdom called McMunchies. McDonald's sued the owner for trademark infringement, claiming that it had the sole right to use the prefix "Mc-." This legal action brought publicity and sympathy to the small sandwich shop owner, who was quoted as saying, "We sell cold sandwiches, cold meats and the odd sausage roll. How can anyone in their right minds confuse us with McDonald's?" In support, the head of the huge Scottish McDonald clan, Lord Godfrey McDonald, even appeared on CBS's "60 Minutes," vowing that if McDonald's continued its suit, he might challenge the corporation's claim of exclusive right to his historic name.[20] Apparently, the court of public opinion can differ greatly from decisions of legal courts.

For another irony, if a product becomes too well-known, this notoriety can create problems; once a trademark becomes part of everyday usage, it loses its protection as a legal trademark. Consider the fate of the terms *aspirin, nylon, kerosene, linoleum,* and *milk of magnesia.* All of them were once the exclusive property of their manufacturers, but they have passed into common language and now anyone can use them. Companies often attempt to counter this threat by advertising that a term is actually a registered trademark. For example, the National Association of Realtors® promotes its name as a federally registered trademark, and Triangle Publications, Inc., has done the same for its TV GUIDE®.

A **patent** guarantees an inventor exclusive rights to an invention for 17 years. Copyrights and patents have a constitutional basis; the U.S. Constitution specifies that the federal government has the power "to promote the progress of science and useful arts, by securing for limited times to authors and inventors the exclusive rights to their respective writings or discoveries." Patent owners sometimes license others to use their patents for negotiated fees.

A **copyright** protects written material such as this textbook, designs, cartoon illustrations, photos, computer software, and so on. Copyrights are filed with the Library of Congress. An author or his or her heirs hold exclusive

Business Directory

bankruptcy the legal nonpayment of financial obligations.

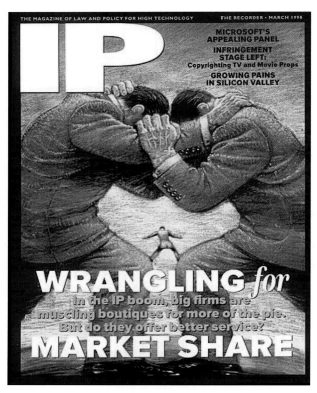

As technology use expands, debate over intellectual property rights has expanded. This online magazine, *IP,* contains information about legal issues and current trends involving technology and intellectual property rights.

rights to published or unpublished works for the author's lifetime, plus 50 years. Works for hire and anonymous or pseudonymous works receive copyright protection for a period of 75 years from publication or 100 years from creation, whichever is shorter.

As firms do more business overseas, the law regarding trademarks, patents, and copyrights is growing more complex. Despite legal registration and protection in the United States, they may be fair game in other countries. Federal and industry surveys estimate the annual cost of counterfeited products to U.S. companies at $200 billion. As many as 5 percent of products sold worldwide may be counterfeit. Countries such as Russia, China, Vietnam, and Korea are involved in producing fake products as diverse as videos and computer software, watches, purses and luggage, and T-shirts and caps. Designer labels are especially prone to fakes because of their high price tags. In another twist, importers bring products to the United States without their logos (called "blanks") and have the logos attached in illegal workrooms. The products are then sold in small shops and flea markets. Ten of the most popular product fakes sold in the United States are:

- ▼ Nike baseball caps
- ▼ Tag Heuer Ladies' watches
- ▼ Oakley sunglasses
- ▼ Moschino handbags
- ▼ Tommy Hilfiger T-shirts
- ▼ Versace scarves
- ▼ Coach mini belt purses
- ▼ Dooney & Bourke drawstring bags
- ▼ Chanel purses
- ▼ Louis Vuitton roll-on hand luggage[21]

Efforts to combat these illegal activities have grown to global proportions. The spread of new technology and the Internet has made copying and distribution of copyrighted and patented materials possible—and relatively easy. There is increasing interest worldwide in protecting **intellectual property,** such as inventions; trademarks; and literary, musical, artistic, photographic, and audiovisual works. The World Intellectual Property Organization (WIPO) is attempting to protect inventors' and creators' rights around the globe through treaties and other agreements.[22]

www www.wipo.org

TAX LAW

A branch of law that affects every business, employee, and consumer in the United States is tax law. **Taxes** are the assessments by which government units raise revenue. Federal, state, and local governments and special taxing authorities all levy taxes.

Business Directory

intellectual property   industrial property, such as trademarks and inventions, and copyrights, such as those of literary, musical, artistic, photographic, and audiovisual works.

taxes   the assessments used to raise revenue for government units.

Federal taxes currently account for about a 20 percent share of the United States gross domestic product (GDP); this figure has fluctuated between 18 and 20 percent since 1960. The share of GDP consumed by state and local taxes has remained stable at roughly 12 percent since the early 1970s.[23]

HOW TAXES ARE LEVIED

Some taxes are paid by individuals and some by businesses. Both have decided impacts on contemporary business. Business taxes reduce profits, and personal taxes cut the disposable incomes that individuals can spend on the products of businesses. Governments spend their revenue from taxes to buy industry's goods and services. Governments also act as transfer agents, moving tax revenue to other consumers and transferring Social Security taxes from the working population to retired or disabled persons.

Governments can levy taxes on several different bases: income, sales, business receipts, property, assets, and so on. The type of tax varies from one taxing authority to the other. The individual income tax is the biggest source of revenue for the federal government. Many states rely on sales taxes. In addition to sales taxes, some cities collect taxes on earnings. Finally, many community college districts get the bulk of their revenue from real estate or property taxes.

TEN BUSINESS TERMS YOU NEED TO KNOW

law	negotiable instrument
business law	agency
judiciary	bankruptcy
contract	taxes
sales law	intellectual property

Other Important Business Terms

common law	damages
statutory law	tort
international law	product liability
trial court	trademark
appellate court	patent
breach of contract	copyright

ASSIGNMENTS

1. U.S. Air Flight 427 crashed while approaching Pittsburgh International Airport on the evening of September 8, 1994, killing all 132 people aboard. Just a few days later the first lawsuit was filed. Arthur Alan Wolk, a Philadelphia lawyer specializing in air crash litigation, predicted that financial settlements could top $200 million. Wolk remarked, "It will be a blockbuster of a case." The only limits on legal claims would involve people flying on international itineraries. Treaties limit damages to $75,000 for international passengers. Families of domestic passengers could expect seven-digit settlements for their losses. However, lawyers working for what are called *contingency fees* would pocket one-third to one-half of the settlements.[24]

   a. Should the law set limits on settlements resulting from domestic air crashes? Why or why not?
   b. Should the law set limits on contingency fees charged by lawyers? Explain your viewpoint.

2. Earlier, this appendix mentioned a breach of contract lawsuit brought by Sun Microsystems against Microsoft. The U.S. Justice Department recently announced that it would broaden its ongoing investigation into Microsoft to include the modifications to Sun's Java language. Sun has said that its "write once, run anywhere" goal is to ensure that all computer users can use and run Java programs. Microsoft has a near monopoly in the personal computer market with its Windows operating system. Since the Java programs can run on any operating system and are especially useful in tying together different computer systems on a network (Internet, intranet, or extranet), some industry observers claim that Microsoft is attempting to squash a potential threat to its near-monopoly.[25] Consider the following questions:

   a. Do you think that Sun Microsystems has the right to control modifications that companies make to its patented program? Why or why not?
   b. Microsoft was recently ordered by a U.S. District Court to remove Sun's Java logo from its marketing materials. At this point, the company says that it will continue to claim that its software products are "Java compatible." Do you think removal of Sun's trademark is enough?
   c. Why do you think the Justice Department is concerned over new software products? Does Microsoft's dominant position in personal com-

puters help or hurt customers in the long run? In the short run? List the advantages and disadvantages you can think of.

   d. Look up the most recent developments in this case—either on the Internet or in newspapers or magazines. What has happened since this text was written? What legal issues are involved?

3. Privately owned companies are becoming more common in China. At the same time, the number of bankruptcies in that country has also grown.[26] Explain the relationship, if any, between these two facts. What purpose does bankruptcy law serve? Explain your answer.

4. Customers' views of counterfeit products have been mixed. The public generally does not see a big threat in fake T-shirts, sports apparel, or watches. But businesses claim that theft of their logos is stealing profits from products that they have spent a long time and a lot of money to build up. Part of the cost of their products goes to pay back those investments. What steps could the U.S. government take to help U.S. business both here and abroad? Consider the impact of technology in your answer.

5. United States bankruptcy law permits bankrupt parties to retain a good deal of personal property. Discuss the concept behind this exemption.

Notes

CHAPTER 1

1. Dell Jones and Lorrie Grant, "What Caused Levi's Blues?" *USA Today,* February 23, 1999, pp. B1, B2; Rachel Beck, "Levi's to Close 11 Plants," *Mobile Register,* February 23, 1999, p. B9; Stephanie Stoughton and Leslie Walker, "Manufacturers' Online Stores Upset Their Retailers," *Washington Post,* accessed online at www.washingtonpost.com, February 9, 1999, p. A1; Luisa Kroll, "Digital Denim," *Forbes,* December 28, 1998, pp. 102–103; Steve Rosenbush, "Personalizing Service on Web," *USA Today,* November 16, 1998, p. 15E; and Alice Z. Cuneo, "Levi's Plans to Get Personal in Bid to Halt Share Declines," *Advertising Age,* November 9, 1998, p. 90.
2. Information in this section comes from John M. Berry, "Knowing the Numbers, Knowing the Economy," *Washington Post,* May 25, 1997, p. H1; Bill Montague, "Consumer Confidence at 28-Year High," *USA Today,* May 28, 1997, p. 1A; Glenn Somerville, "Economic Data Suggest Steady Growth Ahead," *Washington Post,* August 27, 1997, p. C10; and Melanie Wells, "Expert's Prediction: Ad Spending Could Hit $186B This Year," *USA Today,* June 18, 1997, p. 2B.
3. Kevin Shinkle, "Newspaper Industry Bounding Back as Profits Surge," *San Diego Union Tribune,* September 30, 1997, p. C1.
4. John R. Thelin, "Not All the Non-Profits Are Charity Cases," *Lexington Herald-Leader,* June 29, 1997, p. B1.
5. Kathryn Kranhold, "L.A. Art Museum Chief Gets Down to Business," *The Wall Street Journal,* July 30, 1997, p. C2.
6. Brad Edmonson, "Nonprofits Wake Up to the Future," *Forecast,* May 1997, downloaded from www.demographics.com., September 28, 1997.
7. Lee Neville, "Database: First Kiss," *U.S. News & World Report,* September 22, 1997, p. 12.
8. Frank Green, "Wind," *San Diego Union Tribune,* September 23, 1997, p. I1.
9. Phaedra Hise, "Industry Bottoms Out, Disposes of Diaper Service," *Inc.,* June 1997, p. 32.
10. Bernie Herlihy, "A Little Strategy," *Marketing Tools,* September 1997, p. 34.
11. Richard C. Morais, "The Age of Aquarius?" *Forbes,* September 8, 1997, p. 60.
12. Bruce Upbin, "A Touch of Schizophrenia," *Forbes,* July 7, 1997, p. 57.
13. Daniel Gross, *Forbes' Greatest Business Stories of All Time* (New York: John Wiley & Sons, 1996), pp. 23-38 and 41-57.
14. "Steel versus Silicon," *Forbes,* July 7, 1997.
15. David A. Aaker, *Building Strong Brands* (New York: Free Press, 1996), pp. 38-51.
16. Leon L. Berry, "Relationship Marketing of Services—Growing Interest, Emerging Perspectives," *Journal of the Academy of Marketing Science,* Fall 1995, p. 2.
17. Don Peppers and Martha Rogers, *Enterprise One to One* (New York: Doubleday, 1997), p. 211.
18. Elyse M. Friedman, "The New Economy Almanac," *Inc Special Issue: The State of Small Business,* 1997, p. 108.
19. "20 Million Americans Consider the Internet to Be Indispensable," *Open Market,* downloaded from www.openmarket.com, September 15, 1997.
20. Friedman, "New Almanac," p. 108.
21. "Reintermediated," *Wired,* September 1997, p. 208.
22. Rodney J. Moore, "Downhill from Here," *Marketing Tools,* September 1997, p. 10.
23. Frederick F. Reichheld, *The Loyalty Effect* (Cambridge, Mass.: Harvard Business School Press, 1996), p. 33.
24. Martha Rogers, "Attention to MVCs Pays Off for Hickory Farms," *Inside 1:1,* September 11, 1997, p. 1.
25. Alan M. Webber and Heath Row, "How You Can Help Them," *Fast Company,* November/December 1997, p. 128.
26. David Carnoy et al., "Create and Destroy," *Success,* January/February 1997, p. 29.
27. Paul Klebnikov, "Mercedes Benz's Bold Niche Strategy," *Forbes,* September 8, 1997, p. 68.
28. "How You Help"
29. "Top Ten Countries with which the U.S. Trades," U.S. Census Bureau, Foreign Trade Division, downloaded from www.census.gov/foreign-trade/www/balance.html.
30. David Wallechnisky, "Are We Still Number One?" *Parade,* April 18, 1997, p. 5.
31. Seth Godin, ed., *Information Please Business Almanac 1997* (Boston: Houghton Mifflin, 1997).
32. Wendy M. Beech, "Building a Successful Home-Based Business," *Black Enterprise,* September 1997, p. 92.
33. Godin, *Almanac 1997,* p. 398.
34. "If Europeans Worked More . . . ," *Business Week,* July 14, 1997, p. 18.
35. Tamara Henry, "Study: USA Losing Competitive Edge," *USA Today,* April 25, 1997, downloaded from www.usatoday.com.
36. Michael Kinsman, "Retail Bhain Eager to Hire the Gen Xers," *San Diego Union Tribune,* September 14, 1997, p. C1.
37. Amy Saltzman, "Making It in a Sizzling Economy," *U.S. News & World Report,* June 23, 1997, p. 50.
38. Debra Nussbaum, "For Many Small Businesses, the Labor Pool Is Shallow," *New York Times,* August 24, 1997, p. F11.
39. Elain McShulskis, "Job Tenure Short for Men and Women," *HR Magazine,* May 1997, p. 20.
40. Bill Birchard, "Hire Great People Fast," *Fast Company,* August/September 1997, p. 132.
41. Maureen Minehan, "The Fastest-Growing U.S. Ethnic Groups," *HR Magazine,* May 1997, p. 160.
42. "Pushing the Envelope at GM," *Next Step,* Winter 1997, p. 51.
43. Maggie Jackson, "Working at Home Catches On in U.S.," *San Diego Union Tribune,* July 3, 1997, p. C1.
44. Sue Shellenbarger, "Work Gets Wilder as Employees Insist on Stable Family Life," *The Wall Street Journal,* July 16, 1997, p. B1.
45. Elain McShulskis, "Record Number of Companies Say They're Understaffed," *HR Magazine,* April 1997, p. 26.
46. Marianne Kolbasuk McGee, "US Airways to Outsource IT to Sabre," *Informationweek,* September 1, 1997, p. 28.
47. Gayle Sato Stodder, "How to Build a Million-Dollar Business," *Entrepreneur,* September 1997, p. 100.
48. Howard Schultz, "Starbucks' Secret Weapon," *Fortune,* September 29, 1997, p. 268.

49. Gail Robinson and Kathleen Dechant, "Building a Business Case for Diversity," *Academy of Management Executive,* August 1997, p. 21.

50. Christine Foster, "A Life in Spice," *Forbes,* May 19, 1997, p. 78.

51. Jose Aguayo, "Control Freak," *Forbes,* May 19, 1997, p. 128.

52. John J. Kao, "The Art & Discipline of Business Creativity," *Strategy & Leadership,* July/August 1997, p. 6.

53. Bob Filipczak, "It Takes All Kinds: Creativity in the Work Force," *Training,* May 1997, p. 32.

54. David Sheff, "Levis Changes Everything," *Fast Company: New Rules of Business Special Edition,* 1997, p. 24.

55. Larry Ponemon, "Ethics Programs: Make Them Real," *Management Accounting,* July 1997, p. 14.

56. Steven Berglas, "Liar, Liar, Pants on Fire," *Inc.,* August 1997, p. 33.

57. Stephen Butler, "Business Ethics and Corporate Responsibility: Good for the Bottom Line," *Vital Speeches of the Day,* July 1, 1997, p. 559.

58. Shosana Alexander, *Women's Ventures, Women's Visions* (Freedom, Calif.: Crossing Press, 1997), p. 147.

59. John Grossman, "Education First," *Sky,* May 1997.

CHAPTER 2

1. Joseph Nocera, "Witnesses in Wonderland," *Fortune,* March 1, 1999, pp. 168–180; Rajiv Chandrasekaran, "Microsoft Executive Tells of Restrictions on Net Firms," *Washington Post,* February 9, 1999, p. E1; Doug Levy and Paul Davidson, "Sun Microsystems: Microsoft Flooded Us Out of Market," *USA Today,* December 2, 1998, p. 5B; and Susan Garland, "Nailing Microsoft Means Proving Harm Was Done," *Business Week,* November 16, 1998, p. 50.

2. Rex Dalton, "Tainted Harvest (Part 2)," *San Diego Union Tribune,* September 28, 1997.

3. Kay Paine, "Corporate Raiders: Some Employees Rationalize 'Everybody's Doing It,'" *Amarillo Globe News,* October 9, 1997.

4. Maggie Johnson, "Nearly Half of Workers Take Unethical Actions, Cite Pressures," *Detroit News,* April 5, 1997.

5. Robert McGarvey, "Do the Right Thing," *Entrepreneur,* April 1994, pp. 64–66.

6. John W. De Pauw, "Ethical Fitness," *Executive Excellence,* June 1997, p. 6.

7. Michele Marchetti, "Whatever It Takes," *Sales & Marketing Management,* December 1997, pp. 28–38.

8. John Parker, "Ex-U.S. Worker Faces Prison for Taking Bribe," *The Oklahoman,* October 21, 1997.

9. Phoebe Zerwick, "Ethical?" *Winston-Salem Journal,* March 23, 1997, p. A1.

10. Stephanie Armour, "Companies Rate Honesty as Best Worker Policy," *Des Moines Register,* May 4, 1997, p. 1.

11. Victoria Sonshine Pasher, "Judge Orders Nationwide to Testify," *National Underwriter Property & Casualty-Risk & Benefits Management,* February 24, 1997, p. 1.

12. Janet P. Near and Marcia P. Miceli, "Whistle-Blowing: Myth and Reality," *Journal of Management,* Fall 1996, p. 507.

13. Dawn Marie Driscoll and W. Michael Hoffman, "Spot the Red Flags in Your Organization," *Workforce,* June 1997, pp. 135–136.

14. Johnson, "Nearly Half."

15. Nigel Richardson and Megan Barry, "Minding Your Ps and Qs at Nortel," *CMA Magazine,* May 1997, pp. 20–22.

16. Michael I. Roth, "Good Ethics Equals Good Business," *National Underwriter,* July 21, 1997, p. 45.

17. Laura Keller, "Dilbert Does Ethics," *Successful Meetings,* June 1997, p. 19.

18. Johnson, "Nearly Half."

19. Richardson and Barry, "Minding Ps and Qs."

20. Steve Hamm, Susan B. Garland, and Owen Ullmann, "Going after Gates," *Business Week,* November 3, 1997, pp. 34–35.

21. Brian O'Reilly, "Transforming the Power Business," *Fortune,* September 29, 1997, pp. 142–156.

22. Tim Clark and Margie Wylie, "Clinton Sets Course for Internet," *C/Net News.Com,* July 1, 1997; and Margie Wylie, "Business Wins, Consumers Lose?" *C/Net News. Com,* July 1, 1997.

23. Quoted in David L. Kurtz and Louis E. Boone, *Marketing,* 3rd ed. (Fort Worth, Tex.: Dryden Press, 1987), pp. 41–42.

24. Examples reported in Thomas A. Fogarty, "Corporations Use Causes for Effect," *USA Today,* November 10, 1997, p. 7B.

25. Anastasia Toufexis, "Know What You Eat," *Time,* May 9, 1994, p. 68.

26. Caroline Waxler, "I Boycott, Therefore I Am," *Forbes,* September 8, 1997, p. 39.

27. "The Cool 'Habit' of Youth," *Business & Health: What Cigarettes Do to American Business,* August 1997, p. 15.

28. M. L. Stein, "Paper Picketed," *Editor & Publisher,* July 25, 1997, p. 13.

29. "Tobacco Settlement Is a Done Deal," *USA Today,* November 20, 1998, p. A1; Joseph P. Shapiro, "Industry Foes Fume over the Tobacco Deal," *U.S. News & World Report,* November 30, 1998, p. 30; and Ira Teinowitz, "Tobacco Pact Creates Potential Print Windfall," *Advertising Age,* November 23, 1998, p. 4.

30. Jonathan Friedland, "Oil Companies Strive to Turn a New Leaf to Save Rain Forest," *The Wall Street Journal,* July 17, 1997.

31. Ross Kerber, "For Sale: Environmentally Correct Electricity," *The Wall Street Journal,* July 23, 1997, p. B1.

32. Earle Eldride, "Alternative Power Not for Everyone," *USA Today,* June 5, 1997, p. B1.

33. Wade Davis, "The Rubber Industry's Biological Nightmare," *Fortune,* August 4, 1997, pp. 86–98; J. Taylor Buckley, "New Spins Make Use of Old Tires," *USA Today,* May 27, 1997, p. 11A; Kevin Krajick, "Mining the Scrap Heap for Treasure," *Smithsonian,* May 1997, pp. 34–45.

34. Pearlman Group/Roper Worldwide survey reported in *Promo,* February 1997, p. 49.

35. D. Rose, "Enova Chief Grilled on Diversity at Merger Hearing," *San Diego Union-Tribune,* September 18, 1997, p. C1.

36. Tim Vercellotti, "Companies Turn to 'Strategic Giving,'" *Philanthropy Journal Online,* September 22, 1997.

37. Jennifer Mulen, "Performance-Based Corporate Philanthropy: How 'Giving Smart' Can Further Corporate Goals," *Public Relations Quarterly,* Summer 1997, p. 42.

38. Ibid.

39. Michael A. Lipton and Cathy Free, "Many Happy Returns," *People,* July 21, 1997, p. 63.

40. Keith Alexander, "Jury: Dow Chemical 'Negligent,'" *USA Today,* August 19, 1997, p. 1.

41. "Commission Still Investigating Hair-Eating Dolls," *Lubbock Avalanche Journal,* December 31, 1996, downloaded from www.lubbockonline.com, September 26, 1997.

42. "2.5 Million Mountain Bikes Being Recalled," *Orange County Register,* July 11, 1997.

43. Lynne Carrier, "Foodmaker Tackles Safety Issues," *San Diego Daily Transcript,* February 17, 1995, downloaded from http://sddt.com, October 20, 1997.

44. Noelle Knox, "FTC May Penalize Auto Industry," *Detroit News,* April 22, 1997.

45. Lauran Neergaard, "FDA Eases Restrictions on TV Drug Advertising," *Detroit News,* August 9, 1997.

46. "Sears Ordered to Pay $100 Million in Suit," *San Diego Union-Tribune,* June 5, 1997, p. C4.

47. John D. McClain, "Consumers' League Unveils Internet Fraud Web Page," *Business Today.com,* September 10, 1997.

48. "Phone Orders Go Unanswered," Council of Better Business Bureaus press release, September 15, 1997.

49. Gretchen Morgenson, "On Sleazy Street," *Forbes,* June 16, 1997, p. 262.

50. Don Peppers and Martha Rogers, *Enterprise One to One* (New York: Currency Doubleday, 1997), p. 157.

51. Anne Fisher, "Danger Zone," *Fortune,* September 8, 1997, p. 165.

52. Keith H. Hammonds, Roy Furchgott, Steve Hamm, and Paul C. Judge, "Work and Family," *Business Week,* September 15, 1997, p. 96.

53. Ibid.

54. Ibid.

55. "Changing Corporate Culture: The CoreStates Experience," *Next Step,* Winter 1997, p. 44.

56. Margaret Jacobs, "Men's Club," *The Wall Street Journal,* June 9, 1994, pp. A1, A8.

57. Frances Lynch, *Draw the Line: A Sexual Harassment-Free Workplace* (Grants Pass, Ore.: Oasis Press/ PSI Research, 1995), p. 18.

58. "Facts about Sexual Harassment," U.S. Equal Employment Opportunity Commission, downloaded from www.eeoc.gov/facts/fs-sex.html, October 5, 1997.

59. De'Ann Weimer and Emily Thornton, "Slow Healing at Mitsubishi," *Business Week,* September 22, 1997, p. 74.

60. "Women's Groups, Lawmakers Call for End to Pay Inequity," *Augusta Chronicle,* April 12, 1997.

61. Patricia Dingh, "Shades of Gray in the Global Marketplace," *HR Magazine,* April 1997, pp. 90–98.

62. Cyndee Miller, "Marketers Weigh Effects of Sweatshop Crackdown," *Marketing News,* May 12, 1997, p. 1.

63. "Nike Severs Ties with Factories," *San Diego Union Tribune,* October 3, 1997, p. C1.

64. Aaron Bernstein, "Corporate America's Sweatshop Police," *Business Week,* October 20, 1997, p. 39. See also Aaron Bernstein, "A Potent Weapon in the War against Sweatshops," *Business Week,* December 1, 1997.

CHAPTER 3

1. "Pathways to Success: The Welfare to Work Partnership," UPS Web site, accessed at www.community.ups.com, February 9, 1999; "UPS Delivers Education to Midnight-Shift Workers," *The Bergen Record Online* (NJ), Bergen Record Corp., February 8, 1999, accessed at www.bergen.com; Keith H. Hammonds, "Welfare-to-Work: A Good Start," *Business Week,* June 1, 1998, p. 102; and Roy Furchgott, "UPS's Package Deal for Workers," *Business Week,* June 1, 1998, p. 104.

2. Jim Carlton, "Cheaper PCs Start to Attract New Customers," *The Wall Street Journal,* January 25, 1998, pp. B1, B8.

3. Peter Coy, Gary McWilliams, and John Rossant, "The New Economics of Oil," *Business Week,* November 3, 1997, pp. 140–144.

4. Micheline Maynard, "Sales Slump Forces Saturn to Cut Production," *USA Today,* January 21, 1998, p. B1.

5. Scott Kilman, "Free Market Comes to the Farm," *The Wall Street Journal,* June 16, 1997, p. A1.

6. Ronald B. Lieber, "Beating the Odds," *Fortune,* March 31, 1997, p. 82.

7. Thomas Peterson, "The Cartels Are Finally Crumbling," *Business Week,* February 2, 1998, p. 52.

8. Patricia Kranz, "Boris' Young Turks," *Business Week,* April 28, 1997, p. 52.

9. Dexter Roberts, Mark L. Clifford, and Matt Miller, "Overhauling China Inc.?" *Business Week,* August 25, 1997, p. 54.

10. A. M. Doro, "Les Affaires," *Across the Board,* July-August 1997, p. 44.

11. Michael Kepp, "Privatization of Brazil Railway Completed," *American Metal Market,* August 8, 1997, p. 4.

12. Information downloaded from http://william-king.www. drexel.edu, October 1997.

13. Michael J. Mandel, "The Zero Inflation Economy," *Business Week,* January 19, 1998, pp. 28–31.

14. "The 1998 CPI Revision: Changes in Available Data Series," U.S. Bureau of Labor Statistics report, downloaded from http://stats.bls.gov/cpi1998a.htm; see also John Stamper, "Cost of Living Index Gets Reshaped for 21st Century," *Mobile Register,* February 26, 1998, p. 8B.

15. Anne Kates Smith, "Bye-Bye Inflation," *U.S. News & World Report,* December 8, 1997, p. 74.

16. Peter Brimelow, "Freedom Pays," *Forbes,* June 16, 1997, p. 142–143.

17. "Tracking the National Debt," *San Diego Union Tribune,* December 10, 1997, p. B9.

18. Michael Mandel, Keith Naughton, Greg Burns, Stephen Baker, "How Long Can It Last?" *Business Week,* May 19, 1997, p. 33.

19. Paula Kriner, "Gourmet Baked Goods? Give In to Bobbi's Sweet Surrender," *San Diego Union Tribune,* December 10, 1997, p. C1.

20. Smith, "Bye-Bye Inflation."

21. "Why Layoffs Are Getting Lighter," *Fortune,* March 2, 1998, p. 224

22. Mike McNamee and Dean Foust, "How Growth Could End the Budget Wars," *Business Week,* May 19, 1997, p. 32.

23. Don Tapscott, *The Digital Economy* (New York: McGraw-Hill, 1996), p. 7.

24. Kim Clark, "These Are the Good Old Days," *Fortune,* June 9, 1997, pp. 74–87.

25. Michael J. Mandel, "The New Business Cycle," *Business Week,* March 31, 1997, pp. 58–68.

26. Clark, "Good Old Days."

27. Mandel, "New Business Cycle."

28. Ibid.
29. M. Sharon Baker, "Effort to Salvage Virtual i-O Fails," *Puget Sound Business Journal,* May 23, 1997, p. 1.
30. Hal Plotkin, "Seeking Quality, Juicer Squeezes Out Franchisees," *Inc.,* July 1997, p. 25.
31. Don Peppers, "How You Can Help Them," *Fast Company,* October/November 1997, p. 25.
32. Anne Fisher, "What Labor Shortage?" *Fortune,* June 23, 1997, p. 154.
33. Holstein, "New Economy."
34. Fisher, "Labor Shortage?"
35. "What Asia—and the World—Must Do," *Business Week,* January 28, 1998, p. 108; and Gary S. Becker, "Asia May Be Shaken But It's No House of Cards," *Business Week,* February 2, 1998.

CHAPTER 4

1. "Volkswagen Beetle: Old and New," accessed at nbcin.nbcll-news.com, March 3, 1999; "Buggin': Everyone is Antsy for the New Beetle," *Rolling Stone,* January 7, 1999, p. 78; Jean Halliday, "Marketer of the Year," *Advertising Age,* December 14, 1998, pp. 1ff; and Janet Guyon, "Getting the Bugs Out at VW," *Fortune,* March 29, 1999, pp. 96–102.
2. Sabrata N. Chakravarty and John R. Hayes, "The Pure-Play Syndrome," *Forbes,* October 20, 1997, pp. 209–215.
3. Rebecca Blumenstein, "While Going Global, GM Slips at Home," *The Wall Street Journal,* January 8, 1997, p. B1.
4. Rebecca Blumenstein, "GM Is Building Plants in Developing Nations to Woo New Markets," *The Wall Street Journal,* August 4, 1997, p. A1.
5. Patricia Kranz, "How Do You Say 'Fore' in Russian?" *Business Week,* October 6, 1997, p. 162.
6. "Clinton: Mr. Global Economy?" *Investor's Business Daily,* November 10, 1997; "Fast Track–Fast Growth," *Investor's Business Daily,* October 31, 1997; and "Free-Trade Tax Cut," *Investor's Business Daily,* September 18, 1997.
7. "Big Emerging Markets: India," *Big Emerging Markets: Outlook and Sourcebook,* U.S. Department of Commerce, downloaded from www.stat-usa.gov/bems/bemsind/bemsind.html.
8. Stephane Garelli, "Executive Summary," *World Competitiveness Yearbook 1997,* International Institute for Management Development, downloaded from www.imd.ch/wcy/approach/summary.html.
9. "Bell Canada Outlines Investments in Brazil," *South American Business Information,* May 13, 1997.
10. Paul Simao, "Canada's Economy Seen Leading 67 Nations," *Reuters Business Report,* April 30, 1997.
11. Geri Smith and Elizabeth Malkin, "The Border," *Business Week,* May 12, 1997, pp. 64–74.
12. Stanley Reed, Julia Flynn, and Heidi Dawley, "Britain's Boom," *Business Week International,* April 14, 1997, p. 18.
13. Gail Edmondson, "Go West, Young Frenchman," *Business Week,* March 9, 1998, p. 52.
14. "Big Emerging Markets: Poland," *Big Emerging Markets: Outlook and Sourcebook 1996,* U.S. Department of Commerce, downloaded from www.stat-usa.gov/bems/bemspol/bemspol.html; and "U.S. Exports, Imports, and Merchandise Trade Balances by Country: 1992–1996," *Statistical Abstract of the United States, 1997,* 117th ed. (Washington, D.C.: Bureau of the Census, 1997), p. 805.
15. *The Central Intelligence Agency's Handbook of International Economic Statistics, 1997,* updated January 12, 1998, downloaded from www.odci.gov/cia/publications/hies97/b/tab6.htm.
16. Paul Krugman, "Asia: What Went Wrong," *Fortune,* March 2, 1998, pp. 32–34; Tim Rohwer, "Asia's Meltdown," *Fortune,* February 16, 1998, pp. 84–90; and Brian Bremner and Pete Engardio, "What to Do about Asia," *Business Week,* January 26, 1998, pp. 26–31.
17. "Going Global: East Asia-Pacific Rim," *Inc. Special Issue: The State of Small Business,* 1997.
18. Adrienne Fox, "China Challenges U.S. Makers as Exports Lead Robust Growth," *Investor's Business Daily,* April 10, 1997.
19. "Latin American Business Must, in Its Own Way, Play the Global Game," *The Economist,* December 6, 1997.
20. "MS Touts Latin American Market," *Reuters News Service,* November 25, 1997.
21. Geri Smith, Elisabeth Malkin, Ian Katz, Andrea Mandel-Campbell, and John Pearson, "The Corporation: The New Latin Corporation," *Business Week,* October 27, 1997, p. 71.
22. "U.S. Trade Deficit Worst in Nine Years," *USA Today,* February 20, 1998, p. B1.
23. Matthew Miller, "Don't Worry, Be Happy," *U.S. News & World Report,* February 23, 1998, pp. 53–54.
24. "U.S. International Trade in Goods and Services: November 1997," Report FT900 (CB-98-13), Bureau of the Census, Foreign Trade Division.
25. Dexter Roberts, "Big Bird Heads for Shanghai," *Business Week,* November 10, 1997, p. 66.
26. Cacilie Rohweddeer, "Ein Popcorn, Bitte: Hollywood Studios Invade Europe," *The Wall Street Journal,* November 5, 1997, p. B1.
27. Jeffrey D. Zbar, "Kids' Networks Mature into Global Programming Force," *Advertising Age International,* March 1997, p. I6; and Jeffrey D. Zbar, "Niche Audiences Are Growing," *Advertising Age International,* July 1997, p. I18.
28. Helen Cooper and Scott Killman, "Trade Wars Aside, U.S. and Europe Buy More of Each Others' Foods," *The Wall Street Journal,* November 4, 1997, p. A1.
29. Steve Glain, "A Whole New Wave of Japanese Exports Is Headed Westward," *The Wall Street Journal,* November 14, 1997, p. A1.
30. Steven Butler, "Die Hard: Japan's Trade Surplus," *U.S. News & World Report,* May 19, 1997, p. 46; and "Key Currency Cross Rates," *The Wall Street Journal,* February 13, 1998, p. C15.
31. "Quotable," *Sales & Marketing Management,* September 1996, p. 23.
32. Yumiko Ono, "Will Good Housekeeping Translate into Japanese?" *The Wall Street Journal,* December 30, 1997, pp. B1, B6.
33. Jeff Walters, "Have Brands, Will Travel," *Brandweek,* October 6, 1997, p. 22.
34. Carl Quintanilla, "Despite Setbacks, Whirlpool Pursues Overseas Markets," *The Wall Street Journal,* December 9, 1997, p. B4; and Carl Quintanilla, "Whirlpool Net Doubled in 4th Quarter," *The Wall Street Journal,* February 4, 1998, p. A6.

35. Nicole Crawford, "When in Ghana, Hold the Flowers," *Promo,* September 1997, p. 132.

36. "Nike on Sacrilegious Shoe: Just Dump It," *U.S. News & World Report,* July 7, 1997, p. 63.

37. Penni Crabtree, "Qualcomm Lays Off 700 Amid Asia Woes," *San Diego Union-Tribune,* February 6, 1998, p. A1; Michael Kinsman and Ernesto Portillo, Jr., "Vans Cuts 165 Workers in Vista, Cites Asia," *San Diego Union-Tribune,* January 14, 1998, p. C1; and Mark L. Clifford, "Job Shock," *Business Week,* December 22, 1997, pp. 48–49.

38. Joyce Barnathan, "Hong Kong: The New Economy," *Business Week,* June 9, 1997, pp. 44–49; and Ian Buruma, "Hong Kong, Feeling Flu-ish," *New York Times,* February 1, 1998, pp. 38–42.

39. "In the Eye of the Hurricane," *Business Week,* February 16, 1998, pp. 50–52; Dorinda Elliott, "Painting the Town Red," *Newsweek,* July 7, 1997, pp. 36–39; and Caspar Weinberger, "Six Months after China's Takeover," *Forbes,* December 29, 1997, p. 37.

40. Paul Blustein, "Pact to Bar Bribery Is Reached," *Washington Post,* May 24, 1997, p. F1.

41. Thomas Omestad, "Bye-Bye to Bribes," *U.S. News & World Report,* December 22, 1997, pp. 39–44.

42. Michael Dorgan, "Rewriting the Laws of the Information Age," *San Jose Mercury News,* August 8, 1997; and Erik Eckholm, "China Draws the Line on Internet Use," *San Diego Union-Tribune,* January 1, 1998, p. A21.

43. Dexter Roberts, "Cheated in China," *Business Week,* October 6, 1997, pp. 142–143.

44. "MS Touts Latin American Market," *Reuters News Service,* November 25, 1997.

45. Michael R. Czinkota and Ilkka A. Ronkainen, *International Marketing,* 5th ed. (Forth Worth, Tex.: Dryden Press, 1998), pp. 38–40.

46. "WTO Telecoms Deal Will Ring in the Changes on 5 February 1998," *World Trade Organization,* January 26, 1998.

47. Jay Solomon, "World Bank Says It Was Wrong on Indonesia," *The Wall Street Journal,* February 5, 1998, pp. A17, A18.

48. Steven Butler, Thomas Omestad, and Kenneth T. Walsh, "The Year of the IMF," *U.S. News & World Report,* January 12, 1998, pp. 42–43.

49. Phillip J. Longman and Shaheena Ahmad, "The Bailout Backlash," *U.S. News & World Report,* February 2, 1998, pp. 37–38; and Rich Miller, "When It Comes to Global Policy, Everyone's a Critic," *USA Today,* February 9, 1998, pp. B1, B2.

50. Don M. Ings, "NAFTA Boosts Our Region's Economy," *San Diego Union-Tribune,* August 6, 1997, p. B7.

51. Helene Cooper, "Expert's View of NAFTA's Economic Impact: It's a Wash," *The Wall Street Journal,* June 17, 1997, p. A20.

52. Ibid.

53. Tim Loughran, "Stocks, Peso Rally as Voters Clobber PRI," *San Diego Union Tribune,* July 8, 1997, pp. C1, C2.

54. Lawrence Ingrassia, "One Dollar Is Worth One Dollar, But That Wasn't Always So," *The Wall Street Journal,* January 13, 1998, pp. A1, A10.

55. Paul Blustein, "U.S. in Talks with EU on Easing Trade Curbs," *Washington Post,* February 4, 1998, p. C13; and William J. McDonough, "The EMU Will Be Good for the U.S.," *The Wall Street Journal,* February 6, 1998, p. A22.

56. Steve Barth, "Free to Trade," *World Trade,* January 1998, pp. 27–29.

57. Johnathan Friedland and Louise Lee, "Foreign Aisles," *The Wall Street Journal,* October 8, 1997, p. A1; and Zellner et al., "Wal-Mart Spoken Here."

58. Tonia L. Shakespeare, "Business Opportunities in Jamaica," *Black Enterprise,* May 1997.

59. Ian Jones, "A Purse from a Sow's Ear," *World Trade,* August 1997, pp. 90–91.

60. Personal interview with Michael Rivkin, owner of Famous Trails, January 27, 1998.

61. John R. Engen, "Rolling in Dough," *Success,* June 1997, p. 31.

62. "Wal-Mart to Expand in Mexico," *San Diego Union-Tribune,* June 4, 1997, p. C1.

63. "Cross Border Deals," *World Trade,* August 1997, p. 92.

64. Erran Carmel, "The Explosion of Global Software Teams," *Computerworld Global Innovators,* December 8, 1997, p. 6; and Srikumar S. Rao, "Silicon Valley Goes East—Way East," *Forbes,* November 17, 1997, p. 158.

65. "AT&T, STET/Telecom Italia and Unisource Announce Far-Reaching Agreement," *Cambridge Telecom Report,* July 7, 1997.

66. Andrew Tanzer, "Stepping Stones to a New China?" *Forbes,* January 27, 1997, p. 78.

67. Damon Darlin, "Maquiladora-ville," *Forbes,* May 6, 1996, pp. 111–112.

68. William J. Holstein, "Ford: The Road Ahead," *U.S. News & World Report,* March 10, 1997, p. 45; and Micheline Maynard, "Ford, GM Confront European Challenges," *USA Today,* May 27, 1997, p. 3B.

69. Brent Schindler, "Microsoft: First America, Now the World," *Fortune,* August 18, 1997, pp. 214–216.

CHAPTER 5

1. NewsHour forum, accessed at www.pbs.org, February 18, 1999; Heather Green, "Not So Odd a Couple after All," *Business Week*, December 21, 1998, pp. 77–78; "Ink Dries on AOL's $10 Billion Netscape Deal," *Mobile Register,* March 18, 1999, p. 7B; and Russ Mitchell, "Why AOL Really Clicks," *U.S. News & World Report*, December 7, 1998, pp. 52–53.

2. Small Business Administration, "Starting Your Business," (Washington, D.C.: U.S. Government Printing Office, 1998), p. 1.

3. Tim Talevich and Tershia d'Elgin, "Taking on the Giants," *The Costco Connection,* August 1997, p. 22.

4. "Notebook," *Time,* August 4, 1997, p. 17.

5. Personal interview with Becky Busath, May 1997.

6. Luisa Kroll, "My Partner, My Father," *Forbes,* June 2, 1997, pp. 66–70.

7. "Top 10 Ways to Start Your Homebased Business Off Right," *Business Start-Ups,* September 1997, p. 38; and Daniel H. Pink, "Free Agent Nation," *Fast Company,* December/January 1998, p. 132.

8. Mo Krochmal, "Teaming Up against Technology Giants," *TechWeb,* January 22, 1998, p. 1.

9. "Tiny, But Mighty," *Business Start-Ups,* March 1998, p. 5.

10. Jeffrey A. Tannenbaum, "Worker Satisfaction Found to Be Higher at Small Companies," *The Wall Street Journal,* May 5,

1997, p. B3; and "Facts about Small Business," SBA Office of Advocacy, 1997.

11. Joel Kotkin, "The 4 Best Small-Business Neighborhoods," *Inc.: The State of Small Business,* 1997, pp. 58–72.

12. Erik Schonfeld, "Atcom/Info: Internet Kiosks," *Fortune,* July 7, 1997, p. 88.

13. "Facts about Small Business," SBA Office of Advocacy, 1998. See also Karen Roy, "Team Effort," *Business Start-Ups,* April 1998, pp. 40–43.

14. Chris Woodyard, "Virtual Tailors Fashion Apparel," *USA Today,* February 16, 1998, p. 3B.

15. Jill Andresky Fraser, "Hire Finance," *Inc.,* January 1998, pp. 87–91.

16. Personal interview with Joel McIntosh, January 1998.

17. Sharon Nelton, "Coming to Grips with Growth," *Nation's Business,* February 1998, pp. 26–32.

18. Carolyn Z. Lawrence, "Know Your Competition," *Business Start-Ups,* April 1997, pp. 51–56.

19. "Many Healthy Returns," *Business Week,* January 12, 1998, p. 72.

20. "Facts about Small Business," SBA Office of Advocacy, 1998.

21. "Small Business Answer Card 1997," SBA Office of Advocacy, 1998.

22. "Banks Big on Small-Business Loans," *Business Start-Ups,* January 1998, p. 48.

23. "It Took a Laundry to Clean the Area," *Mobile Register,* February 13, 1998, p. 2A.

24. Debra Phillips, "Good Advice," *Entrepreneur,* November 1997, p. 60.

25. Karen Gutloff, "Five Alternative Ways to Finance Your Business," *Black Enterprise,* March 1998, pp. 81–85.

26. Jan Norman, "How to Finance Your Business," *Business Start-Ups,* January 1998.

27. Nelton, "Coming to Grips."

28. Nancy Hatch Woodward, "A Place to Grow," *Business Start-Ups,* January 1998, pp. 42–45.

29. Hal Plotkin, "Wal-Mart Throws the Book at Small-Biz Vendors," *Inc.,* January 1997, p. 29. See also Heather Page, "United We Stand," *Entrepreneur,* April 1998, pp. 122–125.

30. "Firms Owned by Women of Color Show Growth in Non-Traditional Sectors," *NFWBO News,* 3rd Quarter, 1997, pp. 1–3.

31. "Women in Businesses of Their Own," *The Wall Street Journal Almanac* (New York: Ballantine Books, 1998), p. 232.

32. "Home Based Business Success Story: Friendly Auto Glass Is Launched with a Micro Loan," *Online Women's Business Center,* downloaded from www.onlinewbc.org, January 20, 1998.

33. Karin Moeller, "For Women Only," *Business Start-Ups,* March 1998, p. 4.

34. Carolyn Brown, "More than Just Window Dressing?" *Black Enterprise,* September 1994, pp. 103–112.

35. Roy S. Johnson, "The New Black Power," *Fortune,* August 4, 1997, pp. 46–47.

36. Mark Richard Moss, "A Fish Tale of Success," *Nation's Business,* January 1998, pp. 50–51.

37. Leslie Brokaw, "Minding the Store," *Inc.,* November 1993, pp. 66–75.

38. Paula M. White, "Reaching a McMilestone," *Black Enterprise,* March 1998, p. 18.

39. Charlotte Mulhern, "In the Ranking," *Entrepreneur,* March 1998, p. 38.

40. Roberta Maynard, "Trade Links Via the Internet," *Nation's Business,* December 1997, pp. 51–53.

41. "News and Notes," *The Licensing Letter,* April 1, 1997, p. 3.

42. Jill Andresky Fraser, "Perfect Form," *Inc.,* December 1997, pp. 155–156.

43. Carolyn Z. Lawrence, "Partner Problems: What to Do When a Partnership Turns Sour," *Business97,* August/September 1997, p. 40.

44. Ibid.

45. "Forbes 500 Annual Directory," *Forbes,* April 21, 1997, p. 181.

46. Jill Andresky Fraser, "Perfect Form," *Inc.,* December 1997, pp. 155–158.

47. Carolyn T. Geer, "Turning Employees into Stakeholders," *Forbes,* December 1, 1997, p. 154.

48. Susan Chandler, "United: The Dubious Joys of Ownership," *Business Week,* January 27, 1997, p. 33.

49. "The Olympic Partnership," *Fortune,* February 2, 1998, pp. 114–134.

50. James Aley and Matt Siegel, "The Fallout from Merger Mania," *Fortune,* March 2, 1998, pp. 26–27.

51. *The Wall Street Journal Almanac 1998* (New York: Ballantine Books, 1998), p. 184.

CHAPTER 6

1. Amazon.com culture page, accessed at www.amazon.com, March 9, 1999; "Amazon Gets into Drugstore," *CNN Financial News,* February 24, 1999, accessed at www.cnnfn.com; "Amazon.com Invests in Geoworks Stake," Reuters Limited, February 17, 1999; "Sun Entertainment Becomes Part of Amazon.com Associates Network," Sun Entertainment press release, Business Wire, February 17, 1999; "Amazon Seeks New Products," *CNN Financial News,* Ferbruary 1, 1999, accessed at www.cnnfn.com; "Amazon Flows in Europe," *CNN Financial News,* October 15, 1998, accessed at www.cnnfn.com; Joshua Macht, "Amazon.com: A Moving Target," *Inc.,* October 1998, p. 18.

2. Rieva Lesonsky, "The Right Path?" *Entrepreneur,* March 1997, p. 6.

3. "The Evolution of the Professional Entrepreneur," *Inc., Special Issue: The State of Small Business 1997,* July 20, 1997, p. 52.

4. Telephone interview with Marianne Sullivan, Administrative Director, Center for Entrepreneurial Leadership, June 1, 1995.

5. Gianna Jacobson, "A Jolt of Inspiration," *Success,* January/February 1997, p. 21.

6. Leslie Brokaw, "Turnaround Entrepreneur: Case in Point," *Inc.,* December 1995, p. 88.

7. Dale D. Buss, "Coping with Faster Change," *Nation's Business,* March 1995, p. 27.

8. Vivian Marino, "Entrepreneurship Abounds among Today's Youngsters," *Mobile Register,* June 1, 1997, p. 4-F.

9. "CEOs' Top Reasons for Starting a Company," *Inc. 500 Almanac,* October 22, 1996, p. 24.

10. Michael Barrier, "Entrepreneurs Who Excel," *Nation's Business,* August 1996, p. 19.

11. Gary M. Stern, "Young Entrepreneurs Make Their Mark," *Nation's Business,* August 1996, pp. 49–51.

12. Andrew Serwer, "Paths to Wealth in the New Economy," *Fortune,* February 20, 1995, p. 56.

13. Ibid.

14. Gene Koretz, "Big Payoffs from Layoffs," *Business Week,* February 24, 1997, p. 30.

15. Tariq K. Muhammad, "From Buppies to Biz-wiz: Forget Corporate America—Generation X Is Choosing the Entrepreneurial Path to Success," *Black Enterprise,* January 1997, p. 44.

16. Karin Moeller, "It's Just a State of Mind," *Business Start-Ups,* July 1997, p. 4.

17. Mitchell Stern and Wilma Randle, "The Best Way to Start a Business . . . May Be to Buy One," *Working Woman,* March 1996, p. 33.

18. Nina Muck and Suzanne Oliver, "Women of the Valley," *Forbes,* December 30, 1996, p. 105.

19. Tom Richman, "Creators of the New Economy," *Inc. Special Issue: The State of Small Business 1997,* July 20, 1997, p. 46.

20. "Small Talk," *Inc. Special Issue: The State of Small Business 1996,* May 21,1996, p. 18.

21. Fred Hapgood, "Foreign Exchange," *Inc.* Tech 1997, pp. 85–86.

22. David Carnoy, "Global Entrepreneur: Teaming Up," *Success,* April 1997, p. 20.

23. Katherine S. Mangan, "Many Business Schools Add Classes on Entrepreneurship," *The Chronicle of Higher Education* 43 (January 24, 1997), p. A8.

24. Heather Page, "Wired for Success," *Entrepreneur,* May 1997, pp. 132–139.

25. Kristin Dunlop Godsey, "Spoil Them Rotten," *Success,* September 1997, p. 22.

26. Janean Chun, "Search for Tomorrow," *Entrepreneur,* May 1997, p. 112.

27. Ibid., p. 120.

28. John Case, "Is America Really Different?" *Inc. Special Issue: The State of Small Business 1996,* May 21, 1996, pp. 108–109.

29. Dana Milbank, "Tough Business: Polish Entrepreneurs Revitalize Economy but Battle Huge Odds," *The Wall Street Journal,* March 30, 1995, pp. A1, A6.

30. Jerry Useem, "Start a Company, Save the World," *Inc.,* May 1997, p. 18.

31. "Small Beginnings," *The Economist,* November 23, 1996, p. S13.

32. Marc Ballon, "Giving Unternehmers a Good Name," *Inc.,* June 1997, p. 29.

33. "Female Entrepreneurs Soaring around the World," *USA Today,* December 1994, p. 10.

34. Gayle Sato Stodder, "How to Build a Million-Dollar Company," *Entrepreneur,* September 1997, p. 106.

35. "Southwest Airlines, A Tale of Two Men, One Airline, and a Cocktail Napkin."

36. Michael Hopkins, "Help Wanted," *Inc. Special Issue: The State of Small Business 1997,* July 20, 1997, pp. 35–36; and Adam Savage, "Entrepreneurship Programs Must Change with Times," *Marketing Educator,* Spring 1997, p. 4.

37. Muhammad, "From Buppies to Biz-wiz," p. 44.

38. Alfredo J. Estrada, "Entrepreneurial Opportunities," *Hispanic,* June 1997, p. 62.

39. Earl G. Graves, "New Enterprise," *Black Enterprise,* September 1996, p. 9; and Elyse M. Friedman, ed., "The New-Economy Almanac," *Inc. Special Issue: The State of Small Business 1997,* July 20, 1997, p. 118.

40. Heather Page, "Like Father, Like Son?" *Entrepreneur,* May 1997, p. 20; and Gene Koretz, "What Makes an Entrepreneur: Parental Example Is a Big Factor," *Business Week,* December 9, 1996, p. 32.

41. Michael Barrier, "Entrepreneurs Who Excel."

42. This discussion is based on Donald F. Kuratko and Richard M. Hodgetts, *Entrepreneurship: A Contemporary Approach,* 4th ed. (Fort Worth, Tex.: Dryden Press, 1998), pp. 101–106.

43. Bill Gates, *The Road Ahead* (New York: Penguin Books, 1995), p. 18.

44. Andrew E. Serwer, "Paths to Wealth in the New Economy."

45. Kathleen Allen, "What Do Women Want?" *Inc.,* September 1996, p. 27.

46. Dan Hager, "Technology and Tenacity," *Nation's Business,* August 1996, pp. 14, 16.

47. Alessandra Bianchi, "What's Love Got to Do with It?" *Inc.,* May 1996, pp. 76–85.

48. Clint Willis, "Try, Try Again," *Forbes ASAP,* June 2, 1997, pp. 59–64.

49. Carol Steinberg, "Young and Restless," *Success,* April 1997, pp. 73–75.

50. Robert McGarvey, "Words from the Wise," *Entrepreneur,* May 1997, pp. 154–155.

51. Michael Warshaw, ed., "Never Say Die: Spectacular Stories of Triumph," downloaded from http://www.successmagazine.com/archives.html/AUG.html/Comeback.html, July 9, 1997.

52. Tom Stein, "No Experience Required: How the Youngest Entrepreneurs Are Creating Big Companies and Changing the Future," *Success,* March 1996, p. 36.

53. Jackie Bazan, "Happiness Is a Screening Process," *Nation's Business,* July 1997, p. 6.

54. Frank Demmler, "Getting On with Your Life's Work," downloaded from http://www.enterprise.org/enet/reflections/fdlife.html on July 7, 1997; Kylo-Patrick Hart, "A Smart Idea: Found Something You Like to Do? Make It Your Business!" *Business Start-Ups,* June 1997, pp. 74–78; Danielle Kennedy, "Get Smart," *Entrepreneur,* March 1997, pp. 88–91; and Laura M. Litvan, "The Hot Zones for Entrepreneurs," *Nation's Business,* June 1996, pp. 42–43.

55. John Simons, "The Youth Movement," *U.S. News & World Report,* September 23, 1996, p. 65.

56. Fred Vogelstein and David Brindley, "No More Wrapping and Rolling," *U.S. News & World Report,* April 21, 1997, pp. 85, 87; and William G. Flanagan and Alexandra Alger, "It's Found Money," *Forbes,* February 10, 1997, pp. 214, 216.

57. Stern and Randle, "Best Way to Start," p. 33.

58. T. Trent Gegax, "Fast-Food Fast Tracker," *Newsweek,* May 26, 1997, p. 57.

59. Amar Bhide, "How Entrepreneurs Craft Strategies that Work," *Harvard Business Review,* March–April 1994, p. 150.

60. Stern, "Young Entrepreneurs," pp. 49–51.

61. "Seed Capital," *Inc. 500 Almanac,* October 22, 1996, p. 23.

62. Peter Speigel, "Batter Up!" *Forbes,* June 2, 1997, pp. 126, 128.

63. David Evanson, "Capital Questions," *Entrepreneur,* March 1997, pp. 62–65.

64. Gianna Jacobson, "Do or Die! Get a Cash Infusion from a High-Powered Angel Network," *Success,* April 1997, p. 18; and Stephanie Gruner, "Conversations with Angels," *Inc.,* October 1996, p. 86.

65. Perspective given by L. D. DeSimone, 3M chairman and CEO, in "How Can Big Companies Keep the Entrepreneurial Spirit Alive?" *Harvard Business Review,* November–December 1995, pp. 184–185.
66. Perspective given by William F. O'Brien, president and CEO of Starlight Telecommunications, in "How Can Big Companies Keep the Entrepreneurial Spirit Alive?" *Harvard Business Review,* November–December, 1995, pp. 185–186.
67. Ibid.
68. Phaedra Hise, "New Recruitment Strategy: Ask Your Best Employees to Leave," *Inc.,* July 1997, p. 28.

CHAPTER 7

1. "Time Warner Eyes New Internet Stakes," *InternetNews.com,* January 22, 1999, accessed at www.internews.com; Eben Shapiro, "Time Warner Builds Internet Superstore," *The Wall Street Journal,* September 14, 1998, p. B1; and Michael Krantz, "Click Till You Drop," *Time.com,* July 20, 1998, accessed at cgi.pathfinder.com/time/magazine.
2. Linda Grant, "Monsanto's Bet: There's Gold in Going Green," *Fortune,* April 14, 1997, p. 116; and "Growth through Global Sustainability: An Interview with Monsanto's CEO Robert B. Shapiro," *Harvard Business Review,* January/February 1997, p. 78.
3. Patricia Sellers, "Sears: The Turnaround Is Ending, the Revolution Has Begun," *Fortune,* April 28, 1997, p. 106.
4. Joe Griffith, *Speaker's Library of Business Stories, Anecdotes, and Humor* (Englewood Cliffs, N.J.: Prentice Hall, 1990), p. 9.
5. Lisa Pemberton-Butler, "Expanding Too Quickly was Todo's Unwrapping," *Seattle Times,* April 27, 1997, downloaded from *Seattle Times* Web site at http://www.seattletimes.com, August 10, 1997.
6. Ronald B. Lieber, "Flying High, Going Global," *Fortune,* July 7, 1997, p. 195.
7. Christine Sparta, "Fergie's Ads Yanked Due to 'Paparazzi' Line," *USA Today,* September 3, 1997, p. 2D.
8. Mickie Valentine, "Bebis Asks Investors for Patience," *The Tampa Tribune,* March 4, 1997, downloaded from *Tampa Tribune* Web site at http://tampatrib.com, August 9, 1997.
9. Mike Troy, "JumboSports Shoots for the Big Time," *Discount Store News,* March 3, 1997, p. 3.
10. "A Letter from the President, Stephen Bebis," company document, downloaded from company Web site at http://www.jumbosports.com, August 5, 1997.
11. Ibid.
12. Ibid.
13. Ibid.
14. Nicole Harris, "Home Depot: Beyond Do-It-Yourselfers," *Business Week,* June 30, 1997, p. 86.
15. Rick Mullin, "Taking Customer Relations to the Next Level," *Journal of Business Strategy,* January/February 1997, p. 22.
16. Meryl Davids, "Unleashing a Shared Brand," *Journal of Business Strategy,* March/April 1997, p. 56.
17. Linda Grant, "GE's 'Smart Bomb' Strategy," *Fortune,* July 21, 1997, p. 109.
18. Gary Heil, Tom Parket, and Deborah C. Stephens, *One Size Fits One* (New York: International Thomson Publishing/Van Nostrand Reinhold, 1997), p. 124.
19. Daniel McGinn and Tara Weingarten, "Oh, What a Feeling," *Newsweek,* July 28, 1997, p. 51.
20. Nichole M. Christian, "One Weekend, 52 Jeeps, a Chance to Bond," *The Wall Street Journal,* May 13, 1997, p. B1.
21. "Jeep Takes the Canyon Into the City with an Off-Highway Driving Course," Chrysler Corp. press release, June 19, 1997.
22. Don Peppers and Martha Rogers, "Oxford Health Takes a Big Step Toward 1:1," Inside 1:1 newsletter, downloaded from Web at http//www.marketing1to1.com, July 31, 1997.
23. Bruce Kasanoff, "Kingsway Paper: Bagging Customer Loyalty," Inside 1:1 newsletter, downloaded from Web at http://www.marketing1to1.com, July 31, 1997.
24. Tim W. Ferguson, "A Revolution That Has a Long Way to Go," *Forbes,* August 11, 1997, p. 106.
25. Robert N. Stone and J. Barry Mason, "Relationship Management: Strategic Marketing's Next Source of Competitive Advantage," *Journal of Marketing Theory and Practice,* Spring 1997, p. 8.
26. Jim McCraw, "Motorcycle Wars: Japan's Latest Shots at Fortress Harley," *The New York Times,* July 20, 1997, Sec. 11, p. 1.
27. Brigid McMenamin, "Internet Philanthropy," *Forbes,* August 11, 1997, p. 46.
28. Anne Faircloth, "One-on-One Shopping," *Fortune,* July 7, 1997, p. 235.
29. Mark Henricks, "Extra Credit," *Entrepreneur,* February 1997, p. 80.
30. Don Peppers and Martha Rogers, *Enterprise One to One* (New York: Currency/Doubleday, 1997), p. 42.
31. "Three Retailers Experiment with Recognition and Rewards," *Colloquy,* Issue 1, 1997, p. 1.
32. "Hallmark Cares Enough to Recognize and Reward Its 'Very Best'," *Colloquy,* Issue 1, 1997, p. 10.
33. "Golf Cards' Marketing Bogey," *Credit Card Management,* February 1997, p. 6.
34. Steve Gelsi, "GM Dealing for Hilfiger, Karan Cars," *Brandweek,* March 3, 1997, p. 4.
35. "Co-Branding," *Restaurant Business Brand Power Supplement,* 1997, p. 26.
36. Sean Mehegan, "Nestlé Links with Frito-Lay for $8M Launch of Chocolate Pretzels," *Brandweek,* March 24, 1997, p. 3.
37. Sean Mehegan, "Playskool Puts Stamp on SunBlocks," *Brandweek,* February 17, 1997, p. 14.
38. Irwin Teich, "Holding on to Customers: The Bottom-Line Benefits of Relationship Building," *Bank Marketing,* February 1997, p. 12.
39. Personal interview with Steve Lauer, Subway franchise owner, Ft. Collins, Colorado, August 8, 1997.
40. Example from Marketing 1:1 Web page, "Best Practices," at http://www.marketing1to1.com, downloaded August 8, 1997.
41. John H. Seridan, "Bonds of Trust," *Industry Week,* March 17, 1997, p. 52.
42. Julie Sullivan, "Nice Pants," *Wired,* August 1997, p. 131.
43. Russell Redman, "Beneficial Connects with Customers via Net, Phone," *Bank Systems & Technology,* July 1997, p. 46.

44. John Foley, "Market of One: Ready, Aim, Sell!" *Information Week,* February 17, 1997, p. 34.

45. "The Colonel's Bold Campaign," *Chain Store Age,* June 1997, p. A12.

46. Calmetta Y. Coleman, "Finally, Supermarkets Find Ways to Increase Their Profit Margins," *The Wall Street Journal,* May 29, 1997, p. A1.

47. Laura Bird and Wendy Bounds, "Stores' Demands Squeeze Apparel Companies," *The Wall Street Journal,* July 15, 1997, pp. B1, B3.

48. Ibid.

49. "Business Process Outsourcing," *Directors & Boards,* Spring 1997, p. 37.

50. "Preventive Maintenance Via Outsourcing," *Chain Store Age,* July 1997, p. T6.

51. "USPS Makes Better Service a Priority," *Purchasing,* June 5, 1997, p. 75.

52. Kelly J. Andrews, "Strategic Alliances Fuel Faster Growth Among High-Tech Companies," *Entrepreneurial Edge Online,* downloaded from Web at http://www.edgeonline.com, August 13, 1997.

53. David Ernst and Andy Steinhubl, "Picking a Partner," *Oil & Gas Investor,* July 1997, p. 40.

54. Ginger Conlon, "Selling With the Enemy," *Sales & Marketing Management,* May 1997, p. 113.

55. Mark Hamstra, "Beyond Tokyo: Operators Scour Japan for Lower-Cost Growth Opportunities," *Nation's Restaurant News,* May 26, 1997, p. 35.

56. Rosabeth Moss Kanter, "The Power of Partnering," *Sales & Marketing Management,* June 1997, p. 26.

CHAPTER 8

1. Sun Microsystems Web site, accessed at www.sun.com, March 15, 1999; Janet Rae-Dupree, "Sun Microsystems' Chief: A Mission Against 'Dark Side,'" *San Jose Mercury News,* January 26, 1998, accessed at www.sjmercury.com; Brent Schlender, "Javaman: The Adventures of Scott McNealy," *Fortune,* October 13, 1997, accessed at www.pathfinder.com/fortune; Robert D. Hof, Kathy Rebello, and Peter Burrows, "Scott McNealy's Rising Sun," *Business Week,* updated June 14, 1997, accessed at www.businessweek.com.

2. Linda Wilson, "Know It All," *Computerworld Internet Careers,* December 8, 1997, p. 13.

3. Alessandra Bianchi, "Mission Improbable," *Inc.,* September 1996, pp. 69–75.

4. Gary McWilliams, "Power Play," *Business Week,* February 9, 1998, pp. 90–97; and Compaq press release, "Compaq to Acquire Digital for $9.6 Billion," January 26, 1998.

5. Hal Lancaster, "Managing Your Time in Real-World Chaos Takes Real Planning," *The Wall Street Journal,* August 19, 1997, p. B1.

6. Bob Nelson, "Try Praise," *Inc.,* September 1996, p. 115.

7. David Molnar, "Seven Keys to International Management," *HR Focus,* May 1997, pp. 11–12.

8. Brian Dumaine, "Don't Be an Ugly-American Manager," *Fortune,* October 16, 1995, p. 225.

9. Robert Lenzner and Carrie Shook, "The Battle of the Bottoms," *Forbes,* March 24, 1997, pp. 98–103.

10. Vivian Pospisil, "Gut Feeling or Skilled Reasoning?" *Industry Week,* March 3, 1997, p. 12.

11. Michael Warshaw, "Guts and Glory," *Success,* March 1997, pp. 27–32.

12. Ronald A. Heifetz and Donald L. Laurie, "The Work of Leadership," *Harvard Business Review,* January/February 1997, pp. 124–134.

13. Thomas A. Stewart, "Why Leadership Matters," *Fortune,* March 2, 1998, pp. 71–82; Allen R. Myerson, "Air Herb," *New York Times Magazine,* November 9, 1997, pp. 36–39; and Jesse Katz, "Is This the Perfect Place to Work?" *Reader's Digest,* June 1997, pp. 33–41.

14. Michael A. Verespej, "Widespread Responsibility," *Industry Week,* January 19, 1998, pp. 31–35.

15. John Case, "Corporate Culture," *Inc.,* November 1996, pp. 42–53.

16. Ibid., p. 52.

17. Nina Munk and Suzanne Oliver, "Think Fast," *Forbes,* March 24, 1997, pp. 146–152; and Case, "Corporate Culture," pp. 42–48.

18. Bill Harris, "How Can Big Companies Keep the Entrepreneurial Spirit Alive?", *Harvard Business Review,* November/December 1995, p. 188. (Harris is executive vice president of Intuit.)

CHAPTER 9

1. Mike Hogan, "Symantec: Doing Well Is the Best Revenge," *PC World News,* March 2, 1999, accessed at www.pcworld.com; Symantec Web site, accessed at www.symantec.com, March 9, 1999; Career Mosaic Web site, accessed at www.careermosaic.com, March 9, 1999; Tom Abate, "A Software Survivor, Symantec's CEO Says the Thrill Isn't Gone," *San Francisco Chronicle,* August 27, 1998, accessed at www.symantec.com.

2. Carolyn Hirschman, "All Aboard: The Boom in Employee Leasing May Bring Great Career Opportunities for HR Professionals," *HRMagazine,* September 1997, pp. 80–85.

3. Linda Thornburg, "Employers and Graduates Size Each Other Up," *HRMagazine,* May 1997, pp. 76–79.

4. Christopher Woodall, "Play It Again, Sam," *HRMagazine,* May 1997, pp. 84–87.

5. Patricia Nakache, "Cisco's Recruiting Edge," *Fortune,* September 29, 1997, pp. 275–276.

6. Sherri Eng, "Computer Savvy Helping Hunters to Snare Best Jobs," *Computerlink,* March 18, 1997, p. 19.

7. Michael Barrier, "Lawsuits Gone Wild," *Nation's Business,* February 1998, pp. 12–18.

8. Robert W. Thompson, "HR Issues Fill Congress In Box," *HRMagazine,* January 1998, pp. 70–80.

9. "HR Can Ease the Pain of Discrimination Suits," *HR Focus,* October 1997, p. S5.

10. Carol Hacker, "The Cost of Poor Hiring Decisions . . . And How to Avoid Them," *HR Focus,* October 1997, p. S13.

11. Sarah Schafer, "Putting IT to the Test," *Inc. Technology,* March 18, 1997, pp. 74–75.

12. Carl Quintanilla, "Getting Fired," *The Wall Street Journal,* May 27, 1997, p. A1.

13. Barrier, "Lawsuits Gone Wild," p. 17.
14. Karen Lowry Miller, "Without Training, I Can't Start My Real Life," *Business Week,* September 16, 1996, p. 60; and "Training Competitiveness," *Journal of European Industrial Training,* June1995, p. 16.
15. Linda Thornburg, "Investment in Training Technology Yields Good Returns," *HRMagazine,* January 1998, pp. 37–41.
16. Anne Field, "Class Act," *Inc. Technology,* March 18, 1997, pp. 55–59.
17. Martha Cooley, "HR in Russia: Training for Long-Term Success," *HRMagazine,* December 1997, pp. 98–106.
18. Stephanie Gruner, "Feedback from Everyone," *Inc.,* February 1997, pp. 102–103.
19. Daniel Kadlec, "How CEO Pay Got Away," *Time,* April 28, 1997, p. 59; and Jennifer Reingold, "Executive Pay," *Business Week,* April 21, 1997, pp. 58–66.
20. Luisa Kroll, "Catching Up," *Forbes,* May 19, 1997, pp. 162–163; and Stewart Pinkerton, "The Itch to Get Rich," *Forbes,* April 21, 1997, p. 132.
21. Michelle Neely Martinez, "The Proof Is in the Profits," *Working Mother,* May 1997, pp. 27–30.
22. Jeffrey C. Thurmond, "Section 125: Cafeteria Plans and Public Accountants," *National Public Accountant,* August 1996, pp. 10, 12.
23. Donna Fenn, "Managing Generation X," *Inc.,* August 1996, p. 91; and Lynne S. Dumas, "The New Flexibility," *Working Mother,* July/August 1996, pp. 28–32.
24. Ken Terry, "Who Benefits?" *Inc.,* February 1997, p. 101.
25. Lynn Asinoff, "Click & Shift: Workers Control Their Benefits On-Line," *The Wall Street Journal,* November 21, 1997, pp. C1, C28.
26. Michelle Neely Martinez, "Flexible Work Options: Work-Life Programs Reap Business Benefits," *HRMagazine,* June 1997, pp. 110–114.
27. Ibid., pp. 112–113.
28. "Hiring Telecommuters," *San Diego Union-Tribune,* January 5, 1998, p. C1.
29. Nancy Hatch Woodward, "Beyond Basic Benefits," *HRMagazine,* September 1997, pp. 53–56.
30. Quintanilla, "Getting Fired."
31. Gene Koretz, "The Downside of Downsizing," *Business Week,* April 28, 1997, p. 26; John Byrne et al., "Can Walter Fix AT&T?" *Business Week,* March 10, 1997, pp. 27–30; and Dominic Bencivenga, "Employers and Workers Come to Terms," *HRMagazine,* June 1997, pp. 91–97.
32. Anne Fisher, "The 100 Best Companies to Work for in America," *Fortune,* January 12, 1998, p. 69.
33. Dominic Bencivenga, "Forces behind the Emerging New Pact," *HRMagazine,* June 1997, pp. 94–95.
34. Ibid., p. 94.
35. Bencivenga, "Come to Terms," pp. 92–93.
36. Linda Grant, "Happy Workers, High Returns," *Fortune,* January 12, 1998, p. 81.
37. "Helping Foreign Workers Feel More at Home," *Nation's Business,* June 1997, p. 11.
38. G. Pascal Zachary, "The New Search for Meaning in 'Meaningless' Work," *The Wall Street Journal,* January 9, 1997, pp. B1, B2.
39. Douglas McGregor, *The Human Side of Enterprise* (New York: McGraw-Hill, 1960), pp. 33–48.
40. "A Few Ideas from the Trenches," *Costco Connection,* September 1997, p. 43; and Kerry A. Dolan, "When Money Isn't Enough," *Forbes,* November 18, 1996, pp. 165–166.
41. Society for Human Resource Management, "Workplace Visions," November/December 1997, downloaded from www.shrm.org/issues.htm, February 2, 1998.
42. Robert McGarvey, "X Appeal," *Entrepreneur,* May 1997, pp. 87–89.
43. Ibid., p. 87.
44. "A Few Ideas"; and Dolan, "When Money," p. 165.

CHAPTER 10

1. Emory Mulling, "Valued Employees Pay Like Happy Customers," *Austin Business Journal,* March 8, 1999, accessed at www.amcity.com; W. L. Gore & Associates Web site, accessed at www.gore.com, March 9, 1999; Shelly Branch, "America's Top Employers," *Fortune,* January 11, 1999, accessed at www.pathfinder.com/fortune; Michael Kaplan, "You Have No Boss," *Fast Company,* no. 11, October/November 1997, p. 226.
2. Jeffrey L. Seglin, "The Happiest Workers in the World," *Inc. Special Issue: The State of Small Business,* May 21, 1996, pp. 62–74.
3. Christopher Palmeri, "Believe in Yourself, Believe in the Merchandise," *Forbes,* September 8, 1997, pp. 118–124.
4. Thomas Petzinger Jr., "Forget Empowerment, This Job Requires Constant Brainpower," *The Wall Street Journal,* October 17, 1997, p. B1.
5. Steve Kaufman, "ESOPs' Appeal on the Increase," *Nation's Business,* June 1997, pp. 43–44; and Joan Szabo, "Share the Wealth," *Entrepreneur,* February 1997, pp. 72–75.
6. Kaufman, "ESOPs' Appeal," p. 43.
7. Ibid., p. 44.
8. Justin Martin, "So, You Want to Work for the Best . . . ,"*Fortune,* January 12, 1998, pp. 77–78.
9. Sherri Eng, "Team Spirit: It Can Be a Winner at Work, But It Takes Practice, Practice, Practice," *San Diego Union-Tribune,* November 10, 1997, pp. D1, D3.
10. Rebecca Blumenstein, "That's Why I Like My Job . . . I Have an Impact on Quality," *The Wall Street Journal,* August 28, 1997, pp. B1, B2.
11. Richard Daft, *Management,* 4th ed. (Fort Worth, Tex.: Dryden Press, 1997), pp. 596–598.
12. Charles C. Snow et al., "Use Transnational Teams to Globalize Your Company," *Organizational Dynamics,* Spring 1996, p. 50.
13. Michael A. Verespej, "Lead, Don't Manage," *Industry Week,* March 4, 1996, pp. 55–60.
14. George Taninecz, "Team Players," *Industry Week,* July 15, 1996, pp. 28–32.
15. Adapted from Daft, *Management,* pp. 600–601.
16. Sylvia Odenwald, "Global Work Teams," *Training & Development,* February 1996, pp. 54–57.
17. Thomas Love, "Keeping the Business Going When an Executive Is Absent," *Nation's Business,* March 1998, p. 10.
18. Nina Munk and Suzanne Oliver, "Women of the Valley," *Forbes,* December 30, 1996, pp. 102–108.

19. Robert McGarvey, "Joining Forces," *Entrepreneur,* September 1996, pp. 80–83.
20. Michele Marchetti, "Why Teams Fail," *Sales & Marketing Management,* June 1997, p. 91.
21. Ibid.
22. Ibid.
23. "Work Week," *The Wall Street Journal,* November 28, 1995, p. A1.
24. Adapted from Daft, *Management,* pp. 602–603.
25. Ronald B. Lieber, "Cool Offices," *Fortune,* December 9, 1996, pp. 204–210.
26. Kenneth Labich, "Elite Teams," *Fortune,* February 19, 1996, pp. 90–99.
27. Hugh McCann, "Straight Talk in Teamland," *Ward's Auto World,* February 1996, pp. 27–30.
28. Jack Robertiello, "Buehler Uses Feedback to Nourish Its Meal Plans," *Supermarket News,* February 3, 1997, pp. 23–24.
29. Louis E. Boone, *Quotable Business* (New York: Random House, 1992), p. 69.
30. Alexander Lucia, "Leaders Know How to Listen," *HRFocus,* April 1997, p. 25.
31. For examples of well-written letters, see Jerry Fischer, "Letter Perfect," *Entrepreneur,* July 1994, pp. 214–216.
32. William R. Pape, "Remote Control," *Inc. Technology,* September 17, 1996, pp. 25–26.
33. Ginger Trumfio, "More than Words," *Sales & Marketing Management,* April 1994, p. 55.
34. Edward T. Hall, *The Silent Language* (Garden City, N.Y.: Doubleday, 1952), p. 209; cited in Louis E. Boone, David L. Kurtz, and Judy R. Block, *Contemporary Business Communication,* 2nd ed. (Englewood Cliffs, N.J.: Prentice-Hall, 1997), p. 71.
35. Roberta Maynard, "Sharing the Wealth—of Information," *Nation's Business,* September 1997, p. 15.
36. Michael Adams, "Mixed Messages," *Sales & Marketing Management,* June 1997, pp. 73–76.
37. Sarah Schafer, "E-Mail Grows Up," *Inc. Technology,* March 18, 1997, pp. 87–88.
38. Barb Cole-Gomolski, "What Overload? IS Thrives on E-Mail," *Computerworld,* December 8, 1997, pp. 1, 14.
39. Based on Daft, *Management,* pp. 575–576.
40. "Five-Year Corporate Study Concludes Fax Prevails over E-Mail," *Business Wire,* April 23, 1996.
41. Stephanie Gruner, "Image Building," *Inc.,* August 1996, p. 87.
42. Norm Leaper, "Ahh . . . the Pitfalls of International Communication," *Communication World,* June–July 1996, pp. 58–60.
43. Martha Cooley, "HR in Russia: Training for Long-Term Success," *HRMagazine,* December 1997, pp. 98–106.
44. Leaper, "Pitfalls of International."

CHAPTER 11
1. AFL-CIO Web site, accessed at www.aflcio.org, March 18, 1999; David Whitford, "Labor's Lost Chance," *Fortune,* September 18, 1998, accessed at www.pathfinder.com/fortune.
2. Steven Greenhouse, "Union Membership Drops Worldwide, U.N. Reports," *New York Times,* November 4, 1997, p. A8.
3. James Worsham, "Labor's New Assault," *Nation's Business,* June 1997, pp. 16–23.

4. "Union Members Summary," January 31, 1997, downloaded from stats.bls.gov/news.release/union2.nws.htm, January 6, 1998.
5. Glen Burkins, "Nursing Homes Are Labor's New Target in Its Promised Return," *The Wall Street Journal,* July 8, 1997, pp. A1, A8.
6. Worsham, "New Assault," p. 20.
7. "Down to the Wire," *Time,* September 16, 1996, p. 68.
8. Bill Vlasic and William C. Symmonds, "Sweet Deal," *Business Week,* September 30, 1996, pp. 32–33.
9. David Woodruff, "'The German Worker Is Making a Sacrifice,'" *Business Week,* July 28, 1997, pp. 46–47.
10. James Bennett, "President Intervenes to Block Strike Next Month at Amtrak," *New York Times,* August 22, 1997, p. A21.
11. Clifford J. Levy, "Panel Upholds Giuliani Offer on Police Pay," *New York Times,* September 5, 1997, pp. B1, B5.
12. "Loss for Third Quarter," UPS press release, November 13, 1997; Jacob M. Schlesinger and Bernard Wysocki, "UPS Pact Fails to Shift Balance of Power Back toward U.S. Workers," *The Wall Street Journal,* August 20, 1997, pp. A1, A6; Aaron Bernstein, "At UPS, Part-Time Work Is a Full-Time Issue," *Business Week,* June 16, 1997, pp. 88–92; and "Strike Out," *CQ Researcher,* June 28, 1996, p. 570.
13. David J. Lynch, "Downsizing Grips Europe: Labor Unions Losing Ground," *USA Today,* September 29, 1997, pp. 1B, 2B.
14. Aaron Bernstein, "'Working Capital': Labor's New Weapon?" *Business Week,* September 29, 1997, pp. 110–112; "Steelworkers Ratify Contract," Wheeling-Pittsburgh Steel press release, August 12, 1997; and Stephen Baker, "Why This Steel Chief Has Such an Iron Will," *Business Week,* May 19, 1997, p. 90.
15. Aaron Bernstein, "'Disaster' for Motown Papers?" *Business Week,* August 4, 1997, pp. 38–40; Jane Slaughter, "Business (as Usual) Unionism in Detroit," *The Nation,* April 14, 1997, p. 10; and Thomas Frank, "Killing News in Motor City," *The Nation,* November 26, 1996, pp. 19–23.
16. Michael A. Verespej, "Wounded & Weaponless," *Industry Week,* September 16, 1996, pp. 46–58.
17. Bob Chase, "President's Viewpoint: Paradigm Lost," *NEA Today,* March 1997, p. 2.
18. Aaron Bernstein, "Look Who's Pushing Productivity," *Business Week,* April 7, 1997, pp. 72–76.
19. Ibid., p. 76.
20. Edward Baig, "When It's Time to Do Battle with Your Company," *Business Week,* February 10, 1997, pp. 130–131.
21. Del Jones, "Firms Fighting, Winning to Keep Unions at Bay," *USA Today,* September 19, 1997, pp. 1B, 2B.
22. "The Trouble with South Korea," *The Economist,* January 18, 1997, pp. 35–37.
23. Gene Epstein, "Lincoln Electric: Highly Motivated," *Barron's,* November 25, 1996, p. 24.
24. Greenhouse, "Union Membership Drops."
25. Verespej, "Wounded & Weaponless," p. 47.
26. Ibid., pp. 51–52.
27. Worsham, "Labor's New Assault," p. 17.
28. Aaron Bernstein, "Sweeney's Blitz," *Business Week,* February 17, 1997, pp. 56–62.
29. Worsham, "Labor's New Assault," p. 16.

30. Aaron Bernstein, "Big Labor Invites a Few Friends Over," *Business Week,* April 21, 1997, p. 44.

31. Worsham, "Labor's New Assault," p. 17.

32. Andrea Andelson, "Union for Doctors to Join Forces with Government Workers," *New York Times,* August 27, 1997, p. A18.

33. Kenneth Jost, "Labor Movement's Future," June 28, 1996, pp. 553–576; and Worsham, "Labor's New Assault," pp. 21–22.

CHAPTER 12

1. Betsy Streisand, "Savoring Private Ryan," *U.S. News & World Report,* February 22, 1999, pp. 49–51; "Between the Lines: The Design and Style of 'The Prince of Egypt,'" Film Ink, accessed March 12, 1999, at www.film-ink.com/reports/1998/december/princeofegypt.shtml; Susan Wloszczyna, "Following 'Prince of Egypt' from Scripture to Script," *USA Today,* December 18, 1998, p. 8E; Chris Woodyard, "DreamWorks Puts 'Prince' to Test," *USA Today,* November 25, 1998, p. 1B.

2. "Development Time Is Money," *Business Week,* January 27, 1997, p. 6. Data from the Product Development & Management Association.

3. "Caterpillar Sets U.S. Export Record," Caterpillar press release, February 27, 1998; and Robert Rose, "Plowing Ahead," *The Wall Street Journal,* October 4, 1994, pp. A1, A12.

4. Print advertisement, ©A. M. Castle & Co. 1997.

5. GM press release, March 13, 1998; and Alex Taylor III, "New Idea from Europe's Automakers," *Fortune,* pp. 159–172.

6. David Hage and Linda Grant, "How to Make America Work," *U.S. News & World Report,* December 6, 1993, pp. 48–54.

7. Mary J. Cronin, "Intranets Reach the Factory Floor," *Fortune,* August 18, 1997, p. 208.

8. John R. Hayes, "Watch Out, Dell," *Forbes,* March 24, 1997, p. 84.

9. Terry Useem, "Company Goes Crazy Over Partnerships, Gets Committed," *Inc.,* June 1997, p. 24.

10. Mark Hendricks, "On the Spot," *Entrepreneur,* May 1997, p. 80.

11. This classic story is told in Michael Hammer, "Reengineering Work: Don't Automate, Obliterate," *Harvard Business Review,* July/August 1990, pp. 104–112.

12. William M. Carley, "To Keep GE's Profits Rising, Welch Pushes Quality-Control Plan," *The Wall Street Journal,* January 13, 1997, pp. A1, A8.

CHAPTER 13

1. "Hollywood Memorabilia Now Showing on eBay," PRNewswire, March 12, 1999; "Onsale Hits Milestone with Ten-Millionth Bid," BusinessWire, March 8, 1999; Richard Chang, "'Click,' Online Auctions Win in Collectibles Frenzy," Reuters Limited, March 5, 1999; David Doran, "Bidding War," *Entrepreneur,* December 1998, p. 24; "Electronic Auction House eBay Draws Big Crowds," *USA Today,* November 15, 1998, p. 8E; and Katharine Mieszkowski, "Wanna Buy? What Am I Bid?" *Fast Company,* November 1998, pp. 288ff.

2. Danielle Kennedy, "The Service Solution," *Entrepreneur,* March 1998, pp. 90–92.

3. Douglas MacDonald, "A Conversation with Dr. Val Feigenbaum," *Tenneco Symposium,* Summer 1992, pp. 20–24.

4. "Information Builders," *InfoWorld,* March 9, 1998, p. 18.

5. Michael McLaughlin, "Now Are You Satisfied?" *Fortune,* February 16, 1998, pp. 161–168.

6. Ian P. Murphy, "Amex Looks beyond Satisfaction, Sees Growth," *Marketing News,* May 12, 1997, pp. 6, 22.

7. Kelly Shermach, "Build a Web Site, and They Will Come," *Marketing News,* May 12, 1997, pp. 6, 12.

8. Judy Sutton, "Hard-to-Reach Ethnic," *Marketing News,* January 5, 1998, p. 2; and Roz Ayers-Williams, "The Changing Face of Nonprofits," *Black Enterprise,* May 1998, pp. 110–114.

9. Laura Koss Feder, "Branding Culture," *Marketing News,* January 5, 1998, pp. 1, 26.

10. Betsy Spethmann, "Cause Celebre," *Promo,* February 1998, pp. 31–32, 126–130.

11. Ibid.

12. Rick Klein, "Eli Lilly Joins Consumer Ad Trend for Diabetes Drugs," *Advertising Age,* June 23, 1997, p. 11.

13. Patrick M. Reilly, "Rich Marketing Alliances Keep Music Stars Glowing," *The Wall Street Journal,* January 22, 1998, pp. B1, B6.

14. Maria Atanasov, "In Moscow, 'Red October' Means Chocolate," *Fortune,* June 9, 1997, p. 40.

15. Justin Martin, "Give 'Em *Exactly* What They Want," *Fortune,* November 10, 1997, pp. 283–285; and information accessed at www.thecustomfoot.com, April 2, 1998.

16. Juliana Koranteng, "Reebok Finds Its Second Wind as It Pursues Global Presence," *Ad Age International,* January 1998, p. 18.

17. S. C. Gwynne, "Thriving on Health Food," *Time,* February 23, 1998, p. 53.

18. Skip Wollenberg, "Tobacco Deal Ends One Battle," *Mobile Register* (November 21, 1998), p. 7B; and Ira Teinowitz, "Tobacco Pact Creates Potential Print Windfall," *Advertising Age* (November 23, 1998), p. 4.

19. Mir Maqbool Alam Khan, "Indian Court Tells Lever to Clean Up Ad Claims," *Ad Age International,* January 1998, p. 32.

20. Jean Halliday, "Mercury Cougar Turns to Internet," *Advertising Age,* January 12, 1998, p. 39.

21. Melanie Berger, "It's Your Move," *Sales & Marketing Management,* March 1998, pp. 45–53.

22. Alexia Parks, "Online Focus Groups Reshape Market Research Industry," *Marketing News,* May 12, 1997, p. 28.

23. Laurie Freeman, "Marketing the Market," *Marketing News,* March 2, 1998, pp. 1, 14.

24. Julie Bort, "Getting Your Data Mart in Shape," *Infoworld,* March 16, 1998, pp. 77–78.

25. Peter Coy, "He Who Mines Data May Strike Fool's Gold," *Business Week,* June 16, 1997, p. 40.

26. Elizabeth Lesly Stevens and Ronald Grover, "The Entertainment Glut," *Business Week,* February 16, 1998, pp. 88–95.

27. Jack Neff, "P&G Reaches Out to Women at Work," *Advertising Age,* November 10, 1997, p. S4.

28. Nicole Crawford, "It's Culture, Not Color," *Promo,* January 1998, pp. 47–50, 132–134; and James B. Arndorfer, "Bank of America Campaign Aims for Asian Americans," *Advertising Age,* June 9, 1997, p. 6.

29. David Leonhardt, "Two-Tier Marketing," *Business Week,* March 17, 1997, pp. 82–90.

30. Freeman, "Marketing the Market."
31. Geoffrey Brewer, "The Customer Stops Here," *Sales & Marketing Management,* March 1998, pp. 31–35.

CHAPTER 14

1. PriceSCAN Web site, accessed at www.pricescan.com, March 12, 1999; "Useful Site of the Day," www.pricescan.com, March 12, 1999; Scott Woolley, "Price War!" *Forbes,* December 14, 1998, pp. 182, 184; "Useful Site of the Day," *Yahoo Internet Life,* May 8, 1997, accessed at www.zdnet.com.
2. Kimberly Patch and Eric Smalley, "Speech Recognition Makes Some Noise," *InfoWorld,* February 2, 1998, pp. 69–74.
3. Philip E. Ross, "Redefining the Term 'User-Friendly,'" *Forbes,* July 7, 1997, pp. 252–260.
4. Kristin Dunlap Godsey, "Terminal Velocity," *Success,* October 1997, p. 12.
5. Ellen Neuborne, "MMM! Cereal for Dinner," *Business Week,* November 24, 1997, pp. 105–106.
6. Gertrude Chavez, "The Buzz: Jollibee Hungers to Export Filipino Tastes, Dominate Asian Fast-Food," *Ad Age International,* March 9, 1998, p. 14.
7. Keith Naughton and Bill Vlasic, "The Nostalgia Boom," *Business Week,* March 23, 1998, pp. 58–64.
8. Bill Vlasic, "Too Many Models, Too Little Focus," *Business Week,* December 1, 1997, p. 148.
9. Susan Jackson, "Batteries Not Included—Ever," *Business Week,* December 8, 1997, p. 46.
10. Stan Crock, "Pilotless Planes: Not Cleared for Takeoff?" *Business Week,* December 8, 1997, pp. 106–111.
11. Constance Gustke, "Built to Last," *Sales & Marketing Management,* August 1997, pp. 78–83.
12. Paul Lukas, "The Ghastliest Product Launches," *Fortune,* March 16, 1998, p. 44.
13. Jack Neff, "Clorox Price Hike Tests Brand's Power," *Advertising Age,* September 27, 1997, pp. 3, 51.
14. Sara Hammel, "What's in a Name? For the Pros, Big Bucks," *U.S. News & World Report,* October 13, 1997, p. 50.
15. Robert McMatch and Thom Forbes, "Look before You Leap," *Entrepreneur,* April 1998, pp. 135–139.
16. Judann Pollack and Jack Neff, "Marketer Decree: Be a Top Brand or Begone," *Advertising Age,* September 15, 1997, pp. 1, 82.
17. Sarah Lorge, "Better Off Branded," *Sales & Marketing Management,* March 1998, pp. 39–42.
18. Gerry Khermouch, "Read This. It's Free," *Brandweek,* June 15, 1997, p. 42.
19. Eric Hall, "Music Retailer Finds Commerce in Communities," *InfoWorld,* February 2, 1998, p. 46.
20. Louis E. Boone, C. M. Kochunny, and Dianne Wilkins, "Applying the Brand Equity Concept to Major League Baseball," *Sports Marketing Quarterly,* Fall 1995, p. 34.
21. Jack Neff, "P&G Redefines the Brand Manager," *Advertising Age,* October 13, 1997, pp. 1, 18, 20.
22. Laurel Wentz, "Brand Management Goes Regional at Ford," *Ad Age International,* October 1997, p. I2.
23. Cyndee Miller, "Marketers Hail Proposed Census Changes," *Marketing News,* April 8, 1996, pp. 1, 6.
24. Gerry Khermouch, Stephanie Thompson, and Karen Benezra,

"Marketers' Pack-a-Day Habit," *Brandweek,* July 7, 1997, pp. 12–20.
25. Lynn Beresford, "It's a Wrap," *Entrepreneur,* March 1997, p. 40.
26. Louise Kramer, "Coca-Cola Updating Core Brand Graphics," *Advertising Age,* January 12, 1998, p. 10.
27. Marilyn Chase, "Pretty Soon the Word 'Organic' on Foods Will Mean One Thing," *The Wall Street Journal,* August 18, 1997, p. B1.
28. Rachel Beck, "Retailers Protest Item Pricing Laws," *Marketing News,* September 15, 1997, p. 35.
29. Jeff Bailey and Scott Kilman, "Here's What's Driving Some Lenders Crazy: Borrowers Who Think," *The Wall Street Journal,* February 20, 1998, pp. A1, A8; and Keven J. Clancy, "At What Profit Price?" *Brandweek,* June 23, 1997, pp. 24–28.
30. Peter Burrows, Larry Armstrong, and Gary McWilliams, "Uh-Oh, They're Going Like Hotcakes," *Business Week,* October 13, 1997, pp. 55, 58; and Ira Sager and Peter Burrows, "I'm Not Gonna Pay a Lot for This Aptiva," *Business Week,* October 13, 1997, p. 59.
31. Dave Casey, "How Low Can You Go?" *Mobile Register,* February 9, 1998, pp. F1, F2.
32. Katherine Bruce, "The Missionary of Pantyhose," *Forbes,* December 15, 1997, pp. 116–118.
33. Michael Czinkota and Ilkka Ronkainen, *International Marketing* (Fort Worth, Tex.: Dryden Press, 1998), pp. 373–378.

CHAPTER 15

1. "Supermarket Highway," *TechWeb,* accessed at www.techweb.com, March 24, 1999; Streamline Web site, accessed at www.streamline.com, March 24, 1999; Christine Eng, "Home Delivery: A Slowly Growing Channel," *Retail Info Systems News,* February 1999, accessed at www.risnews.com; Carol Memmott, "Web Site Streamlines Your Errands," *USA Today,* November 16, 1998, p. 5E; James Lardner, "Please Don't Squeeze the Tomatoes Online," *U.S. News Online,* November 9, 1998, accessed at www.usnews.com; Eric Ransdell, "How Do You Win on the Web?" *Fast Company,* August 1998, pp. 152–165; "Streamline Inc.—Learning Relationship with Customers," *Total Learning & Performance,* 1997, accessed at www.totalearning.com.
2. Marianne Detwiler, "Beyond Beverages: Urban Juice Turns Soda into a Trendy Tonic," *Entrepreneurial Edge* 1 (1998), pp. 60–63.
3. Sarah Schafer, "Have It Your Way," *Entrepreneurial Edge* 1 (1998), pp. 57–64.
4. Wendy Zellner, "A Warehouse Full of Woes at Fleming," *Business Week,* March 3, 1997, pp. 88–90.
5. Damon Darlin, "Channel Change," *Forbes,* August 25, 1997, p. 80.
6. Robert Carey, "Replacing Reps with Middlemen," *Sales & Marketing Management,* February 1997, p. 34.
7. Peter Galuszka, "The $9 Billion Company Nobody Knows," *Business Week,* March 3, 1997, pp. 88–90.
8. Tom Dellecave, Jr., "Beating a Path to Your Door," *Sales & Marketing Management,* May 1997, pp. 124–127.
9. Thomas Petzinger, Jr., "Gasket Salesman Uses E-Mail, Fax,

the Web, and Shoe Leather," *The Wall Street Journal,* April 4, 1997, p. B1.

10. Susan Jackson and Tim Smart, "Mom and Pop Fight Back," *Business Week,* April 14, 1997, p. 46.

11. William J. Holstein and Kerry Hannon, "They Drop Till You Shop," *U.S. News & World Report,* July 21, 1997, p. 51.

12. Anthony Bianco, "Virtual Bookstores Start to Get Real," *Business Week,* October 27, 1997, pp. 146–148.

13. Luisa Kroll, "Good Service Sells," *Forbes,* January 12, 1998, pp. 198–200.

14. Ronald J. Alsop, ed., *The Wall Street Journal Almanac 1998* (New York: Ballantine Books, 1997), p. 281.

15. Ibid., p. 282.

16. Louis E. Boone and David L. Kurtz, *Contemporary Marketing 1999* (Fort Worth, Tex.: Dryden Press, 1999), p. 520.

17. Elizabeth Weise, "Shopping the Superhighway," *USA Today,* December 10, 1997, p. D1.

18. Heather Green, Gail DeGeorge, and Amy Barrett, "The Virtual Mall Gets Real," *Business Week,* January 26, 1998, pp. 90–91.

19. Pete Hisey, "Wal-Mart Seeks Shoppers with Online Service," *Discount Store News,* August 19, 1996, pp. 1, 54.

20. Beth Snyder, "Stores Battle Publishers for Online Gift Registries," *Advertising Age,* March 16, 1998, p. 34.

21. National Automatic Merchandising Association, www.vending.org, January 1998.

22. Company literature from Kmart Web site, accessed at www.kmart.com, March 23, 1998.

23. William C. Symonds, "Talbots Drops the 'Funkier Stuff,'" *Business Week,* October 6, 1997, pp. 164–166.

24. Calmetta Y. Coleman, "Selling Jewelry, Dolls, and TVs next to Corn Flakes," *The Wall Street Journal,* November 11, 1997, p. B1.

25. Christopher Palmeri, "Wicked Screwdriver Guys," *Forbes,* September 22, 1997, pp. 150–151.

26. Ann Marsh and Scott Woolley, "The Customer Is Always Right? Not at Fry's," *Forbes,* November 2, 1997, pp. 86–90.

27. Gloria Lau, "Know Thy Customers," *Forbes,* July 7, 1997, p. 76.

28. International Council of Shopping Centers, accessed at www.icsc.org, March 18, 1998.

29. Ibid.

30. Susan Reda, "Chains Find that In-Town Locations Answer Shopper Demands for Convenience and Newness While Avoiding the Sameness of Malls," *Store,* November 1997, accessed at www.store.org, March 23, 1998.

31. Ibid.

32. Eric Ransdell, "REI: Adventures in Retailing," *Fast Company,* December/January 1998, pp. 182–191.

33. Cacilie Rohwedder, "U.S. Catalog Firms Go after Europeans," *The Wall Street Journal,* January 6, 1998, p. A15.

34. James Cox, "Catalogers Expand in Asia," *USA Today,* October 18, 1996, p. 4B.

35. Tara Parker-Pope, "Why the Veterinarian Really Recommends that 'Designer' Chow," *The Wall Street Journal,* November 3, 1997, p. A1.

36. Carrie Shook, "Making Haste Slowly," *Forbes,* September 22, 1997, pp. 220–222.

37. "Apple Lifts Two Distributors, Cuts Three," *Newsbytes News Network,* accessed at www.newsbytes.com, November 3, 1997.

38. Lisa Rauck, "Made in the U.S.A.," *Entrepreneurial Edge* 1 (1998), pp. 70–71.

39. Gina M. Larson, "Suddenly Sneakers," *Entrepreneurial Edge* 1 (1998), pp. 61–63.

40. Tim W. Ferguson, "A Revolution that Has a Long Way to Go," *Forbes,* August 11, 1997, pp. 106–112.

41. Linda Himelstein, "Levi's Is Hiking Up Its Pants," *Business Week,* December 1, 1997, pp. 70–75.

42. Richard Behar, "Why Subway Is the Biggest Problem in Franchising," *Fortune,* March 16, 1998, pp. 126–134.

43. Bernard Warner, "Selling on Site," *AdWeek,* September 29, 1997, pp. 43–44.

44. Clinton Wilder, "Emerging E-Commerce—Supply Chain: Middlemen Beware?" *Information Week,* October 20, 1997, p. 94.

45. Robert Mottley, "How The Gap Fills Its Gaps in Logistics," *American Shipper,* January 1997, pp. 36–39.

46. "How Mickey Mouse Ears Make Their Way to the Magic Kingdom," *Modern Materials Handling,* accessed at www.manufacturing.net, July 1997.

47. James Flanigan, "Delivering the Goods: Moving Merchandise is Shaping Up to Be a Hot Southland Industry," *Los Angeles Times,* April 2, 1997, p. D1.

48. Chris Gillis, "Logistics and Marketing," *American Shipper,* March 1997, pp. 42–46.

49. Tom Andel, "Carrier Selection Tools: Open a Window to Service," *Transportation & Distribution,* July 1996, pp. 27–32.

50. American Association of Railroads, downloaded from www.aar.org, March 23, 1998.

51. Gregory Morris, "Keeping the Gateways Open: Shippers Try to Maintain Options," *Chemical Week,* September 24, 1997, p. 31.

52. Ibid.

53. Boone and Kurtz, *Contemporary Marketing 1999,* p. 542.

54. Gillis, "Logistics and Marketing."

55. Karen Auguston Field and Gary Forger, "Delivering the Magic of Disney World," *Modern Materials Handling,* July 1, 1997, accessed at www.manufacturing.net, March 19, 1998.

56. Tom Feare, "Lennox's New DC Turns Up Heat on Competitors," *Modern Materials Handling,* December 1, 1997, accessed at www.manufacturing.net, March 1998.

57. Mottley, "Fills Gaps."

58. Gary Forger, "Alberto-Culver Washes Inefficiency Out of Its Warehouses," *Modern Materials Handling,* September 1, 1997, accessed at www.manufacturing.net, March 26, 1998.

CHAPTER 16

1. "Chief Underpants Officer," *Fast Company,* "Job Titles of the Future," accessed at www.timeslink.com, March 24, 1999; Barbara Flanagan, "Underneath It All, the Name Counts," *New York Times,* February 4, 1999, p. F3; John Greenwood, "Dang, I Forgot to Put My Underwear On," *National Post,* January 23, 1999, p. D1; Susan Carpenter, "Fashion Forward Vending Machine Undies," *Los Angeles Times,* December 16, 1998, p. E2; and T.L. Stanley, "Guerilla Marketers of the Year," *Brandweek,* November 23, 1998, pp. 18–26.

2. "Cliffhanger," *Adweek,* July 21, 1997, p. 37.
3. "Airing Your Underwear," *Promo,* September 1997, p. 12; and "Brief Marketing," *Marketing News,* September 16, 1997, p. 2.
4. "Be Your Own Rock," *Adweek,* July 21, 1997, p. 41.
5. "Some Customers Are King," *Business Week,* November 17, 1997, pp. 2–3.
6. Dottie Enrico, "AT&T Makes Connection with Ad Campaign," *USA Today,* May 19, 1997, p. 6B.
7. Robert Langreth, "Three Drug Makers, Helped by Ads, Post Higher Profits," *The Wall Street Journal,* October 22, 1997, p. B4; and Catherine Arnst, "Is Good Marketing Bad Medicine?" *Business Week,* April 13, 1998, pp. 62–63.
8. Laura Tiffany, "Here's the Scoop," *Business Start-Ups,* December 1997, p. 32.
9. "Don't Mess with Dinner," *Adweek,* July 21, 1997, p. 39.
10. Ian P. Murphy, "Bowling Industry Rolls Out Unified Marketing Plan," *Marketing News,* January 20, 1997, p. 2.
11. "100 Leaders by U.S. Advertising Spending," *Advertising Age,* September 21, 1997, p. S4.
12. Ellen Neuborne, "More Bang for the Super Bowl Bucks," *Business Week,* February 2, 1998, p. 70.
13. Yumiko Ono, "Pore Strips Clean Up with Grimy Pitches," *The Wall Street Journal,* January 23, 1998, pp. B1, B5.
14. James B. Arndorfer, "AmEx Takes Another Swipe at Visa in New Commercials," *Advertising Age,* June 16, 1997, p. 59.
15. "Too Much Good Stuff," *Adweek,* July 24, 1997, p. 43.
16. Jan D. Markman, "5-Year Outlook," *Adweek,* September 8, 1997, p. 38.
17. "Newspapers Find Net Friendly, Not a Rival," *San Diego Union-Tribune,* March 17, 1998, p. 11.
18. Richard Katz, "Network TV: Eroding but Not Going Away," *Adweek,* September 8, 1997, p. 8.
19. Jill Goldsmith, "New System Eases Ad Buying on Cable TV," *The Wall Street Journal,* March 12, 1998, p. B10; and Ronald Grover, "Is It Prime Time for Cable?" *Business Week,* September 8, 1997, pp. 94–98.
20. Melanie Wells, "Networks Pay when Viewers Stay Away," *USA Today,* October 10, 1997, pp. 1B–2B.
21. Roy Furchgott, "Turning Shower Scum into Gold," *Business Week,* November 17, 1997, pp. 8–10.
22. Susan Headden, "The Junk Mail Deluge," *U.S. News & World Report,* December 8, 1997, pp. 40–48.
23. Barbara Martinez, "Catalogers Hope Smarter Mailings Bring Better Results as Holiday Rush Begins," *The Wall Street Journal,* December 1, 1997, p. B10.
24. Sally Goll Beatty, "Billboard Firms Ease into Smokeless Era," *The Wall Street Journal,* October 30, 1997, p. B6.
25. Joshua Levine, "Zap-Proof Advertising," *Forbes,* September 22, 1997, pp. 146–147.
26. Richard Covington, "Companies Find the Net Helps Trap Surprising Sources of Revenue," *International Herald Tribune,* February 23, 1998, accessed at http://www.iht.com.
27. "Online Ads Generate $1 Billion," *Reuters,* December 4, 1997.
28. Al Urbanski, "Sweet Site," *Promo,* September 1997, pp. 31–33.
29. Alice Ann Love, "Companies Want to Cut Coupons, but Consumers Demand Bargains," *Marketing News,* May 12, 1997, p. 15.

30. "Excedrin Program Provides Headache Relief," *Brandweek,* May 5, 1997, p. 58.
31. "Where Merchandise Carries the Message," *Promo,* August 1997, p. 10.
32. Michele Marchetti, "Hey Buddy, Can You Spare $113.25?" *Sales & Marketing Management,* August 1997, p. 70.
33. Michele Marchetti, "Is Cold Calling Worth It?" *Sales & Marketing Management,* August 1997, p. 103.
34. Karren Mills, "Wilson Getting Piece of Growth Consulting Action," *Lexington Herald-Leader,* November 17, 1997, accessed at http://www.newsworks.com.
35. Sarah Schafer, "Supercharged Sell," *Inc. Tech 1997,* pp. 42–51.
36. Jeremy Schlosberg, "Closing the Sale," *VAR Business,* February 1, 1997, accessed at http://www.techweb.com.
37. Kristin Hussey, "New Phone Scams Result in Unauthorized Charges," *The Capital,* March 2, 1998, accessed at http://www.newsworks.com.
38. Marchetti, "Can You Spare?"
39. Erika Rasmussen, "The Check's in the Mail," *Sales & Marketing Management,* June 1997, p. 16.
40. Schafer, "Supercharged Sell."
41. "Companies Will Spend 13% More on Sponsorships," *Marketing News,* February 2, 1998, p. 7.
42. Patrick M. Reilly, "Rich Marketing Alliances Keep Music Stars Glowing," *The Wall Street Journal,* January 22, 1998, pp. B1, B6.
43. Ellen Neuborne, "This Exhibit Is Brought to You By . . . ," *Business Week,* November 10, 1997, pp. 91–94.
44. Kate Fitzgerald, "Samples Go on Tour," *Advertising Age,* May 5, 1997, p. 37.
45. Kevin Helliker, "Old Fashioned PR Gives General Mills Advertising Bargains," *The Wall Street Journal,* March 20, 1997, pp. A1, A6.
46. Melanie Wells, "The Quest for Free Ink, Free Air," *USA Today,* May 19, 1997, p. 3B.
47. Dottie Enrico, "Free Publicity Sometimes Can Be a Touchy Issue," *USA Today,* May 19, 1997, p. 7B.
48. Kate Fitzgerald, "Nintendo," *Advertising Age,* June 30, 1997, p. 20.
49. James Collins, "Gross and Grosser," *Time,* March 23, 1998, pp. 75–76; and Ronald Grover, "If These Shows Are Hits, Why Do They Hurt So Much?" *Business Week,* April 13, 1998, p. 36.

CHAPTER 17

1. Rubric Web site, accessed at www.rubricsoft.com, March 24, 1999; "Rubric and Vantive Partner to Deliver Integrated Front Office Applications to Build Customer Relationships," company press release, Business Wire, March 23, 1999; "BEA WebLogic Supports Real-Time Application for Fortune 1,000 and E-Commerce Customers," *Java Industry Connection,* February 18, 1999; and Elizabeth Weise, "Start-Up Bets Big on Computer Age," *USA Today,* November 16, 1998, pp. 18E–19E.
2. G. Christian Hill, "Bringing It Home," *The Wall Street Journal,* June 16, 1997, pp. R1, R4.
3. Jeffrey Young and Julie Pitta, "Wal-Mart or Western Union?" *Forbes,* July 7, 1997, pp. 244–246.

4. Bill Meyers, "Digital Devices Becoming 12th Man on the Team," *USA Today,* October 10, 1997, pp. 1A, 2A.

5. Hill, "Bringing It Home," p. R4.

6. Africa Gordon, "Technology Permeates Life on Many Campuses," *USA Today,* June 17, 1997, p. 12E; "IBM/CollegeNET Alliance Accelerates WWW Revolution in Applying to College," Universal Algorithms press release, July 29, 1997.

7. Martha Rogers, "Transforming the Selling Process to Strengthen Customer Relationships," *Inside 1to1,* October 23, 1997, distributed via e-mail.

8. Thomas Hoffman, "Linking Business Partners," *Computer-World Intranets,* June 23, 1997, pp. 2–3.

9. R. F. Sharp, "Flowing with Technology," *Lexington Herald-Leader,* September 28, 1997.

10. Bruce Schwartz, "Power of the Byte Drives Transition to Innovation Age," *USA Today,* June 17, 1997, p. 1E; and Mike Snider, "The Digital Frontier," *USA Today,* June 17, 1997, pp. 1E–2E.

11. Tapscott, *The Digital Economy* (New York: McGraw-Hill, 1996), p. 9.

12. Henry Goldblatt, "Your Next Phone Call May Be via the Net," *Fortune,* June 23, 1997, pp. 139-140; and Mark Winter, "The Mouse that Roared over IP," International Data Corp., July 17, 1997, downloaded from www.idcresearch.com, August 24, 1997.

13. Tapscott, *The Digital Economy,* pp. 222, 225.

14. Gerry McGovern, "Sharing," *New Thinking,* September 16, 1997.

15. Amy Cortese, "Why Microsoft Is Glued to the Tube," *Business Week,* September 22, 1997, pp. 96–102.

16. "Why Internet Advertising?" *Brandweek,* May 5, 1997, p. 10.

17. Vince Matthews, "Disney Shows off D-mail," C|Net News.com, June 19, 1997, downloaded from www.news.com, October 7, 1997; and Jeff Pelline, "Disney Buys Family Planet Site," C|Net News.com, April 18, 1997, downloaded from www.news.com, October 7, 1997.

18. Robert J. Hawkins, "That Rumble Is 'Tanarus' Ready to Roll," *San Diego Union Tribune ComputerLink,* November 18, 1997, p. 4; Michael Kanellos, "Sony to Put Web Browsing in Planes," C|Net News.com, October 1, 1997, downloaded from www.news.com, October 8, 1997.

19. Judy Artunian, "Telemedicine Moves into the Mainstream," *Case Review,* Fall 1997.

20. Steven Hepker, "Technology on the 'Mooooo've," *Jackson Citizen Patriot,* July 20, 1997.

21. "The Future of IT: A Gartner Group Report," *Forbes* special supplement, September 22, 1997, pp. 5–6.

22. Peter Burrows, "HP Pictures the Future," *Business Week,* July 7, 1997, pp. 100–109; and Tim Clark, "HP Now an E-Commerce Power," C|Net News.com, April 24, 1997, downloaded from www.news.com, August 4, 1997.

23. Simon Barker-Benfield, "Automation Replacing Mortgage Banking Jobs," *Jacksonville (Florida) Times-Union,* May 19, 1997; and Ellen Neuborne, "Productivity Jumps; Technology Gets Credit," *USA Today,* June 19, 1997, p. B1.

24. David H. Freedman, "Steel Edge," *Forbes ASAP,* October 6, 1997, pp. 52–53.

25. Jim Bair, "Knowledge Management: The Era of Shared Ideas," in "Future of IT," p. 28.

26. Jennifer Tanaka, "There's No Place Like Home, Unless It's the Office," *Newsweek,* July 7, 1997, p. 14; and "Telecommuting on the Rise," *Reuters News Service,* October 8, 1997.

27. Neuborne, "Productivity Jumps."

28. Freedman, "Steel Edge," p. 47.

29. Joan O'C. Hamilton, "When Science Fiction Becomes Social Reality," *Business Week,* March 10, 1997, pp. 84–85.

30. "Internet Domain Survey, July 1997," downloaded from www.nw.com, September 26, 1997; and "NUA Internet Surveys Review and Analysis," March/April 1997 and May/June 1997, downloaded from www.nua.ie, September 7, 1997.

31. Amy Cortese, "A Census in Cyberspace," *Business Week,* May 5, 1997, p. 84.

32. Jube Shiver, Jr., "The New Marketplace," *Los Angeles Times,* September 9, 1997.

33. David M. Halbfinger, "Computer Kiosks Ease Dealing with Bureaucracy," *New York Times,* September 9, 1997.

34. Christina Valdez Diaz, "Buyers, Sellers Connect Online," *USA Today,* June 17, 1997, p. 9E.

35. J. D. Mosley-Mathcett, "Show Me the (Cyber) Money!" *Marketing News,* June 9, 1997, p. 18.

36. Tim Clark, "Business E-Commerce to Top $8 Billion," C|Net News.com, July 29, 1997, downloaded from www.news.com, July 29, 1997.

37. Nick Wrede, "E-Commerce Goes from EDI to Extranets," August 15, 1997, downloaded from http://webtech.com, October 8, 1997.

38. David Wilson, "Net Gain," *San Jose Mercury News,* October 12, 1997.

39. Shiver, "New Marketplace."

40. Annette Hamilton, "How the Web Was Won," *ZDNet Anchor Desk,* November 17, 1997; and Valdez Diaz, "Buyers, Sellers Connect."

41. Mitch Wagner and Sharon Gaudin, "Keeping Sites Open," and "While E-Commerce Firms Sweat Out Shaky Net Reliability . . . ," *ComputerWorld,* July 28, 1997, p. 14.

42. Tim Clark, "Privacy Group Promotes Compliance Logo," C|Net News.com, June 26, 1997, downloaded from www.news.com, August 30, 1997.

43. Jeff Carlson, "Making Sense of the Web Process," downloaded from www.thunderlizard.com, September 24, 1997.

44. David Noack, "Choosing the Right Path to the Net," *Nation's Business,* March 1997, p. 16.

45. Mark Halper, "So Does Your Web Site Pay?" *Forbes ASAP,* August 25, 1997, p. 117; and Del Jones, "High Web Site Pay Doesn't Reflect Revenue," *USA Today,* July 16, 1997, p. 4B.

46. Howard Millman, "WebMaker: MCI, Intel, and Vanstar Find the Right Balance," *Infoworld,* March 31, 1997, p. 44B.

47. Kerr Pechter, "Intel Wants to be 'Nike of Computer Business' in China," *Ad Age International,* June 1997, pp. I2, I6.

48. Sharon Machlis, "Europe's Dreaming of an E-Christmas," *ComputerWorld,* November 10, 1997, p. 29.

49. "Ameritech to Buy 42% of Danish Phone Company," *The Wall Street Journal,* October 28, 1997.

50. "NUA Internet Surveys Review and Analysis," March-April 1997, downloaded from www.nua.ie, September 7, 1997.

51. Kevin Maney, "Technology Is 'Demolishing' Time, Distance," *USA Today,* April 24, 1997, pp. 1B, 2B.

52. Lynn Beresford, "Global Smarts: Toy Story," *Entrepreneur,* February 1997, p. 38.

53. Michael Tarsala, "IBM's Plan for Home, Sweet Cyberhome," *Investor's Business Daily,* June 6, 1997.

54. Janet Purdy Levaux, "Medicine 2010: Will Computers Be a Panacea?" *Investor's Business Daily,* March 6, 1997.

55. "Defense Department to Make Deep Cuts in Civilian Personnel," *The Wall Street Journal,* November 11, 1997, p. A20.

56. Predictions based on information in Neil Gross, "Into the Wild Frontier," *Business Week,* June 23, 1997, pp. 72–84; and Peter Schwartz and Peter Leyden, "The Long Boom," *Wired,* July 1997, pp. 116–173.

CHAPTER 18

1. Xerox Web site, accessed at www.xerox.com, March 25, 1999; "Xerox Ships DocuShare 2.0, Creates Powerful Knowledge Sharing Platform," company news release, March 9, 1999, accessed at www.xerox.com; Marc Ferranti, "Xerox Fashions Raft of Products as Digital 'Portals,'" *InfoWorld Electric,* November 19, 1998, accessed at www.infoworld.com; "What Else Would You Like to Know about Encanto?" company news release, January 27, 1998, accessed at www.encanto.com.

2. Robert S. Boyd, "Science Agency Worries about an Information Glut," *San Jose Mercury News,* February 11, 1998, pp. 1C, 6C.

3. Alessandra Bianchi, "A Line on Benefits," *Inc. Technology,* November 15, 1997, p. 112.

4. Elaine M. Cummings and Miryam Williamson, "Tools of the Trade," *CIO,* July 1997, pp. 70–72.

5. Jay Finegan, "Joining Forces," *CIO Web Business,* December 1, 1997, pp. 42–44.

6. See Sarah Schafer, "Beyond Horsepower," *Inc. Technology,* March 18, 1997, p. 74; and Heather Page, "Have It Your Way," *Entrepreneur,* January 1997, p. 20.

7. Tariq K. Muhammad, "Rex in Effect," *Black Enterprise,* February 1998, p. 60.

8. Len Strazewski, "Take Office Along—in a Pocket," *Crain's Small Business,* June 1997, p. T1.

9. Miguel Helft, "Java's New Reality," *San Jose Mercury News,* February 9, 1998, pp. 1E, 4E.

10. Alessandra Bianchi, "At Your Service," *Inc. Technology,* November 15, 1997, p. 113.

11. Jenny C. McCune, "E-Mail Etiquette," *Management Review,* April 1997, pp. 14–15.

12. William R. Pape, "Group Insurance," *Inc. Technology,* June 15, 1997, pp. 29, 31.

13. Emily Kay, "Hello Mr. Chips! Multimedia in the Classroom," *Inside Technology Training,* June 1997, pp. 19–20, 22.

14. Sarah Schafer, "Supercharged Sell," *Inc. Technology,* June 15, 1997, pp. 42–45.

15. James A. Crapko, "Chrysler Shifts Gears," *Inside Technology Training,* January 1998, pp. 32–33.

16. Anne Field, "Class Act," *Inc. Technology,* March 18, 1997, pp. 55–57, 59.

17. Derek Slater, "Wary of Groupware?" *CIO Enterprise,* November 15, 1997, p. 74.

18. Sarah Schafer, "Is Your Data Safe?" *Inc. Technology,* June 15, 1997, pp. 93–97.

19. Tom Field, "Getting in Touch with Your Inner Web," *CIO,* January 15, 1997, pp. 38–39.

20. Debby Young, "AT&T's Intranet Reaches Out to Touch Everyone," *CIO Web Business,* October 1, 1997, p. 78.

21. E. B. Baatz, "Net Results," *CIO,* February 1, 1997, accessed at www.cio.com.

22. Thomas E. Ricks and John Simons, "FBI Probes Break-ins at Military Computers," *The Wall Street Journal,* February 26, 1998, p. B8; and "Computer Crime Getting Worse, Says U.S. Watchdog Group," Reuters Limited, March 4, 1998.

23. Sarah Schafer, "Is Your Data Safe?" *Inc. Technology,* June 15, 1997, pp. 93–97.

24. Greg Beaubien, "Computer Ripoffs on the Rise," *Crain's Small Business,* June 1997, p. T6.

25. Robert McGarvey, "Good Medicine," *Entrepreneur,* March 1997, p. 28.

26. Joshua Macht, "A River Runs through It," *Inc. Technology,* June 17, 1997, p. 21.

CHAPTER 19

1. Johnson & Johnson Web site, accessed at www.jnj.com, April 8, 1999; Stephen H. Wildstrom, "Surfing for Annual Reports," *Business Week,* April 14, 1997, p. 22; and Richard J. Koreto, "When the Bottom Line Is Online," *Journal of Accountancy,* March 1997, pp. 63–65.

2. "Employment and Earnings," U.S. Department of Labor, Bureau of Labor Statistics, January 1997.

3. Sarah Fuhrmann, "Putting Fun into Finance," *Monsanto Magazine,* 1997, pp. 24–26; and John Case, "The Open Book Revolution," *Inc.,* June 1995, pp. 26–43.

4. Richard J. Koreto, "New Technology Helps the Older Client: A Practical Site Reaps Marketing Rewards," *Journal of Accountancy,* January 1997, pp. 69–71.

5. Sean Flynn, "Beverage Isle," *Boston Magazine,* March 1997, p. 23; and Katrina Burger, "A Drink with an Attitude," *Forbes,* February 10, 1997.

6. Lee Berton, "Big Six's Shift to Consulting Accelerates," *The Wall Street Journal,* September 21, 1995, p. B1.

7. Dan McGraw, "One Plus One Leaves Five," *U.S. News & World Report,* September 29, 1997, p. 66; Jill Andresky Fraser, "How Many Accountants Does It Take to Change an Industry?" *Inc.,* April 1997, pp. 63–69; and Ernst & Young's Web site for Management Consulting Services, www.eyi.com.

8. William L. Reeb and Michaelle Camero, "Getting Beyond Counting," *Journal of Accountancy,* December 1996, pp. 69–72.

9. Ibid., p. 71.

10. Ellen DePasquale, "Winning Numbers," *Inc. Technology,* September 1996, pp. 84–87.

11. Dennis Keeling, "A Buyers' Guide: High-End Accounting Software," *Journal of Accountancy,* December 1996, pp. 43–52.

12. Ibid., p. 44.

13. Tania Chau, Jon Goldstein, Anita Hamilton, and Melissa Scram, "Cyber Elite," *Time Digital,* September 15, 1997, p. 30; "Corporate Scoreboard," *Business Week,* May 12, 1997, p. 144; and Michael K. Ozanian and Kurt Badenhausen, "The 100 Best Growth Companies," *Financial World,* January 21, 1997, p. 53.

14. Ralph Ortina, "Continuous Budgeting at the HON Company," *Management Accounting,* January 1996, p. 20.

15. John S. McClenahen, "A Pocketful of Euro-Change," *Industry Week,* May 5, 1997, pp. 21–24.

16. "Global Accounting's Roadblock," *The Economist,* April 27, 1996, pp. 79–80.

CHAPTER 20

1. David Bank, "Making a Map of the Internet Universe," *The Wall Street Journal,* April 8, 1999, accessed at www.nrstg1s.djnr.com; SEC Web site, accessed at www.sec.gov, April 8, 1999; Michael Collins, "Enhanced EDGAR on the Way," *CBS MarketWatch,* April 4, 1999, accessed at cbs.marketwatch.com; Randall W. Forsyth, "These Web sites Let You Grab Data to Play with Later," *Barron's,* March 29, 1999, p. 45, accessed at nrstg1s.djnr.com; Jonathan Oatis, "Edgar II: This Time It's Commercial," Reuters Limited, March 28, 1999; Jeff Harrington, "SEC Polices Internet to Combat Fraud," *Knight-Ridder Tribune Business News,* March 27, 1999, accessed at nrstg1s.djnr.com.

2. C. Meyrick Payne et al., "The Route to the Top," *Chief Executive,* December 1995, p. 24; and Louis E. Boone, Janelle Emmert Goodnight, and Jeanne Harris, "Leading Corporate America in an Era of Change: A Statistical Profile of Chief Executive Officers," *USA Working Papers,* 1995.

3. Dan Sewell, "Hand-Picked Successor Expected to Replace Goizueta at Coke," *The Sheboygan Press,* October 20, 1997, p. A10.

4. Ronald B. Lieber, "Secrets of the Superstars," *Fortune,* September 29, 1997, pp. 81–82; and "About Sylvan Learning Systems, Inc.," downloaded from www.educate.com, October 16, 1997.

5. Kelly Greene, "Losses, Delays Plague Internet Bank," *The Wall Street Journal,* May 28, 1997, p. 54.

6. Jill Andresky Fraser, "I Need a Bank That Can Handle Our International Business," *Inc.,* February 1997, p. 98.

7. U.S. Treasury Department Web page, downloaded November 14, 1997; "Multimillion-Dollar Push," *Mobile Press Register,* March 2, 1996, p. 7B; and "Coming Soon: Big Ben. Later: Ample Abe," *U.S. News & World Report,* October 9, 1995, p. 18.

8. "The Cashless Society," *The Economist,* March 15, 1997, pp. 77–78; and Bill Powell, "How to Survive in the Sour Cream Economy," *Newsweek,* November 11, 1996, p. 55.

9. Elaine Pofeldt, "The Self-Made Woman," *Success,* June 1997, pp. 37–46.

10. Tariq K. Muhammad, "The Branding of BET," *Black Enterprise,* June 1997, pp. 156–171.

11. Seth Lubove, "The Pickled Palm Man," *Forbes,* August 12, 1996, pp. 86–87.

12. Steven F. Riggs, "Other People's Money," *Self-Employed Professional,* September/October 1997, pp. 24–31.

13. Ibid., p. 24.

14. Nina Munk and Suzanne Oliver, "Women of the Valley," *Forbes,* December 30, 1996, pp. 102–108.

15. Riggs, "Other People's Money," p. 24.

16. Ibid., pp. 30–31; and Jill Andresky Fraser, "The Deal," *Inc.,* October 1996, pp. 56–64.

17. "Fortune 1000 Ranked within Industries," *Fortune,* April 28, 1997, p. F-46.

18. Peter Galauszka, David Lindorff, and Carol Marlack, "Are ATMs Still Money in the Bank?" *Business Week,* June 9, 1997, pp. 96, 98.

19. Ibid.

20. Ellen Benoit, "Slouching toward the Checkless Society," *Institutional Investor,* November 1996, p. 23; and "Corporate America Not Yet Paperless," *Bank Systems & Technology,* June 1996, p. 12.

21. Janet Novak, "The Check Is Not in the Mail," *Forbes,* September 9, 1996, p. 140.

22. Margaret Mannix, "Keeping a Check on Debit Card Liability," *U.S. News & World Report,* September 8, 1997, p. 23; and Christine Dugas, "Debit Card Convenience Comes with Caveat," *USA Today,* May 30, 1997, p. 5B.

23. Tariq K. Muhammad, "Electronic Commerce and the Future of Money," *Black Enterprise,* June 1997, p. 257; and Nikhil Deogun, "The Smart Money Is on the Smart Cards, but Electronic Cash Seems Dumb to Some," *The Wall Street Journal,* August 5, 1996, pp. B1, B8.

24. Nicholas Retsinas, "What Does the Future Hold for the Thrift Industry?" *American Banker,* November 14, 1996, p. 3.

25. Telephone interview with Bob Loftus, National Credit Union Administration, January 7, 1997.

26. Eileen Gunn, "How to Maximize Your Pension Payout," *Fortune,* October 28, 1996, p. 233.

27. Diane Harris, "Smart Ways to Shop the New Financial Supermarkets," *Money,* June 1997, pp. 101–113.

28. The discussion of the Federal Reserve's monetary tools is based on *The Story of Monetary Policy,* Federal Reserve Bank of New York, Public Information Department, 1996.

29. David Connor, "Home and Away," *The Banker,* February 1996, pp. 44–48.

30. "The Fortune Global 500 Ranked within Industries," *Fortune,* August 4, 1997, pp. F16–F17.

31. James Kraus, "Hibernia to Advise Belize Government on Project Finance," *American Banker,* January 2, 1997, p. 7.

CHAPTER 21

1. Ameritrade Web site, accessed at www.ameritrade.com, April 16, 1999; Andrew Cave, "City: US Broker's $8bn Web Feat," *The Daily Telegraph,* April 16, 1999, accessed at nrstg1p.djnr.com; Rebecca Buckman, "Heard on the Street: Ameritrade Rockets as Online Trading Surges," *The Wall Street Journal,* April 15, 1999, accessed at www.wsj.doc; "Profit-Taking Hits Highflying Online Brokerage Sector," *Dow Jones Business News,* April 15, 1999, accessed at nrstg1p.djnr.com; "Ameritrade Posts Record Profits, New Accounts Soar," Reuters Limited, April 14, 1999; Douglas Gerlach, "Trading Places: The Top Online Brokers," *PC World,* February 1999, accessed at www.pcworld.com; Kathleen Ohlson, "Complaints by Online Traders Skyrocket," *Computerworld,* January 28, 1999, accessed at www.computerworld.com; Jack Reerink, "Interview—Ameritrade Aims for Rapid Growth," *Money* magazine, April 29, 1998, accessed at www.pathfinder.com.

2. James A. Anderson, "Taking Your Company Public," *Black Enterprise,* June 1997, pp. 237–243; Jennifer Westhaven,

"January Effect May Rescue IPOs Temporarily," *Money,* December 31, 1997, www.pathfinder.com.money, January 28, 1998.

3. "VimpelCom Reports 41% Increase in Second Quarter Earnings; 110% Year-to-Year Subscriber Growth," company press release, August 27, 1997.

4. Stephen D. Solomon, "Follow the Money," *Inc.,* June 1997, pp. 80–81.

5. David R. Evanson, "Direct Hit," *Entrepreneur,* June 1997, pp. 68–71; and Stephanie Gruner, "When Mom & Pop Go Public," *Inc.,* December 1996, pp. 56–73.

6. Michael Krantz, "Moguls by the Million," *Time,* September 29, 1997, pp. 43–44.

7. J. Schulz, "Offerings Online," *Worth,* Special Issue, July 1997, pp. 75–79.

8. Gary Hamel, "Killer Strategies That Make Shareholders Rich," *Fortune,* June 23, 1997, pp. 70–80.

9. "Gimme 500 IBM and a Cheese Danish," *Time,* November 10, 1997, p. 27.

10. Suzanne Woolley, "The Booming Big Board," *Business Week,* August 4, 1997, pp. 58–64.

11. Ibid., p. 62.

12. Eileen P. Gunn, "Emerging Markets," *Fortune,* August 18, 1997, pp. 168–173.

13. Steve Zwick, "GLOBEX Wins, Loses a Few," *Futures: Magazine of Commodities & Options,* May 1993, p. 12.

14. Leah Nathans Spiro and Linda Himelstein, "With the World Wide Web, Who Needs Wall Street?" *Business Week,* April 29, 1996, pp. 120–121.

15. Matthew Schifrin, "Cyber-Schwab," *Forbes,* May 5, 1997, pp. 42–43.

16. Daniel Strachman, "NationsBanc's Trading Software Slashes Compliance Costs," *American Banker,* March 28, 1994, p. A4.

17. Woolley, "Booming Big Board," p. 61; and David Nusbaum, "An Automated Argument," *Futures: Magazine of Commodities & Options,* February 1994, p. 52.

18. Woolley, "Booming Big Board," p. 60.

19. Kerry Hannon, "Who Needs Brokers Anyway?" *U.S. News & World Report,* July 21, 1997, p. 60.

20. Ibid. See also Daniel Kadlec, "The Company Store," *Time,* October 6, 1997, p. 60.

21. Anne Kates Smith, "NYSE and Nasdaq: Dollar and Common Cents," *U.S. News & World Report,* June 16, 1997, p. 54, and Marcy Gordon, "Big Board Dumping Stock-Price Fractions," *Mobile Register,* June 6, 1997, p. 7B.

22. "Four Stocks to Be Changed in Dow Industrials," *The Wall Street Journal,* March 13, 1997, pp. C1, C15.

23. Lauren Young, "Socially Responsible Investors Appear Set to Chalk Up Another Strong Year," *The Wall Street Journal,* December 23, 1996, p. A5.

24. "A Bull Market in Stock Fraud," *Maclean's,* September 26, 1997, p. 56; and Marcy Gordon, "SEC Vows Renewed Effort to Counter Stock Fraud," *Milwaukee Journal Sentinel,* September 23, 1997, p. 3D.

25. Anne Kates Smith, "Betrayers of Trust," *U.S. News & World Report,* July 7, 1997, pp. 72–75.

26. Gordon, "Renewed Effort."

27. "What Are the Best Uses of My Dividends?" *The American Funds Investor,* Fall/Winter 1997, p. 16.

APPENDIX A

1. VIEWnet, Inc., "Virtual Job Fairs," accessed May 7, 1998, at www.viewnetinc.com/VIEWnet/vjfconst.htm; Rebecca Quick, "Your Cyber Career: Using the Internet to Find a Job, *The Wall Street Journal,* March 5, 1998, p. B8; "Recruiting on the Internet," Datamation, August 1, 1995, pp. 39–41; M. Loeb, "Getting Hired by Getting Wired," *Fortune,* November 13, 1995, p. 252; "William Bulkeley, "Replaced by Technology: Job Interviews," *The Wall Street Journal,* August 22, 1994, pp. B1, B4; "Dial a Job Interview," *Chain Store Age Executive with Shopping Center Age,* July 1994, p. 35; Carrie Goerne, "Software 'Interviewers' Screen Job Hopefuls," *Marketing News,* March 2, 1992, p. 14; and Stephen Piontek, " 'Intelligent' System Licks Agent Turnover Problem," *National Underwriter Life & Health—Financial Services Edition,* May 15, 1992, p. 4.

2. Louis Richman, "The New Work Force Builds Itself," *Fortune,* June 27, 1994, pp. 68–76.

3. "Americans' Changing Opportunities," *Money,* December 1993, p. 145.

4. Thomas Kirkpatrick and Chad Lewis, *Effective Supervision* (Fort Worth, Tex.: Dryden Press, 1995), pp. 395–398.

5. Career Center Online, accessed May 11, 1998, at www.jobweb.org.

6. Stratford Sherman, "Leaders Learn to Heed the Voice within," *Fortune,* August 22, 1994, pp. 92–100.

7. Caryne Browne, "Have I Got a Career for You," *Black Enterprise,* February 1993, pp. 145–152.

8. Richman, "New Work Force"; and Lee Smith, "Landing that First Real Job," *Fortune,* May 16, 1994, pp. 58–60.

APPENDIX B

1. CDC AIDS Information, 1997-1998, www.cdc.gov; "CDC Tackles Surge in Sexual Diseases," www.redribbon.net/cdc/cdcdaily.htm, March 26, 1998; and John Carey and Naomi Freundlich, "Is the AIDS News as Good as It Looks?" *Business Week,* May 19, 1997, p. 42.

2. Bryan Chitwood, "Malden Mills' Recovery Strong," *Outdoor Retailer,* 1997; Tom Weisand, "Malden Mills Gets $1M Retraining Grant," June 26, 1997, Business Today.com; Shelley Donald Coolidge,"Corporate Decency Prevails at Malden Mills," *The Christian Science Monitor,* March 28, 1996; "Out of the Ashes," UNITE home page.

3. Personal interview with Boyd Allen, manager, Geosciences, Foster Wheeler Environmental Corp., March 30, 1998.

4. "Pacifica Homeowners Must Move It or Lose It," *CNN,* March 3, 1998; Edward Epstein, "Agencies in Bay Area Preparing for El Niño." *The San Francisco Chronicle,* September 5, 1997. Kevin Chappell, "Boss, I Feel Lousy. Where's My Check?" *U.S. News & World Report,* July 29, 1991, p. 25.

5. "Same Sex Harassment Ruling Creates Profound Challenges for Employers," *Business Wire,* March 6, 1998.

6. Mark D. Fefer, "Tailored Health Plans Take off," *Fortune,* June 27, 1994, p. 12.

7. Steven Findlay, "85 Percent of American Workers Using HMOs," *USA Today,* January 20, 1998, p. 3A.

8. "The Wrong Medicine," *Money,* June 1997.

9. Brian O'Reilly, "Taking on the HMOs," *Fortune,* February 16, 1998.

10. Findlay, "85 Percent of American Workers."
11. "Websure SM Becomes First Web Site to Offer Life Products Direct to Consumers," *Business Wire,* March 9, 1998.

APPENDIX C

1. "Oprah to Take on Texas Cattlemen Again," *Reuters Limited,* April 17, 1998; Mary Brophy Marcus, "Oprah Takes the Bull by the Horns," *U.S. News & World Report,* January 26, 1998, p. 15; Sue Anne Pressley, "Oprah Winfrey Wins Case Filed by Cattlemen," *Washington Post,* February 27, 1998, p. A3; Adam Cohen, "Trial of the Savory," *Time,* February 2, 1998, p. 77; Chip Chandler, "Winfrey Wins One for Free Speech," *Amarillo Globe-News,* February 27,1998; Jeff Franks, "Cattleman to Appeal Verdict in Winfrey Lawsuit," Reuters Limited, February 27, 1998; Scott Parks, "Oprah Hails Free Speech after Verdict," *The Dallas Morning News,* February 27, 1998; Scott Parks, "Lawyers for Oprah, Cattlemen Clash Over Accuracy of Show," January 22, 1998, pp. 1A and 17A.
2. International Trade Law Monitor, "UNIDROIT, The International Institute for the Unification of Private Law: Work Program for the 1996–98 Triennium," September 10, 1997, accessed at http://itl.irv.uit.no/trade_law/papers/unidroit.html.
3. "Microsoft Says U.S. View Makes No Sense," Reuters Limited, March 10, 1998, 6:38 AM EST; Joshua Quittner, "Mr. Gates Goes to Washington," *Time,* March 16, 1998, vol. 151, No. 10.
4. Reinhardt Krause and Carol Haber, "Court Books TI/Cyrix Suit to Texas Turf," *Electronic News,* March 28, 1994, p. 1; "Delaware Chancery Court Is 'Key' to QVC's Chances of Buying Paramount," *Communications Daily,* November 12, 1993, p. 9; "Delaware Chancery Court," *The Oil and Gas Journal,* January 25, 1993, p. 50; and Michael Armstrong, "Small Wonder Delaware State Is Good Place to Incorporate," *Philadelphia Business Journal,* January 25, 1993, p. 4B.
5. "FTC Wants More Details on Compaq–Digital Deal," Reuters Limited, March 10, 1998, 6:38 AM EST; Bonnie Jansen, "FTC Judge Upholds Charges against Toys 'R' Us," FTC File No. 941 0040, Docket No. 9278, September 30, 1997; Valerie Marchant, "Tough Guys in the Toy Dept.," *Time,* October 13, 1997, vol. 150, No. 15.
6. Dan Goodin, "Sun, Microsoft Trade Java Barbs," CNET News.com, February 27, 1998, 12:05 PM PT; "Sun Sues Microsoft for Breach of Java™ Contract," Sun Microsystems press release, October 7, 1997.
7. John Allison and Robert A. Prentice, *Business Law: Text and Cases in the Legal Environment* (Fort Worth, Tex.: Dryden Press, 1994), p. 81.
8. Ibid., pp. 301–302.
9. Ibid., pp. 628–629.
10. Ibid., p. 160.
11. "Coffee Appeal," *USA Today,* October 14, 1994, p. 3A.
12. Allison and Prentice, *Business Law,* pp. 447–450.
13. "Chrysler to Recall '95 Sedans after Losing Appeal over Safety," *The Chicago Tribune,* March 22, 1998, Section 1, p. 11; "Chrysler Fighting to Block Recall, Avoid Fine," The Associated Press, March 17, 1998, 12:26 PM EST; "NHTSA Makes Final Decision, Orders Recall: 1995 Chrysler Cirrus, Dodge Stratus Do Not Meet Safety Standard for Seat Belt Achorages," press release, Office of the Assistant Secretary for Public Affairs, U.S. Department of Transportation, June 4, 1996.
14. See, for example, *The New Shorter Oxford English Dictionary,* 4th ed., ed. by Lesley Brown, vol. 1 (Oxford: Oxford University Press, 1993), p. 179.
15. Jonathan Foreman, "The Freedom to Fail," *Audacity,* Winter 1994, pp. 28–37.
16. Some of the information is from Michele Galen, "If Personal Bankruptcy Is Your Only Way Out," *Business Week,* January 21, 1991, pp. 90–91.
17. David Corder, "Harsh Medicine," *Kansas City Business Journal,* May 20, 1994, p. 16; and Rosalind Resnick, "The Deadbeat State," *Forbes,* July 8, 1991, p. 62.
18. January 1998 consumer credit statistics from "Consumer Credit Outstanding," Federal Reserve Statistical Release G.19, Historical Data, March 12, 1998, accessed at www.bog.frb.fed.us; Kim Clark, "Why So Many Americans Are Going Bankrupt," *Fortune,* August 4, 1997, pp. 24–25; Joshua Wolf Shenk, "In Debt All the Way Up to Their Nose Rings," *U.S. News & World Report,* June 9, 1997, pp. 38–39.
19. Foreman, "Freedom to Fail."
20. "Scots Chief to Defend His Clan: Lord McDonald Set to Challenge McDonald's Burger Chain over Use of the Ancient Name," *The Herald (UK),* October 7, 1996, accessed at http://www.mcspotlight.org/media/press/herald_7oct96.html; "Corner Shop Faces McDonald's Writ," *The Times (UK),* September 24, 1996, accessed at http://www.mcspotlight.org/media/press/times_24sep96.html.
21. William Green and Katherine Bruce, "Riskless Crime?" *Forbes,* August 11, 1997; David Stipp and Sheree R. Curry, "Farewell, My Logo," *Fortune,* May 27, 1996.
22. World Intellectual Property Organization Web site, accessed March 18, 1998, at http://www.wipo.org.
23. William Baumol and Alan Blinder, *Economics: Principles and Policy,* 7th ed. (Fort Worth, Tex.: Dryden Press, 1997), pp. 470–471.
24. Tony Mauro, "Crash Settlements Could Be Staggering," *USA Today,* September 12, 1994, p. 3A.
25. Don Clark, "Sun Microsystems Still Has Legion of Java Believers," *The Wall Street Journal,* March 23, 1998, p. B4; David Bank and John R. Wilke, "Microsoft Probe Now Includes Java Software," *The Wall Street Journal,* March 17, 1998, p. B8.
26. "Special Article Reviews Results of Bankruptcy Law," *China Intelligence Report,* May 11, 1994.

Credits

FIGURE CREDITS

Figure 1.5 Reported in "Freedom to Connect," *Wired,* August 1997.

Figure 1.6 U.S. Census Bureau, Foreign Trade Division.

Figure 3.6A(Left) Photograph courtesy of Hibernia Management and Development Company, Ltd.

Figure 3.6B(Right) Photo by Jay Rusovich, Courtesy of Anadarko Petroleum Corporation.

Figure 3.10 Data from the U.S. Bureau of Labor Statistics. Reprinted from Michael J. Mandel, "The Zero Inflation Economy," *Business Week*, January 19, 1998, p. 30.

Figure 3.11 U.S. Bureau of Labor Statistics, downloaded from http://stats.bls.gov/cpi1998g.htm.

Figure 3.13 Data downloaded from www.house.gov/chriscox, February 2, 1998; see also "Clinton Unveils $1.73 Trillion Budget," *USA Today*, February 4, 1998, p. A1.

Figure 3.15 White House, Congressional Budget Office, and *Business Week* data reported in Mike McNamee and Dean Foust, "How Growth Could End the Budget Wars," *Business Week*, May 19, 1997, pp. 33–34.

Figure 4.1 *Beverage Digest* data reported in Sabrata N. Chakravarty and John R. Hayes, "The Pure-Play Syndrome," *Forbes*, October 20, 1997, pp. 212, 214. Reprinted by permission of Forbes Magazine © Forbes, Inc., 1997.

Figure 4.2 U.S. Trade Administration, Department of Commerce, downloaded from www.stat-usa.gov/itabems.html.

Figure 4.9 © Greg Gibson–AP/WIDE WORLD PHOTOS.

Figure 4.12 Transparency International Corruption Perception Index reported in *U.S. News & World Report,* December 22, 1997, pp. 39–44. Reprinted by permission of *U.S. News and World Report.*

Figure 4.19 Data reported in "On My Mind," *Forbes,* March 10, 1997, p. 23.

Figure 5.2 "1997 Small Business Profile," Small Business Administration, downloaded from www.sbaonline.sba.gov/ADVO/stats/profiles/ February 17, 1998.

Figure 5.3 "Small Business Economic Indicators," Office of Advocacy, Small Business Administration, July 1997, pp. 1–21.

Figure 5.11 "How Many Businesses Are There?" SBA Office of Advocacy, 1997.

Figure 5.15 From *Pride*, Chapter 4, "The Forms of Business Ownership," p. 118.

Figure 6.1 Percentages are based on a survey conducted by the National Federation of Independent Business and Wells Fargo Bank, and reported in Karin Moeller, "It's Just a State of Mind," *Business Start-Ups*, July 1997, p. 4.

Figure 7.3 © Beckman Instruments, Inc., 1997.

Figure 9.3 Courtesy of Cisco Systems, Inc.

Figure 9.6 Reprinted by permission, *Nation's Business*, February 1998. *Employee Benefits 1997 Edition*, U.S. Chamber of Commerce.

Figure 9.9 Anne Fisher, "The 100 Best Companies to Work for in America," *Fortune*, January 12, 1998, pp. 68–95; Sarah Shafer, "Battling a Labor Shortage? It's All in Your Imagination," *Inc.*, August 1997, p. 24; Randall Lane, "Pampering the Customers, Pampering the Employees," *Forbes*, October 14, 1996, pp. 74–80; and Robert Levering and Milton Moskowitz, *The 100 Best Companies to Work for in America* (New York: Bantam Doubleday, 1993), p. 470.

Figure 9.10 Adapted from William G. Ouchi and Alfred M. Jaeger, "Type Z Organizations: Stability in the Midst of Mobility," *Academy of Management Review* 3 (1978), 308–314.

Figure 9.11 Reprinted with permission from *The Journal of Accountancy*, September 1997, p. 20. Copyright © 1997 by American Institute of CPAs. Opinions of the authors are their own and do not necessarily reflect policies of the AICPA.

Figure 10.1 Illustration by Rodica Prato © 1993.

Figure 11.1 *Nation's Business*, June 1997, p. 22.

Figure 11.6 Courtesy of NEA TODAY/ National Education Association.

Figure 13.21 Data from Frederick Reichheld, *The Loyalty Effect* (Cambridge, Mass. Harvard Business School Press).

Figure 16.2 © 1997 Fruit of the Loom, Inc. Reprinted with permission.

Figure 16.8 Courtesy of the Coca-Cola Company.

Figure 16.13 Courtesy of Taco Bell Corp. © 1998.

Figure 17.1(Left) The material is reprinted, written permission from Tandy Corporation.

Figure 17.1(Right) Courtesy of Gilbarco Inc. Greensboro, NC.

Figure 17.9 Compiled by NUA Internet Surveys; downloaded from www.nua.ie/surveys/how_many_online.html, January 13, 1997.

Figure 17.10 Find/SVP 1997 American Internet User Survey, downloaded from http://etrg.findsvp.com/internet, September 25, 1997.

Figure 17.13(Left) ©1997 Quaker State Corporation. Used with permission.

Figure 17.13(Top Right) Photograph reproduced with permission of Motorola, Inc.

Figure 17.13(Bottom Right) Courtesy of Ohio Department of Human Services.

Figure 17.14 Data from Mara der Hovanesian, "Technology Can Be Strategic Ally for Small Firms," *San Diego Union-Tribune Computer Link*, September 9, 1997, p. 21.

Figure 17.15 "What Works on the Web?" *IntelliGram,* downloaded from www.intelliquest.com, September 30, 1997.

APPENDIX A

Figure A.1 Source: "Employment and Total Job Openings, 1996–2006, and 1996 Median Weekly Earnings by Education and Training Category," Bureau of Labor Statistics Web Site at www.bls.gov/news.release/ecopro.table5.htm, December 8, 1997.

Figure A.6 Source: "Rebecca Smith's eResumes and Resources," accessed at www.eresume.com, May 11, 1998, originally from Rebecca Smith, "NetKnocking," *Computer Bits*, January 1997, vol. 7, no. 1.

PHOTO CREDITS

Page 5 AP/Wide World Photos.

Page 12 © Gamma Liaison.

Page 15 © Tony Larkin/Rex Features.

Page 21 Courtesy of Hickory Farms of Ohio.

Page 22 © Andreas Bottcher.

Page 27 © David Woo.

Page 28 © Blair Jensen.

Page 49 Courtesy of Northern Telecom.

Page 65 © *U.S. News & World Report.*

Page 81 © AP/Wide World Photos.

Page 117 © Courtesy of Volkswagen of America, Inc. and Arnold Communications.

Page 144 © John Chiasson/Gamma Liaison.

Page 161 "America Online" and "AOL" are registered trademarks of America Online, Inc.

Name Index

Subject Index

Absolute advantage, in international trade, 125

Accessory equipment, as business products, 453

Accommodating style, of conflict resolution, 337

Accountant, virtual, 636–637

Accounting, 629–631, 630. *See also* listings under Financial

  business activities involving, 632–633

  financial statements and, 638–640

  international, 646–647

  unethical, 632

  use of information from, 631–632

Accounting equation, 637–638.

Accounting process, 635–636

Accounting professionals, 633–635

Accounting system, 636–638

  accounting equation and, 637–638

  GAAP and, 637

Achievement needs, of entrepreneurs, 210

Acquisition, 190–191

  AOL and Internet, 161–162

  in international trade, 144

  in oil industry, 192

ACSI. *See* American Customer Satisfaction Index (ACSI)

Active listening, 341

Activity ratio, 643, 644–645

Adaptation

  and international marketing, 428–429

  of strategic plans, 238–239

Adaptive planning, 231, 233

Address lists, for direct mail, 534

Administered vertical marketing system, 509

Administrative agencies, A28

Administrative trade barriers, 137–138

ADR. *See* Alternative dispute resolution (ADR)

Advertising, 525, 528–529

  brand recognition and, 466–467

  cooperative, 553

  ethics in, 554

  by Levi Strauss, 6

  product/institutional categories of, 529–530

  and product life cycle, 529–530

  puffery and deception in, 554–555

  regulation of, 64

  revenue generation and Web, 585

  for sales stabilization, 527

  socially responsible, 56

  top ten advertising spenders by industry, 529

  types of, 529

  for union membership, 376

Advertising media, 530–537

  comparison of, 531

  cost and, 531–532

  direct mail, 534

  infomercials and specialized media, 536–537

  interactive media, 535–536

  magazines, 533–534

  newspapers, 531

  outdoor advertising, 534–535

  radio, 533

  television, 531–533

Advertorials, 554

Advocacy advertising (cause advertising), **529**

Affinity program, 250

Affirmative action, 297–299

AFL-CIO, 355–356, 359

  organizational changes in, 362–363

  rebuilding unions and, 375–376, 377

African-Americans

  BET cable TV programming and, 664–666

  business social responsibility and, 61

  small business ownership by, 178

  startups by, 209

  workforce diversity and, 27

Age, in demographic segmentation, 438

Age Discrimination in Employment Act (1968), 68, 69

Agency, law of, **A31**

Agency shop, 362

Agent, 493, A31

Agent/distributor services, 150

Aging population

  economic effect of, 106–107, 108

  workforce and, 24–25

Agribusiness, new technology in, 574–575

Agricultural industry, Dole and Japan's, 100, 104

AIDS

  business responsibility and, 56–57

  insurance industry and, A13–A14

  patients in workforce, 316

AIO statements, 439

Airline Deregulation Act (1978), 52–53, 91

Airline industry

  as oligopoly, 91

  and physical distribution, 513

Air pollution, 57

Alcohol, advertising of, 56

Algeria, 96

Alien corporation, 187

Alliances. *See also* Strategic alliance

  among workers, 376

Alternative dispute resolution (ADR), 374

Amalgamated Clothing Workers, 358

Amazon region, social responsibility in, 57

American Automobile Labeling Act, 50

American Customer Satisfaction Index (ACSI), 421

American Dental Association (ADA), logo usage of, 427

American Federation of Labor (AFL), 358–359. *See also* AFL-CIO

American Institute of Certified Public Accountants (AICPA), 633

American Medical Association (AMA)

  medical ethics and, 52

sale of logo and, 426–427

American Postal Workers Union, 360

American Society of Quality Control, ACSI of, 421

American Stock Exchange (AMEX), 697

Americans with Disabilities Act (1990), 68, 69, 297

  disabled in workforce and, 314

Analysis. *See* Forecasting

Analytic production system, 388

Angel investors, 217, 668

Animated films, production of, 383–384

Annual reports, 629

Antidrug campaigns, 529

Antitrust Division, of Department of Justice, 51

Antitrust suit, against Microsoft, 41–42, 51

Appellate courts, A27–A28

Applications software, 611

Apprenticeship programs, 300–301

Arbitration

  of labor-management disputes, 369–370

  for nonunion employees, 374

Art industry, and not-for-profit marketing, 423

Arts sponsorships, 549

ASEAN (Association of South East Asian Nations), 139

Asia, 21

  cyber-companies and trade in, 122–123

  economic recession in, 6

  global economic impact of, 110

  as market, 124

Asians, workforce diversity and, 27

Assembly line, 386, 387

Assessment, of competitive position, 234–237

Asset, 637

Assistance programs, for female-owned businesses, 177

Associates, at W.L. Gore, 323–324

Athletic shoe industry, customer relations in, 241

Atmospherics (store), 503–504

ATMs. *See* Automated teller machines (ATMs)

Attitudes, termination and, 306

Auction houses, 494

Auctions

  formats of, 413

  online, 413–414

Audience

  in communication process, 338

  measurement of promotional, 553

Autocratic leadership, 276

Automated teller machines (ATMs), usage fees, 671–672

Automatic merchandising, 497–498

Automobile industry

  and back-to-the-future marketing strategy, 459

  in China, 94

  Chrysler digital prototyping and, 390–391

International Index